11th EDITION

Criminology
Theories, Patterns, and Typologies

LARRY J. SIEGEL

University of Massachusetts, Lowell

WADSWORTH
CENGAGE Learning·

Australia • Brazil • Japan • Korea • Mexico • Singapore • Spain • United Kingdom • United States

Criminology: Theories, Patterns, and Typologies, **Eleventh Edition**
Larry J. Siegel

Senior Publisher: Linda Ganster

Senior Acquisitions Editor: Carolyn Henderson Meier

Senior Developmental Editor: Shelley Murphy

Assistant Editor: Rachel McDonald

Editorial Assistant: Virginette Acacio

Media Editor: Ting Jian Yap

Senior Marketing Manager: Michelle Williams

Marketing Assistant: Jack Ward

Senior Marketing Communications Manager: Heather Baxley

Senior Content Project Manager: Christy Frame

Creative Director: Rob Hugel

Senior Art Director: Maria Epes

Senior Print Buyer: Judy Inouye

Rights Acquisitions Account Manager: Dean Dauphinais

Production Service: Linda Jupiter, Jupiter Productions

Photo Researcher: Kim Adams Fox

Text Designer: Lisa Buckley

Copy Editor: Kay Mikel

Proofreader: Mary Kanable

Indexer: Katherine Stimson

Cover Designer: Riezebos Holzbaur/Brie Hattey

Cover Image: © Diana Ong/Superstock

Compositor: PreMediaGlobal

For product information and technology assistance, contact us at **Cengage Learning Customer & Sales Support, 1-800-354-9706.**

For permission to use material from this text or product, submit all requests online at **www.cengage.com/permissions.**
Further permissions questions can be e-mailed to **permissionrequest@cengage.com.**

Library of Congress Control Number: 2011936818

Student Edition:

ISBN-13: 978-1-133-04964-7

ISBN-10: 1-133-04964-8

Wadsworth
20 Davis Drive
Belmont, CA 94002-3098
USA

Cengage Learning is a leading provider of customized learning solutions with office locations around the globe, including Singapore, the United Kingdom, Australia, Mexico, Brazil, and Japan. Locate your local office at **www.cengage.com/global.**

Cengage Learning products are represented in Canada by Nelson Education, Ltd.

To learn more about Wadsworth, visit **www.cengage.com/wadsworth**

Purchase any of our products at your local college store or at our preferred online store **www.cengagebrain.com.**

This book is dedicated to my kids, Eric, Andrew, Julie, and Rachel, and to my grandkids, Jack, Kayla, and Brooke. It is also dedicated to Jason Macy (thanks for marrying Rachel) and Therese J. Libby (thanks for marrying me).

SOCIOLOGICAL THEORY

ORIGIN 1897

FOUNDERS Émile Durkheim, Robert Ezra Park, Ernest Burgess, Clifford Shaw, Walter Reckless, Frederic Thrasher

MOST IMPORTANT WORKS Durkheim, *The Division of Labor in Society* (1893), and *Suicide: A Study in Sociology* (1897); Park, Burgess, and John McKenzie, *The City* (1925); Thrasher, *The Gang* (1926); Shaw et al., *Delinquency Areas* (1925); Edwin Sutherland, *Criminology* (1924)

CORE IDEAS A person's place in the social structure determines his or her behavior. Disorganized urban areas are the breeding ground of crime. A lack of legitimate opportunities produces criminal subcultures. Socialization within the family, the school, and the peer group controls behavior.

MODERN OUTGROWTHS Strain Theory, Cultural Deviance Theory, Social Learning Theory, Social Control Theory, Social Reaction Theory, Labeling

Émile Durkheim

Corbis/Bettmann

Harvard Law School Library

Sheldon and Eleanor Glueck

MULTIFACTOR/INTEGRATED THEORY

ORIGIN About 1930

FOUNDERS Sheldon and Eleanor Glueck

MOST IMPORTANT WORKS Sheldon and Eleanor Glueck: *Five Hundred Delinquent Women* (1934); *Later Criminal Careers* (1937); *Criminal Careers in Retrospect* (1943); *Juvenile Delinquents Grown Up* (1940); *Unraveling Juvenile Delinquency* (1950)

CORE IDEAS Crime is a function of environmental, socialization, physical, and psychological factors. Each makes an independent contribution to shaping and directing behavior patterns. Deficits in these areas of human development increase the risk of crime. People at risk for crime can resist antisocial behaviors if these traits and conditions can be strengthened.

MODERN OUTGROWTHS Developmental Theory, Life Course Theory, Latent Trait Theory

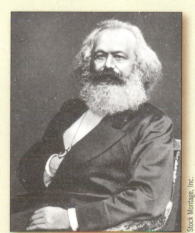
Karl Marx

Stock Montage, Inc.

About the Author

LARRY J. SIEGEL was born in the Bronx in 1947. While living on Jerome Avenue and attending City College of New York in the 1960s, he was swept up in the social and political currents of the time. He became intrigued with the influence contemporary culture had on individual behavior: Did people shape society or did society shape people? He applied his interest in social forces and human behavior to the study of crime and justice. After graduating CCNY, he attended the newly opened program in criminal justice at the State University of New York at Albany, earning both his M.A. and Ph.D. degrees there. After completing his graduate work, Dr. Siegel began his teaching career at Northeastern University, where he was a faculty member for nine years. After leaving Northeastern, he held teaching positions at the University of Nebraska–Omaha and Saint Anselm College in New Hampshire. He is currently a professor at the University of Massachusetts–Lowell. Dr. Siegel has written extensively in the area of crime and justice, including books on juvenile law, delinquency, criminology, criminal justice, and criminal procedure. He is a court certified expert on police conduct and has testified in numerous legal cases. The father of four and grandfather of three, Larry Siegel and his wife, Terry, now reside in Bedford, New Hampshire, with their two dogs, Watson and Cody.

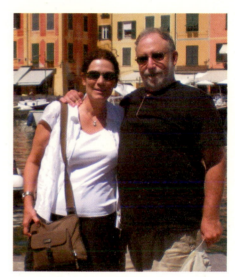

The author with his wife, Therese, in Italy.

Preface

I have studied and taught criminology for more than 40 years and sometimes think I have seen and heard everything, but every so often I encounter a case or an incident that is so unsettling I cannot get it out of my mind. "How can this have happened?" I think. "How can people treat others in such a callous fashion?" Such was the case of the Norway attacks that occurred on July 22, 2011. Anders Behring Breivik, a right-wing extremist, first set off a car bomb explosion at the executive government quarter of Oslo, outside the office of Prime Minister Jens Stoltenberg, killing eight people and wounded many others. Then, dressed as a police officer, he went to a youth camp organized by the liberal Norwegian Labour Party on the island of Utøya and mercilessly gunned down 69 people, mostly young teens. When police finally arrived, the 32-year-old Breivik quickly surrendered.

At first glance Breivik's actions would appear to be the product of a mind with a serious defect, but his violent shooting spree was carefully planned and executed. Months earlier he had traveled to Prague to purchase weapons, having read on the Internet that it was easy to obtain automatic weapons in the Czech Republic. Having failed to obtain weaponry abroad, Breivik worked at obtaining valid gun permits in Norway and took shooting lessons at a local gun club. Just before carrying out his murderous rampage, Breivik published a long manifesto on the Internet explaining his views and motivations: he wanted to end Muslim influence in Norway by destroying the future of the liberal, pro-immigration Labour Party; he hoped to spark a race war in Europe between Christians and Muslims. Was he deranged? Although his acts were extreme—he purchased high-powered weapons, loaded them with exploding ammunition, disguised himself as a police officer, methodically stalked his prey, and surrendered to police even though he still had ammunition left in his guns—these acts seem more calculating and shrewd than random and disorganized.

Criminologists devote their careers to understanding human nature, both good and bad. They ask this fundamental question: Why do people behave the way they do? How can someone like Breivik kill more than 70 innocent people, shooting wounded teens in the head to make sure they were dead? Breivik was not the product of poverty or a gang member in a disorganized neighborhood; he was a farmer whose parents, though separated, were both wealthy and educated. How can his behavior ever be explained?

Anders Behring Breivik shooting a rifle while preparing for his attack

AP Photo/via Scanpix

The general public is greatly concerned by criminal acts such as the Norway massacre. I share this concern and have been able to channel my personal interest into a career as a teacher of criminology. My goal in writing this text is to help students generate the same curiosity about issues of crime and justice. What could be more important or fascinating than a field of study that deals with such wide-ranging topics as the effects of violent media on young people, drug abuse, and organized crime? Criminology is a dynamic field, changing constantly due to the release of major research studies, Supreme Court rulings, and government policy decisions. This dynamism and diversity make it an important and engrossing area of study.

This text is designed to review ongoing issues and to cover the field of criminology in an organized and comprehensive manner. It is meant as a broad overview of the field, designed to whet the reader's appetite and encourage further and more in-depth exploration. Several major themes recur throughout the book:

- **Competing Viewpoints.** In every chapter an effort is made to introduce students to the diversity of thought that characterizes this academic discipline. One reason the study of criminology is so important is that debates continue over the nature and extent of crime and the causes and prevention of criminality. Some experts view criminal offenders as society's victims, unfortunate people who are forced to violate the law because they lack hope for legitimate opportunity; criminals are a "product of their environment." Others view antisocial behavior as a product of mental and physical abnormalities, present at birth or soon after, that are stable over the life course; is it possible that criminals are "born and not made"? Still another view is that crime is a rational choice of greedy, selfish people who can be deterred only through the threat of harsh punishments; therefore, if "you do the crime, you do the time." We explore these and other views of crime causation. To help students understand these competing viewpoints, Concept Summary boxes synthesize the main points and outlook of each theoretical model.

■ **Critical Thinking.** It is important for students to think critically about law and justice and to develop a critical perspective toward the social institutions and legal institutions entrusted with crime control. Throughout the book, students are asked to critique featured material and to think outside the box. To aid in this task, each chapter features "Thinking Like a Criminologist: An Ethical Dilemma," which presents a scenario students can analyze with the help of material found in the chapter.

■ **Diversity.** Diversity is a key issue in criminology, and racial, ethnic, gender, and cultural diversity issues are integrated throughout the text. Material on international issues are presented, such as the use of the death penalty abroad, as well as gender issues, such as the rising rate of female criminality. Race, Culture, Gender, and Criminology feature boxes highlight diversity issues.

■ **Currency and Immediacy.** Throughout the book, every attempt is made to use the most current research and to cover the most immediate topics, highlighting the major trends in criminological research and justice policy. Most people who use the book have told me that this is one of its strongest features. I present current research in a balanced fashion, though this sometimes can be frustrating to students. For example, some experts find that biological traits and conditions promote crime, but other criminologists conclude that this research is spurious and that biology and crime are unrelated. Which position is correct? Although it is comforting to reach a definite conclusion about an important topic, sometimes that is simply not possible. In an effort to be objective and fair, each side of important criminological debates is presented in full. Throughout the text, The Criminological Enterprise boxes review important research in criminology, such as the one in Chapter 2 that discusses research that helps to explain why crime rates rise and fall.

■ **Social Policy.** The focus on social policy throughout the book helps students learn how criminological theory has been translated into crime prevention

programs. Policy and Practice in Criminology features show how criminological ideas and research can be put into action.

■ In sum, the primary goals in writing this text are as follows:

1. To provide students with a thorough knowledge of criminology and show its diversity and intellectual content
2. To be as thorough and up to date as possible
3. To be objective and unbiased
4. To describe current theories, crime types, and methods of social control, and analyze their strengths and weaknesses
5. To show how criminological thought has influenced social policy

TOPIC AREAS

The 11th edition has been thoroughly revised and updated. Chapter 13, **Enterprise Crime: White-Collar and Green-Collar Crime**, now includes extensive coverage of green crimes, ranging from illegal fishing to environmental pollution and dumping. Chapter 15, **Crimes of the New Millennium: Cybercrime and Transnational Organized Crime**, is also new and covers emerging areas of criminality made possible by technological advances such as the Internet and instant communication. Crime is going global and so, too, is criminology.

The text is divided into three main sections or topic areas.

Part One provides a framework for studying criminology. Chapter 1 defines the field and discusses its most basic concepts: the definition of crime, the component areas of criminology, the concept of criminal law, and the ethical issues that confront the field. Chapter 2 covers criminological research methods, and the nature, extent, and patterns of crime. Chapter 3 is devoted to the concept of victimization, including the nature of victims, theories of victimization, and programs designed to help crime victims.

Part Two contains six chapters that cover criminological theory: Why do people behave the way they do? Why do they commit crimes? These views focus on choice (Chapter 4), biological and psychological traits (Chapter 5), social structure and culture (Chapter 6), social process and socialization (Chapter 7), social conflict and critical criminology (Chapter 8), and human development (Chapter 9).

Part Three is devoted to the major forms of criminal behavior. The chapters in this section cover violent crime (Chapter 10); political crime and terrorism (Chapter 11); common theft offenses (Chapter 12); enterprise crimes, including white-collar and green-collar crimes (Chapter 13); public order crimes, including sex offenses and substance abuse (Chapter 14); and cybercrime and transnational organized crime (Chapter 15).

GOALS AND OBJECTIVES

The 11th edition has been carefully structured to cover relevant material in a comprehensive, balanced, and objective fashion. Every attempt has been made to present material in an interesting and contemporary style. No single political or theoretical position dominates the text; instead, the many diverse views contained within criminology and that characterize its interdisciplinary nature are presented in an unbiased and even-handed fashion. Analysis of the most important scholarly works and scientific research reports is balanced by a great deal of topical information on recent cases and events, ranging from new millennium cybercrimes to the violence of the Zeta gang, the "muscle" formed to protect Mexican drug cartels.

WHAT'S NEW IN THIS EDITION

- **Chapter 1 (Crime and Criminology)** revisits the case of Natalie Holloway, the 18-year-old girl from Birmingham, Alabama, who disappeared in 2005 and is alleged to have been murdered while on holiday on the island of Aruba. The reason: in 2010, Joran van der Sloot, long a suspect in the case, is alleged to have killed another young girl. The Race, Culture, Gender, and Criminology feature "Crime in Other Cultures" has been updated. A new Policy and Practice in Criminology feature asks the question, "Are Sex Offender Registration Laws Effective?" The Thinking Like a Criminologist | An Ethical Dilemma box considers the case of Cody Watson, a star NFL quarterback involved in a dog-fighting ring. A new section covers "The Law in Contemporary Society." In Profiles in Crime, "Conspiracy Does Not Pay," we delve into the story of three Philadelphia police officers indicted for their involvement in a drug conspiracy. Another new section, "Legalizing Marijuana," reviews efforts to decriminalize the use of medical marijuana.
- **Chapter 2 (The Nature and Extent of Crime)** begins with the love triangle between George Zinkhan, Marie Bruce, and Thomas Tanner that led to murder. Profiles in Crime, "A Pain in the Glass," highlights a couple who used the "waiter, there is glass in my food" ruse in restaurants and supermarkets stretching from Boston to Washington, D.C., to fraudulently obtain thousands of dollars. A new exhibit considers the question, "Why Do Victims Report Crime?" A recent study of more than 100 retired New York Police Department captains and higher-ranking officers found that officers were under intense pressure to reduce crime and may have manipulated crime statistics to show that their efforts were successful. This chapter now covers a self-report technique called the life event calendar (LEC). A Policy and Practice in Criminology feature, "The CATCH Program," describes a program that supports local law enforcement agencies' efforts to analyze crime series and patterns.

- **Chapter 3 (Victims and Victimization)** highlights updated victim data using the latest surveys. A new section on "Vicarious Fear" examines why people who are not personally victimized but who observe, or are exposed to, violence on a routine basis become fearful. The section "Crime in Schools" explains that crime is shockingly common because schools are populated by one of the most dangerous segments of society—teenage males. A Profiles in Crime feature, "Online Predator," tells the story of Jonathan Wryn Vance, 24, of Auburn, Alabama, who used the Internet for interstate extortion. New material on lifestyle and victimization points out that people who belong to groups that have an extremely risky lifestyle—homeless, runaways, drug users—are at high risk for victimization; the more time they are exposed to street life, the greater their risk of becoming crime victims. The Criminological Enterprise, "Escalation or Desistance: The Effect of Victimization on Criminal Careers," looks at what happens when a criminal experiences victimization. A new section on "Crisis Intervention" discusses programs that refer victims to specific services to help them recover from their ordeal. The Thinking Like a Criminologist | An Ethical Dilemma box examines "Stand Your Ground" laws.
- **Chapter 4 (Rational Choice Theory)** now covers the development and history of rational choice/classical theory, most closely identified with the thoughts of 18th-century Italian social philosopher Cesare Beccaria and his famous treatise, "On Crimes and Punishment." A new section, "Why Crime?" looks at why some people choose to commit crime even though the consequences of crime can be painful, costly, and embarrassing. The Criminological Enterprise, "Drug Dealer Retaliation," examines the rational way drug dealers retaliate for perceived wrongdoing. A new Profiles in Crime, "Let Them Swim Home," describes the case of Eugene Temkin, who tried to hire a hit man to kill his partner in a deal gone bad.
- **Chapter 5 (Trait Theories)** now begins with the history and development of trait theories, including the work of Cesare Lombroso. A new exhibit illustrates the elements of the scientific method. A discussion of the dyslogic syndrome, first proposed by psychologist

Robert Rimland, provides another explanation for the actions of troubled children. A new section on "Smoking and Drinking" shows how maternal alcohol abuse and/or smoking during gestation has long been linked to prenatal damage and subsequent antisocial behavior in adolescence. A section on "Lead Ingestion" covers recent research studies suggesting lead ingestion is linked to aggressive behaviors on both a macro (group/nation) level and a micro (individual) level. A new section on "Attachment Theory," a view most closely associated with psychologist John Bowlby, who is also connected to the psychodynamic tradition, explores the importance of emotional bonding.

- **Chapter 6 (Social Structure Theories)** begins with a vignette on the MS-13 gang. Profiles in Crime, "MS-13 in Action," explains why MS-13 is considered one of the most fearsome gangs in the United States. There are sections on the development of sociological criminology and on how it has replaced biological positivism as the main focus of criminology. There is an interesting new discussion on how social forces in disadvantaged areas may be so powerful that they overwhelm individual traits. New data on poverty are covered, including the newest trends in child poverty and minority group poverty. Race, Culture, Gender, and Criminology, "More than Just Race," reviews the work of William Julius Wilson, one of the nation's prominent sociologists. There is a new section on "Poverty Concentration," a phenomenon that occurs when working- and middle-class families flee inner-city poverty areas, resulting in the most disadvantaged population being consolidated in the most disorganized urban neighborhoods.

- **Chapter 7 (Social Process Theories: Socialization and Society)** now contains The Criminological Enterprise feature "Family Functioning and Crime," which discusses the work of Rand Conger, one of the nation's leading experts on family life. Profiles in Crime, "But the Water Was Sterile!" discusses a case in which employees at a Texas-based oil company were given fake flu shots.

- **Chapter 8 (Social Conflict, Critical Criminology, and Restorative Justice)** opens with a vignette on the Arab spring and the social conflict that brought political change in Egypt and other nations in the Middle East. There is a significant discussion of "State (Organized) Crime"—acts defined by law as criminal and committed by state officials, both elected and appointed, in pursuit of their jobs as government representatives. The Criminological Enterprise, "Mass Deception," explores Scott Bonn's new book, in which he argues that the Bush administration manufactured public support for war on Iraq by falsely claiming that its leader, Saddam Hussein, was involved in the terrorist attacks of 9/11 and that Iraq possessed weapons of mass destruction. There is a new section covering "Illegal Domestic Surveillance" and another on "Human Rights Violations," as well as a

section on "Crime and Social Institutions." The sections on "Left Realism" have been updated and expanded, and a new Criminological Enterprise feature, "Left Realism and Terrorism," has been added. Profiles in Crime, "Russia's Death Squads," discusses how Russia crushed the separatist rebel groups in Chechnya. A Policy and Practices in Criminology feature reviews "Victim Offender Reconciliation in Denver, Colorado."

- **Chapter 9 (Developmental Theories: Life Course, Latent Trait, and Trajectory)** has been completely reorganized and now includes an independent section on "Trajectory Theories" and the different "Pathways to Crime." The chapter begins with a vignette on the murder of Californians Thomas and Jackie Hawks by a group of criminals who decided to steal their yacht. There is a new section on the "Foundations of Developmental Theory" and also new material on gender and persistence and desisting from crime, including material on cognition and desistence and identity and desistance. Profiles in Crime discusses "The Xbox Killers." The Criminological Enterprise feature, "Love, Sex, Marriage, and Crime," reviews research by sociologists Bill McCarthy and Teresa Casey, examining the association between romance and delinquency in a sample of teens. The section on "Trajectory Theories" features new material on offense specialization and generalization and recruiters versus lone wolves.

- **Chapter 10 (Interpersonal Violence)** begins with a new vignette on the high-profile case of Casey Anthony, a young Florida mother accused of killing her daughter. We ask, "Are Humans Instinctively Violent?" and explore sociologist Randall Collins's theory of violence, which states that humans are inherently passive and that violence is a function of social interaction. There also is a new section on "Handguns and Firearms." Profiles in Crime focuses on "The Duke Rape Case," and a new Criminological Enterprise feature discusses "Rape in America." The case of Dominique Strauss-Kahn, the French diplomat accused of rape, is also discussed. A new section, "Deliberate Indifference Murder," explains how a person can be held criminally liable for the death of another even if that person did not intend to injure the victim but exhibited *deliberate indifference* to the danger his or her actions might cause. The robbery sections have been updated with new material on "Planning to Rob." The Criminological Enterprise, "Following the Script," looks at research showing that robbers worry more about victims' reactions than about law enforcers. After all, an uncooperative victim could alter the course of events, threaten valued goals, or put all involved in physical danger. There is a new section on sex and murder. A new Profiles in Crime, "Bound by Hate," describes how 17-year-old Jeffrey Conroy and six other Long Island, New York, teenagers decided to hunt for Hispanic men to assault, which led to murder.

- **Chapter 11 (Political Crime and Terrorism)** begins with the life story and death of the world's most notorious terrorist, Osama bin Laden, and a new exhibit lists some "Notable Terror Prosecutions." The case of the Russian spy group of sleeper agents that unraveled in 2010 with 10 people arrested is also examined. Thinking Like a Criminologist | An Ethical Dilemma deals with the provocative topic of whether to torture a suspected terrorist. A section now covers how terror groups are financed, and another explains how socialization and friendship influence the choice of becoming a terrorist. In addition, Brian Michael Jenkins, a noted expert on the topic, identifies the strategic principles he believes are key to countering terror in contemporary society.

- **Chapter 12 (Property Crime)** includes a section on overzealous enforcement in retail theft, which can result in countersuits being filed. A recent case is reviewed in which federal authorities uncovered the largest credit card scam in history: 11 people stole 40 million credit and debit card numbers from major retailers by installing "sniffer" programs designed to capture credit card numbers, passwords, and account information as they moved through the retailers' card processing networks. A new section on "Car Cloning" describes a recent form of professional auto theft. The chapter covers confidence games run by swindlers who aspire to separate a victim (or "sucker") from his or her hard-earned money. Another new section, "Third-Party Fraud," examines the costs when the "victim" is a third party, such as an insurance company, forced to pay for false claims.

- **Chapter 13 (Enterprise Crime: White-Collar and Green-Collar Crime)** now includes both white-collar and green-collar crimes. The chapter begins with the story of Robert Allen Stanford, a financier on the tropical island of Antigua who liked to be called "Sir Robert." Stanford committed one of the largest enterprise crimes in history, causing people to lose billions. Profiles in Crime, "Dumping a Dumper," tells the story of Larkin Baggett, who owned and operated Chemical Consultants, Inc. and illegally dumped pollutants onto the ground and into a drain that led to a treatment plant in North Salt Lake City, Utah. There is a new section on the "Mortgage Swindles" that threatened to destroy the financial system and another on foreclosure rescue scams, which were designed to prey upon people who obtained mortgages and could not make payments. Profiles in Crime, "Clipping the Hedges," tells of Robert Moffat, a senior executive with International Business Machines Corp. (IBM), who pleaded guilty to securities-related crimes. Half the chapter is now devoted to green crimes, and sections include "Defining Green Crime" and "Forms of Green Crime." Green-collar crime can take many different forms, ranging from deforestation and illegal logging to violations of worker safety. Among those discussed are illegal logging, illegal wildlife exports, illegal fishing, illegal dumping, and illegal polluting. Profiles in Crime, "Hunting the Shark Hunters," describes how the African nation of Mozambique deals with illegal poachers.

- **Chapter 14 (Public Order Crime: Sex and Substance Abuse)** opens with an updated vignette regarding the case of New York Governor Eliot Spitzer, aka Client #9, who was caught paying thousands to a call girl ring. It also covers the Anthony Weiner case, the New York congressman caught in a "sexting" scandal. There is a new section on "The Gay Marriage Crusade," one of the most heated "moral crusades" of our time. An exhibit on John Schools focuses on clients and attempts to steer them away from prostitution through education. A section on "Virtual Kiddie Porn" shows how CGI and other high-tech innovations now make it possible for pornographers to create and distribute pornography using virtual images of children. The case of *United States v. Williams*, which helps define what is considered kiddie porn, is analyzed; and Profiles in Crime, "Kiddie Porn?" discusses the case of Christopher Handley, 39, of Glenwood, Iowa, who was accused of possessing kiddie porn in the form of comic books. Data on drug abuse and use has been updated along with the material on the nature and extent of drug courts.

- **Chapter 15 (Crimes of the New Millennium: Cybercrime and Transnational Organized Crime)** is completely revised and focuses on cybercrime and transnational organized crime. It begins with a new vignette on "Operation Phish Phry," a government crackdown on an international ring fraudulently collecting personal information from victims and using it to defraud financial institutions by creating dummy accounts or bogus credit cards. There is also material covering the Wikileaks scandal. Profiles in Crime, "Operation Joint Hammer," describes an international investigation, begun in Australia, that resulted in the rescue of 14 girls—some as young as 3 years old—who were being sexually abused by pornographers. There is a new section on denial-of-service attacks, and another on Botnets, a software robot (also known as a zombie or drone) that allows an unauthorized user to remotely take control of a host computer without the victim's knowledge or permission. The material on cyberbullying and cyberwar has been updated to reflect recent cases and trends. The sections on "Transnational Organized Crime" cover concepts and activities of contemporary transnational crime groups, including eastern European gangs, Latin American and Mexican drug cartels, and Asian transnational groups. A new section explains how cross-national and transnational gangs are a product of the cyber age. Gang members often use cell phones and the Internet to communicate and to promote their illicit activities. A new Comparative Criminology feature looks at drug production and trafficking in the golden triangle.

FEATURES

This text contains different kinds of pedagogy to help students analyze material in greater depth and to link it to other material in the book:

- **Profiles in Crime** present students with case studies of actual criminals and crimes to help illustrate the position or views within the chapter. By popular demand we have expanded the feature for this edition, presenting even more real-life "from the headlines" criminal cases throughout the text. For example, Chapter 2 presents a Profiles in Crime about the 2009 case of a large Harrisburg, Pennsylvania, prostitution ring that was broken up by federal, state, and county investigators.
- **The Criminological Enterprise** features review important issues in criminology and reflect the major subareas of the field, measuring crime, creating theory, crime typologies, legal theory, and penology. For example, in Chapter 4, The Criminological Enterprise titled "Drug Dealer Retaliation" discusses the recent work of criminologist Scott Jacques, who investigated the forms of drug market retaliation and found they followed a rational pattern. In Chapter 7, The Criminological Enterprise feature discusses the work of Rand Conger, one of the nation's leading experts on family life, who for the past two decades has been involved with four major community studies examining the influence of economic stress on families, children, and adolescents.
- **Policy and Practice in Criminology** features show how criminological ideas and research can be put into action. For example, a Policy and Practice in Criminology box in Chapter 2 discusses "The CATCH Program," an innovative mapping program—the Crime Analysis Tactical Clearing House—that supports local law enforcement agencies in analyzing crime series and patterns using a number of crime mapping and analysis software applications and techniques. Another Policy and Practice in Criminology box in Chapter 8 discusses "Victim Offender Reconciliation in Denver, Colorado," a program designed in response to a summer of violence in the metro Denver area.
- **Race, Culture, Gender, and Criminology** boxes cover issues of racial, sexual, and cultural diversity. For example, in Chapter 2, "On the Run" looks at the life of inner-city kids who spend their time avoiding the police. In Chapter 15, "International Trafficking in Persons" looks at how women are victimized by transnational cartels who force them into the sex trade.
- **Critical Thinking Questions** accompany each of the boxed features except Profiles in Crime, and more questions are presented at the end of each chapter to help students develop their analytical abilities.
- **Connections** are short inserts that help link the material to other areas covered in the book. For example, a Connections box in Chapter 14 links media violence to the material discussed in Chapter 5.
- **Chapter Outlines** provide a roadmap to coverage and serve as a useful review tool.
- **Learning Objectives** spell out what students should learn in each chapter. The chapter **Summary** is now geared to these objectives.
- **Thinking Like a Criminologist | An Ethical Dilemma** present challenging questions or issues for which students must use their criminological knowledge to answer or confront an ethical dilemma. Applying the information learned in the text will help students begin to "think like criminologists."
- Each chapter ends with **Critical Thinking Questions**, which help develop students' critical thinking skills, as well as a list of **Key Terms**.

SUPPLEMENTS

To access additional course materials including CourseMate, please visit www.cengagebrain.com. At the CengageBrain.com home page, search for the ISBN of your title (from the back cover of your book) using the search box at the top of the page. This will take you to the product page where these resources can be found.

An extensive package of supplemental aids accompanies this edition. Many separate items have been developed to enhance the course and to assist instructors and students. Available to qualified adopters. Please consult your local sales representative for details.

For the Instructor

- **Instructor's Resource Manual with Test Bank**
Updated by Tina Freiburger of University of Wisconsin, Milwaukee, to reflect new content in the main text, the manual includes learning objectives, key terms, a detailed chapter outline, a chapter summary, discussion topics, student activities, and a test bank in which 30 percent of the questions have been revised. Each chapter's test bank contains questions in multiple-choice, true/false, fill-in-the-blank, and essay formats—with a full answer key. The test bank is coded to the learning objectives that appear in the main text and includes the page numbers in the main text where the answers can be found. Finally, each test bank question has been carefully reviewed by experienced criminal justice instructors for quality, accuracy, and content coverage. Our Instructor Approved

seal, which appears on the front cover, is our assurance that you are working with an assessment and grading resource of the highest caliber. The manual is available for download on the password-protected instructor book companion website, and a print copy can be obtained by e-mailing your local Cengage Learning representative.

■ **Online Lesson Plans** Revised by Kelly Gould of Sacramento Community College to reflect content in the new edition, the Lesson Plans bring accessible, masterful suggestions to every lesson. This supplement includes a sample syllabus, learning objectives, lecture notes, discussion topics, in-class activities, a detailed lecture outline, assignments, media tools, and "What if . . ." scenarios. Current events and real-life examples in the form of articles, websites, and video links are incorporated into the class discussion topics, activities, and assignments. The lecture outlines are correlated with Microsoft® PowerPoint® slides for ease of classroom use. Lesson Plans are included on the PowerLecture™ resource and are available for download from the password-protected instructor book companion website.

■ **PowerLecture with ExamView®** This one-stop digital library and presentation tool includes preassembled Microsoft PowerPoint lecture slides linked to the learning objectives for each chapter. Also included are an electronic copy of the *Instructor's Resource Manual* with Test Bank, the Student Study Guide, ExamView computerized testing, and more. Based on the learning objectives outlined at the beginning of each chapter, the enhanced PowerLecture lets you bring together text-specific lecture outlines and art from this text, along with new video clips, animations, and learning modules from the Web or your own materials—culminating in a powerful, personalized, media-enhanced presentation. PowerLecture also integrates ExamView—a computerized test bank available for PC and Macintosh computers—software for customizing tests of up to 250 items that can be delivered in print or online. With ExamView you can create, deliver, and customize tests and study guides in minutes. You can easily edit and import your own questions and graphics, change test layouts, and reorganize questions. And, using ExamView's complete word-processing capabilities, you can enter an unlimited number of new questions or edit existing questions.

■ **WebTutor™ on Blackboard® and WebCT®** Jump-start your course with customizable, rich, text-specific content within your Course Management System. Whether you want to web-enable your class or put an entire course online, WebTutor delivers. WebTutor offers a wide array of resources, including media assets, test bank, practice quizzes linked to chapter learning objectives, and additional study aids. Visit www.cengage.com/webtutor to learn more.

■ **Criminal Justice Media Library on WebTutor** Cengage Learning's Criminal Justice Media Library includes nearly 300 media assets on the topics you cover in your courses. Available to stream from any web-enabled computer, the Criminal Justice Media Library's assets include such valuable resources as Career Profile Videos featuring interviews with criminal justice professionals from a range of roles and locations, simulations that enable students to step into various roles and practice their decision-making skills, video clips on current topics from ABC and other sources, animations that illustrate key concepts, interactive learning modules that help students check their knowledge of important topics, and Reality Check exercises that compare expectations and preconceived notions against the real-life thoughts and experiences of criminal justice professionals. Video assets include assessment questions that can be delivered straight to the grade book. The Criminal Justice Media Library can be uploaded and customized within many popular Learning Management Systems. Please contact your Cengage Learning representative for ordering and pricing information.

■ *The Wadsworth Criminal Justice Video Library* So many exciting new videos—so many great ways to enrich your lectures and spark discussion of the material in this text. Your Cengage Learning representative will be happy to provide details on our video policy by adoption size. The library includes these selections and many others.

■ *ABC® Videos*. ABC videos feature short, high-interest clips from current news events as well as historic raw footage going back 40 years. Perfect for discussion starters or to enrich your lectures and spark interest in the material in the text, these brief videos provide students with a new lens through which to view the past and present, one that will greatly enhance their knowledge and understanding of significant events and open up to them new dimensions in learning. Clips are drawn from such programs as *World News Tonight, Good Morning America, This Week, PrimeTime Live, 20/20,* and *Nightline,* as well as numerous ABC News specials and material from the Associated Press Television News and British Movietone News collections.

■ *Cengage Learning's "Introduction to Criminal Justice Video Series"* features videos supplied by the BBC Motion Gallery. These short, high-interest clips from CBS and BBC news programs—everything from nightly news broadcasts and specials to *CBS News Special Reports, CBS Sunday Morning, 60 Minutes,* and more—are perfect classroom discussion starters. Designed to enrich your lectures and spark interest in the material in the text, these brief videos provide students with a new lens through which to view the past and present, one that will greatly enhance their knowledge and understanding of significant events and open up to them new dimensions in learning. Clips are drawn from BBC Motion Gallery.

■ *Films for the Humanities.* Choose from nearly 200 videos on a variety of topics such as elder abuse, supermax prisons, suicide and the police officer, the making of an FBI agent, and domestic violence.

For the Student

■ **CourseMate** Cengage Learning's Criminal Justice CourseMate brings course concepts to life with interactive learning, study, and exam preparation tools that support the printed textbook. CourseMate includes an integrated ebook, quizzes mapped to chapter learning objectives (updated by Paul Klenowski of Clarion University), flashcards, videos, and more, and EngagementTracker, a first-of-its-kind tool that monitors student engagement in the course. The accompanying instructor website offers access to password-protected resources such as an electronic version of the instructor's manual and PowerPoint slides.

■ **Study Guide** An extensive student Study Guide has been developed for this edition by Krista S. Gehring of University of Houston–Downtown. The new Study Guide features a variety of pedagogical aids to help students with diverse learning styles. Students will find learning objectives, chapter outlines and summaries, definitions of major terms, and self-tests with answers. Test questions are correlated to learning objectives in the answer key so students can be sure they are mastering critical course content.

■ **Careers in Criminal Justice Website** *Available bundled with this text at no additional charge.* Featuring plenty of self-exploration and profiling activities, the interactive Careers in Criminal Justice Website helps students investigate and focus on the criminal justice career choices that are right for them. Includes interest assessment, video testimonials from career professionals, resume and interview tips, peripheral skills such as courtroom demeanor and preparation for testimony, effective communication skills, ethics and professionalism, and more.

■ **CLeBook** Cengage Learning's Criminal Justice ebooks allow students to access our textbooks in an easy-to-use online format. Highlight, take notes, bookmark, search your text, and, for most texts, link directly into multimedia. In short, CLeBook combines the best features of paper books and ebooks in one package.

■ *Current Perspectives: Readings from InfoTrac® College Edition* These readers, designed to give students a closer look at special topics in criminal justice, include free access to InfoTrac College Edition. The timely articles are selected by experts in each topic from within InfoTrac College Edition. They are available free when bundled with the text and include the following titles:

Cyber Crime
Victimology
Juvenile Justice
Racial Profiling
White-Collar Crime
Terrorism and Homeland Security
Public Policy and Criminal Justice
Technology and Criminal Justice
Ethics in Criminal Justice
Forensics and Criminal Investigation
Corrections
Law and Courts
Policy in Criminal Justice

ACKNOWLEDGMENTS

The preparation of this text would not have been possible without the aid of my colleagues who helped by reviewing the previous editions and giving me important suggestions for improvement. Reviewers for the 11th edition are:

Donald Alsdurf, Kansas City College Community College
Keith F. Durkin, Ohio Northern University
Lori Guevara, Fayetteville State University
Kathryn D. Morgan, University of Alabama
Jill A. Morrow, Heald College, Concord Campus, California
Laurie Woods, Vanderbilt University

My colleagues at Cengage did their typically outstanding job of aiding me in the preparation of the text and gave me counseling and support. My editor, Carolyn Henderson Meier, is always there for advice, encouragement, and enthusiasm. My BFF Shelley Murphy is simply the world's greatest developmental editor. Kim Adams Fox, the photo editor, is a true professional and is always there with a last-minute photo update. Linda Jupiter, the book's production editor, is always great, terrific, a close friend and confidant. Kay Mikel is the copy editor supreme. and nothing gets past proofreader Mary Kanable. The fabulous Christy Frame somehow pulls everything together as production manager, and Michelle Williams is the fabulous marketing manager. All in all a terrific team!

Larry Siegel
Bedford, New Hampshire

ONE

Concepts of Crime, Law, and Criminology

How is crime defined? How much crime is there, and what are the trends and patterns in the crime rate? How many people fall victim to crime, and who is likely to become a crime victim? How did our system of criminal law develop, and what are the basic elements of crimes? What is the science of criminology all about?

These are some of the core issues that will be addressed in the first three chapters of this text. Chapter 1 introduces students to the field of criminology: its nature, area of study, methodologies, and historical development. Concern about crime and justice has been an important part of the human condition for more than 5,000 years, since the first criminal codes were set down in the Middle East. Although criminology—the scientific study of crime—is considered a modern science, it has existed for more than 200 years. Chapter 1 introduces students to one of the key components of criminology—the development of criminal law. It also discusses the social history of law, the purpose of law, and how law defines crime. Chapter 2 focuses on the acquisition of crime data, crime rate trends, and observable patterns within the crime rate. Chapter 3 is devoted to victims and victimization. Topics include the effects of victimization, the cause of victimization, and efforts to help crime victims.

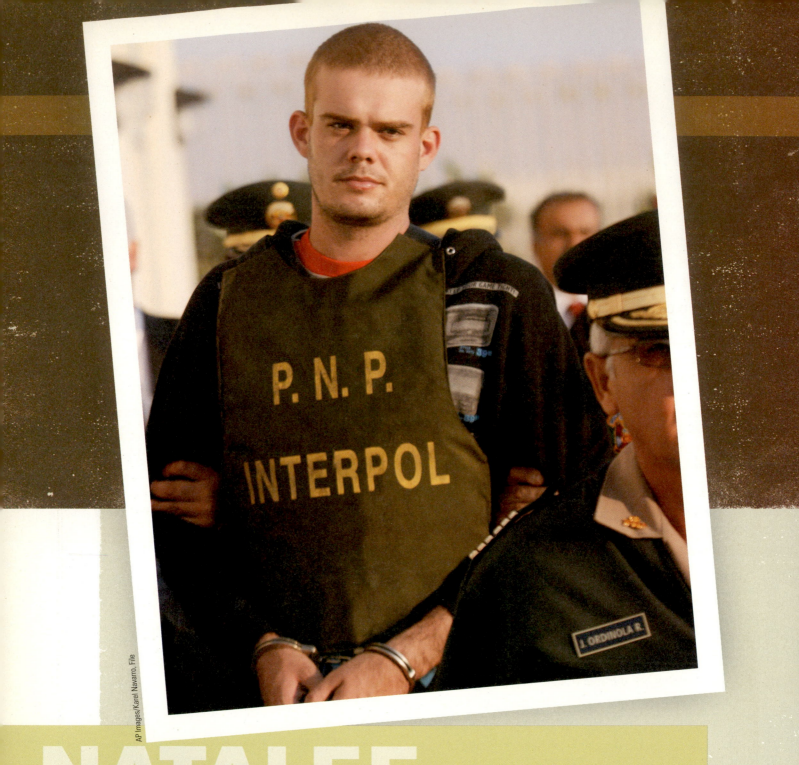

AP Images/Karel Navarro, File

NATALEE

Natalee Holloway, 18, from the Birmingham, Alabama, suburb of Mountain Brook, celebrated her high school graduation by going on a holiday to the Caribbean island of Aruba with about 100 classmates and several parent chaperones. On the night of May 30, 2005, she went to a local bar and was later seen leaving with three men—two brothers from Surinam and a local boy, the son of a high-ranking Dutch judicial official. Holloway never returned to her hotel nor did she appear in any **security camera** footage of the hotel lobby in the course of the night. When she did not show up for the flight home, her passport, luggage, and mobile phone were found in her hotel room.

The three suspects in the case, Joran van der Sloot and brothers Deepak Kalpoe and Satish Kalpoe, were arrested on June 9, 2005. However, the police could not come up with sufficient evidence to make the charges

(continued on page 4)

Crime and Criminology

1

Learning Objectives

1. Understand what is meant by the "field of criminology"
2. Be familiar with the various elements of the criminological enterprise
3. Know the difference between crime and deviance
4. Discuss the three different views of crime
5. Know what constitutes the different categories of law
6. Discuss the different purposes of criminal law
7. Trace the development of criminal law
8. Describe the difference between a felony and a misdemeanor
9. Recognize the relationship between the criminal law and the U.S. Constitution
10. Be familiar with the ethical issues in criminology

stick, and the Kalpoes and Van der Sloot were released. Van der Sloot was required to stay within Dutch territory and he returned to the Netherlands to attend college.

The three young men had told the police that they took Holloway to Arashi Beach, on Aruba's northern tip, and at 2 A.M. dropped her off at her hotel, where they saw her being approached by a security guard as they drove off.[1] This was one of several stories circulating about the case, including claims that Holloway had been sold into sexual slavery and that she had died on the beach and her body was dumped at sea.

The case remains unsolved but not forgotten. In 2010, it was suddenly back on the front page: Van der Sloot approached Natalee Holloway's family in an effort to extort money from them in exchange for information on their daughter, including the location of her body. After being paid $15,000 for information that turned out to be false, Van der Sloot used the cash to travel to Lima, Peru. There, on May 30, 2010, the fifth anniversary of Holloway's disappearance, a local girl, Stephany Tatiana Flores Ramírez, 21, was found dead in the Hotel TAC; the room had been registered in the name of Joran van der Sloot! Witnesses put the unfortunate young woman and Van der Sloot in the hotel together, and a video showed the two playing cards at the same table at a local casino. Ramírez's jewelry, **ID**, and credit cards were missing, as well as over $10,000 she had won earlier that evening at the casino. Captured in Colombia, Van der Sloot was returned to Peru where he remains in a high-security Peruvian prison. He is said to have admitted killing Ramírez because she used his laptop without permission.

How can we explain the behavior of a Joran van der Sloot? What motivates a young man to become a multiple killer? Tall, handsome, educated, and wealthy, he hardly fits the profile of a cold-blooded murderer of young women. He was not a "product of his environment"; his crimes were not "gang related." Is it possible that his violent behavior was a function of some psychological abnormality or biological defect? Yet, those who knew him did not suspect he had a murderous side, nor did the police in Aruba describe him as mentally disturbed or deranged.

The questions about crime and its control raised by the Natalee Holloway/Joran van der Sloot case and other high-profile criminal incidents have spurred interest in **criminology**, an academic discipline that uses the scientific method to study the nature, extent, cause, and control of criminal behavior. Unlike political figures and media commentators—whose opinions about crime may be colored by personal experiences, biases, and election concerns—criminologists remain objective as they study crime and its consequences.[2]

Criminology is a multidisciplinary science. **Criminologists** hold degrees in a variety of diverse fields, most commonly sociology, but also **criminal justice**, political science, psychology, public policy, economics, and the natural sciences.

For most of the twentieth century, criminology's primary orientation was sociological, but today it can be viewed as an integrated approach to the study of criminal behavior.

How this field developed, its major components, and its relationship to crime law and deviance are some of the topics discussed in this chapter.

This text analyzes criminology and its major subareas of inquiry. It focuses on the nature and extent of crime, the causes of crime, and patterns of criminal behavior. This chapter introduces and defines criminology: What are its goals? How do criminologists define crime? How do they conduct research? What ethical issues face those wishing to conduct criminological research?

WHAT IS CRIMINOLOGY?

Criminology is the scientific approach to studying criminal behavior. In their classic definition, preeminent criminologists Edwin Sutherland and Donald Cressey state:

> Criminology is the body of knowledge regarding crime as a social phenomenon. It includes within its scope the processes of making laws, of breaking laws, and of reacting toward the breaking of laws. . . . The objective of criminology is the development of a body of general and verified principles and of other types of knowledge regarding this process of law, crime, and treatment.[3]

Sutherland and Cressey's definition includes some of the most important areas of interest to criminologists:

- *Crime as a social phenomenon.* Although some criminologists believe that individual traits and characteristics may play some role in the cause of criminals' antisocial behavior, most believe that social factors are at the root cause of crime. Even the most disturbed people are influenced by their environment and their social interactions and personal relationships.
- *The processes of making laws.* Sutherland and Cressey's definition recognizes the association between crime and the criminal law and shows how the law defines crime. How and why laws are created and why some are strengthened and others eliminated is of great interest to criminologists.
- *Breaking laws and reacting toward the breaking of laws.* At its core, the purpose of criminology is to understand both the onset of crime and the most effective methods for its elimination. Why do people commit illegal acts, and what can be done to convince them—and others who are contemplating crime—that it is in their best interests to turn their back on criminality? These concepts are naturally bound together: it is impossible to effectively control crime unless we understand its cause.
- *Development of a body of general and verified principles.* Sutherland and Cressey recognize that criminology is a social science and criminologists must use the **scientific method** when conducting research. Criminologists are required to employ valid and reliable experimental designs and sophisticated data analysis techniques or else lose standing in the academic community.

Criminology and Criminal Justice

Although the terms *criminology* and *criminal justice* may seem similar, and people often confuse the two or lump them together, there are major differences between these fields of study. Criminology explains the etiology (origin), extent, and nature of crime in society, whereas criminal justice refers to the study of the agencies of social control—police, courts, and corrections. While criminologists are mainly concerned with identifying the suspected cause of *crime*, criminal justice scholars spend their time identifying effective methods of *crime control*.

Since both fields are crime-related, they do overlap. Some criminologists devote their research to **justice** and social control and are concerned with how the agencies of justice operate, how they influence crime and criminals, and how justice policies shape crime rates and trends. Conversely, criminal justice experts often want to design effective programs of crime prevention or rehabilitation and to do so must develop an understanding of the nature

of crime and its causation. It is common, therefore, for criminal justice programs to feature courses on criminology and for criminology courses to evaluate the agencies of justice.

Criminology and Deviance

Criminology is also related to the study of deviant behaviors—those actions that depart from social norms, values, and beliefs. Included within the broad spectrum of deviant acts are behaviors ranging from violent crimes to joining a nudist colony. However, significant distinctions can be made between these two areas of study because many crimes are not unusual or deviant, and many deviant acts are neither illegal nor criminal.

Take, for instance, substance abuse. Selling and/or possessing recreational drugs, such as marijuana, may be illegal, but can it actually be considered deviant? A significant percentage of the population have used or are using drugs; more than half of all high school students have tried drugs before they graduate.[4] Therefore, it is erroneous to argue that all crimes are deviant behaviors that depart from the norms of society.

Similarly, many deviant acts are not criminal even though they may be both disturbing and shocking to the conscience. Suppose a passerby witnesses someone floundering in the ocean and makes no rescue attempt. Most people would condemn the onlooker's coldhearted behavior as callous, immoral, and deviant. However, no legal action could be taken since a private citizen is not required by law to risk his or her own life to save another's. There is no legal requirement that a person rush into a burning building, brave a flood, or jump into the ocean to save someone from harm. They may be deviant and not share commonly held values, but according to the law, they are not criminals.

In sum, criminologists are concerned with the concept of deviance and its relationship to criminality, whereas those sociologists who study deviant behaviors often want to understand and/or identify the line that separates criminal from merely unusual behaviors. The shifting definition of deviant behavior is closely associated with our concepts of crime. The relationships among criminology, criminal justice, and deviance are illustrated in Concept Summary 1.1.

> The principal purpose of the **Office on National Drug Control Policy (ONDCP)** is to establish policies, priorities, and objectives for the nation's drug control program, the goals of which are to reduce illicit drug use, manufacturing, and trafficking; reduce drug-related crime and violence; and reduce drug-related health consequences. For more information about the United States' program for controlling drugs, visit the Criminal Justice CourseMate at cengagebrain.com, then access the "Web Links" for this chapter.

Criminology: Criminal Justice and Deviance

Criminology

Criminology explores the etiology (origin), extent, and nature of crime in society. Criminologists are concerned with identifying the nature, extent, and cause of crime.

Criminal Justice

Criminal justice refers to the agencies of social control that handle criminal offenders. Criminal justice scholars engage in describing, analyzing, and explaining operations of the agencies of justice, specifically the police departments, courts, and correctional facilities. They seek more effective methods of crime control and offender rehabilitation.

Overlapping Areas of Concern

Criminal justice experts cannot begin to design effective programs of crime prevention or rehabilitation without understanding the nature and cause of crime. They require accurate criminal statistics and data to test the effectiveness of crime control and prevention programs.

Deviance

Deviance refers to the study of behavior that departs from social norms. Included within the broad spectrum of deviant acts are behaviors ranging from violent crimes to joining a nudist colony. Not all crimes are deviant or unusual acts, and not all deviant acts are illegal.

Overlapping Areas of Concern

Under what circumstances do deviant behaviors become crimes? When does sexually oriented material cross the line from merely suggestive to obscene and therefore illegal? If an illegal act becomes a norm, should society reevaluate its criminal status? There is still debate over the legalization and/or decriminalization of abortion, recreational drug use, possession of handguns, and assisted suicide.

WHAT CRIMINOLOGISTS DO: THE CRIMINOLOGICAL ENTERPRISE

Regardless of their theoretical orientation, criminologists are devoted to the study of crime and criminal behavior. As two noted criminologists, Marvin Wolfgang and Franco Ferracuti, put it: "A criminologist is one whose professional training, occupational role, and pecuniary reward are primarily concentrated on a scientific approach to, and study and analysis of, the phenomenon of crime and criminal behavior."[5]

Because criminologists have been trained in diverse fields, several subareas reflecting different orientations and perspectives are now contained within the broader arena of criminology. Taken together, these subareas make up the **criminological enterprise**. Criminologists may specialize in a subarea in the same way that psychologists might specialize in a subfield of psychology, such as cognition, development, perception, personality, psychopathology, or sexuality.

Criminal Statistics and Crime Measurement

The subarea of criminal statistics and crime measurement involves devising valid and reliable measures designed to calculate the amount and trends of criminal activity: How much crime occurs annually? Who commits it? When and where does it occur? Which crimes are the most serious? Criminologists:

- Formulate techniques for collecting and analyzing institutional (police, court, and correctional agency) records and data.
- Develop survey instruments to measure criminal activity not reported to the police by victims. These instruments can by used to estimate the percentage of people who commit crimes but escape detection by the justice system.
- Identify the victims of crime; create surveys designed to have victims report loss and injury that may not have been reported to the police.
- Develop data that can be used to test crime theory. For example, measuring community-level crime rates can help prove whether ecological factors, such as neighborhood poverty and unemployment rates, are related to crime rates.

Those criminologists who devote themselves to criminal statistics engage in a number of different tasks, including:

- Devising accurate methods of collecting crime data
- Using these tested methods to measure the amount and trends of criminal activity
- Using valid crime data to determine who commits crime and where it occurs
- Measuring the effect of social policy and social trends on crime rate changes
- Using crime data to design crime prevention programs and then measuring their effectiveness

The media love to sensationalize crime and report on lurid cases of murder and rape. The general public is influenced by these stories, becoming fearful and altering their behavior to avoid victimization.[6] These news accounts, proclaiming crime waves, are often driven by the need to sell newspapers or increase TV viewership. There is nothing like an impending crime wave or serial killer on the loose to boost readership or viewership. Media accounts therefore can be biased and inaccurate, and it is up to criminologists to set the record straight. Criminologists try to create valid and reliable measurements of criminal behavior. They create techniques to access the records of police and court agencies and use sophisticated statistical methods to understand underlying patterns and trends. They develop survey instruments and then use them with large samples to determine the actual number of crimes being committed and the number of victims who suffer criminal violations: how many people are victims of crime, and what percentage reports the crime to police.

Criminologists are also interested in helping agents of the criminal justice system develop effective crime control policies that rely on accurate measurement of crime rates. By using advanced statistical techniques to calculate where crime will take place, police departments can allocate patrol officers based on these predictions.[7]

The development of valid methods to measure crime and the accuracy of crime data are crucial aspects of the criminological enterprise. Without valid and reliable crime data sources, efforts to conduct research on crime and create criminological theories would be futile. It is also important to determine why crime rates vary across and within regions in order to gauge the association between social and economic forces and criminal activity.

About 10.5 million crimes were reported in 2009, a drop of more than 4 million reported crimes since the 1991 peak, and this despite a boost of about 50 million in the general population. Are the crime trends and patterns experienced in the United States unique or do they occur in other cultures as well? This issue is explored in the accompanying Race, Culture, Gender, and Criminology feature.

Sociology of Law, Law and Society, Socio-Legal Studies

The sociology of law, also referred to as the study of law and society, is a subarea of criminology concerned with the role social forces play in shaping criminal law and, concomitantly, the role of criminal law in shaping society. Criminologists interested in studying the social aspects of law focus on such topics as:

- The history of legal thought
- How social forces shape the definition and content of the law
- The impact of legal change on society
- The relationship between law and social control
- The effect of criminalization/legalization on behaviors

Some criminologists who study law and society consider the role of law in the context of criminological theory. They try to understand how legal decision making influences individuals, groups, and the criminal justice system. Others try to identify alternatives to traditional legal process—for example, by designing nonpunitive methods of dispute resolution. Some seek to describe the legal system and identify and explain patterns of behavior that guide its operation. Others use the operations of law as a perspective for understanding culture and social life.[8]

Because the law is constantly evolving, criminologists are often asked to determine whether legal change is required and what shape it should take. Criminologists may use their research skills to assess the effects of a proposed legal change. Take for instance the crime of obscenity. Typically, there is no uniform standard of what is considered obscene; material that to some people is lewd and offensive may be considered a work of art by others. How far should the law go in curbing "adult films" and literature? Criminologists might conduct research aimed at determining the effect the proposed law will have on curbing access to obscene material such as child pornography. Other relevant research issues might include analysis of the harmful effects of viewing pornography: Are people who view pornography more likely to commit violent crime than non-watchers? And what about the effect of virtual porn? Is viewing computer-generated sexual imagery the same as viewing live actors? The answers may one day shape the direction of legislation controlling sexual content on the Internet.

Computer fraud, file sharing, ATM theft, and cyberstalking did not exist when the nation was founded. Consequently, the law must be revised to reflect cultural, societal, and technological changes. In fact, the Supreme Court has often considered empirical research supplied by criminologists on such topics as racial discrimination in the death penalty before it renders an opinion.[9] The research conducted by criminologists then helps shape the direction of their legal decision making. Might the research discussed in the accompanying Policy and Practice in Criminology box influence the shape of the criminal law and how it is applied?

Theory Construction and Testing

Social theory can be defined as a systematic set of interrelated statements or principles that explain some aspect of social life. At their core, theories should serve as models or frameworks for understanding human behavior and the forces that shape its content and direction.

Because, ideally, theories are based on verified *social facts*—readily observed phenomena that can be consistently quantified and measured—criminological theorists use the scientific method to test their theories. They gather data, derive *hypotheses*—testable expectations of behavior that can be derived from the theory—and then test them using valid empirical research methods. For example, social learning theory (see Chapter 7) states that people learn behavior through both observation and experience. If this statement is accurate, then logically there should be a significant association between observing domestic abuse, experiencing child abuse, and becoming an abuser. To test this theory, a number of hypotheses can be derived:

H1: People who are abused as children will grow up to become abusive parents.

H2: People who observe domestic abuse in their childhood will grow up to become abusers themselves.

Although the United States once led the Western world in overall crime, there has been a marked decline in U.S. crime rates, which are now below those of other industrial nations, including England and Wales, Denmark, and Finland.

Making international comparisons is often difficult because the legal definitions of crime vary from country to country. There are also differences in the way crime is measured. For example, in the United States, crime may be measured by counting criminal acts reported to the police or by using victim surveys, whereas in many European countries, the number of cases solved by the police is used as the measure of crime. Despite these problems, valid comparisons can still be made about crime across different countries using a number of reliable data sources. For example, the United Nations Survey of Crime Trends and Operations of Criminal Justice Systems (UNCJS) is one of the best-known sources of information on cross-national data. There is also the United Nations International Study on the Regulation of Firearms. INTERPOL, an international police agency, collects data from police agencies in 179 countries. The World Health Organization (WHO) has conducted surveys on global violence. The *European Sourcebook of Crime and Criminal Justice Statistics* provides data from police agencies in 36 European nations. Finally, the International Crime Victims Survey (ICVS) is conducted in 60 countries and managed by the Ministry of Justice of the Netherlands, the Home Office of the United Kingdom, and the United Nations Interregional Crime and Justice Research Institute, and has become a reliable source of cross-cultural crime and victimization trends.

What do these data sources tell us about crime in other cultures? The ICVS is perhaps the best source today on determining crime and victimization rates and trends. According to the most recent ICVS, an estimated 16 percent of the population in the nations included in the survey have been a victim of at least one of ten common crimes (such as burglary, robbery, theft, assault) in the course of the last year. The countries with the highest scores are Ireland, England and Wales, New Zealand, and Iceland. Lowest overall victimization rates are found in Spain, Japan, Hungary, and Portugal. Similar to the United States, there has been a distinct downward trend in the level of crime and victimization during the past decade. Also, as in the U.S., some cities have much higher crime rates than others: the cities in developed countries with the lowest victimization rates are Hong Kong, Lisbon, Budapest, Athens, and Madrid; highest victimization rates are found in London and Tallinn, Estonia. The drops are most pronounced in property crimes such as vehicle-related crimes (bicycle theft, thefts from cars, and joyriding) and burglary. In most countries, crime rates are back at the level of the late 1980s. One reason is that people around the world are taking precautions to prevent crime. Improved security may well have been one of the main forces behind the universal drop in crimes such as joyriding and household burglary.

What do the cross-national data tell us about individual crimes?

Homicide

Many nations, especially those experiencing social or economic upheaval, have murder rates much higher than the United States. Colombia has about 63 homicides per 100,000 people, and South Africa has 51, compared to fewer than 6 in the United States. During the 1990s, there were more homicides in Brazil than in the United States, Canada, Italy, Japan, Australia, Portugal, Britain, Austria, and Germany combined. Why are murder rates so high in Brazil? Law enforcement officials link the upsurge in violence to drug trafficking, gang feuds, vigilantism, and disputes over trivial matters, in which young, unmarried, uneducated males are involved.

Rape

Violence against women is related to economic hardship and the social status of women. Rates are high in poor nations in which women are oppressed. Where women are more emancipated, the rates of violence against women are lower.

H3: The more serious and prolonged the observed abuse, the more likely those abused will become abusive themselves.

H4: Child abuse and domestic abuse are intergenerational. Abusers are the offspring of abusers and become the parents of abusers.

To test this theory, criminologists might conduct a longitudinal study to determine if (a) people who abuse their spouses and children were abused themselves in childhood and (b) whether the parents of abusers were abused in childhood by their parents.

Sometimes criminologists use innovative methods to test theory. For example, to determine whether abuse is a learned behavior or a function of some biological abnormality, criminologists Tatia M. C. Lee, Siu-Ching Chan, and Adrian Raine used a magnetic resonance imaging (MRI) device to assess brain function of 10 male batterers and then compared the results with those attained from a similar sample of non-abusers. Brain scanning revealed that batterers showed significantly higher neural hyper-responsivity to the threat stimuli in a variety of regions of the brain. This means that when these hypersensitive men experience even mild provocations from their spouses they are hard-wired to

For many women, sexual violence starts in childhood and adolescence and may occur in the home, school, and community. Studies conducted in a wide variety of nations ranging from Cameroon to New Zealand found high rates of reported forced sexual initiation. In some nations, more than 40 percent of adolescent women and 20 percent of adolescent men report sexual coercion at the hands of family members, teachers, boyfriends, or strangers.

Sexual violence has significant health consequences, including suicide, stress, mental illnesses, unwanted pregnancies, sexually transmitted diseases, HIV/AIDS, self-inflicted injuries, and, in the case of child sexual abuse, adoption of high-risk behaviors such as multiple sexual partners and drug use.

Robbery

Countries with more reported robberies than the United States include England and Wales, Portugal, and Spain. Countries with fewer reported robberies include Germany, Italy, and France, as well as Middle Eastern and Asian nations.

Burglary

The United States has lower burglary rates than Australia, Denmark, Finland, England and Wales, and Canada. It has higher reported burglary rates than Spain, Korea, and Saudi Arabia.

Vehicle Theft

Australia, England and Wales, Denmark, Norway, Canada, France, and Italy now have higher rates of vehicle theft than the United States.

Child Abuse

A World Health Organization report found that child physical and sexual abuse takes a significant toll around the world. In a single year, about 57,000 children under 15 years of age are murdered. The homicide rates for children aged 0 to 4 years were over twice as high as rates among children aged 5 to 14 years. Many more children are subjected to nonfatal abuse and neglect; 8 percent of male and 25 percent of female children up to age 18 experience sexual abuse of some kind.

Gun Crimes

There has been a common assumption that the United States is the most heavily armed nation on earth, but there is new evidence that people around the world are arming themselves in record numbers. Residents in the 15 countries of the European Union have an estimated 84 million firearms. Of these, 67 million (80 percent) are in civilian hands. With a total population of 375 million people, this amounts to 17 guns for every 100 people.

CRITICAL THINKING

1. Although risk factors at all levels of social and personal life contribute to youth violence, young people in all nations who experience change in societal-level factors—such as economic inequalities, rapid social change, and the availability of firearms, alcohol, and drugs—seem the most likely to get involved in violence. Can anything be done to help alleviate these social problems?

2. The United States is notorious for employing much tougher penal measures than European nations. Do you believe our tougher measures would work abroad and should be adopted there as well? Is there a downside to putting lots of people in prison?

SOURCES: Jan van Dijk, John van Kesteren, and Paul Smit, "Criminal Victimisation in International Perspective: Key Findings from the 2004–2005 ICVS and EU ICS, 2008," http://rechten.uvt.nl/icvs/pdffiles/ICVS2004_05.pdf (accessed October 29, 2010); Virendra Kumar and Sarita Kanth, "Bride Burning," Lancet 364 (2004): 18–19; Etienne Krug, Linda Dahlberg, James Mercy, Anthony Zwi, and Rafael Lozano, World Report on Violence and Health, (Geneva: World Health Organization, 2002); Graeme Newman, Global Report on Crime and Justice, (New York: Oxford University Press, 1999).

respond with violence. Rather than being a learned behavior, Lee and his associates conclude there is a neurobiological predisposition to spouse abuse in some men.[10]

Criminal Behavior Systems and Crime Typologies

Criminologists who study criminal behavior systems and crime typologies focus their research on specific criminal types and patterns: violent crime, theft crime, public order crime, and organized crime. Numerous attempts have been made to describe and understand particular crime types. Marvin Wolfgang's famous 1958 study, *Patterns in Criminal Homicide*—considered a landmark analysis of the nature of homicide and the relationship between victim and offender—found that victims often precipitate the incident that results in their death.[11] Edwin Sutherland's analysis of business-related offenses helped coin a new phrase—white-collar crime—to describe economic crime activities.

Criminologists also conduct research on the links between different types of crime and criminals. This is known as a **crime typology**. Some typologies focus on the criminal, suggesting the existence of offender groups, such as

Are Sex Offender Registration Laws Effective?

Criminologists interested in legal studies also evaluate the impact new laws have on society after they have been in effect for awhile. Take for instance the practice of sex offender registration, which requires convicted sex offenders to register with local law enforcement agencies when they move into a community. These are often called Megan's Laws in memory of 7-year-old Megan Kanka, killed in 1994 by sex offender Jesse Timmendequas, who had moved unannounced into her New Jersey neighborhood. Megan's Laws require law enforcement authorities to make information available to the public regarding registered sex offenders, including the offender's name, picture, address, incarceration date, and nature of crime. The information can be published in newspapers or put on a sex offender website.

In *Connecticut Dept. of Public Safety v. Doe* (2003), the U.S. Supreme Court upheld the legality of sex offender registration when it ruled that persons convicted of sexual offenses may be required to register with a state's Department of Public Safety and then be listed on a sex offender registry on the Internet containing registrants' names, addresses, photographs, and descriptions. In a 9–0 opinion upholding the plan, the Court reasoned that, because the law was based on the fact that a defendant had been convicted of a sex offense, disclosing their names on the registry without a hearing did not violate due process.

But while sex offender registration laws may be constitutional and pervasive (they are used in all 50 states), appeal to politicians who may be swayed by media crusades against child molesters (i.e., "To Catch a Predator" on *Dateline NBC*), and appease the public's desire to "do something" about child predators, do they actually work? Does registration deter future sex offenses and reduce the incidence of predatory acts against children?

To answer this question, criminologists Kristen Zgoba and Karen Bachar recently (2009) conducted an in-depth study of the effectiveness of New Jersey's registration law and found that while expensive to maintain, the system did not produce effective results. On the one hand, sex offense rates in New Jersey were in a steep decline before the system was installed and the rate of decline actually slowed down after 1995 when the law took effect. Zgoba and Bachar's data show that the greatest rate of decline in sex offending occurred prior to the passage and implementation of Megan's Law. On the other hand, passage and implementation of Megan's Law did not reduce the number of rearrests for sex offenses, nor did it have any demonstrable effect on the time between when sex offenders were released from prison and the time they were rearrested for any new offense, such as a drug, theft, or another sex offense.

In another effort, Jill Levenson, Elizabeth Letourneau, Kevin Armstrong, and Kristen Zgoba investigated the relationship between failure to register (FTR) as a sex offender and subsequent recidivism with a sample of 3,000 people convicted of sexually related crimes. Levenson and her associates found that there was no significant difference in the proportion of sexual recidivists and nonrecidivists with registration violations nor did FTR predict sexual recidivism. And when there was recidivism, there was no significant difference in time to recidivism when comparing those who failed to register (2.9 years) with compliant registrants (2.8 years).

These results challenge the effectiveness of sex offender registration laws. Rather than deter crime, sex offender laws may merely cause sex offenders to be more cautious while giving parents a false sense of security. For example, offenders may target victims in other states or communities where they are not registered and parents are less cautious.

CRITICAL THINKING

1. Considering the findings of Zgoba and Bachar, would you advocate abandoning sex offender registration laws because they are ineffective? Or might there be other reasons to keep them active?

2. What other laws do you think should be the topic of careful scientific inquiry to see if they actually work as advertised?

SOURCES: Jill Levenson, Elizabeth Letourneau, Kevin Armstrong, and Kristen Zgoba, "Failure to Register as a Sex Offender: Is It Associated with Recidivism?" *Justice Quarterly* 27 (2010): 305–331; *Connecticut Dept. of Public Safety v. Doe*, 538 U.S. 1 (2003); Kristen Zgoba and Karen Bachar, "Sex Offender Registration and Notification: Research Finds Limited Effects in New Jersey," National Institute of Justice, April 2009, www.ncjrs.gov/pdffiles1/nij/225402.pdf (accessed October 29, 2010).

professional criminals, psychotic criminals, amateur criminals, and so on. Others focus on the crimes, clustering them into categories such as property crimes, sex crimes, and so on. While 50 years ago they might have focused their attention on rape, murder, and burglary, they now may be looking at stalking, cybercrime, terrorism, and hate crimes. For example, a number of criminologists are now doing research on terrorism, trying to determine if there is such a thing as a "terrorist personality." Among the findings:

- Mental illness is not a critical factor in explaining terrorist behavior. Also, most terrorists are not "psychopaths."
- There is no "terrorist personality," nor is there any accurate profile—psychologically or otherwise—of the terrorist.

- Histories of childhood abuse and trauma and themes of perceived injustice and humiliation often are prominent in terrorist biographies, but do not really help to explain terrorism.[12]

Research on criminal behavior systems and crime types is important because it enables criminologists to understand why people commit specific sorts of crime, and using this information, gives them the tools to devise crime reduction strategies.

According to the consensus view, crimes are behaviors believed to be repugnant to all elements of society. Do you agree with the artist's implied sentiment that spraying graffiti on a wall is not really a crime? Why do you think this remains an outlawed behavior?

Punishment, Penology, and Social Control

Criminologists also are involved in creating effective crime policies, developing methods of social control, and the correction and control of known criminal offenders; it is this segment of criminology that overlaps criminal justice. Criminologists conduct research that is designed to evaluate justice initiatives in order to determine their efficiency, effectiveness, and impact. For example, should capital punishment continue to be employed or is its use simply too risky? To explore this issue, Samuel Gross and his colleagues looked at death row inmates who were later found to be innocent. The sample of 340 death row inmates (327 men and 13 women), exonerated after having served years in prison, indicated that about half (144 people) were cleared by DNA evidence. Collectively, they had spent more than 3,400 years in prison for crimes they did not commit—an average of more than 10 years each. Gross and his colleagues found that exonerations from death row are more than 25 times more frequent than exonerations for other prisoners convicted of murder, and more than 100 times more frequent than for all imprisoned felons.[13] How many wrongful convictions might be uncovered if all criminal convictions were given the same degree of scrutiny as death penalty cases? The Gross research illustrates how important it is to evaluate penal measures in order to determine their effectiveness and reliability.

Victimology: Victims and Victimization

In two classic criminological studies, one by Hans von Hentig and the other by Stephen Schafer, the critical role of the victim in the criminal process was first identified. These authors were the first to suggest that victim behavior is often a key determinant of crime and that victims' actions may actually precipitate crime. Both men believe that the study of crime is not complete unless the victim's role is considered.[14] For those studying the role of the victim in crime, these areas are of particular interest:

- Using victim surveys to measure the nature and extent of criminal behavior not reported to the police
- Calculating the actual costs of crime to victims
- Measuring the factors that increase the likelihood of becoming a crime victim
- Studying the role of the victim in causing or precipitating crime
- Designing services for the victims of crime, such as counseling and compensation programs

The study of victims and victimization has uncovered some startling results. For one thing, criminals have been found to be at greater risk for victimization than noncriminals.[15] Rather than being the passive receptors of criminal acts who are in the "wrong place at the wrong time," crime victims may engage in high-risk lifestyles that increase their own chance of victimization and make them highly vulnerable to crime.

The various elements of the criminological enterprise are summarized in Concept Summary 1.2.

CONNECTIONS

In recent years, criminologists have devoted ever-increasing attention to the victim's role in the criminal process. It has been suggested that a person's lifestyle and behavior may actually increase the risk that he or she will become a crime victim. Some have suggested that living in a high-crime neighborhood increases risk; others point at the problems caused by associating with dangerous peers and companions. For a discussion of victimization risk, see Chapter 3.

The Criminological Enterprise

These subareas constitute the discipline of criminology:

Criminal Statistics and Research Methodology

Gathering valid crime data. Devising new research methods; measuring crime patterns and trends.

The Sociology of Law/Law and Society

Determining the origin of law. Measuring the forces that can change laws and society.

Theory Construction and Testing

Predicting individual behavior. Understanding the cause of crime rates and trends.

Criminal Behavior Systems and Crime Typologies

Determining the nature and cause of specific crime patterns. Studying violence, theft, organized, white-collar, and public order crimes.

Penology and Social Control

Studying the correction and control of criminal behavior. Using scientific methods to assess the effectiveness of crime control and offender treatment programs.

Victimology/Victims and Victimization

Studying the nature and cause of victimization. Aiding crime victims; understanding the nature and extent of victimization; developing theories of victimization risk.

HOW CRIMINOLOGISTS VIEW CRIME

Professional criminologists usually align themselves with one of several schools of thought or perspectives in their field. Each perspective maintains its own view of what constitutes criminal behavior and what causes people to engage in criminality. This diversity of thought is not unique to criminology; biologists, psychologists, sociologists, historians, economists, and natural scientists disagree among themselves about critical issues in their fields. Considering the multidisciplinary nature of the field of criminology, fundamental issues such as the nature and definition of crime itself are cause for disagreement among criminologists.

A criminologist's choice of orientation or perspective depends, in part, on his or her definition of crime. This section discusses the three most common concepts of crime used by criminologists.

The Consensus View of Crime

According to the **consensus view**, crimes are behaviors believed to be repugnant to all elements of society. The substantive criminal law, which is the written code that defines crimes and their punishments, reflects the values, beliefs, and opinions of society's mainstream. The term *consensus* is used because it implies that there is general agreement among a majority of citizens on what behaviors should be outlawed by the criminal law and henceforth viewed as crimes. As the eminent criminologists Edwin Sutherland and Donald Cressey put it:

> Criminal behavior is behavior in violation of the criminal law.... [I]t is not a crime unless it is prohibited by the criminal law [which] is defined conventionally as a body of specific rules regarding human conduct which have been promulgated by political authority, which apply uniformly to all members of the classes to which the rules refer, and which are enforced by punishment administered by the state.[16]

This approach to crime implies that it is a function of the beliefs, morality, and rules established by the existing legal power structure. According to Sutherland and Cressey's statement, criminal law is applied "uniformly to all members of the classes to which the rules refer." This statement reveals the authors' faith in the concept of an "ideal legal system" that deals adequately with all classes and types of people. Laws prohibiting theft and violence may be directed at the neediest members of society, whereas laws that sanction economic acts such as insider trading, embezzlement, and corporate price-fixing are aimed at controlling the wealthiest. The reach of the criminal law is not restricted to any single element of society.

Social Harm The consensus view of crime links illegal behavior to the concept of **social harm**. Though people generally enjoy a great deal of latitude in their behavior, it is agreed that behaviors that are harmful to other people and society in general must be controlled. Social harm is what sets strange, unusual, or **deviant behavior**—or any other action that departs from social norms—apart from criminal behaviors.[17]

CONNECTIONS

The associations among crime, social harm, and morality are best illustrated in efforts to criminalize acts considered dangerous to the public welfare because they involve behaviors that offend existing social values. These so-called public order crimes include pornography, prostitution, and drug use. Though "victims" are often willing participants, some people believe it is society's duty to save them from themselves. To read more about crime, morality, and social harm, see Chapter 14.

This position is not without controversy. Although it is clear that rape, robbery, and murder are inherently harmful and their control justified, behaviors such as drug use and prostitution are more problematic because the harm they inflict is only on those who are willing participants. According to the consensus view, society is justified in controlling these so-called victimless crimes because public opinion holds that they undermine the social fabric and threaten the general well-being of society. Society has a duty to protect all its members—even those who choose to engage in high-risk behaviors. But are victims always people and how far should we go to protect non-humans? That is the topic addressed in the Thinking like a Criminologist feature.

The Conflict View of Crime

The **conflict view** depicts society as a collection of diverse groups—business owners, workers, professionals, students—who are in constant and continuing conflict. Groups able to assert their political power use the law and the criminal justice system to advance their economic and social position. Criminal laws, therefore, are viewed as acts created to protect the haves from the have-nots. Critical criminologists often compare and contrast the harsh penalties exacted on the poor for their "street crimes" (burglary, robbery, and larceny) with the minor penalties the wealthy receive for their white-collar crimes (securities violations and other illegal business practices), though the latter may cause considerably more social harm. While the poor go to prison for minor law violations, the wealthy are given lenient sentences for even the most serious breaches of law. Rather than being class neutral, criminal law reflects and protects established economic, racial, gendered, and political power and privilege.

Crime, according to this definition, is a political concept designed to protect the power and position of the upper classes at the expense of the poor. Even crimes prohibiting violent acts, such as armed robbery, rape, and murder, may have political undertones. Banning violent acts ensures domestic tranquility and guarantees that the anger of the poor and disenfranchised classes will not be directed at their wealthy capitalist exploiters. According to this conflict view of crime, "real" crimes would include the following acts:

- Violations of human rights due to racism, sexism, and imperialism
- Unsafe working conditions
- Inadequate child care
- Inadequate opportunities for employment and education
- Substandard housing and medical care
- Crimes of economic and political domination
- Pollution of the environment
- Price-fixing
- Police brutality
- Assassinations and war-making
- Violations of human dignity
- Denial of physical needs and necessities, and impediments to self-determination
- Deprivation of adequate food
- Blocked opportunities to participate in political decision making

Cody Watson

On January 10, 2011, Cody Watson, the star quarterback of the Los Angeles Hawks pleaded guilty to charges of criminal conspiracy stemming from his involvement in a dog-fighting ring. Watson had been accused of torturing and executing dogs who lost their matches at his arena. While dog lovers demand that Watson receive the harshest punishment possible, others complain that harsh treatment is uncalled for and unfair. During the sentencing hearing, Watson's lawyer observed that people eat steaks and cheeseburgers all the time. "Isn't it a bit hypocritical to consume the flesh of dead animals, killed for our pleasure, and condemn the behavior of someone accused of killing animals for another purpose?" The attorney went on to note, "Many people are hunters who routinely shoot and kill moose and deer. Why is it legal to hunt and kill defenseless animals if we are so concerned about animal welfare?" He then pointed out such unsavory and brutal activities as fox hunting, raising minks and chinchillas for fur coats, bull fighting, and boiling lobsters alive, all of which are perfectly legal. He addressed the

jokllica/Fotalia

court with this summation, "Why were these practices, which involve the killing of innocent creatures, legal while dog fighting is condemned and its practitioners imprisoned? While some have argued that it is the method of killing that counts, I am not sure that the victims would agree." Despite his plea, Cody Watson was sentenced to 23 months in prison and suspended from his team.

» **The commissioner of the NFL has asked your research team to advise him on whether Watson should be reinstated to the NFL after he completes his sentence. To provide an unbiased account, divide your team into two groups, and have each one make a presentation to the commissioner on Watson's case, one supporting his reinstatement, the other opposed. Address such issues as whether his actions really cause social harm. Is what he did worse than the euthanizing of abandoned dogs because no one stepped forward in time for their adoption?**

The Interactionist View of Crime

The **interactionist view** of crime traces its antecedents to the symbolic interaction school of sociology, first popularized by pioneering sociologists George Herbert Mead, Charles Horton Cooley, and W. I. Thomas.[18] This position holds that (a) people act according to their own interpretations of reality, through which they assign meaning to things; (b) they observe the way others react, either positively or negatively; and (c) they reevaluate and interpret their own behavior according to the meaning and symbols they have learned from others.

According to this perspective, there is no objective reality. People, institutions, and events are viewed subjectively and labeled either good or evil according to the interpretation of the evaluator. Some people might consider the hit film *Borat: Cultural Learnings of America for Make Benefit Glorious Nation of Kazakhstan* as obscene, degrading, and offensive, while others view the same film as a laugh riot. The same interactions help define crime:

- The content of the criminal law and consequently the definition of crime often depend on human interaction and perceptions. Alcohol is legal, marijuana is not. It could easily be the other way around. Gay marriage is legal in some jurisdictions, illegal in others.
- Deciding whether an individual act is considered a crime is also a function of interaction and labeling. When an argument results in the death of one of the participants, a jury may be asked to decide whether the act was murder, self-defense, or merely an accidental fatality. Each person on the jury may have his or her own interpretation of what took place, and whether the act is labeled a crime and the actor a criminal depends on the juror's interpretation of events.

The process in which people are defined or labeled as criminal is also subjective. One person is viewed as an unrepentant hard-core offender and sent to a maximum security prison. Another, who has committed essentially the same crime, is considered remorseful and repentant and given probation in the community. Though their acts are similar, the treatment they receive is quite different. In a classic statement, sociologist Howard Becker argued, "The deviant is one to whom that label has successfully been applied; deviant behavior is behavior people so labeled."[19] According to the interactionist view, the definition of crime reflects the preferences and opinions of people who hold social power in a particular legal jurisdiction. These **moral entrepreneurs** wage campaigns (*moral crusades*) to control behaviors they view as immoral and wrong (e.g., abortion) or, conversely, to legalize behaviors they consider harmless social eccentricities (e.g., carrying a handgun for self-protection; smoking pot). Because drug use offends their moral sense, it is currently illegal to purchase marijuana and hashish, while liquor and cigarettes are sold openly, even though far more people die of alcoholism and smoking than from drug abuse each year.[20] Even the definition of serious violent offenses, such as rape and murder, depends on the prevailing moral values of those who shape the content of the criminal law. For example, Florida has implemented a "stand your ground law" that legalizes the killing of an unarmed thief or intruder if the person is found in the owner's parked car; in other states, shooting an unarmed person merely because he or she was sitting in your car might be considered murder. Fifty years ago, a man could not be prosecuted for raping his wife; today, every state criminalizes marital rape. In sum, the definition of crime is more reflective of prevailing moral values than of any objective standard of right and wrong.

The interactionist view of crime is similar to the conflict perspective; both suggest that behavior is outlawed and considered criminal when it offends people who hold social, economic, and political power. However, unlike the conflict view, the interactionist perspective does not attribute capitalist economic and political motives to the process of defining crime. Laws against pornography, prostitution, and drugs are believed to be motivated more by moral crusades than by economic values.

The three main views of crime are summarized in Concept Summary 1.3.

Defining Crime

It is possible to take elements from each school of thought to formulate an integrated definition of crime, such as this one:

> Crime is a violation of societal rules of behavior as interpreted and expressed by a criminal legal code

CONCEPT SUMMARY 1.3

The Definition of Crime

The definition of crime affects how criminologists view the cause and control of illegal behavior and shapes their research orientation.

Conflict View
- The law is a tool of the ruling class.
- Crime is a politically defined concept.
- "Real crimes" are not outlawed.
- The law is used to control the underclass.

Consensus View
- The law defines crime.
- The law reflects public opinion.
- Agreement exists on outlawed behavior.
- Laws apply to all citizens equally.

Interactionist View
- Moral entrepreneurs define crime.
- Crimes are illegal because society defines them that way.
- The definition of crime evolves according to the moral standards of those in power.

created by people holding social and political power. Individuals who violate these rules are subject to sanctions by state authority, social stigma, and loss of status.

This definition combines the consensus position that the criminal law defines crimes with the conflict perspective's emphasis on political power and control and the interactionist concept of labeling and stigma. Thus crime, as defined here, is a political, social, and economic function of modern life.

CRIME AND THE LAW

No matter which definition of crime we embrace, criminal behavior is tied to the law. It is therefore important for all criminologists to have some understanding of the development of law, its objectives, its elements, and how it has evolved.

A Brief History of the Law

The concept of criminal law has been recognized for more than 3,000 years. Hammurabi (1792–1750 BCE), the sixth king of Babylon, created the most famous set of written laws of the ancient world, known today as the Code of Hammurabi. Preserved on basalt rock columns, the code established a system of crime and punishment based on physical retaliation ("an eye for an eye"). The severity of punishment depended on class standing: if convicted of an unprovoked assault, a slave would be killed, whereas a freeman might lose a limb.

More familiar is the Mosaic Code of the Israelites (1200 BCE). According to tradition, God entered into a covenant or contract with the tribes of Israel in which they agreed to obey his law (the 613 laws of the Old Testament, including the Ten Commandments), as presented to them by Moses, in return for God's special care and protection. The Mosaic Code is not only the foundation of Judeo-Christian moral teachings but also a basis for the U.S. legal system. Prohibitions against murder, theft, and perjury preceded by several thousand years the same laws found in the modern United States.

Though ancient formal legal codes were lost during the Dark Ages, early German and Anglo-Saxon societies developed legal systems featuring monetary compensation for criminal violations. Guilt was determined by two methods. One was compurgation, in which the accused person swore an oath of innocence with the backing of 12 to 25 oath helpers, who would attest to his or her character and claims of innocence. The second was trial by ordeal, which was based on the principle that divine forces would not allow an innocent person to be harmed. It involved such measures as having the accused place his or her hand in boiling water or hold a hot iron. If the wound healed, the person was found innocent; if the wound did not heal, the accused was deemed guilty. Another version, trial by combat, allowed the accused to challenge his accuser to a duel, with the outcome determining the legitimacy of the accusation. Punishments included public flogging, branding, beheading, and burning.

Common Law

After the Norman conquest of England in 1066, royal judges began to travel throughout the land, holding court in each shire several times a year. When court was in session, the royal administrator, or judge, would summon a number of citizens who would, on their oath, tell of the crimes and serious breaches of the peace that had occurred since the judge's last visit. The royal judge would then decide what to do in each case, using local custom and rules of conduct as his guide. Courts were bound to follow the law established in previous cases unless a higher authority, such as the king or the pope, overruled the law.

The present English system of law came into existence during the reign of Henry II (1154–1189), when royal judges began to publish their decisions in local cases. Judges began to use these written decisions as a basis for their decision making, and eventually a fixed body of legal rules and principles was established. If a new rule was successfully applied in a number of different cases, it would become a precedent. These precedents would then be commonly applied in all similar cases—hence the term **common law**. Crimes such as murder, burglary, arson, and rape are common-law crimes whose elements were initially defined by judges. They are referred to as *mala in se*, inherently evil and depraved. When the situation required it, the English Parliament enacted legislation to supplement the judge-made common law. These were referred to as statutory or *mala prohibitum* crimes, which reflected existing social conditions. English common law evolved constantly to fit specific incidents that the judges encountered. For example, in the *Carriers* case (1473), an English court ruled that a merchant who had been hired to transport merchandise was guilty of larceny (theft) if he kept the goods for his own purposes.[21] Before the *Carriers* case, it was not considered a crime under the common law when people kept something that was voluntarily placed in their possession, even if the rightful owner had only given them temporary custody of the merchandise. Breaking with legal tradition, the court acknowledged that the commercial system could not be maintained unless the laws of theft were expanded. The definition of larceny was altered in order to meet the needs of a growing free enterprise economic system. The definition of theft was changed to include the taking of goods not only by force or stealth but also by embezzlement and fraud.

The Law in Contemporary Society

In contemporary U.S. society, the law governs almost all phases of human enterprise, including commerce, family life, property transfer, and the regulation of interpersonal conflict. It contains elements that control personal relationships between individuals and public relationships between individuals and the government. The former is known as *civil law*, and the latter is called *criminal law*. The law then can generally be divided into four broad categories:

- *Substantive criminal law.* The branch of the law that defines crimes and their punishment is known as **substantive criminal law**. It involves such issues as the mental and physical elements of crime, crime categories, and criminal defenses.
- *Procedural criminal law.* Those laws that set out the basic rules of practice in the criminal justice system are **procedural criminal laws**. Some elements of the law of criminal procedure are the rules of evidence, the law of arrest, the law of search and seizure, questions of appeal, jury selection, and the right to counsel.
- *Civil law.* The set of rules governing relations between private parties, including both individuals and organizations (such as business enterprises or corporations), is known as **civil law**. The civil law is used to resolve, control, and shape such personal interactions as contracts, wills and trusts, property ownership, and commerce. Contained within the civil law is tort law discussed in Exhibit 1.1.
- *Public or administrative law.* The branch of law that deals with the government and its relationships with individuals or other governments is known as **public law**. It governs the administration and regulation of city, county, state, and federal government agencies.

The four categories of the law can be interrelated. A crime victim may file a tort action against a criminal defendant and sue for damages in a civil court. Under tort law, a crime victim may sue even if the defendant is found not guilty because the evidentiary standard in a civil action is less than is needed for a criminal conviction (preponderance of the evidence versus beyond a reasonable doubt). In some instances, the government has the option to pursue a legal matter through the criminal process, file a tort action, or bring the matter before an administrative court. White-collar crimes often involve criminal, administrative, and civil penalties.

Shaping the Criminal Law

Before the American Revolution, the colonies, then under British rule, were subject to the common law. After the colonies won their independence, state legislatures standardized common-law crimes such as murder, burglary, arson, and rape by putting them into statutory form in criminal codes. As in England, whenever common law proved inadequate to deal with changing social and moral issues, the states and Congress supplemented it with legislative statutes. Similarly, statutes prohibiting such offenses as the sale and possession of narcotics or the pirating of DVDs have been passed to control human behavior unknown at the time the common law was formulated. Today, criminal behavior is defined primarily by statute. With few exceptions, crimes are removed, added, or modified by the legislature of a particular jurisdiction.

The content of the law may also be shaped by judicial decision making. A criminal statute may be no longer enforceable when an appellate judge rules that it is vague, deals with an act no longer of interest to the public, or is an unfair exercise of state control over an individual. Conversely, a judicial ruling may expand the scope of an existing criminal law, thereby allowing control over behaviors that heretofore were beyond its reach. In a famous 1990 case, 2 Live Crew (made up of Luther Campbell, Christopher Wong Won, Mark Ross, and David Hobbs), a prominent rap group, found its sales restricted in Florida as police began arresting children under 18 for purchasing the band's sexually explicit CD *As Nasty as They Want to Be*. The hit single "Me So Horny" was banned from local radio stations. Prosecutors tried but failed to get a conviction after group members were arrested at a concert. If members of the Crew had in fact been found guilty and the conviction had been upheld by the state's highest appellate court, obscenity laws would have been expanded to cover people singing (or rapping) objectionable music lyrics.

Constitutional Limits   Regardless of its source, all criminal law in the United States must conform to the rules and dictates of the U.S. Constitution.[22] Any criminal law that even appears to conflict with the various provisions and articles of the Constitution must reflect a compelling need to protect public safety or morals.[23]

Criminal laws have been interpreted as violating constitutional principles if they are too vague or too broad to give clear meaning of their intent. A law forbidding adults to engage

---

EXHIBIT 1.1

Types of Torts

1. *Intentional torts* are injuries that the person knew or should have known would occur through his or her actions—e.g., a person attacks and injures another (assault and battery) after a dispute.
2. *Negligent torts* are injuries caused because a person's actions were unreasonably unsafe or careless—e.g., a traffic accident is caused by a reckless driver.
3. *Strict liability torts* are injuries that occur because a particular action causes damage prohibited by statute—e.g., a victim is injured because a manufacturer made a defective product.

in "immoral behavior" could not be enforced because it does not use clear and precise language or give adequate notice as to which conduct is forbidden.[24] The Constitution also prohibits laws that make a person's status a crime. Becoming or being a heroin addict is not a crime, although laws can forbid the sale, possession, and manufacture of heroin.

The Constitution limits laws that are overly cruel and/or capricious. Whereas the use of the death penalty may be constitutionally approved, capital punishment would be forbidden if it were used for lesser crimes such as rape or employed in a random, haphazard fashion.[25] Cruel ways of executing criminals that cause excessive pain are likewise forbidden. One method used to avoid "cruelty" is lethal injection. In the 2008 case *Baze and Bowling v. Rees*, the Court upheld the use of lethal injection unless there is a "substantial risk of serious harm" that the drugs will not work effectively.[26]

One of the categories described in Exhibit 1.2 are so-called inchoate or incomplete crimes, such as attempt, solicitation, and conspiracy. The accompanying Profiles in Crime feature discusses the crime of conspiracy.

EXHIBIT 1.2

Definitions of Common-Law Crimes

Crime	Definition	Example
Crimes Against the Person		
First-degree murder	Unlawful killing of another human being with malice aforethought and with premeditation and deliberation.	A woman buys poison and pours it into a cup of coffee her husband is drinking, intending to kill him for the insurance benefits.
Voluntary manslaughter	Intentional killing committed under extenuating circumstances that mitigate the killing, such as killing in the heat of passion after being provoked.	A husband coming home early from work finds his wife in bed with another man. The husband goes into a rage and shoots and kills both lovers with a gun he keeps by his bedside.
Battery	Unlawful touching of another with intent to cause injury.	A man seeing a stranger sitting in his favorite seat in a cafeteria, goes up to that person and pushes him out of the seat.
Assault	Intentional placing of another in fear of receiving an immediate battery.	A student aims an unloaded gun at her professor and threatens to shoot. He believes the gun is loaded.
Rape	Unlawful sexual intercourse with a female without her consent.	After a party, a man offers to drive a female acquaintance home. He takes her to a wooded area and, despite her protests, forces her to have sexual relations with him.
Robbery	Wrongful taking and carrying away of personal property from a person by violence or intimidation.	A man armed with a loaded gun approaches another man on a deserted street and demands his wallet.
Inchoate (Incomplete) Offenses		
Attempt	An intentional act for the purpose of committing a crime that is more than mere preparation or planning of the crime. The crime is not completed, however.	A person places a bomb in the intended victim's car so that it will detonate when the ignition key is used. The bomb is discovered before the car is started. Attempted murder has been committed.
Conspiracy	Voluntary agreement between two or more persons to achieve an unlawful object or to achieve a lawful object using means forbidden by law.	A doctor conspires with a con man to fake accidents and then bring the false "victims" to his office so he can collect medical fees from an insurance company.
Solicitation	With the intent that another person engage in conduct constituting a felony, a person solicits, requests, commands, or otherwise attempts to cause that person to engage in such conduct.	A terrorist approaches a person he believes is sympathetic to his cause and asks him to join in a plot to blow up a government building.
Crimes Against Property		
Burglary	Trespassory breaking and entering of a dwelling house of another in the nighttime with the intent to commit a felony.	Intending to steal some jewelry and silver, a young man breaks a window and enters another's house at 10 P.M.
Arson	Intentional burning of a dwelling house of another.	A worker, angry that her boss did not give her a raise, goes to her boss's house and sets it on fire.
Larceny	Taking and carrying away the personal property of another with the intent to keep and possess the property.	While shopping, a woman sees a diamond ring displayed at the jewelry counter. When no one is looking, the woman takes the ring, places it in her pocket, and walks out of the store without paying.

SOURCE: Developed by Therese J. Libby, J.D.

Robert Snyder

James Venziale

Mark Williams

On July 13, 2010, three Philadelphia police officers, Robert Snyder, Mark Williams, and James Venziale, were indicted for their involvement in a drug conspiracy. The scheme was put in play in April when Venziale met with reputed drug dealer Angel "Fat Boy" Ortiz near the North Philadelphia Amtrak station. Venziale and Ortiz discussed a plan to steal, with the illegal assistance of Philadelphia police officers, 300 grams of heroin from Miguel Santiago, their supplier. On

May 14, 2010, immediately after Santiago's drug courier delivered 300 grams of heroin to Ortiz, Officers Williams and Venziale—who were on duty and in uniform—stopped Ortiz's vehicle and seized the shipment. Williams and Venziale faked arresting Ortiz and handcuffed him outside his car, while Santiago's men looked on in disgust. The fake arrest made it appear as if they were seizing the heroin, thereby protecting Ortiz from retaliation. The deal was facilitated by

a fourth conspirator, Christal Snyder, Robert Snyder's wife, who passed information, via telephone or text message, between Ortiz and the police officers. In return for getting the 300 grams of heroin without payment to Santiago, Ortiz paid Williams and Venziale approximately $6,000, and paid Christal Snyder an additional amount. Unfortunately for all those involved, Ortiz sold the stolen heroin to a drug dealer and money launderer who turned out to be a Drug Enforcement Administration (DEA) undercover agent. Conspiracies of this magnitude are not punished lightly, and the sentences the conspirators face range from 44 years (Robert Snyder) to 212 years ("Fat Boy" Ortiz) in prison.

SOURCE: Matt Flegenheimer and Robert Moran, "3 City Officers Charged in Heroin Scheme," *Philadelphia Inquirer*, July 13, 2010, www.philly.com/philly/news/breaking/98344124.html (accessed October 30, 2010).

The Substantive Criminal Law

The substantive criminal law defines crime and punishment. Each state and the federal government has its own substantive criminal code, developed over many generations and incorporating moral beliefs, social values, and political, economic, and other societal concerns.

Criminal laws are divided into felonies and misdemeanors. The distinction is based on seriousness: a felony is a serious offense; a misdemeanor is a minor or petty crime. Crimes such as murder, rape, and burglary are felonies; they are punished with long prison sentences or even death. Crimes such as unarmed assault and battery, petty larceny, and disturbing the peace are misdemeanors; they are punished with a fine or a period of incarceration in a county jail.

Regardless of their classification, acts prohibited by the criminal law constitute behaviors considered unacceptable and impermissible by those in power. People who engage in these acts are eligible for severe sanctions. By outlawing these behaviors, the government expects to achieve a number of social goals:

- *Enforcing social control.* Those who hold political power rely on criminal law to formally prohibit behaviors

believed to threaten societal well-being or to challenge their authority. For example, U.S. criminal law incorporates centuries-old prohibitions against the following behaviors harmful to others: taking another person's possessions, physically harming another person, damaging another person's property, and cheating another person out of his or her possessions. Similarly, the law prohibits actions that challenge the legitimacy of the government, such as planning its overthrow, collaborating with its enemies, and so on.

- *Discouraging revenge.* By punishing people who infringe on the rights, property, and freedom of others, the law shifts the burden of revenge from the individual to the state. As Oliver Wendell Holmes stated, this prevents "the greater evil of private retribution."[27] Although state retaliation may offend the sensibilities of many citizens, it is greatly preferable to a system in which people would have to seek justice for themselves.

- *Expressing public opinion and morality.* Criminal law reflects constantly changing public opinions and moral values. *Mala in se* crimes, such as murder and forcible rape, are almost universally prohibited; however, the prohibition of legislatively created *mala prohibitum* crimes, such as traffic offenses and gambling violations, changes according to social conditions and attitudes. Criminal law is used to codify these changes.

- *Deterring criminal behavior.* Criminal law has a social control function. It can control, restrain, and direct human behavior through its sanctioning power. The threat of punishment associated with violating the law is designed to prevent crimes before they occur. During the Middle Ages, public executions drove this point home. Today criminal law's impact is felt through news accounts of long prison sentences and an occasional execution.

- *Punishing wrongdoing.* The deterrent power of criminal law is tied to the authority it gives the state to sanction or punish offenders. Those who violate criminal law are subject to physical coercion and punishment.

- *Maintaining social order.* All legal systems are designed to support and maintain the boundaries of the social system they serve. In medieval England, the law protected the feudal system by defining an orderly system of property transfer and ownership. Laws in some socialist nations protect the primacy of the state by strictly curtailing profiteering and individual enterprise. Our own capitalist system is also supported and sustained by criminal law. In a sense, the content of criminal law is more a reflection of the needs of those who control the existing economic and political system than a representation of some idealized moral code.

- *Providing restoration.* Victims deserve restitution or compensation for their pain and loss. The criminal law can be used to restore to victims what they have lost. Because we believe in equity and justice, it is only fair that the guilty help repair the harm they have caused others by their crimes. Punishments such as fines, forfeiture, and restitution are connected to this legal goal.

Some of the elements of the contemporary criminal law are discussed in The Criminological Enterprise feature "The Elements of Criminal Law."

The Evolution of Criminal Law

The criminal law is constantly evolving in an effort to reflect social and economic conditions. Sometimes legal changes are prompted by highly publicized cases that generate fear and concern. A number of highly publicized cases of celebrity stalking, including Robert John Bardo's fatal shooting of actress Rebecca Schaeffer on July 18, 1989, prompted more than 25 states to enact **stalking statutes** that prohibit "the willful, malicious, and repeated following and harassing of another person."[28] Similarly, after 7-year-old Megan Kanka of Hamilton Township, New Jersey, was killed in 1994 by a repeat sexual offender who had moved into her neighborhood, the federal government passed legislation requiring that the general public be notified of local pedophiles (sexual offenders who target children).[29] California's sexual predator law, which took effect on January 1, 1996, allows

people convicted of sexually violent crimes against two or more victims to be committed to a mental institution after their prison terms have been served.[30]

The criminal law may also change because of shifts in culture and social conventions, reflecting a newfound tolerance of behavior condemned only a few years before. In an important 2003 case, *Lawrence v. Texas*, the Supreme Court declared that laws banning sodomy were unconstitutional because they violated the due process rights of citizens because of their sexual orientation. In its decision, the Court said:

> Although the laws involved . . . here . . . do not more than prohibit a particular sexual act, their penalties and purposes have more far-reaching consequences, touching upon the most private human conduct, sexual behavior, and in the most private of places, the home. They seek to control a personal relationship that, whether or not entitled to formal recognition in the law, is within the liberty of persons to choose without being punished as criminals. The liberty protected by the Constitution allows homosexual persons the right to choose to enter upon relationships in the confines of their homes and their own private lives and still retain their dignity as free persons.

As a result of the decision, all sodomy laws in the United States are now unconstitutional and therefore unenforceable.[31]

What are some of the new laws that are being created and old ones that have been eliminated?

Stalking Laws More than 25 states have enacted stalking statutes, which prohibit and punish acts described typically as "the willful, malicious, and repeated following and harassing of another person."[32] Stalking laws were originally formulated to protect women terrorized by former husbands and boyfriends, although celebrities are often plagued by stalkers as well. In celebrity cases, these laws often apply to stalkers who are strangers or casual acquaintances of their victims.

Prohibiting Assisted Suicide Some laws are created when public opinion turns against a previously legal practice. Physician-assisted suicide became the subject of a national debate when Dr. Jack Kevorkian began practicing what he calls *obitiatry*, helping people take their own lives.[33] In an attempt to stop Kevorkian, Michigan passed a statutory ban on assisted suicide, reflecting what lawmakers believed to be prevailing public opinion.[34] Kevorkian was released on June 1, 2007, on parole due to good behavior. He died on June 3, 2011; he was 83 years old. Forty-four states now disallow assisted suicide either by statute or common law, including Michigan.[35]

Registering Sex Offenders Some legal changes have been prompted by public outrage over a particularly heinous crime. One of the most well known is Megan's Law, named after 7-year-old Megan Kanka of Hamilton Township,

Although each state and the federal government have unique methods of defining crime, there are significant uniformities and similarities that shape the essence of almost all criminal law codes. Although the laws of California, Texas, and Maine may all be somewhat different, the underlying concepts that guide and shape their legal systems are universal. The question remains: regardless of jurisdictional boundaries, what is the legal definition of a crime and how does the criminal law deal with it?

Legal Definition of a Crime

Today, in all jurisdictions, the legal definition of a crime involves the elements of the criminal acts that must be proven in a court of law if the defendant is to be found guilty. For the most part, common criminal acts have both mental and physical elements, both of which must be present if the act is to be considered a legal crime. In order for a crime to occur, the state must show that the accused committed the guilty act, or *actus reus*, and had the *mens rea*, or criminal intent, to commit the act. The *actus reus* may be an aggressive act, such as taking someone's money, burning a building, or shooting someone; or it may be a failure to act when there is a legal duty to do so, such as a parent neglecting to seek medical attention for a sick child. The *mens rea* (guilty mind) refers to an individual's state of mind at the time of the act or, more specifically, the person's intent to commit the crime.

Actus Reus

To satisfy the requirements of *actus reus*, guilty actions must be voluntary. Even though an act may cause harm or damage, it is not considered a crime if it was done by accident or was an involuntary act. For example, it would not be a crime if a motorist obeying all the traffic laws hit a child who ran into the street. If the same motorist were drinking or speeding, then his action would be considered a vehicular crime because it was a product of negligence. Similarly, it would not be considered a crime if a babysitter accidentally dropped a child and the child died. However, it would be considered manslaughter if the sitter threw the child down in anger or frustration and the blow caused the child's death. In some circumstances of *actus reus*, the use of words is considered criminal. In the crime of sedition, the words of disloyalty constitute the *actus reus*. If a person falsely yells "fire" in a crowded theater and people are injured in the rush to exit, that person is held responsible for the injuries, because the use of the word in that situation constitutes an illegal act.

Typically, the law does not require people to aid others in distress, such as entering a burning building to rescue people trapped by a fire. However, failure to act is considered a crime in certain instances:

- *Relationship of the parties based on status.* Some people are bound by relationship to give aid. These relationships include parent/child and husband/wife. If a husband finds his wife unconscious because she took an overdose of sleeping pills, he is obligated to save her life by seeking medical aid. If he fails to do so and she dies, he can be held responsible for her death.
- *Imposition by statute.* Some states have passed laws requiring people to give aid. For example, a person who observes a broken-down automobile in the desert but fails to stop and help the other parties involved may be committing a crime.
- *Contractual relationships.* These relationships include lifeguard and swimmer, doctor and patient, and babysitter or au pair and child. Because lifeguards have been hired to ensure the safety of swimmers, they have a legal duty to come to the aid of drowning persons. If a lifeguard knows a swimmer is in danger and does nothing about it and the swimmer drowns, the lifeguard is legally responsible for the swimmer's death.

Mens Rea

In most situations, for an act to constitute a crime, it must be done with criminal intent, or *mens rea*. Intent, in the legal sense, can mean carrying out an act intentionally, knowingly, and willingly. However, the definition also encompasses situations in which recklessness or negligence establishes the required criminal intent.

New Jersey, who was killed in 1994. Charged with the crime was a convicted sex offender, who, unknown to the Kankas, lived across the street. On May 17, 1996, President Bill Clinton signed Megan's Law, which contained two components:

1. *Sex offender registration.* A revision of the 1994 Jacob Wetterling Act, which had required the states to register individuals convicted of sex crimes against children, also established a community notification system.
2. *Community notification.* States were compelled to make private and personal information on registered sex offenders available to the public.

Variations of Megan's Law have been adopted by all 50 states. Although civil libertarians have expressed concern that notification laws may interfere with an offender's post-release privacy rights, recent research indicates that registered offenders find value in Megan's Law because it helps deter future abuse. When DNA collection is included in the law, it helps reduce false accusations and convictions.[36]

Clarifying Rape Sometimes laws are changed to clarify the definition of crime and to quell public debate over the boundaries of the law. When does bad behavior cross

Criminal intent also exists if the results of an action, although originally unintended, are certain to occur. When Timothy McVeigh planted a bomb in front of the Murrah Federal Building in Oklahoma City, he did not intend to kill any particular person in the building. Yet the law would hold that McVeigh or any other person would be substantially certain that people in the building would be killed in the blast, and McVeigh therefore had the criminal intent to commit murder.

Strict Liability

Though common-law crimes require that both the *actus reus* and the *mens rea* must be present before a person can be convicted of a crime, several crimes defined by statute do not require *mens rea*. In these cases, the person accused is guilty simply by doing what the statute prohibits; intent does not enter the picture. These strict liability crimes, or public welfare offenses, include violations of health and safety regulations, traffic laws, and narcotic control laws. For example, a person stopped for speeding is guilty of breaking the traffic laws regardless of whether he or she intended to go over the speed limit or did it by accident. The underlying purpose of these laws is to protect the public; therefore, intent is not required.

Criminal Defenses

When people defend themselves against criminal charges, they must refute one or more of the elements of the crime of which they have been accused. A number of different approaches can be taken to create this defense.

First, defendants may deny the *actus reus* by arguing that they were falsely accused and that the real culprit has yet to be identified. Second, defendants may claim that although they engaged in the criminal act of which they are accused, they lacked the *mens rea* (intent) needed to be found guilty of the crime.

If a person whose mental state is impaired commits a criminal act, it is possible for the person to excuse his or her criminal actions by claiming that he or she lacked the capacity to form sufficient intent to be held criminally responsible. Insanity, intoxication, and ignorance are types of excuse defenses. A defendant might argue that because he suffered from a mental impairment that prevented him from understanding the harmfulness of his acts, he lacked sufficient *mens rea* to be found guilty as charged.

Another type of defense is justification. Here the individual usually admits committing the criminal act but maintains that he or she should not be held criminally liable because the act was justified. Among the justification defenses are necessity, duress, self-defense, and entrapment. A battered wife who kills her mate might argue that she acted out of duress; her crime was committed to save her own life.

Persons standing trial for criminal offenses may thus defend themselves by claiming that they did not commit the act in question, that their actions were justified under the circumstances, or that their behavior can be excused by their lack of *mens rea*. If either the physical or mental elements of a crime cannot be proven, then the defendant cannot be convicted.

CRITICAL THINKING

1. Should the concept of the "guilty mind" be eliminated from the criminal law and replaced with a strict liability standard? (If you do the crime, you do the time.)

2. Some critics believe that current criminal defenses, such as the battered wife defense or the insanity defense, allow people to go free even though they committed serious criminal acts and are actually guilty as charged. Do you agree?

SOURCES: Joshua Dressler, *Cases and Materials on Criminal Law* (American Casebook Series) (Eagan, MN: West Publishing, 2003); Joel Samaha, *Criminal Law* (Belmont, CA: Wadsworth Publishing, 2001).

the line into criminality, and when does it remain merely bad behavior? An example of the former can be found in changes to the law of rape. In seven states, including California, it is now considered rape if the victim consents to sex, the sex act begins, the victim changes his/her mind during the act and tells his/her partner to stop, and the partner refuses and continues. The fact that the victim initially consented to and participated in a sexual act does not bar him/her from withdrawing that consent. However, the victim must communicate the withdrawal of consent in such a manner that the accused knew or reasonably should have known that the consent was withdrawn. Before the legal change, such a circumstance was not considered rape but merely aggressive sex.[37]

Controlling Technology   Changing technology and the ever-increasing role of technology in people's daily lives will require modifications of the criminal law. Such technologies as automatic teller machines and cellular phones have already spawned a new generation of criminal acts involving theft of access numbers and software piracy. For example, a modification to Virginia's Computer Crimes Act that took effect in 2005 makes *phishing*—sending out bulk e-mail messages designed to trick consumers into revealing bank

AP Images, Jane Roseberg

Cheng Chui Ping was one of the most powerful underworld figures in New York. Known as "the Mother of all Snakeheads"—meaning she was top dog in the human smuggling trade—to her friends in Chinatown she was "Sister Ping."

Cheng was an illegal immigrant herself. Born in 1949 in the poor farming village of Shengmei in Fujian province, she left her husband and family behind and set out for the West, traveling via Hong Kong and Canada before ending up in New York in 1981.

She opened a grocery store and started other ventures that became fronts for her people-trafficking business. For more than a decade, Cheng smuggled as many as 3,000 illegal immigrants from her native China into the United States—charging upwards of $40,000 per person. To ensure her clients paid their smuggling fees, Sister Ping hired members of the Fuk Ching, Chinatown's most feared gang, to transport and guard them in the United States.

In addition to running her own operation, Sister Ping helped other smugglers by financing large vessels designed for human cargo. She also ran a money transmitting business out of her Chinatown variety store. She used this business to collect smuggling fees from family members of her own "customers," and also collected ransom money on behalf of other alien smugglers.

Conditions aboard the smuggling vessels were often inhumane. The voyages were dangerous, and on at least one occasion a boat capsized while offloading people to a larger vessel, and 14 of her "customers" drowned. The *Golden Venture*, a smuggling ship Sister Ping helped finance for others, was intentionally grounded off the coast of Rockaway, Queens, when the offloading vessel failed to meet it in the open sea. Many of the passengers could not swim, and 10 people drowned.

Cheng Chui Ping was indicted when members of the Fuk Ching gang cooperated with federal agents. After her indictment, Cheng fled to China, where she continued to run a smuggling operation. Hong Kong police arrested her at the airport. Cheng fought extradition but was eventually delivered to the United States. She was convicted in New York less than two years later on multiple counts, including money laundering, conspiracy to commit alien smuggling, and other smuggling-related offenses, and was sentenced to 35 years in prison.

The activities of Sister Ping illustrate how the law must evolve to confront newly emerging social problems such as illegal immigration. Other areas include cybercrime, drug importation, and terrorism. Unfortunately, the law is sometimes slow to change, and change comes only after conditions have reached a crisis. How might laws be changed to reduce illegal immigration? Should people caught entering the country illegally be charged with a felony and imprisoned?

SOURCES: FBI News release, "Sister Ping Sentenced to 35 Years in Prison for Alien Smuggling, Hostage Taking, Money Laundering and Ransom Proceeds Conspiracy," March 16, 2006, http://www.justice.gov/usao/nys/pressreleases/March06/sisterpingsentencingpr.pdf (accessed October 31, 2010); BBC news, "Cheng Chui Ping: 'Mother of Snakeheads,'" http://news.bbc.co.uk/2/hi/americas/4816354.stm (accessed October 31, 2010).

account passwords, Social Security numbers, and other personal information—a felony. Those convicted of selling the data or using the data to commit another crime, such as identity theft, now face twice the prison time.

Protecting the Environment In response to the concerns of environmentalists, the federal government has passed numerous acts designed to protect the nation's well-being. The Environmental Protection Agency has successfully prosecuted significant violations of these and other new laws, including data fraud cases (e.g., private laboratories submitting false environmental data to state and federal environmental agencies); indiscriminate hazardous waste dumping that resulted in serious injuries and death; industrywide ocean dumping by cruise ships; oil spills that caused significant damage to waterways, wetlands, and beaches; and illegal handling of hazardous substances such as pesticides and asbestos that exposed children, the poor, and other especially vulnerable groups to potentially serious illness.[38]

Legalizing Marijuana A number of states are now exploring the legalization of marijuana for medical purposes. For example, New Jersey Senate Bill 119, signed into law on January 18, 2010, is typical of changes in the law. The bill protects "patients who use marijuana to alleviate suffering from debilitating medical conditions, as well as their physicians, primary caregivers, and those who are authorized to produce marijuana for medical purposes" from "arrest, prosecution, property forfeiture, and criminal and other penalties." It also provides for the creation of alternative treatment centers, "at least two each in the northern, central, and southern regions of the state. The first two centers issued a permit in each region shall be nonprofit entities, and centers subsequently issued permits may be nonprofit or for-profit entities." The bill allows marijuana to be prescribed for a variety of illnesses ranging from severe chronic pain, nausea, and vomiting to terminal illnesses such as cancer. Physicians determine how much marijuana a patient needs and give written instructions to be presented to an alternative treatment center. The maximum amount for a 30-day period is two ounces.[39] According to the Drug Policy Alliance, Alaska, California, Colorado, Hawaii, Maine, Michigan, Montana, Nevada, New Mexico, Oregon, Rhode Island, Vermont, and Washington have created laws that effectively remove state-level criminal penalties for growing and/or possessing medical marijuana. Another ten states, plus the District of Columbia, have symbolic medical marijuana laws (laws that support medical marijuana but do not provide patients with legal protection under state law).[40]

While providing medical marijuana has strong public support, the federal government still criminalizes any use of marijuana, and federal agents can arrest users even if they have prescriptions from doctors in states where medical marijuana is legal. The Supreme Court ruled in 2005 in *Gonzales v. Raich* that the federal government can prosecute medical marijuana patients, even in states with compassionate use laws.[41] The Court ruled that under the Commerce Clause of the United States Constitution, which allows the United States Congress "To regulate Commerce . . . among the several States," Congress may ban the use of cannabis even where states approve its use for medicinal purposes. The reasoning: because of high demand, marijuana grown for medical reasons would find its way into the hands of ordinary drug users. So while the law may change on a local or state level, federal rules take precedent.

Responding to Terrorism   The criminal law has also undergone extensive change in both substance and procedure in the aftermath of the September 11, 2001, terrorist attacks. These acts will be discussed further in Chapter 18.

The future direction of U.S. criminal law remains unclear. Certain actions, such as crimes by corporations and political corruption, will be labeled as criminal and given more attention. Other offenses, such as recreational drug use, may be reduced in importance or removed entirely from the criminal law system. The globalization of crime will present even more challenges, as described in the Profiles in Crime feature "The Mother of All Snakeheads."

ETHICAL ISSUES IN CRIMINOLOGY

A critical issue facing students of criminology involves recognizing the field's political and social consequences. All too often, criminologists forget the social responsibility they bear as experts in the area of crime and justice. When government agencies request their views of issues, their pronouncements and opinions become the basis for sweeping social policy. The lives of millions of people can be influenced by criminological research data.

Debates over gun control, capital punishment, and mandatory sentences are ongoing and contentious. Some criminologists have successfully argued for social service, treatment, and rehabilitation programs to reduce the crime rate, but others consider them a waste of time, suggesting instead that a massive prison construction program coupled with tough criminal sentences can bring the crime rate down. By accepting their roles as experts on law-violating behavior, criminologists place themselves in a position of power; the potential consequences of their actions are enormous. Therefore, they must be aware of the ethics of their profession and be prepared to defend their work in the light of public scrutiny. Major ethical issues include these:

- What to study?
- Whom to study?
- How to study?

What to Study?

Under ideal circumstances, when criminologists choose a subject for study, they are guided by their own scholarly interests, pressing social needs, the availability of accurate data, and other similar concerns. Nonetheless, in recent years, a great influx of government and institutional funding has influenced the direction of criminological inquiry. Major sources of monetary support include the Justice Department's National Institute of Justice, the National Science Foundation, and the National Institute of Mental Health. Private foundations, such as the Edna McConnell Clark Foundation, have also played an important role in supporting criminological research.

Though the availability of research money has spurred criminological inquiry, it has also influenced the direction research has taken. State and federal governments provide a significant percentage of available research funds, and they may also dictate the areas that can be studied. In recent years, for example, the federal government has spent millions of dollars funding long-term cohort studies of criminal careers. Consequently, academic research has recently focused on criminal careers. Other areas of inquiry may be ignored because there is simply not enough funding to pay for or sponsor the research.

A potential conflict of interest may arise when the institution funding research is itself one of the principal subjects of the research project. Governments may be reluctant to fund research on fraud and abuse of power by government officials. They may also exert a not-so-subtle influence on the criminologists seeking research funding: if criminologists are too critical of the government's efforts to reduce or counteract crime, perhaps they will be barred from receiving further financial help. This situation is even more acute when we consider that criminologists typically work for universities or public agencies and are under pressure to bring in a steady flow of research funds or to maintain the continued viability of their agency. Even when criminologists maintain discretion of choice, the direction of their efforts may not be truly objective. The objectivity of research may be questioned if studies are funded by organizations that have a vested interest in the outcome of the research. For example, a study on the effectiveness of the defensive use of handguns to stop crime may be tainted if the funding for the project comes from a gun manufacturer whose sales may be affected by the research findings. Efforts to show that private prisons are more effective than state correctional facilities might be tainted if the researchers received a research grant from a corporation that maintains private prisons.

Whom to Study?

A second major ethical issue in criminology concerns who will be the subject of inquiries and study. Too often, criminologists focus their attention on the poor and minorities while ignoring the middle-class criminal who may be committing white-collar crime, organized crime, or government crime. Critics have charged that by "unmasking" the poor and desperate, criminologists have justified any harsh measures taken against them. For example, a few social scientists have suggested that criminals have lower intelligence quotients than the average citizen, and that because minority group members have lower than average IQ scores, their crime rates are high.[42] This was the conclusion reached in *The Bell Curve*, a popular though highly controversial book written by Richard Herrnstein and Charles Murray.[43] Although such research is often methodologically unsound, it brings to light the tendency of criminologists to focus on one element of the community while ignoring others. The question that remains is whether it is ethical for criminologists to publish biased or subjective research findings, paving the way for injustice.

How to Study?

Ethics are once again questioned in cases where subjects are misled about the purpose of the research. When white and African American individuals are asked to participate in a survey of their behavior or an IQ test, they are rarely told in advance that the data they provide may later be used to prove the existence of significant racial differences in their self-reported crime rates. Should subjects be told about the true purpose of a survey? Would such disclosures make meaningful research impossible? How far should criminologists go when collecting data? Is it ever permissible to deceive subjects to collect data? Criminologists must take extreme care when they select subjects for their research studies to ensure that they are selected in an unbiased and random manner.[44]

When criminological research efforts involve experimentation and treatment, care must be taken to protect those subjects who have been chosen for experimental and control groups. For example, it may be unethical to provide a special treatment program for one group while depriving others of the same opportunity. Conversely, criminologists must be careful to protect subjects from experiments that may actually cause them harm. An examination of the highly publicized Scared Straight program, which brought youngsters into contact with hard-core prison inmates who gave them graphic insights into prison life (to scare them out of a life of crime), discovered that the young subjects may have been harmed by their experience. Rather than being frightened into conformity, subjects actually increased their criminal behavior.[45]

SUMMARY

1. **Understand what is meant by the "field of criminology"**
   - Criminology is the scientific approach to the study of criminal behavior and society's reaction to law violations and violators. It is an academic discipline that uses the scientific method to study the nature, extent, cause, and control of criminal behavior. Criminology is an interdisciplinary science. Criminologists hold degrees in a variety of fields, most commonly sociology, but also criminal justice, political science, psychology, economics, engineering, and the natural sciences. Criminology is a fascinating field, encompassing a wide variety of topics that have both practical application and theoretical importance.

2. **Be familiar with the various elements of the criminological enterprise**
   - The various subareas included within the scholarly discipline of criminology, taken as a whole, define the field of study. The subarea of criminal statistics/crime measurement involves calculating the amount of, and trends in, criminal activity. Sociology of law/law and society/socio-legal studies is a subarea of criminology concerned with the role that social forces play in shaping criminal law and the role of criminal law in shaping society. Criminologists also explore the causes of

crime. Another subarea of criminology involves research on specific criminal types and patterns: violent crime, theft crime, public order crime, organized crime, and so on. The study of penology, correction, and sentencing involves the treatment of known criminal offenders. Criminologists recognize that the victim plays a critical role in the criminal process and that the victim's behavior is often a key determinant of crime.

3. **Know the difference between crime and deviance**
   - Criminologists devote themselves to measuring, understanding, and controlling crime and deviance. Deviance includes a broad spectrum of behaviors that differ from the norm, ranging from the most socially harmful to the relatively inoffensive. Criminologists are often concerned with the concept of deviance and its relationship to criminality.

4. **Discuss the three different views of crime**
   - According to the consensus view, crimes are behaviors that all elements of society consider repugnant. This view holds that the majority of citizens in a society share common values and agree on what behaviors should be defined as criminal. The conflict view depicts criminal behavior as being defined by those in power to protect and advance their own self-interest. According to the interactionist view, those with social power are able to impose their values on society as a whole, and these values then define criminal behavior.

5. **Know what constitutes the different categories of law**
   - Substantive criminal law involves such issues as the mental

and physical elements of crime, crime categories, and criminal defenses. Procedural criminal law sets out the basic rules of practice in the criminal justice system. It includes the rules of evidence, the law of arrest, the law of search and seizure, questions of appeal, jury selection, and the right to counsel. The civil law governs relations between private parties, including both individuals and organizations (such as business enterprises and/or corporations), and is used to resolve, control, and shape such personal interactions as contracts, wills and trusts, property ownership, personal disputes (torts), and commerce. Administrative laws are enforced by governmental agencies such as the IRS or EPA.

6. **Discuss the different purposes of criminal law**
   - The criminal law serves several important purposes. It represents public opinion and moral values. It enforces social controls. It deters criminal behavior and wrongdoing. It punishes transgressors. It creates equity and abrogates the need for private retribution.

7. **Trace the development of criminal law**
   - The criminal law used in U.S. jurisdictions traces its origin to the English system. At first the law of precedent was used to decide conflicts on a case-by-case basis during the middle ages. Judges began to use these written decisions as a basis for their decision making, and eventually a fixed body of legal rules and principles was established. If a new rule was successfully applied in a number of different cases, it would become a precedent. These precedents would then be commonly

applied in all similar cases—hence the term *common law*. In the U.S. legal system, lawmakers have codified common-law crimes into state and federal penal codes.

8. **Describe the difference between a felony and a misdemeanor**
   - A felony is a serious offense that carries a penalty of imprisonment, usually for one year or more, and may entail loss of political rights. A misdemeanor is a minor crime usually punished by a short jail term and/or a fine.

9. **Recognize the relationship between the criminal law and the U.S. Constitution**
   - All criminal law in the United States must conform to the rules and dictates of the U.S. Constitution. Criminal laws have been interpreted as violating constitutional principles if they are too vague or too broad to give clear meaning of their intent. The Constitution also prohibits laws that make a person's status a crime. The Constitution limits laws that are overly cruel or capricious.

10. **Be familiar with the ethical issues in criminology**
   - Ethical issues arise when information-gathering methods appear biased or exclusionary. These issues may cause serious consequences because research findings can significantly affect individuals and groups. Criminologists must be concerned about the topics they study. Another ethical issue in criminology revolves around the selection of research subjects. A third area of concern involves the methods used in conducting research.

KEY TERMS

criminology (4)
criminologists (4)
criminal justice (4)
scientific method (5)
justice (5)
criminological enterprise (6)
crime typology (9)

consensus view (12)
social harm (12)
deviant behavior (12)
conflict view (13)
interactionist view (14)
moral entrepreneurs (14)
common law (15)

mala in se (15)
mala prohibitum (15)
substantive criminal law (16)
procedural criminal law (16)
civil law (16)
public law (16)
stalking statutes (19)

CRITICAL THINKING QUESTIONS

1. Beccaria argued that the threat of punishment controls crime. Are there other forms of social control? Aside from the threat of legal punishments, what else controls your own behavior?

2. What research method would you employ if you wanted to study drug and alcohol abuse at your own school?

3. Would it be ethical for a criminologist to observe a teenage gang by "hanging" with them, drinking, and watching as they steal cars? Should he or she report that behavior to the police?

4. Can you identify behaviors that are deviant but not criminal? What about crimes that are illegal but not deviant?

5. Do you agree that some of the most damaging acts in society are not punished as crimes? If so, what are they?

6. If you could change the criminal law, what behaviors would you legalize? What would you criminalize? What might be the consequences of your actions—in other words, are there any hidden drawbacks?

NOTES

1. CNN, "Missing Teen's Mother Leaves Aruba," August 1, 2005, www.cnn.com/2005/LAW/07/31/aruba.missing (accessed October 31, 2010).

2. John Hagan and Alberto Palloni, "Sociological Criminology and the Mythology of Hispanic Immigration and Crime," *Social Problems* 46 (1999): 617–632.

3. Edwin Sutherland and Donald Cressey, *Principles of Criminology*, 6th Ed. (Philadelphia: J. B. Lippincott, 1960), p. 3.

4. Monitoring the Future, "Teen Marijuana Use Tilts Up, While Some Drugs Decline in Use," December 14, 2009, http://monitoringthefuture.org/pressreleases/09drugpr_complete.pdf (accessed October 31, 2010).

5. Marvin Wolfgang and Franco Ferracuti, *The Subculture of Violence* (London: Social Science Paperbacks, 1967), p. 20.

6. Mirka Smolej and Janne Kivivuori, "The Relation between Crime News and Fear of Violence," *Journal of Scandinavian Studies in Criminology and Crime Prevention* 7 (2006): 211–227.

7. Jacqueline Cohen, Wilpen Gorr, and Andreas Olligschlaeger, "Leading Indicators and Spatial Interactions: A Crime-Forecasting Model for Proactive Police Deployment," *Geographical Analysis* 39 (2007): 105–127.

8. The Sociology of Law Section of the American Sociological Association, www.departments.bucknell.edu/soc_anthro/soclaw/textfiles/Purpose_soclaw.txt (accessed October 31, 2010).

9. Rosemary Erickson and Rita Simon, *The Use of Social Science Data in Supreme Court Decisions* (Champaign, IL: University of Illinois Press, 1998).

10. Tatia M. C. Lee, Siu-Ching Chan, and Adrian Raine, "Hyperresponsivity to Threat Stimuli in Domestic Violence Offenders: A Functional Magnetic Resonance Imaging Study," *Journal of Clinical Psychiatry* 70 (2009): 36–45.

11. Marvin Wolfgang, *Patterns in Criminal Homicide* (Philadelphia: University of Pennsylvania Press, 1958).

12. Randy Borum, *Psychology of Terrorism* (Tampa: University of South Florida, 2004). Available at www.ncjrs.gov/pdffiles1/nij/grants/208552.pdf (accessed October 31, 2010).

13. Samuel Gross, Kristen Jacoby, Daniel Matheson, Nicholas Montgomery, and Sujata Patil, "Exonerations in the United States, 1989 through 2003," *Journal of Criminal Law and Criminology* 95 (2005): 523–559.

14. Hans von Hentig, *The Criminal and His Victim* (New Haven: Yale University Press, 1948); Stephen Schafer, *The Victim and His Criminal* (New York: Random House, 1968).

15. Linda Teplin, Gary McClelland, Karen Abram, and Darinka Mileusnic, "Early Violent Death among Delinquent Youth: A Prospective Longitudinal Study," *Pediatrics* 115 (2005): 1586–1593.

16. Edwin Sutherland and Donald Cressey, *Criminology*, 6th Ed. (Philadelphia: J. B. Lippincott, 1960), p. 8.

17. Charles McCaghy, *Deviant Behavior* (New York: MacMillan, 1976), pp. 2–3.

18. See Herbert Blumer, *Symbolic Interactionism* (Englewood Cliffs, NJ: Prentice Hall, 1969).

19. Howard Becker, *Outsiders: Studies in the Sociology of Deviance* (New York: Free Press, 1963), p. 9.

20. The National Council on Alcoholism and Drug Dependence, www.ncadd.org (accessed October 31, 2010).

21. *Carriers* Case, 13 Edward IV 9.pL.5 (1473).

22. See John Weaver, *Warren—The Man, the Court, the Era* (Boston: Little, Brown, 1967); see also "We the People," *Time*, July 6, 1987, p. 6.

23. *Kansas v. Hendricks*, 117 S.Ct. 2072 (1997); *Chicago v. Morales*, 119 S.Ct. 246 (1999).

24. *City of Chicago v. Morales et al.*, 527 U.S. 41 (1999).

25. Daniel Suleiman, "The Capital Punishment Exception: A Case for Constitutionalizing the Substantive Criminal Law," *Columbia Law Review* 104 (2004): 426–458.

26. *Baze and Bowling v. Rees*, 553 U.S. ___ (2008).

27. Oliver Wendell Holmes, *The Common Law*, ed. Mark De Wolf (Boston: Little, Brown, 1881), p. 36.

28. National Institute of Justice, *Project to Develop a Model Anti-Stalking Statute* (Washington, DC: National Institute of Justice, 1994).

29. "Clinton Signs Tougher 'Megan's Law,'" *CNN News Service*, May 17, 1996.

30. Associated Press, "Judge Upholds State's Sexual Predator Law," *Bakersfield Californian*, October 2, 1996.

31. *Lawrence et al. v. Texas*, No. 02-102. June 26, 2003.

32. National Institute of Justice, *Project to Develop a Model Anti-Stalking Statute*.

33. Marvin Zalman, John Strate, Denis Hunter, and James Sellars, "Michigan Assisted Suicide Three Ring Circus: The Intersection of Law and Politics," *Ohio Northern Law Review* 23 (1997): 863–903.

34. 1992 P.A. 270, as amended by 1993 P.A.3, M.C. L. ss. 752.1021 to 752. 1027.

35. Michigan Code of Criminal Procedure, "Assisting a Suicide," Section 750.329a.

36. Sarah Welchans, "Megan's Law: Evaluations of Sexual Offender Registries," *Criminal Justice Policy Review* 16 (2005): 123–140.

37. Matthew Lyon, "No Means No? Withdrawal of Consent During Intercourse and the Continuing Evolution of the Definition of Rape," *Journal of Criminal Law and Criminology* 95 (2004): 277–314.

38. Environmental Protection Agency, Criminal Enforcement Division, www.epa.gov/compliance/criminal/ (accessed October 31, 2010).

39. State of New Jersey 213th Legislature, Senate Bill 119, http://medicalmarijuana.procon.org/sourcefiles/NJS119.pdf (accessed October 31, 2010).

40. Drug Policy Alliance Network, Medical Marijuana, www.drugpolicy.org/marijuana/medical/ (accessed October 31, 2010).

41. *Gonzales v. Raich*, 545 U.S. 1, 2005.

42. See, for example, Michael Hindelang and Travis Hirschi, "Intelligence and Delinquency: A Revisionist Review," *American Sociological Review* 42 (1977): 471–486.

43. Richard Herrnstein and Charles Murray, *The Bell Curve* (New York: Free Press, 1994).

44. Victor Boruch, Timothy Victor, and Joe Cecil, "Resolving Ethical and Legal Problems in Randomized Experiments," *Crime and Delinquency* 46 (2000): 330–353.

45. Anthony Petrosino, Carolyn Turpin-Petrosino, and James Finckenauer, "Well-Meaning Programs Can Have Harmful Effects! Lessons from Experiments of Programs Such as Scared Straight," *Crime and Delinquency* 46 (2000): 354–379.

AP Images/*The Athens Banner-Herald* Athens, David Manning

ON April 25, 2009, George Zinkhan, 57, killed his wife, Marie Bruce, and two other people, Thomas Tanner and Ben Teague, as they exited a reunion picnic of the Town and Gown Players theater group in Athens, Georgia. Zinkhan then fled the scene and eluded a police manhunt until his body was located in a rural area two weeks later. It seems that Zinkhan had dug a shallow grave, covered himself with twigs and leaves, and then committed suicide by shooting himself in the head. At first the shootings seemed inexplicable, but news reports later indicated that George and Marie were having marital problems and that George suspected Tanner, a Clemson University economics professor, of being romantically involved with Marie; the third victim, Ben Teague, was simply "at the wrong place, at the wrong time."

The Nature and Extent of Crime

2

Chapter Outline

Learning Objectives

1. Be familiar with the various forms of crime data
2. Know the problems associated with collecting data
3. Be able to discuss recent trends in the crime rate
4. Be familiar with the factors that influence crime rates
5. Compare crime rates under different ecological conditions
6. Be able to discuss the association between social class and crime
7. Know what is meant by the term *aging out process*
8. Recognize that there are gender and racial patterns in crime
9. Be familiar with Wolfgang, Figlio, and Sellin's pioneering research on chronic offending
10. Understand the suspected causes of chronicity

Although romantic triangles have been the basis of violence for quite some time (when Catherine Howard cheated on her husband, Henry VIII, with his friend Thomas Culpeper, he had them both beheaded), what made this case unusual was the social and educational standing of those involved. George Zinkhan received his Ph.D. from the University of Michigan, became a distinguished professor of marketing at the University of Georgia, had authored numerous books and scholarly articles, and was serving as editor of a prestigious business journal. Marie Bruce, his wife, was a highly regarded attorney in Athens, Georgia. Thomas Tanner had earned a master's degree in economics at Iowa State University in Ames, Iowa, and his Ph.D. in economics at the University of Georgia; he was director of the Center for Economic Modeling at Clemson University.[1]

Stories such as the Athens shooting, splashed across the media and rehashed on nightly talk shows, help convince most Americans that we live in a violent society. If a well-known professor kills three people, including his wife, is anyone safe? When people read headlines about a violent crime spree, they begin to fear crime and take steps to protect themselves, perhaps avoiding public places and staying at home in the evening.[2] When asked if they fear walking in their neighborhood at night, more than one third of all American citizens say yes.[3] About one quarter say they bought a gun for self-protection, and more than 10 percent claim they carry guns for defense.[4]

Are Americans justified in their fear of violent crime? Should they barricade themselves behind armed guards? Are crime rates actually rising or falling? Where do most crimes occur and who commits them? To answer these and similar questions, criminologists have devised elaborate methods of crime data collection and analysis. Without accurate data on the nature and extent of crime, it would not be possible to formulate theories that explain the onset of crime or to devise social policies that facilitate its control or elimination. Accurate data collection is also critical in assessing the nature and extent of crime, tracking changes in the crime rate, and measuring the individual and social factors that may influence criminality.

In this chapter, we review how crime data are collected on criminal offenders and offenses and what this information tells us about crime patterns and trends. We also examine the concept of criminal careers and discover what available crime data can tell us about the onset, continuation, and termination of criminality.

PRIMARY SOURCES OF CRIME DATA

We begin with a discussion of the primary sources of crime data routinely used by criminologists around the globe, including official records and national surveys collected, compiled, and analyzed by government agencies such as the federal government's Bureau of Justice Statistics and the Federal Bureau of Investigation (FBI). Criminologists use these techniques to measure the nature and extent of criminal behavior and the personality, attitudes, and background of criminal offenders. It is important to understand how these data are collected to gain insight into how professional criminologists approach various problems and questions in their field. What are these primary sources, how are they collected, and how valid are their findings?

Official Records: The Uniform Crime Report

In order to understand more about the nature and extent of crime, criminologists use the records of government agencies such as police departments, prisons, and courts. Official record data can be used to examine crime rates and trends. They can also be analyzed to uncover the individual and social forces that affect crime: to study the relationship between crime and poverty, for example, criminologists might use income and family data from the United States Census Bureau and then cross-reference this information with crime data collected by local police departments. The most important crime record data are collected from local law enforcement agencies by the Federal Bureau of Investigation (FBI) and published yearly in their **Uniform Crime Report (UCR)**.

> For access to the **Bureau of Justice Statistics'** web page, visit the Criminal Justice CourseMate at cengagebrain.com, then access the "Web Links" for this chapter.

The UCR includes both crimes reported to local law enforcement departments and the number of arrests made by police agencies. The UCR is the best known and most widely cited source of official criminal statistics.[5] The FBI receives and compiles records from more than 17,000 police departments serving a majority of the U.S. population. Its major unit of analysis involves **index crimes**, or **Part I crimes**: murder and nonnegligent manslaughter, forcible rape, robbery, aggravated assault, burglary, larceny, arson, and motor vehicle theft. Exhibit 2.1 defines these crimes.

The FBI tallies and annually publishes the number of reported offenses by city, county, standard metropolitan statistical area, and geographical divisions of the United States. In addition to recording crimes reported to the police, the UCR also collects data on the number and characteristics (age, race, and gender) of individuals who have been arrested for committing a crime. Included in the arrest data are people who have committed Part I crimes and people who have been arrested for all other crimes, known collectively as **Part II crimes**. This latter group includes such criminal acts as sex crimes, drug trafficking, and vandalism.

EXHIBIT 2.1

Part I (Index) Crime Offenses

Criminal Homicide
Murder and Nonnegligent Manslaughter   The willful (nonnegligent) killing of one human being by another. Deaths caused by negligence, attempts to kill, assaults to kill, suicides, accidental deaths, and justifiable homicides are excluded. Justifiable homicides are limited to (a) the killing of a felon by a law enforcement officer in the line of duty and (b) the killing of a felon, during the commission of a felony, by a private citizen.

Manslaughter by Negligence   The killing of another person through gross negligence. Traffic fatalities are excluded. Although manslaughter by negligence is a Part I crime, it is not included in the crime index.

Forcible Rape
The carnal knowledge of a female forcibly and against her will. Included are rapes by force and attempts or assaults to rape. Statutory offenses (no force used—victim under age of consent) are excluded.

Robbery
The taking or attempting to take anything of value from the care, custody, or control of a person or persons by force or threat of force or violence and/or by putting the victim in fear.

Aggravated Assault
An unlawful attack by one person upon another for the purpose of inflicting severe or aggravated bodily injury. This type of assault usually is accompanied by the use of a weapon or by means likely to produce death or great bodily harm. Simple assaults are excluded.

Burglary/Breaking or Entering
The unlawful entry of a structure to commit a felony or a theft. Attempted forcible entry is included.

Larceny/Theft (except motor vehicle theft)
The unlawful taking, carrying, leading, or riding away of property from the possession or constructive possession of another. Examples are thefts of bicycles or automobile accessories, shoplifting, pocket picking, or the stealing of any property or article that is not taken by force and violence or by fraud. Attempted larcenies are included. Embezzlement, con games, forgery, worthless checks, and so on are excluded.

Motor Vehicle Theft
The theft or attempted theft of a motor vehicle. A motor vehicle is self-propelled and runs on the surface and not on rails. Specifically excluded from this category are motorboats, construction equipment, airplanes, and farming equipment.

Arson
Any willful or malicious burning or attempt to burn, with or without intent to defraud, a dwelling house, public building, motor vehicle, or aircraft, personal property of another, or the like.

SOURCE: FBI, Uniform Crime Report, Crime in the United States, 2009.

Compiling the Uniform Crime Report

The methods used to compile the UCR are quite complex. Each month law enforcement agencies report the number of index crimes known to them. These data are collected from records of all crime complaints that victims, officers who discovered the infractions, or other sources reported to these agencies.

Whenever criminal complaints are found through investigation to be unfounded or false, they are eliminated from the actual count. However, the number of actual offenses known is reported to the FBI whether or not anyone is arrested for the crime, the stolen property is recovered, or prosecution ensues.

The UCR uses three methods to express crime data. First, the number of crimes reported to the police and arrests made are expressed as raw figures. For example, an estimated 15,241 persons were murdered nationwide in 2009. Second, crime rates per 100,000 people are computed. That is, when the UCR indicates that the murder rate was 5.0 in 2009, it means about 5 people in every 100,000 were murdered between January 1 and December 31 of 2009. This is the equation used:

$$\frac{\text{Number of Reported Crimes}}{\text{Total U.S. Population}} \times 100{,}000 = \text{Rate per } 100{,}000$$

Third, the FBI computes changes in rate of crime over time. The 15,241 murders in 2009 was a 7.3 percent decrease from the 2008 figure, a 9 percent decrease from the 2005 figure, and a 2.2 percent decrease from the 2000 estimate.[6]

Clearance Rates In addition, each month law enforcement agencies also report how many crimes were **cleared**. Crimes are cleared in two ways: (1) when at least one person is arrested, charged, and turned over to the court for prosecution; or (2) by exceptional means, when some element beyond police control precludes the physical arrest of an offender (i.e., the offender leaves the country). Data on the number of clearances involving the arrest of only juvenile offenders, data on the value of property stolen and recovered in connection with Part I offenses, and detailed information pertaining to criminal homicide are also reported.

Traditionally, slightly more than 20 percent of all reported index crimes are cleared by arrest each year, including about 45 percent of violent crimes and 17 percent of property crimes.

Not surprisingly, as Figure 2.1 shows, the most serious crimes such as murder and rape are cleared at much higher rates than less serious property crimes such as larceny. What factors account for this clearance rate differential?

- The media gives more attention to serious violent crimes and as a result local and state police departments are more likely to devote time and spend more resources in their investigations.
- There is more likely to be a prior association between victims of violent/serious crimes and their attackers, a fact that aids police investigations.
- Even if they did not know one another beforehand, violent crime victims and offenders interact so that identification is facilitated.

- Serious violent crimes often produce physical evidence—blood, body fluids, fingerprints—that can be used to identify suspects.

The Profiles in Crime feature shows how one atypical crime was solved.

Are the Uniform Crime Reports Valid?

Despite criminologists' continued reliance on the UCR, its accuracy has been suspect. The three main areas of concern are reporting practices, law enforcement practices, and methodological problems.

Reporting Practices Some criminologists claim that victims of many serious crimes do not report these incidents to police; therefore, these crimes do not become part of the UCR. The reasons for not reporting vary. Some victims do not trust the police or have confidence in their ability to solve crimes. Others do not have property insurance and therefore believe it is useless to report theft. In other cases, victims fear reprisals from an offender's friends or family or, in the case of family violence, from their spouse, boyfriend, and/or girlfriend.[7]

According to surveys of crime victims, less than 40 percent of all criminal incidents are reported to the police. Some of these victims justify not reporting by stating that the incident was "a private matter," that "nothing could be done," or that the victimization was "not important enough."[8] These findings indicate that the UCR data may significantly underreport the total number of annual criminal events. Some of the reasons crime victims decide to report crime are set out in Exhibit 2.2.

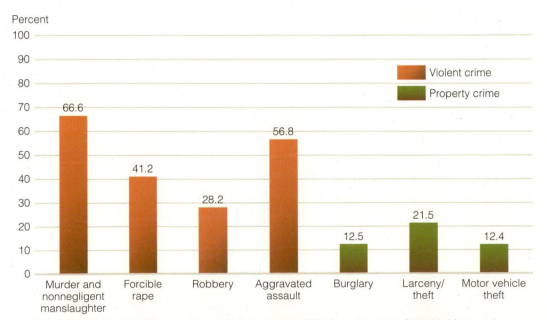

FIGURE 2.1
Crimes Cleared by Arrest

Percentage of crimes cleared by arrest or exceptional means, 2009.

SOURCE: Crime in the United States, 2009, www2.fbi.gov/ucr/cius2009/offenses/clearances/index.html (accessed November 1, 2010).

Profiles in Crime
A Pain in the Glass

From 1997 to 2005, Ronald and Mary Evano turned dining in restaurants into a profitable (albeit illegal) scam. They used the "waiter, there is glass in my food" ruse in restaurants and supermarkets stretching from Boston to Washington, D.C. While crude, their efforts paid big dividends. They allegedly swindled insurance companies out of $200,000 and conned a generous helping of food establishments and hospitals along the way. And to top it off, in order to look authentic, the Evanos actually did eat glass.

How did the Evanos pull off their scam? After ordering or buying food at restaurants, hotel bars, or supermarkets, either Ronald or Mary would "discover" glass in his or her food. They would then report the incident to management and fill out a report. After leaving the food establishment, they would check into the emergency room at the local

hospital complaining of severe stomach pain. After presenting fake IDs and Social Security cards to hospital staff, they'd allow doctors to examine them. In some cases, x-rays would show actual pieces of glass in their stomachs (but none of it came from the food they purchased). Once released from the hospital, the couple would continue getting medical treatment for stomach pain. After racking up several thousand dollars in bills, they would file an insurance claim for their extensive "pain and suffering."

The scheme unraveled when the Insurance Fraud Bureau of Massachusetts noticed a pattern of glass-eating claims in the state. The private industry organization eventually realized that most claims were being filed by the same couple and contacted federal authorities who then traced

the couple's trail of insurance fraud across three states and the District of Columbia.

On March 16, 2006, the Evanos were indicted on mail fraud, identity theft, Social Security fraud, and making false statements on health care matters. In 2007, Ronald Evano pleaded guilty and was sentenced to 63 months imprisonment; Mary Evano became a fugitive until 2010 when she was caught and pleaded guilty.

SOURCES: Press release, United States Attorney's Office, District of Massachusetts, "Woman Pleads Guilty in Glass-Eating Fraud Scheme," www.justice.gov/usao/ma/Press%20Office%20-%20Press%20Release%20Files/Sept2010/EvanoMaryPleaPR.html (accessed November 23, 2010); *Insurance Journal*, "Mass. Couple Charged in Glass-Eating Insurance Fraud," April 16, 2006, www.insurancejournal.com/news/east/2006/04/17/67327.htm (accessed November 1, 2010).

EXHIBIT 2.2

Why Do Victims Report Crime?

- *Seriousness*. The more serious the crime, the more likely it is to be reported. How do victims judge seriousness? If they are injured, especially if a weapon was involved, they are more likely to consider the incident serious and report it to the police. If the crime was completed, and the criminal got away with their wallet, purse, car, or package, reporting is more likely to occur.
- *Social support*. The more support victims have from family, friends and social service agencies, the more likely they are to report crime.
- *Victim-offender relationship*. Crimes involving strangers are more likely to be reported than those involving friends and relatives. One exception to this rule: if the crime was committed by an ex-husband or ex-wife, the police are more likely to be called than if it was committed by a stranger.
- *Dirty hands*. People who are themselves involved in criminal activities are less likely to report crime than those whose "hands are clean." The dirty hands may not be related to criminal activity: people who cheat on their wives, drink excessively, or have other skeletons in the closet are less likely to call the police than their less deviant peers.

SOURCE: Andrew Karmen, *Crime Victims: An Introduction to Victimology* (Belmont, CA: Wadsworth, 2009).

Law Enforcement Practices The way police departments record and report criminal and delinquent activity also affects the validity of UCR statistics. Some police departments define crimes loosely—reporting a trespass as a burglary or an assault on a woman as an attempted rape—whereas others pay strict attention to FBI guidelines. These reporting practices may help explain inter-jurisdictional differences in crime.[9] Changes in reporting can shape the crime trends reported in the UCR. When Eric Baumer and Janet Lauritsen examined data from 1973 to 2005, their findings showed that changes in victims' crime-reporting practices can have a significant impact on crime rate.[10] So what may be viewed as a significant change in crime rates may in fact represent a change in victims' behavior more than in criminals' behavior. Arson is seriously under-reported because many fire departments do not report to the FBI, and those that do define many fires that may well have been set by arsonists as "accidental" or "spontaneous."[11]

Some local police departments make systematic errors in UCR reporting. They may count an arrest only after a formal booking procedure, although the UCR requires arrests to be counted if the suspect is released without a formal charge. One survey of arrests found an error rate of about 10 percent in every Part I offense category.[12]

More serious allegations claim that in some cases police officials may deliberately alter reported crimes to improve their department's public image. Police administrators interested in lowering the crime rate may falsify crime reports by classifying a burglary as a nonreportable trespass.[13] An audit of the Atlanta Police Department, which included confidential interviews with police officers, concluded that the department consistently under-reported crimes for years. The reason? To improve the city's image for tourism.[14] A recent study of more than a hundred retired New York Police Department captains and higher-ranking officers by John Eterno and Eli Silverman found that police commanders, under intense pressure to reduce crime by hard-charging police commissioners such as William Bratton, manipulated crime statistics in order to show that their efforts were working.[15] How did they cheat? One method was to check eBay and other websites to find prices for items that had been reported stolen that were actually lower than the value provided by the crime victim. They would then use the lower values to reduce felony grand larcenies, crimes that are in the UCR, to misdemeanor petit larcenies that go unrecorded. Some commanders reported sending officers to crime scenes to persuade victims not to file complaints or alter crimes so they did not have to be reported to the FBI. For example, an attempted burglary must be reported, but an illegal trespass does not. While it is possible that the New York police administrators were under more pressure to reduce crime than their counterparts around the country, the fact that members of the largest police department in the United States may have fudged UCR data is disturbing. In response to the report, on January 6, 2011, the New York City police commissioner chose three former federal prosecutors to review the department's crime-reporting system.

Crime rates also may be altered based on the way law enforcement agencies process UCR data. As the number of employees assigned to dispatching, record keeping, and criminal incident reporting increases, so too will national crime rates. What appears to be a rising crime rate may be simply an artifact of improved police record-keeping ability.[16]

Methodological Issues   Methodological issues also contribute to questions pertaining to the UCR's validity. The most frequent issues include the following:

- No federal crimes are reported.
- Reports are voluntary and vary in accuracy and completeness.
- Not all police departments submit reports.
- The FBI uses estimates in its total crime projections.
- According to the "Hierarchy Rule," in a multiple-offense incident, only the most serious crime is counted. Thus if an armed bank robber commits a robbery, assaults a patron as he flees, steals a car to get away, and damages property during a police chase, only the robbery is reported because it is the most serious offense. Consequently, many lesser crimes go unreported.
- Each act is listed as a single offense for some crimes but not for others. If a man robbed six people in a bar, the offense is listed as one robbery; but if he assaulted or

murdered them, it would be listed as six assaults or six murders.

- Incomplete acts are lumped together with completed ones.
- Important differences exist between the FBI's definition of certain crimes and those used in a number of states.[17]

In addition to these issues, the complex scoring procedure used in the UCR program means that many serious crimes are not counted. If during an armed bank robbery the robber strikes a teller with the butt of a handgun, then runs from the bank and steals an automobile at the curb, he has technically committed robbery, aggravated assault, and motor vehicle theft, which are three Part I offenses. However, the UCR only records the most serious crime; the robbery would be the only one recorded in the UCR.[18]

The National Incident-Based Reporting System (NIBRS)

Clearly there must be a more reliable source for crime statistics than the UCR as it stands today. Beginning in 1982, a five-year redesign effort was undertaken to provide more comprehensive and detailed crime statistics. The effort resulted in the **National Incident-Based Reporting System (NIBRS)**, a program that collects data on each reported crime incident. Instead of submitting statements of the kinds of crime that individual citizens report to the police and summary statements of resulting arrests, the new program requires local police agencies to provide at least a brief account of each incident and arrest, including the incident, victim, and offender information. Under NIBRS, law enforcement authorities provide information to the FBI on each criminal incident involving one or more of 46 specific offenses, including the 8 Part I crimes, that occur in their jurisdiction; arrest information on the 46 offenses plus 11 lesser offenses is also provided in NIBRS. These expanded crime categories include numerous additional crimes, such as blackmail, embezzlement, drug offenses, and bribery; this allows a national database on the nature of crime, victims, and criminals to be developed. Other collected information includes statistics gathered by federal law enforcement agencies, as well as data on hate or bias crimes. When fully implemented, NIBRS will provide:

- Expansion of the number of offense categories included
- Detail on individual crime incidents (offenses, offenders, victims, property, and arrests)
- Linkage between arrests and clearances to specific incidents or offenses
- Inclusion of all offenses in an incident rather than only the most serious offense
- The ability to distinguish between attempted and completed crimes
- Linkages between offense, offender, victim, property, and arrestee variables that permit examination of interrelationships[19]

Thus far, more than 20 states have implemented their NIBRS program, and 12 others are in the process of finalizing their data collections. When this program is fully implemented and adopted across the nation, it should bring about greater uniformity in cross-jurisdictional reporting and improve the accuracy of official crime data. Whether it can capture cases missing in the UCR remains to be seen.[20]

A number of academic institutes are devoted to **survey research**, including the Princeton University Survey Research Center (SRC). For more information about this topic, visit the Criminal Justice CourseMate at cengagebrain.com, then access the "Web Links" for this chapter.

For more information about **NIBRS**, visit the Criminal Justice CourseMate at cengagebrain.com, then access the "Web Links" for this chapter.

Survey Research

The second primary source of crime/victimization measurement is through surveys in which people are asked about their attitudes, beliefs, values, and characteristics, as well as their experiences with crime and victimization.

Surveys typically involve **sampling**, which refers to the process of selecting for study a limited number of subjects who are representative of entire groups sharing similar characteristics, called the **population**. To understand the social forces that produce crime, a criminologist might interview a sample of 3,000 prison inmates drawn from the population of more than 2 million inmates in the United States; in this case, the sample represents the entire population of U.S. inmates. It is assumed that the characteristics of people or events in a carefully selected sample will be quite similar to those of the population at large. If the sampling was done correctly, the responses of the 3,000 inmates should represent the entire population of inmates.

In some circumstances, criminologists may want the survey to be representative of all members of society; this is referred to as a **cross-sectional survey**. A survey of all students who attend the local public high school would be considered a cross-sectional survey since all members of the community, both rich and poor, male and female, go to high school. Cross-sectional surveys are a useful and cost-effective technique for measuring the characteristics of large numbers of people:

- Because questions and methods are standardized for all subjects, uniformity is unaffected by the perceptions or biases of the person gathering the data.
- Carefully drawn samples enable researchers to generalize their findings from small groups to large populations.
- Though surveys measure subjects at a single point in their life span, questions can elicit information on subjects' past behavior as well as expectations of future behaviors.[21]

The National Crime Victimization Survey (NCVS)

Because more than half of all victims do not report their experiences to the police, the UCR cannot measure all the annual criminal activity. To address the nonreporting issue, the federal government's Bureau of Justice Statistics sponsors the **National Crime Victimization Survey (NCVS)**, a comprehensive, nationwide survey of victimization in the United States. Begun in 1973, the NCVS provides a detailed picture of crime incidents, victims, and trends.[22]

CONNECTIONS

Victim surveys provide information not only about criminal incidents that have occurred, but also about the individuals who are most at risk of falling victim to crime, and where and when they are most likely to become victimized. Data from recent NCVS surveys will be used in Chapter 3 to draw a portrait of the nature and extent of victimization in the United States.

How the NCVS Is Conducted U.S. Census Bureau personnel interview household members in a nationally representative sample of approximately 38,000 households (about 68,000 people). People are interviewed twice a year, so that approximately 136,000 interviews of persons age 12 or older are conducted annually. Households stay in the sample for three years. New households are rotated into the sample on an ongoing basis. The NCVS collects information on crimes suffered by individuals and households, whether or not those crimes were reported to law enforcement. It estimates the proportion of each crime type reported to law enforcement, and it summarizes the reasons that victims give for reporting or not reporting. In 1993, the survey was redesigned to provide detailed information on the frequency and nature of the crimes of rape, sexual assault, personal robbery, aggravated and simple assault, household burglary, theft, and motor vehicle theft.

The survey provides information about victims (age, sex, race, ethnicity, marital status, income, and educational level), offenders (sex, race, approximate age, and victim–offender relationship), and the crimes (time and place of occurrence, use of weapons, nature of injury, and economic consequences). Questions also cover the experiences of victims with the criminal justice system, self-protective measures used by victims, and possible substance abuse by offenders. Supplements are added periodically to the survey to obtain detailed information on topics like school crime.

NCVS: Advantages and Problems The greatest advantage of the NCVS over official data sources such as the UCR is that it can estimate the total amount of annual crimes and not only those that are reported to police. Nonreporting is a significant issue: typically, less than half of all violent victimizations and about 40 percent of all property crimes are reported to the police. As a result, the NCVS data provides a more complete picture of the nation's crime problem. Also, because some crimes are significantly underreported, the NCVS is an indispensable measure of their occurrence. Take for example the crimes of rape and sexual assault, of which slightly more than half of incidents are reported to police. The UCR shows that in 2009 slightly more than 88,000 rapes or attempted rapes occurred, as compared to the 126,000 uncovered by the NCVS. In addition, the NCVS helps us understand why crimes are not reported to police and whether the type and nature of the criminal event influences whether the police will ever know it occurred. With the crime of rape, research shows that victims are much more likely to report rape if it is accompanied by another crime such as robbery than they are if it is a stand-alone event. Official data alone cannot provide that type of information.[23]

While its utility and importance is unquestioned, the NCVS may also suffer from some methodological problems. As a result, its findings must be interpreted with caution. Among the potential problems are the following:

- Over reporting due to victims' misinterpretation of events. A lost wallet may be reported as stolen, or an open door may be viewed as a burglary attempt.
- Under-reporting due to the embarrassment of reporting crime to interviewers, fear of getting in trouble, or simply forgetting an incident.
- Inability to record the personal criminal activity of those interviewed, such as drug use or gambling; murder is also not included, for obvious reasons.
- Sampling errors, which produce a group of respondents who do not represent the nation as a whole.
- Inadequate question format that invalidates responses. Some groups, such as adolescents, may be particularly susceptible to error because of question format.[24]

The Future of the NCVS For the past 30 years, the NCVS (along with the UCR) has served as one of the two major indicators of crime and victimization in the United States.

It now faces some important challenges. A recent analysis conducted by the National Research Council found that its effectiveness has been undermined by budget limitations.[25]

In order to keep going in light of tight resources, the survey's sample size and methods of data collection have been altered. Although the current sample size is still valid for its purpose, victimization is still a relatively rare event so that when contacted many respondents do not have incidents to report. Consequently the NCVS now has to combine multiple years of data in order to comment on change over time, which is less desirable than an annual measure of year-to-year change.

Reflecting these issues, in 2006 significant changes were made to the way the NCVS is collected so that victimization estimates are not totally comparable to previous years. The methodological changes included: a new sampling method, a change in the method of handling first-time interviews with households, and a change in the method of interviewing. Some selected areas were dropped from the sample while others were added. Finally, computer-assisted personal interviewing (CAPI) replaced paper and pencil interviewing (PAPI). While these issues are critical, there is no substitute available that provides national information on crime and victimization with extensive detail on victims and the social context of the criminal event.

Self-Report Surveys

While the NCVS is designed to measure victimization directly and criminal activity indirectly, participants in **self-report surveys** are asked to describe, in detail, their recent and lifetime participation in criminal activity. Self-reports are generally given anonymously in groups, so that the people being surveyed are assured that their responses will remain private and confidential. Secrecy and anonymity are essential to maintain the honesty and validity of responses. Self-report survey questions might ask:

- How many times in the past year have you taken something worth more than $50?
- How many times in the past year did you hurt someone so badly that they needed medical care?
- How many times in the past year did you vandalize or damage school property?
- How many times in the past year did you use marijuana?

While most self-report studies have focused on juvenile delinquency and youth crime, they can also be used to examine the offense histories of select groups such as prison inmates, drug users, and even police officers.[26]

In addition to crime-related items, most self-report surveys contain questions about attitudes, values, and behaviors. There may be questions about participants' substance abuse history, arrest history, and their family relations, such as "Did your parents ever strike you with a stick or a belt?" By correlating the responses, criminologists are able to analyze the relationship between personal factors and criminal behaviors. Statistical analysis of the responses can be used to determine whether people who report being abused as children are also more likely to use drugs as adults. When psychologist Christiane Brems and her associates used this approach to collect data from 274 women and 556 men receiving drug detoxification services, they found that 20 percent of men and more than 50 percent of women reported childhood physical or sexual abuse. Individuals who report an *abuse* history also reported earlier age of onset of drinking, more problems associated with use of alcohol/drugs, more severe psychopathology, and more lifetime arrests.[27]

ACE STOCK LIMITED/Alamy

Self-report surveys can be used to assess the "dark figures of crime," offenses that would never otherwise be counted in the official crime data. Self-reports have been used to measure trends and patterns in teen substance abuse, something that official data would never be able to assess.

Self-Report Patterns   One of the most important sources of self-report data is the Monitoring the Future (MTF) study, which researchers at the University of Michigan Institute for Social Research (ISR) have been conducting annually since 1978. This national survey typically involves more than 2,500 high school seniors.[28] The MTF is considered the national standard to measure substance abuse trends among American teens.

abuse, false ID use, shoplifting or larceny under $50, fighting, marijuana use, or damage to the property of others. Furthermore, self-reports dispute the notion that criminals and delinquents specialize in one type of crime or another; offenders seem to engage in a mixed bag of crime and deviance.[29]

Validity of Self-Reports   Critics of self-report studies frequently suggest that it is unreasonable to expect people to candidly admit illegal acts. This is especially true of those with official records, who may be engaging in the most criminality. At the same time, some people may exaggerate their criminal acts, forget some of them, or be confused about what is being asked. Some surveys contain an overabundance of trivial offenses, such as shoplifting small items or using false identification to obtain alcohol, often lumped together with serious crimes to form a total crime index. Consequently, comparisons between groups can be highly misleading.

The "missing cases" phenomenon is also a concern. Even if 90 percent of a school population voluntarily participate in a self-report study, researchers can never be sure whether the few who refuse to participate or are absent that day comprise a significant portion of the school's population of persistent high-rate offenders. Research indicates that offenders with the most extensive prior criminality are also the most likely "to be poor historians of their own crime commission rates."[30] It is also unlikely that the most serious chronic offenders in the teenage population are willing to cooperate

CONNECTIONS

MTF data on patterns and trends in teenage substance abuse will be analyzed in Chapter 14. Despite public perception to the contrary, teen drug use seems to be on the decline.

🔴 For more information about the **Monitoring the Future** website, visit the Criminal Justice CourseMate at cengagebrain.com, then access the "Web Links" for this chapter.

The MTF data indicate that the number of people who break the law is far greater than the number projected by official statistics. Almost everyone questioned is found to have violated a law at some time, including truancy, alcohol

with criminologists administering self-report tests.[31] Institutionalized youths, who are not generally represented in the self-report surveys, are not only more delinquent than the general youth population, but are also considerably more misbehaving than the most delinquent youths identified in the typical self-report survey.[32] Consequently, self-reports may measure only nonserious, occasional delinquents while ignoring hardcore chronic offenders who may be institutionalized and unavailable for self-reports.

CONNECTIONS

Criminologists suspect that a few high-rate offenders are responsible for a disproportionate share of all serious crime. Results would be badly skewed if even a few of these chronic offenders were absent or refused to participate in schoolwide self-report surveys. For more on chronic offenders, see the sections at the end of this chapter.

There is also evidence that reporting accuracy differs among racial, ethnic, and gender groups. It is possible that some groups are more worried about image than others and less willing to report crime, deviance, and/or victimization for fear that it would make them or their group look bad. Take these cases, for instance:

- One recent study found that while girls were usually more willing than boys to disclose drug use, Latino girls significantly under-report their drug usage. Such gender and ethnic-based differences in reporting might provide a skewed and inaccurate portrait of criminal and/or delinquent activity—in this case, the self-report data would falsely show that Latino girls use fewer drugs than other females.[33]
- African Americans have been found to be less willing to report traffic stops than Caucasians, a phenomenon that prevents accurate assessments of racial profiling by police. Because of this reluctance to report stops that have occurred, it is possible that the "driving while black" phenomenon is worse than research surveys indicate.[34]

To address these criticisms, various techniques have been used to verify self-report data.[35] The "known group" method compares youths who are known to be offenders with those who are not to see whether the former report more delinquency. Research shows that when kids are asked if they have ever been arrested or sent to court, their responses accurately reflect their true life experiences.[36] New techniques are also being developed to more accurately measure past behaviors. The life event calendar (LEC), for example, is an instrument designed to help people recall the timing and sequencing of life experiences and events such as committing crime. The LEC is organized in a calendar format (Table 2.1), with time demarcations positioned horizontally and life events vertically. It is hoped that the LEC technique now allows

TABLE 2.1 The Life Event Calendar

2005	December Christmas	January New Year	February Valentine's Day
Got arrested			
Where living			
Employment			
Violent victimization			
Used drugs			
Went to court			

researchers to extract and record data in a manner that mimics the way people store and organize their memories.[37]

While these studies are supportive, self-report data must be interpreted with some caution. Asking subjects about their past behavior may capture more serious crimes but miss minor criminal acts—that is, people remember armed robberies and rapes better than they do minor assaults and altercations.[38] In addition, some classes of offenders, such as substance abusers, may have a tough time accounting for their prior misbehavior.[39]

Evaluating the Primary Sources of Crime Data

The UCR, NCVS, and self-reports are the standard sources of data used by criminologists to track trends and patterns in the crime rate. Each has its own strengths and weaknesses. The UCR contains information on the number and characteristics of people arrested, information that the other data sources lack. Some recent research indicates that for serious crimes, such as drug trafficking, arrest data can provide a meaningful measure of the level of criminal activity in a particular neighborhood environment, which other data sources cannot provide. It is also the source of information on particular crimes such as murder, which the other data sources cannot provide.[40] It remains the standard unit of analysis upon which most criminological research is based. However, UCR data omits many criminal incidents victims choose not to report to police, and it is subject to the reporting caprices of individual police departments.

The NCVS includes unreported crime and important information on the personal characteristics of victims. However, the data consist of estimates made from relatively limited samples of the total U.S. population, so that even narrow fluctuations in the rates of some crimes can have a major impact on findings. It also relies on personal recollections that may be inaccurate. The NCVS does not include data on important crime patterns, including murder and drug abuse.

Self-report surveys can provide information on the personal characteristics of offenders—such as their attitudes, values, beliefs, and psychological profiles—that is unavailable from any other source. Yet, at their core, self-reports rely on the honesty of criminal offenders and drug abusers, a population not generally known for accuracy and integrity.

Although their tallies of crimes are certainly not in sync, the crime patterns and trends they record are often quite similar (see Concept Summary 2.1).[41] Each of the sources of crime data agree about the personal characteristics of serious criminals (such as age and gender) and where and when crime occurs (such as urban areas, nighttime, and summer months). In addition, the problems inherent in each source are consistent over time. Therefore, even if the data sources are incapable of providing an exact, precise, and valid count of crime at any given time, they are reliable indicators of changes and fluctuations in yearly crime rates.

SECONDARY SOURCES OF CRIME DATA

In addition to these main sources of crime data, a number of other techniques are used by criminologists to gather data on specific crime problems and trends, to examine the lives of criminal offenders, and to assess the effectiveness of crime control efforts:

Cohort Research

Cohort research involves observing a group of people who share a like characteristic over time. Researchers might select all girls born in Albany, New York, in 1970 and then follow their behavior patterns for 20 years. The research data might include their school experiences, arrests, hospitalizations, and information about their family life (divorces, parental relations). The subjects might be given repeated intelligence and physical exams; their diets might be monitored.

Data may be collected directly from the subjects during interviews and meetings with family members. Criminologists might also examine records of social organizations, such as hospitals, schools, welfare departments, courts, police departments, and prisons. School records contain data on students' academic performance, attendance, intelligence, disciplinary problems, and teacher ratings. Hospitals record incidents of drug use and suspicious wounds, which may be indicative of child abuse. Police files contain reports of criminal activity, arrest data, personal information on suspects, victim reports, and actions taken by police officers. Court records enable researchers to compare the personal characteristics of offenders with the outcomes of their court appearances, conviction rates, and types of sentence. Prison records contain information on inmates' personal characteristics, adjustment problems, disciplinary records, rehabilitation efforts, and length of sentence served. If the cohort is carefully drawn, it may be possible to determine which life experiences produce criminal careers.

Because it is extremely difficult, expensive, and time-consuming to follow a cohort over time, another approach is to take an intact cohort from the past and collect data from their educational, family, police, and hospital records. This format is known as a **retrospective cohort study**.[42] For example, a cohort of girls who were in grade school in 1970 could be selected from school attendance records. A criminologist might then acquire their police and court records over the following four decades to determine (a) which ones developed a criminal record and (b) whether school achievement predicts adult criminality.

CONNECTIONS

Some critical criminological research has been based on cohort studies, such as the important research conducted by University of Pennsylvania criminologist Marvin Wolfgang and his colleagues. Their findings have been instrumental in developing an understanding about the onset and development of a criminal career. Wolfgang's cohort research, which is discussed later in this chapter, helped identify the chronic criminal offender.

Experimental Research

Sometimes criminologists are able to conduct controlled experiments to collect data on the cause of crime. They may wish to directly test whether (a) watching a violent TV show will (b) cause viewers to act aggressively. This test requires experimental research. To conduct experimental research, criminologists manipulate or intervene in the lives of their subjects to see the outcome or the effect of the intervention. True experiments usually have three elements: (1) random selection of subjects, (2) a control or comparison group, and (3) an experimental condition. Using this approach to find out the effects of viewing violent media content, a criminologist might have one group of randomly chosen subjects watch an extremely violent and gory film (*Resident Evil* or *The Human Centipede*) while another randomly selected group viewed something more mellow (*The Princess Diaries* or *Happy Feet*). If the subjects who watched the violent film were significantly more aggressive than those who watched the nonviolent film, an association between media content and behavior would be supported. The fact that both groups were randomly selected would prevent some preexisting condition from invalidating the results of the experiment.

Because it is sometimes impossible to randomly select subjects or manipulate conditions, criminologists may be forced to rely on what is known as a *quasi-experimental design*. A criminologist may want to measure whether kids who were abused as children are more likely to become violent as teens. Of course, it is impossible to randomly select youth, assign them to two independent groups, and then purposely abuse members of one group in order to gauge their reactions. To get around this dilemma, a criminologist may follow a group of kids who were abused and compare them with a matched group who though similar in every other respect were never abused in order to discover if the battered kids were more likely to become violent teens. Because the subjects were not randomly assigned, it is impossible to know whether there was something in the abused group that made them more crime prone than the unabused kids.

True criminological experiments are relatively rare because they are difficult and expensive to conduct; they involve manipulating subjects' lives, which can cause ethical and legal roadblocks; and they require long follow-up periods to verify results. Nonetheless, they have been an important source of criminological data.

Observational and Interview Research

Sometimes criminologists focus their research on relatively few subjects, interviewing them in depth or observing them as they go about their activities. This research often results in the kind of in-depth data absent in large-scale surveys. In one such effort, Claire Sterk-Elifson focused on the lives of middle-class female drug abusers.[43] The 34 interviews she conducted provide insight into a group whose behavior might not be captured in a large-scale survey. Sterk-Elifson found that these women were introduced to cocaine at first "just for fun": "I do drugs," one 34-year-old lawyer told her, "because I like the feeling. I would never let drugs take over my life."[44] Unfortunately, many of these subjects succumbed to the power of drugs and suffered both emotional and financial stress.

Another common criminological method is to observe criminals firsthand to gain insight into their motives and activities. This may involve going into the field and participating in group activities; this was done in sociologist William Whyte's famous study of a Boston gang, *Street Corner Society*.[45] Other observers conduct field studies but remain in the background, observing but not being part of the ongoing activity.[46]

Criminologists observe people in their home setting and interview them in order to gain insight into their behavior, attitudes, and values. Some specialize in gang research. Here, members of the Pico Norte 19th Street Gang flash their hand signs in El Paso, Texas. The gang, an offshoot of the Los Juaritos gang from Ciudad Juarez, Mexico, has become the most notorious gang in the city, with some 60 active members. The gang is known for being a "clean gang"—not involved in drug trafficking or part of older gangs that have become involved in large organized crime schemes. Some 650 known gang members, the majority of Hispanic origin, operate in El Paso. When interviewed, members say they joined the gang to gain respect among their peers and to protect themselves against other gangs; they consider the group a part of their family. Interviews can provide information unavailable with other research methods.

© Hector Mata/AFP/Getty Images

Meta-Analysis and Systematic Review

Meta-analysis involves gathering data from a number of previous studies. Compatible information and data are extracted and pooled together. When analyzed, the grouped data from several different studies provide a more powerful and valid indicator of relationships than the results provided from a single study. A **systematic review** is another widely accepted means of evaluating the effectiveness of public policy interventions. It involves collecting the findings from previously conducted scientific studies that address a particular problem, appraising and synthesizing the evidence, and using the collective evidence to address a particular scientific question.

Through these well-proven techniques, criminologists can identify what is known and what is not known about a particular problem and use the findings as a first step for carrying out new research. Criminologists David Farrington and Brandon Welsh used a systematic review and a meta-analysis to study the effects of street lighting on crime.[47] After identifying and analyzing 13 relevant studies, Farrington and Welsh found evidence showing that neighborhoods that improve their street lighting do in fact experience a reduction in crime rates. Their findings should come as no great surprise: it seems logical that well-lit streets would have fewer robberies and thefts because (a) criminals could not conceal their efforts under the cover of darkness, and (b) potential victims could take evasive action if they saw a suspicious-looking person lurking about. However, their analysis produced an unusual finding: improving lighting caused the crime rate to go down during the day just as much as it did during the night! Obviously, the crime-reducing effect of streetlights had little to do with illuminating the streets. Farrington and Welsh speculate that improved street lighting increases community pride and solidarity, and the result of this newfound community solidarity is a lowered crime rate, during both the day and evening.

Data Mining

A relatively new criminological technique, data mining, uses multiple advanced computational methods, including artificial intelligence (the use of computers to perform logical functions), to analyze large data sets usually involving one or more data sources. The goal is to identify significant and recognizable patterns, trends, and relationships that are not easily detected through traditional analytical techniques alone.[48] Criminologists then use this information for various purposes, such as the prediction of future events or behaviors.

Data mining might be employed to help a police department allocate resources to combat crime based on offense patterns. To determine if such a pattern exists, a criminologist might employ data mining techniques with a variety of sources including calls for service data, crime or incident reports, witness statements, suspect interviews, tip information, telephone toll analysis, or Internet activity.

Data mining permits proactive or "risk-based" deployment of police resources, a procedure that can increase public safety by optimizing the allocation of resources. For example, Richmond, Virginia, has experienced frequent random gunfire on New Year's Eve that has long presented a challenge to local law enforcement agencies. Through the use of data mining, the Richmond Police Department identified and targeted locations associated with increased random gunfire during the previous New Year's Eve holiday and deployed additional police resources to these areas. The results were extremely positive: there was a 49 percent reduction in the number of random gunfire complaints, with a concomitant increase in seized weapons of 246 percent. Using data mining to target resources, the Richmond Police Department required fewer police personnel than originally anticipated, which permitted the release of approximately 50 sworn employees. Data mining yielded a cost savings of approximately $15,000 during the eight-hour initiative. The Richmond Police Department's initiative demonstrated the ability to do more with less through the use of data mining and risk-based deployment strategies in the public safety arena.[49]

Crime Mapping

Criminologists are now using crime maps to create graphic representations of the spatial geography of crime. Computerized crime maps allow criminologists to analyze and correlate a wide array of data to create immediate, detailed visuals of crime patterns. The most simple maps display crime locations or concentrations and can be used, for example, to help law enforcement agencies increase the effectiveness of their patrol efforts. More complex maps can be used to chart trends in criminal activity. For example, criminologists might be able to determine if certain neighborhoods in a city have significantly higher crime rates than others—so-called hot spots of crime.[50] Figure 2.2 illustrates a crime map generated in Providence, Rhode Island. How mapping is used by police is the topic of the accompanying Policy and Practice in Criminology feature.

CRIME TRENDS

Crime is not new to this century.[51] Studies have indicated that a gradual increase in the crime rate, especially in violent crime, occurred from 1830 to 1860. Following the Civil War, this rate increased significantly for about 15 years. Then, from 1880 up to the time of the First World War,

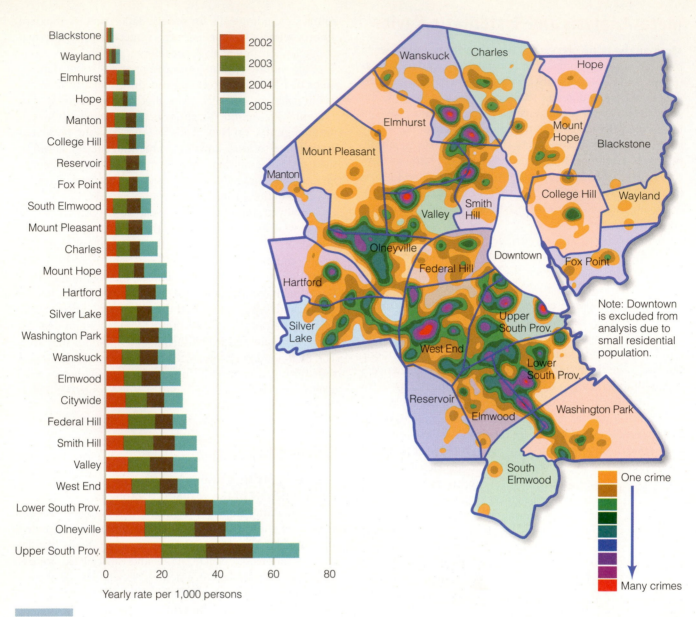

Legend: 2002, 2003, 2004, 2005

Bar chart categories (top to bottom): Blackstone, Wayland, Elmhurst, Hope, Manton, College Hill, Reservoir, Fox Point, South Elmwood, Mount Pleasant, Charles, Mount Hope, Hartford, Silver Lake, Washington Park, Wanskuck, Elmwood, Citywide, Federal Hill, Smith Hill, Valley, West End, Lower South Prov., Olneyville, Upper South Prov.

X-axis: 0, 20, 40, 60, 80
Yearly rate per 1,000 persons

Map labels: Wanskuck, Charles, Hope, Elmhurst, Mount Hope, Blackstone, Mount Pleasant, College Hill, Wayland, Manton, Valley, Smith Hill, Olneyville, Downtown, Fox Point, Hartford, Federal Hill, Silver Lake, Upper South Prov., West End, Lower South Prov., Reservoir, Elmwood, Washington Park, South Elmwood

Note: Downtown is excluded from analysis due to small residential population.

Map legend: One crime → Many crimes

FIGURE 2.2

Police Crime Map: Providence, Rhode Island

SOURCE: The Providence Plan, www.provplan.org.

with the possible exception of the years immediately preceding and following the war, the number of reported crimes decreased. After a period of readjustment, the crime rate steadily declined until the Depression (about 1930), when another crime wave was recorded. As measured by the UCR, crime rates increased gradually following the 1930s until the 1960s, when the growth rate became much greater. The homicide rate, which had actually declined from the 1930s to the 1960s, also began a sharp increase that continued through the 1970s.

By 1991, police recorded about 14.6 million crimes. Since then, the number of crimes has been in decline; in 2009, about 10.5 million crimes were reported to the police,

a drop of 4 million recorded crimes from the peak despite an increasing national population.

During the same period, the number of victimizations reported to the NCVS also showed a significant downturn. For example, in 2009, the NCVS recorded about 4 million violent crimes (rapes or sexual assaults, robberies, aggravated assaults, and simple assaults), 15.5 million property crimes (burglaries, motor vehicle thefts, and household thefts), and 133,000 personal thefts (picked pockets and snatched purses).[52] This number has dropped by half since 1991, when 43 million crimes were reported, including more than 10 million violent crimes. The victimization rate for violence was more than 50 incidents per 1,000 population, while today it

One innovative mapping program, CATCH—the Crime Analysis Tactical Clearing House—supports local law enforcement agencies in analyzing crime series and patterns. CATCH staff use a number of crime mapping and analysis software applications and techniques to help agencies analyze identified crime series. CATCH is based on next-event forecasting, which differs from geographic profiling. Geographic profiling analyzes the locations of a series of crimes to determine where the offender most likely resides. Next-event forecasting looks at where previous crimes occurred to predict where the next crime will happen. So far CATCH has had several successes. In one case, the Savannah-

Chatham, Georgia, police department was baffled by a series of nine kidnappings and rapes. CATCH staff mapped the crime locations along with other variables and created a timeline. Because the victims were kidnapped and then taken to isolated locations and assaulted, the mapping was complex. Using movement-analysis techniques, CATCH team members projected probable locations where the offender had targeted the victims and provided a list of recommendations for disrupting the series. These forecasts and recommendations backed up conclusions by the Savannah authorities, who initiated a public awareness campaign about the crimes. The Savannah-Chatham Police

Department arrested the offender following an attack in an area targeted for increased surveillance.

CRITICAL THINKING

Do you believe that it is possible to predict where crime will take place in the future? It sounds like the film *Minority Report* using computers. Is there a downside to this type of prediction?

SOURCES: *TechBeat*, National Law Enforcement and Corrections Technology Center, "A Good Catch," www.justnet.org/TechBeat%20Files/AGoodCatch.pdf (accessed November 1, 2010).

---

is less than 20; in 1991, victims reported more than 300 incidents of property crime per 1,000 population, while today it is less than 150.[53] Between 2008 and 2009 all crime types recorded significant declines.

Violent and property crime rates in 2009 remained at the lowest levels recorded since 1973, the first year that such data were collected. The rate of every major violent and property crime measured by the Bureau of Justice Statistics fell between 2000 and 2009. The overall violent crime rate fell 39 percent, and the property crime rate declined by 29 percent during the last 10 years.

Figure 2.3 illustrates serious violent crime rate trends over that past 30 years as measured by four separate indicators and readily shows the welcome drop in the overall crime rate.

The crime drop has affected both violent and property crimes. About 1.3 million violent crimes are now being reported to police, a rate of about 450 per 100,000 inhabitants. As Table 2.2 shows, the number and rate of violent crimes have dropped significantly for almost two decades, while the population has increased by 50 million. Table 2.3 shows similar trends for the number and rate of property crimes (larceny, motor vehicle theft, and arson), which have also declined for most of the

past two decades. Preliminary UCR data indicate that this trend continued between 2009 and 2010 when the number of violent crimes dropped 6 percent and the number of property crimes dropped about 3 percent.

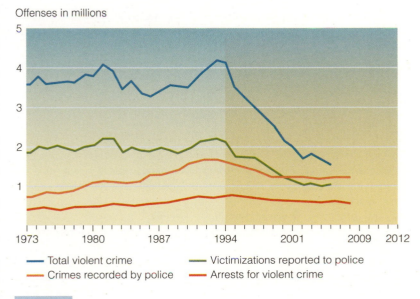

FIGURE 2.3
Four Measures of Serious Violent Crime

SOURCE: Bureau of Justice Statistics, http://bjs.ojp.usdoj.gov/content/glance/cv2.cfm (accessed November 1, 2010).

The Criminological Enterprise
Factors that Influence Crime Trends

Crime experts have identified a variety of social, economic, personal, and demographic factors that influence crime rate trends. Although crime experts are still uncertain about how these factors impact these trends, directional change seems to be associated with changes in crime rates.

Age Structure

As a general rule, the crime rate follows the proportion of teens in the population: more kids, more crime! Crime rates skyrocketed in the 1960s when the baby boomers became teens and the 13 to 19 population grew rapidly. Crime rate drops since 1993 can be explained in part by an aging society: the elderly commit relatively few crimes.

Immigration

Immigration has a suppressor effect on crime. Research shows that immigrants are less crime prone than the general population, so that as the number of immigrants increases per capita crime rates decline. During the past two decades, cities with the largest increases in immigration have experienced the largest decreases in crime rates, especially homicides and robberies.

Economy

The general public believes that crime rates increase as the economy turns down and unemployment rises. However, there is little correlation between these indicators of economic prosperity and crime rates. Unemployed people do not suddenly join gangs or commit armed robberies. Criminals are usually unemployed or underemployed and therefore not affected by short-term economic conditions.

Crime rates may, however, be influenced by other types of economic factors. The decline in the burglary rate over the past decade may be explained in part by the abundance and subsequent decline in price of commonly stolen merchandise such as iPods, laptops, cell phones, flat screen TVs, and digital cameras. On the other hand, new targets may increase crime rates; subway crime increased in New York when thieves began targeting people carrying iPods and expensive cell phones such as the iPhone.

Abortion

There is evidence that the recent drop in the crime rate is linked to the availability of legalized abortion. In 1973, *Roe v. Wade* legalized abortion nationwide, and the drop in the crime rate began approximately 18 years later, in 1991. Crime rates began to decline when the first groups of potential offenders affected by the abortion decision began reaching the peak age of criminal activity. It is possible that the link between crime rates and abortion is the result of two mechanisms: (1) selective abortion on the part of women most at risk to have children who would engage in criminal activity, and (2) improved childrearing or environmental circumstances caused by better maternal, familial, or fetal care because women are having fewer children.

Gun Availability

The availability of firearms may influence the crime rate: as the number of guns in the population increases, so do violent crime rates. Handguns are especially dangerous if they fall into the hands of teens. Surveys of high school students indicate that between 6 and 10 percent carry guns at least some of the time. Guns also cause escalation in the seriousness of crime. As the number of gun-toting students increases, so too does the seriousness of violent crime as a school yard fight turns into murder.

Gangs

Another factor that affects crime rates is the explosive growth in teenage gangs. Surveys indicate that there are about 800,000 gang members in the United States. Data collected by the National Youth Gang Center show that gang members are responsible for a large proportion of all violent offenses committed during the adolescent years.

Boys who are members of gangs are far more likely to possess guns than non-gang members; criminal activity increases when kids join gangs. Gangs involved in the urban drug trade recruit juveniles because they work cheaply, are immune from heavy criminal penalties, and are daring and willing to take risks. Arming themselves for protection, these drug-dealing children present a menace to their community, which persuades non–gang-affiliated neighborhood adolescents to arm themselves for protection. The result is an arms race that produces an increasing spiral of violence. As gangs become more organized, so too does their level of violence and drug dealing. Without gang influence, the crime rate might be much lower.

Drug Use

Some experts tie increases in the violent crime rate between 1985 and 1993 to the crack epidemic, which swept the nation's largest cities, and to drug-trafficking gangs that fought over drug turf. These well-armed gangs did not hesitate to use violence to control territory, intimidate rivals, and increase market share. As the crack epidemic subsided, so too did the violence rates in New York City and other metropolitan areas where crack use was rampant. A sudden increase in drug use on the other hand may be a harbinger of future increases in the crime rate, especially if guns are easily obtained and fall into the hands of gang members.

Media

Some experts argue that violent media can influence the direction of crime rates. As the availability of media with a violent theme skyrocketed with the introduction of home video players, DVDs, cable TV, computer and video games, and so on, so too did teen violence rates. Efforts to curb violence on TV may help account for a declining crime rate.

Medical Technology

Some crime experts believe that the presence and quality of health care can have a significant impact on murder rates. Murder rates might be up to five times higher than they are today without medical breakthroughs in treating victims of violence developed over the past 40 years. The big breakthrough occurred in the 1970s when technology developed to treat injured soldiers in Vietnam was applied to trauma care in the nation's hospitals. Since then, fluctuations in the murder rate can be linked to the level and availability of emergency medical services.

Justice Policy

Some law enforcement experts have suggested that a reduction in crime rates may be attributed to adding large numbers of police officers and using them in aggressive police practices that target "quality of life" crimes such as panhandling, graffiti, petty drug dealing, and loitering. By showing that even the smallest infractions will be dealt with seriously, aggressive police departments may be able to discourage potential criminals from committing more serious crimes. Cities employing aggressive, focused police work may be able to lower homicide rates in the area.

It is also possible that tough laws imposing lengthy prison terms on drug dealers and repeat offenders can affect crime rates. The fear of punishment may inhibit some would-be criminals and place a significant number of potentially high-rate offenders behind bars, lowering crime rates. As the nation's prison population expanded, the crime rate has fallen.

However, justice policy can sometimes backfire and actually lift crime rates. Take for instance the long-term effect of incarceration. The imprisonment boom has resulted in more than 2 million people behind bars. While this policy may take some dangerous offenders off the street, eventually most get out. About 600,000 inmates are now being released each year, and many return to their communities without marketable skills or resources. The number of releasees will rise for the foreseeable future as more and more sentences bestowed during the high crime rate 1990s are completed. The recidivism rate of paroled inmates is quite high, averaging about 40 percent for those released from federal penitentiaries and 67 percent for those released from state custody. Inmates reentering society may have a significant effect on local crime rates.

Social and Cultural Change

International scholar Martin Kilias notes that crime trends can be influenced by sudden "breaches"—that is, new opportunities for offending that open as a result of changes in the technological or social environment. As an example he shows that violence among men has decreased since 1850 in some countries because the concept of "honor" has lost most of its importance. There is evidence, he finds, that it was common in the past for a small argument to end in a duel or at least a brawl if a person's personal or family honor was impugned or questioned. Today, honor-based killings can still be found, such as areas of Turkey where any critical remark about a person's reputation is dealt with by aggression against the source of "rumors."

While maintaining honor and saving face are still important factors in contemporary society, other cultural macro-level conditions such as the number of single-parent families, high school dropout rates, racial conflict, and the prevalence of teen pregnancies also exert a powerful influence on crime rates. High levels of race- and ethnicity-based income inequality have been shown to have an impact on crime rates. Areas where there is both within and between group inequality experience more violent crimes than neighborhoods in which most residents are doing equally well.

CRITICAL THINKING

While crime rates have been declining in the United States, they have been increasing in Europe. Is it possible that factors that correlate with crime rate changes in the United States have little utility in predicting changes in other cultures? What other factors may increase or reduce crime rates?

SOURCES: Tim Wadsworth, "Is Immigration Responsible for the Crime Drop? An Assessment of the Influence of Immigration on Changes in Violent Crime Between 1990 and 2000," *Social Science Quarterly* 91 (2010): 531–553; Amy Anderson and Lorine Hughes, "Exposure to Situations Conducive to Delinquent Behavior: The Effects of Time Use, Income, and Transportation," *Journal of Research in Crime and Delinquency* 46 (2009): 5–34; the National Gang Intelligence Center, *National Gang Threat Assessment, 2009*, www.justice.gov/ndic/pubs32/32146/gangs.htm (accessed November 23, 2010); Ramiro Martinez, Jr., and Matthew Amie Nielsen, "Local Context and Determinants of Drug Violence in Miami and San Diego: Does Ethnicity and Immigration Matter?" *International Migration Review* 38 (2004): 131–157; Richard Rosenfeld, Robert Fornango, and Andres Rengifo, "The Impact of Order-Maintenance Policing on New York City Homicide and Robbery Rates: 1988–2001," *Criminology* 45 (2007): 355–384; National Youth Gang Center, "What Proportion of Serious and Violent Crime Is Attributable to Gang Members," www.nationalgangcenter.gov/About/FAQ#R50 (accessed November 1, 2010); Martin Killias, "The Opening and Closing of Breaches: A Theory on Crime Waves, Law Creation and Crime Prevention," *European Journal of Criminology* 3 (2006): 11–31; Alfred Blumstein, "The Crime Drop in America: An Exploration of Some Recent Crime Trends" *Journal of Scandinavian Studies in Criminology and Crime Prevention* 7 (2006): 17–35; Steven Levitt, "Understanding Why Crime Fell in the 1990s: Four Factors that Explain the Decline and Six that Do Not," *Journal of Economic Perspectives* 18 (2004): 163–190; Brad Bushman and Craig Anderson, "Media Violence and the American Public," *American Psychologist* 56 (2001): 477–489; Anthony Harris, Stephen Thomas, Gene Fisher, and David Hirsch, "Murder and Medicine: The Lethality of Criminal Assault 1960–1999," *Homicide Studies* 6 (2002): 128–167; John J. Donohue and Steven D. Levitt, "The Impact of Legalized Abortion on Crime," *Quarterly Journal of Economics* 116 (2001): 379–420.

TABLE 2.2 Number of Violent Crimes and Violence Rates

Year	Population	Number of Violent Crimes	Rate per 100,000
1992	255,029,699	1,932,274	757.7
2000	281,421,906	1,425,486	506.5
2004	293,656,842	1,360,088	463.2
2009	307,006,550	1,318,398	429.4

SOURCE: FBI, Uniform Crime Reports, http://www2.fbi.gov/ucr/cius2009/data/table_01.html (accessed November 1, 2010).

TABLE 2.3 Number of Property Crimes and Property Crime Rates

Year	Population	Number of Property Crimes	Rate per 100,000
1992	255,029,699	12,505,917	2,903.7
2000	281,421,906	10,182,584	3,618.3
2004	293,656,842	10,319,386	3,514.1
2009	307,006,550	9,320,971	3,036.1

SOURCE: FBI, Uniform Crime Reports,http://www2.fbi.gov/ucr/cius2009/data/table_01.html (accessed November 1, 2010).

TABLE 2.4 Survey of Criminal Activity of High School Seniors, 2009 (Percentage Engaging in Offenses)

Crime	Committed at Least Once	Committed More than Once
Set fire on purpose	2	1
Damaged school property	6	5
Damaged work property	2	3
Auto theft	3	3
Auto part theft	2	2
Break and enter	11	12
Theft, less than $50	11	13
Theft, more than $50	4	5
Shoplift	11	14
Gang fight	9	8
Hurt someone badly enough to require medical care	6	6
Used force or a weapon to steal	2	2
Hit teacher or supervisor	1	2
Participated in serious fight in school or at work	6	5

SOURCE: *Monitoring the Future, 2009* (Ann Arbor, MI: Institute for Social Research, 2009).

Even teenage criminality, a source of national concern, has been in decline during this period. The proportion of serious violent crimes committed by juveniles has generally declined since 1993. Victims perceived that between one-fifth and one-quarter of violent crimes were committed by juveniles. According to the victim's perception of the age of the offender, the number of serious violent offenses committed by persons ages 12 to 17 declined more than 60 percent since 1993.

Trends in Self-Reporting

Self-report results appear to be more stable than the UCR and NCVS data indicate. When the results of recent self-report surveys are compared with various studies conducted over a 20-year period, a uniform pattern emerges. The use of drugs and alcohol increased markedly in the 1970s, leveled off in the 1980s, increased until the mid-1990s, and have been in decline ever since. Theft, violence, and damage-related crimes seem more stable. Although a self-reported crime wave has not occurred, neither has there been any visible reduction in self-reported criminality.

Table 2.4 contains data from the most recent MTF survey.

It should be noted that if the MTF data are accurate, the crime problem is much greater than FBI and NCVS data would lead us to believe. There are approximately 40 million youths between the ages of 10 and 18. According to MTF findings, this group accounts for more than 100 percent of all theft offenses reported in the UCR. More than 3 percent of the students said they used a knife or a gun in a robbery. At this rate, high school students commit 1.2 million armed robberies per year. In comparison, the UCR tallied about 200,000 armed robberies for all age groups. The MTF indicates that a great deal of crime is hidden from public view and not reported by victims.

The factors that help explain the upward and downward movement in crime rates, such as the one we have experienced for the past two decades, are discussed in The Criminological Enterprise feature "Factors that Influence Crime Trends" on page 44.

WHAT THE FUTURE HOLDS

It is risky to speculate about the future of crime trends because current conditions can change rapidly. It's possible that crime rates may rise in the future if the unemployment rate remains high for a prolonged period of time and the current generation of teens lose hope of ever gaining legitimate employment. Gang membership may increase and those involved in gangs may remain in them longer. However, as

Profiles in Crime
"Clever," "Kalgon," and "Prince" Go to Prison

While prostitution arrests and prosecutions are in decline, that does not mean all major traffickers escape detection. In 2009, a large Harrisburg, Pennsylvania, based prostitution ring was broken up by federal, state, and county investigators that may be typical of the large-scale prostitution rings operating in the United States. The group ran a highly organized ring that set predetermined prices for sexual services and then wired the money they earned to co-conspirators in other states. The conspirators engaged in extensive interstate travel and transportation of women and girls for prostitution and openly discussed their illegal activities. One of the men was overheard bragging to another, "I love pimping." The men used violence and intimidation to recruit and control the women and girls being prostituted by them; one described beating prostitutes so brutally that "both my hands were swelled up."

At least nine of the women were minors under the age of 18 when they were enticed, persuaded, or coerced into lives of prostitution. The youngest of these girls was only 12 when she was prostituted by the ring.

Rather than confine their activities to one state, the ring operated in several, including Pennsylvania, Ohio, Michigan, Indiana, Illinois, Arkansas, Virginia, Georgia, Maryland, Tennessee, the District of Columbia, California, Florida, Nevada, Texas, and Louisiana. Investigators found that this prostitution enterprise had been operating in the Harrisburg area for almost a decade. Despite their colorful nicknames, those indicted and convicted were cruel, violent, and amoral:

Robert Scott II, aka "Lil' Rob" and "Clever"
Kenneth Britton, aka "KB" and "Kalgon"
Franklin Robinson, aka "Silk" and "Silky Red"

Eric Hayes, aka "International Ross" and "Ross"
Derek Maes, aka "Prince"
Derick Price, aka "Coleone" and "Toone"
Dawan Oliver, aka "Thug" and "Finesse"
Terrence Williams, aka "Sleazy T"
Shimon Maxwell, aka "Smooth"
Eric Pennington, aka "Escalade"
Kory Barham, aka "Cutty Blue" and "Cuttlas Y. Blue"
Robert Scott, Sr., aka "Big Rob"
Atlas Aquarius, aka "Large"
Melissa Jacobs, aka "Storm"
Tana Adkins, aka "Sapphire"

SOURCE: U.S. Department of Justice, "Two Men Sentenced to a Combined Total 396 Months for Their Role in Multistate Prostitution and Money Laundering Ring," January 12, 2009, www.justice.gov/usao/pam/press_releases/2009%20archive/ProstitutionRing_01_12_09.htm (accessed November 2, 2010).

---

economist Steven Levitt comments, if teens commit more crime in the future, their contribution may be offset by the aging of the population, which will produce a large number of senior citizens and elderly, a group with a relatively low crime rate.[54] The immigrant population is also increasing, another factor that may reduce crime rates.

Such prognostications are reassuring, but there is, of course, no telling what changes are in store that may influence crime rates. Technological developments such as e-commerce on the Internet have created new classes of crime that are not recorded by any of the traditional methods of crime measurement. It's possible that some crimes such as fraud, larceny, prostitution, obscenity, vandalism, stalking, and harassment have increased over the Internet while falling under the radar of official crime data. For example, the number of people arrested for prostitution has declined 17 percent during the past decade. It's possible that (a) there are simply fewer prostitutes, (b) police are less likely to arrest prostitutes than they were a decade ago, or (c) prostitution is booming, but because it's being conducted via the Internet, prostitutes are more likely now to avoid detection (though as the accompanying Profiles in Crime feature indicates, some do get caught). Nonetheless, the rate of traditional violent crimes has also decreased significantly, indicating that the growth of high-tech crimes cannot alone explain the crime drop in America.

> ### CONNECTIONS
> The topic of e-crime will be discussed in detail in Chapter 15. It seems logical that falling common-law crime rates may reflect increases in e-crime.

CRIME PATTERNS

Criminologists look for stable crime rate patterns to gain insight into the nature of crime. The cause of crime may be better understood by examining the rate. If, for example, criminal statistics consistently show that crime rates are higher in poor neighborhoods in large urban areas, then the cause of crime may be related to poverty and neighborhood decline. If, in contrast, crime rates are spread evenly across society, and rates are equal in poor and affluent neighborhoods, this would provide little evidence that crime has an economic basis. Instead, crime might be linked to socialization, personality, intelligence, or some other trait unrelated to class position or income. In this section, we examine traits and patterns that may influence the crime rate.

Crime rates are higher in urban areas, in the south, and during the summer months. Two exceptions to this trend are murders and robberies, which occur frequently in December and January. Here, in a security camera photo provided by the Nashville, Tennessee, Police Department, two men with guns rob a convenience store in Nashville, December 12, 2006. Police say the men killed two people and critically injured another.

AP Images/Nashville Police Department

point (85 degrees) when it may be too hot for any physical exertion.[56] However, criminologists continue to debate this issue:

- Some believe that crime rates rise with temperature (i.e., the hotter the day, the higher the crime rate).[57]
- Others have found evidence that the curvilinear model is correct.[58]
- Some research shows that a rising temperature will cause some crimes to continually increase (e.g., domestic assault), while others (e.g., rape) will decline after temperatures rise to an extremely high level.[59]

If in fact there is an association between temperature and crime, how can it be explained? The relationship may be due to the stress and tension caused by extreme temperatures. The human body generates stress hormones (adrenaline and testosterone) in response to excessive heat; hormonal activity has been linked to aggression.[60]

One way to combat the temperature–crime association: turn off your air conditioner! James Rotton and Ellen Cohn found that assaults in air-conditioned settings increased as the *temperature rose;* assaults in non-air-conditioned settings declined after peaking at moderately high temperatures.[61]

Regional Differences   Large urban areas have by far the highest violence rates; rural areas have the lowest per capita crime rates. Exceptions to this trend are low population resort areas with large transient or seasonal populations, such as Atlantic City, New Jersey. Typically, the western and southern states have had consistently higher crime rates than the Midwest and Northeast (Figure 2.4). This pattern has convinced some criminologists that regional cultural values influence crime rates; others believe that regional differences can be explained by economic differences.

Use of Firearms

Firearms play a dominant role in criminal activity. According to the UCR, about two-thirds of all murders and 40 percent of robberies involve firearms; most of these weapons are handguns.

Because of these findings, there is an ongoing debate over gun control. International criminologists Franklin Zimring and Gordon Hawkins believe the proliferation of handguns and the high rate of lethal violence they cause is the single most significant factor separating the crime problem in the United States from the rest of the developed world.[62] Differences between the United States and Europe in nonlethal crimes are only modest at best—and getting smaller over time.[63]

In contrast, some criminologists believe that personal gun use can actually be a deterrent to crime. Gary Kleck and Marc

The Ecology of Crime

Patterns in the crime rate seem to be linked to temporal and ecological factors. Some of the most important of these are discussed here.

Day, Season, and Climate   Most reported crimes occur during the warm summer months of July and August. During the summer, teenagers, who usually have the highest crime levels, are out of school and have greater opportunity to commit crime. People spend more time outdoors during warm weather, making themselves easier targets. Similarly, homes are left vacant more often during the summer, making them more vulnerable to property crimes. Two exceptions to this trend are murders and robberies, which occur frequently in December and January (although rates are also high during the summer).

Crime rates also may be higher on the first day of the month than at any other time. Government welfare and Social Security checks arrive at this time, and with them come increases in such activities as breaking into mailboxes and accosting recipients on the streets. Also, people may have more disposable income at this time, and the availability of extra money may relate to behaviors associated with crime such as drinking, partying, gambling, and so on.[55]

Temperature   Weather effects (such as temperature swings) may have an impact on violent crime rates. Traditionally, the association between temperature and crime was thought to resembles an inverted U-shaped curve: crime rates increase with rising temperatures and then begin to decline at some

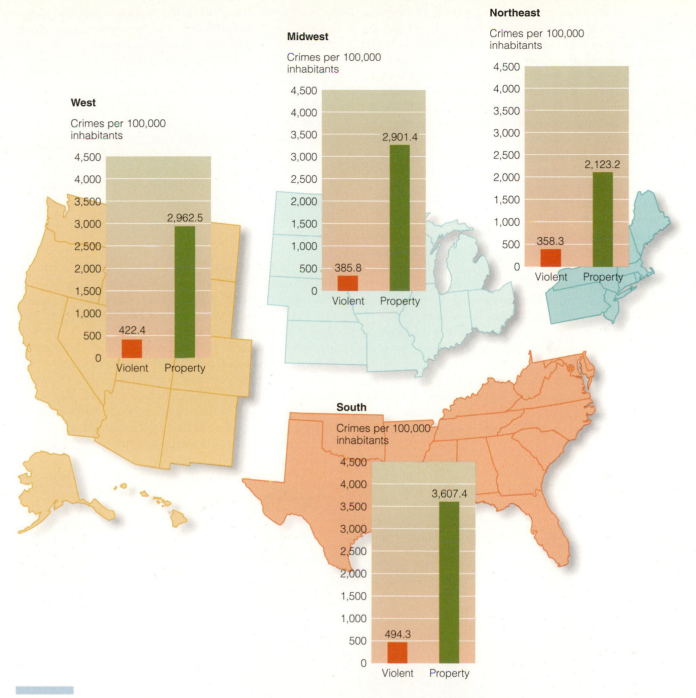

FIGURE 2.4

Regional Crime Rates, Violent and Property Crimes per 100,000 Inhabitants

SOURCE: FBI, *Crime in the United States, 2009*, www2.fbi.gov/ucr/cius2009/offenses/standard_links/regional_estimates.html (accessed November 23, 2010).

Gertz have found that as many as 400,000 people per year use guns in situations in which they later claim that the guns almost "certainly" saved lives. Even if these estimates are off by a factor of 10, it means that armed citizens may save 40,000 lives annually. Although Kleck and Gertz recognize that guns are involved in murders, suicides, and accidents, which claim more than 30,000 lives per year, they believe their benefit as a crime prevention device should not be overlooked.[64]

Social Class, Socioeconomic Conditions, and Crime

It makes sense that crime is inherently a lower-class phenomenon. After all, people at the lowest rungs of the social structure have the greatest incentive to commit crimes, and people who are undergoing financial difficulties are the ones most likely to become their targets.[65] It seems logical that people who are outside the economic mainstream and therefore are unable to obtain desired goods and services legally will resort to illegal activities—such as selling narcotics—to obtain a share of the "American Dream": if you can't afford a car, steal it; if you cannot afford designer clothes, become a drug dealer. **Instrumental crimes** are those committed by indigent people to compensate for the lack of legitimate economic opportunity. People living in poverty are also believed to engage in disproportionate amounts of **expressive crimes**, such as rape and assault, as a result of their anger and frustration against society, a condition fueled by alcohol and drug abuse, common in impoverished areas.[66]

When measured with UCR data, official statistics indicate that crime rates in inner-city, high-poverty areas are generally higher than those in suburban or wealthier areas.[67] Surveys of prison inmates consistently show that prisoners were members of the lower class and unemployed or underemployed in the years before their incarceration. These are empirical indicators of a class–crime connection.

While the association between class and crime seems logical, it is not accepted by all criminologists. An alternative explanation is that the relationship between official crime and social class is a function of law enforcement practices, not actual criminal behavior patterns. Police may devote more resources to poor areas, and consequently apprehension rates may be higher there. Similarly, police may be more likely to formally arrest and prosecute lower-class citizens, especially racial and ethnic minorities, while giving those in the middle and upper classes more lenient treatment, such as handling their law violations with a warning. Police behavior and not actual behavior may account for the lower class's over-representation in official statistics and the prison population. This explanation is supported by self-report data that does not find a direct relationship between social class and crime.[68] The conclusion: if the poor have more extensive criminal records than the wealthy, this difference is attributable to differential law enforcement and not to class-based behavior differences. That is, police may be more likely to arrest lower-class offenders and treat the affluent more leniently.[69]

Evaluating the Class–Crime Association

While the true relationship between class and crime is difficult to determine, the weight of recent evidence seems to suggest that serious, official crime such as rape, murder, and burglary is more prevalent among the lower classes, whereas less serious and self-reported crime is spread more evenly throughout the social structure.[70] Income inequality, poverty, and resource deprivation are all associated with the most serious violent crimes, including homicide and assault.[71] Members of the lower class are more likely to suffer psychological abnormality, including high rates of anxiety and conduct disorders, conditions that may promote criminality.[72]

Research consistently shows that community-level indicators of social inequality are significantly related to crime rates. People living in communities that lack economic and social opportunities are more likely to commit crime than their more affluent neighbors.[73] Community poverty has a significant influence on residents' psychological well-being: people living in substandard areas feel relatively deprived, a condition that produces anger, strain, and frustration.[74] Family life is disrupted, and law-violating youth groups thrive in a climate that undermines adult supervision.[75] So while poverty alone cannot explain crime, debate is far from over. Although crime rates may be higher in lower-class areas, poverty alone cannot explain why a particular individual becomes a chronic violent criminal (if it could, the crime problem would be much worse than it is now). Nevertheless, socioeconomic conditions may influence some people to break the law.[76]

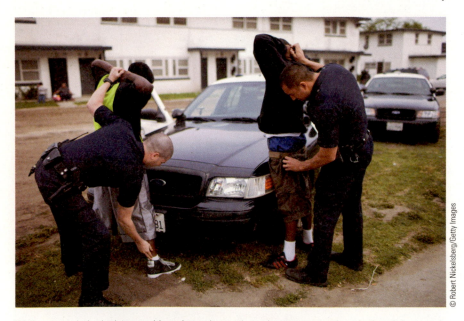

© Robert Nickelsberg/Getty Images

While most criminologists consider crime a lower-class phenomenon, others believe it is spread more evenly across the social structure. Official crime data show that the most serious crimes are committed in lower-class environments. Here, on April 15, 2010, police officers with the Los Angeles Police Department's gang unit search two young men in the Nickerson Gardens Housing Project in the South East police division of Los Angeles, California. The housing project is a traditional street gang neighborhood controlled by the Bounty Hunter Bloods, associated with the nationwide Bloods gang. Lower-class areas are more likely to experience gang activity than more affluent neighborhoods.

Crime and the Economy One of the enduring controversies in the class–crime association is the effect of uneconomic conditions such as unemployment on crime. The association seems logical: if class and crime are related, crime rates should peak during tough economic times when people are out of work and the poor are hard-pressed to find jobs. However, research shows that aggregate crime rates and aggregate unemployment rates seem weakly related. In other words, crime rates sometimes rise during periods of economic prosperity and fall during periods of economic decline.[77]

There are four diverging views on the association between the economy and crime rates:

- *Bad economy means higher crime rates.* When the economy turns down, people who are underemployed or unemployed will become motivated to commit property crimes to obtain desperately needed resources. In contrast, a strong economy, such as the one we had in the 1990s, will bring the crime rate down. When people perceive that the economy is doing well, i.e., there is positive consumer sentiment, the rate of property crimes such as burglary, larceny, and motor vehicle theft declines.[78]

- *Good economy means higher crime rates.* A good economy requires that more people be hired, including teens. Unfortunately, kids with after-school jobs are more likely to engage in antisocial activities. Since teens commit more crimes than adults, high teenage employment will actually increase the overall crime rate.[79]

- *Bad economy means lower crime rate.* During an economic downturn, unemployed parents are at home to supervise children and guard their possessions. When people are unemployed, they have less money on hand and purchase fewer things worth stealing. They may even sell their valuables to raise cash, reducing suitable targets for burglars and thieves.

- *Crime and the economy are unrelated.* It is also possible that the state of the economy and crime rates are unrelated. It seems unlikely that middle-class workers will suddenly join gangs or become bank robbers when they lose their jobs. Research conducted by Gary Kleck and Ted Chiricos shows that the relationship between unemployment and crime rates is insignificant. Unemployed people are neither likely to stick up gas stations, banks, and drug stores, nor are they more likely to engage in nonviolent property crimes, including shoplifting, residential burglary, theft of motor vehicle parts, and theft of automobiles, trucks, and motorcycles.[80] Also, conditions that influence crime rates may counter economic trends. For example, when crime rates are high, voters complain, prompting state and local officials to pour money into police, courts, and correctional services, thereby lowering the crime rate. Since such measures are costly, when crime rates decline and fear temporarily abates, taxpayers will turn their anger toward the high cost of government, thereby convincing state officials to lower taxes and cut back on justice spending. When crime rates increase, as they inevitably do, there are renewed calls for police protection. Because these cycles parallel but do not necessarily coincide with economic conditions, crime rates and crime prevention spending may be high when the economy is working and in decline during an economic downturn or vice versa. The economy has been in turmoil for quite some time, both during the boom years in the 1990s and after the markets crashed and unemployment peaked in the new millennium.

One reason for all this confusion may simply be methodological: measuring the associations among variables such as jobs, the economy, and crime is often quite difficult. There are significant economic differences at the state, county, community, and neighborhood level. While people in one area of the city are doing quite well, their neighbors living in another part of town may be suffering unemployment. Crime rates may even vary by street, an association that is difficult to detect.

Criminologist Shawn Bushway has recently argued that there is no natural or optimum rate of crime and that crime rates go up and down in long, slow trajectories that vary considerably from period to period. These trajectories may be influenced by massive changes in the economy since 1960. Women have joined the workforce in large numbers; union influence has shrunk; manufacturing has moved overseas; and computers and the Internet have changed the way that resources are created and distributed. As manufacturing has moved overseas, less-educated, untrained male workers have been frozen out of the job market. These workers may find themselves competing in illegal markets: selling drugs may be more profitable than working in a fast food restaurant. Similarly, people may find prostitution and/or sex work more lucrative relative to minimum wage jobs in the legitimate market. When the economy turns, drug dealers do not suddenly quit the trade and get a job with GE or IBM. Hence, argues Bushway, labor markets, rather than unemployment rates, are the economic engine that shapes the crime rate and creates incentives for individuals to participate in illegal activities.[81]

So the association between economic factors and crime is quite complex and cannot be explained with a simple linear relationship (i.e., the higher the unemployment rate, the more crime).[82] Class and economic conditions may affect some crimes and some people differently than they affect others. Some subgroups in the population (e.g., women, African Americans) seem more deeply influenced by economic factors than others (e.g., men, whites).[83] There may also be cultural factors involved: while class is related to crime rates in the United States, the effect may be less significant in other cultures, especially those that place less emphasis on the accumulation of material goods.[84]

CONNECTIONS

If class and crime are unrelated, then the causes of crime must be found in factors experienced by members of all social classes—psychological impairment, family conflict, peer pressure, school failure, and so on. Theories that view crime as a function of problems experienced by members of all social classes are reviewed in Chapter 7.

Age and Crime

There is general agreement that age is inversely related to criminality. Criminologists Travis Hirschi and Michael Gottfredson state, "Age is everywhere correlated with crime. Its effects on crime do not depend on other demographic correlates of crime."[85] Regardless of economic status, marital status, race, sex, and so on, younger people commit crime more often than their older peers. Research shows that on average, kids who are persistent offenders begin committing crime in their childhood, rapidly increase their offending activities in late adolescence and then begin a slowdown in adulthood. Early starters tend to commit more crime and are more likely to continue to be involved in criminality over a longer period of time.[86] While it has been long assumed that most kids commit crime in groups, and that peer support encourages offending in adolescence, the most recent research disputes the "co-offending" hypothesis and suggests the great bulk of youth crime is a solo act.[87] Kids who assume an outlaw persona find that their antisocial acts bring them increased social status among peers who admire their risk-taking behaviors. Young criminals may be looking for an avenue of behavior that improves their peer group standing.[88] Hence, they commit more crime in adolescence.

CONNECTIONS

Hirschi and Gottfredson have used their views on the age–crime relationship as a basis for their General Theory of Crime. This important theory holds that the factors that produce crime change little after birth and that the association between crime and age is constant. For more on this view, see the section on the General Theory of Crime in Chapter 9.

Official statistics tell us that young people are arrested at a disproportionate rate to their numbers in the population; victim surveys generate similar findings for crimes in which assailant age can be determined. Whereas youths under 18

collectively make up about 6 percent of the total U.S. population, they account for about 25 percent of serious crime arrests and 17 percent of arrests for all crimes. As a general rule, the peak age for property crime is believed to be 16, and for violence, 18. In contrast, adults 45 and over, who make up about a third of the population, account for only 7 percent of serious crime arrests. The elderly are particularly resistant to the temptations of crime; they make up more than 14 percent of the population and less than 1 percent of arrests. Elderly males 65 and over are predominantly arrested for alcohol-related matters (e.g., public drunkenness and drunk driving) and elderly females for larceny (e.g., shoplifting). The elderly crime rate has remained stable for the past 20 years.[89]

Aging Out of Crime

Most criminologists agree that people commit less crime as they age.[90] Crime peaks in adolescence and then declines rapidly thereafter. According to criminologist Robert Agnew, this peak in criminal activity can be linked to essential features of adolescence in modern, industrial societies. Because adolescents are given most of the privileges and responsibilities of adults in these cultures, they also experience:

- A reduction in supervision
- An increase in social and academic demands
- Participation in a larger, more diverse, peer-oriented social world
- An increased desire for adult privileges
- A reduced ability to cope in a legitimate manner and increased incentive to solve problems in a criminal manner[91]

Adding to these incentives is the fact that young people, especially the indigent and antisocial, tend to discount the future.[92] They are impatient, and because their future is uncertain, they are unwilling or unable to delay gratification. As they mature, troubled youths are able to develop a long-term life view and resist the need for immediate gratification.[93] **Aging out** of crime may be a function of the natural history of the human life cycle.[94] Deviance in adolescence is fueled by the need for money and sex and reinforced by close relationships with peers who defy conventional morality. At the same time, teenagers are becoming independent from parents and other adults who enforce conventional standards of morality and behavior. They have a new sense of energy and strength and are involved with peers who are similarly vigorous and frustrated.

In adulthood, people strengthen their ability to delay gratification and forgo the immediate gains that law violations bring. They also start wanting to take responsibility for their behavior and to adhere to conventional mores.[95] Getting married, raising a family, and creating long-term family ties provide the stability that helps people desist from crime.[96]

CONNECTIONS

Some criminologists argue that although most people age out of crime, a small group continues into old age as chronic or persistent offenders. It is possible that the population may contain different sets of criminal offenders: one group whose criminality declines with age; another whose criminal behavior remains constant through maturity. This issue will be discussed in greater detail in Chapter 9.

Gender and Crime

Male crime rates are much higher than those of females. Victims report that their assailant was male in more than 80 percent of all violent personal crimes. The most recent Uniform Crime Report arrest statistics indicate that males account for more than 80 percent of all arrests for serious violent crimes and almost 70 percent of the arrests for serious property crimes; murder arrests are 8 males to 1 female. MTF data also show that young men commit more serious crimes, such as robbery, assault, and burglary, than their female peers.

Even though gender differences in the crime rate have persisted over time, there seems little question that females are now involved in more crime than ever before and that there are more similarities than differences between male and female offenders.[97] UCR arrest data shows that over the past decade, while male arrest rates have declined by 9 percent, female arrest rates have increased by 9 percent. Most notable have been increased female arrests for serious crimes such as robbery (up 10 percent) and burglary (up 15 percent). So during a period of slowing overall growth in crime rates, women have increased their participation in crime.

Explaining Gender Differences in the Crime Rate

Early criminologists pointed to emotional, physical, and psychological differences between males and females to explain the differences in crime rates. Cesare Lombroso's 1895 book, *The Female Offender*, argued that a small group of female criminals lacked "typical" female traits of "piety, maternity, undeveloped intelligence, and weakness."[98] In physical appearance as well as in their emotional makeup, delinquent females appeared closer to men than to other women. Lombroso's theory became known as the **masculinity hypothesis**; in essence, a few "masculine" females were responsible for the handful of crimes women commit.

Another early view of female crime focused on the supposed dynamics of sexual relationships. Female criminals were viewed as either sexually controlling or sexually naive, either manipulating men for profit or being manipulated by them. The female's criminality was often masked because criminal justice authorities were reluctant to take action

against a woman.[99] This perspective is known as the **chivalry hypothesis**, which holds that much female criminality is hidden because of the culture's generally protective and benevolent attitude toward women.[100] In other words, police are less likely to arrest, juries are less likely to convict, and judges are less likely to incarcerate female offenders.

Although these early writings are no longer taken seriously, some criminologists still believe that gender-based traits are a key determinant of crime rate differences. Among the suspected differences include physical strength and hormonal influences. According to this view, male sex hormones (androgens) account for more aggressive male behavior, and gender-related hormonal differences explain the gender gap in the crime rate.[101]

CONNECTIONS

Gender differences in the crime rate may be a function of androgen levels because these hormones cause areas of the brain to become less sensitive to environmental stimuli, making males more likely to seek high levels of stimulation and to tolerate more pain in the process. Chapter 5 discusses the biosocial causes of crime and reviews this issue in greater detail.

Socialization and Development

Although there are few gender-based differences in aggression during the first few years of life, girls are socialized to be less aggressive than boys and are supervised more closely by parents.[102] Differences in aggression become noticeable between ages 3 and 6 when children are first socialized into organized peer groups such as the daycare center or school. Males are more likely then to display physical aggression while girls display relational aggression—excluding disliked peers from playgroups, gossiping, and interfering with social relationships.

Males are taught to be more aggressive and assertive and are less likely to form attachments to others. They often view their aggression as a gender-appropriate means to gain status and power, either by joining deviant groups and gangs or engaging in sports. Even in the middle-class suburbs, they may seek approval by knocking down or running through peers on the playing field, while females literally cheer them on. The male search for social approval through aggressive behavior may make them more susceptible to criminality, especially when the chosen form of aggression is antisocial or illegal. Recent research by Jean Bottcher found that young boys perceive their roles as being more dominant than young girls.[103] Male perceptions of power, their ability to have freedom and hang with their friends, helped explain the gender differences in crime and delinquency.

In contrast, girls are encouraged to care about other people and avoid harming them; their need for sensitivity and understanding may help counterbalance the effects of poverty and family problems. And because they are more verbally proficient, many females may develop social skills that help them deal with conflict without resorting to violence. Females are taught to be less aggressive and to view belligerence as a lack of self-control—a conclusion that is unlikely to be reached by a male.

Girls are usually taught—directly or indirectly—to respond to provocation by feeling anxious and depressed, whereas boys are encouraged to retaliate. Overall, when they are provoked, females are much more likely to feel distressed than males—experiencing sadness, anxiety, and uneasiness. Although females may get angry as often as males, many have been taught to blame themselves for harboring such negative feelings. Females are therefore much more likely than males to respond to anger with feelings of depression, anxiety, fear, and shame. Although females are socialized to fear that their anger will harm valued relationships, males react with "moral outrage," looking to blame others for their discomfort.[104]

Cognitive Differences   Psychologists note significant cognitive differences between boys and girls that may impact on their antisocial behaviors. Girls have been found to be superior to boys in verbal ability, while boys test higher in visual-spatial performance. Girls acquire language faster, learning to speak earlier and faster with better pronunciation. Girls are far less likely to have reading problems than boys, while boys do much better on standardized math tests. (This difference is attributed by some experts to boys receiving more attention from math teachers.) In most cases these cognitive differences are small, narrowing, and usually attributed to cultural expectations. When given training, girls demonstrate an ability to increase their visual-spatial skills to the point where their abilities become indistinguishable from the ability of boys.

Cognitive differences may contribute to behavioral variations. Even at an early age, girls are found to be more empathic than boys—that is, more capable of understanding and relating to the feelings of others.[105] Empathy for others may help shield girls from antisocial acts because they are more likely to understand a victim's suffering. Girls are more concerned with relationship and feeling issues, and they are less interested than boys are in competing for material success. Boys who are not tough and aggressive are labeled sissies and cry babies. In contrast, girls are given different messages; they are expected to form closer bonds with their friends and share feelings. Their superior verbal skills may allow girls to talk rather than fight. When faced with conflict, women might be more likely to attempt to negotiate, rather than to either respond passively or to physically resist, especially when they perceive increased threat of harm or death.[106]

Feminist Views   In the 1970s, **liberal feminist theory** focused attention on the social and economic role of women in society and its relationship to female crime rates.[107] This view suggested that the traditionally lower crime rate for women could be explained by their "second-class" economic and social position. As women's social roles changed and their lifestyles became more like men's, it was believed that their crime rates would converge. Criminologists, responding to this research, began to refer to the "new female criminal." The rapid increase in the female crime rate, especially in what had traditionally been male-oriented crimes (such as burglary and larceny), supports the feminist view. In addition, self-report studies seem to indicate that (a) the pattern of female criminality, if not its frequency, is quite similar to that of male criminality, and (b) the factors that predispose male criminals to crime have an equal impact on female criminals.[108]

CONNECTIONS

Critical criminologists view gender inequality as stemming from the unequal power of men and women in a capitalist society and the exploitation of females by fathers and husbands. This perspective is considered more fully in Chapter 8.

Is Convergence Likely?   Although male arrest rates are still considerably higher than female rates, female arrest rates seem to be increasing at a faster pace; it is possible that they may eventually converge. Women are committing more crime, and young girls are joining gangs in record numbers.[109]

While these trends indicate that gender differences in the crime rate may be eroding, some criminologists remain skeptical about the data. They find that gender-based crime rate differences are still significant; the "emancipation of women" may have had relatively little influence on female crime rates.[110] For one thing, many female criminals come from the socioeconomic class least affected by the women's movement; their crimes seem more a function of economic inequality than women's rights. For another, the offense patterns of women are still quite different from those of men. While males still commit a disproportionate share of serious crimes such as robbery, burglary, murder, and assault, most female criminals are still engaging in less serious crimes than their male counterparts.[111] How then can gender-based arrest rates be explained? According to Darrell Steffensmeier and his associates, these arrest trends may be explained more by changes in police activity than in criminal activity. Police today may be more willing to arrest girls for minor crimes; police are making more arrests for crimes that occur at school and in the home; police are responding more vigorously to public demands for action and are therefore less likely to use their discretion to help females.[112] Police may also be abandoning their traditional deference toward women in an effort to be "gender neutral." In addition, changing laws such as dual arrest laws in domestic cases that mandate both parties be taken into custody, result in more women suffering arrest in domestic incidents.[113]

Race and Crime

Official crime data indicate that minority group members are involved in a disproportionate share of criminal activity. African Americans make up about 12 percent of the general population, yet they account for almost 40 percent of Part I violent crime arrests and 30 percent of property crime arrests. They also are responsible for a disproportionate number of Part II arrests (except for alcohol-related arrests, which detain primarily white offenders).

Are these data a reflection of true racial differences in the crime rate, or do they reflect racial bias in the justice process? We can evaluate this issue by comparing racial differences in self-report data with those found in official delinquency records. Charges of racial discrimination in the justice process would be substantiated if whites and blacks self-reported equal numbers of crimes, but minorities were arrested and prosecuted far more often.

Early efforts by noted criminologists found virtually no relationship between race and self-reported delinquency, a finding that supported racial bias in the arrest decision process.[114] Other, more recent self-report studies that use large national samples of youths have also found little evidence of racial disparity in self-reported crimes committed.[115] These and other self-report studies seem to indicate that the delinquent behavior rates of black and white teenagers are generally similar and that differences in arrest statistics may indicate a differential selection policy by police.[116] Suspects who are poor, minority, or male are more likely to be formally arrested than suspects who are white, affluent, or female.[117]

Evidence of racial bias in the arrest process can be found in the use of racial profiling to stop African Americans and search their cars without probable cause or reasonable suspicion. Police officers, some social commentators note, have created a form of traffic offense called DWB, "driving while black."[118] National surveys of driving practices show that young black and Latino males are more likely to be stopped by police and suffer citations, searches, and arrests, as well as be the target of force even though they are no more likely to be in the possession of illegal contraband than white drivers.[119]

Although the official statistics, such as UCR arrest data, may reflect discriminatory justice system practices, African Americans are arrested for a disproportionate amount of serious violent crime, such as robbery and murder, and some criminologists find it improbable that police discretion and/or bias *alone* could account for these proportions. It is doubtful that police routinely release white killers, robbers, and rapists while arresting violent black offenders who commit the same offenses.[120] If these racial differences in serious crimes exist how can they be explained?

System Bias   Race-based differences in the crime rate can be explained in part as an effect of unequal or biased treatment by the justice system. There are a number of indications that system bias exists and penalizes racial minorities. According to what is known as the **racial threat hypothesis**,

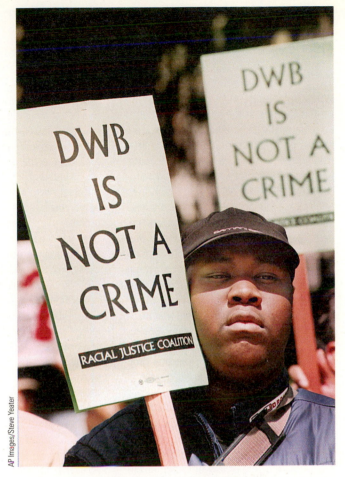

Empirical evidence shows that, in at least some jurisdictions, young African American males are treated more harshly by the criminal and juvenile justice systems than are members of any other group. Elements of institutional racism have become so endemic that terms such as "DWB" (driving while black) are now part of the vernacular, used to signify the fact that young African American motorists are routinely stopped by police.

as the percentage of minorities in the population increases, so too does the amount of social control that police direct at minority group members.[121] Police are more likely to aggressively patrol minority neighborhoods; suspect, search, and arrest minority group members; and make arrests for minor infractions, helping to raise the minority crime rate.[122] For example, when Malcolm Holmes and his colleagues studied law enforcement actions in southwestern border communities, they found that as the numbers of poor Hispanics increase, affluent Anglos demand greater levels of police protection.[123] The result is a stepped-up effort to control and punish minority citizens, which segregates minorities from the economic mainstream and reinforces the physical and social isolation of the barrio.[124]

The "racial threat" effect is not the only evidence of system bias. There are some indications that the justice system treats minority defendants differently from members of the white majority. Black, Latino, and American Indian youth

When sociologist Alice Goffman was an undergraduate at the University of Pennsylvania, she tutored a high school student named Aisha. She later met Aisha's brother Ronny, age 15, when he came home from a juvenile detention center, and Ronny introduced her to Mike, who was 21, and then Mike's best friend Chuck, age 18, who also came home from county jail. Chuck, Mike, and Ronny were part of a loose group of about 15 young men who grew up around 6th Street in Philadelphia, most of whom were unemployed and trying to make it outside of the formal economy. Some worked as low-level crack dealers; others sold marijuana, "wet" (PCP and/or embalming fluid), or pills like Xanax. Some of the men occasionally made money by robbing other drug dealers. One earned his keep by exotic dancing and offering sex to women.

Through her connections to these young people, Goffman was able to draw an understanding of life in the Philadelphia underclass, the burdens faced by the urban poor, and the role of law enforcement in everyday life. On 6th Street, the constant threat of arrest and incarceration shaped behavior and values and became an integral part of everyday behavior.

In these neighborhoods, children learn at an early age to watch out for the police and to prepare to run when they see them in the neighborhood. The first topic of the day focused on who had been taken into custody the night before and who had outrun the cops and gotten away. The young men discussed how the police identified and located the people they were looking for, what the charges were likely to be, what physical harm had been done to the man as he was caught and arrested, and what property the police had taken and what had been wrecked or lost during the chase.

In the 6th Street neighborhood, a significant portion of the young men were "on the run," some because they were suspects in actual street crimes, but most because there were outstanding arrest warrants for minor infractions such as shoplifting or possession of recreational drugs. Young men were constantly worried that they would be picked up by the police and taken into custody even when they did not have a warrant out for their arrest. Those on probation or parole, on house arrest, or going through a trial expressed concern that they would soon be picked up and taken into custody for some violation that would "come up in the system." People on the run make a concerted effort to thwart their discovery and apprehension.

Goffman found that once a man finds that he may be stopped by the police and taken into custody, he discovers that people, places, and relations he formerly relied on, and that are integral to maintaining a respectable identity, get redefined as paths to confinement. Public places and institutions are seen as threatening. When Alex and his girlfriend, Donna, both age 22, drove to the hospital for the birth of their son, two police officers came into the room and arrested Alex for violating parole. After Alex was arrested, other young men expressed hesitation to go to the hospital when their babies were born. Equally scary was a job in the legitimate economy where the police knew your schedule in advance and traps could be set, resulting in arrest and confinement.

People learn to avoid calling upon the justice system for help, especially if they have a criminal record. Goffman noted numerous instances in which members of the group contacted the police when they were injured, robbed, or threatened. These men were either in good standing with the courts or had no pending legal constraints. She did not observe any person with a warrant call the police or voluntarily make use of the courts during the six years she spent there. Young men with warrants seemed to see the authorities only as a threat to their safety. This has two important implications:

- Because they steered clear of the law, young men with criminal records are vulnerable to criminals looking for an easy score.
- Because they could not call the police, wanted people were more likely to use

are treated more severely in juvenile court than their white counterparts. They may be more likely to be detained, have formal charges (petitions) filed, and be removed from their homes and placed in secure confinement.[125]

As adults, minority group members, especially those who are indigent or unemployed, continue to receive disparate treatment. Black and Latino adults are less likely to receive bail in violent crime cases than whites, and consequently more likely to be kept in detention pending trial.[126] They also receive longer prison sentences than whites who commit similar crimes and have similar criminal histories. Take for instance the use of habitual offender statutes that provide very long sentences for a second or third conviction ("three strikes and you're out"). One recent study (2008) by Matthew Crow and Kathrine Johnson looked at the use of habitual sentencing practices in Florida and reached the conclusion that race and ethnicity still matter: minority drug and violent offenders are viewed as particular threats to dominant, mainstream values and are more likely to be charged as habitual offenders than are European Americans.[127] Nor is this solely a state court problem. After reviewing sentences in the federal court system, Jill Doerner and Stephen Demuth found that particularly harsh punishments are focused disproportionately on the youngest Hispanic and black male defendants. Young Hispanic male defendants have the highest odds of incarceration, and young black male defendants receive the longest sentences.[128] Yet when African Americans are victims of crime, their predicaments receive less public concern and

violence to protect themselves or to get back at others. This kind of self-help crime is typically carried out when the police and the courts are unavailable because people have warrants out for their arrest and may be held in custody if they contact the authorities.

Like going to the hospital or using the police and the courts, even more intimate relations—friends, family, and romantic partners—may pose a threat and thus have to be avoided or at least carefully navigated. In some instances, the police are used as agents of social control and as a form of direct retaliation. When Michelle, age 16, got pregnant, she claimed that 17-year-old Reggie was the father. Reggie denied he had gotten her pregnant until he was in jail and was forced to admit he was the father in order to buy the silence of Michelle and her aunt.

While family members, partners, or friends of a wanted man occasionally call the police on him to control his behavior or to punish him for a perceived wrong, close kin or girlfriends also link young men to the police because the police compel them to do so. It is common practice for the police to put pressure on friends, girlfriends, and family members to provide information, particularly when these people have their own warrants, are serving probation or parole, or have a pending trial. Family members and

friends who are not themselves caught up in the justice system may be threatened with eviction or with having their children taken away.

In this world, maintaining a secret and unpredictable routine decreases the chance of arrest: it is easier for the police to find a person through his last known address if he comes home at around the same time to the same house every day. Finding a person at work is easier if he works a regular shift in the same place every day. Cultivating secrecy and unpredictability, then, serves as a general strategy to avoid confinement. The "secret life" also provides an excuse for failure: "I could not lead a respectable life because it would lead me to jail." This explains social and economic failure in a culturally acceptable manner.

The presence of the criminal justice system in the lives of the poor, Goffman found, cannot simply be measured by the number of people sent to prison or the number who return home with felony convictions. The recent rise in imprisonment has fostered a climate of fear and suspicion in poor communities—a climate in which family members and friends are pressured to inform on one another and young men live as suspects and fugitives, with the daily fear of confinement. One strategy for coping with these risks is to avoid dangerous places, people, and interactions entirely.

A young man thus does not attend the birth of his child or seek medical help when he is badly beaten. He avoids the police and the courts, even if it means using violence when he is injured or becoming the target of others who are looking for someone to rob. A second strategy is to cultivate unpredictability—to remain secretive and to work outside the economic mainstream. To ensure that those close to him will not inform on him, a young man comes and goes in irregular and unpredictable ways, remaining elusive and untrusting, sleeping in different beds, and deceiving those close to him about his life. Considering this burden, is it surprising that young men raised in this environment find themselves on the run and outside the law?

CRITICAL THINKING

Goffman paints a pretty bleak picture of underclass life and the social forces that shape its existence. Should the United States intervene in other countries in attempts at "nation building" or to develop democracy abroad in third-world nations when there are so many problems here at home?

SOURCE: Alice Goffman, "On the Run: Wanted Men in a Philadelphia Ghetto," *American Sociological Review* 74 (2009): 339–357.

media attention than that afforded white victims.[129] Murders involving whites (and females) are much more likely to be punished with death than those whose victims are black males, a fact not lost on the minority population.[130]

Disparities in justice policy result in the widely disproportionate makeup of the prison population. As Figure 2.5 shows, the percentage of minority men and women who are behind bars is far higher than the percentage of European Americans. It is not surprising that African Americans of all social classes hold negative attitudes toward the justice system and view it as an arbitrary and unfair institution.[131]

The Race, Culture, Gender and Criminology feature discusses the associations between the threat of arrest, incarceration, poverty, and culture in the minority community.

Cultural Bias

Another explanation of racial differences in the crime rate rests on the legacy of racial discrimination based on personality and behavior.[132] The fact that U.S. culture influences African American crime rates is underscored by the fact that black violence rates are much lower in other nations—both those that are predominantly white, such as Canada, and those that are predominantly black, such as Nigeria.[133]

Some criminologists view black crime as a function of socialization in a society where the black family was torn apart and black culture destroyed in such a way that recovery has proven impossible. Early experiences, beginning with slavery, have left a wound that has been deepened by

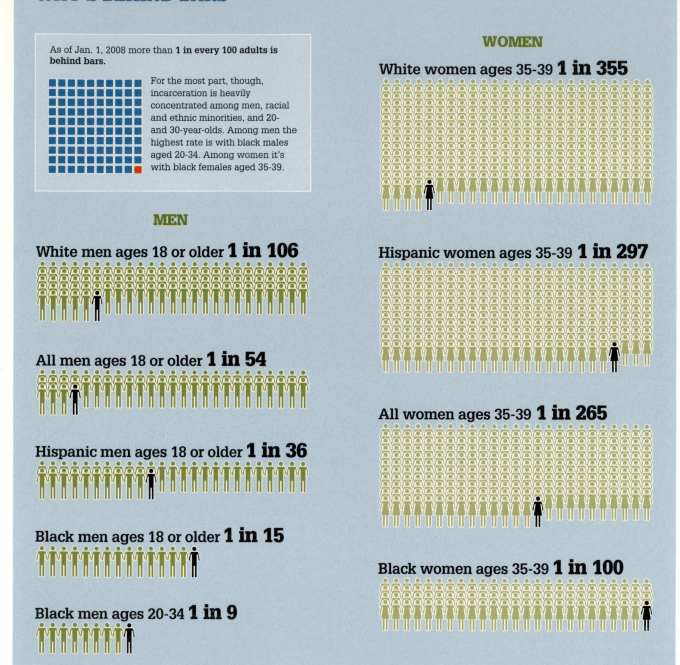

WHO'S BEHIND BARS

As of Jan. 1, 2008 more than **1 in every 100 adults is behind bars.**

For the most part, though, incarceration is heavily concentrated among men, racial and ethnic minorities, and 20- and 30-year-olds. Among men the highest rate is with black males aged 20-34. Among women it's with black females aged 35-39.

MEN

White men ages 18 or older **1 in 106**

All men ages 18 or older **1 in 54**

Hispanic men ages 18 or older **1 in 36**

Black men ages 18 or older **1 in 15**

Black men ages 20-34 **1 in 9**

WOMEN

White women ages 35-39 **1 in 355**

Hispanic women ages 35-39 **1 in 297**

All women ages 35-39 **1 in 265**

Black women ages 35-39 **1 in 100**

FIGURE 2.5
Who's Behind Bars

SOURCE: The Pew Center on the States, "One in 100: Behind Bars in America 2008," Pew Foundation, Washington, D.C., www.pewcenteronthestates.org/uploadedFiles/One%20in%20100.pdf (accessed November 2, 2010).

racism and lack of opportunity.[134] Children of the slave society were thrust into a system of forced dependency and ambivalence and antagonism toward one's self and group.

In an important work, *All God's Children: The Bosket Family and the American Tradition of Violence,* crime reporter Fox Butterfield chronicles the history of the Boskets, a black family, through five generations.[135] He focuses on Willie Bosket, who is charming, captivating, and brilliant. He is also one of the worst criminals in the New York State penal system. By the time he was in his teens, he had committed more than 200 armed robberies and 25 stabbings. Butterfield shows how the early struggles in the South, with its violent slave culture, led directly to Willie Bosket's rage and violence on the streets of New York City. Beginning in South Carolina in the 1700s, the southern slave society was a place where white notions of honor demanded immediate retaliation for the smallest slight. According to Butterfield, contemporary black violence is a tradition inherited from white southern violence. The need for respect has turned into a cultural mandate that can provoke retaliation at the slightest hint of insult.

Structural Bias

A third view is that racial differences in the crime rate are a function of disparity in the social and economic structure of society. William Julius Wilson, one of the nation's most prominent sociologists, provides a description of the plight of the lowest levels of the underclass, which he labels the truly disadvantaged, most often minority group members who dwell in urban inner cities, occupy the bottom rung of the social ladder, and are the victims of discrimination. Because the truly disadvantaged rarely come into contact with the actual source of their oppression, they direct their anger and aggression at those with whom they are in close contact, such as neighbors, businesspeople, and landlords. Plagued by under- or unemployment, they begin to lose self-confidence, a feeling exacerbated by the plight of kin and friendship groups who also experience extreme economic marginality. Self-doubt is a neighborhood norm that threatens to overwhelm those forced to live in areas of concentrated poverty. Most adults in inner-city ghetto neighborhoods are not working during a typical week and are therefore not affected by short-term economic trends. Poverty in these inner-city areas is pervasive and unchanging—if anything, it is steadily worsening as residents are further shut out of the economic mainstream.

Wilson focuses on the plight of the African American community, which had enjoyed periods of relative prosperity in the 1950s and 1960s. He suggests that as difficult as life was for African Americans in the 1940s and 1950s, they at least had a reasonable hope of steady work. Now, because of the globalization of the economy, those opportunities have evaporated. In the past, growth in the manufacturing sector fueled upward mobility and formed the foundation of today's African American middle class. Those opportunities no longer exist, because manufacturing plants have been moved to inaccessible rural and overseas locations where the cost of doing business is lower. With manufacturing opportunities all but obsolete in the United States, service and retail establishments that depended on blue-collar spending have similarly disappeared, leaving behind an economy based on welfare and government supports. In less than 20 years, formerly active African American neighborhoods have become crime-infested inner-city ghettos.

In his most recent work, *More than Just Race: Being Black and Poor in the Inner City*, Wilson tries to explain the persistence of poverty in black neighborhoods. He finds that both culture and structure play a role in crime. For example, a law and order political philosophy and fear of racial conflict have led to high incarceration rates among African American males. While black women can get jobs in service industries, employers are less likely to hire black men, especially those with a criminal record. As a result, there has been a decline in the ability of black men to be providers, adding further stress to the stability of the African American family. Here we can see how structure and culture intertwine to produce stress in the African American community.[136]

Economic and Social Disparity   Racial and ethnic differentials in crime rates may also be tied to economic and social disparity. Racial and ethnic minorities are often forced to live in high-crime areas where the risk of victimization is significant. People who witness violent crime and are victimized may themselves engage in violence.[137]

Racial and ethnic minorities face a greater degree of social isolation and economic deprivation than the white majority, a condition that has been linked by empirical research to high violence rates.[138] Not helping the situation is the fact that during tough economic times, blacks and whites may find themselves competing for shrinking job opportunities. As economic competition between the races grows, interracial homicides do likewise; economic and political rivalries lead to greater levels of interracial violence.[139]

Even during times of economic growth, lower-class African Americans are left out of the economic mainstream, a fact that meets with a growing sense of frustration and failure.[140] As a result of being shut out of educational and economic opportunities enjoyed by the rest of society, this population may be prone to the lure of illegitimate gain and criminality. African Americans living in lower-class inner-city areas may be disproportionately violent because they are exposed to more violence in their daily lives than other racial and economic groups.[141] Many black youths are forced to attend essentially segregated schools that are underfunded and deteriorated, a condition that elevates the likelihood of their being incarcerated in adulthood.[142]

CONNECTIONS

The concept of relative deprivation refers to the fact that people compare their success to those with whom they are in immediate contact. Even if conditions improve, they still may feel as if they are falling behind. A sense of relative deprivation, discussed in Chapter 6, may lead to criminal activity.

Family Dissolution   Family dissolution in the minority community may be tied to low employment rates among African American males, which places a strain on marriages. The relatively large number of single-female-headed households in these communities may be tied to the high mortality rate among African American males, caused by disease and violence.[143] When families are weakened or disrupted, their social control is compromised. It is not surprising, then, that divorce and separation rates are significantly associated with homicide rates in the African American community.[144]

CONNECTIONS

According to some criminologists, racism has created isolated subcultures that espouse violence as a way of coping with conflict situations. Exasperation and frustration among minority group members who feel powerless to fit into middle-class society are manifested in aggression. This view is discussed further in Chapter 10, which reviews the subculture of violence theory.

Is Convergence Possible?   Race differences in family structure, economic status, education achievement, and other social factors persist. Does that mean that racial differences in the crime rate will persist, or is convergence possible? One argument is that if and when economic conditions improve in the minority community, differences in crime rates will eventually disappear.[145] Another view is that the trend toward residential integration, under way since 1980, may also help reduce crime rate differentials.[146] An important study (2010) by Gary LaFree and his associates tracked race-specific homicide arrest differences in 80 large U.S. cities from 1960 to 2000, and found substantial convergence in black/white homicide arrest rates over time.[147]

Homicide rate differences narrowed in cities with a growing black population and also where there was little race-based difference in the number of intact families. In other words, where the percentage of families led by a single parent were equal in the black and white communities, crime rates went down. Conversely, homicide ratios expanded in cities where African Americans were involved in more drug-related crimes than whites. This finding indicates that crime rate convergence may be linked to social factors. Positive factors, such as equality in family structure, will reduce race-based differences; negative factors, such as drug use differentials, will enhance race-based differences. In sum, the weight of the evidence shows that although there is little difference in the self-reported crime rates of racial groups, Hispanics and African Americans are more likely to be arrested for serious violent crimes. The causes of minority crime have been linked to poverty, racism, hopelessness, lack of opportunity, and urban problems experienced by all too many African American citizens.

Immigration and Crime

There is a prevailing view that illegal immigrants are dangerous and violent people and that areas that house illegal immigrants experience a spike in their crime rates. This view culminated in the passage in Arizona of a new law—the Support Our Law Enforcement and Safe Neighborhoods Act—that creates new crimes and enables police officers to stop, detain, and arrest people for what they perceive as immigration violation—reasonable suspicion that they are in the country without documentation.[148] This law makes it a crime to lack immigration papers and requires police to determine whether people they encounter are in the country illegally.[149] Some elements of this law have been challenged in the courts. In April 2011, the 9th Circuit Court of Appeals in San Francisco rejected an appeal by Arizona Governor Jan Brewer seeking to lift an injunction imposed by a federal judge in Phoenix, Arizona, the day before the controversial law was to take effect July 29, 2010. The appeals court ruled Arizona cannot require local police to demand documentation from suspected illegal immigrants.[150]

Some critics call for tough new laws limiting immigration and/or strictly enforcing immigration laws because immigrants are crime prone and represent a social threat. How true are their perceptions? Not very true, according to the report "Crime, Corrections, and California: What Does Immigration Have to Do with It?" released by the Public Policy Institute of California.[151] According to the data, immigrants are far less likely than the average U.S. native to commit crime. Significantly lower rates of incarceration and institutionalization among foreign-born adults suggest that long-standing fears of immigration as a threat to public safety are unjustified. Among the key findings:

- People born outside the United States make up about 35 percent of California's adult population but represent about 17 percent of the state prison population.
- U.S.-born adult men are incarcerated in state prisons at rates up to 3.3 times higher than foreign-born men.
- Among men ages 18 to 40—the age group most likely to commit crime—those born in the United States are 10 times more likely than immigrants to be in county jail or state prison.
- Noncitizen men from Mexico ages 18 to 40—a group disproportionately likely to have entered the United States illegally—are more than 8 times *less* likely than U.S.-born men in the same age group to be in a correctional setting (0.48 percent versus 4.2 percent).

The findings are striking because immigrants in California are more likely than the U.S.-born to be young and male and to have low levels of education—all characteristics associated with higher rates of crime and incarceration. Yet the report shows that institutionalization rates of young male immigrants with less than a high school diploma are extremely low, particularly when compared with U.S.-born men with low levels of education.

The California report is not unique. A number of research studies have concluded that immigrants have lower crime rates than the norm. For example, a recent examination by Ramiro Martinez of homicide rates in Texas found that counties on the Mexican border have significantly *lower* homicide rates than non-border counties, and Texas counties with *higher* levels of immigration concentration had lower levels of homicide. Not only are Latino homicide rates lower in these areas, so are those of non-Latino whites and blacks. No compelling support was found for the claim that border areas are more violent due to proximity or immigration.[152]

The low rates of criminal involvement by immigrants may be due in part to current U.S. immigration policy, which screens immigrants for criminal history and assigns extra penalties to noncitizens who commit crimes.

Chronic Offenders/ Criminal Careers

Crime data show that most offenders commit a single criminal act and upon arrest discontinue their antisocial activity. Others commit a few less serious crimes. A small group of criminal offenders, however, account for a majority of all criminal offenses. These persistent offenders are referred to as **career criminals** or **chronic offenders**. The concept of the chronic or career offender is most closely associated with the research efforts of Marvin Wolfgang, Robert Figlio, and Thorsten Sellin.[153] In their landmark 1972 study, *Delinquency in a Birth Cohort*, they used official records to follow the criminal careers of a cohort of 9,945 boys born in Philadelphia in 1945 from the time of their birth until they reached 18 years of age in 1963. Official police records were used to identify delinquents. About one-third of the boys (3,475) had some police contact. The remaining two-thirds (6,470) had none. Each delinquent was given a seriousness weight score for every delinquent act.[154] The weighting of delinquent acts allowed the researchers to differentiate between a simple assault requiring no medical attention for the victim and serious battery in which the victim needed hospitalization. The best-known discovery of Wolfgang and his associates was that of the so-called chronic offender. The cohort data indicated that 54 percent (1,862) of the sample's delinquent youths were repeat offenders, whereas the remaining 46 percent (1,613) were one-time offenders. The repeaters could be further categorized as nonchronic recidivists and chronic recidivists. The former consisted of 1,235 youths who had been arrested more than once but fewer than

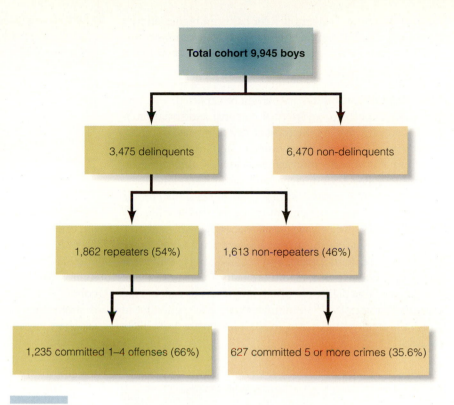

FIGURE 2.6
Distribution of Offenses in the Philadelphia Cohort

SOURCE: Marvin Wolfgang, Robert Figlio, and Thorsten Sellin, *Delinquency in a Birth Cohort* (Chicago: University of Chicago Press, 1972). Reprinted with permission of University of Chicago Press.

five times and who made up 35.6 percent of all delinquents. The latter were a group of 627 boys arrested five times or more, who accounted for 18 percent of the delinquents and 6 percent of the total sample of 9,945. (See Figure 2.6.)

The chronic offenders (known today as "the chronic 6 percent") were involved in the most dramatic amounts of delinquent behavior: they were responsible for 5,305 offenses, or 51.9 percent of all the offenses committed by the cohort. Even more striking was the involvement of chronic offenders in serious criminal acts. Of the entire sample, the chronic 6 percent committed 71 percent of the homicides, 73 percent of the rapes, 82 percent of the robberies, and 69 percent of the aggravated assaults.

Wolfgang and his associates found that arrests and court experience did little to deter the chronic offender. In fact, punishment was inversely related to chronic offending: the more stringent the sanction chronic offenders received, the more likely they would be to engage in repeated criminal behavior.

In a second cohort study, Wolfgang and his associates selected a new, larger birth cohort, born in Philadelphia in 1958, which contained both male and female subjects.[155] Although the proportion of delinquent youths was about the same as that in the 1945 cohort, they again found a similar pattern of chronic offending. Chronic female delinquency was relatively rare—only 1 percent of the females in the survey were chronic offenders. Wolfgang's pioneering effort to identify the chronic career offender has been replicated by a number of other researchers in a variety of locations in the United States.[156] The chronic offender has also been found abroad.[157]

What Causes Chronicity?   As might be expected, kids who have been exposed to a variety of personal and social problems at an early age are the most at risk to repeat offending, a concept referred to as **early onset**. One important study of delinquent offenders in Orange County, California, conducted by Michael Schumacher and Gwen Kurz, found several factors (see Exhibit 2.3) that characterized the chronic offender, including problems in the home and at school.[158] Other research studies have found that early involvement in criminal activity (getting arrested before age 15), relatively low intellectual development, and parental drug involvement were key predictive factors for chronicity.[159] Offenders who accumulate large debts, use drugs, and resort to violence are more likely to persist.[160] In contrast, those who spend time in a juvenile facility and later in an adult prison are more likely to desist.[161]

EXHIBIT 2.3

Characteristics that Predict Chronic Offending

School Behavior/Performance Factor
- Attendance problems (truancy or a pattern of skipping school)
- Behavior problems (recent suspensions or expulsion)
- Poor grades (failing two or more classes)

Family Problem Factor
- Poor parental supervision and control
- Significant family problems (illness, substance abuse, discord)
- Criminal family members
- Documented child abuse, neglect, or family violence

Substance Abuse Factor
- Alcohol or drug use (by minors in any way but experimentation)

Delinquency Factor
- Stealing pattern of behavior
- Runaway pattern of behavior
- Gang member or associate

SOURCE: Michael Schumacher and Gwen Kurz, *The 8% Solution: Preventing Serious Repeat Juvenile Crime* (Thousand Oaks, CA: Sage, 1999).

CONNECTIONS

It is evident that chronic offenders suffer from a profusion of social problems. Some criminologists believe that accumulating a significant variety of these social deficits is the key to understanding criminal development. For more on this topic, see the discussion on problem behavior syndrome in Chapter 9.

Persistence: The Continuity of Crime   One of the most important findings from the cohort studies is that persistent juvenile offenders are the ones most likely to continue their criminal careers into adulthood.[162] Paul Tracy and Kimberly Kempf-Leonard followed up all subjects in the second 1958 cohort and found that two-thirds of delinquent offenders desisted from crime, but those who started their delinquent careers early and who committed serious violent crimes throughout adolescence were the most likely to persist as adults.[163] This phenomenon is referred to as **persistence** or the **continuity of crime**.[164]

Children who are found to be disruptive and antisocial as early as age 5 or 6 are the most likely to exhibit stable, long-term patterns of disruptive behavior throughout adolescence.[165] They have measurable behavior problems in areas such as learning and motor skills, cognitive abilities, family relations, and other areas of social, psychological, and physical functioning.[166] Youthful offenders who persist are more likely to abuse alcohol, get into trouble while in military service, become economically dependent, have lower aspirations, get divorced or separated, and have a weak employment record.[167] They do not specialize in one type of crime; rather, they engage in a variety of criminal acts, including theft, use of drugs, and violent offenses.

Implications of the Chronic Offender Concept   The findings of the cohort studies and the discovery of the chronic offender have revitalized criminological theory. If relatively few offenders become chronic, persistent criminals, then perhaps they possess some individual trait that is responsible for their behavior. Most people exposed to troublesome social conditions, such as poverty, do not become chronic offenders, so it is unlikely that social conditions alone can cause chronic offending. Traditional theories of criminal behavior have failed to distinguish between chronic and occasional offenders. They concentrate more on explaining why people begin to commit crime and pay scant attention to why people stop offending. The discovery of the chronic offender 30 years ago forced criminologists to consider such issues as persistence and desistance in their explanations of crime; more recent theories account for not only the onset of criminality but also its termination.

Does Tough Love Work?

The planning director for the State Department of Juvenile Justice has asked for your advice on how to reduce the threat of chronic offenders. Some of the more conservative members of her staff seem to believe that these kids need a strict dose of rough justice if they are to be turned away from a life of crime. They believe juvenile delinquents who are punished harshly are less likely to recidivate than youths who receive lesser punishments, such as community corrections or probation. In addition, they believe that hardcore, violent offenders deserve to be punished; excessive concern for offenders and not their acts ignores the rights of victims and society in general.

The planning director is unsure whether such an approach is ethical. Is it ethical to use tough punishment with kids because

Iuoman/iStockphoto

it may produce deviant identities that lock kids into a criminal way of life? She is concerned that a strategy stressing punishment is not only unethical, but it will have relatively little impact on chronic offenders and, if anything, may cause escalation in serious criminal behaviors.

>> **The director has asked you for your professional advice on this ethical dilemma. Write a two-page memorandum: On the one hand, the system must be sensitive to the adverse effects of stigma and labeling. On the other hand, the need for control and deterrence must not be ignored. Is it possible to reconcile these two opposing views?**

The chronic offender has become a central focus of crime control policy. Apprehension and punishment seem to have little effect on the offending behavior of chronic offenders, and most repeat their criminal acts after their correctional release.[168] Because chronic offenders rarely learn from their mistakes, sentencing policies designed to incapacitate chronic offenders for long periods of time without hope of probation or parole have been established. Incapacitation rather than rehabilitation is the goal. Among the policies spurred by the chronic offender concept are mandatory sentences for violent or drug-related crimes, "**three strikes**" policies, which require people convicted of a third felony offense to serve a mandatory life sentence, and "truth in sentencing" policies, which require that convicted felons spend a significant portion of their sentence behind bars. Whether such policies can reduce crime rates or are merely "get tough" measures designed to placate conservative voters remains to be seen.

SUMMARY

1. **Be familiar with the various forms of crime data**
   - The Federal Bureau of Investigation collects data from local law enforcement agencies and publishes that information yearly in its Uniform Crime Report (UCR). The National Incident-Based Reporting System (NIBRS) is a program that collects data on each reported crime incident. The National Crime Victimization Survey (NCVS) is a nationwide survey of victimization in the United States. Self-report surveys ask people to describe, in detail, their recent and lifetime participation in criminal activity.

2. **Know the problems associated with collecting data**
   - Many serious crimes are not reported to police and therefore are not counted by the UCR. The NCVS may have problems due to victims' misinterpretation of events and under-reporting prompted by the embarrassment of reporting crime to interviewers, fear of getting in trouble, or simply forgetting an incident. And respondents in self-report studies may exaggerate their criminal acts, forget some of them, or be confused about what is being asked.

3. **Be able to discuss recent trends in the crime rate**
   - Crime rates peaked in 1991 when police recorded almost 15 million crimes. Since then, the number of crimes has been in decline. About 10.5 million crimes were reported in 2009, a drop of 4 million reported crimes since the 1991 peak, despite an increase of about 50 million in the general population. NCVS data show that criminal victimizations have declined significantly during the past 30 years: in 1973, an estimated 44 million victimizations were recorded, compared to 20 million today.

4. **Be familiar with the factors that influence crime rates**
   - The age composition of the population, the number of immigrants, the availability of legalized abortion, the number of guns, drug use, availability of emergency medical services, numbers of police officers, the state of the economy, cultural change, and criminal opportunities all influence crime rates.

5. **Compare crime rates under different ecological conditions**
   - Patterns in the crime rate seem to be linked to temporal and ecological factors. Most reported crimes occur during July and August. Large urban areas have by far the highest rates of violent crimes, and rural areas have the lowest per capita.

6. **Be able to discuss the association between social class and crime**
   - People living in poverty engage in disproportionate amounts of expressive crimes, such as rape and assault. Crime rates in inner-city, high-poverty areas are generally higher than those in suburban or wealthier areas.

7. **Know what is meant by the term *aging-out process***
   - Regardless of economic status, marital status, race, sex, and other factors, younger people commit crime more often than older people, and this relationship has been stable across time. Most criminologists agree that people commit less crime as they age.

8. **Recognize that there are gender and racial patterns in crime**
   - Male crime rates are much higher than those of females. Gender differences in the crime rate have persisted over time, but there is little question that females are now involved in more crime than ever before and that there are more similarities than differences between male and female offenders. Official crime data indicate that minority group members are involved in a disproportionate share of criminal activity. Racial and ethnic differentials in crime rates may be tied to economic and social disparity.

9. **Be familiar with Wolfgang, Figlio, and Sellin's pioneering research on chronic offending**
   - The concept of the chronic or career offender is most closely associated with the research efforts of Marvin Wolfgang, Robert Figlio, and Thorsten Sellin. Chronic offenders are involved in significant amounts of delinquent behavior and tend later to become adult criminals. Unlike most offenders, they do not age out of crime.

10. **Understand the suspected causes of chronicity**
    - Kids who have been exposed to a variety of personal and social problems at an early age are the most at risk to repeat offending. Chronic offenders often have problems in the home and at school, relatively low intellectual development, and parental drug involvement.

KEY TERMS

Uniform Crime Report (UCR) (30)
index crimes (30)
Part I crimes (30)
Part II crimes (30)
cleared crimes (32)
National Incident-Based Reporting System (NIBRS) (34)
sampling (35)
population (35)
cross-sectional survey (35)

National Crime Victimization Survey (NCVS) (35)
self-report survey (36)
cohort (39)
retrospective cohort study (39)
meta-analysis (41)
systematic review (41)
instrumental crimes (50)
expressive crimes (50)
aging out (52)

masculinity hypothesis (53)
chivalry hypothesis (53)
liberal feminist theory (54)
racial threat hypothesis (55)
career criminal (61)
chronic offender (61)
early onset (62)
persistence (62)
continuity of crime (62)
three strikes (63)

CRITICAL THINKING QUESTIONS

1. Would you answer honestly if a national crime survey asked you about your criminal behavior, including drinking and drug use? If not, why not? If you would not answer honestly, do you question the accuracy of self-report surveys?

2. How would you explain gender differences in the crime rate? Why do you think males are more violent than females?

3. Assuming that males are more violent than females, does that mean crime has a biological rather than a social basis (because males and females share a similar environment)?

4. The UCR reports that crime rates are higher in large cities than in small towns. What does that tell us about the effects of TV, films, and music on teenage behavior?

5. What social and environmental factors do you believe influence the crime rate? Do you think a national emergency would increase or decrease crime rates?

NOTES

1. Fox News, "Georgia Professor Who Killed Wife, 2 Others Was Targeting Her Male Friend," May 12, 2009, www.foxnews.com/story/0,2933,519897,00.html (accessed November 3, 2010).

2. Mirka Smolej and Janne Kivivuori, "The Relation Between Crime News and Fear of Violence," *Journal of Scandinavian Studies in Criminology and Crime Prevention* 7 (2006): 211–227.

3. The Gallup Organization, Inc., *The Gallup Poll* [Online]. Available at www.gallup.com/poll/1603/Crime.aspx (accessed November 3, 2010).

4. Data provided by the Sourcebook of Criminal Justice, *Sourcebook of Criminal Justice Statistics*, Hindelang Criminal Justice Research Center University at Albany, 2008, www.albany.edu/sourcebook/pdf/t2402007.pdf (accessed November 3, 2010).

5. Federal Bureau of Investigation, *Crime in the United States, 2009* (Washington, DC: U.S. Government Printing Office, 2010), www2.fbi.gov/ucr/cius2009/index.html (accessed November 3, 2010). Herein cited in notes as FBI.

6. FBI, *Crime in the United States, 2009*, www2.fbi.gov/ucr/cius2009/offenses/violent_crime/murder_homicide.html (accessed November 3, 2010).

7. Richard Felson, Steven Messner, Anthony Hoskin, and Glenn Deane, "Reasons for Reporting and Not Reporting Domestic Violence to the Police," *Criminology* 40 (2002): 617–648.

8. Shannan Catalano, *Criminal Victimization 2003* (Washington, DC: Bureau of Justice Statistics, 2004). Herein cited as NCVS, 2003.

9. Duncan Chappell, Gilbert Geis, Stephen Schafer, and Larry Siegel, "Forcible Rape: A Comparative Study of Offenses Known to the Police in Boston and Los Angeles," in *Studies in the Sociology of Sex*, ed. James Henslin (New York: Appleton Century Crofts, 1971), pp. 169–193.

10. Eric Baumer and Janet Lauritsen, "Reporting Crime to the Police, 1973–2005: A Multivariate Analysis of Long-Term Trends in the National Crime Survey (NCVS)," *Criminology* 48 (2010): 131–185.

11. Patrick Jackson, "Assessing the Validity of Official Data on Arson," *Criminology* 26 (1988): 181–195.

12. Lawrence Sherman and Barry Glick, "The Quality of Arrest Statistics," *Police Foundation Reports* 2 (1984): 1–8.

13. David Seidman and Michael Couzens, "Getting the Crime Rate Down: Political Pressure and Crime Reporting," *Law and Society Review* 8 (1974): 457.

14. Ariel Hart, "Report Finds Atlanta Police Cut Figures on Crimes," *New York Times*, February 21, 2004, p. A3; William K. Rashbaum, "Retired Officers Raise Questions on Crime Data," *New York Times*, February 6, 2010.

15. John Eterno and Eli B. Silverman, "The NYPD's Compstat: Compare Statistics or Compose Statistics," *International Journal of Police Science and Management* 12 (2010, in press). See also John A. Eterno and Eli. B. Silverman, *Unveiling Compstat: The Global Policing Revolution's Naked Truths* (London: CRC Press/Taylor and Francis Group, 2012, forthcoming).

16. Robert O'Brien, "Police Productivity and Crime Rates: 1973–1992," *Criminology* 34 (1996): 183–207.

17. Leonard Savitz, "Official Statistics," in *Contemporary Criminology*, ed. Leonard Savitz and Norman Johnston (New York: Wiley, 1982), pp. 3–15.

18. FBI, *UCR Handbook* (Washington, DC: U.S. Government Printing Office, 1998), p. 33.

19. National Archive of Criminal Justice Data, *National Incident-Based Reporting System Resource Guide*, www.icpsr.umich.edu/NACJD/NIBRS/ (accessed November 3, 2010).

20. Lynn Addington, "The Effect of NIBRS Reporting on Item Missing Data in Murder Cases," *Homicide Studies* 8 (2004): 193–213.

21. Michael Gottfredson and Travis Hirschi, "The Methodological Adequacy of Longitudinal Research on Crime," *Criminology* 25 (1987): 581–614.

22. Bureau of Justice Statistics, "The Nation's Two Crime Measures," http://bjs.ojp.usdoj.gov/content/pub/pdf/ntcm.pdf (accessed November 3, 2010).

23. Lynn A. Addington and Callie Marie Rennison, "Rape Co-occurrence: Do Additional Crimes Affect Victim Reporting and Police Clearance of Rape?" *Journal of Quantitative Criminology* 24 (2008): 205–226.

24. L. Edward Wells and Joseph Rankin, "Juvenile Victimization: Convergent Validation of Alternative Measurements," *Journal of Research in Crime and Delinquency* 32 (1995): 287–307.

25. Robert M. Groves and Daniel L. Cork, *Surveying Victims: Options for Conducting the National Crime Victimization Survey* (Washington, DC: National Research Council, 2008), www.nap.edu/catalog/12090.html (accessed November 3, 2010).

26. Saul Kassin, Richard Leo, Christian Meissner, Kimberly Richman, Lori Colwell, Amy-May Leach, and Dana La Fon, "Police Interviewing and Interrogation: A Self-Report Survey of Police Practices and Beliefs," *Law and Human Behavior* 31 (2007): 381–400.

27. Christiane Brems, Mark Johnson, David Neal, and Melinda Freemon, "Childhood Abuse History and Substance Use Among Men and Women Receiving Detoxification Services," *American Journal of Drug and Alcohol Abuse* 30 (2004): 799–821.

28. Lloyd Johnston, Patrick O'Malley, and Jerald Bachman, *Monitoring the Future, 2006* (Ann Arbor, MI: Institute for Social Research, 2006).

29. D. Wayne Osgood, Lloyd Johnston, Patrick O'Malley, and Jerald Bachman, "The Generality of Deviance in Late Adolescence and Early Adulthood," *American Sociological Review* 53 (1988): 81–93.

30. Leonore Simon, "Validity and Reliability of Violent Juveniles: A Comparison of Juvenile Self-Reports with Adult Self-Reports Incarcerated in Adult Prisons," paper presented at the annual meeting of the American Society of Criminology, Boston, November 1995, p. 26.

31. Stephen Cernkovich, Peggy Giordano, and Meredith Pugh, "Chronic Offenders: The Missing Cases in Self-Report Delinquency Research," *Journal of Criminal Law and Criminology* 76 (1985): 705–732.

32. Terence Thornberry, Beth Bjerregaard, and William Miles, "The Consequences of Respondent Attrition in Panel Studies: A Simulation Based on the Rochester Youth Development Study," *Journal of Quantitative Criminology* 9 (1993): 127–158.

33. Julia Yun Soo Kim, Michael Fendrich, and Joseph S. Wislar, "The Validity of Juvenile Arrestees' Drug Use Reporting: A Gender Comparison," *Journal of Research in Crime and Delinquency* 37 (2000): 419–432.

34. Donald Tomaskovic-Devey, Cynthia Pfaff Wright, Ronald Czaja, and Kirk Miller, "Self-Reports of Police Speeding Stops by Race: Results from the North Carolina Reverse Record Check Survey," *Journal of Quantitative Criminology* 22 (2006): 279–297.

35. See Spencer Rathus and Larry Siegel, "Crime and Personality Revisited: Effects of MMPI Sets on Self-Report Studies," *Criminology* 18 (1980): 245–251; John Clark and Larry Tifft, "Polygraph and Interview Validation of Self-Reported Deviant Behavior," *American Sociological Review* 31 (1966): 516–523.

36. Mallie Paschall, Miriam Ornstein, and Robert Flewelling, "African-American Male Adolescents' Involvement in the Criminal Justice System: The Criterion Validity of Self-Report Measures in Prospective Study," *Journal of Research in Crime and Delinquency* 38 (2001): 174–187.

37. Nancy Morris and Lee Ann Slocum, "The Validity of Self-Reported Prevalence, Frequency, and Timing of Arrest: An Evaluation of Data Collected Using a Life Event Calendar," *Journal of Research in Crime and Delinquency* 47 (2010): 210–240.

38. Jennifer Roberts, Edward Mulvey, Julie Horney, John Lewis, and Michael Arter, "A

Test of Two Methods of Recall for Violent Events," *Journal of Quantitative Criminology* 21 (2005): 175–193.

39. Lila Kazemian and David Farrington, "Comparing the Validity of Prospective, Retrospective, and Official Onset for Different Offending Categories," *Journal of Quantitative Criminology* 21 (2005): 127–147.

40. Barbara Warner and Brandi Wilson Coomer, "Neighborhood Drug Arrest Rates: Are They a Meaningful Indicator of Drug Activity? A Research Note," *Journal of Research in Crime and Delinquency* 40 (2003): 123–139.

41. Alfred Blumstein, Jacqueline Cohen, and Richard Rosenfeld, "Trend and Deviation in Crime Rates: A Comparison of UCR and NCVS Data for Burglary and Robbery," *Criminology* 29 (1991): 237–248. See also Michael Hindelang, Travis Hirschi, and Joseph Weis, *Measuring Delinquency* (Beverly Hills: Sage, 1981).

42. See, generally, David Farrington, Lloyd Ohlin, and James Q. Wilson, *Understanding and Controlling Crime* (New York: Springer-Verlag, 1986), pp. 11–18.

43. Claire Sterk-Elifson, "Just for Fun? Cocaine Use among Middle-Class Women," *Journal of Drug Issues* 26 (1996): 63–76.

44. Ibid., p. 63.

45. William F. Whyte, *Street Corner Society* (Chicago: University of Chicago Press, 1955).

46. Herman Schwendinger and Julia Schwendinger, *Adolescent Subcultures and Delinquency* (New York: Praeger, 1985).

47. David Farrington and Brandon Welsh, "Improved Street Lighting and Crime Prevention," *Justice Quarterly* 19 (2002): 313–343.

48. Colleen McCue, Emily Stone, and Teresa Gooch, "Data Mining and Value-Added Analysis," *FBI Law Enforcement Bulletin* 72 (2003): 1–6.

49. Colleen McCue, "Using Data Mining to Predict and Prevent Violent Crimes," presentation made to SPSS Incorporated, 2004.

50. Jerry Ratcliffe, "Aoristic Signatures and the Spatio-Temporal Analysis of High Volume Crime Patterns," *Journal of Quantitative Criminology* 18 (2002): 23–43.

51. Clarence Schrag, *Crime and Justice: American Style* (Washington, DC: U.S. Government Printing Office, 1971), p. 17.

52. Bureau of Justice Statistics News Release, "Violent Crime Rate Remained Unchanged While Theft Rate Declined in 2008," September 2, 2009, http://bjs.ojp.usdoj.gov/content/pub/press/cv08pr.cfm (accessed November 3, 2010).

53. Kathleen Maguire and Ann Pastore, *Sourcebook of Criminal Justice Statistics, 1995* (Albany, NY: Hindelang Research Center, 1996), www.druglibrary.org/schaffer/govpubs/sourcebook/1995/ (accessed November 3, 2010).

54. Steven Levitt, "The Limited Role of Changing Age Structure in Explaining Aggregate Crime Rates," *Criminology* 37 (1999): 581–599.

55. Ellen Cohn, "The Effect of Weather and Temporal Variations on Calls for Police Service," *American Journal of Police* 15 (1996): 23–43.

56. R. A. Baron, "Aggression as a Function of Ambient Temperature and Prior Anger Arousal," *Journal of Personality and Social Psychology* 21 (1972): 183–189.

57. Brad Bushman, Morgan Wang, and Craig Anderson, "Is the Curve Relating Temperature to Aggression Linear or Curvilinear? Assaults and Temperature in Minneapolis Reexamined," *Journal of Personality and Social Psychology* 89 (2005): 62–66.

58. Paul Bell, "Reanalysis and Perspective in the Heat-Aggression Debate," *Journal of Personality and Social Psychology* 89 (2005): 71–73.

59. Ellen Cohn, "The Prediction of Police Calls for Service: The Influence of Weather and Temporal Variables on Rape and Domestic Violence," *Journal of Environmental Psychology* 13 (1993): 71–83.

60. John Simister and Cary Cooper, "Thermal Stress in the U.S.A.: Effects on Violence and on Employee Behaviour," *Stress and Health* 21 (2005): 3–15.

61. James Rotton and Ellen Cohn, "Outdoor Temperature, Climate Control, and Criminal Assault," *Environment and Behavior* 36 (2004): 276–306.

62. See, generally, Franklin Zimring and Gordon Hawkins, *Crime Is Not the Problem: Lethal Violence in America* (New York: Oxford University Press, 1997).

63. Ibid., p. 36.

64. Gary Kleck and Marc Gertz, "Armed Resistance to Crime: The Prevalence and Nature of Self-Defense with a Gun," *Journal of Criminal Law and Criminology* 86 (1995): 219–249.

65. Felipe Estrada and Anders Nilsson, "Segregation and Victimization: Neighbourhood Resources, Individual Risk Factors and Exposure to Property Crime," *European Journal of Criminology* 5 (2008): 193–216.

66. Robert Nash Parker, "Bringing 'Booze' Back In: The Relationship between Alcohol and Homicide," *Journal of Research in Crime and Delinquency* 32 (1995): 3–38.

67. Victoria Brewer and M. Dwayne Smith, "Gender Inequality and Rates of Female Homicide Victimization across U.S. Cities," *Journal of Research in Crime and Delinquency* 32 (1995): 175–190.

68. James Short and F. Ivan Nye, "Extent of Unrecorded Juvenile Delinquency, Tentative Conclusions," *Journal of Criminal Law, Criminology, and Police Science* 49 (1958): 296–302.

69. Charles Tittle, Wayne Villemez, and Douglas Smith, "The Myth of Social Class and Criminality: An Empirical Assessment of the Empirical Evidence," *American Sociological Review* 43 (1978): 643–656.

70. Judith Blau and Peter Blau, "The Cost of Inequality: Metropolitan Structure and Violent Crime," *American Sociological Review* 147 (1982): 114–129; Richard Block, "Community Environment and Violent Crime," *Criminology* 17 (1979): 46–57; Robert Sampson, "Structural Sources of Variation in Race-Age-Specific Rates of Offending across Major U.S. Cities," *Criminology* 23 (1985): 647–673.

71. Chin-Chi Hsieh and M. D. Pugh, "Poverty, Income Inequality, and Violent Crime: A Meta-Analysis of Recent Aggregate Data Studies," *Criminal Justice Review* 18 (1993): 182–199.

72. Richard Miech, Avshalom Caspi, Terrie Moffitt, Bradley Entner Wright, and Phil Silva, "Low Socioeconomic Status and Mental Disorders: A Longitudinal Study of Selection and Causation during Young Adulthood," *American Journal of Sociology* 104 (1999): 1,096–1,131; Marvin Krohn, Alan Lizotte, and Cynthia Perez, "The Interrelationship between Substance Use and Precocious Transitions to Adult Sexuality," *Journal of Health and Social Behavior* 38 (1997): 87–103, at 88; Richard Jessor, "Risk Behavior in Adolescence: A Psychosocial Framework for Understanding and Action," in *Adolescents at Risk: Medical and Social Perspectives*, ed. D. E. Rogers and E. Ginzburg (Boulder, CO: Westview, 1992).

73. Ramiro Martinez, Jacob Stowell, and Jeffrey Cancino, "A Tale of Two Border Cities: Community Context, Ethnicity, and Homicide," *Social Science Quarterly* 89 (2008): 1–16.

74. Robert Agnew, "A General Strain Theory of Community Differences in Crime Rates," *Journal of Research in Crime and Delinquency* 36 (1999): 123–155.

75. Bonita Veysey and Steven Messner, "Further Testing of Social Disorganization Theory: An Elaboration of Sampson and Groves's Community Structure and Crime," *Journal of Research in Crime and Delinquency* 36 (1999): 156–174.

76. Alan Lizotte, Terence Thornberry, Marvin Krohn, Deborah Chard-Wierschem, and David McDowall, "Neighborhood Context and Delinquency: A Longitudinal Analysis," in *Cross National Longitudinal Research on Human Development and Criminal Behavior*, ed. E. M. Weitekamp and H. J. Kerner (Stavernstr, Netherlands: Kluwer, 1994), pp. 217–227.

77. Steven Messner, Lawrence Raffalovich, and Richard McMillan, "Economic Deprivation and Changes in Homicide Arrest Rates for White and Black Youths, 1967–1998: A National Time Series Analysis," *Criminology* 39 (2001): 591–614.

78. Richard Rosenfeld and Robert Fornango, "The Impact of Economic Conditions on Robbery and Property Crime: The Role of Consumer Sentiment," *Criminology* 45 (2007): 735–769.

79. Robert Apel, Shawn Bushway, Robert Brame, Amelia M. Haviland, Daniel S. Nagin, and Ray Paternoster, "Unpacking the Relationship Between Adolescent Employment and Antisocial Behavior: A Matched Samples Comparison," *Criminology* 45 (2007): 67–97.

80. Gary Kleck and Ted Chiricos, "Unemployment and Property Crime: A Target-Specific Assessment of Opportunity and Motivation as Mediating Factors," *Criminology* 40 (2002): 649–680.

81. Shawn Bushway, "Economy and Crime," *The Criminologist* 35 (2010): 1–5.

82. Douglas Smith and Laura Davidson, "Interfacing Indicators and Constructs in Criminological Research: A Note on the Comparability of Self-Report Violence Data for Race and Sex Groups," *Criminology* 24 (1986): 473–488.

83. R. Gregory Dunaway, Francis Cullen, Velmer Burton, and T. David Evans, "The Myth of Social Class and Crime Revisited: An Examination of Class and Adult Criminality," *Criminology* 38 (2000): 589–632.

84. Olena Antonaccio, Charles Tittle, Ekaterina Botchkovar, and Maria Kranidioti, "The Correlates of Crime and Deviance: Additional Evidence," *Journal of Research in Crime and Delinquency* 47 (2010): 297–328, http://jrc.sagepub.com/content/47/3/297.full.pdf+html (accessed November 3, 2010).

85. Travis Hirschi and Michael Gottfredson, "Age and the Explanation of Crime," *American Journal of Sociology* 89 (1983): 552–584, at 581.

86. Misaki Natsuaki, Xiaojia Ge, and Ernst Wenk, "Continuity and Changes in the Developmental Trajectories of Criminal Career: Examining the Roles of Timing of First Arrest and High School Graduation," *Journal of Youth and Adolescence* 37 (2008): 431–444.

87. Lisa Stolzenberg and Stewart D'Alessio, "Co-offending and the Age-Crime Curve," *Journal of Research in Crime and Delinquency* 45 (2008): 65–86.

88. Derek Kreager, "When It's Good to Be 'Bad': Violence and Adolescent Peer Acceptance," *Criminology* 45 (2007): 893–923.

89. For a comprehensive review of crime and the elderly, see Kyle Kercher, "Causes and Correlates of Crime Committed by the Elderly," in *Critical Issues in Aging Policy*, ed. E. Borgatta and R. Montgomery (Beverly Hills: Sage, 1987), pp. 254–306; Darrell Steffensmeier, "The Invention of the 'New' Senior Citizen Criminal," *Research on Aging* 9 (1987): 281–311.

90. Hirschi and Gottfredson, "Age and the Explanation of Crime."

91. Robert Agnew, "An Integrated Theory of the Adolescent Peak in Offending," *Youth and Society* 34 (2003): 263–302.

92. Margo Wilson and Martin Daly, "Life Expectancy, Economic Inequality, Homicide, and Reproductive Timing in Chicago Neighbourhoods," *British Journal of Medicine* 314 (1997): 1,271–1,274.

93. Edward Mulvey and John LaRosa, "Delinquency Cessation and Adolescent Development: Preliminary Data," *American Journal of Orthopsychiatry* 56 (1986): 212–224.

94. James Q. Wilson and Richard Herrnstein, *Crime and Human Nature* (New York: Simon and Schuster, 1985), pp. 126–147.

95. Ibid., p. 219.

96. Ryan King, Michael Massoglia, and Ross MacMillan, "The Context of Marriage and Crime: Gender, the Propensity to Marry, and Offending in Early Adulthood," *Criminology* 45 (2007): 33–65.

97. Paul Tracy, Kimberly Kempf-Leonard, and Stephanie Abramoske-James, "Gender Differences in Delinquency and Juvenile Justice Processing: Evidence from National Data," *Crime and Delinquency* 55 (2009): 171–215.

98. Cesare Lombroso, *The Female Offender* (New York: Appleton, 1920), p. 122.

99. Otto Pollack, *The Criminality of Women* (Philadelphia: University of Pennsylvania, 1950).

100. For a review of this issue, see Darrell Steffensmeier, "Assessing the Impact of the Women's Movement on Sex-Based Differences in the Handling of Adult Criminal Defendants," *Crime and Delinquency* 26 (1980): 344–357.

101. Alan Booth and D. Wayne Osgood, "The Influence of Testosterone on Deviance in Adulthood: Assessing and Explaining the Relationship," *Criminology* 31 (1993): 93–118.

102. This section relies on the following sources: Kristen Kling, Janet Shibley Hyde, Carolin Showers, and Brenda Buswell, "Gender Differences in Self-Esteem: A Meta Analysis," *Psychological Bulletin* 125 (1999): 470–500; Anne Campbell, *Men, Women and Aggression* (New York: Basic Books, 1993); Ann Beutel and Margaret Mooney Marini, "Gender and Values," *American Sociological Review* 60 (1995): 436–448; John Gibbs, Velmer Burton, Francis Cullen, T. David Evans, Leanne Fiftal Alarid, and R. Gregory Dunaway, "Gender, Self-Control, and Crime," *Journal of Research in Crime and Delinquency* 35 (1998): 123–147.

103. Jean Bottcher, "Social Practices of Gender: How Gender Relates to Delinquency in the Everyday Lives of High-Risk Youths," *Criminology* 39 (2001): 893–932.

104. Daniel Mears, Matthew Ploeger, and Mark Warr, "Explaining the Gender Gap in Delinquency: Peer Influence and Moral Evaluations of Behavior," *Journal of Research in Crime and Delinquency* 35 (1998): 251–266.

105. Lisa Broidy, Elizabeth Cauffman, and Dorothy Espelage, "Sex Differences in Empathy and Its Relation to Juvenile Offending," *Violence and Victims* 18 (2003): 503–516.

106. Debra Kaysen, Miranda Morris, Shireen Rizvi, and Patricia Resick, "Peritraumatic Responses and Their Relationship to Perceptions of Threat in Female Crime Victims," *Violence Against Women* 11 (2005): 1,515–1,535.

107. Freda Adler, *Sisters in Crime* (New York: McGraw-Hill, 1975); Rita James Simon, *The Contemporary Woman and Crime* (Washington, DC: U.S. Government Printing Office, 1975).

108. David Rowe, Alexander Vazsonyi, and Daniel Flannery, "Sex Differences in Crime: Do Mean and Within-Sex Variation Have Similar Causes?" *Journal of Research in Crime and Delinquency* 32 (1995): 84–100; Michael Hindelang, "Age, Sex, and the Versatility of Delinquency Involvements," *Social Forces* 14 (1971): 525–534; Martin Gold, *Delinquent Behavior in an American City* (Belmont, CA: Brooks/Cole, 1970); Gary Jensen and Raymond Eve, "Sex Differences in Delinquency: An Examination of Popular Sociological Explanations," *Criminology* 13 (1976): 427–448.

109. Finn-Aage Esbensen and Elizabeth Piper Deschenes, "A Multisite Examination of Youth Gang Membership: Does Gender Matter?" *Criminology* 36 (1998): 799–828.

110. Darrell Steffensmeier and Renee Hoffman Steffensmeier, "Trends in Female Delinquency," *Criminology* 18 (1980): 62–85; see also Darrell Steffensmeier and Renee Hoffman Steffensmeier, "Crime and the Contemporary Woman: An Analysis of Changing Levels of Female Property Crime, 1960–1975," *Social Forces* 57 (1978): 566–584; Joseph Weis, "Liberation and Crime: The Invention of the New Female Criminal," *Crime and Social Justice* 1 (1976): 17–27; Carol Smart, "The New Female Offender: Reality or Myth," *British Journal of Criminology* 19 (1979): 50–59; Steven Box and Chris Hale, "Liberation/Emancipation, Economic Marginalization or Less Chivalry," *Criminology* 22 (1984): 473–478.

111. Anne Campbell, Steven Muncer, and Daniel Bibel, "Female–Female Criminal Assault: An Evolutionary Perspective," *Journal of Research in Crime and Delinquency* 35 (1998): 413–428.

112. Darrell Steffensmeier, Jennifer Schwartz, Hua Zhong, and Jeff Ackerman, "An Assessment of Recent Trends in Girls' Violence Using Diverse Longitudinal Sources: Is the Gender Gap Closing?" *Criminology* 43 (2005): 355–406.

113. Susan Miller, Carol Gregory, and Leeann Iovanni, "One Size Fits All? A Gender-Neutral Approach to a Gender-Specific Problem: Contrasting Batterer Treatment Programs for Male and Female Offenders," *Criminal Justice Policy Review* 16 (2005): 336–359.

114. Leroy Gould, "Who Defines Delinquency: A Comparison of Self-Report and Officially Reported Indices of Delinquency for Three Racial Groups," *Social Problems* 16 (1969): 325–336; Harwin Voss, "Ethnic

Differentials in Delinquency in Honolulu," *Journal of Criminal Law, Criminology, and Police Science* 54 (1963): 322–327; Ronald Akers, Marvin Krohn, Marcia Radosevich, and Lonn Lanza-Kaduce, "Social Characteristics and Self-Reported Delinquency," in *Sociology of Delinquency*, ed. Gary Jensen (Beverly Hills: Sage, 1981), pp. 48–62.

115. David Huizinga and Delbert Elliott, "Juvenile Offenders: Prevalence, Offender Incidence, and Arrest Rates by Race," *Crime and Delinquency* 33 (1987): 206–223. See also Dale Dannefer and Russell Schutt, "Race and Juvenile Justice Processing in Court and Police Agencies," *American Journal of Sociology* 87 (1982): 1,113–1,132.

116. Paul Tracy, "Race and Class Differences in Official and Self-Reported Delinquency," in *From Boy to Man, from Delinquency to Crime*, ed. Marvin Wolfgang, Terence Thornberry, and Robert Figlio (Chicago: University of Chicago Press, 1987), p. 120.

117. Miriam Sealock and Sally Simpson, "Unraveling Bias in Arrest Decisions: The Role of Juvenile Offender Type-Scripts," *Justice Quarterly* 15 (1998): 427–457.

118. Nicola Persico and Petra Todd, "The Hit Rates Test for Racial Bias in Motor-Vehicle Searches," *Justice Quarterly* 25 (2008): 37–53.

119. Robin Shepard Engel and Jennifer Calnon, "Examining the Influence of Drivers' Characteristics during Traffic Stops with Police: Results from a National Survey," *Justice Quarterly* 21 (2004): 49–90.

120. Daniel Georges-Abeyie, "Definitional Issues: Race, Ethnicity and Official Crime/Victimization Rates," in *The Criminal Justice System and Blacks*, ed. D. Georges-Abeyie (New York: Clark Boardman, 1984), p. 12; Robert Sampson, "Race and Criminal Violence: A Demographically Disaggregated Analysis of Urban Homicide," *Crime and Delinquency* 31 (1985): 47–82.

121. Hurbert Blalock, Jr., *Toward a Theory of Minority-Group Relations* (New York: Capricorn Books, 1967).

122. Engel and Calnon, "Examining the Influence of Drivers' Characteristics during Traffic Stops with Police."

123. Malcolm Holmes, Brad Smith, Adrienne Freng, and Ed Muñoz, "Minority Threat, Crime Control, and Police Resource Allocation in the Southwestern United States," *Crime and Delinquency* 54 (2008): 128–152.

124. Bradley Keen and David Jacobs, "Racial Threat, Partisan Politics, and Racial Disparities in Prison Admissions," *Criminology* 47 (2009): 209–238.

125. Nancy Rodriguez, "Outcomes and Why Preadjudication Detention Matters: The Cumulative Effect of Race and Ethnicity in Juvenile Court," *Journal of Research in Crime and Delinquency* 47 (2010): 391–413, http://jrc.sagepub.com/

content/47/3/391.full.pdf+html (accessed November 3, 2010).

126. Michael Leiber and Kristan Fox, "Race and the Impact of Detention on Juvenile Justice Decision Making," *Crime and Delinquency* 51 (2005): 470–497; Traci Schlesinger, "Racial and Ethnic Disparity in Pretrial Criminal Processing," *Justice Quarterly* 22 (2005): 170–192.

127. Matthew Crow and Kathrine Johnson, "Race, Ethnicity, and Habitual-Offender Sentencing: A Multilevel Analysis of Individual and Contextual Threat," *Criminal Justice Policy Review* 19 (2008): 63–83.

128. Jill Doerner and Stephen Demuth, "The Independent and Joint Effects of Race/Ethnicity, Gender, and Age on Sentencing Outcomes in U.S. Federal Courts," *Justice Quarterly* 27 (2010): 1–27.

129. Alexander Weiss and Steven Chermak, "The News Value of African-American Victims: An Examination of the Media's Presentation of Homicide," *Journal of Crime and Justice* 21 (1998): 71–84.

130. Jefferson Holcomb, Marian Williams, and Stephen Demuth, "White Female Victims and Death Penalty Disparity Research," *Justice Quarterly* 21 (2004): 877–902.

131. Ronald Weitzer and Steven Tuch, "Race, Class, and Perceptions of Discrimination by the Police," *Crime and Delinquency* 45 (1999): 494–507.

132. Barry Sample and Michael Philip, "Perspectives on Race and Crime in Research and Planning," in *The Criminal Justice System and Blacks*, ed. Georges-Abeyie, pp. 21–36.

133. Ruth Peterson, Lauren Krivo, and Mark Harris, "Disadvantage and Neighborhood Violent Crime: Do Local Institutions Matter?" *Journal of Research in Crime and Delinquency* 37 (2000): 31–63.

134. James Comer, "Black Violence and Public Policy," in *American Violence and Public Policy*, ed. Lynn Curtis (New Haven, CT: Yale University Press, 1985), pp. 63–86.

135. Fox Butterfield, *All God's Children: The Bosket Family and the American Tradition of Violence* (New York: Avon, 1996).

136. William Julius Wilson, *More than Just Race: Being Black and Poor in the Inner City* (New York: Norton, 2009); William Julius Wilson and Richard Taub, *There Goes the Neighborhood: Racial, Ethnic, and Class Tensions in Four Chicago Neighborhoods and Their Meaning for America* (New York: Knopf, 2006); William Julius Wilson, *The Truly Disadvantaged* (Chicago: University of Chicago Press, 1987); *When Work Disappears: The World of the Urban Poor* (New York: Knopf, 1996); *The Bridge over the Racial Divide: Rising Inequality and Coalition Politics*, Wildavsky Forum Series, 2 (Berkeley: University of California Press, 1999).

137. Joanne Kaufman, "Explaining the Race/Ethnicity–Violence Relationship: Neigh-

borhood Context and Social Psychological Processes," *Justice Quarterly* 22 (2005): 224–251.

138. Karen Parker and Patricia McCall, "Structural Conditions and Racial Homicide Patterns: A Look at the Multiple Disadvantages in Urban Areas," *Criminology* 37 (1999): 447–469.

139. David Jacobs and Katherine Woods, "Interracial Conflict and Interracial Homicide: Do Political and Economic Rivalries Explain White Killings of Blacks or Black Killings of Whites?" *American Journal of Sociology* 105 (1999): 157–190.

140. Melvin Thomas, "Race, Class and Personal Income: An Empirical Test of the Declining Significance of Race Thesis, 1968–1988," *Social Problems* 40 (1993): 328–339.

141. Mallie Paschall, Robert Flewelling, and Susan Ennett, "Racial Differences in Violent Behavior among Young Adults: Moderating and Confounding Effects," *Journal of Research in Crime and Delinquency* 35 (1998): 148–165.

142. Gary LaFree and Richard Arum, "The Impact of Racially Inclusive Schooling on Adult Incarceration Rates among U.S. Cohorts of African Americans and Whites Since 1930," *Criminology* 44 (2006): 73–103.

143. R. Kelly Raley, "A Shortage of Marriageable Men? A Note on the Role of Cohabitation in Black–White Differences in Marriage Rates," *American Sociological Review* 61 (1996): 973–983.

144. Julie Phillips, "Variation in African-American Homicide Rates: An Assessment of Potential Explanations," *Criminology* 35 (1997): 527–559.

145. Roy Austin, "Progress toward Racial Equality and Reduction of Black Criminal Violence," *Journal of Criminal Justice* 15 (1987): 437–459.

146. Reynolds Farley and William Frey, "Changes in the Segregation of Whites from Blacks During the 1980s: Small Steps toward a More Integrated Society," *American Sociological Review* 59 (1994): 23–45.

147. Gary LaFree, Eric Baumer, and Robert O'Brien, "Still Separate and Unequal? A City-Level Analysis of the Black–White Gap in Homicide Arrests Since 1960," *American Sociological Review* 75 (2010): 75–100.

148. Arizona SB 1070, §1 (2010).

149. Ramiro Martínez, Jr., "Crime and Immigration," *The Criminologist* 35 (2010): 16–17.

150. Albor Ruiz, "Ray of Hope for Immigrants as Court Buries Arizona Law," NYDailyNews.com, April 13, 2011, www.nydailynews.com/ny_local/2011/04/13/2011-04-13_ray_of_hope_for_immigrants_as_court_buries_arizona_law.html (accessed October 21, 2011).

151. Kristin F. Butcher and Anne Morrison Piehl, "Crime, Corrections, and California: What Does Immigration Have to Do with

It?" Public Policy Institute of California, 2008, www.ppic.org/main/publication.asp?i=776 (accessed November 3, 2010).

152. Martínez, Jr. "Crime and Immigration."

153. Marvin Wolfgang, Robert Figlio, and Thorsten Sellin, *Delinquency in a Birth Cohort* (Chicago: University of Chicago Press, 1972).

154. See Thorsten Sellin and Marvin Wolfgang, *The Measurement of Delinquency* (New York: Wiley, 1964), p. 120.

155. Paul Tracy and Robert Figlio, "Chronic Recidivism in the 1958 Birth Cohort," paper presented at the annual meeting of the American Society of Criminology, Toronto, October 1982; Marvin Wolfgang, "Delinquency in Two Birth Cohorts," in *Perspective Studies of Crime and Delinquency*, ed. Katherine Teilmann van Dusen and Sarnoff Mednick (Boston: Kluwer-Nijhoff, 1983), pp. 7–17. The following sections rely heavily on these sources.

156. Lyle Shannon, *Criminal Career Opportunity* (New York: Human Sciences Press, 1988).

157. D. J. West and David P. Farrington, *The Delinquent Way of Life* (London: Hienemann, 1977).

158. Michael Schumacher and Gwen Kurz, *The 8% Solution: Preventing Serious Repeat Juvenile Crime* (Thousand Oaks, CA: Sage, 1999).

159. Peter Jones, Philip Harris, James Fader, and Lori Grubstein, "Identifying Chronic Juvenile Offenders," *Justice Quarterly* 18 (2001): 478–507.

160. Lila Kazemian and Marc LeBlanc, "Differential Cost Avoidance and Successful Criminal Careers," *Crime and Delinquency* 53 (2007): 38–63.

161. Rudy Haapanen, Lee Britton, and Tim Croisdale, "Persistent Criminality and Career Length," *Crime and Delinquency* 53 (2007): 133–155.

162. See, generally, Wolfgang, Thornberry, and Figlio, eds., *From Boy to Man, from Delinquency to Crime.*

163. Paul Tracy and Kimberly Kempf-Leonard, *Continuity and Discontinuity in Criminal Careers* (New York: Plenum Press, 1996).

164. Kimberly Kempf-Leonard, Paul Tracy, and James Howell, "Serious, Violent, and Chronic Juvenile Offenders: The Relationship of Delinquency Career Types to Adult Criminality," *Justice Quarterly* 18 (2001): 449–478.

165. R. Tremblay, R. Loeber, C. Gagnon, P. Charlebois, S. Larivee, and M. LeBlanc, "Disruptive Boys with Stable and Unstable High Fighting Behavior Patterns during Junior Elementary School," *Journal of Abnormal Child Psychology* 19 (1991): 285–300.

166. Jennifer White, Terrie Moffitt, Felton Earls, Lee Robins, and Phil Silva, "How Early Can We Tell? Predictors of Childhood Conduct Disorder and Adolescent Delinquency," *Criminology* 28 (1990): 507–535.

167. John Laub and Robert Sampson, "Unemployment, Marital Discord, and Deviant Behavior: The Long-Term Correlates of Childhood Misbehavior," paper presented at the annual meeting of the American Society of Criminology, Baltimore, November 1990; rev. version.

168. Michael Ezell and Amy D'Unger, "Offense Specialization among Serious Youthful Offenders: A Longitudinal Analysis of a California Youth Authority Sample" (Durham, NC: Duke University, 1998, unpublished report).

AP Images/Tina Fineberg

On February 25, 2006, Imette St. Guillen stopped in for a late night drink at The Falls bar, a popular New York City nightspot. Later that evening, the bar's manager asked the bouncer, Darryl Littlejohn, to escort St. Guillen out after she stayed past the 4 A.M. closing time.[1] Later he recalled hearing the pair argue before they disappeared through a side door. Sometime during the next 17 hours, St. Guillen was raped and killed and her bound body left on the side of a desolate Brooklyn roadway. Police investigators soon set their sights on Littlejohn, a felon with prior convictions for robbery, drugs, and gun possession. He was indicted for murder when blood found on plastic ties that were used to bind St. Guillen's hands behind her back matched Littlejohn's DNA.

(continued on page 72)

Victims and Victimization

3

Learning Objectives

1. Describe the victim's role in the crime process
2. Know the greatest problems faced by crime victims
3. Know what is meant by the term *cycle of violence*
4. Be familiar with the ecology of victimization risk
5. Describe the victim's household
6. Describe the most dominant victim characteristics
7. Be familiar with the concept of repeat victimization
8. Be familiar with the most important theories of victimization
9. Discuss programs dedicated to caring for the victim
10. Be familiar with the concept of victims' rights

Imette St. Guillen was a brilliant and beautiful young woman loved by her family and friends. She attended the Boston Latin School in Massachusetts and graduated magna cum laude from George Washington University in 2003 as a member of Phi Beta Kappa. At the time of her death, she was a graduate student at John Jay College of Criminal Justice in New York City, where she would have completed her master's degree in May 2006. "New York was Imette's home," her sister, Alejandra St. Guillen, told reporters. "She loved the city and its people . . . Imette was a good person, a kind person. Her heart was full of love. With Imette's death, the world lost someone very special too soon."[2]

On July 8, 2009, Littlejohn faced Kings County Supreme Court Justice Abraham Gerges at his sentencing hearing. He heard members of Imette's family tearfully address the court. "I will never share another birthday with her," her mother, Maureen St. Hilaire, told the judge. Her sister Alejandra accused Littlejohn of robbing her of "my one sister and my dearest friend." "I'll never see my sister marry," she said. "I'll never hold Imette's children in my arms. Imette's loss is with me forever." "The last thing she did before she left, she turned around and waved," Maureen St. Guillen said. "[She] mouthed, 'I love you, mom.'" After hearing all testimony, Judge Gerges called Littlejohn an unrepentant "predator" who should never taste freedom again. "If there were truly justice in this world, I would have the power to bring her back to you," Gerges told Maureen and Alejandra, who sobbed in the courtroom. "To my great sorrow, that is not possible."

The St. Guillen murder case illustrates the importance of understanding the victim's role in the crime process. Why do people become targets of predatory criminals? Do people become victims because of their lifestyle and environment? Did Imette contribute to her attack by staying out late at night, drinking, and being alone? Imette's friends, who had been with her earlier in the evening, had left her in the early morning hours because they considered The Falls bar neighborhood safe. If Imette had been with friends to guard her, would she be alive today? And is this a matter of unfairly "blaming the victim" for her risky behavior? Can someone actually deflect or avoid criminal behavior or is it a matter of fate and chance? What can be done to protect victims, for instance, if a convicted violent criminal is employed in a bar and asked to escort patrons? And, failing that, what can be done to help them in the aftermath of crime?

Criminologists who focus their attention on crime victims refer to themselves as **victimologists**. This chapter examines victims and their relationship to the criminal process. First, using available victim data, we analyze the nature and extent of **victimization**. We then discuss the relationship between victims and criminal offenders. During this discussion, we look at the various theories of victimization that attempt to explain the victim's role in the crime problem. Finally, we examine how society has responded to the needs of victims and discuss the special problems they still face.

PROBLEMS OF CRIME VICTIMS

The National Crime Victimization Survey (NCVS) indicates that the annual number of victimizations in the United States is about 20 million.[3] Being the target or victim of a rape, robbery, or assault is a terrible burden that can have considerable long-term consequences.[4] The costs of victimization can include such things as damaged property, pain and suffering to victims, and the involvement of the police and other agencies of the justice system. In this section, we explore some of the effects of these incidents.

Economic Loss

When the costs of goods taken during property crimes is added to productivity losses caused by injury, pain, and emotional trauma, the cost of victimization is estimated to be in the hundreds of billions of dollars.

System Costs The American taxpayer is burdened with the costs of crime and justice. While it is difficult to pinpoint the exact costs of crime, criminologists using methods similar to those employed to determine civil damages find that over the lifetime of their careers in crime the typical criminal costs society about $2 million.[5] Using this form of analysis, violent crime by juveniles alone costs the United States more than $160 billion each year.[6] This estimate includes some of the costs incurred by federal, state, and local governments to assist victims of juvenile violence, such as medical treatment for injuries and services for victims, which amounts to about $30 billion. The remaining $130 billion is due to losses suffered by victims, such as lost wages, pain, suffering, and reduced quality of life. Not included in these figures are the costs incurred trying to reduce juvenile violence, which include early prevention programs, services for juveniles, and the juvenile justice system.

Juvenile violence is only one part of the crime picture. If the cost of the justice system, legal costs, treatment costs, and so on are included, the total loss due to crime amounts to $450 billion annually, or about $1,800 per U.S. citizen. Crime produces social costs that must be paid by nonvictims as well. For example, heroin abuse may cost the nation up to $20 billion per year, including the medical complications of heroin addiction, primarily treatment for HIV/AIDS and psychiatric care, as well as paying for the cost of incarceration, policing, legal adjudication, and the cost to crime victims. There is also the cost of lost productivity—heroin addicts are less than half as likely to have a full-time job as compared with the national average—and the treatment of heroin addiction in clinics and hospitals.[7]

Individual Costs   In addition to these societal costs, victims may suffer long-term losses in earnings and occupational attainment. Victim costs resulting from an assault are as high as $14,000, and costs are even higher for rape and arson; the average murder costs more than $4 million.[8] Research by Ross Macmillan shows that Americans who suffer a violent victimization during adolescence earn about $110,000 less than nonvictims during their lifetime; Canadian victims earn $300,000 less. Macmillan reasons that victims bear psychological and physical ills that inhibit first their academic achievement and later their economic and professional success.[9]

Some victims are physically disabled as a result of serious wounds sustained during episodes of random violence, including a growing number who suffer paralyzing spinal cord injuries. If victims have no insurance, the long-term effects of the crime may have devastating financial as well as emotional and physical consequences.[10]

Suffering Stress and PTSD

Victims may suffer stress and anxiety long after the incident is over and the justice process has been completed. **Post-traumatic stress disorder (PTSD)**—a condition whose symptoms include depression, anxiety, and self-destructive behavior—is a common problem especially when the victim does not receive adequate support from family and friends.[11] To shield themselves, some victims deny the attack occurred or question whether they were "really raped." But denial only goes so far and does not shield victims from the long-term effects of sexual assault.[12]

Men may be particularly susceptible to post-rape PTSD, believing that their situation is both unique and somehow "unmanly." Knowing the effect of a sexual assault on men, rape has become an interrogation tool in some theaters of war. Sexual assault was routinely used during the civil war in Yugoslavia to terrorize male prisoners. The Croats, Serbs, and Bosnians who were attacked suffered from a variety of traumatic reactions, including sleep disturbances, concentration difficulties, nightmares and flashbacks, feelings of hopelessness, constant headaches, profuse sweating, and rapid heartbeat.[13]

Adolescent Stress   It is widely assumed that younger children are less likely to be injured in attacks than older teens and adults, but in fact the opposite may be true.[14] Recent research by David Finkelhor and his colleagues at the University of New Hampshire Crimes Against Children Research Center found that younger children's victimization by peers and siblings was similar to that experienced by older youth. Both groups suffered similar injuries, were just as likely to be hit with an object that could cause injury, and were victimized on multiple occasions.[15]

These younger victims are also more prone to suffer stress. Adolescent victims are particularly at risk to PTSD.[16] Kids who have undergone traumatic sexual experiences later suffer psychological deficits.[17] Mark Shelvin and his associates found that a history of childhood trauma, including rape and molestation, was significantly associated with visual, auditory, and tactile hallucinations. Kids who were repeatedly traumatized increased their experience with the three types of hallucinations, clearly indicating that childhood abuse can have a devastating effect on long-term mental health.[18]

Many run away to escape their environment, which puts them at risk for juvenile arrest and involvement with the justice system.[19] Others suffer posttraumatic mental problems, including acute stress disorders, depression, eating disorders, nightmares, anxiety, suicidal ideation, and other psychological problems.[20] Stress, however, does not end in childhood. Children who are psychologically, sexually, or physically abused are more likely to suffer low self-esteem and be more suicidal as adults.[21] They are also placed at greater risk to be re-abused as adults than those who escaped childhood victimization.[22] The re-abused carry higher risks for psychological and physical problems, ranging from sexual promiscuity to increased HIV infection rates.[23] Abuse as a child may lead to despair, depression, and even homelessness as an adult. One study of homeless women found that they were much more likely than other women to report childhood physical abuse, childhood sexual abuse, adult physical assault, previous sexual assault in adulthood, and a history of mental health problems.[24]

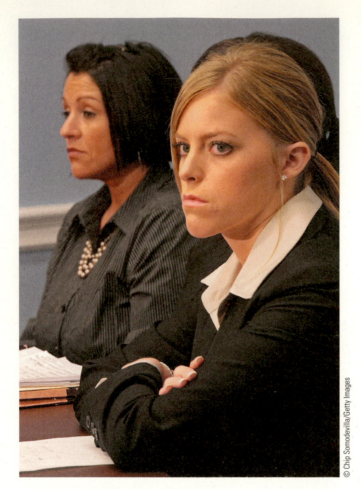

After being the target of violent crime, victims often display long-term fear and anxiety, including posttraumatic stress disorder. Here, former Halliburton/KBR employees Tracy Barker (left) and Jamie Leigh Jones participate in a news conference on Capitol Hill, December 19, 2007, in Washington, D.C. Barker said she was sexually assaulted in 2005 by a State Department employee while working for KBR, Inc., a large U.S. contractor, at a company-run camp in Basra, Iraq. Jones says that she was raped by co-workers and held against her will while working for KBR at Camp Hope in Baghdad. Many victims of sexual assault suffer psychological pain long after their physical injuries have healed.

Relationship Stress Spousal abuse takes a particularly heavy toll on victims. Numerous research efforts show that victims of spousal abuse suffer an extremely high prevalence of psychological problems, including but not limited to depression, generalized anxiety disorder (GAD), panic disorder, substance use disorders, borderline personality disorder, antisocial personality disorder, posttraumatic stress disorder (an emotional disturbance following exposure to stresses outside the range of normal human experience), anxiety disorder, and **obsessive-compulsive disorder** (an extreme preoccupation with certain thoughts and compulsive performance of certain behaviors).[25] One reason may be that abusive spouses are as likely to abuse their victims psychologically with threats and intimidation as they are to use physical force; psychological abuse can lead to depression and other long-term disabilities.[26]

Fear

Many people fear crime, especially the elderly, the poor, and minority group members.[27] Their fear is escalated by lurid news accounts of crime and violence.[28]

While hearing about crime causes fear, those who experience it are even more likely to be fearful and change their behaviors. Victims of violent crime are the most deeply affected, fearing a repeat of their attack. Many go through a fundamental life change, viewing the world more suspiciously and as a less safe, controllable, and meaningful place. Some develop a generalized fear of crime and worry about being revictimized. For example, if they have been assaulted, they may develop fears that their house will be burglarized.[29] These people are more likely to suffer psychological stress for extended periods of time.[30]

Crime can have devastating effects on its victims, who may take years to recover from the incident. In a moving book, *Aftermath: Violence and the Remaking of a Self*, rape victim Susan Brison recounts the difficult time she had recovering from her ordeal. The trauma disrupted her memory, cutting off events that happened before the rape from those that occurred afterward, and eliminated her ability to conceive of a happy or productive future. Although sympathizers encouraged her to forget the past, she found that confronting it could be therapeutic.[31]

The **National Organization for Victim Assistance** is a private, nonprofit organization of victim and witness assistance programs and practitioners, criminal justice agencies and professionals, mental health professionals, researchers, former victims and survivors, and others committed to the recognition and implementation of victim rights and services. For more information about victim assistance, visit the Criminal Justice CourseMate at cengagebrain.com, then access the "Web Links" for this chapter.

Vicarious Fear Even if people are not personally victimized, those who observe or are exposed to violence on a routine basis become fearful.[32] Hearing about another's victimization may make people timid and cautious.[33] If they don't fear for themselves, they become concerned for others—their wives or husbands, children, elderly parents, and siblings.[34] Not only are people likely to move out of their neighborhood if they become crime victims, but they are also likely to relocate if they hear that a friend or neighbor has suffered a break-in or burglary.[35]

Vicarious fear is escalated by lurid news accounts of crime and violence.[36] Matthew Lee and Erica DeHart found that news stories about serial killers on a rampage can cause a chill felt throughout the city. About half the people they surveyed who had read or heard about serial killers experienced an increase in their fear of crime that prompted them to protect themselves and their family by implementing some sort of protective measure, such as carrying mace or pepper spray or adding a security device to their home.[37]

Antisocial Behavior

Does victimization produce antisocial behaviors? Is it possible that people who are victimized strike back at others, becoming antisocial themselves? Is it possible then that criminals and victims are not two separate and distinct groups but rather one and the same?[38] The abuse–crime phenomenon is referred to as the **cycle of violence**.[39] Research shows that both boys and girls are more likely to engage in violent behavior if they were the targets of physical abuse and were exposed to violent behavior among adults they know or live with or were exposed to weapons.[40]

> The mission of the **National Center for Victims of Crime** is to help victims of crime rebuild their lives: "We are dedicated to serving individuals, families, and communities harmed by crime." Learn more by visiting the Criminal Justice CourseMate at cengagebrain.com, then access the "Web Links" for this chapter.

People who were physically or sexually abused, especially young males, are much more likely to smoke, drink, and take drugs than are non-abused youth. As adults, victims are more likely to commit crimes themselves.[41]

Given the evidence pointing to a link between victimization and crime, how can the association be explained?

- *Victimization causes social problems.* People who are crime victims experience long-term negative consequences, including problems with unemployment and developing personal relationships, factors related to criminality. Some young victims may run away from home, taking to the streets and increasing their risk of becoming a crime victim.[42]
- *Victimization causes stress and anger.* Victimization may produce anger, stress, and strain. Known offenders report significant amounts of posttraumatic stress disorder as a result of prior victimization, which may in part explain their violent and criminal behaviors.[43]
- *Victimization prompts revenge.* Victims may seek revenge against the people who harmed them or whom they believe are at fault for their problems. In some cases, these feelings become generalized to others who share the same characteristics of their attackers (e.g., men, Hispanics).[44] As a result, their reactions become displaced, and they may lash out at people who are not their attackers. They may take drastic measures, fearing revictimization, and arm themselves for

self-protection.[45] In some cultures, retaliation is an expected and accepted response to victimization.[46]
- *Spurious association.* It is also possible that the association between victimization and crime is spurious and that victims and criminals are actually two separate groups. The personal traits that produce violent criminals, such as impulsive personality, may not be the same ones that produce victims.[47] There may appear to be a connection because both criminals and victims tend to have the same lifestyle and live in the same neighborhoods, making it seem they are one and the same.

THE NATURE OF VICTIMIZATION

How many crime victims are there in the United States, and what are the trends and patterns in victimization? As noted in Chapter 2, about 21 million criminal victimizations now occur each year.[48] While this total is significant, it represents almost a 20-year decline in criminal victimization from a peak of more than 40 million reported victimizations. Figures 3.1 and 3.2 demonstrate changes in violent and property victimizations between 1998 and 2009, a period when violence rates dropped 41 percent and property victimizations dropped 32 percent.

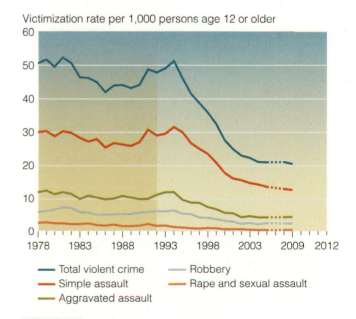

FIGURE 3.1
Violent Crime Victimization Trends

SOURCE: Jennifer Truman and Michael Rand, *Criminal Victimization, 2009* (Washington, DC: Bureau of Justice Statistics, 2010), http://bjs.ojp.usdoj.gov/content/pub/pdf/cv09.pdf (accessed January 5, 2010).

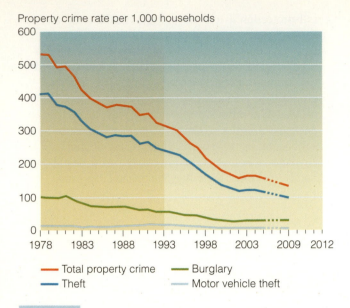

Property crime rate per 1,000 households

Legend:
— Total property crime
— Theft
— Burglary
— Motor vehicle theft

FIGURE 3.2
Property Crime Victimization Trends

SOURCE: Jennifer Truman and Michael Rand, *Criminal Victimization, 2009* (Washington, DC: Bureau of Justice Statistics, 2010), http://bjs.ojp. usdoj.gov/content/pub/pdf/cv09.pdf (accessed January 5, 2010).

While the number and rate of victimization have declined, patterns in the victimization survey findings are stable and repetitive, suggesting that victimization is not random but is a function of personal and ecological factors. The stability of these patterns allows us to make judgments about the nature of victimization; policies can then be created in an effort to reduce the victimization rate. Who are victims? Where does victimization take place? What is the relationship between victims and criminals? The following sections discuss some of the most important victimization patterns and trends.

The Social Ecology of Victimization

The NCVS shows that violent crimes are slightly more likely to take place in an open, public area (such as a street, a park, or a field), in a school building, or at a commercial establishment such as a tavern during the daytime or early evening hours than in a private home during the morning or late evening hours. The more serious violent crimes, such as rape and aggravated assault, typically take place after 6 P.M. Approximately two-thirds of rapes and sexual assaults occur at night—6 P.M. to 6 A.M. Less serious forms of violence, such as unarmed robberies and personal larcenies like purse snatching, are more likely to occur during the daytime. Neighborhood characteristics affect the chances of victimization. Those living in the central city have significantly higher rates of theft and violence than suburbanites; people living in rural areas have a victimization rate almost

half that of city dwellers. The risk of murder for both men and women is significantly higher in disorganized inner-city areas where gangs flourish and drug trafficking is commonplace.

Crime in Schools   Schools unfortunately are the locale of a great deal of victimization because they are populated by one of the most dangerous segments of society, teenage males. During before- and after-school activities, adult supervision is minimal, and hallways and locker rooms are typically left unattended. Kids who participate in school sports may leave their valuables in locker rooms that make attractive targets; others may congregate in unguarded places, making them attractive targets for predators who come on school grounds.[49] Currently:

- Among students ages 12 to 18, there are about 1.7 million victims of nonfatal crimes at school, including 900,000 thefts and 800,000 violent crimes (simple assault and serious violent crime).
- About 8 percent of students in grades 9 to 12 report being threatened or injured with a weapon in the previous 12 months, and 22 percent report that illegal drugs were made available to them on school property.
- About 86 percent of public schools report that at least one violent crime, theft, or other crime occurred at their school during the past 12 months.[50]

The Victim's Household

The NCVS tells us that within the United States, larger homes, African American homes, urban homes, and those in the West are the most vulnerable to crime. In contrast, rural homes, white homes, and those in the Northeast are the least likely to contain crime victims or be the target of theft offenses, such as burglary or larceny. People who own their homes are less vulnerable than renters.

Recent population movement and changes may account for decreases in crime victimization. U.S. residents have become extremely mobile, moving from urban areas to suburban and rural areas. In addition, family size has been reduced; more people than ever before are living in single-person homes (about one-quarter of the population). It is possible that the decline in household victimization rates during the past decades can be explained by the fact that smaller households in less populated areas have a lower victimization risk.

Victim Characteristics

Social and demographic characteristics also distinguish victims and nonvictims. The most important of these factors are gender, age, social status, and race.

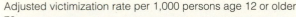

Adjusted victimization rate per 1,000 persons age 12 or older

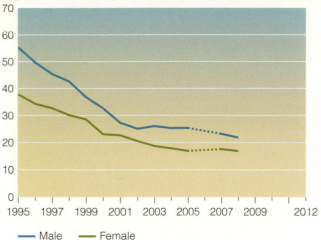

Rate per 1,000 persons in age group

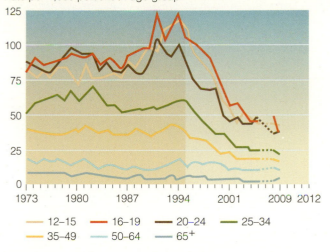

FIGURE 3.3

Violent Crime Rates by Gender of Victim

NOTE: Violent crimes included are homicide, rape, robbery, and both simple and aggravated assault.

SOURCE: Bureau of Justice Statistics data, 2010, http://bjs.ojp.usdoj.gov/content/glance/vsx2.cfm (accessed November 5, 2010).

FIGURE 3.4

Violent Crime Rates by Age of Victim

NOTE: Violent crimes included are homicide, rape, robbery, and both simple and aggravated assault.

SOURCE: Bureau of Justice Statistics data, http://bjs.ojp.usdoj.gov/content/glance/vage.cfm (accessed November 5, 2010) updated.

Gender   As Figure 3.3 shows, gender affects victimization risk. Except for the crimes of rape and sexual assault, males are more likely than females to be the victims of violent crime. Men are almost twice as likely as women to experience robbery. Women, however, are six times more likely than men to be victims of rape, domestic violence, and sexual assault. Although males are more likely to be victimized than females, the gender differences in the victimization rate have narrowed significantly over time.

One significant gender difference is that women are much more likely to be victimized by someone they know or with whom they live. Of those offenders victimizing females, about two-thirds were described as someone the victim knew or was related to. In contrast, fewer than half of male victims were attacked by a friend, relative, or acquaintance.

While women are more likely to be the target of domestic assaults, intimate partner violence seems to be declining. One reason may be an increasing amount of economic and political opportunities for women: research shows that economic inequality is significantly related to female victimization rates. As more laws or acts favorable to women are passed and more economic opportunities become available, the lower their rates of violent victimization.[51]

Age   Victim data reveal that young people face a much greater victimization risk than do older persons. Even the youngest kids are not immune: David Finkelhor and his colleagues found that when compared to older siblings, younger children were just as likely to be hit with an object that could cause injury and were just as likely to be victimized on multiple occasions and suffer similar injuries.[52]

Victim risk diminishes rapidly after age 25: teens 16 to 19 suffer 45 violent crimes per 1,000, whereas people over

65 experience only 2 per 1,000. As shown in Figure 3.4, teens and young adults experience the highest rates of violent crime. Violent crime rates declined in recent years for most age groups.

Elderly Victims   Although the elderly are less likely to become crime victims than the young, they are most often the victims of a narrow band of criminal activities from which the young are more immune. Frauds and scams, purse snatching, pocket picking, stealing checks from the mail, and committing crimes in long-term care settings claim more older than younger victims. The elderly are especially susceptible to fraud schemes because they have insurance, pension plans, proceeds from the sale of homes, and money from Social Security and savings that make them attractive financial targets. Because many elderly live by themselves and are lonely, they remain more susceptible to telephone and mail fraud. Unfortunately, once victimized, the elderly have more limited opportunities either to recover their lost money or to earn enough to replace what they have lost.[53]

Another emerging problem is the rising number of elderly living in long-term care facilities. There is much that is unknown about the abuse and criminal victimization of adults living in residential care facilities, but what is known is troubling. While a national survey of elderly care facilities is being planned for the future, there is little question that the environment at many residential care facilities across the country warrants the attention of all individuals working to help adults live with dignity and respect. Available data suggest that adults are victimized at an alarming rate, and often have much more difficulty participating in the criminal justice system and receiving the help they need.[54]

Elder abuse is a particularly important issue because of shifts in the U.S. population; the Bureau of the Census predicts that by 2030 the population over age 65 will nearly triple to more than 70 million people, and older people will make up more than 20 percent of the population (up from 12.3 percent in 1990). The saliency of elder abuse is underscored by reports from the National Center on Elder Abuse, which show an increase of 150 percent in reported cases of elder abuse nationwide since 1986.[55]

CONNECTIONS

The association between age and victimization is undoubtedly tied to lifestyle: adolescents often stay out late at night, go to public places, and hang out with other kids who have a high risk of criminal involvement. Teens also face a high victimization risk because they spend a great deal of time in the most dangerous building in the community—the local school. As Chapter 2 indicated, adolescents have the highest crime rates. It is not surprising that people who associate with these high-crime-rate individuals (other adolescents) have the greatest victimization risk.

Social Status The poorest Americans are also the most likely victims of violent and property crime. For example, homeless people, who are among the poorest individuals in America, suffer very high rates of assault.[56] This association occurs across all gender, age, and racial groups. Although the poor are more likely to suffer violent crimes, the wealthy are more likely targets of personal theft crimes such as pocket picking and purse snatching. Perhaps the affluent—sporting more expensive attire and driving better cars—attract the attention of thieves.

Marital Status Marital status also influences victimization risk. Never-married males and females are victimized more often than married people. Widows and widowers have the lowest victimization risk. This association between marital status and victimization is probably influenced by age, gender, and lifestyle:

- Adolescents and teens, who have the highest victimization risk, are too young to have been married.
- Young single people go out in public more often and sometimes interact with high-risk peers, increasing their exposure to victimization.
- Widows and widowers suffer much lower victimization rates because they are older, interact with older people, and are more likely to stay home at night and to avoid public places.

Race and Ethnicity As Figure 3.5 shows, (a) African Americans are more likely than whites to be victims of violent crime, and (b) serious violent crime rates have declined in recent years for both blacks and whites.

Why do these discrepancies exist? Because of income inequality, racial and minority group members are often forced to live in deteriorated urban areas beset by alcohol and drug abuse, poverty, racial discrimination, and violence. Consequently, their lifestyle places them in the most at-risk population group. However, as Figure 3.5 shows, the rate of black victimization has been in steep decline, and the racial gap in victimization rates seems to be narrowing.

Repeat Victimization Does prior victimization enhance or reduce the chances of future victimization? Individuals who have been crime victims have a significantly higher chance of future victimization than people who have not been victims.[57] Households that have experienced victimization in the past are the ones most likely to experience it again in the future.[58]

What factors predict **chronic victimization**? Most repeat victimizations occur soon after a previous crime has occurred, suggesting that repeat victims share some personal characteristic that makes them a magnet for predators.[59] For example, children who are shy, physically weak, or socially isolated may be prone to being bullied in the school yard.[60] David Finkelhor and Nancy Asigian have found that three specific types of characteristics increase the potential for victimization:

- *Target vulnerability.* The victims' physical weakness or psychological distress renders them incapable of resisting or deterring crime and makes them easy targets.
- *Target gratifiability.* Some victims have some quality, possession, skill, or attribute that an offender wants to obtain, use, have access to, or manipulate. Having attractive possessions such as a leather coat may make one vulnerable to predatory crime.
- *Target antagonism.* Some characteristics increase risk because they arouse anger, jealousy, or destructive impulses in potential offenders. Being gay or effeminate, for example, may bring on undeserved attacks in the street; being argumentative and alcoholic may provoke barroom assaults.[61]

Repeat victimization may occur when the victim does not take defensive action. For example, if an abusive husband finds out that his battered wife will not call the police, he repeatedly victimizes her; or if a hate crime is committed and the police do not respond to reported offenses, the perpetrators learn they have little to fear from the law.[62] Women who fight back and/or use self-protective action during the first incident of sexual battering reduce their likelihood of being a recurrent victim.[63]

Of course, not all victims are repeaters. Some take defensive measures to lessen their chance of future victimizations. Some may change their lifestyle, take fewer risks, and cut back on associating with dangerous people; once burnt, twice shy.[64]

Victims and Their Criminals

The victim data also tell us something about the relationship between victims and criminals. Males are more likely to be violently victimized by a stranger, and females are more likely to be victimized by a friend, an acquaintance, or an intimate. As the Profiles in Crime feature shows, what it means to be victimized by an acquaintance may take on a whole different meaning in the Internet age.

Victims report that most crimes are committed by a single offender over age 20. Crime tends to be intraracial: black offenders victimize blacks, and whites victimize whites. However, because the country's population is predominantly white, it stands to reason that criminals of all races will be more likely to target white victims. Victims

AP Images/Sam Horton

Victims tend to be young males. Minorities and city dwellers are much more likely to be victimized than older women living in rural areas. Here, people come to the aid of an unidentified victim at the scene where at least five people were shot and two suspects were taken into custody in a shooting incident along the Mardi Gras parade route in New Orleans, February 24, 2009.

report that substance abuse is involved in about one-third of violent crime incidents.[65]

Although many violent crimes are committed by strangers, a surprising number of violent crimes are committed by relatives or acquaintances of the victims. In fact, more than half of all nonfatal personal crimes are committed by people who are described as being known to the victim. Women are especially vulnerable to people they know. More than 60 percent of rape or sexual assault victims state the offender was an intimate, a relative, a friend, or an acquaintance. Women are more likely than men to be robbed by a friend or acquaintance; most males report that the people who robbed them were strangers.

THEORIES OF VICTIMIZATION

For many years, criminological theory focused on the actions of the criminal offender; the role of the victim was virtually ignored. But more than 50 years ago, scholars

Adjusted victimization rate per 1,000 persons age 12 or older

```
50
40
30
20
10
0
  1978  1983  1988  1993  1998  2003  2009  2012
```

— Blacks   — Whites

FIGURE 3.5
Race and Victimization

SOURCE: Bureau of Justice Statistics, http://bjs.ojp.usdoj.gov/content/glance/race.cfm (accessed November 5, 2010).

Profiles in Crime
Online Predator

On August 13, 2009, Jonathan Wryn Vance, 24, of Auburn, Alabama, was convicted in a federal court and sentenced to 18 years in prison on charges of interstate extortion and interstate transportation in aid of extortion. More specifically, Vance used the Internet and a number of different online screen names, including "metascape" and "manescape 22," to transmit threatening communications to more than 50 minor females and young women in Alabama between 2006 and 2007.

Vance gained access to his victims via social networking sites, where he used false pretenses that let him into their circle of "friends" online. He met some of his victims at social events at local churches and others at Auburn University where he had attended school. Vance would at first pretend to be a family member, friend, or acquaintance of his female victims in order to gain their trust. He sometimes accomplished this by initiating a game in which he would pose as an anonymous long-lost friend or secret admirer who would only reveal his true identity if the recipient truthfully answered

a series of 10 questions. The questions allegedly asked for body measurements and details, past sexual experiences, and current sexual fantasies, and were designed to elicit intimate and embarrassing personal information from the victims. As soon as he had acquired the information, Vance would demand that the victims provide him with their confidential sign-on information for various interactive computer services, such as Facebook, MySpace, Hotmail, and Yahoo, and/or digital still images or webcam video of themselves in various states of undress, exposing themselves, or engaging in sexually explicit conduct. He allegedly told victims that if they did not comply with his demands, he would injure their reputations by transmitting the intimate and embarrassing personal information about them to other people, including their peers, church members, and employers. Vance sometimes approached his victims by posing as one of their own family members, friends, or online contacts. Under that guise, Vance would allegedly send an e-mail or instant message to one victim using another victim's account, pretending that the sender

could not access her Facebook or MySpace account and needed to borrow the recipient's account sign-on information in order to address the problem. Once he had obtained access to his victims' accounts, Vance would change the passwords, effectively holding the accounts hostage. He would then inform the victims of the trick and demand that they send him digital images or webcam video transmissions of themselves in various states of undress, nude, or engaging in sexually explicit conduct, in order to regain access to their accounts. Some victims complied with Vance's demands, though others did not. Most of the threatening communications were allegedly sent via the America Online (AOL) Instant Messenger service (AIM).

SOURCES: Patrick Hickerson, "Alabama Predator Sentenced to 18 Years for Facebook Extortion Attempts: How He Got Access," *Birmingham News*, April 17, 2009, http://blog.al.com/spotnews/2009/04/auburn_alabama_predator_senten.html (accessed November 5, 2010); U.S. Department of Justice News Release, "Auburn Man Indicted for Online Extortion," www.justice.gov/criminal/cybercrime/vanceIndict.pdf (accessed November 5, 2010).

began to realize that the victim is not a passive target in crime, but someone whose behavior can influence his or her own fate, someone who "shapes and molds the criminal."[66] These early works helped focus attention on the role of the victim in the crime problem and led to further research efforts that have sharpened the image of the crime victim. Today a number of different theories attempt to explain the causes of victimization; the most important are discussed here.

Victim Precipitation Theory

According to **victim precipitation theory**, some people may actually initiate the confrontation that eventually leads to their injury or death. Victim precipitation can be either active or passive.

Active precipitation occurs when victims act provocatively, use threats or fighting words, or even attack first.[67]

In 1971, Menachem Amir suggested female rape victims often contribute to their attacks by dressing provocatively or pursuing a relationship with the rapist.[68] Although Amir's findings are controversial, courts have continued to return not-guilty verdicts in rape cases if a victim's actions can in any way be construed as consenting to sexual intimacy.[69]

Passive precipitation occurs when the victim exhibits some personal characteristic that unknowingly either threatens or encourages the attacker. Although the victim may never have met the attacker or even know of his or her existence, the attacker feels menaced and acts accordingly.[70] In some instances, the crime can occur because of personal conflict—for example, when two people compete over a job, promotion, love interest, or some other scarce and coveted commodity. A woman may become the target of domestic violence when she increases her job status and her success results in a backlash from a jealous spouse or partner.[71]

Passive precipitation may also occur when the victim belongs to a group whose mere presence threatens the attacker's reputation, status, or economic well-being. For example, hate-crime violence may be precipitated by immigrant group members arriving in the community to compete for jobs and housing. Research indicates that passive precipitation is related to power: if the target group can establish themselves economically or gain political power in the community, their vulnerability will diminish. They are still a potential threat, but they become too formidable a target to attack; they are no longer passive precipitators.[72] By implication, economic power reduces victimization risk.

Victim Impulsivity Perhaps there is something about victims' personality traits that incite attacks. A number of research efforts have found that both male and female victims have an impulsive personality that might render them abrasive and obnoxious, characteristics that might incite victimization.[73] People who are impulsive and lack self-control are less likely to have a high tolerance for frustration and a physical rather than mental orientation; they are less likely to practice risk avoidance. It is possible that impulsive people are not only antagonistic and therefore more likely to become targets, but they also are risk takers who get involved in dangerous situations and fail to take precautions.[74]

Lifestyle Theory

Some criminologists believe people may become crime victims because their lifestyle increases their exposure to criminal offenders. Victimization risk is increased by such behaviors as associating with young men, going out in public places late at night, and living in an urban area. Conversely, one's chances of victimization can be reduced by staying home at night, moving to a rural area, staying out of public places, earning more money, and getting married. The basis of **lifestyle theory** is that crime is not a random occurrence but rather a function of the victim's lifestyle. For example, due to their lifestyle and demographic makeup, college campuses contain large concentrations of young women who may be at greater risk for rape and other forms of sexual assault than women in the general population. Single women who drink frequently and have a prior history of being sexually assaulted are most likely to be assaulted on campus.[75]

Though females are more likely to be victimized by a friend, an acquaintance, or an intimate, some are harmed by strangers. In a case that made national headlines, ESPN reporter Erin Andrews was stalked and spied upon by a deranged admirer who used a spy cam to take nude photographs of her that he then placed on the Internet. Her attacker, Michael David Barrett, pleaded guilty and was sentenced to 2.5 years in prison.

Image of Sport/Newscom

People who belong to groups that have an extremely risky life—homeless, runaways, drug users—are at high risk for victimization; the more time they are exposed to street life, the greater their risk of becoming crime victims.[76] When Kimberly Tyler and Morgan Beal interviewed more than 100 homeless youth in midwestern cities, they found that personal and behavioral characteristics helped put them in danger for physical and sexual abuse. Those who ran away at an earlier age, did it more often, slept on the street, panhandled, and hung out with deviant peers rather than protective family members were the ones most likely to suffer physical victimization. Sexual victimization risk was elevated if the homeless youth was a female, had an unkempt and disheveled appearance, and had friends who were willing to trade sex for money.[77] Tyler and Beal's research shows that not only does lifestyle promote victimization, but there is significant behavioral variation within lifestyle groupings that can elevate victimization risk even more.

Others are exposed to risk because of their status. Teenage males have an extremely high victimization risk because their lifestyle places them at risk both at school and once they leave the school grounds.[78] They spend a great deal of time hanging out with friends and pursuing recreational fun.[79] Their friends may give them a false ID so they can go drinking in the neighborhood bar, or they may hang out in taverns at night, which places them at risk because many fights and assaults occur in places that serve liquor.

College Lifestyle College students maintain a high-risk lifestyle—partying, taking recreational drugs—that makes them victimization prone.[80] Bonnie Fisher and her colleagues surveyed thousands of college students and found that college women face the risk of sexual assault at a higher rate than women in the general population.[81] Fisher and her colleagues found that 90 percent of the victims knew the person who sexually victimized them. Most often this was a boyfriend, ex-boyfriend, classmate, friend, acquaintance, or coworker; college professors were not identified as committing any rapes or sexual coercions. The vast majority of sexual victimizations occurred in the evening (after 6:00 P.M.), typically (60 percent) in the students' living quarters; many were connected to drinking. Other common crime scenes were other living quarters on campus and fraternity houses (about 10 percent). Off-campus sexual victimizations, especially rapes, also occurred in residences. Incidents where women were threatened or touched also took place in settings such as bars, dance clubs or nightclubs, and work settings. Research confirms that young women who involve themselves in substance abuse and come into contact with men who are also substance abusers increase the likelihood that they will be sexual assault victims.[82]

> The **Office for Victims of Crime (OVC)** was established by the 1984 Victims of Crime Act (VOCA) to oversee diverse programs that benefit victims of crime. The OVC provides substantial funding to state victim assistance and compensation programs and supports training designed to educate criminal justice and allied professionals regarding the rights and needs of crime victims. Learn more about assistance to victims of crime by visiting the Criminal Justice CourseMate at cengagebrain.com, then access the "Web Links" for this chapter.

Criminal Lifestyle Not surprisingly, getting involved in criminality also increases the chance of victimization. The perils of a deviant lifestyle do not end in adolescence and haunt risk takers through their life. Kids with a history of family violence and involvement in crime increase their chances of becoming the victims of homicide as adults.[83] Kids who take drugs and carry weapons in their adolescence maintain a greater chance of being shot and killed as adults.[84]

Take for instance gang boys, a group at high risk for victimization. The gang lifestyle—engaging in serious crime and delinquency, carrying guns, selling drugs, retaliating against perceived slights or disrespect—typifies behaviors that significantly increase the chances of becoming the victim of violent crimes. Protecting the gang's turf and engaging in retaliatory vendettas to maintain the gang's reputation also increase the risk of personal victimization.[85] Gang boys are much more likely to own guns and associate with violent peers than nonmembers.[86] Those who choose aggressive or violent friends are more likely to begin engaging in antisocial behavior themselves and suffer psychological deficits.[87] Experiencing victimization brings on retaliation, creating a never-ending cycle of violence begetting even more violence.[88]

The association between victimization and criminal lifestyle may be more one of risk than propensity: people who are involved in crime are constantly exposed to dangerous people who elevate their victimization risk. Considering the risk criminals take and the likelihood they will become victims themselves, what impact does victimization have on a criminal career? Does it encourage more crime and bloody retaliation or does it result in rethinking the dangers of a criminal way of life? The Criminological Enterprise feature helps answer this question.

Deviant Place Theory

According to **deviant place theory**, the greater their exposure to dangerous places, the more likely people will become victims of crime and violence.[89] Victims do not encourage crime, but are victim prone because they reside in socially disorganized high-crime areas where they have the greatest risk of coming into contact with criminal offenders, irrespective of their own behavior or lifestyle.[90] The more often victims visit dangerous places, the more likely they will be exposed to crime and violence.[91] Neighborhood crime levels, then, may be more important for determining the chances of victimization than individual characteristics. Consequently, there may be little reason for residents in lower-class areas to alter their lifestyle or take safety precautions because personal behavior choices do not influence the likelihood of victimization.[92]

Deviant places are poor, densely populated, highly transient neighborhoods in which commercial and residential property exist side by side.[93] The commercial property provides criminals with easy targets for theft crimes, such as shoplifting and larceny. Successful people stay out of these stigmatized areas; they are homes for "demoralized kinds of people" who are easy targets for crime: the homeless, the addicted, the retarded, and the elderly poor.[94] People who live in more affluent areas and take safety precautions significantly lower their chances of becoming crime victims; the effect of safety precautions is less pronounced in poor areas. Residents of poor areas have a much greater risk of becoming victims because they live near many motivated offenders; to protect themselves, they have to try harder to be safe than the more affluent.[95]

Sociologist William Julius Wilson has described how people who can afford to leave dangerous areas do so. He suggests that affluent people realize that criminal victimization can be avoided by moving to an area with greater law enforcement and lower crime rates. Because there are significant interracial income differences, white residents are able to flee inner-city high-crime areas, leaving members of racial minorities behind to suffer high victimization rates.[96]

The Criminological Enterprise
Escalation or Desistance: The Effect of Victimization on Criminal Careers

What happens when a criminal experiences victimization? Does it encourage further criminal activities or, conversely, might the experience help convince a career criminal to choose another career?

Recent research by Scott Jacques and Richard Wright shows that for at least one set of criminal offenders—drug dealers—becoming a crime victim sets the stage for their breaking away from their chosen profession and transitioning into a new life course. This unexpected life event is a "break from the customary" and may lead to "a disturbance of habit in which a customary behavior can no longer be maintained," namely, drug dealing. They find that serious victimizations help drug dealers realize that they better begin thinking about transitioning out of crime. Terminating drug dealing is an adaptation that allows them to gain control over their lives and to reduce the probability of future victimization.

Jacques and Wright tested their views with interviews with two drug sellers, Pete and Christian. Both were in their early 20s, enrolled in college, and had never been arrested. Each told about the incident that resulted in their terminating their drug-dealing careers. Pete was robbed and beaten. He was forced to show up at a family member's funeral battered and sporting a black eye. When Pete's extended family saw his black eye at the funeral and consoled him, Pete experienced regret and shame. As Pete puts it, "That's the thing in my life that I regret most in my life ever, having my whole entire family having to see me all beat up because I was selling weed." Shame and regret related to victimization and drug dealing strengthened his bond to his family and thereby reduce the probability of future drug dealing.

Just before he was victimized, Christian recognized that he had lost control of his life and said to himself, "Why . . . am I doing this? I'm about to get robbed. Why am I doing this?" Christian could not find the strength to stop himself from doing a drug deal that he predicted would result in his own victimization. He thought about finding his attacker and getting revenge, but Christian did not want to take the chance of getting shot. He wasn't into physical violence, so he did not find the adaptation of retaliation to be an attractive option. Although victimization did not result in Christian instantly terminating his illicit activity, the desistance process was set in motion because he started to reevaluate the benefits and costs of dealing in relation to alternative lines of available action. Christian considered that he was 18 years of age and thus no longer a minor, that he was going to college soon, that the profit of dealing was not large enough to offset the risks, and that it was time for him to go and make something of himself. In the end, Christian decided that dealing was too hazardous and that termination was the best course of action.

CRITICAL THINKING

Jacques and Wright find that for some criminals, victimization is an eye-opening event, helping them choose to desist from crime. This transition is aided by a number of factors ranging from attachment to family and friends, to belief that there are alternatives to criminality. However, it is the victimization event that is the catalyst for the decision to transition out of crime. Do you agree with their assessment? Or might victimization breed anger, resentment, and vengeance?

SOURCE: Scott Jacques and Richard Wright, "The Victimization–Termination Link," *Criminology* 46 (2008): 47–91.

Routine Activities Theory

Routine activities theory was first articulated in a series of papers by Lawrence Cohen and Marcus Felson.[97] They concluded that the volume and distribution of predatory crime (violent crimes against a person and crimes in which an offender attempts to steal an object directly) are closely related to the interaction of three variables that reflect the routine activities of the typical American lifestyle (see Figure 3.6):

- The availability of **suitable targets**, such as homes containing easily salable goods
- The absence of **capable guardians**, such as police, homeowners, neighbors, friends, and relatives
- The presence of **motivated offenders**, such as a large number of unemployed teenagers

The presence of these components increases the likelihood that a predatory crime will take place. Targets are more likely to be victimized if they are poorly guarded and exposed to a large group of motivated offenders, such as teenage boys.[98] As targets increase in value and availability, so too should crime rates. Conversely, as the resale value of formerly pricey goods such as iPods and cell phones declines, so too should burglary rates.[99]

Increasing the number of motivated offenders and placing them in close proximity to valuable goods will increase victimization levels. Even after-school programs, designed to reduce criminal activity, may produce higher crime rates because they lump together motivated offenders—teen boys—with vulnerable victims (other teen boys).[100] Young women who drink to excess in bars and frat houses may

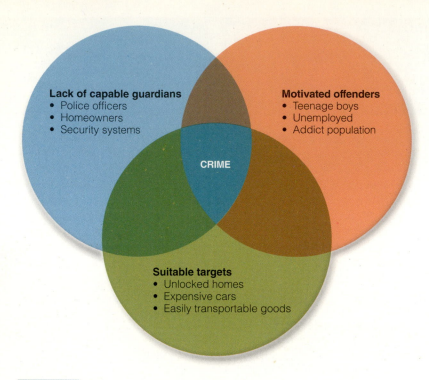

Lack of capable guardians
• Police officers
• Homeowners
• Security systems

Motivated offenders
• Teenage boys
• Unemployed
• Addict population

CRIME

Suitable targets
• Unlocked homes
• Expensive cars
• Easily transportable goods

FIGURE 3.6

Routine Activities Theory: The Interaction of Three Factors

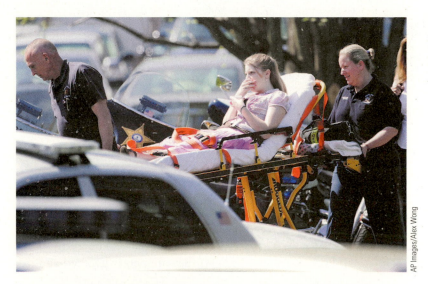

AP Images/Alex Wong

A young woman is carried out by emergency rescuers after collapsing during the funeral service of Virginia Tech shooting victim Reema Samaha on April 23, 2007. Samaha graduated from Westfield High School, the same school attended by gunman Seung-Hui Cho. How would routine activities theory explain the Virginia Tech shooting? What aspects of the theory could be applied to such a seemingly senseless killing?

elevate their risk of **date rape** because (a) they are perceived as easy targets, and (b) their attackers can rationalize the attack because they view intoxication as a sign of immorality ("She's loose, so I didn't think she'd care").[101]

Conversely, people can reduce their chances of victimization if they adopt a lifestyle that limits their exposure to danger: by getting married, having children, and moving to a small town.[102]

Guardianship Even the most motivated offenders may ignore valuable targets if they are well guarded. Despite containing valuable commodities, private homes and/or public businesses may be considered off-limits by seasoned criminals if they are well protected by capable guardians and efficient security systems.[103]

Criminals are also aware of police guardianship. In order to convince them that crime does not pay, more cops can be put on the street. Proactive, aggressive law enforcement officers who quickly get to the scene of the crime help deter criminal activities.[104]

Hot Spots Motivated people—such as teenage males, drug users, and unemployed adults—are the ones most likely to commit crime. If they congregate in a particular neighborhood, it becomes a "hot spot" for crime and violence. People who live in these hot spots elevate their chances of victimization. For example, people who live in public housing projects may have high victimization rates because their fellow residents, mostly indigent, are extremely motivated to commit crime.[105] Yet motivated criminals must have the opportunity to find suitable undefended targets before they commit crime. Even the most desperate criminal might hesitate to attack a well-defended target, whereas a group of teens might rip off an unoccupied home on the spur of the moment.[106] In hot spots for crime, therefore, an undefended yet attractive target becomes an irresistible objective for motivated criminals. Given these principles, it is not surprising that people who (a) live in high-crime areas and (b) go out late at night (c) carrying valuables such as an expensive watch and (d) engage in risky behavior such as drinking alcohol, (e) without friends or family to watch or help them, have a significant chance of becoming crime victims.[107]

The Criminological Enterprise feature shows how changes in lifestyle can contribute to victimization.

Support for Routine Activities Theory Research supports many facets of routine activities theory. Cohen and Felson themselves found that crime rates increased between

The Criminological Enterprise
Crime and Everyday Life

According to Marcus Felson, crime began to increase in the United States as the country changed from a nation of small villages and towns to one of large urban environments. Because metropolitan areas provide a critical population mass, predatory criminals are better able to hide and evade apprehension. After committing crime, criminals can blend into the crowd, disperse their loot, and make a quick escape using the public transportation system.

As the population became more urban, the middle class, fearing criminal victimization, fled to the suburbs. Rather than being safe from crime, the suburbs produced a unique set of routine activities that promote victimization risk. In many families, both parents are likely to commute to work, leaving teens unsupervised. Affluent kids own or drive cars, date, and socialize with peers in unsupervised settings, all behaviors that are related to both crime and victimization.

The downtown shopping district was replaced by the suburban shopping mall. Here, strangers converge in large numbers and youths hang out. The interior is filled with people, so drug deals can be concealed in the pedestrian flow. Stores have attractively displayed goods, encouraging shoplifting and employee pilferage. Substantial numbers of cars are parked in areas that make larceny and car theft virtually undetectable. Cars that carry away stolen merchandise have an undistinguished appearance: who notices people placing items in a car in a shopping mall lot? Also, shoppers can be attacked in parking lots as they walk in isolation to and from their cars. As car ownership increases, teens have greater access to transportation outside parental control. So while victimization rates in urban areas are still higher, routine activities in the suburbs may also produce the risk of victimization. Felson has set out the factors that increase the likelihood of victimization as the features of metropolitan living have spread to the suburbs:

- It has become more difficult to protect people from criminal entry because homes have been dispersed over larger areas, huge parking lots have been created, and building heights lowered.
- By spreading people and vehicles over larger areas as they travel and park, people are more exposed to attack.
- There are fewer people in each household and consequently less intrapersonal and intrafamily supervision.

- As shopping, work, and socializing are spread further from home, people are forced to leave their immediate neighborhood, and, as strangers, they become more vulnerable to attack.
- By spreading vast quantities of retail goods throughout huge stores and malls, with fewer employees to watch over them, the divergent metropolis creates a retail environment that invites people of all ages to shoplift.
- Commuting to the inner city for work requires that millions of dollars' worth of vehicles be left in parking lots without supervision.

CRITICAL THINKING

Does routine activities theory merely describe why people become victims rather than get at the heart of the matter: why are there motivated offenders? If people are motivated to commit crime, where does their motivation come from?

SOURCE: Marcus Felson and Rachel Boba, *Crime and Everyday Life: Insights and Implications for Society,* 4th Ed. (Thousand Oaks, CA: Sage, 2009).

1960 and 1980 because the number of adult caretakers at home during the day (guardians) decreased as a result of increased female participation in the workforce. While mothers are at work and children in day care, homes are left unguarded. Similarly, with the growth of suburbia and the decline of the traditional neighborhood, the number of such familiar guardians as family, neighbors, and friends diminished.[108] Steven Messner and his associates found that as adult unemployment rates *increase*, juvenile homicide arrest rates *decrease*. One possible reason for this phenomenon: it is possible that juvenile arrests decrease because unemployed adults are at home to supervise their children and make sure they do not get in trouble or join gangs.[109] The availability and cost of easily transportable goods has also been shown to influence victimization rates: as the costs of goods such as mobile phones and camcorders declined, so too did burglary rates.[110]

Routine Activities and Lifestyle   Routine activities theory and the lifestyle approach have a number of similarities. They both assume that a person's living arrangements can affect victim risk and that people who live in unguarded areas are at the mercy of motivated offenders. These two theories both rely on four basic concepts: (1) proximity to criminals, (2) time of exposure to criminals, (3) target attractiveness, and (4) guardianship.[111]

Based on the same basic concepts, these theories share five predictions: People increase their victimization risk if they (1) live in high-crime areas, (2) go out late at night, (3) carry valuables such as an expensive watch, (4) engage in risky behavior such as drinking alcohol, and (5) are without friends or family to watch or help them.[112]

The various theories of victimization are summarized in Concept Summary 3.1.

Victimization Theories

	Major Premise	Strengths of the Theory	Research Focus of the Theory
Victim precipitation	The major premise of victim precipitation theory is that victims trigger criminal acts by their provocative behavior. Active precipitation involves fighting words or gestures. Passive precipitation occurs when victims unknowingly threaten their attacker.	The strength of the theory is that it explains multiple victimizations: if people precipitate crime, it follows that they will become repeat victims if their behavior persists over time.	The research focuses of the theory are the victim's role, crime provocation, and the victim–offender relationship.
Lifestyle	The major premise of lifestyle theory is that victimization risk is increased when people have a high-risk lifestyle. Placing oneself at risk by going out to dangerous places results in increased victimization.	The strength of the theory is that it explains victimization patterns in the social structure. Males, young people, and the poor have high victimization rates because they have a higher-risk lifestyle than females, the elderly, and the affluent.	The research focuses of the theory are personal activities, peer relations, place of crime, and type of crime.
Deviant place	The major premise of deviant place theory is that victims do not encourage crime but are victim prone because they reside in socially disorganized high-crime areas where they have the greatest risk of coming into contact with criminal offenders, irrespective of their own behavior or lifestyle.	The strength of the theory is that it shows why people with conventional lifestyles become crime victims in high-risk areas. Victimization is a function of place and location, not lifestyle and risk taking.	The research focus of the theory is victimization in high-crime, disorganized neighborhoods.
Routine activities	The major premise of routine activities theory is that crime rates can be explained by the availability of suitable targets, the absence of capable guardians, and the presence of motivated offenders.	The strengths of the theory are that it can explain crime rates and trends, it shows how victim behavior can influence criminal opportunity, and it suggests that victimization risk can be reduced by increasing guardianship and/or reducing target vulnerability.	The research focuses of the theory are opportunity to commit crime, effect of police and guardians, population shifts, and crime rates.

CARING FOR THE VICTIM

National victim surveys indicate that almost every American age 12 and over will one day become the victim of a common-law crime, such as larceny or burglary, and in the aftermath suffer financial problems, mental stress, and physical hardship.[113] Surveys show that more than 75 percent of the general public has been victimized by crime at least once in their life; as many as 25 percent of the victims develop posttraumatic stress disorder, and their symptoms last for more than a decade after the crime occurred.[114] The long-term effects of sexual victimization can include years of problem avoidance, social withdrawal, and self-criticism. Helping these victims adjust and improve their coping techniques can be essential to their recovery.[115] Law enforcement agencies, courts, and correctional and human service systems have come to realize that due process and human rights exist for both the defendant and the victim of criminal behavior.

The Government's Response to Victimization

Because of public concern over violent personal crime, President Ronald Reagan created a Task Force on Victims of Crime in 1982.[116] This group suggested that a balance be achieved between recognizing the victim's rights and providing the defendant with due process. Recommendations included providing witnesses and victims with protection from intimidation, requiring restitution in criminal cases, developing guidelines for fair treatment of crime victims and witnesses, and expanding programs of victim compensation.[117] Consequently, the Omnibus Victim and Witness Protection Act was passed, which required the use of victim impact statements at sentencing in federal criminal cases, greater protection for witnesses, more stringent bail laws, and the use of restitution in criminal cases.

In 1984, the Comprehensive Crime Control Act and the Victims of Crime Act authorized federal funding for state victim compensation and assistance projects.[118] With these acts, the federal government began to address the plight of the victim and make victim assistance an even greater concern of the public and the justice system. In 2004, the Justice for All Act modified existing federal law and created a new set of rights for victims (Exhibit 3.1), including the right to be protected from the accused in their case and to be informed of their release. Legal expert Michael O'Hear finds that the Crime Victims' Rights Act of 2004 can be viewed as an effort to promote victims' rights as a counterweight to defendants' rights, illustrating both the public's hostility to defendants and its skepticism of the traditional lawyer- and judge-dominated legal system, which they feel is too liberal.[119]

Due to this recognition of the needs of victims, an estimated 2,000 **victim-witness assistance programs** have developed around the United States.[120] Victim-witness assistance programs are organized on a variety of governmental levels and serve a variety of clients. We will look at the most prominent forms of victim services operating in the United States.[121]

Victim Compensation   One of the primary goals of victim advocates has been to lobby for legislation creating crime **victim compensation** programs.[122] As a result of such legislation, the victim ordinarily receives compensation from the state to pay for damages associated with the crime. Rarely are two compensation schemes alike, however, and many state programs suffer from lack of both adequate funding and proper organization within the criminal justice system. Compensation may be made for medical bills, loss of wages, loss of future earnings, and counseling. In the case of death, the victim's survivors can receive burial expenses and aid for loss of support.[123] Awards are typically in the $100 to $15,000 range. Occasionally programs will provide emergency assistance to indigent victims until compensation is available. Emergency assistance may come in the form of food vouchers or replacement of prescription medicines.

In 1984, the federal government created the Victims of Crime Act (VOCA), which grants money to state compensation boards derived from fines and penalties imposed on federal offenders. The money is distributed each year to the states to fund both their crime victim compensation programs and their victim assistance programs, such as rape crisis centers and domestic violence shelters. Victims of child abuse and victims of domestic violence receive most of the funds. VOCA money goes to support victims' medical expenses, gives them economic support for lost wages, helps to compensate for the death of loved ones, and provides mental health counseling.[124] Currently, this assistance amounts to $400 million per year.[125]

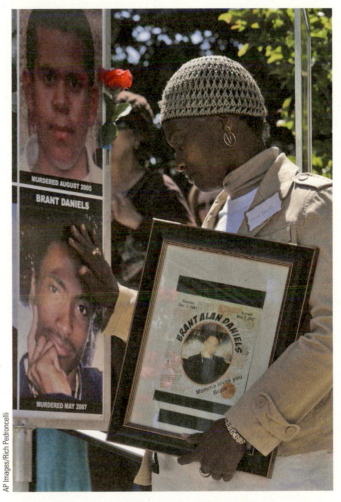

AP Images/Rich Pedroncelli

National victim surveys indicate that almost every American age 12 and over will one day become the victim of some crime, including serious violent crimes such as rape and murder. Victims and their families suffer financial problems, mental stress, and physical hardship. There have been nationwide efforts to help survivors cope with their loss. Here, on April 16, 2008, Leona Daniels touches a photograph of her son, murder victim Brant Daniels, during the 19th Annual Victims March on the Capitol in Sacramento, California. Daniels was among several hundred family members and friends of murder victims who attended the rally to call for tougher anticrime laws. Brant Daniels, a student at Fresno City College from Los Angeles, was murdered in a dispute over a video game in Fresno, May 7, 2007.

Victim Advocates   Ensuring victims' rights can involve an eclectic group of advocacy groups, some independent, others government sponsored, and some self-help. Advocates can be especially helpful when victims need to interact with the agencies of justice. For example, advocates can lobby police departments to keep investigations open as well as request the return of recovered stolen property. They can demand from prosecutors and judges protection from harassment and reprisals by, for example, making "no contact" a condition of bail. They can help victims make statements during sentencing hearings as well as probation and parole revocation procedures. Victim advocates can also interact with news media, making sure that reporting is accurate and that victim privacy is not violated. Victim advocates can be part of an independent agency similar to a legal aid society. If successful, top-notch advocates may eventually open private offices, similar to attorneys, private investigators, or jury consultants.

Some programs assign advocates to help victims understand the operations of the justice system and guide them through the process. Victims of sexual assault may be assigned the assistance of a rape victim advocate to stand by their side as they negotiate the legal and medical systems that must process their case. Research shows that rape survivors who had the assistance of an advocate were significantly more likely to have police reports taken, were less likely to be treated negatively by police officers, and reported less distress from their medical contact experiences.[126]

Court advocates prepare victims and witnesses by explaining court procedures: how to be a witness, how bail works, and what to do if the defendant makes a threat. Lack of such knowledge can cause confusion and fear, making some victims reluctant to testify in court procedures.

Many victim programs also provide transportation to and from court, and advocates may remain in the courtroom during hearings to explain procedures and provide support. Court escorts are particularly important for elderly and disabled victims, victims of child abuse and assault, and victims who have been intimidated by friends or relatives of the defendant. These types of services may be having a positive effect since recent research shows that victims may now be less traumatized by a court hearing than previously believed.[127]

Victim Counseling   Numerous programs provide counseling and psychological support to help victims recover from the long-term trauma associated with a violent victimization. Clients are commonly referred to the local network of public and private social service agencies that can provide emergency and long-term assistance with transportation, medical care, shelter, food, and clothing. In addition, more than half of victim programs provide **crisis intervention** to victims, many of whom feel isolated, vulnerable, and in need of immediate services. Some programs counsel at their offices, and others visit victims' homes, the crime scene, or a hospital. Helping victims adjust is often a difficult process, and recent research has found little evidence that counseling efforts are as successful as previously hoped.[128]

Public Education   More than half of all victim programs include public education to help familiarize the general public with their services and with other agencies that assist crime victims. In some instances, these are primary education programs, which teach methods of dealing with conflict without resorting to violence. For example, school-based programs present information on spousal and dating abuse followed by discussions of how to reduce violent incidents.[129]

Crisis Intervention   Most victim programs refer victims to specific services to help them recover from their ordeal. Clients are commonly referred to the local network of public and private social service agencies that provide emergency and long-term assistance with transportation, medical care, shelter, food, and clothing. In addition, more than half of all victim programs provide crisis intervention for victims who feel isolated, vulnerable, and in need of immediate services. Some programs counsel at their offices; others visit victims in their homes, at the crime scene, or in the hospital. For example, the Good Samaritans program in Mobile County, Alabama, unites law enforcement and faith-based and community organizations to train and mobilize volunteers who can help crime victims. Good Samaritan volunteers provide services such as:

- Making repairs to a home after a break-in
- Conducting home safety inspections to prevent revictimization
- Accompanying victims to court
- Supplying "victim care kits" or other support[130]

Victim–Offender Reconciliation Programs

Victim–offender reconciliation programs (VORPs) use mediators to facilitate face-to-face encounters between victims and their attackers. The aim is to engage in direct negotiations that lead to **restitution agreements** and, possibly, reconciliation between the two parties involved.[131] Hundreds of programs are currently in operation, and they handle thousands of cases per year. Designed at first to address routine misdemeanors such as petty theft and vandalism, programs now commonly hammer out restitution agreements in more serious incidents such as residential burglary and even attempted murder.

The **Victim–Offender Reconciliation Program (VORP)** Information and Resource Center provides information on programs and training and provides technical assistance. For more information about restorative justice, visit the Criminal Justice CourseMate at cengagebrain.com, then access the "Web Links" for this chapter.

CONNECTIONS

Reconciliation programs are based on the concept of restorative justice, which rejects punitive correctional measures in favor of viewing crimes of violence and theft as interpersonal conflicts that need to be settled in the community through noncoercive means. See Chapter 8 for more on this approach.

Victim Impact Statements   Every state jurisdiction allows victims to make an impact statement before the sentencing judge. Victim impact information is part of the Federal Crime Act of 1994, in which Congress gave federal victims of violent crime or sexual assault the right to speak at sentencing. Through the Child Protection Act of 1990, child victims of federal crimes are allowed to submit victim impact statements that are "commensurate with their age and cognitive development," which can include drawings, models, etc.[132]

This gives the victim an opportunity to tell of his or her experiences and describe the ordeal. In the case of a murder trial, the surviving family can recount the effect the crime has had on their lives and well-being.[133]

The effect of victim/witness statements on sentencing has been the topic of some debate. Some research finds that victim statements result in a higher rate of incarceration, but others find that the statements are insignificant.[134] One recent study by Joel Caplan found that the use of victim statements at parole hearings had little influence on the decision process, and inmate release was based more on factors such as measures of institutional behavior, crime severity, and criminal history.[135]

Those who favor the use of impact statements argue that because the victim is harmed by the crime, he or she has the right to influence the outcome of the case. After all, the public prosecutor is allowed to make sentencing recommendations because the public has been harmed by the crime. Logically, the harm suffered by the victim legitimizes his or her right to make sentencing recommendations.[136]

Victims and Self-Protection

Although the general public mostly approves of the police, fear of crime and concern about community safety have prompted some to become their own "police force," taking an active role in community protection and citizen crime control groups.[137] The more crime in an area, the greater the amount of fear and the more likely residents will be to engage in self-protective measures.[138]

Research indicates that a significant number of crimes may not be reported to police simply because victims prefer to take matters into their own hands.[139] One manifestation of this trend is the concept of **target hardening**, or making one's home and business crime-proof through locks, bars, alarms, and other devices.[140] Other commonly used crime prevention techniques include a fence or barricade at the entrance; a doorkeeper, guard, or receptionist in an apartment building; an intercom or phone to gain access to the building; surveillance cameras; window bars; warning signs; and dogs chosen for their ability to guard the house. The use of these measures is inversely proportional to perception of neighborhood safety: people who fear crime are more likely to use crime prevention techniques. Although the true relationship is still unclear, there is mounting evidence that people who protect their homes are less likely to be victimized by property crimes.[141] One study conducted in the Philadelphia area found that people who install burglar alarms are less likely to suffer burglary than those who forgo similar preventive measures.[142]

Fighting Back   Some people take self-protection to its ultimate end by preparing to fight back when criminals attack them. How successful are victims when they resist? Research indicates that victims who fight back often frustrate their attackers but also face increased odds of being physically harmed during the attack.[143] In some cases, fighting back decreases the odds of a crime being completed but increases the victim's chances of injury.[144] Resistance may draw the attention of bystanders and make a violent crime physically difficult to complete, but it can also cause offenders to escalate their violence.[145]

What about the use of firearms for self-protection? Again, there is no clear-cut answer. Each year, 2.5 million times, victims use guns for defensive purposes, a number that is not surprising considering that about one-third of U.S. households contain guns.[146] Gary Kleck has estimated that armed victims kill between 1,500 and 2,800 potential felons each year and wound between 8,700 and 16,000. Kleck's research shows, ironically, that by fighting back victims kill far more criminals than the estimated 250 to 1,000 killed annually by police.[147] Kleck has found that the risk of collateral injury is relatively rare and that potential victims should be encouraged to fight back.[148] In a recent study conducted with colleague Jongyeon Tark, Kleck reviewed more than 27,000 contact crime incidents and found that when compared to nonresistance, self-protection significantly reduced the likelihood of property loss and injury and that the most forceful tactics, including resistance with a gun, appear to have the strongest effects in reducing the risk of injury. Importantly, the research indicated that resistance did not contribute to injury in any meaningful way. The conclusion: it is better to fight than flee.[149]

The Thinking Like a Criminologist feature concerns efforts to give victims greater leeway to "fight back."

Community Organization

Not everyone is capable of buying a handgun or semiautomatic weapon and doing battle with predatory criminals. An alternative approach has been for communities to organize on the neighborhood level against crime. Citizens have been working independently and in cooperation with local police agencies in neighborhood patrol and block watch programs. These programs organize local citizens in urban areas to patrol neighborhoods, watch for suspicious people, help secure the neighborhood, lobby for improvements (such as increased lighting), report crime to police, put out community newsletters, conduct home security surveys, and serve as a source for crime information or tips.[150] Although such programs are welcome additions to police services, there is little evidence that they appreciably affect the crime rate. There is also concern that their effectiveness is spottier in low-income, high-crime areas, which need the most crime prevention assistance.[151] Block watches and neighborhood patrols seem more successful when they are part of general-purpose or multi-issue community groups rather than when they focus directly on crime problems.[152]

Victims' Rights

More than 30 years ago, legal scholar Frank Carrington suggested that crime victims have legal rights that should assure them of basic services from the government.[153] According to Carrington, just as the defendant has the right to counsel and a fair trial, society is also obliged to ensure basic rights for law-abiding citizens. These rights range from adequate protection from violent crimes to victim compensation and assistance from the criminal justice system.

Because of the influence of victims' rights advocates, every state now has a set of legal rights for crime victims in its code of laws, often called a Victims' Bill of Rights.[154] These generally include the right:

- To be notified of proceedings and the status of the defendant
- To be present at criminal justice proceedings
- To make a statement at sentencing and to receive restitution from a convicted offender
- To be consulted before a case is dismissed or a plea agreement entered
- To a speedy trial
- To keep the victim's contact information confidential

Not only has the victims' rights movement caught on in the United States, it has also had an impact in Europe. The European Union member nations have agreed in principle to a

Profiles in Crime
Jesse Timmendequas and Megan's Law

Richard and Maureen Kanka thought that their 7-year-old daughter Megan was safe in their quiet, suburban neighborhood in Hamilton Township, New Jersey. Then, on July 29, 1994, their lives were shattered when Megan went missing. Maureen Kanka searched the neighborhood and met 33-year-old Jesse Timmendequas, who lived across the street. Timmendequas told her that he had seen Megan earlier that evening while he was working on his car. The police were called in and soon focused their attention on Timmendequas's house when they learned that he and two other residents were convicted sex offenders who had met at a treatment center and decided to live together upon their release. Timmendequas, who appeared extremely nervous when questioned, was asked to accompany police back to their headquarters, where he confessed to luring Megan into his home by inviting her to see a puppy, then raping her and strangling her to death.

Timmendequas had served six years in prison for aggravated assault and attempted sexual assault on another child. The fact that a known sex offender was living anonymously in the Kankas' neighborhood turned Megan's death into a national crusade to develop laws that require sex offenders to register with local police when they move into a neighborhood and require local authorities to provide community notification of the sex offender's presence. New York State's Sex Offender Registration Act is typical of these efforts, commonly known as Megan's Law. Becoming effective on January 21, 1996, the statute requires that sex offenders in New York are classified by the risk of reoffense. A court determines whether an offender is a level 1 (low risk), 2 (moderate risk), or 3 (high risk). The court also determines whether an offender should be given the designation of a sexual predator, sexually violent offender, or predicate sex offender. Offenders are required to be registered for 20 years or life. Level 1 offenders with no designation must register for 20 years. Level 1 offenders with a designation, as well as level 2 and level 3 offenders regardless of whether they have a designation, must register for life. Local law enforcement agencies are notified whenever a sex offender moves into their jurisdiction. That agency may notify schools and other "entities with vulnerable populations" about the presence of a level 2 or level 3 offender if the offender poses a threat to public safety. The act established a toll-free telephone information line that citizens can call to inquire whether a person is listed in the registry and access information on sex offenders living in their neighborhoods. On the federal level, the Jacob Wetterling Crimes Against Children Law, passed in May 1996, requires states to pass some version of Megan's Law or lose federal aid. At least 47 states plus the District of Columbia have complied. Jesse Timmendequas was sentenced to death on June 20, 1997, and is currently on death row.

The case of Megan Kanka illustrates both the risk children face from sexual predators and the efforts being made by the justice system to limit that risk. To some civil liberty groups, such as the American Civil Liberties Union, registration laws go too far because they will not prevent sex offenders from committing crimes and because they victimize rehabilitated ex-offenders and their families. Should the rights of the victim take precedent over the privacy of the offender?

SOURCES: New York State Sex Offender Registry and the Sex Offender Registration Act (SORA), http://criminaljustice.state.ny.us/nsor/ (accessed November 6, 2010), New York State Correction Law Article 6-C (Section 168 et seq.).

---

set of rules that creates minimum standards for the protection of victims of crime. These guarantee that all victims should:

- Be treated with respect
- Have their entitlement to a real and appropriate role in criminal proceedings recognized
- Have the right to be heard during proceedings and to supply evidence
- Receive information on: the type of support available; where and how to report an offence; criminal proceedings and their role in them; access to protection and advice; entitlement to compensation; and, if they wish, the outcomes of their complaints, including sentencing and release of the offender
- Have communication safeguards: that is, member states should take measures to minimize communication difficulties in criminal proceedings
- Have access to free legal advice concerning their role in the proceedings and, where appropriate, legal aid
- Receive payment of expenses incurred as a result of participation in criminal proceedings

- Receive reasonable protection, including protection of privacy
- Receive compensation in the course of criminal proceedings
- Receive penal mediation in the course of criminal proceedings where appropriate
- Benefit from various measures to minimize the difficulties faced where victims are resident in another member state, especially when organizing criminal proceedings[155]

A final, albeit controversial, element of the victims' rights movement is the development of offender registration laws that require that the name and sometimes addresses of known sex offenders be posted by law enforcement agencies. Today almost every state has adopted sex offender laws and the federal government runs a National Sex Offender Public Registry with links to every state.[156] Sex offender registration is indelibly linked to the death of Megan Kanka, an incident described in the Profiles in Crime feature "Jesse Timmendequas and Megan's Law."

SUMMARY

1. **Describe the victim's role in the crime process**
   - Victims may influence criminal behavior by playing an active role in a criminal incident. The discovery that victims play an important role in the crime process has prompted the scientific study of victims, or victimology. Criminologists who focus their attention on crime victims refer to themselves as victimologists.

2. **Know the greatest problems faced by crime victims**
   - The costs of victimization can include such things as damaged property, pain and suffering to victims, and the involvement of the police and other agencies of the justice system. The pain and suffering inflicted on an individual can result in the need for medical care, the loss of wages from not being able to go to work, and reduced quality of life from debilitating injuries and/or fear of being victimized again, which can result in not being able to go to work, long-term medical care, and counseling.

3. **Know what is meant by the term *cycle of violence***
   - People who are crime victims may be more likely to commit crime themselves. Some may seek revenge against the people who harmed them. The abuse–crime phenomenon is referred to as the cycle of violence.

4. **Be familiar with the ecology of victimization risk**
   - Violent crimes are slightly more likely to take place in an open, public area, such as a street, a park, or a field. The more serious violent crimes, such as rape and aggravated assault, typically take place after 6:00 P.M. Those living in the central city have significantly higher rates of theft and violence than suburbanites;

people living in rural areas have a victimization rate almost half that of city dwellers. Schools unfortunately are the site of a great deal of victimization because they are populated by one of the most dangerous segments of society, teenage males.

5. **Describe the victim's household**
   - The NCVS tells us that within the United States, larger, African American, western, and urban homes are the most vulnerable to crime. In contrast, rural, European American homes in the Northeast are the least likely to contain crime victims or be the target of theft offenses, such as burglary and larceny. People who own their homes are less vulnerable than renters.

6. **Describe the most dominant victim characteristics**
   - Except for the crimes of rape and sexual assault, males are more likely than females to be the victims of violent crime. Victim data reveal that young people face a much greater victimization risk than older persons. The poorest Americans are the most likely to be victims of violent and property crime. This association occurs across all gender, age, and racial groups. African Americans are about twice as likely as European Americans to be victims of violent crime. Never-married males and females are victimized more often than married people.

7. **Be familiar with the concept of repeat victimization**
   - Individuals who have been crime victims have a significantly higher chance of future victimization than people who have remained nonvictims. Households that have experienced victimization in the past are the ones most likely to

experience it again in the future. One reason: some victims' physical weakness or psychological distress renders them incapable of resisting or deterring crime and makes them easy targets.

8. **Be familiar with the most important theories of victimization**
   - According to victim precipitation theory, some people may actually initiate the confrontation that eventually leads to their injury or death. Victim precipitation can be either active or passive. Some criminologists believe that people may become crime victims because their lifestyle increases their exposure to criminal offenders. People who have high-risk lifestyles—drinking, taking drugs, getting involved in crime—have a much greater chance of victimization. According to deviant place theory, the greater their exposure to dangerous places, the more likely people are to become victims of crime and violence. So-called deviant places are poor, densely populated, highly transient neighborhoods in which commercial and residential properties exist side by side. Routine activities theory links victimization to the availability of suitable targets, the absence of capable guardians, and the presence of motivated offenders.

9. **Discuss programs dedicated to caring for the victim**
   - Victim-witness assistance programs are government programs that help crime victims and witnesses; they may include compensation, court services, and/or crisis intervention. Such programs often include victim compensation—financial aid awarded to crime victims to

repay them for their loss and injuries; this assistance may cover medical bills, loss of wages, loss of future earnings, and/or counseling. Some programs assign counselors to victims to serve as advocates to help them understand the operation of the justice system and guide them through the process. Most jurisdictions allow victims to make an impact statement before the sentencing judge. Most victim programs refer victims to specific services to help them recover from their ordeal.

10. **Be familiar with the concept of victims' rights**
    - Every state now has a set of legal rights for crime victims in its code of laws, often called a Victims' Bill of Rights. These generally include the victim's right to be notified of proceedings and the status of the defendant, to be present at criminal justice proceedings and to make statements at trials, to receive restitution from a convicted offender, and to be consulted about trial procedures, such as when a plea is offered.

KEY TERMS

victimologists (72)
victimization (72)
posttraumatic stress disorder (PTSD) (73)
obsessive-compulsive disorder (74)
cycle of violence (75)
elder abuse (78)
chronic victimization (78)

victim precipitation theory (80)
active precipitation (80)
passive precipitation (80)
lifestyle theory (81)
deviant place theory (82)
routine activities theory (83)
suitable targets (83)
capable guardians (83)

motivated offenders (83)
date rape (84)
victim-witness assistance programs (87)
victim compensation (87)
crisis intervention (88)
restitution agreements (89)
target hardening (89)

CRITICAL THINKING QUESTIONS

1. Considering what we learned in this chapter about crime victimization, what measures can you take to better protect yourself from crime?

2. Do you agree with the assessment that schools are some of the most dangerous locations in the community? Did you find your high school to be a dangerous environment?

3. Does a person bear some of the responsibility for his or her victimization if the person maintains a lifestyle that contributes to the chances of becoming a crime victim? In other words, should we "blame the victim"?

4. Have you ever experienced someone "precipitating" crime? If so, did you do anything to help the situation?

NOTES

1. *New England News*, "Authorities Develop Case Against Bouncer in Grad Student Slaying," March 24, 2006.
2. Ibid.
3. Michael Rand, *Criminal Victimization, 2008* (Washington, DC: Bureau of Justice Statistics, 2009).
4. Arthur Lurigio, "Are All Victims Alike? The Adverse, Generalized, and Differential Impact of Crime," *Crime and Delinquency* 33 (1987): 452–467.
5. Brandon Welsh, Rolf Loeber, Bradley Stevens, Magda Stouthamer-Loeber, Mark Cohen, and David Farrington, "Costs of Juvenile Crime in Urban Areas: A Longitudinal Perspective," *Youth Violence and Juvenile Justice* 6 (2008): 3–27. Data adjusted for inflation.
6. Children's Safety Network Economics and Insurance Resource Center, "State Costs of Violence Perpetrated by Youth," www.childrenssafetynetwork.org/publications_resources/index.asp (accessed November 8, 2010).
7. National Institute of Drug Abuse, Heroin Abuse and Addiction, http://drugabuse.gov/ResearchReports/heroin/heroin.html (accessed November 9, 2010).
8. Ted R. Miller, Mark A. Cohen, and Brian Wiersema, *Victim Costs and Consequences: A New Look* (Washington, DC: National Institute of Justice, 1996), p. 9, Table 2. Adjusted for inflation.
9. Ross Macmillan, "Adolescent Victimization and Income Deficits in Adulthood: Rethinking the Costs of Criminal Violence from a Life-Course Perspective," *Criminology* 38 (2000): 553–588. Adjusted for inflation.
10. James Anderson, Terry Grandison, and Laronistine Dyson, "Victims of Random Violence and the Public Health Implication: A Health Care or Criminal Justice Issue?" *Journal of Criminal Justice* 24 (1996): 379–393.
11. Angela Scarpa, Sara Chiara Haden, and Jimmy Hurley, "Community Violence Victimization and Symptoms of Posttraumatic Stress Disorder: The Moderating Effects of Coping and Social Support," *Journal of Interpersonal Violence* 21 (2006): 446–469.
12. Heather Littleton and Craig Henderson, "If She Is Not a Victim, Does That Mean She Was Not Traumatized? Evaluation of

Predictors of PTSD Symptomatology Among College Rape Victims," *Violence Against Women* 15 (2009): 148–167.

13. Mladen Loncar, Neven Henigsberg, and Pero Hrabac, "Mental Health Consequences in Men Exposed to Sexual Abuse During the War in Croatia and Bosnia," *Journal of Interpersonal Violence* 25 (2010): 191–203.

14. Dean Kilpatrick, Benjamin Saunders, and Daniel Smith, *Youth Victimization: Prevalence and Implications* (Washington, DC: National Institute of Justice, 2003).

15. David Finkelhor, Heather Turner, and Richard Ormrod, "Kid's Stuff: The Nature and Impact of Peer and Sibling Violence on Younger and Older Children," *Child Abuse and Neglect* 30 (2006): 1,401–1,421.

16. Catherine Grus, "Child Abuse: Correlations with Hostile Attributions," *Journal of Developmental and Behavioral Pediatrics* 24 (2003): 296–298.

17. Kim Logio, "Gender, Race, Childhood Abuse, and Body Image among Adolescents," *Violence Against Women* 9 (2003): 931–955.

18. Mark Shevlin, Martin Dorahy, and Gary Adamson, "Childhood Traumas and Hallucinations: An Analysis of the National Comorbidity Survey," *Journal of Psychiatric Research* 41 (2007): 222–228.

19. Jeanne Kaufman and Cathy Spatz Widom, "Childhood Victimization, Running Away, and Delinquency," *Journal of Research in Crime and Delinquency* 36 (1999): 347–370.

20. N. N. Sarkar and Rina Sarkar, "Sexual Assault on Woman: Its Impact on Her Life and Living in Society," *Sexual and Relationship Therapy* 20 (2005): 407–419.

21. Michael Wiederman, Randy Sansone, and Lori Sansone, "History of Trauma and Attempted Suicide among Women in a Primary Care Setting," *Violence and Victims* 13 (1998): 3–11; Susan Leslie Bryant and Lillian Range, "Suicidality in College Women Who Were Sexually and Physically Abused and Physically Punished by Parents," *Violence and Victims* 10 (1995): 195–215; William Downs and Brenda Miller, "Relationships between Experiences of Parental Violence During Childhood and Women's Self-Esteem," *Violence and Victims* 13 (1998): 63–78; Sally Davies-Netley, Michael Hurlburt, and Richard Hough, "Childhood Abuse as a Precursor to Homelessness for Homeless Women with Severe Mental Illness," *Violence and Victims* 11 (1996): 129–142.

22. Jane Siegel and Linda Williams, "Risk Factors for Sexual Victimization of Women," *Violence Against Women* 9 (2003): 902–930.

23. Michael Miner, Jill Klotz Flitter, and Beatrice Robinson, "Association of Sexual Revictimization with Sexuality and Psychological Function," *Journal of Interpersonal Violence* 21 (2006): 503–524.

24. Lana Stermac and Emily Paradis, "Homeless Women and Victimization: Abuse and Mental Health History among Homeless Rape Survivors," *Resources for Feminist Research* 28 (2001): 65–81.

25. Gregory Stuart, Todd M. Moore, Kristina Coop Gordon, Susan Ramsey, and Christopher Kahler, "Psychopathology in Women Arrested for Domestic Violence," *Journal of Interpersonal Violence* 21 (2006): 376–389; Caron Zlotnick, Dawn Johnson, and Robert Kohn, "Intimate Partner Violence and Long-Term Psychosocial Functioning in a National Sample of American Women," *Journal of Interpersonal Violence* 21 (2006): 262–275.

26. K. Daniel O'Leary, "Psychological Abuse: A Variable Deserving Critical Attention in Domestic Violence," *Violence and Victims* 14 (1999): 1–21.

27. Ron Acierno, Alyssa Rheingold, Heidi Resnick, and Dean Kilpatrick, "Predictors of Fear of Crime in Older Adults," *Journal of Anxiety Disorders* 18 (2004): 385–396.

28. Mirka Smolej and Janne Kivivuori, "The Relation Between Crime News and Fear of Violence," *Journal of Scandinavian Studies in Criminology and Crime Prevention* 7 (2006): 211–227.

29. Pamela Wilcox Rountree, "A Reexamination of the Crime–Fear Linkage," *Journal of Research in Crime and Delinquency* 35 (1998): 341–372.

30. Robert Davis, Bruce Taylor, and Arthur Lurigio, "Adjusting to Criminal Victimization: The Correlates of Postcrime Distress," *Violence and Victimization* 11 (1996): 21–34.

31. Susan Brison, *Aftermath: Violence and the Remaking of a Self* (Princeton, NJ: Princeton University Press, 2001).

32. Chris Gibson, Zara Morris, and Kevin Beaver, "Secondary Exposure to Violence During Childhood and Adolescence: Does Neighborhood Context Matter?" *Justice Quarterly* 26 (2009): 30–57.

33. Susan Popkin, Victoria Gwlasda, Dennis Rosenbaum, Jean Amendolla, Wendell Johnson, and Lynn Olson, "Combating Crime in Public Housing: A Qualitative and Quantitative Longitudinal Analysis of the Chicago Housing Authority's Anti-Drug Initiative," *Justice Quarterly* 16 (1999): 519–557.

34. Karen Snedker, "Altruistic and Vicarious Fear of Crime: Fear for Others and Gendered Social Roles," *Sociological Forum* 21 (2006): 163–195.

35. Min Xie and David McDowall, "Escaping Crime: The Effects of Direct and Indirect Victimization on Moving," *Criminology* 46 (2008): 809–840.

36. Smolej and Kivivuori, "The Relation Between Crime News and Fear of Violence."

37. Matthew Lee and Erica DeHart, "The Influence of a Serial Killer on Changes in Fear of Crime and the Use of Protective Measures: A Survey-Based Case Study of Baton Rouge," *Deviant Behavior* 28 (2007): 1–28.

38. Alex R. Piquero, John MacDonald, Adam Dobrin, Leah E. Daigle, and Francis T. Cullen, "Self-Control, Violent Offending, and Homicide Victimization: Assessing the General Theory of Crime," *Journal of Quantitative Criminology* 25 (2005): 55–71.

39. Cathy Spatz Widom, *The Cycle of Violence* (Washington, DC: National Institute of Justice, 1992), p. 1.

40. Steve Spaccarelli, J. Douglas Coatsworth, and Blake Sperry Bowden, "Exposure to Serious Family Violence among Incarcerated Boys: Its Association with Violent Offending and Potential Mediating Variables," *Violence and Victims* 10 (1995): 163–180; Jerome Kolbo, "Risk and Resilience among Children Exposed to Family Violence," *Violence and Victims* 11 (1996): 113–127.

41. Timothy Ireland and Cathy Spatz Widom, *Childhood Victimization and Risk for Alcohol and Drug Arrests* (Washington, DC: National Institute of Justice, 1995).

42. Min Jung Kim, Emiko Tajima, Todd I. Herrenkohl, and Bu Huang, "Early Child Maltreatment, Runaway Youths, and Risk of Delinquency and Victimization in Adolescence: A Mediational Model," *Social Work Research* 33 (2009): 19–28.

43. Brigette Erwin, Elana Newman, Robert McMackin, Carlo Morrissey, and Danny Kaloupek, "PTSD, Malevolent Environment, and Criminality among Criminally Involved Male Adolescents," *Criminal Justice and Behavior* 27 (2000): 196–215.

44. Ulrich Orth, Leo Montada, and Andreas Maercker, "Feelings of Revenge, Retaliation Motive, and Posttraumatic Stress Reactions in Crime Victims," *Journal of Interpersonal Violence* 21 (2006): 229–243.

45. Chris Melde, Finn-Aage Esbensen, and Terrance Taylor, "'May Piece Be with You': A Typological Examination of the Fear and Victimization Hypothesis of Adolescent Weapon Carrying," *Justice Quarterly* 26 (2009): 348–376.

46. Charis Kubrin and Ronald Weitzer, "Retaliatory Homicide: Concentrated Disadvantage and Neighborhood Culture," *Social Problems* 50 (2003): 157–180.

47. Christopher Schreck, Eric Stewart, and D. Wayne Osgood, "A Reappraisal of the Overlap of Violent Offenders and Victims," *Criminology* 46 (2008): 872–906.

48. Victim data used in these sections are from Rand, *Criminal Victimization, 2008.*

49. Pamela Wilcox, Marie Skubak Tillyer, and Bonnie S. Fisher, "Gendered Opportunity? School-Based Adolescent Victimization," *Journal of Research in Crime and Delinquency* 46 (2009): 245–269.

50. Bureau of Justice Statistics, *Indicators of School Crime and Safety: 2008*, http://bjs.ojp.usdoj.gov/content/pub/pdf/iscs08.pdf (accessed December 11, 2010).

51. Victoria Titterington, "A Retrospective Investigation of Gender Inequality and Female Homicide Victimization," *Sociological Spectrum* 26 (2006): 205–231.

52. David Finkelhor, Heather Turner, and Richard Ormrod, "Kid's Stuff: The Nature and Impact of Peer and Sibling Violence on Younger and Older Children," *Child Abuse and Neglect* 30 (2006): 1,401–1,421.

53. Lamar Jordan, "Law Enforcement and the Elderly: A Concern for the 21st Century," *FBI Law Enforcement Bulletin* 71 (2002): 20–24.

54. National Organization for Victim Assistance, "Adult Victims of Crime and Abuse in Residential Care Facilities," www.trynova.org/victiminfo/elderly/ (accessed November 6, 2010).

55. Robert C. Davis and Juanjo Medina-Ariza, *Results from an Elder Abuse Prevention Experiment in New York* (Washington, DC: National Institute of Justice, September 2001).

56. Tracy Dietz and James Wright, "Age and Gender Differences and Predictors of Victimization of the Older Homeless," *Journal of Elder Abuse and Neglect* 17 (2005): 37–59.

57. Karin Wittebrood and Paul Nieuwbeerta, "Criminal Victimization During One's Life Course: The Effects of Previous Victimization and Patterns of Routine Activities," *Journal of Research in Crime and Delinquency* 37 (2000): 91–122; Janet Lauritsen and Kenna Davis Quinet, "Repeat Victimizations among Adolescents and Young Adults," *Journal of Quantitative Criminology* 11 (1995): 143–163.

58. Denise Osborn, Dan Ellingworth, Tim Hope, and Alan Trickett, "Are Repeatedly Victimized Households Different?" *Journal of Quantitative Criminology* 12 (1996): 223–245.

59. Graham Farrell, "Predicting and Preventing Revictimization," in *Crime and Justice: An Annual Review of Research*, Vol. 20, ed. Michael Tonry and David Farrington (Chicago: University of Chicago Press, 1995), pp. 61–126.

60. Ibid., p. 61.

61. David Finkelhor and Nancy Asigian, "Risk Factors for Youth Victimization: Beyond a Lifestyles/Routine Activities Theory Approach," *Violence and Victimization* 11 (1996): 3–19.

62. Graham Farrell, Coretta Phillips, and Ken Pease, "Like Taking Candy: Why Does Repeat Victimization Occur?" *British Journal of Criminology* 35 (1995): 384–399.

63. Bonnie S. Fisher, Leah E. Daigle, and Francis T. Cullen, "What Distinguishes Single from Recurrent Sexual Victims? The Role of Lifestyle-Routine Activities and First-Incident Characteristics," *Justice Quarterly* 27 (2010): 102–129.

64. Graham C. Ousey, Pamela Wilcox, and Bonnie S. Fisher, "Something Old, Something New: Revisiting Competing Hypotheses of the Victimization–Offending Relationship Among Adolescents," *Journal of Quantitative Criminology*, published online, July 2010.

65. Christopher Innes and Lawrence Greenfeld, *Violent State Prisoners and Their Victims* (Washington, DC: Bureau of Justice Statistics, 1990).

66. Hans von Hentig, *The Criminal and His Victim: Studies in the Sociobiology of Crime* (New Haven: Yale University Press, 1948), p. 384.

67. Marvin Wolfgang, *Patterns of Criminal Homicide* (Philadelphia: University of Pennsylvania Press, 1958).

68. Menachem Amir, *Patterns in Forcible Rape* (Chicago: University of Chicago Press, 1971).

69. Susan Estrich, *Real Rape* (Cambridge, MA: Harvard University Press, 1987).

70. Martin Daly and Margo Wilson, *Homicide* (New York: Aldine de Gruyter, 1988).

71. Edem Avakame, "Female's Labor Force Participation and Intimate Femicide: An Empirical Assessment of the Backlash Hypothesis," *Violence and Victim* 14 (1999): 277–283.

72. Rosemary Gartner and Bill McCarthy, "The Social Distribution of Femicide in Urban Canada, 1921–1988," *Law and Society Review* 25 (1991): 287–311.

73. Wilcox, Tillyer, and Fisher, "Gendered Opportunity?"

74. Christopher Schreck, Eric Stewart, and Bonnie Fisher, "Self-Control, Victimization, and Their Influence on Risky Lifestyles: A Longitudinal Analysis Using Panel Data," *Journal of Quantitative Criminology* 22 (2006): 319–340.

75. Bonnie Fisher, Francis Cullen, and Michael Turner, *The Sexual Victimization of College Women* (Washington, DC: National Institute of Justice, 2001).

76. Dan Hoyt, Kimberly Ryan, and Mari Cauce, "Personal Victimization in a High-Risk Environment: Homeless and Runaway Adolescents," *Journal of Research in Crime and Delinquency* 36 (1999): 371–392.

77. Kimberly Tyler and Morgan Beal, "The High-Risk Environment of Homeless Young Adults: Consequences for Physical and Sexual Victimization," *Violence and Victims* 25 (2010): 101–115.

78. See, generally, Gary Gottfredson and Denise Gottfredson, *Victimization in Schools* (New York: Plenum Press, 1985).

79. Gary Jensen and David Brownfield, "Gender, Lifestyles, and Victimization: Beyond Routine Activity Theory," *Violence and Victims* 1 (1986): 85–99.

80. Bonnie Fisher, John Sloan, Francis Cullen, and Chunmeng Lu, "Crime in the Ivory Tower: The Level and Sources of Student Victimization," *Criminology* 36 (1998): 671–710.

81. Fisher, Cullen, and Turner, *The Sexual Victimization of College Women*.

82. Elizabeth Reed, Hortensia Amaro, Atsushi Matsumoto, and Debra Kaysen, "The Relation Between Interpersonal Violence and Substance Use Among a Sample of University Students: Examination of the Role of Victim and Perpetrator Substance Use," *Addictive Behaviors* 34 (2009): 316–318.

83. Michael Ezell and Emily Tanner-Smith, "Examining the Role of Lifestyle and Criminal History Variables on the Risk of Homicide Victimization," *Homicide Studies* 13 (2009): 144–173; Rolf Loeber, Mary DeLamatre, George Tita, Jacqueline Cohen, Magda Stouthamer-Loeber, and David Farrington, "Gun Injury and Mortality: The Delinquent Backgrounds of Juvenile Offenders," *Violence and Victim* 14 (1999): 339–351; Adam Dobrin, "The Risk of Offending on Homicide Victimization: A Case Control Study," *Journal of Research in Crime and Delinquency* 38 (2001): 154–173.

84. Loeber et al., "Gun Injury and Mortality"; Dobrin, "The Risk of Offending on Homicide Victimization."

85. James Howell, "Youth Gang Homicides: A Literature Review," *Crime and Delinquency* 45 (1999): 208–241.

86. Alan Lizotte and David Sheppard, *Gun Use by Male Juveniles* (Washington, DC: Office of Juvenile Justice and Delinquency Prevention, 2001); Daneen Deptula and Robert Cohen, "Aggressive, Rejected, and Delinquent Children and Adolescents: A Comparison of Their Friendships," *Aggression and Violent Behavior* 9 (2004): 75–104.

87. Sylvie Mrug, Betsy Hoza, and William Bukowski, "Choosing or Being Chosen by Aggressive-Disruptive Peers: Do They Contribute to Children's Externalizing and Internalizing Problems?" *Journal of Abnormal Child Psychology* 32 (2004): 53–66.

88. Daniel Neller, Robert Denney, Christina Pietz, and R. Paul Thomlinson, "Testing the Trauma Model of Violence," *Journal of Family Violence* 20 (2005): 151–159.

89. Maryse Richards, Reed Larson, and Bobbi Viegas Miller, "Risky and Protective Contexts and Exposure to Violence in Urban African American Young Adolescents," *Journal of Clinical Child and Adolescent Psychology* 33 (2004): 138–148.

90. James Garofalo, "Reassessing the Lifestyle Model of Criminal Victimization," in *Positive Criminology*, ed. Michael Gottfredson and Travis Hirschi (Newbury Park, CA: Sage, 1987), pp. 23–42.

91. Richards, Larson, and Miller, "Risky and Protective Contexts and Exposure to Violence in Urban African American Young Adolescents."

92. Terance Miethe and David McDowall, "Contextual Effects in Models of Criminal Victimization," *Social Forces* 71 (1993): 741–759.

93. Rodney Stark, "Deviant Places: A Theory of the Ecology of Crime," *Criminology* 25 (1987): 893–911.

94. Ibid., p. 902.

95. Pamela Wilcox Rountree, Kenneth Land, and Terance Miethe, "Macro–Micro Integration in the Study of Victimization: A Hierarchical Logistic Model Analysis Across Seattle Neighborhoods," paper presented at the annual meeting of the American Society of Criminology, Phoenix, November 1993.

96. William Julius Wilson, *The Truly Disadvantaged* (Chicago: University of Chicago Press, 1990); see also Allen Liska and Paul Bellair, "Violent-Crime Rates and Racial Composition: Convergence Over Time," *American Journal of Sociology* 101 (1995): 578–610.

97. Lawrence Cohen and Marcus Felson, "Social Change and Crime Rate Trends: A Routine Activities Approach," *American Sociological Review* 44 (1979): 588–608.

98. Teresa LaGrange, "The Impact of Neighborhoods, Schools, and Malls on the Spatial Distribution of Property Damage," *Journal of Research in Crime and Delinquency* 36 (1999): 393–422.

99. Melanie Wellsmith and Amy Burrell, "The Influence of Purchase Price and Ownership Levels on Theft Targets: The Example of Domestic Burglary," *British Journal of Criminology* 45 (2005): 741–764.

100. Denise Gottfredson and David Soulé, "The Timing of Property Crime, Violent Crime, and Substance Use Among Juveniles," *Journal of Research in Crime and Delinquency* 42 (2005): 110–120.

101. Georgina Hammock and Deborah Richardson, "Perceptions of Rape: The Influence of Closeness of Relationship, Intoxication, and Sex of Participant," *Violence and Victimization* 12 (1997): 237–247.

102. Wittebrood and Nieuwbeerta, "Criminal Victimization during One's Life Course," pp. 112–113.

103. Brandon Welsh and David Farrington, "Surveillance for Crime Prevention in Public Space: Results and Policy Choices in Britain and America," *Criminology and Public Policy* 3 (2004): 701–730.

104. Richard Timothy Coupe and Laurence Blake, "The Effects of Patrol Workloads and Response Strength on Arrests at Burglary Emergencies," *Journal of Criminal Justice* 33 (2005): 239–255.

105. Don Weatherburn, Bronwyn Lind, and Simon Ku, "'Hotbeds of Crime?' Crime and Public Housing in Urban Sydney," *Crime and Delinquency* 45 (1999): 256–271.

106. Andy Hochstetler, "Opportunities and Decisions: Interactional Dynamics in Robbery and Burglary Groups," *Criminology* 39 (2001): 737–763.

107. Richard Felson, "Routine Activities and Involvement in Violence as Actor, Witness, or Target," *Violence and Victimization* 12 (1997): 209–223.

108. Lawrence Cohen, Marcus Felson, and Kenneth Land, "Property Crime Rates in the United States: A Macrodynamic Analysis, 1947–1977, with Ex-ante Forecasts for the Mid-1980s," *American Journal of Sociology* 86 (1980): 90–118.

109. Steven Messner, Lawrence Raffalovich, and Richard McMillan, "Economic Deprivation and Changes in Homicide Arrest Rates for White and Black Youths, 1967–1998: A National Time Series Analysis," *Criminology* 39 (2001): 591–614.

110. Melanie Wellsmith and Amy Burrell, "The Influence of Purchase Price and Ownership Levels on Theft Targets: The Example of Domestic Burglary," *British Journal of Criminology* 45 (2005): 741–764.

111. Terance Miethe and Robert Meier, *Crime and Its Social Context: Toward an Integrated Theory of Offenders, Victims, and Situations* (Albany, NY: State University of New York Press, 1994).

112. Richard Felson, "Routine Activities and Involvement in Violence as Actor, Witness, or Target," *Violence and Victimization* 12 (1997): 209–223.

113. Patricia Resnick, "Psychological Effects of Victimization: Implications for the Criminal Justice System," *Crime and Delinquency* 33 (1987): 468–478.

114. Dean Kilpatrick, Benjamin Saunders, Lois Veronen, Connie Best, and Judith Von, "Criminal Victimization: Lifetime Prevalence, Reporting to Police, and Psychological Impact," *Crime and Delinquency* 33 (1987): 479–489.

115. Cassidy Gutner, Shireen Rizvi, Candice Monson, and Patricia Resick, "Changes in Coping Strategies, Relationship to the Perpetrator, and Posttraumatic Distress in Female Crime Victims," *Journal of Traumatic Stress* 19 (2006): 813–823.

116. U.S. Department of Justice, *Report of the President's Task Force on Victims of Crime* (Washington, DC: U.S. Government Printing Office, 1983).

117. Ibid., pp. 2–10; "Review on Victims/Witnesses of Crime," *Massachusetts Lawyers Weekly*, April 25, 1983, p. 26.

118. Robert Davis, *Crime Victims: Learning How to Help Them* (Washington, DC: National Institute of Justice, 1987).

119. Michael M. O'Hear, "Punishment, Democracy, and Victims," *Federal Sentencing Reporter* 19 (2006): 1.

120. Peter Finn and Beverly Lee, *Establishing a Victim-Witness Assistance Program* (Washington, DC: U.S. Government Printing Office, 1988).

121. This section leans heavily on Albert Roberts, "Delivery of Services to Crime Victims: A National Survey," *American Journal of Orthopsychiatry* 6 (1991): 128–137; see also Albert Roberts, *Helping Crime Victims: Research, Policy, and Practice* (Newbury Park, CA: Sage, 1990).

122. Randall Schmidt, "Crime Victim Compensation Legislation: A Comparative Study," *Victimology* 5 (1980): 428–437.

123. Ibid.

124. National Association of Crime Victim Compensation Boards, www.nacvcb.org (accessed November 6, 2010).

125. Office for Victims of Crime, 2010 Crime Victims Fund Compensation and Assistance Allocations, www.ojp.usdoj.gov/ovc/grants/cvfa2010.html (accessed December 11, 2010).

126. Rebecca Campbell, "Rape Survivors' Experiences with the Legal and Medical Systems: Do Rape Victim Advocates Make a Difference?" *Violence Against Women* 12 (2006): 30–45.

127. Ulrich Orth and Andreas Maercker, "Do Trials of Perpetrators Retraumatize Crime Victims?" *Journal of Interpersonal Violence* 19 (2004): 212–228.

128. Barbara Sims, Berwood Yost, and Christina Abbott, "The Efficacy of Victim Services Programs," *Criminal Justice Policy Review* 17 (2006): 387–406.

129. Pater Jaffe, Marlies Sudermann, Deborah Reitzel, and Steve Killip, "An Evaluation of a Secondary School Primary Prevention Program on Violence in Intimate Relationships," *Violence and Victims* 7 (1992): 129–145.

130. Good Samaritans Program, www.ojp.usdoj.gov/ovc/publications/infores/Good_Samaritans/ (accessed November 6, 2010).

131. Andrew Karmen, "Victim–Offender Reconciliation Programs: Pro and Con," *Perspectives of the American Probation and Parole Association* 20 (1996): 11–14.

132. Information provided by the National Center for the Victims of Crime, www.ncvc.org (accessed November 6, 2010).

133. Rachelle Hong, "Nothing to Fear: Establishing an Equality of Rights for Crime Victims Through the Victims' Rights Amendment," *Notre Dame Journal of Legal Ethics and Public Policy* (2002): 207–225; see also *Payne v. Tennessee*, 111 S.Ct. 2597, 115 L.Ed.2d 720 (1991).

134. Robert Davis and Barbara Smith, "The Effects of Victim Impact Statements on Sentencing Decisions: A Test in an Urban Setting," *Justice Quarterly* 11 (1994): 453–469; Edna Erez and Pamela Tontodonato, "The Effect of Victim Participation in Sentencing on Sentence Outcome," *Criminology* 28 (1990): 451–474.

135. Joel Caplan, "Parole Release Decisions: Impact of Positive and Negative Victim and Nonvictim Input on a Representative Sample of Parole-Eligible Inmates," *Violence and Victims* 25 (2010): 224–242.

136. Douglas E. Beloof, "Constitutional Implications of Crime Victims as Participants," *Cornell Law Review* 88 (2003): 282–305.

137. Sara Flaherty and Austin Flaherty, *Victims and Victims' Risk* (New York: Chelsea House, 1998).

138. Pamela Wilcox Rountree and Kenneth Land, "Burglary Victimization, Perceptions of Crime Risk, and Routine Activities: A Multilevel Analysis across Seattle Neighborhoods and Census Tracts," *Journal of Research in Crime and Delinquency* 33 (1996): 1,147–1,180.

139. Leslie Kennedy, "Going It Alone: Unreported Crime and Individual Self-Help," *Journal of Criminal Justice* 16 (1988): 403–413.

140. Ronald Clarke, "Situational Crime Prevention: Its Theoretical Basis and Practical Scope," in *Annual Review of Criminal Justice Research*, ed. Michael Tonry and Norval Morris (Chicago: University of Chicago Press, 1983).

141. See, generally, Dennis P. Rosenbaum, Arthur J. Lurigio, and Robert C. Davis, *The Prevention of Crime: Social and Situational Strategies* (Belmont, CA: Wadsworth, 1998).

142. Andrew Buck, Simon Hakim, and George Rengert, "Burglar Alarms and the Choice Behavior of Burglars," *Journal of Criminal Justice* 21 (1993): 497–507; for an opposing view, see James Lynch and David Cantor, "Ecological and Behavioral Influences on Property Victimization at Home: Implications for Opportunity Theory," *Journal of Research in Crime and Delinquency* 29 (1992): 335–362.

143. Alan Lizotte, "Determinants of Completing Rape and Assault," *Journal of Quantitative Criminology* 2 (1986): 213–217.

144. Polly Marchbanks, Kung-Jong Lui, and James Mercy, "Risk of Injury from Resisting Rape," *American Journal of Epidemiology* 132 (1990): 540–549.

145. Caroline Wolf Harlow, *Robbery Victims* (Washington, DC: Bureau of Justice Statistics, 1987).

146. Gary Kleck, "Guns and Violence: An Interpretive Review of the Field," *Social Pathology* 1 (1995): 12–45, at 17.

147. Ibid.

148. Gary Kleck, "Rape and Resistance," *Social Problems* 37 (1990): 149–162.

149. Jongyeon Tark and Gary Kleck, "Resisting Crime: The Effects of Victim Action on the Outcomes of Crimes," *Criminology* 42 (2004): 861–909.

150. James Garofalo and Maureen McLeod, *Improving the Use and Effectiveness of Neighborhood Watch Programs* (Washington, DC: National Institute of Justice, 1988).

151. Peter Finn, *Block Watches Help Crime Victims in Philadelphia* (Washington, DC: National Institute of Justice, 1986).

152. Ibid.

153. See Frank Carrington, "Victim's Rights Litigation: A Wave of the Future," in *Perspectives on Crime Victims*, ed. Burt Galaway and Joe Hudson (St. Louis: Mosby, 1981).

154. National Center for Victims of Crime, www.ncvc.org/policy/issues/rights/ (accessed November 6, 2010).

155. "Council Framework Decision of 15 March 2001 on the Standing of Victims in Criminal Proceedings," http://eur-lex.europa.eu/LexUriServ/LexUriServ.do?uri=OJ:L:2001:082:0001:0004:EN:PDF (accessed November 6, 2010); "Proposal for a Council Directive on Compensation to Crime Victims," http://ec.europa.eu/civiljustice/comp_crime_victim/comp_crime_victim_ec_en.htm (accessed December 11, 2010).

156. U.S. Department of Justice, Dru Sjodin National Sex Offender Public Registry, www.nsopr.gov (accessed November 6, 2010).

TWO

Theories of Crime Causation

An important goal of the criminological enterprise is to create valid and accurate theories of crime causation. A theory can be defined as an abstract statement that explains why certain phenomenon or things do (or do not) happen. A valid theory must (a) have the ability to be able to predict future occurrences or observations of the phenomenon in question and (b) have the ability to be validated or tested through experiment or some other form of empirical observation. So, for example, if a theory states that watching violent TV shows leads to aggressive behavior, it can be considered valid only if careful and empirically sound tests can prove that kids who watch a lot of violent TV in the present will one day become violent in the future.

Criminologists have sought to collect vital facts about crime and interpret them in a scientifically meaningful fashion. By developing empirically verifiable statements, or hypotheses, and organizing them into theories of crime causation, they hope to identify the causes of crime.

Since the late nineteenth century, criminological theory has pointed to various underlying causes of crime. The earliest theories generally attributed crime to a single underlying cause: atypical body build, genetic abnormality, insanity, physical anomalies, socialization, or poverty. More recent theoretical efforts are more dynamic, incorporating multiple personal and social factors into a complex web to explain the onset, continuation, and eventual desistance from a criminal career.

In this section, theories of crime causation are grouped into six chapters. Chapters 4 and 5 focus on theories that view crime as based on individual traits. They hold that crime is either a free will choice made by an individual, a function of personal psychological or biological abnormality, or both. Chapters 6, 7, and 8 investigate theories based in sociology and political economy. These theories portray crime as a function of the structure, process, and conflicts of social living. Chapter 9 is devoted to theories that combine or integrate a number of concepts that explain criminal behavior over the life course, otherwise known as developmental views of crime.

REUTERS/Jeff Zelevansky/Landov

JUST

Just before Christmas in 2004, more than 150,000 fax machines around the country spat out a mysterious message, addressed to a "Dr. Mitchel," that had been written by a financial planner named "Chris." Though it was clearly the wrong number, a lot of people were intrigued because the note was about a hot stock that "Chris" wanted the doctor to buy immediately: "I have a stock for you that will triple in price just like the last stock I gave you 'SIRI' did. I can't get you on either phone. Either call me, or call Linda to place the new trade. We need to buy IFLB now."

Soon after the mystery fax was sent, shares of IFLB (Infinium Labs, a video gaming company) started to increase, jumping 160 percent in four days and trading at six times its previous volume. Unfortunately for the investors who jumped on the tip, there was no "Dr. Mitchel," no "Chris," no "Linda," and no real stock tip.

(continued on page 102)

Rational Choice Theory

4

Learning Objectives

1. Describe the development of rational choice theory
2. Describe the concepts of rational choice
3. Discuss how offenders structure criminality
4. Describe how criminals structure crime
5. Develop knowledge showing that crime is rational
6. Know what is meant by the term *seductions of crime*
7. Discuss the elements of situational crime prevention
8. Be familiar with the elements of general deterrence
9. Discuss the basic concepts of specific deterrence
10. Understand the pros and cons of an incapacitation strategy to reduce crime

It was all part of a scam: the phony fax sender bought shares of Infinium Labs in advance while prices were cheap, blanketed the nation with bogus faxes, and pocketed a tidy profit after the prices rose when people started to buy the shares. It all worked according to plan: in less than two months, the conspiracy resulted in a net gain of more than $400,000.

Eventually the Securities and Exchange Commission opened an investigation, tracing the fax calls to a Florida company run by Michael Pickens, who in July 2005 was arrested and charged with securities fraud; Pickens pleaded guilty and on December 20, 2007, was sentenced to five years of probation and ordered to take part in a substance abuse program and pay $1.2 million in restitution. Ironically, Pickens is the son of multi-billionaire oil investor T. Boone Pickens, one of the nation's richest men.[1]

The "pump and dump" stock market scheme orchestrated by Michael Pickens involved knowledge, planning, and ingenuity. Some law violators carefully plan their activities, buy the proper equipment, try to avoid detection, and then attempt to squirrel away their criminal profits in some hidden bank account. Their calculated actions suggest that the decision to commit crime can involve rational and detailed planning and decision making, designed to maximize personal gain and avoid capture and punishment. Some criminologists go as far as suggesting that the source of all criminal violations—committing a robbery, selling drugs, attacking a rival, or filing a false tax return—rests upon rational decision making. Such a decision may be based on a variety of personal reasons, including greed, revenge, need, anger, lust, jealousy, thrill-seeking, or vanity. But the final decision to commit a crime is only made after the potential offender carefully weighs the potential benefits and consequences of their planned action and decides that the benefits of crime are greater than its consequences:

- The jealous suitor concludes that the risk of punishment is worth the satisfaction of punching a rival in the nose.
- The greedy shopper considers the chance of apprehension by store detectives so small that she takes a "five-finger discount" on a new sweater.
- The drug dealer concludes that the huge profit from a single shipment of cocaine far outweighs the possible costs of apprehension.
- The school yard bully carefully selects his next victim—someone who is weak, unpopular, and probably won't fight back.
- The college student downloads a program that allows her to illegally copy music onto her iPod.

But can all crimes be a function of planning and calculation? While we can easily assume that international drug dealers, white-collar criminals such as Michael Pickens, and organized crime figures use planning, organization, and rational decision making to commit their crimes, can we also assume that such common crimes as theft, fraud, and even murder are a function of detailed planning and decision making? Before the college students take music off the Web, they must first not only acquire expertise and skill, but also decide that the money they save is worth the risk of detection. But what about the college student who gets into a bar fight or decides to have sex with an unconscious girl at a frat party? Are these crimes calculated and shrewd or random and senseless? Some criminologists would answer that they believe all criminal behavior, no matter how destructive or seemingly irresponsible, is actually a matter of thought and decision making. As a group, they are referred to as **rational choice** theorists.

This chapter reviews the philosophical underpinnings of rational choice theory, tracing it back to the classical school of criminology. We then turn to more recent theoretical models that flow from the concept of choice. These models hold that because criminals are rational, their behavior can be controlled or deterred by the fear of punishment; desistance can then be explained by a growing and intense fear of criminal sanctions. These views include situational crime control, general deterrence theory, specific deterrence theory, and incapacitation. Finally, the chapter briefly reviews how choice theory has influenced criminal justice policy.

THE DEVELOPMENT OF RATIONAL CHOICE

During the early Middle Ages (1200–1400), superstition and fear of satanic possession dominated thinking. People who violated social norms or religious practices were believed to be witches or possessed by demons and not rational decision makers. St. Thomas Aquinas (1225–1274) argued that there was a God-given "natural law" that was based on people's natural tendency to do good. People who were evil were manifesting original sin and a fall from grace, similar to that experienced by Adam and Eve when they were expelled from the Garden of Eden.

The prescribed method for dealing with the possessed was burning at the stake, a practice that survived into the seventeenth century. Beginning in the mid-thirteenth century, the jurisdiction of central governments reached a significantly broader range of social behaviors. Human problems and conflicts began to be dealt with in a formalized and legal manner.[2] Nonetheless, superstition and harsh punishments did not end quickly. The authorities were on guard against Satan's offspring, who engaged in acts ranging from witchcraft to robbery. Between 1581 and 1590, Nicholas Remy, head of the Inquisition in the French province of Lorraine, ordered 900 sorcerers and witches burned to death; likewise, Peter Binsfield, the bishop of the German city of Trier, ordered the death of 6,500 people. An estimated 100,000 people were prosecuted throughout Europe for witchcraft during the sixteenth and seventeenth centuries. It was also commonly believed that some families produced offspring who were unsound or unstable and that social misfits were inherently damaged by reason of their "inferior blood."[3] It was common practice to use cruel tortures to extract confessions, and those convicted of violent or theft crimes suffered extremely harsh penalties, including whipping, branding, maiming, and execution. Almost all felons were punished with death; the law made little distinction between thieves and murderers.

This rather fantastical vision of deviant behavior and its control began to wane as new insights were developed about human nature and behavior during the Renaissance. One influential authority, philosopher Thomas Hobbes (1588–1678), suggested the existence of a "social contract" between people and the state: people naturally pursue their own self-interests but are rational enough to realize that selfishness will produce social chaos, so they agree to give up their own selfish interests as long as everyone else does the same thing. Not all agree to the social contract, and therefore the state became empowered with the right to use force to maintain the contract.

Development of Classical Criminology

During the eighteenth-century **Enlightenment** period, social philosophers such as Jeremy Bentham (1748–1833) began to embrace the view that human behavior was a result of rational thought processes.

According to Bentham's "utilitarian calculus," people choose to act when, after weighing costs and benefits, they believe that their actions will bring them an increase in pleasure and a reduction of pain. It stands to reason that criminal behavior could be eliminated or controlled if would-be law violators could be convinced that the pain of punishment exceeds the benefits of crime.[4] The purpose of law is to produce and support the total happiness of the community it serves. Because punishment is in itself harmful, its existence is justified only if it promises to prevent greater evil than it creates. Punishment, therefore, has four main objectives:

1. To prevent all criminal offenses
2. When it cannot prevent a crime, to convince the offender to commit a less serious crime
3. To ensure that a criminal uses no more force than is necessary
4. To prevent crime as cheaply as possible[5]

Cesare Beccaria

The development of rational classical criminology is most closely identified with the thoughts of Italian social philosopher Cesare Beccaria (1738–1794), and his famous treatise, "On Crimes and Punishment" in which he called for fair and certain punishment to deter crime. He believed people are egotistical and self-centered, and therefore they must be motivated by the fear of punishment, which provides a tangible motive for them to obey the law and suppress the "despotic spirit" that resides in every person.[6] Beccaria suggested that (a) people choose all behavior, including criminal behavior; (b) their choices are designed to bring them pleasure and reduce pain; (c) criminal choices can be controlled by fear of punishment; and (d) the *more severe, certain, and swift the punishment*, the greater its ability to control criminal behavior.

While necessary, Beccaria also believed that punishment must be proportional to the seriousness of crime; if not, people would be encouraged to commit more serious offenses. For example, if robbery, rape, and murder were all punished by death, robbers or rapists would have little reason to refrain from killing their victims to eliminate them as witnesses to the crime. Today, this is referred to as the concept of **marginal deterrence**—if petty offenses were subject to the same punishment as more serious crimes, offenders would choose the more serious crime because the resulting punishment would be about the same.[7]

Beccaria also suggested that the extremely harsh punishments of the day and routine use of torture were inappropriate and excessive. To deter crime, the pain of punishment must be administered in a fair, balanced, and proportionate amount, just enough to counterbalance the pleasure obtained from crime. Beccaria stated his famous theorem like this:

> In order for punishment not to be in every instance, an act of violence of one or many against a private citizen, it must be essentially public, prompt, necessary, the least possible in the given circumstances, proportionate to the crimes, and dictated by the laws.[8]

Classical Criminology

The writings of Beccaria and his followers form the core of what today is referred to as **classical criminology**. As originally conceived in the eighteenth century, classical criminology theory had several basic elements:

- In every society, people have free will to choose criminal or lawful solutions to meet their needs or settle their problems.
- Criminal solutions can be very attractive because for little effort they hold the promise of a huge payoff.
- A person will choose not to commit crime only if he or she believes that the pain of expected punishment is greater than the promise of reward. This is the principle of deterrence.
- In order to be an effective crime deterrent, punishment must be severe, certain, and swift enough to convince potential criminals that "crime does not pay."

This classical perspective influenced penal practices for more than 200 years. The law was made proportionate to crime so that the most serious offenses earned the harshest punishments. Executions were still widely used but slowly began to be employed for only the most serious crimes. The catchphrase was "let the punishment fit the crime."

Beccaria's ideas and writings inspired social thinkers to believe that criminals choose to commit crime and that crime can be controlled by judicious punishment. His vision was widely accepted throughout Europe and the United States.[9]

This vision was embraced by France's postrevolutionary Constituent Assembly (1789) in its Declaration of the Rights of Man:

> [T]he law has the right to prohibit only actions harmful to society. . . . The law shall inflict only such punishments as are strictly and clearly necessary . . . no person shall be punished except by virtue of a law enacted and promulgated previous to the crime and applicable to its terms.

Similarly, a prohibition against cruel and unusual punishment was incorporated in the Eighth Amendment to the U.S. Constitution.

Beccaria's writings have been credited as the basis of the elimination of torture and severe punishment in the nineteenth century. The practice of incarcerating criminals and structuring prison sentences to fit the severity of crime was a reflection of his classical criminology.

By the end of the nineteenth century, the popularity of the classical approach began to decline, and by the middle of the twentieth century, this perspective was neglected by mainstream criminologists. During this period, criminologists focused on internal and external factors—poverty, IQ, education, home life—which were believed to be the true causes of criminality. Because these conditions could not be easily manipulated, the concept of punishing people for behaviors beyond their control seemed both foolish and cruel. Although classical principles still controlled the way police, courts, and correctional agencies operated, most criminologists rejected classical criminology as an explanation of criminal behavior.

Contemporary Choice Theory Emerges

Beginning in the mid-1970s, there was renewed interest in the classical approach to crime. First, the rehabilitation of known criminals came under attack. According to liberal criminology, if crime was caused by some social or psychological problem, such as poverty, then crime rates could be reduced by providing good jobs and economic opportunities. Despite some notable efforts to provide such opportunities, a number of national surveys (the best known being Robert Martinson's "What Works?") failed to find examples of rehabilitation programs that prevented future criminal activity.[10] A well-publicized book, *Beyond Probation*, by Charles Murray and Louis Cox, went as far as suggesting that punishment-oriented programs could suppress future criminality much more effectively than those that relied on rehabilitation and treatment efforts.[11]

A significant increase in the reported crime rate, as well as serious disturbances in the nation's prisons, frightened the general public. The media depicted criminals as callous and dangerous rather than as needy people deserving of public sympathy. Some criminologists began to suggest that it made more sense to frighten these cold calculators with severe punishments than to waste public funds by futilely trying to improve entrenched social conditions linked to crime, such as poverty.[12]

Thinking About Crime   Beginning in the late 1970s, a number of criminologists began producing books and monographs expounding the theme that criminals are rational actors who plan their crimes, fear punishment, and deserve to be penalized for their misdeeds. In a 1975 book that came to symbolize renewed interest in classical views, *Thinking about Crime*, political scientist James Q. Wilson debunked the view that crime was a function of external forces, such as poverty, that could be altered by government programs. Instead, he argued, efforts should be made to reduce criminal opportunity by deterring would-be offenders and incarcerating known criminals. People who are likely to commit crime, he maintained, lack inhibition against misconduct, value the excitement and thrills of breaking the law, have a low stake in conformity, and are willing to take greater chances than the average person. If they could be convinced that their actions will bring severe punishment, only the totally irrational would be willing to engage in crime.[13] Wilson made this famous observation:

> Wicked people exist. Nothing avails except to set them apart from innocent people. And many people, neither

wicked nor innocent, but watchful, dissembling, and calculating of their chances, ponder our reaction to wickedness as a clue to what they might profitably do.[14]

Here Wilson is saying that unless we react forcefully to crime, those "sitting on the fence" will get a clear message—crime pays.

> To read a famous talk given by **James Wilson, "Two Nations,"** the 1997 Francis Boyer lecture delivered at the annual dinner of the American Enterprise Institute, visit the Criminal Justice CourseMate at cengagebrain.com, then access the "Web Links" for this chapter.

The Seductions of Crime   Another influential work was sociologist Jack Katz's *Seductions of Crime*. Katz argues that there are immediate benefits to criminality. These seductions of crime are situational inducements that directly precede the commission of a crime and draw offenders into law violations. For example, someone challenges their authority and they vanquish their opponent with a beating; or they want to do something exciting, so they break into and vandalize a school building.

According to Katz, choosing crime can help satisfy personal needs. For some people, shoplifting and vandalism are attractive because getting away with crime is a thrilling demonstration of personal competence; Katz calls this "sneaky thrills." Even murder can have an emotional payoff. Killers behave like the avenging gods of mythology, choosing to have life-or-death control over their victims.

Katz finds that crimes can help soothe the strain produced by emotional upheaval. For example, when a person is rebuked for his or her behavior, violence may be a method for restoring the person's self-esteem. When a person gets drunk and rowdy at a party and is told by a rival to tone it down, the aggrieved person may respond, "So, I'm acting like a fool, am I?" and attack. Public embarrassment leads to action; the person must "sacrifice" or injure the body of the victim to maintain his or her "honor." A number of research studies have supported Katz's view that situational inducements play an important role in causing adolescent misbehavior. People are most likely to be "seduced" if they fear neither the risk of apprehension nor its social consequences. People who either (a) fear losing the respect of their peers or (b) suffer legal punishment are most likely to forgo the seductions of crime.

Impact on Crime Control   Coinciding with the publication of Wilson's book was a conservative shift in U.S. public policy, which resulted in Ronald Reagan's election to the presidency in 1980. Political decision makers embraced Wilson's ideas as a means to bring the crime rate down. Tough new laws were passed, creating mandatory prison sentences for drug offenders; the nation's prison population skyrocketed. Critics decried the disproportionate number of young minority men being locked up for drug law violations.[15] Today, about 65 percent of the prison population is African American or Hispanic.[16] Despite liberal anguish, conservative views of crime control have helped shape criminal justice policy for the past two decades.[17] Many Americans, some of whom are passionate opponents of abortion on the grounds that it takes human life, became, ironically, ardent supporters of the death penalty![18] This "get tough" attitude was supported by the fact that while the prison population has grown to new heights, the crime rate has been in a steep decline.

> Even if the **death penalty** were an effective deterrent, some critics believe it presents ethical problems that make its use morally dubious. For more information about what the American Civil Liberties Union has to say, visit the Criminal Justice CourseMate at cengagebrain.com, then access the "Web Links" for this chapter.

From these roots, a more contemporary version of classical theory has evolved. It is based on intelligent thought processes and criminal decision making.[19] This new view of rational choice is somewhat different from the original classical theory that portrayed criminals as people who tried to maximize their pleasure and minimize pain. If they were caught committing crime it was because they were sloppy thinkers and imperfect in their decision making. In contrast, this contemporary version views the decision to commit crime as being shaped by human emotions and thought processes. It recognizes that other influences have an impact on criminal decision making, including social relationships, individual traits and capabilities, and environmental characteristics. So, this new version of rational choice theory assumes that human behavior is both "willful and determined."[20]

THE CONCEPTS OF RATIONAL CHOICE

According to the contemporary rational choice approach, law-violating behavior occurs when an offender decides to risk breaking the law after considering both personal factors (i.e., the need for money, revenge, thrills, and entertainment) and situational factors (i.e., how well a target is protected and the efficiency of the local police force). People who believe that the risks of crime outweigh the rewards may decide to go straight. If they think they are likely to be arrested and punished, they are more likely to seek treatment and turn their lives around than risk criminal activities.[21]

Why Crime?

The core premise of rational choice theory is that some people choose crime under some circumstances. Why is that so when the consequences can be painful, costly, and embarrassing? Nonetheless, for some people choosing crime is actually an easy decision to make. Take adolescents, who regularly violate the law. The criminal lifestyle fits well with this group, whose membership routinely organize their life around risk taking and partying. Criminal events provide money for drugs and serve as an ideal method for displaying courage and fearlessness to one's running mates. Rather than create overwhelming social problems, a criminal way of life can be extremely beneficial, helping kids overcome the problems and stress they face in their daily lives.

Crime helps some people achieve a sense of control or mastery over their environment.[22] Adolescents in particular may find themselves feeling out of control because society limits their opportunities and resources. Antisocial behavior gives them the opportunity to exert control over their own lives and destinies, by helping them avoid situations they find uncomfortable or repellant (e.g., running away from an abusive home) or obtain resources for desired activities and commodities (e.g., stealing or selling drugs to buy stylish outfits).[23] Crime may also help them boost their self-esteem by attacking perceived enemies (e.g., they vandalize the property of an adult who has called the cops on them). Drinking and drug taking may help some kids ward off depression and compensate for a lack of positive experiences; they learn how to self-medicate themselves. Some, angry at their mistreatment, may turn to violence to satisfy a desire for revenge or retaliation.[24]

Engaging in risky behavior helps some people feel alive and competent. Some turn to substance abuse to increase their sense of personal power, to become more assertive, and reduce tension and anxiety.[25] Others embrace a deviant lifestyle to compensate for their feelings of powerlessness or ordinariness. There is also evidence that antisocial acts can provide positive solutions to problems. Violent kids, for example, may have learned that being aggressive with others is a good means to control the situation and get what they want; counterattacks may be one means of controlling people who are treating them poorly.[26]

Considering its benefits, why do people age out of crime? While crime as a short-run problem-solving solution may be appealing to adolescents, it becomes less attractive as people mature and begin to appreciate the dangers of using crime to solve problems.[27] Going to a drunken frat party may sound appealing to sophomores who want to improve their social life, but the risks involved to safety and reputation make them off limits as they grow older. As people mature, their thinking extends farther into the future, and risky behavior is a threat to long-range plans.

Choosing Crime

Even those who decide to enter a criminal way of life do not commit crime all the time. People who commit crime go to school, church, or work, they have family time, engage in romances, play sports, and go to movies. Why do they choose to commit a particular crime at a particular time?

Before choosing to commit a crime, **reasoning criminals** evaluate the risk of apprehension, the seriousness of expected punishment, the potential value of the criminal enterprise, and their immediate need for criminal gain; their behavior is systematic and selective. For example, burglars choose targets based on their value, novelty, and resale potential. A relatively new piece of electronic gear such as the newest iPhone or iPad may be a prime target, because it has not yet saturated the market and still retains high value.[28]

Risk evaluations may cover a wide range of topics: What's the chance of getting caught? How difficult will it be to commit the crime? Is the profit worth the effort? Should I risk committing crime in my own neighborhood where I know the territory, or is it worth traveling to a strange place in order to increase my profits?[29]

People who decide to get involved in crime weigh up the chances of arrest (based on their past experiences), plus the subjective psychic rewards of crime including the excitement and social status it brings and perceived opportunities for easy gains. If the rewards are great, the perceived risk small, and the excitement high, the likelihood of committing additional crimes increases.[30] Successful thieves say they will do it again in the future; past experience has taught them the rewards of illegal behavior.[31]

Criminals, then, are people who share the same ambitions as conventional citizens but have decided to cut corners and use illegal means to achieve their goals (see the Profiles in Crime feature "Looting the Public Treasury"). Many criminal offenders retain conventional American values of striving for success, material attainment, and hard work.[32] When Philippe Bourgois studied crack dealers in East Harlem in New York City, he found that their motivations were not dissimilar from the average citizen: they were upwardly mobile, scrambling around to obtain their "piece of the pie."[33] If they commit crime, it is because they have chosen an illegal path to obtain the goals that might otherwise have been out of reach.

In contrast, the decision to forgo crime is reached when the potential criminal believes that risks outweigh rewards. People will forgo crime if after a careful evaluation of the circumstances they conclude that:

- They stand a good chance of being caught and punished.
- They fear the consequences of punishment.
- They risk losing the respect of their peers, damaging their reputations, and experiencing feelings of guilt or shame.[34]
- The risk of apprehension outweighs the profit and/or pleasure of crime.[35]

Profiles in Crime
Looting the Public Treasury

After graduating from UCLA, Albert Robles served terms as mayor, councilman, and deputy city manager of South Gate, California, an industrial community about 12 miles outside downtown Los Angeles. Soon after Robles became city treasurer in 1997, he plotted to rule the city purely for his own benefit. He even proclaimed himself "King of South Gate" and referred to the city as his "fiefdom." Once in power, Robles got involved in a number of convoluted illegal schemes, including:

- Using the city's treasury as his "private piggy bank for himself, his family, and his friends" (according to acting U.S. Attorney George Cardona), costing South Gate more than $35 million and bringing it to the verge of bankruptcy
- Firing city hall employees at will, replacing them with supporters who had little experience
- Recruiting and bankrolling unqualified local supporters for city council until he controlled the council
- Threatening anyone who stood in his way (suspiciously, one of his adversaries on the city council was shot in the head)

Robles and his corrupt cronies then cooked up schemes to line their own pockets with the public's cash. In one such scheme, Robles coerced businesses to hire a financial consultant named Edward Espinoza in order to win various city contracts, including senior housing and sewer rehabilitation projects. As part of this plan, Robles and Espinoza set up a shell corporation that raked in some $2.4 million—more than $1.4 million of which went straight into Robles's pockets. He used part of the money to buy a $165,000 beach condo in Baja for his mother; he also forked over $55,000 for "platinum membership" in a motivational group. In another scheme, Robles steered a $48 million refuse and recycling contract to a company in exchange for more than $30,000 in gifts and campaign contributions.

In February 2003, Robles was targeted by a federal grand jury looking into the handling of federal loans and grants. FBI and IRS investigators pored over city records to uncover his illegal schemes. The citizens of South Gate ultimately voted Robles and his cronies out of office (but not before he racked up huge legal bills at the city's expense), and he was convicted at trial in July 2005. Two of his business associates—including Espinoza—also went to prison.

Robles's illegal acts were the product of careful plotting and planning. They were

AP Images/Nick Ut

motivated by greed and not need. To some criminologists, stories like these confirm the fact that many crimes are a matter of rational choice.

SOURCES: Federal Bureau of Investigation, "Corruption in City Hall: The Crooked Reign of 'King' Albert," January 8, 2007, www2.fbi.gov/page2/jan07/cityhall010807.htm (accessed November 8, 2010); Hector Becerra, "Robles Sentenced to 10 Years," *Los Angeles Times*, November 29, 2006, p. 1.

CONNECTIONS

Lack of conventional opportunity is a persistent theme in sociological theories of crime. The frustration caused by a perceived lack of opportunity explains the high crime rates in lower-class areas. Chapter 6 discusses strain and cultural deviance theories, which provide alternative explanations of how lack of opportunity is associated with crime.

Offense and Offender

Rational choice theorists view crime as both offense- and offender-specific.[36] That a crime is **offense-specific** means that offenders will react selectively to the characteristics of

an individual criminal act. Take for instance the decision to commit a burglary. The thought process might include:

- Evaluating the target yield
- Probability of security devices
- Police patrol effectiveness
- Availability of a getaway car
- Ease of selling stolen merchandise
- Presence of occupants
- Neighbors who might notice a break-in
- Presence of guard dogs
- Presence of escape routes
- Entry points and exits

The fact that a crime is **offender-specific** means that criminals are not robots who engage in unthinking, unplanned random acts of antisocial behavior. Before deciding to commit crime, individuals must decide whether they have the prerequisites to commit a successful criminal act. These might include evaluation of:

- Whether they possess the necessary skills to commit the crime
- Their immediate need for money or other valuables
- Whether legitimate financial alternatives to crime exist, such as a high-paying job
- Whether they have available resources to commit the crime

- Their fear of expected apprehension and punishment
- Availability of alternative criminal acts, such as selling drugs
- Physical ability, including health, strength, and dexterity

Note the distinction made here between crime and criminality.[37] Crime is an event; **criminality** is a personal trait. Professional criminals do not commit crime all the time, and even ordinary citizens may, on occasion, violate the law. Some people considered high risk because they are indigent or disturbed may never violate the law, whereas others who are seemingly affluent and well adjusted may risk criminal behavior given enough provocation and/or opportunity. What conditions promote crime and enhance criminality?

Structuring Criminality

A number of personal factors condition people to choose crime. Among the more important factors are economic opportunity, learning and experience, and knowledge of criminal techniques.

Economic Opportunity
Boston Magazine ran an article recently about a university lecturer with a master's degree from Yale and a doctorate in cultural anthropology who took another job to pay the bills: call girl.[38] Rather than living on the meager teaching salary she was offered, the "Ivy League hooker" chose to make the tax-free $140 per hour for her services (she charged $200, handing over $60 to the escort service that arranged her dates). She left the business when she became financially self-sufficient.

The Ivy League hooker is not alone. Perceptions of economic opportunity influence the decision to commit crime. Some people may engage in criminal activity simply because they need the money to support their lifestyle and perceive few other potential income sources. Sociologists Christopher Uggen and Melissa Thompson found that people who begin taking hard drugs also increase their involvement in crime, taking in from $500 to $700 per month. Once they become cocaine and heroin users, the benefits of other criminal enterprises become overwhelmingly attractive: how else can a drug user earn enough to support his or her habit?[39]

Crime also becomes attractive when an individual becomes convinced that it will result in excessive profits with few costs. Research shows that criminals may be motivated to commit crime when they know others who have made big scores and are quite successful at crime. Although the prevailing wisdom is that crime does not pay, a small but significant subset of criminals actually enjoy earnings of close to $50,000 per year from crime, and their success may help motivate other would-be offenders.[40] However, offenders are likely to desist from crime if they believe that their future criminal earnings will be relatively low and that attractive and legal opportunities to generate income

© Francesco Guidicini/ZUMA Press

Some people commit crime simply for economic reasons: it is convenient and easy to make financial gain through illegal activity. Dr. Brooke Magnanti, shown here, is a research scientist, blogger, and writer who, until her identity was revealed in November 2009, was known by the pen name Belle de Jour. While completing her doctoral studies in England, between 2003 and 2004, Magnanti supported her income by working as a prostitute. Her diary, published as the anonymous blog *Belle de Jour: Diary of a London Call Girl,* became increasingly popular as speculation surrounded the identity of Belle de Jour and whether the diary was even real. Remaining anonymous, Magnanti went on to have her experiences published in 2005 in *The Intimate Adventures of a London Call Girl* and in a 2006 follow-up, *The Further Adventures of a London Call Girl.* In 2007, Belle's blogs and books were adapted into a television series, *Secret Diary of a Call Girl.* Having written as a newspaper columnist, Belle also moved into fiction publishing. In November 2009, reportedly fearing an ex-boyfriend was about to expose her real identity, Magnanti revealed to a newspaper her real name and current occupation as a researcher in child health at Bristol University. Why do you think highly educated women such as Brooke Magnanti get into prostitution? Is it solely for the money?

are available.[41] In this sense, rational choice is a function of a person's perception of conventional alternatives and opportunities.

Learning and Experience Learning and experience may be important elements in structuring the choice of crime.[42] Career criminals may learn the limitations of their powers; they know when to take a chance and when to be cautious. Experienced criminals may turn from a life of crime when they develop a belief that the risk of crime is greater than its potential profit.[43] Patricia Morgan and Karen Ann Joe's three-city study (San Francisco, San Diego, and Honolulu) of female drug abusers found that experience helped dealers avoid detection. One dealer, earning $50,000 per year, explained her strategy this way:

> I stayed within my goals, basically . . . I don't go around doing stupid things. I don't walk around telling people I have drugs for sale. I don't have people sitting out in front of my house. I don't have traffic in and out of my house . . . I control the people I sell to.[44]

Morgan and Joe found that these female dealers consider drug distribution a positive experience that gives them economic independence, self-esteem, increased ability to function, professional pride, and the ability to maintain control over their lives. These women often seemed more like yuppies opening a boutique than out-of-control addicts:

> I'm a good dealer. I don't cut my drugs, I have high-quality drugs insofar as it's possible to get high-quality drugs. I want to be known as somebody who sells good drugs, but doesn't always have them, as opposed to someone who always has them and sometimes the drugs are good.[45]

Here we see how experience in the profession shapes criminal decision making.

Knowledge of Criminal Techniques Criminals report learning techniques that help them avoid detection, a sure sign of rational thinking and planning. Some are specialists, who learn to be professional car thieves or bad-check artists. Others are generalists who sell drugs one day and commit burglaries the next. In his studies of drug dealers, criminologist Bruce Jacobs found that crack dealers learn how to stash crack cocaine in some undisclosed location so that they are not forced to carry large amounts of product on their persons. Dealers carefully evaluate the security of their sales area before setting up shop.[46] Most consider the middle of a long block the best place for drug deals because they can see everything in both directions; police raids can be spotted before they develop.[47] If a buyer seems dangerous or unreliable, the dealer would require that they do business in spaces between apartment buildings or in back lots. Although dealers lose the tactical edge of being on a public street, they gain a measure of protection because their associates can watch over the deal and come to the rescue if the buyer tries to "pull something."[48] Similar detection avoidance schemes were found by Gordon Knowles in his study of crack dealers in Honolulu, Hawaii. Knowles found that drug dealers often use pornographic film houses as their base of operations because they offer both privacy and convenience.[49]

When Jacobs, along with Jody Miller, studied female crack dealers, they discovered a variety of defensive moves used by the dealers to avoid detection.[50] One of these techniques, called stashing, involved learning how to hide drugs on their person, in the street, or at home. One dealer told Jacobs and Miller how she hid drugs in the empty shaft of a curtain rod; another wore hollow earmuffs to hide crack. Because only female officers may conduct body cavity searches on women, the dealers often had time to get rid of their drugs before they got to the station house. Dealers are aware of legal definitions of possession. One said she stashed her drugs 250 feet from her home because that was beyond the distance (150 feet) police considered a person legally to be in "constructive possession" of drugs.

Criminals who learn the proper techniques may be able to prolong their criminal careers. Jacobs found that these offenders use specific techniques to avoid being apprehended by police. They play what they call the "peep game" before dealing drugs, scoping out the territory to make sure the turf is free from anything out of place that could be a potential threat (such as police officers or rival gang members).[51] One crack dealer told Jacobs:

> There was this red Pontiac sittin' on the corner one day with two white guys inside. They was just sittin' there for an hour, not doin' nothin'. Another day, diff'rent people be walkin' up and down the street you don't really recognize. You think they might be kin of someone but then you be askin' around and they [neighbors] ain't never seen them before neither. When ya' see strange things like that, you think somethin' be goin' on [and you don't deal].[52]

Drug dealers told Jacobs that they also carefully consider whether they should deal alone or in groups; large groups draw more attention from police but can offer more protection. Drug-dealing gangs and groups can help divert the attention of police: if their drug dealing is noticed by detectives, a dealer can slyly walk away or dispose of evidence while confederates distract the cops.[53]

Structuring Crime

Criminal decision making is not only based on an assessment of personal needs and capabilities, but also on a rational assessment of the criminal event. Decisions must be made about what, where, when, and whom to target:

Choosing the Type of Crime   The choice of crime may be dictated by market conditions. Generalists may alter their criminal behavior according to shifting opportunity structures: they may rob the elderly on the first of the month when they know that Social Security checks have been cashed, switch over to shoplifting if a new fence moves into the neighborhood, and, if a supply becomes available, sell a truckload of hijacked cigarettes to neighborhood convenience stores.

Sometimes the choice of crime is structured by the situational factors. Eric Baumer and his associates found that cities whose population of crack cocaine users is on the increase also experience an increase in their robbery rates and a corresponding decrease in burglary rates. Baumer reasons that crack users need a quick influx of cash to purchase drugs and are in no position to plan a burglary and take the time to sell their loot; street robberies are designed to provide a quick influx of cash that meets their lifestyle needs.[54]

Choosing the Time and Place of Crime   There is also evidence that criminal choice is structured by the time and place. Interviews with burglars show that they prefer "working" between 9 A.M. and 11 A.M. and in mid-afternoon, when parents are either at work or dropping off or picking up kids at school.[55] Burglars avoid Saturdays because most families are at home; Sunday morning during church hours is considered a prime time for weekend burglaries.[56] Some find out which families have star high school athletes because those that do are sure to be at the weekend game, leaving their houses unguarded.[57]

The place of crime is also carefully chosen. Because criminals often go on foot or use public transportation, they are unlikely to travel long distances to commit crimes and are more likely to drift toward the center of a city than move toward outlying areas.[58] Some may occasionally commute to distant locations to commit crimes if they believe the payoff is greater, but most prefer to stay in their own neighborhood where they are familiar with the terrain.[59] They will only travel to unfamiliar areas if they believe the new location contains a worthy target and lax law enforcement. They may be encouraged to travel when the police are cracking down in their own neighborhood and the "heat is on."[60] Predatory criminals are in fact aware of law enforcement capabilities and consider them closely before deciding to commit crimes. Communities with the reputation of employing aggressive crime-fighting cops are less likely to attract potential offenders than areas perceived to have passive law enforcers.[61]

Selecting the Target of Crime   Criminals may also be well aware of target vulnerability. When they choose targets, they may shy off if they sense danger. In a series of interviews with career property offenders, Kenneth Tunnell found that burglars avoid targets if they feel there are police in the area or if "nosy neighbors" might be suspicious and cause trouble.[62] Paul Bellair found that robbery levels are relatively low in neighborhoods where residents keep a watchful eye on their neighbors' property.[63]

Predatory criminals seek out easy targets who can't or won't fight back and avoid those who seem menacing and dangerous. Not surprisingly, they tend to shy away from potential victims whom they believe are armed and dangerous.[64] The search for suitable victims may bring them in contact with people who themselves engage in deviant or antisocial behaviors.[65] Perhaps predatory criminals sense that people with "dirty hands" make suitable targets because they are unlikely to want to call the police or get entangled with the law.

In some instances, however, targets are chosen in order to send a message rather than to generate capital. Bruce Jacobs and Richard Wright used in-depth interviews with street robbers who target drug dealers and found that their crimes are a response to one of three types of violations.[66]

- *Market-related* violations emerge from disputes involving partners in trade, rivals, or generalized predators.
- *Status-based* violations involve encounters in which the grievant's essential character or normative sensibilities have been challenged.
- *Personalistic* violations flow from incidents in which the grievant's autonomy or belief in a just world have been jeopardized.

Robbery in this instance is an instrument used to settle scores, display dominance, and stifle potential rivals. Retaliation certainly is rational in the sense that actors who lack legitimate access to the law and who prize respect above everything else will often choose to resolve their grievances through a rough and ready brand of self-help.

IS CRIME RATIONAL?

It is relatively easy to show that some crimes are the product of rational, objective thought, especially when they involve an ongoing criminal conspiracy centered on economic gain. When prominent bankers in the savings and loan industry were indicted for criminal fraud, their elaborate financial schemes exhibited not only signs of rationality but brilliant, though flawed, financial expertise.[67] The stock market manipulations of Enron and WorldCom executives, the drug dealings of international cartels, and the gambling operations of organized crime bosses all demonstrate a reasoned analysis of market conditions, interests, and risks. Even small-time wheeler-dealers, such as the female drug dealers discussed earlier in the chapter, are guided by their rational assessment of the likelihood of apprehension and take pains to avoid detection. But what about common crimes of theft and violence? Are these rational acts or unplanned, haphazard, and spontaneous?

Is Theft Rational?

Some common theft-related crimes—larcenies, shoplifting, purse snatchings—seem more likely to be random acts of criminal opportunity than well-thought-out conspiracies. However, there is evidence that even these seemingly unplanned events may be the product of careful risk assessment, including environmental, social, and structural factors. For example, there are professional shoplifters, referred to as **boosters**, who use complex methods in order to avoid detection. They steal with the intention of reselling stolen merchandise to professional fences, another group of criminals who use cunning and rational decision making in their daily activities.

Burglars seem to be motivated by rational choice and show evidence of planning and thought. They carefully choose the neighborhood location of their crimes. They seem to avoid areas where residents protect their homes with alarms, locks, and other methods of "target hardening" or where residents watch out for one another and try to control unrest or instability in their communities.[68] Most burglars prefer to commit crimes in **permeable neighborhoods**, those with a greater than usual number of access streets from traffic arteries into the neighborhood.[69] These areas are chosen for theft and break-ins because they are familiar and well traveled, they appear more open and vulnerable, and they offer more potential escape routes.[70] Burglars appear to monitor car and pedestrian traffic and avoid selecting targets on heavily traveled streets.[71] Corner homes, usually near traffic lights or stop signs, are the ones most likely to be burglarized: stop signs give criminals a legitimate reason to stop their cars and look for an attractive target.[72] Secluded homes, such as those at the end of a cul-de-sac or surrounded by wooded areas, make suitable targets.[73] Professionals also report being concerned about target convenience. They are more apt to choose familiar burglary sites that are located in easily accessible and open areas.[74]

Burglars are choosy when they select targets. They avoid freestanding buildings because they can more easily be surrounded by police; they like to select targets that are known to do a primarily cash business, such as bars, supermarkets, and restaurants.[75] Burglars also seem to know the market and target goods that are in demand. Police in England report that carefully planned burglaries seem to be on the decline, presumably because goods that were the target a few years back—such as video recorders and DVD players—are now so cheap that they are not worth stealing; in English terms, they are barely worth "nicking." Flat-screen TVs may be valuable, but those that are the most valuable have become so large that they are impractical to steal.[76] As a result, the planned professional burglary is on a decline in Britain at the same time that street muggings are on the rise.

Is Drug Use Rational?

Did Lindsay Lohan make an objective, rational choice to abuse alcohol and potentially sabotage her career? Did the terrific young actor Heath Ledger make a rational choice when he abused prescription drugs to the point that it killed him? Is it possible that drug users and dealers, a group not usually associated with clear thinking, make rational choices?

Research does in fact show that from its onset drug use is controlled by rational decision making. Users report that they begin taking drugs when they believe that the benefits of substance abuse outweigh its costs (e.g., they believe that drugs will provide a fun, exciting, thrilling experience). Their entry into substance abuse is facilitated by their perception that valued friends and family members endorse and encourage drug use and abuse substances themselves.[77]

In adulthood, heavy drug users and dealers show signs of rationality and cunning in their daily activity, approaching drug dealing as a business proposition. Research conducted by Leanne Fiftal Alarid and her partners shows that women drawn into dealing drugs learn the trade in a businesslike manner. One young dealer told them how she learned the techniques of the trade from an older male partner:

> He taught me how to "recon" [reconstitute] cocaine, cutting and repacking a brick from 91 proof to 50 proof, just like a business. He treats me like an equal partner, and many of the friends are business associates. I am a catalyst. . . . I even get guys turned on to drugs.[78]

Note the business terminology used. This coke dealer could be talking about an IT training course at a major corporation! If criminal acts are treated as business decisions, in which profit and loss potential must be carefully calculated, then crime must indeed be a rational event. The Criminological Enterprise feature discusses the rational aspects of drug dealing.

The way drug dealers retaliate for perceived wrongdoing shows a great deal of rationality. We can observe this rational behavior when dealers seek to retaliate for perceived or real wrongdoing or when they compete for markets or seek retaliation for drug deals gone bad. Because participants in illicit drug markets are beyond the law and their respectability (i.e., status) is relatively low, disputes are unlikely to be settled by police or courts; they must "take care of business" themselves.

Recently, criminologist Scott Jacques investigated the forms of drug market retaliation and found they followed a rational pattern. After interviewing a sample of experienced drug dealers, Jacques found that dispute resolution can take four different forms, two involving nonviolent means and two violent.

Nonviolent Retaliation

- *Stealth retaliation* is defined as nonviolent revenge gained through resource confiscation without interaction between the retaliator and wrongdoer during the transfer. Stealth retaliation can involve any kind of resource, such as drugs, money, or jewelry, and the amount confiscated can vary widely, from one gram to a kilo of drugs, or tens to thousands of dollars. If a dealer feels he or she may have been ripped off, the dealer may break into the victim's apartment and take his plasma TV and a kilo of drugs.
- *Fraudulent retaliation* is defined as nonviolent retribution accomplished using deception to trick a wrongdoer into an unfair trade. After being short-changed in a drug deal, fraudulent retaliation could involve selling their rival a gram or pound of fake drugs, as an instant revenge for the perceived wrongdoing. Some fraudulent retaliation schemes involve immediate payback or may involve an elaborate scam that evolves over a matter of days, weeks, or even months.

Violent Retaliation

- *Violent confiscation* is defined as retaliation that involves both violence and resource confiscation. Violent confiscation can involve taking money in amounts ranging from $1 to $1 million, one ounce or many pounds of drugs, and using violence to do so, ranging from a slap to the face to a murder. It can be immediate, such as a retaliatory robbery or take weeks—for example, during a retaliatory kidnapping
- *Pure fight* is defined as violent vengeance that does not involve resource transfer between disputants. A pure fight may occur when a drug dealer feels a rival is poaching on his territory and decides to kill him in order to protect his turf and maintain his tough guy rep.

In some cases, victims use a tit-for-tat strategy. Dave, a drug dealer, was victimized in an act of stealth retaliation and turned the tables on his victimizer. He told Jacques:

Dave: There was one time when somebody didn't pay me back, it was just about $300, and I had trusted the kid for a long time. He wasn't paying upfront, I was just giving him the bud [marijuana] and he would sell it and give me the money later, and then it took about three weeks once, he still hadn't given it to me, and I was trying to call him and get it from him . . . [A]nd another week or two passed and I started talking to a lot of people and I was putting some time into it trying to figure out what was going on, and

Is Violence Rational?

Brandon Wilson, 21, slashed the throat of Matthew Cecchi, a 9-year-old California boy, then stabbed him in the back and left him to bleed to death on the floor of a public restroom. At trial, he claimed that he was not responsible for his actions, that he was high on LSD, and that the voice of God told him to kill a child. After his conviction on murder charges, Wilson told the jury that he would "do it again in a second if I had the chance." When the jury later met to consider the death penalty, Wilson told them, "My whole purpose in life is to help destroy your society. You people are here as representatives of that society. As such, you should do everything in your power to rid the world of me, execute me." Granting his wish, the jury foreman told reporters, "If there was ever a case that deserved the death penalty, this one fits."[79]

Though Brandon Wilson was seemingly a demented child killer, the jury concluded that he was a rational and calculating killer who may have carefully chosen his victim. Is it possible that violent acts, through which the offender gains little material benefit, are the product of reasoned decision making? Yes, it is. There are a number of indicators that suggest violence has rational elements. When Trevor Bennett and Fiona Brookman conducted interviews with English offenders with a history of violence, they found that some motivations were cultural, such as maintaining one's status and honor, and others might be visceral, such as excitement and getting a buzz from dangerous pursuits. There were also rational elements to violent acts, such as calculating that the engagement would be successful or the perceived need to mete out informal justice to an enemy.[80] Crime experts such as Richard Felson argue that violence is a matter of choice and serves specific goals:

they all said he wasn't going to pay me, and the way he was talking about it was just really disrespectful. I just went over to his place with a couple of other kids that I know to do shit like this, but I don't do shit like this unless someone has my money.

Interviewer: Do shit like what?

Dave: What I'm about to tell you. Well, basically, we just went up to his house and knocked on it for a little bit, but the music was so loud they couldn't hear us, I guess his mom was out of town, and I saw that his car was right there, and I opened up his car door and stole his TV that he had actually stolen from somebody else.

William's story, below, illustrates how a drug dealer took revenge by violently confiscating the wrongdoer's resources:

William: I was on probation . . . and I had a PO [parole officer] meeting and so I had just picked up about six or seven thousand dimes [Valiums] and my buddy was driving me as I didn't have a license. So I'm not gonna walk in there with two cargo pockets bulging out huge, you know I wasn't that stupid at the time. Yeah, selling drugs on probation wasn't smart. So I left it on my friend's seat, and this was a friend in my group of 50, I'd say. He gave me a ride, I gave him 10 dimes for giving me a ride and so I put it in his car, went in there. Probation was never fast at that place . . . it was never a fast process, you were there 45 minutes to an hour. I came out, my buddy dropped me off . . . I counted them and tallied them and I don't remember exactly how much I was supposed to have, but I was about 300 to 400 short, but out of a bag of six or seven thousand Valiums you're not gonna be able to tell 300, you just can't tell. So I guess he probably had a couple of handfuls out of each bag . . . [S]o my friend [and I], we showed up at his house, beat the hell out of him and took every dollar he had, you know, just two guys on one. We weren't gonna bloody him up or anything, just kind of beat the hell out of him, held him, took all the DVDs we could find, obviously he had sold some, probably got about $600 back. I gave my friend $200 [and] I took $400.

Each form of retaliation depends upon a number of personal and situational conditions. For example, stealth retaliation is only possible if a wrongdoer physically separates from his or her wealth, while fraudulent retaliation and violent confiscation are only possible if a wrongdoer has contact with his or her wealth. Pure violence can take place regardless of whether the perceived wrongdoer has wealth. Stealth retaliation is possible when fraudulent retaliation and violent confiscation are not possible, and vice versa.

CRITICAL THINKING

Jacques's research clearly suggests that drug dealers are rational decision makers whose choice of retaliation styles depends on personal and situational factors. Can you offer another explanation for their behavior that does not rely on rational choice? (Hint: Think of culture and environment.)

SOURCES: Scott Jacques, "The Necessary Conditions for Retaliation: Toward a Theory of Non-Violent and Violent Forms in Drug Markets," *Justice Quarterly* 27 (2010): 186–205.

- *Control.* The violent person may want to control his or her victim's behavior and life.
- *Retribution.* The perpetrator may want to punish someone without calling the police or using the justice system to address his or her grievances. The person takes the law into his or her own hands.
- *Deterrence.* The attacker may want to stop someone from repeating acts that he or she considers hostile or provocative.
- *Reputation.* An attack may be motivated by the need to enhance reputation and create self-importance in the eyes of others.

Felson also recognizes that the violent act may have multiple goals. But in any case, even violence may be a product of rational decision making.[81]

Rational Robbers Street robbers also are likely to choose victims who are vulnerable, have low coercive power, and do not pose any threat.[82] In their survey of violent felons, James Wright and Peter Rossi found that robbers avoid victims who may be armed and dangerous. About three-fifths of all felons interviewed were more afraid of armed victims than of police; about two-fifths had avoided a victim because they believed the victim was armed; and almost one-third reported that they had been scared off, wounded, or captured by armed victims.[83] It comes as no surprise that cities with higher than average gun-carrying rates generally have lower rates of unarmed robbery.[84]

Robbers also tend to pick the time and day of crimes carefully. When they rob a commercial establishment, they choose the time when there is the most cash on hand to increase their take from the crime. For example, robbery rates increase in the winter partly because the Christmas shopping season means more money in the cash registers of potential targets.[85] Targets are generally found close to

Brandon Wilson, the accused killer of 9-year-old Matthew Cecchi, stands handcuffed in felony arraignment court in Vista, California. Can such violent acts ever be considered "rational"? Before you answer, remember that Wilson could have attacked a Marine, police officer, or kung fu expert, but instead "chose" a defenseless child.

AP Images/Lenny Ignelzi

Even serial murderers, outwardly the most irrational of all offenders, tend to pick their targets with care. Most choose victims who are defenseless or who cannot count on police protection: prostitutes, gay men, hitchhikers, children, hospital patients, the elderly, and the homeless. Rarely do serial killers target weightlifters, martial arts experts, or any other potentially powerful group.[91]

Are killers rational and calculating? Read the Profiles in Crime feature and judge for yourself.

Rational Sex Criminals? One might think that sex crimes are highly irrational, motivated by hate, lust, revenge, emotions that defy rational planning. But sex criminals report using rational thought and planning when carrying out their crimes. Serial rapists rationally choose their targets. They travel, on average, three miles from their homes to commit their crimes in order to avoid victims who might recognize them later. The desire to avoid detection supersedes the wish to obtain a victim with little effort. Older, more experienced rapists who have extensive criminal histories are willing to travel farther; younger rapists who have less experience committing crimes travel less and are therefore more at risk of detection.[92]

Child molesters/rapists report that they volunteer or seek employment in day care centers and other venues where victims can be found. They use their status to gain the trust of children and to be seen as nonthreatening to the child. Within the context of this work environment they can then use subtle strategies of manipulation, such as giving love and attention to gain their victims' trust (e.g., spending a lot of time with them), and they can gradually desensitize the children and gain their cooperation in sexual activity (e.g., through nonsexual touching).[93] These efforts obviously display planning and rationality.

robbers' homes or in areas in which they routinely travel. Familiarity with the area gives them ready knowledge of escape routes; this is referred to as their "awareness space."[86] A familiar location allows them to blend in, not look out of place, and not get lost when returning home with their loot.[87]

Rational Killers? Hollywood likes to portray deranged people killing innocent victims at random, but people who carry guns and are ready to use them typically do so for more rational reasons. They may perceive that they live in a dangerous environment and carry a weapon for self-protection. Some are involved in dangerous illegal activities such as drug dealing and carry weapons as part of the job.[88] Even in apparently senseless killings among strangers, the conscious motive is typically revenge for a prior dispute or disagreement among the parties involved or their families.[89] Many homicides are motivated by offenders' desire to avoid retaliation from a victim they assaulted or to avoid future prosecutions by getting rid of witnesses.[90] Although some killings are the result of anger and aggression, others are the result of rational planning.

ELIMINATING CRIME

For many people, then, crime is attractive; it brings rewards, excitement, prestige, or other desirable outcomes without lengthy work or effort.[94] Whether the motive is economic gain, revenge, or hedonism, crime has an allure that some people cannot resist.[95] Some law violators describe the adrenaline rush that comes from successfully executing illegal activities in dangerous situations as **edgework**, the "exhilarating, momentary integration of danger, risk, and skill" that motivates people to try a variety of dangerous criminal and noncriminal behaviors.[96] Crime is not some random act, but a means that can provide both pleasure and solutions to vexing personal problems. As Michael Gottfredson and Travis Hirschi put it, these criminals derive satisfaction from "money without work, sex without courtship, revenge without court delays."[97]

Eugene Temkin loaned his old buddy Michael Hershman $500,000 to invest in a casino in Equatorial Guinea, Africa. When the casino didn't do well, Hershman was unable to repay Temkin, who had taken the money from a second mortgage on an apartment building he owned. When the money was lost, Temkin couldn't make payments on the property and eventually lost it to foreclosure. He then sued Hershman for $900,000 and was awarded $450,000, but much of it went to paying attorneys. Despite the lawsuit's resolution, Temkin was relentless, demanding more money and refusing any attempts at compromise. Hershman even offered more cash and a job, but Temkin declined. The two took out mutual restraining orders against one another.

For some people, that would have been the end of the story, but not for Eugene Temkin: he wanted revenge. He began asking people about hiring a hit man until someone who knew of his plotting informed police detectives of the plan. Over the following several months, undercover law enforcement personnel, posing as professional killers for hire, met with Temkin to discuss how to carry out the plot. Temkin wanted the hit man to first force Hershman to pay up and then have him killed.

On July 8, 2010, Temkin met with an undercover agent in Encino, California, and paid him the first installment of a $30,000 fee to carry out the murders. According to the plan, the murders were to be carried out in Santo Domingo, the Dominican Republic, when Hershman was on vacation. Temkin chose the Dominican Republic because "assassination in a third world country is . . . just another day in the park, and then it's clean—it's all over."

Temkin bragged that he knew some local guys there who could "scoop up" the victim and keep him "hog-tied in a basement." Another crew could "scoop up" the victim's wife and children as leverage, and hold them as hostages. After being intimidated by the hit man, Hershman was to wire $5 million to an untraceable bank account. The murder would take place after the money was handed over, though Temkin hadn't figured out exactly how Hershman would "meet his final destiny." The pseudo hit man recommended making the death look like a suicide, to which Temkin responded, "Suicide is a beautiful thing." Another plan was to drop Hershman into the sea 10 miles from shore, giving the victim a chance at survival because, as Temkin told detectives, "[Y]ou know, what doesn't kill you makes

you stronger. Well, I'm just making him stronger." He then said, "Well, let him swim home. It'll be a very, very, very good workout. An extremely good workout."

Temkin provided the undercover agent photographs of the victims, as well as other identifying information. He also gave the undercover agent the information he would need to deposit the money into a bank account Temkin established in his name in Montevideo, Uruguay.

On July 27, 2010, Temkin was indicted on one count of soliciting a crime of violence, one count of attempting to interfere with interstate commerce by threats and violence, and one count of using interstate facilities in the commission of a murder-for-hire. If convicted, he faces a statutory maximum sentence of 50 years in prison.

SOURCES: FBI Los Angeles, "Goleta Man Indicted in Connection with Murder-for-Hire Plot Targeting Bel Air Resident and Others," July 27, 2010, http://losangeles.fbi.gov/pressrel/pressrel10/la072710.htm (accessed November 8, 2010); Chris Meagher, "Goleta Man Charged with Murder-for-Hire Plot, Allegedly Tried to Pay a Hit Man to Extort and Kill Former Business Partner," *Santa Barbara Independent*, July 30, 2010, www.independent.com/news/2010/jul/30/goleta-man-charged-murder-hire-plot/ (accessed November 8, 2010).

Considering its allure, how can crime be prevented or eliminated? It seems logical that if crime is rational and people choose to commit crime after weighing its rewards and benefits and factoring in their needs and abilities, then it can be controlled or eradicated by convincing potential offenders that:

- Crime is a poor choice that will not bring them rewards, but instead lead to hardship and deprivation.
- Crime is not worth the effort. It is easier to work at a legitimate job than to evade police, outwit alarms, and avoid security.
- Crime brings pain that is not easily forgotten. People who experience the pains of punishment will not readily commit more crimes.

The following sections discuss each of these crime reduction or control strategies in some detail.

SITUATIONAL CRIME PREVENTION

Desperate people may contemplate crime, but only the truly irrational would attack a well-defended, inaccessible target and risk strict punishment. Crime prevention can be achieved by reducing the opportunities people have to commit particular crimes, a practice known as **situational crime prevention**. According to this concept, in order to reduce criminal activity, planners must be aware of the characteristics of sites and situations that are at risk to crime; the things that draw or push people toward these sites and situations; what equips potential criminals to take advantage of illegal opportunities offered by these sites and situations; and what constitutes the immediate triggers for criminal actions.[98] Criminal acts will be avoided if (a) potential targets are guarded securely, (b) the means to commit crime are controlled, and (c) potential offenders are carefully monitored.

Situational crime prevention was first popularized in the United States in the early 1970s by Oscar Newman, who coined the term **defensible space**. This term signifies that crime can be prevented or displaced through the use of residential architectural designs that reduce criminal opportunity, such as well-lit housing projects that maximize surveillance.[99] C. Ray Jeffery wrote *Crime Prevention through Environmental Design*, which extended Newman's concepts and applied them to nonresidential areas, such as schools and factories.[100] According to this view, mechanisms such as security systems, deadbolt locks, high-intensity street lighting, and neighborhood watch patrols should reduce criminal opportunity.[101]

In 1992, Ronald Clarke published *Situational Crime Prevention*, which compiled the best-known strategies and tactics to reduce criminal incidents.[102] Criminologists have suggested using a number of situational crime prevention efforts that might reduce crime rates. One approach is not to target a specific crime but to create an environment that can reduce the overall crime rate by limiting the access to tempting targets for a highly motivated offender group (such as high school students).[103]

Targeting Specific Crimes

Situational crime prevention can also involve developing tactics to reduce or eliminate a specific crime problem (such as shoplifting in an urban mall or street-level drug dealing). According to Derek Cornish and Ronald Clarke, situational crime prevention efforts may be divided into five strategies:[104]

- Increase the effort needed to commit crime
- Increase the risks of committing crime
- Reduce the rewards for committing crime
- Reduce provocation/induce guilt or shame for committing crime
- Reduce excuses for committing crime

Increase Efforts   Some of the tactics to increase efforts include target-hardening techniques such as putting unbreakable glass on storefronts, locking gates, and fencing yards. Technological advances can make it more difficult to commit crimes; for example, having an owner's photo on credit cards should reduce the use of stolen cards. The development of new products, such as steering locks on cars, can make it more difficult to commit crimes. Empirical evidence indicates that steering locks have helped reduce car theft in the United States, Britain, and Germany.[105] Installing a locking device on cars that prevents inebriated drivers from starting the vehicle (breath-analyzed ignition interlock device) significantly reduces drunk-driving rates among people with a history of driving while intoxicated.[106] Removing

visibility-blocking signs from store windows, installing brighter lights, and instituting a pay-first policy can help reduce thefts from gas stations and convenience stores.[107]

Another way to increase effort is to reduce opportunities for criminal activity. Many cities have established curfew laws in an effort to limit the opportunity juveniles have to engage in antisocial behavior.[108] However, curfew laws have not met with universal success.[109] So another approach has been to involve kids in after-school programs that take up their time and reduce their opportunity to get in trouble. An example of this type of program is the Doorsteps Neighbourhood Program in Toronto, Ontario, which is designed to help children in high-risk areas complete their schoolwork as well as providing them with playtime that helps improve their literacy and communication skills. Children who are part of this program enter into routines that increase the effort they must make if they want to get involved in after-school crime and nuisance activities.[110]

Reduce Rewards   Target reduction strategies are designed to reduce the value of crime to the potential criminal. These include making car radios removable so they can be kept in the home at night, marking property so that it is more difficult to sell when stolen, and having gender-neutral phone listings to discourage obscene phone calls. Tracking systems, such as those made by the LoJack Corporation, help police locate and return stolen vehicles.

Increase Risk   If criminals believe that committing crime is very risky, only the most foolhardy would attempt to commit criminal acts. Managing crime falls into the hands of people Marcus Felson calls **crime discouragers**.[111] These discouragers can be grouped into three categories: guardians, who monitor targets (such as store security guards); handlers, who monitor potential offenders (such as parole officers and parents); and managers, who monitor places (such as homeowners and doorway attendants). If crime discouragers do their job correctly, the potential criminal will be convinced that the risk of crime outweighs any potential gains.[112]

Crime discouragers have different levels of responsibility, ranging from highly personal involvement, such as the homeowner protecting her house and the parent controlling his children, to the most impersonal general involvement, such as a stranger who stops someone from shoplifting in the mall (Exhibit 4.1).

Research indicates that crime discouragers can have an impact on crime rates. An evaluation of a police initiative in Oakland, California, found that an active working partnership with residents and businesspeople who have a stake in maintaining order in their places of work or residences can reduce levels of drug dealing while at the same time increasing civil behavior. Collective action and cooperation in solving problems were effective in controlling crime, whereas individual action (such as calling 911) seemed to have little effect.[113]

EXHIBIT 4.1

Crime Discouragers

Level of responsibility	Types of Supervisors and Objects of Supervision		
	Guardians (monitoring suitable targets)	Handlers (monitoring likely offenders)	Managers (monitoring amenable places)
Personal (owners, family, friends)	Student keeps eye on own book bag	Parent makes sure child gets home	Homeowner monitors area near home
Assigned (employees with specific assignment)	Store clerk monitors jewelry	Principal sends kids back to school	Doorman protects building
Diffuse (employees with general assignment)	Accountant notes shoplifting	School clerk discourages truancy	Hotel maid impairs trespasser
General (strangers, other citizens)	Bystander inhibits shoplifting	Stranger questions boys at mall	Customer observes parking structure

SOURCE: From "Crime and Place," page 59, edited by John E. Eck and David Weisburd. Copyright 2010 by Lynne Rienner Publishers, Inc. Used with permission by the publisher.

In addition to crime discouragers, it may be possible to raise the risks of committing crime by creating mechanical devices that increase the likelihood that a criminal will be observed and captured. The Policy and Practice in Criminology feature "Reducing Crime through Surveillance" discusses a recent evaluation of such methods in Great Britain and other nations.

Increase Shame/Reduce Provocation   Crime may be reduced or prevented if we can communicate to people the wrongfulness of their behavior and how it is harmful to society. We may tell them to "say no to drugs" or that "users are losers." By making people aware of the shamefulness of their actions we hope to prevent their criminal activities even if chances of detection and punishment are slight.

Some efforts to make people ashamed of their acts are personal and provocative. Recently, a judge in Hudson, Kansas, ordered a man who admitted to molesting an 11-year-old boy to post "A Sex Offender Lives Here" signs on all four sides of his home and "A Sex Offender in this Car" in bold yellow lettering on the sides of his automobile.[114] This order is typical for judges who have ordered people convicted of socially unacceptable crimes to advertise their guilt in the hope that they will be too ashamed to recidivate. "John lists" have also been published to shame men involved in hiring prostitutes.

Other methods of inducing guilt or shame might include such techniques as posting signs or warnings to embarrass potential offenders or creating mechanisms to identify perpetrators and/or publicize their crimes. For example, Ronald Clarke reports how caller ID in New Jersey resulted in significant reductions in the number of obscene phone calls.[115] Megan's Laws require sex offender registration and notification systems. While these systems have been used for more than a decade, there is little evidence that they reduce sex crimes: research shows that sex offender registration does not have a statistically significant effect on the number of rapes reported at the state level.[116]

Some crimes are the result of extreme provocation (e.g., road rage). It might be possible to reduce provocation by creating programs that reduce conflict. Creating an early closing time in local bars might limit assaults that are the result of late night drinking, such as conflicts in pubs at closing time. Posting guards outside of schools at recess might prevent childish taunts from escalating into full-blown brawls. Antibullying programs that have been implemented in schools are another method of reducing provocation.

Remove Excuses   Crime may be reduced by making it difficult for people to excuse their criminal behavior by saying things like "I did not know that was illegal" or "I had no choice." Some municipalities have set up roadside displays that electronically flash cars' speed rate as they drive by, so that when stopped by police, drivers cannot say they did not know how fast they were going. Litter boxes, brightly displayed, can eliminate the claim that "I just did not know where to throw my trash." Reducing or eliminating excuses also makes it physically easy for people to comply with laws and regulations, thereby reducing the likelihood they will choose crime.

Reducing Crime through Surveillance

Brandon Welsh and David Farrington have been using systematic review and meta-analysis to assess the comparative effectiveness of situational crime prevention techniques. Recently, they evaluated the effectiveness of closed-circuit television (CCTV) surveillance cameras and improved street lighting, techniques that are currently being used around the world.

They find that CCTV surveillance cameras serve many functions and are used in both public and private settings. CCTV can deter would-be criminals who fear detection and apprehension. They can also aid police in the detection and apprehension of suspects, aid in the prosecution of alleged offenders, improve police officer safety and compliance with the law (through, for instance, cameras mounted on the dashboard of police cruisers to record police stops, searches, and so on), and aid in the detection and prevention of terrorist activities. Nowhere is the popularity of CCTV more apparent than in Great Britain, where an estimated 4.2 million CCTV cameras, or 1 for every 14 citizens, are in operation. It has been estimated that the average Briton is caught on camera 300 times each day.

After reviewing 41 studies conducted around the world, Welsh and Farrington found that CCTV interventions (a) have a small but significant desirable effect on crime, (b) are most effective in reducing crime in car parks (parking lots), (c) are most effective in reducing vehicle crimes, and (d) are more effective in reducing crime in the United Kingdom than in other countries.

They found that effectiveness was significantly correlated with the degree of coverage of the CCTV cameras, which was greatest in car parks. However, the effect was most pronounced in parking lots that also employed other situational crime prevention interventions, such as improved lighting and security officers.

Notably, Welsh and Farrington found that CCTV schemes in the U.K. showed a sizable (19 percent) and significant desirable effect on crime, whereas those in other countries showed no desirable effect on crime. One reason was that all of the sites that used other interventions alongside CCTV were in England. It is possible that CCTV on its own is not sufficient to influence an offender's decision whether to commit a crime and thus has to be buttressed by other methods, such as security fences or guards.

Another important issue is cultural context. In the U.K., there is a high level of public support for the use of CCTV cameras in public settings to prevent crime. In America and other nations, the public is less accepting of surveillance technology and more apprehensive about its "Big Brother" connotations. Furthermore, in America, resistance to the use of CCTV in public places also takes the form of legal action and constitutional challenges under the U.S. Constitution's Fourth Amendment prohibition against unreasonable searches and seizures. In Sweden, surveillance cameras are highly regulated in public places, and in nearly all instances their use requires a permit from the county administrative board.

In Norway, there is a high degree of political scrutiny of public CCTV schemes run by the police.

It could very well be that the overall poor showing of CCTV schemes in countries other than Britain is due in part to a lack of public support (and maybe even of political support) for these schemes, which in turn may result in reduced program funding, the police assigning lower priority to CCTV, and negative media reactions. Each of these factors could undermine the effectiveness of CCTV schemes. In contrast, the British Home Office, who funded many of the British evaluations, wanted to show that CCTV was effective because it had invested so much money in these schemes.

Welsh and Farrington conclude that CCTV reduces crime in some circumstances. In light of the mixed results, future CCTV schemes should be carefully implemented in different settings and should employ high-quality evaluation designs with long follow-up periods.

CRITICAL THINKING

Would you be willing to have a surveillance camera set up in your home or dorm in order to prevent crime, knowing that your every move was being watched and recorded?

SOURCE: Brandon C. Welsh and David P. Farrington, *Making Public Places Safer: Surveillance and Crime Prevention* (New York: Oxford University Press, 2008).

Situational Crime Prevention: Costs and Benefits   Some attempts at situational crime prevention have proven highly successful while others have not met their goals. However, it is now apparent that the approach brings with it certain nontransparent or hidden costs and benefits that can either increase effectiveness or undermine success. Before the overall success of this approach can be evaluated, these costs and benefits must be considered. Among the hidden benefits of situational crime control efforts are:

■ *Diffusion.* Sometimes efforts to prevent one crime help prevent another; in other instances, crime control efforts in one locale reduce crime in another area.[117] This effect is referred to as **diffusion of benefits**. Diffusion may be produced by two independent effects. Crime control efforts may deter criminals by causing them to fear apprehension. Video cameras set up in a mall to reduce shoplifting can also reduce property damage because would-be vandals fear they will be caught on camera. One recent police program targeting drugs in areas of Jersey City, New Jersey, also reduced public morals crimes because potential offenders were aware of increased police patrols.[118]

- *Discouragement.* Sometimes crime control efforts targeting a particular locale help reduce crime in surrounding areas and populations; this is referred to as **discouragement**. In her study of the effects of the SMART program (a drug enforcement program in Oakland, California, that enforces municipal codes and nuisance abatement laws), criminologist Lorraine Green found that not only did drug dealing decrease in targeted areas, but improvement was found in adjacent areas as well. She suggests that the program most likely discouraged buyers and sellers who saw familiar hangouts closed. This sign that drug dealing would not be tolerated probably decreased the total number of people involved in drug activity even though they did not operate in the targeted areas.[119] Another example of this effect can be found in evaluations of the LoJack auto protection system. LoJack uses a hidden radio transmitter to track stolen cars. As the number of LoJack installations rises, police notice that the sale of stolen auto parts declines. It appears that people in the illegal auto parts business (that is, chop shops) close down because they fear that the stolen cars they buy might contain LoJack.[120] A device designed to protect cars from theft also has the benefit of disrupting the sale of stolen car parts.

While there are hidden benefits to situational crime prevention, there may also be costs that limit their effectiveness:

- *Displacement.* A program that seems successful because it helps lower crime rates at specific locations or neighborhoods may simply be redirecting offenders to alternative targets; this is known as **displacement**, as crime is not prevented but deflected or displaced.[121] Beefed-up police patrols in one area may shift crimes to a more vulnerable neighborhood.[122]
- *Extinction.* Sometimes crime reduction programs may produce a short-term positive effect, but benefits dissipate as criminals adjust to new conditions. They learn to dismantle alarms or avoid patrols; they may try new offenses they had previously avoided. And elimination of one crime may encourage commission of another: if every residence in a neighborhood has a foolproof burglar alarm system, motivated offenders may be forced to turn to armed robbery, a riskier and more violent crime.
- *Encouragement.* Crime reduction programs may boomerang and increase rather than decrease the potentiality for crime. For example, some situational efforts rely on increasing the risk of crime by installing street lighting, assuming that rational criminals will avoid areas where their criminal activities are more visible. However, as Brandon Welsh and David Farrington

note, in some cases street lighting improvement efforts can backfire and increase opportunities for crime. Well-lighted areas may bring a greater number of potential victims and potential offenders into the same physical space. The increased visibility may allow potential offenders to make better judgments of target vulnerability and attractiveness (e.g., they can spot people with jewelry and other valuables). Lighting may make an area more attractive and increase social activity; increasing the number of unoccupied homes makes them available for burglary. Increased illumination may make it easier for offenders to commit crimes and to escape.[123]

Before the effectiveness of situational crime prevention can be accepted, these hidden costs and benefits must be weighed and balanced.

GENERAL DETERRENCE

According to the rational choice view, motivated, rational people will violate the law if left free and unrestricted. **General deterrence** theory holds that crime rates are influenced and controlled by the threat and/or application of criminal punishment. If people fear being apprehended and punished, they will not risk breaking the law. An inverse relationship should then exist between crime rates and the fear of legal sanctions. If, for example, the punishment for a crime is increased and the effectiveness and efficiency of the criminal justice system are improved, then the number of people willing to risk committing crime should decline.

The severity, certainty, and speed of punishment are interrelated. If a particular crime—say, robbery—is punished severely, but few robbers are ever caught or punished, the severity of punishment for robbery will probably not deter people from robbing. However, if the certainty of apprehension and conviction is increased by modern technology, more efficient police work, or some other factor, then even minor punishment might deter the potential robber.

Deterrence theorists tend to believe that the certainty of punishment seems to have a greater impact than its severity or speed. In other words, people will more likely be deterred from crime if they believe that they will get caught; what happens to them after apprehension seems to have less impact.[124] Nonetheless, all three elements of the deterrence equation are important, and it would be a mistake to emphasize one at the expense of the others. For example, if all resources were given to police agencies to increase the probability of arrest, crime rates might increase because there were insufficient funds for swift prosecution and effective correction.[125]

AP Images/*The Minnesota Daily*/Lauren Desteno

Police officers in riot gear take control of State Street in downtown Madison, Wisconsin, after the city's annual Halloween bash. According to the theory of general deterrence, aggressive police action will reduce the likelihood that would-be criminals (in this case, rioters) would dare to violate the law.

Perception and Deterrence

According to deterrence theory, not only does the actual chance of punishment influence criminality, so too does the *perception of punishment*.[126] A central theme of deterrence theory is that people who perceive they will be punished for crimes in the future will avoid doing those crimes in the present.[127] The *actual likelihood* of being arrested or imprisoned will have little effect on crime rates if criminals believe that they have only a small chance of suffering apprehension and punishment.[128]

To prove the association between perception and deterrence empirically, Canadian criminologists Etienne Blais and Jean-Luc Bacher conducted an interesting experiment: they had insurance companies send a written threat to a random sample of insured persons reminding them of the punishment for insurance fraud, and then compared the claims they filed with a control group of people who did not get the threatening letter. Blais and Bacher found that those who got the letter were less likely to pad their claims than were those in the control group.[129] Clearly the written warning that offenders will be caught and punished for insurance fraud deterred illegal activity.

Certainty of Punishment and Deterrence

According to **deterrence theory**, if the probability of arrest, conviction, and sanctioning increases, crime rates should decline. As the certainty of punishment increases, even

the most motivated criminal may desist because the risks of crime outweigh its rewards.[130] If people believe that their criminal transgressions will result in apprehension and punishment, then only the truly irrational will commit crime.[131] Considering this association, it is common for crime control efforts to be aimed at convincing rational criminals to avoid the risk of crime. Take for instance Project Safe Neighborhoods, which was the centerpiece of the government's crime policy in President George W. Bush's first term. Safe Neighborhoods relied on media campaigns aimed at convincing people that carrying handguns was a serious crime for which they would be caught, prosecuted, and severely punished with mandatory prison sentences. Evaluations suggest that the program worked and gun crimes declined after the program was instituted.[132]

The Tipping Point Unfortunately for deterrence theory, punishment is not very certain. Only 10 percent of all serious offenses result in apprehension (half go unreported, and police make arrests in about 20 percent of reported crimes). Police routinely do not arrest suspects in personal disputes even when they lead to violence.[133] As apprehended offenders are processed through all the stages of the criminal justice system, the odds of their receiving serious punishment diminish. As a result, some offenders believe they will not be severely punished for their acts and consequently have little regard for the law's deterrent power.

Criminologists maintain that if the certainty of punishment could be increased to a critical level, the so-called tipping point, then the deterrent effect would kick in and crime rates would decline.[134] Crime persists because we have not reached the tipping point, and most criminals believe that (a) there is only a small chance they will be arrested for committing a particular crime, (b) police officers are sometimes reluctant to make arrests even when they are aware of crime, and (c) even if apprehended there is a good chance of either getting off totally or receiving a lenient punishment such as probation.[135]

One way of increasing the tipping point may be to add police officers. As the number of active, aggressive, crime-fighting cops increases, arrests and convictions should likewise increase, and would-be criminals will be convinced that the risk of apprehension outweighs the benefits they can gain from crime.[136]

While adding cops seems a logical way of reducing crime, this assumption has been questioned ever since a famous experiment was conducted in the early 1970s by the Kansas City, Missouri, Police Department.[137] To evaluate the effectiveness of police patrols, 15 independent Kansas City police beats or districts were divided into three groups. The first (active) retained a normal police patrol; the second (proactive) was supplied with two to three times the normal number of patrol forces; the third (reactive) eliminated its preventive patrol entirely, and police officers responded only when summoned by citizens to the scene of a crime.

Surprisingly, these variations in patrol techniques had little effect on the crime patterns. Variations in police patrol techniques also appeared to have little effect on citizens' attitudes toward the police, their satisfaction with police, or their fear of future criminal behavior. It is possible that as people traveled around the city they noticed a large number of police officers in one area and relatively few in another; the two effects may have cancelled each other out!

While subsequent research using sophisticated methodological tools found evidence that increased police levels does over time reduce the level of criminal activity, it has been hard to shake the influence of the Kansas City study.[138] It had convinced criminologists that the mere presence of patrol officers on the street did not have a deterrent effect. Just recently, in fact, John Worrall and Tomislav Kovandzic found that cities that increased the size of their patrol force were the ones most likely to experience a reduction in crime. Perhaps the findings of the Kansas City study had created a "rush to judgment"?[139]

One reason for this disconnect may be found in the manner in which police officers approach their job. What happens if police officers engage in aggressive, focused crime-fighting initiatives, targeting specific crimes such as murder or robbery? Would such activities result in more arrests and a greater deterrent effect?[140] To answer this question, some police departments have instituted **crackdowns**—sudden changes in police activity designed to increase the communicated threat or actual certainty of punishment. For example, a police task force might target street-level narcotics dealers by using undercover agents and surveillance cameras in known drug-dealing locales. Crackdown efforts have met with mixed reviews.[141] In one well-known study, Lawrence Sherman found that while crackdowns initially deterred crime, crime rates returned to earlier levels once the crackdown ended.[142] Other research efforts have also found that while at first successful as a crime suppression technique, the initial effect of the crackdown soon wore off after high-intensity police activity ended.[143]

Although these results are troubling, there is some evidence that when police combine crackdowns with the use of aggressive problem-solving and community improvement techniques, such as increasing lighting and cleaning vacant lots, crackdowns may be successful in reducing some forms of crime.[144] When the Dallas Police Department established a policy of aggressively pursuing truancy and curfew enforcement, they found that the effort actually lowered rates of gang violence.[145] A month-long crackdown and cleanup initiative in Richmond, Virginia, in seven city neighborhoods found that crime rates declined by 92 percent; the effects persisted up to six months after the crackdown ended, and no displacement was observed.[146] Police seem to have more luck deterring crime when they use more focused approaches, such as aggressive problem-solving and community improvement techniques.[147] Merely saturating an area with police may not deter crime, but focusing efforts on a particular problem area has a deterrent effect.

Severity of Punishment and Deterrence

According to general deterrence theory, as the severity of punishment increases, crime rates should decrease. Does this equation hold water? The evidence is decidedly mixed. While some studies have found that increasing sanction levels can control common criminal behaviors, others have not achieved a positive result.[148]

Take the case of enhancing punishment: in order to control handguns, a state might add five years to a sentence if a handgun was used during the crime. However, it is often difficult to determine if such measures actually work. When Daniel Kessler and Steven Levitt evaluated the deterrent effect of California's sentencing enhancement act, they found that it did in fact lower crime rates.[149] However, gun crimes went down in other states that did not enhance or increase their sentences![150] What appears to be a deterrent effect may be the result of some other factor, such as an improved economy.

It stands to reason that if severity of punishment can deter crime, then fear of the death penalty, the ultimate legal deterrent, should significantly reduce murder rates. Because no one denies its emotional impact, failure of the death penalty to deter violent crime would jeopardize the validity of the entire deterrence concept. Because this topic is so important, it is featured in The Criminological Enterprise.

CONNECTIONS

Even if capital punishment proves to be a deterrent, many experts still question its morality, fairness, and legality. Chapters 14 and 16 provide further discussion that can help you decide whether the death penalty is an appropriate response to murder.

Shame and Humiliation   Fear of shame and embarrassment can be a powerful deterrent to crime. Those who fear being rejected by family and peers are reluctant to engage in deviant behavior.[151] These factors manifest themselves in two

The Criminological Enterprise
Does Capital Punishment Deter Murder?

According to deterrence theory, the death penalty—the ultimate deterrent—should deter murder—the ultimate crime. Most Americans approve of the death penalty, including, as Norma Wilcox and Tracey Steele found, convicted criminals who are currently behind bars. But is the public's approval warranted? Does the death penalty actually deter murder?

Empirical research on the association between capital punishment and murder can be divided into three types: immediate impact studies, comparative research, and time-series analysis.

Immediate Impact

If capital punishment is a deterrent, the reasoning goes, then its impact should be greatest after a well-publicized execution. Robert Dann began testing this assumption in 1935 when he chose five highly publicized executions of convicted murderers in different years and determined the number of homicides in the 60 days before and after each execution. Each 120-day period had approximately the same number of homicides, as well as the same number of days on which homicides occurred. Dann's study revealed that an average of 4.4 more homicides occurred during the 60 days following an execution than during those preceding it, suggesting that the overall impact of executions might actually be an increase in the incidence of homicide. Seventy years later when Lisa Stolzenberg and Stewart D'Alessio examined the effect of the death penalty on the murder rate in Houston, Texas, they also found that even when executions were highly publicized in the local press, they still had little influence on the murder rate.

Comparative Research

Another type of research compares the murder rates in jurisdictions that have abolished the death penalty with the rates of those that employ the death penalty. Studies using this approach have found little difference in the murder rates of adjacent states, regardless of their use of the death penalty; capital punishment did not appear to influence the reported rate of homicide. Research conducted in 14 nations around the world found little evidence that countries with a death penalty have lower violence rates than those without; homicide rates actually decline after capital punishment is abolished, a direct contradiction to its supposed deterrent effect.

Time-Series Studies

Time-series studies look at the long-term association between capital sentencing and murder. If capital punishment is a deterrent, then periods that have an upswing in executions should also experience a downturn in violent crime and murder. Most research efforts have failed to show such a relationship. One test of the deterrent effect of the death penalty in Texas by Jon Sorenson and his colleagues found no association between the frequency of execution and murder rates during the years 1984 to 1997. Matt Breverlin used data gathered from 1974 to 2001 in all 50 states to demonstrate that the death penalty for juveniles has no statistically significant deterrent effect. His conclusion is that state-level economic conditions, population density, and incarceration rates have a much greater impact on the juvenile murder rate than the deterrent impact of the death penalty. These findings seem to indicate that the threat and/or reality of

execution has relatively little influence on murder rates. Although it is still uncertain why the threat of capital punishment fails as a deterrent, the cause may lie in the nature of homicide itself. Murder is often an expressive "crime of passion" involving people who know each other and who may be under the influence of drugs and alcohol. Those who choose to take a life may be less influenced by the threat of punishment, even death, than those who commit crime for economic gain.

Rethinking the Deterrent Effect of Capital Punishment

In contrast to these results, some recent studies have concluded that executing criminals may, in fact, bring the murder rate down. Those who still maintain that an association exists between capital punishment and murder rate believe that the relationship has been masked or obscured by faulty research methods. Newer studies, using sophisticated data analysis, have been able to uncover a more significant association. For example, criminologist Steven Stack has conducted a number of research studies that show that the immediate impact of a well-publicized execution can lower the murder rate during the following month. James Yunker, using a national data set, has found evidence that there is a deterrent effect of capital punishment now that the pace of executions has accelerated. Economists Hashem Dezhbakhsh, Paul H. Rubin, and Joanna M. Shepherd performed an advanced statistical analysis on county-level homicide data in order to calculate the effect of each execution on the number of homicides that would otherwise have occurred. Using a

---

ways: (1) personal shame over violating the law and (2) the fear of public humiliation if the deviant behavior becomes public knowledge. People who say that their involvement in crime would cause them to feel ashamed are less likely to offend than people who deny fears of embarrassment.[152]

People who are afraid that significant others—such as parents, peers, neighbors, and teachers—will disapprove

of their behavior are less likely to commit crime.[153] While shame can be a powerful deterrent, offenders also seem to be influenced by forgiveness and acceptance. They are less likely to repeat their criminal activity if victims are willing to grant them forgiveness.[154]

The fear of exposure and consequent shaming may vary according to the cohesiveness of community structure and variety of models (for example, the effect of an execution conducted today on reducing homicides in five years, and so on), they found that each execution leads to an average of 18 fewer murders. In another study, Shepherd claims that the reason some research has not found a deterrent effect is because capital punishment may have differing influence depending on where and how it is used. Calculating each state's murder rate separately and lumping all state data together masks the deterrent effect of the death penalty. She found that the use of capital punishment deterred murder in states that conducted more executions than the norm. In contrast, in states that conducted relatively few executions (one or two per year), the average execution either increased the murder rate or had no effect. Shepherd concludes that each execution has two opposing effects. It can contribute to a climate of brutal violence (i.e., the brutalization effect) that tells people it is okay to kill in revenge. It can also act as a deterrent and show potential criminals that the state is willing to use the ultimate penalty to punish crimes. However, only if a state routinely uses executions does the deterrent effect take place; only then do potential criminals become convinced that the state is serious about the punishment, so that the criminals start to reduce their criminal activity.

These efforts contradict findings that capital punishment fails as a deterrent. So on the one hand, the most recent research indicates that the death penalty is being used more frequently, it is possible that the tipping point has been reached, and it is now an effective deterrent measure. On the other hand, capital punishment still carries significant baggage: since 1976,

more than 100 people have been wrongfully convicted and sentenced to death in the United States. And according to research sponsored by the Pew Foundation, a majority of death penalty convictions have been overturned, many due to "serious, reversible error," including egregiously incompetent defense counsel, suppression of exculpatory evidence, false confessions, racial manipulation of the jury, "snitch" and accomplice testimony, and faulty jury instructions.

After years of study, the death penalty remains a topic of considerable criminological debate.

CRITICAL THINKING

Even if effective, there is no question the death penalty can cause problems. For example, when Geoffrey Rapp studied the effect of the death penalty on the safety of police officers, he found that the introduction of capital punishment actually created an extremely dangerous environment for law enforcement officers. Because the death penalty does not have a deterrent effect, criminals are more likely to kill police officers when the death penalty is in place. Tragically, the death penalty may lull officers into a false sense of security, causing them to let down their guard—killing fewer citizens but getting killed more often themselves. Given Rapp's findings, should we still maintain the death penalty?

SOURCES: Jeffrey Fagan, "Death and Deterrence Redux: Science, Law and Causal Reasoning on Capital Punishment," *Ohio State Journal of Criminal Law* 4 (2006): 255–320; Pew Foundation, Death Penalty, www.pewtrusts.

org/our_work_detail.aspx?id=322 (accessed November 9, 2010); Joanna Shepherd, "Deterrence versus Brutalization: Capital Punishment's Differing Impacts Among States," *Michigan Law Review* 104 (2005): 203–253; Matt Beverlin, "A Study of the Deterrence Effect of the Juvenile Death Penalty," paper presented at the Southern Political Science Association annual meeting, New Orleans, 2005, 1–34; John Donohue and Justin Wolfers, "Uses and Abuses of Empirical Evidence in the Death Penalty Debate," *Stanford Law Review* 58 (2005): 791–845; Lisa Stolzenberg and Stewart D'Alessio, "Capital Punishment, Execution Publicity, and Murder in Houston, Texas," *Journal of Criminal Law and Criminology* 94 (2004): 351–380; Geoffrey Rapp, "The Economics of Shootouts: Does the Passage of Capital Punishment Laws Protect or Endanger Police Officers?" *Albany Law Review* 65 (2002): 1,051–1,084; Robert Dann, "The Deterrent Effect of Capital Punishment," *Friends Social Service Series 29* (1935); Thorsten Sellin, *The Death Penalty* (Philadelphia: American Law Institute, 1959); Walter Reckless, "Use of the Death Penalty," *Crime and Delinquency* 15 (1969): 43–51; Dane Archer, Rosemary Gartner, and Marc Beittel, "Homicide and the Death Penalty: A Cross-National Test of a Deterrence Hypothesis," *Journal of Criminal Law and Criminology* 74 (1983): 991–1,014; Jon Sorenson, Robert Wrinkle, Victoria Brewer, and James Marquart, "Capital Punishment and Deterrence: Examining the Effect of Executions on Murder in Texas," *Crime and Delinquency* 45 (1999): 481–931; Norma Wilcox and Tracey Steele, "Just the Facts: A Descriptive Analysis of Inmate Attitudes Toward Capital Punishment," *Prison Journal* 83 (2003): 464–483; Zhiqiang Liu, "Capital Punishment and the Deterrence Hypothesis: Some New Insights and Empirical Evidence," *Eastern Economic Journal* (Spring 2004); Steven Stack, "The Effect of Well-Publicized Executions on Homicide in California," *Journal of Crime and Justice* 21 (1998): 1–12; James Yunker, "A New Statistical Analysis of Capital Punishment Incorporating U.S. Postmoratorium Data," *Social Science Quarterly* 82 (2001): 297–312; Hashem Dezhbakhsh, Paul H. Rubin, and Joanna M. Shepherd, "Does Capital Punishment Have a Deterrent Effect? New Evidence from Postmoratorium Panel Data," *American Law and Economics Review* 5 (2003): 344–376.

---

the type of crime. **Informal sanctions** may be most effective in highly unified areas where everyone knows one another and the crime cannot be hidden from public view. The threat of informal sanctions seems to have the greatest influence on instrumental crimes, which involve planning, and not on impulsive or expressive criminal behaviors or those associated with substance abuse.[155]

Speed (Celerity) of Punishment and Deterrence

The third leg of Beccaria's equation involves the celerity or speed of punishment: the faster punishment is applied and the more closely it is linked to the crime, the more likely it will serve as a deterrent.[156] The deterrent effect of the law

Year of execution	Number executed	Average elapsed time in months from sentence to execution for all inmates
2000	85	137
2001	66	142
2002	71	127
2003	65	131
2004	59	132
2005	60	147
2006	53	145

SOURCE: Bureau of Justice Statistics, *Capital Punishment, 2006—Statistical Tables,* bjs.ojp.usdoj.gov/content/pub/html/cp/2006/cp06st.pdf (accessed November 8, 2010).

may be neutralized if there is a significant lag between apprehension and punishment. In the American justice system, court delays brought by numerous evidentiary hearings and requests for additional trial preparation time are common trial tactics. As a result, the criminal process can be delayed to a point where the connection between crime and punishment is broken. Take for instance how the death penalty is employed. As Table 4.1 shows, more than 10 years typically elapse between the time a criminal is convicted for murder and his or her execution. During that period, many death row inmates have repented, matured, and turned their lives around, only to be taken out and executed. Delay in its application may mitigate or neutralize the potential deterrent effect of capital punishment.

The threat of punishment may also be neutralized by the belief that even if caught criminals can avoid severe punishment through plea negotiations. The fact that killers can avoid the death penalty by bargaining for a life sentence may also undermine the deterrent effect of the law.[157]

Research indicates that, in general, the deterrence and retributive value of a given criminal sanction steadily decreases as the lag between crime and punishment lengthens. Because criminals discount punishments that lag behind their crimes, how and when punishment is applied can alter its effect. A criminal who is apprehended, tried, and convicted soon after committing a crime will be more deeply affected than one who experiences a significant lag between crime and punishment.[158] Criminologist Raymond Paternoster found that adolescents, a group responsible for a disproportionate amount of crime, may be well aware that the juvenile court is generally lenient about imposing meaningful sanctions on even the most serious juvenile offenders.[159] Even those accused of murder are often convicted of lesser offenses and spend relatively short amounts of time behind bars.[160] Not surprisingly, the more experience a kid has with the juvenile justice system, the less deterrent effect it has: crime-prone youth, ones

who have a long history of criminality, know that crimes provide immediate gratification, whereas the threat of punishment is far in the future.[161]

Restrictive/Partial Deterrence   Deterrence is rarely an all or nothing proposition: some crimes are more deterrable than others; some criminals are more deterrable. Deterrence measures may not eliminate crime but reduce or restrict its occurrence. Deterrence measures may not totally convince criminals that crime does not pay, but might help increase their sensitivity to the risks involved in crime and thereby alter or shape their decision making. For example, criminologist Bruce Jacobs has identified the concept of restrictive deterrence, a phenomenon that occurs when deterrence measures convince would-be criminals that the risk of committing a particular crime is just too great. Potential criminals then find ways to adapt to this perceived threat:

1. The offender reduces the number of crimes he or she commits during a particular period of time.
2. The offender commits less-serious crimes, assuming that even if he or she is apprehended, the punishment will not be as severe for a more minor infraction (thus, an offender shoplifts a $100 pair of jeans instead of robbing a convenience store for the same monetary reward).
3. The offender takes actions to reduce the chance that he or she will be caught and to increase the chance that the contemplated offense will be undertaken without risk of detection (e.g., wearing a disguise to avoid being identified by the victim).
4. Recognizing danger, the offender commits the same crime at a different place or time.[162]

Analyzing General Deterrence

Some experts believe that the purpose of the law and justice system is to create a "threat system."[163] That is, the threat of legal punishment should, on the face of it, deter lawbreakers through fear. Nonetheless, as we have already discussed, the relationship between crime rates and deterrent measures is far less clear than choice theorists might expect. Despite efforts to punish criminals and make them fear crime, there is little evidence that the fear of apprehension and punishment alone can reduce crime rates. How can this discrepancy be explained?

Rationality   Deterrence theory assumes a rational offender who weighs the costs and benefits of a criminal act before deciding on a course of action. In many instances, criminals are desperate people who suffer from personality disorders that impair their judgment and render them incapable of making truly rational decisions.[164] It is doubtful that any deterrent measure could have influenced an irrational Jared Loughner when he attempted to assassinate U.S. Representative Gabrielle Giffords on January 8, 2011. They may be impulsive and imprudent rather than reasoning and calculating.

Compulsion   We know that a relatively small group of chronic offenders commits a significant percentage of all serious crimes. Some psychologists believe this select group suffers from an innate or inherited emotional state that renders them both incapable of fearing punishment and less likely to appreciate the consequences of crime.[165] Research shows that people who are easily aroused sexually also say that they will be more likely to act in a sexually aggressive fashion and not consider the legal consequences of their actions.[166] Their heightened emotional state negates the deterrent effect of the law.

Need   Many offenders are members of what is referred to as the underclass—people cut off from society, lacking the education and skills they need to be in demand in the modern economy.[167] Such desperate people may not be deterred from crime by fear of punishment because, in reality, they perceive few other options for success. Among poor, high-risk groups, such as teens living in economically depressed neighborhoods, the threat of formal sanctions is irrelevant.[168] Young people in these areas have less to lose because their opportunities are few, and they have little attachment to social institutions such as school or family. In their environment, they see many people who appear relatively well off (the neighborhood drug dealer) committing crimes without getting caught or punished.[169]

Greed   Some may be immune to deterrent effects because they believe the profits from crime are worth the risk of punishment; it may be their only significant chance for gain and profit. When criminologists Alex Piquero and George Rengert studied active burglars, they found that the lure of criminal profits outweighed their fears of capture and subsequent punishment. Perceived risk of punishment may deter some potential and active criminal offenders, but only if they doubt that they can make a "big score" from committing a crime.[170]

Greed may encourage some law violators to overestimate the rewards of crime that in reality are often quite meager. When Steven Levitt and Sudhir Alladi Venkatesh studied the financial rewards of being in a drug gang, they found that despite enormous risks to health, life, and freedom, average gang members earned only slightly more than what they could in the legitimate labor market (about $6 to $11 per hour).[171] Why then did they stay in the gang? Members believed that there was a strong potential for future riches if they stayed in the drug business and earned a "management" position (i.e., gang leaders earned a lot more). Deterrence is neutralized because the gang boys' greed causes them to overestimate the potential for future criminal gain versus the probability of apprehension and punishment.[172]

Some People Are More Deterrable than Others   Not every crime can be discouraged, nor is every criminal deterrable. Research shows that deterrent measures may have greater impact on some people and a lesser effect on others.[173] Some people may be suffering from personality disorders and mental infirmity, which make them immune to the deterrent power of the law.[174] However, for some crimes, where a small group of chronic offenders (for example, dealers in illegal firearms) are responsible for a great majority of the criminal activity, a targeted strategy that directs a surge of law enforcement activity against repeat offenders may help reduce crime even in the most disorganized neighborhoods.[175]

It also appears that it is easier to deter offenders from some crimes than from others. A recent (2009) meta-analysis of the existing literature shows that the most significant deterrent effects can be achieved on minor petty criminals, whereas more serious offenders such as murderers are harder to discourage.[176] Because criminals may more readily deterred from committing some crimes—such as tax noncompliance, speeding, and illegal parking—future research should be directed at identifying and targeting these preventable offenses.[177]

SPECIFIC DETERRENCE

The theory of **specific deterrence** (also called special or particular deterrence) holds that after experiencing criminal sanctions that are swift, sure, and powerful, known criminals will never dare repeat their criminal acts. While general deterrence relies on the perception of future punishments, specific deterrence relies on its application:

- The drunk driver whose sentence is a substantial fine and a week in the county jail should be convinced that the price to be paid for drinking and driving is too great to consider future violations.
- The burglar who spends five years in a tough maximum security prison will find his enthusiasm for theft dampened.
- The tax cheat who is assessed triple damages will think twice before filing a false return.

In principle, punishment works if a connection can be established between the planned action and memories of its consequence; if these recollections are adequately intense, the action will be unlikely to occur again.[178] Yet, the connection between experiencing punishment and fearing future punishment is not always as strong as expected.[179]

At first glance, specific deterrence does not seem to work because a majority of known criminals are not deterred by their punishment. Arrest and punishment seem to have little effect on experienced criminals and may even increase the likelihood that first-time offenders will commit new crimes.[180] A sentence to a juvenile justice facility does little to deter a persistent delinquent from becoming an adult criminal.[181] Most prison inmates had prior records of arrest and conviction before their current offenses.[182] About two-thirds of all convicted felons are rearrested within three years of their release from prison, and those who have been punished in the past are the most likely to recidivate.[183] Incarceration may sometimes slow down or delay recidivism in the short term, but the overall probability of rearrest does not change following incarceration.[184]

According to the theory of specific deterrence, the harsher the punishment, the less likely the chances of recidivism. But research shows that this is not always the case. Offenders sentenced to prison do not have lower rates of recidivism than those receiving more lenient community sentences for similar crimes. White-collar offenders who receive prison sentences are as likely to recidivate as those who receive community-based sanctions.[185]

In some instances, rather than reducing the frequency of crime, severe punishments may actually increase reoffending rates.[186] Some states are now employing high-security "supermax" prisons that use bare minimum treatment and 23-hours-a-day lockdown. Certainly such a harsh regimen should deter future criminality. But a recent study in the state of Washington showed that upon release supermax prisoners had significantly higher felony recidivism rates when compared to a matched sample of traditional inmates.[187] There are a number of factors that might help explain why severe punishments promote rather than restrict criminality:

- Offenders may believe they have learned from their experiences, and now know how to beat the system and get away with crime.[188]
- Severely punished offenders may represent the "worst of the worst," who will offend again no matter what punishments they experience.[189]
- Punishment may bring defiance rather than deterrence. People who are harshly treated may want to show that they cannot be broken by the system. Punishment might be perceived to be capricious, unjust, or unfair, which causes sanctioned offenders to commit additional crimes as a way to lash out and retaliate.
- Harsh treatment labels and stigmatizes offenders, locking them into a criminal career.
- Criminals who are punished may also believe that the likelihood of getting caught twice for the same type of crime is remote: "Lightning never strikes twice in the same spot," they may reason; no one is that unlucky.[190]

The Domestic Violence Studies

While these results are not encouraging, there are research studies that show that arrest and conviction may under some circumstances lower the frequency of reoffending, a finding that supports specific deterrence.[191] The most famous of these involve arrest and punishment for domestic violence.

Yet, they also show that achieving specific deterrent effects may sometimes be elusive. In the classic study, Lawrence Sherman and Richard Berk had police officers in Minneapolis, Minnesota, randomly assign one of three outcomes to domestic assault cases they encountered on their beats:[192]

- Advice and mediation only
- Remove the assailant from the home for a period of eight hours
- Formally arrest the assailant

According to deterrence theory, arrest should have a greater impact than advice and mediation, and in this case it did. Sherman and Berk found that when police took formal action (arrest), the chance of recidivism was substantially less than with less punitive measures, such as warning offenders or ordering offenders out of the house for a cooling-off period. A six-month follow-up found that only 10 percent of those who were arrested repeated their violent behavior, while 19 percent of those advised and 24 percent of those sent away repeated their offenses. Sherman and Berk concluded that a formal arrest was the most effective means of controlling domestic violence, regardless of what happened to the offender in court, and the specific deterrent effect of arrest produced positive long-term outcomes.

The Minneapolis experiment deeply affected police operations around the nation. Atlanta, Chicago, Dallas, Denver, Detroit, New York, Miami, San Francisco, and Seattle, among other large cities, adopted policies encouraging arrests in domestic violence cases. A number of states adopted legislation mandating that police either take formal action in domestic abuse cases or explain in writing their failure to act. Nonetheless, replicating the Minneapolis experiment in five other locales—including Omaha, Nebraska, and Charlotte, North Carolina—failed to duplicate the original results.[193] In these locales, formal arrest was not a greater deterrent to domestic abuse than warning or advising the assailant.

More recent efforts to link punishment and deterrence in domestic violence cases have also produced inconclusive results. One recent examination conducted by Andrew Klein and Terri Tobin of the abuse and criminal careers of 342 men arraigned in the Quincy, Massachusetts, District Court found that batterers were undeterred by arrest, prosecution, probation supervision, incarceration, and treatment. Although only a minority of the men in the study reabused (32 percent) or were arrested for any crime (43 percent) within a year of their first involvement with the justice system, over the next decade, the majority (60 percent) were involved in a second incident and almost three-fourths were rearrested for a domestic abuse or nondomestic abuse crime. The implications of the domestic violence research is that even if punishment can produce a short-term specific deterrent effect, it fails to produce longer-term behavior change.[194]

INCAPACITATION

It stands to reason that if more criminals are sent to prison, the crime rate should go down. Because most people age out of crime, the duration of a criminal career is limited. Placing offenders behind bars during their prime crime years should lessen their lifetime opportunity to commit crime. The shorter the span of opportunity, the fewer offenses they can commit during their lives; hence crime is reduced. This theory, known as the **incapacitation effect**, seems logical, but does it work? The most recent data indicate that nationwide more than 1.6 million are in prison and that the inmate population has nearly tripled in 30 years; another 700,000 people are in local jails. Because the number of American adults is about 230 million, this means that one in every 100 adults is behind bars.[195] Advocates of incapacitation suggest that this growth in the prison/jail population is directly responsible for the decade-long decline in the crime rate: by putting dangerous felons under lock and key for longer periods of time, the opportunity they have to commit crime is significantly reduced and so too is the crime rate.

Belief that a strict incarceration policy can shape criminal choice and reduce crime rates has encouraged states to adopt tough sentencing laws such as the "three strikes and you're out" policy. This sentencing model mandates that people convicted of three felony offenses serve a mandatory life term without parole. Many states already employ habitual offender laws that provide long (or life) sentences for repeat offenders. Three strikes supporters credit the law for a significant drop in California's crime rate, among the sharpest decline in any state. At least 2 million fewer criminal incidents have occurred, including 6,700 fewer homicides, since the state's three strikes law took effect.[196]

Does Incarceration Control Crime?

The fact that crime rates have dropped while the prison population has boomed supports incapacitation as an effective crime control policy. This assumption seems logical considering how much crime chronic offenders commit each year and the fact that criminal opportunities are ended once they are behind bars. While it is difficult to measure precisely, there is at least some evidence that crime rates and incarceration rates are interrelated.[197] Economist Steven Levitt concludes that each person put behind bars results in a decrease of 15 serious crimes per year. He argues that the social benefits associated with crime reduction equal or exceed the social and financial costs of incarceration.[198]

CONNECTIONS

Chapter 2 discussed the factors that control crime rates. What appears to be an incapacitation effect may actually reflect the effect of some other legal phenomena and not the incarceration of so many criminals. If, for example, the crime rate drops as more people are sent to prison, it would appear that incapacitation works. However, crime rates may really be dropping because potential criminals now fear punishment and are being deterred from crime. What appears to be an incapacitation effect may actually be an effect of general deterrence. Similarly, people may be willing to build new prisons because the economy is robust. If the crime rate drops, it may be because of economic effects and not because of prison construction.

AP Images/Robert E. Klein

Paul J. Leahy, 39, of East Bridgewater, Massachusetts, (left) stands with his lawyer, Frank H. Spillane of Easton, Massachusetts, during Leahy's arraignment in the Brockton District Court on July 18, 2002. Leahy was arraigned on charges including murder, kidnapping, and armed robbery in the stabbing death of Alexandra Zapp, 30, of Newport, Rhode Island, which took place at a rest stop on Route 24 in Bridgewater, Massachusetts. Leahy, a repeat sex offender, was found guilty of first-degree murder on September 24, 2003, and sentenced to life without parole. Should repeat sex offenders be incapacitated for life before their behavior spirals out of control? Or can everyone be rehabilitated if given proper treatment?

While Levitt's argument is persuasive, not all criminologists buy into the incapacitation effect:

- There is little evidence that incapacitating criminals will deter them from future criminality and even more reason to believe they may be more inclined to commit crimes upon release. The more prior incarceration experiences inmates have, the more likely they are to recidivate (and return to prison) within 12 months of their release.[199]
- By its nature, the prison experience exposes young, first-time offenders to higher-risk, more experienced inmates who can influence their lifestyle and help shape their attitudes. Novice inmates also run an increased risk of becoming infected with AIDS and other health hazards, and that exposure reduces their life chances after release.[200] The short-term crime reduction effect of incapacitating criminals is negated if the prison experience has the long-term effect of escalating frequency of criminal behavior upon release.
- The economics of crime suggest that if money can be made from criminal activity, there will always be someone to take the place of the incarcerated offender. New criminals will be recruited and trained, offsetting any benefit accrued by incarceration. Imprisoning established offenders may likewise open new opportunities for competitors who were suppressed by more experienced criminals. Incarcerating gang members or organized crime figures may open crime and illegal drug markets to new groups and gangs who are even hungrier and more aggressive than the gangs they replaced
- Most criminal offenses are committed by teens and very young adult offenders who are unlikely to be sent to prison for a single felony conviction. Aging criminals are already past the age when they are likely to commit crime. As a result, a strict incarceration policy may keep people in prison beyond the time they are a threat to society while a new cohort of high-risk adolescents is on the street.[201]
- An incapacitation strategy is terribly expensive. The prison system costs billions of dollars each year. Even if incarceration could reduce the crime rate, the costs would be enormous. Are U.S. taxpayers willing to spend billions more on new prison construction and annual maintenance fees? A strict incarceration policy would result in a growing number of elderly inmates whose maintenance costs, estimated at about $70,000 per year, are three times higher than those of younger inmates. Estimates are that about 16 percent of the prison population is over age 50.[202]
- Relying on incapacitation as a crime control mechanism has resulted in an ever-expanding prison population. Eventually most inmates return to society in a process referred to as reentry. In most states, prison inmates, especially those convicted of drug crimes, have come from comparatively few urban inner-city areas. Their return may contribute to family disruption, undermine social

institutions, and create community disorganization. Rather than act as a crime suppressant, incarceration may have the long-term effect of accelerating crime rates.[203]

Three Strikes Laws   So while on an individual level there is evidence that a stay in prison can reduce the length of a criminal career, there is some question whether increasing the size of the prison population can have a dramatic effect on crime rates.[204] Take the "three strikes and you're out" laws, which require the state courts to hand down mandatory periods of incarceration of up to life in prison to persons who have been convicted of a serious criminal offense on three or more separate occasions. While a policy of placing people convicted of a third felony behind bars for life is politically compelling, many criminologists believe these laws will not work for these reasons:

- Most three-time losers are on the verge of aging out of crime, so why waste money by keeping them behind bars?
- Current sentences for violent crimes are already severe.
- An expanding prison population will drive up already high prison costs.
- There would be racial disparity in sentencing.
- Police would be in danger because two-time offenders would violently resist a third arrest knowing they face a life sentence.
- The prison population probably already contains the highest-frequency criminals.[205]

Concept Summary 4.1 outlines the various methods of crime control and their effects. The accompanying Thinking Like a Criminologist feature addresses this issue.

> **CONNECTIONS**
>
> The problems of inmate reentry are discussed in detail in Chapter 17. As millions of former inmates reenter their old neighborhoods, they may become a destabilizing force, driving up crime rates.

PUBLIC POLICY IMPLICATIONS OF CHOICE THEORY

From the origins of classical theory to the development of modern rational choice views, the belief that criminals choose to commit crime has influenced the relationships among law, punishment, and crime. Although research on the core principles of choice theory and deterrence theories produces mixed results, these models have had an important impact on crime prevention strategies.

When police patrol in well-marked cars, it is assumed that their presence will deter would-be criminals. When the harsh realities of prison life are portrayed in movies and TV shows, the lesson is not lost on potential criminals. Nowhere is the idea that the threat of punishment can control crime more evident than in the implementation of tough mandatory criminal sentences to control violent crime and drug trafficking.

Despite the ongoing debate about its deterrent effect, some advocates argue that the death penalty can effectively restrict criminality; at least it ensures that convicted criminals never again get the opportunity to kill. Many observers are dismayed because people who are convicted of murder sometimes kill again when released on parole. One study of 52,000 incarcerated murderers found that 810 had been previously convicted of murder and had killed 821 people following their previous release from prison.[206] About 9 percent of all inmates on death row have had prior convictions for homicide. Death penalty advocates argue that if these criminals had been executed for their first offenses, hundreds of people would be alive today.[207] And the recent evidence indicating that if used a lot capital punishment can reduce a state's murder rate has encouraged some members of the moral and legal community to suggest that capital punishment is justified because it is a life-saving social policy. Writing in the *Stanford Law Review*, Cass Sunstein and Adrian Vermeule conclude that "a government that settles upon a package of crime-control policies that does *not* include capital punishment might well seem, at least prima facie, to be both violating the rights and reducing the welfare of its citizens—just as would a state that failed to enact simple environmental measures promising to save a great many lives."[208]

Just Desert

The concept of criminal choice has also prompted the creation of justice policies referred to as **just desert**. The just desert position has been most clearly spelled out by criminologist Andrew Von Hirsch in his book *Doing Justice*.[209] Von Hirsch suggests the concept of desert as a theoretical model to guide justice policy. This utilitarian view purports that punishment is needed to preserve the social equity disturbed by crime. Nonetheless, he claims, the severity of punishment should be commensurate with the seriousness of the crime.[210] Von Hirsch's views can be summarized in these three statements:

1. Those who violate others' rights deserve to be punished.
2. We should not deliberately add to human suffering; punishment makes those punished suffer.
3. However, punishment may prevent more misery than it inflicts; this conclusion reestablishes the need for desert-based punishment.[211]

Desert theory is also concerned with the rights of the accused. It alleges that the rights of the person being punished should not be unduly sacrificed for the good of others (as with deterrence). The offender should not be treated as more (or less) **blameworthy** than is warranted by the character of his or her offense. For example, Von Hirsch asks the following question: if two crimes, A and B, are equally serious, but if severe penalties are shown to have a deterrent

No Frills

The governor is running on a law and order plank. He claims that prisons don't work because they are too lenient. He proposes ending hot meals, education programs, counseling, and phone privileges. Television and other recreation would be curtailed, as well as visitation. His reasoning is that if prison was just an awful experience,

Lou Oates/Shutterstock

few inmates would risk returning and therefore would be afraid to commit new crimes.

>> **Write a brief position paper giving your take on the plan. Would it work? If not, what might be some problems with the governor's proposed "no frills" approach?**

---

effect only with respect to A, would it be fair to punish the person who has committed crime A more harshly simply to deter others from committing the crime? Conversely, imposing a light sentence for a serious crime would be unfair because it would treat the offender as less blameworthy than he or she is.

If deterrence is not a proper basis, then how do we determine how much punishment is fitting for a particular crime? In other words, how do we assess blame? According to legal scholar Richard Frase, two basic elements determine an offender's degree of blameworthiness: the nature and seriousness of the harm caused or threatened by the crime and the offender's degree of fault in committing the crime. In contemporary society, fault is measured by a number of factors: the offender's intent (e.g., deliberate wrongdoing is considered more serious than criminal negligence); his or her capacity to obey the law (e.g., blameworthiness is tempered by such conditions as mental disease or defect, chemical dependency, or situational factors such as threats or other strong inducements to commit the crime); the offender's motives for committing the crime (which may mitigate

or aggravate culpability); and, for multidefendant crimes, the defendant's role in the offense as instigator, leader, follower, primary actor, or minor player.[212] According to Frase, fairness is brought to the justice process by assessing blame in a fair and even-handed manner: fairness to the victim and the victim's family (i.e., otherwise they might seek vengeance on their own), fairness to law-abiding persons (who refrained from committing this offense), and fairness to the defendant (who has a right to be punished in proportion to his blameworthiness).

In sum, the just desert model suggests that retribution justifies punishment because people deserve what they get for past deeds. Punishment based on deterrence or incapacitation is wrong because it involves an offender's future actions, which cannot accurately be predicted. Punishment should be the same for all people who commit the same crime. Criminal sentences based on individual needs or characteristics are inherently unfair because all people are equally blameworthy for their misdeeds. The influence of Von Hirsch's views can be seen in sentencing models that give the same punishment to all people who commit the same type of crime.

SUMMARY

1. **Describe the development of rational choice theory**
   - Rational choice theory has its roots in the classical school of criminology developed by the eighteenth-century Italian social thinker Cesare Beccaria. James Q. Wilson observed that people who are likely to commit crime are unafraid of breaking the law because they value the excitement and thrills of crime, have a low stake in conformity, and are willing to take greater chances than the average person.

2. **Describe the concepts of rational choice**
   - Law-violating behavior is the product of careful thought and planning. People who commit crime believe that the rewards of crime outweigh the risks. If they think they are likely to get arrested and punished, people will not risk criminal activities. Before choosing to commit a crime, reasoning criminals carefully select targets, and their behavior is systematic and

selective. Rational choice theorists view crime as both offense- and offender-specific.

3. **Discuss how offenders structure criminality**
   - Criminals consider their needs and capabilities before committing crimes. One important decision that is made before someone enters a life of crime is the need for money. Personal experience may be an important element in structuring criminality. Before committing crimes, criminals report, they actually learn techniques to help them avoid detection while making profits.

4. **Describe how criminals structure crime**
   - Criminals carefully choose where they will commit their crime. Evidence of rational choice may be found in the way criminals locate their targets. Rational choice involves both shaping criminality and structuring crime. If a target appears dangerous, they will choose another.

5. **Develop knowledge showing that crime is rational**
   - There is evidence that theft-related crimes are the product of careful risk assessment, including environmental, social, and structural factors. Target selection seems highly rational. Even drug use is controlled by rational decision making. Users report that they begin taking drugs when they believe the benefits of substance abuse outweigh its costs. Evidence confirms that even violent criminals select suitable targets by picking people who are vulnerable and lack adequate defenses. In some instances, targets are chosen in order to send a message rather than to generate capital.

6. **Know what is meant by the term *seductions of crime***
   - In his book *Seductions of Crime*, Jack Katz argues that there are immediate benefits to criminality. According to Katz, choosing crime can help satisfy personal needs. Katz finds that crimes can help soothe the strain produced by emotional upheaval. People are most likely to be "seduced" if they fear neither the risk of apprehension nor its social consequences.

7. **Discuss the elements of situational crime prevention**
   - Situational crime prevention involves developing tactics to reduce or eliminate a specific crime problem. These include tactics to increase the effort required to commit crime, such as putting unbreakable glass on storefronts, locking gates, and fencing yards. It can also involve increasing the risks of crime through better security efforts. Reducing the rewards of crime is designed to lessen the value of crime to the potential criminal. Crime may be reduced or prevented if we can communicate to people the wrongfulness of their behavior and how it is harmful to society. Crime may be reduced by making it difficult for people to excuse their criminal behavior by saying things like "I didn't know that was illegal" or "I had no choice."

8. **Be familiar with the elements of general deterrence**
   - Crime can be controlled by increasing the real or perceived threat of criminal punishment. According to deterrence theory, not only does the actual chance of punishment influence criminality, so too does the *perception of punishment*. A central theme of deterrence theory is that people who perceive they will be punished for crimes will avoid doing those crimes. According to general deterrence theory, if the certainty of arrest, conviction, and sanctioning increases, crime rates should decline. The threat of severe punishment should also bring the crime rate down. The faster punishment is applied and the more closely it is linked to the crime, the more likely it will serve as a deterrent. The factors of severity, certainty, and speed of punishment may also influence one another.

9. **Discuss the basic concepts of specific deterrence**
   - The theory of specific deterrence holds that criminal sanctions should be so powerful that known criminals will never repeat their criminal acts. Research on specific deterrence does not provide any clear-cut evidence that punishing criminals is an effective means of stopping them from committing future crimes. Punishment may bring defiance rather than deterrence. People who are harshly treated may want to show that they cannot be broken by the system. The stigma of harsh treatment labels people and helps lock offenders into a criminal career instead of convincing them to avoid one.

10. **Understand the pros and cons of an incapacitation strategy to reduce crime**
    - The more criminals are sent to prison, the more the crime rate should go down. Placing offenders behind bars during their prime crime years should reduce their lifetime opportunity to commit crime. The shorter the span of opportunity, the fewer offenses they can commit during their lives; hence, crime is reduced. However, there is little evidence that incapacitating criminals will deter them from future criminality and reason to believe they may be more inclined to commit even more crimes upon release.

KEY TERMS

rational choice (102)
Enlightenment (103)
marginal deterrence (103)
classical criminology (104)
reasoning criminal (106)
offense-specific crime (107)
offender-specific crime (107)
criminality (108)
boosters (111)

permeable neighborhood (111)
edgework (114)
situational crime prevention (115)
defensible space (116)
crime discouragers (116)
diffusion of benefits (118)
discouragement (119)
displacement (119)
general deterrence (119)

deterrence theory (120)
crackdowns (121)
informal sanctions (123)
specific deterrence (125)
incapacitation effect (127)
just desert (129)
blameworthy (129)

CRITICAL THINKING QUESTIONS

1. Are criminals rational decision makers, or are they motivated by uncontrollable psychological and emotional drives?

2. Would you want to live in a society where crime rates are low because criminals are subjected to extremely harsh punishments, such as flogging for vandalism?

3. If you were caught by the police while shoplifting, which would you be more afraid of: receiving criminal punishment or having to face your friends or relatives?

4. Is it possible to create a method of capital punishment that would actually deter murder—for example, by televising executions? What might be some of the negative consequences of such a policy?

NOTES

1. Reuters News Service, "T. Boone Pickens' Son Gets Probation in Fraud Case," December 10, 2007, www.cnbc.com/id/22183588/ (accessed November 6, 2010); FBI, "Hot Stock Tip, Anyone? The Case of the Phony Faxes," November 20, 2006, www2.fbi.gov/page2/nov06/stock_scam112006.htm (accessed November 6, 2010).

2. Alan Harding, *Medieval Law and the Foundations of the State* (New York: Oxford University Press, 2002).

3. Eugen Weber, *A Modern History of Europe* (New York: W. W. Norton, 1971), p. 398.

4. Jeremy Bentham, *A Fragment on Government and an Introduction to the Principle of Morals and Legislation*, ed. Wilfred Harrison (Oxford: Basil Blackwell, 1967).

5. Ibid., p. xi.

6. Ibid.

7. George J. Stigler, "The Optimum Enforcement of Laws," *Journal of Political Economy* 78 (1970): 526–528.

8. Marvin Wolfgang, *Patterns in Criminal Homicide* (Philadelphia: University of Pennsylvania Press, 1958).

9. Bob Roshier, *Controlling Crime* (Chicago: Lyceum Books, 1989), p. 10.

10. Robert Martinson, "What Works? Questions and Answers about Prison Reform," *Public Interest* 35 (1974): 22–54.

11. Charles Murray and Louis Cox, *Beyond Probation* (Beverly Hills: Sage, 1979).

12. Ronald Bayer, "Crime, Punishment, and the Decline of Liberal Optimism," *Crime and Delinquency* 27 (1981): 190.

13. James Q. Wilson, *Thinking about Crime*, rev. ed. (New York: Vintage Books, 1983), p. 260.

14. Ibid., p. 128.

15. Michael Tonry, *Malign Neglect: Race, Crime and Punishment in America* (New York: Oxford University Press, 1995).

16. William J. Sabol, Heather Couture, and Paige M. Harrison, *Prisoners in 2006* (Washington, DC: Bureau of Justice Statistics, 2007).

17. John Irwin and James Austin, *It's About Time: America's Imprisonment Binge* (Belmont, CA: Wadsworth, 1997).

18. Kimberly Cook, "A Passion to Punish: Abortion Opponents Who Favor the Death Penalty," *Justice Quarterly* 15 (1998): 329–346.

19. See, generally, Derek Cornish and Ronald Clarke, eds., *The Reasoning Criminal: Rational Choice Perspectives on Offending* (New York: Springer Verlag, 1986); Philip Cook, "The Demand and Supply of Criminal Opportunities," in *Crime and Justice*, Vol. 7, ed. Michael Tonry and Norval Morris (Chicago: University of Chicago Press, 1986), pp. 1–28; Ronald Clarke and Derek Cornish, "Modeling Offenders' Decisions: A Framework for Research and Policy," in *Crime and Justice*, Vol. 6, ed. Michael Tonry and Norval Morris (Chicago: University of Chicago Press, 1985), pp. 147–187; and Morgan Reynolds, *Crime by Choice: An Economic Analysis* (Dallas: Fisher Institute, 1985).

20. David A. Ward, Mark C. Stafford, and Louis N. Gray, "Rational Choice, Deterrence, and Theoretical Integration," *Journal of Applied Social Psychology* 36 (2006): 571–585.

21. Hung-en Sung and Linda Richter, "Rational Choice and Environmental Deterrence in the Retention of Mandated Drug Abuse Treatment Clients," *International Journal of Offender Therapy and Comparative Criminology* 51 (2007): 686–702.

22. Timothy Brezina, "Delinquent Problem-Solving: An Interpretive Framework for Criminological Theory and Research," *Journal of Research in Crime and Delinquency* 37 (2000): 3–30.

23. Bill McCarthy and John Hagan, "Mean Streets: The Theoretical Significance of Situational Delinquency Among Homeless Youths," *American Journal of Sociology* 3 (1992): 597–627.

24. Andy Hochstetler, "Opportunities and Decisions: Interactional Dynamics in Robbery and Burglary Groups," *Criminology* 39 (2001): 737–763.

25. Jeff Ferrell, "Criminological Verstehen: Inside the Immediacy of Crime," *Justice Quarterly* 14 (1997): 3–23.

26. Peter Wood, Walter Gove, James Wilson, and John Cochran, "Nonsocial Reinforcement and Habitual Criminal Conduct: An Extension of Learning," *Criminology* 35 (1997): 335–366.

27. Christopher Birkbeck and Gary LaFree, "The Situational Analysis of Crime and Deviance," *American Review of Sociology* 19 (1993): 113–137.

28. Melanie Wellsmith and Amy Burrell, "The Influence of Purchase Price and Ownership Levels on Theft Targets: The Example of Domestic Burglary," *British Journal of Criminology* 45 (2005): 741–764.

29. Carlo Morselli and Marie-Noële Royer, "Criminal Mobility and Criminal Achievement," *Journal of Research in Crime and Delinquency* 45 (2008): 4–21.

30. Ross Matsueda, Derek Kreager, and David Huizinga, "Deterring Delinquents: A Rational Choice Model of Theft and Violence," *American Sociological Review* 71 (2006): 95–122.

31. Jeffrey Bouffard, "Predicting Differences in the Perceived Relevance of Crime's Costs and Benefits in a Test of Rational Choice Theory," *International Journal of Offender Therapy and Comparative Criminology* 51 (2007): 461–485.

32. Christopher Uggen and Melissa Thompson, "The Socioeconomic Determinants of Ill-Gotten Gains: Within-Person Changes in Drug Use and Illegal Earnings," *American Journal of Sociology* 109 (2003): 146–187.

33. Philippe Bourgois, *In Search of Respect: Selling Crack in El Barrio* (Cambridge: Cambridge University Press, 1995), p. 326.

34. Bouffard, "Predicting Differences in the Perceived Relevance of Crime's Costs and Benefits in a Test of Rational Choice Theory."

35. George Rengert and John Wasilchick, *Suburban Burglary: A Time and Place for Everything* (Springfield, IL: Charles C Thomas, 1985).

36. Derek Cornish and Ronald Clarke, "Understanding Crime Displacement: An Application of Rational Choice Theory," *Criminology* 25 (1987): 933–947.

37. Michael Gottfredson and Travis Hirschi, *A General Theory of Crime* (Stanford, CA: Stanford University Press, 1990).

38. Jeannette Angell, "Confessions of an Ivy League Hooker," *Boston Magazine*, August 2004, pp. 120–134.

39. Uggen and Thompson, "The Socioeconomic Determinants of Ill-Gotten Gains."

40. Pierre Tremblay and Carlo Morselli, "Patterns in Criminal Achievement: Wilson and Abrahamse Revisited," *Criminology* 38 (2000): 633–660.

41. Liliana Pezzin, "Earnings Prospects, Matching Effects, and the Decision to Terminate a Criminal Career," *Journal of Quantitative Criminology* 11 (1995): 29–50.

42. Ronald Akers, "Rational Choice, Deterrence, and Social Learning Theory in Criminology: The Path Not Taken," *Journal of Criminal Law and Criminology* 81 (1990): 653–676.

43. Neal Shover, *Aging Criminals* (Beverly Hills: Sage, 1985).

44. Patricia Morgan and Karen Ann Joe, "Citizens and Outlaws: The Private Lives and Public Lifestyles of Women in the Illicit Drug Economy," *Journal of Drug Issues* 26 (1996): 125–142, at 132.

45. Ibid., p. 136.

46. Bruce Jacobs, "Crack Dealers' Apprehension Avoidance Techniques: A Case of Restrictive Deterrence," *Justice Quarterly* 13 (1996): 359–381.

47. Ibid., p. 367.

48. Ibid., p. 372.

49. Gordon Knowles, "Deception, Detection, and Evasion: A Trade Craft Analysis of Honolulu, Hawaii's Street Crack Cocaine Traffickers," *Journal of Criminal Justice* 27 (1999): 443–455.

50. Bruce Jacobs and Jody Miller, "Crack Dealing, Gender, and Arrest Avoidance," *Social Problems* 45 (1998): 550–566.

51. Jacobs, "Crack Dealers' Apprehension Avoidance Techniques."

52. Ibid., p. 367.

53. Ibid., p. 368.

54. Eric Baumer, Janet Lauritsen, Richard Rosenfeld, and Richard Wright, "The Influence of Crack Cocaine on Robbery, Burglary, and Homicide Rates: A Cross-City, Longitudinal Analysis," *Journal of Research in Crime and Delinquency* 35 (1998): 316–340.

55. George Rengert and John Wasilchick, *Space, Time, and Crime: Ethnographic Insights into Residential Burglary* (Washington, DC: National Institute of Justice, 1989); see also Rengert and Wasilchick, *Suburban Burglary*.

56. Paul Cromwell, James Olson, and D'Aunn Wester Avary, *Breaking and Entering, an Ethnographic Analysis of Burglary* (Newbury Park, CA: Sage, 1989), pp. 30–32.

57. Ibid., p. 24.

58. Michael Costanzo, William Halperin, and Nathan Gale, "Criminal Mobility and the Directional Component in Journeys to Crime," in *Metropolitan Crime Patterns*, ed. Robert Figlio, Simon Hakim, and George Rengert (Monsey, NY: Criminal Justice Press, 1986), pp. 73–95.

59. Morselli and Royer, "Criminal Mobility and Criminal Achievement."

60. Joseph Deutsch and Gil Epstein, "Changing a Decision Taken Under Uncertainty: The Case of the Criminal's Location Choice," *Urban Studies* 35 (1998): 1,335–1,344.

61. Robert Sampson and Jacqueline Cohen, "Deterrent Effects of the Police on Crime: A Replication and Theoretical Extension," *Law and Society Review* 22 (1988): 163–188.

62. Kenneth Tunnell, *Choosing Crime* (Chicago: Nelson-Hall, 1992), p. 105.

63. Paul Bellair, "Informal Surveillance and Street Crime: A Complex Relationship," *Criminology* 38 (2000): 137–167.

64. Gary Kleck and Don Kates, *Armed: New Perspectives on Guns* (Amherst, NY: Prometheus Books, 2001).

65. Elizabeth Ehrhardt Mustaine and Richard Tewksbury, "Predicting Risks of Larceny Theft Victimization: A Routine Activity Analysis Using Refined Lifestyle Measures," *Criminology* 36 (1998): 829–858.

66. Bruce A. Jacobs and Richard Wright, "Researching Drug Robbery," *Crime and Delinquency*, December 2007, online edition, http://cad.sagepub.com/cgi/rapidpdf/0011128707307220v1 (accessed September 20, 2010).

67. Associated Press, "Thrift Hearings Resume Today in Senate," *Boston Globe*, January 2, 1991, p. 10.

68. Pamela Wilcox, Tamara Madensen, and Marie Skubak Tillyer, "Guardianship in Context: Implications for Burglary Victimization Risk and Prevention," *Criminology* 45 (2007): 771–803.

69. Garland White, "Neighborhood Permeability and Burglary Rates," *Justice Quarterly* 7 (1990): 57–67.

70. Ibid., p. 65.

71. Matthew Robinson, "Lifestyles, Routine Activities, and Residential Burglary Victimization," *Journal of Criminal Justice* 22 (1999): 27–52.

72. Cromwell, Olson, and Avary, *Breaking and Entering*.

73. Andrew Buck, Simon Hakim, and George Rengert, "Burglar Alarms and the Choice Behavior of Burglars: A Suburban Phenomenon," *Journal of Criminal Justice* 21 (1993): 497–507.

74. Ralph Taylor and Stephen Gottfredson, "Environmental Design, Crime, and Prevention: An Examination of Community Dynamics," in *Communities and Crime*, ed. Albert Reiss and Michael Tonry (Chicago: University of Chicago Press, 1986), pp. 387–416.

75. John Gibbs and Peggy Shelly, "Life in the Fast Lane: A Retrospective View by Commercial Thieves," *Journal of Research in Crime and Delinquency* 19 (1982): 229–230.

76. "The Decline of the English Burglary," *The Economist* 371 (2004): 59.

77. John Petraitis, Brian Flay, and Todd Miller, "Reviewing Theories of Adolescent Substance Use: Organizing Pieces in the Puzzle," *Psychological Bulletin* 117 (1995): 67–86.

78. Leanne Fiftal Alarid, James Marquart, Velmer Burton, Francis Cullen, and Steven Cuvelier, "Women's Roles in Serious Offenses: A Study of Adult Felons," *Justice Quarterly* 13 (1996): 431–454, at 448.

79. Ben Fox, "Jury Recommends Death for Convicted Child Killer," *Boston Globe*, October 6, 1999, p. 3.

80. Trevor Bennett and Fiona Brookman, "The Role of Violence in Street Crime: A Qualitative Study of Violent Offenders," *International Journal of Offender Therapy and Comparative Criminology* 53 (2009): 617–633.

81. Richard B. Felson, *Violence and Gender Reexamined* (Washington, DC: American Psychological Association, 2002).

82. Richard Felson and Steven Messner, "To Kill or Not to Kill? Lethal Outcomes in Injurious Attacks," *Criminology* 34 (1996): 519–545, at 541.

83. James Wright and Peter Rossi, *Armed and Considered Dangerous: A Survey of Felons and Their Firearms* (Hawthorne, NY: Aldine De Gruyter, 1983), pp. 141–159.

84. Gary Kleck and Marc Gertz, "Carry Guns for Protection: Results from the National Self-Defense Survey," *Journal of Research in Crime and Delinquency* 35 (1998): 193–224.

85. Peter van Koppen and Robert Jansen, "The Time to Rob: Variations in Time and Number of Commercial Robberies," *Journal of Research in Crime and Delinquency* 36 (1999): 7–29.

86. William Smith, Sharon Glave Frazee, and Elizabeth Davison, "Furthering the Integration of Routine Activity and Social Disorganization Theories: Small Units of Analysis and the Study of Street Robbery as a Diffusion Process," *Criminology* 38 (2000): 489–521.

87. Wim Bernasco and Paul Nieuwbeerta, "How Do Residential Burglars Select Target Areas? A New Approach to the Analysis of Criminal Location Choice," *British Journal of Criminology* 45 (2005): 296–315.

88. Alan Lizotte, Marvin Krohn, James Howell, Kimberly Tobin, and Gregory Howard, "Factors Influencing Gun Carrying Among Young Urban Males Over the Adolescent–Young Adult Life Course," *Criminology* 38 (2000): 811–834.

89. Scott Decker, "Deviant Homicide: A New Look at the Role of Motives and Victim–Offender Relationships," *Journal of Research in Crime and Delinquency* 33 (1996): 427–449.

90. Felson and Messner, "To Kill or Not to Kill?"

91. Eric Hickey, *Serial Murderers and Their Victims* (Pacific Grove, CA: Brooks/Cole, 1991), p. 84.

92. Janet Warren, Roland Reboussin, Robert Hazlewood, Andrea Cummings, Natalie Gibbs, and Susan Trumbetta, "Crime Scene and Distance Correlates of Serial Rape," *Journal of Quantitative Criminology* 14 (1998): 35–58.

93. Benoit Leclerc, Jean Proulx, and André McKibben, "Modus Operandi of Sexual Offenders Working or Doing Voluntary Work with Children and Adolescents," *Journal of Sexual Aggression* 11 (2005): 187–195.

94. Christopher Birkbeck and Gary LaFree, "The Situational Analysis of Crime and Deviance," *American Review of Sociology* 19 (1993): 113–137; Karen Heimer and Ross Matsueda, "Role-Taking, Role Commitment, and Delinquency: A Theory of Differential Social Control," *American Sociological Review* 59 (1994): 400–437.

95. Peter Wood, Walter Gove, James Wilson, and John Cochran, "Nonsocial Reinforcement and Habitual Criminal Conduct: An Extension of Learning," *Criminology* 35 (1997): 335–366.

96. Ferrell, "Criminological Verstehen," p. 12.

97. Gottfredson and Hirschi, *A General Theory of Crime.*

98. Patricia Brantingham, Paul Brantingham, and Wendy Taylor, "Situational Crime Prevention as a Key Component in Embedded Crime Prevention," *Canadian Journal of Criminology and Criminal Justice* 47 (2005): 271–292.

99. Oscar Newman, *Defensible Space: Crime Prevention through Urban Design* (New York: Macmillan, 1973).

100. C. Ray Jeffery, *Crime Prevention through Environmental Design* (Beverly Hills: Sage, 1971).

101. See also Pochara Theerathorn, "Architectural Style, Aesthetic Landscaping, Home Value, and Crime Prevention," *International Journal of Comparative and Applied Criminal Justice* 12 (1988): 269–277.

102. Ronald Clarke, *Situational Crime Prevention: Successful Case Studies* (Albany, NY: Harrow and Heston, 1992).

103. Marcus Felson, "Routine Activities and Crime Prevention," in *National Council for Crime Prevention, Studies on Crime and Crime Prevention, Annual Review*, Vol. 1 (Stockholm: Scandinavian University Press, 1992), pp. 30–34.

104. Derek Cornish and Ronald Clarke, "Opportunities, Precipitators and Criminal Decisions: A Reply to Wortley's Critique of Situational Crime Prevention," *Crime Prevention Studies* 16 (2003): 41–96; Ronald Clarke and Ross Homel, "A Revised Classification of Situational Prevention Techniques," in *Crime Prevention at a Crossroads*, ed. Steven P. Lab (Cincinnati: Anderson Publishing, 1997).

105. Barry Webb, "Steering Column Locks and Motor Vehicle Theft: Evaluations for Three Countries," in *Crime Prevention Studies*, ed. Ronald Clarke (Monsey, NY: Criminal Justice Press, 1994), pp. 71–89.

106. Barbara Morse and Delbert Elliott, "Effects of Ignition Interlock Devices on DUI Recidivism: Findings from a Longitudinal Study in Hamilton County, Ohio," *Crime and Delinquency* 38 (1992): 131–157.

107. Nancy LaVigne, "Gasoline Drive-Offs: Designing a Less Convenient Environment," in *Crime Prevention Studies*, Vol. 2, ed. Ronald Clarke (New York: Criminal Justice Press, 1994), pp. 91–114.

108. Eric Fritsch, Tory Caeti, and Robert Taylor, "Gang Suppression through Saturation Patrol, Aggressive Curfew, and Truancy Enforcement: A Quasi-Experimental Test of the Dallas Anti-Gang Initiative," *Crime and Delinquency* 45 (1999): 122–139.

109. Kenneth Adams, "The Effectiveness of Juvenile Curfews at Crime Prevention," *The Annals of the American Academy of Political and Social Science* 587 (May 2003): 136–159.

110. Brantingham, Brantingham, and Taylor, "Situational Crime Prevention as a Key Component in Embedded Crime Prevention."

111. Marcus Felson, "Those Who Discourage Crime," in *Crime and Place, Crime Prevention Studies*, Vol. 4, ed. John Eck and David Weisburd (New York: Criminal Justice Press, 1995), pp. 53–66; John Eck, "Drug Markets and Drug Places: A Case-Control Study of the Spatial Structure of Illicit Drug Dealing," Ph.D. dissertation, University of Maryland, College Park, 1994.

112. Eck, "Drug Markets and Drug Places," p. 29.

113. Lorraine Green Mazerolle, Colleen Kadleck, and Jan Roehl, "Controlling Drug and Disorder Problems: The Role of Place Managers," *Criminology* 36 (1998): 371–404.

114. "Pervert's Tough Sign-tence," *The Sun*, March 26, 2008, www.thesun.co.uk/sol/homepage/news/article960199.ece (accessed November 6, 2010).

115. Ronald Clarke, "Deterring Obscene Phone Callers: The New Jersey Experience," *Situational Crime Prevention*, ed. Ronald Clarke (Albany, NY: Harrow and Heston, 1992), pp. 124–132.

116. Bob Edward Vásquez, Sean Maddan, and Jeffery T. Walker, "The Influence of Sex Offender Registration and Notification Laws in the United States: A Time-Series Analysis," *Crime and Delinquency* 54 (2008): 175–192.

117. Ronald Clarke and David Weisburd, "Diffusion of Crime Control Benefits: Observations of the Reverse of Displacement," in *Crime Prevention Studies*, Vol. 2, ed. Ronald Clarke (New York: Criminal Justice Press, 1994).

118. David Weisburd and Lorraine Green, "Policing Drug Hot Spots: The Jersey City Drug Market Analysis Experiment," *Justice Quarterly* 12 (1995): 711–734.

119. Lorraine Green, "Cleaning Up Drug Hot Spots in Oakland, California: The Displacement and Diffusion Effects," *Justice Quarterly* 12 (1995): 737–754.

120. Ian Ayres and Steven D. Levitt, "Measuring Positive Externalities from Unobservable Victim Precaution: An Empirical Analysis of LoJack," *Quarterly Journal of Economics* 113 (1998): 43–78.

121. Robert Barr and Ken Pease, "Crime Placement, Displacement, and Deflection," in *Crime and Justice, A Review of Research*, Vol. 12, ed. Michael Tonry and Norval Morris (Chicago: University of Chicago Press, 1990), pp. 277–319.

122. Clarke, *Situational Crime Prevention*, p. 27.

123. Brandon Welsh and David Farrington, "Crime Prevention and Hard Technology: The Case of CCTV and Improved Street Lighting," in *The New Technology of Crime, Law, and Social Control*, ed. James Byrne and Donald Rebovich (Monsey, NY: Criminal Justice Press, 2007).

124. Daniel Nagin and Greg Pogarsky, "An Experimental Investigation of Deterrence: Cheating, Self-Serving Bias, and Impulsivity," *Criminology* 41 (2003): 167–195.

125. Silvia Mendes, "Certainty, Severity, and Their Relative Deterrent Effects: Questioning the Implications of the Role of Risk in Criminal Deterrence Policy," *Policy Studies Journal* 32 (2004): 59–74.

126. Robert Apel, Greg Pogarsky, and Leigh Bates, "The Sanctions–Perceptions Link in a Model of School-Based Deterrence," *Journal of Quantitative Criminology* 25 (2009): 201–226.

127. Nagin and Pogarsky, "Integrating Celerity, Impulsivity, and Extralegal Sanction Threats into a Model of General Deterrence."

128. Robert Bursik, Harold Grasmick, and Mitchell Chamlin, "The Effect of Longitudinal Arrest Patterns on the Development of Robbery Trends at the Neighborhood Level," *Criminology* 28 (1990): 431–450; Theodore Chiricos and Gordon Waldo, "Punishment and Crime: An Examination of Some Empirical Evidence," *Social Problems* 18 (1970): 200–217.

129. Etienne Blais and Jean-Luc Bacher, "Situational Deterrence and Claim Padding: Results from a Randomized Field Experiment," *Journal of Experimental Criminology* 3 (2007): 337–352.

130. R. Steven Daniels, Lorin Baumhover, William Formby, and Carolyn Clark-Daniels, "Police Discretion and Elder Mistreatment: A Nested Model of Observation, Reporting, and Satisfaction," *Journal of Criminal Justice* 27 (1999): 209–225.

131. Daniel Nagin and Greg Pogarsky, "Integrating Celerity, Impulsivity, and Extralegal Sanction Threats into a Model of General Deterrence: Theory and Evidence," *Criminology* 39 (2001): 865–892.

132. Timothy O'Shea, "Getting the Deterrence Message Out: The Project Safe Neighborhoods Public–Private Partnership," *Police Quarterly* 10 (2007): 288–306.

133. David Klinger, "Policing Spousal Assault," *Journal of Research in Crime and Delinquency* 32 (1995): 308–324.

134. Charles Tittle and Alan Rowe, "Certainty of Arrest and Crime Rates: A Further Test of the Deterrence Hypothesis," *Social Forces* 52 (1974): 455–462.

135. Daniels, Baumhover, Formby, and Clark-Daniels, "Police Discretion and Elder Mistreatment."

136. David Bayley, *Policing for the Future* (New York: Oxford, 1994).

137. George Kelling, Tony Pate, Duane Dieckman, and Charles Brown, *The Kansas City Preventive Patrol Experiment: A Summary Report* (Washington, DC: Police Foundation, 1974).

138. Tomislav V. Kovandzic and John J. Sloan, "Police Levels and Crime Rates Revisited, A County-Level Analysis from Florida (1980–1998)," *Journal of Criminal Justice* 30 (2002): 65–76; Steven Levitt, "Using Electoral Cycles in Police Hiring to Estimate the Effect of Police on Crime," *American Economic Review* 87 (1997): 70–91; Marvell and Moody, "Specification Problems, Police Levels, and Crime Rates."

139. John Worrall and Tomislav Kovandzic, "Police Levels and Crime Rates: An Instrumental Variables Approach," *Social Science Research* 39 (2010): 506–516.

140. Michael White, James Fyfe, Suzanne Campbell, and John Goldkamp, "The Police Role in Preventing Homicide: Considering the Impact of Problem-Oriented Policing on the Prevalence of Murder," *Journal of Research in Crime and Delinquency* 40 (2003): 194–226.

141. Kenneth Novak, Jennifer Hartman, Alexander Holsinger, and Michael Turner, "The Effects of Aggressive Policing of Disorder on Serious Crime," *Policing* 22 (1999): 171–190.

142. Lawrence Sherman, "Police Crackdowns," *NIJ Reports* (March/April 1990): 2–6, at 2.

143. Jacqueline Cohen, Wilpen Gorr, and Piyusha Singh, "Estimating Intervention Effects in Varying Risk Settings: Do Police Raids Reduce Illegal Drug Dealing at Nuisance Bars?" *Criminology* 42 (2003): 257–292.

144. Anthony Braga, David Weisburd, Elin Waring, Lorraine Green Mazerolle, William Spelman, and Francis Gajewski, "Problem-Oriented Policing in Violent Crime Places: A Randomized Controlled Experiment," *Criminology* 37 (1999): 541–580.

145. Fritsch, Caeti, and Taylor, "Gang Suppression through Saturation Patrol, Aggressive Curfew, and Truancy Enforcement."

146. Michael Smith, "Police-Led Crackdowns and Cleanups: An Evaluation of a Crime Control Initiative in Richmond, Virginia," *Crime and Delinquency* 47 (2001): 60–68.

147. Braga et al., "Problem-Oriented Policing in Violent Crime Places."

148. Nagin and Pogarsky, "Integrating Celerity, Impulsivity, and Extralegal Sanction Threats into a Model of General Deterrence," pp. 884–885.

149. Daniel Kessler and Steven D. Levitt, "Using Sentence Enhancements to Distinguish Between Deterrence and Incapacitation," *Journal of Law and Economics* 42 (1999): 343–363.

150. Cheryl Marie Webster, Anthony Doob, and Franklin Zimring, "Proposition 8 and Crime Rates in California: The Case of the Disappearing Deterrent," *Criminology and Public Policy* 5 (2006): 417–448.

151. Donald Green, "Past Behavior as a Measure of Actual Future Behavior: An Unresolved Issue in Perceptual Deterrence Research," *Journal of Criminal Law and Criminology* 80 (1989): 781–804, at 803; Matthew Silberman, "Toward a Theory of Criminal Deterrence," *American Sociological Review* 41 (1976): 442–461; Linda Anderson, Theodore Chiricos, and Gordon Waldo, "Formal and Informal Sanctions: A Comparison of Deterrent Effects," *Social Problems* 25 (1977): 103–114. See also Maynard Erickson and Jack Gibbs, "Objective and Perceptual Properties of Legal Punishment and Deterrence Doctrine," *Social Problems* 25 (1978): 253–264; and Daniel Nagin and Raymond Paternoster, "Enduring Individual Differences and Rational Choice Theories of Crime," *Law and Society Review* 27 (1993): 467–485.

152. Harold Grasmick and Robert Bursik, "Conscience, Significant Others, and Rational Choices: Extending the Deterrence Model," *Law and Society Review* 24 (1990): 837–861, at 854.

153. Harold Grasmick, Robert Bursik, and Karyl Kinsey, "Shame and Embarrassment as Deterrents to Noncompliance with the Law: The Case of an Anti-Littering Campaign," paper presented at the annual meeting of the American Society of Criminology, Baltimore, November 1990, p. 3.

154. Harry Wallace, Julie Juola Exline, and Roy Baumeister, "Interpersonal Consequences of Forgiveness: Does Forgiveness Deter or Encourage Repeat Offenses?" *Journal of Experimental Social Psychology* 44 (2008): 453–460.

155. Thomas Peete, Trudie Milner, and Michael Welch, "Levels of Social Integration in Group Contexts and the Effects of Informal Sanction Threat on Deviance," *Criminology* 32 (1994): 85–105.

156. Richard D. Clark, "Celerity and Specific Deterrence: A Look at the Evidence," *Canadian Journal of Criminology* 30 (1988): 109–122.

157. Charles N. W. Keckler, "*Life v. Death:* Who Should Capital Punishment Marginally Deter?" *Journal of Law, Economics and Policy* 2 (2006): 101–161.

158. Yair Listokin, "Crime and (with a Lag) Punishment: The Implications of Discounting for Equitable Sentencing," *American Criminal Law Review* 44 (2007): 115–140.

159. Raymond Paternoster, "Decisions to Participate in and Desist from Four Types of Common Delinquency: Deterrence and the Rational Choice Perspective," *Law and Society Review* 23 (1989): 7–29.

160. James Williams and Daniel Rodeheaver, "Processing of Criminal Homicide Cases in a Large Southern City," *Sociology and Social Research* 75 (1991): 80–88.

161. Greg Pogarsky, KiDeuk Kim, and Ray Paternoster, "Perceptual Change in the National Youth Survey: Lessons for Deterrence Theory and Offender Decision-Making," *Justice Quarterly* 22 (2005): 1–29.

162. Bruce A. Jacobs, "Deterrence and Deterrability," *Criminology* 48 (2010): 417–442.

163. Ernest van Den Haag, "The Criminal Law as a Threat System," *Journal of Criminal Law and Criminology* 73 (1982): 709–785.

164. James A. Swartz and Arthur J. Lurigio, "Serious Mental Illness and Arrest: The Generalized Mediating Effect of Substance Use," *Crime and Delinquency* 53 (2007): 581–604.

165. David Lykken, "Psychopathy, Sociopathy, and Crime," *Society* 34 (1996): 30–38.

166. George Lowenstein, Daniel Nagin, and Raymond Paternoster, "The Effect of Sexual Arousal on Expectations of Sexual Forcefulness," *Journal of Research in Crime and Delinquency* 34 (1997): 443–473.

167. Ken Auletta, *The Under Class* (New York: Random House, 1982).

168. Foglia, "Perceptual Deterrence and the Mediating Effect of Internalized Norms among Inner-City Teenagers"; Paternoster, "Decisions to Participate in and Desist from Four Types of Common Delinquency"; Raymond Paternoster, "Examining Three-Wave Deterrence Models: A Question of Temporal Order and Specification," *Journal of Criminal Law and Criminology* 79 (1988): 135–163; Raymond Paternoster, Linda Saltzman, Gordon Waldo, and Theodore Chiricos, "Estimating Perceptual Stability and Deterrent Effects: The Role of Perceived Legal Punishment in the Inhibition of Criminal Involvement," *Journal of Criminal Law and Criminology* 74 (1983): 270–297; M. William Minor and Joseph Harry, "Deterrent and Experiential Effects in Perceptual Deterrence Research: A Replication and Extension," *Journal of Research in Crime and Delinquency* 19 (1982): 190–203; Lonn Lanza-Kaduce, "Perceptual Deterrence and Drinking and Driving Among College Students," *Criminology* 26 (1988): 321–341.

169. Foglia, "Perceptual Deterrence and the Mediating Effect of Internalized Norms Among Inner-City Teenagers," pp. 419–443.

170. Alex Piquero and George Rengert, "Studying Deterrence with Active Residential Burglars," *Justice Quarterly* 16 (1999): 451–462.

171. Steven Levitt and Sudhir Alladi Venkatesh, "An Economic Analysis of a Drug-Selling Gang's Finances," NBER Working Papers 6592 (Cambridge, MA: National Bureau of Economic Research, Inc., 1998).

172. Bill McCarthy, "New Economics of Sociological Criminology," *Annual Review of Sociology* (2002): 417–442.

173. Greg Pogarsky, "Identifying 'Deterrable' Offenders: Implications for Deterrence Research," *Justice Quarterly* 19 (2002): 431–452.

174. Nagin and Pogarsky, "Integrating Celerity, Impulsivity, and Extralegal Sanction Threats into a Model of General Deterrence: Theory and Evidence."

175. Anthony Braga, "Pulling Levers Focused Deterrence Strategies and the Prevention of Gun Homicide," *Journal of Criminal Justice* 36 (2008): 332–343.

176. Dieter Dolling, Horst Entorf, Dieter Hermann, and Thomas Rupp, "Deterrence Effective? Results of a Meta-Analysis of Punishment," *European Journal on Criminal Policy and Research* 15 (2009): 201–224.

177. Michael Tonry, "Learning from the Limitations of Deterrence Research," *Crime and Justice: A Review of Research* 37 (2008): 279–311.

178. James Q. Wilson and Richard Herrnstein, *Crime and Human Nature* (New York: Simon & Schuster, 1985), p. 494.

179. Alicia Sitren and Brandon Applegate, "Testing the Deterrent Effects of Personal and Vicarious Experience with Punishment and Punishment Avoidance," *Deviant Behavior* 28 (2007): 29–55.

180. Christina Dejong, "Survival Analysis and Specific Deterrence: Integrating Theoretical and Empirical Models of Recidivism," *Criminology* 35 (1997): 561–576.

181. Paul Tracy and Kimberly Kempf-Leonard, *Continuity and Discontinuity in Criminal Careers* (New York: Plenum Press, 1996).

182. Lawrence Greenfeld, *Examining Recidivism* (Washington, DC: U.S. Government Printing Office, 1985).

183. Allen Beck and Bernard Shipley, *Recidivism of Prisoners Released in 1983* (Washington, DC: Bureau of Justice Statistics, 1989).

184. Dejong, "Survival Analysis and Specific Deterrence," p. 573.

185. David Weisburd, Elin Waring, and Ellen Chayet, "Specific Deterrence in a Sample of Offenders Convicted of White-Collar Crimes," *Criminology* 33 (1995): 587–607.

186. Dejong, "Survival Analysis and Specific Deterrence"; Raymond Paternoster and Alex Piquero, "Reconceptualizing Deterrence: An Empirical Test of Personal and Vicarious Experiences," *Journal of Research in Crime and Delinquency* 32 (1995): 251–258.

187. David Lovell, L. Clark Johnson, and Kevin Cain, "Recidivism of Supermax Prisoners in Washington State," *Crime and Delinquency* 53 (2007): 633–656.

188. Peter Wood, "Exploring the Positive Punishment Effect Among Incarcerated Adult Offenders," *American Journal of Criminal Justice* 31 (2007): 8–22.

189. Jacobs, "Deterrence and Deterrability."

190. Greg Pogarsky and Alex R. Piquero, "Can Punishment Encourage Offending? Investigating the 'Resetting' Effect," *Journal of Research in Crime and Delinquency* 40 (2003): 92–117.

191. Doris Layton MacKenzie and Spencer De Li, "The Impact of Formal and Informal Social Controls on the Criminal Activities of Probationers," *Journal of Research in Crime and Delinquency* 39 (2002): 243–276.

192. Lawrence Sherman and Richard Berk, "The Specific Deterrent Effects of Arrest for Domestic Assault," *American Sociological Review* 49 (1984): 261–272.

193. Christopher Maxwell, Joel H. Garner, and Jeffrey A. Fagan, *The Effects of Arrest in Intimate Partner Violence: New Evidence from the Spouse Assault Replication Program* (Washington, DC: National Institute of Justice, 2001); J. David Hirschel, Ira Hutchison, and Charles Dean, "The Failure of Arrest to Deter Spouse Abuse," *Journal of Research in Crime and Delinquency* 29 (1992): 7–33; Franklyn Dunford, David Huizinga, and Delbert Elliott, "The Role of Arrest in Domestic Assault: The Omaha Experiment," *Criminology* 28 (1990): 183–206.

194. Andrew Klein and Terri Tobin, "A Longitudinal Study of Arrested Batterers, 1995–2005: Career Criminals," *Violence Against Women* 14 (2008): 136–157.

195. Pew Charitable Trust, *One in 100: Behind Bars in America 2008* (Washington, DC: Pew Charitable Trusts, 2008), www.pewcenteronthestates.org/uploadedFiles/One%20in%20100.pdf (accessed November 6, 2010).

196. Bobby Caina Calvan, "Calif. Initiative Seeks to Rewrite Three-Strikes Law," *Boston Globe*, July 12, 2004, p. 1.

197. William Spelman, "Specifying the Relationship Between Crime and Prisons," *Journal of Quantitative Criminology* 24 (2008): 149–178.

198. Steven Levitt, "Why Do Increased Arrest Rates Appear to Reduce Crime: Deterrence, Incapacitation, or Measurement Error?" *Economic Inquiry* 36 (1998): 353–372; see also Thomas Marvell and Carlisle Moody, "The Impact of Prison Growth on Homicide," *Homicide Studies* 1 (1997): 205–233.

199. John Wallerstedt, *Returning to Prison, Bureau of Justice Statistics Special Report* (Washington, DC: U.S. Department of Justice, 1984).

200. James Marquart, Victoria Brewer, Janet Mullings, and Ben Crouch, "The Implications of Crime Control Policy on HIV/AIDS-

Related Risk Among Women Prisoners," *Crime and Delinquency* 45 (1999): 82–98.

201. Jose Canela-Cacho, Alfred Blumstein, and Jacqueline Cohen, "Relationship Between the Offending Frequency of Imprisoned and Free Offenders," *Criminology* 35 (1997): 133–171.

202. Kate King and Patricia Bass, "Southern Prisons and Elderly Inmates: Taking a Look Inside," paper presented at the annual meeting of the American Society of Criminology, San Diego, November, 1997.

203. James Lynch and William Sabol, "Prisoner Reentry in Perspective," Urban Institute, www.urban.org/publications/410213.html (accessed November 6, 2010).

204. Rudy Haapanen, Lee Britton, and Tim Croisdale, "Persistent Criminality and Career Length," *Crime and Delinquency* 53 (2007): 133–155.

205. Marc Mauer, testimony before the U.S. Congress, House Judiciary Committee, on "Three Strikes and You're Out," March 1, 1994.

206. Stephen Markman and Paul Cassell, "Protecting the Innocent: A Response to the Bedeau-Radelet Study," *Stanford Law Review* 41 (1988): 121–170, at 153.

207. James Stephan and Tracy Snell, *Capital Punishment, 1994* (Washington, DC: Bureau of Justice Statistics, 1996), p. 8.

208. Cass R. Sunstein and Adrian Vermeule, "Is Capital Punishment Morally Required? Acts, Omissions, and Life-Life Tradeoffs," *Stanford Law Review* 58 (2006): 703–750, at 749.

209. Andrew von Hirsch, *Doing Justice* (New York: Hill and Wang, 1976).

210. Ibid., pp. 15–16.

211. Ibid.

212. Richard Frase, "Punishment Purposes," *Stanford Law Review* 67 (2005): 67–85.

On Monday, April 16, 2007, 23-year-old Seung-Hui Cho methodically took the lives of 32 people—27 students and 5 professors—at Virginia Tech before taking his own life.[1] In the aftermath of the tragedy, Cho was described as a loner unable to make social connections. He had been involuntarily institutionalized in a mental health facility. He became fixated on several female students who eventually complained to the police because he was showing up at their rooms and bombarding them with instant messages.[2] In a creative writing class, he read one of his poems in class, and its sinister content so frightened classmates that some did not show up the next time the class met.[3] Ten months later, on February 14, 2008, another tragedy occurred at Northern Illinois University. Steven Kazmierczak, a former student, who was currently enrolled in the school of social work at the University of Illinois at Urbana-Champaign, entered Cole Hall, a large

(continued on page 140)

Trait Theories

5

Chapter Outline

Learning Objectives

1. Be familiar with the development of trait theory
2. Discuss the biochemical conditions that produce crime
3. Be familiar with the neurophysiological conditions associated with crime
4. Link genetics to crime
5. Explain the evolutionary view of crime
6. Discuss the elements of the psychodynamic perspective
7. Link behavioral theory to crime
8. Know the cognitive processes related to crime
9. Discuss the elements of personality related to crime
10. Be aware of the controversy over the association between intelligence and crime

auditorium-style lecture hall on the NIU campus, armed with a shotgun and three handguns. Standing on the stage, he methodically began shooting into the crowded classroom, killing 5 and wounding 16 others before taking his own life. In the aftermath of the incident, Kazmierczak was described as "an outstanding student" who suffered from depression and anxiety. His girlfriend, Jessica Baty, later said, "He was anything but a monster," Baty said. "He was probably the nicest, most caring person ever."[4] In a more recent tragedy, on January 8, 2011, Jared Lee Loughner opened fire in a supermarket parking lot in Tucson, Arizona, killing 6 and wounding 19 in a misguided attempt to assassinate Congresswoman Gabrielle Giffords.

Senseless tragedies such as these help convince some criminologists that the root cause of crime may be linked to mental or physical abnormality. How could young men such as Cho, Loughner, and Kazmierczak engage in mass murder unless they were suffering from some form of mental instability or collapse? In the aftermath of the killings, there seemed to be ample evidence that all three were under severe psychological stress, yet no one was able to foresee or predict their violent actions.

This vision is neither new nor unique. The image of a disturbed, mentally ill offender seems plausible because more than one generation of Americans has grown up on films and TV shows that portray violent criminals as mentally deranged and physically abnormal. Beginning with Alfred Hitchcock's film *Psycho*, producers have made millions depicting the ghoulish acts of people who at first seem normal and even friendly but turn out to be demented and dangerous. Lurking out there are fanatical patients (*Saw I* through *Saw VI*, plus *Saw 3D*), crazed babysitters (*The Hand that Rocks the Cradle*), frenzied airline passengers (*Red Eye*; *Turbulence*), deranged roommates (*Single White Female*), cracked neighbors (*Disturbia*; *Last House on the Left*), psychotic tenants (*Pacific Heights*), demented secretaries (*The Temp*), unhinged police (*Maniac Cop*), mad cab drivers (*The Bone Collector*), irrational fans (*The Fan*; *Misery*), abnormal girlfriends (*Obsessed*; *Fatal Attraction*) and boyfriends (*Fear*), unstable husbands (*Enough*; *Sleeping with the Enemy*) and wives (*Black Widow*), loony fathers (*The Stepfather*), mothers (*Friday the 13th, Part 1*), and grandmothers (*Hush*), unbalanced crime victims (*I Know What You Did Last Summer*), maniacal children (*The Good Son*; *Children of the Corn*), manic hotel owners (*Psycho*; *Hostel* and *Hostel: Part II*), lunatic high school friends (*Scream*) and college classmates (*Scream II*), possessed dolls (*Child's Play 1–3*) and their mates (*Bride of Chucky*), and nutsy teenaged admirers (*The Crush*). Sometimes they even try to kill each other (*Freddy vs. Jason*), and some are not even totally human (*Twilight*; *I Am Legend*). No one can ever be safe when doctors, psychologists, and psychiatrists who should be treating these disturbed people turn out to be demonic murderers themselves (*The Human Centipede*; *Hannibal*; *Silence of the Lambs*). Is it any wonder

that we respond to a particularly horrible crime by saying of the perpetrator, "That guy must be crazy" or "She is a monster!"

The view that criminals bear physical and/or mental traits that make them different and abnormal is not restricted to the movie going public. Since the nineteenth century, criminologists have suggested that biological and psychological traits have the power to influence behavior. People develop physical or mental traits at birth or soon after that affect their social functioning over the life course and influence their behavior choices. Because these mental and physical traits are rare and occur infrequently, only a few people in any social environment embark on criminal careers. As you may recall, only a small percentage of all offenders go on to become persistent repeaters. It makes logical sense that what sets these chronic offenders apart from the "average" criminal is an abnormal biochemical makeup, brain structure, genetic constitution, or some other personal trait.[5] The fact that each of us has a unique physical makeup and personality structure explains why, when faced with the same life situations, one person commits crime and becomes a chronic offender, whereas another attends school, church, and neighborhood functions and obeys the laws of society.

To understand this view of crime causation, we begin with a brief review of the development of trait theories.

FOUNDATIONS OF TRAIT THEORY

During the late nineteenth century, the scientific method was beginning to take hold in Europe. Rather than relying on pure thought and reason, scientists began to use careful observation and analysis of natural phenomena in their experiments. This movement inspired new discoveries in biology, astronomy, and chemistry. Charles Darwin's (1809–1882) discoveries on the evolution of man encouraged a nineteenth-century "cult of science." Darwin's discoveries encouraged other scholars to be certain that all human activity could be verified by scientific principles. If the scientific method could be applied to the study of the natural world, then why not use it to study human behavior?

Auguste Comte (1798–1857), considered the founder of sociology, applied scientific methods to the study of society. According to Comte, societies pass through stages that can be grouped on the basis of how people try to understand the world in which they live. People in primitive societies consider inanimate objects as having life (for example, the sun is a god); in later social stages, people embrace a rational, scientific view of the world. Comte called this final stage the positive stage, and those who followed his writings became known as positivists. As we understand it today, **positivism** has two main elements:

- All true knowledge is acquired through direct observation and not through conjecture or belief. Statements that cannot be backed up by direct observation—for instance, "all babies are born innocent"—are invalid and worthless.
- The scientific method must be used if research findings are to be considered valid. This involves such steps as identifying problems, collecting data, forming hypotheses, conducting experiments, and interpreting results (see Exhibit 5.1).

According to the positivist tradition, social processes are a product of the measurable interaction between relationships and events. Human behavior therefore is a function of a variety of forces. Some are social, such as the effect of wealth and class; others are political and historical, such as war and famine. Other forces are more personal and psychological, such as an individual's brain structure and his or her biological makeup or mental ability. Each of these influences and shapes human behavior. People are neither born "good" nor "bad," and are neither "saints" nor "sinners." They are a product of their social and psychological traits, influenced by their upbringing and environment.

Biological Positivism

The earliest "scientific" studies applying the positivist model to criminology were conducted by physiognomists, such as J. K. Lavater (1741–1801), who studied the facial features of criminals to determine whether the shape of ears, nose, and eyes and the distance between them were associated with antisocial behavior. Phrenologists, such as Franz Joseph Gall (1758–1828) and Johann K. Spurzheim (1776–1832), studied the shape of the skull and bumps on the head to determine whether these physical attributes were linked to criminal behavior. Phrenologists believed that external cranial characteristics dictate which areas of the brain control physical activity. The brain, they suggested, has 30 different areas or faculties that control behavior. The size of a brain could be determined by inspecting the contours of the skull—the larger the organ, the more active it was. The relative size of brain organs could be increased or decreased through exercise and self-discipline.[6] Though phrenology techniques and methods are no longer practiced or taken seriously, these efforts were an early attempt to use a "scientific" method to study crime.

By the early nineteenth century, abnormality in the human mind was being linked to criminal behavior patterns.[7] Philippe Pinel (1745–1826), one of the founders of French psychiatry, claimed that some people behave abnormally even without being mentally ill. He coined the phrase *manie sans delire* to denote what today is referred to as a **psychopathic personality**. In 1812, an American, Benjamin Rush (1745–1813), described patients with an "innate preternatural moral depravity."[8] Another early criminological pioneer, English physician Henry Maudsley (1835–1918), believed that insanity and criminal behavior were strongly linked. He stated: "Crime is a sort of outlet in which their unsound tendencies are discharged; they would go mad if they were not criminals, and they do not go mad because they are criminals."[9] These early research efforts shifted attention to brain functioning and personality as the keys to criminal behavior. When Sigmund Freud's (1856–1939) work on the unconscious gained worldwide notoriety, the psychological basis of behavior was forever established.

Cesare Lombroso

In Italy, Cesare Lombroso (1835–1909), a physician who served much of his career in the Italian army, was studying the cadavers of executed criminals in an effort to scientifically

---

EXHIBIT 5.1

Elements of the Scientific Method

Observation
Identify problem and collect data and facts.

Hypothesis
Develop a reasonable explanation to account for or predict the data observed and the facts collected.

Test Hypothesis
Test hypothesis using control groups and experimental methods.

Interpretation
Analyze data using accepted statistical techniques.

Conclusion
Interpret data and verify or disprove accuracy of hypothesis.

determine whether law violators were physically different from people of conventional values and behavior.[10] Lombroso believed that serious offenders—those who engaged in repeated assault- or theft-related activities—were "born criminals" who had inherited a set of primitive physical traits that he referred to as **atavistic anomalies**. Physically, born criminals were throwbacks to more primitive savage people. Among the crime-producing traits Lombroso identified were enormous jaws and strong canine teeth common to carnivores and savages who devour raw flesh. These criminogenic traits can be acquired through *indirect heredity*, from a degenerate family whose members suffered from such ills as insanity, syphilis, and alcoholism, or *direct heredity*—being the offspring of criminal parents.

Lombroso's version of criminal anthropology was brought to the United States via articles and textbooks that adopted his ideas. He attracted a circle of followers who expanded on his vision of **biological determinism** and helped stimulate interest in what is referred to as **criminal anthropology**.[11] Ironically, Lombroso's research was more popular in the United States than it was in Europe, and by the turn of the century, American social thinkers were discussing "the science of penology" and "the science of criminology."[12]

Lombroso's Contemporaries Lombroso was not alone in his views on the biological basis of crime. A contemporary, Raffaele Garofalo (1852–1934), shared the belief that certain physical characteristics indicate a criminal nature: "a lower degree of sensibility to physical pain, seems to be demonstrated by the readiness with which prisoners submit to the operation of tattooing."[13] Enrico Ferri (1856–1929) added a social dimension to Lombroso's work and argued that criminals should not be held personally or morally responsible for their actions because forces outside their control caused criminality.[14]

Advocates of the **inheritance school**, such as Henry Goddard, Richard Dugdale, and Arthur Estabrook, traced several generations of crime-prone families (referred to by pseudonyms such as the "Jukes" and the "Kallikaks"), finding evidence that criminal tendencies were based on genetics.[15] Their conclusion: traits deemed socially inferior could be passed down from generation to generation through inheritance. Modern scholars point out that these families lived in severe poverty so that social rather than biological factors may have been at the root of their problems.[16]

The body build or **somatotype** school, developed more than 50 years ago by William Sheldon, held that criminals manifest distinct physiques that make them susceptible to particular types of antisocial behavior. Three types of body builds were identified:

- *Mesomorphs* have well-developed muscles and an athletic appearance. They are active, aggressive, sometimes violent, and the most likely to become criminals.
- *Endomorphs* have heavy builds and are slow moving. They are known for lethargic behavior, rendering them

unlikely to commit violent crime and more willing to engage in less strenuous criminal activities such as fencing stolen property.
- *Ectomorphs* are tall, thin, and less social and more intellectual than the other types. These types are the least likely to commit crime.[17]

Sheldon recognized that pure types are rare and that most people have elements of all three types. He identified a Dionysian temperament, a person who has an excess of mesomorphy with a deficiency in ectomorphic restraint, thereby rendering them impulsive and into self-gratification, a condition that would produce crime.

The Legacy of Biological Criminology

The work of Lombroso and his contemporaries is regarded today as a historical curiosity, not scientific fact. Strict biological determinism is no longer taken seriously (later in his career even Lombroso recognized that not all criminals were biological throwbacks). Early biological determinism has been discredited because it is methodologically flawed; most studies did not use control groups from the general population to compare results, a violation of the scientific method. Many of the traits assumed to be inherited are not really genetically determined but could be caused by deprivation in surroundings and diet. Even if most criminals shared some biological traits, they might be products not of heredity but of some environmental condition, such as poor nutrition or health care. Unusual appearance, and not behavior, may have prompted people to be labeled and punished by the justice system.

Because of these deficiencies the validity of a purely biological/psychological explanation of criminality became questionable and is no longer considered valid. Today, criminologists believe that environmental conditions interact with human traits and conditions to influence behavior. Hence, the term **biosocial theory** has been coined to reflect the assumed link between physical and mental traits, the social environment, and behavior.

Sociobiology

What seems no longer tenable at this juncture is any theory of human behavior which ignores biology and relies exclusively on socio-cultural learning. . . . Most social scientists have been wrong in their dogmatic rejection and blissful ignorance of the biological parameters of our behavior.[18]

At midcentury, sociology dominated the study of crime and scholarship and any suggestion that antisocial behavior may have an individual-level cause was treated with enmity.[19] Some criminologists label this position as **biophobia**, the view that no serious consideration should be given to biological factors when attempting to understand human nature.[20]

Then in the early 1970s, spurred by the publication of *Sociobiology*, by biologist Edmund O. Wilson, the biological basis for crime once again emerged into the limelight.[21] **Sociobiology** differs from earlier theories of behavior in that it stresses that biological and genetic conditions affect how social behaviors are learned and perceived. These perceptions, in turn, are linked to existing environmental structures. Sociobiologists view the gene as the ultimate unit of life that controls all human destiny. Although they believe environment and experience also have an impact on behavior, their main premise is that most actions are controlled by a person's "biological machine." Most important, people are controlled by the innate need to have their genetic material survive and dominate others. Consequently, they do everything in their power to ensure their own survival and that of others who share their gene pool (relatives, fellow citizens, and so forth). Even when they come to the aid of others, which is called **reciprocal altruism**, people are motivated by the belief that their actions will be reciprocated and that their gene survival capability will be enhanced.

Contemporary Trait Theories

The study of sociobiology revived interest in finding a biological basis for crime and delinquency. If, as it suggests, biological (genetic) makeup controls human behavior, it follows that it should also be responsible for determining whether a person chooses law-violating or conventional behavior. This view of crime causation is referred to as **trait theory**.

Trait theorists today do not suggest that a single biological or psychological attribute is thought to adequately explain all criminality. Rather, each offender is considered unique, physically and mentally; consequently, there must be different explanations for each person's behavior. Some may have inherited criminal tendencies, others may be suffering from nervous system (neurological) problems, and still others may have a blood chemistry disorder that heightens their antisocial activity. Criminologists who focus on the individual see many explanations for crime, because, in fact, there are many differences among criminal offenders.

Trait theorists are not overly concerned with legal definitions of crime; they do not try to explain why people violate particular statutory laws such as car theft or burglary. To them, these are artificial legal concepts based on arbitrary boundaries (i.e., speeding may be arbitrarily defined as exceeding 65 miles per hour in some areas, 70 in others). Instead, trait theorists focus on basic human behavior and drives—attachment, aggression, violence, impulsivity—that are linked to antisocial behavior patterns. They also recognize that human traits may not alone produce criminality and that crime-producing interactions involve both personal traits—such as intelligence, personality, and chemical and genetic makeup—and environmental factors, such as family life, educational attainment, economic factors, and neighborhood conditions. Physical or mental traits are, therefore, but one part of a large pool of environmental, social, and personal factors that account for criminality. Some people may have a predisposition toward aggression, but environmental stimuli can either suppress or trigger antisocial acts.

Environment, Traits, and Crime   Even the most committed trait theorists recognize that environmental conditions in disadvantaged inner-city areas may have a powerful influence on antisocial behavior. Many people who reside in these areas experience poverty, racism, frustration, and anger, yet relatively few become delinquents and even fewer mature into adult criminals. Because not all humans are born with equal potential to learn and achieve (**equipotentiality**), the combination of physical traits and the environment produces individual behavior patterns. In fact, what may appear to some as the effect of environment and socialization actually may be linked to genetically determined physical and/or mental traits. Psychologist Bernard Rimland, for one, argues that while childhood behavior problems are commonly linked to poor environment, disrupted socialization, or inadequate parenting, they actually stem from an abnormal trait: neurological damage linked to diet and chemical contamination. In his 2008 book, *Dyslogic Syndrome*, Rimland disputes the notion that bad or ineffective parenting is to blame for troubled or disobedient children:

> . . . most "bad" children . . . suffer from toxic physical environments, often coupled with genetic vulnerability, rather than toxic family environments. . . . research clearly shows that the culprits primarily responsible for the dyslogical behavior of millions of America's children are not their parents, but rather the poor-quality food substitutes they eat, the pollutants in the air they breathe, the chemically contaminated water they drink, and other less well-known physical insults that cause malfunctioning brains and bodies. Many of these children are labeled "hyperactive" or "attention disordered." Some are labeled "conduct disordered." Some are labeled "oppositional." Thousands are labeled "depressed" or "bipolar." And many are simply dismissed as hopelessly warped or evil. They struggle at school, they struggle through life, and in their wake they leave a trail of misery—of disrupted and saddened lives. But it's not truly their fault, and it's rarely their parents' fault.[22]

So according to Rimland and others who share his beliefs, it is personal traits and biological makeup in combination with the social environment that explains behavioral choices.[23] As criminologists Anthony Walsh and Lee Ellis conclude, "If there is one takeaway lesson from studying biological bases of behavior, it is that the more we study them the more we realize how important the environment is."[24]

Contemporary trait theories can be divided into two major subdivisions: one that stresses psychological functioning and another that stresses biological (biosocial) makeup. Although there is often overlap between these views (i.e., brain functioning may have a biological basis), each branch has its unique characteristics and will be discussed separately.

BIOSOCIAL THEORY

Rather than viewing the criminal as a person whose behavior is controlled solely by conditions determined at birth, most biocriminologists believe that physical, environmental, and social conditions work in concert to produce human behavior; this integrated approach is commonly referred to as biosocial theory. The following subsections will examine some of the more important schools of thought within

AP Images/Mike Derer, Pool

Eric Hunt stands in Superior Court in Somerville, New Jersey, accused of attacking Nobel laureate and Holocaust scholar Elie Wiesel in San Francisco on February 1, 2007. Hunt, a Holocaust denier, was convicted and sentenced to two years, but was given credit for time served and good behavior; he was released and ordered to undergo psychological treatment. Are troubled people like Hunt the "victim" of some personal trait or condition that prevents them from understanding the wrongfulness of their behavior? Or if they do understand, are they able to control their antisocial thoughts?

biosocial theory.[25] First, we look at the biochemical factors that are believed to affect behavior. Then the relationship of brain function and crime will be considered, followed by an analysis of genetics and crime. Finally, evolutionary views of crime causation are evaluated.

Biochemical Conditions and Crime

Some trait theorists believe biochemical conditions, including both those that are genetically predetermined and those acquired through diet and environment, control and influence antisocial behavior.[26] The influence of damaging chemical and biological contaminants may begin before birth if the mother's diet either lacks or has an excess of important nutrients (such as manganese) that may later cause developmental problems in her offspring.[27] In sum, exposure to harmful chemicals and poor diet *in utero*, at birth, and beyond may then affect people throughout their life course. Some of the more important biochemical factors that have been linked to criminality are set out in detail here.

Smoking and Drinking Maternal alcohol abuse and/or smoking during gestation have long been linked to prenatal damage and subsequent antisocial behavior in adolescence.[28] When Lisa Gatzke-Kopp and Theodore Beauchaine examined relations between maternal smoking and child behavior, they found that exposure to smoke was associated with increased psychopathology in offspring and that exposure to secondhand cigarette smoke during pregnancy predicted later conduct disorder.[29] Having a smoking parent had a greater affect on behavior than other influences, including prematurity, low birth weight, and poor parenting practices.

Research now shows that people who start drinking by the age of 14 are five times more likely to become alcoholics than people who hold off on drinking until the age of 21. It is possible that early exposure of the brain to alcohol may short-circuit the growth of brain cells, impairing the learning and memory processes that protect against addiction. Thus, early ingestion of alcohol will have a direct influence on behavior.[30]

Exposure to Chemicals and Minerals Biosocial criminologists maintain that minimum levels of minerals and chemicals are needed for normal brain functioning and growth, especially in the early years of life. Research conducted over the past decade shows that an over- or undersupply of certain chemicals and minerals—including sodium, mercury potassium, calcium, amino acids, monoamines, and peptides—can lead to depression, mania, cognitive problems, memory loss, and abnormal sexual activity.[31] Common food additives such as calcium propionate, which is used to preserve bread, have been linked to problem behaviors.[32] Even some commonly used medicines may have detrimental side effects. There has been recent research linking sildenafil, more commonly known as Viagra, with aggressive and violent behavior. While the cause is still unknown, it is possible that sildenafil exerts various biochemical and physiologic effects in the brain and that it affects information processing.[33]

Research shows that excessive intake of certain metals such as iron and manganese may be linked to neurological dysfunctions such as intellectual impairment and attention deficit hyperactivity disorder (ADHD). These neurological conditions are believed to be a precursor of delinquent and criminal behaviors.[34] In a recent international study, Hong Kong researchers, D. K. L. Cheuk and Virginia Wong measured the blood mercury levels of 52 children diagnosed with ADHD and compared them to another group of 59 non-ADHD adolescents. After controlling for numerous personal and social factors, Cheuk and Wong found that the ADHD sample had significantly higher mercury levels than controls. While the sample size they used was small, they were able to conclude that mercury poisoning, both prenatal and after birth, can have a detrimental effect on cognitive functions and cause behavioral problems later in life that have been associated with crime and delinquency.[35]

Diet and Crime

If biochemical makeup can influence behavior, then it stands to reason that food intake and diet are related to crime.[36] Those biocriminologists who believe in a diet–aggression association claim that in every segment of society there are violent, aggressive, and amoral people whose improper food, vitamin, and mineral intake may be responsible for their antisocial behavior.[37] If diet could be improved, they believe, the frequency of violent behavior would be reduced.[38]

In some instances, the absence in the diet of certain chemicals and minerals—including sodium, potassium, calcium, amino acids, magnesium, monoamines, and peptides—can lead to depression, mania, cognitive problems, memory loss, and abnormal sexual activity.[39] In contrast, research shows that excessive amounts of harmful substances such as food dyes and artificial colors and/or flavors seem to provoke hostile, impulsive, and otherwise antisocial behaviors.[40] Take for instance a study that tested 153 3-year-olds and 144 children between the ages of 8 and 9 by exposing them to three different drink combinations:

- Mix A contained the additives sunset yellow, carmoisine, tartrazine, ponceau 4R, and sodium benzoate, chemicals typically found in two single-serving bags of candy.
- Mix B contained sunset yellow, carmoisine, quinoline yellow, allura red, and sodium benzoate equal to what is in two to four bags of candy.
- There was also a placebo with no additives.

Using a carefully planned experimental design, the researchers found that Mix A markedly worsened the younger children's hyperactivity scores, and that both Mix A and Mix B affected older children adversely.[41]

Diet can have a long-term influence on behavior. Adrian Raine and his colleagues charted the long-term effects of a two-year diet enrichment program for 3-year-olds in the African nation of Mauritania. One hundred randomly selected children were placed in the program, which provided them with nutritious lunches, physical exercise, and enhanced education. They were then compared with a control group made up of children who did not participate in the program. By age 17, kids who had been malnourished before they entered the nutrition program had higher scores on physical and psychological well-being than malnourished kids who had not been in the program. By age 23, the malnourished kids who had been in the program 20 years earlier still did better on personality tests and had lower levels of self-reported crimes than the malnourished children who had not been placed in the program. Overall, the results showed that providing children with nutritious diets and enriched environments is associated with greater mental health and reduced antisocial activities later in life.[42]

Sugar Intake

One area of diet that has received a great deal of attention is the association between high intakes of carbohydrates and sugar and antisocial behavior. Experiments have been conducted in which children's diets were altered so that sweet drinks were replaced with fruit juices, table sugar with honey, molasses substituted for sugar in cooking, and so on; results indicate that these changes can reduce aggression levels.[43] Although these results are impressive, a number of biologists have questioned this association, and some recent research efforts have failed to find a link between sugar consumption and violence.[44] In one important study, a group of researchers had 25 preschool children and 23 school-age children described as sensitive to sugar follow a different diet for three consecutive three-week periods. One diet was high in sucrose, the second substituted aspartame (NutraSweet) for a sweetener, and the third relied on saccharin. Careful measurement of the subjects found little evidence of cognitive or behavioral differences that could be linked to diet. If anything, sugar seemed to have a calming effect on the children.[45]

In sum, while some research efforts allege a sugar–violence association, others suggest that many people who maintain diets high in sugar and carbohydrates are not violent or crime prone. In some cases, in fact, sugar intake has been found to possibly reduce or curtail violent tendencies.[46]

Glucose Metabolism/Hypoglycemia

Research shows that persistent abnormality in the way the brain metabolizes glucose (sugar) can be linked to antisocial behaviors such as substance abuse.[47] **Hypoglycemia** occurs when glucose in the blood falls below levels necessary for normal and efficient brain functioning. The brain is sensitive to the lack of blood sugar because it is the only organ that obtains its energy solely from the combustion of carbohydrates. Thus, when the brain is deprived of blood sugar, it has no alternate food supply to call upon, and brain metabolism slows down, impairing function. Symptoms of hypoglycemia include irritability, anxiety, depression, crying spells, headaches, and confusion.

Research studies have linked hypoglycemia to outbursts of antisocial behavior and violence.[48] Several studies have related assaults and fatal sexual offenses to hypoglycemic reactions.[49] Hypoglycemia has also been connected with a syndrome characterized by aggressive and assaultive behavior, glucose disturbance, and brain dysfunction. Some attempts have been made to measure hypoglycemia using subjects with a known history of criminal activity. Studies of jail and prison inmate populations have found a higher than normal level of hypoglycemia.[50] High levels of reactive hypoglycemia have been found in groups of habitually violent and impulsive offenders.[51]

Hormonal Influences

Criminologist James Q. Wilson, in his book *The Moral Sense*, concludes that hormones, enzymes, and neurotransmitters may be the keys to understanding human behavior. According to Wilson, they help explain gender differences in the crime rate. Males, he writes, are biologically and naturally more aggressive than females, while women are naturally more nurturing due to the fact they are the ones who bear and raise children.[52] Hormone levels also help explain the aging-out process. Levels of testosterone, the principal male steroid hormone, decline during the life cycle and may explain why violence rates diminish over time.[53]

A number of biosocial theorists are now evaluating the association between violent behavior episodes and hormone levels, and the findings suggest that abnormal levels of male sex hormones (**androgens**) do in fact produce aggressive behavior.[54] In particular, one recent study by Lee Ellis and his associates found that self-reported violent criminality was positively correlated with masculine mannerisms, masculine body appearance, physical strength, strength of sex drive, low/deep voice, upper body strength, lower body strength, and amount of body hair.[55] Other androgen-related male traits include sensation seeking, impulsivity, dominance, and lesser verbal skills; all of these androgen-related male traits are related to antisocial behaviors.[56] There is a growing body of evidence suggesting that hormonal changes are also related to mood and behavior and, concomitantly, that adolescents experience more intense mood swings, anxiety, and restlessness than their elders.[57] An association between hormonal activity and antisocial behavior is suggested because rates of both factors peak in adolescence.[58]

One area of concern has been **testosterone**, the most abundant androgen, which controls secondary sex characteristics, such as facial hair and voice timbre. Excessive levels of testosterone have been linked to violence and aggression.[59] Studies of prisoners show that testosterone levels are higher in men who commit violent crimes than in the general population.

Hormonal differences may be a key to understanding gender differences in the crime rate. Females may be biologically protected from deviant behavior in the same way they are immune from some diseases that strike males.[60] Girls who have high levels of testosterone or are exposed to testosterone *in utero* may become more aggressive in adolescence.[61] Conversely, boys who were prenatally exposed to steroids that decrease androgen levels display decreased aggressiveness in adolescence. Gender differences in the crime rate then may be explained by the relative difference in androgens between the two sexes.

Hormonal changes may also be able to explain regional and temporal differences in the crime rate. We know that violent crime rates vary from month to month in a seasonal pattern peaking in the summer, and that crime rates are higher in the warmer West and South regions than the cooler Northeast and Midwest. Evidence also shows that impulsive work-related behavior such as strikes and quitting jobs are more likely to occur during the summer. How can these phenomena be explained? It is possible they are due to the side effects of stress hormones such as adrenaline, which the body generates to cope with thermal heat stress. As heat rises, people get irritable, and the body produces excess hormones, which are directly related to aggression and antisocial behaviors.[62]

How Hormones Influence Behavior

Hormones cause areas of the brain to become less sensitive to environmental stimuli. High androgen levels require people to seek excess stimulation and to be willing to tolerate pain in their quest for thrills. Androgens are linked to brain seizures that, under stressful conditions, can result in emotional volatility. Androgens affect the brain structure itself. They influence the left hemisphere of the **neocortex**, the part of the brain that controls sympathetic feelings toward others.[63] Here are some of the physical reactions produced by hormones that have been linked to violence:

- A lowering of average resting arousal under normal environmental conditions to a point where individuals are motivated to seek unusually high levels of environmental stimulation and are less sensitive to harmful aftereffects resulting from this stimulation
- A lowering of seizure thresholds in and around the limbic system, increasing the likelihood that stressful environmental factors will trigger strong and impulsive emotional responses
- A rightward shift in neocortical functioning, resulting in an increased reliance on the brain hemisphere that is most closely integrated with the limbic system and is least prone to reason in logical-linguistic forms or to respond to linguistic commands[64]

These effects promote violence and other serious crimes by causing people to seek greater levels of environmental stimulation and to tolerate more punishment, increasing impulsivity, emotional volatility, and antisocial emotions.[65]

Drugs that decrease testosterone levels are now being used to treat male sex offenders.[66] The female hormones, estrogen and progesterone, have been administered to sex offenders to decrease their sexual potency.[67] The long-term side effects of this treatment and the potential danger are still unknown.[68]

Premenstrual Syndrome Hormonal research has not been limited to male offenders. The suspicion has long existed that the onset of the menstrual cycle triggers excessive amounts of the female sex hormones, which affect antisocial, aggressive behavior. This condition is commonly referred to as **premenstrual syndrome**, or **PMS**.[69] The link between PMS and delinquency was first popularized more than 35 years ago by Katharina Dalton, whose studies of English women indicated that females are more likely to commit suicide and be aggressive and otherwise antisocial just before or during menstruation.[70] Based on her findings, lawyers began using PMS as a legal criminal defense that was accepted in courts in England and the United States.[71]

Dalton's research is often cited as evidence of the link between PMS and crime, but methodological problems make it impossible to accept her findings at face value. There is still significant debate over any link between PMS and aggression. Some doubters argue that the relationship is spurious; it is equally likely that the psychological and physical stress of aggression brings on menstruation and not vice versa.[72]

Diana Fishbein, a noted expert on biosocial theory, concludes that there is in fact an association between elevated levels of female aggression and menstruation. Research efforts, she argues, show (a) that a significant number of incarcerated females committed their crimes during the premenstrual phase and (b) that at least a small percentage of women appear vulnerable to cyclical hormonal changes, which makes them more prone to anxiety and hostility.[73] While the debate is ongoing, it is important to remember that the overwhelming majority of females who do suffer anxiety reactions prior to and during menstruation do not actually engage in violent criminal behavior; so any link between PMS and crime is tenuous at best.[74]

Allergies Allergies are defined as unusual or excessive reactions of the body to foreign substances.[75] For example, hay fever is an allergic reaction caused when pollen cells enter the body and are fought or neutralized by the body's natural defenses. The result of the battle is itching, red eyes and active sinuses.

Cerebral allergies cause an excessive reaction in the brain, whereas **neuroallergies** affect the nervous system. Neuroallergies and cerebral allergies are believed to cause the allergic person to produce enzymes that attack wholesome foods as if they were dangerous to the body.[76] They may also cause swelling of the brain and produce sensitivity in the central nervous system, conditions linked to mental, emotional, and behavioral problems. Research indicates a connection between allergies and hyperemotionality, depression, aggressiveness, and violent behavior.[77]

Neuroallergy and cerebral allergy problems have also been linked to hyperactivity in children, a condition also linked to antisocial behavior. The foods most commonly involved in producing such allergies are cow's milk, wheat, corn, chocolate, citrus, and eggs; however, about 300 other foods have been identified as allergens. The potential seriousness of the problem has been raised by studies linking the average consumption of one suspected cerebral allergen, corn, to cross-national homicide rates.[78]

Environmental Contaminants When the Centers for Disease Control and Prevention conducted a very extensive evaluation of chemical and mineral contamination in the United States just a few years ago, it found that despite some significant improvements there are still many dangerous substances in the environment, including lead, copper, cadmium, mercury, and inorganic gases such as chlorine and nitrogen dioxide.[79] Prolonged exposure to these substances can cause severe illness or death; at more moderate levels, they have been linked to emotional and behavioral disorders.[80] Among the suspects that have been linked to developmental delays and emotional problems are chemicals used in the agricultural business in insecticides and pesticides. Another suspected cause with dysfunctional behavior is phthalates, industrial chemicals widely used as solvents and ingredients in plastics. Thousands of household items, from shampoos to flooring products, contain phthalates, and research shows that exposure is related to childhood misbehavior and improper functioning.[81] One such substance, chlorpyrifos, is now banned for residential use but is still allowed for agriculture and commercial enterprises. Recent research by Virginia Rauh and her colleagues found that children exposed to large amounts of chlorpyrifos before birth maintain an increased risk for personal problems such as attention deficit hyperactivity disorder (highly exposed children were significantly more likely to score lower on measures of psychomotor and mental development).[82] These outcomes have been linked to antisocial behavior.

CONNECTIONS

The link between neurological deficiencies such as ADHD and antisocial behavior will be discussed more fully later in this chapter.

Lead Ingestion A number of recent research studies have suggested that lead ingestion is linked to aggressive behaviors on both a macro- or group/nation level and on a micro- or individual case level.[83]

On a macro-level, areas with the highest concentrations of lead also report the highest levels of homicide.[84] Examining changes in lead levels in the United States, Britain,

Canada, France, Australia, Finland, Italy, West Germany, and New Zealand (lead levels changed when nations phased out lead-containing paint and gasoline), economist Rick Nevin found that long-term worldwide trends in crime levels correlate significantly with changes in environmental levels of lead. Nevin discovered that children exposed to higher levels of lead during the preschool developmental years engaged in higher rates of offending when they reached their late teens and early twenties. His conclusion: 65 to 90 percent or more of the substantial variation in violent crime in all these countries was explained by lead. In the United States, juvenile arrest rates skyrocketed in the 1960s, an increase that tracked the increase in the use of leaded gas usage after World War II. As the use of leaded gas declined, so too did crime rates.[85]

On a micro-level, research finds that even limited exposure to lead can have a deleterious influence on a child's development and subsequent behavior and correlates significantly with neurological conditions such as hyperactivity.[86] Delinquents are almost four times more likely to have high bone-lead levels than children in the general population.[87] Criminologist Deborah Denno investigated the behavior of more than 900 African American youths and found that lead poisoning was one of the most significant predictors of male delinquency and persistent adult criminality.[88] Herbert Needleman and his associates have conducted a number of studies indicating that youths who had high lead concentrations in their bones were much more likely to report attention problems, delinquency, and aggressiveness than those who were lead free.[89] Recent research shows that almost any elevated level of lead ingestion is related to lower IQ scores, a factor linked to

aggressive behavior.[90] There is also evidence linking lead exposure to mental illnesses, such as schizophrenia, which have been linked to antisocial behaviors.[91]

The CDC survey found that among children ages 1 to 5, the average blood lead level was about 2.2 percent, which was down from 4.4 percent a decade ago. While the improvement is welcome, exposure of children to lead in homes containing lead-based paint and lead-contaminated dust remains a serious public health concern.[92] Research also shows that lead effects may actually begin in the womb due to the mother's dietary consumption of foods, such as seafood, that are high in lead content.[93] Improved prenatal care may help mothers avoid the danger of lead exposure and reduce long-term crime rates.

Neurophysiological Conditions and Crime

Some researchers focus their attention on **neurophysiology**, the study of brain activity.[94] They believe neurological and physical abnormalities are acquired as early as the fetal or prenatal stage or through birth delivery trauma and that they control behavior throughout the life span.[95]

Studies conducted in the United States and in other nations have indicated that the relationship between impairment in executive brain functions (such as abstract reasoning, problem-solving skills, and motor behavior skills) and aggressive behavior is significant.[96] Children who suffer from measurable neurological deficits at birth are believed to also suffer from a number of antisocial traits throughout their life course, ranging from habitual lying to antisocial violence.[97]

The association between neurological disorder and antisocial behaviors may take a number of different paths:

- *Direct association.* Neurological deficits may be a direct cause of antisocial behavior, including violent offending.[98] The presence of brain abnormality causes irrational and destructive behaviors. Clinical analysis of convicted murderers by Peer Briken and colleagues found that a significant number (31 percent) showed evidence of brain abnormalities, including epilepsy, traumatic brain injury, childhood encephalitis, or meningitis causing brain damage, genetic disorders, and unspecified brain damage.[99] In addition, the subjects with brain abnormalities were significantly more likely to commit multiple murders.

Benita Nahimana (foreground left), 3, plays with her sister Sophia and neighbor Gloria on the chipped-paint wood floor in their old apartment as parents Regina and Razaro watch. Now in a new home, Benita is still recovering from being exposed to lead poisoning in the apartment. Some criminologists believe that early and prolonged exposure to lead is related to antisocial behavior in adolescence.

AP Images/Jim Cole

- *Indirect association.* Being in possession of a neurological impairment leads to the development of personality traits that are linked to antisocial behaviors. For example, impulsivity and lack of self-control have been linked to antisocial behavior. While the prevailing wisdom is that self-control is a product of socialization and upbringing, there is now evidence that self-control may in fact be regulated and controlled by the prefrontal cortex of the brain.[100] Under this scenario, neurological impairment reduces impulse- and self-control, which leads to damaging behavioral choices.
- *Interactive cause.* Neurological deficits may interact with another trait or social condition to produce antisocial behaviors. Take for instance the research conducted by Adrian Raine, which found that kids who had experienced birth complications indicative of neurological impairment and had also experienced maternal rejection as they matured were more likely to engage in criminal offending than boys who did not experience these symptoms.[101] The combination of neurological dysfunction and maternal rejection had a more powerful influence on behavior than either of these conditions alone.

Measuring Neurological Impairment

There are numerous ways to measure neurological functioning, including memorization and visual awareness tests, short-term auditory memory tests, and verbal IQ tests. These tests have been found to distinguish criminal offenders from noncriminal control groups.[102]

Traditionally, the most important measure of neurophysiological functioning is the **electroencephalograph** (**EEG**), which records the electrical impulses given off by the brain.[103] It represents a signal composed of various rhythms and transient electrical discharges, commonly called brain waves, which can be recorded by electrodes placed on the scalp. The frequency is given in cycles per second, measured in hertz (Hz), and usually ranges from 0.5 to 30 Hz. Studies using the EEG find that violent criminals have far higher levels of abnormal EEG recordings than nonviolent or one-time offenders. Although about 5 percent of the general population have abnormal EEG readings, about 50 to 60 percent of adolescents with known behavior disorders display abnormal recordings.[104] Behaviors highly correlated with abnormal EEG include poor impulse control, inadequate social adaptation, hostility, temper tantrums, and destructiveness.[105] Studies of adults have associated slow and bilateral brain waves with hostile, hypercritical, irritable, nonconforming, and impulsive behavior.[106]

Newer brain scanning techniques, using electronic imaging such as positron emission tomography (PET), brain electrical activity mapping (BEAM), single photon emission computed tomography (SPECT), and the superconducting quantum interference device (SQUID) have made it possible to assess which areas of the brain are directly linked to antisocial behavior.[107] Violent criminals have been found to have impairment in the prefrontal lobes, thalamus, hypothalamus, medial temporal lobe, superior parietal, and left angular gyrus areas of the brain.[108] Some research using PET shows that domestic violence offenders have lower metabolism in the right hypothalamus and decreased correlations between cortical and subcortical brain structures than a group of control subjects.[109] Daniel Amen and his colleagues employed SPECT to test a sample of people convicted of an impulsive murder. They found that these offenders suffered from a condition that reduced blood flow to a region of the brain involved with planning and self-control. Because this area of the brain is believed to control anger management, those who suffer reduced blood flow may be limited in their self-control, planning, and understanding of future consequences when challenged or forced to concentrate.[110]

It is possible that antisocial behavior is influenced by what is referred to as prefrontal dysfunction, a condition that occurs when demands on brain activity overload the prefrontal cortex and result in a lack of control over antisocial behaviors. Because the prefrontal lobes have not fully developed in adolescence, it is not surprising that this is the time that violent behavior peaks.[111]

Minimal Brain Dysfunction

Minimal brain dysfunction (**MBD**) is related to an abnormality in cerebral structure. It has been defined as an abruptly appearing, maladaptive behavior that interrupts an individual's lifestyle and life flow. In its most serious form, MBD has been linked to serious antisocial acts, an imbalance in the urge-control mechanisms of the brain, and chemical abnormality. Included in the category of minimal brain dysfunction are several abnormal behavior patterns: dyslexia, visual perception problems, hyperactivity, poor attention span, temper tantrums, and aggressiveness. One type of minimal brain dysfunction is manifested through episodic periods of explosive rage. This form of the disorder is considered an important cause of such behavior as spouse beating, child abuse, suicide, aggressiveness, and motiveless homicide. One perplexing feature of this syndrome is that people who are afflicted with it often maintain warm and pleasant personalities between episodes of violence. Some studies measuring the presence of MBD in offender populations have found that up to 60 percent exhibit brain dysfunction on psychological tests.[112] Criminals have been characterized as having a dysfunction of the dominant hemisphere of the brain.[113] Researchers using brain wave data have predicted with 95 percent accuracy the recidivism of violent criminals.[114] More sophisticated brain scanning techniques, such as PET, have also shown that brain abnormality is linked to violent crime.[115]

Learning Disabilities

One specific type of MBD that has generated considerable interest is **learning disability** (**LD**), a disorder in one or more of the basic psychological processes involved in understanding or using spoken or written languages. Learning-disabled children usually exhibit poor motor coordination (for example, problems with poor hand-eye coordination, trouble climbing stairs, clumsiness), have behavior problems (lack of emotional control, hostility, cannot stay on task), and have improper auditory and vocal responses (do not seem to hear, cannot differentiate sounds and noises).[116] Though learning disabilities are quite common (approximately 10 percent of all youths have some form of learning disorders), estimates of LD among kids who engage in antisocial behavior is far higher.[117]

What is the association between learning disabilities and crime? There are two popular explanations:

- *Susceptibility rationale* argues that the link is caused by certain side effects of learning disabilities, such as impulsiveness, poor ability to learn from experience, and inability to take social cues.
- *School failure rationale* assumes that the frustration caused by the LD produces poor school performance leading to a negative self-image and acting-out behavior.

Some recent research conducted by Tomer Einat and Amela Einat in Israel might help settle this issue. They found that a far higher percentage of Israeli prison inmates (69.6 percent) were characterized as learning disabled, as opposed to an estimated 10 to 15 percent of the general Israeli population. Among the inmates, learning disabilities were correlated both with low level of education (dropping out of school at an early age) and early age of criminal onset. Their conclusion: people with learning disabilities who give up school at early stages due to their disabilities are more likely to initiate a criminal career at an early age, as compared to individuals—with or without learning disabilities—who do not leave school. Helping LD kids adjust to school may also help them avoid criminal careers.[118]

Attention Deficit Hyperactivity Disorder (ADHD) Many parents have noticed that their children do not pay attention to them—they run around and do things in their own way. Sometimes this inattention is a function of age; in other instances, it is a symptom of **attention deficit hyperactivity disorder** (**ADHD**), in which a child shows a developmentally inappropriate lack of attention, impulsivity, and hyperactivity. The various symptoms of ADHD are described in Exhibit 5.2.

About 3 percent of U.S. children (most often boys, but the condition can also affect girls) are believed to suffer from this disorder, and it is the most common reason children are referred to mental health clinics. ADHD has been associated with poor school performance, grade retention, placement in special needs classes, bullying, stubbornness, and lack of response to discipline. Although the origin of ADHD is still unknown, suspected causes include neurological damage, prenatal stress, and even reactions to food additives and chemical allergies. Some psychologists believe that the syndrome is essentially a chemical problem, specifically, an impairment in the chemical system that supports rapid and efficient communication in the brain's management system.[119]

EXHIBIT 5.2

Symptoms of Attention Deficit Hyperactivity Disorder (ADHD)

Lack of Attention

- Frequently fails to finish projects
- Does not seem to pay attention
- Does not sustain interest in play activities
- Cannot sustain concentration on schoolwork or related tasks
- Is easily distracted

Impulsivity

- Frequently acts without thinking
- Often "calls out" in class
- Does not want to wait his or her turn in lines or games
- Shifts from activity to activity
- Cannot organize tasks or work
- Requires constant supervision

Hyperactivity

- Constantly runs around and climbs on things
- Shows excessive motor activity while asleep
- Cannot sit still; is constantly fidgeting
- Does not remain in his or her seat in class
- Is constantly on the go like a "motor"

SOURCE: Adapted from American Psychiatric Association, *Diagnostic and Statistical Manual of Mental Disorders,* 4th Ed. (Washington, DC: American Psychiatric Press, 1994).

There are also ties to family turmoil: parents of ADHD children are more likely to be divorced or separated, and ADHD children are much more likely to move to new locales than non-ADHD children.[120] It may be possible, then, that emotional turmoil either produces symptoms of ADHD or, if they already exist, causes them to intensify.

A series of research studies now links ADHD to the onset and sustenance of a delinquent career.[121] Children with ADHD are more likely than non-ADHD youths to use illicit drugs, alcohol, and cigarettes in adolescence; to be arrested; to be charged with a felony; and to have multiple arrests.

Many ADHD children also suffer from **conduct disorder** (**CD**) and continually engage in aggressive and antisocial behavior in early childhood. The disorders are sustained over the life course: children diagnosed with ADHD are more likely to be suspended from school and engage in criminal behavior as adults. This ADHD–crime association is important because symptoms of ADHD seem stable through adolescence into adulthood.[122]

In addition to adolescent misbehavior, hyperactive or ADHD children are at greater risk for antisocial activity and drug use/abuse that persists into adulthood.[123] There is some evidence that ADHD youths who also exhibit early signs of MBD and conduct disorder (such as fighting) are the most at risk for persistent antisocial behaviors continuing into adulthood. For example, Jason Fletcher and Barbara Wolfe evaluated data on nearly 14,000 individuals participating in the National Longitudinal Study of Adolescent Health (also known as Add Health) and found that children with ADHD are at a heightened risk for criminality as adults. The data showed that participants with the inattentive type of ADHD were 6.5 percent more likely to commit a crime than their non-ADHD peers, while those with impulsive symptoms were 11 percent more likely and those with a combination of both inattention and hyperactivity were 5 percent more likely to report participating in criminal activities as young adults.[124] Another recent study by Patricia Westmoreland and her associates, which assessed more than 300 randomly selected prison inmates, found that more than 20 percent could be diagnosed with ADHD, and these inmates were more likely to report problems with emotional and social functioning and to have higher suicide risk scores than non-sufferers. The ADHD groups also had higher rates of mood, anxiety, psychotic, antisocial, and borderline personality disorders.[125]

How is ADHD treated? Today, the most typical treatment is doses of stimulants, such as Ritalin, which ironically help control emotional and behavioral outbursts. Other therapies, such as altering diet and food intake, are now being investigated.[126] However, treatment is not always effective. While some treated children with ADHD improve, many do not and continue to show a greater occurrence of externalizing (acting-out) behaviors and significant deficits in areas such as social skills, peer relations, and academic performance over the life course. A recent study by Stephen Hinshaw and his associates compared groups of ADHD and non-ADHD girls and found that even after treatment about four-fifths of the ADHD girls required social services such as special education, tutoring, or psychotherapy, compared to only one-seventh of the comparison girls; 50 percent of the ADHD girls exhibited oppositional defiant disorder, compared to only 7 percent of the control group.[127]

Tumors, Lesions, Injury, and Disease

The presence of brain tumors and lesions has also been linked to a wide variety of psychological problems, including personality changes, hallucinations, and psychotic episodes.[128] Persistent criminality has been linked to lesions in the frontal and temporal regions of the brain, which play an important role in regulating and inhibiting human behavior, including formulating plans and controlling intentions.[129] Clinical evaluation of depressed and aggressive psychopathic subjects showed a significant number (more than 75 percent)

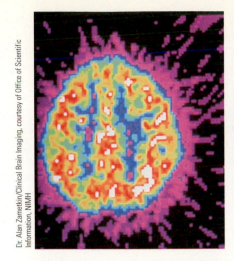
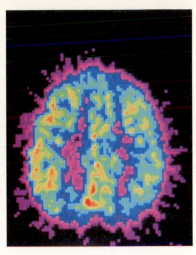

Dr. Alan Zametkin/Clinical Brain Imaging, courtesy of Office of Scientific Information, NIMH

This scan compares a normal brain (left) and an ADHD brain (right). Areas of orange and white demonstrate a higher rate of metabolism, while areas of blue and green represent an abnormally low metabolic rate. Why is ADHD so prevalent in the United States today? Some experts believe that our immigrant forebears, risk takers who impulsively left their homelands for life in a new world, may have brought with them a genetic predisposition for ADHD.

had dysfunction of the temporal and frontal regions of the brain.[130]

There is evidence that people with tumors are prone to depression, irritability, temper outbursts, and even homicidal attacks. Clinical case studies of patients suffering from brain tumors indicate that previously docile people may undergo behavior changes so great that they attempt to seriously harm their families and friends. When the tumor is removed, their behavior returns to normal.[131] In addition to brain tumors, head injuries caused by accidents, such as falls or auto crashes, have been linked to personality reversals marked by outbursts of antisocial and violent behavior.[132]

A variety of central nervous system diseases have also been linked to personality changes. Some of these conditions include cerebral arteriosclerosis, epilepsy, senile dementia, Wernicke-Korsakoff's syndrome, and Huntington's chorea. Associated symptoms of these diseases are memory deficiency, orientation loss, and affective (emotional) disturbances dominated by rage, anger, and increased irritability.[133]

Brain Chemistry

Neurotransmitters are chemical compounds that influence or activate brain functions. Those studied in relation to aggression include dopamine, norepinephrine, serotonin, monoamine oxidase, and GABA.[134] Evidence exists that abnormal levels of these chemicals are associated with aggression. For example, several researchers have reported inverse correlations between serotonin concentrates in the blood and impulsive and/or suicidal behavior.[135] Recent studies of habitually violent Finnish criminals show that low serotonin (5-hydroxytryptamine, 5-HT) levels are associated with poor impulse control and hyperactivity.

In addition, a relatively low concentration of 5-hydroxyin-doleactic acid (5-HIAA) is predictive of increased irritability, sensation seeking, and impaired impulse control.[136]

What is the link between brain chemistry and crime? Prenatal exposure of the brain to high levels of androgens can result in a brain structure that is less sensitive to environmental inputs. Affected individuals seek more intense and varied stimulation and are willing to tolerate more adverse consequences than individuals not so affected.[137] Such exposure also results in a rightward shift in (brain) hemispheric functioning and a concomitant diminution of cognitive and emotional tendencies. One result of this tendency is that left-handers are disproportionately represented in the criminal population since the movement of each hand tends to be controlled by the hemisphere of the brain on the opposite side of the body.

It has also been suggested that individuals with a low supply of the enzyme monoamine oxidase (known either by the acronym MOMA or MAO) engage in behaviors linked with violence and property crime, including defiance of punishment, impulsivity, hyperactivity, poor academic performance, sensation seeking and risk taking, and recreational drug use.[138] Abnormal levels of MAO may explain both individual and group differences in the crime rate. For example, females have higher levels of MAO than males, a condition that may explain gender differences in the crime rate.[139]

The brain and neurological system can produce natural or endogenous opiates that are chemically similar to the narcotics opium and morphine. It has been suggested that the risk and thrills involved in crime cause the neurological system to produce increased amounts of these natural narcotics. The result is an elevated mood state, perceived as an exciting and rewarding experience that acts as a positive reinforcement for crime.[140] The brain then produces its own natural high as a reward for risk-taking behavior. Some people achieve this high by rock climbing and skydiving; others engage in crimes of violence.

Because this linkage has been found, it is not uncommon for violence-prone people to be treated with antipsychotic drugs such as Haldol, Stelazine, Prolixin, and Risperdal, which help control levels of neurotransmitters (such as serotonin/dopamine); these are sometimes referred to as **chemical restraints** or **chemical straitjackets**.

Arousal Theory

It has long been suspected that obtaining thrills is a crime motivator. Adolescents may engage in crimes such as shoplifting and vandalism simply because they offer the attraction of "getting away with it"; from this perspective, delinquency is a thrilling demonstration of personal competence.

According to **arousal theory**, for a variety of genetic and environmental reasons, some people's brains function differently in response to environmental stimuli. All of us

seek to maintain a preferred or optimal level of arousal: too much stimulation leaves us anxious and stressed out; too little makes us feel bored and weary. There is, however, variation in the way people's brains process sensory input. Some nearly always feel comfortable with little stimulation, whereas others require a high degree of environmental input to feel comfortable. The latter are "sensation seekers," who seek out stimulating activities, which may include aggressive, violent behavior patterns.[141]

Evidence that some people may have lower levels of arousal comes from studies on resting heart rate levels conducted by Adrian Raine and his associates, who found that antisocial children have lower resting heart rates than the general population. Raine speculates that some people lack fear and are nonresponsive to the threat of punishment, a condition that allows them to feel relatively comfortable while engaging in antisocial encounters. People who have low arousal levels will seek out risky situations and become more involved with criminal behavior as an avenue toward thrill seeking. Because lack of fear and thrill-seeking behavior are characteristics of adult psychopaths, antisocial children might therefore develop into psychopaths as adults.[142]

The factors that determine a person's level of arousal are not fully determined, but suspected sources include:

- *Brain chemistry (and brain structure).* Some people have brains with many more nerve cells with receptor sites for neurotransmitters than others.
- *Heart rate.* Another view is that people with low heartbeat rates are more likely to commit crime because they seek stimulation to increase their feelings of arousal to normal levels.[143]
- *Autonomic nervous system.* Some biosocial theorists link arousal to the autonomic nervous system as measured by skin conductance response. People with abnormally exaggerated skin conductivity may react with above average negative emotional intensity to stimulus that would have little effect on the average person. As a result, provocations that some people might merely shrug off are viewed as highly confrontational, inflammatory, insulting, and deserving of an aggressive reply.[144]

In sum, brain structure, chemistry, and development are believed to exert a strong influence on human behavior.

Genetics and Crime

On July 14, 1955, Richard Franklin Speck broke into a dormitory and systematically tortured, raped, and murdered eight student nurses in one of the most horrific cases of mass murder in the nation's history. Genetic testing showed that Speck had an abnormal XYY chromosomal structure (XY is normal in males), a finding that provoked a national frenzy: was it possible that all people with XYYs were potential killers? Civil libertarians expressed fear that all XYYs could be labeled dangerous and violent regardless of whether they had engaged in violent activities.[145] Interest in the XYY theory dissipated when it was disclosed that Speck did not actually have an extra Y chromosome.[146] However, the Speck case drew researchers' attention to looking for a genetic basis of crime. Contemporary biosocial theorists are interested in the role genetics plays in shaping human behavior and want to uncover if the propensity to commit crime is an inherited trait passed down from one generation to the next.[147]

The relationship between inherited traits and crime may be either direct or indirect:

- *Direct association.* Possessing a particular genetic structure makes a person prone to aggression, violence, and antisocial behavior.[148] Regardless of environmental influences, people with a particular genetic code get involved in antisocial behaviors. This explains deviant behavior among the rich and famous, some of whom may be the product of a damaged genetic package; it also explains why the majority of those who are poor and desperate are still neither violent nor crime prone, since the environment plays only a secondary role in the production of deviant behaviors.
- *Indirect association.* Possessing a particular genetic makeup is associated with behaviors, attitudes, and personality traits that are also linked to antisocial behavior. Personality conditions linked to aggression such as psychopathy, impulsivity, and neuroticism have been found to be heritable.[149] Genetics shapes the way kids view their family relationships; whether they believe they have a strong attachment to parental socialization is also a strong predictor of crime and delinquency.[150]

Testing Genetic Theory   If criminal tendencies are inherited, then it stands to reason that the children of criminal parents should be more likely to become law violators than the offspring of conventional parents. A number of studies have found that parental criminality and deviance do, in fact, have a powerful influence on delinquent behavior.[151] Some of the most important data on parental deviance have been gathered as part of a long-term study of English youth called the Cambridge Study in Delinquent Development (CSDD). This research has followed a group of about 1,000 males from the time they were 8 years old until today, when they are in their adulthood. The males in the study have been repeatedly interviewed and their school and police records evaluated. These cohort data indicate that a significant number of delinquent youths have criminal fathers.[152] While 8.4 percent of the sons of noncriminal fathers eventually became chronic offenders, about 37 percent of youths with criminal fathers were multiple offenders.[153] More recent analysis of the data confirms that delinquent youths grow up to become the parents of antisocial children.[154] One specific form of aggressive behavior that seems to be inherited is school yard bullying: bullies have children who bully others, and these second-generation bullies grow up to become the fathers of children who are also bullies, in a never-ending cycle.[155]

The Cambridge findings are not unique. Data from the Rochester Youth Development Study (RYDS), a longitudinal analysis that has been monitoring the behavior of 1,000 upstate New York area youths since 1988, also finds an intergenerational continuity in antisocial behavior.[156]

It is possible, of course, that the genetic effect of parental deviance may be exaggerated by mating practices. For example, if an antisocial male partners with an antisocial female and breeds antisocial children, it appears to be a genetic effect. But it is also possible that this "antisocial" family consists of people who have suffered labeling and stigma, isolating them from the mainstream and increasing their chances of criminality. While it may appear that they produce children who are genetically predisposed to crime, it is also possible that what appears to be a genetic effect is actually the product of social processes.[157]

Sibling Similarities   It stands to reason that if the cause of crime is in part genetic, then the behavior of siblings should be similar because they share genetic material. Research does show that if one sibling engages in antisocial behavior, so do his/her brothers and sisters. The effect is greatest among same-sex siblings.[158] Sibling pairs who report warm, mutual relationships and share friends are the most likely to behave in a similar fashion; those who maintain a close relationship also have similar rates of crime and drug abuse.[159]

While the similarity of siblings' behavior seems striking, what appears to be a genetic effect may also be explained by other factors:

- Siblings who live in the same environment are influenced by similar social and economic factors.
- Deviant siblings may grow closer because of shared interests.
- Younger siblings who admire their older siblings may imitate the elders' behavior.
- The deviant sibling forces or threatens the brother or sister into committing criminal acts.
- Siblings living in a similar environment may develop similar types of friends; it is peer behavior that is the critical influence. The influence of peers may negate any observed interdependence of sibling behavior.[160]

Twin Behavior   As mentioned above, because siblings are usually brought up in the same household and share common life experiences, any similarity in their antisocial behavior might be a function of environmental influences and experiences and not genetics at all. To guard against this, biosocial theorists have compared the behavior of same-sex twins and again found concordance in their behavior patterns.[161]

However, an even more rigorous test of genetic theory involves comparison of the behavior of identical monozygotic (MZ) twins with fraternal dizygotic (DZ) twins; while the former have an identical genetic makeup, the latter share only about 50 percent of their genetic combinations.

Research has shown that MZ twins are significantly closer in their personal characteristics, such as intelligence, than are DZ twins.[162]

The earliest studies conducted on the behavior of twins detected a significant relationship between the criminal activities of MZ twins and a much lower association between those of DZ twins. A review of relevant studies conducted between 1929 and 1961 found that 60 percent of MZ twins shared criminal behavior patterns (if one twin was criminal, so was the other), whereas only 30 percent of DZ twin behavior was similarly related.[163] These findings may be viewed as powerful evidence that a genetic basis for criminality exists.

One famous study of twin behavior still under way is the Minnesota Twin Family Study. This research compares the behavior of MZ and DZ twin pairs who were raised together with others who were separated at birth and in some cases did not even know of each other's existence. The study shows some striking similarities in behavior and ability for twin pairs raised apart. An MZ twin reared away from a co-twin has about as good a chance of being similar to the co-twin in terms of personality, interests, and attitudes as one who has been reared with his or her co-twin. The conclusion: similarities between twins are due to genes, not the environment.[164]

Evaluating Genetic Research

Twin studies also have their detractors. Some opponents suggest that available evidence provides little conclusive proof that crime is genetically predetermined. Not all research efforts have found that MZ twin pairs are more closely related in their criminal behavior than DZ or ordinary sibling pairs, and some that have found an association note that it is at best "modest."[165] Those who oppose the genes–crime relationship point to the inadequate research designs and weak methodologies of supporting research. The newer, better-designed research studies, critics charge, provide less support than earlier, less methodically sound studies.[166]

Even if the behavior similarities between MZ twins are greater than those between DZ twins, the association may be explained by environmental factors. MZ twins are more likely to look alike and to share physical traits than DZ twins, and they are more likely to be treated similarly. Similarities in their shared behavior patterns may therefore be a function of socialization and/or environment and not heredity.[167]

It is also possible that what appears to be a genetic effect picked up by the twin research is actually the effect of sibling influence on criminality, referred to as the **contagion effect**: genetic predispositions and early experiences make some people, including twins, susceptible to deviant behavior, which is transmitted by the presence of antisocial siblings in the household.[168]

The contagion effect may explain in part the higher concordance of deviant behaviors found in identical twins as compared to fraternal twins or mere siblings. The relationship between identical twins may be stronger and more enduring than other sibling pairs so that contagion and not genetics explains their behavioral similarities. According to Marshall Jones and Donald Jones, the contagion effect may also help explain why the behavior of twins is more similar in adulthood than in adolescence.[169] Youthful misbehavior is influenced by friends and peer group relationships. As adults, the influence of peers may wane as people marry and find employment. In contrast, twin influence is everlasting; if one twin is antisocial, it legitimizes and supports the criminal behavior in his or her co-twin. This effect may grow even stronger in adulthood because twin relations are more enduring than any other. What seems to be a genetic effect may actually be the result of sibling interaction with a brother or sister who engages in antisocial activity.

Adoption Studies

One way of avoiding the pitfalls of twin studies is to focus attention on the behavior of adoptees. It seems logical that if the behavior of adopted children is more closely aligned to that of their biological parents than to that of their adoptive parents, then the idea of a genetic basis for criminality would be supported. If, on the other hand, adoptees are more closely aligned to the behavior of their adoptive parents than their biological parents, an environmental basis for crime would seem more valid.

Several studies indicate that some relationship exists between biological parents' behavior and the behavior of their children, even when their contact has been nonexistent.[170] One analysis of Swedish adoptees also found that genetic factors are highly significant, accounting for 59 percent of the variation in their petty crime rates. Boys who had criminal parents were significantly more likely to violate the law. Environmental influences and economic status were significantly less important, explaining about 19 percent of the variance in crime. Nonetheless, having a positive environment, such as being adopted into a more affluent home, helped inhibit genetic predisposition.[171]

The genes–crime relationship is controversial because it implies that the propensity to commit crime is present at birth and cannot be altered. It raises moral dilemmas: if *in utero* genetic testing could detect a gene for violence, and a violence gene was found to be present, what could be done as a precautionary measure?

Evolutionary Theory

Some criminologists believe the human traits that produce violence and aggression are produced through the long process of human evolution.[172] According to this evolutionary view, the competition for scarce resources has influenced and shaped the human species.[173] Over the course of human existence, people whose personal characteristics enable them to accumulate more than others are the most likely to breed and dominate the species. People have been shaped to engage in actions that promote their well-being and ensure the survival and reproduction of their genetic line. Males who are impulsive risk-takers may be able to father more children because they are reckless in their social relationships and have sexual encounters with numerous partners. If, according to evolutionary theories, such behavior patterns are inherited, impulsive behavior becomes intergenerational, passed down from father to son. It is not surprising, then, that human history has been marked by war, violence, and aggression.

Violence and Evolution   In their classic book *Homicide*, Martin Daly and Margo Wilson suggest that violent offenses are often driven by evolutionary and reproductive factors. High rates of spouse abuse in modern society may be a function of aggressive men seeking to control and possess mates. When females are murdered by their spouses, the motivating factor is typically fear of infidelity and the threat of attachment to a new partner. Infidelity challenges male dominance and future reproductive rights. It comes as no surprise that in some cultures, including our own, sexual infidelity discovered in progress by the aggrieved husband is viewed legally as a provocation that justifies retaliatory killing.[174] Men who feel most threatened over the potential of losing mates to rivals are the ones most likely to engage in sexual violence. Research shows that women in common-law marriages, especially those who are much younger than their husbands, are at greater risk than older married women. Abusive males may fear the potential loss of their younger mates, especially if they are not bound by a marriage contract, and may use force for purposes of control and possession.[175] Armed robbery is another crime that may have evolutionary underpinnings. Though most robbers are caught and severely punished, it remains an alluring pursuit for men who want to both show their physical prowess and display resources with which to conquer rivals and attract mates. Violent episodes are far more common among men who are unemployed and unmarried—in other words, those who may want to demonstrate their allure to the opposite sex but who are without the benefit of position or wealth.[176]

Gender and Evolution   Evolutionary concepts have been linked to gender-based differences in the crime rate. To ensure survival of the gene pool (and the species), it is beneficial for a male of any species to mate with as many suitable females as possible since each can bear his offspring. In contrast, because of the long period of gestation, females require a secure home and a single, stable, nurturing partner to ensure their survival. Because of these differences in mating patterns, the most aggressive males mate most often and have the greatest number of offspring. Therefore, over the history of the human species, aggressive males have had the greatest impact on the gene pool. The descendants of these aggressive males now account for the disproportionate amount of male aggression and violence.[177]

Crime rate differences between the genders, then, may be less a matter of socialization than inherent differences in mating patterns that have developed over time.[178] Among young men, reckless, life-threatening "risk-proneness" is especially likely to evolve in cultures that force males to find suitable mates to ensure their ability to reproduce. Unless they are aggressive with potential mates and potential rivals for those suitable mates, they are doomed to remain childless.[179]

Other evolutionary factors may have influenced gender differences. Feminists have suggested that with the advent of agriculture and trade in prehistory, women were forced into a position of high dependence and limited power. They began to compete among themselves to secure partners who could provide necessary resources. As a result of these early evolutionary developments, intergender competition became greatest during periods of resource deprivation—times when women become most dependent on a male for support. These trends can still be observed. For example, during times of high female unemployment, female–female aggression rates increase as women compete with each other for men who can provide them with support. In contrast, as rates of social welfare increase, female–female aggression rates diminish because the state serves as a readily available substitute for a male breadwinner.[180]

Evaluation of the Biosocial Branch of Trait Theory

Biosocial perspectives on crime have raised some challenging questions. Critics find some of these theories to be racist and dysfunctional. If there are biological explanations for street crimes, such as assault, murder, or rape, the argument goes, and if, as the official crime statistics suggest, the poor and minority-group members commit a disproportionate number of such acts, then by implication biological theory says that members of these groups are biologically different, flawed, or inferior.

Some biological explanations for the geographic, social, and temporal patterns in the crime rate are problematic. Furthermore, biological theory seems to divide people into criminals and noncriminals on the basis of their genetic and physical makeup, ignoring self-reports indicating that almost everyone has engaged in some type of illegal activity during his or her lifetime.

Biosocial theorists counter that their views should not be confused with Lombrosian, deterministic biology. Rather than suggest that there are born criminals and noncriminals, they maintain that some people carry the potential to be violent or antisocial and that environmental conditions can sometimes trigger antisocial responses.[181] This would explain why some otherwise law-abiding citizens engage in a single, seemingly unexplainable antisocial act, and conversely, why some people with long criminal careers often engage in conventional behavior. It also explains why there are geographic and temporal patterns in the crime rate: people who are predisposed to crime may simply have more opportunities to commit illegal acts in the summer in Los Angeles and Atlanta than in the winter in Bedford, New Hampshire, and Minot, North Dakota, or perhaps their hormonal levels become activated as the temperature rises.

The biosocial view is that behavior is a product of interacting biological and environmental events.[182] Physical impairments may make some people "at risk" to crime, but it is when they are linked to social and environmental problems, such as family dysfunction, that they trigger criminal acts.[183] For example, Avshalom Caspi and his associates found that girls who reach physical maturity at an early age are the ones most likely to engage in delinquent acts. This finding might suggest a relationship between biological traits (hormonal activity) and crime. However, the Caspi research found that the association may also have an environmental basis. Physically mature girls are the ones most likely to have prolonged contact with a crime-prone group: older adolescent boys.[184] Here, the combination of biological change, social relationships, and routine opportunities may predict crime rates.

The most significant criticism of biosocial theory has been the lack of adequate empirical testing. In most research efforts, sample sizes are relatively small and nonrepresentative. A great deal of biosocial research is conducted with samples of adjudicated offenders who have been placed in clinical treatment settings. Methodological problems make it impossible to determine whether findings apply only to offenders who have been convicted of crimes and placed in treatment or to the population of criminals as a whole.[185] More research is needed to clarify the relationships proposed by biosocial researchers and to silence critics.

Concept Summary 5.1 summarizes the various biosocial theories of crime.

PSYCHOLOGICAL TRAIT THEORIES

Andrew Luster, an heir to the Max Factor cosmetic fortune, lived a privileged life of sun and fun in a beach house in an exclusive community near Santa Barbara. However, Andrew had a darker side, which came to light on July 17, 2000, when he was arrested after a young woman accused him of drugging her with the "date rape" drug GHB and then having sex with her while she was unconscious. When police served a warrant on his home, they found tapes indicating Luster had a habit of drugging women and raping them while they were comatose. Halfway through the trial, Luster jumped bail, disappeared, and was declared a fugitive

---

from justice. In his absence, the jury found him guilty on 86 of the 87 counts, and he was eventually sentenced to more than 100 years in prison. Five months later, he was captured in the resort town of Puerto Vallarta, Mexico, by bounty hunter Duane "Dog" Chapman. On July 3, 2003, an appellate court denied Luster's appeal of his guilty verdicts because he had jumped bail.

How can we explain the bizarre behavior of Andrew Luster? Why would a wealthy, handsome man drug and rape unsuspecting women? Could his acts possibly be the result of calculation and planning, or are they the product of some mental aberration or personality disturbance? What drives people who seem to have everything to commit bizarre crimes?

The second branch of trait theories focuses on the psychological aspects of crime, including the associations among intelligence, personality, learning, and criminal behavior.

Psychological theories of crime have a long history. In *The English Convict*, Charles Goring (1870–1919) studied the mental characteristics of 3,000 English convicts.[186] He found little difference in the physical characteristics of criminals and noncriminals, but he uncovered a significant relationship between crime and a condition he referred to as **defective intelligence**, which involves such traits as feeblemindedness, epilepsy, insanity, and defective social instinct.[187] Goring believed criminal behavior was inherited and could, therefore, be controlled by regulating the reproduction of families who produced mentally defective children.

Gabriel Tarde (1843–1904) is the forerunner of modern-day learning theorists.[188] Tarde believed people learn from one another through a process of imitation. Tarde's ideas are similar to modern social learning theorists who believe that both interpersonal and observed behavior, such as a movie or television, can influence criminality.

Since the pioneering work of people like Tarde and Goring, psychologists, psychiatrists, and other mental health professionals have long played an active role in formulating criminological theory. In their quest to understand and treat all varieties of abnormal mental conditions, psychologists have encountered clients whose behavior falls within categories society has labeled as criminal, deviant, violent, and antisocial.

This section is organized along the lines of the predominant psychological views most closely associated with the causes of criminal behavior. Some psychologists view antisocial behavior from a **psychoanalytic** or **psychodynamic perspective**: their focus is on early childhood experience and its effect on personality. In contrast, **behaviorism** stresses social learning and behavior modeling as the keys to criminality. **Cognitive theory** analyzes human perception and how it affects behavior.

Psychodynamic Theory

Psychodynamic (or psychoanalytic) psychology was originated by Viennese psychiatrist Sigmund Freud (1856–1939) and has since remained a prominent segment of psychological theory.[189]

For a collection of links to libraries, museums, and biographical materials related to **Sigmund Freud and his works**, visit the Criminal Justice CourseMate at cengagebrain.com, then access the "Web Links" for this chapter.

Freud believed that we all carry with us residue of the most significant emotional attachments of our childhood, which then guide future interpersonal relationships. Today the term *psychodynamic* refers to a broad range of theories that focus on the influence of instinctive drives and forces and the importance of developmental processes in shaping personality. Contemporary psychodynamic theory places greater emphasis on conscious experience and its interaction with the unconscious, in addition to the role that social factors play in development. Nonetheless, it still focuses on the influence of early childhood experiences on the development of personality, motivation, and drives.

Elements of Psychodynamic Theory According to the classic version of the theory, the human personality contains a three-part structure. The **id** is the primitive part of an individual's mental makeup present at birth. It represents unconscious biological drives for sex, food, and other life-sustaining necessities. The id follows the **pleasure principle**: it requires instant gratification without concern for the rights of others.

The **ego** develops early in life, when a child begins to learn that his or her wishes cannot be instantly gratified. The ego is that part of the personality that compensates for the demands of the id by helping the individual guide his or her actions to remain within the boundaries of social convention. The ego is guided by the **reality principle**: it takes into account what is practical and conventional by societal standards.

The **superego** develops as a result of incorporating within the personality the moral standards and values of parents, community, and significant others. It is the moral aspect of an individual's personality; it passes judgments on behavior. The superego is divided into two parts: **conscience** and **ego ideal**. Conscience tells what is right and wrong. It forces the ego to control the id and directs the individual into morally acceptable and responsible behaviors, which may not be pleasurable. Exhibit 5.3 summarizes Freud's personality structure.

EXHIBIT 5.3

Freud's Model of the Personality Structure

Personality Structure	Guiding Principle	Description
Id	Pleasure principle	Unconscious biological drives; requires instant gratification
Ego	Reality principle	Helps the personality refine the demands of the id; helps person adapt to conventions
Superego	The conscience	The moral aspect of the personality

Psychosexual Stages of Human Development The most basic human drive present at birth is **eros**, the instinct to preserve and create life. The other is the death instinct (**thanatos**), which is expressed as aggression.

Eros is expressed sexually. Consequently, very early in their development, humans experience sexuality, which is expressed by seeking pleasure through various parts of the body. During the first year of life, a child attains pleasure by sucking and biting; Freud called this the **oral stage**. During the second and third years of life, the focus of sexual attention is on the elimination of bodily wastes—the **anal stage**. The **phallic stage** occurs during the third year, when children focus their attention on their genitals. Males begin to have sexual feelings for their mothers (the **Oedipus complex**) and girls for their fathers (the **Electra complex**). **Latency** begins at age 6. During this period, feelings of sexuality are repressed until the genital stage begins at puberty; this marks the beginning of adult sexuality.

If conflicts are encountered during any of the psychosexual stages of development, a person can become **fixated** at that point. This means, as an adult, the fixated person will exhibit behavior traits characteristic of those encountered during infantile sexual development. For example, an infant who does not receive enough oral gratification during the first year of life is likely as an adult to engage in such oral behavior as smoking, drinking, or drug abuse or to be clinging and dependent in personal relationships. Thus, according to Freud, the roots of adult behavioral problems can be traced to problems developed in the earliest years of life.

The Psychodynamics of Antisocial Behavior Psychologists have long linked criminality to abnormal mental states produced by early childhood trauma. For example, Alfred Adler (1870–1937), the founder of individual psychology, coined the term **inferiority complex** to describe people who have feelings of inferiority and compensate for them with a drive for superiority. Controlling others may help reduce personal inadequacies. Erik Erikson (1902–1984) described the **identity crisis**—a period of serious personal questioning people undertake in an effort to determine their own values and sense of direction. Adolescents undergoing an identity crisis might exhibit out-of-control behavior and experiment with drugs and other forms of deviance.

The psychoanalyst whose work is most closely associated with criminality is August Aichorn.[190] After examining many delinquent youths, Aichorn concluded that societal stress, though damaging, could not alone result in a life of crime unless a predisposition existed that psychologically prepared youths for antisocial acts. This mental state, which he labeled **latent delinquency**, is found in youngsters whose personality requires them to act in these ways:

- Seek immediate gratification (to act impulsively)
- Consider satisfying their personal needs more important than relating to others
- Satisfy instinctive urges without considering right and wrong (that is, they lack guilt)

The psychodynamic model of the criminal offender depicts an aggressive, frustrated person dominated by events that occurred early in childhood. Perhaps because they may have suffered unhappy experiences in childhood or had families that could not provide proper love and care, criminals suffer from weak or damaged egos that make them unable to cope with conventional society. Weak egos are associated with immaturity, poor social skills, and excessive dependence on others. People with weak egos may be easily led into crime by antisocial peers and drug abuse. Some offenders have underdeveloped superegos and consequently lack internalized representations of those behaviors that are punished in conventional society. They commit crimes because they have difficulty understanding the consequences of their actions.[191]

Offenders may suffer from a garden variety of mood and/or behavior disorders. They may be histrionic, depressed, antisocial, or narcissistic.[192] They may suffer from conduct disorders, which include long histories of antisocial behavior, or mood disorders characterized by disturbance in expressed emotions. Among the latter is **bipolar disorder**, in which moods alternate between periods of wild elation and deep depression.[193] Some offenders are driven by an unconscious desire to be punished for prior sins, either real or imaginary. As a result, they may violate the law to gain attention or to punish their parents.

According to this view, crime is a manifestation of feelings of oppression and people's inability to develop the proper psychological defenses and rationales to keep these feelings under control. Criminality enables troubled people to survive by producing positive psychic results: it helps them to feel free and independent, and it gives them the possibility of excitement and the chance to use their skills and imagination. Crime also provides them with the promise of positive gain; it allows them to blame others for their predicament (for example, the police), and it gives them a chance to rationalize their sense of failure ("If I hadn't gotten into trouble, I could have been a success").[194]

Attachment Theory

Attachment theory, a view most closely associated with psychologist John Bowlby, is also connected to the psychodynamic tradition. Bowlby believed that the ability to form attachments—that is, emotionally bond to another person— has important lasting psychological implications that follow people across the life span. Attachments are formed soon after birth, when infants bond with their mothers. They will become frantic, crying and clinging, to prevent separation or to re-establish contact with a missing parent. Bowlby noted that this behavior is not restricted to humans and occurs in all mammals, indicating that separation anxiety may be instinctual or evolutionary. After all, attachment figures, especially the mother, provide support and care, and without attachment an infant would be helpless and could not survive. Bowlby also challenged Freud's view of the development of the ego and superego, claiming that at birth these were bound up in the relationship with one's mother.[195]

Bowlby's most important finding was that to grow up mentally healthy, "the infant and young child should experience a warm, intimate, and continuous relationship with his mother (or permanent mother substitute) in which both find satisfaction and enjoyment."[196]

According to this view, failing to develop proper attachment may cause people to fall prey to a number of psychological disorders. Psychologists believe that children with attachment problems lack trust and respect for others. They often display many psychological symptoms, some of which resemble attention deficit hyperactivity disorder (ADHD). They may be impulsive and have difficulty concentrating, and consequently experience difficulty in school. As adults, they often have difficulty initiating and sustaining relationships with others and find it difficult to sustain romantic relationships. Criminologists have linked people having detachment problems with a variety of antisocial behaviors, including sexual assault and child abuse.[197] It has been suggested that boys disproportionately experience disrupted attachment and that these disruptions are causally related to disproportionate rates of male offending.[198]

Mental Disorders and Crime

According to the psychodynamic tradition, traumatic life events can bring about severe mental disorders that have been linked to the onset of crime and deviance. Mental disorders typically involve a psychological condition that disrupts thinking, feeling, and other important psychological processes. They may cause people to deviate from social expectations and impair their everyday functioning. A less severe form are mood disorders—prolonged and intense emotional upheavals that shape and color a person's psychic life. A more severe mental disorder is referred to as psychosis and is characterized by derangement of personality and loss of contact with reality, thereby causing deterioration of normal social functioning. These are discussed more fully below.

Mood Disorders and Crime   Psychologists recognize a variety of mental disorders that may be linked to antisocial behavior. Adolescents who are frequently uncooperative and hostile and who seem to be much more difficult than other children the same age may be suffering from a psychological condition known as *disruptive behavior disorder (DBD)*, which can take on two distinct forms: *oppositional defiant disorder (ODD)* and *conduct disorder (CD)*.[199] Children suffering from ODD experience an ongoing pattern of uncooperative, defiant, and hostile behavior toward authority figures that seriously interferes with the youngsters' day-to-day functioning. Symptoms of ODD may include frequent loss of temper and constant arguing with adults; defying adults or refusing adult requests or rules; deliberately annoying

others; blaming others for mistakes or misbehavior; being angry and resentful; being spiteful or vindictive; swearing or using obscene language; or having low self-esteem. The person with ODD is moody and easily frustrated and may abuse drugs as a form of self-medication.[200]

CD is typically considered a more serious group of behavioral and emotional problems.[201] Children and adolescents with CD have great difficulty following rules and behaving in socially acceptable ways. They are often viewed by other children, adults, and social agencies as severely antisocial. Research shows that they are frequently involved in such activities as bullying, fighting, committing sexual assaults, and cruelty to animals.

What causes CD? Numerous biosocial and psychological factors are suspected. There is evidence, for example, that interconnections between the frontal lobes and other brain regions may influence CD. There is also research showing that levels of serotonin can influence the onset of CD and that CD has been shown to aggregate in families, suggesting a genetic basis of the disorder.[202]

ODD and CD are not the only mood disorders associated with antisocial behavior. Some people find it impossible to cope with feelings of oppression or depression. Research shows that people who are clinically depressed are more likely to engage in a garden variety of illegal acts.[203] Some people suffer from **alexithymia**, a deficit in emotional cognition that prevents them from being aware of their feelings or being able to understand or talk about their thoughts and emotions; they seem robotic and emotionally dead.[204] Others may suffer from eating disorders and are likely to use fasting, vomiting, and drugs to lose weight or to keep from gaining weight.[205]

Psychosis and Crime   The most serious forms of psychological disturbance will result in mental illness referred to as **psychosis**, which includes severe mental **disorders**, such as depression, bipolar disorder (manic depression), and **schizophrenia**—characterized by extreme impairment of a person's ability to think clearly, respond emotionally, communicate effectively, understand reality, and behave appropriately. Schizophrenics may hear nonexistent voices, hallucinate, and make inappropriate behavioral responses. People with severe mental disorders exhibit illogical and incoherent thought processes and a lack of insight into their behavior. For example, they may see themselves as agents of the devil, avenging angels, or the recipients of messages from animals and plants.

David Berkowitz (the "Son of Sam" or the "44-calibre killer"), a noted serial killer who went on a rampage from 1976 to 1977, exhibited these traits when he claimed that his killing spree began when he received messages from a neighbor's dog. **Paranoid schizophrenics** suffer complex behavior delusions involving wrongdoing or persecution—they think everyone is out to get them.

There is evidence that law violators suffer from a disproportionate amount of severe mental health problems.[206] Female offenders seem to have more serious mental health symptoms, including schizophrenia, paranoia, and obsessive behaviors, than male offenders.[207] It is not surprising, then, that abusive mothers have been found to have mood and personality disorders and a history of psychiatric diagnoses.[208] Juvenile murderers have been described in clinical diagnosis as "overtly hostile," "explosive or volatile," "anxious," and "depressed."[209] Studies of men accused of murder found that 75 percent could be classified as having some mental illness, including schizophrenia.[210] Also, the reported substance abuse among the mentally ill is significantly higher than that of the general population.[211] Kids growing up in homes where parents suffer mental illness are much more likely to be at risk for family instability, poverty, and other factors that are related to future delinquency and crime. So not only may mental illness be a cause of crime, but its effect may be intergenerational.[212]

The diagnosed mentally ill appear in arrest and court statistics at a rate disproportionate to their presence in the population.[213] There is also evidence that the mentally ill are prone to attack their caregivers: doctors working with mental patients are significantly more likely to be attacked by patients than any other health care provider.[214]

Nor is this relationship unique to the United States. Forensic criminologist Henrik Belfrage studied mental patients in Sweden and found that 40 percent of those discharged from institutional care had a criminal record as compared to less than 10 percent of the general public.[215] Another Swedish study found that about 1 in 20 serious crimes in that country were committed by people with severe mental illness. Australian men diagnosed with schizophrenia are four times more likely than the general population to be convicted for serious violence.[216] And a recent Danish study found a significant positive relationship between mental disorders such as schizophrenia and criminal violence.[217] Similarly, a study of German inmates found a significant amount of mental illness in both male and female prisoners.[218]

In sum, people who suffer psychosis, including paranoid or delusional feelings, and who believe others wish them harm or that their mind is dominated by forces beyond their control, seem to be violence prone.[219]

The **National Mental Health Association (NMHA)** is the country's oldest and largest nonprofit organization addressing all aspects of mental health and mental illness. It is dedicated to improving the mental health of all individuals and achieving victory over mental illnesses. For more information, visit the Criminal Justice CourseMate at cengagebrain.com, then access the "Web Links" for this chapter.

Is the Link Valid? Despite this evidence, there are still questions about whether mental disorder is a direct cause of crime and violence. The mentally ill may be more likely to withdraw or harm themselves than to act aggressively toward others.[220] Mentally disordered inmates who do recidivate upon release appear to do so for the same reasons as the mentally sound—extensive criminal histories, substance abuse, and family dysfunction—rather than as a result of their illness.[221]

It is also possible that the link between mental disorder and crime is spurious and an artifact of some intervening factor: the factors that cause mental turmoil also cause antisocial behaviors. People who suffer child abuse are more likely to have mental anguish and commit violent acts; child abuse is the actual cause of both problems.[222]

Mentally ill people may be more likely to lack financial resources than the mentally sound. Living in a stress-filled, urban environment may produce symptoms of both mental illness and crime.[223] It is not surprising that mentally ill people, forced to live in deteriorated neighborhoods, are much more likely to be crime victims than the mentally sound.[224]

A recent Swedish study found that schizophrenic patients are very likely to live in neighborhoods characterized by high levels of disorder, fear of crime, and victimization. The association was circular: the presence of large numbers of mentally ill people helped increase neighborhood fear, leading to neighborhood deterioration, lowered values, and the influx of more diagnosed mentally ill people seeking cheap housing. Segregating the mentally ill may result in worsening of the illness as well as increasing the deterioration of local areas.[225]

The link between mental disorder and crime may also be related to the treatment of the mentally ill: the police may be more likely to arrest the mentally ill, giving the illusion that they are crime prone.[226] However, some recent research by Paul Hirschfield and his associates gives only mixed support to this view. Although some mental health problems increase the risk of arrest, others bring out more cautious or compassionate police responses that may result in treatment rather than arrest.[227] Further research is needed to clarify this important relationship.

It is also possible that a lack of resources may inhibit the mentally ill from obtaining the proper treatment, which, if made available, would result in reduced criminality. For example, a recent study conducted in North Carolina compared the outcomes for mentally ill patients who received outpatient treatment with an untreated comparison group; treatment significantly reduced arrest probability (12 percent versus 45 percent).[228]

The Thinking Like a Criminologist feature considers the ethical dilemma of mental health defenses in criminal proceedings.

To access a site devoted to the relationship between mental illness and crime, visit the Criminal Justice CourseMate at cengagebrain.com, then access the "Web Links" for this chapter.

Something Snapped

The American Psychiatric Association (APA) believes a person should not be held legally responsible for a crime if his or her behavior meets the following standard developed by legal expert Richard Bonnie:

> A person charged with a criminal offense should be found not guilty by reason of insanity if it is shown that as a result of mental disease or mental retardation he was unable to appreciate the wrongfulness of his conduct at the time of the offense.

As used in this standard, the terms *mental disease* and *mental retardation* include only those severely abnormal mental conditions that grossly and demonstrably impair a person's perception or understanding of reality and that are not attributable primarily to the voluntary ingestion of alcohol or other psychoactive substances.

crabshack photos/Fotalia

>> You are part of a research team with expertise on forensic criminology. Your team has been asked by the judge to investigate the case of Bill W., a young man who has murdered his father, and to make a written sentencing recommendation. You discover that Bill has a history of horrendous sexual and physical abuse at the hands of his father. When interviewed, Bill admits that "it is wrong to kill," but that something just "snapped" when he saw his dad with his arm around his younger brother, who also had cuts and bruises. Have one half of the research team write a brief recommending that Bill's behavior be excused because of his prior history of mistreatment. Have the other half write an opinion supporting a criminal conviction because he fails to meet the test of insanity according to the APA definition. Have each group make an oral presentation of their findings and have the team leader choose the most persuasive argument to present to the judge.

Behavioral Theory

Psychological behavior theory maintains that human actions are developed through learning experiences. Rather than focusing on unconscious personality traits or cognitive development patterns produced early in childhood, behavior theorists are concerned with the actual behaviors people engage in during the course of their daily lives. The major premise of behavior theory is that people alter their behavior according to the reactions it receives from others. Behavior is supported by rewards and extinguished by negative reactions or punishments. Behavioral theory is quite complex with many different subareas. With respect to criminal activity, the behaviorist views crimes, especially violent acts, as learned responses to life situations that do not necessarily represent psychologically abnormal responses.

Social Learning Theory   **Social learning** is the branch of behavior theory most relevant to criminology.[229] Social learning theorists, most notably Albert Bandura, argue that people are not actually born with the ability to act violently, but that they learn to be aggressive through their life experiences.

> To read about the life and work of **Albert Bandura**, visit the Criminal Justice CourseMate at cengagebrain.com, then access the "Web Links" for this chapter.

These experiences include personally observing others acting aggressively to achieve some goal or watching people being rewarded for violent acts on television or in movies. People learn to act aggressively when, as children, they model their behavior after the violent acts of adults. Later in life, these violent behavior patterns persist in social relationships. For example, the boy who sees his father repeatedly strike his mother with impunity is the one most likely to grow up to become a battering parent and husband.

Though social learning theorists agree that mental or physical traits may predispose a person toward violence, they believe that activating a person's violent tendencies is achieved by factors in the environment. The specific forms that aggressive behavior takes, the frequency with which it is expressed, the situations in which it is displayed, and the specific targets selected for attack are largely determined by social learning. However, people are self-aware and engage in purposeful learning. Their interpretations of behavior outcomes and situations influence the way they learn from experiences. One adolescent who spends a weekend in jail for drunk driving may find it the most awful experience of her life—one that teaches her to never drink and drive again. Another person, however, may find it an exciting experience about which he can brag to his friends.

Social Learning and Violence   Social learning theorists view violence as something learned through a process called **behavior modeling**. In modern society, aggressive acts are usually modeled after three principal sources:

Does the media influence behavior? Does broadcast violence cause aggressive behavior in viewers? This has become a hot topic because of the persistent theme of violence on television and in films. Critics have called for drastic measures, ranging from banning TV violence to putting warning labels on heavy metal albums out of fear that listening to hard-rock lyrics produces delinquency.

If there is in fact a TV–violence link, the problem is indeed alarming: Marketing research indicates that adolescents ages 11 to 14 view violent horror movies at a higher rate than any other age group. Children this age use older peers and siblings and apathetic parents to gain access to R-rated films. Most U.S. households now have cable TV, which features violent films and shows unavailable on broadcast networks. Even children's programming is saturated with violence.

The fact that children watch so much violent TV is not surprising considering the findings of a well-publicized study conducted by UCLA researchers who found that at least 10 network shows made heavy use of violence. Of the 161 television movies monitored (every one that aired that season), 23 raised concerns about their use of violence, violent theme, violent title, or inappropriate portrayals of a scene. Of the 118 theatrical films monitored (every one that aired that season), 50 raised concerns about their use of violence.

On-air promotions also reflect a continuing, if not worsening, problem. Some series may contain several scenes of violence, each of which is appropriate within its context. An advertisement for that show, however, will feature only those violent scenes without any of the context. Even some children's television programming had worrisome signs, featuring "sinister combat" as the theme of the show. The characters are usually happy to fight and frequently do so with little provocation.

There have been numerous anecdotal cases of violence linked to TV and films. For example, in a famous incident, John Hinckley shot President Ronald Reagan due to his obsession with actress Jodie Foster, which developed after he watched her play a prostitute in the violent film *Taxi Driver*. Hinckley viewed the film at least 15 times.

While not all experts believe that media violence is a direct *cause* of violent behavior (because if it was, there would be millions of daily incidents in which viewers imitated the aggression they watched on TV or in movies), many do agree that media violence *contributes* to aggression. Developmental psychologist John Murray carefully reviewed existing research on the effect of TV violence on children and reached the conclusion that viewing media violence is related to both short- and long-term increases in aggressive attitudes, values, and behaviors; the effects of media violence are both real and strong. Similarly, Brad Bushman and Craig Anderson have found that watching violence on TV is correlated to aggressive behaviors.

There is also evidence that kids who watch TV are more likely to persist in aggressive behavior as adults. A recent study conducted by researchers at Columbia University found that kids who watch more than an hour of TV each day show an increase in assaults, fights, robberies, and other acts of aggression later in life and into adulthood. One reason is that TV viewing may create changes in personality and cognition that produce long-term behavioral changes. Dimitri Christakis and his associates found that for every hour of television watched daily between the ages of 1 and 3, the risk of developing attention problems increased by 9 percent over the life course; attention problems have been linked to antisocial behaviors.

There are several explanations for the effects of television and film violence on behavior:

- Media violence can provide aggressive "scripts" that children store in memory. Repeated exposure to these scripts can increase their retention and lead to changes in attitudes.
- Children learn from what they observe. In the same way they learn cognitive and social skills from their parents and friends, children learn to be violent from television.
- Television violence increases the arousal levels of viewers and makes them more prone to act aggressively. Studies measuring the galvanic skin response of subjects—a physical indication of arousal based on the amount of electricity conducted across the palm of the

---

- *Family interaction.* Studies of family life show that aggressive children have parents who use similar tactics when dealing with others. For example, the children of wife batterers are more likely to use aggressive tactics themselves than children in the general population, especially if the victims (their mothers) suffer psychological distress from the abuse.
- *Environmental experiences.* People who reside in areas in which violence is a daily occurrence are more likely to act violently than those who dwell in low-crime areas whose norms stress conventional behavior.

- *Mass media.* Films and television shows commonly depict violence graphically. Moreover, violence is often portrayed as an acceptable behavior, especially for heroes who never have to face legal consequences for their actions.

The Criminological Enterprise feature "Violent Media/ Violent Behavior?" has more on the effects of the media and violent behavior.

Social learning theorists have tried to determine what triggers violent acts. One position is that a direct, pain-producing physical assault will usually trigger a violent

hand—show that viewing violent television shows led to increased arousal levels in young children.

- Watching television violence promotes such negative attitudes as suspiciousness and the expectation that the viewer will become involved in violence. Those who watch television frequently come to view aggression and violence as common and socially acceptable behavior.

- Television violence allows aggressive youths to justify their behavior. It is possible that, instead of causing violence, television helps violent youths rationalize their behavior as a socially acceptable and common activity.

- Television violence may disinhibit aggressive behavior, which is normally controlled by other learning processes. *Disinhibition* takes place when adults are viewed as being rewarded for violence and when violence is seen as socially acceptable. This contradicts previous learning experiences in which violent behavior was viewed as wrong.

Debating the Media–Violence Link

While this research is quite persuasive, not all criminologists accept that watching TV and movies or playing violent video games actually leads to interpersonal violence. Just because kids who are exposed to violent media also engage in violent behaviors is not proof of a causal connection. It is also possible that kids who are violent later seek out violent media: what would we expect violent gang boys to watch on TV?

Hannah Montana? There is little evidence that areas that experience the highest levels of violent TV viewing also have rates of violent crime that are above the norm. Millions of children watch violence every night but do not become violent criminals. If violent TV shows did, indeed, cause interpersonal violence, then there should be few ecological and regional patterns in the crime rate, but there are many. Put another way, how can regional differences in the violence rate be explained considering the fact that people all across the nation watch the same TV shows and films? Nor can the media–violence link explain recent crime trends. Despite a rampant increase in violent TV shows, films, and video games, the violence rate among teens has been in a significant decline.

One reason for the ongoing debate may be that media violence may affect one subset of the population but have relatively little effect on others. Sociologist George Comstock has identified attributes that make some people especially prone to the effects of media violence:

- Predisposition for aggressive or antisocial behavior
- Rigid or indifferent parenting
- Unsatisfactory social relationships
- Low psychological well-being
- Having been diagnosed as suffering from disruptive behavior disorders (DBDs)

So if the impact of media on behavior is not in fact universal, it may have the greatest effect on those who are the most socially and psychologically vulnerable.

CRITICAL THINKING

1. Should the government control the content of TV shows and limit the amount of weekly violence? How could the national news be shown if violence were omitted? What about boxing matches or hockey games?

2. How can we explain the fact that millions of kids watch violent TV shows and remain nonviolent? If there is a TV–violence link, how can we explain the fact that violence rates may have been higher in the Old West than they are today? Do you think violent gang kids stay home and watch TV shows?

SOURCES: George Comstock, "A Sociological Perspective on Television Violence and Aggression," *American Behavioral Scientist* 51 (2008): 1,184–1,211; John Murray, "Media Violence: The Effects Are Both Real and Strong," *American Behavioral Scientist* 51 (2008): 1,212–1,230; Tom Grimes and Lori Bergen, "The Epistemological Argument Against a Causal Relationship Between Media Violence and Sociopathic Behavior Among Psychologically Well Viewers," *American Behavioral Scientist* 51 (2008): 1,137–1,154; Craig Anderson and Brad J. Bushman, "The Effects of Media Violence on Society," *Science* 295 (2002): 2,377–2,379; Brad Bushman and Craig Anderson, "Media Violence and the American Public," *American Psychologist* 56 (2001): 477–489; UCLA Center for Communication Policy, *Television Violence Monitoring Project* (Los Angeles, CA).

response. Yet the relationship between painful attacks and aggressive responses has been found to be inconsistent. Whether people counterattack in the face of physical attack depends, in part, on their skill in fighting and their perception of the strength of their attackers. Verbal taunts and insults have also been linked to aggressive responses. People who are predisposed to aggression by their learning experiences are likely to view insults from others as a challenge to their social status and to react with violence. Still another violence-triggering mechanism is a perceived reduction in one's life conditions. Prime examples of this phenomenon are riots and demonstrations in poverty-stricken ghetto areas. Studies have shown that discontent also produces aggression in the more successful members of lower-class groups who have been led to believe they can succeed but then have been thwarted in their aspirations. While it is still uncertain how this relationship is constructed, it is apparently complex. No matter how deprived some individuals are, they will not resort to violence. It seems evident that people's perceptions of their relative deprivation have different effects on their aggressive responses.

In summary, social learning theorists have said that the following four factors may contribute to violent and/or aggressive behavior:

- *An event that heightens arousal.* Such as a person frustrating or provoking another through physical assault or verbal abuse.
- *Aggressive skills.* Learned aggressive responses picked up from observing others, either personally or through the media.
- *Expected outcomes.* The belief that aggression will somehow be rewarded. Rewards can come in the form of reducing tension or anger, gaining some financial reward, building self-esteem, or gaining the praise of others.
- *Consistency of behavior with values.* The belief, gained from observing others, that aggression is justified and appropriate, given the circumstances of the current situation.

Cognitive Theory

One area of psychology that has received increasing recognition in recent years has been the cognitive school. Psychologists with a cognitive perspective focus on mental processes and how people perceive and mentally represent the world around them and solve problems. The pioneers of this school were Wilhelm Wundt (1832–1920), Edward Titchener (1867–1927), and William James (1842–1920). Today, there are several subdisciplines within the cognitive area. The **moral development** branch is concerned with the way people morally represent and reason about the world. **Humanistic psychology** stresses self-awareness and "getting in touch with feelings." The **information processing** branch focuses on the way people process, store, encode, retrieve, and manipulate information to make decisions and solve problems.

Moral and Intellectual Development Theory
The moral and intellectual development branch of cognitive psychology is perhaps the most important for criminological theory. Jean Piaget (1896–1980), the founder of this approach, hypothesized that people's reasoning processes develop in an orderly fashion, beginning at birth and continuing until they are 12 years old and older.[230] At first, children respond to the environment in a simple manner, seeking interesting objects and developing their reflexes. By the fourth and final stage, the formal operations stage, they have developed into mature adults who can use logic and abstract thought.

Lawrence Kohlberg first applied the concept of moral development to issues in criminology.[231] He found that people travel through stages of moral development during which their decisions and judgments on issues of right and wrong are made for different reasons. It is possible that serious offenders have a moral orientation that differs from that of law-abiding citizens. Kohlberg classified people according

to the stage on this continuum at which their moral development ceased to grow. Kohlberg and his associates conducted studies in which criminals were found to be significantly lower in their moral judgment development than noncriminals of the same social background.[232] Since his pioneering efforts, researchers have continued to show that criminal offenders are more likely to be classified in the lowest levels of moral reasoning (Stages 1 and 2), whereas noncriminals have reached a higher stage of moral development (Stages 3 and 4).[233]

Recent research indicates that the decision not to commit crimes may be influenced by one's stage of moral development. People at the lowest levels report that they are deterred from crime because of their fear of sanctions. Those in the middle consider the reactions of family and friends. Those at the highest stages refrain from crime because they believe in duty to others and universal rights.[234]

Moral development theory suggests that people who obey the law simply to avoid punishment or have outlooks mainly characterized by self-interest are more likely to commit crimes than those who view the law as something that benefits all of society. Those at higher stages of moral reasoning tend to sympathize with the rights of others and are associated with conventional behaviors, such as honesty, generosity, and nonviolence. Subsequent research has found that a significant number of noncriminals display higher stages of moral reasoning than criminals and that engaging in criminal behavior leads to reduced levels of moral reasoning, which in turn produces more delinquency in a never-ending loop.[235]

CONNECTIONS

The deterrent effect of informal sanctions and feelings of shame discussed in Chapter 4 may hinge on the level of a person's moral development. The lower one's state of moral development, the less impact informal sanctions may have; increased moral development and informal sanctions may be better able to control crime.

Information Processing
When cognitive theorists who study information processing try to explain antisocial behavior, they do so in terms of mental perception and how people use information to understand their environment. When people make decisions, they engage in a sequence of cognitive thought processes:

1. Encode information so that it can be interpreted.
2. Search for a proper response.
3. Decide on the most appropriate action.
4. Act on the decision.[236]

Not everyone processes information in the same way, and the differences in interpretation may explain the development of radically different visions of the world.

According to this cognitive approach, people who use information properly, who are better conditioned to make reasoned judgments, and who can make quick and reasoned decisions when facing emotion-laden events are the ones best able to avoid antisocial behavior choices.[237] In contrast, crime-prone people may have cognitive deficits and use information incorrectly when they make decisions.[238] Law violators may lack the ability to perform cognitive functions in a normal and orderly fashion.[239] Some may be sensation seekers who are constantly looking for novel experiences, whereas others lack deliberation and rarely think through problems. Some may give up easily, whereas others act without thinking when they get upset.[240]

People with inadequate cognitive processing perceive the world as stacked against them; they believe they have little control over the negative events in their life.[241] Chronic offenders come to believe that crime is an appropriate means to satisfy their immediate personal needs, which take precedence over more distant social needs such as obedience to the law.[242] They have a distorted view of the world that shapes their thinking and colors their judgments. Because they have difficulty making the right decision while under stress, they pursue behaviors that they perceive as beneficial and satisfying, but that turn out to be harmful and detrimental.[243] They may take aggressive action because they wrongly believe that a situation demands forceful responses when it actually does not. They find it difficult to understand or sympathize with other people's feelings and emotions, which leads them to blame their victims for their problems.[244] Thus, the sexual offender believes his target either led him on or secretly wanted the forcible sex to occur: "She was asking for it."[245]

Shaping Perceptions   People whose cognitive processes are skewed or faulty may be relying on mental scripts learned in childhood that tell them how to interpret events, what to expect, how they should react, and what the outcome of the interaction should be.[246] Hostile children may have learned improper scripts by observing how others react to events; their own parents' aggressive and inappropriate behavior would have considerable impact. Some may have had early and prolonged exposure to violence (for example, child abuse), which increases their sensitivity to slights and maltreatment. Oversensitivity to rejection by their peers is a continuation of sensitivity to rejection by their parents.[247] Violent behavior responses learned in childhood become a stable behavior because the scripts that emphasize aggressive responses are repeatedly rehearsed as the child matures.[248]

To violence-prone kids, people seem more aggressive than they actually are and seem to intend them ill when there is no reason for alarm. According to information processing theory, as these children mature, they use fewer cues than most people to process information. Some use violence in a calculating fashion as a means of getting what they want; others react in an overly volatile fashion to the slightest provocation. Aggressors are more likely to be vigilant, on edge, or suspicious. When they attack victims, they may believe they are defending themselves, even though they are misreading the situation.[249]

Adolescents who use violence as a coping technique with others are also more likely to exhibit other social problems, such as drug and alcohol abuse.[250] There is also evidence that delinquent boys who engage in theft are more likely to exhibit cognitive deficits than nondelinquent youth. For example, they have a poor sense of time, leaving them incapable of dealing with or solving social problems in an effective manner.[251] Information processing theory has been used to explain the occurrence of date rape. Sexually violent males believe that when their dates say no to sexual advances the women are really "playing games" and actually want to be taken forcefully.[252]

Errors in cognition and information processing have been used to explain the behavior of child abusers. Distorted thinking patterns abusers express include the following:

Zachariah Blanton, 17, is led into the Jackson County Courthouse in Brownstown, Indiana, by sheriff's deputies on July 26, 2006. Blanton was tried on charges of murder, attempted murder, and criminal recklessness for a series of highway shootings that killed a man in southern Indiana. Blanton had been on a hunting trip with relatives but got into an argument and drove off in anger shortly before the attacks. He drove to a nearby overpass, aimed his rifle over the trunk of his vehicle, and fired at trucks on Interstate 65. Can such incidents of random and seemingly unprovoked violence be a product of watching too much violent media in which shooting is made to look routine and ordinary?

AP Images/Michael Conroy

- *Child as a sexual being.* Children are perceived as being able to and wanting to engage in sexual activity with adults.[253]
- *Nature of harm.* The offender perceives that sexual activity does not cause harm (and may in fact be beneficial) to the child.
- *Entitlement.* The child abuser perceives that he is superior and more important than others and hence is able to have sex with whomever and whenever he wants.
- *Dangerous world.* An offender perceives that others are abusive and rejecting, and he must fight to be safe.
- *Uncontrollable.* The world is perceived as uncontrollable, and circumstances are outside of his control.

Treatment based on how people process information takes into account that people are more likely to respond aggressively to a provocation because thoughts tend to intensify the insult or otherwise stir feelings of anger. Cognitive therapists, during the course of treatment, attempt to teach explosive people to control aggressive impulses by viewing social provocations as problems demanding a solution rather than retaliation. Programs are aimed at teaching problem-solving skills that may include self-disclosure, role-playing, listening, following instructions, joining in, and using self-control.[254]

Therapeutic interventions designed to make people better problem solvers may involve such measures as (a) enhancing coping and problem-solving skills; (b) enhancing relationships with peers, parents, and other adults; (c) teaching conflict resolution and communication skills and methods for resisting peer pressure related to drug use and violence; (d) teaching consequential thinking and decision-making abilities; (e) modeling prosocial behaviors, including cooperation with others, self-responsibility, respecting others, and public speaking efficacy; and (f) teaching empathy.[255]

Treatment interventions based on learning social skills are relatively new, but there are some indications that this approach can have long-term benefits for reducing criminal behavior.[256]

The various psychological theories of crime are set out in Concept Summary 5.2.

PSYCHOLOGICAL TRAITS AND CHARACTERISTICS

In addition to creating theories of behavior and development, psychologists also study psychological traits and characteristics that define an individual and shape how he or she functions in the world. Certain traits have become associated

CONCEPT SUMMARY 5.2

Psychological Trait Theories

Psychodynamic
- The major premise of the theory is that the development of the unconscious personality early in childhood influences behavior for the rest of the person's life. Criminals have weak egos and damaged personalities.
- The strengths of the theory are that it explains the onset of crime and why crime and drug abuse cut across class lines.
- The research focuses of the theory are on mental disorders, personality development, and unconscious motivations and drives.

Behavioral
- The major premise of the theory is that people commit crime when they model their behavior after others they see being rewarded for similar acts. Behavior is reinforced by rewards and extinguished by punishment.
- The strengths of the theory are that it explains the role of significant others in the crime process; it shows how the media can influence crime and violence.
- The research focuses of the theory are the media and violence, as well as the effects of child abuse.

Cognitive
- The major premise of the theory is that individual reasoning processes influence behavior. Reasoning is influenced by the way people perceive their environment.
- The strengths of the theory are that it shows why criminal behavior patterns change over time as people mature and develop their reasoning powers. It may explain the aging-out process.
- The research focuses of the theory are perception and cognition.

with psychological problems and the development of antisocial behavior trends. Two of the most critical—personality and intelligence—are discussed in detail in the following sections.

Personality and Crime

Personality can be defined as the reasonably stable patterns of behavior, including thoughts and emotions, that distinguish one person from another.[257] One's personality reflects a characteristic way of adapting to life's demands and problems. The way we behave is a function of how our personality enables us to interpret life events and make appropriate behavioral choices. Can the cause of crime be linked to personality?

The association between personality traits and crime has a long history. Sheldon Glueck and Eleanor Glueck identified a number of personality traits that they believe characterize antisocial youth:[258]

self-assertiveness	lack of concern for others
defiance	
extroversion	feeling unappreciated
ambivalence	distrust of authority
impulsiveness	poor personal skills
narcissism	mental instability
suspicion	hostility
destructiveness	resentment
sadism	

Psychologist Hans Eysenck linked personality to crime when he identified two traits that he associated with antisocial behavior: *extroversion-introversion* and *stability-instability*. Extreme introverts are overaroused and avoid sources of stimulation; in contrast, extreme extroverts are unaroused and seek sensation. Introverts are slow to learn and be conditioned; extroverts are impulsive individuals who lack the ability to examine their own motives and behaviors. Those who are unstable, a condition Eysenck calls "neuroticism," are anxious, tense, and emotionally unstable.[259] People who are both neurotic and extroverted lack self-insight and are impulsive and emotionally unstable; they are unlikely to have reasoned judgments of life events. While extrovert neurotics may act self-destructively (e.g., abusing drugs), more stable people will be able to reason that such behavior is ultimately harmful and life threatening. Eysenck believes that personality is controlled by genetic factors and is heritable.

A number of research efforts have found an association between the personality traits identified by Eysenck and repeat and chronic criminal offending.[260] Other suspected traits include impulsivity, hostility, and aggressiveness.[261] Callous, unemotional traits in very young children can be a warning sign for future psychopathy and antisocial behavior.[262] Personality defects have been linked not only to aggressive antisocial behaviors such as assault and rape, but also to white-collar and business crimes.[263]

According to this view, the personality is the key to understanding antisocial behavior. The more severe the disorder, the greater the likelihood that the individual will engage in serious and repeated antisocial acts.[264] Take for instance **sadistic personality disorder**, defined as a repeating pattern of cruel and demeaning behavior. People suffering from this type of extreme personality disturbance seem prone to engage in serious violent attacks, including homicides motivated by sexual sadism.[265]

The Antisocial Personality The Diagnostic and Statistical Manual of the American Psychiatric Association (APA) defines the antisocial personality as a pervasive pattern of disregard for, and violation of, the rights of others that begins in childhood or early adolescence and continues into adulthood. In addition, those suffering from this disease usually exhibit at least three of the following behaviors:

- Failure to conform to social norms with respect to lawful behaviors as indicated by repeatedly performing acts that are grounds for arrest
- Deceitfulness, as indicated by repeatedly lying, use of aliases, or conning others for personal profit or pleasure
- Impulsivity or failure to plan ahead
- Irritability and aggressiveness, as indicated by repeated physical fights or assaults
- Reckless disregard for safety of self or others
- Consistent irresponsibility, as indicated by repeated failure to sustain consistent work behavior or honor financial obligations
- Lack of remorse, as indicated by being indifferent to or rationalizing having hurt, mistreated, or stolen from another[266]

The terms **psychopath** and **sociopath** are commonly used to describe people who have an antisocial personality (though the APA considers the terms antiquated and obsolete). People with these traits have been involved in some of the nation's most notorious crimes (see the accompanying Profiles in Crime feature).

Though these terms are often used interchangeably, some psychologists distinguish between sociopaths and psychopaths, suggesting that the former are a product of a destructive home environment whereas the latter are a product of an inherited genetic defect.[267] This condition is discussed in The Criminological Enterprise feature "The Psychopath" on page 170.

Research on Personality Since maintaining a deviant personality has been related to crime and delinquency, numerous attempts have been made to devise accurate measures of personality and determine whether they can predict antisocial behavior. One of the most widely used psychological tests is the **Minnesota Multiphasic Personality Inventory**, commonly called the MMPI. This test has subscales designed to measure many different personality traits, including psychopathic deviation (Pd scale), schizophrenia (Sc),

A young Robert Chambers arrives in court in 1986.

Chambers, now 41 and showing the effects of narcotics abuse, is led to court in 2007 to face drug charges.

Her friends described Jennifer Levin as outgoing, pretty, and having a good sense of style. She may have had her wild side, gaining entrance to the New York club scene though she was only 17 years old. It was at a club called Dorrian's that she spotted Robert Chambers. Standing 6'4" and weighing 200 pounds, movie-star-handsome Chambers seemed like the ideal man. What Levin and her friends didn't realize was that Chambers had his own dark side, doing poorly in school, committing burglaries, and selling and using drugs. He had attended Boston University, but got kicked out when he stole someone's credit card.

On the night of August 25, 1986, he hooked up with an adoring Jennifer Levin and they left the bar together. The next morning her body was found in Central Park. When questioned, Chambers claimed that Levin had attacked him sexually: she tied him up, groped him, and insisted on sex. While fending off her advances, he pushed her away and she died by accident; he was defending himself against rape. Chambers's defense counsel placed the blame squarely on Levin, claiming her loose, dissolute life caused her death. The media fed the flames and proclaimed her enjoyment of "rough sex." Referred to as the "Preppie Murder Case," it became one of the most notorious murders in New York City history. The case dragged on for two years before trial and while the jury deadlocked for nine days, Chambers decided to plead guilty in exchange for a sentence of 5 to 15 years in prison.

What the jury did not know was that between his arrest and trial Chambers was out and about, attending parties and having a grand time. At one event, a friend taped Chambers as he put on a woman's wig and choked himself with his own hands as he gagged loudly. He picked up a doll and twisted its neck. Chambers spoke in a high female voice as he said, "My name is . . ."

The head of the doll suddenly came off the body. "Oops," he said in a maniacal voice, "I think I killed it!"

The public was shocked when the outrageous tape was played on TV and opinion turned against Chambers. All of a sudden, people realized how incredible it was to believe that Chambers had been attacked by Jennifer Levin, who stood 5'3" and weighed 120 pounds. Levin's mother mounted a campaign to keep Chambers behind bars, and he served the maximum sentence, 15 years. After release in 2003, he led a dissolute life, dealing drugs with an old girlfriend until busted by an undercover agent. On August 11, 2008, Chambers pleaded guilty to selling drugs. On September 2, 2008, he was sentenced to 19 years on the drug charges.

Jennifer Levin had the misfortune of running into a young man who displayed many of the characteristics of the classic sociopath/psychopath. He was callous, lacked empathy, was constantly involved in antisocial activities, and experienced uncontrolled rage. He did not learn from his mistakes because he could never believe he made any; Jennifer Levin's death was her fault and not his.

SOURCES: Linda Wolfe, "Wasted: The Preppie Murder" (New York, iUniverise, 2000).

---

and hypomania (Ma).[268] Research studies have detected an association between scores on the Pd scale and criminal involvement.[269] Another frequently administered personality test, the **California Personality Inventory (CPI)**, has also been used to distinguish deviants from nondeviant groups.[270] The **Multidimensional Personality Questionnaire (MPQ)** allows researchers to assess such personality traits as control, aggression, alienation, and well-being.[271] Evaluations using this scale indicate that adolescent offenders who are crime prone maintain "negative emotionality," a tendency to experience aversive affective states, such as anger, anxiety, and irritability. They also are predisposed to weak personal constraints, and they have difficulty controlling impulsive behavior urges. Because they are both impulsive and aggressive, crime-prone people are quick to take action against perceived threats.

Evidence that personality traits predict crime and violence is important because it suggests that the root cause of crime can be found in the forces that influence human development at an early stage of life. If these results are valid, rather than focus on job creation and neighborhood improvement, crime control efforts might be better focused on helping families raise children who are reasoned and reflective and enjoy a safe environment.

Intelligence and Crime

Intelligence refers to a person's ability to reason, comprehend ideas, solve problems, think abstractly, understand complex ideas, learn from experience, and discover solutions to complex problems. It was long believed that people who maintain a below-average intelligence quotient (IQ) were at risk to criminality. Criminals were believed to have inherently substandard intelligence, and thus, they seemed naturally inclined to commit more crimes than more intelligent persons. Furthermore, it was thought that if authorities could determine which individuals had low IQs, they might identify potential criminals before they committed socially harmful acts.

Social scientists had a captive group of subjects in juvenile training schools and penal institutions, and they began to measure the correlation between IQ and crime by testing adjudicated offenders. Thus, inmates of penal institutions were used as a test group around which numerous theories about intelligence were built, leading ultimately to the nature-versus-nurture controversy that is still going on today. These concepts are discussed in some detail in the following sections.

Nature Theory   **Nature theory** argues that intelligence is largely determined genetically, that ancestry determines IQ, and that low intelligence, as demonstrated by low IQ, is linked to criminal behavior. When the newly developed IQ tests were administered to inmates of prisons and juvenile training schools in the first decades of the twentieth century, the nature position gained support because a very large proportion of the inmates scored low on the tests. During his studies in 1920, Henry Goddard found that many institutionalized persons were what he considered "feebleminded"; he concluded that at least half of all juvenile delinquents were mental defectives.[272] In 1926, William Healy and Augusta Bronner tested groups of delinquent boys in Chicago and Boston and found that 37 percent were subnormal in intelligence. They concluded that delinquents were five to ten times more likely to be mentally deficient than normal boys.[273] These and other early studies were embraced as proof that low IQ scores identified potentially delinquent children and that a correlation existed between innate low intelligence and deviant behavior. IQ tests were believed to measure the inborn genetic makeup of individuals, and many criminologists accepted the idea that individuals with substandard IQs were predisposed toward delinquency and adult criminality.

Nurture Theory   The rise of culturally sensitive explanations of human behavior in the 1930s led to the nurture school of intelligence. **Nurture theory** states that intelligence must be viewed as partly biological but primarily sociological. Because intelligence is not inherited, low-IQ parents do not necessarily produce low-IQ children.[274] Nurture theorists discredited the notion that people commit crimes because they have low IQs. Instead, they postulated that environmental stimulation from parents, relatives, social contacts, schools, peer groups, and innumerable others create a child's IQ level and that low IQs result from an environment that also encourages delinquent and criminal behavior. Thus, if low IQ scores are recorded among

criminals, these scores may reflect criminals' cultural background, not their mental ability. Studies challenging the assumption that people automatically committed criminal acts because they had below-average IQs began to appear as early as the 1920s. In 1926, John Slawson studied 1,543 delinquent boys in New York institutions and compared them with a control group of New York City boys.[275] Slawson found that although 80 percent of the delinquents achieved lower scores in abstract verbal intelligence, delinquents were about normal in mechanical aptitude and nonverbal intelligence. These results indicated the possibility of cultural bias in portions of the IQ tests. He also found that there was no relationship between the number of arrests, the types of offenses, and IQ.

Though many early criminologists believed there was a link between intelligence and crime, in 1931, Edwin Sutherland evaluated IQ studies of criminals and delinquents and noted significant variation in the findings, which disproved any notion that criminals were "feebleminded."[276] The IQ–crime link was all but forgotten in the criminological literature.

More than 40 years later, the respected criminologists Travis Hirschi and Michael Hindelang resurrected the IQ–crime debate. They reexamined existing research data and concluded that the weight of evidence shows that IQ is a more important factor than race and socioeconomic class for predicting criminal and delinquent involvement.[277] Rejecting the notion that IQ tests are race and class biased, they concluded that major differences exist between criminals and noncriminals within similar racial and socioeconomic class categories. They proposed the idea that low IQ increases the likelihood of criminal behavior through its effect on school performance. That is, youths with low IQs do poorly in school, and school failure and academic incompetence are highly related to delinquency and later to adult criminality.

Hirschi and Hindelang's inferences have been supported by research conducted by both U.S. and international scholars.[278] *The Bell Curve*, Richard Herrnstein and Charles Murray's influential albeit controversial book on intelligence, comes down firmly for an IQ–crime link. Their extensive review of the available literature shows that people with lower IQs are more likely to commit crime, get caught, and be sent to prison.[279]

Some studies have found a direct IQ–delinquency link among samples of adolescent boys.[280] When Alex Piquero examined violent behavior among groups of children in Philadelphia, he found that scores on intelligence tests were the best predictors of violent behavior and could be used to distinguish between groups of violent and nonviolent offenders.[281] Others find that the IQ–crime link is an indirect one: low intelligence leads to poor school performance, which enhances the chances of criminality.[282] The IQ–crime relationship has also been found in cross-national studies conducted in a number of countries, including Sweden, Denmark, and Canada.[283]

The Criminological Enterprise
The Psychopath

Some violent offenders may have a disturbed character structure commonly referred to as psychopathy, sociopathy, or antisocial personality. Although they may exhibit superficial charm and above-average intelligence, this often masks a disturbed personality that makes them incapable of forming enduring relationships with others and continually involves them in such deviant behaviors as violence, risk taking, substance abuse, and impulsivity.

From an early age, many psychopaths have had home lives that were filled with frustration, bitterness, and quarreling. Antisocial youths exhibit low levels of guilt and anxiety and persistently violate the rights of others. Their intelligence may alter their criminal career development, and render it quite different from that of nonpsychopathic criminals; high intelligence appears to enhance the destructive potential of a psychopath, while intelligence may mediate the criminality of the nonpsychopath.

As a result of this instability and frustration, these individuals developed personalities that became unreliable, unstable, demanding, and egocentric. Most psychopaths are risk-taking, sensation seekers who are constantly involved in a garden variety of antisocial behaviors. Some may become almost addicted to thrill seeking, resulting in repeated and dangerous risky behaviors. They are often described as grandiose, egocentric, manipulative, forceful, and cold-hearted, with shallow emotions and the inability to feel remorse, empathy with others, or anxiety over their misdeeds. When they commit antisocial acts, they are less likely to feel shame or empathize with their victims.

Hervey Cleckley, a leading authority on psychopathy, described them as follows:

> [Psychopaths are] chronically antisocial individuals who are always in trouble, profiting neither from experience nor punishment, and maintaining no real loyalties to any person, group, or code. They are frequently callous and hedonistic, showing marked emotional immaturity, with lack of responsibility, lack of judgment and an ability to rationalize their behavior so that it appears warranted, reasonable and justified.

Considering these personality traits, it is not surprising that research studies show that people evaluated as psychopaths are significantly more prone to criminal and violent behavior when compared to nonpsychopathic control groups. Psychopaths tend to continue their criminal careers long after other offenders burn out or age out of crime. They are continually in trouble with the law and, therefore, are likely to wind up in penal institutions. After reviewing available data, forensic psychologist James Blair and his colleagues conclude that approximately 15 to 25 percent of U.S. prison inmates meet diagnostic criteria for psychopathy. Once they are released, former inmates who suffer from psychopathy are three times more likely to reoffend within a year of release than other prisoners, and four times more likely to reoffend violently.

The Cause of Psychopathy

Though psychologists are still not certain of the cause of psychopathy, a number of factors are believed to contribute to its development.

Traumatic Socialization

Some explanations focus on family experiences, suggesting that the influence of an unstable parent, parental rejection, lack of love during childhood, and inconsistent discipline may be related to psychopathy. Children who lack the opportunity to form an attachment to a mother figure in the first three years of life, who suffer sudden separation from the mother figure, or who see changes in the mother figure are most likely to develop psychopathic personalities. According to this view, the path runs from antisocial parenting to psychopathy to criminality. Psychologist David Lykken suggests that psychopaths have an inherited "low fear quotient," which inhibits their fear of punishment. All people have a natural or innate fear of certain stimuli, such as spiders, snakes, fires, or strangers. Psychopaths, as a rule, have few fears. Normal socialization processes depend on punishing antisocial behavior to inhibit future transgressions. Someone who does not fear punishment is simply harder to socialize.

IQ and Crime Reconsidered   The Hirschi-Hindelang research increased interest and research on the association between IQ and crime, but the issue is far from settled and is still a matter of significant debate. While the studies cited above found an IQ–crime association, others suggest that IQ level has negligible influence on criminal behavior.[284] An evaluation of existing knowledge on intelligence conducted by the American Psychological Association concluded that the strength of an IQ–crime link was "very low."[285] Those who question the IQ–crime link suggest that any association may be based on spurious data and inadequate research methodologies:

- IQ tests are biased and reflect middle-class values. As a result, socially disadvantaged people do poorly on IQ tests, and members of that group are also the ones most likely to commit crime. The low IQ–crime association is spurious: people who suffer disadvantages such as poverty and limited educational resources do poorly on IQ tests and also commit crime.
- The measurement of intelligence is often varied and haphazard, and results may depend on the particular method used. The correlation between intelligence and antisocial behavior using IQ tests as a measure of aptitude is slight; it is stronger if attendance in special programs or special schools is used as an indicator of intellectual ability.[286]
- People with low IQs are stigmatized and negatively labeled by middle-class decision makers such as

Neurological Disorder

Psychopaths may suffer from lower than normal levels of arousal. Research studies show that psychopaths have lower skin conductance levels and fewer spontaneous responses than normal subjects. There may be a link between psychopathy and autonomic nervous system (ANS) dysfunction. The ANS mediates physiological activities associated with emotions and is manifested in such measurements as heartbeat rate, blood pressure, respiration, muscle tension, capillary size, and electrical activity of the skin (called galvanic skin resistance). Psychopaths may be less capable of regulating their activities than other people. While some people may become anxious and afraid when facing the prospect of committing a criminal act, psychopaths in the same circumstances feel no such fear. James Ogloff and Stephen Wong conclude that their reduced anxiety levels result in behaviors that are more impulsive and inappropriate and in deviant behavior, apprehension, and incarceration.

Brain Structure

Another view is that psychopathy is related to abnormal brain structures. Consequently, psychopaths may need greater than average stimulation to bring them up to comfortable levels (similar to arousal theory, discussed earlier).

Another view is that psychopathy is bound up in an impairment of the amygdala, that part of the brain that plays a crucial role in processing emotions. As James Blair and his colleagues suggest, amygdala dysfunction gives rise to impairments in aversive conditioning, instrumental learning, and the processing of fearful and sad expressions. These impairments interfere with socialization; people with impaired amygdalea do not learn to avoid actions that cause harm to other individuals. Because of this deficiency, psychopaths have problems distinguishing and processing people's facial expressions. When Quentin Deeley and his colleagues compared facial recognition ability of psychopaths with a control group, they found that the former were significantly less likely to recognize and emotionally respond to facial and other signals of distress. This inability may help explain the lack of emotional empathy observed among people with antisocial personalities.

Chronic Offending

The antisocial personality concept seems to jibe with what is known about chronic offending. As many as 80 percent of these high-end chronic offenders exhibit sociopathic behavior patterns. Though comprising about 4 percent of the total male population and less than 1 percent of the total female population, they are responsible for half of all serious felony offenses committed annually. Not all high-rate chronic offenders are sociopaths, but enough are to support a strong link between personality dysfunction and long-term criminal careers.

CRITICAL THINKING

1. Should people diagnosed as psychopaths be separated and treated even if they have not yet committed a crime?

2. Should psychopathic murderers be spared the death penalty because they lack the capacity to control their behavior?

SOURCES: Cengiz Basoglu, Umit Semiz, Ozgur Oner, Huseyin Gunay, Servet Ebrinc, Mesut Cetin, Onur Sildiroglu, Ayhan Algul, Alpay Ates, and Guner Sonmez, "A Magnetic Resonance Spectroscopy Study of Antisocial Behaviour Disorder, Psychopathy and Violent Crime Among Military Conscripts" *Acta Neuropsychiatrica* 20 (2008): 72–77; Rolf Holmqvist, "Psychopathy and Affect Consciousness in Young Criminal Offenders," *Journal of Interpersonal Violence* 23 (2008): 209–224; James Blair, Derek Mitchell, and Karina Blair, *The Psychopath: Emotion and the Brain* (New York: Blackwell Publishing, 2005); Quinton Deeley, Eileen Daly, Simon Surguladze, Nigel Tunstall, Gill Mezey, Dominic Beer, Anita Ambikapathy, Dene Robertson, Vincent Giampietro, Michael Brammer, Amory Clarke, John Dowsett, Tom Fahy, Mary L. Phillips, and Declan G. Murphy, "Facial Emotion Processing in Criminal Psychopathy," *British Journal of Psychiatry* 189 (2006): 533–539; Gisli Gudjonsson, Emil Einarsson, Ólafur Örn Bragason, and Jon Fridrik Sigurdsson, "Personality Predictors of Self-Reported Offending in Icelandic Students," *Psychology, Crime and Law* 12 (2006): 383–393; David Lykken, "Psychopathy, Sociopathy, and Crime," *Society* 34 (1996): 30–38; Hervey Cleckley, "Psychopathic States," in *American Handbook of Psychiatry*, ed. S. Aneti (New York: Basic Books, 1959), pp. 567–569.

police officers, teachers, and guidance counselors. It is not a low IQ that causes criminal behavior, but the reaction to negative labels: alienation, stigma, and resentment.

- Research using official record data may be flawed. It's possible that criminals with high IQ are better able to avoid detection and punishment than low-IQ people. Research using data from arrestees may omit the more intelligent members of the criminal subclass. And even if they are caught, high-IQ offenders are less likely to be convicted and punished. Because their favorable treatment helps higher-IQ offenders avoid the pains of criminal punishment, it lessens their chances of recidivism.

- Maintaining a low IQ may influence some criminal patterns, such as arson and sex crimes, but not others, further clouding the waters.[287]

Even if it can be shown that known offenders have lower IQs than the general population, it is difficult to explain many patterns in the crime rate. Why are there more male than female criminals? (Are females smarter than males?) Why do crime rates vary by region, time of year, and even weather patterns? Why does aging out occur? IQs do not increase with age, so why should crime rates fall?

While some research shows that people who act aggressively in social settings also have lower IQ scores than their peers, other findings suggest that the association between intelligence and crime is insignificant. Should mentally challenged offenders be punished in the same manner as those who are not intellectually impaired? Here, Daryl Atkins walks into the York-Poquoson Courtroom in York, Virginia. Atkins, whose case led the U.S. Supreme Court to bar execution of the mentally retarded as unconstitutionally cruel, remained on death row years after the landmark ruling.

To read all about **IQ testing and intelligence**, visit the Criminal Justice CourseMate at cengagebrain. com, then access the "Web Links" for this chapter.

PUBLIC POLICY IMPLICATIONS OF TRAIT THEORY

For most of the twentieth century, biological and psychological views of criminality have influenced crime control and prevention policy. The result has been front-end or **primary prevention programs** that seek to treat personal problems before they manifest themselves as crime. To this end, thousands of family therapy organizations, substance abuse clinics, and mental health associations operate throughout the United States. Teachers, employers, relatives, welfare agencies, and others make referrals to these facilities. These services are based on the premise that if a person's problems can be treated before they become overwhelming, some future crimes will be prevented. **Secondary prevention programs** provide treatment such as psychological counseling to youths and adults who are at risk for law violation. **Tertiary prevention programs** may be a requirement of a probation order, part of a diversionary sentence, or aftercare at the end of a prison sentence.

Biologically oriented therapy is also being used in the criminal justice system. Programs have altered diets, changed lighting, compensated for learning disabilities, treated allergies, and so on.[288] More controversial has been the use of mood-altering chemicals, such as lithium, pemoline, imipramine, phenytoin, and benzodiazepines, to control behavior. Another practice that has elicited concern is the use of psychosurgery (brain surgery) to control antisocial behavior. Surgical procedures have been used to alter the brain structure of convicted sex offenders in an effort to eliminate or control their sex drives. Results are still preliminary, but some critics argue that these procedures are without scientific merit.[289]

Numerous psychologically based treatment methods range from individual counseling to behavior modification. For example, treatment based on how people process information takes into account that people are more likely to respond aggressively to provocation if thoughts intensify the insult or otherwise stir feelings of anger. Cognitive therapists attempt to teach explosive people to control aggressive impulses by viewing social provocations as problems demanding a solution rather than retaliation. Therapeutic interventions designed to make people better problem solvers may involve measures that enhance:

- Coping and problem-solving skills
- Relationships with peers, parents, and other adults
- Conflict resolution and communication skills, and methods for resisting peer pressure related to drug use and violence
- Consequential thinking and decision-making abilities
- Prosocial behaviors, including cooperation with others, self-responsibility, respecting others, and public-speaking efficacy
- Empathy[290]

While it is often difficult to treat people with severe mental and personality disorders, there is evidence that positive outcomes can be achieved with the right combination of treatment modalities.[291]

SUMMARY

1. **Be familiar with the development of trait theory**
   - The view that criminals have physical or mental traits that make them different began with the Italian physician and criminologist Cesare Lombroso. In the early 1970s, spurred by the publication of *Sociobiology: The New Synthesis*, by Edmund O. Wilson, biological explanations of crime once again emerged. Trait theorists today recognize that crime-producing interactions involve both personal traits and environmental factors. If only a few offenders become persistent repeaters, what sets them apart from the rest of the criminal population may be some crime-producing trait.

2. **Discuss the biochemical conditions that produce crime**
   - Biochemical conditions influence antisocial behavior. Biocriminologists maintain that an improper diet can cause chemical and mineral imbalance and lead to cognitive and learning deficits and problems, and these factors in turn are associated with antisocial behaviors. Abnormal levels of male sex hormones (androgens) can produce aggressive behavior. Exposure to lead has been linked to emotional and behavioral disorders.

3. **Be familiar with the neurophysiological conditions associated with crime**
   - Inherited or acquired neurological and physical abnormalities control behavior throughout the life span. Neurological impairment may also lead to the development of personality traits linked to antisocial behaviors. According to arousal theory, a need for high levels of environmental stimulation may lead to aggressive, violent behavior patterns.

4. **Link genetics to crime**
   - Another biosocial theme is that the human traits associated with criminality have a genetic basis. According to this view, (1) antisocial behavior is inherited, (2) the genetic makeup of parents is passed on to children, and (3) genetic abnormality is linked to a variety of antisocial behaviors.

5. **Explain the evolutionary view of crime**
   - Human traits that produce violence and aggression have been advanced by the long process of human evolution. According to evolutionary theory, behavior patterns are inherited, impulsive behavior becomes intergenerational, passed down from parents to children.

6. **Discuss the elements of the psychodynamic perspective**
   - The id is the primitive part of people's mental makeup, the ego is shaped by learning and experience, and the superego reflects the morals and values of parents and significant others. Criminals are id-driven people who suffer from weak or damaged egos. Crime is a manifestation of feelings of oppression and the inability to develop the proper psychological defenses and rationales to keep these feelings under control.

7. **Link behavioral theory to crime**
   - People are not born with the ability to act violently; rather, they learn to be aggressive through their life experiences. These experiences include personally observing others acting aggressively to achieve some goal or observing people being rewarded for violent acts.

8. **Know the cognitive processes related to crime**
   - Crime-prone people may have cognitive deficits and use information incorrectly when they make decisions. They view crime as an appropriate means to satisfy their immediate personal needs, which take precedence over more distant social needs such as obedience to the law.

9. **Discuss the elements of personality related to crime**
   - Sociopathic, psychopathic, or antisocial people cannot empathize with others, and are shortsighted and hedonistic. These traits make them prone to problems ranging from psychopathology to drug abuse, sexual promiscuity, and violence. Factors related to personality problems include improper socialization, having a psychopathic parent, experiencing parental rejection and lack of love during childhood, and receiving inconsistent discipline.

10. **Be aware of the controversy over the association between intelligence and crime**
    - Proponents of nature theory argue that intelligence is largely determined genetically, that ancestry determines IQ, and that low intelligence is linked to criminal behavior. Proponents of nurture theory argue that intelligence is not inherited and that low-IQ parents do not necessarily produce low-IQ children. The IQ–criminality debate is unlikely to be settled soon. Measurement is beset by many methodological problems.

KEY TERMS

positivism (141)
psychopathic personality (141)
atavistic anomalies (142)
biological determinism (142)
criminal anthropology (142)
inheritance school (142)
somatotype (142)
biosocial theory (142)
biophobia (142)
sociobiology (143)
reciprocal altruism (143)
trait theory (143)
equipotentiality (143)
hypoglycemia (145)
androgens (146)
testosterone (146)
neocortex (146)
premenstrual syndrome, or PMS (147)
cerebral allergies (147)
neuroallergies (147)
neurophysiology (148)
electroencephalograph (EEG) (149)
minimal brain dysfunction (MBD) (149)
learning disability (LD) (149)
attention deficit hyperactivity disorder (ADHD) (150)
conduct disorder (CD) (150)

chemical restraints or chemical straitjackets (152)
arousal theory (152)
contagion effect (154)
defective intelligence (157)
psychoanalytic or psychodynamic perspective (157)
behaviorism (157)
cognitive theory (157)
id (157)
pleasure principle (157)
ego (157)
reality principle (157)
superego (157)
conscience (157)
ego ideal (157)
eros (158)
thanatos (158)
oral stage (158)
anal stage (158)
phallic stage (158)
Oedipus complex (158)
Electra complex (158)
latency (158)
fixated (158)
inferiority complex (158)
identity crisis (158)
latent delinquency (158)

bipolar disorder (158)
attachment theory (158)
alexithymia (159)
psychosis (159)
disorders (159)
schizophrenia (159)
paranoid schizophrenics (159)
social learning (161)
behavior modeling (161)
moral development (164)
humanistic psychology (164)
information processing (164)
personality (166)
sadistic personality disorder (167)
psychopath (167)
sociopath (167)
Minnesota Multiphasic Personality Inventory (167)
California Personality Inventory (CPI) (168)
Multidimensional Personality Questionnaire (MPQ) (168)
intelligence (168)
nature theory (169)
nurture theory (169)
primary prevention programs (172)
secondary prevention programs (172)
tertiary prevention programs (172)

CRITICAL THINKING QUESTIONS

1. What should be done with the young children of violence-prone criminals if in fact research could show that the tendency to commit crime is inherited?

2. After considering the existing research on the subject, would you recommend that young children be forbidden from eating foods with a heavy sugar content?

3. Knowing what you do about trends and patterns in crime, how would you counteract the assertion that people who commit crime are physically or mentally abnormal? For example, how would you explain the fact that crime is more likely to occur in western and urban areas than in eastern or rural areas?

4. Aside from becoming a criminal, what other career paths are open to psychopaths?

5. Research shows that kids who watch a lot of TV in adolescence are more likely to behave aggressively in adulthood. This has led some to conclude that TV watching is responsible for adult violence. Can this relationship be explained in another way?

NOTES

1. Ian Urbina and Manny Fernardez, "Memorial Services Held in U.S. and Around World," *New York Times*, April 21, 2007.
2. Raymond Hernandez, "A Friend, a 'Good Listener' and a Victim in a Day of Tragedy," *New York Times*, April 17, 2007.
3. Ibid.
4. Abbie Boudreau and Scott Zamost, "Girlfriend: Shooter Was Taking Cocktail of 3 Drugs," CNN, February 20, 2008, www.cnn.com/2008/CRIME/02/20/shooter.girlfriend/ (accessed November 9, 2010).
5. Israel Nachshon, "Neurological Bases of Crime, Psychopathy, and Aggression," in *Crime in Biological, Social and Moral Contexts*, ed. Lee Ellis and Harry Hoffman (New York: Praeger, 1990), p. 199. Herein cited as *Crime in Biological Contexts*.

6. Nicole Rafter, "The Murderous Dutch Giddler: Criminology, History and the Problem of Phrenology," *Theoretical Criminology* 9 (2005): 65–97.

7. Nicole Rafter, "The Unrepentant Horse-Slasher: Moral Insanity and the Origins of Criminological Thought," *Criminology* 42 (2004): 979–1,008.

8. Described in David Lykken, "Psychopathy, Sociopathy, and Crime," *Society* 34 (1996): 29–38.

9. See Peter Scott, "Henry Maudsley," in *Pioneers in Criminology*, ed. Hermann Mannheim (Montclair, NJ: Prentice Hall, 1981).

10. To read about Lombroso, go to http://jah-sonic.com/Lombroso.html (accessed November 9, 2010).

11. Nicole Hahn Rafter, "Criminal Anthropology in the United States," *Criminology* 30 (1992): 525–547.

12. Ibid., p. 535.

13. Raffaele Garofalo, *Criminology*, trans. Robert Miller (Boston: Little, Brown, 1914), p. 92.

14. Enrico Ferri, *Criminal Sociology* (New York: D. Appleton, 1909).

15. See Richard Dugdale, *The Jukes* (New York: Putnam, 1910); Arthur Estabrook, *The Jukes in 1915* (Washington, DC: Carnegie Institute of Washington, 1916); Henry H. Goddard, *The Kallikak Family: A Study in the Heredity of Feeble-Mindedness* (New York: Macmillan, 1912).

16. Stephen Jay Gould, *The Mismeasure of Man*, rev. ed. (New York: Norton, 1996).

17. William Sheldon, *Varieties of Delinquent Youth* (New York: Harper Bros., 1949).

18. Pierre van den Bergle, "Bringing the Beast Back In: Toward a Biosocial Theory of Aggression," *American Sociological Review* 39 (1974): 779.

19. John Laub and Robert Sampson, "The Sutherland-Glueck Debate: On the Sociology of Criminological Knowledge," *American Journal of Sociology* 96 (1991): 1,402–1,440.

20. Lee Ellis, "A Discipline in Peril: Sociology's Future Hinges on Curing Biophobia," *American Sociologist* 27 (1996): 21–41.

21. Edmund O. Wilson, *Sociobiology* (Cambridge, MA: Harvard University Press, 1975).

22. Bernard Rimland, *Dyslogic Syndrome: Why Today's Children Are "Hyper," Attention Disordered, Learning Disabled, Depressed, Aggressive, Defiant, or Violent—and What We Can Do About It* (London: Jessica Kingsley Publishers, 2008).

23. Anthony Walsh, "Behavior Genetics and Anomie/Strain Theory," *Criminology* 38 (2000): 1,075–1,108.

24. Anthony Walsh and Lee Ellis, "Shoring Up the Big Three: Improving Criminological Theories with Biosocial Concepts," paper presented at the annual meeting of the American Society of Criminology, San Diego, November 1997, p. 16.

25. Leonard Hippchen, "Some Possible Biochemical Aspects of Criminal Behavior," *Journal of Behavioral Ecology* 2 (1981): 1–6; Sarnoff Mednick and Jan Volavka, "Biology and Crime," in *Crime and Justice*, ed. Norval Morris and Michael Tonry (Chicago: University of Chicago Press, 1980), pp. 85–159; Saleem Shah and Loren Roth, "Biological and Psychophysiological Factors in Criminality," in *Handbook of Criminology*, ed. Daniel Glazer (Chicago: Rand McNally, 1974), pp. 125–140.

26. See, generally, Adrian Raine, *The Psychopathology of Crime* (San Diego: Academic Press, 1993); see also Leonard Hippchen, *The Ecologic-Biochemical Approaches to Treatment of Delinquents and Criminals* (New York: Van Nostrand Reinhold, 1978).

27. Jonathon Ericson, Francis Crinella, K. Alison Clarke-Stewart, Virginia Allhusen, Tony Chan, and Richard T. Robertson, "Prenatal Manganese Levels Linked to Childhood Behavioral Disinhibition," *Neurotoxicology and Teratology* 29 (2007): 181–187; Joseph Hibbeln, John Davis, Colin Steer, Pauline Emmett, Imogen Rogers, Cathy Williams, and Jean Golding, "Maternal Seafood Consumption in Pregnancy and Neurodevelopmental Outcomes in Childhood (ALSPAC Study): An Observational Cohort Study," *The Lancet* 369 (2007): 578–585.

28. Lauren Wakschlag, Kate Pickett, Kristen Kasza, and Rolf Loeber, "Is Prenatal Smoking Associated with a Developmental Pattern of Conduct Problems in Young Boys?" *Journal of the American Academy of Child and Adolescent Psychiatry* 45 (2006): 461–467; "Diet and the Unborn Child: The Omega Point," *The Economist*, January 19, 2006.

29. Lisa M. Gatzke-Kopp and Theodore Beauchaine, "Direct and Passive Prenatal Nicotine Exposure and the Development of Externalizing Psychopathology," *Child Psychiatry and Human Development* 38 (2007): 255–269.

30. F. T. Crews, A. Mdzinarishvili, D. Kim, J. He, and K. Nixon, "Neurogenesis in Adolescent Brain Is Potently Inhibited by Ethanol," *Neuroscience* 137 (2006): 437–445.

31. K. Murata, P. Weihe, E. Budtz-Jorgensen, P. J. Jorgensen, and P. Grandjean, "Delayed Brainstem Auditory Evoked Potential Latencies in 14-Year-Old Children Exposed to Methylmercury," *Journal of Pediatrics* 144 (2004): 177–183; Eric Konofal, Samuele Cortese, Michel Lecendreux, Isabelle Arnulf, and Marie Christine Mouren, "Effectiveness of Iron Supplementation in a Young Child with Attention-Deficit/Hyperactivity Disorder," *Pediatrics* 116 (2005): 732–734.

32. Sue Dengate and Alan Ruben, "Controlled Trial of Cumulative Behavioural Effects of a Common Bread Preservative," *Journal of Pediatrics and Child Health* 38 (2002): 373–376.

33. Harold Milman and Suzanne Arnold, "Neurologic, Psychological, and Aggressive Disturbances with Sildenafil," *Annals of Pharmacotherapy* 36 (2002): 1,129–1,134.

34. Gail Wasserman, Xinhua Liu, Faruque Parvez, Habibul Ahsan, Diane Levy, Pam Factor-Litvak, Jennie Kline, Alexander van Geen, Vesna Slavkovich, Nancy J. Lolacono, Zhongqi Cheng, Yan Zheng, and Joseph Graziano, "Water Manganese Exposure and Children's Intellectual Function in Araihazar, Bangladesh," *Environmental Health Perspectives* 114 (2006): 124–129; Eric Konofal, Michel Lecendreux, Isabelle Arnulf, and Marie-Christine Mouren, "Iron Deficiency in Children with Attention-Deficit/Hyperactivity Disorder," *Archives of Pediatric and Adolescent Medicine* 158 (2004): 1,113–1,115; Konofal et al., "Effectiveness of Iron Supplementation in a Young Child with Attention-Deficit/Hyperactivity Disorder."

35. D. K. L. Cheuk and Virginia Wong, "Attention Deficit Hyperactivity Disorder and Blood Mercury Level: A Case-Control Study in Chinese Children," *Neuropediatrics*, 37 (2006): 234–240.

36. Alexandra Richardson and Paul Montgomery, "The Oxford-Durham Study: A Randomized Controlled Trial of Dietary Supplementation with Fatty Acids in Children with Developmental Coordination Disorder," *Pediatrics* 115 (2005): 1,360–1,366.

37. Ap Zaalberg, Henk Nijman, Erik Bulten, Luwe Stroosma, and Cees van der Staak, "Effects of Nutritional Supplements on Aggression, Rule-Breaking, and Psychopathology Among Young Adult Prisoners," *Aggressive Behavior* 35 (2009): 1–10.

38. Ronald Prinz and David Riddle, "Associations Between Nutrition and Behavior in 5-Year-Old Children," *Nutrition Reviews Supplement* 44 (1986): 151–158.

39. M. Mousain-Bosc, M. Roche, A. Polge, D. Pradai-Prat, J. Rapin, and J. P. Bali, "Improvement of Neurobehavioral Disorders in Children Supplemented with Magnesium-Vitamin B6, Part I, Attention Deficit Hyperactivity Disorder," *Magnesium Research* 19 (2006): 46–52.

40. Karen Lau, W. Graham McLean, Dominic P. Williams, and C. Vyvyan Howard "Synergistic Interactions Between Commonly Used Food Additives in a Developmental Neurotoxicity Test," *Toxicological Science* 90 (2006): 178–187.

41. Donna McCann, Angelina Barrett, Alison Cooper, Debbie Crumpler, Lindy Dalen, Kate Grimshaw, Elizabeth Kitchin, Kris Lok, Lucy Porteous, Emily Prince, Edmund Sonuga-Barke, John O Warner, and Jim Stevenson, "Food Additives and Hyperactive Behaviour in 3-Year-Old and

8/9-Year-Old Children in the Community: A Randomised, Double-Blinded, Placebo-Controlled Trial," *The Lancet* 370 (2007): 1,560–1,567.

42. Adrian Raine, Kjetil Mellingen, Jianghong Liu, Peter Venables, and Sarnoff Mednick, "Effects of Environmental Enrichment at Age Three to Five Years on Schizotypal Personality and Antisocial Behavior at Ages Seventeen and Twenty-Three Years," *American Journal of Psychiatry* 160 (2003): 1–9.

43. Stephen Schoenthaler and Walter Doraz, "Types of Offenses Which Can Be Reduced in an Institutional Setting Using Nutritional Intervention," *International Journal of Biosocial Research* 4 (1983): 74–84.

44. H. Bruce Ferguson, Clare Stoddart, and Jovan Simeon, "Double-Blind Challenge Studies of Behavioral and Cognitive Effects of Sucrose-Aspartame Ingestion in Normal Children," *Nutrition Reviews Supplement* 44 (1986): 144–158; Gregory Gray, "Diet, Crime and Delinquency: A Critique," *Nutrition Reviews Supplement* 44 (1986): 89–94.

45. Mark Wolraich, Scott Lindgren, Phyllis Stumbo, Lewis Steginik, Mark Appelbaum, and Mary Kiritsy, "Effects of Diets High in Sucrose or Aspartame on the Behavior and Cognitive Performance of Children," *New England Journal of Medicine* 330 (1994): 303–306.

46. Dian Gans, "Sucrose and Unusual Childhood Behavior," *Nutrition Today* 26 (1991): 8–14.

47. Diana Fishbein, "Neuropsychological Function, Drug Abuse, and Violence, a Conceptual Framework," *Criminal Justice and Behavior* 27 (2000): 139–159.

48. D. Hill and W. Sargent, "A Case of Matricide," *The Lancet* 244 (1943): 526–527.

49. E. Podolsky, "The Chemistry of Murder," *Pakistan Medical Journal* 15 (1964): 9–14.

50. J. A. Yaryura-Tobias and F. Neziroglu, "Violent Behavior, Brain Dysrhythmia and Glucose Dysfunction: A New Syndrome," *Journal of Orthopsychiatry* 4 (1975): 182–188.

51. Matti Virkkunen, "Reactive Hypoglycemic Tendency Among Habitually Violent Offenders," *Nutrition Reviews Supplement* 44 (1986): 94–103.

52. James Q. Wilson, *The Moral Sense* (New York: Free Press, 1993).

53. Walter Gove, "The Effect of Age and Gender on Deviant Behavior: A Biopsychosocial Perspective," in *Gender and the Life Course*, ed. A. S. Rossi (New York: Aldine, 1985), pp. 115–144.

54. Alan Booth and D. Wayne Osgood, "The Influence of Testosterone on Deviance in Adulthood: Assessing and Explaining the Relationship," *Criminology* 31 (1993): 93–118.

55. Lee Ellis, Shyamal Das, and Hasan Buker, "Androgen-Promoted Physiological Traits and Criminality: A Test of the Evolutionary Neuroandrogenic Theory," *Personality and Individual Differences* 44 (2008): 701–711.

56. Anthony Walsh, "Genetic and Cytogenetic Intersex Anomalies: Can They Help Us to Understand Gender Differences in Deviant Behavior?" *International Journal of Offender Therapy and Comparative Criminology* 39 (1995): 151–166.

57. Christy Miller Buchanan, Jacquelynne Eccles, and Jill Becker, "Are Adolescents the Victims of Raging Hormones? Evidence for Activational Effects of Hormones on Moods and Behavior at Adolescence," *Psychological Bulletin* 111 (1992): 62–107.

58. Alex Piquero and Timothy Brezina, "Testing Moffitt's Account of Adolescent-Limited Delinquency," *Criminology* 39 (2001): 353–370.

59. Booth and Osgood, "The Influence of Testosterone on Deviance in Adulthood."

60. Walsh, "Genetic and Cytogenetic Intersex Anomalies: Can They Help Us to Understand Gender Differences in Deviant Behavior?"

61. Celina Cohen-Bendahan, Jan Buitelaar, Stephanie van Goozen, Jacob Orlebeke, and Peggy Cohen-Kettenis, "Is There an Effect of Prenatal Testosterone on Aggression and Other Behavioral Traits? A Study Comparing Same-Sex and Opposite-Sex Twin Girls," *Hormones and Behavior* 47 (2005): 230–237.

62. John Simister and Cary Cooper, "Thermal Stress in the U.S.A.: Effects on Violence and on Employee Behaviour," *Stress and Health: Journal of the International Society for the Investigation of Stress* 21 (2005): 3–15.

63. Lee Ellis, "Evolutionary and Neurochemical Causes of Sex Differences in Victimizing Behavior: Toward a Unified Theory of Criminal Behavior and Social Stratification," *Social Science Information* 28 (1989): 605–636.

64. For a general review, see Lee Ellis and Phyllis Coontz, "Androgens, Brain Functioning, and Criminality: The Neurohormonal Foundations of Antisociality," in *Crime in Biological Contexts*, pp. 162–193.

65. Ibid., p. 181.

66. Robert Rubin, "The Neuroendocrinology and Neuro-Chemistry of Antisocial Behavior," in *The Causes of Crime, New Biological Approaches*, ed. Sarnoff Mednick, Terrie Moffitt, and Susan Stack (Cambridge: Cambridge University Press, 1987), pp. 239–262.

67. J. Money, "Influence of Hormones on Psychosexual Differentiation," *Medical Aspects of Nutrition* 30 (1976): 165.

68. Mednick and Volavka, "Biology and Crime."

69. For a review of this concept, see Anne E. Figert, "The Three Faces of PMS: The Professional, Gendered, and Scientific Structuring of a Psychiatric Disorder," *Social Problems* 42 (1995): 56–72.

70. Katharina Dalton, *The Premenstrual Syndrome* (Springfield, IL: Charles C Thomas, 1971).

71. M. S. Zeedyk and F. E. Raitt, "Biology in the Courtroom: PMS in Legal Defenses," *Psychology, Evolution and Gender* 1 (1999): 123–143.

72. Julie Horney, "Menstrual Cycles and Criminal Responsibility," *Law and Human Nature* 2 (1978): 25–36.

73. Diana Fishbein, "Selected Studies on the Biology of Antisocial Behavior," in *New Perspectives in Criminology*, ed. John Conklin (Needham Heights, MA: Allyn & Bacon, 1996), pp. 26–38.

74. Ibid.; Karen Paige, "Effects of Oral Contraceptives on Affective Fluctuations Associated with the Menstrual Cycle," *Psychosomatic Medicine* 33 (1971): 515–537.

75. H. E. Amos and J. J. P. Drake, "Problems Posed by Food Additives," *Journal of Human Nutrition* 30 (1976): 165.

76. Ray Wunderlich, "Neuroallergy as a Contributing Factor to Social Misfits: Diagnosis and Treatment," in *Ecologic-Biochemical Approaches to Treatment of Delinquents and Criminals*, ed. Leonard Hippchen (New York: Van Nostram Reinhold, 1978), pp. 229–253.

77. See, for example, Paul Marshall, "Allergy and Depression: A Neurochemical Threshold Model of the Relation between the Illnesses," *Psychological Bulletin* 113 (1993): 23–39.

78. A. R. Mawson and K. J. Jacobs, "Corn Consumption, Tryptophan, and Cross-National Homicide Rates," *Journal of Orthomolecular Psychiatry* 7 (1978): 227–230.

79. Centers for Disease Control and Prevention, "CDC Releases Most Extensive Assessment Ever of Americans' Exposure to Environmental Chemicals," press release, January 31, 2003.

80. Núria Ribas-Fitó, Maties Torrent, Daniel Carrizo, Jordi Júlvez, Joan O. Grimalt, and Jordi Sunyer, "Exposure to Hexachlorobenzene During Pregnancy and Children's Social Behavior at 4 Years of Age," *Environmental Health Perspectives* 115 (2007): 447–450.

81. Stephanie M. Engel, Amir Miodovnik, Richard Canfield, Chenbo Zhu, Manori Silva, Antonia Calafat, and Mary Wolff, "Prenatal Phthalate Exposure Is Associated with Childhood Behavior and Executive Functioning," *Environmental Health Perspectives* 118 (2010): 565–571.

82. Virginia Rauh, Robin Garfinkel, Frederica Perera, Howard Andrews, Lori Hoepner, Dana Barr, Ralph Whitehead, Deliang Tang, and Robin Whyatt, "Impact of Prenatal Chlorpyrifos Exposure on Neurodevelopment in the First 3 Years of Life

Among Inner-City Children," *Pediatrics* 118 (2006): 1,845–1,859.

83. Kelly P. K. Olympio, Pedro V. Oliveira, Juliana Naozuka, Maria R. A. Cardoso, Antonio F. Marques, Wanda M. R. Günther, and Etelvino J. H. Bechara, "Surface Dental Enamel Lead Levels and Antisocial Behavior in Brazilian Adolescents," *Neurotoxicology and Teratology* 32 (2010): 273–279; David C. Bellinger, "Lead," *Pediatrics* 113 (2004): 1,016–1,022.

84. Paul Stretesky and Michael Lynch, "The Relationship Between Lead Exposure and Homicide," *Archives of Pediatric Adolescent Medicine* 155 (2001): 579–582.

85. Rick Nevin, "Understanding International Crime Trends: The Legacy of Preschool Lead Exposure," *Environmental Research* 104 (2007): 315–336.

86. Joel Nigg, G. Mark Knottnerus, Michelle Martel, Molly Nikolas, Kevin Cavanagh, Wilfried Karmaus, and Marsha D. Rappley, "Low Blood Lead Levels Associated with Clinically Diagnosed Attention-Deficit/Hyperactivity Disorder and Mediated by Weak, Cognitive Control," *Biological Psychiatry* 63 (2008): 325–331.

87. Jeff Evans, "Asymptomatic, High Lead Levels Tied to Delinquency," *Pediatric News* 37 (2003): 13.

88. Deborah Denno, "Considering Lead Poisoning as a Criminal Defense," *Fordham Urban Law Journal* 20 (1993): 377–400.

89. Herbert Needleman, Christine McFarland, Roberta Ness, Stephen Fienberg, and Michael Tobin, "Bone Lead Levels in Adjudicated Delinquents: A Case Control Study," *Neurotoxicology and Teratology* 24 (2002): 711–717; Herbert Needleman, Julie Riess, Michael Tobin, Gretchen Biesecker, and Joel Greenhouse, "Bone Lead Levels and Delinquent Behavior," *Journal of the American Medical Association* 275 (1996): 363–369.

90. Todd A. Jusko, Charles R. Henderson, Jr., Bruce P. Lanphear, Deborah A. Cory-Slechta, Patrick J. Parsons, and Richard L. Canfield, "Blood Lead Concentrations <10 μg/dL and Child Intelligence at 6 Years of Age," *Environ Health Perspectives* 116 (2008): 243–248.

91. Mark Opler, Alan Brown, Joseph Graziano, Manisha Desai, Wei Zheng, Catherine Schaefer, Pamela Factor-Litvak, and Ezra S. Susser, "Prenatal Lead Exposure, [Delta]-Aminolevulinic Acid, and Schizophrenia," *Environmental Health Perspectives* 112 (2004): 548–553.

92. Centers for Disease Control and Prevention, "CDC Releases Most Extensive Assessment Ever of Americans' Exposure to Environmental Chemicals."

93. Emily Oken, Robert O. Wright, Ken P. Kleinman, David Bellinger, Chitra J. Amarasiriwardena, Howard Hu, Janet W. Rich-Edwards, and Matthew W. Gillman, "Maternal Fish Consumption, Hair Mercury, and Infant Cognition in a U.S. Cohort," *Environmental Health Perspectives* 113 (2005): 1,376–1,380.

94. Terrie Moffitt, "The Neuropsychology of Juvenile Delinquency: A Critical Review," in *Crime and Justice, An Annual Review*, Vol. 12, ed. Norval Morris and Michael Tonry (Chicago: University of Chicago Press, 1990), pp. 99–169.

95. Terrie Moffitt, Donald Lynam, and Phil Silva, "Neuropsychological Tests Predicting Persistent Male Delinquency," *Criminology* 32 (1994): 277–300; Elizabeth Kandel and Sarnoff Mednick, "Perinatal Complications Predict Violent Offending," *Criminology* 29 (1991): 519–529; Sarnoff Mednick, Ricardo Machon, Matti Virkkunen, and Douglas Bonett, "Adult Schizophrenia Following Prenatal Exposure to an Influenza Epidemic," *Archives of General Psychiatry* 44 (1987): 35–46; C. A. Fogel, S. A. Mednick, and N. Michelson, "Hyperactive Behavior and Minor Physical Anomalies," *Acta Psychiatrica Scandinavia* 72 (1985): 551–556.

96. Jean Seguin, Robert Pihl, Philip Harden, Richard Tremblay, and Bernard Boulerice, "Cognitive and Neuropsychological Characteristics of Physically Aggressive Boys," *Journal of Abnormal Psychology* 104 (1995): 614–624; Deborah Denno, "Gender, Crime and the Criminal Law Defenses," *Journal of Criminal Law and Criminology* 85 (1994): 80–180.

97. Yaling Yang, Adrian Raine, Todd Lencz, Susan Bihrle, Lori Lacasse, and Patrick Colletti, "Prefrontal White Matter in Pathological Liars," *British Journal of Psychiatry* 187 (2005): 320–325.

98. Nathaniel Pallone and James Hennessy, "Brain Dysfunction and Criminal Violence," *Society* 35 (1998): 21–27, at 25.

99. Peer Briken, Niels Habermann, Wolfgang Berner, and Andreas Hill, "The Influence of Brain Abnormalities on Psychosocial Development, Criminal History and Paraphilias in Sexual Murderers," *Journal of Forensic Sciences* 50 (2005): 1–5.

100. Kevin Beaver, John Paul Wright, and Matthew Delisi, "Self-Control as an Executive Function: Reformulating Gottfredson and Hirschi's Parental Socialization Thesis," *Criminal Justice and Behavior* 34 (2007): 1,345–1,361.

101. Adrian Raine, P. Brennan, and S. Mednick, "Interaction Between Birth Complications and Early Maternal Rejection in Predisposing to Adult Violence: Specificity to Serious, Early Onset Violence," *American Journal of Psychiatry* 154 (1997): 1,265–1,271.

102. Deborah Denno, *Biology, Crime and Violence: New Evidence* (Cambridge: Cambridge University Press, 1989).

103. Diana Fishbein and Robert Thatcher, "New Diagnostic Methods in Criminology: Assessing Organic Sources of Behavioral Disorders," *Journal of Research in Crime and Delinquency* 23 (1986): 240–267.

104. See, generally, David Rowe, *Biology and Crime* (Los Angeles: Roxbury Press, 2001).

105. R. W. Aind and T. Yamamoto, "Behavior Disorders of Childhood," *Electroencephalography and Clinical Neurophysiology* 21 (1966): 148–156.

106. See, generally, Jan Volavka, "Electroencephalogram Among Criminals," in *The Causes of Crime, New Biological Approaches*, ed. Sarnoff Mednick, Terrie Moffitt, and Susan Stack (Cambridge: Cambridge University Press, 1987), pp. 137–145; Z. A. Zayed, S. A. Lewis, and R. P. Britain, "An Encephalographic and Psychiatric Study of 32 Insane Murderers," *British Journal of Psychiatry* 115 (1969): 1,115–1,124.

107. Nathaniel Pallone and James Hennessy, "Brain Dysfunction and Criminal Violence," *Society* 35 (1998): 21–27; P. F. Goyer, P. J. Andreason, and W. E. Semple, "Positronic Emission Tomography and Personality Disorders," *Neuropsychopharmacology* 10 (1994): 21–28.

108. Adrian Raine, Monte Buchsbaum, and Lori LaCasse, "Brain Abnormalities in Murderers Indicated by Positron Emission Tomography," *Biological Psychiatry* 42 (1997): 495–508.

109. David George, Robert Rawlings, Wendol Williams, Monte Phillips, Grace Fong, Michael Kerich, Reza Momenan, John Umhau, and Daniel Hommer, "A Select Group of Perpetrators of Domestic Violence: Evidence of Decreased Metabolism in the Right Hypothalamus and Reduced Relationships Between Cortical/Subcortical Brain Structures in Positron Emission Tomography," *Psychiatry Research: Neuroimaging* 130 (2004): 11–25.

110. Daniel G. Amen, Chris Hanks, Jill Prunella, and Aisa Green, "An Analysis of Regional Cerebral Blood Flow in Impulsive Murderers Using Single Photon Emission Computed Tomography," *Journal of Neuropsychiatry and Clinical Neurosciences* 19 (2007): 304–309.

111. Adrian Raine, "The Role of Prefrontal Deficits, Low Autonomic Arousal, and Early Health Factors in the Development of Antisocial and Aggressive Behavior in Children," *Journal of Child Psychology and Psychiatry* 43 (2002): 417–434.

112. D. R. Robin, R. M. Starles, T. J. Kenney, B. J. Reynolds, and F. P. Heald, "Adolescents Who Attempt Suicide," *Journal of Pediatrics* 90 (1977): 636–638.

113. R. R. Monroe, *Brain Dysfunction in Aggressive Criminals* (Lexington, MA: D.C. Heath, 1978).

114. L. T. Yeudall, *Childhood Experiences as Causes of Criminal Behavior* (Senate of Canada, Issue No. 1, Thirteenth Parliament, Ottawa, 1977).

115. Raine, Buchsbaum, and LaCasse, "Brain Abnormalities in Murderers Indicated by Positron Emission Tomography."

116. Cited in Charles Post, "The Link Between Learning Disabilities and Juvenile Delinquency: Cause, Effect, and 'Present Solutions,'" *Juvenile and Family Court Journal* 31 (1981): 59.

117. Joel Zimmerman, William Rich, Ingo Keilitz, and Paul Broder, "Some Observations on the Link Between Learning Disabilities and Juvenile Delinquency," *Journal of Criminal Justice* 9 (1981): 9–17; J. W. Podboy and W. A. Mallory, "The Diagnosis of Specific Learning Disabilities in a Juvenile Delinquent Population," *Juvenile and Family Court Journal* 30 (1978): 11–13.

118. Tomer Einat and Amela Einat, "Learning Disabilities and Delinquency: A Study of Israeli Prison Inmates," *International Journal of Offender Therapy and Comparative Criminology*, October 1, 2007 (online publication), http://ijo.sagepub.com/cgi/rapidpdf/0306624X07307352v1 (accessed November 9, 2010).

119. Thomas Brown, *Attention Deficit Disorder: The Unfocused Mind in Children and Adults* (New Haven, CT: Yale University Press, 2005).

120. Leonore Simon, "Does Criminal Offender Treatment Work?" *Applied and Preventive Psychology* (Summer 1998).

121. Terrie Moffitt and Phil Silva, "Self-Reported Delinquency, Neuropsychological Deficit, and History of Attention Deficit Disorder," *Journal of Abnormal Child Psychology* 16 (1988): 553–569.

122. Elizabeth Hart et al., "Criterion Validity of Informants in the Diagnosis of Disruptive Behavior Disorders in Children: A Preliminary Study," *Journal of Consulting and Clinical Psychology* 62 (1994): 410–414.

123. Russell Barkley, Mariellen Fischer, Lori Smallish, and Kenneth Fletcher, "Young Adult Follow-Up of Hyperactive Children: Antisocial Activities and Drug Use," *Journal of Child Psychology and Psychiatry* 45 (2004): 195–211; Molina Pelham, Jr., "Childhood Predictors of Adolescent Substance Use in a Longitudinal Study of Children with ADHD," *Journal of Abnormal Psychology* 112 (2003): 497–507; Peter Muris and Cor Meesters, "The Validity of Attention Deficit Hyperactivity and Hyperkinetic Disorder Symptom Domains in Nonclinical Dutch Children," *Journal of Clinical Child and Adolescent Psychology* 32 (2003): 460–466.

124. Jason Fletcher and Barbara Wolfe, "Long-Term Consequences of Childhood ADHD on Criminal Activities," *Journal of Mental Health Policy and Economics* 12 (2009): 119–138.

125. Patricia Westmoreland, Tracy Gunter, Peggy Loveless, Jeff Allen, Bruce Sieleni, and Donald Black, "Attention Deficit Hyperactivity Disorder in Men and Women Newly Committed to Prison," *International Journal of Offender Therapy and Comparative Criminology* 54 (2010): 361–377.

126. Karen Harding, Richard Judah, and Charles Gant, "Outcome-Based Comparison of Ritalin[R] versus Food-Supplement Treated Children with AD/HD," *Alternative Medicine Review* 8 (2003): 319–330.

127. Stephen Hinshaw, Elizabeth Owens, Nilofar Sami, and Samantha Fargeon, "Prospective Follow-Up of Girls with Attention-Deficit/Hyperactivity Disorder into Adolescence: Evidence for Continuing Cross-Domain Impairment," *Journal of Consulting and Clinical Psychology* 74 (2006): 489–499.

128. Rita Shaughnessy, "Psychopharmacotherapy of Neuropsychiatric Disorders," *Psychiatric Annals* 25 (1995): 634–640.

129. Lorne Yeudall, "A Neuropsychosocial Perspective of Persistent Juvenile Delinquency and Criminal Behavior," paper presented at the New York Academy of Sciences, September 26, 1979, p. 4; F. A. Elliott, "Neurological Aspects of Antisocial Behavior," in *The Psychopath: A Comprehensive Study of Antisocial Disorders and Behaviors*, ed. W. H. Reid (New York: Brunner/Mazel, 1978), pp. 146–189.

130. Ibid., p. 177.

131. H. K. Kletschka, "Violent Behavior Associated with Brain Tumor," *Minnesota Medicine* 49 (1966): 1,853–1,855.

132. V. E. Krynicki, "Cerebral Dysfunction in Repetitively Assaultive Adolescents," *Journal of Nervous and Mental Disease* 166 (1978): 59–67.

133. C. E. Lyght, ed., *The Merck Manual of Diagnosis and Therapy* (West Point, FL: Merck, 1966).

134. Albert Reiss and Jeffrey Roth, eds., *Understanding and Preventing Violence* (Washington, DC: National Academy Press, 1993), p. 119.

135. M. Virkkunen, M. J. DeJong, J. Bartko, and M. Linnoila, "Psychobiological Concomitants of History of Suicide Attempts Among Violent Offenders and Impulsive Fire Starters," *Archives of General Psychiatry* 46 (1989): 604–606.

136. Matti Virkkunen, David Goldman, and Markku Linnoila, "Serotonin in Alcoholic Violent Offenders," *The Ciba Foundation Symposium, Genetics of Criminal and Antisocial Behavior* (Chichester, England: Wiley, 1995).

137. Lee Ellis, "Left- and Mixed-Handedness and Criminality: Explanations for a Probable Relationship," in *Left-Handedness, Behavioral Implications and Anomalies*, ed. S. Coren (Amsterdam: Elsevier, 1990): 485–507.

138. M. Skondras, M. Markianos, A. Botsis, E. Bistolaki, and G. Christodoulou, "Platelet Monoamine Oxidase Activity and Psychometric Correlates in Male Violent Offenders Imprisoned for Homicide or Other Violent Acts," *European Archives of Psychiatry and Clinical Neuroscience* 254 (2004): 380–386.

139. Lee Ellis, "Monoamine Oxidase and Criminality: Identifying an Apparent Biological Marker for Antisocial Behavior," *Journal of Research in Crime and Delinquency* 28 (1991): 227–251.

140. Walter Gove and Charles Wilmoth, "Risk, Crime and Neurophysiologic Highs: A Consideration of Brain Processes that May Reinforce Delinquent and Criminal Behavior," in *Crime in Biological Contexts*, pp. 261–293.

141. Lee Ellis, "Arousal Theory and the Religiosity-Criminality Relationship," in *Contemporary Criminological Theory*, ed. Peter Cordella and Larry Siegel (Boston: Northeastern University, 1996), pp. 65–84.

142. Adrian Raine, Patricia Brennan, and Sarnoff Mednick, "The Interaction Between Birth Complications and Early Maternal Rejection in Predisposing to Adult Violence: Specificity to Serious, Early Onset Violence," *American Journal of Psychiatry* 154 (1997): 1,265–1,271.

143. Adrian Raine, Peter Venables, and Sarnoff Mednick, "Low Resting Heart Rate at Age 3 Years Predisposes to Aggression at Age 11 Years: Evidence from the Mauritius Child Health Project," *Journal of the American Academy of Adolescent Psychiatry* 36 (1997): 1,457–1,464.

144. Daniel Hart, Nancy Eisenberg, and Carlos Valiente, "Personality Change at the Intersection of Autonomic Arousal and Stress," *Psychological Science* 18 (2007): 492–497.

145. T. R. Sarbin and L. E. Miller, "Demonism Revisited: The XYY Chromosome Anomaly," *Issues in Criminology* 5 (1970): 195–207.

146. Mednick and Volavka, "Biology and Crime," p. 93.

147. Anita Thapar, Kate Langley, Tom Fowler, Frances Rice, Darko Turic, Naureen Whittinger, John Aggleton, Marianne van den Bree, Michael Owen, and Michael O'Donovan, "Catechol O-methyltransferase Gene Variant and Birth Weight Predict Early-Onset Antisocial Behavior in Children with Attention-Deficit/Hyperactivity Disorder," *Archives of General Psychiatry* 62 (2005): 1,275–1,278.

148. Brian Boutwell and Kevin Beaver, "A Biosocial Explanation of Delinquency Abstention," *Criminal Behaviour and Mental Health* 18 (2008): 59–74.

149. Gregory Carey and David DiLalla, "Personality and Psychopathology: Genetic Perspectives," *Journal of Abnormal Psychology* 103 (1994): 32–43.

150. Kevin M. Beaver, "The Effects of Genetics, the Environment, and Low Self-Control on Perceived Maternal and Paternal Socialization: Results from a Longitudinal Sample

of Twins," *Journal of Quantitative Criminology*, published online July 9, 2010, and available at www.springerlink.com/content/1579675h65435717/ (accessed November 9, 2010).

151. For an early review, see Barbara Wooton, *Social Science and Social Pathology* (London: Allen & Unwin, 1959); John Laub and Robert Sampson, "Unraveling Families and Delinquency: A Reanalysis of the Glueck's' Data," *Criminology* 26 (1988): 355–380.

152. D. J. West and D. P. Farrington, eds., "Who Becomes Delinquent?" in *The Delinquent Way of Life* (London: Heinemann, 1977); D. J. West, *Delinquency, Its Roots, Careers, and Prospects* (Cambridge, MA: Harvard University Press, 1982).

153. West, *Delinquency*, p. 114.

154. Carolyn Smith and David Farrington, "Continuities in Antisocial Behavior and Parenting across Three Generations," *Journal of Child Psychology and Psychiatry* 45 (2004): 230–247.

155. David Farrington, "Understanding and Preventing Bullying," in *Crime and Justice*, Vol. 17, ed. Michael Tonry (Chicago: University of Chicago Press, 1993), pp. 381–457.

156. Terence Thornberry, Adrienne Freeman-Gallant, Alan Lizotte, Marvin Krohn, and Carolyn Smith, "Linked Lives: The Intergenerational Transmission of Antisocial Behavior," *Journal of Abnormal Child Psychology* 31 (2003): 171–185.

157. Smith and Farrington, "Continuities in Antisocial Behavior and Parenting across Three Generations."

158. Abigail Fagan and Jake Najman, "Sibling Influences on Adolescent Delinquent Behaviour: An Australian Longitudinal Study," *Journal of Adolescence* 26 (2003): 547–559.

159. David Rowe and Bill Gulley, "Sibling Effects on Substance Use and Delinquency," *Criminology* 30 (1992): 217–232; see also David Rowe, Joseph Rogers, and Sylvia Meseck-Bushey, "Sibling Delinquency and the Family Environment: Shared and Unshared Influences," *Child Development* 63 (1992): 59–67.

160. Dana Haynie and Suzanne Mchugh, "Sibling Deviance in the Shadows of Mutual and Unique Friendship Effects?" *Criminology* 41 (2003): 355–393.

161. Louise Arseneault, Terrie Moffitt, Avshalom Caspi, Alan Taylor, Fruhling Rijsdijk, Sara Jaffee, Jennifer Ablow, and Jeffrey Measelle, "Strong Genetic Effects on Cross-Situational Antisocial Behaviour Among 5-Year-Old Children According to Mothers, Teachers, Examiner-Observers, and Twins' Self-Reports," *Journal of Child Psychology and Psychiatry* 44 (2003): 832–848.

162. David Rowe, "Sibling Interaction and Self-Reported Delinquent Behavior: A Study of 265 Twin Pairs," *Criminology* 23 (1985): 223–240; Nancy Segal, "Monozygotic and Dizygotic Twins: A Comparative Analysis of Mental Ability Profiles," *Child Development* 56 (1985): 1,051–1,058.

163. Ibid.

164. Thomas Bouchard, "Genetic and Environmental Influences on Intelligence and Special Mental Abilities," *American Journal of Human Biology* 70 (1998): 253–275; some findings from the Minnesota study can be accessed from the website www.psych.umn.edu/psylabs/mtfs/ (accessed November 9, 2010).

165. Gregory Carey, "Twin Imitation for Antisocial Behavior: Implications for Genetic and Family Environment Research," *Journal of Abnormal Psychology* 101 (1992): 18–25; David Rowe and Joseph Rodgers, "The Ohio Twin Project and ADSEX Studies: Behavior Genetic Approaches to Understanding Antisocial Behavior," paper presented at the annual meeting of the American Society of Criminology, Montreal, Canada, November 1987.

166. Glenn Walters, "A Meta-Analysis of the Gene–Crime Relationship," *Criminology* 30 (1992): 595–613.

167. Alice Gregory, Thalia Eley, and Robert Plomin, "Exploring the Association Between Anxiety and Conduct Problems in a Large Sample of Twins Aged 2–4," *Journal of Abnormal Child Psychology* 32 (2004): 111–123.

168. Marshall Jones and Donald Jones, "The Contagious Nature of Antisocial Behavior," *Criminology* 38 (2000): 25–46.

169. Ibid., p. 31.

170. R. J. Cadoret, C. Cain, and R. R. Crowe, "Evidence for a Gene–Environment Interaction in the Development of Adolescent Antisocial Behavior," *Behavior Genetics* 13 (1983): 301–310.

171. Lawrence Cohen and Richard Machalek, "A General Theory of Expropriative Crime: An Evolutionary Ecological Approach," *American Journal of Sociology* 94 (1988): 465–501.

172. For a general review, see Martin Daly and Margo Wilson, "Crime and Conflict: Homicide in Evolutionary Psychological Theory," in *Crime and Justice, An Annual Edition*, ed. Michael Tonry (Chicago: University of Chicago Press, 1997), pp. 51–100.

173. Ibid.

174. Martin Daly and Margo Wilson, *Homicide* (New York: Aldine de Gruyter, 1988), p. 194.

175. Margo Wilson, Holly Johnson, and Martin Daly, "Lethal and Nonlethal Violence against Wives," *Canadian Journal of Criminology* 37 (1995): 331–361.

176. Daly and Wilson, *Homicide*, pp. 172–173.

177. Lee Ellis, "The Evolution of Violent Criminal Behavior and Its Nonlegal Equivalent," in *Crime in Biological, Social, and Moral Contexts*, ed. Lee Ellis and Harry Hoffman (New York: Praeger, 1990), pp. 63–65.

178. David Rowe, Alexander Vazsonyi, and Aurelio Jose Figuerdo, "Mating-Effort in Adolescence: A Conditional Alternative Strategy," *Personal Individual Differences* 23 (2002): 105–115.

179. Ibid.

180. Anne Campbell, Steven Muncer, and Daniel Bibel, "Female–Female Criminal Assault: An Evolutionary Perspective," *Journal of Research in Crime and Delinquency* 35 (1998): 413–429.

181. Deborah Denno, "Sociological and Human Developmental Explanations of Crime: Conflict or Consensus," *Criminology* 23 (1985): 711–741.

182. Israel Nachshon and Deborah Denno, "Violence and Cerebral Function," in *The Causes of Crime, New Biological Approaches*, ed. Sarnoff Mednick, Terrie Moffitt, and Susan Stack (Cambridge: Cambridge University Press, 1987), pp. 185–217.

183. Raine, Brennan, Mednick, and Mednick, "High Rates of Violence, Crime, Academic Problems, and Behavioral Problems in Males with Both Early Neuromotor Deficits and Unstable Family Environments."

184. Avshalom Caspi, Donald Lynam, Terrie Moffitt, and Phil Silva, "Unraveling Girls' Delinquency: Biological, Dispositional, and Contextual Contributions to Adolescent Misbehavior," *Developmental Psychology* 29 (1993): 283–289.

185. Glenn Walters and Thomas White, "Heredity and Crime: Bad Genes or Bad Research," *Criminology* 27 (1989): 455–486, at 478.

186. Charles Goring, *The English Convict: A Statistical Study, 1913* (Montclair, NJ: Patterson Smith, 1972).

187. Edwin Driver, "Charles Buckman Goring," in *Pioneers in Criminology*, ed. Hermann Mannheim (Montclair, NJ: Patterson Smith, 1970), p. 440.

188. Gabriel Tarde, *Penal Philosophy*, trans. R. Howell (Boston: Little, Brown, 1912).

189. See, generally, Donn Byrne and Kathryn Kelly, *An Introduction to Personality* (Englewood Cliffs, NJ: Prentice Hall, 1981).

190. August Aichorn, *Wayward Youth* (New York: Viking Press, 1935).

191. See, generally, D. A. Andrews and James Bonta, *The Psychology of Criminal Conduct* (Cincinnati: Anderson, 1994), pp. 72–75.

192. Paige Crosby Ouimette, "Psychopathology and Sexual Aggression in Nonincarcerated Men," *Violence and Victimization* 12 (1997): 389–397.

193. Robert Krueger, Avshalom Caspi, Phil Silva, and Rob McGee, "Personality Traits Are Differentially Linked to Mental Disorders: A Multitrait-Multidiagnosis Study of an Adolescent Birth Cohort," *Journal of*

Abnormal Psychology 105 (1996): 299–312.

194. Seymour Halleck, *Psychiatry and the Dilemmas of Crime* (Berkeley: University of California Press, 1971).

195. John Bowlby, "Maternal Care and Mental Health," *World Health Organization Monograph* (WHO Monographs Series No. 2). Geneva: World Health Organization, 1951, p. 53.

196. Ibid., p. 13.

197. Eric Wood and Shelley Riggs, "Predictors of Child Molestation: Adult Attachment, Cognitive Distortions, and Empathy," *Journal of Interpersonal Violence* 23 (2008): 259–275.

198. Karen L. Hayslett-McCall and Thomas J. Bernard, "Attachment, Masculinity, and Self-Control: A Theory of Male Crime Rates," *Theoretical Criminology* 6 (2002): 5–33.

199. Jeffrey Burke, Rolf Loeber, and Boris Birmaher, "Oppositional Defiant Disorder and Conduct Disorder: A Review of the Past 10 Years, Part II," *Journal of the American Academy of Child and Adolescent Psychiatry* 41 (2002): 1,275–1,294.

200. Ellen Kjelsberg, "Gender and Disorder Specific Criminal Career Profiles in Former Adolescent Psychiatric In-Patients," *Journal of Youth and Adolescence* 33 (2004): 261–270.

201. Richard Rowe, Julie Messer, Robert Goodman, and Howard Meltzer, "Conduct Disorder and Oppositional Defiant Disorder in a National Sample: Developmental Epidemiology," *Journal of Child Psychology and Psychiatry and Allied Disciplines* 45 (2004): 609–621.

202. Paul Rohde, Gregory N. Clarke, David E. Mace, Jenel S. Jorgensen, and John R. Seeley, "An Efficacy/Effectiveness Study of Cognitive-Behavioral Treatment for Adolescents with Comorbid Major Depression and Conduct Disorder," *Journal of the American Academy of Child and Adolescent Psychiatry* 43 (2004): 660–669.

203. Minna Ritakallio, Riittakerttu Kaltiala-Heino, Janne Kivivuori, Tiina Luukkaala, and Matti Rimpelä, "Delinquency and the Profile of Offences among Depressed and Non-depressed Adolescents,"*Criminal Behaviour and Mental Health* 16 (2006): 100–110.

204. Grégoire "Zimmermann, Delinquency in Male Adolescents: The Role of Alexithymia and Family Structure," *Journal of Adolescence* 29 (2006): 321–332.

205. Ching-hua Ho, J. B Kingree, and Martie Thompson, "Associations between Juvenile Delinquency and Weight-Related Variables: Analyses from a National Sample of High School Students," *International Journal of Eating Disorders* 39 (2006): 477–483.

206. Michael Pullmann, Jodi Kerbs, Nancy Koroloff, Ernie Veach-White, Rita Gaylor, and DeDe Sieler, "Juvenile Offenders with Mental Health Needs: Reducing Recidivism Using Wraparound," *Crime and Delinquency* 52 (2006): 375–397; Jennifer Beyers and Rolf Loeber, "Untangling Developmental Relations between Depressed Mood and Delinquency in Male Adolescents," *Journal of Abnormal Child Psychology* 31 (2003): 247–267.

207. Dorothy Espelage, Elizabeth Cauffman, Lisa Broidy, Alex Piquero, Paul Mazerolle, and Hans Steiner, "A Cluster-Analytic Investigation of MMPI Profiles of Serious Male and Female Juvenile Offenders," *Journal of the American Academy of Child and Adolescent Psychiatry* 42 (2003): 770–777.

208. Richard Famularo, Robert Kinscherff, and Terence Fenton, "Psychiatric Diagnoses of Abusive Mothers, A Preliminary Report," *Journal of Nervous and Mental Disease* 180 (1992): 658–660.

209. James Sorrells, "Kids Who Kill," *Crime and Delinquency* 23 (1977): 312–320.

210. Richard Rosner, "Adolescents Accused of Murder and Manslaughter: A Five-Year Descriptive Study," *Bulletin of the American Academy of Psychiatry and the Law* 7 (1979): 342–351.

211. Richard Wagner, Dawn Taylor, Joy Wright, Alison Sloat, Gwynneth Springett, Sandy Arnold, and Heather Weinberg, "Substance Abuse among the Mentally Ill," *American Journal of Orthopsychiatry* 64 (1994): 30–38.

212. Susan Phillips, Alaattin Erkanli, Gordon Keeler, Jane Costello, and Adrian Angold, "Disentangling the Risks: Parent Criminal Justice Involvement and Children's Exposure to Family Risks," *Criminology and Public Policy* 5 (2006): 677–702.

213. Bruce Link, Howard Andrews, and Francis Cullen, "The Violent and Illegal Behavior of Mental Patients Reconsidered," *American Sociological Review* 57 (1992): 275–292; Ellen Hochstedler Steury, "Criminal Defendants with Psychiatric Impairment: Prevalence, Probabilities and Rates," *Journal of Criminal Law and Criminology* 84 (1993): 354–374.

214. Richard Friendman, "Violence and Mental Illness—How Strong Is the Link?" *New England Journal of Medicine* 355 (2006): 2,064–2,066.

215. Henrik Belfrage, "A Ten-Year Follow-Up of Criminality in Stockholm Mental Patients: New Evidence for a Relation between Mental Disorder and Crime," *British Journal of Criminology* 38 (1998): 145–155.

216. C. Wallace, P. Mullen, P. Burgess, S. Palmer, D. Ruschena, and C. Browne, "Serious Criminal Offending and Mental Disorder. Case Linkage Study," *British Journal of Psychiatry* 174 (1998): 477–484.

217. Patricia Brennan, Sarnoff Mednick, and Sheilagh Hodgins, "Major Mental Disorders and Criminal Violence in a Danish Birth Cohort," *Archives of General Psychiatry* 57 (2000): 494–500.

218. Stefan Watzke, Simone Ullrich, and Andreas Marneros, "Gender- and Violence-Related Prevalence of Mental Disorders in Prisoners," *European Archives of Psychiatry and Clinical Neuroscience* 256 (2006): 414–421.

219. John Monahan, *Mental Illness and Violent Crime* (Washington, DC: National Institute of Justice, 1996).

220. Robin Shepard Engel and Eric Silver, "Policing Mentally Disordered Suspects: A Reexamination of the Criminalization Hypothesis," *Criminology* 39 (2001): 225–352; Marc Hillbrand, John Krystal, Kimberly Sharpe, and Hilliard Foster, "Clinical Predictors of Self-Mutilation in Hospitalized Patients," *Journal of Nervous and Mental Disease* 182 (1994): 9–13.

221. James Bonta, Moira Law, and Karl Hanson, "The Prediction of Criminal and Violent Recidivism among Mentally Disordered Offenders: A Meta-Analysis," *Psychological Bulletin* 123 (1998): 123–142.

222. Eric Silver, "Mental Disorder and Violent Victimization: The Mediating Role of Involvement in Conflicted Social Relationships," *Criminology* 40 (2002): 191–212.

223. Stacy DeCoster and Karen Heimer, "The Relationship between Law Violation and Depression: An Interactionist Analysis," *Criminology* 39 (2001): 799–837.

224. Alexander McFarlane, Geoff Schrader, Clara Bookless, and Derek Browne, "Prevalence of Victimization, Posttraumatic Stress Disorder and Violent Behaviour in the Seriously Mentally Ill," *Australian and New Zealand Journal of Psychiatry* 40 (2006): 1,010–1,015; Eric Silver, "Extending Social Disorganization Theory: A Multilevel Approach to the Study of Violence among Persons with Mental Illness," *Criminology* 38 (2000): 1,043–1,074.

225. B. Lögdberg, L. L. Nilsson, M. T. Levander, and S. Levander, "Schizophrenia, Neighbourhood, and Crime," *Acta Psychiatrica Scandinavica* 110 (2004): 92–97.

226. Courtenay Sellers, Christopher Sullivan, Bonita Veysey, and Jon Shane, "Responding to Persons with Mental Illnesses: Police Perspectives on Specialized and Traditional Practices," *Behavioral Sciences and the Law* 23 (2005): 647–657.

227. Paul Hirschfield, Tina Maschi, Helene Raskin White, Leah Goldman Traub, and Rolf Loeber, "Mental Health and Juvenile Arrests: Criminality, Criminalization, or Compassion?" *Criminology* 44 (2006): 593–630.

228. Jeffrey Wanson, Randy Borum, Marvin Swartz, Virginia Hidaym, H. Ryan Wagner, and Barbara Burns, "Can Involuntary Outpatient Commitment Reduce Arrests among Persons with Severe Mental Illness?" *Criminal Justice and Behavior* 28 (2001): 156–189.

229. This discussion is based on three works by Albert Bandura: *Aggression: A Social Learning Analysis* (Englewood Cliffs, NJ: Prentice Hall, 1973), *Social Learning Theory* (Englewood Cliffs, NJ: Prentice Hall, 1977), and "The Social Learning Perspective: Mechanisms of Aggression," in *Psychology of Crime and Criminal Justice*, ed. Hans Toch (New York: Holt, Rinehart & Winston, 1979), pp. 198–236.

230. See, generally, Jean Piaget, *The Moral Judgment of the Child* (London: Kegan Paul, 1932).

231. Lawrence Kohlberg, *Stages in the Development of Moral Thought and Action* (New York: Holt, Rinehart & Winston, 1969).

232. L. Kohlberg, K. Kauffman, P. Scharf, and J. Hickey, *The Just Community Approach in Corrections: A Manual* (Niantic, CT: Connecticut Department of Corrections, 1973).

233. Scott Henggeler, *Delinquency in Adolescence* (Newbury Park, CA: Sage, 1989), p. 26.

234. Carol Veneziano and Louis Veneziano, "The Relationship between Deterrence and Moral Reasoning," *Criminal Justice Review* 17 (1992): 209–216.

235. Quinten Raaijmakers, Rutger Engels, and Anne van Hoof, "Delinquency and Moral Reasoning in Adolescence and Young Adulthood," *International Journal of Behavioral Development* 29 (2005): 247–258; Scott Henggeler, *Delinquency in Adolescence* (Newbury Park, CA: Sage, 1989), p. 26.

236. K. A. Dodge, "A Social Information Processing Model of Social Competence in Children," in *Minnesota Symposium in Child Psychology*, Vol. 18, ed. M. Perlmutter (Hillsdale, NJ: Erlbaum, 1986), pp. 77–125.

237. Adrian Raine, Peter Venables, and Mark Williams, "Better Autonomic Conditioning and Faster Electrodermal Half-Recovery Time at Age 15 Years as Possible Protective Factors against Crime at Age 29 Years," *Developmental Psychology* 32 (1996): 624–630.

238. Jean Marie McGloin and Travis Pratt, "Cognitive Ability and Delinquent Behavior among Inner-City Youth: A Life-Course Analysis of Main, Mediating, and Interaction Effects," *International Journal of Offender Therapy and Comparative Criminology* 47 (2003): 253–271.

239. Elizabeth Cauffman, Laurence Steinberg, and Alex Piquero, "Psychological, Neuropsychological, and Physiological Correlates of Serious Antisocial Behavior in Adolescence: The Role of Self-Control," *Criminology* 43 (2005): 133–176.

240. Donald Lynam and Joshua Miller, "Personality Pathways to Impulsive Behavior and Their Relations to Deviance: Results from Three Samples," *Journal of Quantitative Criminology* 20 (2004): 319–341.

241. Shadd Maruna, "Desistance from Crime and Explanatory Style: A New Direction in the Psychology of Reform," *Journal of Contemporary Criminal Justice* 20 (2004): 184–200.

242. Tony Ward and Claire Stewart, "The Relationship Between Human Needs and Criminogenic Needs," *Psychology, Crime and Law* 9 (2003): 219–225.

243. David Ward, Mark Stafford, and Louis Gray, "Rational Choice, Deterrence, and Theoretical Integration," *Journal of Applied Social Psychology* 36 (2006): 571–585.

244. Coralijn Nas, Bram Orobio de Castro, and Willem Koops, "Social Information Processing in Delinquent Adolescents," *Psychology, Crime and Law* 11 (2005): 363–375.

245. Elizabeth Kubik and Jeffrey Hecker, "Cognitive Distortions About Sex and Sexual Offending: A Comparison of Sex Offending Girls, Delinquent Girls, and Girls from the Community," *Journal of Child Sexual Abuse* 14 (2005): 43–69.

246. L. Huesman and L. Eron, "Individual Differences and the Trait of Aggression," *European Journal of Personality* 3 (1989): 95–106.

247. Rolf Loeber and Dale Hay, "Key Issues in the Development of Aggression and Violence from Childhood to Early Adulthood," *Annual Review of Psychology* 48 (1997): 371–410.

248. Judith Baer and Tina Maschi, "Random Acts of Delinquency: Trauma and Self-Destructiveness in Juvenile Offenders," *Child and Adolescent Social Work Journal* 20 (2003): 85–99.

249. J. E. Lochman, "Self and Peer Perceptions and Attributional Biases of Aggressive and Nonaggressive Boys in Dyadic Interactions," *Journal of Consulting and Clinical Psychology* 55 (1987): 404–410.

250. Kathleen Cirillo, B. E. Pruitt, Brian Colwell, Paul M. Kingery, Robert S. Hurley, and Danny Ballard, "School Violence: Prevalence and Intervention Strategies for At-Risk Adolescents," *Adolescence* 33 (1998): 319–331.

251. Leilani Greening, "Adolescent Stealers' and Nonstealers' Social Problem-Solving Skills," *Adolescence* 32 (1997): 51–56.

252. D. Lipton, E. C. McDonel, and R. McFall, "Heterosocial Perception in Rapists," *Journal of Consulting and Clinical Psychology* 55 (1987): 17–21.

253. Vincent Marziano, Tony Ward, Anthony Beech, and Philippa Pattison, "Identification of Five Fundamental Implicit Theories Underlying Cognitive Distortions in Child Abusers: A Preliminary Study," *Psychology, Crime and Law* 12 (2006): 97–105.

254. Reiss and Roth, *Understanding and Preventing Violence*, p. 389.

255. Cirillo et al., "School Violence."

256. See, generally, Walter Mischel, *Introduction to Personality*, 4th Ed. (New York: Holt, Rinehart & Winston, 1986).

257. D. A. Andrews and J. Stephen Wormith, "Personality and Crime: Knowledge and Construction in Criminology," *Justice Quarterly* 6 (1989): 289–310; Donald Gibbons, "Comment—Personality and Crime: Non-Issues, Real Issues, and a Theory and Research Agenda," *Justice Quarterly* (1989): 311–324.

258. Sheldon Glueck and Eleanor Glueck, *Unraveling Juvenile Delinquency* (Cambridge, MA: Harvard University Press, 1950).

259. See, generally, Hans Eysenck, *Personality and Crime* (London: Routledge and Kegan Paul, 1977); Hans Eysenck and M. W. Eysenck, *Personality and Individual Differences* (New York: Plenum, 1985).

260. Catrien Bijleveld and Jan Hendriks, "Juvenile Sex Offenders: Differences between Group and Solo Offenders," *Psychology, Crime and Law* 9 (2003): 237–246; Joshua Miller and Donald Lynam, "Personality and Antisocial Behavior," *Criminology* 39 (2001): 765–799; Edelyn Verona and Joyce Carbonell, "Female Violence and Personality," *Criminal Justice and Behavior* 27 (2000): 176–195.

261. Eysenck and Eysenck, *Personality and Individual Differences*.

262. Essi Viding, James Blair, Terrie Moffitt, and Robert Plomin, "Evidence for Substantial Genetic Risk for Psychopathy in 7-Year-Olds," *Journal of Child Psychology and Psychiatry* 46 (2005): 592–597.

263. Gerhard Blickle, Alexander Schlegel, Pantaleon Fassbender, and Uwe Klein, "Some Personality Correlates of Business White-Collar Crime," *Applied Psychology: An International Review* 55 (2006): 220–233.

264. Andreas Hill, Niels Habermann, Wolfgang Berner, and Peer Briken, "Sexual Sadism and Sadistic Personality Disorder in Sexual Homicide," *Journal of Personality Disorders* 20 (2006): 671–684.

265. Ibid.

266. American Psychiatric Association, *Diagnostic and Statistical Manual of Mental Disorders* (Washington, DC: American Psychiatric Association, 1994).

267. See, generally, R. Starke Hathaway and Elio Monachesi, *Analyzing and Predicting Juvenile Delinquency with the MMPI* (Minneapolis: University of Minnesota Press, 1953).

268. R. Starke Hathaway, Elio Monachesi, and Lawrence Young, "Delinquency Rates and Personality," *Journal of Criminal Law, Criminology, and Police Science* 51 (1960): 443–460; Michael Hindelang and Joseph Weis, "Personality and Self-Reported Delinquency: An Application of Cluster Analysis," *Criminology* 10 (1972): 268; Spencer Rathus and Larry Siegel, "Crime and Personality Revisited," *Criminology* 18 (1980): 245–251.

269. See, generally, Edward Megargee, *The California Psychological Inventory*

Handbook (San Francisco: Jossey-Bass, 1972).

270. Avshalom Caspi, Terrie Moffitt, Phil Silva, Magda Stouthamer-Loeber, Robert Krueger, and Pamela Schmutte, "Are Some People Crime-Prone? Replications of the Personality–Crime Relationship Across Countries, Genders, Races and Methods," *Criminology* 32 (1994): 163–195.

271. Edwin Sutherland, "Mental Deficiency and Crime," in *Social Attitudes*, ed. Kimball Young (New York: Henry Holt, 1931).

272. William Healy and Augusta Bronner, *Delinquency and Criminals: Their Making and Unmaking* (New York: Macmillan, 1926).

273. Joseph Lee Rogers, H. Harrington Cleveland, Edwin van den Oord, and David Rowe, "Resolving the Debate over Birth Order, Family Size and Intelligence," *American Psychologist* 55 (2000): 599–612.

274. John Slawson, *The Delinquent Boys* (Boston: Budget Press, 1926).

275. Edwin Sutherland, "Mental Deficiency and Crime," in *Social Attitudes*, ed. Kimball Young (New York: Henry Holt, 1931), Chap. 15.

276. Travis Hirschi and Michael Hindelang, "Intelligence and Delinquency: A Revisionist Review," *American Sociological Review* 42 (1977): 471–586.

277. Ibid.

278. Donald Lynam, Terrie Moffitt, and Magda Stouthamer-Loeber, "Explaining the Relation Between IQ and Delinquency: Class, Race, Test Motivation, School Failure or Self-Control," *Journal of Abnormal Psychology* 102 (1993): 187–196.

279. Susan Pease and Craig T. Love, "Optimal Methods and Issues in Nutrition Research in the Correctional Setting," *Nutrition Reviews Supplement* 44 (1986): 122–131.

280. Alex Piquero, "Frequency, Specialization, and Violence in Offending Careers," *Journal of Research in Crime and Delinquency* 37 (2000): 392–418.

281. James Q. Wilson and Richard Herrnstein, *Crime and Human Nature* (New York: Simon & Schuster, 1985), p. 148.

282. Ibid., p. 171.

283. Lorne Yeudall, Delee Fromm-Auch, and Priscilla Davies, "Neuropsychological Impairment of Persistent Delinquency," *Journal of Nervous and Mental Diseases* 170 (1982): 257–265; Hakan Stattin and Ingrid Klackenberg-Larsson, "Early Language and Intelligence Development and Their Relationship to Future Criminal Behavior," *Journal of Abnormal Psychology* 102 (1993): 369–378; H. D. Day, J. M. Franklin, and D. D. Marshall, "Predictors of Aggression in Hospitalized Adolescents," *Journal of Psychology* 132 (1998): 427–435.

284. Camilla Hagelstam and Helinä Häkkänen, "Adolescent Homicides in Finland: Offence and Offender Characteristics," *Forensic Science International* 164 (2006): 110–115.

285. Richard Herrnstein and Charles Murray, *The Bell Curve, Intelligence and Class Structure in American Life* (New York: Free Press, 1994).

286. Murray Simpson, M. K Simpson, and J. Hogg, "Patterns of Offending Among People with Intellectual Disability: A Systematic Review Part I: Methodology and Prevalence Data," *Journal of Intellectual Disability Research* 45 (2001): 384–396.

287. Ibid.

288. Mark O'Callaghan and Douglas Carroll, "The Role of Psychosurgical Studies in the Control of Antisocial Behavior," in *The Causes of Crime: New Biological Approaches*, ed. Sarnoff Mednick, Terrie Moffitt, and Susan Stack (Cambridge: Cambridge University Press, 1987), pp. 312–328.

289. Reiss and Roth, *Understanding and Preventing Violence*, p. 389.

290. Cirillo, Pruitt, Colwell, Kingery, Hurley, and Ballard, "School Violence."

291. Martin Olsson, Kjell Hansson, and Marianne Cederblad, "A Long-Term Follow-Up of Conduct Disorder Adolescents into Adulthood," *Nordic Journal of Psychiatry* 60 (2006): 469–479.

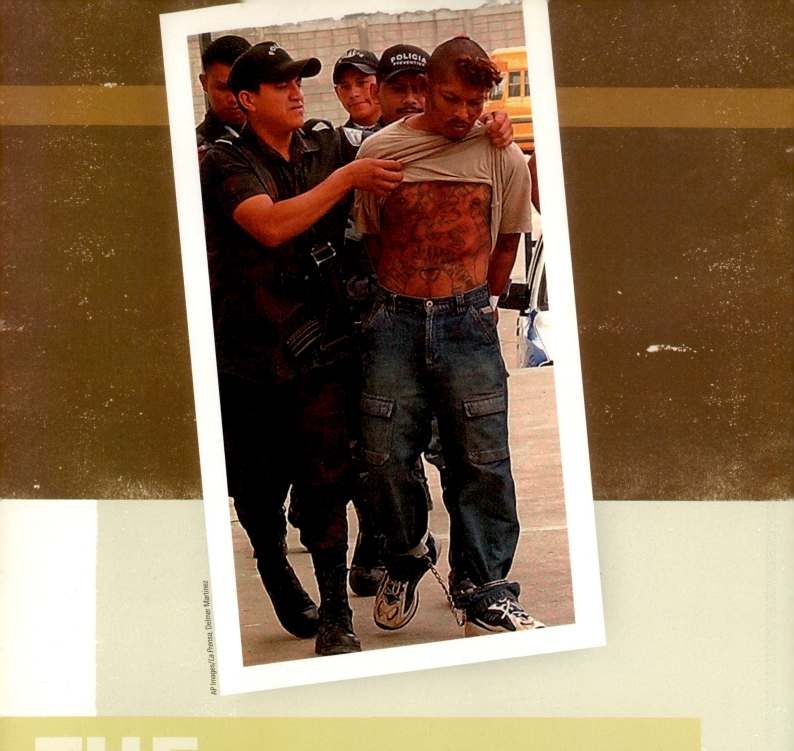

AP Images/*La Prensa*, Delmer Martinez

THE The tiny country of El Salvador (population 7.2 million) is home to more than 40,000 gang members. Rather than being a homegrown phenomenon, gangs are actually a U.S. import. How did this happen? In the early 1990s, hundreds of members of two of Los Angeles's largest gangs, the 18th Street Gang and the MS-13 gang, who had illegally made their home in the United States, were deported back to El Salvador. The deportees brought L.A. gang culture with them to a country already swamped with weapons from an ongoing civil war. Now on their home turf, gang boys recruited thousands of local teenagers into their reconstituted gangs. Joining a gang gave these poor, urban teenagers a powerful sense of identity and belonging. They were also free now to show their courage and manhood by engaging in a never-ending turf war with one another.

(*continued on page 186*)

Social Structure Theories

6

Learning Objectives

1. Be familiar with the different elements of the social structure
2. Describe the association between social structure and crime
3. Know the elements of social disorganization theory
4. Be familiar with the views of Shaw and McKay
5. Know the various elements of ecological theory
6. Be able to discuss the association between collective efficacy and crime
7. Discuss what is meant by the concept of strain
8. Know what Merton meant by the term *anomie*
9. Discuss the concept of negative affective states
10. Discuss the elements of cultural deviance theory

Ironically, both gangs were started in Los Angeles by Salvadorans fleeing a civil war. When they first arrived in L.A. they were preyed upon by preexisting Mexican gangs. The MS-13 gang was formed as a means of self-protection. The gang's name—Mara Salvatrucha—most likely comes from *mara*, slang for "army ant," and *salvatrucha*, local slang for tough, streetwise Salvadorans; the "13" is a common L.A. gang reference. Over time, both gangs' ranks grew and members entered a variety of rackets, from extortion to drug trafficking. When law enforcement cracked down and deported members, the deportees quickly created outposts in El Salvador and throughout Central America. The Salvadoran government has responded by criminalizing gang membership and arresting thousands. But government efforts have not stemmed the tide of recruitment, and the gangs appear to be more popular than ever.[1]

MS-13 operates in at least 42 states and the District of Columbia and has about 6,000 to 10,000 members nationwide. Its members engage in a wide range of criminal activity, including drug distribution, murder, rape, prostitution, robbery, home invasions, immigration offenses, kidnapping, carjackings/auto thefts, and vandalism. MS-13 is expanding its membership through recruitment and migration. New members are recruited by experienced gang boys who glorify the gang lifestyle (often on the Internet, complete with pictures and videos) and by absorbing smaller gangs. MS-13 members supplement their illegal income by working for legitimate businesses (often by presenting false documentation). They primarily pick employers that don't scrutinize employment documents, especially in the construction, restaurant, delivery service, and landscaping industries.

MS-13 originated in Los Angeles, but when members migrated eastward, they began forming cliques that for the most part operated independently. These cliques, though, often maintain regular contact with members in other regions to coordinate recruitment/criminal activities and to prevent conflicts.[2]

Some experts believe that the 10,000-member MS-13 is now the nation's most dangerous gang, while the 18th Street Gang, with over 20,000 members, is the largest.

Both MS-13 and the 18th Street Gang are part of a significant national gang population that has spread across the nation. Teen gangs have become an ever-present fixture of the American urban experience. Gang members are heavily armed, dangerous, and more violent than nonmembers. They are about 10 times more likely to carry handguns than nongang members, and gun-toting gang members commit about 10 times more violent crimes than nonmembers; gang homicides seem to be on an upswing. The most recent national survey finds that gangs exist in all levels of the social strata, from rural counties to metropolitan areas.[3]

To criminologists it comes as no surprise that gangs develop in poor, deteriorated urban neighborhoods. Many kids in these areas grow up hopeless and alienated, believing that they have little chance of being part of the American Dream.[4] Joining a gang holds the promise of economic rewards and status enhancements, which the conventional world simply cannot provide. The Profiles in Crime feature discusses a recent case of gang activity in Virginia that shows the routine use of violence and the national scope of the problem.

This association between social conditions and crime is not lost on criminologists, many of whom conclude that criminals are indigent and desperate people rather than abnormal, calculating, or evil. Raised in deteriorated parts of town, they lack the social support and economic resources available to more affluent members of society. According to this view, it is *social forces*—and not individual traits—that cause crime. Social forces in disadvantaged areas may be so powerful that they overwhelm individual choice. In disadvantaged neighborhoods, residents develop a feeling of fatalism and adopt a "nothing to lose" attitude. Regardless of personal traits or characteristics, these factors force individuals to take advantage of criminal opportunities. While in a middle-class environment, people who maintain an antisocial or impulsive personality may find the support they need to resist (or desist) the lure of antisocial activities; in the most disorganized inner-city areas of the city, *everyone* is susceptible to crime.[5] According to this

AP Images/Luis Romero

MS-13 is considered one of the most fearsome gangs in the United States, and the events of July 29, 2009, give clear support to this view. On that day, three MS-13 members—Adolfo Amaya Portillo, Eris Ramon Arguera, and Alcides Umaña—posed as potential customers to lure a pimp, Carlos Luna, and one of his "girls" to Manor Road in Alexandria, Virginia. Once Luna and the prostitute arrived at Manor Road, they were quickly subdued by the heavily armed MS-13 members. When the gang bangers demanded extortion payments from Luna, he refused to pay. A struggle ensued during which Luna attempted to grab Portillo's handgun. The boys cut his throat and shot him three times but left the young woman unharmed. Portillo, Arguera, and Umaña fled after taking the money that Luna and the prostitute had earned that day. The young woman then flagged down a police car and called for help. An investigation was initiated by the local police departments, and federal agencies, including the FBI and the U.S. Immigration and Customs Enforcement office of investigations, leading to the arrest of the three MS-13 members. Convicted of murder, Portillo was sentenced to 480 months in prison followed by five years of supervised release. Arguera was sentenced to 324 months in prison, and Umaña was sentenced to 240 months.

The case illustrates that gang members routinely use violence as a tool, taking someone's life in what might be considered a minor dispute over money. It also shows the effects of gang migration: a gang formed in Los Angeles is now active in Virginia.

SOURCE: News release, U.S. Attorney's Office for the Eastern District of Virginia, "MS-13 Member Sentenced to 40 Years for Murdering Pimp in July 2009," August 6, 2010, www.justice.gov/usao/vae/Pressreleases/08-AugustPDFArchive/10/20100806portillonr.html (accessed November 12, 2010).

---

view, rather than focusing on individual choice or traits to understand the root cause of criminal behavior, we must analyze the influence of these destructive social forces. In this chapter, we trace the origin of sociological criminology and then focus on how a person's place in the social structure determines and shapes his or her behavior.

DEVELOPMENT OF SOCIOLOGICAL CRIMINOLOGY

At the same time that biological positivists were conducting their experiments, others were using social data to scientifically study the major changes that were taking place in nineteenth-century society and in so doing helping to create the field of sociology.

Sociology seemed an ideal perspective from which to study society. After thousands of years of stability, the world was undergoing a population explosion: the population estimated at 600 million in 1700 had risen to 900 million by 1800. People were flocking to cities in ever-increasing numbers. Manchester, England, had 12,000 inhabitants in 1760 and 400,000 in 1850; during the same period, the population of Glasgow, Scotland, rose from 30,000 to 300,000.

The development of machinery such as power looms had doomed cottage industries and given rise to a factory system in which large numbers of people toiled for extremely low wages. The spread of agricultural machines increased the food supply while reducing the need for a large rural workforce; these excess laborers further swelled city populations. At the same time, political, religious, and social traditions continued to be challenged by the scientific method.

Quetelet and Durkheim

The application of sociological concepts to criminology can be traced to the works of pioneering sociologists L. A. J. (Adolphe) Quetelet (1796–1874) and (David) Émile Durkheim (1858–1917). Quetelet instigated the use of data and statistics in performing criminological research. Durkheim, considered one of the founders of sociology, defined crime as a normal and necessary social event.[6] These two perspectives have been extremely influential on modern criminology.

Quetelet was a Belgian mathematician who began (along with a Frenchman, André-Michel Guerry) what is known as the cartographic school of criminology.[7] This approach made use of social statistics that were being developed in Europe in the early nineteenth century. Statistical data provided important demographic information on the population, including density, gender, religious affiliations, and wealth.

Quetelet studied data gathered in France (called the *Comptes generaux de l'administration de la justice*) to investigate the influence of social factors on the propensity to commit crime. In addition to finding a strong influence of age and sex on crime, Quetelet also uncovered evidence that season, climate, population composition, and poverty were related to criminality. More specifically, he found that crime rates were greatest in the summer, in southern areas, among heterogeneous populations, and among the poor and uneducated. He also found crime rates to be influenced by drinking habits.[8] Quetelet identified many of the relationships between crime and social phenomena that still serve as a basis for criminology today. His findings that crime had a social basis was a direct challenge to Lombrosian biological determinism.

According to Émile Durkheim's vision of social positivism, crime is part of human nature because it has existed during periods of both poverty and prosperity.[9] Crime is *normal* because it is virtually impossible to imagine a society in which criminal behavior is totally absent. Such a society would almost demand that all people be and act exactly alike. Durkheim believed that the inevitability of crime is linked to the differences (heterogeneity) within society. Since people are so different from one another and employ such a variety of methods and forms of behavior to meet their needs, it is not surprising that some will resort to criminality. Even if "real" crimes were eliminated, human weaknesses and petty vices would be elevated to the status of crimes. As long as human differences exist, then, crime is inevitable and one of the fundamental conditions of social life.

Durkheim argued that crime can even be useful and, on occasion, healthy for society. He held that the existence of crime paves the way for social change and indicates that the social structure is not rigid or inflexible. Put another way, if such differences did not exist, it would mean that everyone behaved the same way and agreed on what is right and wrong. Such universal conformity would stifle creativity and independent thinking. To illustrate this concept, Durkheim offered the example of the Greek philosopher Socrates, who was considered a criminal and put to death for corrupting the morals of youth simply because he expressed ideas that were different from what people believed at that time.

Durkheim reasoned that another benefit of crime is that it calls attention to social ills. A rising crime rate can signal the need for social change and promote a variety of programs designed to relieve the human suffering that may have caused crime in the first place. In his influential book, *The Division of Labor in Society*, Durkheim described the consequences of the shift from a small, rural society, which he labeled "mechanical," to the more modern "organic" society with a large urban population, division of labor, and personal isolation.[10] From this shift flowed anomie, or norm and role confusion, a powerful sociological concept that helps describe the chaos and disarray accompanying the loss of traditional values in modern society. Durkheim's research on suicide indicated that anomic societies maintain high suicide rates; by implication, anomie might cause other forms of deviance as well.

The Chicago School and Beyond

The primacy of sociological positivism as the intellectual basis of criminology was secured by research begun in the early twentieth century by Albion W. Small (1854–1926), who organized the famed sociology department at the University of Chicago. Referred to as the Chicago School, urban sociologists such as W. I. Thomas (1863–1947), Robert Ezra Park (1864–1944), Ernest W. Burgess (1886–1966), and Louis Wirth (1897–1952) pioneered research on the social ecology of the city. In 1915, Robert Ezra Park called for anthropological methods of description and observation to be applied to urban life.[11] He was concerned with how neighborhood structure developed, how isolated pockets of poverty formed, and what social policies could be used to alleviate urban problems. In response, Chicago School sociologists carried out an ambitious program of research and scholarship on urban topics, including criminal behavior patterns. Harvey Zorbaugh's *The Gold Coast and the Slum*, Frederick Thrasher's *The Gang*, and Louis Wirth's *The Ghetto*[12] are classic examples of objective, highly descriptive accounts of urban life. Park, with Ernest Burgess, studied the social ecology of the city and found that some neighborhoods form so-called natural areas of wealth and affluence, while others suffered poverty and disintegration.[13] Regardless of their race, religion, or ethnicity, the everyday behavior of people living in these areas was controlled by the social and ecological climate.

This body of research inspired a generation of scholars to conclude that social forces operating in urban areas create "natural areas" for crime.[14] These urban neighborhoods maintain such a high level of poverty that critical institutions of socialization and control, such as the school and the family, begin to break down. While normally these social institutions can apply the social control necessary to restrain the neighborhood youth, their weakness means that kids are now free to engage in exciting and enticing law-violating behaviors. As crime rates soar and residents are afraid to leave their homes at night, the neighborhood becomes *socially disorganized*—unable to apply social control on its residents. It can no longer muster the cohesion needed to protect its residents from crime, drug abuse, and violence. Criminal behavior is not then a function of personal traits or choice, but is linked to environmental conditions that fail to provide residents with proper human relations and development.

The Chicago School sociologists initiated the view that crime and social ecological conditions were linked. Neighborhood conditions, and not individual pathology, influence and shape the direction of crime rates. Their writings became the core of sociological criminology, and the social environment and its influence on human behavior have remained the primary focus of criminology. Their authority was such that most criminologists have been trained in sociology, and criminology courses are routinely taught in departments of sociology. What is their vision and how do they connect criminality with a person's place in the social structure?

SOCIOECONOMIC STRUCTURE AND CRIME

People in the United States live in a **stratified society**. Social strata are created by the unequal distribution of wealth, power, and prestige. Social classes are segments of the population whose members have a relatively similar portion of desirable things and who share attitudes, values, norms, and an identifiable lifestyle. In U.S. society, it is common to identify people as upper-, middle-, and lower-class citizens, with a broad range of economic variations existing within each group. The upper-upper class is reserved for a small number of exceptionally well-to-do families who maintain enormous financial and social resources. The top 20 percent of households earn more than $90,000 per year while the bottom 20 percent averages about $19,000. The "super rich"—the top one-tenth of 1 percent (0.1 percent)—averages about $1.6 million in income each year.[15] The very top, the 400 highest-earning U.S. households, reported an average of $345 million in income in a single year (2007); the average income reported by the top 400 earners more than doubled from $131.1 million in 2001.

Nor is the wealth concentration effect unique to the United States; it is a worldwide phenomenon. According to the most recent World Wealth Report, there are about 6 million high net worth individuals in the world today (people with more than $1 million in assets excluding their primary residence); they have a collective net worth of more than $30.8 trillion, and their numbers are steadily growing.[16]

In contrast, the indigent have scant, if any, resources and suffer socially and economically as a result. And while the United States is the richest country in the world, the most recent federal data indicate that the number and rate of people living in poverty has risen since 2000.[17] (See Figure 6.1.) Almost 40 million Americans now live in poverty.

Lower-class areas are scenes of inadequate housing and health care, disrupted family lives, underemployment, and despair. Members of the lower class also suffer in other ways. They are more prone to depression, less likely to have achievement motivation, and less likely to put off immediate gratification for future gain. For example, they may be less willing to stay in school because the rewards for educational achievement are in the distant future.

The poor are constantly bombarded by the media with advertisements linking material possessions to self-worth, but they are often unable to attain desired goods and services through conventional means. Though they are members of a society that extols material success above any other, they are unable to satisfactorily compete for such success with members of the upper classes. As a result, they may turn to illegal solutions to their economic plight: they may deal drugs for profit, steal cars and sell them to "chop shops," or commit armed robberies for desperately needed funds. They may become so depressed that they take alcohol and drugs as a form of self-tranquilization, and because of their poverty, they may acquire the drugs and alcohol through illegal channels.

The Underclass

In 1966, sociologist Oscar Lewis argued that the crushing lifestyle of lower-class areas produces a **culture of poverty**, which is passed from one generation to the next.[18] Apathy, cynicism, helplessness, and mistrust of social institutions such as schools, government agencies, and the police mark the culture of poverty. This mistrust prevents members of the lower class from taking advantage of the meager opportunities available to them. Lewis's work was the first of a group that described the plight of **at-risk** children and adults. In 1970, Swedish economist Gunnar Myrdal described a worldwide **underclass** that was cut off from society, its members lacking the education and skills needed to be effectively in demand in modern society.[19]

Economic disparity will continually haunt members of the underclass and their children over the course of their life span. Even if they value education and other middle-class norms, their desperate life circumstances (e.g., high unemployment and nontraditional family structures) may

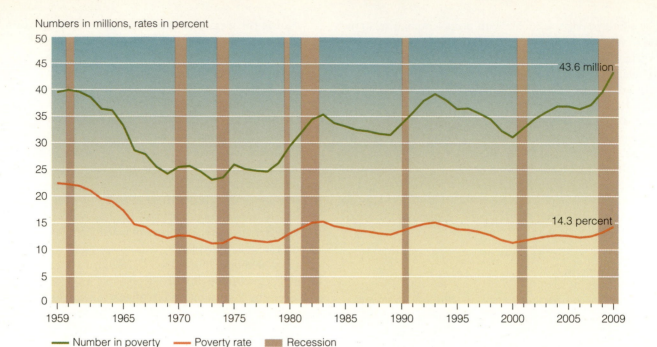

Numbers in millions, rates in percent

FIGURE 6.1
Number in Poverty and Poverty Rate

SOURCE: U.S. Census Bureau, Current Population Survey, 1960 to 2009 Annual Social and Economic Supplements, www.census.gov/hhes/www/poverty/data/incpovhlth/2009/pov09fig04.pdf (accessed December 15, 2010).

prevent them from developing the skills, habits, and lifestyles that lead first to educational success and later to success in the workplace.[20] Their ability to maintain social ties in the neighborhood become weak and attenuated, further weakening a neighborhood's cohesiveness and its ability to regulate the behavior of its citizens.[21]

Child Poverty

The timing of poverty also seems to be relevant. Findings suggest that poverty during early childhood may have a more severe impact on behavior than poverty during adolescence and adulthood.[22] This is particularly important today because, as Figure 6.2 shows, children have a higher poverty rate, 19 percent, than any other age group.

Children are hit especially hard by poverty. Hundreds of studies have documented the association between family poverty and children's health, achievement, and behavior impairments.[23] Children who grow up in low-income homes are less likely to achieve in school and are less likely to complete their schooling than children with more affluent parents.[24] Poor children are also more likely to suffer from health problems and to receive inadequate health care. The number of U.S. children covered by health insurance is declining and will continue to do so for the foreseeable future.[25] Without health benefits or the means to afford medical care, these children are likely to have health problems

that impede their long-term development. Children who live in extreme poverty or who remain poor for multiple years appear to suffer the worst outcomes.

Besides their increased chance of physical illness, poor children are much more likely than wealthy children to suffer various social and physical ills, ranging from low birth weight to a limited chance of earning a college degree. Many live in substandard housing—high-rise, multiple-family dwellings—which can have a negative influence on their long-term psychological health.[26] Adolescents in the worst neighborhoods share the greatest risk of dropping out of school and becoming teenage parents.

Kids Count, a project of the Annie E. Casey Foundation, is a national and state-by-state effort to track the relative status of children in the United States. For more information, visit the Criminal Justice CourseMate at cengagebrain.com, then access the "Web Links" for this chapter.

Minority Group Poverty

The burdens of underclass life are often felt most acutely by minority group members. As Table 6.1 shows, there is real disparity in the annual income of Asian ($65,469), white ($54,461), Hispanic ($38,039), and black ($32,584) households.[27]

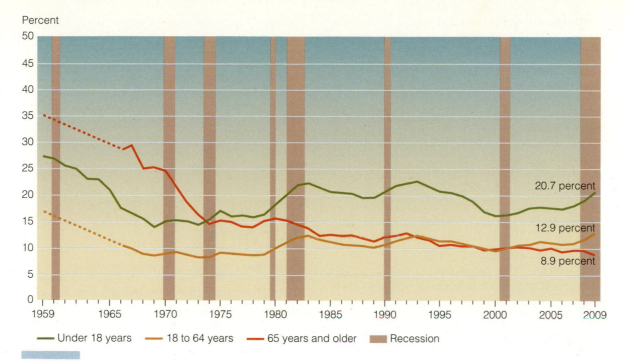

Percent

FIGURE 6.2
Poverty Rates by Age

SOURCE: U.S. Census Bureau, Current Population Survey, 1960 to 2009 Annual Social and Economic Supplements, www.census.gov/hhes/www/poverty/data/incpovhlth/2009/pov09fig05.pdf (accessed December 15, 2010).

TABLE 6.1	Race and Income		
Race and Hispanic Origin of Householder	2008	2009	Change
White	$52,113	$51,861	−0.5%
White, not Hispanic	$55,319	$54,461	−1.6%
Black	$34,088	$32,584	−4.4%
Asian	$65,388	$65,469	0.1%
Hispanic origin (any race)	$37,769	$38,039	0.7%

SOURCE: U.S. Census Bureau, "Income, Poverty and Health Insurance Coverage in the United States: 2009," www.census.gov/newsroom/releases/archives/income_wealth/cb10-144.html (accessed December 15, 2010).

The share of young black men without jobs has climbed relentlessly, with only a slight pause during the economic peak of the late 1990s. Today, the African American unemployment rate is significantly higher than the white unemployment rate.[28] About 25 percent of African Americans and 22 percent of Hispanics live in poverty as compared to 8 percent of non-Hispanic whites and 11 percent of Asians.[29] These problems are not only experienced by adults: the rates of child poverty in the United States also vary significantly by race and ethnicity. Latino and African American children are more than twice as likely to be poor as Asian and white children. Minority children are four times less likely to have health insurance as other kids. There are large ethnic disparities in the amount of time preschool-age children spend in structured preschool settings. Clearly, minority children begin life with significant social and educational deficits.[30]

Race-based economic disparity can take a terrific toll. While whites use their economic, social, and political advantages to live in sheltered gated communities protected by security guards and police, minorities are denied similar protections and privileges.[31] In contrast, a significant proportion of minority group members are relegated to living in inner-city areas, where they are hit hard by race-based disparity such as income inequality and institutional racism.[32]

Black crime rates, more so than white, seem to be influenced by the shift of high-paid manufacturing jobs overseas and their replacement with lower-paid service sector jobs.[33] In desperation, some turn to crime and drug dealing as a means of economic survival. More often than not, these desperate acts go awry, and the result is gunplay and death. And because victims may be white, there appears to be a racial motivation. However, what appear to be racially motivated crimes may be more a function of economic factors (i.e., the shift of jobs overseas) rather than interracial hate or antagonism.[34]

Race, Income, and Crime Minority group problems are exacerbated by the lack of meaningful social effort to integrate communities, resulting in neighborhoods that are all black, all white, all Hispanic, and so on. There is also the perception in the minority community that the police are overzealous in their duties, leading to feelings of injustice; in some neighborhoods a significant portion—up to half—of all minority males are under criminal justice system control.[35] The costs of crime, such as paying for lawyers and court costs, perpetuate poverty by depriving families and children of this money.[36] Among recent findings about the plight suffered by young minority males are the following:

- If they do commit crime, minority youth are more likely to be officially processed to the juvenile court than Caucasian youths, helping them develop an official record at an early age, an outcome that may increase their chances of incarceration as adults.[37]

- According to a recent report by the Pew Foundation, while 1 in 30 men between the ages of 20 and 34 is behind bars, for black males in that age group the figure is 1 in 9. One in 100 black women in their mid- to late-30s are incarcerated compared to 1 in 355 European American women.[38] One reason may be that the justice system routinely provides less favorable outcomes for minority youth, increasing the chances they will develop an official criminal record at an early age.

- While dropout rates have declined, about 6 percent of white, 11 percent of black, and 22 percent of Hispanic students drop out of high school each year. In the inner cities, more than half of all black men do not finish high school.[39]

- These differentials are critical because interracial crime rate differentials may be explained by differences in standard of living: if interracial economic disparity would end, so too might differences in the crime rate.[40]

The issue of minority poverty is explored further in the Race, Culture, Gender, and Criminology feature "More than Just Race," which discusses the works of William Julius Wilson, one of the nation's leading experts on race and culture.

> The **World Wealth Report** provides information on global income trends. For more information, visit the Criminal Justice CourseMate at cengagebrain.com, then access the "Web Links" for this chapter.

SOCIAL STRUCTURE THEORIES

The problems caused by poverty and income inequality are not lost on criminologists. They recognize that the various sources of crime data show that crime rates are highest in neighborhoods characterized by poverty and social disorder. Although members of the middle and upper classes sometimes engage in crime, these are generally nonviolent acts, such as embezzlement and fraud, which present little danger to the general public. In contrast, lower-class crime is often the violent, destructive product of youth gangs and marginally and underemployed young adults. The real crime problem is essentially a lower-class phenomenon, which breeds criminal behavior that begins in youth and continues into young adulthood. Kids growing up poor and living in households that lack economic resources are much more likely to get involved in serious crime than their wealthier peers.[41] To explain this phenomenon, criminologists have formulated **social structure theories**. As a group, they suggest that social and economic forces operating in deteriorated lower-class areas are the key determinant of criminal behavior patterns. Social forces begin to affect people while they are relatively young and continue to influence them throughout their lives. Though not all youthful offenders become adult criminals, those who are exposed to a continual stream of violence in deteriorated inner-city neighborhoods are the ones most likely to persist in their criminal careers.[42]

Social structure theorists challenge those who suggest that crime is an expression of some personal trait or individual choice. They argue that people living in equivalent social environments tend to behave in a similar, predictable fashion. If the environment did not influence human behavior, then crime rates would be distributed equally across the social structure, which they are not.[43] Because crime rates are higher in lower-class urban centers than

© Kevin Fleming/Corbis

About 25 percent of children in the United States live in poverty. These children are less likely to achieve in school or to complete their education. They are more likely to have health problems and to receive inadequate health care. Children living in poverty suffer a variety of social and physical ills, ranging from low birth weight to dropping out of school to becoming teenage parents.

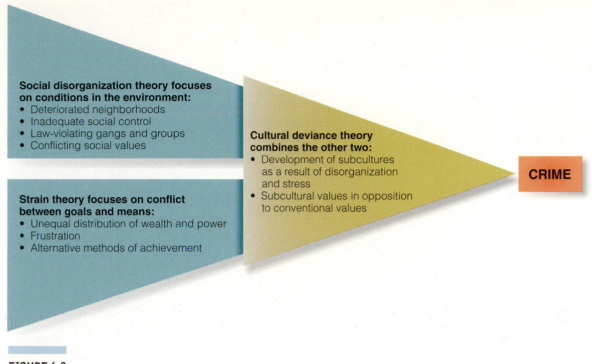

FIGURE 6.3
The Three Branches of Social Structure Theory

in middle-class suburbs, social forces must be operating in blighted urban areas that influence or control behavior.[44]

There are three independent yet overlapping branches within the social structure perspective—social disorganization, strain theory, and cultural deviance theory (outlined in Figure 6.3):

- **Social disorganization theory** focuses on the conditions within the urban environment that affect crime rates. A disorganized area is one in which institutions of social control—such as the family, commercial establishments, and schools—have broken down and can no longer carry out their expected or stated functions. Indicators of social disorganization include high unemployment, school dropout rates, deteriorated housing, low-income levels, and large numbers of single-parent households. Residents in these areas experience conflict and despair, and, as a result, antisocial behavior flourishes.

- **Strain theory** holds that crime is a function of the conflict between the goals people have and the means they can use to obtain them legally. Most people in the United States desire wealth, material possessions, power, prestige, and other life comforts. And although these social and economic goals are common to people in all economic strata, strain theorists insist that the ability to obtain these goals is class dependent. Members of the lower class are unable to achieve these symbols of success through conventional means. Consequently, they feel anger, frustration, and resentment, which is referred to as **strain**. Lower-class citizens can

either accept their condition and live out their days as socially responsible, if unrewarded, citizens, or they can choose an alternative means of achieving success, such as theft, violence, or drug trafficking.

- **Cultural deviance theory**, the third variation of structural theory, combines elements of both strain and social disorganization. According to this view, because of strain and social isolation, a unique lower-class culture develops in disorganized neighborhoods. These independent **subcultures** maintain a unique set of values and beliefs that are in conflict with conventional social norms. Criminal behavior is an expression of conformity to lower-class subcultural values and traditions and not a rebellion from conventional society. Subcultural values are handed down from one generation to the next in a process called **cultural transmission.**

Although each of these theories is distinct in critical aspects, each approach has at its core the view that socially isolated people, living in disorganized neighborhoods, are the ones most likely to experience crime-producing social forces. Each branch of social structure theory will now be discussed in some detail.

Social Disorganization Theory

Social disorganization theory links crime rates to neighborhood ecological characteristics. Communities where the fabric of social life has become frayed and torn are unable

William Julius Wilson, one of the nation's most prominent sociologists, has produced an impressive body of work that details racial problems and racial politics in American society. In 1987, he provided a description of the plight of the lowest levels of the underclass, which he labeled the **truly disadvantaged**. Wilson portrayed members of this group as socially isolated people who dwell in urban inner cities, occupy the bottom rung of the social ladder, and are the victims of discrimination. They live in areas in which the basic institutions of society—family, school, housing—have long since declined. Their decline triggers similar breakdowns in the strengths of inner-city areas, including the loss of community cohesion and the ability of people living in the area to control the flow of drugs and criminal activity. For example, in a more affluent area, neighbors might complain to parents that their children were acting out. In distressed areas, this element of informal social control may be absent because parents are under stress or all too often absent. These effects magnify the isolation of the underclass from mainstream society and promote a ghetto culture and behavior.

Because the truly disadvantaged rarely come into contact with the actual source of their oppression, they direct their anger and aggression at those with whom they are in close and intimate contact, such as neighbors, businesspeople, and landlords. Members of this group, plagued by under- or unemployment, begin to lose self-confidence, a feeling supported by the plight of kin and friendship groups who also experience extreme economic marginality. Self-doubt is a neighborhood norm, overwhelming those forced to live in areas of concentrated poverty.

In his important book, *When Work Disappears*, Wilson assesses the effect of joblessness and underemployment on residents in poor neighborhoods on Chicago's south side. He argues that for the first time since the nineteenth century, most adults in inner-city ghetto neighborhoods are not working during a typical week. He finds that inner-city life is only marginally affected by changes in the nation's economy and unaffected by technological development. Poverty in these inner-city areas is eternal and unchanging and, if anything, worsening as residents are further shut out of the economic mainstream.

Wilson focuses on the plight of the African American community, which had enjoyed periods of relative prosperity in the 1950s and 1960s. He suggests that as difficult as life was in the 1940s and 1950s for African Americans, they at least had a reasonable hope of steady work. Now, because of the globalization of the economy, those opportunities have evaporated. Though in the past racial segregation had limited opportunity, growth in the manufacturing sector fueled upward mobility and provided the foundation of today's African American middle class. Those opportunities no longer exist as manufacturing plants have moved to inaccessible rural and overseas locations where the cost of doing business is lower. With manufacturing opportunities all but obsolete in the United States, service and retail establishments, which depended on blue-collar spending, have similarly disappeared, leaving behind an economy based on welfare and government supports. In less than 20 years, formerly active African American communities have become crime-infested inner-city neighborhoods.

The hardships faced by residents in Chicago's south side are not unique to that community. Beyond sustaining inner-city poverty, the absence of employment opportunities has torn at the social fabric of the nation's inner-city neighborhoods. Work helps socialize young people into the wider society, instilling in them such desirable values as hard work, caring, and respect for others. When work becomes scarce, however, the discipline and structure it provides are absent. Community-wide underemployment destroys social cohesion, increasing the presence of neighborhood social problems ranging from drug use to educational failure. Schools in these areas are unable to teach basic skills and because desirable employment is lacking, there are few adults to serve as role models. In contrast to more affluent suburban households where daily life is organized around job and career demands, children in inner-city areas are not socialized in the workings of the mainstream economy.

In *The Bridge over the Racial Divide: Rising Inequality and Coalition Politics,* Wilson expands on his views of race in contemporary society. He argues that there is a growing inequality in American society, and ordinary families, of all races and ethnic origins, are suffering. Whites, Latinos, African Americans, Asians, and Native Americans must therefore begin to put aside their differences and concentrate more on what they have in common—their aspirations, problems, and hopes. There needs to be mutual cooperation across racial lines.

to provide essential services to their residents, such as education, health care, and proper housing. Residents in these crime-ridden neighborhoods want to flee the area at the earliest opportunity. Because they want out, they become uninterested in community matters. As a result, these neighborhoods are destabilized. There is constant population turnover; people are not interested in investing in these communities. Soon streets are littered and untidy, housing becomes deteriorated, and the neighborhood is rezoned for mixed-use (i.e., residential and commercial property exist side by side).

Because the area is undergoing stress, the normal sources of *social control* common to most neighborhoods—the family, school, neighbors, business owners, the church, law enforcement, and social service agencies—become ineffective, weak, and disorganized. Personal relationships are strained because

One reason for this set of mutual problems is that the government tends to aggravate rather than ease the financial stress being placed on ordinary families. Monetary policy, trade policy, and tax policy are harmful to working-class families. A multiracial citizens' coalition could pressure national public officials to focus on the interests of ordinary people. As long as middle- and working-class groups are fragmented along racial lines, such pressure is impossible.

Wilson finds that racism is becoming more subtle and harder to detect. Whites believe that blacks are responsible for their inferior economic status because of their cultural traits. Because even affluent whites fear corporate downsizing, they are unwilling to vote for governmental assistance to the poor because it means more taxes and lower corporate profits, a condition that threatens their jobs. Whites are continuing to be suburban dwellers, further isolating poor minorities in central cities and making their problems distant and unimportant. Wilson continues to believe that the changing marketplace, with its reliance on sophisticated computer technologies, is continually decreasing demand for low-skilled workers, which impacts African Americans more negatively than other better educated and affluent groups.

Wilson argues for a cross-race, class-based alliance of working- and middle-class Americans to pursue policies that will benefit them rather than the affluent. These include full employment, programs to help families and workers in their private lives, and a reconstructed "affirmative opportunity" program that benefits African Americans without antagonizing whites.

In *There Goes the Neighborhood*, Wilson, along with Richard Taub, assesses racial relations in four Chicago neighborhoods. The picture he paints is quite bleak. He finds that racism is still an active part of people's lives though its motif is changing. People are unusually hostile when outsiders move into their enclave. If they have a choice, they move; if not, they are angry and sullen. In a white middle-class neighborhood, people are angry when black and Latino newcomers arrive, believing they threaten property values and neighborhood stability. Whites and Latinos are able to reach common ground on only one social issue: preventing kids from being bused to a black school district. People seem unfazed about using offensive racist language to express their feelings and feel superior to other groups and races. Racism seems to cloak social anxiety: people worried about jobs and health care take their frustrations out on others. Wilson as always comes up with a prescription for positive change: strengthen neighborhood social organizations and people will be less likely to flee. Race relations can be improved if people from diverse backgrounds can come together to reach common goals such as school improvement. Society as a whole must be willing to help out and repair inner-city ghetto areas. Without such help, racial and class tensions spread throughout the city.

In his most recent work, *More than Just Race: Being Black and Poor in the Inner City*, Wilson tries to explain the persistence of poverty in black neighborhoods: is it cultural (family, personal values) or structural (segregation, racism)? He finds that both factors play a role. For example, a law-

and-order political philosophy and fear of racial conflict have led to high incarceration rates among African American males. While black women can get jobs in service industries, employers are less likely to hire black men, especially those with a criminal record. As a result, there has been a decline in the ability of black men to be providers and further stress on the stability of the African American family. Here we can see how structure and culture intertwine to produce stress in the African American community. In an era of 10 percent unemployment, the picture Wilson paints is not encouraging.

CRITICAL THINKING

1. Is it unrealistic to assume that a government-sponsored public works program can provide needed jobs in this era of budget cutbacks?

2. What are some of the hidden costs of unemployment in a community setting?

3. How would a biocriminologist explain Wilson's findings?

SOURCES: William Julius Wilson, *More than Just Race: Being Black and Poor in the Inner City* (New York: Norton, 2009); William Julius Wilson and Richard Taub, *There Goes the Neighborhood: Racial, Ethnic, and Class Tensions in Four Chicago Neighborhoods and Their Meaning for America* (New York: Knopf, 2006); William Julius Wilson, *The Truly Disadvantaged* (Chicago: University of Chicago Press, 1987); *When Work Disappears: The World of the Urban Poor* (New York: Alfred Knopf, 1996); *The Bridge over the Racial Divide: Rising Inequality and Coalition Politics* (Wildavsky Forum Series, 2) (Berkeley: University of California Press, 1999).

neighbors are constantly relocating to better areas. Resident turnover further weakens communication and blocks the establishment of common goals. The result: any attempt at community-level problem solving ends in frustration.[45]

The problems encountered in this type of disorganized area take the form of a contagious disease, destroying the inner workings that enable neighborhoods to survive; the community becomes "hollowed out."[46] Crime and violence take the form of a "slow epidemic," spreading to surrounding areas and infecting them with inner-city problems.[47]

Gang Formation   Because social institutions are frayed or absent, law-violating youth groups and gangs form and are free to recruit neighborhood youth. Both boys and girls who feel detached and alienated from their social world are at risk to become gang members.[48]

Not surprisingly, then, there are now more than 27,000 gangs such as MS-13 in the United States, containing about 800,000 members.[49] Nor is ganging unique to the United States. In his recent book, *A World of Gangs* (2008), John Hagedorn, a leading authority on the topic, shows there are now more than a billion people who live in urban slums around the world. Gangs are a common feature in these disorganized areas. They engage in a variety of activities, including drug dealing and crime and in some areas are involved in political violence. While gangs may be organized by race, their true purpose is to provide a platform for members to confront poverty, racism, and conflict. They have their own culture language (i.e., gangsta rap), and members espouse a philosophy of survival by any means necessary. Gangs will flourish and expand if globalization continues to produce masses of the very poor and a few super-rich.[50]

The elements of social disorganization theory are shown in Figure 6.4.

Poverty
- Development of isolated lower-class areas
- Lack of conventional social opportunities
- Racial and ethnic discrimination

Social disorganization
- Breakdown of social institutions and organizations such as school and family
- Lack of informal and formal social control

Breakdown of traditional values
- Development of law-violating gangs and groups
- Deviant values replace conventional values and norms

Criminal areas
- Neighborhood becomes crime prone
- Stable pockets of crime develop
- Lack of external support and investment

Cultural transmission
Adults pass norms (focal concerns) to younger generation, creating stable lower-class culture

Criminal careers
Most youths age out of delinquency, marry, and raise families, but some remain in life of crime

FIGURE 6.4
Social Disorganization Theory

Foundations of Social Disorganization Theory   Social disorganization theory was first popularized by the work of two Chicago sociologists, Clifford R. Shaw and Henry D. McKay, who linked life in disorganized, transitional urban areas to neighborhood crime rates. Shaw and McKay began their pioneering work on crime in Chicago during the early 1920s while working as researchers for a state-supported social service agency.[51] They were heavily influenced by Chicago School sociologists Ernest Burgess and Robert Park, who had pioneered the ecological analysis of urban life.

Shaw and McKay began their analysis during a period in the city's history that was fairly typical of the transition that was taking place in many other urban areas. Chicago had experienced a mid-nineteenth-century population expansion, fueled by a dramatic influx of foreign-born immigrants and, later, migrating southern families. Congregating in the central city, the newcomers occupied the oldest housing areas and therefore faced numerous health and environmental hazards.

Sections of the city started to physically deteriorate. This condition prompted the city's wealthy, established citizens to become concerned about the moral fabric of Chicago society. The belief was widespread that immigrants from Europe and the rural South were crime prone and morally dissolute. In fact, local groups were created with the very purpose of "saving" the children of poor families from moral decadence.[52] It was popular to view crime as the property of inferior racial and ethnic groups.

Transitional Neighborhoods   Shaw and McKay explained crime and delinquency within the context of the changing urban environment and ecological development of the city. They saw that Chicago had developed into distinct neighborhoods (natural areas), some affluent and others wracked by extreme poverty. These poverty-ridden, **transitional neighborhoods** suffered high rates of population turnover and were incapable of inducing residents to remain and defend the neighborhoods against criminal groups.

Low rents in these areas attracted groups with different racial and ethnic backgrounds. Newly arrived immigrants from Europe and the South congregated in these transitional neighborhoods. Their children were torn between assimilating into a new culture and abiding by the traditional values of their parents. They soon found that informal social control mechanisms that had restrained behavior in the "old country" or rural areas were disrupted. These urban areas were believed to be the spawning grounds of young criminals.

In transitional areas, successive changes in the population composition, disintegration of traditional cultures, diffusion of divergent cultural standards, and gradual industrialization of the area result in dissolution of neighborhood culture and organization. The continuity of conventional neighborhood traditions and institutions is broken, leaving children feeling displaced and without a strong or definitive set of values.

Concentric Zones Shaw and McKay identified the areas in Chicago that had excessive crime rates. Using a model of analysis pioneered by Ernest Burgess, they noted that distinct ecological areas had developed in the city, comprising a series of five concentric circles, or zones, and that there were stable and significant differences in interzone crime rates (Figure 6.5). The areas of heaviest concentration of crime appeared to be the transitional inner-city zones, where large numbers of foreign-born citizens had recently settled.[53] The zones furthest from the city's center had correspondingly lower crime rates.

Analysis of these data indicated a surprisingly stable pattern of criminal activity in the various ecological zones over a 65-year period. Shaw and McKay concluded that, in the transitional neighborhoods, multiple cultures and diverse values, both conventional and deviant, coexist. Children growing up in the street culture often find that adults who have adopted a deviant lifestyle are the most financially successful people in the neighborhood: for example, the gambler, the pimp, or the drug dealer. Required to choose between conventional and deviant lifestyles, many inner-city kids saw the value in opting for the latter. They join with other like-minded youths and form law-violating gangs and cliques. The development of teenage law-violating groups is an essential element of youthful misbehavior in lower-class areas. The values that inner-city youths adopt are often in conflict with existing middle-class norms, which demand strict obedience to the legal code. Consequently, a value conflict occurs that sets the delinquent youth and his or her peer group even further apart from conventional society. The result is a more solid embrace of deviant goals and behavior. To justify their choice of goals, these youths seek support by recruiting new members and passing on the delinquent tradition.

Shaw and McKay's statistical analysis confirmed their theoretical suspicions. Even though crime rates changed, they found that the highest rates were always in Zones I and II (central city and a transitional area). The areas with the highest crime rates retained high rates even when their ethnic composition changed (in the areas Shaw and McKay examined, from German and Irish to Italian and Polish).[54]

The Legacy of Shaw and McKay Social disorganization concepts articulated by Shaw and McKay have remained a prominent fixture of criminological scholarship and thinking for more than 75 years. While cultural and social conditions have changed and American society today is much more heterogeneous and mobile than during Shaw and

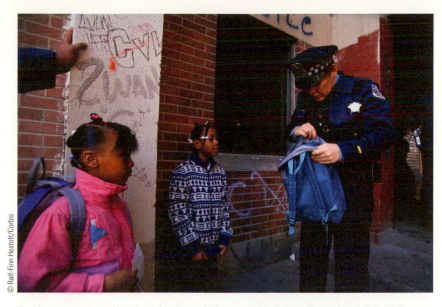

© Ralf-Finn Hestoft/Corbis

A policewoman searches the schoolbag of a young girl in the graffiti-covered Cabrini Green Housing Project. Because socially disorganized areas are undergoing stress, the normal sources of social control common to most neighborhoods—the family, school, personal ties, interest of the business community, law enforcement, and social service agencies—become weak and disorganized. When social control can be maintained, the likelihood of crime and violence decreases.

McKay's time, the most important elements of their findings still hold up:[55]

- Crime rates are sensitive to the destructive social forces operating in lower-class urban neighborhoods.
- Environmental factors, rather than individual differences, are the root cause of crime. Personal abnormality or inferiority has little to do with crime rates.
- Crime is a constant fixture in poverty areas regardless of racial or ethnic makeup.
- Neighborhood disintegration and the corresponding erosion of social control are the primary causes of criminal behavior; community values, norms, and cohesiveness affect individual behavior choices.

Despite these noteworthy achievements, the validity of some of Shaw and McKay's positions have been challenged. Some critics have faulted their assumption that neighborhoods are essentially stable, suggesting that there is a great deal more fluidity and transition than assumed by Shaw and McKay.[56] There is also concern about their reliance on police records to calculate neighborhood crime rates. Relying on official data means that findings may be more sensitive to the validity of police-generated data than they are true interzone crime rate differences. Numerous studies indicate that police use extensive discretion when arresting people and that social status is one factor that influences their decisions.[57] It is possible that people in middle-class neighborhoods commit many criminal acts that never show up in official statistics, whereas people in lower-class areas face a far greater chance of arrest and court adjudication.[58]

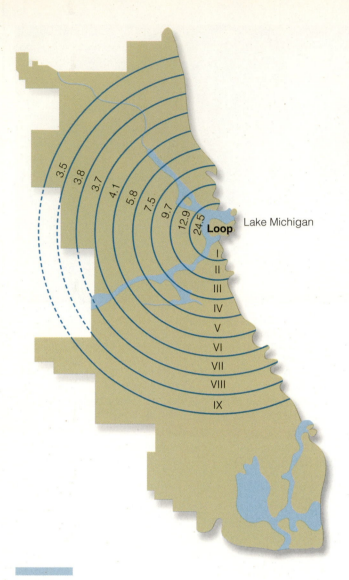

FIGURE 6.5
Shaw and McKay's Concentric Zones Map of Chicago

NOTE: Arabic numerals represent the rate of male delinquency.
SOURCE: Clifford R. Shaw et al., *Delinquency Areas* (Chicago: University of Chicago Press, 1929), p. 99.

The relationship between ecology and crime rates, therefore, may reflect police behavior more than criminal behavior.

These criticisms aside, the concept of social disorganization provides a valuable contribution to our understanding of the causes of criminal behavior. By introducing a new variable—the ecology of the city—to the study of crime, Shaw and McKay paved the way for a whole generation of criminologists to focus on the social influences of criminal and delinquent behavior.

The Social Ecology School

About 30 years ago, a group of criminologists began to re-examine ecological conditions that support criminality.[59] Contemporary social ecologists developed a "purer" form of structural theory that emphasizes the association of community deterioration and economic decline to criminality, but places less emphasis on the value and norm conflict that lay at the core of Shaw and McKay's vision. According to this more contemporary view, living in deteriorated, crime-ridden neighborhoods exerts a powerful influence over behavior that is strong enough to neutralize the positive effects of a supportive family and close social ties. If individual or family status influences criminality and violence, it is because of the nature of the communities in which disadvantaged persons and families reside and not the strength of family relationships themselves.[60] In the following sections, some of the more recent social ecological research is discussed in detail.

Community Deterioration   Social ecologists have focused their attention on the association between crime rates and community deterioration: disorder, poverty, alienation, disassociation, and fear of crime.[61] They find that neighborhoods with a high percentage of deserted houses and apartments experience high crime rates; abandoned buildings serve as a "magnet for crime."[62] Areas in which houses are in poor repair, boarded up, and burned out, and whose owners are best described as "slumlords," are also the location of the highest violence rates and gun crime.[63] These are neighborhoods in which retail establishments often go bankrupt, are abandoned, and deteriorate physically.[64]

Poverty Concentration   William Julius Wilson describes how working- and middle-class families flee inner-city poverty areas, resulting in a poverty **concentration effect** in which the most disadvantaged population is consolidated in the most disorganized urban neighborhoods. Poverty concentration has been associated with income and wealth disparities, nonexistent employment opportunities, inferior housing patterns, and unequal access to health care.[65] Urban areas marked by concentrated poverty become isolated and insulated from the social mainstream and more prone to criminal activity, violence, and homicide.[66]

How does neighborhood poverty concentration produce high crime rates? White families are more likely to leave an area when they perceive that the surrounding neighborhoods have become predominantly minority.[67] As the working and middle classes move out to the suburbs, they take with them their financial and institutional resources and support, undermining the community's level of informal social control.[68] People left behind are socially isolated and have even a tougher time managing urban decay and conflict and/or controlling youth gangs and groups; after all, the most successful people in the community have left for "greener pastures."[69] Businesses are disinclined to locate in poverty areas; banks become reluctant to lend money for new housing or businesses.[70]

In sum, inner-city crime motivates middle-class flight to the suburbs, isolating the poor in central-city ghettos and barrios, concentrating poverty and creating an environment within which criminal behavior becomes normative, and leading impressionable youth to adopt criminal lifestyles. The resulting deterioration in social capital in high-poverty areas reduces community social control, opening the door forever to expanding community crime rates.[71]

Chronic Unemployment The association between unemployment and crime is still unsettled: aggregate crime rates and aggregate unemployment rates seem weakly related. In other words, crime rates sometimes rise during periods of economic prosperity and fall during periods of economic decline.[72] Yet, as Shaw and McKay claimed, neighborhoods that experience chronic unemployment also encounter social disorganization and crime.[73] How can these divergent trends be explained?

One possibility is that even though short-term national economic trends may have little effect on crime, long-term *local unemployment* rates may have a more significant impact on conditions at the community or neighborhood level.[74] How does job loss lead to crime? Unemployment destabilizes households, and unstable families are the ones most likely to produce children who put a premium on violence and aggression as a means of dealing with limited opportunity. This lack of opportunity perpetuates higher crime rates, especially when large groups or cohorts of people of the same age compete for relatively scant resources.[75]

Limited employment opportunities also reduce the stabilizing influence of parents and other adults, who may have once been able to counteract the allure of youth gangs. Sociologist Elijah Anderson's analysis of Philadelphia neighborhood life found that "old heads" (i.e., respected neighborhood residents) who at one time played an important role in socializing youth have been displaced by younger street hustlers and drug dealers. While the old heads complain that these newcomers may not have earned or worked for their fortune in the "old-fashioned way," the old heads also admire and envy these kids whose gold chains and luxury cars advertise their wealth amid poverty.[76] The old heads may admire the fruits of crime, but they disdain the violent manner in which they were acquired.

Community Fear In neighborhoods where people help one another, residents are less likely to fear crime and be afraid of becoming a crime victim.[77] When people feel distant from one another, disconnected from others in the community, they are more likely to view their environment as a dangerous place.[78]

People feel safe in neighborhoods that are orderly and in repair.[79] In contrast, those living in neighborhoods that suffer social and physical **incivilities**—rowdy youth, trash and litter, graffiti, abandoned storefronts, burned-out buildings, littered lots, strangers, drunks, vagabonds, loiterers, prostitutes, noise, congestion, angry words, dirt, and stench—are much more likely to be fearful. Put another way, disorder breeds fear.[80]

Fear is based on experience. Residents who have already been victimized are more fearful of the future than those who have escaped crime.[81] People become afraid when

they are approached by someone in the neighborhood selling drugs. They become afraid when they see neighborhood kids hanging out in community parks and playgrounds or when gangs proliferate in the neighborhood.[82] They may fear that their children will also be approached and seduced into the drug life.[83] The presence of such incivilities, especially when accompanied by relatively high crime rates, convinces residents that their neighborhood is dangerous; becoming a crime victim seems inevitable.[84] Eventually they become emotionally numb, and as their exposure to crime increases, they experience indifference to the suffering of others.[85]

Fear can become contagious. People tell others when they have been victimized, spreading the word that the neighborhood is getting dangerous and that the chances of future victimization are high.[86] They dread leaving their homes at night and withdraw from community life.

CONNECTIONS

Fear of repeat victimization may be both instinctual and accurate. Remember that in Chapter 3 we discussed the fact that some people may be "victim prone" and fated to suffer repeated victimization over the life course.

When people live in areas where the death rates are high and life expectancies are short, they may alter their behavior out of fear. They may feel, "Why plan for the future when there is a significant likelihood that I may never see it?" In such areas, young boys and girls may psychologically assimilate by taking risks and discounting the future. Teenage birthrates soar and so do violence rates.[87] For these children, the inevitability of death skews their perspective of how they live their lives.

When fear grips a neighborhood, business conditions begin to deteriorate, population mobility increases, and a "criminal element" begins to drift into the area.[88] In essence, the existence of fear incites more crime, increasing the chances of victimization, producing even more fear, in a never-ending loop.[89] Fear is often associated with other community-level factors:

1. *Race and fear.* Fear of crime is also bound up in anxiety over racial and ethnic conflicts. Fear becomes most pronounced in areas undergoing rapid and unexpected racial and age-composition changes, especially when they are out of proportion to the rest of the city.[90] Whites become particularly fearful when they sense that they are becoming a racial minority in their neighborhood.[91]

   The fear experienced by whites may be based on racial stereotypes, but it may also be caused by the premonition that they will become less well protected because police do not provide adequate services in predominantly African American neighborhoods.[92]

   Whites are not the only group to experience race-based fear. Minority group members may experience greater levels of fear than whites, perhaps because they may have fewer resources to address ongoing social problems.[93] Fear can be found among other racial and ethnic groups, especially when they believe they are in the minority and vulnerable to attack. In their study of race relations in Florida, Ted Chiricos and his associates found that whites feel threatened by Latinos and blacks but only in South Florida where whites are outnumbered by those two groups; in contrast, Latinos are threatened by blacks but only outside of South Florida where Latinos are the minority.[94]

2. *Gangs and fear.* Gangs flourish in deteriorated neighborhoods with high levels of poverty, lack of investment, high unemployment rates, and population turnover.[95] Unlike any other crime, however, gang activity is frequently undertaken out in the open, on the public ways, and in full view of the rest of the community.[96] Brazen criminal activity undermines community solidarity because it signals that the police must be either corrupt or inept. The fact that gangs are willing to openly engage in drug sales and other types of criminal activity shows their confidence that they have silenced or intimidated law-abiding people in their midst. The police and the community alike become hopeless about their ability to restore community stability, producing greater levels of community fear.

3. *Mistrust and fear.* People who report living in neighborhoods with high levels of crime and civil disorder become suspicious and mistrusting.[97] They develop a sense of powerlessness, which amplifies the effect of neighborhood disorder and increases levels of mistrust. Some residents become so suspicious of authority that they develop a **siege mentality** in which the outside world is considered the enemy out to destroy the neighborhood. Elijah Anderson found that residents in the African American neighborhoods he studied believed in the existence of a secret plan to eradicate the population by such strategies as permanent unemployment, police brutality, imprisonment, drug distribution, and AIDS.[98] White officials and political leaders were believed to have hatched this conspiracy, and it was demonstrated by the lax law enforcement efforts in poor areas. Residents felt that police cared little about black-on-black crime because it helped reduce the population. Rumors abounded that federal government agencies, such as the CIA, controlled the drug trade and used profits to fund illegal overseas operations.

This siege mentality results in mistrust of critical social institutions, including business, government, and schools. Government officials seem arrogant and haughty. Residents become self-conscious, worried about garnering any respect, and are particularly attuned to anyone who disrespects them. Considering this feeling of mistrust, when police ignore crime in poor areas or, conversely, when they are violent and corrupt, anger flares, and people take to the streets and react in violent ways.[99] When people are fearful, they may demand more aggressive police protection, with sometimes unexpected results. This is the topic of the accompanying Thinking Like a Criminologist feature.

Community Change

In our postmodern society, the urban areas undergoing rapid structural changes in racial and economic composition also seem to experience the greatest change in crime rates. In contrast, stable neighborhoods, even those with a high rate of poverty, experience relatively low crime rates and have the strength to restrict substance abuse and criminal activity.[100]

Recent studies recognize that change, not stability, is the hallmark of inner-city areas. A neighborhood's residents, wealth, density, and purpose are constantly evolving. Even disorganized neighborhoods acquire new identifying features. Some may become multiracial, while others become racially homogeneous. Some areas become stable and family oriented, while in others, mobile, never-married people predominate.[101]

As areas decline, some residents flee to safer, more stable localities. Those who cannot leave because they cannot afford to live in more affluent communities face an increased risk of victimization. Those who can move to more affluent neighborhoods find that their lifestyles and life chances improve immediately and continue to do so over their life span.[102] Take for instance the Gautreaux Program, a major initiative ordered by the courts in 1976 to provide a metropolitan-wide remedy for racial discrimination in Chicago's public housing program. The program helped inner-city families relocate to more affluent white suburbs. Research on the effects of the Gautreaux program shows that most families who moved to Chicago's suburbs were still living in those suburbs 10 and even 20 years later. Despite some race-based problems, children's attitudes toward school improved and their grades did not drop. Moreover, as children in these Gautreaux families grew up and left home, they moved to neighborhoods that were far safer and more affluent than the inner-city neighborhoods their families had left behind.[103]

High population turnover can have a devastating effect on community culture because it thwarts communication and information flow.[104] In response to this turnover, a culture may develop that dictates standards of dress, language, and behavior to neighborhood youth that are in opposition to those of conventional society. All these factors are likely to produce increased crime rates.

The Cycles of Community Change

During periods of population turnover, communities may undergo changes that undermine their infrastructure. Urban areas seem to have life cycles, which begin with building residential dwellings and are followed by a period of decline, with marked decreases in socioeconomic status and increases in population density.[105] Later stages in this life cycle include changing racial or ethnic makeup, population thinning, and finally, a renewal stage in which obsolete housing is replaced and upgraded (**gentrification**). Areas undergoing such change seem to experience an increase in their crime rates.[106]

Operation Hammerhead

A number of citizen complaints have been filed against Northtown police officers Donald Libby and Karen O'Brien, each of whom have more than 15 years on the force. The problems began soon after Chief Wayne Goldner, under pressure from the media to "do something" about the gang problem in the central city area, initiated Operation Hammerhead. Designed to bring about immediate change in the area, Hammerhead created an independent gang control unit made up of 12 officers who were to act independently under supervision of a lieutenant. The Hammerhead squad created files on known gang members and gang locales, and ran a group of informers to generate intelligence on gang activity. The squad was to respond quickly to emergencies and calls for assistance pertaining to gang activity. One of their assignments was to displace gang members who hung out on corners, harassed passersby, exhorted money from merchants, and actively sold drugs.

After a few months on the job, two members of the team, Libby and O'Brien, were the target of numerous complaints, which centered on their treatment of neighborhood youth. They were charged with roughing up neighborhood kids, slapping some of them around, and being disrespectful. In the most serious incident, they used a nightstick on the head of a 15-year-old they suspected of being a member of the local 13th Street gang and who was seen selling

Catherine Yeulet/iStockphoto

drugs openly on the street. The youth suffered a broken arm and concussion and required hospitalization. When interviewed by the Internal Affairs Bureau, the officers claimed they were "only doing their job" and that the boy had been aggressive and disrespectful when apprehended. Besides, they argued, Hammerhead's commanding officer knew they were using aggressive tactics, community leaders had demanded results, and—most importantly—gang activity had declined 22 percent in the area since Hammerhead was instituted. So while the two readily admit to all the allegations lodged against them, they contend that they were justified under the circumstances. The boy and his parents have also filed suit, claiming that the amount of force used was unnecessary and violated his civil rights.

» **You have been hired as a consultant to advise the mayor on how to handle this delicate issue. He wants you to send him a three-page memo outlining how you would deal with the situation. Would you have him back the police and applaud the results they are getting from this aggressive gang control unit? Or do you believe the ends do not justify the means and suggest that he sanction the officers or even end the program and substitute another method of gang control? If so, what approach would you suggest?**

As communities go through cycles, neighborhood deterioration precedes increasing rates of crime and delinquency.[107] Neighborhoods most at risk for crime rate increases contain large numbers of single-parent families and unrelated people living together, have gone from having owner-occupied to renter-occupied units, and have an economic base that has lost semiskilled and unskilled jobs (indicating a growing residue of discouraged workers who are no longer seeking employment).[108] These ecological disruptions strain existing social control mechanisms and inhibit their ability to control crime and delinquency.

Racial Threat Community change may also have racial overtones. Because of racial differences in economic well-being, those "left behind" are all too often minority citizens.[109] Those who cannot move find themselves surrounded by a constant influx of new residents. Whites may feel threatened as the number of minorities in the population increases and competes with them for jobs and political power.[110] According to the racial threat hypothesis, as the percentage of minority group members in the population increases, so too does the crime rate. Why does this phenomenon occur? In changing neighborhoods, adults may actually encourage the law-violating behavior of youths. They may express attitudes

that justify violence as a means of protecting their property and way of life by violently resisting newcomers.[111] They may also demand more money be spent on police and other justice agencies. As racial prejudice increases, the call for law and order aimed at controlling the minority population grows louder.[112]

Collective Efficacy

Cohesive communities, whether urban or rural, with high levels of social control and social integration, where people know one another and develop interpersonal ties, may also develop **collective efficacy**: mutual trust, a willingness to intervene in the supervision of children, and the maintenance of public order.[113] It is the cohesion among neighborhood residents combined with shared expectations for informal social control of public space that promotes collective efficacy.[114] Residents in these areas are able to enjoy a better life because the fruits of cohesiveness can be better education, health care, and housing opportunities.[115]

In contrast, residents of socially disorganized neighborhoods find that efforts at social control are weak and attenuated. People living in economically disadvantaged areas are significantly more likely to perceive their immediate surroundings in more negative terms (i.e., higher levels of incivilities) than those living in areas that maintain collective efficacy.[116] When community social control efforts are blunted, crime rates increase, further weakening neighborhood cohesiveness.[117] There are actually three forms of collective efficacy: informal, institutional, and public social control.

Informal Social Control

Some elements of collective efficacy operate on the primary or private level and involve peers, families, and relatives. These sources exert informal control by either awarding or withholding approval, respect, and admiration. Informal control mechanisms include direct criticism, ridicule, ostracism, desertion, or physical punishment.[118] Because they already have a propensity to commit crime without informal social controls, some people will be unable to avoid entanglements in antisocial behaviors.[119]

The most important wielder of informal social control is the family, which may keep at-risk kids in check through such mechanisms as corporal punishment, withholding privileges, or ridiculing lazy or disrespectful behavior. The importance of the family to apply informal social control takes on greater importance in neighborhoods with few social ties among adults and limited collective efficacy. In these areas, parents cannot call upon neighborhood resources to take up the burden of controlling children and face the burden of providing adequate supervision.[120]

The family is not the only force of informal social control. In some neighborhoods, people are committed to preserving their immediate environment by confronting destabilizing forces such as teen gangs.[121] By helping neighbors become more resilient and self-confident, adults in these areas provide the external support systems that enable youth to desist from crime. Residents teach one another that they have moral and social obligations to their fellow citizens; children learn to be sensitive to the rights of others and to respect differences.

In some areas, neighborhood associations and self-help groups form.[122] The threat of skyrocketing violence rates may draw people together to help each other out. While criminologists believe that crime rates are lower in cohesive neighborhoods, it is also possible that an escalating crime rate may bring people closer together to fight a common problem.[123] Some neighbors may get involved in informal social control through surveillance practices, for example, by keeping an eye out for intruders when their neighbors go out of town. Informal surveillance has been found to reduce the levels of some crimes such as street robberies; however, if robbery rates remain high, surveillance may be terminated because people become fearful for their safety.[124]

Institutional Social Control

Social institutions such as schools and churches cannot work effectively in a climate of alienation and mistrust. Unsupervised peer groups and gangs, which flourish in disorganized areas, disrupt the influence of those neighborhood control agents that do exist.[125]

People who reside in these neighborhoods find that involvement with conventional social institutions, such as schools and afternoon programs, is often attenuated or blocked.[126] Children are at risk for recruitment into gangs and law-violating groups when there is a lack of effective public services. Gangs become an attractive alternative when adolescents have little to do after school and must rely on out-of-home care rather than more structured school-based programs.[127] As a result, crime may flourish and neighborhood fear increases, conditions that decrease a community's cohesion and thwart the ability of its institutions to exert social control over its residents.[128]

To combat these influences, communities that have collective efficacy attempt to utilize their local institutions to control crime. Sources of institutional social control include businesses, stores, schools, churches, and social service and volunteer organizations.[129] When these institutions are effective, crime rates decline.[130] Some institutions, such as recreation centers for teens, have been found to lower crime rates because they exert a positive effect; others, such as taverns and bars, can help destabilize neighborhoods and increase the rate of violent crimes such as rape and robbery.[131]

Public Social Control

Stable neighborhoods are also able to arrange for external sources of social control. If they can draw on outside help and secure external resources—a process referred to as public social control—they are better able to reduce the effects of disorganization and maintain lower levels of crime and victimization.[132] Racial differences in crime and violence rates may be explained in part by the ability of citizens in affluent, predominantly white neighborhoods to use their economic resources, and the political power they bring, to their own advantage. They demand and receive a level of protection in their communities that is not enjoyed in less affluent minority communities.[133]

The level of policing, one of the primary sources of public social control, may vary from neighborhood to neighborhood. The police presence is typically greatest when community organizations and local leaders have sufficient political clout to get funding for additional law enforcement personnel. An effective police presence sends a message that the area will not tolerate deviant behavior. Because they can respond vigorously to crime, the police prevent criminal groups from gaining a toehold in the neighborhood.[134] Criminals and drug dealers avoid such areas and relocate to easier and more appealing targets.[135] In contrast, crime rates are highest in areas where police are mistrusted because they engage in misconduct, such as use of excessive force, or because they are seemingly indifferent to neighborhood problems.[136]

In more disorganized areas, the absence of political powerbrokers limits access to external funding and protection.[137] Without outside funding, a neighborhood may lack the ability to get back on its feet.[138] In these areas, there are fewer police, and those that do patrol the area are less motivated and their resources are stretched tighter. These communities cannot mount an effective social control effort because as neighborhood disadvantage increases, the level of informal social control decreases.[139]

The government can also reduce crime by providing economic and social supports through publicly funded social support and welfare programs. Though welfare is often criticized by conservative politicians as being a government handout, there is evidence of a significant association between the amount of welfare money people receive and lowered crime rates.[140] Government assistance may help people improve their social status by providing them with the financial resources to clothe, feed, and educate their children while at the same time reducing stress, frustration, and anger. Using government subsidies to reduce crime is controversial and not all research has found that it actually works as advertised.[141]

People living in disorganized areas may also be able to draw on resources from their neighbors in more affluent surrounding communities, helping to keep crime rates down.[142] This phenomenon may explain, in part, why violence rates are high in poor African American neighborhoods cut off from outside areas for support.[143]

The Effect of Collective Efficacy In areas where collective efficacy remains high, children are less likely to become involved with deviant peers and engage in problem behaviors.[144] In these more stable areas, kids are able to use their wits to avoid violent confrontations and to feel safe in their own neighborhood, a concept referred to as **street efficacy**.[145] This association is important because adolescents living in communities with high levels of efficacy are less likely to resort to violence themselves or to associate with delinquent peers.[146]

In contrast, adolescents who live in neighborhoods with concentrated disadvantage and low collective efficacy begin to lose confidence in their ability to avoid violence. They perceive, and rightly so, that the community cannot provide the level of social control needed to neutralize or make up for what individuals lack in personal self-control.[147] The lack of community controls may convince them to take matters in their own hands—for example, joining a gang or carrying a weapon for self-protection.

Collective efficacy has other benefits. When residents are satisfied that their neighborhoods are good places to live, they feel a sense of obligation to maintain order themselves and are more willing to work hard to encourage informal social control. In areas where social institutions and processes—such as police protection—are working adequately, residents are willing to intervene personally to help control unruly children and uncivil adults.[148]

In contrast, in disorganized areas, the population is transient and people want to leave as soon as they can afford to find better housing. Interpersonal relationships remain superficial, and people are less willing to help out neighbors or exert informal controls over their own or neighbors' children. Social institutions such as schools and churches cannot work effectively in a climate of alienation and mistrust.[149] Children who live in these neighborhoods find that involvement with conventional social institutions, such as schools and afternoon programs, is blocked; they are instead at risk for recruitment into gangs.[150] These problems are stubborn and difficult to overcome. And even when an attempt is made to revitalize a disorganized neighborhood by creating institutional support programs such as community centers and better schools, the effort may be countered by the ongoing drain of deep-rooted economic and social deprivation.[151]

According to the social ecology school, then, the quality of community life, including levels of change, fear, incivility, poverty, and deterioration, has a direct influence on an area's crime rate. It is not some individual property or trait that causes people to commit crime, but the quality and ambience of the community in which they reside. Conversely, in areas that have high levels of social control and collective efficacy, crime rates have been shown to decrease—no matter what the economic situation. Concept Summary 6.1 sets out the features of social disorganization theory.

> To read a famous *Atlantic Magazine* article titled "Broken Windows," which discusses the concept of **community deterioration and crime**, visit the Criminal Justice CourseMate at cengagebrain.com, then access the "Web Links" for this chapter.

CONCEPT SUMMARY 6.1

Social Disorganization Theories

Theory	Major Premise	Strengths	Research Focus
Shaw and McKay's concentric zones theory	Crime is a product of transitional neighborhoods that manifest social disorganization and value conflict.	Identifies why crime rates are highest in slum areas. Points out the factors that produce crime. Suggests programs to help reduce crime.	Poverty; disorganization, gangs, neighborhood change; community context of crime.
Social ecology theory	The conflicts and problems of urban social life and communities, including fear, unemployment, deterioration, and siege mentality, influence crime rates.	Accounts for urban crime rates and trends. Identifies community-level factors that produce high crime rates.	Social control; fear; collective efficacy; unemployment.

STRAIN THEORIES

As a group, strain theorists believe that most people share similar values and goals. They want to earn money, have a nice home, drive a great car, and wear stylish clothes. They also want to care for their families and educate their children. Unfortunately, the ability to achieve these personal goals is stratified by socioeconomic class. While the affluent may live out the American Dream, the poor are shut out from achieving their goals. Because they can't always get what they want, they begin to feel frustrated and angry, a condition that is referred to as strain.

Strain is related to criminal motivation. People who feel economically and socially humiliated may perceive the right to humiliate others in return.[152] Psychologists warn that under these circumstances those who consider themselves "losers" begin to fear and envy "winners" who are doing very well at their expense. If they fail to take risky aggressive tactics, they are surely going to lose out in social competition and have little chance of future success.[153] These generalized feelings of **relative deprivation** are precursors to high crime rates.[154]

According to the strain view, sharp divisions between the rich and poor create an atmosphere of envy and mistrust that may lead to violence and aggression.[155] People who feel deprived because of their race or economic class standing eventually develop a sense of injustice and discontent. The less fortunate begin to distrust the society that has nurtured social inequality and obstructed their chances of progressing by legitimate means. The constant frustration that results from these feelings of inadequacy produces pent-up aggression and hostility and, eventually, leads to violence and crime. The effect of inequality may be greatest when the impoverished population believes they are becoming less able to compete in a society where the balance of economic and social power is shifting further toward the already affluent. Under these conditions, the likelihood that the poor will choose illegitimate life-enhancing activities increases.[156] The basic components of strain theory are set out in Figure 6.6.

Strain theories come in two distinct formulations:

- *Structural strain*. Using a sociological lens, structural strain suggests that economic and social sources of strain shape collective human behavior.
- *Individual strain*. Using a psychological reference, individual strain theories suggest that individual life experiences cause some people to suffer pain and misery, feelings that are then translated into antisocial behaviors.

The Concept of Anomie

The roots of strain theories can be traced to Émile Durkheim's notion of **anomie** (from the Greek *a nomos*, "without norms"). According to Durkheim, an anomic society is one in which rules of behavior (i.e., values, customs, and norms) have broken down or become inoperative during periods of rapid social change or social crisis such as war or famine. Anomie is most likely to occur in societies that are moving from a preindustrial society, which is held together by traditions, shared values, and unquestioned beliefs (i.e., **mechanical solidarity**) to a postindustrial social system, which is highly developed and dependent upon the division of labor. In this modern society, people are connected by their interdependent needs for one another's services and production (i.e., **organic solidarity**). The shift in traditions and values creates social turmoil. Established norms begin to erode and lose meaning. If a division occurs between what the population expects and what the economic and productive forces of society can realistically deliver, a crisis situation develops that can manifest itself in normlessness or anomie. This condition can be found in modern day Russia as it shifts from a Communist system to a free enterprise system without the social support and guarantees the population has come to expect.[157]

Anomie undermines society's social control function. Every society works to limit people's goals and desires. If a society becomes anomic, it can no longer establish and maintain control over its population's wants and desires. Because

John Ziebell yells at Immigration Day protest marchers as they pass by his home in New Haven, Connecticut, on May 1, 2007. Ziebell was angry because, he said, he was unemployed and has been unable to find a job. According to strain theory, conflict results when, because of rapid changes in society, a gulf develops between personal goals and the means available to achieve them. The result: alienation and conflict.

AP Images/Bob Child

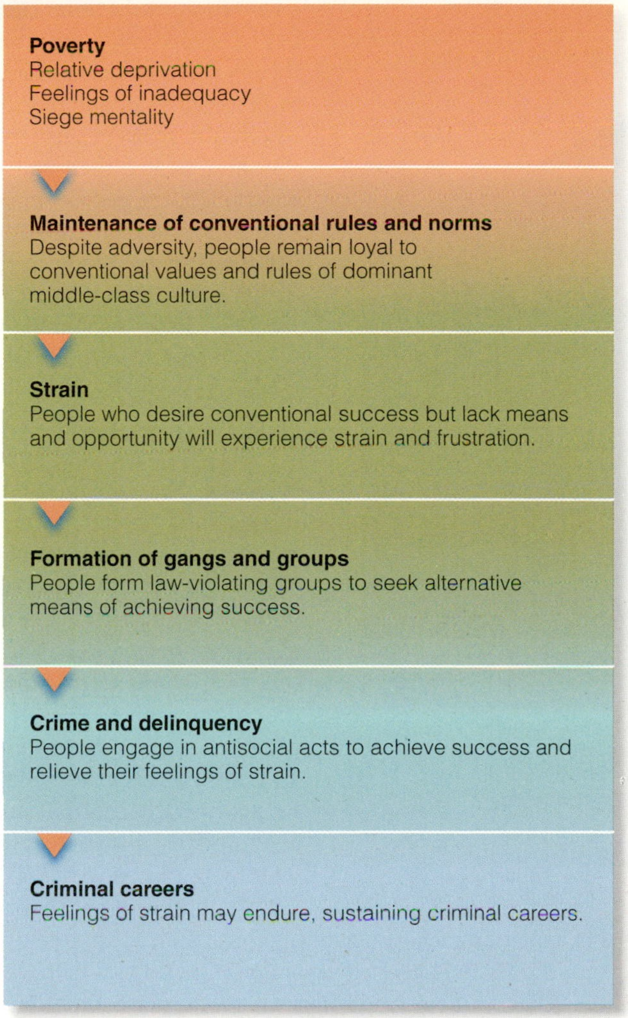

Poverty
Relative deprivation
Feelings of inadequacy
Siege mentality

▼

Maintenance of conventional rules and norms
Despite adversity, people remain loyal to
conventional values and rules of dominant
middle-class culture.

▼

Strain
People who desire conventional success but lack means
and opportunity will experience strain and frustration.

▼

Formation of gangs and groups
People form law-violating groups to seek alternative
means of achieving success.

▼

Crime and delinquency
People engage in antisocial acts to achieve success and
relieve their feelings of strain.

▼

Criminal careers
Feelings of strain may endure, sustaining criminal careers.

FIGURE 6.6
The Basic Components of Strain Theory

people find it difficult to control their appetites, their demands become unlimited. Under these circumstances, obedience to legal codes may be strained, and alternative behavior choices, such as crimes, may be inevitable.

Merton's Theory of Anomie

Durkheim's ideas were applied to criminology by sociologist Robert Merton in his **theory of anomie**.[158] Merton used a modified version of the concept of anomie to fit social, economic, and cultural conditions found in modern U.S. society.[159] He found that two elements of culture interact to produce potentially anomic conditions: culturally defined goals and socially approved means for obtaining them. Contemporary society stresses the goals of acquiring wealth, success, and power. Socially permissible means include hard work, education, and thrift.

In the United States, Merton argued, legitimate means to acquire wealth are stratified across class and status lines. Those with little formal education and few economic resources soon find that they are denied the ability to legally acquire wealth—the preeminent success symbol. When socially mandated goals are uniform throughout society and access to legitimate means is bound by class and status, the resulting strain produces anomie among those who are locked out of the legitimate opportunity structure. Consequently, they may develop criminal or delinquent solutions to the problem of attaining goals.

Social Adaptations   Merton argued that each person has his or her own concept of the goals of society and the means at his or her disposal to attain them. Table 6.2 shows Merton's diagram of the hypothetical relationship between social goals, the means for getting them, and the individual actor. Here is a brief description of each of these modes of adaptation:

- *Conformity*. Conformity occurs when individuals both embrace conventional social goals and also have the means at their disposal to attain them. The conformist desires wealth and success and can obtain them through education and a high paying job. In a balanced, stable society, this is the most common social adaptation. If a majority of its people did not practice conformity, the society would cease to exist.
- *Innovation*. Innovation occurs when an individual accepts the goals of society but rejects or is incapable of attaining them through legitimate means. Many people desire material goods and luxuries but lack the financial ability to attain them. The resulting conflict forces them to adopt innovative solutions to their dilemma: they steal, sell drugs, or extort money. Of the five adaptations, innovation is most closely associated with criminal behavior.

If successful, innovation can have serious, long-term social consequences. Criminal success helps convince otherwise law-abiding people that innovative means work better and faster than conventional ones. The prosperous drug dealer's expensive car and flashy clothes give out the message that crime pays. Merton claims, "The process thus enlarges the extent of anomie within the system, so that others, who did not respond in the form of deviant behavior to the relatively slight anomie which they first obtained, come to do so as anomie is spread and is intensified."[160] This explains why crime is initiated and sustained in certain low-income ecological areas.

- *Ritualism*. Ritualists have gained the tools to accumulate wealth—for example, they are educated and informed—but reject established cultural goals of contemporary society. These are people who enjoy the routine of work without having the ambition to climb to the top of their profession; they are not risk takers. Some may enjoy being mid-level government bureaucrats. They are the professors who want to get

Merton describes a number of adaptations to the anomie caused by the disjunction of goals and means. Here, children stand among the tents set up in a shantytown being built in the Liberty City neighborhood in Miami, Florida, October 24, 2006. Several organizations and individuals occupied the public land to build the shantytown to serve the needs of the poor African American community in the wake of a government housing scandal. The lot had been vacant for years since the city of Miami purchased, and subsequently demolished, the low-rent apartment complex that had been located at the site. Which of Merton's adaptations best describes this social action?

Evaluation of Anomie Theory According to anomie theory, social inequality leads to perceptions of anomie. To resolve the goals–means conflict and relieve their sense of strain, some people innovate by stealing or extorting money, others retreat into drugs and alcohol, others rebel by joining revolutionary groups, and still others get involved in ritualistic behavior by joining a religious cult.

Merton's view of anomie has been one of the most enduring and influential sociological theories of criminality. By linking deviant behavior to the success goals that control social behavior, anomie theory attempts to pinpoint the cause of the conflict that produces personal frustration and consequent criminality. By acknowledging that society unfairly distributes the legitimate means to achieving success, anomie theory helps explain the existence of high-crime areas and the apparent predominance of delinquent and criminal behavior among the lower class. By suggesting that social conditions, not individual personalities, produce crime, Merton greatly influenced the direction taken to reduce and control criminality during the latter half of the twentieth century.

A number of questions are left unanswered by anomie theory.[161] Merton does not explain why people choose to commit certain types of crime. For example, why does one anomic person become a mugger and another deal drugs?

tenure, but do not strive to become chairperson of the department. Some ritualists gain pleasure from practicing traditional ceremonies regardless of whether they have a real purpose or goal. The rules and customs in religious orders, clubs, and college fraternities are appealing to ritualists. Ritualists should have the lowest level of criminal behavior because they have abandoned the success goal, which is at the root of criminal activity.

- *Retreatism.* Retreatists reject both the goals and the means of society. Merton suggests that people who adjust in this fashion are "in the society but not of it." Included in this category are "psychotics, psychoneurotics, chronic autists, pariahs, outcasts, vagrants, vagabonds, tramps, chronic drunkards, and drug addicts." Because such people are morally or otherwise incapable of using both legitimate and illegitimate means, they attempt to escape their lack of success by withdrawing, either mentally or physically.

- *Rebellion.* Rebellion involves substituting an alternative set of goals and means for conventional ones. Revolutionaries who wish to promote radical change in the existing social structure and who call for alternative lifestyles, goals, and beliefs are engaging in rebellion. Rebellion may be a reaction against a corrupt and hated government or an effort to create alternate opportunities and lifestyles within the existing system.

TABLE 6.2 Typology of Individual Modes of Adaptation

Modes of Adaptation	Cultural Goals	Institutionalized Means
I. Conformity	+	+
II. Innovation	+	−
III. Ritualism	−	+
IV. Retreatism	−	−
V. Rebellion	±	±

SOURCE: Reprinted with the permission of Free Press, a Division of Simon & Schuster, Inc., from *Social Theory and Social Structure* by Robert K. Merton. Copyright © 1957 by The Free Press. Copyright renewed © 1985 by Robert K. Merton. All rights reserved.

Anomie may be used to explain differences in crime rates, but it cannot explain why most young criminals desist from crime as adults. Does this mean that perceptions of anomie dwindle with age? Is anomie short-lived?

Critics have also suggested that people pursue a number of different goals, including educational, athletic, and social success. Juveniles may be more interested in immediate goals, such as having an active social life or being a good athlete, than in long-term "ideal" achievements, such as monetary success. Achieving these goals is not a matter of social class alone; other factors, including athletic ability, intelligence, personality, and family life, can either hinder or assist goal attainment.[162] Anomie theory also assumes that all people share the same goals and values, which is false.[163]

Some contemporary theories are grounded on Merton's visionary concepts. Some of these are macro-level theories that hold that the success goal integrated within American society influences the nature and extent of the aggregate crime rate. There are also individual micro-level versions of the theory, which focus on how an individual is affected by feelings of alienation and strain.

Macro-Level Strain Theory: Institutional Anomie Theory

An important addition to the strain literature is the book *Crime and the American Dream*, by Steven Messner and Richard Rosenfeld.[164] Their macro-level version of anomie theory views antisocial behavior as a function of cultural and institutional influences in U.S. society, a model they refer to as **institutional anomie theory**. Messner and Rosenfeld agree with Merton's view that the success goal is pervasive in American culture. They refer to this as the **American Dream**, a term they employ as both a goal and a process. As a goal, the American Dream involves accumulating material goods and wealth via open individual competition. As a process, it involves both being socialized to pursue material success and believing that prosperity is an achievable goal in American culture. In the United States, the capitalist system encourages innovation in pursuit of monetary rewards. Businesspeople such as Bill Gates, Warren Buffett, and Donald Trump are considered national heroes and leaders. Anomic conditions occur because the desire to succeed at any cost drives people apart, weakens the collective sense of community, fosters ambition, and restricts desires to achieve anything that is not material wealth. Achieving a "good name" and respect is not sufficient. Capitalist culture "exerts pressures toward crime by encouraging an anomic cultural environment, an environment in which people are encouraged to adopt an 'anything goes' mentality in the pursuit of personal goals . . . the anomic pressures inherent in the American Dream are nourished and sustained by an institutional balance of power dominated by the economy."[165]

What is distinct about American society, according to Messner and Rosenfeld, and what most likely determines the exceedingly high national crime rate, is that anomic conditions have been allowed to "develop to such an extraordinary degree."[166] There do not seem to be any alternatives that would serve the same purpose or strive for the same goal.

Impact of Anomie Why does anomie pervade American culture? According to Messner and Rosenfeld, it is because capitalist culture promotes intense pressures for economic success. Prosocial, noneconomic institutions that might otherwise control the exaggerated emphasis on financial success, such as religious or charitable institutions, have been rendered powerless or obsolete. As a result, the value structure of society is dominated by economic realities that weaken institutional social control. In other words, people are so interested in making money that their behavior cannot be controlled by the needs of family or the restraints of morality.

There are three reasons social institutions have been undermined. First, noneconomic functions and roles have been devalued. Performance in other institutional settings—the family, school, or community—is assigned a lower priority than the goal of financial success. Few students go to college to study the classics; most want to major in a field with good job prospects. Second, when conflicts emerge, noneconomic roles become subordinate to and must accommodate economic roles. The schedules, routines, and demands of the workplace take priority over those of the home, the school, the community, and other aspects of social life. A parent given the opportunity for a promotion thinks nothing of uprooting his family and moving them to another part of the country. And third, economic language, standards, and norms penetrate into noneconomic realms. Economic terms become part of the common vernacular. People want to get to the "bottom line"; spouses view themselves as "partners" who "manage" the household. Retired people say they want to "downsize" their household; we "outsource" home repairs instead of doing them ourselves. Corporate leaders run for public office promising to "run the country like a business." People join social clubs to make connections and "network," not to make close friends.

According to Messner and Rosenfeld, the relatively high U.S. crime rates can be explained by the interrelationship between culture and institutions. The dominance of the American Dream mythology ensures that many people will develop wishes and desires for material goods that cannot be satisfied by legitimate means. People are willing to do anything to get ahead, from cheating on tests to get higher grades to engaging in corporate fraud and tax evasion.[167] Those who cannot succeed become willing to risk everything, including a prison sentence.

The American Dream mythos may have a different effect on people depending on their place in the social structure. In their analysis of survey data, Stephen Cernkovich and his associates found that the American Dream mythology had a greater effect on whites than African Americans. Cernkovich reasons that whites may have greater expectations of material success than African Americans, whose aspirations have been tempered by a long history of racial and economic deprivation. When whites experience strain, they are more apt to react with anger and antisocial behavior.[168]

Institutional Effects   At the institutional level, the dominance of economic concerns weakens the informal social control exerted by the family, church, and school. These institutions have lost their ability to regulate behavior and have instead become a conduit for promoting material success. Parents push their kids to succeed at any cost; schools encourage kids to get into the best colleges; religious institutions promote their wealth and power.[169] Crime rates may rise even in a healthy economy because national prosperity heightens the attractiveness of monetary rewards, encouraging people to gain financial success by any means possible, including illegal ones. Meanwhile, the importance of social institutions as a means of exerting social control is reduced. In this "culture of competition," self-interest prevails and generates amorality, acceptance of inequality, and disdain for the less fortunate.[170]

The Messner-Rosenfeld version of anomie strain may be a blueprint for crime-reduction strategies: if citizens are provided with an economic safety net, they may be able to resist the influence of economic deprivation and commit less crime. Nations that provide such resources—welfare, pension benefits, health care—have significantly lower crime rates.[171] In contrast, crime and violence rates are highest in nations that experience high levels of income inequality.[172]

Micro-Level Strain Theory: General Strain Theory

Sociologist Robert Agnew's **general strain theory (GST)** helps identify the micro-level or individual influences of strain. Whereas Merton explains social class differences in the crime rate, Agnew explains why individuals who feel stress and strain are more likely to commit crimes. Agnew also offers a more general explanation of criminal activity among all elements of society rather than restricting his views to lower-class crime.[173]

Multiple Sources of Stress   Agnew suggests that criminality is the direct result of **negative affective states**—the anger, frustration, and adverse emotions that emerge in the wake of negative and destructive social relationships. He finds that negative affective states are produced by a variety of sources of strain (Figure 6.7):

- *Failure to achieve positively valued goals.* This category of strain, similar to what Merton speaks of in his theory of anomie, is a result of the disjunction between aspirations and expectations. This type of strain occurs when people aspire for wealth and fame, but, lacking financial and educational resources, assume that such goals are impossible to achieve. These people, wracked by despair, who feel few opportunities for success, are at risk for crime.[174]
- *Disjunction of expectations and achievements.* Strain can also be produced when there is a disjunction between expectations and achievements. When people compare themselves to peers who seem to be doing a lot better financially or socially (such as making more money or getting better grades), even those doing relatively well feel strain. For example, when a high school senior is accepted at a good college but not a "prestige school" like some of her friends, she will feel strain. Perhaps she is not being treated fairly because the "playing field" is tilted against her; "other kids have connections," she may say. Perceiving inequity may result in adverse reactions, ranging from running away from its source to

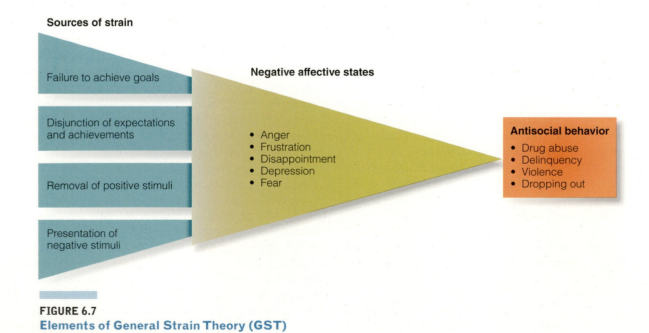

FIGURE 6.7
Elements of General Strain Theory (GST)

lowering the benefits of others through physical attacks or vandalizing their property.

- *Removal of positively valued stimuli.* Strain may occur because of the actual or anticipated removal or loss of a positively valued stimulus from the individual. Divorce can produce strain, as can the death of a loved one, moving to a new neighborhood, or getting a new job. The loss of positive stimuli may lead to criminality when a person tries to prevent the loss, retrieve what has been lost, obtain substitutes, or seek revenge against those responsible for the loss.[175]

The effect of removal of positive stimuli may be class bound. Middle-class people are less able to cope with the removal of positive stimuli. When you are expected to succeed because of your class position, failure may be harder to swallow; those who have limited opportunities and lower expectations may be able to take failure in stride.[176]

- *Presentation of negative stimuli.* While the GST recognizes that the removal of positive stimuli produces strain, it relies more heavily on the effects of negative or noxious stimuli. Included within this category are such pain-inducing social interactions as child abuse and neglect, crime victimization, physical punishment, family and peer conflict, school failure, and interaction with stressful life events ranging from family breakup, unemployment, moving, feelings of dissatisfaction with friends and school to verbal threats and air pollution.[177] Becoming the target of racism and discrimination may also trigger the anger and aggression predicted by Agnew.[178]

Another important source of negative stimuli is to experience violent crime firsthand. Agnew himself found evidence that the strain associated with becoming a crime victim and anticipating future victimization may cause people to embrace antisocial behavior.[179] People who are victims of violent crimes may develop angry emotionality that translates into anger and subsequent antisocial behaviors.[180]

The effect of negative stimuli is not always a one-shot deal but may be ongoing. Some people who feel constantly picked on and maltreated by others will become detached and sullen. And even though they are angry and disengaged, they may be forced to interact with the source of strain, such as their boss, on a regular basis. Because this is unpleasant, they get angry and frustrated and plan corrective action: they can assault or seek revenge against the source of their strain or even self-medicate by using drugs and alcohol.[181]

According to Agnew, the greater the intensity and frequency of strain experiences, the greater their impact and the more likely they are to cause criminality. Each type of strain will increase the likelihood of experiencing such negative emotions as disappointment, depression, fear, and, most important, anger. Anger increases perceptions of being wronged and produces a desire for revenge, energizes individuals to take action, and lowers inhibitions. Violence and aggression seem justified if you have been wronged and are righteously angry.

Because it produces these emotions, strain can be considered a predisposing factor for criminality when it is chronic and repetitive and creates a hostile, suspicious, and aggressive attitude. Individual strain episodes may serve as a situational event or trigger that produces crime, such as when a particularly stressful event ignites a violent reaction. Strain may predispose people toward antisocial behaviors rather than cause them to commit a specific act to relieve strain. So the person who feels strain because of financial need may be as likely to beat up a rival as he is to rob a liquor store.[182]

Sources of Strain

There are a variety of sources of strain. Sometimes it can be a particular individual who is causing problems, such as a peer group rival. When individuals identify a target to blame for their problems, they are more likely to respond with retaliatory action (for example, "Joe stole my wife away by lying about me, so I beat him up!"). Sometimes the source of strain is difficult to pinpoint (for example, "I feel depressed because of the way the world is going"); this type of ambiguous strain is unlikely to produce an aggressive response.[183]

Social Sources of Strain People may begin to feel strain because of their membership in a peer or social group. The relationship may be reciprocal. People who report feelings of stress and anger are more likely to interact with others who are similarly stressed out.[184] Peer group membership has its benefits, such as friendship, companionship, and support, but such groups also force members into behavior patterns (such as using drugs) that can be the source of unwelcome stress. Feelings of strain and being overwhelmed may become magnified as individuals attempt to comply with peer group demands. People may, for example, get involved in an unwanted shoplifting spree to pay for drugs, creating even more stress in their lives.[185] Experiments show that people who perceive strain because they are being treated unfairly report (1) high levels of situational anger that lead to (2) higher levels of theft from an employer.[186] People who live in strain-producing social conditions are more likely to cope with their negative emotions through crime.[187]

People who perceive strain because their success goals are blocked are more likely to engage in criminal activities.[188] This association is universal: research efforts conducted in foreign locales (such as Italy and South Korea) have found support for an association between strain and involvement in criminal acts.[189] Though some culture-based differences have been found, the basic premises of the GST do not seem culture bound.[190]

Community Sources of Strain The GST generally focuses on individual-level sources of strain, yet there are distinct ecological variations in the crime rate. Some regions, cities, and neighborhoods are more crime prone than others. Can ecological differences produce "negative affective states" in large segments of the population, which account for these differences? Agnew suggests that there are, in fact, community-level factors, such as blocked opportunities and lack of social support, that produce feelings of strain. According to Agnew, communities contribute to strain in several ways:

- They influence the goals people pursue and the ability people have to meet these goals.
- They influence feelings of relative deprivation and exposure to aversive stimuli, including family conflict, incivility, and economic deprivation.
- They influence the likelihood that angry, strain-filled individuals will interact with one another.

Consequently, not only does GST predict deviance on an individual level, but it can also account for community-level differences in the crime rate.

Coping with Strain

Not all people who experience strain fall into a life of crime and eventually resort to criminality. Some are able to marshal their emotional, mental, and behavioral resources to cope with the anger and frustration produced by strain. Coping ability may be a function of both individual traits and personal experiences over the life course. Personal temperament, prior learning of antisocial attitudes and behaviors, and association with criminal peers who reinforce anger are among other factors affecting the ability to cope. People who are impulsive and lack attachments to others are less able to cope than those who are bonded to others and maintain higher levels of self-control.[191] Those high in negative emotionality and low in constraint will be more likely to react to strain with antisocial behaviors.[192] In contrast, those people who can call on family, friends, and social institutions for help and support are better able to cope with strain.[193]

Although it may be socially disapproved, criminality can provide relief and satisfaction for someone living an otherwise stress-filled life. Using violence for self-protection may increase feelings of self-worth among those who feel inadequate or intellectually insecure.[194]

Some defenses are cognitive; individuals may be able to rationalize frustrating circumstances. Not getting the career they desire is "just not that important"; they may be poor, but the "next guy is worse off"; and if things didn't work out, then they "got what they deserved." Others seek behavioral solutions: they run away from adverse conditions or seek revenge against those who caused the strain. Others will try to regain emotional equilibrium with techniques ranging from physical exercise to drug abuse.

Strain and Criminal Careers While some people can effectively cope with strain, how does GST explain both chronic offending and the stability of crime over the life course? GST recognizes that certain people have traits that may make them particularly sensitive to strain. These include an explosive temperament, being overly sensitive or emotional, low tolerance for adversity, and poor problem-solving skills.[195]

Aggressive people who have these traits are likely to have poor interpersonal skills and are more likely to be treated negatively by others; their combative personalities make them feared and disliked. These people are likely to live in families whose caretakers share similar personality traits. They are also more likely to reject conventional peers and join deviant groups. Such individuals are subject to a high degree of strain over the course of their lives.

Crime peaks during late adolescence because this is a period of social stress caused by the weakening of parental supervision and the development of relationships with a diverse peer group. Peers may help soften the blow of strainful events or may exacerbate their impact. Kids who find themselves the target of stressful life events may be at greater risk to crime when they turn to peers who themselves are involved in criminality.[196] Agnew created the concept of storylines to help explain how people deal with the stressors of everyday life. This concept is discussed in The Criminological Enterprise.

Many kids going through the trauma of family breakup and frequent changes in family structure find themselves feeling a high degree of strain. They may react by becoming involved in precocious sexuality or by turning to substance abuse to mask the strain. For example, research shows that young girls of any social class are more likely to bear out-of-wedlock children if they themselves experienced an unstable family life.[197] Adolescence is also a period during which hormone levels peak, and the behavior moderating aspects of the brain have not fully developed—two factors that make adolescent males susceptible to environmental sources of strain.[198]

As they mature, children's expectations increase; some find that they are unable to meet academic and social demands. Adolescents are very concerned about their standing with peers. Those deficient in these areas may find they are social outcasts, another source of strain. In adulthood, crime rates drop because these sources of strain are reduced, new sources of self-esteem emerge, and adults seem more likely to bring their goals in line with reality.

CONNECTIONS

Explaining continuity and change in offending rates over the life course has become an important goal of criminologists. Analysis of latent trait and life course theories in Chapter 9 provides some recent thinking on this topic.

The Criminological Enterprise
Storylines

Criminologist Robert Agnew has identified a concept—storylines—to help explain why people commit crimes. He finds that when criminals are asked why they offend, they typically tell a story explaining why they engaged in crime. These stories describe the stressful events and conditions leading up to the crime and how they dealt with the pressure and strain. Very often it is some unusual or unplanned event that led them to feel strain and resort to criminal actions to solve their problems: they were insulted by a rival and sought revenge; they lost money gambling and, needing to pay off their debt, had to commit a burglary; some guy was hitting on their girl so they were forced to give them a beatdown. A storyline is a temporally limited, interrelated set of events and conditions that increases the likelihood that individuals will engage in a crime or a series of related crimes.

Storylines begin with a particular event; that is, "something happens" that is upsetting. This event affects the characteristics of the individual, leads to increased feelings of strain, and alters their associations and interactions. The feeling was temporary; they may claim "that's not really like me." They turn into a new person—jealous, angry, desperate, violent—that is out of character. The storyline ends when some event restores the individual's normal level of functioning, ending the temporary drama in their lives.

What are some typical stories that are told?

- *A Desperate Need for Money.* Offenders often report that they engage in crime during those periods when something has happened that creates a temporary but desperate need for money, and the individual believes that there are no good legitimate options for obtaining such money. Usually cited for this turn of events are unexpected expenses, poor budgeting between paydays, temporary employment problems, the temporary loss of other sources of financial support, demands that debts be repaid, gambling losses, drug binges, or the pressure to pay legal fines or fees. So this storyline might go: "I knew the Knicks were going to beat the Celtics, so I borrowed $500 for a bet, and then they lost on a lucky shot. I had to pay the loan back so I stole my brother-in-law's plasma TV and sold it on the street."

- *An Unresolved Dispute.* This storyline begins when someone does or says something that the individual does not like, or challenges and/or threatens a core identity value or status. The individual experiences one or more negative emotions, such as anger and humiliation, and then finds someone to blame for this negative treatment. This type of storyline often has a romantic twist: "I thought someone was hitting on my girl, because she was acting very strange. I thought she was trying to hook up with someone and I was really upset. Then I saw this guy with her. I was afraid she was going to be unfaithful, so I hit him in the face with a pipe."

- *A Brief but Close Involvement with a Criminal Other(s).* Individuals often develop close associations with criminal others over long periods of time, but sometimes the associations are more fleeting—lasting only hours, days, or weeks. This storyline can have a number of elements. The individual gets involved with another individual or group who entices them into committing a crime they would never have committed on their own. Success in a crime might lead to invitations for other crimes. Using this storyline, a person might say, "I was in a bar drinking when these guys I met told me that I could get some great weed for only $100 an ounce. I usually don't do things like that, but the price seemed so good I couldn't pass it up."

- *A Brief, Tempting Opportunity for Crime.* Individuals may develop or encounter tempting opportunities for crime that last from several hours to weeks. Being tempted means that the cost of crime is perceived as being low while the benefits are high and that this advantaged circumstance will persist for some time. This storyline might be, "I know this guy who is working as a security guard in an electronics store. He will sell me video games for $10 each that I know I can peddle on the street for $30. He can get me 50 games next week. Why pass up an easy $1,000? And besides, I can't get in trouble because I didn't really take the stuff myself."

Of course, individuals may experience more than one storyline at a time, each one contributing to or influencing another: a kid runs away from home, creating a desperate need for money; this gets him into disputes with other kids on the street, putting him in temporary contact with antisocial peers, and creates tempting opportunities for crime.

Agnew believes that storylines are the key to understanding the immediate cause of crime. The ebb and flow of storylines, partly a function of luck and chance, help explain why some people commit crime, then stop, only to start again. They also help us understand the context of crime, why it occurs in some situations and not others. A person may commit a violent act when he or she is in the midst of a domestic crisis, but resolve the same situation peacefully at another point in his or her life.

CRITICAL THINKING

1. What storylines do college students use when they cheat on tests? Smoke pot? Get drunk at a frat party? Are they similar to Agnew's vision?

2. If people use storylines to get involved in crime, are there ones that prevent or inhibit illegal activities?

SOURCES: Robert Agnew, "Storylines as a Neglected Cause of Crime," *Journal of Research in Crime and Delinquency* 43 (2006): 119–147.

Strain Theories

Theory	Major Premise	Strengths	Research Focus
Anomie theory	People who adopt the goals of society but lack the means to attain them seek alternatives, such as crime.	Points out how competition for success creates conflict and crime. Suggests that social conditions and not personality can account for crime. Explains high lower-class crime rates.	Frustration; anomie; effects of failure to achieve goals.
Institutional anomie theory	The desire to accumulate wealth and material goods pervades all aspects of American life.	Explains why crime rates are so high in American culture.	Frustration; effects of materialism.
General strain theory	Strain has a variety of sources. Strain causes crime in the absence of adequate coping mechanisms.	Identifies the complexities of strain in modern society. Expands on anomie theory. Shows the influence of social events on behavior over the life course. Explains middle-class crimes.	Strain; inequality; negative affective states; influence of negative and positive stimuli.

Evaluating GST

Agnew's work is important because it both clarifies the concept of strain and directs future research agendas. The model has been shown to predict crime and deviance within a number of subject, racial, gender, and age groups.[199] It also addresses the dynamic nature of criminal behavior: levels of strain vary over the life course and so do crime rates. As levels of strain increase, so does involvement in antisocial activities; as strain levels decrease, so do individual crime rates. Feelings of strain then appear to play a key role in offending continuity and change.[200]

One of the biggest question marks about GST is its ability to adequately explain gender differences in the crime rate. Females experience as much or more strain, frustration, and anger as males, but their crime rate is much lower. Is it possible that there are gender differences either (a) in the relationship between strain and criminality or (b) in the ability to cope with the effects of strain? Not all sources of strain produce the anger envisioned by Agnew.[201] Although females may experience more strain, males may be more deeply affected by interpersonal stress.[202]

There is evidence that stress influences both males and females equally; however, the degree to which it leads to criminal behavior is much higher among males than females.[203] When presented with similar types of strain, males and females respond with a different constellation of negative emotions.[204] Females may be socialized to internalize stress, blaming themselves for their problems; males may take the same type of strain and relieve it by striking out at others and deflecting criticism with aggression.[205] Consequently, males may resort to criminality in the face of stressors of any magnitude, but only extreme levels of strain produce violent reactions from women.[206] Males may also seek out their peers when they are faced with strain, whereas females are less inclined to confide in others. Male bonding with peers may actually increase their involvement with deviant behavior, a risk that is avoided by females. More effort is certainly needed to understand the cross-gender impact of strain.[207]

These issues aside, general strain theory has proven to be an enduring vision of the cause of criminality. Researchers have continued to show that people who perceive strain are the ones most likely to engage in delinquent activity.[208] Concept Summary 6.2 sets out the features of strain theory.

To read more about the work of **Émile Durkheim**, go to the Criminal Justice CourseMate at cengagebrain. com, then access the "Web Links" for this chapter.

CULTURAL DEVIANCE THEORIES

The third branch of social structure theory combines the effects of social disorganization and strain to explain how people living in deteriorated neighborhoods react to social isolation and economic deprivation. Because their lifestyle is draining, frustrating, and dispiriting, members of the lower class create an independent subculture with its own set of rules and values. Middle-class culture stresses hard work,

delayed gratification, formal education, and being cautious; the lower-class
subculture stresses excitement, toughness, risk taking, fearlessness, immediate gratification, and "street smarts." The
lower-class subculture is an attractive
alternative because the urban poor find
that it is impossible to meet the behavioral demands of middle-class society.

Unfortunately, subcultural norms often clash with conventional values. People who have close personal ties to the
neighborhood, especially when they are
to deviant networks such as gangs and
criminal groups, may find that community norms interfere with their personal
desire for neighborhood improvement.
So when the police are trying to solve a
gang-related killing, neighbors may find
that their loyalty to the gang boy and
his family outweighs their desire to create a more stable crime-free community
by giving information to the police.[209]
Figure 6.8 outlines the elements of cultural deviance theory.

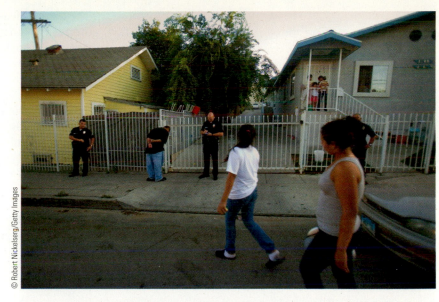

According to cultural deviance theory, gangs flourish in an environment where there is strain
and social disorganization. They provide an alternative for neighborhood kids who feel they
can never make it in the legitimate world. Here, Los Angeles police officers question a
17-year-old gang member caught associating with another member and violating his
probation. The boy was handcuffed and taken to the Rampart police station for a hearing
with a probation officer. Local residents have a deep-seated resentment of the LAPD. The
area is known for its violent gangs, which compete for the lucrative drug trade. Los Angeles's
violent crime rates, traditionally among the highest in California, have recently fallen as
gangs have shifted to outlying counties where real estate prices are more affordable. Does
that mean that crime-producing inner-city norms and values will be spreading to
surrounding areas and infecting them with inner-city problems?

Conduct Norms

The concept that the lower class develops a unique culture
in response to strain can be traced to Thorsten Sellin's classic
1938 work, *Culture Conflict and Crime*, a theoretical attempt
to link cultural adaptation to criminality.[210] Sellin's main
premise is that criminal law is an expression of the rules of
the dominant culture. The content of the law, therefore, may
create a clash between conventional, middle-class rules and
splinter groups, such as ethnic and racial minorities who are
excluded from the social mainstream. These groups maintain their own set of **conduct norms**—rules governing the
day-to-day living conditions within these subcultures.[211]
Conduct norms can be found in almost any culture and are
not the property of any particular group, culture, or political
structure.

Complicating matters is the fact that most of us belong
to several social groups. In a complex society, the number
of groups people belong to—family, peer, occupational, and
religious—is quite large. "A conflict of norms is said to exist when more or less divergent rules of conduct govern the
specific life situation in which a person may find himself."[212]
According to Sellin, **culture conflict** occurs when the rules
expressed in the criminal law clash with the demands
of group conduct norms. To make his point, Sellin cited
the case of a Sicilian father in New Jersey who killed the
16-year-old boy who seduced his daughter and then expressed surprise at being arrested. He claimed that he had
"merely defended his family honor in a traditional way."[213]

Focal Concerns

In his classic 1958 paper, "Lower Class Culture as a Generating Milieu of Gang Delinquency," Walter Miller identified
the unique value system that defines lower-class culture.[214]
Conformance to these **focal concerns** dominates life among
the lower class. According to Miller, clinging to lower-class
focal concerns promotes illegal or violent behavior. Toughness may mean displaying fighting prowess; street smarts
may lead to drug deals; excitement may result in drinking,
gambling, or drug abuse. Focal concerns do not necessarily represent a rebellion against middle-class values; rather,
these values have evolved specifically to fit conditions in
lower-class areas. The major lower-class focal concerns are
set out in Exhibit 6.1.[215] The Profiles in Crime feature "A
Life in the Drug Trade" illustrates how lower-class focal concerns shape behavior in the inner city.

It is this adherence to the prevailing cultural demands
of lower-class society that causes urban crime. Research, in
fact, shows that members of the lower class value toughness and want to show they are courageous in the face of
provocation.[216] A reputation for toughness helps them acquire social power while at the same time insulating them
from becoming victims. Violence is also seen as a means to
acquire the accouterments of wealth (nice clothes, flashy
cars, or access to clubs), control or humiliate another person, defy authority, settle drug-related "business" disputes,

Poverty
Lack of opportunity
Anomie

Socialization
Lower-class youths are socialized to value middle-class goals and ideas. However, their environment inhibits future success.

Subculture
Blocked opportunities prompt formation of groups with alternative lifestyles and values.

Deviant values
The new subculture maintains values considered deviant by the normative culture.

Crime and delinquency
Obeying subcultural values involves youth in criminal behaviors such as drug use and violence.

Criminal careers
Some gang members can parlay their status into criminal careers; others become drug users or commit violent assault.

FIGURE 6.8
Elements of Cultural Deviance Theory

attain retribution, satisfy the need for thrills or risk taking, and respond to challenges to one's manhood.[217]

To some criminologists, the influence of lower-class focal concerns and culture seems as relevant today as when first identified by Miller almost 50 years ago. The Race, Culture, Gender, and Criminology feature "The Code of the Streets" discusses a recent version of the concept of cultural deviance.

Theory of Delinquent Subcultures

Albert Cohen first articulated the theory of delinquent subcultures in his classic 1955 book, *Delinquent Boys*.[218] Cohen's central position was that delinquent behavior of lower-class youths is actually a protest against the norms and values of middle-class U.S. culture. Because social conditions make them incapable of achieving success legitimately, lower-class youths experience a form of culture conflict that Cohen

labels **status frustration**.[219] As a result, many of them join together in gangs and engage in behavior that is "nonutilitarian, malicious, and negativistic."[220]

Cohen viewed the delinquent gang as a separate subculture, possessing a value system directly opposed to that of the larger society. He describes the subculture as one that "takes its norms from the larger culture, but turns them upside down. The delinquent's conduct is right by the standards of his subculture precisely because it is wrong by the norms of the larger cultures."[221]

EXHIBIT 6.1

Miller's Lower-Class Focal Concerns

Trouble
In lower-class communities, people are evaluated by their actual or potential involvement in making trouble. Getting into trouble includes such behavior as fighting, drinking, and sexual misconduct. Dealing with trouble can confer prestige—for example, when a man establishes a reputation for being able to handle himself well in a fight. Not being able to handle trouble, and having to pay the consequences, can make a person look foolish and incompetent.

Toughness
Lower-class males want local recognition of their physical and spiritual toughness. They refuse to be sentimental or soft and instead value physical strength, fighting ability, and athletic skill. Those who cannot meet these standards risk getting a reputation for being weak, inept, and effeminate.

Smartness
Members of the lower-class culture want to maintain an image of being streetwise and savvy, using their street smarts, and having the ability to outfox and out-con the opponent. Though formal education is not admired, knowing essential survival techniques, such as gambling, conning, and outsmarting the law, is a requirement.

Excitement
Members of the lower class search for fun and excitement to enliven an otherwise drab existence. The search for excitement may lead to gambling, fighting, getting drunk, and sexual adventures. In between, the lower-class citizen may simply "hang out" and "be cool."

Fate
Lower-class citizens believe their lives are in the hands of strong spiritual forces that guide their destinies. Getting lucky, finding good fortune, and hitting the jackpot are all slum dwellers' daily dreams.

Autonomy
Being independent of authority figures, such as the police, teachers, and parents, is required. Losing control is an unacceptable weakness, incompatible with toughness.

SOURCE: Walter Miller, "Lower-Class Culture as a Generating Milieu of Gang Delinquency," *Journal of Social Issues* 14 (1958): 5–19.

Profiles in Crime

A Life in the Drug Trade

In summer 2004, a dramatic murder trial took place in New York City that aptly illustrates how lower-class cultural concerns—the code of the streets—clash with the rules and values of American culture and how deviant cultures can exist side by side with middle-class culture.

Two Bronx men, Alan Quiñones and Diego Rodriguez, were accused of heroin trafficking and killing a police informant. The trial hinged on the testimony of one of their confederates—Hector Vega, a key government witness who had previously pleaded guilty to taking part in the murder. He described in vivid detail how he watched the defendants beat the victim, Edwin Santiago, as he lay handcuffed on the floor of a Bronx apartment. He told the jury how the defendants Quiñones and Rodriguez spit in Santiago's face to show what they thought of police informants. Santiago's body was found mutilated and burned beyond recognition on June 28, 1999.

During the trial, Vega gave the jury a detailed lesson in retail drug operations. In the Bronx, beatings, slashings, and shootings are routinely used to enforce what he called "the drug law": "If people deserved it, I beat them up." He showed them a tattoo on his upper right arm that meant "Money, Power, Respect." Vega, 31, also told the jury that he headed a group of heroin vendors who did business from his "spot," his sales area, between Daly and Honeywell Avenues in the Bronx. He said he had learned the trade from a stepfather, a building superintendent who he said had a second job as a narcotics entrepreneur: "I always knew about the drug business. I was raised around it."

As a mid-level drug dealer, Vega received heroin on consignment from big-time drug wholesalers and turned it over in $100 packages to people he called his "managers," who in turn found "runners" to sell it on the street. His job was to "make sure everybody is working, and I will make sure everything is running correctly." Vega received a "commission" of about 35 percent of all sales in his organization; he estimated that he made a total of at least $500,000 in the five years before his arrest.

Vega told how he used strict rules to run his organization. He did not sell between 1 and 3 P.M. because of "school hours." He did not allow anyone to sell at his spot without his approval, or steal drugs from him, or pass him a counterfeit bill, or taint the quality of drugs sold under his name. If that happened, he said, "I'd be looking like a fool. The drug spot will go down." When Manny, one of his workers, stole one package of heroin, Vega slashed his face with a box cutter. When the wound did not immediately bleed, "I didn't see nothing cut, I didn't see anything I did, so I did it a second time," he said, until he saw blood. Angered by a counterfeit bill he received from a crack addict, "I punched him in the face, I kicked him, I threw him on the floor and kicked him again." He disciplined one stranger who cheated him by hitting the man in the back of the head with a three-foot tree branch. Police informants were given special treatment. "In the drug world, in the drug law, we say that snitches get stitches," he said. "In jail, you cut their face. In the street, you beat them. You kill them."

Vega testified that the defendants Quiñones and Rodriguez were heroin wholesalers and that he began buying drugs from them a few months before Santiago's death. After he learned that Quiñones suspected Santiago of working undercover for the police, he helped him lure Santiago to the apartment of a girlfriend where the beatings and murder took place. For his cooperation, Vega faced a 15-year sentence rather than the death penalty.

SOURCE: Julia Preston, "Witness Gives Details of Life as Drug Dealer," *New York Times*, July 12, 2004.

According to Cohen, the development of the delinquent subculture is a consequence of socialization practices found in the ghetto or inner-city environment. These children lack the basic skills necessary to achieve social and economic success in the demanding U.S. society. They also lack the proper education and therefore do not have the skills upon which to build a knowledge or socialization foundation. He suggests that lower-class parents are incapable of teaching children the necessary techniques for entering the dominant middle-class culture. The consequences of this deprivation include developmental handicaps, poor speech and communication skills, and inability to delay gratification.

Middle-Class Measuring Rods One significant handicap that lower-class children face is the inability to positively impress authority figures, such as teachers, employers, or supervisors. Cohen calls the standards set by these authority figures **middle-class measuring rods**. The conflict and frustration lower-class youths experience when they fail to meet these standards is a primary cause of delinquency. For example, the fact that a lower-class student is deemed by those in power to be substandard or below the average of what is expected can have an important impact on his or her future life chances. A school record may be reviewed by juvenile court authorities and by the military. Because a military record can influence whether or not someone is qualified for certain jobs, it is quite influential.[222] Negative evaluations become part of a permanent file that follows an individual for the rest of his or her life. When he or she wants to improve, evidence of prior failures is used to discourage advancement.

A widely cited view of the interrelationship of culture and behavior is Elijah Anderson's concept of the "code of the streets." He sees that life circumstances are tough for the "ghetto poor"—lack of jobs that pay a living wage, stigma of race, fallout from rampant drug use and drug trafficking, and alienation and lack of hope for the future. Living in such an environment places young people at special risk of crime and deviant behavior.

There are two cultural forces running through the neighborhood that shape their reactions. *Decent values* are taught by families committed to middle-class values and representing mainstream goals and standards of behavior. Though they may be better off financially than some of their street-oriented neighbors, they are generally "working poor." They value hard work and self-reliance and are willing to sacrifice for their families; they harbor hopes for a better future for their children. Most go to church and take a strong interest in education. Some see their difficult situation as a test from God and derive great support from their faith and from the church community.

In opposition, *street values* are born in the despair of inner-city life and are in opposition to those of mainstream society. The street culture has developed what Anderson calls a code of the streets, a set of informal rules setting down both proper attitudes and ways to respond if challenged. If the rules are violated, there are penalties and sometimes violent retribution.

At the heart of the code is the issue of respect—loosely defined as being "treated right." The code demands that disrespect be punished or hard-won respect will be lost. With the right amount of respect, a person can avoid being bothered in public. If he is bothered, not only may he be in physical danger, but he has been disgraced or "dissed" (disrespected). Some forms of dissing, such as maintaining eye contact for too long, may seem pretty mild. But to street kids who live by the code, these actions become serious indications of the other person's intentions and a warning of imminent physical confrontation.

These two orientations—decent and street—socially organize the community. Their coexistence means that kids who are brought up in decent homes must be able to successfully navigate the demands of the street culture. Even in decent families, parents recognize that the code must be obeyed or at the very least negotiated; it cannot simply be ignored.

The Respect Game

Young men in poor inner-city neighborhoods build their self-image on the foundation of respect. Having "juice" (as respect is sometimes called on the street) means that they can take care of themselves even if it means resorting to violence. For street youth, losing respect on the street can be damaging and dangerous. Once they have demonstrated that they can be insulted, beaten up, or stolen from, they become an easy target. Kids from decent families may be able to keep their self-respect by getting good grades or a scholarship. Street kids do not have that luxury. With nothing to fall back on, they cannot walk away from an insult. They must retaliate with violence.

One method of preventing attacks is to go on the offensive. Aggressive, violence-prone people are not seen as easy prey. Robbers do not get robbed, and street fighters are not the favorite targets of bullies. A youth who communicates an image of not being afraid to die and not being afraid to kill has given himself a sense of power on the street.

Anderson's work has been well received by the criminological community. A number of researchers have found that the "code of the streets" does in fact exist and that Anderson's observations are in fact valid. Jeffery Fagan's interviews with 150 young men who had experiences with violent crimes while living in some of New York City's toughest neighborhoods found that many alternated their demeanor between "decent" and "street" codes of behavior. Both orientations existed side by side within the same individuals. The street code's rules for getting and maintaining respect through aggressive behavior forced many "decent" youths to situationally adopt a tough demeanor and perhaps behave violently in order to survive an otherwise hostile and possibly dangerous environment.

CRITICAL THINKING

1. Does the code of the street, as described by Anderson, apply in the neighborhood in which you were raised? That is, is it universal?

2. Is there a form of "respect game" being played out on college campuses? If so, what is the substitute for violence?

SOURCES: Elijah Anderson, *Code of the Street: Decency, Violence, and the Moral Life of the Inner City* (New York: Norton, 2000); Elijah Anderson, "Violence and the Inner-City Street Code," in *Violence and Children in the Inner City*, ed. Joan McCord (New York: Cambridge University Press, 1998), pp. 1–30; Elijah Anderson, "The Code of the Streets," *Atlantic Monthly* 273 (May 1994): 80–94; Timothy Brezina, Robert Agnew, Francis T. Cullen, and John Paul Wright, "The Code of the Street: A Quantitative Assessment of Elijah Anderson's Subculture of Violence Thesis and Its Contribution to Youth Violence Research," *Youth Violence and Juvenile Justice* 2 (2004): 303–328; Jeffrey Fagan, *Adolescent Violence: A View from the Street*, NIJ Research Preview (Washington, DC: National Institute of Justice, 1998).

The Formation of Deviant Subcultures   Cohen believes lower-class boys who suffer rejection by middle-class decision makers usually elect to join one of three existing subcultures: the corner boy, the college boy, or the delinquent boy. The **corner boy** role is the most common response to middle-class rejection. The corner boy is not a chronic delinquent, but may be a truant who engages in petty or status offenses, such as precocious sex and recreational drug abuse. His main loyalty is to his peer group, on which he depends for support, motivation, and interest. His values, therefore, are those of the group with which he is in close personal contact. The corner boy, well aware of his failure to achieve the standards of the American Dream, retreats into the comforting world of his lower-class peers and eventually becomes a stable member of his neighborhood, holding a menial job, marrying, and remaining in the community.

The **college boy** embraces the cultural and social values of the middle class. Rather than scorning middle-class measuring rods, he actively strives to be successful by those standards. Cohen views this type of youth as one who is embarking on an almost hopeless path, since he is ill-equipped academically, socially, and linguistically to achieve the rewards of middle-class life.

The **delinquent boy** adopts a set of norms and principles in direct opposition to middle-class values. He engages in short-run hedonism, living for today and letting "tomorrow take care of itself."[223] Delinquent boys strive for group autonomy. They resist efforts by family, school, or other sources of authority to control their behavior. They may join a gang because it is perceived as autonomous, independent, and the focus of "attraction, loyalty, and solidarity."[224] Frustrated by their inability to succeed, these boys resort to a process Cohen calls **reaction formation**. Symptoms of reaction formation include overly intense responses that seem disproportionate to the stimuli that trigger them. For the delinquent boy, this takes the form of irrational, malicious, and unaccountable hostility to the enemy, which in this case are "the norms of respectable middle-class society."[225] Reaction formation causes delinquent boys to overreact to any perceived threat or slight. They sneer at the college boy's attempts at assimilation and scorn the corner boy's passivity. The delinquent boy is willing to take risks, violate the law, and flout middle-class conventions.

Cohen's work helps explain the factors that promote and sustain a delinquent subculture. By introducing the concepts of status frustration and middle-class measuring rods, Cohen makes it clear that social forces and not individual traits promote and sustain a delinquent career. By introducing the corner boy, college boy, delinquent boy triad, he helps explain why many lower-class youth fail to become chronic offenders: there is more than one social path open to indigent youth.[226] His work is a skillful integration of strain and social disorganization theories and has become an enduring element of the criminological literature.

Theory of Differential Opportunity

In their classic work *Delinquency and Opportunity*, written 50 years ago, Richard Cloward and Lloyd Ohlin combined strain and social disorganization principles into a portrayal of a gang-sustaining criminal subculture.[227] Cloward and Ohlin agreed with Cohen and found that independent delinquent subcultures exist within society. They consider a delinquent subculture to be one in which certain forms of delinquent activity are essential requirements for performing the dominant roles supported by the subculture.[228]

Youth gangs are an important part of the delinquent subculture. Although not all illegal acts are committed by gang youth, they are the source of the most serious, sustained, and costly criminal behaviors. Delinquent gangs spring up in disorganized areas where youths lack the opportunity to gain success through conventional means.

True to strain theory principles, Cloward and Ohlin portray inner-city kids as individuals who want to conform to middle-class values but lack the means to do so.[229]

Differential Opportunities The centerpiece of the Cloward and Ohlin theory is the concept of **differential opportunity**, which states that people in all strata of society share the same success goals but that those in the lower class have limited means of achieving them. People who perceive themselves as failures within conventional society will seek alternative or innovative ways to gain success. People who conclude that there is little hope for advancement by legitimate means may join with like-minded peers to form a gang. Gang members provide the emotional support to handle the shame, fear, or guilt they may develop while engaging in illegal acts. Delinquent subcultures then reward these acts that conventional society would punish. The youth who is considered a failure at school and is only qualified for a menial job at a minimum wage can earn thousands of dollars plus the respect of his or her peers by joining a gang and engaging in drug deals or armed robberies.

Cloward and Ohlin recognize that the opportunity for both successful conventional and criminal careers is limited. In stable areas, adolescents may be recruited by professional criminals, drug traffickers, or organized crime groups. Unstable areas, however, cannot support flourishing criminal opportunities. In these socially disorganized neighborhoods, adult role models are absent, and young criminals have few opportunities to join established gangs or to learn the fine points of professional crime. Cloward and Ohlin's most important finding, then, is that all opportunities for success, both illegal and conventional, are closed for the most "truly disadvantaged" youth.

Because of differential opportunity, kids are likely to join one of three types of gangs:

- *Criminal gangs.* Criminal gangs exist in stable lower-class areas in which close connections among adolescent, young adult, and adult offenders create an environment for successful criminal enterprise.[230] Youths are recruited into established criminal gangs that provide a training ground for a successful criminal career. Gang membership provides a learning experience in which the knowledge and skills needed for success in crime are acquired. During this "apprenticeship stage," older, more experienced members of the criminal subculture hold youthful "trainees" on tight reins, limiting activities that might jeopardize the gang's profits (for example, engaging in nonfunctional, irrational violence). Over time, new recruits learn the techniques and attitudes of the criminal world and how to "cooperate

© Spencer Platt/Getty Images

Kids may join gangs because they are looking for acceptance and respect. The gang may serve as a surrogate family. By providing an alternative, community programs hope to entice kids away from gangs. Some programs have a religious theme. Here, the Venerable Khon Sao, a Buddhist monk, teaches Cambodian youths, many of them gang members, how to pray at a Buddhist temple in Lowell, Massachusetts. In conjunction with the police department, the temple has begun a program that teaches teens the fundamentals of Buddhist thought two evenings a week. In the classes, the youths learn how to pray, meditate, and act peacefully.

tried crime or violence but are too clumsy, weak, or scared to be accepted in criminal or violent gangs. They then retreat into a role on the fringe of society. Members of the retreatist subculture constantly search for ways of getting high—alcohol, pot, heroin, unusual sexual experiences, music. They are always "cool," detached from relationships with the conventional world. To feed their habit, retreatists develop a "hustle"— pimping, conning, selling drugs, and committing petty crimes. Personal status in the retreatist subculture is derived from peer approval.

Evaluating Social Structure Theories

The social structure approach has significantly influenced both criminological theory and crime-prevention strategies. Its core concepts seem to be valid in view of the relatively high crime and delinquency rates and gang activity occurring in the deteriorated inner-city areas of the nation's largest cities.[234] The public's image of the disorganized inner city includes roaming bands of violent teenage gangs, drug users, prostitutes, muggers, and similar frightening examples of criminality. All of these are present today in inner-city areas.

Critics of the approach charge that we cannot be sure that it is lower-class culture itself that promotes crime and not some other force operating in society. They deny that residence in urban areas alone is sufficient to cause people to violate the law.[235] It is possible, they counter, that lower-class crime rates may be an artifact of bias in the criminal justice system. Lower-class areas seem to have higher crime rates because residents are arrested and prosecuted by agents of the justice system who, as members of the middle class, exhibit class bias.[236] Class bias is often coupled with discrimination against minority group members, who have long suffered at the hands of the justice system.

Even if the higher crime rates recorded in lower-class areas are valid, it is still true that most members of the lower class are not criminals. The discovery of the chronic offender indicates that a significant majority of people living in lower-class environments are not criminals and that a relatively small proportion of the population commits most crimes. If social forces alone could be used to explain crime, how can we account for the vast number of urban poor who remain honest and law abiding? Given these circumstances, law violators must be motivated by some individual mental, physical, or social process or trait.[237]

successfully with others in criminal enterprises."[231] To become a fully accepted member of the criminal gang, novices must prove themselves reliable and dependable in their contacts with their criminal associates.

- *Conflict gangs.* Conflict gangs develop in communities unable to provide either legitimate or illegitimate opportunities. These highly disorganized areas are marked by transient residents and physical deterioration. Crime in this area is "individualistic, unorganized, petty, poorly paid, and unprotected."[232] There are no successful adult criminal role models from whom youths can learn criminal skills. When such severe limitations on both criminal and conventional opportunity intensify frustrations of the young, violence is used as a means of gaining status. The image of the conflict gang member is the swaggering, tough adolescent who fights with weapons to win respect from rivals and engages in unpredictable and destructive assaults on people and property. Conflict gang members must be ready to fight to protect their own and their gang's integrity and honor. By doing so, they acquire a "rep," which provides them with a means for gaining admiration from their peers and consequently helps them develop their own self-image. Conflict gangs, according to Cloward and Ohlin, "represent a way of securing access to the scarce resources for adolescent pleasure and opportunity in underprivileged areas."[233]
- *Retreatist gangs.* Retreatists are double failures, unable to gain success through legitimate means and unwilling to do so through illegal ones. Some retreatists have

Cultural Deviance Theories

Theory	Major Premise	Strengths	Research Focus
Miller's focal concern theory	Citizens who obey the street rules of lower-class life (focal concerns) find themselves in conflict with the dominant culture.	Identifies the core values of lower-class culture and shows their association to crime.	Cultural norms; focal concerns.
Cohen's theory of delinquent gangs	Status frustration of lower-class boys, created by their failure to achieve middle-class success, causes them to join gangs.	Shows how the conditions of lower-class life produce crime. Explains violence and destructive acts. Identifies conflict of lower class with middle class.	Gangs; culture conflict; middle-class measuring rods; reaction formation.
Cloward and Ohlin's theory of opportunity	Blockage of conventional opportunities causes lower-class youths to join criminal, conflict, or retreatist gangs.	Shows that even illegal opportunities are structured in society. Indicates why people become involved in a particular type of criminal activity. Presents a way of preventing crime.	Gangs; cultural norms; culture conflict; effects of blocked opportunity.

It is also questionable whether a distinct lower-class culture actually exists. Several researchers have found that gang members and other delinquent youths seem to value middle-class concepts, such as sharing, earning money, and respecting the law, as highly as middle-class youths. Criminologists contend that lower-class youths also value education as highly as middle-class students do.[238] Public opinion polls can also be used as evidence that a majority of lower-class citizens maintain middle-class values. National surveys find that people in the lowest income brackets want tougher drug laws, more police protection, and greater control over criminal offenders.[239] These opinions seem similar to conventional middle-class values rather than representative of an independent, deviant subculture. While this evidence contradicts some of the central ideas of social structure theory, the discovery of stable patterns of lower-class crime, the high crime rates found in disorganized inner-city areas, and the rise of teenage gangs and groups support a close association between crime rates and social class position. Concept Summary 6.3 sets out the features of cultural deviance theories.

PUBLIC POLICY IMPLICATIONS OF SOCIAL STRUCTURE THEORY

Social structure theory has had a significant influence on public policy. If the cause of criminality is viewed as a schism between lower-class individuals and conventional goals, norms, and rules, it seems logical that alternatives

to criminal behavior can be provided by giving inner-city dwellers opportunities to share in the rewards of conventional society.

One approach is to give indigent people direct financial aid through welfare programs that assist needy families. Although welfare has been curtailed through the Federal Welfare Reform Act of 1996, research shows that crime rates decrease when families receive supplemental income through public assistance payments.[240]

There are also efforts to reduce crime by improving the community structure in high-crime inner-city areas. Crime-prevention efforts based on social structure precepts can be traced back to the Chicago Area Project, supervised by Clifford R. Shaw. This program attempted to organize existing community structures to develop social stability in otherwise disorganized lower-class neighborhoods. The project sponsored recreation programs for children in the neighborhoods, including summer camping. It campaigned for community improvements in such areas as education, sanitation, traffic safety, physical conservation, and law enforcement. Project members also worked with police and court agencies to supervise and treat gang youth and adult offenders. In a 25-year assessment of the project, Solomon Kobrin found that it was successful in demonstrating the feasibility of creating youth welfare organizations in high-delinquency areas.[241] Kobrin also discovered that the project made a distinct contribution to ending the isolation of urban males from the mainstream of society.

Social structure concepts, especially Cloward and Ohlin's views, were a critical ingredient in the Kennedy and Johnson administrations' "War on Poverty," begun in the early 1960s. Rather than organizing existing community structures, as Shaw's Chicago Area Project had done, this later effort called for an all-out attack on the crime-producing structures of inner-city areas. War on Poverty programs included the Job Corps, VISTA (the urban Peace Corps), Head Start and Upward Bound (educational enrichment programs), Neighborhood Legal Services, and the largest community organizing effort, the Community Action Program. War on Poverty programs were sweeping efforts to change the social structure of the inner-city area. They sought to reduce crime by developing a sense of community pride and solidarity in poverty areas and by providing educational and job opportunities for crime-prone youths. Some War on Poverty programs—Head Start, Neighborhood Legal Services, and the Community Action Program—have continued to help people.

Today, Operation Weed and Seed is the foremost structural theory–based crime-reduction strategy. Its aim is to prevent, control, and reduce violent crime, drug abuse, and gang activity in targeted high-crime neighborhoods across

the country. Weed and Seed sites range in size from several neighborhood blocks to 15 square miles.[242] The strategy involves a two-pronged approach. First, law enforcement agencies and prosecutors cooperate in "weeding out" criminals who participate in violent crime and drug abuse, and attempt to prevent their return to the targeted area. Then, participating agencies begin "seeding," which brings human services to the area, encompassing prevention, intervention, treatment, and neighborhood revitalization. A community-oriented policing component bridges weeding and seeding strategies. Officers obtain helpful information from area residents for weeding efforts while they aid residents in obtaining information about community revitalization and seeding resources. Operation Weed and Seed is an example of a modern-day crime-control approach that relies on changing neighborhood structure to reduce crime rates.

SUMMARY

1. **Be familiar with the different elements of the social structure**
   - People in the United States live in a stratified society; social strata are created by the unequal distribution of wealth, power, and prestige. There are now 40 million Americans living in poverty. The crushing lifestyle of lower-class areas produces a culture of poverty that is passed from one generation to the next and is stained by apathy, cynicism, helplessness, and mistrust of social institutions. Children in these areas are hit especially hard by poverty. The burdens of underclass life are often felt most acutely by minority group members. Almost 25 percent of African Americans and 22 percent of Latino Americans still live in poverty, compared to less than 10 percent of whites.

2. **Describe the association between social structure and crime**
   - According to social structure theory, the root cause of crime can be traced directly to the socioeconomic disadvantages that have become embedded in American society. Lower-class

people are driven to desperate measures, such as crime and substance abuse, to cope with their economic plight. Aggravating this dynamic is the constant media bombardment linking material possessions to self-worth.

3. **Know the elements of social disorganization theory**
   - Crime occurs in disorganized areas where institutions of social control, such as the family, commercial establishments, and schools, have broken down and can no longer perform their expected or stated functions. Indicators of social disorganization include high unemployment and school dropout rates, deteriorated housing, low income levels, and large numbers of single-parent households. Residents in these areas experience conflict and despair, and, as a result, antisocial behavior flourishes.

4. **Be familiar with the views of Shaw and McKay**
   - Shaw and McKay explained crime and delinquency within the context of the changing

urban environment and ecological development of the city. Poverty-ridden transitional neighborhoods suffered high rates of population turnover and were incapable of inducing residents to remain and defend the neighborhoods against criminal groups. The values that slum youths adopt often conflict with existing middle-class norms, which demand strict obedience to the legal code. Consequently, a value conflict further separates the delinquent youth and his or her peer group from conventional society; the result is a more solid embrace of deviant goals and behavior.

5. **Know the various elements of ecological theory**
   - Crime rates and the need for police services are associated with community deterioration: disorder, poverty, alienation, disassociation, and fear of crime. In larger cities, neighborhoods with a high percentage of deserted houses and apartments experience high crime rates. In disorganized neighborhoods that suffer social and physical

incivilities that cause fear, as fear increases, quality of life deteriorates. People who live in neighborhoods that experience high levels of crime and civil disorder become suspicious and mistrusting and may develop a "siege mentality." As areas decline, residents flee to safer, more stable localities.

6. **Be able to discuss the association between collective efficacy and crime**
   - Cohesive communities develop collective efficacy: mutual trust, a willingness to intervene in the supervision of children, and the maintenance of public order. Some elements of collective efficacy operate on the primary, or private, level and involve peers, families, and relatives. Communities that have collective efficacy attempt to use their local institutions to control crime. Stable neighborhoods are also able to arrange for external sources of social control, such as more police on patrol, that further reduce crime rates.

7. **Discuss what is meant by the concept of strain**
   - Strain theorists argue that although social and economic goals are common to people in all economic strata, the ability to obtain these goals is class dependent. Most people in the United States desire wealth, material possessions, power, prestige, and other life comforts. Members of the lower class are unable to achieve these symbols of success through conventional means. Consequently, they feel anger, frustration, and resentment, referred to collectively as strain.

8. **Know what Merton meant by the term** *anomie*
   - Merton argues that in the United States legitimate means to acquire wealth are stratified across class and status lines. Some people have inadequate means of attaining success; others who have the means reject societal goals. To resolve the goals–means conflict and relieve their sense of strain, some people innovate by stealing or extorting money; others retreat into drugs and alcohol; some rebel by joining revolutionary groups; and still others get involved in ritualistic behavior by joining a religious cult.

9. **Discuss the concept of negative affective states**
   - Agnew suggests that criminality is the direct result of negative affective states—the anger, frustration, and adverse emotions that emerge in the wake of destructive social relationships. He finds that negative affective states are produced by a variety of sources of strain, including the failure to achieve success, application of negative stimuli, and removal of positive stimuli.

10. **Discuss the elements of cultural deviance theory**
    - Cultural deviance theory combines elements of both strain and social disorganization theories. A unique lower-class culture has developed in disorganized neighborhoods. These independent subcultures maintain unique values and beliefs that conflict with conventional social norms. Criminal behavior is an expression of conformity to lower-class subcultural values and traditions, not a rebellion from conventional society. Subcultural values are handed down from one generation to the next in a process called cultural transmission.

KEY TERMS

CRITICAL THINKING QUESTIONS

1. Is there a "transition" area in your town or city? Does the crime rate remain constant in this neighborhood regardless of the racial, ethnic, or cultural composition of its residents?

2. Do you believe a distinct lower-class culture exists? Do you know anyone who has the focal concerns Miller talks about? Did you experience elements of these focal concerns while you were in high school? Will forms of communication such as the Internet reduce cultural differences and create a more homogenous society, or are subcultures resistant to such influences?

3. Do you agree with Agnew that there is more than one cause of strain? If so, are there other sources of strain that he did not consider?

4. How would a structural theorist explain the presence of middle-class crime?

5. How would biosocial theories explain the high levels of violent crime in lower-class areas?

NOTES

1. Arian Campo-Flores, "The Most Dangerous Gang in the United States," *Newsweek*, March 28, 2006; Ricardo Pollack, "Gang Life Tempts Salvador Teens," BBC News, http://news.bbc.co.uk/1/hi/world/americas/4201183.stm (accessed May 30, 2007).

2. FBI, "The MS-13 Threat, A National Assessment," January 14, 2008, www.fbi.gov/page2/jan08/ms13_011408.html (accessed September 20, 2010).

3. Arlen Egley, Jr., and Christina E. Ritz, *Highlights of the 2004 National Youth Gang Survey* (Washington, DC: Office of Juvenile Justice and Delinquency Prevention, 2006).

4. Steven Messner and Richard Rosenfeld, *Crime and the American Dream* (Belmont, CA: Wadsworth, 1994), p. 11.

5. Gregory M. Zimmerman, "Impulsivity, Offending, and the Neighborhood: Investigating the Person–Context Nexus," *Journal of Quantitative Criminology*, published online June 3, 2010.

6. See, generally, Robert Nisbet, *The Sociology of Émile Durkheim* (New York: Oxford University Press, 1974).

7. L. A. J. Quetelet, *A Treatise on Man and the Development of His Faculties* (Gainesville, FL: Scholars' Facsimiles and Reprints, 1969), pp. 82–96.

8. Ibid., p. 85.

9. Émile Durkheim, *Rules of the Sociological Method*, reprint ed., trans. W. D. Halls (New York: Free Press, 1982).

10. Émile Durkheim, *The Division of Labor in Society*, reprint ed. (New York: Free Press, 1997).

11. Robert E. Park, "The City: Suggestions for the Investigation of Behavior in the City Environment," *American Journal of Sociology* 20 (1915): 579–583.

12. Harvey Zorbaugh, *The Gold Coast and the Slum* (Chicago: University of Chicago Press, 1929); Frederick Thrasher, *The Gang* (Chicago: University of Chicago Press, 1927); Louis Wirth, *The Ghetto* (Chicago: University of Chicago Press, 1928).

13. Robert Park, Ernest Burgess, and Roderic McKenzie, *The City* (Chicago: University of Chicago Press, 1925).

14. Ibid.

15. United States Census Bureau, *Income, Poverty, and Health Insurance Coverage in the United States: 2008*, www.census.gov/prod/2009pubs/p60-236.pdf (accessed September 19, 2010).

16. Capgemini and Merrill Lynch, 2009 World Wealth Report, www.ml.com/media/113831.pdf (accessed September 19, 2010).

17. United States Census Bureau, *Income, Poverty, and Health Insurance Coverage in the United States: 2008*.

18. Oscar Lewis, "The Culture of Poverty," *Scientific American* 215 (1966): 19–25.

19. Gunnar Myrdal, *The Challenge of World Poverty* (New York: Vintage Books, 1970).

20. James Ainsworth-Darnell and Douglas Downey, "Assessing the Oppositional Culture Explanation for Racial/Ethnic Differences in School Performances," *American Sociological Review* 63 (1998): 536–553.

21. Barbara Warner, "The Role of Attenuated Culture in Social Disorganization Theory," *Criminology* 41 (2003): 73–97.

22. Jeanne Brooks-Gunn and Greg J. Duncan, "The Effects of Poverty on Children," *Future of Children* 7 (1997): 34–39.

23. Ibid.

24. Greg Duncan, W. Jean Yeung, Jeanne Brooks-Gunn, and Judith Smith, "How Much Does Childhood Poverty Affect the Life Chances of Children?" *American Sociological Review* 63 (1998): 406–423.

25. Ibid., p. 409.

26. Gary Evans, Nancy Wells, and Annie Moch, "Housing and Mental Health: A Review of the Evidence and a Methodological and Conceptual Critique," *Journal of Social Issues* 59 (2003): 475–501.

27. U.S. Census Bureau, "Income, Poverty and Health Insurance Coverage in the United States: 2009," www.census.gov/newsroom/releases/archives/income_wealth/cb10-144.html (accessed December 15, 2010).

28. U.S. Department of Labor, "Employment and Unemployment in Families by Race and Hispanic or Latino Ethnicity, 2008–09 Annual Averages," www.bls.gov/news.release/famee.t01.htm (accessed September 20, 2010).

29. United States Census Bureau, *Income, Poverty, and Health Insurance Coverage in the United States: 2008*.

30. UCLA Center for Health Policy Research, "The Health of Young Children in California: Findings from the 2001 California Health Interview Survey" (Los Angeles: UCLA Center for Health Policy Research, 2003).

31. Maria Velez, Lauren Krivo, and Ruth Peterson, "Structural Inequality and Homicide: An Assessment of the Black-White Gap in Killings," *Criminology* 41 (2003): 645–672.

32. Karen Parker and Matthew Pruitt, "Poverty, Poverty Concentration, and Homicide," *Social Science Quarterly* 81 (2000): 555–582.

33. Karen Parker, "Industrial Shift, Polarized Labor Markets, and Urban Violence: Modeling the Dynamics Between the Economic Transformation and Disaggregated Homicide," *Criminology* 42 (2004): 619–645.

34. Tim Wadsworth and Charis Kubrin, "Structural Factors and Black Interracial Homicide: A New Examination of the Causal Process," *Criminology* 42 (2004): 647–672.

35. John Hagan, Carla Shedd, and Monique Payne, "Race, Ethnicity, and Youth Perceptions of Criminal Injustice," *American Sociological Review* 70 (2005): 381–407.

36. Eric Lotke, "Hobbling a Generation: Young African-American Men in Washington, D.C.'s Criminal Justice System—Five Years Later," *Crime and Delinquency* 44 (1998): 355–366.

37. Michael Leiber and Joseph Johnson, "Being Young and Black: What Are Their Effects

on Juvenile Justice Decision Making?" *Crime and Delinquency* 54 (2008): 560–581.

38. Pew Foundation, *One in 100: Behind Bars in America 2008*, www.pewcenteronthestates.org/uploadedFiles/8015PCTS_Prison08_FINAL_2-1-1_FORWEB.pdf (accessed September 20, 2010).

39. National Center for Education Statistics, 2008, http://nces.ed.gov/fastfacts/display.asp?id=16; Ronald Mincy, ed., *Black Males Left Behind* (Washington, DC: Urban Institute, 2006); Erik Eckholm, "Plight Deepens for Black Men, Studies Warn," *New York Times*, March 20, 2006.

40. Thomas McNulty and Paul Bellair, "Explaining Racial and Ethnic Differences in Serious Adolescent Violent Behavior," *Criminology* 41 (2003): 709–748; Julie A. Phillips, "White, Black, and Latino Homicide Rates: Why the Difference?" *Social Problems* 49 (2002): 349–374.

41. David Bjerk, "Measuring the Relationship Between Youth Criminal Participation and Household Economic Resources," *Journal of Quantitative Criminology* 23 (2007): 23–39.

42. Justin Patchin, Beth Huebner, John McCluskey, Sean Varano, and Timothy Bynum, "Exposure to Community Violence and Childhood Delinquency," *Crime and Delinquency* 52 (2006): 307–332.

43. David Brownfield, "Social Class and Violent Behavior," *Criminology* 24 (1986): 421–438.

44. See Charles Tittle and Robert Meier, "Specifying the SES/Delinquency Relationship," *Criminology* 28 (1990): 271–295, at 293.

45. See Ruth Kornhauser, *Social Sources of Delinquency* (Chicago: University of Chicago Press, 1978), p. 75.

46. Jonathan Crane, "The Epidemic Theory of Ghettos and Neighborhood Effects on Dropping Out and Teenage Childbearing," *American Journal of Sociology* 96 (1991): 1,226–1,259; see also Rodrick Wallace, "Expanding Coupled Shock Fronts of Urban Decay and Criminal Behavior: How U.S. Cities Are Becoming 'Hollowed Out,'" *Journal of Quantitative Criminology* 7 (1991): 333–355.

47. Jeffrey Fagan and Garth Davies, "The Natural History of Neighborhood Violence," *Journal of Contemporary Criminal Justice* 20 (2004): 127–147.

48. Kerryn E. Bell, "Gender and Gangs: A Quantitative Comparison," *Crime and Delinquency* 55 (2009): 363–387.

49. Arlen Egley and Christina O'Donnell, *Highlights of the 2007 National Youth Gang Survey* (Washington, DC: Office of Juvenile Justice and Delinquency Prevention, 2009), www.nationalgangcenter.gov/documents/2007-survey-highlights.pdf (accessed September 20, 2010).

50. John M. Hagedorn, *A World of Gangs: Armed Young Men and Gangsta Culture* (Minneapolis: University of Minnesota Press, 2008).

51. Clifford R. Shaw and Henry D. McKay, *Juvenile Delinquency and Urban Areas*, rev. ed. (Chicago: University of Chicago Press, 1972).

52. Anthony Platt, *The Child Savers: The Invention of Delinquency* (Chicago: University of Chicago Press, 1968).

53. Shaw and McKay, *Juvenile Delinquency and Urban Areas*, p. 52.

54. Ibid., p. 171.

55. Claire Valier, "Foreigners, Crime and Changing Mobilities," *British Journal of Criminology* 43 (2003): 1–21.

56. For a discussion of these issues, see Robert Bursik, "Social Disorganization and Theories of Crime and Delinquency: Problems and Prospects," *Criminology* 26 (1988): 521–539.

57. Robert Sampson, "Effects of Socioeconomic Context of Official Reaction to Juvenile Delinquency," *American Sociological Review* 51 (1986): 876–885.

58. Jeffrey Fagan, Ellen Slaughter, and Eliot Hartstone, "Blind Justice? The Impact of Race on the Juvenile Justice Process," *Crime and Delinquency* 33 (1987): 224–258; Merry Morash, "Establishment of a Juvenile Police Record," *Criminology* 22 (1984): 97–113.

59. For a general review, see James Byrne and Robert Sampson, eds., *The Social Ecology of Crime* (New York: Springer Verlag, 1985).

60. Stacy De Coster, Karen Heimer, and Stacy Wittrock, "Neighborhood Disadvantage, Social Capital, Street Context, and Youth Violence," *Sociological Quarterly* (2006): 723–753.

61. See, generally, Bursik, "Social Disorganization and Theories of Crime and Delinquency," pp. 519–551.

62. William Spelman, "Abandoned Buildings: Magnets for Crime?" *Journal of Criminal Justice* 21 (1993): 481–493.

63. Keith Harries and Andrea Powell, "Juvenile Gun Crime and Social Stress: Baltimore, 1980–1990," *Urban Geography* 15 (1994): 45–63.

64. Ellen Kurtz, Barbara Koons, and Ralph Taylor, "Land Use, Physical Deterioration, Resident-Based Control, and Calls for Service on Urban Streetblocks," *Justice Quarterly* 15 (1998): 121–149.

65. Gregory Squires and Charis Kubrin, "Privileged Places: Race, Uneven Development and the Geography of Opportunity in Urban America," *Urban Studies* 42 (2005): 47–68; Matthew Lee, Michael Maume, and Graham Ousey, "Social Isolation and Lethal Violence Across the Metro/Nonmetro Divide: The Effects of Socioeconomic Disadvantage and Poverty Concentration on Homicide," *Rural Sociology* 68 (2003): 107–131.

66. Lee, Maume, and Ousey, "Social Isolation and Lethal Violence Across the Metro/Nonmetro Divide"; Charis E. Kubrin, "Structural Covariates of Homicide Rates: Does Type of Homicide Matter?" *Journal of Research in Crime and Delinquency* 40 (2003): 139–170; Darrell Steffensmeier and Dana Haynie, "Gender, Structural Disadvantage, and Urban Crime: Do Macrosocial Variables Also Explain Female Offending Rates?" *Criminology* 38 (2000): 403–438.

67. Kyle Crowder and Scott South, "Spatial Dynamics of White Flight: The Effects of Local and Extralocal Racial Conditions on Neighborhood Out-Migration," *American Sociological Review* 73 (2008): 792–812.

68. Paul Jargowsky and Yoonhwan Park, "Cause or Consequence? Suburbanization and Crime in U.S. Metropolitan Areas," *Crime and Delinquency* 55 (2009): 28–50.

69. Edward S. Shihadeh, "Race, Class, and Crime: Reconsidering the Spatial Effects of Social Isolation on Rates of Urban Offending," *Deviant Behavior* 30 (2009): 349–378.

70. Jeffrey Morenoff, Robert Sampson, and Stephen Raudenbush, "Neighborhood Inequality, Collective Efficacy, and the Spatial Dynamics of Urban Violence," *Criminology* 39 (2001): 517–560.

71. Jargowsky and Park, "Cause or Consequence?"

72. Steven Messner, Lawrence Raffalovich, and Richard McMillan, "Economic Deprivation and Changes in Homicide Arrest Rates for White and Black Youths, 1967–1998: A National Time Series Analysis," *Criminology* 39 (2001): 591–614.

73. Steven Messner and Kenneth Tardiff, "Economic Inequality and Levels of Homicide: An Analysis of Urban Neighborhoods," *Criminology* 24 (1986): 297–317.

74. Adam Dobrin, Daniel Lee, and Jamie Price, "Neighborhood Structure Differences Between Homicide Victims and Nonvictims," *Journal of Criminal Justice* 33 (2005): 137–143; G. David Curry and Irving Spergel, "Gang Homicide, Delinquency, and Community," *Criminology* 26 (1988): 381–407; Darrell Steffensmeier and Dana Haynie, "Gender, Structural Disadvantage, and Urban Crime: Do Macrosocial Variables Also Explain Female Offending Rates?" *Criminology* 38 (2000): 403–438; Richard McGahey, "Economic Conditions, Organization, and Urban Crime," in *Communities and Crime*, ed. Albert Reiss and Michael Tonry (Chicago: University of Chicago Press, 1986), pp. 231–270.

75. Scott Menard and Delbert Elliott, "Self-Reported Offending, Maturational Reform, and the Easterlin Hypothesis," *Journal of Quantitative Criminology* 6 (1990): 237–268.

76. Elijah Anderson, *Streetwise: Race, Class and Change in an Urban Community* (Chicago: University of Chicago Press, 1990), pp. 243–244.

77. Matthew Lee and Terri Earnest, "Perceived Community Cohesion and Perceived Risk

of Victimization: A Cross-National Analysis," *Justice Quarterly* 20 (2003): 131–158.

78. John Hipp, "Micro-Structure in Micro-Neighborhoods: A New Social Distance Measure, and Its Effect on Individual and Aggregated Perceptions of Crime and Disorder," *Social Networks* 32 (2010): 148–159.

79. Joseph Schafer, Beth Huebner, and Timothy Bynum, "Fear of Crime and Criminal Victimization: Gender-Based Contrasts," *Journal of Criminal Justice* 34 (2006): 285–301.

80. Xu Yili, Mora Fiedler, and Karl Flaming, "Discovering the Impact of Community Policing," *The Journal of Research in Crime and Delinquency* 42 (2005): 147–186.

81. Stephanie Greenberg, "Fear and Its Relationship to Crime, Neighborhood Deterioration, and Informal Social Control," in *The Social Ecology of Crime*, ed. James Byrne and Robert Sampson (New York: Springer Verlag, 1985), pp. 47–62.

82. Pamela Wilcox, Neil Quisenberry, and Shayne Jones, "The Built Environment and Community Crime Risk Interpretation," *Journal of Research in Crime and Delinquency* 40 (2003): 322–345.

83. C. L. Storr, C.-Y. Chen, and J. C. Anthony, "'Unequal Opportunity': Neighborhood Disadvantage and the Chance to Buy Illegal Drugs," *Journal of Epidemiology and Community Health* 58 (2004): 231–238.

84. Pamela Wilcox Rountree and Kenneth Land, "Burglary Victimization, Perceptions of Crime Risk, and Routine Activities: A Multilevel Analysis Across Seattle Neighborhoods and Census Tracts," *Journal of Research in Crime and Delinquency* 33 (1996): 147–180.

85. Tim Phillips and Philip Smith, "Emotional and Behavioural Responses to Everyday Incivility," *Journal of Sociology* 40 (2004): 378–399.

86. Wesley Skogan, "Fear of Crime and Neighborhood Change," in *Communities and Crime*, ed. Albert Reiss and Michael Tonry (Chicago: University of Chicago Press, 1986), pp. 191–232.

87. Margo Wilson and Martin Daly, "Life Expectancy, Economic Inequality, Homicide, and Reproductive Timing in Chicago Neighborhoods," *British Journal of Medicine* 314 (1997): 1,271–1,274.

88. Skogan, "Fear of Crime and Neighborhood Change."

89. Ibid.

90. Ralph Taylor and Jeanette Covington, "Community Structural Change and Fear of Crime," *Social Problems* 40 (1993): 374–392.

91. Ted Chiricos, Michael Hogan, and Marc Gertz, "Racial Composition of Neighborhood and Fear of Crime," *Criminology* 35 (1997): 107–131.

92. Ibid., p. 125.

93. Jodi Lane and James Meeker, "Social Disorganization Perceptions, Fear of Gang Crime, and Behavioral Precautions Among Whites, Latinos, and Vietnamese," *Journal of Criminal Justice* 32 (2004): 49–62.

94. Ted Chiricos, Ranee McEntire, and Marc Gertz, "Social Problems, Perceived Racial and Ethnic Composition of Neighborhood and Perceived Risk of Crime," *Social Problems* 48 (2001): 322–341.

95. Curry and Spergel, "Gang Homicide, Delinquency, and Community."

96. Lawrence Rosenthal, "Gang Loitering and Race," *Journal of Criminal Law and Criminology* 91 (2000): 99–160.

97. Catherine E. Ross, John Mirowsky, and Shana Pribesh, "Powerlessness and the Amplification of Threat: Neighborhood Disadvantage, Disorder, and Mistrust," *American Sociological Review* 66 (2001): 568–580.

98. Anderson, *Streetwise: Race, Class, and Change in an Urban Community*, p. 245.

99. William Terrill and Michael Reisig, "Neighborhood Context and Police Use of Force," *Journal of Research in Crime and Delinquency* 40 (2003): 291–321.

100. Bridget Freisthler, Elizabeth Lascala, Paul Gruenewald, and Andrew Treno, "An Examination of Drug Activity: Effects of Neighborhood Social Organization on the Development of Drug Distribution Systems," *Substance Use and Misuse* 40 (2005): 671–686.

101. Finn-Aage Esbensen and David Huizinga, "Community Structure and Drug Use: From a Social Disorganization Perspective," *Justice Quarterly* 7 (1990): 691–709.

102. Micere Keels, Greg Duncan, Stefanie Deluca, Ruby Mendenhall, and James Rosenbaum, "Fifteen Years Later: Can Residential Mobility Programs Provide a Long-Term Escape from Neighborhood Segregation, Crime, and Poverty?" *Demography* 42 (2005): 51–72.

103. Northwestern University, Institute for Policy Research, "IPR Research on Gautreaux and Other Public Housing Mobility Programs," www.northwestern.edu/ipr/publications/Gautreaux.html (accessed August 25, 2010).

104. Wesley Skogan, *Disorder and Decline: Crime and the Spiral of Decay in American Neighborhoods* (New York: Free Press, 1990), pp. 15–35.

105. Robert Bursik and Harold Grasmick, "Decomposing Trends in Community Careers in Crime," paper presented at the annual meeting of the American Society of Criminology, Baltimore, November 1990.

106. Ralph Taylor and Jeanette Covington, "Neighborhood Changes in Ecology and Violence," *Criminology* 26 (1988): 553–589.

107. Leo Scheurman and Solomon Kobrin, "Community Careers in Crime," in *Communities and Crime*, ed. Albert Reiss and Michael Tonry (Chicago: University of Chicago Press, 1986), pp. 67–100.

108. Ibid.

109. Allen Liska and Paul Bellair, "Violent-Crime Rates and Racial Composition: Convergence over Time," *American Journal of Sociology* 101 (1995): 578–610.

110. Patricia McCall and Karen Parker, "A Dynamic Model of Racial Competition, Racial Inequality, and Interracial Violence," *Sociological Inquiry* 75 (2005): 273–294.

111. Janet Heitgerd and Robert Bursik, "Extracommunity Dynamics and the Ecology of Delinquency," *American Journal of Sociology* 92 (1987): 775–787.

112. Steven Barkan and Steven Cohn, "Why Whites Favor Spending More Money to Fight Crime: The Role of Racial Prejudice," *Social Problems* 52 (2005): 300–314.

113. Jeffrey Michael Cancino, "The Utility of Social Capital and Collective Efficacy: Social Control Policy in Nonmetropolitan Settings," *Criminal Justice Policy Review* 16 (2005): 287–318; Chris Gibson, Jihong Zhao, Nicholas Lovrich, and Michael Gaffney, "Social Integration, Individual Perceptions of Collective Efficacy, and Fear of Crime in Three Cities," *Justice Quarterly* 19 (2002): 537–564.

114. Robert J. Sampson and Stephen W. Raudenbush, *Disorder in Urban Neighborhoods: Does It Lead to Crime?* (Washington, DC: National Institute of Justice, 2001).

115. Andrea Altschuler, Carol Somkin, and Nancy Adler, "Local Services and Amenities, Neighborhood Social Capital, and Health," *Social Science and Medicine* 59 (2004): 1,219–1,230.

116. Michael Reisig and Jeffrey Michael Cancino, "Incivilities in Nonmetropolitan Communities: The Effects of Structural Constraints, Social Conditions, and Crime," *Journal of Criminal Justice* 32 (2004): 15–29.

117. Robert Sampson, Jeffrey Morenoff, and Felton Earls, "Beyond Social Capital: Spatial Dynamics of Collective Efficacy for Children," *American Sociological Review* 64 (1999): 633–660.

118. Donald Black, "Social Control as a Dependent Variable," in *Toward a General Theory of Social Control*, ed. D. Black (Orlando: Academic Press, 1990).

119. Shayne Jones and Donald R. Lynam, "In the Eye of the Impulsive Beholder: The Interaction Between Impulsivity and Perceived Informal Social Control on Offending," *Criminal Justice and Behavior* 36 (2009): 307–321.

120. Jennifer Beyers, John Bates, Gregory Pettit, and Kenneth Dodge, "Neighborhood Structure, Parenting Processes, and the Development of Youths' Externalizing Behaviors: A Multilevel Analysis," *American Journal of Community Psychology* 31 (2003): 35–53.

121. Ralph Taylor, "Social Order and Disorder of Street Blocks and Neighborhoods: Ecology, Microecology, and the Systemic Model of Social Disorganization," *Journal of Research in Crime and Delinquency* 34 (1997): 113–155.

122. April Pattavina, James Byrne, and Luis Garcia, "An Examination of Citizen Involvement in Crime Prevention in High-Risk versus Low- to Moderate-Risk Neighborhoods," *Crime and Delinquency* 52 (2006): 203–231.

123. Steven Messner, Eric Baumer, and Richard Rosenfeld, "Dimensions of Social Capital and Rates of Criminal Homicide," *American Sociological Review* 69 (2004): 882–905.

124. Paul Bellair, "Informal Surveillance and Street Crime: A Complex Relationship," *Criminology* 38 (2000): 137–170.

125. Skogan, *Disorder and Decline.*

126. Robert Sampson and W. Byron Groves, "Community Structure and Crime: Testing Social Disorganization Theory," *American Journal of Sociology* 94 (1989): 774–802; Denise Gottfredson, Richard McNeill, and Gary Gottfredson, "Social Area Influences on Delinquency: A Multilevel Analysis," *Journal of Research in Crime and Delinquency* 28 (1991): 197–206.

127. Jodi Eileen Morris, Rebekah Levine Coley, and Daphne Hernandez, "Out-of-School Care and Problem Behavior Trajectories Among Low-Income Adolescents: Individual, Family, and Neighborhood," *Child Development* 75 (2004): 948–965.

128. Ruth Triplett, Randy Gainey, and Ivan Sun, "Institutional Strength, Social Control, and Neighborhood Crime Rates," *Theoretical Criminology* 7 (2003): 439–467; Fred Markowitz, Paul Bellair, Allen Liska, and Jianhong Liu, "Extending Social Disorganization Theory: Modeling the Relationships Between Cohesion, Disorder, and Fear," *Criminology* 39 (2001): 293–320.

129. Robert Bursik and Harold Grasmick, "The Multiple Layers of Social Disorganization," paper presented at the annual meeting of the American Society of Criminology, New Orleans, November 1992.

130. George Capowich, "The Conditioning Effects of Neighborhood Ecology on Burglary Victimization," *Criminal Justice and Behavior* 30 (2003): 39–62.

131. Ruth Peterson, Lauren Krivo, and Mark Harris, "Disadvantage and Neighborhood Violent Crime: Do Local Institutions Matter?" *Journal of Research in Crime and Delinquency* 37 (2000): 31–63.

132. Maria Velez, "The Role of Public Social Control in Urban Neighborhoods: A Multi-Level Analysis of Victimization Risk," *Criminology* 39 (2001): 837–864.

133. Velez, Krivo, and Peterson, "Structural Inequality and Homicide."

134. David Klinger, "Negotiating Order in Patrol Work: An Ecological Theory of Police Response to Deviance," *Criminology* 35 (1997): 277–306.

135. Rodney Stark, "Deviant Places: A Theory of the Ecology of Crime," *Criminology* 25 (1987): 893–911.

136. Robert Kane, "Compromised Police Legitimacy as a Predictor of Violent Crime in Structurally Disadvantaged Communities," *Criminology* 43 (2005): 469–498.

137. Robert Sampson, "Neighborhood and Community," *New Economy* 11 (2004): 106–113.

138. Robert Bursik and Harold Grasmick, "Economic Deprivation and Neighborhood Crime Rates, 1960–1980," *Law and Society Review* 27 (1993): 263–278.

139. Delbert Elliott, William Julius Wilson, David Huizinga, Robert Sampson, Amanda Elliott, and Bruce Rankin, "The Effects of Neighborhood Disadvantage on Adolescent Development," *Journal of Research in Crime and Delinquency* 33 (1996): 389–426.

140. James DeFronzo, "Welfare and Homicide," *Journal of Research in Crime and Delinquency* 34 (1997): 395–406.

141. John Worrall, "Reconsidering the Relationship Between Welfare Spending and Serious Crime: A Panel Data Analysis with Implications for Social Support Theory," *Justice Quarterly* 22 (2005): 364–391.

142. Sampson, Morenoff, and Earls, "Beyond Social Capital."

143. Thomas McNulty, "Assessing the Race–Violence Relationship at the Macro Level: The Assumption of Racial Invariance and the Problem of Restricted Distribution," *Criminology* 39 (2001): 467–490.

144. Delbert Elliott, William Julius Wilson, David Huizinga, Robert Sampson, Amanda Elliott, and Bruce Rankin, "The Effects of Neighborhood Disadvantage on Adolescent Development," *Journal of Research in Crime and Delinquency* 33 (1996): 389–426, at 414.

145. Patrick Sharkey, "Navigating Dangerous Streets: The Sources and Consequences of Street Efficacy," *American Sociological Review* 71 (2006): 826–846.

146. Sampson, Morenoff, and Earls, "Beyond Social Capital."

147. Per-Olof H. Wikström and Kyle Treiber, "The Role of Self-Control in Crime Causation" *European Journal of Criminology* 4 (2007): 237–264.

148. Eric Silver and Lisa Miller, "Sources of Informal Social Control in Chicago Neighborhoods," *Criminology* 42 (2004): 551–585.

149. Bursik and Grasmick, "Economic Deprivation and Neighborhood Crime Rates, 1960–1980."

150. Robert Sampson and W. Byron Groves, "Community Structure and Crime: Testing Social Disorganization Theory," *American Journal of Sociology* 94 (1989): 774–802; Denise Gottfredson, Richard McNeill, and Gary Gottfredson, "Social Area Influences on Delinquency: A Multilevel Analysis," *Journal of Research in Crime and Delinquency* 28 (1991): 197–206.

151. Peterson, Krivo, and Harris, "Disadvantage and Neighborhood Violent Crime."

152. John Braithwaite, "Poverty Power, White-Collar Crime, and the Paradoxes of Criminological Theory," *Australian and New Zealand Journal of Criminology* 24 (1991): 40–58.

153. Wilson and Daly, "Life Expectancy, Economic Inequality, Homicide, and Reproductive Timing in Chicago Neighborhoods."

154. Judith Blau and Peter Blau, "The Cost of Inequality: Metropolitan Structure and Violent Crime," *American Sociological Review* 147 (1982): 114–129.

155. P. M. Krueger, S. A. Huie, R. G. Rogers, and R. A. Hummer, "Neighborhoods and Homicide Mortality: An Analysis of Race/Ethnic Differences," *Journal of Epidemiology and Community Health* 58 (2004): 223–230.

156. Gary LaFree and Kriss Drass, "The Effect of Changes in Intraracial Income Inequality and Educational Attainment on Changes in Arrest Rates for African Americans and Whites, 1957 to 1990," *American Sociological Review* 61 (1996): 614–634; Taylor and Covington, "Neighborhood Changes in Ecology and Violence," p. 582; Richard Block, "Community Environment and Violent Crime," *Criminology* 17 (1979): 46–57; Robert Sampson, "Structural Sources of Variation in Race-Age-Specific Rates of Offending Across Major U.S. Cities," *Criminology* 23 (1985): 647–673; Richard Rosenfeld, "Urban Crime Rates: Effects of Inequality, Welfare Dependency, Region and Race," in *The Social Ecology of Crime*, ed. James Byrne and Robert Sampson (New York: Springer Verlag, 1985), pp. 116–130.

157. Sang-Weon Kim and William Pridemore, "Poverty, Socioeconomic Change, Institutional Anomie, and Homicide," *Social Science Quarterly* 86 (2005): 1,377–1,398.

158. Robert Merton, *Social Theory and Social Structure*, enlarged ed. (New York: Free Press, 1968).

159. For an analysis, see Richard Hilbert, "Durkheim and Merton on Anomie: An Unexplored Contrast in Its Derivatives," *Social Problems* 36 (1989): 242–256.

160. Ibid., p. 243.

161. Albert Cohen, "The Sociology of the Deviant Act: Anomie Theory and Beyond," *American Sociological Review* 30 (1965): 5–14.

162. Robert Agnew, "The Contribution of Social Psychological Strain Theory to the Explanation of Crime and Delinquency," in *Advances in Criminological Theory*, Vol. 6, *The Legacy of Anomie*, ed. Freda Adler and William Laufer (New Brunswick, NJ: Transaction Press, 1995), pp. 111–122.

163. These criticisms are articulated in Messner and Rosenfeld, *Crime and the American Dream*, p. 60.

164. Messner and Rosenfeld, *Crime and the American Dream.*

165. Ibid., p. 61.

166. Steven Messner and Richard Rosenfeld, "An Institutional-Anomie Theory of the Social Distribution of Crime," paper presented at the annual meeting of the American Society of Criminology, Phoenix, November 1993.

167. Lisa Mufti, "Advancing Institutional Anomie Theory," *International Journal of Offender Therapy and Comparative Criminology* 50 (2006): 630–653.

168. Stephen Cernkovich, Peggy Giordano, and Jennifer Rudolph, "Race, Crime, and the American Dream," *Journal of Research in Crime and Delinquency* 37 (2000): 131–170.

169. Jon Gunnar Bernburg, "Anomie, Social Change, and Crime: A Theoretical Examination of Institutional-Anomie Theory," *British Journal of Criminology* 42 (2002): 729–743.

170. John Hagan, Gerd Hefler, Gabriele Classen, Klaus Boehnke, and Hans Merkens, "Subterranean Sources of Subcultural Delinquency Beyond the American Dream," *Criminology* 36 (1998): 309–340.

171. Jukka Savolainen, "Inequality, Welfare State and Homicide: Further Support for the Institutional Anomie Theory," *Criminology* 38 (2000): 1,021–1,042.

172. Kate Pickett, Jessica Mokherjee, and Richard Wilkinson, "Adolescent Birth Rates, Total Homicides, and Income Inequality in Rich Countries," *American Journal of Public Health* 95 (2005): 1,181–1,183.

173. Robert Agnew, "Foundation for a General Strain Theory of Crime and Delinquency," *Criminology* 30 (1992): 47–87.

174. Stephen Baron, "Street Youth, Strain Theory, and Crime," *Journal of Criminal Justice* 34 (2006): 209–223.

175. Cesar Rebellon, "Reconsidering the Broken Homes/Delinquency Relationship and Exploring Its Mediating Mechanism(s)," *Criminology* 40 (2002): 103–135.

176. G. Roger Jarjoura, "The Conditional Effect of Social Class on the Dropout–Delinquency Relationship," *Journal of Research in Crime and Delinquency* 33 (1996): 232–255.

177. Robert Agnew and Helene Raskin White, "An Empirical Test of General Strain Theory," *Criminology* 30 (1992): 475–499; John Hoffman and Alan Miller, "A Latent Variable Analysis of General Strain Theory," *Journal of Quantitative Criminology* 13 (1997): 111–113; Raymond Paternoster and Paul Mazerolle, "General Strain Theory and Delinquency: A Replication and Extension," *Journal of Research in Crime and Delinquency* 31 (1994): 235–263.

178. Ronald Simons, Yi Fu Chen, and Eric Stewart, "Incidents of Discrimination and Risk for Delinquency: A Longitudinal Test of Strain Theory with an African American Sample," *Justice Quarterly* 20 (2003): 827–854.

179. Robert Agnew, "Experienced, Vicarious, and Anticipated Strain: An Exploratory Study on Physical Victimization and Delinquency," *Justice Quarterly* 19 (2002): 603–633.

180. Carter Hay and Michelle Evans, "Violent Victimization and Involvement in Delinquency: Examining Predictions from General Strain Theory," *Journal of Criminal Justice* 34 (2006): 261–274.

181. Sherod Thaxton and Robert Agnew, "The Nonlinear Effects of Parental and Teacher Attachment on Delinquency: Disentangling Strain from Social Control Explanations," *Justice Quarterly* 21 (2004): 763–791.

182. Stacy De Coster and Lisa Kort-Butler, "How General Is General Strain Theory?" *Journal of Research in Crime and Delinquency* 43 (2006): 297–325.

183. Paul Mazerolle and Alex Piquero, "Linking General Strain with Anger: Investigating the Instrumental, Escapist, and Violent Adaptations to Strain," paper presented at the annual meeting of the American Society of Criminology, Boston, November 1995.

184. Paul Mazerolle, Velmer Burton, Francis Cullen, T. David Evans, and Gary Payne, "Strain, Anger, and Delinquent Adaptations Specifying General Strain Theory," *Journal of Criminal Justice* 28 (2000): 89–101; Paul Mazerolle and Alex Piquero, "Violent Responses to Strain: An Examination of Conditioning Influences," *Violence and Victimization* 12 (1997): 323–345.

185. George E. Capowich, Paul Mazerolle, and Alex Piquero, "General Strain Theory, Situational Anger, and Social Networks: An Assessment of Conditioning Influences," *Journal of Criminal Justice* 29 (2001): 445–461.

186. Cesar Rebellon, Nicole Leeper Piquero, Alex Piquero, and Sherod Thaxton, "Do Frustrated Economic Expectations and Objective Economic Inequity Promote Crime? A Randomized Experiment Testing Agnew's General Strain Theory," *European Journal of Criminology* 6 (2009): 47–71.

187. Joanne Kaufman, Cesar Rebellon, Sherod Thaxton, and Robert Agnew, "A General Strain Theory of Racial Differences in Criminal Offending," *Australian and New Zealand Journal of Criminology* 41 (2008): 421–437.

188. Stephen Cernkovich, Peggy Giordano, and Jennifer Rudolph, "Race, Crime and the American Dream," *Journal of Research in Crime and Delinquency* 37 (2000): 131–170.

189. Giacinto Froggio, Nereo Zamaro, and Massimo Lori, "Exploring the Relationship Between Strain and Some Neutralization Techniques," *European Journal of Criminology* 6 (2009): 73–88.

190. Byongook Moon, Merry Morash, Cynthia Perez McCluskey, and Hye-Won Hwang, "A Comprehensive Test of General Strain Theory: Key Strains, Situational- and Trait-Based Negative Emotions, Conditioning Factors, and Delinquency," *Journal of Research in Crime and Delinquency* 46 (2009): 182–212.

191. Hay and Evans, "Violent Victimization and Involvement in Delinquency: Examining Predictions from General Strain Theory."

192. Robert Agnew, Timothy Brezina, John Paul Wright, and Francis T. Cullen, "Strain, Personality Traits, and Delinquency: Extending General Strain Theory," *Criminology* 40 (2002): 43–71.

193. Wan-Ning Bao, Ain Haas, and Yijun Pi, "Life Strain, Coping, and Delinquency in the People's Republic of China," *International Journal of Offender Therapy and Comparative Criminology* 51 (2007): 9–24.

194. Timothy Brezina, "The Functions of Aggression: Violent Adaptations to Interpersonal Violence," paper presented at the annual meeting of the American Society of Criminology, San Diego, November 1997.

195. Agnew, Brezina, Wright, and Cullen, "Strain, Personality Traits, and Delinquency"; Robert Agnew, "Stability and Change in Crime over the Life Course: A Strain Theory Explanation," in *Advances in Criminological Theory*, Vol. 7, *Developmental Theories of Crime and Delinquency*, ed. Terence Thornberry (New Brunswick, NJ: Transaction Books, 1995), pp. 113–137.

196. John Hoffman, "A Life-Course Perspective on Stress, Delinquency, and Young Adult Crime," *American Journal of Criminal Justice* 35 (2010): 105–120.

197. Lawrence Wu, "Effects of Family Instability, Income, and Income Instability on the Risk of Premarital Birth," *American Sociological Review* 61 (1996): 386–406.

198. Anthony Walsh, "Behavior Genetics and Anomie/Strain Theory," *Criminology* 38 (2000): 1,075–1,108.

199. Michael Ostrowsky and Steven Messner, "Explaining Crime for a Young Adult Population: An Application of General Strain Theory," *Journal of Criminal Justice* 33 (2005): 463–476.

200. Lee Ann Slocum, Sally Simpson, and Douglas Smith, "Strained Lives and Crime: Examining Intra-Individual Variation in Strain and Offending in a Sample of Incarcerated Women," *Criminology* 43 (2005): 1,067–1,110.

201. Lisa Broidy, "A Test of General Strain Theory," *Criminology* 39 (2001): 9–36.

202. Robert Agnew and Timothy Brezina, "Relational Problems with Peers, Gender and Delinquency," *Youth and Society* 29 (1997): 84–111.

203. John Hoffmann and S. Susan Su, "The Conditional Effects of Stress on Delinquency and Drug Use: A Strain Theory in Assessment of Sex Differences," *Journal of Research in Crime and Delinquency* 34 (1997): 46–78.

204. Lisa Broidy, "The Role of Gender in General Strain Theory," paper presented at the annual meeting of the American Society of Criminology, Boston, November 1995.

205. Lisa Broidy and Robert Agnew, "Gender and Crime: A General Strain Theory Perspective," *Journal of Research in Crime and Delinquency* 34 (1997): 275–306.

206. Robbin Ogle, Daniel Maier-Katkin, and Thomas Bernard, "A Theory of Homicidal Behavior Among Women," *Criminology* 33 (1995): 173–193.

207. Nicole Leeper Piquero and Miriam Sealock, "Gender and General Strain Theory: A Preliminary Test of Broidy and Agnew's Gender/GST Hypothesis," *Justice Quarterly* 21 (2004): 125–158.

208. Teresa LaGrange and Robert Silverman, "Investigating the Interdependence of Strain and Self-Control," *Canadian Journal of Criminology and Criminal Justice* 45 (2003): 431–464.

209. Christopher Browning, Seth Feinberg, and Robert D. Dietz, "The Paradox of Social Organization: Networks, Collective Efficacy, and Violent Crime in Urban Neighborhoods," *Social Forces* 83 (2004): 503–534.

210. Thorsten Sellin, *Culture Conflict and Crime*, Bulletin No. 41 (New York: Social Science Research Council, 1938).

211. Ibid., p. 22.

212. Ibid., p. 29.

213. Ibid., p. 68.

214. Walter Miller, "Lower-Class Culture as a Generating Milieu of Gang Delinquency," *Journal of Social Issues* 14 (1958): 5–19.

215. Ibid., pp. 14–17.

216. Fred Markowitz and Richard Felson, "Social-Demographic Attitudes and Violence," *Criminology* 36 (1998): 117–138.

217. Jeffrey Fagan, *Adolescent Violence: A View from the Street*, NIJ Research Preview (Washington, DC: National Institute of Justice, 1998).

218. Albert Cohen, *Delinquent Boys* (New York: Free Press, 1955).

219. Ibid., p. 25.

220. Ibid., p. 28.

221. Ibid.

222. Clarence Schrag, *Crime and Justice American Style* (Washington, DC: U.S. Government Printing Office, 1971), p. 74.

223. Cohen, *Delinquent Boys*, p. 30.

224. Ibid., p. 31.

225. Ibid., p. 133.

226. J. Johnstone, "Social Class, Social Areas, and Delinquency," *Sociology and Social Research* 63 (1978): 49–72; Joseph Harry, "Social Class and Delinquency: One More Time," *Sociological Quarterly* 15 (1974): 294–301.

227. Richard Cloward and Lloyd Ohlin, *Delinquency and Opportunity* (New York: Free Press, 1960).

228. Ibid., p. 7.

229. Ibid., p. 85.

230. Ibid., p. 171.

231. Ibid., p. 23.

232. Ibid., p. 73.

233. Ibid., p. 24.

234. Finn-Aage Esbensen and David Huizinga, "Gangs, Drugs and Delinquency in a Survey of Urban Youth," *Criminology* 31 (1993): 565–587.

235. For a general criticism, see Kornhauser, *Social Sources of Delinquency*.

236. Charles Tittle, "Social Class and Criminal Behavior: A Critique of the Theoretical Foundations," *Social Forces* 62 (1983): 334–358.

237. James Q. Wilson and Richard Herrnstein, *Crime and Human Nature* (New York: Simon & Schuster, 1985).

238. Kenneth Polk and F. Lynn Richmond, "Those Who Fail," in *Schools and Delinquency*, ed. Kenneth Polk and Walter Schafer (Englewood Cliffs, NJ: Prentice Hall, 1974), p. 67.

239. Kathleen Maguire and Ann Pastore, *Sourcebook of Criminal Justice Statistics, 1996* (Washington, DC: U.S. Government Printing Office, 1996), pp. 150–166.

240. James DeFronzo, "Welfare and Burglary," *Crime and Delinquency* 42 (1996): 223–230.

241. Solomon Kobrin, "The Chicago Area Project—25-Year Assessment," *Annals of the American Academy of Political and Social Science* 322 (1959): 20–29.

242. Community Capacity Development Office website: www.ojp.usdoj.gov/ccdo/nonflash.html (accessed September 20, 2010).

AP Images/John Bazemore

TEENAGER

Teenager Genarlow Wilson was an honor student and a gifted athlete, attractive, popular, and outgoing. He had a 3.2 grade point average, was all-conference in football, voted 11th-grade prom prince, and his senior year was capped off with a special honor when he was elected Douglas County High's first-ever homecoming king. Instead of going right to his college of choice, Genarlow instead served a sentence in a Georgia prison. His crime: engaging in consensual sex when he was 17 years old with a girl two years younger. Wilson was convicted of aggravated child molestation even though he and the girl were both minors at the time and the sex was clearly consensual.

Wilson engaged in oral sex with the girl during a wild party involving a bunch of kids, marijuana, and alcohol, all captured on videotape. The tapes made it clear the sex was voluntary and not coerced. Though the

(continued on page 230)

Social Process Theories: Socialization and Society

7

Chapter Outline

Learning Objectives

1. Be familiar with the concept of social process and socialization
2. Be able to discuss the differences between social learning, control, and reaction theory
3. Discuss the effect of families and education on crime
4. Be aware of the link between peers and delinquency
5. Be familiar with the association between beliefs and criminality
6. Discuss the main types of social learning theory
7. Be familiar with the principles of control theory
8. Know the basic elements of social reaction or labeling theory
9. Be aware of the effects of labeling
10. Link social process theory to crime prevention efforts

prosecutor favored leniency, Wilson refused a plea bargain because it would mean admitting he was a sexual predator, a charge he vehemently denied and that no one, including the prosecutor, believed was true. Ironically, if the couple had had sexual intercourse, it would have been considered a misdemeanor, but since oral sex was involved, the crime was considered a felony. An additional irony in the case: after Wilson was convicted, the Georgia law was changed, making consensual oral sex between minors a misdemeanor as well. But the new law did not apply retroactively. Instead of using his college scholarship, Wilson was sent to prison.[1]

Genarlow Wilson's case shows how social interactions and process shape crime. He did not consider himself a criminal and even in court denied his culpability. Here is an exchange he had with the prosecutor during the trial:

Wilson: Aggravated child molestation is when like a 60-year-some old man likes messing with 10-year-old girls. I'm 17, the girl was 15, sir. You call that child molestation, two years apart?

Barker: I didn't write the law.

Wilson: I didn't write the law, either.

Barker: That's what the law states is aggravated child molestation, Mr. Wilson, not me.

Wilson: Well, sir, I understand you're just doing your job. I don't blame you. . . . But do you think it's fair? . . . Would you want your son on trial for something like this?[2]

Should Genarlow Wilson have been labeled a "sexual predator"? If he had engaged in a different type of sex act, the case would never have been made public. The law itself was designed to protect young girls from being abused by older men, not members of their own peer group with whom they were socializing freely. And if the act itself was so bad, why was it decriminalized a short time later? The bottom line: if the party had occurred a few months later, Genarlow Wilson would have been playing football at Georgia State University, and not sent to Georgia State Prison!

Genarlow Wilson was in fact labeled a sexual predator and sent to prison because those in power, who define the law and control its process, decided that his behavior constituted a serious crime, a felony. They could have just as easily ignored the action and let him go. It would have been just another case of teens behaving badly. But even powerful decision makers can change their minds and reassess labels. On June 9, 2007, a Georgia judge threw out Genarlow's 10-year sentence and amended it to misdemeanor aggravated child molestation with a 12-month term, plus credit for time served. Under the ruling, Genarlow, who had been behind bars for more than two years, would not be required to register as a sex offender. In making his decision, the Georgia judge stated:

If this court or any court cannot recognize the injustice of what has occurred here, then our court system has lost sight of the goal our judicial system has always strived to accomplish . . . justice being served in a fair and equal manner. . . . The fact that Genarlow Wilson has spent two years in prison for what is now classified as a misdemeanor, and without assistance from this court, will spend eight more years in prison, is a grave miscarriage of justice.[3]

Here we can see how social processes influence both the definition of what is to be considered a crime and who is to be considered a criminal. How people are socialized and how they are perceived by others are critical determinants of a person's status and behavior.

SOCIALIZATION AND CRIME

During the 1930s and 1940s, a group of sociologists began to link social-psychological interactions to criminological behavior. **Sociological social psychology** (also known as psychological sociology) is the study of human interactions and relationships that emphasizes such issues as group dynamics and socialization.

According to this school of thought, an individual's relationship to important social processes, such as education, family life, and peer relations, is the key to understanding human behavior. Poverty and social disorganization alone are not sufficient to cause criminal activity because, after all, many people living in the most deteriorated areas never commit criminal offenses. Something else is needed. Research seemed to show that children who grow up in homes wracked by conflict, attend inadequate schools, and/or associate with deviant peers become exposed to procrime forces.

In this view, the key to understanding crime can be found in human **socialization**—the interactions people have with various organizations, institutions, and processes of society. Most people are influenced by their family relationships, peer group associations, educational experiences, and interactions with authority figures, including teachers, employers, and agents of the justice system. If these relationships are positive and supportive, people can succeed within the rules of society; if these relationships are dysfunctional and destructive, conventional success may be impossible, and criminal solutions may become a feasible alternative. Taken together, this view of crime is referred to as **social process theory**.

The influence of social process theories has endured because the relationship between social class and crime is still uncertain. Most residents of inner-city areas refrain from criminal activity, and few of those who do commit crimes remain persistent chronic offenders into their adulthood. If poverty were the sole cause of crime, then indigent adults would be as criminal as indigent teenagers. The association between economic status and crime has been called problematic because class position alone cannot explain crime rates.[4] Today, more than 40 million Americans live below the poverty line. Even if we were to assume that all criminals come from the lower class—which they do not—it is evident that the great majority of the most indigent Americans do not commit criminal acts even though they may have a great economic incentive to do so. Relatively few adolescents living in the most deteriorated areas become persistent offenders; most kids who do commit crime desist when they reach adulthood despite the continuing pressure of poverty and social decay. Some other force, then, must be at work to explain why the majority of at-risk individuals do not become persistent criminal offenders and to explain why some who have no economic or social reason to commit crime do so anyway.

Criminologists have long studied the critical elements of socialization to determine how they contribute to a burgeoning criminal career. Prominent among these elements are the family, the peer group, and the school.

Family Relations

For some time, family relationships have been considered a major determinant of behavior.[5] In fact, there is abundant evidence that parenting factors, such as the ability to communicate and to provide proper discipline, may play a critical role in determining whether people misbehave as children and even later as adults.

Youths who grow up in households characterized by conflict and tension, and where there is a lack of familial love and support, are susceptible to the crime-promoting forces in the environment.[6] Adolescents who live in this type of environment develop poor emotional well-being, externalizing problems, and antisocial behavior.[7]

Even those children living in so-called high-crime areas will be better able to resist the temptations of the streets if they receive fair discipline, care, and support from parents who provide them with strong, positive role models. Nonetheless, living in a disadvantaged neighborhood places terrific strain on family functioning, especially in single-parent families that experience social isolation from relatives, friends, and neighbors. Children who are raised within such distressed families are at risk for delinquency.[8]

The relationship between family structure and crime is critical when the high rates of divorce and single parents are considered. Today about 32 percent of children live in single-family homes, and there are significant racial differences in family structure (see Table 7.1).[9] Family disruption or change can have a long-lasting impact on children. Research conducted in both the United States and abroad shows that children raised in homes with one or both parents absent may be prone to antisocial behavior.[10] It is not surprising that the number of single-parent households in the population is significantly related to arrest rates.[11]

The Effects of Divorce   Why is the effect of divorce or separation so devastating? Even if single mothers (or fathers) can make up for the loss of a second parent, it is difficult to do so and the chances of failure increase. Single parents may find it difficult to provide adequate supervision, exposing kids to the negative effects of antisocial peers.[12] Poorly supervised kids may be more prone to act impulsively and are therefore less able to employ self-control to restrain their activities.[13]

Living in a single-parent household has been linked to educational failure. Kids living with a single parent may receive less encouragement and less help with schoolwork. Poor school achievement and limited educational aspirations have been associated with delinquent behavior. Also, because they are receiving less attention as a result of having just one parent, these children may be more prone to rebellious acts, such as running away and truancy.[14] Children in two-parent households, on the other hand, are more likely to want to go on to college than kids in single-parent homes.[15]

TABLE 7.1	Children in Single-Parent Families, by Race	
Non-Hispanic white	23%
Black or African American	65%
American Indian	50%
Asian and Pacific Islander	16%
Hispanic or Latino	38%
Total	**32%**

SOURCE: Annie E. Casey Foundation, Kids Count, http://datacenter.kidscount.org/data/acrossstates/Rankings.aspx?ind=107 (accessed December 16, 2010).

The Criminological Enterprise
Family Functioning and Crime

Rand Conger is one of the nation's leading experts on family life. For the past two decades, he has been involved with four major community studies that have examined the influence of economic stress on families, children, and adolescents. In sum, these studies involve almost 1,500 families and over 4,000 individual family members who represent a diverse cross-section of society. The extensive information that has been collected on all of these families over time includes reports by family members, videotaped discussions in the home, and data from schools and other community agencies.

One thing that Conger and his associates have learned is that in all of these different types of families, economic stress appears to have a harmful effect on parents and children. According to his Family Stress Model of economic hardship, such factors as low income and income loss increase parents' sadness, pessimism about the future, anger, despair, and withdrawal from other family members. Economic stress has this impact on parents' social-emotional functioning through the daily pressures it creates for them, such as being unable to pay bills or acquire basic necessities such as adequate food, housing, clothing, and medical care. As parents become more emotionally distressed, they tend to interact with one another and their children in a more irritable and less supportive fashion. These patterns of behavior increase instability in the marriage and also disrupt effective parenting practices, such as monitoring children's activities and using consistent and appropriate disciplinary strategies. Marital instability and disrupted parenting, in turn, increase children's risk of suffering developmental problems, such as depressed mood, substance abuse, and engaging in delinquent behaviors. These economic stress processes also decrease children's ability to function in a competent manner in school and with peers.

The findings also show, however, that parents who remain supportive of one another, and who demonstrate effective problem-solving skills in spite of hardship, can disrupt this negative process and shield their children and themselves from these adverse consequences of economic stress. These parenting skills can be taught and used by human service professionals to assist families experiencing economic pressure or similar stresses in their lives.

CRITICAL THINKING

To help deal with these problems, Conger advocates support for social policies that adequately aid families during stressful times as they recover from downturns in the economy. He also advocates educating parents about effective strategies for managing the economic, emotional, and family relationship challenges they will face when hardship occurs. What would you add to the mix to improve family functioning in America?

SOURCES: Rand Conger and Katherine Conger, "Understanding the Processes Through Which Economic Hardship Influences Families and Children," in *Handbook of Families and Poverty*, ed. D. Russell Crane and Tim B. Heaton (Thousand Oaks, CA: Sage Publications, 2008), pp. 64–81; Iowa State University, Institute for Social and Behavioral Research, the research of Rand Conger, www.isbr.iastate.edu/staff/Personals/rd-conger/ (accessed December 15, 2010).

Because their incomes may decrease substantially in the aftermath of marital breakup, some divorced mothers are forced to move to residences in deteriorated neighborhoods that may place children at risk of crime and drug abuse. In poor neighborhoods, single parents cannot call upon neighborhood resources to take up the burden of controlling children, and, as a result, a greater burden is placed on families to provide adequate supervision.[16] Some groups (i.e., Hispanics, Asians) have been raised in cultures where divorce is rare and parents have less experience in developing child-rearing practices that buffer the effects of family breakup on adolescent problem behavior.[17]

When a mother remarries, it does not seem to mitigate the effects of divorce on youth. Children living with a stepparent exhibit as many problems as youth in single-parent families and considerably more problems than those who are living with both biological parents.[18] The concept of family functioning and crime and the factors that disturb this interaction are discussed in The Criminological Enterprise.

Family Deviance   A number of studies have found that parental deviance has a powerful influence on children's future behavior. Kids look up to and are influenced by their parents, so it comes as no surprise that they are willing to model their behavior along parental lines.[19] When parents drink, take drugs, and commit crimes, the effects can be both devastating and long term. In fact, research shows the effect is intergenerational: the children of deviant parents produce delinquent children themselves.[20]

Some of the most important data on the influence of parental deviance were gathered by British criminologist David Farrington, whose longitudinal research data were gathered in the long-term Cambridge Study in Delinquent Development (CSDD). Some of the most important results include:

- A significant number of delinquent youths have criminal fathers. About 8 percent of the sons of noncriminal fathers became chronic offenders, compared to 37 percent of youths with criminal fathers.[21]

- School yard bullying may be both inter- and intragenerational. Bullies have children who bully others, and these "second-generation bullies" grow up to become the parents of children who are also bullies (see Chapter 9 for more on bullying in the school yard).[22] Thus, one family may have a grandfather, father, and son who are or were school yard bullies.[23]
- Kids whose parents go to prison are much more likely to be at risk for delinquency than children of nonincarcerated parents.[24]

Parental Efficacy   While poor parenting and parental deviance may increase exposure to criminality, children raised by parents who have excellent parenting skills, who are supportive and can effectively control their children in a noncoercive fashion, are more insulated from crime-producing forces in society.[25] Effective parenting can help neutralize the effect of both individual (e.g., emotional problems) and social (e.g., delinquent peers) forces that promote delinquent behaviors.[26] Even kids who are at risk to delinquency because of personality problems or neurological syndromes, such as ADHD, have a much better prognosis if they receive effective, supportive parenting.[27]

Research shows that antisocial behavior will be reduced if parents provide the type of structure that integrates children into families, while giving them the ability to assert their individuality and regulate their own behavior—a phenomenon referred to as **parental efficacy**.[28] In some cultures, emotional support from the mother is critical, whereas in others the father's support remains the key factor.[29]

Numerous studies have uncovered links between the quality of family life and delinquency. Children who feel inhibited with their parents and refuse to discuss important issues with them are more likely to engage in deviant activities. Kids who report having troubled home lives also exhibit lower levels of self-esteem and are more prone to antisocial behaviors.[30] One reason for poor communication is parents who rely on authoritarian disciplinary practices, holding a "my way or the highway" orientation. Telling kids that "as long as you live in my house you will obey my rules" does little to improve communications and may instead produce kids who are rebellious and crime prone.[31]

While the prevailing wisdom is that bad parents produce bad kids, some recent research by David Huh and his colleagues found that the relationship may not be what it seems.

Child Maltreatment   There is also a suspected link between crime and child abuse, neglect, and sexual abuse.[32] Numerous studies conducted in the United States and abroad show that there is a significant association between child maltreatment and serious self-reported and official delinquency, even when taking into account gender, race, and class.[33] Children, both males and females, black or white, who experience abuse, neglect, or sexual abuse are believed to be more crime prone and suffer from other social problems such as depression, suicide attempts, substance abuse,

AP Images/Steve Helber

Children raised by parents who have excellent parenting skills, who are supportive, and who can effectively control their children in a noncoercive fashion are more insulated from crime-producing forces in society. Effective parenting can help neutralize the effect of both individual and social forces that promote delinquent behaviors. Parental efficacy means that parents provide the type of structure that integrates children into families, while giving them the ability to assert their individuality and regulate their own behavior. Bringing children to the library and encouraging them to read is but one method of effective parenting that can neutralize crime-promoting forces in society.

and self-injurious behaviors.[34] The effects of family dysfunction are felt well beyond childhood. Kids who experience high levels of family conflict grow up to lead stressful adult lives, punctuated by periods of depression.[35] Children whose parents are harsh, angry, and irritable are likely to behave in the same way toward their own children, putting their own offspring at risk.[36] Thus the seeds of adult dysfunction are planted early in childhood.

The Chicken or the Egg?   Which comes first, bad parents or bad kids? Does poor parenting cause delinquency or do delinquents undermine their parents' supervisory abilities? In a recent survey, David Huh and his colleagues questioned 500 adolescent girls from eight different schools to determine their perceived parental support and control and whether they engage in problem behaviors such as lying, stealing, running away, or substance abuse. Huh and his colleagues found little evidence that poor parenting is a direct cause of children's misbehavior problems or that it escalates misbehavior. Rather, their results suggest that children's problem behaviors undermine parenting effectiveness. *Increases* in adolescent behavior problems, such as substance abuse, result in a *decrease* in parental control and support. Parental control actually played a small role in influencing children's behavior problems.

Huh suggests it is possible that the parents of adolescents who consistently misbehave may become more tolerant of their behavior and give up on attempts at control. As their kids' behaviors become increasingly threatening and unruly, parents may simply detach from and reject their kids. So in the final analysis, the egg may control the chicken and not vice versa.[37]

Educational Experience

The educational process and adolescent achievement in school have been linked to criminality. Studies show that children who do poorly in school, lack educational motivation, and feel alienated are the most likely to engage in criminal acts.[38] Children who fail in school have been found to offend more frequently than those who are successful in school. These children commit more serious and violent offenses and persist in their offending into adulthood.[39]

Schools contribute to criminality when they label problem youths and set them apart from conventional society. One way in which schools perpetuate this stigmatization is the "track system," which identifies some students as college bound and others as academic underachievers or potential dropouts.[40] Those children placed in tracks labeled advanced placement, college prep, or honors will develop positive self-images and achievement motivation, whereas those assigned to lower level or general courses of study may believe academic achievement is closed to someone of their limited skills.

Dropping Out Another significant educational problem is that many students leave high school without gaining a diploma. Each year, approximately 1.2 million students fail to graduate from high school, more than half of whom are from minority groups. Nationally, about 71 percent of all students graduate from high school, but there are significant differences across racial groups. About half of African American and Hispanic students earn diplomas with their peers; in many states, there is a gap of as many as 40 or 50 percentage points between white and black students. There are also economic differences: a 16- to 24-year-old coming from the highest quartile of family income is about seven times as likely to have completed high school as a 16- to 24-year-old coming from the lowest quartile.[41]

The research on the effect of dropping out is a mixed bag. Some research findings indicate that school dropouts face a significant chance of entering a criminal career, but other efforts using sophisticated methodological tools have failed to find a dropout effect.[42] If there *is* a "dropout effect," it is because those who leave school early already have a long history of poor school performance and antisocial behaviors.[43] In other words, poor school performance predicts both dropping out and antisocial activity. Even if dropping out is not directly related to crime, it reduces earnings and dampens future life achievements.

Peer Relations

Psychologists have long recognized that the peer group has a powerful effect on human conduct and can have a dramatic influence on decision making and behavior choices.[44] Peer influence on delinquent and criminal behavior has been recorded in different cultures and may be a universal norm.[45]

Peer relations can be a double-edged sword. Popular kids who hang out with their friends without parental supervision are at risk for delinquent behaviors mainly because they have more opportunity to get into trouble.[46] Less-popular kids, who are routinely rejected by their peers, are more likely to display aggressive behavior and to disrupt group activities through bickering, bullying, or other antisocial behavior.[47] Those who report inadequate or strained peer relations, and who say they are not popular with the opposite sex, are prone to delinquent behaviors.[48]

Though experts have long debated the exact relationship between peer group interaction and delinquency, there is little question that some kids are particularly susceptible to peer influence.[49] The more antisocial the peer group, the more likely its members will engage in delinquency; nondelinquent friends will help moderate delinquency.[50] One recent study found that kids involved in delinquency are five times more likely than nonoffenders to associate with delinquent peers.[51]

While there is agreement that the association between peers and criminality exists, there is some debate over the path of the relationship:

- Delinquent friends cause law-abiding youth to get in trouble. Kids who fall in with a bad crowd are at risk for delinquency.[52] For girls, a "bad crowd" usually means teenage boys! It may not be surprising that delinquent girls are significantly more likely than their nondelinquent peers to identify males as their closest friends.[53] For girls, hanging out with males may be a precursor to antisocial behavior.[54]
- Antisocial youths seek out and join up with likeminded friends; deviant peers sustain and amplify delinquent careers.[55] Those who choose aggressive or violent friends are more likely to begin engaging in antisocial behavior themselves and suffer psychological deficits.[56] A number of research efforts have found that boys who go through puberty at an early age are more likely to later engage in violence, property crimes, drug use, and precocious sexual behavior.[57] The boys who mature early are the most likely to develop strong attachments to delinquent friends and to be influenced by peer pressure.[58]
- As children move through their life course, antisocial friends help youths maintain delinquent careers and

obstruct the aging-out process.[59] In contrast, noncriminal friends moderate criminality.[60] When (and if) adulthood brings close and sustaining ties to conventional friends, marriage, and family, levels of deviant behavior decline.[61] Troubled kids choose delinquent peers out of necessity rather than desire. The social baggage they cart around prevents them from developing associations with conventional peers. Because they are impulsive, they may join cliques whose members are dangerous and get them into trouble.[62] The most at-risk kids may choose older peers, perhaps because they believe these older, tougher friends can provide some level of protection; their choices may backfire when their more mature companions enmesh them in a deviant subculture.[63] Older peers do not cause straight kids to go bad, but they amplify the likelihood of a troubled kid getting further involved in antisocial behaviors.[64] The fear of punishment is diminished among kids who hang with delinquent friends, and loyalty to delinquent peers may outweigh the fear of punishment.[65]

Religion and Belief

Logic would dictate that people who hold high moral values and beliefs, who have learned to distinguish right from wrong, and who regularly attend religious services should also eschew crime and other antisocial behaviors.[66] Religion binds people together and forces them to confront the consequences of their behavior. Committing crimes would violate the principles of all organized religions.

More than 40 years ago in a now classic study, Travis Hirschi and Rodney Stark found that, contrary to expectations, the association between religious attendance and belief and delinquent behavior patterns is negligible and insignificant.[67] Since the publication of their milestone study, there have been numerous research efforts to review the influence of religion on misbehavior, and a majority have reached an opposite conclusion: maintaining religious beliefs and attending religious services significantly helps reduce crime.[68] Recently, Richard Petts used data from a national survey and found that adolescents residing within two-parent families are less likely to become delinquent and that supportive parenting practices reduce the likelihood of their becoming delinquent even further. However, whether they reside in single-parent or two-parent families, kids who are involved in religion are less likely to engage in delinquency. Religion enhances the effect of parental affection in two-parent homes and also helps kids living in single-parent homes resist the influence of deviant peers. Petts found that religious participation helps reduce deviant behavior involvement throughout the life course, from adolescence until marriage.[69]

Socialization and Crime

To many criminologists, social process, social interaction, and socialization are the chief determinants of criminal behavior. While a person's place in the social structure may contribute to crime, environment alone is not enough to explain criminality. People living in even the most deteriorated urban areas can successfully resist inducements to crime if they have a positive self-image, learn moral values, and have the support of their parents, peers, teachers, and neighbors. The girl with a positive self-image who is chosen for a college scholarship has the warm, loving support of her parents and is viewed by friends and neighbors as someone who is "going places." She is less likely to adopt a criminal way of life than another adolescent who is abused at home, lives with criminal parents, and whose bond to her school and peer group is shattered because she is labeled a troublemaker.[70] The boy who has learned criminal behavior from his parents and siblings and then joins a neighborhood gang is much more likely to become an adult criminal than his next-door neighbor who idolizes his hard-working, deeply religious parents.

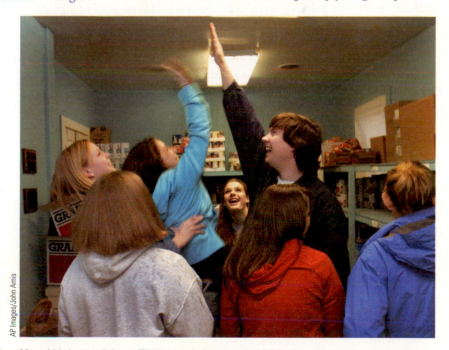

AP Images/John Amis

Many kids have religious affiliations or belong to other institutions that teach moral values that may help shield them from delinquency. Here, Natalie Kruger (15) gives a high-five to youth leader Adrian Martin at a food distribution center in Stone Mountain, Georgia, as other teenagers from Eastminster Presbyterian Church gather around them after the group finished stocking items they brought from their church. The teens joined their peers nationwide for "World Vision," a 30-hour fast during which they also donated food and necessities to organizations that distribute them to the needy.

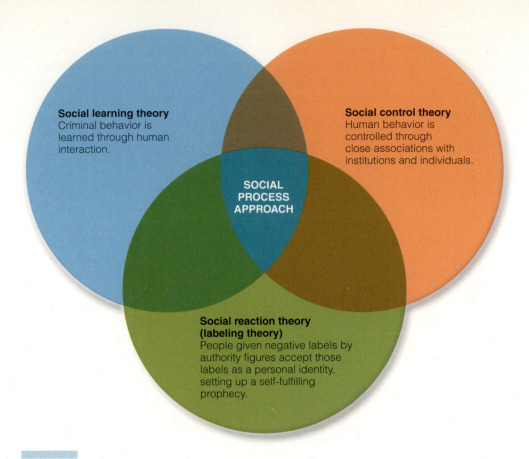

FIGURE 7.1
The Social Processes that Control Human Behavior

Within the figure:

Social learning theory
Criminal behavior is learned through human interaction.

Social control theory
Human behavior is controlled through close associations with institutions and individuals.

SOCIAL PROCESS APPROACH

Social reaction theory (labeling theory)
People given negative labels by authority figures accept those labels as a personal identity, setting up a self-fulfilling prophecy.

It is socialization, not the social structure, that determines life chances. The more social problems encountered during the socialization process, the greater the likelihood that youths will encounter difficulties and obstacles as they mature, such as being unemployed or becoming a teenage mother.

Theorists who believe that an individual's socialization determines the likelihood of criminality adopt the social process approach to human behavior. The social process approach has several independent branches (Figure 7.1):

- **Social learning theory** suggests that people learn the techniques and attitudes of crime from close and intimate relationships with criminal peers; crime is a learned behavior.
- **Social control theory** maintains that everyone has the potential to become a criminal, but that most people are controlled by their bonds to society. Crime occurs when the forces that bind people to society are weakened or broken.
- **Social reaction theory (labeling theory)** says people become criminals when significant members of society label them as such, and they accept those labels as a personal identity.

Put another way, social learning theory assumes people are born good and learn to be bad; social control theory assumes people are born bad and must be controlled in order to be good; social reaction theory assumes that, whether good or bad, people are controlled by the reactions of others. Each of these independent branches will be discussed separately.

> To learn about the **Institute for Child and Family**, whose goal is to stimulate and coordinate the cross-disciplinary work required to make progress on the most difficult child and family policy issues facing the United States, visit the Criminal Justice CourseMate at cengagebrain.com, then access the "Web Links" for this chapter.

SOCIAL LEARNING THEORY

Social learning theorists believe crime is a product of learning the norms, values, and behaviors associated with criminal activity. Social learning can involve the actual techniques of crime—how to hot-wire a car or roll a joint—as well as the psychological aspects of criminality—how to deal with the guilt or shame associated with illegal activities. This section briefly reviews the three most prominent forms of social learning theory: differential association theory, differential reinforcement theory, and neutralization theory.

Differential Association Theory

One of the most prominent social learning theories is Edwin H. Sutherland's **differential association theory**. Often considered the preeminent U.S. criminologist, Sutherland first put forth his theory in his 1939 text, *Principles of Criminology*.[71] The final version of the theory appeared in 1947. When Sutherland died in 1950, Donald Cressey, his longtime associate, continued his work. Cressey was so successful in explaining and popularizing his mentor's efforts that differential association remains one of the most enduring explanations of criminal behavior.

Sutherland's research on white-collar crime, professional theft, and intelligence led him to dispute the notion that crime was a function of the inadequacy of people in the lower classes.[72] To Sutherland, criminality stemmed neither from individual traits nor from socioeconomic position; instead, he believed it to be a function of a learning process that could affect any individual in any culture. Acquiring a behavior is a social learning process, not a political or legal process. Skills and motives conducive to crime are learned as a result of contacts with procrime values, attitudes, and definitions and other patterns of criminal behavior.

Principles of Differential Association
The basic principles of differential association are explained as follows:[73]

- *Criminal behavior is learned.* This statement differentiates Sutherland's theory from prior attempts to classify criminal behavior as an inherent characteristic of criminals. By suggesting that delinquent and criminal behavior is learned, Sutherland implied that it can be classified in the same manner as any other learned behavior, such as writing, painting, or reading.
- *Learning is a by-product of interaction.* Criminal behavior is learned as a by-product of interacting with others. Sutherland believed individuals do not start violating the law simply by living in a criminogenic environment or by manifesting personal characteristics, such as low IQ or family problems, associated with criminality. People—family, friends, peers—have the greatest influence on their deviant behavior and attitude development. Relationships with these influential individuals color and control the way people interpret everyday events. For example, research shows that children who grow up in homes where parents abuse alcohol are more likely to view drinking as being socially and physically beneficial.[74] The intimacy of these associations far outweighs the importance of any other form of communication, such as movies or television. Even on those rare

occasions when violent motion pictures seem to provoke mass criminal episodes, these outbreaks can be more readily explained as a reaction to peer group pressure than as a reaction to the films themselves.

- *Criminal techniques are learned.* Learning criminal behavior involves acquiring the techniques of committing the crime, which are sometimes very complicated and sometimes very simple. This requires learning the specific direction of motives, drives, rationalizations, and attitudes. Some kids may meet and associate with criminal "mentors" who teach them how to be successful criminals and gain the greatest benefits from their criminal activities.[75] They learn the proper way to pick a lock, shoplift, and obtain and use narcotics. In addition, novice criminals learn to use the proper terminology for their acts and then acquire "proper" reactions to law violations. For example, getting high on marijuana and learning the proper way to smoke a joint are behavior patterns usually acquired from more experienced companions. Moreover, criminals must learn how to react properly to their illegal acts, such as when to defend them, rationalize them, or show remorse for them.
- *Perceptions of the legal code influence motives and drives.* The specific direction of motives and drives is learned from perceptions of various aspects of the legal code as being favorable or unfavorable. The reaction to social rules and laws is not uniform across society, and people constantly come into contact with others who maintain different views on the utility of obeying the legal code. Some people they admire may openly disdain or flout the law or ignore its substance. People experience what Sutherland calls *culture conflict* when they are exposed to different and opposing attitudes toward what is right and wrong, moral and immoral. The conflict of social attitudes and cultural norms is the basis for the concept of differential association.
- *Differential associations may vary in frequency, duration, priority, and intensity.* Whether a person learns to obey the law or to disregard it is influenced by the quality of social interactions. Those of lasting *duration* have greater influence than those that are brief. Similarly, *frequent* contacts have greater effect than rare and haphazard contacts. Sutherland did not specify what he meant by *priority*, but Cressey and others have interpreted the term to mean the age of children when they first encounter definitions of criminality. Contacts made early in life probably have a greater and more far-reaching influence than those developed later on. Finally, *intensity* is generally interpreted to mean the importance and prestige attributed to the individual or groups from whom the definitions are learned. For example, the influence of a father, mother, or trusted friend far outweighs the effect of more socially distant figures.
- *The process of learning criminal behavior by association with criminal and anticriminal patterns involves all of the mechanisms involved in any other learning process.* This

suggests that learning criminal behavior patterns is similar to learning nearly all other patterns and is not a matter of mere imitation.

- *Criminal behavior is an expression of general needs and values, but it is not excused by those general needs and values because noncriminal behavior is also an expression of those same needs and values.* This principle suggests that the motives for criminal behavior cannot logically be the same as those for conventional behavior. Sutherland rules out such motives as desire to accumulate money or social status, personal frustration, or low self-concept as causes of crime because they are just as likely to produce noncriminal behavior, such as getting a better education or working harder on a job. It is only the learning of deviant norms through contact with an excess of definitions favorable toward criminality that produces illegal behavior.

A person becomes a criminal when he or she perceives more favorable than unfavorable consequences to violating the law (Figure 7.2). According to Sutherland's theory, individuals become law violators when they are in contact with people, groups, or events that produce an excess of definitions favorable toward criminality and are isolated from counteracting forces. A definition favorable toward criminality occurs, for example, when a person is exposed to friends sneaking into a theater to avoid paying for a ticket or talking about the virtues of getting high on drugs. A definition unfavorable toward crime occurs when friends or parents demonstrate their disapproval of crime. Neutral behavior, such as reading a book, is neither positive nor negative with respect to law violation. Cressey argues that neutral behavior is important; for example, when a child is occupied doing something neutral, it prevents him or her from being in contact with those involved in criminal behaviors.[76]

In sum, differential association theory holds that people learn criminal attitudes and behavior while in their adolescence from close and trusted friends and/or relatives. A criminal career develops if learned antisocial values and behaviors are not at least matched or exceeded by conventional attitudes and behaviors. Criminal behavior, then, is learned in a process that is similar to learning any other human behavior.

Testing Differential Association Theory Numerous research efforts have supported the core principles of differential association. These generally show a correlation between

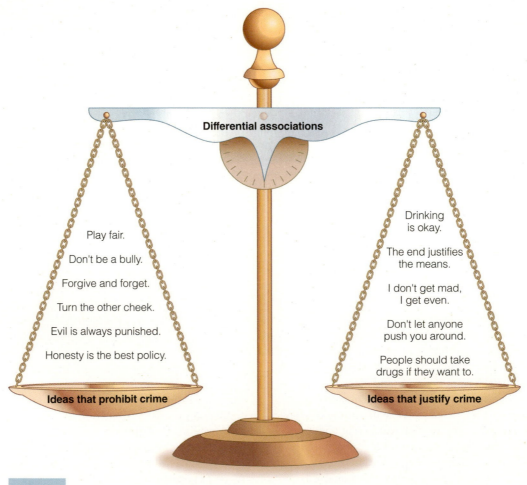

FIGURE 7.2
Differential Associations

(a) having deviant parents and friends, (b) holding deviant attitudes, and (c) committing deviant acts.[77] A recent meta-analysis of the literature by Travis Pratt and his associates found that the association between crime and measures of differential association are "quite strong."[78] Among the most important findings are:

- Crime appears to be intergenerational. Kids whose parents are deviant and criminal are more likely to become criminals themselves and eventually to produce criminal children.

- The more deviant an adolescent's social network and network of affiliations, including parents, peers, and romantic partners, the more likely that adolescent is to engage in antisocial behavior.[79] This finding supports the hypothesis that children learn criminal attitudes from exposure to deviant others, rather than crime being a function of inherited criminal traits.[80]

- People who report having attitudes that support deviant behavior are also likely to engage in deviant behavior.[81] As people mature, having delinquent friends who support criminal attitudes and behavior is strongly related to developing criminal careers. Association with deviant peers has been found to sustain the deviant attitudes.[82]

- The influence of deviant friends is highly supportive of delinquency, regardless of race and/or class.[83] One reason is that within peer groups, high-status leaders will influence and legitimize deviant behavior. In other words, if one of your friends whom you look up to drinks and smokes, it makes it a lot easier for you to engage in those behaviors yourself and to believe they are appropriate.[84]

- Romantic partners who engage in antisocial activities may influence their partner's behavior, which suggests that partners learn from one another.[85] Adolescents with deviant romantic partners are more delinquent than those youths with more prosocial partners, regardless of friends' and parents' behavior.[86]

- Kids who associate and presumably learn from aggressive peers are more likely to behave aggressively themselves.[87] Deviant peers interfere with the natural process of aging out of crime by helping provide the support that keeps kids in criminal careers.[88]

- Differential association is multicultural. Scales measuring differential association have been significantly correlated with criminal behaviors among samples taken in other nations and cultures.[89]

Differential association also seems especially relevant in trying to explain the onset of substance abuse and a career in the drug trade. This requires learning proper techniques and attitudes from an experienced user or dealer.[90] In his interview study of low-level drug dealers, Kenneth Tunnell found that many novices were tutored by a more experienced criminal dealer who helped them make connections with buyers and sellers. One told him:

I had a friend of mine who was an older guy, and he introduced me to selling marijuana to make a few dollars. I started selling a little and made a few dollars. For a young guy to be making a hundred dollars or so, it was a lot of money. So I got kind of tied up in that aspect of selling drugs.[91]

Tunnell found that making connections is an important part of the dealer's world. Adolescent drug users are likely to have intimate relationships with a peer friendship network that supports their substance abuse and teaches them how to deal within the drug world.[92]

Differential association may also be used to explain the gender difference in the crime rate. Males are more likely to socialize with deviant peers than females and, when they do, are more deeply influenced by peer relations.[93] Females are shielded by their unique moral sense, which makes caring about people and avoiding social harm a top priority. Males, in contrast, have a more cavalier attitude toward others and are more interested in their own self-interests. They are therefore more susceptible to the influence of deviant peers.[94]

Analysis of Differential Association Theory   There have been a number of important critiques of the theory. According to the *cultural deviance critique*, differential association is invalid because it suggests that criminals are people "properly" socialized into a deviant subculture; that is, they are taught criminal norms by significant others. Supporters counter that differential association also recognizes that individuals can embrace criminality because they have been improperly socialized into the normative culture.[95]

Differential association theory also fails to explain why one youth who is exposed to delinquent definitions eventually succumbs to them, while another, living under the same conditions, is able to avoid criminal entanglements. It also fails to account for the origin of delinquent definitions: How did the first "teacher" learn delinquent attitudes and definitions in order to pass them on? Who taught the teacher?

Differential association theory assumes that youths learn about crime and then commit criminal acts, but it is also possible that experienced delinquents and criminals seek out like-minded peers after they engage in antisocial acts and that the internalization of deviant attitudes follows, rather than precedes, criminality ("birds of a feather flock together").[96] Research on gang boys shows that they are involved in high rates of criminality before they join gangs, indicating that the group experience facilitates their antisocial behavior rather than playing a role in its creation.[97]

Despite these criticisms, differential association theory maintains an important place in the study of criminal behavior. For one thing, it provides a consistent explanation of all types of delinquent and criminal behavior. Unlike social structure theories, it is not limited to the explanation of a single facet of antisocial activity, such as lower-class gang activity. The theory can also account for the extensive delinquent behavior found even in middle- and upper-class areas, where youths may be exposed to a variety of prodelinquent definitions from such sources as overly opportunistic parents and friends. The theory appears flexible and able to explain current trends in crime and is not bound by those that existed when the theory was first created. For example, Sameer Hinduja and Jason Ingram found that adolescents who pirate music off the Internet are influenced by both personal friends and also online friends they meet in chat rooms and so on. Internet music piracy is not a crime that Sutherland had in mind when he first proposed the theory more than 70 years ago.[98]

Differential Reinforcement Theory

Differential reinforcement theory is another attempt to explain crime as a type of learned behavior. First proposed by Ronald Akers in collaboration with Robert Burgess in 1966, it is a version of the social learning view that employs both differential association concepts along with elements of psychological learning theory.

CONNECTIONS

Psychological learning theories were first discussed in Chapter 5. These trait theories maintain that human actions are developed through learning experiences. Behavior is supported by rewards and extinguished by negative reactions or punishments. In contrast, sociological learning theory holds that behavior is constantly being shaped by life experiences.

According to Akers, the same process is involved in learning both deviant and conventional behavior. People learn to be neither "all deviant" nor "all conforming," but rather strike a balance between the two opposing poles of behavior. This balance is usually stable, but it can undergo revision over time.[99]

A number of learning processes shape behavior. **Direct conditioning**, also called **differential reinforcement**, occurs when behavior is reinforced by being either rewarded or punished while interacting with others. When behavior is punished, this is referred to as **negative reinforcement**. This type of reinforcement can be distributed either by using negative stimuli (punishment) or by loss of a positive reward. Whether deviant or criminal behavior has been initiated or persists depends on the degree to which it has been rewarded or punished and the rewards or punishments attached to its alternatives.

According to Akers, people learn to evaluate their own behavior through their interactions with significant others and groups in their lives. These groups control sources and patterns of reinforcement, define behavior as right or wrong, and provide behaviors that can be modeled through observational learning. The more individuals learn to define

their behavior as good or at least as justified, rather than as undesirable, the more likely they are to engage in it. Adolescents who join a drug-abusing peer group whose members value drugs and alcohol, encourage their use, and provide opportunities to observe people abusing substances will be encouraged, through this social learning experience, to use drugs themselves.

Akers's theory posits that the principal influence on behavior comes from "those groups that control individuals' major sources of reinforcement and punishment and expose them to behavioral models and normative definitions."[100] The important groups are the ones with which a person is in differential association—peer and friendship groups, schools, churches, and similar institutions. Within the context of these critical groups, according to Akers, "deviant behavior can be expected to the extent that it has been differentially reinforced over alternative behavior . . . and is defined as desirable or justified."[101] Once people are indoctrinated into crime, their behavior can be reinforced by being exposed to deviant behavior models—associating with deviant peers—without being subject to negative reinforcements for their antisocial acts. The deviant behavior, originally executed by imitating someone else's behavior, is sustained by social support. For example, kids who engage in computer crime and computer hacking may find their behavior reinforced by peers who are playing the same game.[102]

It is possible that differential reinforcements help establish criminal careers and are a key factor in explaining persistent criminality.

Testing Differential Reinforcement   The principles of differential reinforcement have been subject to empirical review by Akers and other criminologists.[103] In an important test of his theory, Akers and his associates surveyed 3,065 male and female adolescents on drug- and alcohol-related activities and their perception of variables related to social learning and differential reinforcement. Items in the scale included the respondents' perceptions of esteemed peers' attitudes toward drug and alcohol abuse, the number of people they admired who actually used controlled substances, and whether people they admired would reward or punish them for substance abuse. Akers found a strong association between drug and alcohol abuse and social learning variables: those who believed they would be rewarded for deviance by those they respect were the ones most likely to engage in deviant behavior.[104] Aker's efforts have been supported by research showing that kids whose deviant behavior (such as smoking pot) is reinforced by significant others (such as parents or peers) are more likely to accelerate their rates of deviance.[105]

Akers also found that the learning–deviant behavior link is not static. The learning experience continues within a deviant group as behavior is both influenced by and exerts influence over group processes. For example, adolescents may learn to smoke because their friends are smoking

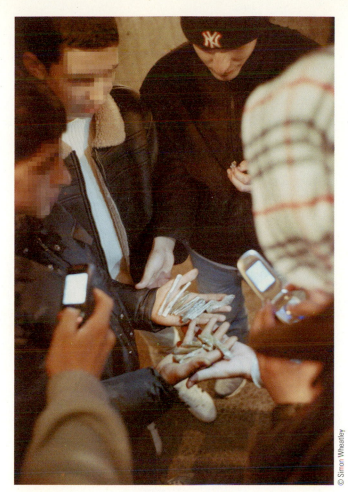

© Simon Wheatley

Differential association theory suggests that people learn the techniques and attitudes necessary to commit crime. Criminal knowledge is gained through experience, and after considering the outcomes of their past experiences, potential offenders decide which criminal acts will be profitable and which are dangerous and should be avoided. Here, a young man is shown photographing a drug deal on his cell phone. Is it possible that he is documenting the experience to learn and keep a record of the best techniques of drug dealing?

and, therefore, approve of this behavior. Over time, smoking influences friendships and peer group memberships as smokers seek out one another for companionship and support.[106]

Differential reinforcement theory is an important perspective that endeavors to determine the cause of criminal activity. It considers how the content of socialization conditions crime. Because not all socialization is positive, it accounts for the fact that negative social reinforcements and experiences can produce criminal results. This concurs with research that demonstrates that parental deviance is related to adolescent antisocial behavior.[107] Parents may reinforce their children's deviant behavior by supplying negative social reinforcements. Akers's work also fits well with rational choice theory because they both suggest that people learn the techniques and attitudes necessary to commit crime. Criminal knowledge is gained through experience. After considering the outcome of their past experiences, potential offenders decide which criminal acts will be profitable and which are dangerous and should be avoided.[108] Integrating these perspectives, people make rational choices about crime because they have learned to balance risks against the potential for criminal gain.

Neutralization Theory

Neutralization theory is identified with the writings of David Matza and his associate Gresham Sykes.[109] They view the process of becoming a criminal as a learning experience in which potential delinquents and criminals master techniques that enable them to counterbalance or neutralize conventional values and drift back and forth between illegitimate and conventional behavior. One reason this is possible is the subterranean value structure of American society. **Subterranean values** are morally tinged influences that have become entrenched in the culture but are publicly condemned. They exist side by side with conventional values and while condemned in public may be admired or practiced in private. Examples include viewing pornographic films, drinking alcohol to excess, and gambling on sporting events. In American culture, it is common to hold both subterranean and conventional values; few people are "all good" or "all bad."

Matza argues that even the most committed criminals and delinquents are not involved in criminality all the time; they also attend schools, family functions, and religious services. Their behavior can be conceived as falling along a continuum between total freedom and total restraint. This process, which he calls **drift**, refers to the movement from one extreme of behavior to another, resulting in behavior that is sometimes unconventional, free, or deviant and at other times constrained and sober.[110] Learning techniques of neutralization enables a person to temporarily "drift away" from conventional behavior and get involved in more subterranean values and behaviors, including crime and drug abuse.[111]

Sykes and Matza base their theoretical model on these observations:[112]

- *Criminals sometimes voice a sense of guilt over their illegal acts.* If a stable criminal value system existed in opposition to generally held values and rules, it would be unlikely that criminals would exhibit any remorse for their acts, other than regret at being apprehended.
- *Offenders frequently respect and admire honest, law-abiding people.* Really honest people are often revered, and if for some reason such people are accused of misbehavior, the criminal is quick to defend their integrity. Those admired may include sports figures, priests and other clergy, parents, teachers, and neighbors.
- *Criminals draw a line between those whom they can victimize and those whom they cannot.* Members of similar

ethnic groups, churches, or neighborhoods are often off limits. This practice implies that criminals are aware of the wrongfulness of their acts.

- *Criminals are not immune to the demands of conformity.* Most criminals frequently participate in many of the same social functions as law-abiding people—for example, in school, church, and family activities.

Because of these factors, Sykes and Matza conclude that criminality is the result of the neutralization of accepted social values through the learning of a standard set of techniques that allow people to counteract the moral dilemmas posed by illegal behavior.[113]

Techniques of Neutralization   Sykes and Matza suggest that people develop a distinct set of justifications for their law-violating behavior (Figure 7.3). These neutralization techniques enable them to temporarily drift away from the rules of the normative society and participate in subterranean behaviors. These techniques of neutralization include the following patterns:

- *Deny responsibility.* Young offenders sometimes claim their unlawful acts were simply not their fault. Criminal acts resulted from forces beyond their control or were accidents.

- *Deny injury.* By denying the wrongfulness of an act, criminals are able to neutralize illegal behavior. For example, stealing is viewed as borrowing; vandalism is considered mischief that has gotten out of hand. Delinquents may find that their parents and friends support their denial of injury. In fact, they may claim that the behavior was merely a prank, helping affirm the offender's perception that crime can be socially acceptable. Since no one was "really hurt" the act was not "really a crime." The Profiles in Crime feature illustrates this element of neutralization.

- *Deny the victim.* Criminals sometimes neutralize wrongdoing by maintaining that the victim of crime "had it coming." Vandalism may be directed against a disliked teacher or neighbor; homosexuals may be beaten up by a gang because their behavior is considered offensive. Denying the victim may also take the form of ignoring the rights of an absent or unknown victim—for example, stealing from the unseen owner of a department store. It becomes morally acceptable for the criminal to commit such crimes as vandalism when the victims, because of their absence, cannot be sympathized with or respected.

- *Condemn condemners.* An offender views the world as a corrupt place with a dog-eat-dog code. Because police and judges are on the take, teachers show favoritism, and parents take out their frustrations on their kids, it is ironic and unfair for these authorities to condemn his or her misconduct. By shifting the blame to others, criminals are able to repress the feeling that their own acts are wrong.

- *Appeal to higher loyalties.* Novice criminals often argue that they are caught in the dilemma of being loyal to their own peer group while at the same time attempting to abide by the rules of the larger society. The needs of the group take precedence over the rules of society because the demands of the former are immediate and localized.

In sum, the theory of neutralization presupposes a condition that allows people to neutralize unconventional norms and values by using such slogans as "I didn't mean to do it," "I didn't really hurt anybody," "They had it coming to them," "Everybody's picking on me," and "I didn't do it for myself." These excuses allow people to drift into criminal modes of behavior.

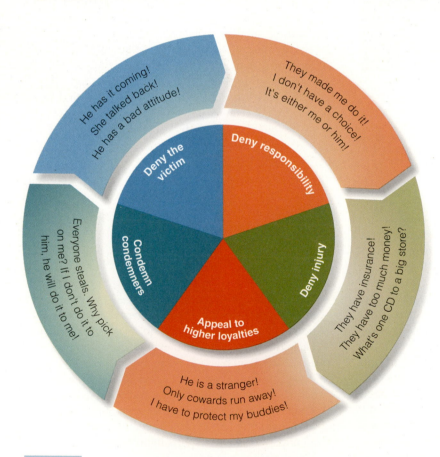

FIGURE 7.3
Techniques of Neutralization

Testing Neutralization Theory   Attempts have been made to verify the assumptions of neutralization theory

Profiles in Crime
But the Water Was Sterile!

Anticipating another tough flu season, some 1,100 employees at a Texas-based oil company lined up to get flu shots during a company-sponsored health fair. Little did they—or their employer—know that after rolling up their sleeves, they'd be injected with water, not vaccine. And they weren't the only ones to receive the fake shots—residents of retirement communities and others in the Houston area got them too.

It was part of an elaborate scam orchestrated over several months by Iyad Abu El Hawa and Martha Denise Gonzales, a pair of Houston-area criminals hoping to cash in on insurance money.

Here's how El Hawa and Gonzales staged their ruse. First, they set up fake health care offices in three different locations, staffed them with unlicensed "medical practitioners," and hired a few unsuspecting licensed nurses to make the offices look legitimate.

Next, Gonzales used her connections from a job as a doctor's office manager to market bogus flu shots and other health care services to doctors, churches, pharmacies, retirement communities, and others in Texas, Louisiana, Ohio, and Colorado.

El Hawa and Gonzales then ordered syringes, vials of sterilized water to serve as the fake vaccine, and other medical supplies from legitimate medical suppliers. To cover their tracks and make the vaccine appear—at least on paper—to be legitimate, they forged invoices and other documents. Since they used sterilized water, they assumed no one would really get hurt; their plan soon went awry.

The nurses hired by the pair unknowingly administered thousands of fake shots. El Hawa and Gonzales also provided syringes prefilled with the fake vaccine to at least one doctor's office. That put the health of some unsuspecting victims at risk, since the pair frequently didn't bother to use proper hygienic methods to fill the syringes. After the shots were given, El Hawa and Gonzales created fake medical records, submitted fraudulent claims to Medicare,

Medicaid, and various insurance companies, and then sat back and waited for the insurance reimbursement checks to start rolling in.

How were they caught? One of the nurses got suspicious and called the FBI after discovering that there were no vials of vaccine and that the couple could not provide the manufacturer tracking numbers for the vaccine. As federal agents closed in, they caught El Hawa trying to discard leftover syringes in a dumpster near his office. He and Gonzales were later convicted and sentenced to up to 10 years in prison.

SOURCES: FBI, "The Case of the Fake Flu Shots: Thousands Injected with Phony Vaccine," October 27, 2006, http://communitydispatch.com/artman/publish/printer_6834.shtml (accessed September 26, 2010); *American Chronicle*, "Texas Man Convicted for Distributing Fake Flu Vaccine," September 11, 2006, www.americanchronicle.com/articles/viewArticle.asp?articleID=13430 (accessed September 26, 2010); Harvey Rice, "Guilty Plea Made in Flu Shot Scam: Phony Doctor Faces Prison for Administering Fake Inoculations," *Houston Chronicle*, September 6, 2006, p. 1.

---

empirically, but the results have been inconclusive.[114] One area of research has been directed at determining whether there really is a need for law violators to neutralize moral constraints. The thinking behind this research is this: if criminals hold values *in opposition* to accepted social norms, then there is really no need to neutralize. So far, the evidence is mixed. Some studies show that law violators approve of criminal behavior, such as theft and violence, and still others find evidence that even though they may be active participants themselves, criminals voice disapproval of illegal behavior.[115] Some studies indicate that law violators approve of social values such as honesty and fairness; others come to the opposite conclusion.[116]

In addition to youthful delinquent behaviors, the adoption of neutralization techniques has also been used to explain the onset of white-collar crime.[117] Businessmen may find it easier to cut corners by claiming that "the government exaggerates dangers to the consumer" (denial of injury) or the "markets are generally safe so the corporate producers should not have to take blame for the few injuries that occur" (denial of responsibility) or "the bottom line is all that matters" (appeal to higher loyalty). The need

to get ahead in the corporate world may help them neutralize the moral constraints that their parents may have taught them in adolescence, such as play fair, don't cheat, take responsibility.

The theory of neutralization, then, is a major contribution to the literature of crime and delinquency. It can account for the aging-out process: youths can forgo criminal behavior as adults because they never really rejected the morality of normative society. It helps explain the behavior of the occasional or nonchronic delinquent, who is able to successfully age out of crime. Because teens are not committed to criminality, as they mature they simply drift back into conventional behavior patterns. While they are young, justifications and excuses neutralize guilt and enable individuals to continue to feel good about themselves.[118] In contrast, people who remain criminals as adults may be using newly learned techniques to neutralize the wrongfulness of their actions and avoid guilt. For example, psychotherapists accused of sexually exploiting their clients blame the victim for "seducing them"; some claim there was little injury caused by the sexual encounter; others seek scapegoats to blame for their actions.[119]

The Criminological Enterprise
When Being Good Is Bad

In their neutralization theory, Sykes and Matza claim that neutralizations provide offenders with a means of preserving a noncriminal self-concept even as they engage in crime and deviance. Sykes and Matza's vision assumes that most criminals believe in conventional norms and values and must use neutralizations in order to shield themselves from the shame attached to criminal activity. Recent research by criminologist Volkan Topalli finds that Sykes and Matza may have ignored the influential street culture that exists in highly disadvantaged neighborhoods. Using data gleaned from 191 in-depth interviews with active criminals in St. Louis, Missouri, Topalli finds that street criminals living in disorganized, gang-ridden neighborhoods "disrespect authority, lionize honor and violence, and place individual needs above those of all others." Rather than having to neutralize conventional values in order to engage in deviant ones, these offenders do not experience guilt that requires neutralizations; they are "guilt free." There is no need for them to "drift" into criminality, Topalli finds, because their allegiance to nonconventional values and lack of guilt perpetually leave them in a state of openness to crime.

Rather than being contrite or ashamed, the offenders Topalli interviewed took great pride in their criminal activities and abilities. Bacca, a street robber who attacked a long-time neighbor without provocation, exemplified such sentiments:

Actually I felt proud of myself just for robbing him, just for doing what I did I felt proud of myself. I didn't feel like I did anything wrong, I didn't feel like I lost a friend 'cause the friends I do have . . . are lost, they're dead. I feel like I don't have anything to lose. I wanted to do just what I wanted to do.

Topalli refers to streetwise offenders such as Bacca as "hardcores," who experience no guilt for their actions and operate with little or no regard for the law. They have little contact with agents of formal social control or conventional norms because their crimes are not directed toward conventional society—they rob drug dealers. Most hardcores maintain no permanent home, staying in various residences as their whim dictates. Their lifestyles are almost entirely dominated by the street ethics of violence, self-sufficiency, and opportunism. Obsessed with a constant need for cash, drugs, and alcohol in order to "keep the party going," on the one hand, and limited by self-defeating and reckless spending habits on the other, they often engage in violent crime to bankroll their street life activities. They do not have to neutralize conventional values, because they have none.

Rather than neutralizing conventional values, hard-core criminals often have to neutralize deviant values: they are expected to be "bad" and have to explain good behavior. Even if they themselves are the victims of crime, they can never help police or even talk to them, a practice defined as snitching and universally despised and discouraged. Smokedog, a carjacker and drug dealer, described the anticipated guilt of colluding with the police in this way, "You know I ain't never told on nobody and I ain't never gonna tell on nobody 'cause I would feel funny in the world if I told on somebody. You know, I would feel funny, I would have regrets about what I did."

Street criminals are also expected to seek vengeance if they are the target of theft or violence. If they don't, their self-image is damaged, and they look weak and ineffective. If they decide against vengeance, they must neutralize their decision by convincing themselves that they are being merciful, respecting direct appeals by their target's family and friends. T-dog, a young drug dealer and car thief, told Topalli how he neutralized the decision not to seek revenge by allowing his uncle to "calm him down." The older man, a robber and drug dealer himself, intervened before T-dog could leave his house armed with two 9mm automatics: "That's basically what he told me, 'Calm down.' He took both my guns and gave me a little .22 to carry when I'm out to put me back on my feet. Gave me an ounce of crack and a pound of weed. That's what made me let it go." In other cases, offenders claimed the target was just not worth the effort, reserving their vengeance for those who were worthy opponents.

Do these findings indicate that neutralization theory is invalid? Topalli concludes that the strength of the theory is its emphasis on cognitive processes that occur prior to offending. He suggests that neutralization theory's current emphasis on a conventional cultural value orientation must be expanded to accommodate the values of the street culture.

CRITICAL THINKING

1. Are there deviant norms and values that you have to neutralize in order to engage in conventional behaviors? What neutralizations have you come up with in order to save face when your friends wanted to engage in some forms of deviance but you decided not to take the risk?

2. Do you agree with Topalli that kids in disorganized neighborhoods shun conventional values? Or do you agree with Sykes and Matza that everyone shares conventional norms and values?

SOURCES: Volkan Topalli, "When Being Good Is Bad: An Expansion of Neutralization Theory," *Criminology* 43 (2005): 797–836.

Are Learning Theories Valid?

Learning theories make a significant contribution to our understanding of the onset of criminal behavior. Nonetheless, the general learning model has been subject to some criticism. One complaint is that learning theorists fail to account for the origin of criminal definitions. How did the first "teacher" learn criminal techniques and definitions? Who came up with the original neutralization technique? And, as The Criminological Enterprise feature suggests, hard core offenders feel little need to neutralize moral restraints—they may not have any!

Learning theories also imply that people systematically learn techniques that enable them to be active and successful criminals, but they fail to adequately explain spontaneous and wanton acts of violence and damage and other expressive crimes that appear to have little utility or purpose. Principles of differential association can easily explain shoplifting, but is it possible that a random shooting is caused by excessive deviant definitions? It is estimated that about 70 percent of all arrestees were under the influence of drugs and alcohol when they committed their crime. Do "crack heads" pause to neutralize their moral inhibitions before mugging a victim? Do drug-involved kids stop to consider what they have "learned" about moral values?[120]

Little evidence exists substantiating that people learn the techniques that enable them to become criminals before they actually commit criminal acts. It is equally plausible that people who are already deviant seek out others with similar lifestyles. Early onset of deviant behavior is now considered a key determinant of criminal careers. It is difficult to see how extremely young adolescents had the opportunity to learn criminal behavior and attitudes within a peer group setting.

Despite these criticisms, learning theories maintain an important place in the study of delinquent and criminal behavior. Unlike social structure theories, these theories are not limited to the explanation of a single facet of antisocial activity—for example, lower-class gang activity; they may be used to explain criminality across all class structures. Even corporate executives may be exposed to a variety of procriminal definitions and learn to neutralize moral constraints.

Edwin H. Sutherland served as the 29th president of the American Sociological Society. His presidential address, "White-Collar Criminality," was delivered at the organization's annual meeting in Philadelphia in December 1939. To read this groundbreaking talk, visit the Criminal Justice CourseMate at cengagebrain.com, then access the "Web Links" for this chapter.

SOCIAL CONTROL THEORY

Social control theories maintain that all people have the potential to violate the law and that modern society presents many opportunities for illegal activity. Criminal activities, such as drug abuse and car theft, are often exciting pastimes that hold the promise of immediate reward and gratification.

Considering the attractions of crime, the question control theorists pose is: why do people obey the rules of society? A choice theorist would respond that it is the fear of punishment; structural theorists would say that obedience is a function of having access to legitimate opportunities; learning theorists would explain that obedience is acquired through contact with law-abiding parents and peers. In contrast, social control theorists argue that people obey the law because behavior and passions are being controlled by internal and external forces. Because they have been properly socialized, most people have developed a strong moral sense, which renders them incapable of hurting others and violating social norms. They develop a **commitment to conformity**, which requires that they obey the rules of society.[121] Properly socialized people believe that getting caught at criminal activity will hurt a dearly loved parent or jeopardize their chance at a college scholarship, or perhaps they feel that their job will be forfeited if they get in trouble with the law. In other words, people's behavior, including criminal activity, is controlled by their attachment and commitment to conventional institutions, individuals, and processes. On the other hand, those who have not been properly socialized, who lack a commitment to others or themselves, are free to violate the law and engage in deviant behavior. Those who are "uncommitted" are not deterred by the threat of legal punishments because they have little to lose.[122]

Self-Concept and Crime

Early versions of control theory speculated that control was a product of social interactions. Maladaptive social relations produced weak self-concept and poor self-esteem, rendering kids at risk to crime. In contrast, youths who felt good about themselves and maintained a positive attitude were able to resist the temptations of the streets. As early as 1951, sociologist Albert Reiss described how delinquents had weak egos.[123] Scott Briar and Irving Piliavin noted that youths who believe criminal activity will damage their self-image and their relationships with others will be most likely to conform to social rules; they have a commitment to conformity. In contrast, those less concerned about their social standing are free to violate the law.[124] In his **containment theory**, pioneering control theorist Walter Reckless argued that a strong self-image insulates a youth from the pressures and pulls of crimi-nogenic influences in the environment.[125] In a series of studies conducted within the school setting, Reckless and his colleagues found that nondelinquent youths are able to maintain a positive self-image in the face of environmental pressures toward delinquency.[126]

It is Travis Hirschi's vision of social control, articulated in his highly influential 1969 book *Causes of Delinquency*, that remains the dominant version of the theory.[127]

Hirschi's Social Bond Theory

In his insightful work, Hirschi links the onset of criminal-ity to the weakening of the ties that bind people to society. He assumes that all individuals are potential law violators, but they are kept under control because they fear that il-legal behavior will damage their relationships with friends, parents, neighbors, teachers, and employers. Without these social ties or bonds, and in the absence of sensitivity to and interest in others, a person is free to commit criminal acts. Hirschi does not view society as containing competing sub-cultures with unique value systems. Most people are aware of the prevailing moral and legal codes. He suggests, how-ever, that in all elements of society people vary in how they respond to conventional social rules and values. Among all ethnic, religious, racial, and social groups, people whose bond to society is weak may fall prey to criminogenic be-havior patterns.

CONNECTIONS

Though his work has achieved a prominent place in criminological literature, Hirschi, along with Michael Gottfredson, has restructured his concept of control by integrating biosocial, psychological, and rational choice theory ideas into a "General Theory of Crime." This the-ory of self-control is discussed more fully in Chapter 9.

Elements of the Social Bond   Hirschi argues that the **so-cial bond** a person maintains with society is divided into four main elements: attachment, commitment, involvement, and belief (Figure 7.4).

- *Attachment.* Attachment refers to a person's sensitivity to and interest in others.[128] Without a sense of attachment, psychologists believe a person becomes a psychopath and loses the ability to relate coherently to the world. The acceptance of social norms and the development of a social conscience depend on attachment to and caring for other human beings. Hirschi views parents, peers, and schools as the important social institutions with which a person should maintain ties. Attachment to parents is the most important. Even if a family is shattered by divorce or separation, a child must retain a strong attachment to one or both parents. Without this attachment, it is unlikely that feelings of respect for oth-ers in authority will develop.

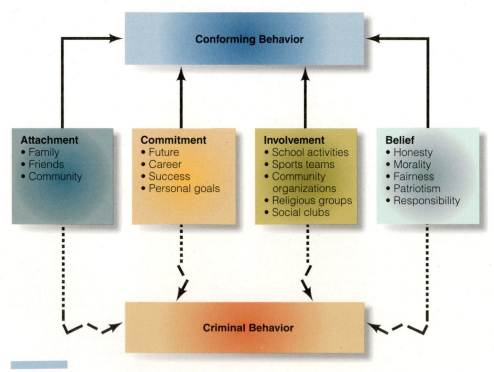

FIGURE 7.4
Elements of the Social Bond

- *Commitment.* Commitment involves the time, energy, and effort expended in conventional lines of action, such as getting an education and saving money for the future. If people build a strong commitment to conventional society, they will be less likely to engage in acts that will jeopardize their hard-won position. Conversely, the lack of commitment to conventional values may foreshadow a condition in which risk-taking behavior, such as crime, becomes a reasonable behavior alternative. The association may be reciprocal. Kids who drink and engage in deviant behavior are more likely to fail in school; kids who fail in school are more likely to later drink and engage in deviant behavior.[129]
- *Involvement.* Heavy involvement in conventional activities leaves little time for illegal behavior. When people become involved in school, recreation, and family, Hirschi believes, it insulates them from the potential lure of criminal behavior, whereas idleness enhances it.
- *Belief.* People who live in the same social setting often share common moral beliefs; they may adhere to such values as sharing, sensitivity to the rights of others, and admiration for the legal code. If these beliefs are absent or weakened, individuals are more likely to participate in antisocial or illegal acts.

Hirschi further suggests that the interrelationship of social bond elements controls subsequent behavior. People who feel kinship and sensitivity to parents and friends should be more likely to adopt and work toward legitimate goals or gain skills that help them avoid antisocial or dangerous behaviors. Girls, for example, who have higher levels of bonding to parents and develop good social skills in adolescence are less likely to experience dating violence as young adults. The reason: a close bond to parents reduces early adolescent alcohol use, a factor that shields girls from victimization.[130]

Testing Social Bond Theory
One of Hirschi's most significant contributions was his attempt to test the principal hypotheses of social bond theory. He administered a detailed self-report survey to a sample of more than 4,000 junior and senior high school students in Contra Costa County, California.[131] In a detailed analysis of the data, Hirschi found considerable evidence to support the control theory model. Among Hirschi's more important findings are the following:

- Youths who were strongly attached to their parents were less likely to commit criminal acts.
- Commitment to conventional values, such as striving to get a good education and refusing to drink alcohol and "cruise around," was indicative of conventional behavior.
- Youths involved in conventional activity, such as homework, were less likely to engage in criminal behavior.
- Youths involved in unconventional behavior, such as smoking and drinking, were more delinquency prone.
- Youths who maintained weak and distant relationships with people tended toward delinquency.

- Those who shunned unconventional acts were attached to their peers.
- Delinquents and nondelinquents shared similar beliefs about society.

Supporting Research
Hirschi's data lent important support to the validity of control theory. Even when the statistical significance of his findings was less than he expected, the direction of his research data was notably consistent. Only in very rare instances did his findings contradict the theory's most critical assumptions.

Hirschi's version of social control theory has been corroborated by numerous research studies, in the United States and abroad, showing that delinquent youth often feel detached from society.[132] Their relationships within the family, peer group, and school often appear strained, indicative of a weakened social bond.[133] Associations among indicators of lack of attachment, belief, commitment, and involvement with measures of delinquency have tended to be positive and significant.[134] In contrast, strong positive attachments help control delinquency.[135]

- *Attachment.* Research indicates that, as Hirschi predicts, kids who are attached to their families, friends, and school are less likely to get involved in a deviant peer group and consequently less likely to engage in criminal activities.[136] Teens who are attached to their parents are also able to develop the social skills that equip them both to maintain harmonious social ties and to escape life stresses such as school failure.[137] In contrast, family detachment—including intrafamily conflict, abuse of children, and lack of affection, supervision, and family pride—are predictive of delinquent conduct.[138]
  Attachment to education is equally important. Youths who are detached from the educational experience are at risk of criminality; those who are committed to school are less likely to engage in delinquent acts.[139] Detachment and alienation from school may be even more predictive of delinquency than school failure and/or educational underachievement.[140]
- *Belief.* There is support for Hirschi's view that holding positive beliefs is inversely related to criminality. Children who are involved in religious activities and hold conventional religious beliefs are less likely to become involved in substance abuse.[141] Kids who live in areas marked by strong religious values and who hold strong religious beliefs themselves are less likely to engage in delinquent activities than adolescents who do not hold such beliefs or who live in less devout communities.[142]
- *Commitment.* As predicted by Hirschi, kids who are committed to future success and achievement are less likely to become involved in delinquent behaviors than those who lack such commitment.[143]
- *Involvement.* Research shows that youths who are involved in conventional leisure activities, such as supervised social activities and noncompetitive sports, are

Profiles in Crime
Alpha Dog

AP Images/Federal Police/HO

In November of 2005, twenty-five-year-old Jesse James Hollywood (that is his real name) was enjoying a comfortable life in Brazil, teaching English and living in a fashionable neighborhood, when he was arrested and sent back to California to face charges of kidnapping and killing a 15-year-old boy.

His story is rather unique. Even though Hollywood had never held a job, he was able, by age 19, to purchase a $200,000 house in West Hills, California, and a Mercedes. His place became a favorite hangout for local kids who came and went at all hours of the day. Jesse was a popular guy, an outgoing kid who, despite being short in stature, was an excellent athlete. How was Jesse able to do all this? Unknown to many, he was a large-scale marijuana dealer.

Jesse's world began to unravel when he came up with a scheme to get money owed to him by Benjamin Markowitz, 22, who was one of his customers. Hollywood and some friends headed for Markowitz's family home on August 6, 2000, planning to kidnap him and hold him for ransom. On the way there, Jesse and his friends spotted Markowitz's 15-year-old stepbrother, Nicholas, whom they kidnapped and held for a few days. Mistakenly believing they would receive life sentences for kidnapping, they forced Nick Markowitz to walk a mile into Los Padres National Forest before being shot and buried in a shallow grave. His body was discovered four days later by hikers.

Four other kids were tried and convicted in the case, but Hollywood escaped and became the subject of an international manhunt, his mug shot plastered on the FBI's website. He wound up in Brazil, where he used fake papers that identified him as Michael Costa Giroux, a native of Rio de Janeiro. Cooperating with the FBI, Brazilian authorities deported him as an illegal alien. On July 8, 2009, a jury found him guilty of kidnapping and first-degree murder with special circumstances; afterward Hollywood was sentenced to life in prison.

The 2006 film *Alpha Dog*, starring Bruce Willis, Justin Timberlake, and Sharon Stone, is based on the case.

SOURCES: Jeremiah Marquez, "Longtime Fugitive Jesse James Hollywood Captured in Brazil," March 11, 2005, http://legacy.signonsandiego.com/news/state/20050310-1604-ca-jesse-jameshollywood.html (accessed September 26, 2010); Amy Silverstein, "Jesse James Hollywood Sentenced to Life," *Santa Barbara Independent*, July 14, 2009, www.independent.com/news/2009/jul/15/jesse-james-hollywood-sentenced-life/ (accessed September 26, 2010).

less likely to engage in delinquency than those who are involved in unconventional leisure activities and unsupervised, peer-oriented social pursuits.[144] One study found that students who engage in a significant amount of extracurricular activities from 8th grade through 12th grade are more likely to experience high academic achievement and prosocial behaviors extending into young adulthood.[145]

Cross-national surveys have also supported the general findings of Hirschi's control theory.[146] For example, one study of Canadian youth found that perception of parental attachment was the strongest predictor of delinquent or law-abiding behavior. Teens who are attached to their parents may develop the social skills that equip them both to maintain harmonious social ties and to escape life stresses such as school failure.[147]

The Profiles in Crime feature describes a case that may rest on a frayed and tattered bond to society.

Opposing Views A great deal of scholarly research has been conducted to corroborate social control theory by replicating Hirschi's original survey techniques.[148] There has been significant empirical support for Hirschi's work, but there are also those who question some or all of its elements.

Here are some elements that have come under criticism and need further study:

- *Friendship.* One significant criticism concerns Hirschi's contention that delinquents are detached loners whose bond to their family and friends has been broken. Some critics have questioned whether delinquents (a) do have strained relations with family and peers and (b) may be influenced by close relationships with deviant peers and family members. A number of research efforts do show that delinquents maintain relationships with deviant peers and are influenced by members of their deviant peer group.[149] Delinquents, however, may not be "lone wolves" whose only personal relationships are exploitive; their friendship patterns seem quite close to those of conventional youth.[150] In fact, some types of offenders, such as drug abusers, may maintain even more intimate relations with their peers than nonabusers.[151] Hirschi would counter that what appears to be a close friendship is really a relationship of convenience and that "birds of a feather flock together" only when it suits their criminal activities. His view is supported by recent research conducted by criminologists Lisa Stolzenberg and Stewart D'Alessio, who found that most juvenile offenses are committed by individuals acting alone and that group offending, when it does occur, is incidental and of little importance to explaining the onset of delinquency.[152]

■ *Not all elements of the bond are equal.* Hirschi makes little distinction between the importance of each element of the social bond, yet research evidence suggests that there may be differences. Some adolescents who report high levels of "involvement," which Hirschi suggests should reduce delinquency, are involved in criminal behavior. As kids get involved in behaviors outside the home, it is possible that parental control weakens, and youths have greater opportunity to commit crime.[153] When asked, children report that concepts such as "involvement" and "belief" have relatively little influence over behavior patterns."[154]

■ *Deviant involvement.* Adolescents who report high levels of involvement, which Hirschi suggests should reduce delinquency, actually report high levels of criminal behavior. Typically, these are kids who are involved in activities outside the home without parental supervision.[155] Kids who spend a lot of time hanging out with their friends, unsupervised by parents and/or other authority figures, and who own cars that give them the mobility to get into even more trouble are the ones most likely to get involved in antisocial acts such as drinking and taking drugs.[156] This is especially true of dating relationships: kids who date, especially if they have multiple partners, are the ones who are likely to get into trouble and engage in delinquent acts.[157] It is possible that although involvement is important, it depends on the behavior in which a person is involved!

■ *Deviant peers and parents.* Hirschi's conclusion that any form of social attachment is beneficial, even to deviant peers and parents, has also been disputed. Rather than deter delinquency attachment to deviant peers, it may support and nurture antisocial behavior. In a now classic study, criminologist Michael Hindelang found that attachment to delinquent peers escalated rather than restricted criminality.[158] In a similar fashion, a number of research efforts have found that youths attached to drug-abusing parents are more likely to become drug users themselves.[159] Attachment to deviant family members, peers, and associates may help motivate youths to commit crime and facilitate their antisocial acts.[160]

■ *Restricted in scope.* There is some question as to whether the theory can explain all modes of criminality (as Hirschi maintains) or is restricted to particular groups or forms of criminality. Control variables seem better able to explain minor delinquency (such as alcohol and marijuana abuse) than more serious criminal acts and associations (such as the association between child abuse and violence).[161] Research efforts have found control variables are more predictive of female than male behavior.[162] Perhaps girls are more deeply influenced by the quality of their bond to society.

■ *Changing bonds.* Social bonds seem to change over time, a phenomenon ignored by Hirschi.[163] It is possible that at one age level, weak bonds (to parents) lead to delinquency, while at another, strong bonds (to peers) lead to delinquency.

■ *Crime and social bonds.* It is possible that Hirschi miscalculated the direction of the relationship between criminality and a weakened social bond.[164] Social bond theory projects that a weakened bond leads to delinquency, but it is possible that the chain of events may flow in the opposite direction: kids who break the law find that their bond to parents, schools, and society eventually becomes weak and attenuated.[165]

Although these criticisms need to be addressed with further research, the weight of existing empirical evidence supports control theory, and it has emerged as one of the preeminent theories in criminology. For many criminologists, it is perhaps the most important way of understanding the onset of youthful misbehavior.

SOCIAL REACTION THEORY

Social reaction theory, commonly called labeling theory (the two terms are used interchangeably here), explains how criminal careers form based on destructive social interactions and encounters. Its roots are found in the **symbolic interaction theory** of sociologists Charles Horton Cooley and George Herbert Mead, and later, Herbert Blumer.[166] Symbolic interaction theory holds that people communicate

AP Images/John Miller

According to labeling theory, perceptions guide behavior. Would you want to invite this guy to lunch with your family? He is The Scary Guy (his real name) and he spends his time teaching students and adults about what they can do to change the world by taking responsibility for their own behavior. His mission is to eliminate hate, violence, and prejudice worldwide. He is shown here hammering home his message at Valencia Middle School in Tucson, Arizona. What do you think of him now?

via symbols—gestures, signs, words, or images—that stand for or represent something else. For example, a gold band on your ring finger conveys many meanings: married; stable; sexually off limits; conventional.

People interpret symbolic gestures from others and incorporate them in their self-image. When a teacher puts an A on your paper, it tells you that you are an excellent student, and the symbol pumps up your self-image. Symbols are used by others to let people know how well they are doing and whether they are liked or appreciated. Wearing a Rolex and driving a Mercedes is a symbolic way of letting people know that you are quite successful. Designer clothes display their symbol to let people know that the wearer has both taste and income. How people view reality then depends on the content of the messages and situations they encounter, the subjective interpretation of these interactions, and how they shape future behavior. There is no objective reality. When someone takes another person's life, it could be self-defense or cold-blooded murder, depending on how people interpret the act. The police officer who punches a suspect may, depending on how people interpret the incident, get a medal for subduing a dangerous criminal or be suspended for police brutality. Because interpretation changes over time, so do the meanings of concepts and symbols.

Social reaction theory picks up on these concepts of *interaction* and *interpretation*.[167] Throughout their lives, people are given a variety of symbolic labels and ways to interact with others. These labels represent behavior and attitude characteristics; labels help define not just one trait but the whole person. People labeled insane are also assumed to be dangerous, dishonest, unstable, violent, strange, and otherwise unsound. Valued labels, including smart, honest, and hard working, suggest overall competence. These labels can improve self-image and social standing. Research shows that people who are labeled with one positive trait, such as being physically attractive, are assumed to maintain other traits, such as being intelligent and competent.[168] In contrast, negative labels—including troublemaker, mentally ill, and stupid—help stigmatize the recipients of these labels and reduce their self-image. Those who have accepted these labels are more prone to engage in deviant behaviors than those whose self-image has not been so tarnished.[169]

Both positive and negative labels involve subjective interpretation of behavior: a troublemaker is merely someone people label as troublesome. There need not be any objective proof or measure indicating that the person is actually a troublemaker. Though a label may be a function of rumor, innuendo, or unfounded suspicion, its adverse impact can be immense.

Patrick Corrigan notes that labeling and **stigma** can harm and diminish both the public and private self. Some groups bear public stigma, and being labeled as part of a stigmatized group "robs people of social opportunities."[170] Public stigma occurs when there is prejudice about a group that stigmatizes members (i.e., sex workers, mental patients) and helps

exclude them from social opportunities, including housing and work. In contrast, self-stigma occurs when negative social attitudes are internalized, subsequently harming a person's self-esteem, and inducing shame. If during the self-stigma process a devalued status is conferred by a significant other—teacher, police officer, elder, parent, or valued peer—the negative label may cause permanent harm. The degree to which a person is perceived as a social deviant may affect his or her treatment at home, at work, at school, and in other social situations. Children may find that their parents consider them a bad influence on younger brothers and sisters. School officials may limit them to classes reserved for people with behavioral problems. Likewise, when adults are labeled as criminal, ex-con, or drug addict, they may find their eligibility for employment severely restricted. Furthermore, if the label is bestowed as the result of conviction for a criminal offense, the labeled person may be subjected to official sanctions ranging from a mild reprimand to incarceration.

FIGURE 7.5
The Labeling Process

Beyond these immediate results, labeling advocates maintain that, depending on the visibility of the label and the manner and severity with which it is applied, a person will have an increasing commitment to a deviant career. They may be watched and become the leading suspect when a similar crime occurs. Labeled people may find themselves turning to others similarly stigmatized for support and companionship. Isolated from conventional society, they may identify themselves as members of an outcast group and become locked into a deviant career. Figure 7.5 illustrates this process. The Thinking Like a Criminologist feature addresses this issue.

Interpreting Crime

Labeling theorists use an interactionist definition of crime. In a defining statement, sociologist Kai Erickson argues, "Deviance is not a property inherent in certain forms of behavior, it is a property conferred upon those forms by the audience which directly or indirectly witnesses them."[171] Crime and deviance, therefore, are defined by the social audience's reaction to people and their behavior and the subsequent effects of that reaction; they are not defined by the moral content of the illegal act itself.[172]

In another famous statement, Howard Becker sums up the importance of the audience's reaction:

> Social groups create deviance by making rules whose infractions constitute deviance, and by applying those rules to particular people and labeling them as outsiders. From this point of view, deviance is not a quality of the act a person commits, but rather a consequence of the application by others of rules and sanctions to an "offender." The deviant is one to whom the label has successfully been applied; deviant behavior is behavior that people so label.[173]

In its purest form, social reaction theory argues that such crimes as murder, rape, and assault are only bad or evil because people label them as such. After all, the difference between an excusable act and a criminal one is often a matter of legal definition, which changes from place to place and from year to year.

Becker refers to people who create rules as *moral entrepreneurs*. An example of a moral entrepreneur today might be members of an ultra-orthodox religious group who target the gay lifestyle and mount a campaign to prevent gays from adopting children or conducting same-sex marriages.[174]

The difference between a forcible rape and a consensual sexual encounter often rests on whom the members of a jury believe and how they interpret the events that took place. The difference between an excusable act and a criminal one is often subject to change and modification. Remember Genarlow Wilson: was he a sex offender or a kid who partied too much? It depends on your viewpoint and the view of those in power. Acts such as performing an abortion, using marijuana, possessing a handgun, and gambling have been legal at some times and places and illegal at others.

Differential Enforcement

An important principle of social reaction theory is that the law is differentially applied, benefiting those who hold economic and social power and penalizing the powerless. The probability of being brought under the control of legal authority is a function of a person's race, wealth, gender, and social standing. A core concept of social reaction theory is that police officers are more likely to suspect, question, search, and arrest males, minority group members, and those in the lower class and to use their discretionary powers to give beneficial treatment to more favored groups.[175] The term **racial profiling** has been used to signify that police suspicion is often directed at minority group males. Minorities and the poor are more likely to be prosecuted for criminal offenses and to receive harsher punishments when convicted.[176] Judges may sympathize with white defendants and help them avoid criminal labels, especially if they seem to come from "good families," whereas minority defendants are not afforded that luxury.[177]

This evidence is used to support the labeling concept that personal characteristics and social interactions are

---

THINKING LIKE A CRIMINOLOGIST 〉 **An Ethical Dilemma**

Bound for College/Bound for Trouble

The principal of the local high school, a big fan of control theory (she used to be in your class), asks for your opinion on a new policy she intends to propose to the school board. She wants to increase students' bond to education and the school experience by creating three tracks of students: one college bound, the other average, and the third for kids who need remedial help. The college-bound would take advanced math and science, the average track would be reserved for those who plan to forgo college, and the remedial track would offer less-challenging course work and be designed to get the students through high school. She argues that the

Chris Schmidt/iStockphoto

college-bound students will be recognized for their achievements and rewarded for their efforts, a process that will solidify their bond to the educational experience, all the while insulating them from more disruptive teens.

〉〉 **Write a memo to the principal commenting on the ethics of this approach: Is it fair to reward one group of students while isolating another? What would be the consequences of such a policy? Would it encourage the better students to achieve or might it damage those who do not fall in the elite group? Would such a policy negatively label and stigmatize kids who were not in the college-bound track?**

more important variables in developing criminal careers than merely violating the law. Social reaction theorists also argue that the content of the law reflects power relationships in society. They point to the evidence that white-collar crimes—economic crimes usually committed by members of the upper class—are most often punished by a relatively small fine and rarely result in a prison sentence. This treatment contrasts with long prison sentences given to those convicted of "street crimes," such as burglary or car theft, which are the province of the lower, powerless classes.[178]

In sum, a major premise of social reaction theory is that the law is differentially constructed and applied, depending on the offenders. It favors the powerful members of society who direct its content and penalizes people whose actions represent a threat to those in control, such as minority group members and the poor who demand equal rights.[179]

Consequences of Labeling

This labeling process is important because once they are stigmatized as troublemakers, adolescents begin to reassess their self-image. Parents who label their children as troublemakers promote deviance amplification. Labeling alienates parents from their children, and negative labels reduce children's self-image and increase delinquency; this process is referred to as **reflected appraisals**.[180] Parental labeling is extremely damaging because it may cause adolescents to seek deviant peers whose behavior amplifies the effect of the labeling.[181]

As they mature, children are in danger of receiving repeated, intensive, official labeling, which has been shown to produce self-labeling and to damage identities.[182] Kids who perceive that they have been negatively labeled by significant others, such as peers and teachers, are also more likely to self-report delinquent behavior and to adopt a deviant self-concept.[183] They are likely to make deviant friends and join gangs, associations that escalate their involvement in criminal activities.[184] If their deviant activities land them in court, the effects can be devastating. An official label increases the risk of their later dropping out of high school. Rather than deterring crime, court intervention increases the likelihood of future criminality.[185] Ironically, the official labeling process may take a greater toll on novice criminals than on more experienced offenders—a consequence that indicates the power of negative labels.[186]

As these youth become adults, the labeling process continues to take its toll. Male drug users labeled as addicts by social control agencies eventually become self-labeled and increase their drug use.[187] People arrested in domestic violence cases, especially those with a low stake in conformity (for example, those who are jobless and unmarried), increase offending after being given official labels.[188] And once in prison, inmates labeled high risk are more likely to have disciplinary problems than those who are spared such negative labels.[189]

Labels are believed to produce stigma. The labeled deviant becomes a social outcast who may be prevented from enjoying a higher education, well-paying jobs, and other social benefits. Such alienation leads to a low self-image.

Joining Deviant Cliques   When people are labeled as deviant, they may join up with similarly outcast delinquent peers who facilitate their behavior.[190] Eventually, antisocial behavior becomes habitual and automatic.[191] The desire to join deviant cliques and groups may stem from a self-rejecting attitude ("at times, I think I am no good at all"), which eventually results in a weakened commitment to conventional values and behaviors. In turn, these people may acquire motives to deviate from social norms. Facilitating this attitude and value transformation is the bond social outcasts form with similarly labeled peers in the form of a deviant subculture.[192]

Membership in a deviant subculture often involves conforming to group norms that conflict with those of conventional society. Deviant behaviors that defy conventional values can serve a number of different purposes. Some acts are designed to show contempt for the source of the negative labels. Other acts are planned to distance the transgressor from further contact with the source of criticism (for example, an adolescent runs away from critical parents).[193]

Retrospective Reading   After someone is labeled because of some unusual or inexplicable act, people begin to reconstruct the culprit's identity so that the act and the label become understandable (e.g., "we always knew there was something wrong with that boy"). It is not unusual for the media to lead the way and interview boyhood friends of an assassin or serial killer. On the 11 o'clock news we can hear them report that the suspect was withdrawn, suspicious, and negativistic as a youth, expressing violent thoughts and ideation, a loner, troubled, and so on. Yet, until now no one was suspicious and nothing was done. This is referred to as **retrospective reading**, a process in which the past of the labeled person is reviewed and reevaluated to fit his or her current status. By conducting a retrospective reading, we can now understand what prompted his current behavior; therefore, the label must be accurate.[194]

Dramatization of Evil   Labels become the basis of personal identity. As the negative feedback of law enforcement agencies, parents, friends, teachers, and other figures amplifies the force of the original label, stigmatized offenders may begin to reevaluate their own identities. If they are not really evil or bad, they may ask themselves, why is everyone making such a fuss? Frank Tannenbaum, a social reaction theory pioneer, referred to this process as the **dramatization of evil**. With respect to the consequences of labeling delinquent behavior, Tannenbaum stated:

> The process of making the criminal, therefore, is a process of tagging, defining, identifying, making conscious and self-conscious; it becomes a way of stimulating, suggesting and evoking the very traits that are

complained of. If the theory of relation of response to stimulus has any meaning, the entire process of dealing with the young delinquent is mischievous insofar as it identifies him to himself or to the environment as a delinquent person. The person becomes the thing he is described as being.[195]

Primary and Secondary Deviance

One of the best-known views of the labeling process is Edwin Lemert's concept of primary deviance and secondary deviance.[196] According to Lemert, **primary deviance** involves norm violations or crimes that have very little influence on the actor and can be quickly forgotten. For example, a college student takes a "five-finger discount" at the campus bookstore. He successfully steals a textbook, uses it to get an A in a course, goes on to graduate, is admitted into law school, and later becomes a famous judge. Because his shoplifting goes unnoticed, it is a relatively unimportant event that has little bearing on his future life.

In contrast, **secondary deviance** occurs when a deviant event comes to the attention of significant others or social control agents who apply a negative label. The newly labeled offender then reorganizes his or her behavior and personality around the consequences of the deviant act. The shoplifting student is caught by a security guard and expelled from college. With his law school dreams dashed and his future cloudy, his options are limited; people who know him say he "lacks character," and he begins to share their opinion. He eventually becomes a drug dealer and winds up in prison (Figure 7.6).

Secondary deviance involves resocialization into a deviant role. The labeled person is transformed into one who,

according to Lemert, "employs his behavior or a role based upon it as a means of defense, attack, or adjustment to the overt and covert problems created by the consequent social reaction to him."[197] Secondary deviance produces a deviance amplification effect. Offenders feel isolated from the mainstream of society and become firmly locked within their deviant role. They may seek out others similarly labeled to form deviant subcultures or groups. Ever more firmly enmeshed in their deviant role, they are locked into an escalating cycle of deviance, apprehension, more powerful labels, and identity transformation. Lemert's concept of secondary deviance expresses the core of social reaction theory: deviance is a process in which one's identity is transformed. Efforts to control the offenders, whether by treatment or punishment, simply help lock them in their deviant role.

Research on Social Reaction Theory

Research on social reaction theory can be classified into two distinct categories. The first focuses on the characteristics of offenders who are chosen for labels. The theory maintains that these offenders should be relatively powerless people who are unable to defend themselves against the negative labeling. The second type of research attempts to discover the effects of being labeled. Labeling theorists predict that people who are negatively labeled should view themselves as deviant and commit increasing amounts of criminal behavior.

Who Gets Labeled? The poor and powerless people are victimized by the law and justice system; labels are not equally distributed across class and racial lines. Critics charge that although substantive and procedural laws govern almost every aspect of the American criminal justice system, discretionary decision making controls its operation at every level. From the police officer's decision on whom to arrest to the prosecutor's decisions on whom to charge and for how many and what kind of charges, to the court's decision on whom to release or on whom to permit bail, to the grand jury's decision on indictment, to the judge's decision on the length of the sentence, discretion works to the detriment of minorities, including African Americans, Latinos, Asian Americans, and Native Americans.[198]

Although these arguments are persuasive, little definitive evidence exists that the justice system is inherently unfair and biased. Procedures such as arrest, prosecution, and sentencing seem to be more often based on legal factors, such as prior record and severity of the crime, than on personal characteristics, such as class and race.[199] However, it is possible that discriminatory practices in the labeling process are subtle and hidden. For example, in a thorough review of sentencing disparity, Samuel Walker, Cassia Spohn, and Miriam DeLone identify what they call **contextual discrimination**. This term refers to judges' practices in some jurisdictions of

FIGURE 7.6
The Process of Creating Secondary Deviance

imposing harsher sentences on African Americans only in some instances, such as when they victimize whites and not other African Americans.[200] They may also be more likely to impose prison sentences on racial minorities in "borderline" cases for which whites get probation. According to their view, racism is very subtle and hard to detect, but it still exerts an influence in the distribution of criminal sanctions.

Labeling Effects   Considerable evidence indicates social sanctions lead to self-labeling and deviance amplification.[201] Children negatively labeled by their parents routinely suffer a variety of problems, including antisocial behavior and school failure.[202] This process has been observed in the United States and abroad, indicating that the labeling process is universal, especially in nations in which a brush with the law brings personal dishonor, such as China and Japan.[203]

Empirical evidence supports the view that labeling plays a significant role in persistent offending.[204] Although labels may not cause adolescents to initiate criminal behaviors, experienced criminals are significantly more likely to continue offending if they believe their parents and peers view them in a negative light; they now have a "damaged identity."[205] Maintaining a damaged identity after official labeling may, along with other negative social reactions from society, produce a "cumulative disadvantage," which provokes some adolescents into repeating their antisocial behaviors.[206] Using longitudinal data obtained from youths ages 13 to 22, Jön Gunnar Bernburg and Marvin Krohn found evidence that, rather than deterring future offending, the "cumulative disadvantage" created by official intervention actually increases the probability that a labeled person will get involved in subsequent antisocial behavior. A label triggers exclusionary processes that limit conventional opportunities, such as educational attainment and employment. Kids who were labeled in adolescence were much more likely to engage in crime in early adulthood unless they were able to overcome labels and do well in school and obtain meaningful employment opportunities.[207]

Is Labeling Theory Valid?

Labeling theory has been the subject of academic debate in criminological circles. Those who criticize it point to its inability to specify the conditions that must exist before an act or individual is labeled deviant—that is, why some people are labeled and others remain "secret deviants."[208]

There is also some question about the real cost of being labeled. In an in-depth analysis of research on the crime-producing effects of labels, criminologist Charles Tittle found little evidence that stigma produces crime.[209] Tittle claims that many criminal careers occur without labeling; that labeling often comes after, rather than before, chronic offending; and that criminal careers may not follow even when labeling takes place. Getting labeled by the justice system and having an enduring criminal record may have little

effect on people who have been burdened with social and emotional problems since birth.[210]

While these criticisms are telling, criminologists Raymond Paternoster and Leeann Iovanni have identified features of the labeling perspective that are important contributions to the study of criminality:[211]

- The labeling perspective identifies the role played by social control agents in the process of crime causation. Criminal behavior cannot be fully understood if the agencies and individuals empowered to control and treat it are neglected.
- Labeling theory recognizes that criminality is not a disease or pathological behavior. It focuses attention on the social interactions and reactions that shape individuals and their behavior.
- Labeling theory distinguishes between criminal acts (primary deviance) and criminal careers (secondary deviance) and shows that these concepts must be interpreted and treated differently.

Labeling theory is also important because of its focus on interaction as well as the situations surrounding the crime. Rather than viewing the criminal as a robot-like creature whose actions are predetermined, it recognizes that crime is often the result of complex interactions and processes. The decision to commit crime involves actions of a variety of people, including peers, the victim, the police, and other key characters. Labels may expedite crime because they guide the actions of all parties involved in these criminal interactions. Actions deemed innocent when performed by one person are considered provocative when someone who has been labeled as deviant engages in them. Similarly, labeled people may be quick to judge, take offense, or misinterpret behavior of others because of past experience.

Labeling theory is also supported by research showing that convicted criminals who are placed in treatment programs aimed at reconfiguring their self-image may be able to develop revamped identities and desist from crime. Some are able to go through "redemption rituals" in which they are able to cast off their damaged identities and develop new ones. As a result, they develop an improved self-concept, which reflects the positive reinforcement they receive while in treatment.[212]

EVALUATING SOCIAL PROCESS THEORIES

The branches of social process theory—social learning, social control, and social reaction—are compatible because they suggest that criminal behavior is part of the socialization process. When interactions with critically important social institutions and processes—the family, schools, justice system, peer groups, employers, and neighbors—are troubled and disturbed, people may turn to criminal solutions for their problems.

Though there is some disagreement about the relative importance of those influences and the form they take, there seems to be little question that social interactions shape the behavior, beliefs, values, and self-image of the offender. People who have learned deviant social values, find themselves detached from conventional social relationships, or are the subject of stigma and labels from significant others will be the most likely to fall prey to criminal behavior. These negative influences can affect people in all walks of life, beginning in their youth and continuing through their majority. The major strength of the social process view is the vast body of empirical data showing that delinquents and criminals are people who grew up in dysfunctional families, who had troubled childhoods, and who failed at school, at work, and in marriage. Prison data show that these characteristics are typical of inmates.

Although persuasive, these theories do not always account for the patterns and fluctuations in the crime rate. If social process theories are valid, for example, people in the West and South must be socialized differently from those in the Midwest and New England because these latter regions have much lower crime rates. How can the fact that crime rates are lower in October than in July be explained if crime is a function of learning or control? How can social processes explain why criminals escalate their activity or why they desist from crime as they age? Once a social bond is broken, how can it be "reattached"? Once crime is "learned," how can it be "unlearned"?

Concept Summary 7.1 sets out the premises, strengths, and research focus of social process theories.

CONCEPT SUMMARY 7.1

Social Process Theories

Theory	Major Premise	Strengths	Research Focus
SOCIAL LEARNING THEORIES			
Differential association theory	People learn to commit crime from exposure to antisocial definitions.	Explains onset of criminality. Explains the presence of crime in all elements of social structure. Explains why some people in high-crime areas refrain from criminality. Can apply to adults and juveniles.	Measuring definitions toward crime; influence of deviant peers and parents.
Differential reinforcement theory	Criminal behavior depends on the person's experiences with rewards for conventional behaviors and punishment for deviant ones. Being rewarded for deviance leads to crime.	Adds psychological learning theory principles to differential association. Links sociological and psychological principles.	The cause of criminal activity; how the content of socialization conditions crime.
Neutralization theory	Youths learn ways of neutralizing moral restraints and periodically drift in and out of criminal behavior patterns.	Explains why many delinquents do not become adult criminals. Explains why youthful law violators can participate in conventional behavior.	Identifying the neutralizations people use to commit crime without jeopardizing their cherished beliefs and values.
SOCIAL CONTROL THEORY			
Hirschi's control theory	A person's bond to society prevents him or her from violating social rules. If the bond weakens, the person is free to commit crime.	Explains the onset of crime; can apply to both middle- and lower-class crime. Explains its theoretical constructs adequately so they can be measured. Has been empirically tested.	Measuring the association between commitment, attachment, involvement, belief, and crime.
SOCIAL REACTION THEORY			
Labeling theory	People enter into law-violating careers when they are labeled for their acts and organize their personalities around the labels.	Explains the role of society in creating deviance. Explains why some juvenile offenders do not become adult criminals. Develops concepts of criminal careers.	Determining whether self-concept is related to crime. Showing how the differential application of labels produces crime; measuring the effect of stigma.

PUBLIC POLICY IMPLICATIONS OF SOCIAL PROCESS THEORY

Social process theories have had a major influence on policy making since the 1950s. Learning theories have greatly influenced the way criminal offenders are dealt with and treated. The effect of these theories has mainly been felt by young offenders, who are viewed as being more salvageable than "hardened" criminals. If people become criminal by learning definitions and attitudes toward criminality, advocates of the social learning approach argue that they can "unlearn" them by being exposed to definitions toward conventional behavior. It is common today for residential and nonresidential programs to offer treatment programs that teach offenders about the harmfulness of drugs, how to forgo delinquent behavior, and how to stay in school. If learning did not affect behavior, such exercises would be futile.

Control theories have also influenced criminal justice and other public policy. Programs have been developed to increase people's commitment to conventional lines of action. Some work at creating and strengthening bonds early in life before the onset of criminality. The educational system has been the scene of numerous programs designed to improve basic skills and create an atmosphere in which youths will develop a bond to their schools. The most famous of these efforts is the Head Start program. Today, Head Start is administered by the Head Start Bureau; the Administration on Children, Youth, and Families (ACYF); the Administration for Children and Families (ACF); and the Department of Health and Human Services (DHHS). It receives annual funding of almost $7 billion, enrolls close to 1 million children, and provides support to more than 1,600 individual programs.[213]

Control theories have focused on the family and have played a key role in putting into operation programs designed to strengthen the bond between parent and child. Others attempt to repair bonds that have been broken and frayed. Examples of this approach are the career, work furlough, and educational opportunity programs being developed in the nation's prisons. These programs are designed to help inmates maintain a stake in society so they will be less willing to resort to criminal activity on their release.

Labeling theorists caution against too much intervention. Rather than ask social agencies to attempt to rehabilitate people having problems with the law, they argue, "less is better." Put another way, the more institutions try to "help" people, the more these people will be stigmatized and labeled. For example, a special education program designed to help problem readers may cause them to label themselves and others as slow or stupid. Similarly, a mental health rehabilitation program created with the best intentions may cause clients to be labeled as crazy or dangerous.

The influence of labeling theory can be viewed in the development of diversion and restitution programs. **Diversion programs** are designed to remove both juvenile and adult offenders from the normal channels of the criminal justice process by placing them in programs designed for rehabilitation. A college student whose drunken driving causes injury to a pedestrian may, before a trial occurs, be placed for six months in an alcohol treatment program. If he successfully completes the program, charges against him will be dismissed. Thus, he avoids the stigma of a criminal label. Such programs are common throughout the nation. Often, they offer counseling, medical advice, and vocational, educational, and family services.

Another label-avoiding innovation that has gained popularity is restitution. Rather than face the stigma of a formal trial, an offender is asked to either pay back the victim of the crime for any loss incurred or do some useful work in the community in lieu of receiving a court-ordered sentence.

Despite their good intentions, stigma-reducing programs have not met with great success. Critics charge that they substitute one kind of stigma for another—for instance, attending a mental health program in place of a criminal trial. In addition, diversion and restitution programs usually screen out violent offenders and repeat offenders. Finally, there is little hard evidence that the recidivism rate of people placed in alternative programs is less than that of people sent to traditional programs.

SUMMARY

1. **Be familiar with the concept of social process and socialization**
Social process theories view criminality as a function of people's interaction with various organizations, institutions, and processes in society. People in all walks of life have the potential to become criminals if they maintain destructive social relationships. Improper socialization is a key component of crime.

2. **Be able to discuss the differences between social learning, control, and reaction theory**
Social learning theory stresses that people learn how to commit crimes and suggests that people learn criminal behaviors much as they learn conventional behavior. Social control theory analyzes the failure of society to control criminal tendencies. Social reaction (labeling) theory maintains that negative labels produce criminal careers.

3. **Discuss the effect of families and education on crime**

Kids growing up in troubled families are crime prone. Parental efficacy reduces crime. Divorce can strain families. School failure is linked to delinquency. Dropping out may influence later criminality. School violence and conflict are also problems.

4. **Be aware of the link between peers and delinquency**

Delinquent peers sustain individual offending patterns. Delinquent friends may help kids neutralize the fear of punishment. The greater the exposure to delinquent peers, the greater the likelihood of criminal behavior.

5. **Be familiar with the association between beliefs and criminality**

People with high moral standards can resist crime. Church attendance is related to low crime rates: the more people attend religious services, the less likely they will engage in antisocial behaviors.

6. **Discuss the main types of social learning theory**

Differential association theory was formulated by Edwin Sutherland. It holds that criminality is a result of a person's perceiving an excess of definitions in favor of crime. Gresham Sykes and David Matza created the theory of neutralization, which stresses that youths learn mental techniques that enable them to overcome societal values and drift into delinquency.

7. **Be familiar with the principles of control theory**

Control theory maintains that all people have the potential to become criminals, but their bonds to conventional society prevent them from violating the law. This view suggests that a person's self-concept aids his or her commitment to conventional action. Travis Hirschi's social control theory describes the social bond as containing elements of attachment, commitment, involvement, and belief. Weakened bonds allow youths to behave antisocially.

8. **Know the basic elements of social reaction or labeling theory**

Social reaction or labeling theory holds that criminality is promoted by becoming negatively labeled by significant others. Such labels as "criminal," "ex-con," and "junkie" isolate people from society and lock them into lives of crime.

9. **Be aware of the effects of labeling**

Labels create expectations that the labeled person will act in a certain way; labeled people are always watched and suspected. Eventually these people begin to accept their labels as personal identities, locking them further into lives of crime and deviance. Edwin Lemert suggests that people who accept labels are involved in secondary deviance while primary deviants are able to maintain an undamaged identity.

10. **Link social process theory to crime prevention efforts**

Social process theories have greatly influenced social policy. They have been applied in treatment orientations as well as community action policies. Some programs teach kids conventional attitudes and behaviors. Others are designed to improve the social bond they have with parents and teachers.

KEY TERMS

sociological social psychology (230)
socialization (231)
social process theory (231)
parental efficacy (233)
social learning theory (236)
social control theory (236)
social reaction theory (labeling theory) (236)
differential association theory (237)

differential reinforcement theory (240)
direct conditioning (240)
differential reinforcement (240)
negative reinforcement (240)
neutralization theory (241)
subterranean values (241)
drift (241)
commitment to conformity (245)
containment theory (245)
social bond (246)

symbolic interaction theory (249)
stigma (250)
racial profiling (251)
reflected appraisals (252)
retrospective reading (252)
dramatization of evil (252)
primary deviance (253)
secondary deviance (253)
contextual discrimination (253)
diversion programs (256)

CRITICAL THINKING QUESTIONS

1. Do negative labels cause crime? Or do people who commit crime become negatively labeled? That is, are labels a cause of crime or a result?

2. Once weakened, can a person's bonds to society become reattached? What social processes might help reattachment?

3. Can you devise a test of Sutherland's differential association theory? How would you go about measuring an excess of definitions toward criminality?

4. Can you think of ways you may have supported your peers' or siblings' antisocial behavior by helping them learn criminal techniques or attitudes?

5. Do you recall neutralizing any guilt you might have felt for committing a criminal or illegal act? Did your neutralizations come before or after you committed the act in question?

NOTES

1. Wright Thompson, "Outrageous Injustice," ESPN Online http://sports.espn.go.com/ espn/eticket/story?page=wilson (accessed September 20, 2010); "Free Genarlow Wilson Now," *New York Times*, December 21, 2006, www.nytimes.com/2006/12/21/ opinion/21thu4.html (accessed September 20, 2010).

2. Chandra Thomas, "Why Is Genarlow Wilson in Prison?" www.refugeesunleashed. net/about4880.html (accessed September 20, 2010).

3. Shannon McCaffrey, "10-Year Sentence for Teen Sex Thrown Out," The Free Library Online, www.thefreelibrary.com/10-year+ sentence+for+teen+sex+thrown+out- a01611363270 (accessed September 20, 2010).

4. Charles Tittle and Robert Meier, "Specifying the SES/Delinquency Relationship," *Criminology* 28 (1990): 271–299, at 274.

5. Sheldon Glueck and Eleanor Glueck, *Unraveling Juvenile Delinquency* (Cambridge, MA: Harvard University Press, 1950); Ashley Weeks, "Predicting Juvenile Delinquency," *American Sociological Review* 8 (1943): 40–46.

6. Diana Formoso, Nancy Gonzales, and Leona Aiken, "Family Conflict and Children's Internalizing and Externalizing Behavior: Protective Factors," *American Journal of Community Psychology* 28 (2000): 175–199.

7. Ming Cui and Rand D. Conger, "Parenting Behavior as Mediator and Moderator of the Association Between Marital Problems and Adolescent Maladjustment," *Journal of Research on Adolescence* 18 (2008): 261–284.

8. Roslyn Caldwell, Jenna Silverman, Noelle Lefforge, and Clayton Silver, "Adjudicated Mexican-American Adolescents: The Effects of Familial Emotional Support on Self-Esteem, Emotional Well-Being, and Delinquency," *American Journal of Family Therapy* 32 (2004): 55–69.

9. Annie E. Casey Foundation, Kids Count, 2006, www.aecf.org/kidscount/sld/com- pare_results.jsp?i=722 (accessed September 20, 2010).

10. Andre Sourander, Henrik Elonheimo, Solja Niemelä, Art-Matti Nuutila, Hans Helenius, Lauri Sillanmäki, Jorma Piha, Tuulk Tamminen, Kirsti Kumpulkinen, Irma Moilanen, and Frederik Almovist, "Childhood Predictors of Male Criminality: A Prospective Population-Based Follow-Up Study from Age 8 to Late Adolescence," *Journal of the American Academy of Child and Adolescent Psychiatry* 45 (2006): 578–586.

11. Jukka Savolainen, "Relative Cohort Size and Age-Specific Arrest Rates: A Conditional Interpretation of the Easterlin Effect," *Criminology* 38 (2000): 117–136.

12. Cesar Rebellon, "Reconsidering the Broken Homes/Delinquency Relationship and Exploring Its Mediating Factors," *Criminology* 40 (2002): 103–136.

13. James Unnever, Francis Cullen, and Robert Agnew, "Why Is 'Bad' Parenting Criminogenic? Implications from Rival Theories," *Youth Violence and Juvenile Justice* 4 (2006): 3–33.

14. L. Edward Wells and Joseph Rankin, "Families and Delinquency: A Meta-Analysis of the Impact of Broken Homes," *Social Problems* 38 (1991): 71–90.

15. Nan Marie Astone and Sara McLanahan, "Family Structure, Parental Practices, and High School Completion," *American Sociological Review* 56 (1991): 309–320.

16. Jennifer Beyers, John Bates, Gregory Pettit, and Kenneth Dodge, "Neighborhood Structure, Parenting Processes, and the Development of Youths' Externalizing Behaviors: A Multilevel Analysis," *American Journal of Community Psychology* 31 (2003): 35–53.

17. En-Ling Pan and Michael Farrell, "Ethnic Differences in the Effects of Intergenerational Relations on Adolescent Problem Behavior in U.S. Single-Mother Families," *Journal of Family Issues* 27 (2006): 1,137–1,158.

18. Paul Amato and Bruce Keith, "Parental Divorce and the Well-Being of Children: A Meta-Analysis," *Psychological Bulletin* 110 (1991): 26–46.

19. Unnever, Cullen, and Agnew, "Why Is 'Bad' Parenting Criminogenic?"

20. Daniel Shaw, "Advancing Our Understanding of Intergenerational Continuity in Antisocial Behavior," *Journal of Abnormal Child Psychology* 31 (2003): 193–199.

21. Donald J. West and David P. Farrington, eds., "Who Becomes Delinquent?" in *The Delinquent Way of Life* (London: Heinemann, 1977); Donald J. West, *Delinquency: Its Roots, Careers, and Prospects* (Cambridge, MA: Harvard University Press, 1982).

22. David Farrington, "Understanding and Preventing Bullying," in *Crime and Justice*, Vol. 17, ed. Michael Tonry (Chicago: University of Chicago Press, 1993), pp. 381–457.

23. Carolyn Smith and David Farrington, "Continuities in Antisocial Behavior and Parenting Across Three Generations," *Journal of Child Psychology and Psychiatry* 45 (2004): 230–247.

24. Joseph Murray and David Farrington, "Parental Imprisonment: Effects on Boys' Antisocial Behaviour and Delinquency Through the Life-Course," *Journal of Child Psychology and Psychiatry* 46 (2005): 1,269–1,278.

25. John Paul Wright and Francis Cullen, "Parental Efficacy and Delinquent Behavior: Do Control and Support Matter?" *Criminology* 39 (2001): 677–706.

26. Christopher Sullivan, "Early Adolescent Delinquency: Assessing the Role of Childhood Problems, Family Environment, and Peer Pressure," *Youth Violence and Juvenile Justice* 4 (2006): 291–313.

27. Andrea Chronis, Heather Jones, Benjamin Lahey, Paul Rathouz, William Pelham, Jr., Stephanie Hall Williams, Barbara Baumann, and Heidi Kipp, "Maternal Depression and Early Positive Parenting Predict

Future Conduct Problems in Young Children with Attention-Deficit/Hyperactivity Disorder," *Developmental Psychology* 43 (2007): 70–82.

28. Carter Hay, "Parenting, Self-Control, and Delinquency: A Test of Self-Control Theory," *Criminology* 39 (2001): 707–736.

29. Sonia Cota-Robles and Wendy Gamble, "Parent-Adolescent Processes and Reduced Risk for Delinquency: The Effect of Gender for Mexican American Adolescents," *Youth and Society* 37 (2006): 375–392.

30. Robert Vermeiren, Jef Bogaerts, Vladislav Ruchkin, Dirk Deboutte, and Mary Schwab-Stone, "Subtypes of Self-Esteem and Self-Concept in Adolescent Violent and Property Offenders," *Journal of Child Psychology and Psychiatry* 45 (2004): 405–411.

31. Jacinta Bronte-Tinkew, Kristin Moore, and Jennifer Carrano, "The Father-Child Relationship, Parenting Styles, and Adolescent Risk Behaviors in Intact Families," *Journal of Family Issues* 27 (2006): 850–881.

32. Murray A. Straus, "Spanking and the Making of a Violent Society: The Short- and Long-Term Consequences of Corporal Punishment," *Pediatrics* 98 (1996): 837–843.

33. Carolyn Smith and Terence Thornberry, "The Relationship Between Childhood Maltreatment and Adolescent Involvement in Delinquency," *Criminology* 33 (1995): 451–479.

34. Kristi Holsinger and Alexander Holsinger, "Differential Pathways to Violence and Self-Injurious Behavior: African American and White Girls in the Juvenile Justice System," *Journal of Research in Crime and Delinquency* 42 (2005): 211–242; Eric Slade and Lawrence Wissow, "Spanking in Early Childhood and Later Behavior Problems: A Prospective Study of Infants and Young Toddlers," *Pediatrics* 113 (2004): 1,321–1,330; Fred Rogosch and Dante Cicchetti, "Child Maltreatment and Emergent Personality Organization: Perspectives from the Five-Factor Model," *Journal of Abnormal Child Psychology* 32 (2004): 123–145.

35. Todd Herrenkohl, Rick Kosterman, David Hawkins, and Alex Mason, "Effects of Growth in Family Conflict in Adolescence on Adult Depressive Symptoms: Mediating and Moderating Effects of Stress and School Bonding," *Journal of Adolescent Health* 44 (2009): 146–152.

36. Rand D. Conger, Institute for Social and Behavioral Research, Iowa State University, www.labome.org/expert/usa/university/conger/rand-d-conger-487510.html (accessed September 20, 2010).

37. David Huh, Jennifer Tristan, Emily Wade, and Eric Stice, "Does Problem Behavior Elicit Poor Parenting? A Prospective Study of Adolescent Girls," *Journal of Adolescent Research* 21 (2006): 185–204.

38. *The Forgotten Half: Pathways to Success for America's Youth and Young Families*

(Washington, DC: William T. Grant Foundation, 1988); Lee Jussim, "Teacher Expectations: Self-Fulfilling Prophecies, Perceptual Biases, and Accuracy," *Journal of Personality and Social Psychology* 57 (1989): 469–480.

39. Eugene Maguin and Rolf Loeber, "Academic Performance and Delinquency," in *Crime and Justice: A Review of Research*, Vol. 20, ed. Michael Tonry (Chicago: University of Chicago Press, 1996), pp. 145–264.

40. Jeannie Oakes, *Keeping Track, How Schools Structure Inequality* (New Haven, CT: Yale University Press, 1985).

41. National Center for Education Statistics, "Dropout and Completion Rates in the United States: 2007," http://nces.ed.gov/pubs2009/dropout07/ (accessed November 18, 2010).

42. Gary Sweeten, Shawn D. Bushway, and Raymond Paternoster, "Does Dropping Out of School Mean Dropping into Delinquency?" *Criminology* 47(2009): 47–91; G. Roger Jarjoura, "Does Dropping Out of School Enhance Delinquent Involvement? Results from a Large-Scale National Probability Sample," *Criminology* 31 (1993): 149–172; Terence Thornberry, Melanie Moore, and R. L. Christenson, "The Effect of Dropping Out of High School on Subsequent Criminal Behavior," *Criminology* 23 (1985): 3–18.

43. Sweeten, Bushway, and Paternoster, "Does Dropping Out of School Mean Dropping into Delinquency?"

44. Irving Janis, *Groupthink: Psychological Studies of Policy Decisions and Fiascoes* (Boston: Houghton Mifflin, 1982).

45. Olena Antonaccio, Charles Tittle, Ekaterina Botchkovar, and Maria Kranidioti, "The Correlates of Crime and Deviance: Additional Evidence," *Journal of Research in Crime and Delinquency*, first published on April 28, 2010, http://jrc.sagepub.com.libproxy.uml.edu/content/early/2010/04/22/0022427810365678.full.pdf+html.

46. Amy Anderson and Lorine Hughes, "Exposure to Situations Conducive to Delinquent Behavior: The Effects of Time Use, Income, and Transportation," *Journal of Research in Crime and Delinquency* 46 (2009): 5–34.

47. Delbert Elliott, David Huizinga, and Suzanne Ageton, *Explaining Delinquency and Drug Use* (Beverly Hills, CA: Sage, 1985); Helene Raskin White, Robert Padina, and Randy La-Grange, "Longitudinal Predictors of Serious Substance Use and Delinquency," *Criminology* 6 (1987): 715–740.

48. Robert Agnew and Timothy Brezina, "Relational Problems with Peers, Gender and Delinquency," *Youth and Society* 29 (1997): 84–111.

49. Maury Nation and Craig Anne Heflinger, "Risk Factors for Serious Alcohol and Drug Use: The Role of Psychosocial Variables in

Predicting the Frequency of Substance Use Among Adolescents," *American Journal of Drug and Alcohol Abuse* 32 (2006): 415–433; Robert Agnew and Timothy Brezina, "Relational Problems with Peers, Gender, and Delinquency," *Youth and Society* 29 (1997). 84–111.

50. Sara Battin, Karl Hill, Robert Abbott, Richard Catalano, and J. David Hawkins, "The Contribution of Gang Membership to Delinquency Beyond Delinquent Friends," *Criminology* 36 (1998): 93–116.

51. Paul Friday, Xin Ren, Elmar Weitekamp, Hans-Jürgen Kerner, and Terrance Taylor, "A Chinese Birth Cohort: Theoretical Implications," *Journal of Research in Crime and Delinquency* 42 (2005): 123–146.

52. Kate Keenan, Rolf Loeber, Quanwu Zhang, Magda Stouthamer-Loeber, and Welmoet van Kammen, "The Influence of Deviant Peers on the Development of Boys' Disruptive and Delinquent Behavior: A Temporal Analysis," *Development and Psychopathology* 7 (1995): 715–726.

53. Brett Johnson Solomon, "Other-Sex Friendship Involvement Among Delinquent Adolescent Females," *Youth Violence and Juvenile Justice* 4 (2006): 75–96.

54. Nation and Heflinger, "Risk Factors for Serious Alcohol and Drug Use: The Role of Psychosocial Variables in Predicting the Frequency of Substance Use Among Adolescents."

55. Terence Thornberry and Marvin Krohn, "Peers, Drug Use, and Delinquency," in *Handbook of Antisocial Behavior*, ed. David Stoff, James Breiling, and Jack Maser (New York: Wiley, 1997), pp. 218–233; Thomas Dishion, Deborah Capaldi, Kathleen Spracklen, and Fuzhong Li, "Peer Ecology of Male Adolescent Drug Use," *Development and Psychopathology* 7 (1995): 803–824.

56. Sylvie Mrug, Betsy Hoza, and William Bukowski, "Choosing or Being Chosen by Aggressive-Disruptive Peers: Do They Contribute to Children's Externalizing and Internalizing Problems?" *Journal of Abnormal Child Psychology* 32 (2004): 53–66.

57. Kevin Beaver and John Paul Wright, "Biosocial Development and Delinquent Involvement," *Youth Violence and Juvenile Justice* 3 (2005): 168–192.

58. Richard Felson and Dana Haynie, "Pubertal Development, Social Factors, and Delinquency Among Adolescent Boys," *Criminology* 40 (2002): 967–989.

59. Mark Warr, "Age, Peers, and Delinquency," *Criminology* 31 (1993): 17–40.

60. Battin et al., "The Contribution of Gang Membership to Delinquency Beyond Delinquent Friends."

61. Mark Warr, "Life-Course Transitions and Desistance from Crime," *Criminology* 36 (1998): 502–536.

62. Stephen W. Baron, "Self-Control, Social Consequences, and Criminal Behavior: Street Youth and the General Theory of

Crime," *Journal of Research in Crime and Delinquency* 40 (2003): 403–425.

63. David Harding, "Violence, Older Peers, and the Socialization of Adolescent Boys in Disadvantaged Neighborhoods," *American Sociological Review* 74 (2009): 445–464.

64. Daneen Deptula and Robert Cohen, "Aggressive, Rejected, and Delinquent Children and Adolescents: A Comparison of Their Friendships," *Aggression and Violent Behavior* 9 (2004): 75–104.

65. Shelley Keith Matthews and Robert Agnew, "Extending Deterrence Theory: Do Delinquent Peers Condition the Relationship Between Perceptions of Getting Caught and Offending?" *Journal of Research in Crime and Delinquency* 45 (2008): 91–118.

66. T. David Evans, Francis Cullen, R. Gregory Dunaway, and Velmer Burton, Jr., "Religion and Crime Reexamined: The Impact of Religion, Secular Controls, and Social Ecology on Adult Criminality," *Criminology* 33 (1995): 195–224.

67. Travis Hirschi and Rodney Stark, "Hellfire and Delinquency," *Social Problems* 17 (1969): 202–213.

68. Colin Baier and Bradley Wright, "If You Love Me, Keep My Commandments: A Meta-Analysis of the Effect of Religion on Crime," *Journal of Research in Crime and Delinquency* 38 (2001): 3–21; Byron Johnson, Sung Joon Jang, David Larson, and Spencer De Li, "Does Adolescent Religious Commitment Matter? A Reexamination of the Effects of Religiosity on Delinquency," *Journal of Research in Crime and Delinquency* 38 (2001): 22–44; Sung Joon Jang and Byron Johnson, "Neighborhood Disorder, Individual Religiosity, and Adolescent Use of Illicit Drugs: A Test of Multilevel Hypothesis," *Criminology* 39 (2001): 109–144.

69. Richard Petts, "Family and Religious Characteristics' Influence on Delinquency Trajectories from Adolescence to Young Adulthood," *American Sociological Review* 74 (2009): 465–483.

70. Walter Miller, *Violence by Youth Gangs and Youth Groups as a Crime Problem in Major American Cities* (Washington, DC: U.S. Government Printing Office, 1975).

71. Edwin H. Sutherland, *Principles of Criminology* (Philadelphia: Lippincott, 1939).

72. See, for example, Edwin Sutherland, "White-Collar Criminality," *American Sociological Review* 5 (1940): 2–10.

73. See Edwin Sutherland and Donald Cressey, *Criminology*, 8th Ed. (Philadelphia: Lippincott, 1970), pp. 77–79.

74. Sandra Brown, Vicki Creamer, and Barbara Stetson, "Adolescent Alcohol Expectancies in Relation to Personal and Parental Drinking Patterns," *Journal of Abnormal Psychology* 96 (1987): 117–121.

75. Carlo Morselli, Pierre Tremblay, and Bill McCarthy, "Mentors and Criminal Achievement," *Criminology* 44 (2006): 17–43.

76. Ibid.

77. Matthew Ploeger, "Youth Employment and Delinquency: Reconsidering a Problematic Relationship," *Criminology* 35 (1997): 659–675.

78. Travis C. Pratt, Francis T. Cullen, Christine S. Sellers, L. Thomas Winfree, Jr., Tamara D. Madensen, Leah E. Daigle, Noelle E. Fearn, and Jacinta M. Gau, "The Empirical Status of Social Learning Theory: A Meta-Analysis" *Informaworld* online e-version, November 2009, www.informaworld.com/smpp/content~db=all~content=a917140010 (accessed September 20, 2010).

79. Robert Lonardo, Peggy Giordano, Monica Longmore, and Wendy Manning, "Parents, Friends, and Romantic Partners: Enmeshment in Deviant Networks and Adolescent Delinquency Involvement," *Journal of Youth and Adolescence* 38 (2009): 367–383.

80. Terence P. Thornberry, "The Apple Doesn't Fall Far from the Tree (Or Does It?): Intergenerational Patterns of Antisocial Behavior—The American Society of Criminology 2008 Sutherland Address," *Criminology* 47 (2009): 297–325; Terence Thornberry, Adrienne Freeman-Gallant, Alan Lizotte, Marvin Krohn, and Carolyn Smith, "Linked Lives: The Intergenerational Transmission of Antisocial Behavior," *Journal of Abnormal Child Psychology* 31 (2003): 171–184.

81. Paul Vowell and Jieming Chen, "Predicting Academic Misconduct: A Comparative Test of Four Sociological Explanations," *Sociological Inquiry* 74 (2004): 226–249.

82. Andy Hochstetler, Heith Copes, and Matt DeLisi, "Differential Association in Group and Solo Offending," *Journal of Criminal Justice* 30 (2002): 559–566.

83. Wesley Church II, Tracy Wharton, and Julie Taylor, "An Examination of Differential Association and Social Control Theory: Family Systems and Delinquency," *Youth Violence and Juvenile Justice* 7 (2009): 3–15.

84. Wesley Younts, "Status, Endorsement and the Legitimacy of Deviance," *Social Forces* 87 (2008): 561–590.

85. Dana Haynie, Peggy Giordano, Wendy Manning, and Monica Longmore, "Adolescent Romantic Relationships and Delinquency Involvement," *Criminology* 43 (2005): 177–210.

86. Lonardo et al., "Parents, Friends, and Romantic Partners."

87. Joel Hektner, Gerald August, and George Realmuto, "Effects of Pairing Aggressive and Nonaggressive Children in Strategic Peer Affiliation," *Journal of Abnormal Child Psychology* 31 (2003): 399–412; Matthew Ploeger, "Youth Employment and Delinquency: Reconsidering a Problematic Relationship," *Criminology* 35 (1997): 659–675; William Skinner and Anne Fream, "A Social Learning Theory Analysis of Computer Crime Among College Students," *Journal of Research in Crime and Delinquency* 34 (1997): 495–518; Denise Kandel and Mark Davies, "Friendship

Networks, Intimacy, and Illicit Drug Use in Young Adulthood: A Comparison of Two Competing Theories," *Criminology* 29 (1991): 441–467.

88. Warr, "Age, Peers, and Delinquency."

89. Clayton Hartjen and S. Priyadarsini, "Gender, Peers, and Delinquency," *Youth and Society* 34 (2003): 387–414.

90. Denise Kandel and Mark Davies, "Friendship Networks, Intimacy, and Illicit Drug Use in Young Adulthood: A Comparison of Two Competing Theories," *Criminology* 29 (1991): 441–467.

91. Kenneth Tunnell, "Inside the Drug Trade: Trafficking from the Dealer's Perspective," *Qualitative Sociology* 16 (1993): 361–381, at 367.

92. Krohn and Thornberry, "Network Theory," pp. 123–124.

93. Daniel Mears, Matthew Ploeger, and Mark Warr, "Explaining the Gender Gap in Delinquency: Peer Influence and Moral Evaluations of Behavior," *Journal of Research in Crime and Delinquency* 35 (1998): 251–266.

94. Ibid.

95. Ronald Akers, "Is Differential Association/Social Learning Cultural Deviance Theory?" *Criminology* 34 (1996): 229–247; for an opposing view, see Travis Hirschi, "Theory Without Ideas: Reply to Akers," *Criminology* 34 (1996): 249–256.

96. Robert Burgess and Ronald Akers, "A Differential Association–Reinforcement Theory of Criminal Behavior," *Social Problems* 14 (1966): 128–147.

97. Mons Bendixen, Inger Endresen, and Dan Olweus, "Joining and Leaving Gangs: Selection and Facilitation Effects on Self-Reported Antisocial Behaviour in Early Adolescence," *European Journal of Criminology* 3 (2006): 85–114.

98. Sameer Hinduja and Jason Ingram, "Social Learning Theory and Music Piracy: The Differential Role of Online and Offline Peer Influences," *Criminal Justice Studies: A Critical Journal of Crime, Law and Society* 22 (2009): 405–420.

99. Ronald Akers, *Deviant Behavior: A Social Learning Approach*, 2nd Ed. (Belmont, CA: Wadsworth, 1977).

100. Ronald Akers, Marvin Krohn, Lonn Lanza-Kaduce, and Marcia Radosevich, "Social Learning and Deviant Behavior: A Specific Test of a General Theory," *American Sociological Review* 44 (1979): 638.

101. Ibid.

102. Robert G. Morris and Ashley G. Blackburn, "Cracking the Code: An Empirical Exploration of Social Learning Theory and Computer Crime," *Journal of Crime and Justice* 32 (2009): 1–34.

103. Marvin Krohn, William Skinner, James Massey, and Ronald Akers, "Social Learning Theory and Adolescent Cigarette Smoking: A Longitudinal Study," *Social Problems* 32 (1985): 455–471.

104. L. Thomas Winfree, Christine Sellers, and Dennis L. Clason, "Social Learning and Adolescent Deviance Abstention: Toward Understanding the Reasons for Initiating, Quitting, and Avoiding Drugs," *Journal of Quantitative Criminology* 9 (1993): 101–125.

105. Jonathan Brauer, "Testing Social Learning Theory Using Reinforcement's Residue: A Multilevel Analysis of Self-Reported Theft and Marijuana Use in the National Youth Survey," *Criminology* 47 (2009): 929–970.

106. Ronald Akers and Gang Lee, "A Longitudinal Test of Social Learning Theory: Adolescent Smoking," *Journal of Drug Issues* 26 (1996): 317–343.

107. Gary Jensen and David Brownfield, "Parents and Drugs," *Criminology* 21 (1983): 543–554.

108. Ronald Akers, "Rational Choice, Deterrence and Social Learning Theory in Criminology: The Path Not Taken," *Journal of Criminal Law and Criminology* 81 (1990): 653–676.

109. Gresham Sykes and David Matza, "Techniques of Neutralization: A Theory of Delinquency," *American Sociological Review* 22 (1957): 664–670; David Matza, *Delinquency and Drift* (New York: Wiley, 1964).

110. Matza, *Delinquency and Drift*, p. 51.

111. Sykes and Matza, "Techniques of Neutralization," pp. 664–670; see also David Matza, "Subterranean Traditions of Youths," *Annals of the American Academy of Political and Social Science* 378 (1961): 116.

112. Sykes and Matza, "Techniques of Neutralization," pp. 664–670.

113. Ibid.

114. Ian Shields and George Whitehall, "Neutralization and Delinquency Among Teenagers," *Criminal Justice and Behavior* 21 (1994): 223–235; Robert A. Ball, "An Empirical Exploration of Neutralization Theory," *Criminologica* 4 (1966): 22–32. See also M. William Minor, "The Neutralization of Criminal Offense," *Criminology* 18 (1980): 103–120; Robert Gordon, James Short, Desmond Cartwright, and Fred Strodtbeck, "Values and Gang Delinquency: A Study of Street Corner Groups," *American Journal of Sociology* 69 (1963): 109–128.

115. Robert Agnew, "The Techniques of Neutralization and Violence," *Criminology* 32 (1994): 555–580; Michael Hindelang, "The Commitment of Delinquents to Their Misdeeds: Do Delinquents Drift?" *Social Problems* 17 (1970): 500–509; Robert Regoli and Eric Poole, "The Commitment of Delinquents to Their Misdeeds: A Reexamination," *Journal of Criminal Justice* 6 (1978): 261–269.

116. Larry Siegel, Spencer Rathus, and Carol Ruppert, "Values and Delinquent Youth: An Empirical Reexamination of Theories of Delinquency," *British Journal of Criminology* 13 (1973): 237–244.

117. Nicole Leeper Piquero, Stephen Tibbetts, and Michael Blankenship, "Examining the Role of Differential Association and Techniques of Neutralization in Explaining Corporate Crime," *Deviant Behavior* 26 (2005): 159–188.

118. John Hamlin, "Misplaced Role of Rational Choice in Neutralization Theory," *Criminology* 26 (1988): 425–438.

119. Mark Pogrebin, Eric Poole, and Amos Martinez, "Accounts of Professional Misdeeds: The Sexual Exploitation of Clients by Psychotherapists," *Deviant Behavior* 13 (1992): 229–252.

120. Eric Wish, *Drug Use Forecasting 1990* (Washington, DC: National Institute of Justice, 1991).

121. Scott Briar and Irving Piliavin, "Delinquency: Situational Inducements and Commitment to Conformity," *Social Problems* 13 (1965–1966): 35–45.

122. Lawrence Sherman and Douglas Smith, with Janell Schmidt and Dennis Rogan, "Crime, Punishment, and Stake in Conformity: Legal and Informal Control of Domestic Violence," *American Sociological Review* 57 (1992): 680–690.

123. Albert Reiss, "Delinquency as the Failure of Personal and Social Controls," *American Sociological Review* 16 (1951): 196–207.

124. Briar and Piliavin, "Delinquency: Situational Inducements and Commitment to Conformity."

125. Walter Reckless, *The Crime Problem* (New York: Appleton-Century-Crofts, 1967), pp. 469–483.

126. Among the many research reports by Reckless and his colleagues are Walter Reckless, Simon Dinitz, and Ellen Murray, "The Good Boy in a High Delinquency Area," *Journal of Criminal Law, Criminology, and Police Science* 48 (1957): 12–26; Frank Scarpitti, Ellen Murray, Simon Dinitz, and Walter Reckless, "The Good Boy in a High Delinquency Area: Four Years Later," *American Sociological Review* 23 (1960): 555–558; Walter Reckless, Simon Dinitz, and Ellen Murray, "Self-Concept as an Insulator Against Delinquency," *American Sociological Review* 21 (1956): 744–746; Walter Reckless and Simon Dinitz, "Pioneering with Self-Concept as a Vulnerability Factor in Delinquency," *Journal of Criminal Law, Criminology, and Police Science* 58 (1967): 515–523; Walter Reckless, Simon Dinitz, and Barbara Kay, "The Self-Component in Potential Delinquency and Potential Non-Delinquency," *American Sociological Review* 22 (1957): 566–570.

127. Travis Hirschi, *Causes of Delinquency* (Berkeley: University of California Press, 1969).

128. Ibid., p. 231.

129. Robert Crosnoe, "The Connection Between Academic Failure and Adolescent Drinking in Secondary School," *Sociology of Education* 79 (2006): 44–60.

130. Carl Maas, Charles Fleming, Todd Herrenkohl, and Richard Catalano, "Childhood Predictors of Teen Dating Violence Victimization," *Violence and Victims* 25 (2010): 131–149.

131. Hirschi, *Causes of Delinquency*, pp. 66–74.

132. Ozden Ozbay and Yusuf Ziya Ozcan, "A Test of Hirschi's Social Bonding Theory," *International Journal of Offender Therapy and Comparative Criminology* 50 (2006): 711–726; Michael Wiatrowski, David Griswold, and Mary K. Roberts, "Social Control Theory and Delinquency," *American Sociological Review* 46 (1981): 525–541.

133. Patricia van Voorhis, Francis Cullen, Richard Mathers, and Connie Chenoweth Garner, "The Impact of Family Structure and Quality on Delinquency: A Comparative Assessment of Structural and Functional Factors," *Criminology* 26 (1988): 235–261.

134. Marc LeBlanc, "Family Dynamics, Adolescent Delinquency, and Adult Criminality," paper presented at the Society for Life History Research conference, Keystone, Colorado, October 1990, p. 6.

135. Bobbi Jo Anderson, Malcolm Holmes, and Erik Ostresh, "Male and Female Delinquents' Attachments and Effects of Attachments on Severity of Self-Reported Delinquency," *Criminal Justice and Behavior* 26 (1999): 435–452.

136. Helen Garnier and Judith Stein, "An 18-Year Model of Family and Peer Effects on Adolescent Drug Use and Delinquency," *Journal of Youth and Adolescence* 31 (2002): 45–56.

137. Teresa LaGrange and Robert Silverman, "Perceived Strain and Delinquency Motivation: An Empirical Evaluation of General Strain Theory," paper presented at the annual meeting of the American Society of Criminology, Boston, November 1995.

138. Van Voorhis et al., "The Impact of Family Structure and Quality on Delinquency."

139. Allison Ann Payne, "A Multilevel Analysis of the Relationships Among Communal School Organization, Student Bonding, and Delinquency," *Journal of Research in Crime and Delinquency* 45 (2008): 429–455.

140. Norman White and Rolf Loeber, "Bullying and Special Education as Predictors of Serious Delinquency," *Journal of Research in Crime and Delinquency* 45 (2008): 380–397.

141. John Cochran and Ronald Akers, "An Exploration of the Variable Effects of Religiosity on Adolescent Marijuana and Alcohol Use," *Journal of Research in Crime and Delinquency* 26 (1989): 198–225.

142. Mark Regnerus and Glen Elder, "Religion and Vulnerability Among Low-Risk Adolescents," *Social Science Research* 32 (2003): 633–658; Mark Regnerus, "Moral Communities and Adolescent Delinquency: Religious Contexts and Community Social Control," *Sociological Quarterly* 44 (2003): 523–554.

143. Michael Cretacci, "Religion and Social Control: An Application of a Modified Social Bond of Violence," *Criminal Justice Review* 28 (2003): 254–277.

144. Robert Agnew and David Peterson, "Leisure and Delinquency," *Social Problems* 36 (1989): 332–348.

145. Jonathan Zaff, Kristin Moore, Angela Romano Papillo, and Stephanie Williams, "Implications of Extracurricular Activity Participation During Adolescence on Positive Outcomes," *Journal of Adolescent Research* 18 (2003): 599–631.

146. Marianne Junger and Ineke Haen Marshall, "The Interethnic Generalizability of Social Control Theory: An Empirical Test," *Journal of Research in Crime and Delinquency* 34 (1997): 79–112; Josine Junger-Tas, "An Empirical Test of Social Control Theory," *Journal of Quantitative Criminology* 8 (1992): 18–29.

147. LaGrange and Silverman, "Perceived Strain and Delinquency Motivation."

148. Kimberly Kempf, "The Empirical Status of Hirschi's Control Theory," in *Advances in Criminological Theory*, ed. Bill Laufer and Freda Adler (New Brunswick, NJ: Transaction Books, 1992).

149. Thomas Vander Ven, Francis Cullen, Mark Carrozza, and John Paul Wright, "Home Alone: The Impact of Maternal Employment on Delinquency," *Social Problems* 48 (2001): 236–257, at 253.

150. Peggy Giordano, Stephen Cernkovich, and M. D. Pugh, "Friendships and Delinquency," *American Journal of Sociology* 91 (1986): 1,170–1,202.

151. Denise Kandel and Mark Davies, "Friendship Networks, Intimacy, and Illicit Drug Use in Young Adulthood: A Comparison of Two Competing Theories," *Criminology* 29 (1991): 441–467.

152. Lisa Stolzenberg and Stewart D'Alessio, "Co-Offending and the Age–Crime Curve," *Journal of Research in Crime and Delinquency* 45 (2008): 65–86.

153. Velmer Burton, Francis Cullen, T. David Evans, R. Gregory Dunaway, Sesha Kethineni, and Gary Payne, "The Impact of Parental Controls on Delinquency," *Journal of Criminal Justice* 23 (1995): 111–126.

154. Kimberly Kempf Leonard and Scott Decker, "The Theory of Social Control: Does It Apply to the Very Young?" *Journal of Criminal Justice* 22 (1994): 89–105.

155. Burton et al., "The Impact of Parental Controls on Delinquency."

156. Amy Anderson and Lorine Hughes, "Exposure to Situations Conducive to Delinquent Behavior: The Effects of Time Use, Income, and Transportation," *Journal of Research in Crime and Delinquency* 46 (2009): 5–34.

157. Patrick Seffrin, Peggy Giordano, Wendy Manning, and Monica Longmore, "The Influence of Dating Relationships on Friendship Networks, Identity Development, and Delinquency," *Justice Quarterly* 26 (2009): 238–267.

158. Michael Hindelang, "Causes of Delinquency: A Partial Replication and Extension," *Social Problems* 21 (1973): 471–487.

159. Gary Jensen and David Brownfield, "Parents and Drugs," *Criminology* 21 (1983): 543–554; see also M. Wiatrowski, D. Griswold, and M. Roberts, "Social Control Theory and Delinquency," *American Sociological Review* 46 (1981): 525–541.

160. Leslie Samuelson, Timothy Hartnagel, and Harvey Krahn, "Crime and Social Control Among High School Dropouts," *Journal of Crime and Justice* 18 (1990): 129–161.

161. Cesar Rebellon and Karen van Gundy, "Can Control Theory Explain the Link Between Parental Physical Abuse and Delinquency? A Longitudinal Analysis," *Journal of Research in Crime and Delinquency* 42 (2005): 247–274; Marvin Krohn and James Massey, "Social Control and Delinquent Behavior: An Examination of the Elements of the Social Bond," *Sociological Quarterly* 21 (1980): 529–543.

162. Jill Leslie Rosenbaum and James Lasley, "School, Community Context, and Delinquency: Rethinking the Gender Gap," *Justice Quarterly* 7 (1990): 493–513.

163. Randy LaGrange and Helene Raskin White, "Age Differences in Delinquency: A Test of Theory," *Criminology* 23 (1985): 19–45.

164. Robert Agnew, "Social Control Theory and Delinquency: A Longitudinal Test," *Criminology* 23 (1985): 47–61.

165. Alan E. Liska and M. D. Reed, "Ties to Conventional Institutions and Delinquency: Estimating Reciprocal Effects," *American Sociological Review* 50 (1985): 547–560.

166. George Herbert Mead, *Mind, Self and Society* (Chicago: University of Chicago Press, 1934); George Herbert Mead, *The Philosophy of the Act* (Chicago: University of Chicago Press, 1938); Charles Horton Cooley, *Human Nature and the Social Order* (New York: Schocken, 1964, first published 1902); Herbert Blumer, *Symbolic Interactionism: Perspective and Method* (Englewood Cliffs, NJ: Prentice Hall, 1969).

167. Bruce Link, Elmer Streuning, Francis Cullen, Patrick Shrout, and Bruce Dohrenwend, "A Modified Labeling Theory Approach to Mental Disorders: An Empirical Assessment," *American Sociological Review* 54 (1989): 400–423.

168. Linda Jackson, John Hunter, and Carole Hodge, "Physical Attractiveness and Intellectual Competence: A Meta-Analytic Review," *Social Psychology Quarterly* 58 (1995): 108–122.

169. Mike Adams, Craig Robertson, Phyllis Gray-Ray, and Melvin Ray, "Labeling and Delinquency," *Adolescence* 38 (2003): 171–186.

170. Patrick Corrigan, "How Stigma Interferes with Mental Health Care," *American Psychologist* 59 (2004): 614–625, at 614.

171. Kai Erickson, "Notes on the Sociology of Deviance," *Social Problems* 9 (1962): 397–414.

172. Edwin Schur, *Labeling Deviant Behavior* (New York: Harper & Row, 1972), p. 21.

173. Howard Becker, *Outsiders, Studies in the Sociology of Deviance* (New York: Macmillan, 1963), p. 9.

174. Laurie Goodstein, "The Architect of the 'Gay Conversion' Campaign," *New York Times*, August 13, 1998, p. A10.

175. Christy Visher, "Gender, Police Arrest Decision, and Notions of Chivalry," *Criminology* 21 (1983): 5–28.

176. Marjorie Zatz, "Race, Ethnicity and Determinate Sentencing," *Criminology* 22 (1984): 147–171.

177. Christina DeJong and Kenneth Jackson, "Putting Race into Context: Race, Juvenile Justice Processing, and Urbanization," *Justice Quarterly* 15 (1998): 487–504.

178. Roland Chilton and Jim Galvin, "Race, Crime and Criminal Justice," *Crime and Delinquency* 31 (1985): 3–14.

179. Joan Petersilia, "Racial Disparities in the Criminal Justice System: A Summary," *Crime and Delinquency* 31 (1985): 15–34.

180. Ross Matsueda, "Reflected Appraisals: Parental Labeling, and Delinquency: Specifying a Symbolic Interactionist Theory," *American Journal of Sociology* 97 (1992): 1,577–1,611.

181. Xiaoru Liu, "The Conditional Effect of Peer Groups on the Relationship Between Parental Labeling and Youth Delinquency," *Sociological Perspectives* 43 (2000): 499–515.

182. Suzanne Ageton and Delbert Elliott, *The Effect of Legal Processing on Self-Concept* (Boulder, CO: Institute of Behavioral Science, 1973).

183. Mike Adams, Craig Robertson, Phyllis Gray-Ray, and Melvin Ray, "Labeling and Delinquency," *Adolescence* 38 (2003): 171–186.

184. Jón Gunnar Bernburg, Marvin Krohn, and Craig Rivera, "Official Labeling, Criminal Embeddedness, and Subsequent Delinquency: A Longitudinal Test of Labeling Theory," *Journal of Research in Crime and Delinquency* 43 (2006): 67–88.

185. Lee Michael Johnson, Ronald Simons, and Rand Conger, "Criminal Justice System Involvement and Continuity of Youth Crime," *Youth and Society* 36 (2004): 3–29.

186. Gary Sweeten, "Who Will Graduate? Disruption of High School Education by Arrest and Court Involvement," *Justice Quarterly* 23 (2006): 462–480.

187. Melvin Ray and William Downs, "An Empirical Test of Labeling Theory Using Longitudinal Data," *Journal of Research in Crime and Delinquency* 23 (1986): 169–194.

188. Sherman and Smith, with Schmidt and Rogan, "Crime, Punishment, and Stake in Conformity."

189. Lawrence Bench and Terry Allen, "Investigating the Stigma of Prison Classification: An Experimental Design," *Prison Journal* 83 (2003): 367–382.

190. Bernburg, Krohn, and Rivera, "Official Labeling, Criminal Embeddedness, and Subsequent Delinquency."

191. Heimer and Matsueda, "Role-Taking, Role-Commitment, and Delinquency."

192. See, for example, Howard Kaplan and Hiroshi Fukurai, "Negative Social Sanctions, Self-Rejection, and Drug Use," *Youth and Society* 23 (1992): 275–298; Howard Kaplan and Robert Johnson, "Negative Social Sanctions and Juvenile Delinquency: Effects of Labeling in a Model of Deviant Behavior," *Social Science Quarterly* 72 (1991): 98–122; Howard Kaplan, Robert Johnson, and Carol Bailey, "Deviant Peers and Deviant Behavior: Further Elaboration of a Model," *Social Psychology Quarterly* 30 (1987): 277–284.

193. Howard Kaplan, *Toward a General Theory of Deviance: Contributions from Perspectives on Deviance and Criminality* (College Station: Texas A&M University, n.d.).

194. John Lofland, *Deviance and Identity* (Englewood Cliffs, NJ: Prentice Hall, 1969).

195. Frank Tannenbaum, *Crime and the Community* (New York: Columbia University Press, 1938), pp. 19–20.

196. Edwin Lemert, *Social Pathology* (New York: McGraw-Hill, 1951).

197. Ibid., p. 75.

198. Bruce Western, *Punishment and Inequality in America* (New York: Russell Sage Foundation, 2006); Sara Steen, Rodney Engen, and Randy Gainey, "Images of Danger and Culpability: Racial Stereotyping, Case Processing, and Criminal Sentencing," *Criminology* 43 (2005): 435–468; Stephanie Bontrager, William Bales, and Ted Chiricos, "Race, Ethnicity, Threat and the Labeling of Convicted Felons," *Criminology* 43 (2005): 589–622.

199. John Wooldredge, "Neighborhood Effects on Felony Sentencing," *Journal of Research in Crime and Delinquency* 44 (2007): 238–263.

200. Samuel Walker, Cassia Spohn, and Miriam DeLone, *The Color of Justice: Race, Ethnicity, and Crime in America* (Belmont, CA: Wadsworth, 1996), pp. 145–146.

201. Howard Kaplan and Robert Johnson, "Negative Social Sanctions and Juvenile Delinquency: Effects of Labeling in a Model of Deviant Behavior," *Social Science Quarterly* 72 (1991): 98–122.

202. Ruth Triplett, "The Conflict Perspective, Symbolic Interactionism, and the Status Characteristics Hypothesis," *Justice Quarterly* 10 (1993): 540–558.

203. Lening Zhang, "Official Offense Status and Self-Esteem Among Chinese Youths," *Journal of Criminal Justice* 31 (2003): 99–105.

204. Charles Tittle, "Two Empirical Regularities (Maybe) in Search of an Explanation: Commentary on the Age/Crime Debate," *Criminology* 26 (1988): 75–85.

205. Robert Sampson and John Laub, "A Life-Course Theory of Cumulative Disadvantage and the Stability of Delinquency," in *Developmental Theories of Crime and Delinquency*, ed. Terence Thornberry (New Brunswick, NJ: Transaction Press, 1997), pp. 133–161; Douglas Smith and Robert Brame, "On the Initiation and Continuation of Delinquency," *Criminology* 4 (1994): 607–630.

206. Sampson and Laub, "A Life-Course Theory of Cumulative Disadvantage and the Stability of Delinquency."

207. Jón Gunnar Bernburg and Marvin Krohn, "Labeling, Life Chances, and Adult Crime: The Direct and Indirect Effects of Official Intervention in Adolescence on Crime in Early Adulthood," *Criminology* 41 (2003): 1,287–1,319.

208. Jack Gibbs, "Conceptions of Deviant Behavior: The Old and the New," *Pacific Sociological Review* 9 (1966): 11–13.

209. Charles Tittle, "Labeling and Crime: An Empirical Evaluation," in *The Labeling of Deviance: Evaluating a Perspective*, ed. Walter Gove (New York: Wiley, 1975), pp. 157–179.

210. Megan Kurlychek, Robert Brame, and Shawn Bushway, "Enduring Risk? Old Criminal Records and Predictions of Future Criminal Involvement," *Crime and Delinquency* 53 (2007): 64–83.

211. Raymond Paternoster and Leeann Iovanni, "The Labeling Perspective and Delinquency: An Elaboration of the Theory and an Assessment of the Evidence," *Justice Quarterly* 6 (1989): 358–394.

212. Shadd Maruna, Thomas Lebel, Nick Mitchell, and Michelle Maples, "Pygmalion in the Reintegration Process: Desistance from Crime Through the Looking Glass," *Psychology, Crime, and Law* 10 (2004): 271–281.

213. Head Start statistics can be found at www.nhsa.org/services/find_a_head_start_program (accessed September 20, 2010).

© Holly Pickett/Redux

ON February 11, 2011, a popular revolt toppled the regime of long-term Egyptian dictator Hosni Mubarak, ushering in a period of turmoil in the Middle East that has become known as the "Arab Spring." Similar protests broke out in Tunisia and Yemen, and a popular uprising aimed at toppling the government of dictator Muammar Khadafi started a civil war in Libya, which resulted in his ouster. However, when protests erupted in Syria against the government of Bashar al-Assad, troops loyal to the ruling party cracked down hard. Researchers from Human Rights Watch, an international civil rights watchdog organization, conducted dozens of interviews inside Syria and found that state security forces killed hundreds of protesters and arbitrarily arrested thousands, many of whom, including children, were beaten and tortured. One youth, 13-year-old Hamza al-Khatib, was brutally tortured and killed by Syrian security forces and became an international symbol of government oppression.

(continued on page 266)

Critical Criminology and Restorative Justice

8

Learning Objectives

1. Be familiar with the ideas that underpin critical criminology
2. Trace the development of critical theory
3. Be able to discuss the difference between structural theory and instrumental theory
4. Link globalization to crime and criminality
5. Define the concept of state (organized) crime
6. Know the goals and findings of critical research
7. Be familiar with the critiques of critical criminology
8. Explain the concept of left realism
9. Know some of the basic ideas of critical feminism
10. Discuss how restorative justice is related to peacemaking criminology

Human Rights Watch concluded that the systematic and deliberate nature and scale of the government's abuses in one area, the Daraa governorate, where more than 400 people were killed and many others tortured, including children, qualified as a crime against humanity. Not surprisingly, Syrian government officials blamed the violence on "terrorist groups" or "armed gangs." Turkish Prime Minister Recep Tayyip Erdoğan denounced the violent crackdown as a "barbarity" that is "inhumane" and "cannot be digested."[1]

The civil rights violations and executions carried out in Syria are extreme examples of the social conflict that dominates and shapes contemporary society. We live in a world rife with political, social, and economic turmoil in nearly every corner of the globe. Conflict comes in many forms, occurs at many levels of society, and involves a whole slew of adversaries: workers and bosses, the United States and its overseas enemies, religious zealots and apostates, citizens and police. It occurs within cities, in neighborhoods, and even within the family.

Social conflict can be destructive when it leads to war, violence, and death; it can be functional when it results in positive social change. Conflict promotes crime by creating a social atmosphere in which the law is a mechanism for controlling dissatisfied, have-not members of society while the wealthy maintain their power. This is why crimes that are the province of the wealthy, such as illegal corporate activities, are sanctioned much more leniently than those, such as burglary, that are considered lower-class activities.

Criminologists who view crime as a function of social conflict and economic rivalry have in the past been known by a number of titles, such as conflict, Marxist, left, or radical criminologists, but today most commonly they are referred to as **critical criminologists** and their field of study as **critical criminology**.

Like their title hints, critical criminologists view themselves as social critics who dig beneath the surface of society to uncover its inequities. They reject the notion that law is designed to maintain a tranquil, fair society and that criminals are malevolent people who wish to trample the rights of others. They believe that the law is an instrument of power, wielded by those who control society in order to maintain their wealth, social position, and class advantage. They consider acts of racism, sexism, imperialism, unsafe working conditions, inadequate child care, substandard housing, pollution of the environment, and war-making used as tools of foreign policy to be the "true crimes." The crimes of the helpless—burglary, robbery, and assault—are expressions of rage over unjust economic conditions more than actual crimes.[2]

Contemporary critical criminologists try to explain crime within economic and social contexts and to express the connection between social class, crime, and social control.[3] They are concerned with issues such as these:

- The role government plays in creating a criminogenic environment

- The relationship between personal or group power and the shaping of criminal law
- The prevalence of bias in justice system operations
- The relationship between a capitalist, free enterprise economy and crime rates

Critical criminologists sometimes reject legal definitions of crime, viewing racism, sexism, and classism as causing greater social harm than burglary, robbery, and rape.[4] Coming from the left, they want to publicize the fact that conservatives work to cut spending on social programs and education and use the money to fund a vast military establishment. The rapid buildup of the prison system and the passage of draconian criminal laws that threaten civil rights and liberties—the death penalty, three strikes laws—are other elements of the conservative agenda. Critical criminologists believe that they are responsible for informing the public about the dangers of these right-wing developments.[5] They scorn mainstream criminologists who accept government funding to carry out research that supports the status quo rather than exposing the hypocrisy rampant in the capitalist system. They find it contemptible that a system of crony capitalism has developed that punishes the poor, unemployed, and desperate and generously rewards corporate executives who fire employees and move jobs overseas.[6]

This chapter reviews the historical development of critical criminology. It covers its principal ideas, and then looks at policies that have been embraced by critical thinkers that focus on peace and restoration rather than punishment and exclusion. Figure 8.1 illustrates the various independent branches of critical theory.

THE HISTORICAL DEVELOPMENT OF CRITICAL CRIMINOLOGY

The roots of critical criminology can be traced to the social philosopher Karl Marx (1818–1883), who identified the economic structures in society that control all human relations. Marx's view of society was shaped by the

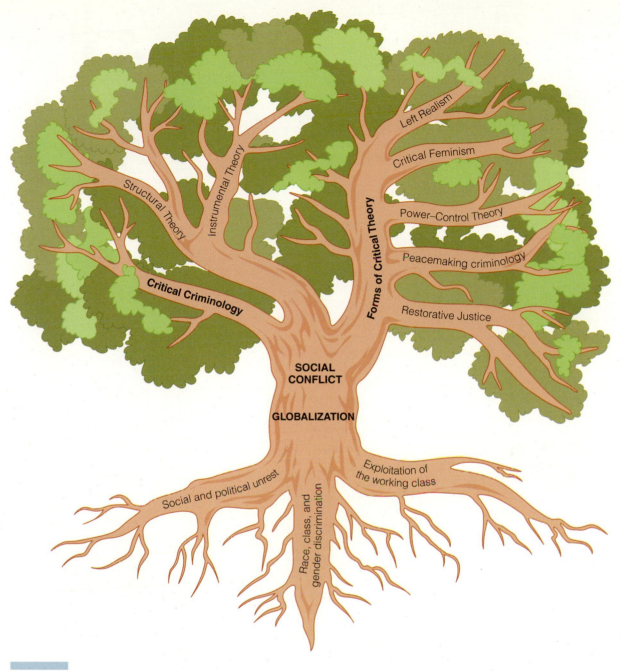

FIGURE 8.1
The Branches Critical Theory

Tree labels:
- Left Realism
- Critical Feminism
- Structural Theory
- Instrumental Theory
- Power–Control Theory
- Critical Criminology
- Forms of Critical Theory
- Peacemaking criminology
- Restorative Justice
- SOCIAL CONFLICT
- GLOBALIZATION
- Social and political unrest
- Race, class, and gender discrimination
- Exploitation of the working class

economic trends and structures of that period. He lived in an era of unrestrained capitalist expansion.[7] The tools of the Industrial Revolution had become regular features of society by 1850. Mechanized factories, the use of coal to drive steam engines, and modern transportation all inspired economic development. Production had shifted from cottage industries to large factories. Industrialists could hire workers on their own terms; as a result, conditions in factories were atrocious. Factory owners and the government enforcement agents in their pay ruthlessly

suppressed trade unions that promised workers salvation from these atrocities.

Marx's early career as a journalist was interrupted by government suppression of the newspaper where he worked because of the paper's liberal editorial policy. He then moved to Paris, where he met Friedrich Engels (1820–1895), who would become his friend and economic patron. By 1847, Marx and Engels had joined with a group of primarily German socialist revolutionaries known as the Communist League.

Productive Forces and Productive Relations

In 1848, Marx issued his famous *Communist Manifesto*, in which he described the oppressive labor conditions prevalent during the rise of industrial capitalism. The exploitation of the working class, he believed, would eventually lead to class conflict and the end of the capitalist system.

Marx focused his attention on the economic conditions perpetuated by the capitalist system. He stated that its development had turned workers into a dehumanized mass who lived an existence that was at the mercy of their capitalist employers. He wrote of the injustice of young children being sent to work in mines and factories from dawn to dusk. He focused on the people who were being beaten down by a system that demanded obedience and cooperation and offered little in return. These oppressive conditions led Marx to conclude that the character of every civilization is determined by its mode of production—the way its people develop and produce material goods (materialism).

Marx identified the economic structures in society that control all human relations. Production has two components: **productive forces**, which include such things as technology, energy sources, and material resources, and **productive relations**, which are the relationships that exist among the people producing goods and services. The most important relationship in industrial culture is between the owners of the means of production, the **capitalist bourgeoisie**, and the people who do the actual labor, the **proletariat**.

Throughout history, society has been organized this way: master–slave, lord–serf, and now capitalist–proletariat. According to Marx, capitalist society is subject to the development of a rigid class structure with the capitalist bourgeoisie at the top, followed by the working proletariat, who actually produce goods and services, and at the bottom, the fringe, nonproductive members who produce nothing and live, parasitically, off the work of others—the **lumpen proletariat** (Figure 8.2).

In Marxist theory, the term *class* does not refer to an attribute or characteristic of a person or a group; rather, it denotes position in relation to others. Thus, it is not necessary to have a particular amount of wealth or prestige to be a member of the capitalist class; it is more important to have the power to exploit others economically, legally, and socially. The political and economic philosophy of the dominant class influences all aspects of life. Consciously or unconsciously, artists, writers, and teachers bend their work to the whims of the capitalist system. The economic system controls all facets of human life; consequently, people's lives revolve around the means of production.

As Marx said:

> In all forms of society, there is one specific kind of production which predominates over the rest, whose relations thus assign rank and influence to the others. It is a general illumination which bathes all the other colours

The owners of production
Capitalist bourgeoisie

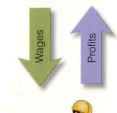

The worker
Proletariat

The nonproductive
Lumpen proletariat

FIGURE 8.2
The Marxist View of Class

and modifies their particularity. It is a particular ether which determines the specific gravity of every being which has materialized within it.[8]

Marx believed societies and their structures were not stable and, therefore, could change through slow evolution or sudden violence. If social conflicts are not resolved, they tend to destabilize society, leading to social change.

The ebb and flow of the capitalist business cycle creates social conflicts that contain the seeds of its own destruction. Marx predicted that from its ashes would grow a socialist state in which the workers themselves would own the means of production. In his analysis, Marx used the **dialectic method**, based on the analysis developed by the philosopher Georg Hegel (1770–1831). Hegel argued that for every idea, or **thesis**, there exists an opposing argument, or **antithesis**. Since neither position can ever be truly accepted, the result is a merger of the two ideas, a **synthesis**. Marx adapted this analytic method for his study of class struggle. History, argued Marx, is replete with examples of two opposing forces whose conflict promotes social change. When conditions are bad enough, the oppressed will rise up to fight the owners and eventually replace them. Thus, in the end, the capitalist system will destroy itself.

A Marxist Vision of Crime

Marx did not write a great deal on the subject of crime, but he mentioned it in a variety of passages scattered throughout his writing. He viewed crime as the product of law enforcement policies in which people are labeled by their experiences with police and are stigmatized and locked into a life of crime.[9] He also saw a connection between criminality and the inequities found in the capitalist system. He reasoned: "There must be something rotten in the very core of a social system which increases in wealth without diminishing its misery, and increases in crime even more rapidly than in numbers."[10]

His collaborator, Friedrich Engels, however, did spend some time on the subject in his work, *The Condition of the Working Class in England in 1844*.[11] Engels portrayed crime as a function of social demoralization—a collapse of people's humanity reflecting a decline in society. Workers, demoralized by capitalist society, are caught up in a process that leads to crime and violence. According to Engels, workers are social outcasts, ignored by the structure of capitalist society and treated as brutes.[12] Left to their own devices, working people commit crime because their choice is a slow death of starvation or a speedy one at the hands of the law. The brutality of the capitalist system, he believed, turns workers into animal-like creatures without a will of their own.

The writings of Karl Marx greatly influenced the development of the view of crime that rested on the concept of social conflict. Even though Marx himself did not write much on the topic of crime, his views on the relationship between crime and the concept of social conflict were first applied to criminology by three distinguished scholars: Willem Bonger, Ralf Dahrendorf, and George Vold. In some instances, their works share the Marxist view that industrial society is wracked by conflict between the proletariat and the bourgeoisie; in other instances, their writings diverge from Marxist dogma. The writing of each of these pioneers is briefly described in Exhibit 8.1.

To read about **Marx and his vision**, go to the Criminal Justice CourseMate at cengagebrain.com, then access the "Web Links" for this chapter.

CREATING A CRITICAL CRIMINOLOGY

The social ferment of the 1960s gave birth to critical criminology. In 1968, a group of British sociologists formed the National Deviancy Conference (NDC). With about 300 members, this organization sponsored several national symposia and dialogues. Members came from all walks of life, but at its core the NDC was a group of academics who were critical of the positivist criminology being taught in British and American universities. More specifically, they rejected the conservative stance of criminologists and their close financial relationship with government funding agencies.

The NDC called attention to ways in which social control might actually cause deviance rather than just respond to antisocial behavior. Many conference members became concerned about the political nature of social control.

In 1973, critical theory was given a powerful academic boost when British scholars Ian Taylor, Paul Walton, and Jock Young published *The New Criminology*.[13] This brilliant, thorough, and well-constructed critique of existing concepts in criminology called for the development of new methods of criminological analysis and critique. *The New Criminology* became the standard resource for scholars critical of both the field of criminology and the existing legal process. Since its publication there has been a tradition for critical criminologists to turn their attention to the field itself, questioning the role criminology plays in supporting the status quo and aiding in the oppression of the poor and powerless.[14]

U.S. scholars were also influenced during the late 1960s and early 1970s by the widespread unrest and social change that shook the world. The war in Vietnam, prison struggles, and the civil rights and feminist movements produced a climate in which criticism of the ruling class seemed a natural by-product. Mainstream, positivist criminology was criticized as being overtly conservative, pro-government, and antihuman. Critical criminologists scoffed when their fellow scholars used statistical analysis of computerized data to describe criminal and delinquent behavior. Several influential scholars embraced the idea that the social conflict produced by the unequal distribution of power and wealth was at the root cause of crime. William Chambliss and Robert Seidman wrote the well-respected treatise *Law, Order and Power*, which documented how the justice system protects the rich and powerful.[15] Chambliss and Seidman's work showed how control of the political and economic system affects the way criminal justice is administered and that the definitions of crime used in contemporary society favor those who control the justice system.

In another influential work, *The Social Reality of Crime*, Richard Quinney also proclaimed that in contemporary society criminal law represents the interests of those who hold power.[16] Where there is conflict between social groups—the wealthy and the poor—those who hold power

will create laws that benefit themselves and keep rivals in check. Law is not an abstract body of rules that represents an absolute moral code; rather, law is an integral part of society, a force that represents a way of life and a method of doing things. Crime is a function of power relations and an inevitable result of social conflict. Criminals are not simply social misfits but people who have come up short in the struggle for success and are seeking alternative means of achieving wealth, status, or even survival.

As a group, these social thinkers began to show how in our postindustrial, capitalist society the economic system invariably produces haves and have-nots.[17] The mode of production shapes social life. Because economic competitiveness is the essence of capitalism, conflict increases and eventually destabilizes both social institutions and social groups.[18]

Contemporary Critical Criminology

From these early roots, a robust critical criminology was formed. At first, these alternative forms of criminology were considered Marxist and radical. They have morphed into a critical criminology that is antiestablishment and questioning of the socioeconomic structures that produce crime and criminality.[19]

Today, critical criminologists devote their attention to a number of important themes and concepts. One is the use and misuse of power, or the ability of persons and groups to determine and control the behavior of others and to shape public opinion to meet their personal interests. Because those in power shape the content of the law, it comes as no surprise that their behavior is often exempt from legal sanctions. Those who deserve the most severe sanctions (wealthy white-collar criminals whose crimes cost society millions of dollars) usually receive lenient punishments, whereas those whose relatively minor crimes are committed out of economic necessity (petty thieves and drug dealers) receive stricter penalties, especially if they are minority group members who lack social and economic power.[20]

Critical criminologists also critique the field of criminology, questioning the role criminologists play in supporting the status quo and aiding in the oppression of the poor and powerless.[21] After all, criminologists may spend their time creating effective crime control mechanisms that swell the nation's prisons with indigent and desperate people while corporate executives make fat profits.

Critical criminologists have also been deeply concerned about the current state of the American political system and the creation of what they consider to be an American empire abroad. Ironically, recent events such as the war in Iraq and the efforts to penalize immigrants and close U.S. borders have energized critical thinkers; their vision seems as pertinent today as it was during its heyday in the 1960s and 1970s.[22] The conservative agenda, they believe, calls for dismantling welfare, health and health programs; lowering labor costs through union busting; increasing tax cuts that favor the wealthy; ending affirmative action; and reducing environmental control and regulation. Some try to show how racism still pervades the American system and manifests itself in a wide variety of social practices ranging from the administration of criminal justice to the "whitening" of the teaching force because recruitment rests on a racially skewed selection process.[23]

Corporations are now more powerful than ever. Spending is being cut on social programs, and the idea of universal health care is attacked because paying for it would cut into corporate profits. The rapid buildup of the prison system and passage of draconian criminal laws that threaten civil rights and liberties—the war on drugs, the death penalty, three strikes laws, and the Patriot Act—are other elements of the conservative agenda. Tax cuts for the wealthy mean less money for social programs. The war on drugs has resulted in millions of people being incarcerated, most of whom are poor and powerless. Critical criminologists believe they are responsible for informing the public about the dangers of these developments.[24]

CONNECTIONS

The USA Patriot Act is discussed further in Chapter 11 within the context of legal efforts to thwart terrorism. Some welcome provisions in the act that make it easier for the government to monitor people considered dangerous, but critical thinkers fear the loss of individual freedom at the expense of state power.

Critical criminologists have turned their attention to the threat competitive capitalism presents to the working class. In addition to perpetuating male supremacy and racism, they believe that modern global capitalism helps destroy the lives of workers in less developed countries. Capitalists hailed China's entry into the World Trade Organization in 2001 as a significant economic event. However, critical thinkers point out that the economic boom has significant costs: the average manufacturing wage in China is 20 to 25 cents per hour; many thousands of workers are killed at work each year and millions more are disabled.[25]

DEFINING CRIME AND JUSTICE

According to critical theorists, crime is a political concept designed to protect the power and position of the upper classes at the expense of the poor. Some, but not all, would include in a list of "real" crimes such acts as violations of human rights due to racism, sexism, and imperialism and other violations of human dignity and physical needs and necessities. Part of the critical agenda, argues criminologist Robert Bohm, is to make the public aware that these behaviors "are crimes just as much as burglary and robbery."[26] Take for instance what Alette Smeulers and Roelof Haveman call **supranational crimes:** war crimes, crimes against humanity, genocide, and other human rights violations. Smeulers and Haveman believe that these types of crimes should merit more attention by criminologists, and therefore they call for a separate specialization.[27]

The nature of a society controls the direction of its criminality; criminals are not social misfits but products of the society and its economic system.[28] According to Michael Lynch and W. Byron Groves, three implications follow from this view:

1. Each society produces its own types and amounts of crime.
2. Each society has its own distinctive ways of dealing with criminal behavior.
3. Each society gets the amount and type of crime that it deserves.[29]

This analysis tells us that criminals are not a group of outsiders who can be controlled by increased law enforcement. Criminality, instead, is a function of social and economic organization. To control crime and reduce criminality, societies must remove the social conditions that promote crime.

In our advanced technological society, those with economic and political power control the definition of crime and the manner in which the criminal justice system enforces the law.[30] Consequently, the only crimes available to the poor are the severely sanctioned "street crimes": rape, murder, theft, and mugging. Members of the middle class cheat on their taxes and engage in petty corporate crime (employee theft), acts that generate social disapproval but are rarely punished severely. The wealthy are involved in acts that should be described as crimes but are not, such as racism, sexism, and profiteering. Although regulatory laws control illegal business activities, these are rarely enforced, and violations are lightly punished. One reason is that an essential feature of capitalism is the need to expand business and create new markets. This goal often conflicts with laws designed to protect the environment and creates clashes with those who seek their enforcement. In our postindustrial society, the need for expansion usually triumphs. For example, corporate spokespeople and their political allies will brand environmentalists as "tree huggers" who stand in the way of jobs and prosperity.[31]

The rich are insulated from street crimes because they live in areas far removed from crime. Those in power use the fear of crime as a tool to maintain their control over society. The poor are controlled through incarceration, and the middle class is diverted from caring about the crimes of the powerful by their fear of the crimes of the powerless.[32] Ironically, they may have more to lose from the economic crimes committed by the rich than the street crimes of the poor. Stock market swindles and savings and loan scams cost the public billions of dollars but are typically settled with fines and probationary sentences.

Because private ownership of property is the true measure of success in American society (as opposed to, say, being a worthy person), the state becomes an ally of the wealthy in protecting their property interests. As a result, theft-related crimes are often punished more severely than are acts of violence because although the former may be interclass, the latter are typically intraclass.

Instrumental vs. Structural Theory

Not all critical thinkers share a similar view of how crime is defined and how society works to control criminal behavior. **Instrumental theorists** view criminal law and the criminal justice system solely as instruments for controlling the poor, have-not members of society. They view the state as the tool of capitalists. In contrast, **structural theorists** believe that the law is not the exclusive domain of the rich; rather, it is used to maintain the long-term interests of the capitalist system and to control members of any class who threaten its existence.

Instrumental Theory   According to the instrumental view, the law and justice system serve the powerful and rich and enable them to impose their morality and standards of behavior on the entire society. Those who wield economic power are able to extend their self-serving definition of illegal or criminal behavior to encompass those who might threaten the status quo or interfere with their quest for ever-increasing profits.[33] The concentration of economic assets in the nation's largest industrial firms translates into the political power needed to control tax laws to limit the firms' tax liabilities.[34] Some have the economic clout to hire top attorneys to defend them against antitrust actions, making them almost immune to regulation.

The poor, according to this branch of critical theory, may or may not commit more crimes than the rich, but they certainly are arrested and punished more often. Under the capitalist system, the poor are driven to crime because a natural frustration exists in a society in which affluence is well publicized but unattainable. When class conflict becomes unbearable, frustration can spill out in riots, such as the one that occurred in Los Angeles on April 29, 1992, which was described as a "class rebellion of the underprivileged against the privileged."[35] Because of class conflict, a deep-rooted hostility is generated among members of the lower class toward a social order they are not allowed to shape and whose benefits are unobtainable.[36]

Instrumental theorists consider it essential to **demystify** law and justice—that is, to unmask its true purpose. Criminological theories that focus on family structure, intelligence, peer relations, and school performance keep the lower classes servile by showing why they are more criminal, less intelligent, and more prone to school failure and family problems than the middle class. Demystification involves identifying the destructive intent of capitalist inspired and funded criminology. Instrumental theory's goal for criminology is to show how capitalist law preserves ruling-class power.[37]

Structural Theory   Structural theorists disagree with the view that the relationship between law and capitalism is unidirectional, always working for the rich and against the poor.[38] If law and justice were purely instruments of the wealthy, why would laws controlling corporate crimes, such as price-fixing, false advertising, and illegal restraint of trade, have been created and enforced?

To a structuralist, the law is designed to keep the system operating efficiently, and anyone, worker or owner, who rocks the boat is targeted for sanction. For example, antitrust legislation is designed to prevent any single capitalist from dominating the system. If the free enterprise system is to function, no single person can become too powerful at the expense of the economic system as a whole. Structuralists would regard the efforts of the U.S. government to break up Microsoft as an example of a conservative government using its clout to keep the system on an even keel. The long prison sentences given to corporate executives who engage in insider trading are a warning to capitalists that they must play by the rules.

THE CAUSE OF CRIME

Critical thinkers believe that the key crime-producing element of modern corporate capitalism is the effort to create **surplus value**—the profits produced by the laboring classes that are accrued by business owners. Once accumulated, surplus value can be either reinvested or used to enrich the owners. To increase the rate of surplus value, workers can be made to toil harder for less pay, be made more efficient, or be replaced by machines or technology. Therefore, economic growth does not benefit all elements of the population, and in the long run it may produce the same effect as a depression or recession.

As the rate of surplus value increases, more people are displaced from productive relationships and the size of the marginal population swells. As corporations downsize to increase profits, high-paying labor and managerial jobs are lost to computer-driven machinery. Displaced workers are forced into service jobs at minimum wage. Many become temporary employees without benefits or a secure position.

As more people are thrust outside the economic mainstream, a condition referred to as **marginalization**, a larger portion of the population is forced to live in areas conducive to crime. Once people are marginalized, commitment to the system declines, producing another criminogenic force: a weakened bond to society.[39] This process is illustrated in Figure 8.3.

The government may be quick to respond during periods of economic decline because those in power assume that poor economic conditions breed crime and social disorder. When unemployment is increasing, public officials assume the worst and devote greater attention to the

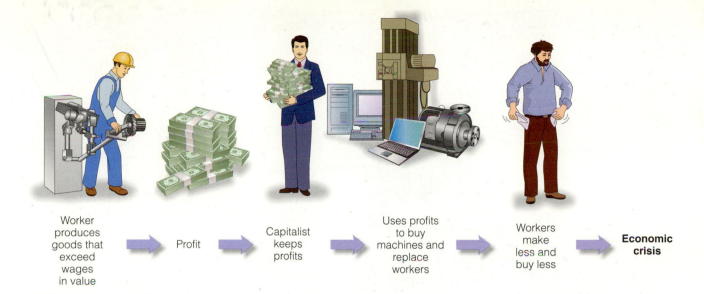

FIGURE 8.3
Surplus Value and Crime

Worker produces goods that exceed wages in value → Profit → Capitalist keeps profits → Uses profits to buy machines and replace workers → Workers make less and buy less → **Economic crisis**

criminal justice system, perhaps building new prisons to prepare for the coming "crime wave."[40] Empirical research confirms that economic downturns are indeed linked to both crime rate increases and government activities such as passing anticrime legislation.[41] As the level of surplus value increases, so too do police expenditures, most likely because of the perceived or real need for the state to control those on the economic margin.[42]

> The theory of **surplus value** can be quite complex. Read more about it at Criminal Justice CourseMate at cengagebrain.com, then access the "Web Links" for this chapter.

Globalization

The new global economy is a particularly vexing development for critical theorists and their use of the concept of surplus value. **Globalization**, which usually refers to the process of creating transnational markets and political and legal systems, has shifted the focus of critical inquiry to a world perspective.

Globalization began when large companies decided to establish themselves in foreign markets by adapting their products or services to the local culture. The process took off with the fall of the Soviet Union, which opened new European markets. The development of China into a super industrial power encouraged foreign investors to take advantage of China's huge supply of workers. As the Internet

and the communication revolution unfolded, companies were able to establish instant communications with their far-flung corporate empires, a technological breakthrough that further aided trade and foreign investments. A series of transnational corporate mergers and takeovers (such as when Ford bought Swedish car maker Volvo in 1999 and then in 2010 sold Volvo to the Chinese car company Geely) produced ever-larger transnational corporations.

Some experts believe globalization can improve the standard of living in third-world nations by providing jobs and training, but critical theorists question the altruism of multinational corporations. Their motives are exploiting natural resources, avoiding regulation, and taking advantage of desperate workers. When these giant corporations set up a factory in a developing nation, it is not to help the local population but to get around environmental laws and take advantage of needy workers who may be forced to labor in substandard conditions. In some instances, transnational companies take advantage of national unrest and calamity in order to engage in profiteering. For example, recent examinations of illegal mineral expropriation in the Democratic Republic of Congo (DRC) highlight the role that transnational corporations and international marketplaces played in the theft of Congolese gold. Although these companies did not directly encourage the conflict or the massive human rights violations and crimes against humanity committed in the region, they took advantage of the existing disorder and violence to make a huge profit.[43]

Globalization has replaced imperialism and colonization as a new form of economic domination and oppression and

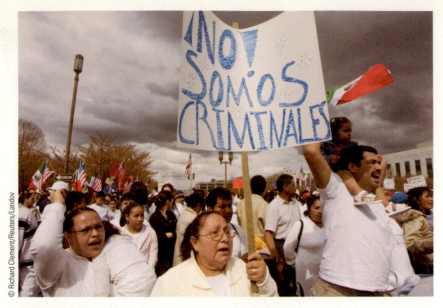

Globalization has changed the traditional ways of doing business, creating prosperity in some nations and chaos in others. People are now moving from nation to nation seeking jobs and a fresh start. Here, supporters of immigration reform rally for immigrants' rights at the state capitol in Salem, Oregon. Several thousand people gathered to support expanding immigrants' rights and to protest a congressional bill that was designed to tighten U.S. immigration. The sign reads, "We are not criminals." Should immigration policies be tightened to protect American jobs, or should immigrants be allowed to enter the United States in order to take part in the "American Dream"?

now presents, according to critical thinkers, a threat to the world economy:

- Growing global dominance and the reach of the free market capitalist system, which disproportionately benefits wealthy and powerful organizations and individuals
- Increasing vulnerability of indigenous people with a traditional way of life to the forces of globalized capitalism
- Growing influence and impact of international financial institutions (such as the World Bank) and the related relative decline of power of local or state-based institutions
- Nondemocratic operation of international financial institutions[44]

Globalization may be responsible for the recent unrest in the financial systems and in so doing has created a fertile ground for contemporary enterprise crimes. By expanding the reach of both criminal and noncriminal organizations, globalization also increases the vulnerability of indigenous people with a traditional way of life.[45] With money and power to spare, criminal enterprise groups can recruit new members, bribe government officials, and even fund private armies. International organized crime has globalized its activities for the same reasons legitimate multinational corporations have expanded around the world: new markets bring new sources of profits. As international crime expert Louise Shelley puts it:

> Just as multinational corporations establish branches around the world to take advantage of attractive labor or raw material markets, so do illicit businesses.

Furthermore, international businesses, both legitimate and illicit, also establish facilities worldwide for production, marketing, and distribution needs. Illicit enterprises are able to expand geographically to take advantage of these new economic circumstances thanks to the communications and international transportation revolution.[46]

Shelley argues that two elements of globalization encourage criminality: one technological, the other cultural. Technological advances such as efficient and widespread commercial airline traffic, improvements in telecommunications (ranging from global cell phone connectivity to the Internet), and the growth of international trade have all aided the growth in illicit transnational activities. These changes have facilitated the cross-border movement of goods and people, conditions exploited by criminals who now use Internet chat rooms to plan their activities. On a cultural level, globalization brings with it an ideology of free markets and free trade. The cultural shift means less intervention and regulation, conditions exploited by crime groups to cross unpatrolled borders and to expand their activities to new regions of the world. Transnational crime groups freely exploit this new freedom to travel to regions where they cannot be extradited, base their operations in countries with ineffective or corrupt law enforcement, and launder their money in countries with bank secrecy or few effective controls. Globalization has allowed both individual offenders and criminal gangs to gain tremendous operational benefits while reducing the risks of apprehension and punishment.

Globalization may have a profound influence on the concept of surplus value. Workers in the United States may be replaced in high-paying manufacturing jobs not by machines but by foreign workers. Instant communication via the Internet and global communications, a development that Marx could not have foreseen, will speed the effect immeasurably. Globalization will have a profound effect both on the economy and eventually on crime rates.

State (Organized) Crime

While mainstream criminologists focus on the crimes of the poor and powerless, critical criminologists focus their attention on the law violations of the powerful. One area of concern is referred to as **state (organized) crime**—acts defined by law as criminal and committed by state officials, both elected or appointed, in pursuit of their jobs as government representatives. Their actions, or in some cases

The Criminological Enterprise
Mass Deception

In his 2010 book, *Mass Deception*, criminologist Scott Bonn argues that the George W. Bush administration manufactured public support for war with Iraq by falsely claiming that its leader, Saddam Hussein, was involved in the terrorist attacks of 9/11 and that Iraq possessed weapons of mass destruction. Bonn explains that the war was a function of a "moral panic" engineered by the Bush administration with the support of the U.S. news media. A moral panic occurs when the general population begins to feel threatened by a person or group even though there may be little actual evidence to support the intensity of feeling expressed by the **population**. Bonn believes that despite overwhelming evidence that the attacks had been solely orchestrated by Osama Bin Laden and al Qaeda, the Bush administration initiated a campaign to link 9/11 to Iraq, Saddam Hussein, and his Ba'ath Party. They convinced the U.S. public and the world that Iraq (a) was involved in the attacks of 9/11, (b) possessed weapons of mass destruction (WMD), and (c) represented a grave and growing threat to U.S. security. In 2002, President Bush proclaimed that "the Iraqi dictator must not be permitted to threaten America and the world with horrible poisons and diseases and gases and atomic weapons." Although the United States was never directly threatened or provoked by Iraq, President Bush declared war allegedly to "disarm Iraq . . . and to defend the world from grave danger." The Bush administration's propaganda campaign was so successful that 70 percent of the U.S. public believed Iraq was directly involved in the attacks of 9/11 when the U.S.-led invasion of Iraq began.

According to Bonn, the cost of Bush's deception was high. Iraq has been embroiled in a civil war, more than 4,000 U.S. soldiers and more than 1 million Iraqis (3.7 percent of the population) have been killed, and the war has cost the American taxpayer $10 billion per month.

Bonn believes that the war in Iraq amounts to state organized crime. It was precipitated by the Bush administration and reinforced by the news media, which exploited preexisting negative stereotypes of Arabs. The Bush administration perpetrated state crimes and war crimes as well as violations of international criminal law when they invaded Iraq. What was the real cause of the war? While the truth may never be known, one possibility is the unfinished Bush family business with Saddam Hussein resulting from the 1991 Persian Gulf War.

Another motivation was the Bush administration's desire to control Iraq's oil production and massive oil reserves.

Bonn critiques the war and the occupation of Iraq as violations of both U.S. and international laws. He believes that despite what amounted to committing war crimes, the Bush administration enjoyed both political and bureaucratic exemptions from prosecution under international law; it is unlikely ever to be held accountable for its actions. Bonn introduces a unique, integrated, and interdisciplinary theory called "critical communication" to explain how and why political elites and the news media periodically create public panics that benefit both parties.

CRITICAL THINKING

Is it fair to brand the war in Iraq as state organized crime? Does Bonn have it right, or were Bush's motives more genuine: to protect the Iraqi people and the world from an evil dictator's ambitions?

SOURCE: Scott A. Bonn, *Mass Deception: Moral Panic and the U.S. War on Iraq* (Rutgers University Press, 2010).

---

failure to act, amount to a violation of the criminal law they are bound by oath or duty to uphold.

Among the most controversial claims made by critical criminologists are those linking the United States to state (organized) crime and violence. The Criminological Enterprise feature reviews a new book that makes just such a claim.

Those who study state crime argue that these antisocial behaviors arise from efforts to either maintain governmental power or to uphold the race, class, and gender advantages of those who support the government. In industrial society, the state will do everything to protect the property rights of the wealthy while opposing the real interests of the poor. They might even go to war to support the capitalist classes who need the wealth and resources of other nations. The desire for natural resources such as rubber, oil, and metals was one of the primary reasons for Japan's invasion of China and other Eastern nations that sparked their entry into World War II. Fifty years later, the United States was accused by many media commentators and political pundits of invading Iraq in order to secure its oil for American use.[47]

There are a number of categories of state crime, and these are set out in some detail below.[48]

Illegal Domestic Surveillance This occurs when government agents listen in on telephone conversations or intercept e-mails without proper approval in order to stifle dissent and monitor political opponents. Sometimes the true purpose of the surveillance is masked by the need for national security while in reality it is illegal organizational policy and practice that has in some cases been sanctioned by heads of state for political purposes. The dangers of illegal surveillance have become magnified because closed-circuit TV cameras are now routinely used by metropolitan police agencies. Many cities, including Washington, D.C., New York, Chicago, and Los Angeles, have installed significant numbers of police-operated cameras trained on public spaces. While ostensibly used to deter crime, once these surveillance facilities are put in place, police departments can use them to record the faces of political demonstrators, to record what people are reading, and to store photographs of people on computer databases without their knowledge or permission. This capability worries both civil libertarians and critical criminologists.[49]

Human Rights Violations

In June 2009, Amnesty International, the civil rights watchdog organization, published a report accusing the Sri Lankan government of a vicious cycle of civil rights abuse in its war against the Tamil Tigers (Liberation Tigers of Tamil Eelam, LTTE), a group that sought to carve out an independent state for the Tamil people, an ethnic/religious minority group. During the conflict the Sri Lankan government was accused of failing to investigate civil rights violations, including disappearances and torture of political suspects. But it was not just the rebels who were hunted and killed. More than 30,000 people considered sympathetic to the Tamil cause disappeared, including businessmen, journalists, and individuals suspected of having terrorist links; even a vice chancellor of a university was a victim. Once they were taken into government hands, people suspected of aiding the rebels often were never seen again. In addition to this outrage, hundreds of thousands of innocent people were displaced from their homes.[50]

Some governments, such as Iran, routinely deny their citizens basic civil rights, holding them without trial and using "disappearances" and summary executions to rid themselves of political dissidents. After students rioted against governmental controls in 1999, more than 70 simply disappeared, another 1,200 to 1,400 were detained, and dozens were killed when security forces broke up demonstrations.[51] Similar violent actions to break up demonstrations took place in June 2009 in the wake of the disputed election that returned President Mahmoud Ahmadinejad to power.

Another state crime involves the operation of the correctional systems in nations that are notorious for depriving detainees of basic necessities and routinely using hard labor and torture to punish political dissidents. The CIA has made use of their brutal regimes to soften up terror suspects for interrogation and sent suspected terror suspects to secret prisons abroad, without trial or indictment. There they can be subject to harsh interrogation tactics forbidden in the United States.[52]

Other human rights violations are directed against migrant laborers. For example, thousands of South Asian migrant workers are now working on a $27 billion island development in the United Arab Emirates. According to Human Rights Watch, to obtain the visas needed to work in the UAE, nearly all workers paid hefty fees to "labor-supply agencies"; many workers sold their homes or land or borrowed money at high rates of interest to pay the agencies' fees. Upon arrival in the UAE, the indebted workers—many of whom are illiterate—were required to sign contracts with the construction companies on much worse terms than they had been promised back home, ensuring that their debts can never be paid off. In the worst cases, they are subjected to what may be considered forced labor or virtual slavery.[53]

State–Corporate Crime

This type of state crime is committed by individuals who abuse their state authority or who fail to exercise it when working with people and organizations in the private sector. For example, a state environmental agency may fail to enforce laws, resulting in the pollution of public waterways. State–corporate crime is particularly alarming, considering that regulatory law aimed at controlling private corporations is being scaled back while globalization has made corporations worldwide entities both in production and in advancing the consumption of their products.[54]

State Violence

Sometimes nations engage in violence to maintain their power over dissident groups. Army or police officers form death squads—armed vigilante groups that kill suspected political opponents or other undesirables. These groups commit assassinations and kidnappings using extremely violent methods to intimidate the population and deter political activity against the government. For example, on January 24, 2009, Manoel Mattos, human rights activist and vice-president of the workers' party in the state of Pernambuco, Brazil, was shot in his own home by intruders. Mattos had received repeated death threats as a result of his work denouncing killings and abuses by death squads across northeast Brazil. Despite the threats, federal police had recently withdrawn the protection he was receiving, allegedly because they felt it was no longer necessary.[55]

The use of death squads is common in third-world countries, but police violence and use of deadly force are not uncommon in Western industrialized nations. In some nations, such as during the civil war in the Russian province of Chechnya, almost all political detainees are subjected to torture, including electric shocks, burnings, and severe beating with boots, sticks, plastic bottles filled with water or sand, and heavy rubber-coated cables. The rest are subject to psychological pressure, such as threats or intimidation of sexual abuse or execution, as well as threats to harm their relatives.[56] The Profiles in Crime box focuses on this abuse.

Crime and Social Institutions

Critical thinkers often focus on contemporary social institutions to show how they operate as instruments of class and racial oppression. Critical scholars find that class bias and racial oppression exist from the cradle to the grave. There are significant race-based achievement differences in education, ranging from scores on standardized tests to dropout and high school completion rates. There are a few high schools, mostly in poverty-stricken inner city neighborhoods, where the high school completion rate is 40 percent or less; these are referred to as **dropout factories**. There are more than 1,700 of these failing schools in the United States. Although they represent only a small fraction of all

Profiles in Crime

Russia's Death Squads

© Konstantin Zavrazhin/Getty Images

Russia's two wars against breakaway province Chechnya went on from the mid-1990s until 2009, when with massive firepower they crushed the separatist rebel groups; hundreds of thousands died during the conflict. As the war raged, Chechen fighters launched suicide attacks against civilians in the Moscow metro and at a rock festival. In 2002, a gang that included 18 female suicide bombers seized more than 800 hostages in a Moscow theatre, 129 of whom died when the Russians pumped poisonous gas into the building on day three of the siege. In 2004, rebels took hundreds of schoolchildren and their relatives hostage in Beslan. After a three-day siege, Russian security forces stormed the school; 334 hostages died, more than half of them children.

Enraged by the Chechen actions, the Russians created death squads made up of elite Russian special forces, commandos who would stop at nothing to find, torture, and kill enemy combatants. In one incident, when a rebel was captured who had been instructing other women to become suicide bombers, death squad commandos tortured her to gain information and then shot her to death. One of the death squad members told reporters, "We disposed of her body in a field. We placed an artillery shell between her legs and one over her chest, added several 200-gram TNT blocks and blew her to smithereens. The trick is to make sure absolutely nothing is left. No body, no proof, no problem." The technique was known as pulverization. The young recruits she was training were taken away by another unit for further interrogation before they, too, were executed. Not only were suspected rebels victimized, but also people close to them were systematically tracked, abducted, tortured, and killed. Intelligence was often extracted by breaking limbs with a hammer, administering electric shocks, and forcing men to perform sexual acts on each other. The bodies were either buried in unmarked pits or pulverized. The scenes would occasionally be filmed and circulated among enemy combatants as a form of psychological warfare.

The Russian government publicly condemned torture and extrajudicial killing and denied that its army committed war crimes in Chechnya. Despite government protestations, the truth seems to be different. Far from being the work of a few ruthless mavericks, these methods were widely used by death squads among the special forces.

SOURCE: *London Times*, April 26, 2009, "Russian Death Squads 'Pulverise' Chechens," www.timesonline.co.uk/tol/news/world/europe/article6168959.ece (accessed May 26, 2011).

---

public high schools in America, they account for about half of all high school dropouts each year.[57]

One reason for these persistent problems may be linked to differences in discipline meted out in poor and wealthy districts. Research shows that African American children receive more disciplinary infractions than children from other racial categories, despite the fact that their behavior is quite similar. Having a higher percentage of black students in a school translates into a greater use of disciplinary tactics, a factor that may explain why minority students fare less well and are more likely to disengage from schools at a younger age than whites.[58] Allison Payne and Kelly Welch recently found that in disadvantaged, urban schools in minority areas, administrators and teachers are more likely to respond to misbehavior in a punitive manner and less likely to respond in a restorative manner as they do in suburban mostly white schools.[59] Critical thinkers might suggest that these class- and race-based burdens make crime inevitable.

The problems faced by underclass kids and racial minorities does not stop at the schoolhouse door. As you may recall, the *racial threat hypothesis* states that as the number of minority group members in the community increases, law enforcement agents become more punitive. There are cries for more "law and order" even when crime rates are declining. As a result, charges of racial profiling have become common. Police are more likely to use racial profiling to stop black motorists as they travel further into the boundaries of predominantly white neighborhoods: black motorists driving in an all-white neighborhood set up a red flag because they are "out of place."[60]

All too often these unwarranted stops lead to equally unfair arrests. In 2011, the team of Tammy Rinehart Kochel, David Wilson, and Stephen Mastrofski thoroughly reviewed the existing literature on police arrest practices, screening more than 4,500 published and unpublished research studies. Their meta-analysis found that minority suspects stopped by police are significantly more likely to be arrested than are white suspects. The chances of a white being arrested was .20, whereas the average probability for a nonwhite was calculated at .26. These findings may be used by critical criminologists as clear evidence of the racial bias they suspect is present in American policing.[61]

Considering this unfair treatment, it is not surprising to critical theorists that police brutality complaints are

Profiles in Crime
Mumia Abu-Jamal

AP Images/Chris Gardner

Mumia Abu-Jamal (born Wesley Cook on April 24, 1954) began his journalism career with the radical Black Panther party in the 1960s. By the time he was 15, Abu-Jamal was appointed minister of information for the Philadelphia branch. After the Panther party disbanded, Abu-Jamal used his writing and speaking talent to become a local broadcaster, even winning a Peabody Award for his coverage of the Pope's visit; in 1980, he became president of the Philadelphia Association of Black Journalists.

Then Mumia Abu-Jamal's life was turned upside down when he was charged with first-degree murder in the killing of Philadelphia police officer Daniel Faulkner. According to authorities, on December 9, 1981, Faulkner, 25, stopped a car for driving the wrong way down the street. Calling for backup, he approached the car and asked the driver, William Cook, to exit the vehicle. A struggle ensued. According to prosecutors, Mumia Abu-Jamal, Cook's older brother, was sitting in a taxicab across the street watching the events unfold. Abu-Jamal approached Officer Faulkner and shot him in the back. Faulkner was able to draw his gun and fire one return shot that struck Abu-Jamal

in the upper abdomen. Having fired this shot, Officer Faulkner fell to the sidewalk. While Faulkner lay helpless, Abu-Jamal approached him and shot him numerous times at close range, killing him instantly.

At trial, four eyewitnesses testified that they saw Abu-Jamal kill Faulkner, experts testified that the gun that killed Faulkner was Abu-Jamal's, and jurors heard that a wounded Abu-Jamal was found at the scene of the crime. He was convicted and sentenced to death. Despite the conviction, the case has become a *cause celebre* for many reasons. Supporters claim that many procedural irregularities occurred during the trial and that the conviction of Abu-Jamal violated his constitutional rights to a fair trial. Among other things, he was denied the right to represent himself at trial. Others claim that Abu-Jamal was targeted and framed because of his radical political activities. The prosecution hid evidence, intimidated witnesses, and illegally excused potential African American jurors.

Abu-Jamal has now been on death row for more than 25 years, and the case has attracted the attention of anti–death penalty activists from all over the world. Abu-Jamal has continued his political activism, published a book titled *Live from Death Row,* completed BA and MA degrees, and made frequent radio broadcasts. The French have made him an honorary citizen of Paris and in 2006 named a street, *Rue Mumia Abu-Jamal,* in his honor. Organizations including Amnesty International, Human Rights Watch, the European Parliament, and the Japanese Diet have demanded that he be awarded a new trial because of the problems in the original case. However, there are also groups who are aghast at the attention paid to someone they consider a cold-blooded cop killer. One group filed a lawsuit

against the City of Paris, which said in part "awarding the honors of a city to a killer of a policeman is an immoral and irresponsible decision."

In 2008, a three-judge panel of the U.S. Third Circuit Court of Appeals upheld the murder conviction but ordered a new capital sentencing hearing over concerns that the jury was improperly instructed. After the United States Supreme Court allowed his July 1982 conviction to stand, the appeals court was ordered to reconsider its decision to rescind the death sentence. On April 26, 2011, the Third Circuit Court of Appeals ordered a new sentencing hearing, finding for a second time that the death-penalty instructions given to the jury at his 1982 trial were potentially misleading; it is still possible that the death sentence will be reimposed. At this time Mumia Abu-Jamal is incarcerated at Pennsylvania's SCI Greene prison.

Critical criminologists view the Mumia Abu-Jamal case as an indicator of the social conflict that infects the nation's social and political systems. People are targeted because of their political views, minorities cannot get a fair trial, and people who are viewed as a threat to the system may find themselves behind bars or even on death row. Conflict rather than consensus rules and shapes society.

SOURCES: Amnesty International, "USA: Mumia Abu-Jamal, Amnesty International Calls for Retrial," February, 17, 2000, http://web.amnesty.org/library/Index/engAMR510202000 (accessed September 25, 2010); Amnesty International, "The Defense: Mumia Abu-Jamal's Legal Representation at Trial," www.mumia.de/special/a%20life%20in%20the%20balance.eng.pdf (accessed August 25, 2011); *Cathy Ceïbe,* "USA Sues Paris: From Death Row, Mumia Stirs Up More Controversy," *L'Humanité, trans. Patrick Bolland, November 13, 2006,* www.humaniteinenglish.com/article423.html (accessed July 11, 2011).

highest in minority neighborhoods, especially those that experience relative deprivation (African American residents earn significantly less money than the European American majority).[62] The conflict between police and the minority community can result in violence and charges of racism,

a topic explored in the Profiles in Crime feature "Mumia Abu-Jamal."

Critical research also shows that racial and economic bias is present in prosecution and punishment. Surveys show that as the numbers of racial and ethnic minorities in the population increase, so too do calls for harsher punishments. Unwarranted fear drives people to believe that a defendant's race and ethnicity should be considered during sentencing.[63] These attitudes then find traction in the justice system: African American defendants are more likely to be prosecuted under habitual offender statutes if they commit crimes where there is a greater likelihood of a white victim—for example, larceny and burglary—than if they commit violent crimes that are largely intraracial; where there is a perceived "racial threat," punishment is enhanced.[64] After conviction, criminal courts also are more likely to dole out harsh punishments to members of powerless, disenfranchised groups.[65] Both white and black offenders have been found to receive stricter sentences if their personal characteristics (single, young, urban, male) show them to be members of the "dangerous classes."[66] Unemployed racial minorities may be perceived as "social dynamite" who present a real threat to society and must be controlled and incapacitated.[67] Critical analysis also shows that despite legal controls the use of the death penalty seems to be skewed against racial minorities.[68]

The rush to punish must be observed through the lens of race: as the percentage of minority group members increases in a population, the imprisonment rate does likewise.[69] States with a substantial minority population have a much higher imprisonment rate than those with predominantly white populations.[70]

Taken in sum, critical criminologists claim that these and other studies underpin the foundations of their view: social institutions are designed to favor the rich and powerful and to oppress those who lack economic power and social standing.

CRITIQUE OF CRITICAL CRIMINOLOGY

Critical criminology has been sharply criticized by some members of the criminological mainstream, who charge that its contribution has been "hot air, heat, but no real light."[71] In turn, critical thinkers have accused mainstream criminologists of being culprits in developing state control over individual lives and selling out their ideals for the chance to receive government funding.

Mainstream criminologists have attacked the substance of critical thought as well. Some argue that critical theory simply rehashes the old tradition of helping the underdog, in which the poor steal from the rich to survive.[72] In reality, most theft is for luxury, not survival. Although the wealthy do commit their share of illegal acts, these are nonviolent and leave no permanent injuries.[73] People do not live in fear of corrupt businessmen and stock traders; they fear muggers and rapists.

Other critics suggest that critical theorists unfairly neglect the capitalist system's efforts to regulate itself—for example, by instituting antitrust regulations and putting violators in jail. Similarly, they ignore efforts to institute social reforms aimed at helping the poor.[74] There seems to be no logic in condemning a system that helps the poor and empowers them to take on corporate interests in a court of law. Even inherently conservative institutions such as police departments have made attempts at self-regulation when they become aware of class- and race-based inequality such as the use of racial profiling in making traffic stops.[75]

Some argue that critical thinkers refuse to address the problems and conflicts that exist in socialist countries, such as the gulags and purges of the Soviet Union under Stalin. Similarly, they fail to explain why some highly capitalist countries, such as Japan, have extremely low crime rates. Critical criminologists are too quick to blame capitalism for every human vice without adequate explanation or regard for other social and environmental factors.[76] In so doing, they ignore objective reality and refuse to acknowledge that members of the lower classes tend to victimize one another. They ignore the plight of the lower classes, who must live in crime-ridden neighborhoods, while condemning the capitalist system from the security of the "ivory tower."

FORMS OF CRITICAL CRIMINOLOGY

Critical criminologists are exploring new avenues of inquiry that fall outside the traditional models of conflict and critical theories. The following sections discuss in detail some recent developments in the conflict approach to crime.

Left Realism

Some critical scholars are now addressing the need for the left wing to respond to the increasing power of right-wing conservatives. They are troubled by the emergence of a strict "law and order" philosophy, which has as its centerpiece such policies as aggressive police patrol, severe sentences for drug offenders, capital punishment, and punishing juveniles in adult court. At the same time, they find the focus of most critical scholarship—the abuse of power by the ruling elite—too narrow. It is wrong, they argue, to ignore inner-city gang crime and violence, which often target indigent people while focusing solely on the depravations of the rich and powerful.[77]

This branch of critical theory, referred to as **left realism**, is most often connected to the writings of British scholars John Lea and Jock Young. In their well-respected 1984 work, *What Is to Be Done About Law and Order?*, they reject the utopian views of idealists who portray street criminals as revolutionaries.[78] They take the more "realistic" approach that street criminals prey on the poor and disenfranchised, thus making the poor doubly abused, first by the capitalist system and then by members of their own class.

Lea and Young's view of crime causation borrows from conventional sociological theory and closely resembles the relative deprivation approach, which posits that experiencing poverty in the midst of plenty creates discontent and breeds crime. As they put it, "The equation is simple: relative deprivation equals discontent; discontent plus lack of political solution equals crime."[79]

In *Crime in Context: A Critical Criminology of Market Societies,* Ian Taylor recognizes that anyone who expects an instant socialist revolution to take place is simply engaging in wishful thinking.[80] He uses data from both Europe and North America to show that the world is currently in the midst of multiple crises that are shaping all human interaction, including criminality. These crises include lack of job creation, social inequality, social fear, political incompetence and failure, gender conflict, and family and parenting issues. These crises have led to a society in which the government seems incapable of creating positive social change: people have become more fearful and isolated from one another and some are excluded from the mainstream because of racism and discrimination; manufacturing jobs have been exported overseas to nations that pay extremely low wages; and fiscal constraints inhibit the possibility of reform. These problems often fall squarely on the shoulders of young black men, who suffer from exclusion and poverty and who now feel the economic burden created by the erosion of manufacturing jobs due to the globalization of the economy. In response, they engage in a form of hypermasculinity, which helps increase their crime rates.[81]

Left Realism and Crime

Left realists view the cause of serious violent crime as a function of economic inequality, community deprivation, and lack of supportive institutions that characterize today's postmodern society. It can even be used to explain terrorism as The Criminological Enterprise feature shows. The economic disparity that puts some citizens at risk of crime and protects others from harm can be directly laid at the feet of crony capitalism. Rewarding CEO's with multimillion-dollar bonuses for firing workers and sending jobs overseas increases corporate profits at the expense of workers pay. As economic disparity increases, so too does drug abuse and crime. Here left realism can be distinguished from traditional liberal criminology, which views criminals as people who have trouble making it in society and see crime as a result of their failures. People commit crime, liberals claim, because their opportunities are blocked. Left realists counter that legitimate opportunities are not blocked because in reality they never actually existed. As legal scholar Elliott Currie claims, our present capitalist socioeconomic system is such that it generates "inequality, injustice, social fragmentation and a 'hard' and unsupportive culture." This view separates left realists from liberal criminologists.[82]

Controlling Crime

Although implementing a socialist economy might help eliminate the crime problem, left realists recognize that something must be done to control crime under the existing system rather than waiting for the development of an ideal society. They argue that crime victims in all classes need and deserve protection; crime control reflects community needs. They do not view police and the courts as inherently evil tools of capitalism whose tough tactics alienate the lower classes. In fact, they recognize that these institutions offer life-saving public services. The left realists wish, however, that police would reduce their use of force and increase their sensitivity to the public.[83] They want the police to be more responsive to community needs, end racial profiling, and improve efforts at self-regulation and enforcement through citizen review boards and other control mechanisms. Left realists call for an end to aggressive policing, arguing that the use of force and formal arrest with minor crimes convinces many people to withhold support and information that the police need to solve much more serious crimes.[84]

Left realists also decry the use of mass incarceration as a crime control device, fearing that it has racial overtones. In her provocative book, *The New Jim Crow: Mass Incarceration in the Age of Colorblindness* (2010), legal scholar Michelle Alexander notes that the number of people in prison has skyrocketed in the past 30 years; there are now more African Americans behind bars than there were slaves at the time of the Civil War. This system of mass incarceration now works as a "tightly networked system of laws, policies, customs, and institutions that operate collectively to ensure the subordinate status of a group defined largely by race."[85] In a sense, the Jim Crow laws, which worked to segregate minorities and prevented them from voting, have been replaced by the War on Drugs, which has placed millions behind bars and restricted their civil rights upon release; existing laws prevent convicted felons from gaining employment, education, housing, obtaining loans, and voting.

In contrast to these harsh measures, left realists believe that community-based efforts hold the greatest promise of crime control. According to left realists, it is possible for community organization efforts to eliminate or reduce crime before police involvement becomes necessary, a process they call preemptive deterrence. The reasoning behind this approach is that if the number of marginalized youths (those who feel they are not part of society and have nothing to lose by committing crime) could be reduced, then delinquency rates would decline.[86]

Surprisingly, this left realist perspective may be gaining traction even in the nation's most conservative states (including Texas), which have begun to reduce their prison expenditures while funding treatment, reentry, and alternatives to incarceration programs. In part this policy shift corresponds

Left realists have focused their attention on street crime and how it affects its targets: lower-class citizens are forced to live in dangerous neighborhoods and communities. Recently, left realist Jennifer Gibbs applied the basic concepts to explain the motivation for terrorist activity. She finds four key elements of left realism that should, if valid, underpin terrorist involvement:

1. People are recruited into terrorist organizations because of relative deprivation
2. Terrorist organizations are subcultures that provide peer support
3. Victims/targets are selected based on opportunity/routine activities
4. "Get tough" policies that create a police state may backfire

Gibbs finds evidence to support proposition (1): terrorists are drawn not from extremely poor populations but from those who realize they have fallen behind other groups. Absolute deprivation (e.g., the inability to provide basic necessities) is not the cause of terrorism; relative deprivation (e.g., being less well off than one's peers) seems to carry more weight, an association predicted by left realism. Feelings of deprivation are exacerbated by the new technology. Advancements like the Internet make communication easier and people can see how much better off others are, increasing the perception of relative deprivation.

Second, left realist theory argues that men who experience stress as a result of relative deprivation and do not have socially appropriate coping mechanisms turn to similarly situated peers, who provide support; they often form subcultures. Likewise, terrorist group members seek peer-support with like-minded people, forming subcultures supportive of these values or ideology. In today's postmodern world, technology has created the opportunity for virtual peer groups and subcultures. Peer support does not necessarily need to be face-to-face within groups but can exist in blogs and chat rooms. Those adhering to a particular ideology may find "peer support" in written communications such as listserves, magazines, and other media.

Gibbs finds weaker support for the role of opportunity in terrorist activities because they tend to be planned rather than spontaneous events. However, there is some evidence that opportunity plays a role in choosing victims: targeting businesses and citizens is easier than targeting government entities or military installations or personnel. Other reasons may include having the "biggest bang for the buck" by targeting businesses—symbolic of capitalism—or civilians, whose deaths generate widespread attention.

The final proposition of left realist theory addressed by Gibbs is that "get tough" policies will not reduce crime. She notes that left realism focuses on individualized or community-focused responses to crime. Get tough policies alienate people and legitimate terrorist organizations. The "war" on terror legitimized groups like al-Qaeda, attracting more terrorism instead of decreasing it. Also, the military response to terrorism is not a deterrent. Military "solutions," in particular, lead to retaliation, generating a cycle of violence because they tend to be reactive rather than proactive. They provide short-term solutions that fail to address the underlying causes that lead to terrorism in the first place. Instead, left realism theory directs policy toward minimal official response and maximizing informal social control. With terrorism, attempting to address the underlying grievances may be helpful.

CRITICAL THINKING

Do you agree with Gibbs's left realist views. If people were motivated to commit terrorist acts because they saw themselves as "relatively deprived," wouldn't there be more terrorists? After all, aside from a few people like Donald Trump, Bill Gates, and JayZ, most of us feel relatively deprived!

SOURCE: Jennifer Gibbs, "Looking at Terrorism Through Left Realist Lenses." *Crime, Law and Social Change* 54 (2010): 171–185.

---

to a change in public opinion: as crime rates have declined and state budgets are in crisis, the public demands low-cost alternatives to the "lock 'em up" policies that have been predominant for the past few decades. It's possible that a more realistic vision of punishment may be on the horizon.[87]

Criticism and Rebuttal Left realism has been criticized by more radical critical thinkers as legitimizing the existing power structure; they want revolution rather than evolution.[88] In rebuttal, left realists say that it is unrealistic to speak of a socialist state lacking a police force or a system of laws and justice. They believe the criminal code does, in fact, represent public opinion and should not be disregarded. According to left realist scholars, Martin Schwartz and Walter DeKeseredy:

What left realists have always believed is that this purposeful inattention to policing, other than waiting for the aftermath of the eventual revolution, also means dooming to misery those women and men who are right now being raped, robbed, beaten and burglarized.[89]

Critical Feminist Theory

Like so many theories in criminology, most of the efforts of critical theorists have been devoted to explaining male criminality.[90] To remedy this theoretical lapse, a number of feminist writers have attempted to explain the cause of crime, gender differences in crime rates, and the exploitation of female victims from a critical perspective.

Critical feminism views gender inequality as stemming from the unequal power of men and women in a capitalist society, which leads to the exploitation of women by fathers, boyfriends, and husbands. Under this system, women are considered a commodity worth possessing, like land or money.[91]

The origin of gender differences can be traced to the development of private property and male domination of the laws of inheritance, which led to male control over property and power.[92] A **patriarchal** system developed in which men's work was valued and women's work was devalued. As capitalism prevailed, the division of labor by gender made women responsible for the unpaid maintenance and reproduction of the current and future labor force, which was derisively called "domestic work." Although this unpaid work done by women is crucial and profitable for capitalists, who reap these free benefits, such labor is exploitative and oppressive for women.[93] Even when women gained the right to work for pay, they were exploited as cheap labor. The dual exploitation of women within the household and in the labor market means that women produce far greater surplus value for capitalists than men.

Patriarchy, or male supremacy, has been and continues to be supported by capitalists. This system sustains female oppression at home and in the workplace.[94] Although the number of traditional patriarchal families is in steep decline, in those that still exist, a wife's economic dependence ties men more securely to wage-earning jobs, further serving the interests of capitalists by undermining potential rebellion against the system.

Patriarchy and Crime Critical feminists link criminal behavior patterns to the gender conflict created by the economic and social struggles common in postindustrial societies. In *Capitalism, Patriarchy, and Crime*, James Messerschmidt argues that capitalist society is marked by both patriarchy and class conflict. Capitalists control the labor of workers, and men control women both economically and biologically.[95] This "double marginality" explains why females in a capitalist society commit fewer crimes than males. Because they are isolated in the family, they have fewer opportunities to engage in elite deviance (white-collar and economic crimes). Although powerful females as well as males will commit white-collar crimes, the female crime rate is restricted because of the patriarchal nature of the capitalist system.[96] Women also are denied access to male-dominated street crimes.

Critical feminists view gender inequality as a function of female exploitation by men. Women have become a "commodity" worth possessing, like land or money. The origin of gender differences can be traced to the development of private property and men's domination over the laws of inheritance, which led to their control over property and power. Are these teen prostitutes—shown here waiting to be booked at the Maricopa, Arizona, jail—a by-product of this view of women as commodities, which was engendered by the capitalist system?

© A. Ramey/PhotoEdit Inc.

Because capitalism renders lower-class women powerless, they are forced to commit less serious, nonviolent, self-destructive crimes, such as abusing drugs. Recent efforts of the capitalist classes to undermine the social support of the poor has hit women particularly hard. The end of welfare, concentration on welfare fraud, and cutbacks to social services all have directly and uniquely affected women.[97]

Powerlessness also increases the likelihood that women will become targets of violent acts.[98] When lower-class males are shut out of the economic opportunity structure, they try to build their self-image through acts of machismo; such acts may involve violent abuse of women. This type of reaction accounts for a significant percentage of female victims who are attacked by a spouse or intimate partner. According to this view, female victimization should decline as women's place in society is elevated and they are able to obtain more power at home, in the workplace, and in government. Empirical research seems to support this view. In nations where the status of women is generally high, sexual violence rates are significantly lower than in nations where women do not enjoy similar educational and occupational opportunities.[99] Women's victimization rates decline as they are empowered socially, economically, and legally.[100]

In *Masculinities and Crime*, Messerschmidt expands on these themes.[101] He suggests that in every culture males try to emulate "ideal" masculine behaviors. In Western culture, this means being authoritative, in charge, combative, and controlling. Failure to adopt these roles leaves men feeling effeminate and unmanly. Their struggle to dominate women in order to prove their manliness is called "doing gender." Crime is a vehicle for men to "do gender" because it separates them from the weak and allows them to demonstrate physical bravery. Violence directed toward women is an especially economical way to demonstrate manhood. Would a weak, effeminate male ever attack a woman?

Feminist writers have supported this view by maintaining that in contemporary society men achieve masculinity at the expense of women. In the best-case scenario, men must convince others that in no way are they feminine or have female qualities. For example, they are sloppy and don't cook or do housework because these are "female" activities. More ominously, men may work at excluding, hurting, denigrating, exploiting, or otherwise abusing women. Even in all-male groups, men often prove their manhood by treating the weakest member of the group as "woman-like" and abusing him accordingly. Men need to defend themselves at all costs from being contaminated with femininity, and these efforts begin in children's playgroups and continue into adulthood and marriage.[102]

Exploitation and Criminality

Critical feminists also focus on the social forces that shape women's lives and experiences to explain female criminality.[103] They attempt to show how the sexual victimization of girls is a function of male socialization because so many young males learn to be aggressive and to exploit women. Males seek out same-sex peer groups for social support; these groups encourage members to exploit and sexually abuse women. On college campuses, peers encourage sexual violence against women who are considered "teasers," "bar pickups," or "loose women." These derogatory labels allow the males to justify their actions; a code of secrecy then protects the aggressors from retribution.[104]

According to the critical feminist view, exploitation triggers the onset of female delinquent and deviant behavior. When female victims run away and abuse substances, they may be reacting to abuse they have suffered at home or at school. Their attempts at survival are labeled as deviant or delinquent behavior.[105] When the exploited girl finds herself in the arms of the justice system, her problems may just be beginning. Boys who get in trouble may be considered "overzealous" youth or kids who just went too far. Young girls who get in trouble are seen as a threat to acceptable images of femininity; their behavior is considered even more unusual and dangerous than male delinquency.[106]

Power–Control Theory

John Hagan and his associates have created a critical feminist model that uses gender differences to explain the onset of criminality.[107] Hagan's view is that crime and delinquency rates are a function of two factors: class position (power) and family functions (control).[108] The link between these two variables is that, within the family, parents reproduce the power relationships they hold in the workplace; a position of dominance at work is equated with control in the household. As a result, parents' work experiences and class position influence the criminality of children.[109]

In **paternalistic families**, fathers assume the traditional role of breadwinners, while mothers tend to have menial jobs or remain at home to supervise domestic matters. Within the paternalistic home, mothers are expected to control the behavior of their daughters while granting greater freedom to sons. In such a home, the parent–daughter relationship can be viewed as a preparation for the "cult of domesticity," which makes girls' involvement in delinquency unlikely, whereas boys are freer to deviate because they are not subject to maternal control. Girls growing up in patriarchal families are socialized to fear legal sanctions more than are males; consequently, boys in these families exhibit more delinquent behavior than their sisters. The result is that boys not only engage in more antisocial behaviors but have greater access to legitimate adult behaviors, such as working at part-time jobs or possessing their own transportation. In contrast, without these legitimate behavioral outlets, girls who are unhappy or dissatisfied with their status are forced to seek out risky **role exit behaviors**, including such desperate measures as running away and contemplating suicide.

In **egalitarian families**—those in which both domestic partners share similar positions of power at home and in the workplace—daughters gain a kind of freedom that reflects reduced parental control. These families produce daughters whose law-violating behavior mirrors their brothers'. In an egalitarian family, girls may have greater opportunity to engage in legitimate adult status behaviors and less need to enact deviant role exits.[110]

Ironically, Hagan believes that these relationships also occur in female-headed households with absent fathers. Hagan and his associates found that when fathers and mothers hold equally valued managerial positions, the similarity between the rates of their daughters' and sons' delinquency is greatest. By implication, girls living in egalitarian households are likely to violate the law because they are less closely controlled than their lower-class counterparts. In homes in which both parents hold positions of power, girls are more likely to have the same expectations of career success as their brothers. Consequently, siblings of both sexes will be socialized to take risks and engage in other behavior related to delinquency.

Evaluating Power–Control Theory

So far, **power–control theory** has received a great deal of attention in the criminological community because it encourages a new approach to the study of criminality, one that includes gender differences, class position, and the structure of the family. Empirical analysis of its premises has generally been supportive. Brenda Sims Blackwell's research supports a key element of power–control theory: females in paternalistic households have learned to fear legal sanctions more than have their brothers.[111]

Not all research is as supportive.[112] Some critics have questioned its core assumption that power and control variables can explain crime.[113] More specifically, critics fail to replicate the finding that upper-class girls are more likely to deviate than their lower-class peers or that class and power interact to produce delinquency.[114] Some researchers have found few gender-based supervision and behavior differences in worker-, manager-, or owner-dominated households.[115] Research indicates that single-mother families may be different than two-parent egalitarian families, though Hagan's theory equates the two.[116]

It is possible that the concept of family employed by Hagan may have to be reconsidered. Power–control theorists should consider the multitude of power and control relationships that are emerging in postmodern society: blended families, families where mothers hold managerial positions and fathers are blue-collar workers, and so forth.[117]

Finally, power and control may interact with other personal traits, such as personality and self-control, to shape behavior.[118] Further research is needed to determine whether power–control can have an independent influence on behavior and can explain gender differences in the crime rate.

Peacemaking Criminology

To members of the **peacemaking** movement, the main purpose of criminology is to promote a peaceful, just society. Rather than standing on empirical analysis of data, peacemaking draws its inspiration from religious and philosophical teachings ranging from Quakerism to Zen.[119] For example, rather than seeing socioeconomic status as a "variable" that is correlated with crime, as do mainstream criminologists, peacemakers view poverty as a source of suffering—almost a crime in and of itself. Poverty enervates people, makes them suffer, and becomes a master status that subjects them to lives filled with suffering. From a peacemaking perspective, a key avenue for preventing crime is, in the short run, diminishing the suffering poverty causes and, in the long run, embracing social policies that reduce the prevalence of economic suffering in contemporary society.[120]

Peacemakers view the efforts of the state to punish and control as crime-encouraging rather than crime-discouraging. These views were first articulated in a series of books with an anarchist theme written by criminologists Larry Tifft and Dennis Sullivan in 1980.[121] Tifft argues, "The violent punishing acts of the state and its controlling professions are of the same genre as the violent acts of individuals. In each instance these acts reflect an attempt to monopolize human interaction."[122]

Sullivan stresses the futility of correcting and punishing criminals in the context of our conflict-ridden society: "The reality we must grasp is that we live in a culture of severed relationships, where every available institution provides a form of banishment but no place or means for

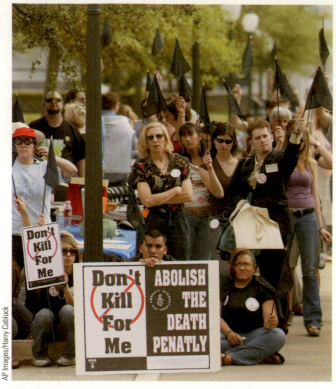

AP Images/Harry Cabluck

Restorative justice advocates want to take coercion out of the justice process, and for that reason they are opposed to the death penalty. At a rally kicking off Amnesty International USA's annual meeting in Austin, Texas, attendees raised black flags in protest and called on Republican Governor Rick Perry and Texas legislators to abolish the death penalty. Can restorative principles be applied to criminals who commit the most violent, heinous crimes, or are they only suitable for petty and first-time offenders?

people to become connected, to be responsible to and for each other."[123] Sullivan suggests that mutual aid rather than coercive punishment is the key to a harmonious society. In *Restorative Justice*, Sullivan and Tifft reaffirm their belief that society must seek humanitarian forms of justice without resorting to brutal punishments:

> By allowing feelings of vengeance or retribution to narrow our focus on the harmful event and the person responsible for it—as others might focus solely on a sin committed and the "sinner"—we tell ourselves we are taking steps to free ourselves from the effects of the harm or the sin in question. But, in fact, we are putting ourselves in a servile position with respect to life, human growth, and the further enjoyment of relationships with others.[124]

Today, advocates of the peacemaking movement, such as Harold Pepinsky and Richard Quinney, try to find humanist solutions to crime and other social problems.[125] Rather than punishment and prison, they advocate such policies as mediation and conflict resolution.[126]

Concept Summary 8.1 summarizes the various emerging forms of critical criminology.

Emerging Forms of Critical Criminology

Theory	Major Premise	Strengths	Research Focus
Left realism	Crime is a function of relative deprivation; criminals prey on the poor.	Represents a compromise between conflict and traditional criminology.	Deterrence; protection.
Critical feminist theory	The capitalist system creates patriarchy, which oppresses women.	Explains gender bias, violence against women, and repression.	Gender inequality; oppression; patriarchy.
Power–control theory	Girls are controlled more closely than boys in traditional male-dominated households. There is gender equity in contemporary egalitarian homes.	Explains gender differences in the crime rate as a function of class and gender conflict.	Power and control; gender differences; domesticity.
Peacemaking criminology	Peace and humanism can reduce crime; conflict resolution strategies can work.	Offers a new approach to crime control through mediation.	Punishment; nonviolence; mediation.

CRITICAL THEORY AND RESTORATIVE JUSTICE

Critical theorists believe that crime will only vanish when there is a reordering of society so that capitalism is destroyed and a socialist state is created. Others call for a more "practical" approach to crime control, making use of inclusionary, nonpunitive strategies for crime prevention and control, an approach known as **restorative justice**.[127] The next sections discuss the foundation and principles of restorative justice.

The Concept of Restorative Justice

The term *restorative justice* is often hard to define because it encompasses a variety of programs and practices. According to a leading restorative justice scholar, Howard Zehr, restorative justice requires that society address victims' harms and needs, hold offenders accountable to put right those harms, and involve victims, offenders, and communities in the process of healing. Zehr maintains that the core value of the restoration process can be translated into respect for all, even those who are different from us, even those who seem to be our enemies. At its core, Zehr argues, restorative justice is a set of principles, a philosophy, an alternate set of guiding questions that provide an alternative framework for thinking about wrongdoing.[128] Restorative justice would reject concepts such as "punishment," "deterrence" and "incarceration" and embrace "apology," "rehabilitation," "reparation," "healing," "restoration," and "reintegration." The Thinking Like a Criminologist feature explores an ethical dilemma that might be produced by a restorative justice program.

Restorative justice has grown out of a belief that the traditional justice system has done little to involve the community in the process of dealing with crime and wrongdoing. What has developed is a system of coercive punishments, administered by bureaucrats, that are inherently harmful to offenders and reduce the likelihood offenders will ever become productive members of society. This system relies on punishment, stigma, and disgrace. In his controversial book, *The Executed God: The Way of the Cross in Lockdown America*, theology professor Mark Lewis Taylor discusses the similarities between this contemporary, coercive justice system and that which existed in imperial Rome when Jesus and many of his followers were executed because they were an inspiration to the poor and slave populations. They represented a threat to the ruling Roman power structure. So, too, is our modern justice system designed to keep the downtrodden in their place. Taylor suggests that there should be a movement to reduce such coercive elements of justice as police brutality and the death penalty before our "lockdown society" becomes the model used around the globe.[129]

Advocates of restorative justice argue that rather than today's lockdown mentality, what is needed is a justice policy that repairs the harm caused by crime and that includes all parties who have suffered from that harm: the victim, the community, and the offender. They have made an ongoing effort to reduce the conflict created by the criminal justice system when it hands out harsh punishments to offenders, many of whom are powerless social outcasts. Based on the principle of reducing social harm, restorative justice advocates argue that the old methods of punishment are a failure: after all, upwards of two-thirds of all prison inmates recidivate soon after their release. And tragically, not all inmates are released. Some are given life sentences for relatively minor crimes under three strikes laws, which mandate such a sentence for a third conviction; some are given sentences of life with no parole, which are in essence death sentences.[130]

Is It a Bribe?

A student wants to discuss a personal matter. It seems that a few weeks ago she was at a party when she was sexually assaulted by a fellow student. The attack was quite traumatic and she suffered both physical and emotional injury. The police were called and the boy charged with rape. Now that a few weeks have passed, she has been contacted by a local program that bills itself as a restorative treatment program. It seems that her attacker is now a client and wants to engage in some form of reconciliation. At an arranged meeting, he professes his regret for the attack and wishes to make amends. He and the program director have worked out a schedule in which the victim will be compensated for her pain and suffering in the amount of $5,000 in exchange for

© Rachael Rush/iStockphoto

her agreeing to a recommendation to the prosecutor that the case be treated informally rather than going to trial. She doesn't know what to do: she needs the money, having missed work after the attack, but at the same time is concerned that people will think she has accepted a bribe to withdraw the charges.

» **Write a paper describing the advice you would give to the student in this situation. How would you suggest that she respond to the program director? Do you consider the payment a bribe or restitution for an evil deed? Can restorative justice be used in a crime such as rape?**

Reintegrative Shaming

One of the key foundations of the restoration movement is contained in John Braithwaite's influential book *Crime, Shame, and Reintegration*.[131] Braithwaite's vision rests on the concept of **shame:** the feeling we get when we don't meet the standards we have set for ourselves or that significant others have set for us. Shame can lead people to believe that they are defective, that there is something wrong with them. Braithwaite notes that countries such as Japan, in which conviction for crimes brings an inordinate amount of shame, have extremely low crime rates. In Japan, criminal prosecution proceeds only when the normal process of public apology, compensation, and the victim's forgiveness breaks down.

Shame is a powerful tool of informal social control. Citizens in cultures in which crime is not shameful, such as the United States, do not internalize an abhorrence for crime because when they are punished, they view themselves as mere victims of the justice system. Their punishment comes at the hands of neutral strangers, such as police and judges, who are being paid to act. In contrast, shaming relies on the victim's participation.[132]

Braithwaite divides the concept of shame into two distinct types. The most common form of shaming typically involves stigmatization, an ongoing process of degradation in which the offender is branded as an evil person and cast out of society. Shaming can occur at a school disciplinary hearing or at a criminal court trial. Bestowing stigma and degradation may have a general deterrent effect: it makes people afraid of social rejection and public humiliation. As a specific deterrent, stigma is doomed to failure; people who suffer humiliation at the hands of the justice system "reject their rejectors" by joining a deviant subculture of

like-minded people who collectively resist social control. Despite these dangers, there has been an ongoing effort to brand offenders and make their shame both public and permanent. For example, most states have passed sex offender registry and notification laws that make public the names of those convicted of sex offenses and warn neighbors of their presence in the community.[133]

But the fear of shame can backfire or be neutralized. When shame is managed well, people acknowledge they made mistakes and suffered disappointments, and try to work out what can be done to make things right; this is referred to as shame management. However, in some cases, to avoid the pain of shaming, people engage in improper shame management, a psychological process in which they deny shame by shifting the blame of their actions to their target or to others.[134] They may blame others, get angry, and take out their frustrations on those whom they can dominate. Improper shame management of this sort has been linked to antisocial acts ranging from school yard bullying to tax evasion.[135]

Massive levels of improper shame management may occur on a societal scale during periods of social upheaval. Because of this, some nations that previously have had low crime rates may experience a surge of antisocial behavior during periods of war and revolution. Rape, an act which may have been unthinkable to most men, suddenly becomes commonplace because of the emergence of narcissistic pride, feeling dominant and arrogant, and developing a sense of superiority over others, in this case your enemy. This sense of hubris fosters aggressive actions and allows combatants to rape women whom they perceive as belonging to an enemy group.[136]

Braithwaite argues that crime control can be better achieved through a policy of **reintegrative shaming**. Here disapproval is extended to the offenders' evil deeds, while at the same time they are cast as respected people who can be reaccepted by society. A critical element of reintegrative shaming occurs when the offenders begin to understand and recognize their wrongdoing and shame themselves. To be reintegrative, shaming must be brief and controlled and then followed by ceremonies of forgiveness, apology, and repentance.

To prevent crime, Braithwaite charges, society must encourage reintegrative shaming. For example, the women's movement can reduce domestic violence by mounting a crusade to shame spouse abusers.[137] Similarly, parents who use reintegrative shaming techniques in their childrearing practices may improve parent–child relationships and ultimately reduce the delinquent involvement of their children.[138] Because informal social controls may have a greater impact than legal or formal ones, it may not be surprising that the fear of personal shame can have a greater deterrent effect than the fear of legal sanctions. It may also be applied to produce specific deterrence. Offenders can meet with victims so that the offenders can experience shame. Family members and peers can be present to help the offender reintegrate.[139] Such efforts can humanize a system of justice that today relies on repression rather than forgiveness as the basis of specific deterrence.

The Process of Restoration

The restoration process begins by redefining crime in terms of a conflict among the offender, the victim, and affected constituencies (families, schools, workplaces, and so forth). Therefore, it is vitally important that the resolution take place within the context in which the conflict originally occurred rather than being transferred to a specialized institution that has no social connection to the community or group from which the conflict originated. In other words, most conflicts are better settled in the community than in a court.

By maintaining "ownership" or jurisdiction over the conflict, the community is able to express its shared outrage about the offense. Shared community outrage is directly communicated to the offender. The victim is also given a chance to voice his or her story, and the offender can directly communicate his or her need for social reintegration and treatment. All restoration programs involve an understanding among all the parties involved in a criminal act: the victim, the offender, and the community. Although processes differ in structure and style, they generally include these elements:

- The offender is asked to recognize that he or she caused injury to personal and social relations along with a determination and acceptance of responsibility (ideally accompanied by a statement of remorse). Only then can the offender be restored as a productive member of the community.
- Restoration involves turning the justice system into a "healing" process rather than being a distributor of retribution and revenge.

- Reconciliation is a big part of the restorative approach. Most people involved in offender–victim relationships actually know one another or were related in some way before the criminal incident took place. Instead of treating one of the involved parties as a victim deserving of sympathy and the other as a criminal deserving of punishment, it is more productive to address the issues that produced conflict between these people.[140]
- The effectiveness of justice ultimately depends on the stake a person has in the community (or in a particular social group). If a person does not value his or her membership in the group, the person will be unlikely to accept responsibility, show remorse, or repair the injuries caused by his or her actions. In contrast, people who have a stake in the community and its principal institutions, such as work, home, and school, find that their involvement enhances their personal and familial well-being.[141]
- The offender must make a commitment to both material (monetary) restitution and symbolic reparation (an apology). A determination must also be made of community support and assistance for both victim and offender.

The intended result of this process is to repair injuries suffered by the victim and the community while ensuring reintegration of the offender.

Restoration Programs Negotiation, mediation, consensus-building, and peacemaking have been part of the dispute resolution process in European and Asian communities for centuries.[142] Native American and Native Canadian people have long used the type of community participation in the adjudication process (for example, sentencing circles, sentencing panels, elders panels) that restorative justice advocates are now embracing.[143]

In some Native American communities, people accused of breaking the law meet with community members, victims (if any), village elders, and agents of the justice system in a **sentencing circle**. Each member of the circle expresses his or her feelings about the act that was committed and raises questions or concerns. The accused can express regret about his or her actions and a desire to change the harmful behavior. People may suggest ways the offender can make things up to the community and those he or she harmed. A treatment program, such as Alcoholics Anonymous, can be suggested, if appropriate.

Restorative justice is now being embraced on many levels within our society and the justice system:

- *Community.* Communities that isolate people and have few mechanisms for interpersonal interaction encourage and sustain crime. Those that implement forms of community dialogue to identify problems and plan tactics for their elimination, guided by restorative justice practices and principles, may create a climate in which violent crime is less likely to occur.[144]

- *Schools.* Some schools have embraced restorative justice practices to deal with students who are involved in drug and alcohol abuse without having to resort to more punitive measures such as expulsion. Schools in Minnesota, Colorado, and elsewhere are now trying to involve students in "relational rehabilitation" programs that strive to improve individuals' relationships with key figures in the community who may have been harmed by their actions.[145]

- *Police.* Restorative justice has been implemented by police when crime is first encountered. The new community policing models are an attempt to bring restorative concepts into law enforcement. Restorative justice relies on the fact that criminal justice policymakers need to listen and respond to the needs of those who are to be affected by their actions, and community policing relies on policies established with input and exchanges between officers and citizens.[146]

- *Courts.* Restorative programs in the courts typically involve diverting the formal court process. These programs encourage meeting and reconciling the conflicts between offenders and victims via victim advocacy, mediation programs, and sentencing circles, in which crime victims and their families are brought together with offenders and their families in an effort to formulate a sanction that addresses the needs of each party.

Victims are given a chance to voice their stories, and offenders can help compensate them financially or provide some service (for example, fixing damaged property).[147] The goal is to enable offenders to appreciate the damage they have caused, to make amends, and to be reintegrated into society.

Restoration programs are being used in court systems around the world. One example is the justice system in Australia, which makes use of a conferencing process to divert offenders from the justice system.[148] This offers offenders the opportunity to attend a conference to discuss and resolve their offense instead of being charged and appearing in court. (Those who deny guilt are not offered conferencing.) The conference, normally lasting one to two hours, is attended by the victims and their supporters, the defendant and his or her supporters, and other concerned parties. The conference coordinator focuses the discussion on condemning the act without condemning the character of the actor. Offenders are asked to tell their side of the story, what happened, how they have felt about the crime, and what they think should be done. The victims and others are asked to describe the physical, financial, and emotional consequences of the crime. This discussion may lead the offenders, their families, and their friends to experience the shame of the act, prompting an apology to the victim. A plan of action is developed and signed by key participants. The plan may include the offender paying compensation to the victim, doing work for the victim or the community, or similar solutions. It is the responsibility of the conference participants to determine the outcomes that are most appropriate for these particular victims and these particular offenders. All eight states and territories in Australia have used the conference model at some time or another.

Reconciliation Restoration has also been used as a national policy to heal internal rifts. For example, after 50 years of oppressive white rule in South Africa, the race-dividing apartheid policy was abolished in the early 1990s, and in 1994 Nelson Mandela, leader of the African National Congress (ANC), was elected president.[149] Some black leaders wanted revenge for the political murders carried out during the apartheid era, but Mandela established the Truth and Reconciliation Commission. Rather than seeking vengeance for the crimes, this government agency investigated the atrocities with the mandate of granting amnesty to those individuals who confessed their roles in the violence and could prove that

Restoration programs can take many forms. Regina Talbert and Anthony Belcher hand out food and clothing on skid row in Los Angeles. The two former addicts are part of the New Directions team, who perform outreach to addicted and alcoholic army, navy, and air force veterans in some of the city's most dangerous neighborhoods. Veterans of U.S. wars, including the current campaigns in Afghanistan and Iraq, are increasingly turning up with alarming signs of PTSD and other serious mental issues. Regina (left), who has been in recovery for nine years, hands out fliers about the New Directions treatment center. Would you consider this a "restoration"-based initiative?

The Victim Offender Reconciliation Program (VORP) of Denver began in 1993 in response to a summer of violence in the metro Denver area. VORP has collaborated with the justice system to provide restorative justice processes for the community as a way of addressing issues overlooked in a more traditional, adversarial justice system. VORP has been a catalyst for long-term answers to crime. Each system has its role and provides part of the solution to the problem of administering justice. The VORP program, steeped in diverse cultural roots, gives an opportunity for reconciling and restoring relationships between victims, offenders, and the community.

Programs are conducted by trained volunteers in restorative justice, mediation, facilitation, cultural competency, and communication. Currently VORP offers victim–offender mediation, community group conferencing, peace circles, and a reparative panel as restorative justice tools. As needed, VORP staff and facilitators also work one on one with victims and offenders of crime.

VORP has three principal aims in furthering its mission:

- Reduce recidivism
- Restore and strengthen community relationships
- Empower victims and the community

The RESTORE Program

One of the Denver VORP programs is designed to help kids who have gotten into trouble by shoplifting from a local store. When a youth is referred by juvenile court, a RESTORE intake form is completed. The youth and a parent or guardian attend two RESTORE sessions and complete a contract, as described below.

Part 1. During this session, the youth and their parents will listen to speakers discuss the impact of shoplifting on the merchant community, as well as the community-at-large. They will also hear other youth speak about how shoplifting has affected them, their peers, and their families.

Part 2. Then, the youth and their parents will meet in smaller groups to talk about the shoplifting incidents they were involved in and how they have been affected by this incident. This group will also include other juvenile shoplifters, their parents, community member, peer representative, and merchant representative, and will be facilitated by RESTORE Volunteers.

Part 3. When the group sessions are complete, each youth and with his/her parent or guardian review and sign a contract to repair the harm to the victim, the community, their family and themselves, including community service. They will sign up for a contract completion date and time to return to the RESTORE Council.

The youth will return in one or two months to present his or her completed contract results and projects, including verification of community service and other contract items. By participating in the RESTORE program, youth can:

- Learn more about shoplifting and how it affects victims and the community
- Repair the harm done by the incident in a meaningful way
- Make choices about the consequences for their actions
- Have their theft charge dismissed upon successful completion of the program

The RESTORE program uses the principles of restorative justice to reintegrate young offenders into community. It is an example of turning theory into action.

CRITICAL THINKING

1. Could you design a program for recreational drug users using the RESTORE model?
2. Do you believe restorative justice programs can work, or are they a method for kids who commit crime to avoid legal responsibility?

SOURCE: Victim Offender Reconciliation Program of Denver, 2009, www.denvervorp.org (accessed August 11, 2011).

---

their actions served some political motive rather than being based on personal factors such as greed or jealousy.

Supporters of the commission believed that this approach would help heal the nation's wounds and prevent years of racial and ethnic strife. Mandela, who had been unjustly jailed for 27 years by the regime, had reason to desire vengeance. Yet he wanted to move the country forward after the truth of what happened in the past had been established. Though many South Africans, including some ANC members, believe that the commission is too lenient, Mandela's attempts at reconciliation have prevailed. The commission is a model of restoration over revenge.

In sum, restoration can be or has been used at the following stages of justice:

- As a form of final warning to young offenders
- As a tool for school officials
- As a method of handling complaints to police
- As a diversion from prosecution
- As a pre-sentencing, post-conviction add-on to the sentencing process
- As a supplement to a community sentence (probation)
- As a preparation for release from long-term imprisonment[150]

The Policy and Practice in Criminology, "Victim Offender Reconciliation in Denver, Colorado," reviews a successful restorative justice program.

The Challenge of Restorative Justice

Restorative justice holds great promise, but there are also some concerns:

- Restorative justice programs must be wary of the cultural and social differences that can be found throughout our heterogeneous society. What may be considered "restorative" in one subculture may be considered insulting and damaging in another.[151]
- There is still no single definition of what constitutes restorative justice.[152] Consequently, many diverse programs that call themselves restorative-oriented pursue objectives that seem remote from the restorative ideal.
- Restorative justice programs face the difficult task of balancing the needs of offenders with those of their victims. If programs focus solely on victims' needs, they may risk ignoring the offenders' needs and increase the likelihood of reoffending. Declan Roache, a lecturer in law at the London School of Economics, makes the argument that the seductive promise of restorative justice may blind admirers to the benefits of traditional methods and prevent them from understanding or appreciating some of the pitfalls of restoration. There is danger, he warns, in a process that is essentially informal, without lawyers, and with little or no oversight on the outcome. The restoration process gives participants unchecked power without the benefit of procedural safeguards.[153]
- Benefits may only work in the short term while ignoring long-term treatment needs. Sharon Levrant and her colleagues suggest that restorative justice programs that feature short-term interactions with victims fail to help offenders learn prosocial ways of behaving. Restorative justice advocates may falsely assume that relatively brief interludes of public shaming will change deeply rooted criminal predispositions.[154]

These are a few of the obstacles that restorative justice programs must overcome to be successful and productive. Yet because the method holds so much promise, criminologists are conducting numerous demonstration projects to find the most effective means of returning the ownership of justice to the people and the community.[155]

SUMMARY

1. **Be familiar with the ideas that underpin critical criminology**
   - Critical criminology is based on the view that crime is a function of the conflict that exists in society. Critical theorists suggest that crime in any society is caused by economic and class conflict. Laws are created by those in power to protect their own rights and to serve their own interests. Criminal law is designed to protect the wealthy and powerful and to control the poor, "have-not" members of society. The poor commit crimes because of their frustration, anger, and need. The wealthy engage in illegal acts because they are used to competition and because they must do so to maintain their position in society.

2. **Trace the development of critical theory**
   - Critical theory has its roots in Marxist thought. Early advocates such as Vold and Bonger believed that all behavior, including criminal acts, has political undertones. The justice system is biased against the poor and designed to protect the wealthy. Social and political oppression produce crime. Crime would disappear if equality rather than discrimination was the norm. These ideas developed during the 1960s when the civil rights, prisoners' rights, and feminist movements encouraged left leaning academics to expose the inequities built into the capitalist system.

3. **Be able to discuss the difference between structural theory and instrumental theory**
   - Critical theorists subscribe to either instrumental theory or structural theory. Instrumental theorists hold that those in authority wield their power to control society and keep the lower classes in check. Structural theorists believe that the justice system is designed to maintain the status quo and is used to punish the wealthy, as well as members of the lower classes, when they break the rules governing capitalism.

4. **Link globalization to crime and criminality**
   - Globalization disproportionately benefits wealthy and powerful organizations and individuals and impoverishes indigenous people. As the influence and impact of international financial institutions increase, there is a related relative decline in power of local or state-based institutions, resulting in the recent unrest in world financial systems. With money and power to spare, global criminal enterprise groups can recruit new members, bribe government officials, and even fund private armies.

5. **Define the concept of state (organized) crime**
   - State crimes involve a violation of citizen trust. They are acts defined by law as criminal and committed by state officials in pursuit of their jobs as government representatives. Some state crimes are committed by individuals who abuse their state authority, or fail to exercise it, when working with people and organizations in the private sector. State–corporate crime involves the deviant activities by which the privileged classes strive to maintain or increase their power.

6. **Know the goals and findings of critical research**
   - Research on critical theory focuses on how the justice system was designed and how it operates to further class interests. It sometimes employs historical analysis to show how the capitalist classes have exerted control over the police, the courts, and correctional agencies. Contemporary research exposes how race and class influence decision making in the criminal justice system.

7. **Be familiar with the critiques of critical criminology**
   - Critical criminology has been criticized by traditional criminologists. Some critics suggest that critical criminologists make fundamental errors in their concepts of ownership and class interest.

8. **Explain the concept of left realism**
   - Left realism sees crime as a function of relative deprivation under capitalism and views the justice system as necessary to protect the lower classes until a socialist society can be developed, which will end crime.

9. **Know some of the basic ideas of critical feminism**
   - Critical feminist writers draw attention to the influence of patriarchal society on crime. According to power–control theory, gender differences in the crime rate can be explained by the structure of the family in a capitalist society.

10. **Discuss how restorative justice is related to peacemaking criminology**
    - Peacemaking criminology brings a call for humanism to criminology. The restorative justice model holds that reconciliation rather than retribution should be applied to prevent and control crime. Restoration programs are now being used around the United States in schools, justice agencies, and community forums. They employ mediation, sentencing circles, and other techniques.

KEY TERMS

critical criminologists (266)
critical criminology (266)
Communist Manifesto (268)
productive forces (268)
productive relations (268)
capitalist bourgeoisie (268)
proletariat (268)
lumpen proletariat (268)
dialectic method (268)
thesis (269)
antithesis (269)
synthesis (269)

imperatively coordinated associations (269)
supranational crimes (271)
instrumental theorists (272)
structural theorists (272)
demystify (272)
surplus value (272)
marginalization (272)
globalization (273)
state (organized) crime (274)
dropout factories (276)
left realism (279)

critical feminism (282)
patriarchal (282)
paternalistic families (283)
role exit behaviors (283)
egalitarian families (283)
power–control theory (283)
peacemaking (284)
restorative justice (285)
shame (286)
reintegrative shaming (286)
sentencing circle (287)

CRITICAL THINKING QUESTIONS

1. How would a conservative reply to a call for more restorative justice? How would a restorative justice advocate respond to a conservative call for more prisons?
2. Considering recent changes in American culture, how would a power–control theorist explain recent drops in the U.S. crime rate?
3. Is conflict inevitable in all cultures? If not, what can be done to reduce the level of conflict in our own society?
4. If Marx were alive today, what would he think about the prosperity enjoyed by the working class in industrial societies? Might he alter his vision of the capitalist system?
5. Has religious conflict replaced class conflict as the most important issue facing modern society? Can anything be done to heal the rifts between people of different faiths?

NOTES

1. Human Rights Watch, "UN: Reject Syria's Human Rights Council Candidacy, Country Under Investigation by Rights Body Not Fit to Join," May 6, 2011, www.hrw.org/en/news/2011/05/06/un-reject-syria-s-human-rights-council-candidacy (accessed August 11, 2011).

2. Michael Lynch and W. Byron Groves, *A Primer in Radical Criminology*, 2nd Ed. (Albany, NY: Harrow & Heston, 1989), pp. 32–33.

3. Michael Lynch, "Rediscovering Criminology: Lessons from the Marxist Tradition," in *Marxist Sociology: Surveys of Contemporary Theory and Research*, ed. Donald McQuarie and Patrick McGuire (New York: General Hall, 1994).

4. Andrew Woolford, "Making Genocide Unthinkable: Three Guidelines for a Critical Criminology of Genocide," *Critical Criminology* 14 (2006): 87–106.

5. Tony Platt and Cecilia O'Leary, "Patriot Acts," *Social Justice* 30 (2003): 5–21.

6. James Defillipis, Robert Fisher, and Eric Shragge, "Radicalizing Community," *Social Policy* 40 (2010): 13–20.

7. See, generally, Karl Marx and Friedrich Engels, *Capital: A Critique of Political Economy*, trans. E. Aveling (Chicago: Charles Kern, 1906); Karl Marx, *Selected Writings in Sociology and Social Philosophy*, trans. P. B. Bottomore (New York: McGraw-Hill, 1956). For a general discussion of Marxist thought, see Lynch and Groves, *A Primer in Radical Criminology*, pp. 6–26.

8. Karl Marx, *Grundrisse: Introduction to the Critique of Political Economy*, trans. Martin Nicolaus (New York: Vintage, 1973), pp. 106–107.

9. Lynch, "Rediscovering Criminology."

10. Karl Marx, "Population, Crime and Pauperism," in *Karl Marx and Friedrich Engels, Ireland and the Irish Question* (Moscow: Progress, 1859, reprinted 1971), p. 92.

11. Friedrich Engels, *The Condition of the Working Class in England in 1844* (London: Allen & Unwin, 1950).

12. Lynch, "Rediscovering Criminology," p. 5.

13. Ian Taylor, Paul Walton, and Jock Young, *The New Criminology: For a Social Theory of Deviance* (London: Routledge & Kegan Paul, 1973).

14. Biko Agozino, "Imperialism, Crime and Criminology: Towards the Decolonisation of Criminology," *Crime, Law and Social Change* 41 (2004): 343–358.

15. William Chambliss and Robert Seidman, *Law, Order, and Power* (Reading, MA: Addison-Wesley, 1971), p. 503.

16. Richard Quinney, *The Social Reality of Crime* (Boston: Little, Brown, 1970).

17. This section borrows heavily from Richard Sparks, "A Critique of Marxist Criminology," in *Crime and Justice*, Vol. 2, ed. Norval Morris and Michael Tonry (Chicago: University of Chicago Press, 1980), pp. 159–208.

18. Barbara Sims, "Crime, Punishment, and the American Dream: Toward a Marxist Integration," *Journal of Research in Crime and Delinquency* 34 (1997): 5–24.

19. Gregg Barak, "Revisionist History, Visionary Criminology, and Needs-Based Justice," *Contemporary Justice Review* 6 (2003): 217–225.

20. John Braithwaite, "Retributivism, Punishment, and Privilege," in *Punishment and Privilege*, ed. W. Byron Groves and Graeme Newman (Albany, NY: Harrow & Heston, 1986), pp. 55–66.

21. Agozino, "Imperialism, Crime and Criminology."

22. Barak, "Revisionist History, Visionary Criminology, and Needs-Based Justice."

23. Kitty Kelley Epstein, "The Whitening of the American Teaching Force: A Problem of Recruitment or a Problem of Racism?" *Social Justice* 32 (2005): 89–102.

24. Tony Platt and Cecilia O'Leary, "Patriot Acts," *Social Justice* 30 (2003): 5–21.

25. Garrett Brown, "The Global Threats to Workers' Health and Safety on the Job," *Social Justice* 29 (2002): 12–25.

26. Robert Bohm, "Radical Criminology: Back to the Basics," paper presented at the annual meeting of the American Society of Criminology, Phoenix, November 1993, p. 2.

27. Alette Smeulers and Roelof Haveman, eds., *Supranational Criminology: Towards a Criminology of International Crimes* (Belgium: Intersentia, 2008).

28. Ibid., p. 4.

29. Lynch and Groves, *A Primer in Radical Criminology*, p. 7.

30. Jeffery Reiman, *The Rich Get Richer and the Poor Get Prison* (New York: Wiley, 1984), pp. 43–44.

31. Rob White, "Environmental Harm and the Political Economy of Consumption," *Social Justice* 29 (2002): 82–102.

32. Sims, "Crime, Punishment, and the American Dream."

33. Gresham Sykes, "The Rise of Critical Criminology," *Journal of Criminal Law and Criminology* 65 (1974): 211–229.

34. David Jacobs, "Corporate Economic Power and the State: A Longitudinal Assessment of Two Explanations," *American Journal of Sociology* 93 (1988): 852–881.

35. Deanna Alexander, "Victims of the L.A. Riots: A Theoretical Consideration," paper presented at the annual meeting of the American Society of Criminology, Phoenix, November 1993.

36. Richard Quinney, "Crime Control in Capitalist Society," in *Critical Criminology*, ed. Ian Taylor, Paul Walton, and Jock Young (London: Routledge & Kegan Paul, 1975), p. 199.

37. Ibid.

38. John Hagan, *Structural Criminology* (New Brunswick, NJ: Rutgers University Press, 1989), pp. 110–119.

39. Michael Lynch, "Assessing the State of Radical Criminology: Toward the Year 2000," paper presented at the annual meeting of the American Society of Criminology, Phoenix, November 1993.

40. Steven Box, *Recession, Crime, and Unemployment* (London: Macmillan, 1987).

41. David Barlow, Melissa Hickman-Barlow, and W. Wesley Johnson, "The Political Economy of Criminal Justice Policy: A Time-Series Analysis of Economic Conditions, Crime, and Federal Criminal Justice Legislation, 1948–1987," *Justice Quarterly* 13 (1996): 223–241.

42. Mahesh Nalla, Michael Lynch, and Michael Leiber, "Determinants of Police Growth in Phoenix, 1950–1988," *Justice Quarterly* 14 (1997): 144–163.

43. Dawn L. Rothe, Jeffrey Ian Ross, Christopher W. Mullins, David Friedrichs, Raymond Michalowski, Gregg Barak, David Kauzlarich, and Ronald C. Kramer, "That Was Then, This Is Now, What About Tomorrow? Future Directions in State Crime Studies," *Critical Criminology* 17 (2009): 3–13.

44. David Friedrichs and Jessica Friedrichs, "The World Bank and Crimes of Globalization: A Case Study," *Social Justice* 29 (2002): 13–36.

45. Ibid.

46. Louise Shelley, "The Globalization of Crime and Terrorism," State Department's Bureau of International Information Programs (IIP), 2006, http://cuwhist.files.wordpress.com/2009/12/the-globalization-of-crime-and-terrorism.pdf (accessed August 11, 2011).

47. Greg Palast, "Secret US Plan for Iraqi Oil, BBC News," March 17, 2005, http://news.bbc.co.uk/1/hi/programmes/newsnight/4354269.stm (accessed August 11, 2011).

48. Jeffrey Ian Ross, *The Dynamics of Political Crime* (Thousand Oaks, CA: Sage, 2003).

49. American Civil Liberties Union, "What's Wrong with Public Video Surveillance? The Four Problems with Public Video Surveillance," www.aclu.org/technology-and-liberty/whats-wrong-public-video-surveillance (accessed August 11, 2011).

50. Amnesty International, "Injustice Fuels Sri Lanka's Cycle of Abuse and Impunity," June 11, 2009, www.amnesty.org/en/news-and-updates/report/injustice-fuels-sri-lankas-cycle-abuse-and-impunity-20090611 (accessed August 11, 2011); Asian Human Rights Commission, "Sri Lanka: A

Disappearance Every Five Hours Is a Result of Deliberate Removal of All Legal Safeguards Against Illegal Detention, Murder and Illegal Disposal of Bodies," February 2, 2007, www.ahrchk.net/statements/mainfile.php/2007statements/912/ (accessed August 11, 2011).

51. BBC News, "Six Days That Shook Iran," July 11, 2000, http://news.bbc.co.uk/2/hi/middle_east/828696.stm (accessed August 11, 2011).

52. MSNBC News, "Bush Acknowledges Secret CIA Prisons," September 6, 2006, www.msnbc.msn.com/id/14689359/ (accessed August 11, 2011); American Civil Liberties Union, "FBI Inquiry Details Abuses Reported by Agents at Guantanamo," January 3, 2007, www.aclu.org/safefree/torture/27816prs20070103.html (accessed August 11, 2011).

53. Human Rights Watch, "UAE: Exploited Workers Building 'Island of Happiness,'" May 19, 2009, www.hrw.org/en/news/2009/05/18/uae-exploited-workers-building-island-happiness (accessed August 11, 2011).

54. Ross, The Dynamics of Political Crime.

55. Amnesty International, "Brazil: One More Human Rights Defender Lost to the Scourge of 'Death-Squads,'" January 26, 2009, www.amnesty.org/en/for-media/press-releases/brazil-one-more-human-rights-defender-lost-scourge-death-squads-20090126 (accessed August 11, 2011).

56. Human Rights Watch, "Chechnya: Research Shows Widespread and Systematic Use of Torture," http://hrw.org/english/docs/2006/11/13/russia14557_txt.htm (accessed August 11, 2011).

57. America's Promise Alliance, "Building a Grad Nation: Progress and Challenge in Ending the High School Dropout Epidemic," November 30, 2010, www.americaspromise.org/Our-Work/Grad-Nation/Building-a-Grad-Nation.aspx (accessed August 11, 2011).

58. Michael Rocques and Raymond Paternoster, "Understanding the Antecedents of the 'School-to-Jail' Link: The Relationship Between Race and School Discipline," Journal of Criminal Law and Criminology 101 (2011): 633–665.

59. Allison Ann Payne and Kelly Welch, "Modeling the Effects of Racial Threat on Punitive and Restorative School Discipline Practices," Criminology 48 (2010): 1019–1062.

60. Albert Meehan and Michael Ponder, "Race and Place: The Ecology of Racial Profiling African American Motorists," Justice Quarterly 29 (2002): 399–431.

61. Tammy Rinehart Kochel, David Wilson, and Stephen Mastrofski, "Effect of Suspect Race on Officers' Arrest Decisions," Criminology 49 (2011): 473–512.

62. Malcolm Homes, "Minority Threat and Police Brutality: Determinants of Civil Rights Criminal Complaints in U.S. Municipalities," Criminology 38 (2000): 343–368.

63. Brian Johnson, Eric Stewart, Justin Pickett, and Marc Gertz, "Ethnic Threat and Social Control: Examining Public Support for Judicial Use of Ethnicity in Punishment," Criminology 49 (2011): 401–441.

64. Charles Crawford, Ted Chiricos, and Gary Kleck, "Race, Racial Threat, and Sentencing of Habitual Offenders," Criminology 36 (1998): 481–511.

65. Darrell Steffensmeier and Stephen Demuth, "Ethnicity and Judges' Sentencing Decisions: Hispanic-Black-White Comparisons," Criminology 39 (2001): 145–178; Alan Lizotte, "Extra-Legal Factors in Chicago's Criminal Courts: Testing the Conflict Model of Criminal Justice," Social Problems 25 (1978): 564–580.

66. Terance Miethe and Charles Moore, "Racial Differences in Criminal Processing: The Consequences of Model Selection on Conclusions about Differential Treatment," Sociological Quarterly 27 (1987): 217–237.

67. Tracy Nobiling, Cassia Spohn, and Miriam DeLone, "A Tale of Two Counties: Unemployment and Sentence Severity," Justice Quarterly 15 (1998): 459–485.

68. Michael Lenza, David Keys, and Teresa Guess, "The Prevailing Injustices in the Application of the Missouri Death Penalty (1978 to 1996)," Social Justice 32 (2005): 151–166.

69. Thomas Arvanites, "Increasing Imprisonment: A Function of Crime or Socioeconomic Factors?" American Journal of Criminal Justice 17 (1992): 19–38.

70. David Greenberg and Valerie West, "State Prison Populations and Their Growth, 1971–1991," Criminology 39 (2001): 615–654.

71. Jack Gibbs, "An Incorrigible Positivist," Criminologist 12 (1987): 2–3.

72. Jackson Toby, "The New Criminology Is the Old Sentimentality," Criminology 16 (1979): 513–526.

73. Richard Sparks, "A Critique of Marxist Criminology," in Crime and Justice, Vol. 2, ed. Norval Morris and Michael Tonry (Chicago: University of Chicago Press, 1980), pp. 159–208.

74. Carl Klockars, "The Contemporary Crises of Marxist Criminology," in Radical Criminology: The Coming Crisis, ed. J. Inciardi (Beverly Hills, CA: Sage, 1980), pp. 92–123.

75. Matthew Petrocelli, Alex Piquero, and Michael Smith, "Conflict Theory and Racial Profiling: An Empirical Analysis of Police Traffic Stop Data," Journal of Criminal Justice 31 (2003): 1–10.

76. Ibid.

77. Anthony Platt, "Criminology in the 1980s: Progressive Alternatives to 'Law and Order,'" Crime and Social Justice 21–22 (1985): 191–199.

78. John Lea and Jock Young, What Is to Be Done About Law and Order? (Harmondsworth, England: Penguin, 1984).

79. Ibid., p. 88.

80. Ian Taylor, Crime in Context: A Critical Criminology of Market Societies (Boulder, CO: Westview Press, 1999).

81. Ibid., pp. 30–31.

82. Elliott Currie, "Plain Left Realism: An Appreciation, and Some Thoughts for the Future," Crime, Law and Social Change 54 (2010): 111–124.

83. Richard Kinsey, John Lea, and Jock Young, Losing the Fight Against Crime (London: Blackwell, 1986).

84. Martin Schwartz and Walter DeKeseredy, "The Current Health of Left Realist Theory," Crime, Law and Social Change 54 (2010): 107–110.

85. Michelle Alexander, The New Jim Crow: Mass Incarceration in the Age of Colorblindness (New York: New Press, 2010), p. 2.

86. Martin Schwartz and Walter DeKeseredy, Contemporary Criminology (Belmont, CA: Wadsworth, 1993), p. 249.

87. Michael Jacobson and Lynn Chancer, "From Left Realism to Mass Incarceration: The Need for Pragmatic Vision in Criminal Justice Policy," Crime, Law and Social Change 55 (2011): 187–196.

88. Martin D. Schwartz and Walter S. DeKeseredy, "Left Realist Criminology: Strengths, Weaknesses and the Feminist Critique," Crime, Law and Social Change 15 (1991): 51–72.

89. Schwartz and DeKeseredy, "The Current Health of Left Realist Theory."

90. For a general review of this issue, see Kathleen Daly and Meda Chesney-Lind, "Feminism and Criminology," Justice Quarterly 5 (1988): 497–538; Douglas Smith and Raymond Paternoster, "The Gender Gap in Theories of Deviance: Issues and Evidence," Journal of Research in Crime and Delinquency 24 (1987): 140–172; and Pat Carlen, "Women, Crime, Feminism, and Realism," Social Justice 17 (1990): 106–123.

91. Herman Schwendinger and Julia Schwendinger, Rape and Inequality (Newbury Park, CA: Sage, 1983).

92. Daly and Chesney-Lind, "Feminism and Criminology."

93. Janet Saltzman Chafetz, "Feminist Theory and Sociology: Underutilized Contributions for Mainstream Theory," Annual Review of Sociology 23 (1997): 97–121.

94. Ibid.

95. James Messerschmidt, Capitalism, Patriarchy, and Crime (Totowa, NJ: Rowman & Littlefield, 1986); for a critique of this work, see Herman Schwendinger and Julia Schwendinger, "The World According to James Messerschmidt," Social Justice 15 (1988): 123–145.

96. Kathleen Daly, "Gender and Varieties of White-Collar Crime," Criminology 27 (1989): 769–793.

97. Gillian Balfour, "Re-imagining a Feminist Criminology," *Canadian Journal of Criminology and Criminal Justice* 48 (2006): 735–752.

98. Jane Roberts Chapman, "Violence Against Women as a Violation of Human Rights," *Social Justice* 17 (1990): 54–71.

99. Carrie Yodanis, "Gender Inequality, Violence Against Women, and Fear," *Journal of Interpersonal Violence* 19 (2004): 655–675.

100. Victoria Titterington, "A Retrospective Investigation of Gender Inequality and Female Homicide Victimization," *Sociological Spectrum* 26 (2006): 205–236.

101. James Messerschmidt, *Masculinities and Crime: Critique and Reconceptualization of Theory* (Lanham, MD: Rowman & Littlefield, 1993).

102. Angela P. Harris, "Gender, Violence, Race, and Criminal Justice," *Stanford Law Review* 52 (2000): 777–810.

103. Suzie Dod Thomas and Nancy Stein, "Criminality, Imprisonment, and Women's Rights in the 1990s," *Social Justice* 17 (1990): 1–5.

104. Walter DeKeseredy and Martin Schwartz, "Male Peer Support and Woman Abuse: An Expansion of DeKeseredy's Model," *Sociological Spectrum* 13 (1993): 393–413.

105. Daly and Chesney-Lind, "Feminism and Criminology." See also Drew Humphries and Susan Caringella-MacDonald, "Murdered Mothers, Missing Wives: Reconsidering Female Victimization," *Social Justice* 17 (1990): 71–78.

106. Kjersti Ericsson and Nina Jon, "Gendered Social Control: 'A Virtuous Girl' and 'a Proper Boy'," *Journal of Scandinavian Studies in Criminology and Crime Prevention* 9 (2006): 126–141.

107. Hagan, *Structural Criminology*.

108. John Hagan, A. R. Gillis, and John Simpson, "The Class Structure and Delinquency: Toward a Power–Control Theory of Common Delinquent Behavior," *American Journal of Sociology* 90 (1985): 1151–1178; John Hagan, John Simpson, and A. R. Gillis, "Class in the Household: A Power–Control Theory of Gender and Delinquency," *American Journal of Sociology* 92 (1987): 788–816.

109. John Hagan, Bill McCarthy, and Holly Foster, "A Gendered Theory of Delinquency and Despair in the Life Course," *Acta Sociologica* 45 (2002): 37–47.

110. Brenda Sims Blackwell, Christine Sellers, and Sheila Schlaupitz, "A Power–Control Theory of Vulnerability to Crime and Adolescent Role Exits—Revisited," *Canadian Review of Sociology and Anthropology* 39 (2002): 199–219.

111. Brenda Sims Blackwell, "Perceived Sanction Threats, Gender, and Crime: A Test and Elaboration of Power–Control Theory," *Criminology* 38 (2000): 439–488.

112. Christopher Uggen, "Class, Gender, and Arrest: An Intergenerational Analysis of Workplace Power and Control," *Criminology* 38 (2001): 835–862.

113. Gary Jensen, "Power–Control versus Social-Control Theory: Identifying Crucial Differences for Future Research," paper presented at the annual meeting of the American Society of Criminology, Baltimore, November 1990.

114. Gary Jensen and Kevin Thompson, "What's Class Got to Do with It? A Further Examination of Power–Control Theory," *American Journal of Sociology* 95 (1990): 1,009–1,023. For some critical research, see Simon Singer and Murray Levine, "Power–Control Theory, Gender and Delinquency: A Partial Replication with Additional Evidence on the Effects of Peers," *Criminology* 26 (1988): 627–648.

115. Kevin Thompson, "Gender and Adolescent Drinking Problems: The Effects of Occupational Structure," *Social Problems* 36 (1989): 30–38.

116. Kristin Mack and Michael Leiber, "Race, Gender, Single-Mother Households, and Delinquency: A Further Test of Power–Control Theory," *Youth and Society* 37 (2005): 115–144.

117. See, generally, Uggen, "Class, Gender, and Arrest."

118. Brenda Sims Blackwell and Alex Piquero, "On the Relationships Between Gender, Power Control, Self-Control, and Crime," *Journal of Criminal Justice* 33 (2005): 1–17.

119. Liz Walz, "One Blood," *Contemporary Justice Review* 6 (2003): 25–36.

120. John F. Wozniak, "Poverty and Peacemaking Criminology: Beyond Mainstream Criminology," *Critical Criminology* 16 (2008): 209–223.

121. See, for example, Dennis Sullivan, and Larry Tifft, *Restorative Justice: Healing the Foundations of Our Everyday Lives* (Monsey, NY: Willow Tree Press, 2005); Dennis Sullivan, *The Mask of Love: Corrections in America, Toward a Mutual Aid Alternative* (Port Washington, NY: Kennikat Press, 1980).

122. Larry Tifft, "Foreword," in Sullivan, *The Mask of Love*, p. 6.

123. Sullivan, *The Mask of Love*, p. 141.

124. Sullivan and Tifft, *Restorative Justice*.

125. Richard Quinney, "The Way of Peace: On Crime, Suffering, and Service," in *Criminology as Peacemaking*, ed. Harold Pepinsky and Richard Quinney (Bloomington: Indiana University Press, 1991), pp. 8–9.

126. For a review of Quinney's ideas, see Kevin B. Anderson, "Richard Quinney's Journey: The Marxist Dimension," *Crime and Delinquency* 48 (2002): 232–242.

127. Kathleen Daly and Russ Immarigeon, "The Past, Present and Future of Restorative Justice: Some Critical Reflections," *Contemporary Justice Review* 1 (1998): 21–45.

128. Howard Zehr, *The Little Book of Restorative Justice* (Intercourse, PA: Good Books, 2002): 1–10.

129. Mark Lewis Taylor, *The Executed God: The Way of the Cross in Lockdown America* (Minneapolis: Fortress Press, 2001).

130. Alfred Villaume, "'Life Without Parole' and 'Virtual Life Sentences': Death Sentences by Any Other Name," *Contemporary Justice Review* 8 (2005): 265–277.

131. John Braithwaite, *Crime, Shame, and Reintegration* (Melbourne, Australia: Cambridge University Press, 1989).

132. Ibid., p. 81.

133. Anthony Petrosino and Carolyn Petrosino, "The Public Safety Potential of Megan's Law in Massachusetts: An Assessment from a Sample of Criminal Sexual Psychopaths," *Crime and Delinquency* 45 (1999): 140–158.

134. Eliza Ahmed, Nathan Harris, John Braithwaite, and Valerie Braithwaite, *Shame Management Through Reintegration* (Cambridge, England: Cambridge University Press, 2001).

135. Eliza Ahmed, "'What, Me Ashamed?' Shame Management and School Bullying," *Journal of Research in Crime and Delinquency* 41 (2004): 269–294.

136. John Braithwaite, "Rape, Shame and Pride," *Journal of Scandinavian Studies in Criminology and Crime Prevention* 7 (2006): 2–16.

137. For more on this approach, see Jane Mugford and Stephen Mugford, "Shame and Reintegration in the Punishment and Deterrence of Spouse Assault," paper presented at the annual meeting of the American Society of Criminology, San Francisco, November 1991.

138. Carter Hay, "An Exploratory Test of Braithwaite's Reintegrative Shaming Theory," *Journal of Research in Crime and Delinquency* 38 (2001): 132–153.

139. Mugford and Mugford, "Shame and Reintegration in the Punishment and Deterrence of Spouse Assault."

140. Gene Stephens, "The Future of Policing: From a War Model to a Peace Model," in *The Past, Present and Future of American Criminal Justice*, ed. Brendan Maguire and Polly Radosh (Dix Hills, NY: General Hall, 1996), pp. 77–93.

141. Rick Shifley, "The Organization of Work as a Factor in Social Well-Being," *Contemporary Justice Review* 6 (2003): 105–126.

142. Kay Pranis, "Peacemaking Circles: Restorative Justice in Practice Allows Victims and Offenders to Begin Repairing the Harm," *Corrections Today* 59 (1997): 74–78.

143. Carol LaPrairie, "The 'New' Justice: Some Implications for Aboriginal Communities," *Canadian Journal of Criminology* 40 (1998): 61–79.

144. Diane Schaefer, "A Disembodied Community Collaborates in a Homicide: Can Empathy Transform a Failing Justice System?" *Contemporary Justice Review* 6 (2003): 133–143.

145. David R. Karp and Beau Breslin, "Restorative Justice in School Communities," *Youth and Society* 33 (2001): 249–272.

146. Paul Jesilow and Deborah Parsons, "Community Policing as Peacemaking," *Policing and Society* 10 (2000): 163–183.

147. Gordon Bazemore and Curt Taylor Griffiths, "Conferences, Circles, Boards, and Mediations: The 'New Wave' of Community Justice Decision Making," *Federal Probation* 61 (1997): 25–37.

148. Heather Strang, "Restorative Justice Programs in Australia," www.criminologyresearchcouncil.gov.au/reports/strang/report.pdf (accessed September 25, 2010).

149. John W. De Gruchy, *Reconciliation: Restoring Justice* (Minneapolis: Fortress, 2002).

150. Lawrence W Sherman and Heather Strang, *Restorative Justice: The Evidence* (London: Smith Institute, 2007), www.sas.upenn.edu/jerrylee/RJ_full_report.pdf (accessed September 25, 2010).

151. David Altschuler, "Community Justice Initiatives: Issues and Challenges in the U.S. Context," *Federal Probation* 65 (2001): 28–33.

152. Lois Presser and Patricia Van Voorhis, "Values and Evaluation: Assessing Processes and Outcomes of Restorative Justice Programs," *Crime and Delinquency* 48 (2002): 162–189.

153. Declan Roche, *Accountability in Restorative Justice* (Clarendon Studies in Criminology) (London: Oxford University Press, 2004).

154. Sharon Levrant, Francis Cullen, Betsy Fulton, and John Wozniak, "Reconsidering Restorative Justice: The Corruption of Benevolence Revisited?" *Crime and Delinquency* 45 (1999): 3–28.

155. Edward Gumz, "American Social Work, Corrections and Restorative Justice: An Appraisal," *International Journal of Offender Therapy and Comparative Criminology* 48 (2004): 449–460.

© ZUMA Press/Newscom

IN In 2004, Californians Thomas and Jackie Hawks decided to sell their yacht, which had been their full-time home, and settle down to spend more time with their grandchild. They were contacted by a proposed buyer, Skylar Deleon, who seemed interested enough to take a test cruise. When Deleon showed up on November 15, 2004, he was accompanied by his wife, Jennifer Henderson, and two male companions, Alonso Machain and John Kennedy. The trio soon overpowered the Hawks and beat, blindfolded, and gagged the terrified couple. Deleon took out a laptop computer and started demanding personal information, including Social Security numbers, dates of birth, and Jackie Hawks's maiden name, so their bank accounts could be looted later. Finally the gang handcuffed the Hawks to the yacht's anchor and sent them hurtling to their deaths in

(*continued on page 298*)

Developmental Theories: Life Course, Latent Trait, and Trajectory

9

Learning Objectives

1. Discuss the history of developmental theory
2. Distinguish between the life course, latent trait, and trajectory theories
3. Be familiar with the principles of the life course theory
4. Explain the term *problem behavior syndrome*
5. Discuss why age of onset is an important factor in crime
6. Know the basic principles of Sampson and Laub's age-graded theory
7. Define the term *latent trait*
8. Be familiar with Wilson and Herrnstein's views on crime and human nature
9. Understand the basic principles of the General Theory of Crime
10. Discuss the concept of criminal trajectories

the ocean. Deleon and the other men then turned the boat around and began an hour-long trip back to the shore, during which they cracked open beers and fished over the side of the boat.

When the police investigated the couple's disappearance, the trail of evidence led directly to the culprits. After the plot unraveled, Jennifer Henderson was tried and convicted of murder and sentenced to life in prison without the possibility of parole. Machain cooperated with the prosecution in a deal to avoid the death penalty; co-conspirator Kennedy was sentenced to death for the crime.

And what of the ringleader Skylar Deleon? Deleon's personal story is as bizarre as his crime was horrific. Born John Julius Jacobson, Jr., he began acting in bit parts in commercials as a child and at age 14 appeared in the series *Mighty Morphin Power Rangers*. At age 20, when his acting career faltered because he had a difficult time remembering lines, he joined the U.S. Marine Corps, but went AWOL 15 days later and received a dishonorable discharge. He drifted into a life of petty and serious crime.

The brutal murder of Tom and Jackie Hawks was not Deleon's first involvement in a capital crime. He also had committed the murder of John Jarvi, whom Deleon baited into traveling to Mexico for an easy-money business deal. Soon after arriving in Mexico, Jarvi was robbed of $50,000, murdered, and his body dumped near a highway. And then there was the attempted murder of witnesses in the Hawks trial. Daniel Elias, a career criminal who met Deleon at the Orange County jail, later testified that Deleon promised him $1 million if he killed witnesses in the upcoming trial. Another bizarre twist: while in jail awaiting trial, Deleon attempted to sever his sexual organs, claiming that the robbery was merely a means to fund a sex change operation.

At his trial, in an effort to spare himself the death penalty, Deleon admitted the murders but claimed that he had suffered a horrific childhood, during which his brutal drug-addicted father exposed him to both physical and sexual abuse. From the time he was 2 years old, Deleon was beaten and abused, including multiple occasions on which his father shoved toothpicks under his fingernails. The claims were backed up by witnesses who described Deleon's father as a control freak, drug addict, and abuser who eventually died of AIDS. The jury was not swayed: they recommended the death penalty, and on April 10, 2009, Deleon was sentenced to death by Orange County Superior Court Judge Frank Fasel.[1]

Career criminals like Skylar Deleon defy what is commonly known about criminal behavior: they do not age out of crime as do most youthful offenders, but persist into their adulthood. Nor do they get involved in a single crime and then forgo illegal activity; they have a long history of antisocial behavior, continually planning and getting involved in criminal acts of greater seriousness until they are captured and imprisoned. Criminologists have struggled to understand the factors that explain the onset and continuation of a criminal career. Some look at a single factor, such as poverty or low intelligence, and suggest that people who maintain this trait are predisposed to crime. Those who study **developmental criminology** attempt to provide a more global vision of a criminal career encompassing its onset, continuation, and termination. This chapter reviews the most important issues in developmental criminology and discusses major concepts and theories in some detail.

FOUNDATIONS OF DEVELOPMENTAL THEORY

During the twentieth century, some criminologists began to integrate sociological, psychological, and economic elements into more complex developmental views of crime causation. Hans Eysenck published *Crime and Personality* in 1964 and proclaimed that antisocial behavior was linked to psychological conditions that were a product of heredity.[2] His controversial theory integrated social, biological, and psychological factors, a vision that upset the sociologists who controlled the field at that time.[3]

However, it is Sheldon (1896–1980) and Eleanor (1898–1972) Glueck who are today considered founders of the developmental branch of criminological theory. While at

Harvard University in the 1930s, they conducted research on the careers of known criminals to determine the factors that predicted persistent offending, making extensive use of interviews and records in their elaborate comparisons of criminals and noncriminals.

The Gluecks' research focused on early onset of delinquency as a harbinger of a criminal career: "[T]he deeper the roots of childhood maladjustment, the smaller the chance of adult adjustment."[4] They also noted the stability of offending careers: children who are antisocial early in life are the most likely to continue their offending careers into adulthood.

The Gluecks identified a number of personal and social factors related to persistent offending, the most important of which was family relations. This factor was considered in terms of quality of discipline and emotional ties with parents. The adolescent raised in a large, single-parent family of limited economic means and educational achievement was the most vulnerable to delinquency. Not restricting their analysis to social variables, the Gluecks measured such biological and psychological traits as body type, intelligence, and personality and found that physical and mental factors also played a role in determining behavior. Children with low intelligence who had a background of mental disease and who had a powerful ("mesomorph") physique were the most likely to become persistent offenders.

Integrating biological, social, and psychological elements, the Gluecks' research suggested that the initiation and continuity of a criminal career was a developmental process influenced by both internal and external situations, conditions, and circumstances. Although impressive, their research was heavily criticized by sociologists such as Edwin Sutherland who wanted to keep criminology within the field of sociology and feared or disparaged efforts to integrate biological or psychological concepts into the field.[5]

In a series of longitudinal research studies, the Gluecks followed the careers of known delinquents to determine the characteristics that predicted persistent offending.[6]

The critical Philadelphia cohort research by Marvin Wolfgang and his associates was another milestone prompting interest in explaining criminal career development.[7] As you may recall, Wolfgang found that while many offenders commit a single criminal act and desist from crime, a small group of chronic offenders engage in frequent and repeated criminal activity and continue to do so across their life span. Wolfgang's research focused attention on criminal careers. Criminologists were now asking this fundamental question: what prompts one person to engage in persistent criminal activity while another, who on the surface suffers the same life circumstances, finds a way to steer clear of crime and travel along a more conventional path?

A 1990 review paper by Rolf Loeber and Marc LeBlanc was another important event that generated interest in developmental theory. In this landmark work, Loeber and LeBlanc proposed that criminologists should devote time and effort to understanding some basic questions about the evolution of criminal careers: Why do people begin committing antisocial acts? Why do some stop while others continue? Why do some escalate the severity of their criminality (that is, go from shoplifting to drug dealing to armed robbery) while others deescalate and commit less serious crimes as they mature? If some terminate their criminal activity, what, if anything, causes them to begin again? Why do some criminals specialize in certain types of crime, whereas others are generalists who engage in a variety of antisocial behavior? According to Loeber and LeBlanc's developmental view, criminologists must pay attention to how a criminal career unfolds, how it begins, why it is sustained, and how it comes to an end.[8]

The Glueck legacy was rediscovered in a series of papers by criminologists Robert Sampson and John Laub, who used modern statistical techniques to reanalyze the Gluecks' carefully drawn empirical measurements. Their findings, published in a series of books and articles, fueled the popularity of what is now referred to as the life course approach.[9]

Life Course, Latent Trait, and Trajectory

These scholarly advances created enormous excitement among criminologists and focused their attention on criminal career research. As research on criminal careers has evolved, three distinct viewpoints have taken shape: life course view, latent trait view, and trajectory view. **Life course theory** views criminality as a dynamic process, influenced by a multitude of individual characteristics, traits, and social experiences. As people travel through the life course, they are constantly bombarded by changing perceptions and experiences, and as a result their behavior will change directions, sometimes for the better and sometimes

CONNECTIONS

Social process theories lay the foundation for assuming that peer, family, educational, and other interactions, which vary over the life course, influence behaviors. See the first few sections of Chapter 7 for a review of these issues. As you may recall from Chapter 2, a great deal of research has been conducted on the relationship of age and crime and the activities of chronic offenders. This scholarship has prompted interest in the life cycle of crime.

for the worse (Figure 9.1). In contrast, **latent trait theories** hold that human development is controlled by a stable propensity or "master trait," present at birth or soon after. As people travel through their life course, this trait is always there, directing their behavior and shaping the course of their life. Because this master trait is enduring, the ebb and flow of criminal behavior is directed by the impact of external forces such as interpersonal interactions and criminal opportunity; though people don't change, their opportunities and experiences do.

A third view, **trajectory theory**, suggests there are multiple trajectories in a criminal career. According to this approach, there are several subgroups within a criminal population that follow distinctively different developmental trajectories that lead them toward a criminal career. Some people may begin antisocial activities early and demonstrate a propensity for crime, whereas others begin later and are influenced by life circumstances. Some specialize in a particular criminal offense; others are generalists who commit a variety of crimes.

Although each of these perspectives seems fundamentally different, they share a common vision: a criminal career is a path down which people travel, some at a different pace, and the destination they reach is never secure, but subject to the whims of the passage.[10] Each of these positions is discussed in detail in the following sections.

LIFE COURSE FUNDAMENTALS

According to the life course view, even as toddlers, people begin relationships and behaviors that will determine their adult life course. At first they must learn to conform to social rules and function effectively in society. Later they are expected to begin to think about careers, leave their parental homes, find permanent relationships, and eventually marry and begin their own families.[11] These transitions are expected to take place in order—beginning with finishing school, then entering the workforce, getting married, and having children.

Some individuals, however, are incapable of maturing in a reasonable and timely fashion because of family, environmental, or personal problems.[12] In some cases, transitions can occur too early—an adolescent girl who engages in precocious sex gets pregnant and is forced to drop out of high school. In other cases, transitions may occur too late—a teenage male falls in with the wrong crowd, goes to prison, and finds it difficult to break into the job market upon release; he puts off getting married because of his diminished economic circumstances. Sometimes interruption of one transition can harm another. A teenager who has family problems may find that her educational and career development is upset or that she suffers from psychological impairments.[13]

Because a transition from one stage of life to another can be a bumpy ride, the propensity to commit crimes is neither stable nor constant: it is a *developmental process*. A positive life experience may help some criminals desist from crime for a while, whereas a negative one

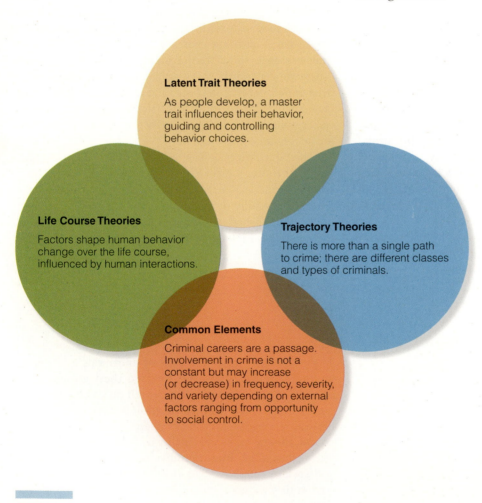

FIGURE 9.1
Developmental Theories

Latent Trait Theories

As people develop, a master trait influences their behavior, guiding and controlling behavior choices.

Life Course Theories

Factors shape human behavior change over the life course, influenced by human interactions.

Trajectory Theories

There is more than a single path to crime; there are different classes and types of criminals.

Common Elements

Criminal careers are a passage. Involvement in crime is not a constant but may increase (or decrease) in frequency, severity, and variety depending on external factors ranging from opportunity to social control.

may cause them to resume their activities. Criminal careers are said to be developmental because people are influenced by the behavior of those around them, and they, in turn, influence others' behavior. A youth's antisocial behavior may turn his more conventional friends against him; their rejection solidifies and escalates his antisocial behavior.[14]

Changing Life Influences

Disruptions in life's major transitions can be destructive and ultimately can promote criminality. Those who are already at risk because of socioeconomic problems or family dysfunction are the most susceptible to these awkward transitions. Criminality, according to this view, cannot be attributed to a single cause, nor does it represent a single underlying tendency.[15] People are influenced by different factors as they mature. Consequently, a factor that may have an important influence at one stage of life (such as delinquent peers) may have little influence later on.[16]

These negative life events can become cumulative: as people acquire more personal deficits, the chances of acquiring additional ones increases.[17] The cumulative impact of these disruptions sustains criminality from childhood into adulthood.[18]

Life course theory also recognizes that as people mature the factors that influence their behavior change.[19] As people make important life transitions—from child to adolescent, from adolescent to adult, from unwed to married—the nature of social interactions changes.[20]

At first, family relations may be most influential; it comes as no shock to life course theorists when research shows that criminality runs in families and that having criminal relatives is a significant predictor of future misbehaviors.[21] In later adolescence, school and peer relations predominate; in adulthood, vocational achievement and marital relations may be the most critical influences. Some antisocial children who are in trouble throughout their adolescence may manage to find stable work and maintain intact marriages as adults; these life events help them desist from crime. In contrast, less fortunate adolescents who develop arrest records and get involved with the wrong crowd may find themselves limited to menial jobs and at risk for criminal careers.

LIFE COURSE CONCEPTS

A view of crime has emerged that incorporates personal change and growth. The factors that produce crime and delinquency at one point in the life cycle may not be relevant at another; as people mature, the social, physical, and environmental influences on their behavior are transformed. People may show a propensity to offend early in their lives, but the nature and frequency of their activities are often affected by forces beyond their control, which elevate and sustain their criminal activity.[22]

The next sections review some of the more important concepts associated with the life course perspective and discuss the most prominent theory of the criminal life course.

Problem Behavior Syndrome

Most criminological theories portray crime as the outcome of social problems. Learning theorists view a troubled home life and deviant friends as precursors of criminality; structural theorists maintain that acquiring deviant cultural values leads to criminality. In contrast, the developmental view is that criminality may best be understood as one of many social problems faced by at-risk youth, a view called **problem behavior syndrome (PBS)**. According to this view, crime is one among a group of interrelated antisocial behaviors that cluster together and typically involve family dysfunction, sexual and physical abuse, substance abuse, smoking, precocious sexuality and early pregnancy, educational underachievement, suicide attempts, sensation seeking, and unemployment.[23] People who suffer from one of these conditions typically exhibit many symptoms of the rest.[24] All varieties of criminal behavior—including violence, theft, and drug offenses—may be part of a generalized PBS, indicating that all forms of antisocial behavior have similar developmental patterns (Exhibit 9.1).[25]

Many examples support the existence of PBS[26]:

- Adolescents with a history of gang involvement are more likely to have been expelled from school, be binge drinkers, test positively for marijuana, have been in

EXHIBIT 9.1

Problem Behaviors

Social
- Family dysfunction
- Unemployment
- Educational underachievement
- School misconduct
- Accident prone
- Medical problems
- Mental disease
- Anxiety
- Eating disorders (bulimia, anorexia)

Personal
- Substance abuse
- Suicide attempts
- Early sexuality
- Sensation seeking
- Early parenthood

Environmental
- High-crime area
- Disorganized area
- Racism
- Exposure to poverty

three or more fights in the past six months, have non-monogamous partners, and test positive for sexually transmitted diseases.[27]

- Kids who gamble and take risks at an early age also take drugs and commit crimes.[28]
- People who exhibit one of these social and personal problems typically exhibit many of the others.[29]

Those who suffer from PBS are prone to more difficulties than the general population.[30] They find themselves with a range of personal dilemmas ranging from drug abuse to being accident prone, requiring more health care and hospitalization, becoming teenage parents, or having mental health problems.[31] PBS has been linked to individual-level personality problems (such as impulsiveness, rebelliousness, and low ego), family problems (such as intrafamily conflict and parental mental disorder), substance abuse, and educational failure.[32] Research shows that social problems such as drug abuse, low income, aggression, single parenthood, residence in isolated urban areas, lack of family support or resources, racism, and prolonged exposure to poverty are all interrelated.[33] Considering the types of problems that cluster together (e.g., mental illness, drug abuse, hospitalization), it is not surprising that people who have a long and varied criminal career are more likely to die early and have greater than average mortality rates. Criminal conduct has been found to increase the chances of premature death due to both natural and unnatural causes, including deaths from accidents, homicide, and suicide. The more crime a person commits, the more likely he or she is to suffer premature death.[34]

In sum, problem behavior syndrome portrays crime as a type of social problem rather than as the product of other social problems.[35] People involved in crime may fall prey to other social problems, ranging from poverty to premature death.[36]

Age of Onset

The life course perspective assumes that the seeds of a criminal career are planted early in life and that early onset of deviance strongly predicts later and more serious criminality.[37] Children who will later become the most serious delinquents begin their deviant careers at a very early (preschool) age, and the earlier the onset of criminality, the more frequent, varied, and sustained the criminal career.[38] If children are aggressive and antisocial during their public school years, they are much more likely to be troublesome and exhibit aggressive behavior in adulthood.[39]

Early-onset criminals seem to be more involved in aggressive acts ranging from cruelty to animals to peer-directed violence.[40] In contrast, late starters are more likely to be involved in nonviolent crimes such as theft.[41]

Recent research by Daniel Nagin and Richard Tremblay shows that late-onset physical aggression is the exception, not the rule, and that the peak frequency of physical aggression occurs during early childhood and generally declines thereafter.[42]

Why is early onset so important? Starting early in delinquent behavior creates a downward spiral in a young person's life.[43] Thereafter, tension may begin to develop with parents and other family members, emotional bonds to conventional peers become weakened and frayed, and opportunities to pursue conventional activities like sports dry up and wither away. Replacing them are closer involvement with more deviant peers and involvement in a delinquent way of life.[44] As they emerge into adulthood, persisters report less emotional support, lower job satisfaction, distant peer relationships, and more psychiatric problems than those who desist.[45]

What causes some kids to begin offending at an early age? Among the suspected root causes are poor parental discipline and monitoring, inadequate emotional support, distant peer relationships, and psychological issues and problems.[46] The psychic scars of childhood are hard to erase.[47]

Children who are improperly socialized by unskilled parents are the most likely to rebel by wandering the streets with deviant peers.[48] Parental influences may be replaced: in middle childhood, social rejection by conventional peers and academic failure sustains antisocial behavior; in later adolescence, commitment to a deviant peer group creates a training ground for crime. While the youngest and most serious offenders may persist in their criminal activity into late adolescence and even adulthood, those who begin their delinquent careers in later adolescence are able to age out of crime or desist.

Gender and Persistence   As they mature, both males and females who have early experiences with antisocial behavior are the ones most likely to persist throughout their life course. Like boys, early-onset girls continue to experience difficulties—increased drug and alcohol use, poor school adjustment, mental health problems, poor sexual health, psychiatric problems, higher rates of mortality, criminal behavior, insufficient parenting skills, relationship dysfunction, lower performance in academic and occupational environments, involvement with social service assistance, and adjustment problems—as they enter young adulthood and beyond.[49]

There are some distinct gender differences as well. For males, the path runs from early onset in childhood to later problems at work and involvement with substance abuse. For females, the path seems somewhat different: early antisocial behavior leads to relationship problems, depression, a tendency to commit suicide, and poor health in adulthood.[50] Males seem to be more deeply influenced by an early history of childhood aggression: males who exhibited chronic physical aggression during the elementary school years exhibit the risk of continued physical violence and delinquency during adolescence. There is less evidence of a linkage between childhood physical aggression and adult aggression among females.[51]

Desisting from Crime

Traditional theories of crime focus on the entry into crime and a criminal career, whereas life course criminology gives equal weight to its termination. As Wolfgang's cohort study found, relatively few of the people who enter into a life of crime persist into and through their adulthood. Most offenders age out of crime, and it is only the most chronic career criminals who continue in a criminal way of life.

Why do people desist from crime? There are a number of views on the process of criminal career termination; some of the more important views are discussed in the following sections.

Cognition and Desistance   In one important work, *Making Good: How Ex-Convicts Reform and Rebuild Their Lives,* criminologist Shadd Maruna interviewed a group of serious criminals in order to understand how they could be reformed. These men, who had been in trouble for most of their lives, were able to turn their lives around even though their background suggests otherwise.

Maruna found that desistance was a process, not an instantaneous event. Desisters undergo a long-term cognitive change in which they begin to see themselves as a "new person" or as having a new outlook on life. They begin to try to understand their past and develop insights into why they behaved the way they did and to understand why and how things went wrong. Desisters begin to feel a sense of fulfillment in engaging in productive behaviors and, in so doing, become agents of their own change. They start feeling in control of their future and have a newfound purpose in life. Rather than running from their past, they view their prior history as a learning experience, finding a silver lining in an otherwise awful situation. As Maruna puts it, "[d]esisting is framed as just another adventure consistent with their life-long personality: They are basically a good person who did some bad things and have learned from their mistakes; desistance fits in with their basic personality structure."[52]

Sociologists Peggy Giordano, Stephen Cernkovich, and Jennifer Rudolph also link desistance to a process of cognitive change. They believe that under some circumstances changes in their environment help some people to construct a kind of psychic "scaffolding" that makes it possible for them to create significant life changes. These behavior changes can include desisting from crime.

To be eligible for desistance, individuals must discard their old bad habits and begin the process of crafting a different way of life. Because at first the new lifestyle is usually only a distant dream or faint possibility, people who want to change must find it within themselves to resonate with, move toward, or select the various environmental catalysts for change.

Giordano and her associates believe there are certain "hooks for change" within the environment. These hooks are positive life experiences that help people turn their lives around; people have to latch onto these opportunities when and if they become available. If he or she can manage to seize the right opportunity, the former offender may undergo a *cognitive transformation*—a process in which the person reshapes his or her thought and behavior patterns into a more conventional and rewarding lifestyle. To desist, the person must be able to envision and begin to fashion an appealing and conventional *replacement self* that can substitute for the older, damaged identity. People can begin to escape their deviant lifestyle only when they begin to believe in their new persona and think, "It is inappropriate for someone like me to do something like that." The new identity must serve as a basis for decision making as the person moves into new and novel situations: "I may have smoked pot as a kid, but now that I am a husband the new me would never take the risk." The concept of a replacement self is critical when the individual faces stressful life circumstances (such as divorce and unemployment) and must make decisions that differ from the ones he or she made in the past (and which turned out to be destructive). What the person did in the past was foolish and destructive: "It is no longer cool to get high, but selfish and destructive." Using these cognitive shifts, the desistance process proceeds from an overall "readiness" to change, to encountering one or more environmental hooks for change, to a shift in identity, and to the maintenance of a positive identity that gradually decreases the desirability of the former deviant behavior.[53]

Identity and Desistance   Recently, criminologists Ray Paternoster and Shawn Bushway linked desistance to changes in a person's identity.[54] Offenders have working identities as persons who have and will commit criminal acts until they are no longer profitable. The process of desistance is gradual and takes over when there is a slow realization that their criminal enterprise is a failure and will probably continue to be so in the future. As the dangers associated with committing crime become too great, the social losses too painful, and the gains less beneficial financially, the working identity of "criminal offender" becomes less and less satisfying. They want to become someone else who fits within the legitimate world. Dissatisfaction with the criminal life coupled with a more optimistic vision of the future provides the initial motivation to break from crime. Unless this initial shift in identity takes place, it is unlikely that the offender will be able to reach out and seek help or aspire to a conventional lifestyle. Desistance then is literally a "break with the past," something has changed and a new person has emerged. Although the development of social networks and the support of romantic partners are undoubtedly important, Paternoster and Bushway find that change must come from within: offenders *first decide to change* and then actually begin to change their sense of who they are. So, according to the identity view, desistance occurs when people decide to change and then seek out others who can aid the process, and not vice versa.

THEORIES OF THE CRIMINAL LIFE COURSE

A number of systematic theories have been formulated that account for onset, continuance, and desistance from crime. As a group they integrate societal level variables such as measures of social control, social learning, and structural models. It is not uncommon for life course theories to interconnect *personal factors* such as personality and intelligence, *social factors* such as income and neighborhood, *socialization factors* such as marriage and military service, *cognitive factors* such as information processing and attention/perception, and *situational factors* such as criminal opportunity, effective guardianship, and apprehension risk into complex multifactor explanations of human behavior. In this sense they are **integrated theories** because they incorporate social, personal, and developmental factors into complex explanations of human behavior. They do not focus on the relatively simple question—why do people commit crime—but on more complex issues: Why do some offenders persist in criminal careers and others desist from or alter their criminal activity as they mature?[55] Why do some people continually escalate their criminal involvement, whereas others slow down and turn their lives around? Are all criminals similar in their offending patterns, or are there different types of offenders and paths to offending? Life course theorists want to know not only why people enter a criminal way of life but why, once they do, they are able to alter the trajectory of their criminal involvement. One of the more important life course theories, Sampson and Laub's **age-graded theory**, is set out in the next section in some detail. Exhibit 9.2 outlines the principles of some other important life course theories.

High-priced call girl, drug abuser, identity thief—Audrey Atlas, 45, of Laguna Hills, California, has been all of these. Now the mother of four, on parole and sober after doing stints at four prisons, she wants to give hope to other troubled women who think there is no hope. For now, at least, she is beating the odds. Shown here, a dinner/meeting at Pastor Lisa Cram's house; Pastor Cram specializes in counseling women. What could cause a chronic offender such as Atlas to turn her life around and step off the criminal path?

Sampson and Laub: Age-Graded Theory

If there are various pathways to crime and delinquency, are there trails back to conformity? In an important 1993 work, *Crime in the Making*, Robert Sampson and John Laub formulated what they called an *age-graded theory of informal social control* (Figure 9.2). In their pioneering research, Laub and Sampson reanalyzed the data originally collected by the Gluecks more than 40 years before. Using modern statistical analysis, Laub and Sampson relied on this data to formulate a life course/developmental view of crime.[56] The principles of age-graded theory include the following:

- Individual traits and childhood experiences are important to understand the onset of delinquent and criminal behavior. But these alone cannot explain the continuity of crime into adulthood.
- Experiences in young adulthood and beyond can redirect criminal transitions or paths. In some cases people can be turned in a positive direction, whereas in others negative life experiences can be harmful and injurious.
- Repeated negative experiences create a condition called **cumulative disadvantage**. Serious problems in adolescence undermine life chances and reduce employability and social relations. People who increase their cumulative disadvantage risk continued offending.

EXHIBIT 9.2

Principal Life Course Theories

Name Social Development Model (SDM)

Principal Theorists J. David Hawkins, Richard Catalano

Major Premise Community-level risk factors make some people susceptible to antisocial behaviors. Preexisting risk factors are either reinforced or neutralized by socialization. To control the risk of antisocial behavior, a child must maintain prosocial bonds. Over the life course, involvement in prosocial or antisocial behavior determines the quality of attachments. Commitment and attachment to conventional institutions, activities, and beliefs insulate youths from the criminogenic influences in their environment. The prosocial path inhibits deviance by strengthening bonds to prosocial others and activities. Without the proper level of bonding, adolescents can succumb to the influence of deviant others.

Name Interactional Theory

Principal Theorists Terence Thornberry and Marvin Krohn, Alan Lizotte, Margaret Farnworth

Major Premise The onset of crime can be traced to a deterioration of the social bond during adolescence, marked by weakened attachment to parents, commitment to school, and belief in conventional values. The cause of crime and delinquency is bidirectional: weak bonds lead kids to develop friendships with deviant peers and get involved in delinquency. Frequent delinquency involvement further weakens bonds and makes it difficult to reestablish conventional ones. Delinquency-promoting factors tend to reinforce one another and sustain a chronic criminal career. Kids who go through stressful life events such as a family financial crisis are more likely to later get involved in antisocial behaviors and vice versa. Criminality is a developmental process that takes on different meaning and form as a person matures. During early adolescence, attachment to the family is critical; by mid-adolescence, the influence of the family is replaced by friends, school, and youth culture; by adulthood, a person's behavioral choices are shaped by his or her place in conventional society and his or her own nuclear family. Although crime is influenced by these social forces, it also influences these processes and associations. Therefore, crime and social processes are interactional.

SOURCES: Terence Thornberry, "Toward an Interactional Theory of Delinquency," *Criminology* 25 (1987): 863–891; Richard Catalano and J. David Hawkins, "The Social Development Model: A Theory of Antisocial Behavior," in *Delinquency and Crime: Current Theories*, ed. J. David Hawkins (New York: Cambridge University Press, 1996), pp. 149–197.

- Positive life experiences and relationships can help a person become reattached to society and allow him or her to *knife off* from a criminal career path.
- Positive life experiences such as gaining employment, getting married, or joining the military create informal social control mechanisms that limit criminal behavior opportunities. These elements of informal social control are called *turning points in crime.*
- Two critical elements of informal social control/turning points are marriage and career. Adolescents who are at risk for crime can live conventional lives if they can find good jobs, achieve successful military careers, or enter into a successful marriage. Turning points may be serendipitous and unexpected: success may hinge on a lucky break; someone takes a chance on them; they win the lottery.
- Another vital feature that helps people desist from crime is "human agency," or the purposeful execution of choice and free will. Former delinquents may choose to go straight and develop a new sense of self and an identity. They can choose to desist from crime and become family men and hard workers.[57]
- While some people persist in crime simply because they find it lucrative or perhaps because it serves as an outlet for their frustrations, others choose not to participate because as human beings they find other, more conventional paths more beneficial and rewarding. Human choice cannot be left out of the equation.

Trajectories, Transitions, and Turning Points One of Laub and Sampson's most important contributions is identifying the life events that enable adult offenders to desist from crime. According to them, trajectories are long-term patterns in life, and transitions are "short-term events embedded in trajectories."[58] Both transitions and trajectories can have a positive or negative connotation. A positive transition, for example, might include graduating from college and getting a good job; a negative trajectory might be joining a gang.

A major concept in the Sampson and Laub theory is that criminal careers are a dynamic process in which an important life event can (a) produce a transition in the life course and (b) change the direction of a person's life course; they refer to these as **turning points**. Some turning points have negative consequences. Youth who join gangs experience significant changes in their emotions, attitudes, and behavior that are hard to shake. Not only are gang boys more likely to engage in crime, they also are more likely to experience long-term negative consequences that extend into early adulthood: getting arrested, dropping out of school, teenage parenthood, and unstable employment. Even short-term gang involvement can have long-lasting consequences.[59]

Some turning points can have a positive effect on people at risk for crime, helping them knife off from criminal careers. Two critical ones are marriage and career: Adolescents who are at risk for crime can live conventional lives if they can find good jobs or achieve successful careers. Even those

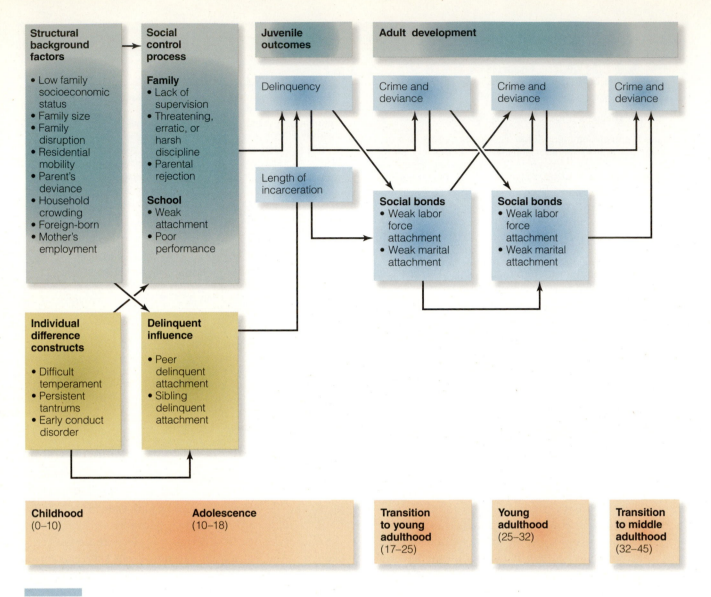

FIGURE 9.2
Sampson and Laub's Age-Graded Theory

SOURCE: Reprinted by permission of the publisher from *Crime in the Making: Pathways and Turning Points Through Life* by Robert Sampson and John Laub, pp. 244–245, Cambridge, Mass.: Harvard University Press, Copyright © 1993 by the President and Fellows of Harvard College. All rights reserved.

who have been in trouble with the law may turn from crime if employers are willing to give them a chance despite their records.

Social Capital   Social scientists recognize that people build **social capital**—positive relations with individuals and institutions that are life sustaining. Laub and Sampson view the development of social capital as essential for desistance. In the same manner that building financial capital improves the chances for personal success, building social capital supports conventional behavior and inhibits deviant behavior. A successful marriage creates social capital when it improves a person's stature, creates feelings of self-worth,

and encourages people to trust the individual. A successful career inhibits crime by creating a stake in conformity; why commit crime when you are doing well at your job? The relationship is reciprocal. If people are chosen to be employees, they return the favor by doing the best job possible; if they are chosen as spouses, they blossom into devoted partners. In contrast, people who fail to accumulate social capital are more prone to commit criminal acts.[60]

The fact that social capital influences a criminal career underscores the life course view that events that occur in later adolescence and adulthood do, in fact, influence behavior choices. Life events that occur in adulthood can help either to terminate or to sustain deviant careers.

Testing Age-Graded Theory A number of research efforts have supported the basic assumptions of age-graded theory:

- Empirical research now shows, as predicted by Sampson and Laub, that people change over the life course and that the factors that predict delinquency in adolescence, such as a weak bond to parents, may have less of an impact on adult crime when other factors, such as marriage and family, take on greater importance.[61]

- Criminality appears to be dynamic and is affected both by the erosion of informal social control and by interaction with antisocial influences. For example, accumulating deviant peers helps sustain criminality: the more deviant friends one accumulates over time, the more likely one is to maintain a criminal career.[62]

- As levels of cumulative disadvantage increase, crime-resisting elements of social life are impaired. Adolescents who are convicted of crime at an early age are more likely to develop antisocial attitudes later in life. They later develop low educational achievement, declining occupational status, and unstable employment records.[63] People who get involved with the justice system as adolescents may find that their career paths are blocked well into adulthood.[64] The relationship is reciprocal: men who are unemployed or underemployed report higher criminal participation rates than employed men.[65]

- Evidence is also available that confirms Sampson and Laub's suspicion that criminal careers can be reversed if life conditions improve and they gain social capital.[66] Kids who have long-term exposure to poverty find that their involvement in crime escalates. Those, however, whose life circumstances improve because their parents are able to escape poverty and move to more attractive environments find that they can be released from criminal involvements. Relocating may place them in a better educational environment where they can have a positive high school experience, facilitated by occupationally oriented course work, small class size, and a positive peer climate. Such children are less likely to become incarcerated as adults than those who do not enjoy these social benefits.[67] Research by Ross Macmillan and his colleagues shows that children whose mothers were initially poor but escaped from poverty were no more likely to develop behavior problems than children whose mothers were never poor.

- Gaining social capital later in life helps erase some of the damage caused by its absence in youth.[68] Delinquents who enter the military, serve overseas, and receive veterans' benefits enhance their occupational status (social capital) while reducing criminal involvement.[69] Kids who have been involved in delinquency during adolescence but are able to somehow find educational success can reverse the course of a criminal career: college attendance and investment in higher education are negatively associated with criminal offending in adulthood.[70] Similarly, people who are fortunate enough to obtain a high-quality job are likely to reduce their criminal activities even though they had a prior history of offending, and even if they have already served a prison sentence.[71]

The Marriage Factor When they achieve adulthood, adolescents who had significant problems with the law are able to desist from crime if they can establish meaningful social ties that provide informal social control. Of these, none is more important than a successful marriage. People who cannot sustain secure marital relations are less likely to desist from crime. People who can find a spouse who supports them despite knowing about their past misdeeds are the ones most likely to steer away from the path of crime. Marriage both transforms people and reduces their opportunity to commit crimes. It helps cut off a person's past, provides new relationships, creates new levels of supervision, and helps the former offender develop structured routines focused on family life. Happy marriages are life sustaining, and marital quality can even improve over time (see the following Criminological Enterprise feature for more on the marriage–crime connection).[72] Spending time in marital and family activities also reduces exposure to deviant peers, which in turn reduces the opportunity to become involved in criminal activities.[73] As Mark Warr states:

> For many individuals, it seems, marriage marks a transition from heavy peer involvement to a preoccupation with one's spouse. That transition is likely to reduce interaction with former friends and accomplices and thereby reduce the opportunities as well as the motivation to engage in crime.[74]

Even people who have a history of criminal activity and have been convicted of serious offenses reduce the frequency of their offending if they live with spouses and maintain employment when they are in the community.[75] The marriage benefit also may be intergenerational: children who grow up in two-parent families are more likely to later have happy marriages themselves than children who are the product of divorced or never-married parents.[76] If people with marital problems are more crime prone, their children will also suffer a greater long-term risk of marital failure and antisocial activity.

Recent research by Ryan Schroeder and his colleagues shows that getting involved in the drug culture has a much more damaging effect on marriage and employment than heavy alcohol abuse.[77] Similarly, joining the military today may have a significantly different meaning and produce significantly different effects than it did for the men in the Glueck sample: recent research indicates that the 12-month prevalence of common mental illnesses in the U.S. military is estimated to be 26 percent, far above the level in the civilian population. Considering this condition, it is difficult to believe that serving in the military today has the same effect it had 60 years ago.[78]

To answer some of these questions, Laub and Sampson contacted the surviving members of the Glueck cohort.

Is it marriage or the promise of romantic love to which it is attached that protects people from crime? When sociologists Bill McCarthy and Teresa Casey examined the association between love, sex, and delinquency in a sample of teens, they found that the closeness offered by adolescent romantic love may fill an important void found between the weakening of bonds with parents and the onset of adult attachments, and it may discourage an array of negative outcomes, including involvement in crime. Adolescent sexual activity without the promise of love increases the likelihood of offending because it is associated with strain created by loveless relationships. McCarthy and Casey find that romantic love has a deterrent effect that encourages youth who have offended to decrease their involvement in crime. It is possible, they speculate, that romantic love discourages offending by strengthening the social bond. By contrast, the association between sex and crime is intensified in relationships short on love. It is possible that kids who engage in sex without love or romance are willing to partake in other risky and/or self-indulgent behaviors, including delinquency and drug use. McCarthy and Casey's research indicates that marriage may help at-risk people knife off from crime, but falling in love with a romantic partner may work just as well.

Researchers Alex Piquero, John Mac-Donald, and Karen Parker tracked 524 men in their late teens and early 20s for seven years after they were paroled from the California Youth Authority during the 1970s and 1980s. They found that former offenders were far less likely to return to crime if they settled down into the routines of a solid marriage. People who get married are more likely to have nine-to-five jobs, come home for dinner, take care of children if they have them, watch television, go to bed, and repeat that cycle over and over again. Single people have a lot of free time to do what they want, especially if they are not employed. There's something about crossing the line of getting married that helps these men stay away from crime.

Marriage may also mark a physical/biological turning point in the life course. Kevin Beaver and his colleagues find that as people mature and go through biological changes, they slow down, prompting them to quit the hectic and strenuous criminal way of life and instead settling into a more comfortable and less taxing marital routine.

Why Do People Have Happy Marriages?

Because the marriage benefit is so great and long-lasting, it is troubling that so many marriages do not succeed; an estimated 40 to 50 percent of first marriages, 67 percent of second marriages, and 74 percent of third marriages end in divorce. Sociologist Rand Conger and his colleagues have discovered that the seeds of divorce are planted early in childhood: kids who grow up with warm, nurturing parents are the ones most likely to have intact marriages. Well-nurtured kids develop into warm and supportive marital partners who produce marriages that are happy, satisfying, and likely to endure. The quality of the parents' marital relationship had no direct influence on the young adult romantic relationship: it is the quality of parenting and not the observation of adult romantic relations that socializes a young person to engage in behaviors likely to promote successful and lasting romantic unions as an adult.

CRITICAL THINKING

1. Do you think marriage is different from merely being in love? Although the McCarthy and Casey research indicates that having a romantic relationship may help reduce crime, can marriage work better?

2. Even if we can show that married people are less likely to commit crime, does that fact prove that getting married is a cause of desistance? Isn't it possible that people who have given up antisocial behaviors are ready to get married and make more attractive mates?

SOURCES: Bill McCarthy and Teresa Casey, "Love, Sex, and Crime: Adolescent Romantic Relationships and Offending," *American Sociological Review* 73 (2008): 944–969; Kevin Beaver, John Paul Wright, Matt Delisi, and Michael Vaughn, "Desistance from Delinquency: The Marriage Effect Revisited and Extended," *Social Science Research* 37 (2008): 736–752; Alex Piquero, John MacDonald, and Karen Parker, "Race, Local Life Circumstances, and Criminal Activity over the Life-Course," *Social Science Quarterly* 83 (2002): 654–671; Pamela Webster, Terri Orbuch, and James House, "Effects of Childhood Family Background on Adult Marital Quality and Perceived Stability," *American Journal of Sociology* 101 (1995): 404–432; Mark Warr, "Life-Course Transitions and Desistance from Crime," *Criminology* 36 (1998): 502–535; Divorce Statistics Collection, www.divorcereform.org/stats.html (accessed August 11, 2011).

Some of their findings are discussed in The Criminological Enterprise feature "Shared Beginnings, Divergent Lives."

To read an **assessment of age-graded theory** by Sampson, Laub, and Gary Sweeten, and also one by Laub and Sampson, go to the Criminal Justice CourseMate at cengagebrain.com, then access the "Web Links" for this chapter.

LATENT TRAIT THEORIES

In a critical 1990 article, David Rowe, D. Wayne Osgood, and W. Alan Nicewander proposed the concept of latent traits to explain the flow of crime over the life cycle. Their model assumes that a number of people in the population have a personal attribute or characteristic that controls their inclination or propensity to commit crimes.[79] This disposition, or **latent trait**, may be present at birth or may be established early in life, and it can remain stable over time. Suspected latent traits include defective intelligence, damaged or impulsive personality, genetic abnormalities, the physical-chemical functioning of the brain, and environmental influences on brain function such as drugs, chemicals, and injuries.[80] Some latent trait theorists maintain that this master trait is inflexible, stable, and unchanging throughout a person's lifetime, whereas others recognize that under some circumstances a latent trait can be altered, influenced, or changed by experiences and interactions.

Regardless of gender or environment, those who maintain one of these suspect traits may be at risk to crime and in danger of becoming career criminals; those who lack the traits have a much lower risk.[81] Because latent traits are stable, people who are antisocial during adolescence are the most likely to persist in crime. The positive association between past and future criminality detected in the cohort studies of career criminals reflects the presence of this underlying stable criminal propensity. That is, if an impulsive personality contributes to delinquency in childhood, it should also cause the same people to offend as adults because personality traits remain stable over the life span.

How Can the Aging Out Process Be Explained? Because latent traits are stable, people who are antisocial during adolescence are the most likely to persist in crime. The positive association between past and future criminality detected in the cohort studies of career criminals reflects the presence of this underlying stable criminal propensity. That is, if an impulsive personality contributes to delinquency in childhood, it should also cause the same people to offend as adults because personality traits remain stable over the life span. According to the concept of **state dependence**, kids who have the propensity to commit crime will find that this latent trait profoundly and permanently disrupts normal socialization. Disruptions in socialization thereafter increase the risk of prolonged antisocial behavior. In this view, early rule breaking increases the probability of future rule breaking because it weakens inhibitions to crime and strengthens criminal motivation. In other words, once kids get a taste of antisocial behavior, they like it and want to continue down a deviant path.[82]

How then can a latent trait theorist explain the well-known fact that people do commit less crime as they mature? It's possible that declining criminal activity may not be a valid indicator of real behavioral change. Why does this illusion exist? Whereas the propensity to commit crime is stable, the opportunity to commit crime fluctuates over time. People may appear to age out of crime as they mature and develop simply because there are fewer opportunities to commit crimes and greater inducements to remain straight. They may marry, have children, and obtain jobs. The former delinquents' newfound adult responsibilities leave them little time to hang with their friends, abuse substances, and get into scrapes with the law. So although their propensity to commit crime remains stable, their opportunity to commit crime has changed.

To understand this concept of stable criminal propensity better, assume that intelligence as measured by IQ tests is a stable latent trait associated with crime. Intelligence remains stable and unchanging over the life course, but crime rates decline with age. How can latent trait theory explain this phenomenon? Teenagers have more opportunity to commit crime than adults, so at every level of intelligence, adolescent crime rates will be higher. As they mature, however, teens with both high and low IQs will commit less crime because their adult responsibilities provide them with fewer criminal opportunities. They may get married and raise a family, get a job, and buy a home. And like most people, as they age they lose strength and vigor, qualities necessary to commit crime. Though their IQ remains stable and their propensity to commit crime is unchanged, their living environment and biological condition have undergone radical change. Even if they wanted to engage in criminal activities, the former delinquents may lack the opportunity and energy to do so.

Crime and Human Nature

Latent trait theorists were encouraged when two prominent social scientists, James Q. Wilson and Richard Herrnstein, published *Crime and Human Nature* in 1985 and suggested that personal traits—such as genetic makeup, intelligence, and body build—may outweigh the importance of social variables as predictors of criminal activity.[83]

According to Wilson and Herrnstein, all human behavior, including criminality, is determined by its perceived consequences. A criminal incident occurs when an individual chooses criminal over conventional behavior (referred to as *noncrime*) after weighing the potential gains and losses of each: "The larger the ratio of net rewards of crime to the net rewards of noncrime, the greater the tendency to commit the crime."[84]

Wilson and Herrnstein's model assumes that both biological and psychological traits influence the crime–noncrime choice. They see a close link between a person's decision to choose crime and such biosocial factors as low intelligence, mesomorphic body type, genetic influences (parental criminality), and possessing an autonomic nervous system that responds too quickly to stimuli. Psychological traits, such as an impulsive or extroverted personality or generalized hostility, also determine the potential to commit crime.

In their focus on the association between these constitutional and psychological factors and crime, Wilson and Herrnstein seem to be suggesting the existence of an elusive latent trait that predisposes people to commit crime.[85] Their vision helped inspire other criminologists to identify the elusive latent trait that causes criminal behavior.[86] The most prominent latent trait theory is Gottfredson and Hirschi's **General Theory of Crime (GTC).**

Why are some delinquents destined to become persistent criminals as adults? John Laub and Robert Sampson have conducted a follow-up to their reanalysis of Sheldon Glueck and Eleanor Glueck's study that matched 500 delinquent boys with 500 non-delinquents. The individuals in the original sample were reinterviewed by the Gluecks at ages 25 and 32. Sampson and Laub located and interviewed the survivors of the delinquent sample, the oldest 70 years old and the youngest 62.

Persistence and Desistance

Laub and Sampson found that delinquency and other forms of antisocial conduct in childhood are strongly related to adult delinquency and drug and alcohol abuse. Former delinquents also suffer consequences in other areas of social life, such as school, work, and family life. For example, delinquents are far less likely to finish high school than are nondelinquents and subsequently are more likely to be unemployed, receive welfare, and experience separation or divorce as adults.

In their latest research, Laub and Sampson address one of the key questions posed by life course theories: is it possible for former delinquents to turn their lives around as adults? They find that most antisocial children do not remain antisocial as adults. For example, of men in the study cohort who survived to age 50, 24 percent had no

arrests for delinquent acts of violence and property after age 17 (6 percent had no arrests for total delinquency); 48 percent had no arrests for predatory delinquency after age 25 (19 percent for total delinquency); 60 percent had no arrests for predatory delinquency after age 31 (33 percent for total delinquency); and 79 percent had no arrests for predatory delinquency after age 40 (57 percent for total delinquency). They conclude that desistance from delinquency is the norm and that most, if not all, serious delinquents desist from delinquency.

Why Do Delinquents Desist?

Laub and Sampson's earlier research indicated that building social capital through marriage and jobs was a key component of desistance from delinquency. However, in this new round of research, Laub and Sampson were able to find out more about long-term desistance by interviewing 52 men as they approached age 70. The follow-up showed a dramatic drop in criminal activity as the men aged. Between the ages of 17 and 24, 84 percent of the men had committed violent crimes; in their 30s and 40s, that number dropped to 14 percent; it fell to just 3 percent as the men reached their 60s and 70s. Property crimes and alcohol- and drug-related crimes also showed significant decreases. They found that men who desisted from crime were rooted in

structural routines and had strong social ties to family and community. Drawing on the men's own words, they found that one important element for "going straight" is the "knifing off" of individuals from their immediate environment and offering the men a new script for the future. Joining the military can provide this knifing-off effect, as does marriage or changing one's residence. One former delinquent (age 69) told them:

> I'd say the turning point was, number one, the Army. You get into an outfit, you had a sense of belonging, you made your friends. I think I became a pretty good judge of character. In the Army, you met some good ones, you met some foul balls. Then I met the wife. I'd say probably that would be the turning point. Got married, then naturally, kids come. So now you got to get a better job, you got to make more money. And that's how I got to the Navy Yard and tried to improve myself.

Former delinquents who went straight were able to put structure into their lives. Structure often led the men to disassociate from delinquent peers, reducing the opportunity to get into trouble. Getting married, for example, may limit the number of nights men can "hang with the guys." As one wife of a former delinquent said, "It is not how

General Theory of Crime

In their important work *A General Theory of Crime,* Michael Gottfredson and Travis Hirschi link the propensity to commit crime to two latent traits: an impulsive personality and a lack of self-control.[87]

Gottfredson and Hirschi attribute the tendency to commit crimes to a person's level of **self-control**. People with limited self-control tend to be impulsive; they are insensitive to other people's feelings, physical (rather than mental), risk takers, shortsighted, and nonverbal.[88] They have a here-and-now orientation and refuse to work for distant goals; they lack diligence, tenacity, and persistence. People

lacking self-control tend to be adventuresome, active, and self-centered. As they mature, they often have unstable marriages, jobs, and friendships.[89] They are less likely to feel shame if they engage in deviant acts and are more likely to find them pleasurable.[90] They also are more likely to engage in dangerous behaviors such as drinking, smoking, and reckless driving; all of these behaviors are associated with criminality (see Exhibit 9.3 for a list of factors that indicate low self-control).[91]

Because those with low self-control enjoy risky, exciting, or thrilling behaviors with immediate gratification, they are more likely to enjoy criminal acts, which require stealth, agility, speed, and power, than conventional acts, which

many beers you have, it's who you drink with." Even multiple offenders who did time in prison were able to desist with the help of a stabilizing marriage.

Former delinquents who can turn their life around, who have acquired a degree of maturity by taking on family and work responsibilities, and who have forged new commitments are the ones most likely to make a fresh start and find new direction and meaning in life. It seems that men who desisted changed their identity as well, and this, in turn, affected their outlook and sense of maturity and responsibility. The ability to change did not reflect a delinquency "specialty": violent offenders followed the same path as property offenders.

Although many former delinquents desisted from delinquency, they still faced the risk of an early and untimely death. Thirteen percent (N=62) of the delinquent as compared to only 6 percent (N=28) of the nondelinquent men died unnatural deaths such as violence, cirrhosis of the liver caused by alcoholism, poor self-care, suicide, and so on. By age 65, 29 percent (N=139) of the delinquent and 21 percent (N=95) of the nondelinquent men had died from natural causes. Frequent delinquent involvement in adolescence and alcohol abuse were the strongest predictors of an early and unnatural death. Although many troubled youth are able to reform, their early excesses may haunt them across their life span.

Policy Implications

Laub and Sampson find that youth problems—delinquency, substance abuse, violence, dropping out, teen pregnancy—often share common risk characteristics. Intervention strategies, therefore, should consider a broad array of antisocial, criminal, and deviant behaviors and not limit the focus to just one subgroup or delinquency type. Because criminality and other social problems are linked, early prevention efforts that reduce delinquency will probably also reduce alcohol abuse, drunk driving, drug abuse, sexual promiscuity, and family violence. The best way to achieve these goals is through four significant life-changing events: marriage, joining the military, getting a job, and changing one's environment or neighborhood. What appears to be important about these processes is that they all involve, to varying degrees, the following items: a knifing off of the past from the present; new situations that provide both supervision and monitoring as well as new opportunities of social support and growth; and new situations that provide the opportunity for transforming identity. Prevention of delinquency must be a policy at all times and at all stages of life.

CRITICAL THINKING

1. Do you believe that the factors that influenced the men in the original Glueck sample are still relevant for change? For example, considering the current high divorce rate, is marriage still a stabilizing force?

2. Recent reports show that male U.S. veterans are twice as likely to die by suicide than people with no military service, and are more likely to kill themselves with a gun than others who commit suicide. Considering this recent finding, do you agree with Laub and Sampson that military service might be beneficial and help troubled kids turn their lives around?

SOURCES: John Laub and Robert Sampson, *Shared Beginnings, Divergent Lives: Delinquent Boys to Age 70* (Cambridge, MA: Harvard University Press, 2003); John Laub and Robert Sampson, "Understanding Desistance from Delinquency," in *Delinquency and Justice: An Annual Review of Research*, Vol. 28, ed. Michael Tonry (Chicago: University of Chicago Press, 2001), pp. 1–71; John Laub and George Vaillant, "Delinquency and Mortality: A 50-Year Follow-Up Study of 1,000 Delinquent and Non-delinquent Boys," *American Journal of Psychiatry* 157 (2000): 96–102.

demand long-term study and cognitive and verbal skills. As Gottfredson and Hirschi put it, they derive satisfaction from "money without work, sex without courtship, revenge without court delays."[92] Many of these individuals who have a propensity for committing crime also engage in other risky, impulsive behaviors such as smoking, drinking, gambling, and illicit sexuality.[93] Although these acts are not illegal, they too provide immediate, short-term gratification.

What Causes Impulsivity? Gottfredson and Hirschi trace the root cause of poor self-control to inadequate childrearing practices that begin soon after birth and can influence neural development. Once experiences are ingrained, the brain establishes a pattern of electrochemical activation that

CONNECTIONS

In his original version of control theory, discussed in Chapter 7, Hirschi focused on the social controls that attach people to conventional society and insulate them from criminality. In this newer work, he concentrates on self-control as a stabilizing force. The two views are connected, however, because both social control (or social bonds) and self-control are acquired through early experiences with effective parenting.

remains for life.[94] Parents who refuse or are unable to monitor a child's behavior, to recognize deviant behavior when it occurs, and to punish that behavior will produce children

The Elements of Impulsivity: Signs That a Person Has Low Self-Control

- Insensitive
- Physical
- Shortsighted
- Nonverbal
- Here-and-now orientation
- Unstable social relations
- Enjoys deviant behaviors
- Risk taker
- Refuses to work for distant goals
- Lacks diligence
- Lacks tenacity
- Adventuresome
- Self-centered
- Shameless
- Imprudent
- Lacks cognitive and verbal skills
- Enjoys danger and excitement

According to Gottfredson and Hirschi's General Theory of Crime, impulsive teens who lack self-control are the ones most often involved in crime. Even if they do not violate the law, they may be risk takers who engage in such hazardous behaviors as drinking, precocious sexuality, smoking, and gambling.

© David Hoffman/UPPA/Photoshot/Newscom

who lack self-control. Children who are not attached to their parents, who are poorly supervised, and whose parents are criminal or deviant themselves are the most likely to develop poor self-control. In a sense, lack of self-control occurs naturally when steps are not taken to stop its development.[95]

The "poor parenting produces low self-control children" model may be intergenerational: parents who themselves manifest low self-control are the ones most likely to use damaging and inappropriate supervision and punishment mechanisms, such as corporal punishment. Inappropriate discipline modes have been linked to lack of self-control in adolescence. These impulsive kids grow up to become poor parents, who use improper discipline, and produce another generation of impulsive kids.[96]

Learning or Biology? The General Theory assumes self-control is a function of socialization and parenting, but some criminologists maintain it may also have a biological basis. Measures of neuropsychological deficits, birth complications, and low birth weight have all been found to have significant direct or indirect effects on levels of self-control.[97] Recent research shows that children who suffer anoxia (oxygen starvation) during birth are the ones most likely to lack self-control later in life, suggesting that impulsivity may have a biological basis.[98] When Kevin Beaver and his associates examined impulsive personality and self-control in twin pairs, they discovered evidence that these traits may be inherited rather than developed.[99] That might explain the stability of these latent traits over the life course.

Crime Rate Variations If individual differences are stable over the life course, why do crime rates vary? Why do people commit less crime as they age? Why are some regions more crime prone than others? Why are some groups more crime prone than others? Does that mean there are between-group differences in self-control? If male crime rates are higher than female rates, does that mean men are more impulsive and lacking in self-control? How does the GTC address these issues?

Gottfredson and Hirschi remind us that criminal propensity and criminal acts are separate concepts (Figure 9.3). On one hand, criminal acts, such as robberies or burglaries, are illegal events or deeds offenders engage in when they perceive them to be advantageous. Burglaries are typically committed by young males looking for cash, liquor, and entertainment; the crime provides "easy, short-term gratification."[100] Crime is rational and predictable; people commit crime when it promises rewards with minimal threat of pain; the threat of punishment can deter crime. If targets are well guarded, crime rates diminish. Only the truly irrational offender would dare to strike under those circumstances.

On the other hand, although criminal offenders are people predisposed to commit crimes, they are not robots who commit crime without restraint; their days are also filled with conventional behaviors, such as going to school, parties, concerts, and church. But given the same set of criminal

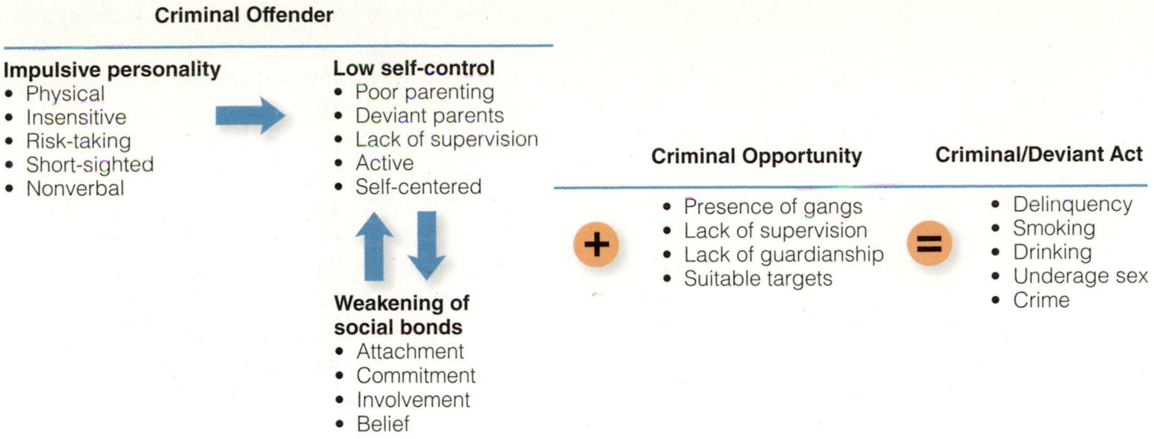

Criminal Offender

Impulsive personality
- Physical
- Insensitive
- Risk-taking
- Short-sighted
- Nonverbal

Low self-control
- Poor parenting
- Deviant parents
- Lack of supervision
- Active
- Self-centered

Weakening of social bonds
- Attachment
- Commitment
- Involvement
- Belief

+

Criminal Opportunity
- Presence of gangs
- Lack of supervision
- Lack of guardianship
- Suitable targets

=

Criminal/Deviant Act
- Delinquency
- Smoking
- Drinking
- Underage sex
- Crime

FIGURE 9.3
Gottfredson and Hirschi's General Theory of Crime

opportunities, such as having a lot of free time for mischief and living in a neighborhood with unguarded homes containing valuable merchandise, crime-prone people have a much higher probability of violating the law than do noncriminals. The propensity to commit crimes remains stable throughout a person's life. Change in the frequency of criminal activity is purely a function of change in criminal opportunity.

If we accept this provision of the GTC, then both criminal propensity and criminal opportunity must be considered to explain criminal participation. Take, for example, the gender differences in the crime rate. According to the GTC, if males commit more crime than females, the cause is their greater impulsivity and sensation seeking, which reduces fear of punishments.[101] But even if we assume that males and females are equally impulsive, the GTC could still explain gender differences by suggesting that males have more opportunity to commit crime. Young teenage girls may be more closely monitored by their parents and therefore lack the freedom to offend. Girls also are socialized to have more self-control than boys: although females get angry as often as males, many have been taught to blame themselves for such feelings. Females are socialized to fear that anger will harm relationships; males are encouraged to react with "moral outrage," blaming others for their discomfort.[102]

Opportunity also can be used to explain ecological variation in the crime rate. How does the GTC explain the fact that crime rates are higher in the summer than in the winter? The number of impulsive people lacking in self-control is no higher in August than it is in December. Gottfredson and Hirschi would argue that seasonal differences are explained by opportunity: during the summer kids are out of school and have more opportunity to commit crime. Similarly, if crime rates are higher in Los Angeles than in Minneapolis, it is because either there are more criminal opportunities in this western city, or because the fast-paced life of L.A. attracts more impulsive people than does the laid-back Midwest.

Environment and Impulsivity The effects of impulsivity and environment may interact in other ways. Recently, criminologist Gregory Zimmerman examined how environment and personality interact in high- and low-crime areas. In high-crime neighborhoods, impulsive people are no more criminal than their nonimpulsive neighbors. In contrast, in safe, low-crime areas, impulsive residents are much more likely to commit crime than their fellow citizens. How can this surprising finding be explained? In disadvantaged neighborhoods, most people tend to possess a feeling of fatalism and adopt a "I have nothing to lose" attitude. These factors cause both nonimpulsive and impulsive individuals to take advantage of criminal opportunities. In these disorganized neighborhoods, nearly everyone commits crime, so having self-control means relatively little. In contrast, in low-crime areas, most people conform, and it's only the most impulsive who risk engaging in crime. Why bother taking a risk when legitimate opportunities abound? In these higher-income neighborhoods, only those totally lacking in self-control are foolish enough to commit crime.[103]

To read an article by Bruce J. Arneklev, Lori Elis, and Sandra Medlicott that tests the **General Theory of Crime**, visit the Criminal Justice CourseMate at cengagebrain.com, then access the "Web Links" for this chapter.

Self-Control and Crime Gottfredson and Hirschi claim that the principles of **self-control theory** can explain all varieties of criminal behavior and all the social and behavioral correlates of crime. That is, such widely disparate crimes as burglary, robbery, embezzlement, drug dealing, murder, rape, and insider trading all stem from a deficiency of self-control. Likewise, gender, racial, and ecological differences in crime rates can be explained by discrepancies in self-control.

Unlike other theoretical models that explain only narrow segments of criminal behavior (e.g., teenage gang formation), Gottfredson and Hirschi argue that self-control applies equally to all crimes, ranging from murder to corporate theft. White-collar crime rates remain low, they claim, because people who lack self-control rarely attain the positions necessary to commit those crimes. However, those few white-collar criminals lack self-control to the same degree and in the same manner as criminals such as rapists and burglars (see the Profiles in Crime feature, "James Paul Lewis, Jr.: 'Crime Against Humanity,'" for an account of someone who may fit this description).

Empirical Support for GTC   Since the publication of *A General Theory of Crime*, numerous researchers have

One criticism of the General Theory of Crime is that people actually do change over their lifetimes. Here, pictures of cofounder of the Crips gang Stanley "Tookie" Williams show him at an early age. Sentenced to prison for the 1979 murders of four people, Williams spent several years involved with violent activities in prison, but around 1993 changed his behavior and became an antigang activist. Williams coauthored such books as *Life in Prison*, which encourages kids to stay out of gangs, and his memoir *Blue Rage, Black Redemption*. Williams was nominated for the Nobel Peace Prize for his efforts. Do you believe that a gang leader like Tookie Williams can really change, or did his changing life circumstances (i.e., being incarcerated) simply prevent him from committing violent criminal acts? Williams was executed in 2005.

attempted to test the validity of Gottfredson and Hirschi's theoretical views.[104] The general consensus of this research is that people with low self-control and poor impulse control are the most likely to engage in serious crime.[105]

One approach has been to identify indicators of impulsiveness and self-control to determine whether these factors correlate with measures of criminal activity. As a group, they suggest that the lower a person's self-control, the more likely he or she is to engage in antisocial behaviors.[106] The lack of self-control may begin early in adolescence and be manifested in aggressive behavior that turn kids into school yard bullies. Aggressive bullies are rejected by other kids, marginalized, and prone to school failure, a path that winds up in a delinquent way of life.[107]

For example, Matt Delisi and Michael Vaughn examined the association between low self-control and criminal careers.[108] They found that compared to non-career offenders, chronic offenders had significantly lower levels of self-control and that the lower the level of a person's self-control, the greater his or her chance of becoming a career criminal. Importantly, Delisi and Vaughn discovered that low self-control was by far the strongest predictor of career criminality, exceeding the impact of age, race, ethnicity, gender, socioeconomic status, mental illness, attention deficit hyperactivity disorder diagnosis, and trauma experience. In a similar fashion, when Alexander Vazsonyi and his associates analyzed self-control and deviant behavior in samples drawn from a number of different countries (Hungary, Switzerland, the Netherlands, the United States, and Japan), they found that low self-control is significantly related to antisocial behavior and that the association can be seen regardless of culture or national settings.[109] Showing that the self-control–crime association is invariant across cultures is a significant contribution to supporting its validity. These results lend strong support to the GTC. Gottfredson and Hirschi's view has become a cornerstone of contemporary criminological theory.

Analyzing the General Theory of Crime   By integrating the concepts of socialization and criminality, Gottfredson and Hirschi help explain why some people who lack self-control can escape criminality, and, conversely, why some people who have self-control might not escape. People who are at risk because they have impulsive personalities may forgo criminal careers because there are no criminal opportunities that satisfy their impulsive needs; instead, they may find other outlets for their impulsive personalities. In contrast, if the opportunity is strong enough, even people with relatively strong self-control may be tempted to violate the law; the incentives to commit crime may overwhelm self-control.

Integrating criminal propensity and criminal opportunity can explain why some children enter into chronic offending while others living in similar environments are able to resist criminal activity. It can also help us understand why the corporate executive with a spotless record gets caught up in business fraud. Even a successful executive may find self-control inadequate if the potential for illegal gain is large.

Profiles in Crime
James Paul Lewis, Jr.: "Crime Against Humanity"

On May 26, 2006, James Paul Lewis, Jr., the former director of Orange County, California–based Financial Advisory Consultants (FAC), was sentenced to 30 years in federal prison for running a massive Ponzi scheme that raised more than $300 million and caused more than 1,600 victims to lose more than $156 million of their hard-earned money.

What exactly did James Lewis do to earn a 30-year prison sentence? He offered investors opportunities to invest in two mutual funds. Through false and fraudulent brochures and other promotional material issued by FAC, he told investors that they would earn annual rates of return of up to 18 percent in an income fund, which claimed to generate revenue from the leasing of medical equipment, commercial lending, and financing insurance premiums, and 40 percent annual returns in a growth fund, which claimed to generate revenue through the purchase and sale of distressed businesses. Instead of investing the investors' money as promised, Lewis used the funds to purchase homes in Villa Park, Laguna Niguel, Palm Desert, San Diego, and Greenwich, Connecticut. He also used investors' money to purchase luxury automobiles for himself, his wife, and his girlfriend. Among other schemes, he used investor money to trade currency futures, managing to lose at least $22 million. To conceal the scheme at FAC, Lewis ran a Ponzi scheme: he took the money of new investors (and new purchases of those who had already bought into the funds) to pay the rates of return promised to investors. In other words, he used the principal to pay the interest—until the money ran out. At one point, nearly 3,300 investors had a total balance of $813,932,080 in the funds, but FAC and Lewis's bank accounts held only slightly more than $2 million.

At Lewis's sentencing hearing, United States District Judge Cormac J. Carney ordered him to pay $156 million in restitution. Because many of his victims were elderly, Judge Carney described the scheme as a "crime against humanity." Several victims told the court about their losses, which included life savings and college funds. Many victims described being forced back to work after losing their retirement savings in the scheme.

How would Gottfredson and Hirschi explain Lewis's ongoing criminal activities? Can someone so calculating lack self-control?

SOURCES: Department of Justice press release, "Operator of Orange County–Based Ponzi Scheme that Caused More than $150 Million in Losses Sentenced to 30 Years in Federal Prison," May 30, 2006, www.justice.gov/usao/cac/pressroom/pr2006/068.html (accessed August 11, 2011); Gillian Flaccus, "California Man Gets 30 Years for Ponzi Scheme," *Washington Post,* May 27, 2006, www.washingtonpost.com/wp-dyn/content/article/2006/05/27/AR2006052700250.html (accessed August 11, 2011).

The driven executive, accustomed to both academic and financial success, may find that the fear of failure can neutralize her self-control. During tough economic times, the impulsive manager who fears dismissal may be tempted to circumvent the law to improve the bottom line.[110]

Although the General Theory seems persuasive, several questions and criticisms remain unanswered. Among the most important are the following:

- *Tautological.* Some critics argue that the theory is tautological or involves circular reasoning: How do we know when people are impulsive? When they commit crimes! Are all criminals impulsive? Of course, or else they would not have broken the law![111]

  Gottfredson and Hirschi counter by saying that impulsivity is not itself a propensity to commit crime but a condition that inhibits people from appreciating the long-term consequences of their behavior. Consequently, if given the opportunity, they are more likely to indulge in criminal acts than their nonimpulsive counterparts.[112] According to Gottfredson and Hirschi, impulsivity and criminality are neither identical nor equivalent. Some impulsive people may channel their reckless energies into noncriminal activity, such as trading on the commodities markets or real estate speculation, and make a legitimate fortune for their efforts. Others, more impulsive, may bend the rules for their own benefit. The Profiles in Crime feature illustrates the crimes of one such impulsive person.

- *Different classes of criminals.* Terrie Moffitt has identified two classes of criminals—adolescent-limited and life course persistent.[113] Researchers have found that there may be different criminal paths or trajectories. People offend at a different pace, commit different kinds of crimes, and are influenced by different external forces.[114] Criminals tend to be "generalists" who engage in a garden variety of criminal acts. However, some people "specialize" in violent crimes and others in theft offenses, and these two groups seem quite different in personality and temperament.[115] This would contradict the GTC vision that a single factor causes crime and that there is a single class of offender. This view will be discussed in more detail later in the chapter.

- *Ecological differences.* The GTC also fails to address individual and ecological patterns in the crime rate. If crime rates are higher in Los Angeles than in Albany, New York, can it be assumed that residents of Los Angeles are more impulsive than residents of Albany? There is little evidence of regional differences in impulsivity or self-control. Can these differences be explained solely by variation in criminal opportunity? Few researchers have tried to account for the influence of culture, ecology, economy, and so on. Gottfredson and Hirschi might counter that crime rate differences may reflect criminal opportunity: one area may have more effective law enforcement, more draconian laws, and higher levels of guardianship. In their view, opportunity is controlled by economy and culture.

- *Racial differences.* Gottfredson and Hirschi explain racial differences in the crime rate as a failure of childrearing practices in the African American community.[116] In so doing, they overlook issues of institutional racism, poverty, and relative deprivation, which have been shown to have a significant impact on crime rate differentials.

- *Moral beliefs.* The General Theory also ignores the moral concept of right and wrong, or "belief."[117] Research by Olena Antonaccio and Charles Tittle found that holding moral values may trump low self-control—that is, high moral standards can inhibit crime even among impulsive individuals.[118]

- *Peer influence.* A number of research efforts show that the quality of peer relations either enhances or controls criminal behavior and that these influences vary over time.[119] As children mature, peer influence continues to grow.[120] Research shows that kids who lack self-control also have trouble maintaining relationships with law-abiding peers. They may either choose or be forced to seek out friends who are similarly limited in their ability to maintain self-control.[120] Similarly, as they mature they may seek out romantic relationships with law-violating boyfriends or girlfriends, and these entanglements enhance the likelihood that they will get further involved in crime (girls seem more deeply influenced by their delinquent boyfriends than boys by their delinquent girlfriends).[122] This finding contradicts the GTC, which suggests the influence of friends should be stable and unchanging and that a relationship established later in life (making deviant friends) should not influence criminal propensity. Gottfredson and Hirschi might counter that it should come as no surprise that impulsive kids, lacking in self-control, seek out peers with similar personality characteristics.

- *People change.* One of the most important questions raised about the GTC concerns its assumption that criminal propensity does not change. Is it possible that human personality and behavior patterns remain unaltered over the life course? Research shows that changing life circumstances, such as starting and leaving school, abusing substances and then getting straight, and starting or ending personal relationships all influence the frequency of offending.[123] Involvement in organized activities such as karate that teach self-discipline and self-regulation have been shown to improve personality traits in at-risk kids, even those diagnosed with oppositional defiance disorder.[124] As people mature, they may

be better able to control their impulsive behavior and reduce their criminal activities.[125]

- *Effective parenting.* Gottfredson and Hirschi propose that children either develop self-control by the end of early childhood or fail to develop it at all. Research shows, however, that some kids who are predisposed toward delinquency may find their life circumstances improved and their involvement with antisocial behavior diminished if they are exposed to positive and effective parenting that appears later in life.[126] Parenting can influence self-control in later adolescence, and kids who receive improved parenting may improve their self-control much later in the life course than predicted by the GTC.[127]

  Some of the most significant research on this topic has been conducted by Ronald Simons and his colleagues. Simons has found that boys who were involved in deviant and oppositional behavior during childhood were able to turn their lives around if they later experienced improved parenting, increased school commitment, and/or reduced involvement with deviant peers. So although early childhood antisocial behavior may increase the chances of later criminality, even the most difficult children are at no greater risk for delinquency than are their conventional counterparts if they later experience positive changes in their daily lives and increased ties with significant others and institutions.[128]

- *Modest relationship.* Some research results support the proposition that self-control is a causal factor in criminal and other forms of deviant behavior, but that the association is at best quite modest.[129] This would indicate that other forces influence criminal behavior and that low self-control alone cannot predict the onset of a criminal or deviant career. Perhaps antisocial behavior is best explained by a condition that either develops subsequent to the development of self-control or is independent of a person's level of impulsivity.[130] This alternative quality, which may be the real stable latent trait, is still unknown.

- *Cross-cultural differences.* There is some evidence that criminals in other countries do not lack self-control, indicating that the GTC may be culturally limited. Otwin Marenin and Michael Resig found equal or higher levels of self-control in Nigerian criminals as in noncriminals.[131] Behavior that may be considered imprudent in one culture may be socially acceptable in another and therefore cannot be viewed as lack of self-control.[132] There is, however, emerging evidence that the GTC may have validity in predicting criminality abroad.[133]

- *Misreads human nature.* According to Francis Cullen, John Paul Wright, and Mitchell Chamlin, the GTC makes flawed assumptions about human character.[134] It assumes that people are essentially selfish, self-serving, and hedonistic and must therefore be controlled lest they gratify themselves at the expense of others. A more plausible view is that humans are inherently generous and kind; selfish hedonists may be a rare exception.

- *One of many causes.* Research shows that even if lack of self-control is a prerequisite to crime, so are other social, neuropsychological, and physiological factors.[135] Social cultural factors have been found to make an independent contribution to criminal offending patterns.[136] Among the many psychological characteristics that set criminals apart from the general population is their lack of self-direction; their behavior has a here-and-now orientation rather than being aimed at providing long-term benefits.[137] Law violators also exhibit lower resting heart rates and perform poorly on tasks that trigger cognitive functions.[138]

- *Some criminals are not impulsive.* Gottfredson and Hirschi assume that criminals are impatient or "present-oriented." They choose to commit crime because the rewards can be enjoyed immediately and the costs or punishments come later or may not come at all. As long as the gains from crime are immediate while the costs of crime are delayed, impulsive present-oriented individuals will commit crimes even if they are not obviously lucrative. However, not all research efforts support this position. As you may recall from Chapter 4, Steven Levitt and Sudhir Alladi Venkatesh found that many young gang boys are willing to wait years to "rise through the ranks" before earning high wages. Their stay in the gang is fueled by the promises of future compensation, a fact that contradicts the GTC. Levitt and Venkatesh conclude that the economic aspects of the decision to join the gang can be viewed as a tournament in which participants vie for large awards that only a small fraction will eventually obtain. Members of the gang accept low wages in the present in the hope that they will advance in the gang and earn well above market wages in the future.[139]

  Moreover, gang members seem acutely aware that they are making an investment in the future by foregoing present gains. As one noted:

  > You think I wanta be selling drugs on the street my whole life? No way, but I know these n— [above me] are making more money. . . . So you know, I figure I got a chance to move up. But if not, s—, I get me a job doin' something else.[140]

  This quotation does not comport with the notion of a super-impulsive young criminal. Even though few gang recruits will ever become gang leaders, they are willing to take the risk in order to earn a future benefit. This finding contradicts Gottfredson and Hirschi's vision of an impulsive criminal who lives for today without worrying about tomorrow.

- *Self-control may waiver.* Gottfredson and Hirschi assume that impulsivity is a singular construct—one is either impulsive or not. However, there may be more than one kind of impulsive personality and it may waiver

over time. Some people may be impulsive because they are sensation seekers who are constantly looking for novel experiences, whereas others lack deliberation and rarely think through problems. Some may give up easily whereas others act without thinking. Some people may have the ability to persist in self-control, but others "get tired" and eventually succumb to their impulses.[141] Think of it this way: a dieter ogles the cheesecake in the fridge all day but has the self-control not to take a slice. Then he wakes hungry in the middle of the night and makes his way into the kitchen thinking, "a little piece of cheesecake won't hurt me." His self-control slips, and his diet goes out the window.

Although there has been criticism of the GTC, it is one of the most important criminological theories of the past few decades. The strength of the GTC lies in its scope and breadth: it attempts to explain all forms of crime and deviance, from lower-class gang delinquency to sexual harassment in the business community.[142] By integrating concepts of criminal choice, criminal opportunity, socialization, and personality, Gottfredson and Hirschi make a plausible argument that all deviant behaviors may originate at the same source. Questions remain, and continued efforts are needed to test the GTC and establish the validity of its core concepts. It remains one of the key developments of modern criminological theory.

TRAJECTORY THEORIES

Trajectory theory is a third developmental approach that combines elements of latent trait and life course theory. The basic premise is that there is more than one path to crime and more than one class of offender; there are different trajectories in a criminal career. All people are different, and one model cannot hope to describe every person's journey through life. Some people are social and have a large peer group, whereas others are loners who make decisions on their own.[143] Because latent trait theories disregard social influences during the life span, and life course theories maintain that social events seem to affect all people equally, they both miss out on the fact that there are different classes and types of offenders.

The reality is that there may be different paths or trajectories to a criminal career. People offend at a different pace, commit different kinds of crimes, and are influenced by different external forces.[144] For example, people who commit violent crimes may be different from nonviolent offenders and may maintain a unique set of personality traits and problem behaviors.[145] This would contradict the GTC vision that a single factor causes delinquency and that there is a single class of offender.

Early, Late, and Non-Starters

According to this view, not all persistent offenders begin at an early age. Some are precocious, beginning their criminal careers early and persisting into adulthood.[146] Others stay out of trouble in adolescence and do not violate the law until their teenage years. Some offenders may peak at an early age, whereas others persist into adulthood. Some people maximize their offending rates at a relatively early age and then reduce their antisocial activity; others persist into their 20s. Some are high-rate offenders; others offend at relatively low rates.[147] There are even different classes of chronic offenders. Some are high-rate offenders, whereas others offend at relatively low frequencies but are persistent in their criminal activities, never really stopping.[148] In sum, there are different types of offenders and different paths to crime.

Both life course and latent trait theories maintain that most persistent offenders are early starters, beginning their delinquent careers in their adolescence and persisting into adulthood. In contrast, trajectory theories hold that people begin their offending careers at different points in their lives and follow different offending trajectories. Those who engage in repeated and sustained involvement with the law in early adolescence are the most likely to continue to violate the law late into their adulthood.[149]

However, not all chronic offenders begin early in life. Some are "late bloomers" who stay out of trouble until relatively late in adolescence.[150] Researchers Sarah Bacon, Raymond Paternoster, and Robert Brame found that late bloomers are actually the teens most likely to get involved in serious adult offending.[151] Because the late bloomer combines psychopathology with risk-taking behavior and poor social skills, their behavior becomes increasingly violent over time.[152] Although these offenders may begin later, they eventually catch up during late adolescence.

There is also a group of abstainers, or non-offenders. Despite the fact that most of their peers engage in a wide variety of antisocial activities, these people never break the law; their conventional behavior makes them deviant because at least some offending is the norm!

Why do some people refrain from antisocial activity of any sort? Who are these folks who never ever shoplifted, smoked pot, got drunk, or had a fight? According to social psychologist Terrie Moffitt, abstainers are social introverts as teens, whose unpopularity shielded them from group pressure to commit delinquent acts.[153] Other experts disagree, suggesting that conformity may be related more to close parental monitoring and involvement with prosocial peer groups than it is to being unpopular.[154]

Offense Specialization/Generalization

Some offenders are specialists, limiting their criminal activities to a cluster of crimes such as theft offenses, including burglary and larceny, or violent offenses such as assault and rape.[155] Others are generalists who engage in a variety of criminal activity such as drug abuse, burglary, and/or rape, depending on the opportunity to commit crime and the likelihood of success.[156] There is an ongoing debate over generalization/specialization: some criminologists believe that most criminals are generalists, whereas others have found evidence that more serious offenders tend to specialize in a narrower range of antisocial activities.[157] The answer may lie in between these two positions; there is evidence for specialization, but it is neither overwhelming nor universal.[158] Some offenders may specialize in the short term but engage in a wider variety of offenses when presented with opportunities to commit crime.[159]

Pathways to Crime

Trajectory theory recognizes that criminals may travel more than a single road. Some may specialize in violence and extortion; some may be involved in theft and fraud; others may engage in a variety of criminal acts.

There is a strong association between parental and children's deviance. In this photo from surveillance videotape in a Bedford, New Hampshire, store, a woman with her daughter (behind the counter) and her son (at left) are shown in the process of stealing more than $2,000 worth of jewelry. The woman turned herself in after Bedford police made the video public.

AP Images/Consignment Gallery release via Bedford, N.H., Police Dept.

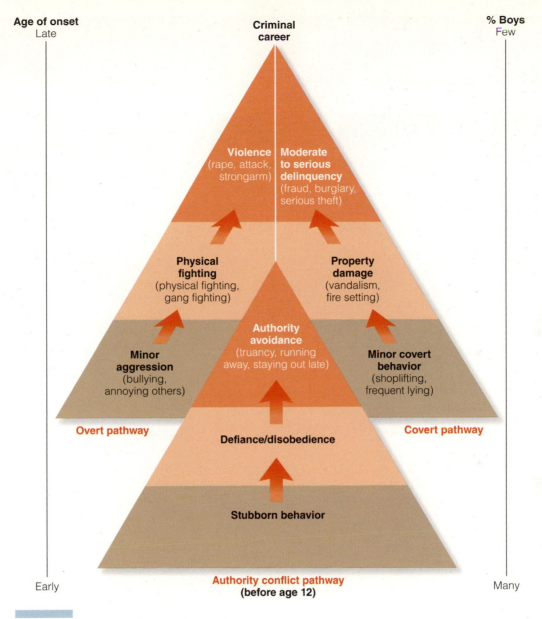

Age of onset
Late

Criminal career

% Boys
Few

Violence (rape, attack, strongarm)

Moderate to serious delinquency (fraud, burglary, serious theft)

Physical fighting (physical fighting, gang fighting)

Property damage (vandalism, fire setting)

Authority avoidance (truancy, running away, staying out late)

Minor aggression (bullying, annoying others)

Minor covert behavior (shoplifting, frequent lying)

Overt pathway

Covert pathway

Defiance/disobedience

Stubborn behavior

Early

Authority conflict pathway (before age 12)

Many

FIGURE 9.4
Loeber's Pathways to Crime

Some of the most important research on delinquent paths or trajectories has been conducted by Rolf Loeber and his associates. Using data from a longitudinal study of Pittsburgh youth, Loeber has identified three distinct paths to a criminal career (Figure 9.4):[160]

- The **authority conflict pathway** begins at an early age with stubborn behavior. This leads to defiance (doing things one's own way, disobedience) and then to authority avoidance (staying out late, truancy, running away).

- The **covert pathway** begins with minor, underhanded behavior (lying, shoplifting) that leads to property

damage (setting nuisance fires, damaging property). This behavior eventually escalates to more serious forms of criminality, ranging from joyriding, pocket picking, larceny, and fencing to passing bad checks, using stolen credit cards, stealing cars, dealing drugs, and breaking and entering.

- The **overt pathway** escalates to aggressive acts beginning with aggression (annoying others, bullying), leading to physical (and gang) fighting, and then to violence (attacking someone, forced theft).

The Loeber research indicates that each of these paths may lead to a sustained deviant career. Some people enter

Troy Victorino

Michael Salas

Jerone Hunter

AP Images/Peter Bauer, Barbara Perez, David Tucker, Pool, File

In the hot summer months of 2004, Troy Victorino and friends Robert Cannon, Jerome Hunter, and Michael Salas were illegally squatting in a Deltona, Florida, home and using it as a "party house." The owners, who were spending the summer in Maine, asked their granddaughter, Erin Belanger, to check up on the property. When she saw what was going on, she called the police to get the squatters removed from the premises. Victorino (who was in jail on an unrelated matter at the time his friends were evicted) left behind an Xbox game system and some clothes, and Belanger took possession of these items. Once he was released from jail on bond, Victorino, feeling disrespected because the police had been called and his stuff confiscated, threatened Belanger and slashed the tires on her car. He warned her that unless she returned the items, he was going to come back and beat her with a baseball bat while she was sleeping. It was not an idle threat. On August 6, 2004, in what is now known either as the *Xbox murders* or the *Deltona massacre*, Victorino, Cannon, Hunter, and

Salas armed themselves with aluminum bats, put on all-black clothing, covered their faces with scarves, kicked in the front door, and attacked Belanger and her roommates as they slept. All six victims, including Erin Belanger, were beaten and stabbed beyond recognition. All six died.

The perpetrators of the deadly attack left a trail of clues that resulted in their quick arrest and indictment on murder charges. It was a pretty sad bunch; they all seemed to have lived troubled lives. Michael Salas was abused even before his birth by his mother, who used drugs during her pregnancy, traded food stamps for cocaine, and left her three sons alone for long periods during the winter. Child Protective Services found cigarette burns on the boys' bodies. Salas's father died of AIDS when Salas was 9. Hunter is a clinically depressed, mentally ill man whose parents were both committed to mental hospitals at the time of the massacre. As early as age 3, Hunter conversed with his identical twin brother Jeremy, who had died from pneumonia at 6 months old. But it was Victorino, a 6-foot-6, 300-pound

career criminal, who most outraged the public. He had spent 8 of the last 11 years before the killings serving prison sentences for a variety of crimes, including auto theft, battery, arson, burglary, and theft. In 1996, he beat a man so severely that doctors needed 15 titanium plates to rebuild the victim's face. Not surprisingly, Victorino also had a long history of physical and sexual abuse that began when he was 2 years old. He suffered from neurological impairment that resulted in poor impulse control and the inability to manage his violent temper.

Despite their personal problems, on August 2, 2006, Victorino and Hunter were sentenced to death by lethal injection, and Cannon and Salas to life in prison without the possibility of parole. Victorino and Hunter remain on death row at the Florida State Prison in Starke because the average length of incarceration of a Florida inmate prior to execution is more than 10 years.

The Xbox killers followed a classic developmental path: early abuse and problems in childhood leading to a long and sustained criminal career. These killers did not age out of crime but persisted and escalated their criminal involvement until it culminated in unspeakable tragedy.

SOURCE: "Deltona Massacre," http://en.academic.ru/dic.nsf/enwiki/6132751 (accessed August 11, 2011); News Journal Online, "Terror at Telford Lane," www.news-journalonline.com/special/deltonadeaths/ (accessed August 11, 2011); CNN, "Probation Officers Fired After 'Xbox Killings'," August 10, 2004, www.cnn.com/2004/LAW/08/09/fla.killing.probation/ (accessed August 11, 2011).

---

two and even three paths simultaneously: they are stubborn, lie to teachers and parents, are bullies, and commit petty thefts. Those taking more than one path are the most likely to become persistent offenders as they mature.

Although some persistent offenders may specialize in one type of behavior, others engage in varied criminal acts and antisocial behaviors as they mature. As adolescents, they cheat on tests, bully kids in the school yard, take drugs, commit burglary, steal a car, and then shoplift from a store.

Later, as adults, some specialize in a particular criminal activity such as drug trafficking, and others are involved in an assortment of deviant acts—selling drugs, committing robberies, and getting involved in break-ins—when the situation arises and the opportunities are present.[161] There may be a multitude of criminal career subgroupings (e.g., prostitutes, drug dealers), each with its own distinctive career path. The Profiles in Crime feature describes the path to murder taken by a band of notorious killers.

Gary Sampson, Spree Killer

Gary L. Sampson, 41, addicted to alcohol and cocaine, was a deadbeat dad, a two-bit thief, and a bank robber with a long history of violence. On August 1, 2001, he turned himself in to the Vermont State Police after fleeing from a string of three murders he committed in Massachusetts and New Hampshire.

Those who knew Sampson speculated that his murders were a desperate finale to a troubled life. During his early life in New England, he once bound, gagged, and beat three elderly women in a candy store, hijacked cars at knifepoint, and had been medically diagnosed as schizophrenic. In 1977, he married a 17-year-old girl he had impregnated; two months later he was arrested and charged with rape for having "unnatural intercourse with a child under 16." Although he was acquitted of that charge, his wife noticed that Sampson was developing a hair-trigger temper and had become increasingly violent; their marriage soon ended. As the years passed, Sampson had at least four failed marriages, was an absentee father to two children, and became an alcoholic and a drug user; he spent nearly half of his adult life behind bars.

Jumping bail after being arrested for theft from an antique store, he headed south to North Carolina and took on a new identity: Gary Johnson, a construction worker. He took up with Ricki Carter, a transvestite, but their relationship was anything but stable. Sampson once put a gun to Carter's head, broke his ribs, and threatened to kill his family. After his breakup with Carter, Sampson moved in with a new girlfriend, Karen Anderson, and began pulling bank jobs. When the police closed in, Sampson fled north. Needing transportation, he carjacked three vehicles and killed the drivers, one a 19-year-old college freshman who had stopped to give Sampson a hand. In December 2003, Sampson received a death sentence from a jury that was not swayed by his claim that he was mentally unfit.

» **The governor is unsettled by the verdict. She wants to grant clemency in the case and reduce Sampson's sentence to life in prison because of the abuse he suffered as a child. She asks you to help her make the judgment. To help her, select two groups, one representing Sampson's interests, the other the prosecution's, and present the governor with a memorandum that will help her decide Sampson's future. Make sure you address the following issue: Would it be fair and ethical to give Sampson clemency?**

Adolescent-Limited Offenders vs. Life Course Persisters

According to psychologist Terrie Moffitt, most young offenders follow one of two paths. **Adolescent-limited offenders** may be considered "typical teenagers" who get into minor scrapes and engage in what might be considered rebellious teenage behavior with their friends.[162] As they reach their mid-teens, adolescent-limited offenders begin to mimic the antisocial behavior of more troubled teens, only to reduce the frequency of their offending as they mature to around age 18.[163] So while it may be cool for some kids to swagger around and get into trouble during their teenage years, they are ready to settle down and assume more conventional roles as they enter young adulthood.

The second path is the one taken by a small group of **life course persisters** who begin their offending career at a very early age and continue to offend well into adulthood.[164] Moffit finds that the seeds of persistence are planted early in life and may combine the effects of abnormal traits, such as neurological deficits, with severe family dysfunction. Persisters are more likely than adolescent-limited offenders to manifest abnormal personal traits such as low verbal ability, impaired reasoning skills, limited learning ability, and weak spatial and memory functions.[165] Individual traits rather than environment seem to have the greatest influence on life course persistence.[166] It is not surprising, then, that many life course persisters display elements of problem behavior syndrome, including mental health problems, psychiatric pathologies, limited school achievement, ADHD, and health issues.[167]

Research shows that the persistence patterns predicted by Moffitt are valid and accurate.[168] Long-term persisters offend more frequently and engage in a greater variety of antisocial acts than other offenders; they also manifest significantly more mental health problems, including psychiatric pathologies, than adolescent-limited offenders.[169]

The Thinking Like a Criminologist feature chronicles the behavior of a life course persister.

Recruiters vs. Lone Wolves

Both life course and latent trait theories often overlook the fact that offenders can be further divided into those who commit crime in groups and "lone wolves," who offend without the help or aid of others. Co-offending most often occurs among younger offenders, ages 10 to 17, after which people begin committing more crimes on their own.[170] After the teen years, solo crimes predominate, which explains why the most recent data suggest that most crimes are committed by lone wolves rather than by criminal groups.[171]

Some lone wolves are content to remain sole practitioners, but others seek out novices to train and mentor: they recruit younger or less experienced people into a criminal way of life. In a recent study, Sarah van Mastrigt and David Farrington found that **recruiters** make up a relatively small (less than 1 percent) portion of the criminal population.[172] These high-rate offenders commit crimes with younger and less-experienced accomplices. Recruiters were more likely than non-recruiters to be older males; to display frequent, long-lasting, and versatile offending behavior; and to be tied to a large number of co-offenders (although they often also offended alone). Even so, recruitment is largely a youthful endeavor, a pattern that refutes the traditional belief that older criminals entice young innocent novices into crime. In fact, van Mastrigt and Farrington found that recruiters and their novices were similar in age and gender, the difference being that recruiters had more offending experience than their "students."

What crimes did recruiters and their "students" commit? Van Mastrigt and Farrington found their crimes to be property-related, in particular, involving theft of and from motor vehicles, shoplifting, and burglary. These offense patterns tended to be stable, suggesting that the recruiters were likely to have influenced the same offenders on more than one occasion, helping them to enter a criminal career.

EVALUATING DEVELOPMENTAL THEORIES

Although the differences between the views presented in this chapter may seem irreconcilable, they share some common ground. They indicate that a criminal career must be understood as a passage along which people travel, that it has a beginning and an end, and that events and life circumstances influence the journey. The factors that affect a criminal career may include structural factors, such as income and status; socialization factors, such as family and peer relations; biological factors, such as size and strength; psychological factors, including intelligence and personality; and opportunity factors, such as free time, inadequate police protection, and a supply of easily stolen merchandise.

Life course theories emphasize the influence of changing interpersonal and structural factors; that is, people change along with the world they live in. Latent trait theories place more emphasis on the fact that behavior is linked less to personal change and more to changes in the surrounding world. Trajectory theories find that there are different classes of offenders who may change at different points of their criminal career.

These perspectives differ in their view of human development. Do people constantly change, as life course theories suggest, or are they stable, constant, and changeless, as the latent trait view indicates? Are the factors that produce criminality different at each stage of life, as the life course view suggests, or does a master trait—such as control balance, self-control, or coercion—steer the course of human behavior? Is there a single path to crime, or are their different paths and different trajectories?

It is also possible that these positions are not mutually exclusive, and each may make a notable contribution to understanding the onset and continuity of a criminal career. In other words, stable individual characteristics (latent traits) may interact with or modify the effects of life course, varying social factors to increase their effect and shape the direction of criminal careers.[173] Is it possible that people take different paths to crime because they have different levels of criminal propensity? Needless to say, measuring these effects is quite complex and relies on sophisticated research techniques. One research effort by Bradley Entner Wright and his associates found evidence supporting both latent trait and life course theories.[174] Their research, conducted with subjects in New Zealand, indicates that low self-control in childhood predicts disrupted social bonds and criminal offending later in life, a finding that supports latent trait theory. They also found that maintaining positive social bonds helps reduce criminality and that maintaining prosocial bonds could even counteract the effect of low self-control. Latent traits are an important influence on crime, but their findings indicate that social relationships that form later in life appear to influence criminal behavior "above and beyond" individuals' preexisting characteristics.[175] This finding may reflect the fact that there are different classes of criminals: a less serious group who are influenced by life events, and a more chronic group whose latent traits insulate them from any positive prosocial relationships; this finding supports trajectory theory concepts.[176]

PUBLIC POLICY IMPLICATIONS OF DEVELOPMENTAL THEORY

A number of policy initiatives have been based on the premises of developmental theory. These typically feature multisystemic treatment efforts designed to provide at-risk kids with personal, social, educational, and family services. For example, one program found that an intervention that promotes academic success, social competence, and educational enhancement during the elementary grades reduced risky sexual practices and their accompanying health consequences in early adulthood.[177]

Other programs are now employing multidimensional strategies and are aimed at targeting children in preschool through the early elementary grades in an attempt to alter the direction of their life course. Many of the most successful programs focus on strengthening children's social-emotional competence and positive coping skills and suppressing the development of antisocial, aggressive behavior.[178] Research evaluations indicate that the most promising multicomponent crime and substance abuse prevention programs for youths, especially those at high risk, are aimed at improving their developmental skills. They may include a school component, an after-school component, and a parent-involvement component. All of these components have the common goal of increasing protective factors and decreasing risk factors in the areas of the family, the community, the school, and the individual.[179] The Boys and Girls Clubs and School Collaborations' Substance Abuse Prevention Program includes a school component called SMART (Skills Mastery and Resistance Training) Teachers, an after-school component called SMART Kids, and a parent-involvement component called SMART Parents. Each component is designed to reduce specific risk factors in the children's school, family, community, and personal environments.[180]

Another successful program, Fast Track, is designed to prevent serious antisocial behavior and related adolescent problems in high-risk children entering first grade.[181] The intervention is guided by a developmental approach that suggests that antisocial behavior is the product of the interaction of multiple social and psychological influences:

- Residence in low-income, high-crime communities places stressors and influences on children and families that increase their risk levels. In these areas, families characterized by marital conflict and instability make consistent and effective parenting difficult to achieve, particularly with children who are impulsive and of difficult temperament.
- Children of high-risk families usually enter the education process poorly prepared for its social, emotional, and cognitive demands. Their parents often are unprepared to relate effectively with school staff, and a poor home–school bond often aggravates the child's adjustment problems. They may be grouped with other children who are similarly unprepared. This peer group may be negatively influenced by disruptive classroom contexts and punitive teachers.
- Over time, aggressive and disruptive children are rejected by families and peers and tend to receive less support from teachers. All of these processes increase the risk of antisocial behaviors in a process that begins in elementary school and lasts throughout adolescence. During this period, peer influences, academic difficulties, and dysfunctional personal identity development can contribute to serious conduct problems and related risky behaviors.

Compared with children in the control group, children in the intervention group displayed significantly less aggressive behavior at home, in the classroom, and on the playground. By the end of the third grade, 37 percent of the intervention group had become free of conduct problems, in contrast with 27 percent of the control group. By the end of elementary school, 33 percent of the intervention group had a developmental trajectory of decreasing conduct problems, as compared with 27 percent of the control group. Furthermore, placement in special education by the end of elementary school was about one-fourth lower in the intervention group than in the control group.

Group differences continued through adolescence. Court records indicate that by eighth grade, 38 percent of the intervention group boys had been arrested, in contrast with 42 percent of the control group. Finally, psychiatric interviews after ninth grade indicate that the Fast Track intervention has reduced serious conduct disorder by over a third, from 27 percent to 17 percent. These effects generalized across gender and ethnic groups and across the wide range of child and family characteristics measured by Fast Track.

SUMMARY

1. **Discuss the history of developmental theory**
   - The foundation of this theory is Sheldon and Eleanor Glueck's integration of biological, psychological, and social factors. Later the Glueck data was rediscovered by criminologists Robert Sampson and John Laub. The Philadelphia cohort research by Marvin Wolfgang and his associates investigated criminal career development. Rolf Loeber and Marc LeBlanc proposed that criminologists should devote time and effort to understanding basic questions about the evolution of criminal careers.

2. **Distinguish between the life course, latent trait, and trajectory theories**
   - Life course theorists view criminality as a dynamic process influenced by a multitude of individual characteristics, traits, and social experiences. Life course theories look at such issues as the onset of crime, the escalation of offenses, the persistence of crime, and desistance from crime. Latent trait theorists believe that human development is controlled by a "master trait" that guides human development and gives some people an increased propensity to commit crime. Trajectory theory holds that there are multiple pathways to crime.

3. **Be familiar with the principles of the life course theory**
   - At an early age, people begin relationships and behaviors that will determine their adult life course. Some individuals are incapable of maturing in a reasonable and timely fashion. A positive life experience may help some criminals desist from crime for a while, but a negative experience may cause them to resume their criminal activities. As people mature, the factors that influence their behavior change. The social, physical, and environmental influences on their behavior are transformed.

4. **Explain the term *problem behavior syndrome***
   - Crime is one of a group of interrelated antisocial behaviors that cluster together. Problem behaviors typically involve family dysfunction, sexual and physical abuse, substance abuse, smoking, precocious sexuality and early pregnancy, educational underachievement, suicide attempts, sensation seeking, and unemployment. People who suffer from one of these conditions typically exhibit many symptoms of the rest.

5. **Discuss why age of onset is an important factor in crime**
   - Early onset of antisocial behavior predicts later and more serious criminality. Adolescent offenders whose criminal behavior persists into adulthood are likely to have begun their deviant careers at a very early (preschool) age. Early-onset kids tend to have poor parental discipline and monitoring, inadequate emotional support, distant peer relationships, and psychological issues and problems.

6. **Know the basic principles of Sampson and Laub's age-graded theory**
   - Sampson and Laub find that the maintenance of a criminal career can be affected by events that occur later in life. They recognize the role of social capital and its influence on the trajectory of a criminal career. When faced with a personal crisis, offenders lack the social supports that can help them reject criminal solutions. Sampson and Laub view criminal careers as a dynamic process in which important life events can change the direction of a person's life course trajectory; these key events are called turning points.

7. **Define the term *latent trait***
   - A number of people in the population have a personal attribute or characteristic that controls their inclination or propensity to commit crimes. A latent trait is a stable feature, characteristic, property, or condition, present at birth or soon after, that makes some people crime prone over the life course. A latent trait may be either present at birth or established early in life, and it can remain stable over time. Suspected latent traits include defective intelligence, damaged or impulsive personality, genetic abnormalities, the physical-chemical functioning of the brain, and environmental influences on brain function, such as drugs, chemicals, and injuries.

8. **Be familiar with Wilson and Herrnstein's views on crime and human nature**
   - According to Wilson and Herrnstein, all human behavior, including criminality, is determined by its perceived consequences. A criminal incident occurs when an individual chooses criminal over conventional behavior. Wilson and Herrnstein assume that both biological and psychological traits influence the choice between crime and noncrime. Wilson and Herrnstein suggest the existence of an elusive latent trait that predisposes people to committing crime.

9. **Understand the basic principles of the General Theory of Crime**
   - Gottfredson and Hirschi link the propensity to commit crime to an impulsive personality and a lack of self-control. People with limited self-control tend to be impulsive; they are insensitive to other people's feelings, predisposed toward physical (rather than mental) activities and solutions, risk takers, shortsighted, and nonverbal. Because those with low self-control enjoy risky, exciting, or thrilling behaviors with immediate gratification, they are more likely to enjoy criminal acts. Gottfredson and Hirschi trace the root cause of poor self-control to inadequate childrearing practices.

10. **Discuss the concept of criminal trajectories**
    - There are different pathways to crime and different types of criminals. Some career criminals may specialize in violence and extortion; some may be involved in theft and fraud; some may engage in a variety of criminal acts. Some offenders begin their careers early in life, whereas others are late bloomers who begin committing crime at about the time when most people desist.

KEY TERMS

developmental criminology (298)
life course theory (299)
latent trait theories (300)
trajectory theory (300)
problem behavior syndrome (PBS) (301)
integrated theories (304)
age-graded theory (304)
cumulative disadvantage (304)

turning points (305)
social capital (306)
latent trait (309)
state dependence (310)
General Theory of Crime (GTC) (311)
self-control (311)
self-control theory (313)
authority conflict pathway (319)

covert pathway (319)
overt pathway (319)
adolescent-limited offenders (321)
life course persisters (321)
recruiters (322)

CRITICAL THINKING QUESTIONS

1. Do you consider yourself to have social capital? If so, what form does it take?

2. Someone you know gets a perfect score on the SAT. What personal, family, and social characteristics do you think this individual has? Another person becomes a serial killer. Without knowing this person, what personal, family, and social characteristics do you think this individual has? If bad behavior is explained by multiple problems, is good behavior explained by multiple strengths?

3. Do you believe it is a latent trait that makes a person crime prone, or is crime a function of environment and socialization?

4. Do you agree with Loeber's multiple pathways model? Do you know people who have traveled down those paths?

5. Do people really change, or do they stay the same but appear to be different because their life circumstances have changed?

NOTES

1. For the most complete account of the case, see Tina Dirmann, *Vanished at Sea: The True Story of a Child TV Actor and Double Murder* (New York: Macmillan, 2008).

2. Hans Eysenck, *Crime and Personality* (London: Methuen, 1964).

3. Nicole Hahn Rafter, "H. J. Eysenck in Fagin's Kitchen: The Return to Biological Theory in 20th-Century Criminology," *History of the Human Sciences* 19 (2006): 37–56.

4. Sheldon Glueck and Eleanor Glueck, *Unraveling Juvenile Delinquency* (Cambridge: Harvard University Press, 1950), p. 48.

5. John Laub and Robert Sampson, "The Sutherland-Glueck Debate: On the Sociology of Criminological Knowledge," *American Journal of Sociology* 96 (1991): 1,402–1,440.

6. See, generally, Sheldon Glueck and Eleanor Glueck, *500 Criminal Careers* (New York: Knopf, 1930); Glueck and Glueck, *One Thousand Juvenile Delinquents* (Cambridge, MA: Harvard University Press, 1934); Glueck and Glueck, *Predicting Delinquency and Crime* (Cambridge, MA: Harvard University Press, 1967), pp. 82–83; Glueck and Glueck, *Unraveling Juvenile Delinquency* (Cambridge, MA: Harvard University Press, 1950).

7. Marvin E. Wolfgang, Robert M. Figlio, and Thorsten Sellin, *Delinquency in a Birth Cohort* (Chicago: University of Chicago Press, 1972).

8. Rolf Loeber and Marc LeBlanc, "Toward a Developmental Criminology," in *Crime and Justice,* Vol. 12, ed. Norval Morris and Michael Tonry (Chicago: University of Chicago Press, 1990), pp. 375–473; Loeber and LeBlanc, "Developmental Criminology Updated," in *Crime and Justice,* Vol. 23, ed. Michael Tonry (Chicago: University of Chicago Press, 1998), pp. 115–198.

9. See, generally, John Laub and Robert Sampson, "The Sutherland–Glueck Debate: On the Sociology of Criminological Knowledge," *American Journal of Sociology* 96 (1991): 1,402–1,440; John Laub and Robert Sampson, "Unraveling Families and Delinquency: A Reanalysis of the Gluecks' Data," *Criminology* 26 (1988): 355–380.

10. Alex Piquero, "Taking Stock of Developmental Trajectories of Criminal Activity over the Life Course," in *The Long View of Crime: A Synthesis of Longitudinal Research*, ed. Akiva Liberman (New York: Springer, 2008), pp. 23–78.

11. Marvin Krohn, Alan Lizotte, and Cynthia Perez, "The Interrelationship between Substance Use and Precocious Transitions to Adult Sexuality," *Journal of Health and Social Behavior* 38 (1997): 87–103, at 88.

12. Jennifer M. Beyers and Rolf Loeber, "Untangling Developmental Relations between Depressed Mood and Delinquency in Male Adolescents," *Journal of Abnormal Child Psychology* 31 (2003): 247–266.

13. Stephanie Milan and Ellen Pinderhughes, "Family Instability and Child Maladjustment Trajectories during Elementary School," *Journal of Abnormal Child Psychology* 34 (2006): 43–56.

14. Bradley Entner Wright, Avshalom Caspi, Terrie Moffitt, and Phil Silva, "The Effects of Social Ties on Crime Vary by Criminal Propensity: A Life-Course Model of Interdependence," *Criminology* 39 (2001): 321–352.

15. Joan McCord, "Family Relationships, Juvenile Delinquency, and Adult Criminality," *Criminology* 29 (1991): 397–417.

16. Paul Mazerolle, "Delinquent Definitions and Participation Age: Assessing the Invariance Hypothesis," *Studies on Crime and Crime Prevention* 6 (1997): 151–168.

17. Peggy Giordano, Stephen Cernkovich, and Jennifer Rudolph, "Gender, Delinquency, and Desistance: Toward a Theory of Cognitive Transformation?" *American Journal of Sociology* 107 (2002): 990–1,064.

18. John Hagan and Holly Foster, "S/He's a Rebel: Toward a Sequential Stress Theory of Delinquency and Gendered Pathways to Disadvantage in Emerging Adulthood," *Social Forces* 82 (2003): 53–86.

19. G. R. Patterson, Barbara DeBaryshe, and Elizabeth Ramsey, "A Developmental Perspective on Antisocial Behavior," *American Psychologist* 44 (1989): 329–335.

20. Robert Sampson and John Laub, "Crime and Deviance in the Life Course," *American Review of Sociology* 18 (1992): 63–84.

21. David Farrington, Darrick Jolliffe, Rolf Loeber, Magda Stouthamer-Loeber, and Larry Kalb, "The Concentration of Offenders in Families, and Family Criminality in the Prediction of Boys' Delinquency," *Journal of Adolescence* 24 (2001): 579–596.

22. Raymond Paternoster, Charles Dean, Alex Piquero, Paul Mazerolle, and Robert Brame, "Generality, Continuity, and Change in Offending," *Journal of Quantitative Criminology* 13 (1997): 231–266.

23. Magda Stouthamer-Loeber and Evelyn Wei, "The Precursors of Young Fatherhood and Its Effect on Delinquency of Teenage Males," *Journal of Adolescent Health* 22 (1998): 56–65; Richard Jessor, John Donovan, and Francis Costa, *Beyond Adolescence: Problem Behavior and Young Adult Development* (New York: Cambridge University Press, 1991); Xavier Coll, Fergus Law, Aurelio Tobias, Keith Hawton, and Joseph Tomas, "Abuse and Deliberate Self-Poisoning in Women: A Matched Case-Control Study," *Child Abuse and Neglect* 25 (2001): 1,291–1,293.

24. Richard Miech, Avshalom Caspi, Terrie Moffitt, Bradley Entner Wright, and Phil Silva, "Low Socioeconomic Status and Mental Disorders: A Longitudinal Study of Selection and Causation during Young Adulthood," *American Journal of Sociology* 104 (1999): 1,096–1,131; Krohn, Lizotte, and Perez, "The Interrelationship between Substance Use and Precocious Transitions to Adult Sexuality," p. 88; Richard Jessor, "Risk Behavior in Adolescence: A Psychosocial Framework for Understanding and Action," in *Adolescents at Risk: Medical and Social Perspectives,* ed. D. E. Rogers and E. Ginzburg (Boulder, CO: Westview Press, 1992).

25. Deborah Capaldi and Gerald Patterson, "Can Violent Offenders Be Distinguished from Frequent Offenders? Prediction from Childhood to Adolescence," *Journal of Research in Crime and Delinquency* 33 (1996): 206–231; D. Wayne Osgood, "The Covariation among Adolescent Problem Behaviors," paper presented at the annual meeting of the American Society of Criminology, Baltimore, November 1990.

26. For an analysis of more than 30 studies, see Mark Lipsey and James Derzon, "Predictors of Violent or Serious Delinquency in Adolescence and Early Adulthood: A Synthesis of Longitudinal Research," in *Serious and Violent Juvenile Offenders: Risk Factors and Successful Interventions,* ed. Rolf Loeber and David Farrington (Thousand Oaks, CA: Sage, 1998).

27. Gina Wingood, Ralph DiClemente, Rick Crosby, Kathy Harrington, Susan Davies, and Edward Hook III, "Gang Involvement and the Health of African American Female Adolescents," *Pediatrics* 110 (2002): 57.

28. David Husted, Nathan Shapira, and Martin Lazoritz, "Adolescent Gambling, Substance Use, and Other Delinquent Behavior," *Psychiatric Times* 20 (2003): 52–55.

29. Krohn, Lizotte, and Perez, "The Interrelationship between Substance Use and Precocious Transitions to Adult Sexuality," p. 88; Jessor, "Risk Behavior in Adolescence."

30. Terence Thornberry, Carolyn Smith, and Gregory Howard, "Risk Factors for Teenage Fatherhood," *Journal of Marriage and the Family* 59 (1997): 505–522; Todd Miller, Timothy Smith, Charles Turner, Margarita Guijarro, and Amanda Hallet, "A Meta-Analytic Review of Research on Hostility and Physical Health," *Psychological Bulletin* 119 (1996): 322–348; Marianne Junger, "Accidents and Crime," in *The Generality of Deviance,* ed. T. Hirschi and M. Gottfredson (New Brunswick, NJ: Transaction Books, 1993).

31. James Marquart, Victoria Brewer, Patricia Simon, and Edward Morse, "Lifestyle Factors among Female Prisoners with Histories of Psychiatric Treatment," *Journal of Criminal Justice* 29 (2001): 319–328; Rolf Loeber, David Farrington, Magda Stouthamer-Loeber, Terrie Moffitt, Avshalom Caspi, and Don Lynam, "Male Mental Health Problems, Psychopathy, and Personality Traits: Key Findings from the First 14 Years of the Pittsburgh Youth Study," *Clinical Child and Family Psychology Review* 4 (2002): 273–297.

32. Robert Johnson, S. Susan Su, Dean Gerstein, Hee-Choon Shin, and John Hoffman, "Parental Influences on Deviant Behavior in Early Adolescence: A Logistic Response Analysis of Age and Gender-Differentiated Effects," *Journal of Quantitative Criminology* 11 (1995): 167–192; Judith Brooks, Martin Whiteman, and Patricia Cohen, "Stage of Drug Use, Aggression, and Theft/Vandalism," in *Drugs, Crime and Other Deviant Adaptations: Longitudinal Studies,* ed. Howard Kaplan (New York: Plenum Press, 1995), pp. 83–96.

33. Helene Raskin White, Peter Tice, Rolf Loeber, and Magda Stouthamer-Loeber, "Illegal Acts Committed by Adolescents under the Influence of Alcohol and Drugs," *Journal of Research in Crime and Delinquency* 39 (2002): 131–153; Candace Kruttschnitt, Jane McLeod, and Maude Dornfeld, "The Economic Environment of Child Abuse," *Social Problems* 41 (1994): 299–312.

34. Paul Nieuwbeerta and Alex Piquero, "Mortality Rates and Causes of Death of Convicted Dutch Criminals 25 Years Later," *Journal of Research in Crime and Delinquency* 45 (2008): 256–286.

35. David Fergusson, L. John Horwood, and Elizabeth Ridder, "Show Me the Child at Seven II: Childhood Intelligence and Later Outcomes in Adolescence and Young Adulthood," *Journal of Child Psychology and Psychiatry and Allied Disciplines* 46 (2005): 850–859.

36. Krysia Mossakowski, "Dissecting the Influence of Race, Ethnicity, and Socioeconomic Status on Mental Health in Young Adulthood," *Research on Aging* 30 (2008): 649–671.

37. Alex R. Piquero and He Len Chung, "On the Relationships between Gender, Early Onset, and the Seriousness of Offending," *Journal of Criminal Justice* 29 (2001): 189–206.

38. David Nurco, Timothy Kinlock, and Mitchell Balter, "The Severity of Preaddiction Criminal Behavior among Urban, Male Narcotic Addicts and Two Nonaddicted Control Groups," *Journal of Research in Crime and Delinquency* 30 (1993): 293–316.

39. Hanno Petras, Nicholas Alongo, Sharon Lambert, Sandra Barrueco, Cindy Schaeffer, Howard Chilcoat, and Sheppard Kellam, "The Utility of Elementary School TOCA-R Scores in Identifying Later Criminal Court Violence Among Adolescent Females," *Journal of the American Academy of Child and Adolescent Psychiatry* 44 (2005): 790–797; Hanno Petras, Howard Chilcoat, Philip Leaf, Nicholas Ialongo, and Sheppard Kellam, "Utility of TOCA-R Scores During the Elementary School Years in Identifying Later Violence among Adolescent Males," *Journal of the American Academy of Child and Adolescent Psychiatry* J43 (2004): 88–96.

40. W. Alex Mason, Rick Kosterman, J. David Hawkins, Todd Herrenkohi, Liliana Lengua, and Elizabeth McCauley, "Predicting Depression, Social Phobia, and Violence in Early Adulthood from Childhood Behavior Problems," *Journal of the American Academy of Child and Adolescent Psychiatry* 43 (2004): 307–315; Rolf Loeber and David Farrington, "Young Children Who Commit Crime: Epidemiology, Developmental

Origins, Risk Factors, Early Interventions, and Policy Implications," *Development and Psychopathology* 12 (2000): 737–762; Patrick Lussier, Jean Proulx, and Marc LeBlanc, "Criminal Propensity, Deviant Sexual Interests and Criminal Activity of Sexual Aggressors Against Women: A Comparison of Explanatory Models," *Criminology* 43 (2005): 249–281.

41. Dawn Jeglum Bartusch, Donald Lynam, Terrie Moffitt, and Phil Silva, "Is Age Important? Testing a General versus a Developmental Theory of Antisocial Behavior," *Criminology* 35 (1997): 13–48.

42. Daniel Nagin and Richard Tremblay, "What Has Been Learned from Group-Based Trajectory Modeling? Examples from Physical Aggression and Other Problem Behaviors," *Annals of the American Academy of Political and Social Science* 602 (2005): 82–117.

43. Mason et al., "Predicting Depression, Social Phobia, and Violence in Early Adulthood from Childhood Behavior Problems"; Ronald Prinz and Suzanne Kerns, "Early Substance Use by Juvenile Offenders," *Child Psychiatry and Human Development* 33 (2003): 263–268.

44. Sarah Bacon, Raymond Paternoster, and Robert Brame, "Understanding the Relationship Between Onset Age and Subsequent Offending During Adolescence," *Journal of Youth and Adolescence* 38 (2009): 301–311.

45. Glenn Clingempeel and Scott Henggeler, "Aggressive Juvenile Offenders Transitioning into Emerging Adulthood: Factors Discriminating Persistors and Desistors," *American Journal of Orthopsychiatry* 73 (2003): 310–323.

46. Mary Campa, Catherine Bradshaw, John Eckenrode, and David Zielinski, "Patterns of Problem Behavior in Relation to Thriving and Precocious Behavior in Late Adolescence," *Journal of Youth and Adolescence* 37 (2008): 627–640; Mason et al., "Predicting Depression, Social Phobia, and Violence in Early Adulthood from Childhood Behavior Problems"; Loeber and Farrington, "Young Children Who Commit Crime"; Lussier, Proulx, and LeBlanc, "Criminal Propensity, Deviant Sexual Interests and Criminal Activity of Sexual Aggressors against Women"; Clingempeel and Henggeler, "Aggressive Juvenile Offenders Transitioning into Emerging Adulthood: Factors Discriminating Persistors and Desistors."

47. David Gadd and Stephen Farrall, "Criminal Careers, Desistance and Subjectivity: Interpreting Men's Narratives of Change," *Theoretical Criminology* 8 (2004): 123–156.

48. G. R. Patterson, L. Crosby, and S. Vuchinich, "Predicting Risk for Early Police Arrest," *Journal of Quantitative Criminology* 8 (1992): 335–355.

49. Holly Hartwig and Jane Myers, "A Different Approach: Applying a Wellness Paradigm to Adolescent Female Delinquents and Offenders," *Journal of Mental Health Counseling* 25 (2003): 57–76.

50. Terrie Moffitt, Avshalom Caspi, Michael Rutter, and Phil Silva, *Sex Differences in Antisocial Behavior: Conduct Disorder, Delinquency, and Violence in the Dunedin Longitudinal Study* (London: Cambridge University Press, 2001).

51. Lisa Broidy, Richard Tremblay, Bobby Brame, David Fergusson, John Horwood, Robert Laird, Terrie Moffitt, Daniel Nagin, John Bates, Kenneth Dodge, Rolf Loeber, Donald Lynam, Gregory Pettit, and Frank Vitaro, "Developmental Trajectories of Childhood Disruptive Behaviors and Adolescent Delinquency: A Six-Site, Cross-National Study," *Developmental Psychology* 39 (2003): 222–245.

52. Shadd Maruna, *Making Good: How Ex-Convicts Reform and Rebuild Their Lives* (Washington, DC: American Psychological Association, 2000), p. 6.

53. Peggy Giordano, Stephen Cernkovich, and Jennifer Rudolph, "Gender, Crime, and Desistance: Toward a Theory of Cognitive Transformation," *American Journal of Sociology* 107 (2002): 990–1,065.

54. Ray Paternoster and Shawn Bushway, "Desistance and the 'Feared Self': Toward an Identity Theory of Criminal Desistance," *Journal of Criminal Law and Criminology* 99 (2009): 1103–1156.

55. Stephen Farrall and Benjamin Bowling, "Structuration, Human Development, and Desistance from Crime," *British Journal of Criminology* 39 (1999): 253–268.

56. Robert Sampson and John Laub, *Crime in the Making: Pathways and Turning Points through Life* (Cambridge, MA: Harvard University Press, 1993); John Laub and Robert Sampson, "Turning Points in the Life Course: Why Change Matters to the Study of Crime," paper presented at the annual meeting of the American Society of Criminology, New Orleans, November 1992.

57. Robert Sampson and John Laub, "A Life-Course View of the Development of Crime," *Annals of the American Academy of Political and Social Science* 602 (2005): 12–45.

58. John Laub, Robert J. Sampson, and Gary Sweeten, "Assessing Sampson and Laub's Life-Course Theory of Crime," in *Taking Stock: The Status of Criminological Theory, Vol. 15, Advances in Criminological Theory*, ed. Francis T. Cullen, John Paul Wright, and Kristie R. Blevins (New Brunswick, NJ: Transaction, 2006), p. 314.

59. Chris Melde and Finn-Aage Esbensen, "Gang Membership as a Turning Point in the Life Course," *Criminology* 49 (2011): 513–552.

60. Daniel Nagin and Raymond Paternoster, "Personal Capital and Social Control: The Deterrence Implications of a Theory of Criminal Offending," *Criminology* 32 (1994): 581–606.

61. Leonore M. J. Simon, "Social Bond and Criminal Record History of Acquaintance and Stranger Violent Offenders," *Journal of Crime and Justice* 22 (1999): 131–146.

62. Raymond Paternoster and Robert Brame, "Multiple Routes to Delinquency? A Test of Developmental and General Theories of Crime," *Criminology* 35 (1997): 49–84.

63. Spencer De Li, "Legal Sanctions and Youths' Status Achievement: A Longitudinal Study," *Justice Quarterly* 16 (1999): 377–401.

64. Shawn Bushway, "The Impact of an Arrest on the Job Stability of Young White American Men," *Journal of Research on Crime and Delinquency* 35 (1999): 454–479.

65. Candace Kruttschnitt, Christopher Uggen, and Kelly Shelton, "Individual Variability in Sex Offending and Its Relationship to Informal and Formal Social Controls," paper presented at the annual meeting of the American Society of Criminology, San Diego, November 1997; Mark Collins and Don Weatherburn, "Unemployment and the Dynamics of Offender Populations," *Journal of Quantitative Criminology* 11 (1995): 231–245.

66. Robert Hoge, D. A. Andrews, and Alan Leschied, "An Investigation of Risk and Protective Factors in a Sample of Youthful Offenders," *Journal of Child Psychology and Psychiatry* 37 (1996): 419–424.

67. Richard Arum and Irenee Beattie, "High School Experience and the Risk of Adult Incarceration," *Criminology* 37 (1999): 515–540.

68. Ross Macmillan, Barbara J. McMorris, and Candace Kruttschnitt, "Linked Lives: Stability and Change in Maternal Circumstances and Trajectories of Antisocial Behavior in Children," *Child Development* 75 (2004): 205–220.

69. Robert Sampson and John Laub, "Socioeconomic Achievement in the Life Course of Disadvantaged Men: Military Service as a Turning Point, circa 1940–1965," *American Sociological Review* 61 (1996): 347–367.

70. Jason Ford and Ryan Schroeder, "Higher Education and Criminal Offending over the Life Course," *Sociological Spectrum* 31 (2011): 32–58.

71. Stephen Tripodia, "The Influence of Social Bonds on Recidivism: A Study of Texas Male Prisoners," *Victims and Offenders* 5 (2010): 354–370; Christopher Uggen, "Ex-Offenders and the Conformist Alternative: A Job Quality Model of Work and Crime," *Social Problems* 46 (1999): 127–151.

72. Terri Orbuch, James House, Richard Mero, and Pamela Webster, "Marital Quality over the Life Course," *Social Psychology*

Quarterly 59 (1996): 162–171; Lee Lillard and Linda Waite, "'Til Death Do Us Part: Marital Disruption and Mortality," *American Journal of Sociology* 100 (1995): 1,131–1,156.

73. Mark Warr, "Life-Course Transitions and Desistance from Crime," *Criminology* 36 (1998): 183–216.

74. Ibid., p. 212.

75. Doris Layton MacKenzie and Spencer De Li, "The Impact of Formal and Informal Social Controls on the Criminal Activities of Probationers," *Journal of Research in Crime and Delinquency* 39 (2002): 243–278.

76. Pamela Webster, Terri Orbuch, and James House, "Effects of Childhood Family Background on Adult Marital Quality and Perceived Stability," *American Journal of Sociology* 101 (1995): 404–432.

77. Ryan Schroeder, Peggy Giordano, and Stephen Cernkovich, "Drug Use and Desistance Processes," *Criminology* 45 (2007): 191–222.

78. James Ridde et al., "Millennium Cohort: The 2001–2003 Baseline Prevalence of Mental Disorders in the U.S. Military," *Journal of Clinical Epidemiology* 60 (2007): 192–201.

79. David Rowe, D. Wayne Osgood, and W. Alan Nicewander, "A Latent Trait Approach to Unifying Criminal Careers," *Criminology* 28 (1990): 237–270.

80. Lee Ellis, "Neurohormonal Bases of Varying Tendencies to Learn Delinquent and Criminal Behavior," in *Behavioral Approaches to Crime and Delinquency*, ed. E. Morris and C. Braukmann (New York: Plenum, 1988), pp. 499–518.

81. David Rowe, Alexander Vazsonyi, and Daniel Flannery, "Sex Differences in Crime: Do Means and Within-Sex Variation Have Similar Causes?" *Journal of Research in Crime and Delinquency* 32 (1995): 84–100.

82. Bacon, Paternoster, and Brame, "Understanding the Relationship Between Onset Age and Subsequent Offending During Adolescence."

83. James Q. Wilson and Richard Herrnstein, *Crime and Human Nature* (New York: Simon & Schuster, 1985).

84. Ibid., p. 44.

85. Ibid., p. 171.

86. David P. Farrington, "Developmental and Life-Course Criminology: Key Theoretical and Empirical Issues," Sutherland Award address presented at the annual meeting of the American Society of Criminology, Chicago, November 2002, revised March 2003; Charles Tittle, *Control Balance: Toward a General Theory of Deviance* (Boulder, CO: Westview Press, 1995); Mark Colvin, *Crime and Coercion: An Integrated Theory of Chronic Criminality* (New York: Palgrave Press, 2000).

87. Michael Gottfredson and Travis Hirschi, *A General Theory of Crime* (Stanford, CA: Stanford University Press, 1990).

88. Ibid., p. 90.

89. Ibid., p. 89.

90. Alex Piquero and Stephen Tibbetts, "Specifying the Direct and Indirect Effects of Low Self-Control and Situational Factors in Offenders' Decision Making: Toward a More Complete Model of Rational Offending," *Justice Quarterly* 13 (1996): 481–508.

91. David Forde and Leslie Kennedy, "Risky Lifestyles, Routine Activities, and the General Theory of Crime," *Justice Quarterly* 14 (1997): 265–294.

92. Gottfredson and Hirschi, *A General Theory of Crime,* p. 112.

93. Ibid.

94. Anthony Walsh and Lee Ellis, "Shoring Up the Big Three: Improving Criminological Theories with Biosocial Concepts," paper presented at the annual meeting of the American Society of Criminology, San Diego, November 1997, p. 15.

95. Dennis Giever, "An Empirical Assessment of the Core Elements of Gottfredson and Hirschi's General Theory of Crime," paper presented at the annual meeting of the American Society of Criminology, Boston, November 1995.

96. Stacey Nofziger, "The "Cause" of Low Self-Control: The Influence of Maternal Self-Control," *Journal of Research in Crime and Delinquency* 45 (2008): 191–224.

97. Marie Ratchford and Kevin Beaver, "Neuropsychological Deficits, Low Self-Control, and Delinquent Involvement: Toward a Biosocial Explanation of Delinquency," *Criminal Justice and Behavior* 36 (2009): 147–162.

98. Kevin Beaver and John Paul Wright, "Evaluating the Effects of Birth Complications on Low-Control in a Sample of Twins," *International Journal of Offender Therapy and Comparative Criminology* 49 (2005): 450–472.

99. Kevin M. Beaver, J. Eagle Shutt, Brian Boutwell, Marie Ratchford, Kathleen Roberts, and J. C. Barnes, "Genetic and Environmental Influences on Levels of Self-Control and Delinquent Peer Affiliation: Results from a Longitudinal Sample of Adolescent Twins," *Criminal Justice and Behavior* 36 (2009): 41–60.

100. Gottfredson and Hirschi, *A General Theory of Crime,* p. 27.

101. Lee Copping, Anne Campbell, and Catherine Cross, "Sex Differences in Impulsivity: A Meta-Analysis," *Psychological Bulletin* 137 (2011): 97–130.

102. For a review of this issue, see Anne Campbell, *Men, Women, and Aggression* (New York: Basic Books, 1993).

103. Gregory Zimmerman, "Impulsivity, Offending, and the Neighborhood: Investigating the Person–Context Nexus," *Journal*

of *Quantitative Criminology* 26 (2010): 301–332.

104. David Brownfield and Ann Marie Sorenson, "Self-Control and Juvenile Delinquency: Theoretical Issues and an Empirical Assessment of Selected Elements of a General Theory of Crime," *Deviant Behavior* 14 (1993): 243–264; Harold Grasmick, Charles Tittle, Robert Bursik, and Bruce Arneklev, "Testing the Core Empirical Implications of Gottfredson and Hirschi's General Theory of Crime," *Journal of Research in Crime and Delinquency* 30 (1993): 5–29; John Cochran, Peter Wood, and Bruce Arneklev, "Is the Religiosity–Delinquency Relationship Spurious? A Test of Arousal and Social Control Theories," *Journal of Research in Crime and Delinquency* 31 (1994): 92–123; Marc LeBlanc, Marc Ouimet, and Richard Tremblay, "An Integrative Control Theory of Delinquent Behavior: A Validation 1976–1985," *Psychiatry* 51 (1988): 164–176.

105. Daniel Nagin and Greg Pogarsky, "Time and Punishment: Delayed Consequences and Criminal Behavior," *Journal of Quantitative Criminology* 20 (2004): 295–317.

106. Christopher Sullivan, Jean Marie McGloin, Travis Pratt, and Alex Piquero, "Rethinking the 'Norm' of Offender Generality: Investigating Specialization in the Short-Term," *Criminology* 44 (2006): 199–233.

107. Norman White and Rolf Loeber, "Bullying and Special Education as Predictors of Serious Delinquency," *Journal of Research in Crime and Delinquency* 45 (2008): 380–397.

108. Matt Delisi and Michael Vaughn, "The Gottfredson-Hirschi Critiques Revisited: Reconciling Self-Control Theory, Criminal Careers, and Career Criminals," *International Journal of Offender Therapy and Comparative Criminology* 52 (2008): 520–537.

109. Alexander Vazsonyi, Janice Clifford Wittekind, Lara Belliston, and Timothy Van Loh, "Extending the General Theory of Crime to 'The East': Low Self-Control in Japanese Late Adolescents," *Journal of Quantitative Criminology* 20 (2004): 189–216; Alexander Vazsonyi, Lloyd Pickering, Marianne Junger, and Dick Hessing, "An Empirical Test of a General Theory of Crime: A Four-Nation Comparative Study of Self-Control and the Prediction of Deviance," *Journal of Research in Crime and Delinquency* 38 (2001): 91–131.

110. Michael Benson and Elizabeth Moore, "Are White-Collar and Common Offenders the Same? An Empirical and Theoretical Critique of a Recently Proposed General Theory of Crime," *Journal of Research in Crime and Delinquency* 29 (1992): 251–272.

111. Ronald Akers, "Self-Control as a General Theory of Crime," *Journal of Quantitative Criminology* 7 (1991): 201–211.

112. Gottfredson and Hirschi, *A General Theory of Crime,* p. 88.

113. Terrie Moffitt, "Adolescence-Limited and Life-Course Persistent Antisocial Behavior: A Developmental Taxonomy," *Psychological Review* 100 (1993): 674–701.

114. Alex Piquero, Robert Brame, Paul Mazerolle, and Rudy Haapanen, "Crime in Emerging Adulthood," *Criminology* 40 (2002): 137–170.

115. Donald Lynam, Alex Piquero, and Terrie Moffitt, "Specialization and the Propensity to Violence: Support from Self-Reports but Not Official Records," *Journal of Contemporary Criminal Justice* 20 (2004): 215–228.

116. Gottfredson and Hirschi, *A General Theory of Crime,* p. 153.

117. Ann Marie Sorenson and David Brownfield, "Normative Concepts in Social Control," paper presented at the annual meeting of the American Society of Criminology, Phoenix, November 1993.

118. Olena Antonaccio and Charles Tittle, "Morality, Self-Control, and Crime," *Criminology* 46 (2008): 479–510.

119. Delbert Elliott and Scott Menard, "Delinquent Friends and Delinquent Behavior: Temporal and Developmental Patterns," in *Crime and Delinquency: Current Theories,* ed. J. David Hawkins (Cambridge: Cambridge University Press, 1996).

120. Graham Ousey and David Aday, "The Interaction Hypothesis: A Test Using Social Control Theory and Social Learning Theory," paper presented at the annual meeting of the American Society of Criminology, Boston, November 1995.

121. Jean Marie McGloin and Lauren O'Neill Shermer, "Self-Control and Deviant Peer Network Structure," *Journal of Research in Crime and Delinquency* 46 (2009): 35–72.

122. Dana Haynie, Peggy Giordano, Wendy Manning, and Monica Longmore, "Adolescent Romantic Relationships and Delinquency Involvement," *Criminology* 43 (2005): 177–210.

123. Julie Horney, D. Wayne Osgood, and Ineke Haen Marshall, "Criminal Careers in the Short-Term: Intra-Individual Variability in Crime and Its Relations to Local Life Circumstances," *American Sociological Review* 60 (1995): 655–673; Martin Daly and Margo Wilson, "Killing the Competition," *Human Nature* 1 (1990): 83–109.

124. Mark Palermo, Massimo Di Luigi, Gloria Dal Forno, Cinzia Dominici, David Vicomandi, Augusto Sambucioni, Luca Proietti, and Patrizio Pasqualetti, "Externalizing and Oppositional Behaviors and Karate-do: The Way of Crime Prevention," *International Journal of Offender Therapy and Comparative Criminology* 50 (2006): 654–660.

125. Charles R. Tittle and Harold G. Grasmick, "Criminal Behavior and Age: A Test of Three Provocative Hypotheses," *Journal of Criminal Law and Criminology* 88 (1997): 309–342.

126. Callie Harbin Burt, Ronald Simons, and Leslie Simons, "A Longitudinal Test of the Effects of Parenting and the Stability of Self-Control: Negative Evidence for the General Theory of Crime," *Criminology* 44 (2006): 353–396.

127. Carter Hay and Walter Forrest, "The Development of Self-Control: Examining Self-Control Theory's Stability Thesis," *Criminology* 44 (2006): 739–774.

128. Ronald Simons, Christine Johnson, Rand Conger, and Glen Elder, "A Test of Latent Trait versus Life-Course Perspectives on the Stability of Adolescent Antisocial Behavior," *Criminology* 36 (1998): 217–244.

129. Carter Hay, "Parenting, Self-Control, and Delinquency: A Test of Self-Control Theory," *Criminology* 39 (2001): 707–736; Douglas Longshore, "Self-Control and Criminal Opportunity: A Prospective Test of the General Theory of Crime," *Social Problems* 45 (1998): 102–114; Finn-Aage Esbensen and Elizabeth Piper Deschenes, "A Multisite Examination of Youth Gang Membership: Does Gender Matter?" *Criminology* 36 (1998): 799–828.

130. Raymond Paternoster and Robert Brame, "The Structural Similarity of Processes Generating Criminal and Analogous Behaviors," *Criminology* 36 (1998): 633–670.

131. Otwin Marenin and Michael Resig, "A General Theory of Crime and Patterns of Crime in Nigeria: An Exploration of Methodological Assumptions," *Journal of Criminal Justice* 23 (1995): 501–518.

132. Bruce Arneklev, Harold Grasmick, Charles Tittle, and Robert Bursik, "Low Self-Control and Imprudent Behavior," *Journal of Quantitative Criminology* 9 (1993): 225–246.

133. Peter Muris and Cor Meesters, "The Validity of Attention Deficit Hyperactivity and Hyperkinetic Disorder Symptom Domains in Nonclinical Dutch Children," *Journal of Clinical Child and Adolescent Psychology* 32 (2003): 460–466.

134. Francis Cullen, John Paul Wright, and Mitchell Chamlin, "Social Support and Social Reform: A Progressive Crime Control Agenda," *Crime and Delinquency* 45 (1999): 188–207.

135. Alex Piquero, John MacDonald, Adam Dobrin, Leah Daigle, and Francis Cullen, "Self-Control, Violent Offending, and Homicide Victimization: Assessing the General Theory of Crime," *Journal of Quantitative Criminology* 21 (2005): 55–71.

136. Ibid.

137. Richard Wiebe, "Reconciling Psychopathy and Low Self-Control," *Justice Quarterly* 20 (2003): 297–336.

138. Elizabeth Cauffman, Laurence Steinberg, and Alex Piquero, "Psychological, Neuropsychological and Physiological Correlates of Serious Antisocial Behavior in Adolescence: The Role of Self-Control," *Criminology* 43 (2005): 133–176.

139. Steven Levitt and Sudhir Alladi Venkatesh, "An Economic Analysis of a Drug-Selling Gang's Finances," *Quarterly Journal of Economics* 13 (2000): 755–789.

140. Ibid., p. 773.

141. Mark Muraven, Greg Pogarsky, and Dikla Shmueli, "Self-Control Depletion and the General Theory of Crime," *Journal of Quantitative Criminology* 22 (2006): 263–277.

142. Kevin Thompson, "Sexual Harassment and Low Self-Control: An Application of Gottfredson and Hirschi's General Theory of Crime," paper presented at the annual meeting of the American Society of Criminology, Phoenix, November 1993.

143. George E. Higgins, Melissa L. Ricketts, Catherine D. Marcum, and Margaret Mahoney, "Primary Socialization Theory: An Exploratory Study of Delinquent Trajectories," *Criminal Justice Studies* 23 (2010): 133–146.

144. Alex Piquero, Robert Brame, Paul Mazerolle, and Rudy Haapanen, "Crime in Emerging Adulthood," *Criminology* 40 (2002): 137–170.

145. Lynam, Piquero, and Moffitt, "Specialization and the Propensity to Violence: Support from Self-Reports but Not Official Records."

146. Ick-Joong Chung, Karl G. Hill, J. David Hawkins, Lewayne Gilchrist, and Daniel Nagin, "Childhood Predictors of Offense Trajectories," *Journal of Research in Crime and Delinquency* 39 (2002): 60–91.

147. Amy D'Unger, Kenneth Land, Patricia McCall, and Daniel Nagin, "How Many Latent Classes of Delinquent/Criminal Careers? Results from Mixed Poisson Regression Analyses," *American Journal of Sociology* 103 (1998): 1,593–1,630.

148. Ibid.

149. Alex Piquero, David Farrington, Daniel Nagin, and Terrie Moffitt, "Trajectories of Offending and Their Relation to Life Failure in Late Middle Age: Findings from the Cambridge Study in Delinquent Development," *Journal of Research in Crime and Delinquency* 47 (2010): 151–173.

150. Chung et al., "Childhood Predictors of Offense Trajectories."

151. Bacon, Paternoster, and Brame, "Understanding the Relationship Between Onset Age and Subsequent Offending During Adolescence."

152. Victor van der Geest, Arjan Blokland, and Catrien Bijleveld, "Delinquent Development in a Sample of High-Risk Youth: Shape, Content, and Predictors of Delinquent Trajectories from Age 12 to 32," *Journal of Research in Crime and Delinquency* 46 (2009): 111–143.

153. Terrie Moffitt, "A Review of Research on the Taxonomy of Life-Course Persistent

versus Adolescence-Limited Antisocial Behavior," in *Taking Stock: The Status of Criminological Theory*, Vol. 15, ed. F. T. Cullen, J. P. Wright, and K. R. Blevins (New Brunswick, NJ: Transaction Publications, 2006), pp. 277–311.

154. Xiaojin Chen and Michele Adam, "Are Teen Delinquency Abstainers Social Introverts? A Test of Moffitt's Theory." *Journal of Research in Crime and Delinquency* 47 (2010): 439–468.

155. Jacqueline Schneider, "The Link Between Shoplifting and Burglary: The Booster Burglar," *British Journal of Criminology* 45 (2005): 395–401.

156. Glenn Deane, Richard Felson, and David Armstrong, "An Examination of Offense Specialization Using Marginal Logit Models," *Criminology* 43 (2005): 955–988.

157. Christopher Sullivan, Jean Marie McGloin, Travis Pratt, and Alex Piquero, "Rethinking the 'Norm' of Offender Generality: Investigating Specialization in the Short-Term," *Criminology* 44 (2006): 199–233.

158. Christopher J. Sullivan, Jean Marie McGloin, James V. Ray, and Michael S. Caudy, "Detecting Specialization in Offending: Comparing Analytic Approaches," *Journal of Quantitative Criminology* 25 (2009): 419–441.

159. Jean Marie McGloin, Christopher J. Sullivan, and Alex R. Piquero, "Aggregating to Versatility? Transitions among Offender Types in the Short Term," *British Journal of Criminology* 49 (2009): 243–264.

160. Rolf Loeber, Phen Wung, Kate Keenan, Bruce Giroux, Magda Stouthamer-Loeber, Wemoet Van Kammen, and Barbara Maughan, "Developmental Pathways in Disruptive Behavior," *Development and Psychopathology* (1993): 12–48.

161. Sheila Royo Maxwell and Christopher Maxwell, "Examining the 'Criminal Careers' of Prostitutes within the Nexus of Drug Use, Drug Selling, and Other Illicit Activities," *Criminology* 38 (2000): 787–809.

162. Alex Piquero and Timothy Brezina, "Testing Moffitt's Account of Adolescent-Limited Delinquency," *Criminology* 39 (2001): 353–370.

163. Moffitt, "Adolescence-Limited and Life-Course Persistent Antisocial Behavior: A Developmental Taxonomy."

164. Terrie Moffitt, "Natural Histories of Delinquency," in *Cross-National Longitudinal Research on Human Development and Criminal Behavior*, ed. Elmar Weitekamp and Hans-Jurgen Kerner (Dordrecht, Netherlands: Kluwer, 1994), pp. 3–65.

165. Adrian Raine, Rolf Loeber, Magda Stouthamer-Loeber, Terrie Moffitt, Avshalom Caspi, and Don Lynam, "Neurocognitive Impairments in Boys on the Life-Course Persistent Antisocial Path," *Journal of Abnormal Psychology* 114 (2005): 38–49.

166. Per-Olof Wikstrom and Rolf Loeber, "Do Disadvantaged Neighborhoods Cause Well-Adjusted Children to Become Adolescent Delinquents? A Study of Male Juvenile Serious Offending, Individual Risk and Protective Factors, and Neighborhood Context," *Criminology* 38 (2000): 1,109–1,142.

167. Alex Piquero, Leah Daigle, Chris Gibson, Nicole Leeper Piquero, and Stephen Tibbetts, "Are Life-Course-Persistent Offenders at Risk for Adverse Health Outcomes?" *Journal of Research in Crime and Delinquency* 44 (2007): 185–207.

168. Andrea Donker, Wilma Smeenk, Peter van der Laan, and Frank Verhulst, "Individual Stability of Antisocial Behavior from Childhood to Adulthood: Testing the Stability Postulate of Moffitt's Developmental Theory," *Criminology* 41 (2003): 593–609.

169. Robert Vermeiren, "Psychopathology and Delinquency in Adolescents: A Descriptive and Developmental Perspective," *Clinical Psychology Review* 23 (2003): 277–318; Paul Mazerolle, Robert Brame, Ray Paternoster, Alex Piquero, and Charles Dean, "Onset Age, Persistence, and Offending Versatility: Comparisons across Sex," *Criminology* 38 (2000): 1,143–1,172.

170. Joan McCord and Kevin P. Conway, *Co-offending and Patterns of Juvenile Crime* (Washington, DC: NIJ Research Bulletin, 2005), www.ncjrs.gov/pdffiles1/nij/210360.pdf (accessed August 11, 2011).

171. Lisa Stolzenberg and Stewart D'Alessio, "Co-offending and the Age-Crime Curve," *Journal of Research in Crime and Delinquency* 45 (2008): 65–86.

172. Sarah van Mastrigt and David Farrington, "Prevalence and Characteristics of Co-Offending Recruiters," *Justice Quarterly* 28 (2011): 325–359.

173. Graham Ousey and Pamela Wilcox, "The Interaction of Antisocial Propensity and Life-Course Varying Predictors of Delinquent Behavior: Differences by Method of Estimation and Implications for Theory," *Criminology* 45 (2007): 313–354.

174. Bradley Entner Wright, Avashalom Caspi, Terrie Moffitt, and Phil Silva, "Low Self-Control, Social Bonds, and Crime: Social Causation, Social Selection, or Both?" *Criminology* 37 (1999): 479–514.

175. Ibid., p. 504.

176. Stephen Cernkovich and Peggy Giordano, "Stability and Change in Antisocial Behavior: The Transition from Adolescence to Early Adulthood," *Criminology* 39 (2001): 371–410.

177. Heather Lonczk, Robert Abbott, J. David Hawkins, Rick Kosterman, and Richard Catalano, "Effects of the Seattle Social Development Project on Sexual Behavior, Pregnancy, Birth, and Sexually Transmitted Disease Outcomes by Age 21 Years," *Archive of Pediatrics and Adolescent Medicine* 156 (2002): 438–447.

178. Kathleen Bodisch Lynch, Susan Rose Geller, and Melinda G. Schmidt, "Multi-Year Evaluation of the Effectiveness of a Resilience-Based Prevention Program for Young Children," *Journal of Primary Prevention* 24 (2004): 335–353.

179. This section leans on Thomas Tatchell, Phillip Waite, Renny Tatchell, Lynne Durrant, and Dale Bond, "Substance Abuse Prevention in Sixth Grade: The Effect of a Prevention Program on Adolescents' Risk and Protective Factors," *American Journal of Health Studies* 19 (2004): 54–61.

180. Nancy Tobler and Howard Stratton, "Effectiveness of School Based Drug Prevention Programs: A Meta-Analysis of the Research," *Journal of Primary Prevention* 18 (1997): 71–128.

181. Information and data can be found at the Fast Track Project website, www.fasttrackproject.org/ (accessed September 1, 2011).

Crime Typologies

Criminologists group criminal offenders and criminal behaviors into categories or typologies so they may be more easily studied and understood. Are there common traits or characteristics that link offenders together and make them distinct from nonoffenders? Are there common areas between seemingly different acts such as murder and rape?

In this section, we focus on crime typologies. They are clustered into six groups: violent crime (Chapter 10), political crime and terrorism (Chapter 11), property crimes involving common theft offenses and arson (Chapter 12), enterprise crimes involving white-collar and green-collar criminals (Chapter 13), public order crimes, such as prostitution and drug abuse (Chapter 14), and cybercrimes and transnational organized crime (Chapter 15). This format groups criminal behaviors by their focus: bringing physical harm to others, misappropriating other people's property, violating laws designed to protect public morals, and using technology to commit crime.

Typologies can be useful in classifying large numbers of criminal offenses or offenders into easily understood categories. This text has grouped offenses and offenders on the basis of their legal definitions and their collective goals, objectives, and consequences.

AP Images/Joe Burbank, Pool

FEW

Few cases in recent history have captivated the media and the public as much as did the story of Casey Anthony, the young mother tried in 2011 for the murder of her 2-year-old daughter, Caylee Marie.[1] The story began when Caylee went missing on June 16, 2008. Casey Anthony failed to report the child's absence to police for 31 days and told people that a baby sitter had taken Caylee on a trip and then kidnapped her to cover up the absence; Caylee's remains were found December 11, 2008, in a wooded lot not far from the Anthony home. The defense team claimed that the baby had accidentally drowned and that Casey and her dad, in a panic, had covered up the accident. Why had Casey gone along with the scheme? The defense claimed she had been sexually abused by her father and had been forced to lie about it her whole life. In contrast, the prosecution argued that Casey had murdered her daughter in cold blood, sedating her with

(continued on page 334)

Interpersonal Violence

10

Learning Objectives

1. Be familiar with the various causes of violent crime
2. Be able to discuss the history of rape and know the different types of rape
3. Discuss the legal issues in rape prosecution
4. Recognize that there are different degrees of murder
5. Be able to discuss the differences among serial killing, mass murder, and spree killing
6. Discuss the concept of murder transaction
7. Be familiar with the nature of assault and battery
8. Know the root causes of child abuse
9. Understand the definition and concept of robbery
10. Be able to discuss newly emerging forms of violence such as hate crimes, workplace violence, and stalking

chloroform, suffocating her with duct tape, and dumping her body in a wooded area. Why did she commit this horrible crime? According to the prosecution, Casey killed her 2-year-old daughter so she could be free to live a life of partying and clubbing. Casey had gotten a tattoo that said "bella vita"—beautiful life—after Caylee had disappeared, a signal to some that she wanted to begin a new and carefree life. What swayed the day was the lack of physical evidence. The body was too decomposed to determine the cause or time of death, nor could evidence be found in the home or in Casey's car, which prosecutors said she had used to transport the body. The jury could not condemn a young woman to death without clear and convincing evidence that she had murdered her child.

The Anthony case illustrates how violent crime has become an ever-present part of American society. It can divide a community, damage reputations, and cause lifelong harm. No matter where people go, they may encounter violent acts, in a back alley or even in their own kitchen. Nor is violence committed solely by gang boys and drug dealers. You can also be attacked by your mother and/or grandfather! No one is immune. Millions of violent crimes occur each year. Some are **expressive violence**—acts that vent rage, anger, or frustration—and some are **instrumental violence**—acts designed to improve the financial or social position of the criminal, for example, through an armed robbery or murder for hire. No matter its cause, interpersonal violence takes a terrible toll. It causes people to live in fear, staying home at night and avoiding dangerous neighborhoods. It also can bring disorder to whole communities, disrupting services and driving down real estate values, further destabilizing areas already reeling from the shock of violent crimes.[2]

This chapter explores the concept of violence in some depth. First, it reviews the suggested causes of violent crime. Then it focuses on specific types of interpersonal violence— rape, homicide, assault and battery, robbery, and newly recognized types of interpersonal violence such as hate crimes, workplace violence, and stalking.

THE CAUSES OF VIOLENCE

What sets off a violent person? Criminologists have a variety of views on this subject. Some believe that violence is a function of human traits and makeup. Others point to improper socialization and upbringing. Violent behavior may be culturally determined and relate to dysfunctional social values.[3] The various sources of violence are set out in Figure 10.1.

Psychological/Biological Abnormality

On March 13, 1995, an ex–Scout leader named Thomas Hamilton took four high-powered rifles into the primary school of the peaceful Scottish town of Dunblane and slaughtered 16 kindergarten children and their teacher before taking his own life. This horrific crime shocked the British Isles into implementing strict controls on all guns.[4] Bizarre outbursts such as Hamilton's support a link between violence and some sort of mental or biological abnormality.

People who are involved in violent episodes may be suffering from severe mental abnormalities.[5] In a classic work, psychologist Dorothy Otnow Lewis showed that kids who

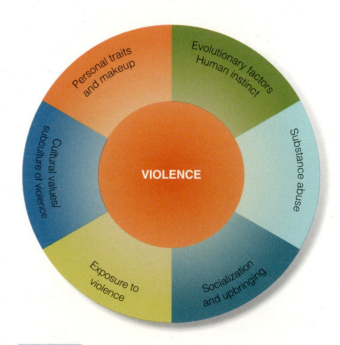

FIGURE 10.1
Sources of Violence

kill may be suffering from multiple symptoms of psychological abnormality: neurological impairment (e.g., abnormal EEGs, multiple psychomotor impairments, and severe seizures), low intelligence, and psychotic symptoms such as paranoia, illogical thinking, and hallucinations.[6] In her book *Guilty by Reason of Insanity*, Lewis found that death row inmates have a history of mental impairment and intellectual dysfunction.[7]

Lewis's research is not unique. Abnormal personality structures, including such traits as depression, impulsivity, aggression, dishonesty, pathological lying, lack of remorse, borderline personality syndrome, and psychopathology, have all been associated with various forms of violence.[8] Violent criminals often manifest early symptoms of a disturbed personality in such behaviors as animal cruelty; some have a long history of torturing and killing animals.[9] It comes as no surprise to psychologists that many murderers kill themselves shortly after committing their crime.[10]

AP Images/Gwen Mayor

While rates of violent crime are higher in the United States than in most other Western nations, violence abroad is not unknown. One of the most catastrophic incidents occurred in the village of Dunblane, Scotland, on July 8, 1996, when heavily armed Thomas Hamilton walked onto the grounds of St. Luke's Infant School and began to methodically shoot children in this kindergarten class. Sixteen children and their teacher were killed. The Dunblane massacre prompted the passage of legislation to control handguns in Scotland and England, which failed to please some critics who felt there should be an outright ban on the possession of guns.

Read more about the **Dunblane Massacre** by visiting the Criminal Justice CourseMate at cengagebrain.com, then access the "Web Links" for this chapter.

There is also evidence that personality disturbance is linked to some physical trait or characteristic. Neuroscientists claim to have found differences in both the limbic system and the prefrontal cortex of the brain that separates aggressive, violent people from the more level headed and reasonable. According to this view, if some defect or injury impairs communication between the limbic system and the frontal cortex, a person might not be entirely able to moderate his or her emotional reactions.[11]

Can treating mental illness reduce violence rates? A recent international survey found a significant relationship between mental health treatment opportunities and violence that may explain trends in crime rates. The survey found that about 5 percent of the decade long drop in the violence rate may be due to expanded mental health treatment.[12]

Human Evolution and Instinct

Some anthropologists trace the roots of violence back to our prehistory, when our ancestors lived in social groups and would fight each other for dominance. The earliest humans would not hesitate to retaliate against aggressors, and it was common for family, tribe, or clan members to protect one another if they were attacked. Tribal/clan leaders attempted to moderate violent outbursts. As humans evolved, they began living in mobile hunting bands, where each member was considered equal, so that there were no dominant peacemakers who could control lethal retaliation. When humans developed agricultural communities, violent retaliation was still routine, but elaborate rules for feuding developed to maintain order.[13]

The presence of violence in early human hunter/gatherer and agricultural communities has convinced some social thinkers that violence is instinctual and a function of human evolution. Sigmund Freud believed that human behavior is shaped by two instinctual drives: *eros*, the life instinct, which drives people toward self-fulfillment and enjoyment, and *thanatos*, the death instinct, which produces self-destruction. Thanatos can be expressed externally (e.g., violence and sadism) or internally (e.g., suicide, alcoholism, or other self-destructive habits).[14]

In his celebrated book *On Aggression*, anthropologist Konrad Lorenz argued that aggressive energy is produced by inbred instincts that are independent of environmental forces.[15] In the animal kingdom, aggression usually serves a productive purpose; for example, it leads members of grazing species such as zebras and antelopes to spread out over available territory to ensure an ample food supply and the survival of the fittest. Lorenz found that humans possess some of the same aggressive instincts as animals. But among lower species, aggression is rarely fatal; when a conflict occurs, the winner is determined through a test of skill or endurance. This inhibition against killing members of their own species protects animals from self-extinction. Humans, lacking this inhibition against fatal violence, are capable of killing their own kind in war or as a result of interpersonal conflicts such as those arising over finding suitable mates.[16]

Lorenz feared that as technology develops and more lethal weapons are produced, the extinction of the human species becomes a significant possibility.

> To read the autobiography of **Konrad Lorenz**, who won the Nobel Prize in medicine in 1973, visit the Criminal Justice CourseMate at cengagebrain.com, then access the "Web Links" for this chapter.

Are Humans Instinctively Violent? In his recent book *Violence: A Micro-sociological Theory*, sociologist Randall Collins proposes a theory of violence that seems diametrically opposed to that of Lorenz: humans are inherently passive, and violence is a function of social interaction. Collins argues that most humans shrink from violent encounters, and even those who talk aggressively are fearful and tense during violent encounters. Humans typically resort to violence only when they have overwhelming superiority over their opponents in terms of arms and numbers. Although the thought of violence makes most people feel weak and scared, a supportive audience helps it become more palatable. Whether it's gang boys acting in a group or terrorists being supported by their leaders, violence is more of a group process than an individual choice.

According to Collins, the myth that humans enjoy bloodshed is perpetuated by media depictions of violence. The barroom brawl, shown in numerous films, is one such example. A fight breaks out in a bar and soon everyone joins in, joyously punching each other and breaking up the premises. When the crowd doesn't join in, they generally make a space for the individuals to fight, cheering and shouting encouragement. Fights are drawn out with two evenly matched opponents punching each other for long periods of combat. Although normative in the movies, Collins points out that these events never actually happen in real life. When a fight does break out, most patrons typically back away to a safe distance and watch, moving away as far as possible. Rather than shouting encouragement, onlookers tend to shrink back vocally as well as physically. And rather than drawn-out brawls, fights are over quickly, typically with a single punch. Most brawlers are willing to quit without a clear-cut victory as soon as a few punches are launched. When there is a group brawl, it's because sides had been chosen beforehand based on social and political views or even sports team loyalty. In these instances, the "free-for-all" that may look

chaotic and unstructured to outsiders is actually carefully organized. Prior organization, group identity, and support, Collins finds, are what enables individuals to overcome their own pervasive fear of violence and confrontation; if it were not well organized, wide-participation group fighting would not be possible.[17]

Substance Abuse

Substance abuse has been associated with violence on both the individual and social levels: substance abusers have higher rates of violence than nonabusers; neighborhoods with high levels of substance abuse have higher violence rates when compared to areas with low use rates.[18] Some research shows that areas with high community levels of addictive drug abuse—crack cocaine and heroin—also experience elevated levels of violent crimes.[19] High use areas also may face social disorganization, poverty, and unemployment, factors that further escalate violence rates.[20] There is a significant association between alcohol abuse and violence, both at the individual and the community level: violence rates are high in neighborhoods that maintain above average access to alcohol via liquor stores, bars, and taverns.[21]

The link between substance abuse and violence appears in three different forms:[22]

- *Psychopharmacological relationship.* Violence may be the direct consequence of ingesting mood-altering substances. Experimental evidence shows that high doses of drugs such as PCP and amphetamines produce violent, aggressive behavior.[23] For example, binge drinking has been closely associated with violent crime rates.[24] Heavy drinking reduces cognitive ability, information processing skills, and the ability to process and react to verbal and nonverbal behavior. As a result, miscommunication becomes more likely and the capacity for rational dialogue is compromised.[25] It is not surprising that males involved in sexual assaults often claim that they were drinking and misunderstood their victims' intentions.[26] Drinking becomes particularly dangerous when abusers have access to firearms; guns and alcohol do not mix well.[27]
- *Economic compulsive behavior.* Drug users resort to violence to obtain the financial resources to support their habit. Studies conducted in the United States and Europe show that addicts commit hundreds of crimes each year.[28]
- *Systemic link.* Violence escalates when drug-dealing gangs flex their muscle to dominate territory and drive out rivals. Studies of gangs that sell drugs show that their violent activities may result in a significant proportion of all urban homicides.[29] Drug dealers/traders also are more likely to carry and use firearms in their daily activities. When Richard Felson and Luke Bonkiewicz studied the drug–violence nexus they found relatively high levels of gun possession among traffickers who

handle stashes of moderately large market value, who have central roles in the trade, and who are members of drug organizations.[30]

Handguns and Firearms

There is a strong and significant association between guns and crime, and some people believe that guns are a cause of lethal violence.[31] Handguns are involved in a significant number of homicides and robberies and are significantly associated with suicide: in any given year, firearms account for over half of all known suicides and two-thirds of all reported homicides. Nonetheless there is no conclusive evidence that guns actually *cause* crime or suicide. It is equally possible that people already intent on killing themselves or someone else choose guns to commit the deed. If guns were not available, they would use some other means: knives, poison, and so forth.

Those who scoff at the guns cause crime argument point to the fact that there are more than 250 million firearms in the United States and that the overwhelming majority of them have not been used for lethal harm. In addition, as the number of firearms rose by more than 40 million between 1990 and 2000, the violence rate showed a significant decline. Criminologist Gary Kleck and some others argue that rather than cause violence, guns may limit bloodshed.[32] He finds that Americans use guns for defensive purposes more than 2 million times a year. Although this figure seems huge, it must be viewed in the context of the total number of guns in the population. Considering these numbers, it is not implausible that 1 percent of the people with access to guns could have used one defensively in a given year.

Guns have other uses. In many assaults, Kleck reasons, the aggressor does not wish to kill but only to scare the victim. Possessing a gun gives aggressors enough killing power so that they may actually be inhibited from attacking. Guns also may enable victims to escape serious injury. Victims may be inhibited from fighting back without losing face; it is socially acceptable to back down from a challenge if the opponent is armed with a gun. Guns then can deescalate a potentially violent situation.[33] Kleck's research has reassured gun advocates who believe that guns can be used for defensive purposes, a belief supported by two recent Supreme Court decisions, *District of Columbia v. Heller* (2008) and *McDonald v. Chicago* (2010), which prohibited states from banning handguns while leaving open regulation.[34]

Of course, the guns–crime debate is unlikely to ever go away. Many criminologists remain skeptical of the benefits of carrying a handgun and question their use as a defensive weapon.[35] They point to research such as that conducted by Tomislav Kovandzic and his colleagues that found that states that have passed "right to carry" laws, which make it easier to own and carry guns, have no lower violence rates than those that strictly control guns.[36]

Socialization and Upbringing

Another view is that improper socialization and upbringing are responsible for the onset of violent acts. Absent or deviant parents, inconsistent discipline, physical abuse, and lack of supervision have all been linked to persistent violent offending.[37]

Although infants demonstrate individual temperaments, who they become may have a lot to do with how they are treated during their early years. Some children are harder to soothe than others; in some cases, difficult infant temperament has been associated with later aggression and behavioral problems.[38] Parents who fail to set adequate limits or to use proper, consistent discipline reinforce a child's coercive behavior.[39] The effects of inadequate parenting and early rejection may affect violent behavior throughout life.[40] There is evidence that children who are maltreated and neglected in early childhood are the ones most likely to be initiated into criminality and thereafter continue or persist in a criminal career.[41]

Children who are subject to even minimal amounts of physical punishment also may be more likely one day to use violence themselves.[42] No one seems to be immune from the effects of exposure to physical abuse during childhood: one recent study found that police officers who had suffered abuse were later abusive to their spouses and children.[43] Sociologist Murray Straus reviewed the concept of discipline in a series of surveys and found a powerful relationship between exposure to physical punishment and later aggression.[44] The effect of physical punishment may be mediated or neutralized to some extent if parents also provide support, warmth, and care. When kids experience physical punishment in the absence of parental involvement, they feel angry and unjustly treated and are more willing to defy their parents and engage in antisocial behavior.[45]

Abused Children Was Caylee Anthony a victim of abuse? Although the jury did not convict, child abuse and its affects are an all too common occurrence. A number of research studies have found that children who are clinically diagnosed as abused later engage in delinquent behaviors, including violence, at a rate significantly greater than that of children who were not abused.[46] Samples of convicted murderers reveal a high percentage of seriously abused youth.[47] The abuse–violence association has been established in many cases in which parents have been killed by their children; sexual abuse is also a constant factor in father (patricide) and mother (matricide) killings.[48] Lewis found in her study of juvenile death row inmates that all had long histories of intense child abuse.[49]

Abuse may have the greatest effect if it is persistent and extends from childhood to adolescence.[50] Children who are physically punished by their parents are likely to physically abuse a sibling and later engage in spouse abuse and other forms of criminal violence.[51] There is evidence that spousal batterers received significantly less love and more punishment from their mothers than did men in a general population comparison group. Abusive childhood experiences may be a key factor in the later development of relationship aggression.[52] Lonnie Athens, a well-known criminologist who links violence to early experiences with child abuse, has coined the phrase **violentization process** to describe how abused kids are turned into aggressive adults.[53] The stages of this process are described in Exhibit 10.1. Athens recognizes that abuse alone is not a sufficient condition to cause someone to become a dangerous violent criminal. One must complete the full cycle of the violentization process—brutalization, belligerence, violent performances, and virulency—to become socialized into violence. Many brutalized children do not go on to become violent criminals, and some later deny that they were abused as youths and redefine their early years as normative.

Exposure to Violence

People who are constantly exposed to violence in the environment may adopt violent methods themselves. Children living in areas marked by extreme violence may eventually become desensitized to the persistent brutality.[54] Much of the difference in violent crime rates between whites and racial minorities can be explained by the fact that the latter are often forced to live in high-crime neighborhoods, which increases their risk of exposure to violence.[55] Areas where people have little confidence in the police and are therefore reluctant to call for help—a condition common in the minority community—may also experience higher levels of violent behavior.[56] Although the racial divide in the United States has narrowed, social and economic inequality still exists, and minority citizens are still forced to live in disorganized neighborhoods, a factor that helps maintain racial and ethnic differences in violence rates.[57]

Social scientist Felton Earls and his associates conducted the Project on Human Development in Chicago Neighborhoods, a government-funded longitudinal study of pathways to violence among 7,000 Chicago area people in 80 randomly selected neighborhoods.[58] Interviews with youths aged 9 to 15 found that large numbers of these children had been victims of or witnesses to violence and that many carry weapons.

Between 30 and 40 percent of the children who reported exposure to violence also displayed significant violent behavior themselves. Earls finds that young teens who witness gun violence are more than twice as likely as non-witnesses to commit violent crime themselves in the following years.[59] Even a single exposure to firearm violence doubles the chance that a young person will later engage in violent behavior.

Children living in these conditions become **crusted over**: they do not let people inside, nor do they express their feelings. They exploit others and in turn are exploited

by those older and stronger; as a result, they develop a sense of hopelessness. They find that parents and teachers focus on their failures and problems, not on their achievements. Consequently, they are vulnerable to the lure of delinquent gangs and groups.[60]

Cultural Values/Subculture of Violence

Violence seems to be concentrated in certain areas of the city that are **hot spots** of crime. Why does this phenomenon occur? To some criminologists the answer involves community level culture and values. Neighborhoods that exhibit collective efficacy—where residents form cohesive groups and where people are willing to intervene when problems occurs—have relatively low violence rates.[61] In contrast, neighborhoods that are disorganized and where poverty is concentrated fail to convey conventional values from one generation to the next. In these areas violence may be the product of cultural beliefs, values, and behaviors that develop to replace those considered conventional.[62]

To explain this phenomenon, criminologists Marvin Wolfgang and Franco Ferracuti formulated the famous concept that some areas contain an independent **subculture of violence**.[63] The norms in the subculture of violence are separate from society's central, dominant value system. In this subculture, a potent theme of violence influences lifestyles, the socialization process, and interpersonal relationships. Even though the subculture's members share some of the dominant culture's values, they expect that violence will be used to solve social conflicts and dilemmas. In some cultural subgroups, then, violence has become legitimized by custom and norms. It is considered appropriate behavior within culturally defined conflict situations in which an individual who has been offended by a negative outcome in a dispute seeks reparations through violent means—a concept referred to as **disputatiousness**.[64]

There is evidence that a subculture of violence may be found in areas that experience concentrated poverty and social disorganization.[65] Though most people abhor violence, income inequality and racial disparity may help instill a sense of hopelessness that nourishes pro-violence norms and values.[66] In these areas people are more likely to carry weapons and to use them in assaults and robberies. Victims are aware of these tactics and are less likely to fight back forcibly when attacked.[67] However, when pressed to the limit, even passive victims may eventually fight back. When Charis Kubrin and Ronald Weitzer studied homicide in St. Louis, Missouri, they discovered that a certain type of killing, referred to as *cultural retaliatory homicide*, is common in neighborhoods that suffer economic disadvantage. In these areas, residents resolve interpersonal conflicts informally—without calling the police—even if it means killing their opponent; neighbors understand and support their violent methods.[68] Because police and other agencies of formal social control are viewed as weak and devalued, understaffed and/or corrupt, people are willing to take matters into their own hands, and violence rates increase accordingly.[69]

The Gang Subculture Criminologists know that violent behavior seems to cluster in particular neighborhoods and communities. Once violence occurs in a neighborhood, the chances for its being repeated skyrockets. One reason for follow-up violence is gang related: once a gang shooting occurs, there is a significant likelihood that retaliation of some sort will occur.[70] It does not come as a surprise, then, that violence rates are highest in urban areas that support teenage gangs.[71] Gang boys are more likely to own guns and other weapons than are non–gang members. They also are more likely to have peers who are gun owners and are more likely to carry guns outside the home.[72]

Many boys are predisposed toward violence before joining a gang, but research shows that once in gangs their violent behavior quickly escalates; after they leave, it significantly declines.[73] Gang members do not kill because they are poor, black, young, or live in a socially disadvantaged neighborhood, but rather because they live in a culture that maintains norms conducive to violent retaliation.[74] When a gang boy kills a rival, murders spread through a process of social contagion as gangs are forced to respond in order to maintain their social status and honor through a display of solidarity. Gang culture associates honor with hypermasculinity and the use of violence to protect reputation. Because formal social control (i.e., the police) is absent in gang areas, violence is condoned or promoted as an acceptable form of social control. The need to conform to cultural values and to protect the gang's rep is more important than individual thoughts and feelings. Although some may link gang violence to "turf wars," disputes that lead to murder are less about a parcel of land than about a gang's status and perceived dominance. The Thinking Like a Criminologist feature focuses on the life of a gang boy and asks the question, "Can he be saved?"

National Values Some nations—including Mexico, Colombia, Angola, Uganda, and Brazil—have relatively high violence rates; others are much more peaceful. A number of national characteristics seem predictive of violence, including approval of violence as a method of retaliation for slights and provocations, a culture that glorifies machismo, political corruption, and an inefficient justice system.[75] Guns are common in these nations because, lacking an efficient justice system, people arm themselves or hire private security forces for protection.[76] In contrast, nations that have a strong communitarian spirit and an emphasis on forgiveness and restorative justice have low violence rates.[77]

Japan has relatively low violence rates because of cultural and economic strengths and a system of exceptionally effective informal social controls that help reduce crime. It also has had a robust economy that may alleviate the stresses that produce violence.[78]

Although the national value argument is persuasive, some criminologists challenge this view, suggesting that nations that have high violence rates also have negative structural factors such as high levels of poverty, income inequality, illiteracy, and high alcohol consumption levels, and its these components, rather than a regional culture of violence, that produce high crime rates.[79] The Race, Culture, Gender, and Criminology feature "The Honor Killing

Can Juan Suarez Be Saved?

The story of prison inmate Juan Suarez is an all-too-familiar account of a life filled with displacement, poverty, and chronic predatory crime. The illegitimate son of a Cuban prostitute in Havana, Suarez was sent to a juvenile reformatory for robbery at the age of 9. After returning home, he lived with his mother and stepfather, who routinely abused him and sold him to child pornographers who used him in sex films with adults. He has told friends that getting a full meal in his childhood was a rare treat.

Suarez emigrated to the United States and soon after became a street thug in Chicago, where he joined the Latin Kings, the city's most notorious gang. After moving to the Bronx, Suarez shot and killed his girlfriend. Sentenced to 20 years to life for aggravated manslaughter, Juan Suarez ended up at Collins Correctional Facility in Helmuth, New York, where he started a New York prison chapter of the Latin Kings. Even while he was in prison segregation, authorities believe he was able to order the leader of the Latin Kings in New York's Rikers Island jail to attack a rival; the victim died after being stabbed. Suarez was then convicted of second-degree murder for ordering the hit.

Suarez now spends 23 hours a day in a 7-by-12-foot cell, allowed one hour to run in a hall outside his cell in a maximum security facility. As his parole date approaches, the head of rehabilitation services at the institution has evaluated Suarez and is convinced that he is above average intelligence and can benefit from community release. In her report, she notes that Suarez is now over 40 years old and has matured and seems ready for change. She recommends that he be made eligible for a program that would allow him to leave the prison grounds for up to 10 hours a day. He would return to the prison at night but would be placed in the general population. If the program is successful, he could be given conditional early parole.

›› **The governor has asked you to investigate the case and make a written recommendation to the parole board. As a criminologist, do you believe that someone like Juan Suarez can change and forgo a life of violence? Would you recommend granting him early release, a special treatment denied to his victims?**

---

of Women and Girls" discusses one type of culturally based violent crime.

American Values Does the United States maintain values that promote violence? According to historian David Courtwright, relatively high violence rates in the United States can be traced to a frontier culture that was characterized by racism and preoccupation with personal honor.[80] Westerners drank heavily and frequented saloons and gambling halls, where petty arguments could become lethal because most patrons carried guns and knives. Violent acts often went unpunished because law enforcement agencies were unable or unwilling to take action. The population of the frontier was mostly young bachelors who were sensitive about honor, morally indifferent, heavily armed, and unchecked by adequate law enforcement. Many died from disease, but others succumbed to drink and violence. Smoking, gambling, and heavy drinking became a cultural imperative, and those who were disinclined to indulge were considered social outcasts. Courtwright claims that over time gender ratios equalized as more men brought families to the frontier and children of both sexes were born. Many men died, returned home, or drifted elsewhere. America's overall male surplus has been disappearing, and a balanced population has helped bring down the violence rate, but remnants of the frontier mentality still exist in contemporary American society.

FORCIBLE RAPE

Rape (from the Latin *rapere,* to take by force) is defined in common law as "the carnal knowledge of a female forcibly and against her will."[81] It is one of the most loathed, misunderstood, and frightening crimes. And, of course, regardless of what form it takes, it can have devastating long-term effects on the victim's emotional and physical well-being.[82]

Under traditional common-law definitions, rape involves nonconsensual sexual intercourse that a male performs against a female he is neither married to nor cohabitating with.[83] There are, of course, other forms of sexual assault, including male on male, female on female, and female on male sexual assaults, but these are not considered within the traditional definition of rape.[84] However, recognizing changing contemporary standards, almost every state has now revised their rape statutes, making them gender neutral.[85] In addition, states now recognize that rape can occur among married couples and people who previously have been sexually intimate.[86]

History of Rape

Rape has been a recognized crime throughout history. It has been the subject of art, literature, film, and theater. Paintings such as the *Rape of the Sabine Women* by Nicolas Poussin,

Race, Culture, Gender, and Criminology
The Honor Killing of Women and Girls

On April 12, 2009, a Jordanian man confessed to stabbing to death his pregnant sister and mutilating her body to protect the family honor. The 28-year-old married woman, who was five months pregnant, was stabbed repeatedly in the face, neck, abdomen, and back and then hacked up with a meat cleaver. She had moved back in with her family after an argument with her husband six months earlier. The brother believed that she had then started seeing other men and had gotten pregnant out of wedlock.

Honor killing and honor crime involve violence against women and girls, including such acts as beating, battering, or killing, by a family member or relative. The attacks are provoked by the belief or perception that an individual's or family's honor has been threatened because of the actual or perceived sexual misconduct of the female. Honor killings are most common in traditional societies in the Middle East, Southwest Asia, India, China, and Latin America. However, the custom is now being exported around the world: in a crime that outraged Germany, a 24-year-old man, identified as Ahmad-Sobair O., killed his sister Morsal on May 15, 2008. He said he had objected to the pretty schoolgirl's lifestyle, her clothing, and her attempts to distance herself from her family. And Germany is not alone. In 2008, Yaser Abdel Said took his two teenaged daughters for a ride in his taxi cab, under the guise of taking them to get something to eat, then drove them to Irving, Texas, where he allegedly shot both girls to death. The reason: they dated boys against

his will. The United Nations estimates that around 5,000 honor killings occur each year, but international women's groups in the Middle East and Southwest Asia suspect there are at least four times that many victims. Most of the victims are young, many are teenagers, slaughtered under a vile tradition that goes back hundreds of years and that now spans half the globe.

Honor killing of a woman or girl by her father, brother, or other male relative may occur because of a suspicion that she engaged in sexual activities before or outside marriage and thus has dishonored the family. Even when rape of a woman or girl has occurred, this may be seen as a violation of the honor of the family for which the female must be killed. Wives' adultery and daughters' premarital "sexual activity," including rape, are seen as extreme violations of the code of behavior and thus may result in the death of the female. Honor killing/crime is based on the shame that a loss of control of the woman or girl brings to the family and to the male head of the family.

According to criminologist Linda Williams, men consider honor killings culturally necessary because any suspicion of sexual activity or suspicion that a girl or a woman was touched by another in a sexual manner is enough to raise questions about the family's honor. Consequently, strict control of women and girls within the home and outside the home is justified. Women are restricted in their activities in the community, religion, and politics. These institutions, in turn, support the control of females. Williams believes the existence of honor killing

is designed to maintain male dominance. Submissiveness may be seen as a sign of sexual purity, and a woman's or girl's attempts to assert her rights can be seen as a violation of the family's honor that needs to be redressed. Rules of honor and threats against females who "violate" such rules reinforce the control of women and have a powerful impact on their lives. Honor killings/crimes serve to keep women and girls from "stepping out of line." The manner in which such behaviors silence women and kill their spirit has led some to label honor killings/crimes more broadly as "femicide."

CRITICAL THINKING

Although we may scoff at honor killings, are there elements of American culture and life that you consider harmful to women that are still tolerated? What can be done to change them?

SOURCES: Robert Fisk, "The Crimewave that Shames the World," *The Independent*, September 7, 2010, www.independent.co.uk/opinion/commentators/fisk/robert-fisk-the-crimewave-that-shames-the-world-2072201.html (accessed August 11, 2011); *Deutsche Welle*, "Afghan-Born German Gets Life for Honor Killing of Sister," February 13, 2009, www.dw-world.de/dw/article/0,,4026518,00.html (accessed June 16, 2009); Dale Gavlak, "Jordan Honor Killing: Man Confesses to Brutally Stabbing to Death Pregnant Sister," *Huffington Post*, April 12, 2009, www.huffingtonpost.com/2009/04/12/jordan-honor-killing-man-_n_185977.html# (accessed August 11, 2011); Linda M. Williams, "Honor Killings," in *Encyclopedia of Interpersonal Violence*, ed. Claire M. Renzetti and Jeffrey I. Edelson (Thousand Oaks, CA: Sage, 2007).

novels such as *Clarissa* by Samuel Richardson, poems such as *The Rape of Lucrece* by William Shakespeare, and films such as *The Accused* and *The Last House on the Left* have sexual violence as their central theme.

In early civilization rape was common. Men staked a claim of ownership on women by forcibly abducting and raping them. This practice led to males' solidification of power and their historical domination of women.[87] Under Babylonian and Hebraic law, the rape of a virgin was a crime

punishable by death. However, if the victim was married, then both she and her attacker were considered equally to blame, and unless her husband intervened, both were put to death.

During the Middle Ages, it was common for ambitious men to abduct and rape wealthy women in an effort to force them into marriage. The practice of "heiress stealing" illustrates how feudal law gave little thought or protection to women and equated them with property.[88] Only in the late

Rape has been the subject of books, poems, and paintings. Here is *The Rape of the Sabine Women* by Nicolas Poussin (1594–1665), which hangs in the Louvre in Paris. In early civilization men staked a claim of ownership on women by forcibly abducting and raping them. This practice led to males' solidification of power and their historical domination of women.

ruling, the surviving Korean women were awarded the equivalent of $2,300 each in compensation.[89] The systematic rape of Bosnian and Kosovar women by Serbian army officers during the civil war in the former Yugoslavia horrified the world during the 1990s. These crimes seemed particularly atrocious because they appeared to be part of an official policy of genocide: rape was deliberately used to impregnate Bosnian women with Serbian children.

On March 9, 1998, Dragoljub Kunarac, 37, a former Bosnian Serb paramilitary commander, admitted before an international tribunal in the Netherlands that he had raped Muslim women during the Bosnian war in 1992. His confession made him the first person to plead guilty to rape as a war crime.[90] Human rights groups have estimated that more than 30,000 women and young girls were sexually abused in the Balkan fighting.

Though shocking, the war crimes discovered in Bosnia have not deterred conquering armies from using rape as a weapon. Pro-government militias in the Darfur region of Sudan were accused of using rape and other forms of sexual violence "as a weapon of war" to humiliate black African women and girls as well as the rebels fighting the Sudanese government in Khartoum.[91] Rape has become epidemic in the Republic of Congo, where the army's notorious 14th brigade has been implicated in many acts of sexual violence, often in the context of massive looting and other attacks on civilians; hundreds of thousands of women are still being raped each year.[92]

fifteenth century, after a monetary economy developed, was forcible sex outlawed. Thereafter, the violation of a virgin caused an economic hardship on her family, who expected a significant dowry for her hand in marriage. However, the law only applied to the wealthy; peasant women and married women were not considered rape victims until well into the sixteenth century. The Christian condemnation of sex during this period was also a denunciation of women as evil, having lust in their hearts, and redeemable only by motherhood. A woman who was raped was almost automatically suspected of contributing to her attack.

Rape and Warfare

The link between warfare and rape is inescapable. Throughout recorded history, soldiers of conquering armies have considered sexual possession of their enemies' women one of the spoils of war. Among the ancient Greeks, rape was socially acceptable within the rules of warfare. During the Crusades, even knights and pilgrims, ostensibly bound by vows of chivalry and Christian piety, took time to rape as they marched toward Constantinople.

The belief that women are part of the spoils of war has continued. During World War II, the Japanese army forced as many as 200,000 Korean women into frontline brothels, where they were repeatedly raped. In a 1998 Japanese

Incidence of Rape

According to the most recent UCR data (2010), about 84,000 rapes or attempted rapes are now being reported to U.S. police each year, a rate of about 60 per 100,000 women in the population.[93] Like other violent crimes, the rape rate has been in a two decade-long decline, and the 2010 totals are significantly below the 84 women per 100,000 whom were rape victims twenty years earlier.

Population density influences the rape rate. Metropolitan areas today have rape rates significantly higher than rural areas; nonetheless, urban areas have experienced a

The Criminological Enterprise
Rape in America

Rape has routinely been considered one of the most underreported crimes, and the data produced by both the NCVS and UCR is problematic. To create a better estimate of rape incidence, Dean Kilpatrick and his research team surveyed more than 5,000 women across the nation. Their data indicate that about 20 million out of 112 million women (18 percent) in the United States have been raped during their lifetime. This includes an estimated 18 million women who have been forcibly raped, nearly 3 million women who have experienced drug-facilitated rape (these rapes occur when the perpetrator deliberately gives the victim drugs without her permission or tries to get her drunk, and then commits an unwanted sexual act), and 3 million women who have experienced incapacitated rape (an unwanted sexual act that occurs after the victim voluntarily used drugs or alcohol). In a single year, more than 1 million women in the United States are raped: more than 800,000 are forcibly raped, nearly 200,000 experience drug-facilitated rape, and about 300,000 experience incapacitated rape. The survey indicates that in contrast to the trends found in official crime sources, rape has not significantly declined in recent decades.

Although co-eds may think they are immune, the survey estimates that more than 11 percent of college women have been raped. In a single year alone, 300,000 college women, 5 percent of total college women, are raped, either forcibly while incapacitated or because they have been drugged.

One of the study's more striking findings is that only 16 percent of all rapes were reported to law enforcement authorities; only 12 percent of the college girls who were raped reported the incident to police. Underreporting helps explain the discrepancy between the survey findings and UCR data. Notably, victims of drug-facilitated or incapacitated rape were somewhat less likely to report it to the authorities than were victims of forcible rape. Major barriers to reporting rape to law enforcement included not wanting others to know about the rape, fear of retaliation, perception of insufficient evidence, uncertainty about how to report, and uncertainty about whether a crime was committed or whether harm was intended.

CRITICAL THINKING

Why do you suppose so few college girls report sexual assaults despite efforts to educate them about rape victimization and its prevention? What can be done to get more victims to report attacks? Would this help lower the number of campus rapes?

SOURCE: Dean G. Kilpatrick, Heidi S. Resnick, Kenneth J. Ruggiero, Lauren M. Conoscenti, and Jenna McCauley, "Drug-facilitated, Incapacitated, and Forcible Rape: A National Study U.S. Department of Justice, 2007," www.ncjrs.gov/pdffiles1/nij/grants/219181.pdf (accessed August 11, 2011).

much greater drop in rape reports than rural areas. The police make arrests in slightly more than half of all reported rape offenses. Of the offenders arrested, typically about half are under 25 years of age, and about two-thirds are white. The racial and age pattern of rape arrests has been fairly consistent for some time. Finally, rape is a warm-weather crime—most incidents occur during July and August, with the lowest rates occurring during December, January, and February.

These data must be interpreted with caution because rape is a traditionally underreported crime. According to the National Crime Victimization Survey (NCVS), almost 125,000 rapes and attempted rapes take place each year, suggesting that many rape incidents are not reported to police.[94] However, as The Criminological Enterprise feature shows, even the NCVS surveys may significantly undercount rape.

Why is rape, one of the most serious violent crimes, also one of the most underreported? Many victims fail to report rapes because they are embarrassed, believe nothing can be done, or blame themselves. Some victims of sexual assaults may even question whether they have really been raped. When the assault involves an acquaintance, such as a boyfriend, and the victim had been drinking or taking drugs, research indicates that the victim is unlikely to label her situation as being a "real" rape.[95] Similarly, if the assault involved oral or digital sex, it is less likely to be labeled a "real" rape. Women are more likely to report rape when it is committed by a stranger who uses a weapon or causes physical injury, or when the rape occurred in a public place—or, if at home, was the result of a "home blitz" (in which an attacker broke in or entered without permission).[96] Therefore, it is likely that many acquaintance rapes and date rapes go unreported.

In addition to victim uncertainty over what constitutes rape, definitions of rape differ between state criminal codes, confusing the issue even further. As a result, using national victim surveys and/or official UCR data to create a valid measure of the true incidence of rape can be problematic.[97] There may be many more rape victims than the official data report.[98] Even if victims fail to acknowledge that their attack was "real" and refuse to report it to the police, the experience can have devastating psychological effects that last long after the attack has been completed.[99]

EXHIBIT 10.2

Varieties of Forcible Rape

- *Anger rape.* This rape occurs when sexuality becomes a means of expressing and discharging pent-up anger and rage. The rapist uses far more brutality than would have been necessary if his real objective had been simply to have sex with his victim. His aim is to hurt his victim as much as possible; the sexual aspect of rape may be an afterthought.
- *Power rape.* This type of rape involves an attacker who does not want to harm his victim as much as he wants to possess her sexually. His goal is sexual conquest, and he uses only the amount of force necessary to achieve his objective. The power rapist wants to be in control, to be able to dominate women and have them at his mercy.
- *Sadistic rape.* This type of rape involves both sexuality and aggression. The sadistic rapist is caught up in ritual—he may torment his victim, bind her, or torture her. Victims are usually related, in the rapist's view, to a personal characteristic that he wants to harm or destroy.

SOURCE: A. Nicholas Groth and Jean Birnbaum, *Men Who Rape* (New York: Plenum Press, 1979).

Types of Rape and Rapists

Some rapes are planned, others are spontaneous; some focus on a particular victim, whereas others occur almost as an afterthought during the commission of another crime, such as a burglary. Some rapists commit a single crime, whereas others are multiple offenders; some attack alone, and others engage in group or gang rapes.[100] Some use force to attack their target, others prey upon those who are incapacitated by drugs and alcohol.[101] Because there is no single type of rape or rapist, criminologists have attempted to define and categorize the vast variety of rape situations.

Criminologists now recognize that there are numerous motivations for rape and as a result various types of rapists. One of the best-known attempts to classify the personalities of rapists was made by psychologist A. Nicholas Groth, an expert on classifying and treating sex offenders. In a now classic study, Groth discovered that every rape encounter contains at least one of these three elements: anger, power, or sadism (Exhibit 10.2).[102] In treating rape offenders, Groth found that about 55 percent were of the power type; about 40 percent, the anger type; and about 5 percent, the sadistic type.[103]

Gang Rape Some research studies estimates that as many as 25 percent or more of rapes involve multiple offenders.[104] There is generally little difference in the demographic characteristics of single- or multiple-victim rapes. However, women who are attacked by multiple offenders are subject to more violence, such as beatings and the use of weapons, and the rapes are more likely to be completed than individual rapes. **Gang rape** victims are more likely to resist and face injury than those attacked by single offenders. They are more likely to call police, to seek therapy, and to contemplate suicide. Gang rapes, then, as might be expected, are more severe in violence and outcome.

Serial Rape Some rapists are one-time offenders, but others engage in multiple or **serial rapes**. Some serial rapists constantly increase their use of force; others do not. Research by Janet Warren and her associates determined that increasers (about 25 percent of serial rapists) tend to be white males who attack multiple victims who are typically older than the norm. During these attacks, the rapist uses excessive profanity and takes more time than during typical rapes. Increasers have a limited criminal history for other crimes, a fact suggesting that their behavior is focused almost solely on sexual violence.[105]

Some serial rapists commit "blitz rapes," in which they attack their victims without warning, whereas others try to "capture" their victims by striking up a conversation or offering them a ride. Others use personal or professional relationships to gain access to their targets.[106]

Acquaintance Rape **Acquaintance rape** involves someone known to the victim, including family members and friends. Included within acquaintance rapes are the subcategories of **date rape**, which involves a sexual attack during a courting relationship; **statutory rape**, in which the victim is underage; and **marital rape**, which is forcible sex between people who are legally married to each other.[107] It is difficult to estimate the ratio between rapes involving strangers and those in which victim and assailant are in some way acquainted because women may be more reluctant to report acts involving acquaintances. By some estimates, about 50 percent of rapes involve acquaintances, a number that is not surprising considering the prevalence of negative attitudes toward women and attitudes that support sexual coercion among some groups of young men.[108] Stranger rapes are typically more violent than acquaintance rapes; attackers are more likely to carry a weapon, threaten the victim, and harm her physically. Stranger rapes also may be less likely to be prosecuted than acquaintance rapes because victims may be more reluctant to recount their ordeal at trial if the attack involved a stranger than if their attacker was someone they knew or had been involved with in an earlier relationship.[109]

Date Rape Date rape was first identified as a significant social problem in the 1980s when Mary Koss conducted surveys finding that a significant number of college-age women had been sexually assaulted by a dating partner; about 27 percent of the respondents were the victim of rape or attempted rape. However, only about a quarter of the women considered what had happened to them "real" rape; the majority either blamed themselves or denied they had really been raped.[110] The Koss research helped identify a social problem that had remained below the radar for far too long.

There is no single form of date rape. Some occur on first dates, others after a relationship has been developing, and still others occur after the couple has been involved for some time. In long-term or close relationships, the male partner may feel he has invested so much time and money in his partner that he is owed sexual relations or that sexual intimacy is an expression that the involvement is progressing. He may make comparisons to other couples who have dated as long and are sexually active.[111] Some use a variety of strategies to coerce sex, including getting their dates drunk, threatening them with termination of the relationship, threatening to disclose negative information, making them feel guilty, or uttering false promises (such as "we'll get engaged") to obtain sex.[112]

Date rape is believed to be frequent on college campuses. It has been estimated that 15 to 30 percent of all college women are victims of rape or attempted rape. A 2006 survey of college women found that 27 percent of the sample had experienced unwanted sexual contact ranging from kissing and petting to sexual intercourse.[113]

The actual incidence of date rape may be even higher than surveys indicate because many victims blame themselves and do not recognize the incident as a rape, saying, for example, "I should have fought back harder" or "I shouldn't have gotten drunk."[114] Victims tend to have a history of excessive drinking and prior sexuality, conditions that may convince them that their intemperate and/or immoderate behavior contributed to their own victimization.[115] Some victims do not report rapes because they do not view their experience as a real rape, which, they believe, involves a strange man "jumping out of the bushes." Other victims are embarrassed and frightened. Many will tell their friends about their rape but refuse to let authorities know what happened; reporting is most common in the most serious cases, such as when a weapon is used; it is less common when drugs and alcohol are involved.[116]

Marital Rape   In 1978, Greta Rideout filed rape charges against her husband, John. This Oregon case grabbed headlines because it was the first in which a husband was prosecuted for raping his wife while sharing a residence with her. John was acquitted, and the couple briefly reconciled; later, continued violent episodes culminated in divorce and a jail term for John.[117]

Traditionally, a legally married husband could not be charged with raping his wife; this was referred to as the **marital exemption**. The origin of this legal doctrine can be traced to the sixteenth-century pronouncement of Matthew Hale, England's chief justice, who wrote:

> But the husband cannot be guilty of rape committed by himself upon his lawful wife, for by their mutual matrimonial consent and contract the wife hath given up herself in this kind unto the husband which she cannot retract.[118]

However, research indicates that many women are raped each year by their husbands as part of an overall pattern of spousal abuse, and these women deserve the protection of the law. Many spousal rapes are accompanied by brutal, sadistic beatings and have little to do with normal sexual interests.[119] Not surprisingly, the marital exemption has undergone significant revision. In 1980, only three states had laws against marital rape; today every state recognizes marital rape as a crime.[120] Piercing the marital exemption is not unique to U.S. courts; more than 100 nations have abolished the marital exemption.[121] However, although marital rape is now recognized, most states do not give wives the same legal protection as they would nonmarried couples, and when courts do recognize marital rape, the perpetrators are sanctioned less harshly than are those accused of nonmarital sexual assaults.[122] For example, in 30 states, a husband is exempt from charges of rape when he does not have to use force; because of the marital contract, a wife's consent is assumed unless she overtly refuses her husband's advances. The existence of some spousal exemptions in the majority of states indicates that rape in marriage is still treated as a lesser crime than other forms of rape.[123]

Statutory Rape   The term *statutory rape* refers to sexual relations between an underage minor and an adult. Although the sex is not forced or coerced, the law says that young people are incapable of giving informed consent, so the act is legally considered nonconsensual. Typically a state's law will define an age of consent above which there can be no criminal prosecution for sexual relations. Although each state is different, most evaluate the age differences between the parties to determine whether an offense has taken place. For example, Indiana law mandates prosecution of men aged 21 or older who have consensual sex with girls younger than 14. In some states, defendants can claim they mistakenly assumed their victims were above the age of consent, whereas in others, "mistake-of-age" defenses are ignored. An American Bar Association (ABA) survey found that prosecution is often difficult in statutory rape cases because the young victims are reluctant to testify. Often parents have given their blessing to the relationships, and juries are reluctant to convict men involved in consensual sex even with young teenage girls.[124]

The Causes of Rape

What factors predispose some men to commit rape? Criminologists' responses to this question are almost as varied as the crime itself. However, most explanations can be grouped into a few consistent categories.

Evolutionary, Biological Factors   One explanation is that rape may be instinctual, developed over the ages as a means of perpetuating the species. In more primitive times, forcible sexual contact may have helped spread genes and maximize offspring. Some believe that these prehistoric drives remain: males still have a natural sexual drive that encourages them to have intimate relations with as many women as possible. The evolutionary view is that the sexual urge corresponds to the unconscious need to preserve the species by spreading one's genes as widely as possible.[125] Men who are sexually aggressive will have a reproductive edge over their more passive peers.[126]

Male Socialization   Some researchers argue that rape is a function of modern male socialization. Some men have been socialized to be aggressive with women and believe that the use of violence or force is legitimate if their sexual advances are rebuffed—that is, "women like to play hard to get and expect to be forced to have sex." Those men who have been socialized to believe that "no means yes" are more likely to be sexually aggressive. The use of sexual violence is aggravated if pro-force socialization is reinforced by peer group members who share similar values.[128]

Diana Russell, a leading expert on sexual violence, suggests that rape is actually not a deviant act but one that conforms to the qualities regarded as masculine in U.S. society.[129] Russell maintains that from an early age boys are taught to be aggressive, forceful, tough, and dominating. Men are taught to dominate at the same time that they are led to believe that women want to be dominated. Russell describes this as the **virility mystique**—the belief that males must separate their sexual feelings from needs for love, respect, and affection. She believes men are socialized to be the aggressors and expect to be sexually active with many women; consequently, male virginity and sexual inexperience are shameful. Similarly, sexually aggressive women frighten some men and cause them to doubt their own masculinity. Sexual insecurity may lead some men to commit rape to bolster their self-image and masculine identity.[130]

Feminists suggest that as the nation moves toward gender equality there may be an immediate increase in rape rates because of increased threats to male virility and dominance. However, in the long term, gender equality will reduce rape rates because there will be an improved social climate toward women.[131]

Psychological Abnormality   Another view is that rapists suffer from some type of personality disorder or mental illness. Research shows that a significant percentage of incarcerated rapists exhibit psychotic tendencies, and many others have hostile, sadistic feelings toward women.[132] A high proportion of serial rapists and repeat sexual offenders exhibit psychopathic personality structures.[133] There is evidence linking rape proclivity with **narcissistic personality disorder**, a pattern of traits and behaviors that indicate infatuation and fixation with one's self to the exclusion of all others and the egotistic and ruthless pursuit of one's gratification, dominance, and ambition.[134]

Social Learning   This perspective submits that men learn to commit rapes much as they learn any other behavior.

For example, sexual aggression may be learned through interaction with peers who articulate attitudes supportive of sexual violence.[135] Nicholas Groth found that 40 percent of the rapists he studied were sexually victimized as adolescents.[136] A growing body of literature links personal sexual trauma with the desire to inflict sexual trauma on others.[137] Watching violent or pornographic films featuring women who are beaten, raped, or tortured has been linked to sexually aggressive behavior in men.[138]

Sexual Motivation   Most criminologists believe rape is a violent act that is not sexually motivated, but it might be premature to dismiss the sexual motive from all rapes.[139] NCVS data reveal that rape victims tend to be young and that rapists prefer younger, presumably more attractive, victims. Data show an association between the ages of rapists and their victims, indicating that men choose rape targets of approximately the same age as consensual sex partners. And, although younger criminals are usually the most violent, older rapists tend to harm their victims more than younger rapists. This pattern indicates that older criminals may rape for motives of power and control, whereas younger offenders may be seeking sexual gratification and therefore be less likely to harm their victims.

Rape and the Law

Unlike other crime victims, women may find that their claim of sexual assault is greeted with some skepticism by police and court personnel.[140] They will soon find they have to prove that they did not engage in sex only to have remorse afterward.[141] Police officers may be hesitant to make arrests and testify in court when the alleged assaults do not yield obvious signs of violence or struggle (presumably showing the victim strenuously resisted the attack). However, police and courts are now becoming more sensitive to the plight of rape victims and are just as likely to investigate acquaintance rapes as they are **aggravated rapes** involving multiple offenders, weapons, and victim injuries. In some jurisdictions, the justice system takes all rape cases seriously and does not ignore those in which victim and attacker have had a prior relationship or those that did not involve serious injury.[142]

Proving Rape   The world was rocked in 2011 when Dominique Strauss-Kahn, the distinguished head of the International Monetary Fund and a leading French politician, was arrested for allegedly raping a hotel maid who had entered his room. Equally stunning was the news of July 1, 2011: the maid had lied about a number of details, throwing the case into disarray and forcing the prosecution to rescind Strauss-Kahn's order of home confinement pending trial. Among the revelations: prosecutors admitted that the victim cleaned another room following the encounter with the French politician and then returned to Strauss-Kahn's room and cleaned that as well before calling the police![143]

Profiles in Crime
The Duke Rape Case

On March 13, 2006, after a "performance" by strippers at a private residence, three members of Duke University's men's lacrosse team allegedly raped one of the women who had been hired to entertain the team. The three players, David Evans, Reade Seligmann, and Collin Finnerty, were charged with first-degree forcible rape, first-degree sexual offense, and kidnapping.

Media outlets had a field day with the case: the young woman was African American and the players were white. The event soon drew national media attention and highlighted racial tensions not only in Durham, North Carolina, where the crime took place, but across the entire nation. The accused boys were wealthy, attractive, and successful. Did they actually believe they could rape a poor young minority woman and get away with the crime because of their power and position? Members of the community demanded justice, the public voiced its outrage, and school officials suspended the accused students, dismissed the coach, and cancelled the lacrosse team's season.

Despite initial shock, public sentiment began to shift as the facts of the case were leaked to the press. There was a lack of physical evidence, the victim's story constantly changed, her character was questioned, there were changes to and inconsistencies in her story, and the second stripper did not back up her story. Most damaging, the press got hold of testimony by a lab director that the prosecutor, Durham District Attorney Mike Nifong, deliberately withheld evidence from the defense that might have cleared the suspects (e.g., DNA from other men, but not the Duke players, was found on the victim's body). On December 22, 2006, Nifong dropped the rape charges against the three indicted players. After ethics charges were filed against him, Nifong asked to be removed, and on January 13, 2007, North Carolina Attorney General Roy Cooper agreed to take over the case. Soon after, Duke University announced that Finnerty and Seligmann had been invited to return to school while they awaited trial and were eligible to rejoin the team (David Evans had already graduated). On April 11, 2007, all remaining charges were dropped against the three players, and in an ironic turnabout, Nifong was brought up on misconduct charges, during which he abruptly resigned his post; he was later stripped of his law license.

The case is troubling because it supports the notion that a great many rape accusations are false, making it more difficult to prosecute and gain conviction in those that are valid.

SOURCES: Susannah Meadows and Evan Thomas, "A Troubled Spring at Duke: A Lacrosse-Team Party Spawns Charges of Rape," *Newsweek*, April 10, 2006, www.highbeam.com/doc/1G1-144103126.html (accessed August 11, 2011); "Duke Lacrosse 'Rape' Accuser Changes Story Again, Says Seligmann Didn't Touch Her," Associated Press, January 12, 2007, www.foxnews.com/story/0,2933,243063,00.html (accessed August 11, 2011); Sal Ruibal, "Rape Allegations Cast Pall at Duke," *USA Today*, March 29, 2006, www.usatoday.com/sports/college/lacrosse/2006-03-29-duke-fallout_x.htm (accessed August 11, 2011).

She lied on her application for citizenship, and mysterious bank deposits kept popping up that may have been linked to criminal activity. In the end, the case went up in smoke. The victim's lack of credibility eventually resulted in the termination of prosecution.

In cases such as this, when the victim's character and behavior seem tainted, proving guilt is extremely challenging for prosecutors. Although the law does not recognize it, jurors are sometimes swayed by the insinuation that the victim lied or that the sexual encounter was consensual or victim precipitated, shifting the blame from rapist to victim. To get a conviction, prosecutors must establish that the act was forced and not voluntary. Consequently, there may be some reluctance to prosecute cases in which questions about the victim's moral character or demeanor and attitude (e.g., she was dressed provocatively) will turn off the jury and undermine the chance of conviction.[144] Prosecutors may be more willing to bring charges in interracial rape cases because they know juries are more likely to believe victims and convict defendants involved in interracial rape than in intraracial rapes.[145]

As well, there is always fear that a frightened and traumatized victim may identify the wrong man, which happened in the case of Dennis Maher, a Massachusetts man freed after spending more than 19 years in prison for rapes he did not commit. Although three victims provided eyewitness identification at trial, DNA testing proved that Maher could not have been the rapist.[146] The Profiles in Crime feature discusses one of the nation's most notorious false rape accusations.

Consent Rape represents a major legal challenge to the criminal justice system for a number of reasons.[147] One issue involves the concept of **consent**. It is essential to prove that the attack was forced and that the victim did not give voluntary consent to her attacker. In a sense, the burden of proof is on the victim to show that her character is beyond question and that she in no way encouraged, enticed, or misled the accused rapist. On the other hand, some states, such as California and Illinois, now recognize that, once given, consent can be withdrawn if a woman changes her mind about sex even after relations have begun. Once she says stop, the act must end or else a rape has occurred.

Proving victim dissent is not a requirement in any other violent crime. For example, robbery victims do not have to prove they did not entice their attackers by flaunting expensive jewelry; yet the defense counsel in a rape case can create reasonable doubt about the woman's credibility. A common defense tactic is to introduce suspicion in the minds of the jury that the woman may have consented to the sexual act and later regretted her decision. Even the appearance of impropriety can undermine a case. When Kobe Bryant was accused of raping a young woman in 2003, the alleged victim was described in the press as being promiscuous, suicidal, mentally ill, a gold digger, on drugs, and so on; she was harassed by Kobe's fans; three men were actually jailed for making threats.[148] When she refused to testify, the charges were dropped; a civil suit was later settled out of court. Research shows that people are more likely to "blame the victim" in a case of sexual assault than they are in other common-law crimes such as armed robbery. Victim blaming is exacerbated if a prior relationship existed or if the victim did not fight back because she was intoxicated, factors that have less impact in other crimes.[149] And even when a defendant is found guilty in a sexual assault case, punishment is significantly reduced if the victim's personal characteristics are viewed as being negative (e.g., transient, hitchhiker, gold digger, or substance abuser).[150] Proving the victim had good character is not a requirement in any other crime.

Conversely, it is difficult for a prosecuting attorney to establish that a woman's character is so impeccable that the absence of consent is a certainty. Such distinctions are important in rape cases because male jurors may be sympathetic to the accused if the victim is portrayed as unchaste. Referring to the woman as "sexually liberated" or "promiscuous" may be enough to result in exoneration of the accused, even if violence and brutality were used in the attack.[151] When Cassia Spohn and David Holleran studied prosecutors' decisions in rape cases, they found that perception of the victim's character was still a critical factor in their decision to file charges. In cases involving acquaintance rape, prosecutors were reluctant to file charges when the victim's character was questioned—for example, when police reports described the victim as sexually active or engaged in a sexually oriented occupation such as stripper. In cases involving strangers, prosecutors were more likely to take action if a gun or knife was used. Spohn and Holleran state that prosecutors are still influenced by perceptions of what constitutes "real rape" and who are "real victims."[152]

Reform   Because of the difficulty rape victims have in obtaining justice, rape laws have been changing around the country. Efforts for reform include changing the language of statutes, dropping the condition of victim resistance, and changing the requirement of use of force to include the threat of force or injury.[153] A number of states and the federal government have replaced rape laws with the more gender-neutral term "crimes of sexual assault."[154] Sexual assault laws outlaw any type of forcible sex, including homosexual rape.[155]

Most states and the federal government have developed **shield laws**, which protect women from being questioned about their sexual history unless it directly bears on the case.

In some instances these laws are quite restrictive, whereas in others they grant the trial judge considerable discretion to admit prior sexual conduct in evidence if it is deemed relevant for the defense. In an important 1991 case, *Michigan v. Lucas*, the U.S. Supreme Court upheld the validity of shield laws and ruled that excluding evidence of a prior sexual relationship between the parties did not violate the defendant's right to a fair trial.[156]

In addition to requiring evidence that consent was not given, the common law of rape required corroboration that the crime of rape actually took place. This involved the need for independent evidence from police officers, physicians, and witnesses that the accused was actually the person who committed the crime, that sexual penetration took place, and that force was present and consent absent. This requirement shielded rapists from prosecution in cases in which the victim delayed reporting the crime or when physical evidence had been compromised or lost. Corroboration is no longer required except under extraordinary circumstances, such as when the victim is too young to understand the crime, has had a previous sexual relationship with the defendant, or gives a version of events that is improbable and self-contradictory.[157]

The federal government may have given rape victims another source of redress when it passed the Violence Against Women Act in 1994. This statute allows rape victims to sue in federal court on the grounds that sexual violence violates their civil rights; the provisions of the act have so far been upheld by appellate courts.[158]

International Trends   Rape reform is not unique to the United States and has become an international movement.[159] A number of nations have made rape a gender-neutral crime. For example, South Africa removed gender from its rape law in 1988, dropping the restriction that perpetrators be male and victims female. The Caribbean nations of Antigua and Barbuda dropped their marital-exclusion clause in 1995, thereafter criminalizing nonconsensual sex between a husband and wife. The kinds of persons and acts subject to and protected by rape laws have expanded dramatically. In Zimbabwe, Article 8 of the 2001 Sexual Offences Act punishes any kind of illegal sexual assault with the same kind of penalties provided by law for rape. With this reform, Zimbabwe greatly increased the range of nonconsensual sexual activities that fall under the umbrella of rape. There has also been an international effort to unify rape laws so that they apply equally to men and women of all classes and statuses. For example, in the South American nation of Paraguay until 1989 Article 315 of that nation's penal code (*Código Penal*) set harsher penalties for the rape of a married woman (four to eight years in prison) than for the rape of an unmarried woman (three to six years), even if the latter were "an honest woman of good name." Why the distinction? It was assumed that the rapist could make things right by marrying his victim if she was an unmarried woman! Today, few codes still include such differential treatments.

To read a report on a **victim-oriented approach to dealing with statutory rape**, visit the Criminal Justice CourseMate at cengagebrain.com, then access the "Web Links" for this chapter.

MURDER AND HOMICIDE

Murder is defined in common law as "the unlawful killing of a human being with malice aforethought."[160] It is the most serious of all common-law crimes and the only one that can still be punished by death. Western society's abhorrence of murderers is illustrated by the fact that there is no statute of limitations in murder cases. Whereas state laws limit prosecution of other crimes to a fixed period, usually 7 to 10 years, accused killers can be brought to justice at any time after their crimes were committed.

To legally prove that a murder has taken place, most state jurisdictions require prosecutors to show that the accused maliciously intended to kill the victim. "Express or actual malice" is the state of mind assumed to exist when someone kills another person in the absence of any apparent provocation. "Implied or constructive malice" is considered to exist when a death results from negligent or unthinking behavior. In these cases, even though the perpetrator did not wish to kill the victim, the killing resulted from an inherently dangerous act and therefore is considered murder. An unusual example of this concept is the attempted murder conviction of Ignacio Perea, an AIDS-infected Miami man who kidnapped and raped an 11-year-old boy. Perea was sentenced to up to 25 years in prison when the jury agreed with the prosecutor's contention that the AIDS virus is a deadly weapon.[161]

Degrees of Murder

There are different levels, or degrees, of homicide.[162] *First-degree murder* occurs when a person kills another after premeditation and deliberation. **Premeditation** means that the killing was considered beforehand and suggests that it was motivated by more than a simple desire to engage in an act of violence. **Deliberation** means the killing was planned after careful thought rather than carried out on impulse: "To constitute a deliberate and premeditated killing, the slayer must weigh and consider the question of killing and the reasons for and against such a choice; having in mind the consequences, he decides to and does kill."[163] The planning implied by this definition need not be a long process; it may be an almost instantaneous decision to take another's life. Also, a killing accompanying a felony, such as robbery or rape, usually constitutes first-degree murder (**felony murder**).

Second-degree murder requires the killer to have malice aforethought but not premeditation or deliberation.

A second-degree murder occurs when a person's wanton disregard for the victim's life and his or her desire to inflict serious bodily harm on the victim, usually with a weapon, results in the victim's death.

Homicide without malice is called **manslaughter** and is usually punished by anywhere from 1 to 15 years in prison. *Voluntary* or **nonnegligent manslaughter** refers to a killing, typically without a weapon, committed in the heat of passion or during a sudden quarrel that provoked violence. Although intent may be present, malice is not. **Involuntary manslaughter,** or **negligent manslaughter,** refers to a killing that occurs when a person's acts are negligent and without regard for the harm they may cause others. Most involuntary manslaughter cases involve motor vehicle deaths—for example, when a drunk driver kills a pedestrian. However, one can be held criminally liable for the death of another in any instance where disregard of safety kills.

Deliberate Indifference Murder Murder is often considered to be an intentional act, but a person can also be held criminally liable for the death of another even if he or she did not intend to injure another person but exhibited *deliberate indifference* to the danger his or her actions might cause. The deliberate indifference standard is met when a person knows of, and yet disregards or ignores, an excessive risk to another's health or safety. For example, during a barroom fight one participant hurls a heavy beer mug at another, missing him but fatally hitting another patron in the head. Though the perpetrator had no intention of killing another person, he should have known that hurling a heavy beer mug could cause a fatal injury.

One of the most famous cases illustrating deliberate indifference murder occurred on January 26, 2001, when Diane Whipple, a San Francisco woman, died after two large dogs attacked her in the hallway of her apartment building. One of the dogs' owners/keepers, Robert Noel, was found guilty of manslaughter, and his wife, Marjorie Knoller, was convicted on charges of second-degree murder because they knew that the dogs were highly dangerous but did little or nothing to control their behavior. Their deliberate indifference put their neighbor at risk with tragic consequences. After a long series of appeals, on June 1, 2007, the California Supreme Court ruled that a dog owner who knows the animal is a potential killer and exposes other people to that danger may be guilty of murder even though he or she did not intend for that particular victim to be injured or killed. In a unanimous decision, the appellate court ruled that Knoller could be convicted of murder because she acted with "conscious disregard of the danger to human life." On September 22, 2008, a California court sentenced Knoller to serve 15 years to life for the death of Diane Whipple.[164]

"Born and Alive" One issue that has received national attention is whether a murder victim can be a fetus that has not yet been delivered; this is referred to as **feticide**. In some instances, fetal harm involves a mother whose behavior endangers an unborn child; in other cases, feticide results from the harmful action of a third party.

Some states have prosecuted women for endangering or killing their unborn fetuses by their drug or alcohol abuse. Some of these convictions have been overturned because the law applies only to a "human being who has been born and is alive."[165] However, in *Whitner v. State*, the Supreme Court of South Carolina ruled that a woman could be held liable for actions during pregnancy that could affect her viable fetus.[166] In holding that a fetus is a "viable person," the court opened the door for a potential homicide prosecution if a mother's action resulted in fetal death. As for third-party actions, only 12 states still follow the common law "born alive" rule: Colorado, Connecticut, Delaware, Hawaii, Montana, New Hampshire, New Jersey, New Mexico, North Carolina, Oregon, Vermont, and Wyoming. In contrast, a number of states have passed legislation creating a separate class of crime that increases criminal penalties when a person causes injury to a woman he or she knows is pregnant, and the injury results in miscarriage or still birth. At the federal level, The Unborn Victims of Violence Act of 2004 makes it a separate crime to harm a fetus during an assault on the mother. If the attack causes death or bodily injury to a child who is *in utero* at the time the conduct takes place, the penalty is the same as that for conduct had the injury or death occurred to the unborn child's mother.

There is still a great deal of state-to-state variation in feticide laws. Some make it a separate crime to kill a fetus or commit an act of violence against a pregnant woman. Others have a viability requirement: feticide can only occur if the unborn child could at the time potentially live outside the mother's body.[167]

The Nature and Extent of Murder

It is possible to track U.S. murder rate trends from 1900 to the present with the aid of coroners' reports and UCR data. The murder rate peaked in 1933, a time of high unemployment and lawlessness, and then fell until 1958. Then the homicide rate began to skyrocket, doubling from the mid-1960s to a peak in 1991, when almost 25,000 people were killed in a single year, a rate of about 10 per 100,000 people. The murder rate has since been in a decline. In 2010, there were about 15,000 murders, a rate of less than 5.5 per 100,000 population.

What else do official crime statistics tell us about murder today? Murder tends to be an urban crime. More than half of homicides occur in cities with a population of 100,000 or more; almost one-quarter of homicides occur in cities with a

population of more than 1 million. Why is homicide an urban phenomenon? Large cities experience the greatest rates of structural disadvantage—poverty, joblessness, racial heterogeneity, residential mobility, family disruption, and income inequality—which are linked to high murder rates.[168] Not surprisingly, large cities are much more commonly the site of drug-related killings and gang-related murders, and relatively less likely to be the location of family-related homicides, including murders of intimates.

Murder victims and offenders tend to be males: about 80 percent of homicide victims and nearly 90 percent of offenders are male. Males are more likely to kill others of similar social standing in more public contexts; women kill family members and intimate partners in private locations.[169]

Murder, like rape, tends to be an intraracial crime: about 90 percent of victims are slain by members of their own race. About half of all murder victims are African Americans. Approximately one-third of murder victims and almost half of the offenders are under the age of 25. As Figure 10.2 shows, the rate per 100,000 peaks in the 18- to 24-year-old age group, while adults over 25 and adolescents suffer similar murder rates.

Some murders involve very young children, a crime referred to as **infanticide** (killing older children is called **filicide**), and others involve senior citizens, referred to as **eldercide**.[170] The UCR indicates that about 350 juveniles are murdered each year. The younger the child, the greater the risk for infanticide. At the opposite end of the age spectrum, less than 5 percent of all homicides involve people age 65 or older. Males age 65 or older are more likely than females of the same age to be homicide victims. Although most of the offenders who committed eldercide were age 50 or younger, elderly females were more likely than elderly males to be killed by an elderly offender.[171]

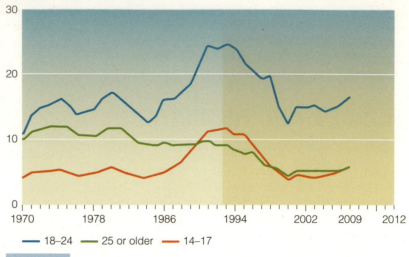

Rate per 100,000

— 18–24 — 25 or older — 14–17

FIGURE 10.2
Homicide Victimization Rate
SOURCE: Bureau of Justice Statistics, http://bjs.ojp.usdoj.gov/content/glance/homage.cfm (accessed August 11, 2011).

Murderers typically have a long involvement in crime; few people begin a criminal career by killing someone. Research shows that people arrested for homicide are significantly more likely to have been in trouble with the law prior to their arrest than people arrested for other crimes.[172]

Today few would deny that some relationship exists between social and ecological factors and murder. The following section explores some of the more important issues related to these factors.

Murderous Relations

One factor that has received a great deal of attention from criminologists is the relationship between the murderer and the victim.[173] A significant number of murders involve people who knew each other beforehand: parents, romantic partners, family members, friends, or acquaintances. In fact, in cases where relationships are known, more people are killed by family members than by strangers. What kind of relationships promote murder and why?

Spousal Relations Even though intramarriage homicide is still commonplace, the rate of homicide among cohabitating couples has declined significantly during the past two decades. One reason may be the shift away from marriage in modern society. There are significant gender differences in homicide trends among unmarried couples. The number of unmarried men killed by their partners has declined (mirroring the overall trend in the murder rate), but the number of women killed by the men they live with has increased dramatically. It is possible that men kill their spouses or partners because they fear losing control and power. Because unmarried people who live together have a legally and socially more open relationship, males in such relationships may be more likely to feel loss of control and exert their power with violence.[174]

Research indicates that most females who kill their mates do so after suffering repeated violent attacks.[175] Perhaps the number of males killed by their partners has declined because alternatives to abusive relationships, such as battered women's shelters, are becoming more prevalent around the United States. Regions that provide greater social support for battered women and that have passed legislation to protect abuse victims also have lower rates of female-perpetrated homicide.[176]

Some people kill their mates because they find themselves involved in a love triangle.[177] Interestingly, women who kill out of jealousy aim their aggression at their partners; in contrast, men are more likely to kill their mates' suitors. Love triangles tend to become lethal when the offenders believe they have been lied to or betrayed. Lethal violence is more common when (a) the rival initiated the affair, (b) the killer knew the spouse was already in a steady relationship outside the marriage, and (c) the killer was repeatedly lied to or betrayed.[178]

CONNECTIONS

It is possible that men who perceive loss of face aim their aggression at rivals who are competing with them for a suitable partner. Biosocial theory (Chapter 5) suggests that this behavior is motivated by the male's instinctual need to replenish the species and protect his place in the gene pool. Killing a rival would help a spouse maintain control over a potential mother for his children.

Personal Relations Most murders occur among people who are acquainted. Although on the surface the killing might have seemed senseless, it often is the result of a long-simmering dispute motivated by revenge, dispute resolution, jealousy, drug deals, racial bias, or threats to identity or status.[179] For example, a prior act of violence, motivated by profit or greed, may generate revenge killing, such as when a buyer robs his dealer during a drug transaction.

How do these murderous relations develop between two people who may have had little prior conflict? In a classic study, David Luckenbill studied *murder transactions* to determine whether particular patterns of behavior are common between the killer and the victim.[180] He found that many homicides follow a sequential pattern. First, the victim makes what the offender considers an offensive move. The offender typically retaliates verbally or physically. An agreement to end things violently is forged with the victim's provocative response. The battle ensues, leaving the victim dead or dying. The offender's escape is shaped by his or her relationship to the victim or the reaction of the audience, if any.

Sexual Relations Some murders are sexually related. The horrific nature of these crimes, especially when they provoke media headlines, create fear that outweigh their actual incidence. Research indicates that sexually related homicide can take a variety of forms:[181]

1. *Interpersonal violence-oriented disputes and assaults.* Interpersonal violence stems from domestic disputes involving husbands and wives, men and women, boyfriends and girlfriends, same-sex couples, and even, on occasion, siblings (they also include love triangle murders, which were discussed earlier). The motive is most often based on elements of rage, hate, anger, jealousy, or revenge.
2. *Rape and/or sodomy-oriented assault.* Rape and/or sodomy-motivated crimes occur under the following circumstances:

   A. The assailant intends to commit a rape or sexual assault but uses excessive force to overcome resistance, resulting in the victim's death.

B. The victim is acquainted with the assailant who uses lethal force to prevent identification.

3. *Deviant-oriented assault, commonly referred to as a lust murder or psychotic killing.* These so-called lust murders are motivated by obsessive sexual fantasies. Lust killers may mutilate parts of the victim's body that they find sexually significant or are the object of their fantasies (e.g., a woman's breasts).

4. *Sexually oriented serial killers.* Not all serial killers have a sexual motivation, but some do. They target a certain type of victim: someone who is vulnerable and easy to control. Their victims are males and females. They may select children, vagrants, prostitutes, or gay men and women. If the victim is female, she may resemble other female victims in some aspect (e.g., long hair, brunette or redhead, coed, nurse, waitress, or female executive).

5. *Vengeance for sexual violence.* In these cases someone enacted vengeance on a sexual-violence perpetrator, either on his or her own behalf or on the behalf of a sexual-violence victim, or potentially out of disgust toward the sexual-violence offender. These cases appear to have an element of planning involved, but the sexual-violence incident occurred prior to the homicide incident.

6. *Self-defense during sexual violence.* In these incidents, sexual violence was taking place and the victim defended herself or himself, resulting in the death of the sexual-violence perpetrator; or another person intervened to defend the sexual-violence victim, and this resulted in the death of the sexual-violence perpetrator.

7. *Escalated argument regarding sexual violence.* Here two or more individuals were engaged in an argument regarding the sexual assault of one of these individuals or another person, and the altercation escalated into violence and the death of one of the parties involved in the dispute.

8. *Third-party death linked to sexual violence.* A homicide that is linked to sexual violence but in which a bystander or third party is the victim of homicide. For example, an intruder breaks into a home, rapes a woman, and kills her husband.

Stranger Relations In the past people tended to kill someone they knew or were related to, but over the past decade the number of stranger homicides has increased. Today more than half of murderers are strangers to their victims, a significant increase from years past. Stranger homicides occur most often as felony murders during rapes, robberies, and burglaries. Others are random acts of urban violence that fuel public fear. For example, a homeowner tells a motorist to move his car because it is blocking the driveway, an argument ensues, and the owner gets a pistol and kills the motorist; or consider a young boy who kills a store manager because, he says, "something came into my head to hurt the lady."[182]

Stranger homicides can result for random gang violence, for example, when someone is killed inadvertently in a drive-by shooting. They also stem from a hate crime directed at a victim merely because of race, class, gender, and so on. For example, when Jeff Gruenewald studied extreme right-wing hate crimes, he found that beating to death homeless persons was a relatively common homicide scenario. The murders of homeless persons typically involved multiple suspects, and all involved non–firearm weapons, including combinations of knives, sticks, boots, and other blunt and bodily weapons (e.g., fists). Who committed these crimes: groups of youth, often loosely organized gangs of skinheads or neo-Nazis, who frequently verbalized their disdain for the homeless, claiming that their victims were lazy and were drains on society (and easy targets).[183]

Why do stranger killings now make up a greater percentage of all murders than in years past? It is possible that tough new sentencing laws, such as the three strikes laws used in California and other habitual criminal statutes, are responsible. These laws mandate that a "three-time loser" be given a life sentence if convicted of multiple felonies. It is possible, as Tomislav Kovandzic and his associates found, that these laws encourage criminals to kill while committing burglaries and robberies. Why hesitate to kill now? If they are caught, they will receive a life sentence anyway.[184]

Student Relations Sadly, violence in schools has become commonplace.[185] According to the latest national survey of crime in schools, more than 2 million nonfatal crimes occur on school grounds each year, including almost 800,000 violent acts. About 10 percent of male and 5 percent of female high school students reported being threatened or injured with a weapon on school property in the past year. Of the violent acts, about 500,000 involved a weapon, including 7,000 physical attacks, 600 robberies, and 4,500 rapes and sexual batteries.

Violence and bullying have become routine; surveys indicate that more than 16 percent of U.S. schoolchildren have been bullied by other students during the current school term, and approximately 30 percent of 6th- through 10th-grade students reported being involved in some aspect of moderate to frequent bullying, either as a bully, the target of bullying, or both. Sometimes violence and bullying can escalate into a school shooting, such as the Columbine High School massacre, which resulted in the deaths of 15 people.

Although relatively rare, these incidents may be expected because up to 10 percent of students report bringing weapons to school on a regular basis.[186] Many of these kids have a history of being abused and bullied; many perceive a lack of support from peers, parents, and teachers.[187] Kids who have been the victims of crime themselves and who hang with peers who carry weapons are most likely to bring guns to school.[188] Troubled kids with little social support and carrying deadly weapons make for an explosive situation.

Research shows that most shooting incidents occur around the start of the school day, the lunch period, or the end of the school day.[189] In most of the shootings (55 percent), a note, threat, or other action indicating risk for violence occurred before the event. Shooters were also likely to have expressed some form of suicidal behavior and to have been bullied by their peers.[190]

Serial Murder

For 31 years, Wichita, Kansas's notorious serial killer, known as BTK (for Bind, Torture, Kill), eluded the police. During his murder spree, the BTK killer sent taunting letters and packages to the police and to the media. Suddenly, after committing gruesome killings in the 1970s he went underground and disappeared from view. After 25 years of silence, he renewed his communications with a local news station. His last communication contained a computer disk, which was traced to 59-year-old Dennis Rader through an FBI analysis of deleted data on the disk. Rader later confessed to 10 murders in an effort to escape the death penalty.

Criminologists consider a **serial killer**, such as Rader, to be a person who kills three or more persons in three or more separate events. In between the murders, the serial killer reverts to his normal lifestyle. Rader worked as a supervisor of the Compliance Department at Park City, Kansas, which put him in charge of animal control, housing problems, zoning, general permit enforcement, and a variety of nuisance cases. A married father of two, he served as a county commissioner, a Cub Scout leader, and a member of Christ Lutheran Church, where he had been elected president of the Congregation Council. Rader's biography and personal life give few clues to his murderous path, which is perhaps why it took more than three decades to track him down.[191]

Types of Serial Killers There are different types of serial killers. Some wander the countryside killing at random; others hide themselves in a single locale and lure victims to their death.[192] Theodore Bundy, convicted killer of three young women and suspected killer of many others, roamed the country in the 1970s, killing as he went. Wayne Gacy, during the same period, killed more than 30 boys and young men without leaving Chicago.

Some serial killers are sadists who gain satisfaction from torturing and killing.[193] Sadists wish to gain complete control over their victims through humiliation, shame, enslavement, and terror. Dr. Michael Swango, who is suspected of killing between 35 and 60 patients, wrote in his diary of the pleasure he obtained from murder. He wrote

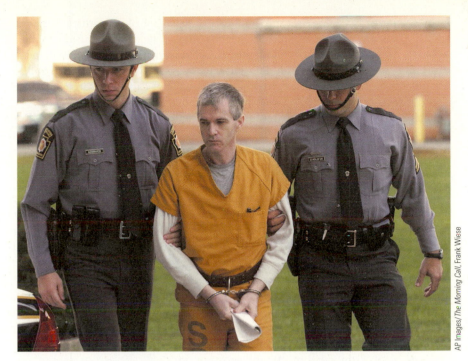

Serial killers keep their identity secret while they engage in their murderous activities. Some may hold trusted positions that shield them from suspicion. Here, former nurse Charles Cullen is led by Pennsylvania state troopers to Lehigh County Court in Allentown, Pennsylvania, November 17, 2004. Cullen pleaded guilty to six murders and three attempted murders. He claimed to have murdered as many as 40 patients during the 16 years he worked at 10 hospitals in New Jersey and Pennsylvania.

of the "sweet, husky, close smell of indoor homicide" and how murders were "the only way I have of reminding myself that I'm still alive."[194]

Swango obtained pleasure from killing, but other health care workers who have committed serial murder rationalize their behavior by thinking they are helping patients end their suffering when they put them to death. Harold Frederick Shipman, Britain's most notorious serial killer, was a general practitioner convicted of 15 murders, most involving elderly patients. After he committed suicide in 2004, further investigation found that he had killed 218 patients and perhaps even more.[195]

Another type, the psychopathic killer, is motivated by a character disorder that causes an inability to experience shame, guilt, sorrow, or other normal human emotions; these murderers are concerned solely with their own needs and passions.

Serial murder experts James Alan Fox and Jack Levin have developed the following typology of serial killer motivations:

- *Thrill killers* strive for either sexual sadism or dominance. This is the most common form of serial murderer.
- *Mission killers* want to reform the world or have a vision that drives them to kill.
- *Expedience killers* are out for profit or want to protect themselves from a perceived threat.[196]

Female Serial Killers An estimated 10 to 15 percent of serial killers are women. A study by criminologists Belea Keeney and Kathleen Heide investigated the characteristics of a sample of 14 female serial killers and found some striking differences between the way male and female killers carried out their crimes.[197] Males were much more likely than females to use extreme violence and torture. Whereas males used a "hands-on" approach, including beating, bludgeoning, and strangling their victims, females were more likely to poison or smother their victims. Men tracked or stalked their victims, but women were more likely to lure victims to their death. There were also gender-based personality and behavior characteristics. Female killers, somewhat older than their male counterparts, abused both alcohol and drugs; males were not likely to be substance abusers. Women were diagnosed as having histrionic, manic-depressive, borderline, dissociative, and antisocial personality disorders; men were more often diagnosed as having antisocial personalities. Aileen Wuornos, executed for killing seven men, was diagnosed with a severe psychopathic personality, a product most likely of her horrific childhood marred by beatings, alcoholism, rape, incest, and prostitution.[198]

The profile of the female serial killer that emerges is a person who smothers or poisons someone she knows. During childhood she suffered from an abusive relationship in a disrupted family. Female killers' education levels are below average, and if they hold jobs, they are in low-status positions.

Why Do Serial Killers Kill? The cause of serial murder eludes criminologists. Such disparate factors as mental illness, sexual frustration, neurological damage, child abuse and neglect, smothering relationships with mothers (David Berkowitz, the notorious Son of Sam, slept in his parents' bed until he was 10), and childhood anxiety are suspected. Most experts view serial killers as sociopaths who from early childhood demonstrate bizarre behavior, such as torturing animals. Some are sadists who enjoy the sexual thrill of murdering and who are both pathological and destructive narcissists.[199]

This behavior extends to the pleasure they reap from killing, their ability to ignore or enjoy their victims' suffering, and their propensity for basking in the media limelight when apprehended for their crimes. Killing provides a way to fill their emotional hunger and reduce their anxiety levels.[200] Wayne Henley, Jr., who along with Dean Corill killed 27 boys in Houston, offered to help prosecutors find the bodies of additional victims so he could break Chicago killer Wayne Gacy's record of 33 murders.[201]

According to experts Fox and Levin, serial killers enjoy the thrill, the sexual gratification, and the dominance they achieve over the lives of their victims. The serial killer rarely uses a gun because this method is too quick and would deprive him of his greatest pleasure, exulting in his victim's suffering. Levin and Fox dispute the notion that serial killers have some form of biological or psychological problems, such as genetic anomalies or schizophrenia. Even the most sadistic serial murderers are not mentally ill or driven by delusions or hallucinations. Instead, they typically exhibit a sociopathic personality that deprives them of pangs of conscience or guilt to guide their behavior. Serial killers are not insane, they claim, but "more cruel than crazy."[202]

Controlling Serial Killers Serial killers come from diverse backgrounds. To date, law enforcement officials have been at a loss to control random killers who leave few clues, constantly move, and have little connection to their victims. Catching serial killers is often a matter of luck. To help local law enforcement officials, the FBI has developed a profiling system to identify potential suspects. Because serial killers often use the same patterns in each attack, they leave a signature that might help in their capture.[203]

In addition, the Justice Department's Violent Criminal Apprehension Program (VICAP), a computerized information service, gathers information and matches offense characteristics on violent crimes around the country.[204] This program links crimes to determine if they are the product of a single culprit.

Mass Murderers

In contrast to serial killings, **mass murder** involves the killing of four or more victims by one or a few assailants within a single event.[205] The murderous incident can last but a few minutes or as long as several hours. In order to qualify as a mass murder, the incident must be carried out by one or a few offenders. Highly organized or institutionalized killings (i.e., war crimes and large-scale acts of political terrorism, as well as certain acts of highly organized crime rings), while atrocious, are not considered mass murder and are motivated by a totally different set of factors. The 2004 brutal and senseless Xbox murders, which involved the killing of six people in Florida by a gang of four men out to avenge the theft of clothes and video games, is a mass murder (see Chapter 9); the genocide of Hitler's Third Reich or a terrorist attack is not.

Mass murderers engage in a single, uncontrollable outburst called "simultaneous killing." Charles Whitman killed 14 people and wounded 30 others from atop the 307-foot tower on the University of Texas campus on August 1, 1966; James Huberty killed 21 people in a McDonald's restaurant in San Ysidro, California, on July 18, 1984; on October 2, 2006, gunman Charles Roberts killed five girls and seriously wounded five others in an Amish schoolhouse in the community of Nickel Mines, Pennsylvania; Seung-Hui Cho killed 32 people and wounded 25 at Virginia Tech on April 16, 2007; and Anders Behring Breivik killed 77 people in and around Oslo, Norway, on July 22, 2011, an act he claimed was motivated by anger against government policies.

Fox and Levin define four types of mass murderers:

- *Revenge killers* seek to get even with individuals or society at large. Their typical target is an estranged wife and "her" children or an employer and "his" employees.

- *Love killers* are motivated by a warped sense of devotion. They are often despondent people who commit suicide and take others, such as a wife and children, with them.
- *Profit killers* are usually trying to cover up a crime, eliminate witnesses, and carry out a criminal conspiracy.
- *Terrorist killers* are trying to send a message. Gang killings tell rivals to watch out; cult killers may actually leave a message behind to warn society about impending doom.[206]

While it often appears that our society has spawned the mass murder, a recent study by Grant Duwe shows that more than 900 mass killings took place between 1900 and 1999 and that mass killings were nearly as common during the 1920s and 1930s as they are today. More of the earlier incidents involved *familicide* (i.e., killing of one's family), and killers were more likely to be older and more suicidal than they are today. The most significant difference between contemporary mass murders and those in the past: more killers use guns today and more incidents involve drug trafficking.[207]

Spree Killers   In 2009, Michael McLendon, 28, killed 10 people in rural Alabama before taking his own life. He had a target list that detectives found in his home. After killing seven members of his family, he drove around the county and killed three more people at random.[208] Spree killers like McLendon engage in a rampage of violence taking place over a period of days or weeks. Unlike mass murderers, their killing is not confined to a single outburst, and unlike serial killers, they don't have a "cooling off" period between murders or return to their "normal" identities in between killings.

Probably the most notorious spree killing to date occurred in October 2002, in the Washington, D.C. area.[209] John Lee Malvo, 17, a Jamaican citizen, and his traveling companion John Allen Muhammad, 41, an Army veteran with an expert's rating in marksmanship, went on a rampage that left more than 10 people dead.

Some spree killers target a specific group or class. John Paul Franklin targeted mixed race couples, African Americans, and Jews, committing more than 20 murders in 12 states in an effort to instigate a race war (Franklin also shot and paralyzed *Hustler* publisher Larry Flynt because he published pictures of interracial sex).[210] Others, like the D.C. snipers Malvo and Muhammad, kill randomly and do not seek out a specific class of victim; their targets included young and old, African Americans and whites, men and women.[211]

ASSAULT AND BATTERY

Although many people mistakenly believe the term *assault and battery* refers to a single act, they are actually two separate crimes. *Battery* requires offensive touching, such as slapping, hitting, or punching a victim. *Assault* requires no actual touching but involves either attempted battery or intentionally frightening the victim by word or deed. Although common law originally intended these twin crimes to be misdemeanors, most jurisdictions now upgrade them to felonies either when a weapon is used or when they occur during the commission of a felony (for example, when a person is assaulted during a robbery). In the UCR, the FBI defines serious assault, or aggravated assault, as "an unlawful attack by one person upon another for the purpose of inflicting severe or aggravated bodily injury"; this definition is similar to the one used in most state jurisdictions.[212]

Under common law, battery required bodily injury, such as broken limbs or wounds. However, under modern law, battery occurs if the victim suffers a temporarily painful blow, even if no injury results. Battery can also involve offensive touching, such as if a man kisses a woman against her will or puts his hands on her body. In some legal jurisdictions, biting someone when infected with AIDS is considered an aggravated assault; some AIDs-infected people have been convicted of aggravated assault for spitting on their victims.[213]

Nature and Extent of Assault

The pattern of criminal assault is similar to that of homicide; one could say that the only difference between the two is that the victim survives.[214] Assaults may be common in our society simply because of common life stresses. Motorists who assault each other have become such a familiar occurrence that the term **road rage** has been coined. There have even been frequent incidents of violent assault among frustrated passengers who lose control while traveling.

Every citizen is bound by the law of assault, even police officers. Excessive use of force can result in criminal charges being filed even if it occurs while police officers are arresting a dangerous felony suspect. Only the minimum amount of force needed to subdue the suspect is allowed by law, and if police use more aggressive tactics than required, they may find themselves the target of criminal charges and civil lawsuits that can run into millions of dollars.[215]

The FBI records about 800,000 assaults each year, a rate of about 275 per 100,000 inhabitants. Like other violent crimes, the number of assaults has been in decline, down about 20 percent in the past decade. People arrested for assault and those identified by victims are usually young, male (about 80 percent), and white, although the number of African Americans arrested for assault (about one-third of the total) is disproportionate to their representation in the population. Assault victims tend to be male, but females also face a significant danger. Assault rates are highest in urban areas, during summer, and in southern and western regions. The most common weapons used in assaults are blunt instruments and hands and feet.

The NCVS indicates that only about half of all serious assaults are reported to the police. The NCVS indicates that the number of assault victimizations has been in steep decline, dropping more than 50 percent during the past decade; even weapon-related assaults have dropped sharply.

Assault in the Home

Violent attacks in the home are one of the most frightening types of assault. Criminologists recognize that intrafamily violence is an enduring social problem in the United States and abroad.

Women are all too often the target of domestic violence, and no one is immune to violent attacks: one recent study found that homicidal injury is a leading cause of death among pregnant and postpartum women in the United States.[216] The United Nation's World Health Organization (WHO) found that around the world, women often face the greatest risk for violence in their own homes and in familiar settings. Almost half the women who die due to homicide are killed by their current or former husbands or boyfriends; in some countries about 70 percent of all female deaths are domestic homicides. It is possible that nearly one in four women will experience violence by an intimate partner in her lifetime, and most of these women are subjected to multiple acts of violence over extended periods of time. In addition to physical abuse, a third to over half of these cases are accompanied by sexual violence; in some countries, up to one-third of adolescent girls report forced sexual initiation.[217] In many places, assaults and even murders occur because men believe that their partners have been defiled sexually, either through rape or sex outside of marriage. In some societies, the only way to cleanse the family honor is by killing the offending female.[218]

Child Abuse One area of intrafamily violence that has received a great deal of media attention is **child abuse**. This term describes any physical or emotional trauma to a child for which no reasonable explanation, such as an accident or ordinary disciplinary practices, can be found.[219] Child abuse can result from actual physical beatings administered to a child by hands, feet, weapons, belts, sticks, burning, and so on. Another form of abuse results from **neglect**—not providing a child with the care and shelter to which he or she is entitled.

Yearly national surveys conducted by the Department of Health and Human Services show that Child Protective Services (CPS) agencies throughout the United States receive more than 3 million referrals each year involving the alleged maltreatment of approximately 6 million children. Of these, approximately 63 percent of the referrals

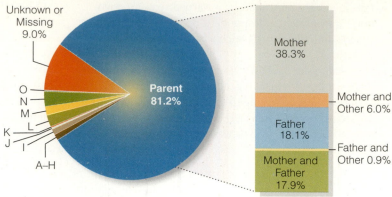

Nonparental

A   Daycare staff 0.5%
B   Foster parent (female relative) 0.0%
C   Foster parent (male relative) 0.0%
D   Foster parent (nonrelative) 0.2%
E   Foster parent (unknown relationship) 0.1%
F   Friend or neighbor 0.4%
G   Legal guardian (female) 0.1%
H   Legal guardian (male) 0.0%

I   More than one nonparental perpetrator 1.1%
J   Other professional 0.1%
K   Partner of parent (female) 0.3%
L   Partner of parent (male) 2.2%
M   Relative (female) 1.7%
N   Relative (male) 3.0%
O   Staff group home 0.2%

FIGURE 10.3

Victims of Child Abuse by Perpetrator Relationship

SOURCE: U.S. Department of Health and Human Services, Administration for Children and Families, Children's Bureau, *Child Maltreatment, 2008* (Washington, DC: U.S. Department of Health and Human Services, 2009), www.acf.hhs.gov/programs/cb/pubs/cm08/index.htm (accessed August 11, 2011).

were screened for investigation or assessment by CPS agencies. In other words, nearly 2 million reports had an investigation or assessment. Of these, approximately 24 percent of the investigations or assessments determined at least one child to be a victim of abuse or neglect, or more than 500,000 per year.[220] Although these numbers seem high, the number of confirmed child abuse/neglect cases has been declining. In 1995, for example, more than 1 million cases were confirmed. According to child maltreatment authority David Finkelor and his colleagues, there are a variety of reasons for the decline, but the easy availability of psychotropic drugs, which may relieve parental anger and stress, might be the greatest contributor to the decline in reported child abuse.[221]

Causes of Child Abuse As Figure 10.3 shows, the great majority of child abuse cases involve parents. Why do parents physically assault their children? Such maltreatment is a highly complex problem with neither a single cause nor a readily available solution. It cuts across ethnic, religious, and socioeconomic lines. Abusive parents cannot be categorized by sex, age, or educational level; they come from all walks of life.[222]

A number of factors have been commonly linked to abuse and neglect:

- Family violence seems to be perpetuated from one generation to another within families. The behavior of abusive parents often can be traced to negative experiences in their own childhood—physical abuse, lack of love, emotional neglect, incest, and so on.
- Blended families, which include children living with an unrelated adult such as a stepparent or another unrelated co-resident, have also been linked to abuse. Children who live with a mother's boyfriend are at much greater risk for abuse than children living with two genetic parents. Some stepparents do not have strong emotional ties to their nongenetic children, nor do they reap emotional benefits from the parent–child relationship.[223]
- Parents may become abusive if they are isolated from friends, neighbors, or relatives who can help in times of crisis. Potentially abusive parents are often alienated from society; they have carried the concept of the shrinking nuclear family to its most extreme form and are cut off from ties of kinship and contact with other people in the neighborhood.[224]

Sexual Abuse   Another aspect of the abuse syndrome is **sexual abuse**—the exploitation of children through rape, incest, and molestation by parents or other adults. It is difficult to estimate the incidence of sexual abuse, but a number of attempts have been made to gauge the extent of the problem. In a classic study, Diana Russell's survey of women in the San Francisco area found that 38 percent had experienced intra- or extrafamilial sexual abuse by the time they reached age 18.[225] Others have estimated that at least 20 percent of females suffer some form of sexual violence; that is, at least one in five girls suffer sexual abuse.[226]

Although sexual abuse is still prevalent, the number of reported cases has been in a significant decline.[227] However, this trend must be interpreted with caution. It is possible that the number of cases is truly in decline due to effective prevention programs, increased prosecution, and public awareness campaigns. However, declines might be the result of more cases being overlooked because of (a) increased evidentiary requirements to substantiate cases, (b) increased caseworker caution due to new legal rights for caregivers, and (c) increasing limitations on the types of cases that agencies accept for investigation.[228]

Sexual abuse is of particular concern because children who have been abused experience a long list of symptoms, including fear, posttraumatic stress disorder, behavior problems, sexualized behavior, and poor self-esteem.[229] Women who were abused as children are also at greater risk of being abused as adults than those who avoided childhood victimization.[230] The amount of force used during the abuse, its duration, and its frequency are all related to the extent of the long-term effects and the length of time needed for recovery.

Regardless of its cause, child abuse can have devastating long-term effects, ranging from depression to loss of self-esteem.[231] Not surprisingly, a history of childhood sexual and physical abuse among persons with severe mental illness is disproportionately high.[232]

Parental Abuse   Parents are sometimes the target of abuse from their own children. Research conducted by Arina Ulman and Murray Straus found the following:

- The younger the child, the higher the rate of child-to-parent violence (CPV).
- At all ages, more children were violent to mothers than to fathers.
- Both boys and girls hit mothers more often than fathers.
- At all ages, slightly more boys than girls hit parents.

Ulman and Straus found that child-to-parent violence was associated with some form of violence by parents, which could either be husband-to-wife, wife-to-husband, corporal punishment of children, or physical abuse. They suggest that if the use of physical punishment could be eliminated or curtailed, then child-to-parent violence would similarly decline.[233]

Spousal Abuse   Spousal abuse has occurred throughout recorded history. Roman men had the legal right to beat their wives for minor acts such as attending public games without permission, drinking wine, or walking outdoors with their faces uncovered.[234] More serious transgressions, such as adultery, were punishable by death. During the later stages of the Roman Empire, the practice of wife beating abated, and by the fourth century, excessive violence on the part of husband or wife was grounds for divorce.[235] During the early Middle Ages, there was a separation of love and marriage.[236] The ideal woman was protected, cherished, and loved from afar. In contrast, the wife, with whom marriage had been arranged by family ties, was guarded jealously and could be punished severely for violating her duties. A husband was expected to beat his wife for "misbehaviors" and might himself be punished by neighbors if he failed to do so.[237]

Through the later Middle Ages and into modern times (from 1400 to 1900), there was little community objection to a man using force against his wife as long as the assault did not exceed certain limits, usually construed as death or disfigurement. By the mid-nineteenth century, severe wife beating fell into disfavor, and accused wife beaters were subject to public ridicule. Nonetheless, limited chastisement was still the rule. By the close of the nineteenth century, England and the United States outlawed wife beating. Yet the long history of husbands' domination of their wives made physical coercion hard to control. Until recent times, the subordinate position of women in the family was believed to give husbands the legal and moral obligation to manage their wives' behavior. Even after World War II, English courts found physical assault a reasonable punishment for a wife who had disobeyed her husband.[238] These ideas form the foundation of men's traditional physical control of women and have led to severe cases of spousal assault.

EXHIBIT 10.3

Factors that Predict Spousal Abuse

- *Presence of alcohol.* Excessive alcohol use may turn otherwise docile husbands into wife abusers.
- *Access to weapons.* A perpetrator's access to a gun and previous threat with a weapon may lead to abuse.
- *Stepchild in the home.* Having a stepchild living in the home may provoke abuse because the parent may have a more limited bond to the child.
- *Estrangement.* Especially from a controlling partner and subsequent involvement with another partner.
- *Hostility toward dependency.* Some husbands who appear docile and passive may resent their dependence on their wives and react with rage and violence; this reaction has been linked to sexual inadequacy.
- *Excessive brooding.* Obsession with a wife's behavior, however trivial, can result in violent assaults.
- *Social learning.* Some males believe society approves of spouse or mate abuse and use these beliefs to justify their violent behavior. Peer support helps shape their attitudes and behaviors.
- *Socioeconomic factors.* Men who fail as providers and are under economic stress may take their frustrations out on their wives.
- *Flashes of anger.* Research shows that a significant amount of family violence results from a sudden burst of anger after a verbal dispute.
- *Military service.* Spouse abuse among men who have served in the military service is extremely high. Similarly, those serving in the military are more likely to assault their wives than civilian husbands. The reasons for this phenomenon may be the violence promoted by military training and the close proximity in which military families live to one another.
- *Having been abused as children.* Husbands who assault their wives were generally battered as children.
- *Unpredictability.* Batterers are unpredictable, unable to be influenced by their wives, and impossible to prevent from battering once an argument has begun.

SOURCES: Christine Sellers, John Cochran, and Kathryn Branch, "Social Learning Theory and Partner Violence: A Research Note," *Deviant Behavior* 26 (2005) 379–395; Jacquelyn Campbell, Daniel Webster, Jane Koziol-McLain, Carolyn Block, Doris Campbell, Mary Ann Curry, Faye Gary, Nancy Glass, Judith McFarlane, Carolyn Sachs, Phyllis Sharps, Yvonne Ulrich, Susan Wilt, Jennifer Manganello, Xiao Xu, Janet Schollenberger, Victoria Frye, and Kathryn Laughon, "Risk Factors for Femicide in Abusive Relationships: Results from a Multisite Case Control Study," *American Journal of Public Health* 93 (2003): 1,089–1,097.

The Nature and Extent of Spousal Abuse   It is difficult to estimate how widespread spousal abuse is today; however, some statistics indicate the extent of the problem. In their classic study of family violence, Richard Gelles and Murray Straus found that 16 percent of surveyed families had experienced husband–wife assaults.[239] In police departments around the country, 60 to 70 percent of evening calls involve domestic disputes.

Not only married women are prone to being victimized by an intimate partner. Dating violence is quite common, and an estimated one in five high school girls may suffer sexual or physical abuse from a boyfriend. Dating violence has been linked to substance abuse, unsafe sex, and eating disorders.[240]

Women are not the only victims of spousal abuse. One recent study of 12,000 male abuse victims serving in the U.S. Army found that abused men were at greater risk for early army discharge and hospitalization than were nonvictims—particularly hospitalizations for depression, alcohol dependence, and mental health problems.[241]

Some of the personal attributes and characteristics of spouse abusers and abusive situations are listed in Exhibit 10.3.

To read more on **dating abuse**, access the Harvard School of Public Health website via the Criminal Justice CourseMate at cengagebrain.com, then access the "Web Links" for this chapter.

ROBBERY

The common-law definition of *robbery* (and the one used by the FBI) is "the taking or attempting to take anything of value from the care, custody or control of a person or persons by force or threat of force or violence and/or by putting the victim in fear."[242] A robbery is considered a violent crime because it involves the use of force to obtain money or goods. Robbery is punished severely because the victim's life is put in jeopardy. In fact, the severity of punishment is based on the amount of force used during the crime, not the value of the items taken.

The FBI records about 400,000 robberies each year, a rate of about 140 per 100,000 population. As with most other violent crimes, there has been a significant reduction in the robbery rate during the past decade; the robbery rate is down almost 40 percent.

Types of Robberies and Robbers

Attempts have been made to *classify and explain* the nature and dynamics of robbery. One approach is to characterize robberies by type, some of which include:

- *Robbery in an open area.* These robberies include street muggings, purse snatchings, and other attacks. Street robbery is most closely associated with mugging, which

This May 18, 2010, security photo shows Michael Mara, a man the FBI nicknamed the "Granddad Bandit," holding a black wallet containing a holdup note. Mara robbed 25 banks in 13 eastern and central states, beginning his crime spree with a robbery in Mobile, Alabama, on January 16, 2009. FBI officials believe he struck three times in Atlanta, Georgia, and twice in Mobile, Alabama. He robbed four banks overall in Alabama, four in Georgia, three in Texas, two in Arkansas, and one each in the other states. Michael Mara's crime spree came to an end with an arrest on August 11, 2010.

refers to grabbing victims from behind and threatening them with a weapon. Street muggers often target unsavory characters, such as drug dealers or pimps who carry large amounts of cash, because these victims would find it awkward to report the crime to the police. Most commit their robberies within a short distance from their homes.

- *Commercial robbery.* This type of robbery occurs in businesses ranging from banks to liquor stores. Banks are among the most difficult targets to rob because they have more personnel and a higher level of security.
- *Robbery on private premises.* This type of robbery involves home invasions while occupants are present.
- *Robbery after a short, preliminary association.* This type of robbery comes after a chance meeting—in a bar, at a party, or after a sexual encounter.
- *Robbery after a longer association between victim and offender.* An example of this type of robbery would be an intimate acquaintance robbing his paramour and then fleeing the jurisdiction.
- *Carjacking.* This is a completed or attempted theft of a motor vehicle by force or threat of force.[243]

It is also possible to distinguish between types of robbers. Among the types of robbers identified by criminologists are these specialties:

- *Professional robbers.* These robbers have a long-term commitment to crime as a source of livelihood. This type of robber plans and organizes crimes prior to committing them and seeks money to support a hedonistic lifestyle. Some professionals are exclusively robbers, whereas others engage in additional types of crimes. Professionals are committed to robbing because it is direct, fast, and profitable. They hold no other steady job and plan three or four "big scores" a year to support themselves. Planning and skill are the trademarks of professional robbers, who often operate in groups with assigned roles. Professionals usually steal large amounts from commercial establishments. After a score, they may stop for a few weeks until "things cool off."
- *Opportunist robbers.* These robbers steal to obtain small amounts of money when an accessible target presents itself. They are not committed to robbery but will steal from cab drivers, drunks, the elderly, and other vulnerable persons if they need some extra spending money. Opportunists are usually teens and gang members who do not plan their crimes. Although they operate within the milieu of the juvenile gang, they are seldom organized and spend little time discussing weapon use, getaway plans, or other strategies.
- *Addict robbers.* These people steal to support their drug habits. They have a low commitment to robbery because of its danger but a high commitment to theft because it supplies needed funds. The addict is less likely to plan crime or use weapons than the professional robber but is more cautious than the opportunist. Addicts choose targets that present minimal risk; however, when desperate for funds, they are sometimes careless in selecting the victim and executing the crime. They rarely think in terms of the big score; they just want enough money to get their next fix.
- *Alcoholic robbers.* These people steal for reasons related to their excessive consumption of alcohol. Alcoholic robbers steal (a) when, in a disoriented state, they attempt to get some money to buy liquor, or (b) when their condition makes them unemployable and they need funds. Alcoholic robbers have no real commitment to robbery as a way of life. They plan their crimes randomly and give little thought to their victim, circumstance, or escape. For that reason, they are the most likely to be caught.[244]

The typical armed robber is unlikely to be a professional who carefully studies targets while planning a crime. People walking along the street, convenience stores, and gas stations are much more likely robbery targets than banks or other highly secure environments. Robbers, therefore, seem to be diverted by modest defensive measures, such as having more than one clerk in a store or locating stores in strip malls; they are more likely to try an isolated store.[245]

Acquaintance Robbery   One type of robber may focus on people they know, a phenomenon referred to as **acquaintance robbery**. This seems puzzling because victims can easily identify their attackers and report them to the police.

However, despite this threat, acquaintance robbery may be attractive for a number of rational reasons:[246]

- Victims may be reluctant to report these crimes because they do not want to get involved with the police. They may be involved in crime themselves (drug dealers, for example), or they may fear retaliation if they report the crime. Some victims may be reluctant to gain the label of "rat" or "fink" if they go to the police.
- Some robberies are motivated by street justice. The robber has a grievance against the victim and settles the dispute by stealing the victim's property. In this instance, robbery may be considered a substitute for an assault: the robber wants retribution and revenge rather than remuneration.[247]
- Because the robber knows the victim personally, the robber has inside information that there will be a "good take." Offenders may target people they know to be carrying a large amount of cash or who just purchased expensive jewelry.
- When a person in desperate need for immediate cash runs out of money, the individual may target people in close proximity simply because they are convenient targets.

When Richard Felson and his associates studied acquaintance robbery, they found that victims were more likely to be injured in acquaintance robberies than in stranger robberies, indicating that revenge rather than reward was the primary motive.[248] Similarly, robberies of family members were more likely to have a bigger payoff than stranger robberies, an indication that the offender was aware that the target had a large amount of cash on hand.

Planning to Rob

Even the most opportunistic robbery is characterized by some evidence of planning and commitment. Robbers bring with them a set of skills, developed over time, that keep the odds of success in their favor.[249] Though they may be concerned about the consequences of their crime, experienced robbers are able to neutralize fear by developing confidence in their ability to maintain control over the situation and to improvise and adapt to unfolding dangers should they arise. Based on experience, they can calculate when the odds are in their favor or when it's best to cut and run.[250]

The time and place of robberies suggest that careful planning takes place before the criminal event: though most crime rates are higher in the summer, robberies seem to peak during the winter months. One reason may be that the cold weather allows robbers a greater opportunity to disguise themselves; another reason is that robbers may be attracted to the high amounts of cash people and merchants carry during the Christmas shopping season.[251] Robbers also may be attracted to the winter because days are shorter, affording them greater concealment in the dark.

Criminologists who interviewed active robbers have found evidence of the planning that takes place before the crime goes down. For one thing, robbers are careful to choose vulnerable victims. For example, both male and female robbers like to target women simply because they believe them to be more vulnerable and likely to offer less resistance.[252] If they have to target males, female robbers use guile to set them up: they pick a victim and show sexual interest to catch them off guard and gain the upper hand.[253]

When Scott Decker and Richard Wright interviewed active robbers in St. Louis, Missouri, they found that robbers carefully plan their crimes beforehand and choose victims who can provide the greatest payoff with the least amount of hassle. Some, surprisingly, target drug dealers, victims who have a lot of cash on hand and who are unlikely to call the police.[254]

Decker and Wright found that robbers have racial, gender, and age preferences in their selection of targets. Some African American robbers prefer white targets because they believe they are too afraid to fight back. Others concentrate on African American victims, who are more likely to carry cash than credit cards. As one interviewee revealed, "White guys can be so paranoid [that] they just want to get away. . . . They're not . . . gonna argue with you." Likewise, intoxicated victims in no condition to fight back were favored targets. Some robbers tend to target women because they feel they are easy subjects; however, others avoid them because they believe they will get emotionally upset and bring unwanted attention. Most agree that the elderly are less likely to put up a fuss than younger, stronger targets.

The Criminological Enterprise feature details the scripts followed by carjackers to minimize risk and manage victim resistance.

EMERGING FORMS OF INTERPERSONAL VIOLENCE

Assault, rape, robbery, and murder are traditional forms of interpersonal violence. As more data become available, criminologists have recognized relatively new subcategories within these crime types, such as serial murder and date rape. Additional new categories of interpersonal violence are now receiving attention in criminological literature; the next sections describe three of these forms of violent crime.

Hate Crimes

Hate crimes usually involve convenient, vulnerable targets who are incapable of fighting back. For example, there have been numerous reported incidents of teenagers attacking vagrants

The Criminological Enterprise
Following the Script

When Heith Copes, Andy Hochstetler, and Michael Cherbonneau interviewed a sample of carjackers, they found that the robbers worried more about the victim's reactions than about law enforcers. An uncooperative victim could alter the course of events, threaten valued goals, or put all involved in physical danger. To get the upper hand, robbers assess the likelihood of a victim fighting back. Fear of victim retaliation leads most carjackers to devote attention to selecting "proper victims": those least likely to resist. Some carjackers steer clear of women drivers, fearing that they will start to yell for help or act erratically under threat of force, making them difficult to control.

Once a victim has been chosen, carjackers carefully execute a line of attack designed to shock the victim into compliance. Some used a blitz method, attacking so rapidly that the target does not have time to respond. Others manipulate their appearance, for example, by posing as a street vendor in order to approach potential victims without causing alarm. Some wait for an opportune moment, lurking in parking lots and approaching inattentive victims as they enter their cars and demand that they surrender their keys.

Establishing Cooperation

To obtain the vehicle, carjackers gained compliance from the victim while controlling his or her conduct through threat or force. Some used extreme force to immobilize victims or used verbal commands to threaten victims into compliance. Others brandished weapons or even administered a forceful blow if no weapon was available. Even if the attack did not incapacitate the victim completely, use of violence made clear the dangers of failing to surrender the car. Though violence was used, most carjackers claimed only to strike victims hard enough to keep them from fighting back, to shock them, or to communicate that their threats were credible. Incapacitating the victim with violence also facilitated his or her removal from the vehicle. In any event, when force was applied, it let the victim know that a robbery was inevitable and reinforced the robbers' message: cooperate or die. Pointing a gun in the victim's face got the message across with a minimum of effort.

Making an Escape

Should the victim be taken or left behind? Although most dumped the driver, a few carjackers chose to abscond with the victims in tow because of the risks that an unmonitored victim posed. The technique was used mainly by those who committed crimes against victims who were not considered to be a physical threat, when victims did not respond quickly to commands, or when the assailant feared the victim could promptly inform the authorities. Nonetheless, few carjackers wanted the victim around longer than necessary and dumped them out of the car as soon as a convenient site presented itself.

Scripts for Crime

The research uncovered the fact that carjackers used and reused scripts when committing their crimes. Scripts for carjacking seem to vary by motivation and location. Those that occurred on drug corners typically involved multiple offenders, were planned in advance, and were aimed at lucrative targets. The "script" called for the carjacker to approach the victim under the guise of being a drug dealer and quickly separate the victim from his or her vehicle, often using a gun. Those operating at shopping malls were more likely to act spontaneously, use verbal commands, and take victims with them when leaving the scene.

Sticking to their scripts enabled carjackers to reduce danger and to use their skills and experience to prevent detection. When things go awry, scripts can be altered to ensure that the same mistake is not made twice. Sticking to the script also prolongs a criminal career. It builds confidence and helps the carjacker act quickly and decisively, analyzing the situation and figuring out what must be done to complete the crime, even if it means altering the script somewhat.

CRITICAL THINKING

Does the fact that carjackers use "scripts" when committing crime and use them repeatedly indicate that even this seemingly random event is a product of thought and deliberation, a finding that supports rational choice theory? If carjacking is in fact planned, what can be done to deter these robbers from committing similar crimes?

SOURCE: Heith Copes, Andy Hochstetler, and Michael Cherbonneau, "Getting the Upper Hand: Scripts for Managing Victim Resistance in Carjackings," published online before print May 3, 2011, *Journal of Research in Crime and Delinquency* (accessed August 11, 2011).

and the homeless in an effort to rid their town or neighborhood of people they consider undesirable.[255] Another group targeted for hate crimes is gay men and women: gay bashing has become common in U.S. cities. The Profiles in Crime feature discusses a highly publicized New York hate crime.

Racial and ethnic minorities have also been the targets of attack. In California, Mexican laborers have been attacked and killed; in New Jersey, Indian immigrants have been the targets of racial hatred.[256] Although hate crimes are often mindless attacks directed toward "traditional" minority victims, political and economic trends may cause this form of violence to be redirected. For example, Asians have been attacked by groups who resent the growing economic power of Japan and Korea as well as the commercial success of

© Stephen Barcelo/Daily News L.P.

On November 8, 2008, 17-year-old Jeffrey Conroy and six other Long Island, New York, teenagers decided to hunt for Hispanic men to assault, an activity they called "Mexican hopping." Around midnight in the parking lot of the Patchogue, Long Island, train station, the boys encountered 37-year-old Marcelo Lucero, a local man who worked in a neighborhood dry cleaning shop. Lucero and another man were walking to a friend's house when they were surrounded, taunted, and attacked with a knife. One of Lucero's arteries was severed, and he bled to death. The gang members were soon identified and arrests made.

Although Conroy admitted to stabbing Lucero when he was interrogated by police, at trial he changed his story and claimed that another boy was responsible. Why did he make a false confession? To protect a friend, Christopher Overton, 17, who was already on probation and facing a long prison sentence as a second-time offender. The jury did not buy Conroy's explanation and found him guilty of manslaughter. Though the jury found that Conroy did not intend to kill Lucero (which would have been second-degree murder), they concluded his reckless actions did cause death; the judge sentenced him to 25 years in prison, the maximum under law.

The Lucero case became a focal point for the tensions that had developed between the Hispanic community and local Anglo residents on Eastern Long Island. Soon after the stabbing, a number of Hispanic residents come forward saying they were the victims of harassment and assaults. The Suffolk County Police Department was criticized for failing to fully investigate complaints of assaults on Latinos.

What would motivate a young man such as Jeffrey Conroy to kill a complete stranger for no apparent reason? His parents and friends saw him as a friendly, athletic teenager in the wrong place at the wrong time. He was no hater, they claimed, having several Hispanics among his closest friends, including the girl he had been dating off and on for years. In contrast, the prosecutors portrayed him as an aggressive teenager with a swastika tattoo on his thigh who stabbed an innocent immigrant out of hate and anger, and then lied in court when he blamed someone else for the crime.

SOURCES: Manny Fernandez, "Youth Recants Confession in Hate Crime Trial," April 8, 2010, *New York Times*, www.nytimes.com/2010/04/09/nyregion/09patchogue.html (accessed August 11, 2011); Manny Fernandez, "In Jail, Hate Crime Killer Says He Isn't So Hateful," *New York Times*, April 29, 2010, www.nytimes.com/2010/04/30/nyregion/30patchogue.html (accessed August 11, 2011); Manny Fernandez, "Long Island Man Gets 25-Year Term in Killing of Immigrant," *New York Times*, May 26, 2010, www.nytimes.com/2010/05/27/nyregion/27patchogue.html (accessed August 11, 2011).

Asian Americans.[257] The factors that precipitate hate crimes are listed in Exhibit 10.4.

The Roots of Hate Why do people commit hate crimes? In their book *Hate Crimes*, Jack McDevitt and Jack Levin identify three motivations for hate crimes: **thrill-seeking hate crimes, reactive (defensive) hate crimes,** and **mission hate crimes:**

- *Thrill-seeking hate crimes.* In the same way some kids like to get together to shoot hoops, hate mongers join forces to have fun by bashing minorities or destroying property. Inflicting pain on others gives them a sadistic thrill.
- *Reactive (defensive) hate crimes.* Perpetrators of these crimes rationalize their behavior as a defensive stand taken against outsiders whom they believe threaten their community or way of life. A gang of teens that attacks a new family in the neighborhood because they are the "wrong" race is committing a reactive hate crime.

EXHIBIT 10.4

Factors that Produce Hate Crimes

- Poor or uncertain economic conditions
- Racial stereotypes in films and on television
- Hate-filled discourse on talk shows or in political advertisements
- The use of racial code language such as "welfare mothers" and "inner-city thugs"
- An individual's personal experiences with members of particular minority groups
- Scapegoating—blaming a minority group for the misfortunes of society as a whole

SOURCE: "A Policymaker's Guide to Hate Crimes," *Bureau of Justice Assistance Monograph* (Washington, DC: Bureau of Justice Assistance, 1997).

- *Mission hate crimes.* Some disturbed individuals see it as their duty to rid the world of evil. Those on a "mission," like skinheads, the Ku Klux Klan (KKK), and white supremacist groups, may seek to eliminate people who threaten their religious beliefs because they are members of a different faith or threaten "racial purity" because they are of a different race.[258]

More recent research by McDevitt and Levin with Susan Bennett used data from the Community Disorders Unit (CDU) of the Boston Police Department to uncover a new category of hate crime: **retaliatory hate crimes**. These offenses are committed in response to a hate crime, whether real or perceived; whether the original incident actually occurred is irrelevant. Their more recent research indicates that most hate crimes can be classified as thrill motivated (66 percent) followed by defensive (25 percent) and retaliatory (8 percent). Few cases were mission-oriented offenders.[259]

In his book *The Violence of Hate*, Levin notes that in addition to the traditional hate mongers, hate crimes can be committed by "dabblers"—people who are not committed to hate but drift in and out of active bigotry. They may be young people who get drunk on Saturday night and assault a gay couple or attack an African American man who happens by; they then go back to work or school on Monday. Some are thrill seekers; others may be reacting to the presence of members of a disliked group in their neighborhood. Levin also notes that some people are "sympathizers": they may not attack African Americans but think nothing of telling jokes with racial themes or agreeing with people who despise gays. Finally, there are "spectators" who may not actively participate in bigotry but who do nothing to stop its course. They may even vote for politicians who are openly bigoted because they agree with their tax policies or some other positions, neglecting to process the fact that their vote empowers prejudice and leads to hate.[260]

Nature and Extent of Hate Crime   According to the FBI, about 7,000 hate-crime incidents involving 8,000 victims occur each year.[261] About half are motivated by racial bigotry and 20 percent by religious intolerance; the rest are the result of a sexual-orientation bias, ethnicity/national origin bias, or bias against a disability.[262] Intimidation was the most common form of hate crime, but about 20 percent involved assault with a weapon and a few led to death.

In crimes in which the victims could identify the culprits, most victims reported that they were acquainted with their attackers or that their attackers were friends, coworkers, neighbors, or relatives.[263] Younger victims were more likely to be victimized by people known to them. Hate crimes can occur in many settings, but most are perpetrated in public settings.

Although 7,000 hate-related incidents each year may seem like a lot, many hate crimes go unreported, so that figure may represent only the tip of the iceberg. Defining hate crimes may differ between legal jurisdictions and so may the incentive to enforce hate-crime laws. In a recent study, Ryan King and his associates investigated the association between past lynchings (1882 to 1930) and contemporary law enforcement responses to hate crimes in the United States. They found that contemporary hate-crime policing and prosecution is less vigorous in areas where lynching was more prevalent prior to 1930, especially if those areas now have large African American populations. That is, past lynching combined with a sizeable black population largely suppresses (a) police compliance with federal hate crime law, (b) police reports of hate crimes that target blacks, and (c) the likelihood of prosecuting a hate-crime case. Their conclusion: social control of intergroup conflict (i.e., hate-related crime) is in part a function of both current racial threat and a long-held cultural tradition of apathy toward the protection of minorities.[264]

Controlling Hate Crimes   Because of the extent and seriousness of the problem, a number of legal jurisdictions have made a special effort to control the spread of hate crimes. Boston maintains the Community Disorders Unit, and the New York City Police Department's Hate Crimes Task Force focuses on apprehending perpetrators of hate crimes.[265]

Specific hate-crime laws originated after the Civil War that were designed to protect the rights of freed slaves.[266] Today, almost every state jurisdiction has enacted some form of legislation designed to combat hate crimes: 39 states have enacted laws against bias-motivated violence and intimidation; 19 states have statutes that specifically mandate the collection of hate-crime data.

Some critics argue that it is unfair to punish criminals motivated by hate any more severely than those who commit similar crimes but are motivated by revenge, greed, or anger. There is also the danger that what appears to be a hate crime, because the target is a minority group member, may actually be motivated by some other factor such as vengeance or monetary gain. In November 2004, Aaron McKinney (who is serving a life sentence for killing Matthew Shepard) told *ABC News* correspondent Elizabeth Vargas that he was high on methamphetamine when he killed Shepard, and that his intent was robbery and not hate. His partner, Russell Henderson, claimed that the killing was simply a robbery gone bad: "It was not because me and Aaron had anything against gays."[267]

However, in his important book *Punishing Hate: Bias Crimes under American Law*, Frederick Lawrence argues that criminals motivated by bias deserve to be punished more severely than those who commit identical crimes for other motives.[268] He suggests that a society dedicated to the equality of all its people must treat bias crimes differently from other crimes and in so doing enhance the punishment of these crimes.[269]

Some criminals choose their victims randomly; others select specific victims, for example, as in crimes of revenge. Bias crimes are different. They are crimes in which (a) distinct identifying characteristics of the victim are critical to the perpetrator's choice of victim, and (b) the individual identity of the victim is irrelevant.[270] Lawrence views a bias crime as one that would not have been committed but for the victim's membership in a particular group.[271] Bias crimes should be punished more severely because the harm caused will exceed that caused by crimes with other motivations:[272]

- Bias crimes are more likely to be violent and involve serious physical injury to the victim.
- Bias crimes will have significant emotional and psychological impact on the victim; they result in a "heightened sense of vulnerability," which causes depression, anxiety, and feelings of helplessness.
- Bias crimes harm not only the victim but also the "target community."
- Bias crimes violate the shared value of equality among citizens and racial and religious harmony in a heterogeneous society.

Recent research by McDevitt and his associates that made use of bias-crime records collected by the Boston police supports Lawrence's position. McDevitt found that the victims of bias crime experience more severe post-crime psychological trauma, for a longer period of time, than do victims of similar crimes that are not motivated by hate or bias. Hate-crime victims are more likely to suffer intrusive thoughts, feelings of danger, nervousness, and depression at a higher level than other crime victims.[273] Considering the damage caused by bias crimes, it seems appropriate that they be punished more severely than typical common-law crimes.

Legal Controls Should symbolic acts of hate such as drawing a swastika or burning a cross be banned, or are they protected by the free speech clause of the First Amendment? The U.S. Supreme Court helped answer this question in the case of *Virginia v. Black* (2003) when it upheld a Virginia statute that makes it a felony "for any person . . . with the intent of intimidating any person or group . . . to burn . . . a cross on the property of another, a highway or other public place," and specifies that "[a]ny such burning . . . shall be prima facie evidence of an intent to intimidate a person or group." The Court ruled that cross burning was intertwined with the Ku Klux Klan and its reign of terror throughout the South. The Court has long held that statements in which the speaker intends to communicate intent to commit an act of unlawful violence to a particular individual or group of individuals is not protected free speech and can be criminalized; the speaker need not actually intend to carry out the threat.[274]

Workplace Violence

In 2006, Dr. Amy Bishop, a Harvard-trained neurobiologist, along with her husband Jim Anderson, invented a portable cell growth incubator designed to replace the old practice of growing cells in a Petri dish. Their highly sophisticated endeavor held much promise, and they were able to raise more than $1 million in start-up money to organize a biotech business. Four

years later, this highly educated woman was in the news for an entirely different reason: while attending a faculty meeting at the University of Alabama's Huntsville campus, Bishop shot to death three of her colleagues and severely wounded three others. The alleged reason: despite her achievements, Bishop was denied tenure (a lifetime academic appointment).

The case soon took on other bizarre twists. According to Massachusetts law enforcement authorities, in 1986 Bishop killed her own brother, Seth Bishop, with a shotgun blast; she was 19 years old. There were suspicions of foul play at the time, but the incident was ruled an accident and Bishop was not charged. In the aftermath of the Huntsville killings, the case was reopened. It seems that Amy Bishop took her father's shotgun, loaded it, and fired a shot in her bedroom, then went downstairs to the kitchen and shot her brother in the chest. She said she accidentally shot him while trying to figure out how to unload the shotgun. However, it turns out that the police never told the district attorney's office that after she supposedly shot her brother by accident, Amy tried to commandeer a getaway car at gunpoint, and that she refused to drop her gun until officers repeatedly ordered her to do so. Another give away: a photo found in her bedroom, where she had loaded the 12-gauge shotgun, showed a *National Enquirer* article describing how a teenager wielding a 12-gauge shotgun killed the parents of actor Patrick Duffy, who played Bobby Ewing on the television show *Dallas*, and then commandeered a getaway car at gunpoint from an auto dealership. Bishop was indicted on her brother's murder on June 16, 2010, and tried to commit suicide two days later.[275] Then it turns out she was also a suspect in another violent incident: a package containing two bombs was sent to the home of Dr. Paul Rosenberg, a professor and doctor at Boston's Children's Hospital, soon after he had criticized her doctoral research.[276] Ironically, at the time Dr. Amy Bishop is heading off to prison, the innovative medical device she created will be heading to market.

It has become commonplace to read of irate employees or former employees attacking coworkers or sabotaging machinery and production lines. **Workplace violence** is now considered one of the leading causes of occupational injury or death.[277] Workplace violence can take a number of different forms:

TYPE 1. Violent acts by criminals who have no other connection with the workplace, but enter to commit robbery or another crime.

TYPE 2. Violence directed at employees by customers, clients, patients, students, inmates, or any others for whom an organization provides services.

TYPE 3. Violence against coworkers, supervisors, or managers by a present or former employee.

TYPE 4. Violence committed in the workplace by someone who doesn't work there, but has a personal relationship with an employee—an abusive spouse or domestic partner.[278]

Who engages in workplace violence? The typical offender is a middle-aged white male who faces termination in a worsening economy. The fear of economic ruin is especially strong in agencies such as the U.S. Postal Service, where long-term employees fear job loss because of automation and reorganization. In contrast, younger workers usually kill while committing a robbery or another felony.

Creating Workplace Violence   A number of factors precipitate workplace violence. One suspected cause is a management style that appears cold and insensitive to workers. As corporations cut their staffs because of an economic downturn or workers are summarily replaced with cost-effective technology, long-term employees may become irate and irrational; their unexpected layoff can lead to violent reactions.[279] The effect is most pronounced when managers are unsympathetic and nonsupportive; their callous attitude may help trigger workplace violence.

Not all workplace violence is triggered by management-induced injustice. In some incidents coworkers have been killed because they refused romantic relationships with the assailants or reported them for sexual harassment. Others have been killed because they got a job the assailant coveted.

Irate clients and customers also have killed because of poor service or perceived slights. Although a hospital is designed to help people deal with their troubles, patients whose demands are not met may attack their caregivers: health care and social services workers have the highest rate of nonfatal assault injuries. Nurses are three times more likely to experience workplace violence than any other professional group.[280] In one Los Angeles incident, a former patient shot and critically wounded three doctors because his demands for painkillers had gone unheeded.[281]

There are a variety of responses to workplace provocations. Some people take out their anger and aggression by attacking their supervisors in an effort to punish the company that dismissed them; this is a form of murder by proxy.[282] Disgruntled employees may attack family members or friends, misdirecting the rage and frustration caused by their work situation. Others are content with sabotaging company equipment; computer databases are particularly vulnerable to tampering. The aggrieved party may do nothing to rectify the situation; this inaction is referred to as **sufferance**. Over time, the unresolved conflict may be compounded by other events that cause an eventual eruption.

The Extent of Workplace Violence   According to security experts Michael Mantell and Steve Albrecht, the cost of workplace violence for American businesses runs to more than $4 billion annually, including lost work time, employee medical benefits, legal expenses, replacing lost employees and retraining new ones, decreased productivity, higher insurance premiums, raised security costs, bad publicity, lost business, and expensive litigation.[283]

These huge costs can be explained by the fact that, on average, 1.7 million people are the victims of violent crime while working or on duty in the United States. An estimated 1.3 million (75 percent) of these incidents are simple assaults and an additional 19 percent are aggravated assaults. Of the occupations examined, police officers, corrections officers, and taxi drivers were victimized at the highest rates. The Bureau of Labor Statistics' Census of Fatal Occupational Injuries (CFOI) reported that about 12,000 workplace homicides have occurred since 1992; like other violent crimes, the number of deaths has been in decline.[284]

Can Workplace Violence Be Controlled?   One approach is to use third parties to mediate disputes. The restorative justice movement (discussed in Chapter 8) advocates the use of mediation to resolve interpersonal disputes. Restorative justice techniques may work particularly well in the workplace, where disputants know one another, and tensions may be simmering over a long period. This may help control the rising tide of workplace violence. Another idea is a human resources approach, with aggressive job retraining and continued medical coverage after layoffs; it is also important to use objective, fair hearings to thwart unfair or biased terminations. Perhaps rigorous screening tests can help identify violence-prone workers so that they can be given anger management training. Most important, employers may want to establish policies restricting weapons in the workplace: recent research shows that workplaces in which guns were specifically permitted are five to seven times more likely to be the site of a worker homicide than those in which all weapons were prohibited.[285]

Stalking

In Wes Craven's popular *Scream* movies, the heroine Sydney (played by Neve Campbell) is pursued by a mysterious adversary who scares her half to death while killing off most of her peer group. Although obviously extreme even by Hollywood standards, the *Scream* movies focus on a newly recognized form of long-term and repeat victimization: **stalking**.[286] Although it is a complex phenomenon, stalking can be defined as a course of conduct directed at a specific person that involves repeated physical or visual proximity, nonconsensual communication, or verbal, written, or implied threats sufficient to cause fear in a reasonable person.[287]

How big a problem is stalking? Kathleen Basile and her associates used a large national sample of almost 10,000 adults to determine the prevalence of stalking in the United States. Analysis showed about 4.5 percent of adults reported having been stalked. Women had a significantly higher prevalence (7 percent) of stalking victimization than did men (2 percent). People who were never married (or who were separated, widowed, or divorced) had significantly higher odds of being stalked than those who were married or had a partner. People aged 55 years or older and those who were retired were least likely to report stalking victimization. In the United States stalking affects nearly 1 in 22 adults, or almost 10 million people, approximately 80 percent of whom are women, at some time during their life.[288]

Although this research is disturbing, it may actually undercount the problem. Bonnie Fisher and her associates found that about 13 percent of the women in a nationally drawn sample of more than 4,000 college women were the victims of stalking. Considering that there are more than 6.5 million women attending college in the United States, about 700,000 women are being stalked each year on college campuses alone.[289] Though students most likely have a lifestyle that increases the risk of stalking compared to women in the general population, these data make it clear that stalking is a very widespread phenomenon.

CONNECTIONS

The Fisher research found that the likelihood of being stalked may be related to the victim's lifestyle and routine activities. Female students who are the victims of stalking tend to date more, go out at night to bars and parties, and live alone. Their lifestyle both brings them into contact with potential stalkers and makes them vulnerable to stalking. For more on routine activities, go to Chapter 3.

Most victims know their stalker. A meta-analysis of existing research conducted by Brian Spitzberg and William Cupach found that most stalking (79 percent) emerged from preexisting relationships and about half of all stalking emerged specifically from romantic relationships.[290]

Women are most likely to be stalked by an intimate partner—a current spouse, a former spouse, someone they lived with, or even a date. In contrast, men typically are stalked by a stranger or an acquaintance. The typical female victim is stalked because her assailant wants to control her, scare her, or keep her in a relationship. Victims of both genders find that there is a clear relationship between stalking and other emotionally controlling and physically abusive behavior. Some psychologists believe that most stalkers are persons with mental illness who create social and public problems due to their violent behavior.[291]

Stalkers behave in ways that induce fear, but they do not always make overt threats against their victims. Many follow or spy upon their victims, some threaten to kill pets, and others vandalize property. Criminologist Mary Brewster found that stalkers who make verbal threats are the ones most likely to later attack their victims.[292] However, it is not uncommon for stalking to end in violence. In their review, Spitzberg and Cupach found that 32 percent of stalking cases involved physical violence and about 12 percent involved sexual violence.[293]

Though stalking is a serious problem, research indicates that many cases are dropped by the courts even though the stalkers often have extensive criminal histories and are frequently the subject of protective orders. A lenient response may be misplaced considering that stalkers tend to repeat their criminal activity within a short time after the lodging of a stalking charge with police authorities.[294] Victims experience its social and psychological consequences long afterward. About one-third seek psychological treatment, and about one-fifth lose time from work; some never return to work.

Why does stalking stop? Most often because the victim moved away or the police got involved or, in some cases, when the stalker met another love interest.

Visit the Criminal Justice CourseMate at cengage-brain.com, then access the "Web Links" for this chapter to:
- examine the **FBI's hate-crime data**
- read more about the **Boston Community Disorder Unit**

SUMMARY

1. **Be familiar with the various causes of violent crime**
   - Violence has become an all-too-common aspect of modern life. Among the various explanations of sources of violent crime are exposure to violence, personal traits and makeup, evolutionary factors and human instincts, cultural values and a subculture of violence, substance abuse, and socialization and upbringing.

2. **Be able to discuss the history of rape and know the different types of rape**
   - Rape, the carnal knowledge of a female forcibly and against her will, has been known throughout history, but the view of rape has evolved. Rape has been an instrument of war for thousands of years. There are numerous forms of rape, including statutory, acquaintance, and date rape.

3. **Discuss the legal issues in rape prosecution**
   - Rape is an extremely difficult charge to prove in court. The victim's lack of consent must be proven; therefore, it almost seems that the victim is on trial. Rape shield laws have been developed to protect victims from having their personal life placed on trial.

4. **Recognize that there are different degrees of murder**
   - Murder is defined as killing a human being with malice aforethought. There are different degrees of murder, and punishments vary accordingly. First-degree murder involves malice and premeditation. Second-degree murder requires malice aforethought but not premeditation or deliberation. Voluntary manslaughter refers to a killing, typically without a weapon, committed in the heat of passion or during a sudden quarrel that provoked violence. Although intent may be present, malice is not. Involuntary or negligent manslaughter refers to a killing that occurs when a person's acts are negligent and without regard for the harm they may cause others.

5. **Be able to discuss the differences among serial killing, mass murder, and spree killing**
   - Murder can involve a single victim or be a serial killing, mass murder, or spree killing that involve multiple victims. The difference between a spree killer and a serial killer is that the latter retains his or her identity and kills secretly. The spree killer abandons his or her normal identity and continues killing until either killed or captured.

6. **Discuss the concept of murder transaction**
   - One important characteristic of murder is that the victim and the criminal often know each other. Murder often involves an interpersonal transaction in which a hostile action by the victim precipitates a murderous relationship. In some instances, it is the victim who initiates the murderous transaction, such as a barroom brawl, and is killed in the aftermath.

7. **Be familiar with the nature of assault and battery**
   - Assault involves physically harming another. Assault requires no actual touching (which is called battery) but involves frightening the victim by word or deed. Assaults often occur in the home, including child abuse and spouse abuse. There also appears to be a trend toward violence within dating couples.

8. **Know the root causes of child abuse**
   - A number of factors have been commonly linked to abuse and neglect. Violence seems to be perpetuated from one generation to another within families. The behavior of abusive parents can often be traced to negative experiences in their own childhood. Blended families, which include children living with an unrelated adult such as a step-parent or another unrelated co-resident, also have been linked to abuse. Parents may become abusive if they are isolated from friends, neighbors, or relatives who can help in times of crisis.

9. **Understand the definition and concept of robbery**
   - The definition of robbery is "the taking or attempting to take anything of value from the care, custody or control of a person or persons by force or threat of force or violence and/or by putting the victim in fear." A robbery is considered a violent crime because it involves the use of force to obtain money or goods. Robbery is punished severely because the victim's life is put in jeopardy. In fact, the severity of punishment is based on the amount of force used during the crime, not the value of the items taken. Robbery that involves people who know each other is acquaintance robbery.

10. **Be able to discuss newly emerging forms of violence such as hate crimes, workplace violence, and stalking**
    - Hate crimes usually involve convenient, vulnerable targets who are incapable of fighting back. People become the target of hate crimes because of their religion, ethnicity, or race, or because they engage in behavior that is considered unacceptable to their attacker, such as being gay. Workplace violence is now considered one of the leading causes of occupational injury or death. It has become commonplace to read of irate employees or former employees attacking coworkers or sabotaging machinery and production lines. Stalking is a course of conduct directed at a specific person that involves repeated physical or visual proximity, nonconsensual communication, or verbal, written, or implied threats sufficient to cause fear in a reasonable person.

KEY TERMS

expressive violence (334)
instrumental violence (334)
violentization process (338)
crusted over (338)
hot spots (339)

subculture of violence (339)
disputatiousness (339)
gang rape (344)
serial rape (344)
acquaintance rape (344)

date rape (344)
statutory rape (344)
marital rape (344)
marital exemption (345)
virility mystique (346)

CRITICAL THINKING QUESTIONS

1. Should different types of rape receive different legal sanctions? For example, should someone who rapes a stranger be punished more severely than someone who is convicted of marital rape or date rape? If your answer is yes, do you also think that someone who kills a stranger should be more severely punished than someone who kills his wife or girlfriend?

2. Is there a subculture of violence in your home city or town? If so, how would you describe its environment and values?

3. There have been significant changes in rape laws regarding issues such as corroboration and shield laws. What other measures would you take to protect the victims of rape when they are forced to testify in court? Should the names of rape victims be published in the press? Do they deserve more protection than those accused of rape?

4. Should hate crimes be punished more severely than crimes motivated by greed, anger, or revenge? Why should crimes be distinguished by the motivations of the perpetrator? Is hate a more heinous motivation than revenge?

5. Do you believe that murder is an interactive event? If so, does that amount to "blaming the victim"? If there is a murder transaction, should we not consider rape, domestic assault, and so forth as "transactions"?

NOTES

1. Lizette Alvarez, "Casey Anthony Not Guilty in Slaying of Daughter," *New York Times*, July 5, 2011, www.nytimes.com/2011/07/06/us/06casey.html (accessed August 11, 2011).

2. George Tita, Tricia Petras, and Robert Greenbaum, "Crime and Residential Choice: A Neighborhood Level Analysis of the Impact of Crime on Housing Prices," *Journal of Quantitative Criminology* 22 (2006): 299–317.

3. Robert Nash Parker and Catherine Colony, "Relationships, Homicides, and Weapons: A Detailed Analysis," paper presented at the annual meeting of the American Society of Criminology, Montreal, November 1987.

4. Stryker McGuire, "The Dunblane Effect," *Newsweek*, October 28, 1996, p. 46.

5. Rokeya Farrooque, Ronnie Stout, and Frederick Ernst, "Heterosexual Intimate Partner Homicide: Review of Ten Years of Clinical Experience," *Journal of Forensic Sciences* 50 (2005): 648–651; Miltos Livaditis, Gkaro Esagian, Christos Kakoulidis, Maria Samakouri, and Nikos Tzavaras, "Matricide by Person with Bipolar Disorder and Dependent Overcompliant Personality," *Journal of Forensic Sciences* 50 (2005): 658–661.

6. Dorothy Otnow Lewis, Ernest Moy, Lori Jackson, Robert Aaronson, Nicholas Restifo, Susan Serra, and Alexander Simos, "Biopsychosocial Characteristics of Children Who Later Murder," *American Journal of Psychiatry* 142 (1985): 1,161–1,167.

7. Dorothy Otnow Lewis, *Guilty by Reason of Insanity* (New York: Fawcett Columbine, 1998).

8. Richard Rogers, Randall Salekin, Kenneth Sewell, and Keith Cruise, "Prototypical Analysis of Antisocial Personality Disorder," *Criminal Justice and Behavior* 27 (2000): 234–255; Amy Holtzworth-Munroe and Gregory Stuart, "Typologies of Male Batterers: Three Subtypes and the Differences among Them," *Psychological Bulletin* 116 (1994): 476–497.

9. Christopher Hensley and Suzanne Tallichet, "Childhood and Adolescent Animal Cruelty Methods and Their Possible Link to Adult Violent Crimes," *Journal of Interpersonal Violence* 24 (2009): 147–158;

Roman Gleyzer, Alan Felthous, and Charles Holzer, "Animal Cruelty and Psychiatric Disorders," *Journal of the American Academy of Psychiatry and the Law* 30 (2002): 257–265.

10. Katherine Van Wormer and Chuk Odiah, "The Psychology of Suicide-Murder and the Death Penalty," *Journal of Criminal Justice* 27 (1999): 361–370.

11. Daniel Strueber, Monika Lueck, and Gerhard Roth, "The Violent Brain," *Scientific American Mind* 17 (2006): 20–27.

12. Dave Marcotte and Sara Markowitz, "A Cure for Crime? Psycho-Pharmaceuticals and Crime Trends," *Journal of Policy Analysis and Management* 30 (2011): 29–56.

13. Christopher Boehm, "Retaliatory Violence in Human Prehistory," *British Journal of Criminology* 51 (2011): 518–534.

14. Sigmund Freud, *Beyond the Pleasure Principle* (London: Inter-Psychoanalytic Press, 1922).

15. Konrad Lorenz, *On Aggression* (New York: Harcourt Brace Jovanovich, 1966).

16. Nigel Barber, "Why Is Violent Crime So Common in the Americas?" *Aggressive Behavior* 32 (2006): 442–450.

17. Randall Collins, *Violence: A Micro-sociological Theory* (Princeton, NJ: Princeton University Press, 2008).

18. Arnie Nielsen, Ramiro Martinez, and Matthew Lee, "Alcohol, Ethnicity, and Violence: The Role of Alcohol Availability for Latino and Black Aggravated Assaults and Robberies," *Sociological Quarterly*, 46 (2005): 479–502.

19. Chris Allen, "The Links Between Heroin, Crack Cocaine and Crime: Where Does Street Crime Fit In?" *British Journal of Criminology* 45 (2005): 355–372.

20. Steven Messner, Glenn Deane, Luc Anselin, and Benjamin Pearson-Nelson, "Locating the Vanguard in Rising and Falling Homicide Rates Across Cities," *Criminology* 43 (2005): 661–696.

21. William Alex Pridemore and Tony Grubesic, "Alcohol Outlets and Community Levels of Interpersonal Violence: Spatial Density, Outlet Type, and Seriousness of Assault," *Journal of Research in Crime and Delinquency*, published online before print May 17, 2011, doi:10.1177/0022427810397952.

22. Paul Goldstein, Henry Brownstein, and Patrick Ryan, "Drug-Related Homicide in New York: 1984–1988," *Crime and Delinquency* 38 (1992): 459–476.

23. Albert Reiss and Jeffrey Roth, *Understanding and Preventing Violence* (Washington, DC: National Academies Press, 1993), pp. 193–194.

24. Robert Brewer and Monica Swahn, "Binge Drinking and Violence," *JAMA: Journal of the American Medical Association* 294 (2005): 16–20.

25. Tomika Stevens, Kenneth Ruggiero, Dean Kilpatrick, Heidi Resnick, and Benjamin Saunders, "Variables Differentiating Singly and Multiply Victimized Youth: Results from the National Survey of Adolescents and Implications for Secondary Prevention," *Child Maltreatment* 10 (2005): 211–223; James Collins and Pamela Messerschmidt, "Epidemiology of Alcohol-Related Violence," *Alcohol Health and Research World* 17 (1993): 93–100.

26. Antonia Abbey, Tina Zawacki, Philip Buck, Monique Clinton, and Pam McAuslan, "Sexual Assault and Alcohol Consumption: What Do We Know about Their Relationship and What Types of Research Are Still Needed?" *Aggression and Violent Behavior* 9 (2004): 271–303.

27. Scott Phillips, Jacqueline Matusko, and Elizabeth Tomasovic, "Reconsidering the Relationship Between Alcohol and Lethal Violence," *Journal of Interpersonal Violence* 22 (2007): 66–84.

28. Martin Grann and Seena Fazel, "Substance Misuse and Violent Crime: Swedish Population Study," *British Medical Journal* 328 (2004): 1,233–1,234; Susanne Rogne Gjeruldsen, Bjørn Myrvang, and Stein Opjordsmoen, "Criminality in Drug Addicts: A Follow-Up Study over 25 Years," *European Addiction Research* 10 (2004): 49–56.

29. Paul Goldstein, Patricia Bellucci, Barry Spunt, and Thomas Miller, "Volume of Cocaine Use and Violence: A Comparison between Men and Women," *Journal of Drug Issues* 21 (1991): 345–367.

30. Richard Felson and Luke Bonkiewicz, "Guns and Trafficking in Crack-Cocaine and Other Drug Markets," *Crime and Delinquency*, published online before print February 10, 2011, doi:10.1177/0011128711398023.

31. Anthony A. Braga and David M. Kennedy, "The Illicit Acquisition of Firearms by Youth and Juveniles," *Journal of Criminal Justice* 29 (2001): 379–388; Jens Ludwig and Philip Cook, "Homicide and Suicide Rates Associated with the Implementation of the Brady Violence Prevention Act," *Journal of the American Medical Association* 284 (2000): 585–591.

32. Gary Kleck and Jongyeon Tark, "Resisting Crime: The Effects of Victim Action on the Outcomes of Crimes," *Criminology* 42 (2005): 861–909.

33. Gary Kleck and Marc Gertz, "Armed Resistance to Crime: The Prevalence and Nature of Self-Defense with a Gun," *Journal of Criminal Law and Criminology* 86 (1995): 150–187.

34. *District of Columbia v. Heller,* 554 U.S. 570 (2008); *McDonald v. Chicago,* 561 U.S. 3025 (2010).

35. John Donohue and Ian Ayres, "Yet Another Refutation of the More Guns, Less Crime Hypothesis—With Some Help From Moody and Marvell," *Econ Journal Watch* 6 (2009): 35–59.

36. Tomislav Kovandzic, Thomas Marvell, and Lynne Vieraitis, "The Impact of 'Shall-Issue' Concealed Handgun Laws on Violent Crime Rates: Evidence from Panel Data for Large Urban Cities," *Homicide Studies* 9 (2005): 292–323; Tomislav Kovandzic and Thomas Marvell, "Right-to-Carry Concealed Handguns and Violent Crime: Crime Control through Gun Control?" *Criminology and Public Policy* 2 (2003): 363–396.

37. Todd Herrenkohl, Bu Huang, Emiko Tajima, and Stephen Whitney, "Examining the Link between Child Abuse and Youth Violence," *Journal of Interpersonal Violence* 18 (2003): 1,189–1,208; Pamela Lattimore, Christy Visher, and Richard Linster, "Predicting Rearrest for Violence among Serious Youthful Offenders," *Journal of Research in Crime and Delinquency* 32 (1995): 54–83.

38. Rolf Loeber and Dale Hay, "Key Issues in the Development of Aggression and Violence from Childhood to Early Adulthood," *Annual Review of Psychology* 48 (1997): 371–410.

39. Deborah Capaldi and Gerald Patterson, "Can Violent Offenders Be Distinguished from Frequent Offenders: Prediction from Childhood to Adolescence," *Journal of Research in Crime and Delinquency* 33 (1996): 206–231.

40. Adrian Raine, Patricia Brennan, and Sarnoff Mednick, "Interaction between Birth Complications and Early Maternal Rejection in Predisposing Individuals to Adult Violence: Specificity to Serious, Early-Onset Violence," *American Journal of Psychiatry* 154 (1997): 1,265–1,271.

41. John Lemmon, "How Child Maltreatment Affects Dimensions of Juvenile Delinquency in a Cohort of Low-Income Urban Youths," *Justice Quarterly* 16 (1999): 357–376.

42. Eric Slade and Lawrence Wissow, "Spanking in Early Childhood and Later Behavior Problems: A Prospective Study of Infants and Young Toddlers," *Pediatrics* 113 (2004): 1,321–1,330.

43. Egbert Zavala, "Testing the Link Between Child Maltreatment and Family Violence Among Police Officers," *Crime and Delinquency*, published online before print November 22, 2010, doi: 10.1177/0011128710389584

44. Murray Straus, "Discipline and Deviance: Physical Punishment of Children and Violence and Other Crime in Adulthood," *Social Problems* 38 (1991): 101–123.

45. Ronald Simons, Chyi-In Wu, Kuei-Hsiu Lin, Leslie Gordon, and Rand Conger, "A Cross-Cultural Examination of the Link between Corporal Punishment and Adolescent Antisocial Behavior," *Criminology* 38 (2000): 47–79.

46. Robert Scudder, William Blount, Kathleen Heide, and Ira Silverman, "Important Links between Child Abuse, Neglect, and Delinquency," *International Journal of Offender Therapy* 37 (1993): 315–323.

47. Dorothy Lewis et al., "Neuropsychiatric, Psychoeducational, and Family Characteristics of 14 Juveniles Condemned to Death in the United States," *American Journal of Psychiatry* 145 (1988): 584–588.

48. Charles Patrick Ewing, *When Children Kill* (Lexington, MA: Lexington Books, 1990), p. 22.

49. Lewis, *Guilty by Reason of Insanity,* pp. 11–35.

50. Timothy Ireland, Carolyn Smith, and Terence Thornberry, "Developmental Issues in the Impact of Child Maltreatment on Later Delinquency and Drug Use," *Criminology* 40 (2002): 359–401.

51. Straus, "Discipline and Deviance."

52. Alan Rosenbaum and Penny Leisring, "Beyond Power and Control: Towards an Understanding of Partner Abusive Men," *Journal of Comparative Family Studies* 34 (2003): 7–26.

53. Lonnie Athens, *The Creation of Dangerous Violent Criminals* (Urbana: University of Illinois Press, 1992), pp. 27–80.

54. Eric Stewart, Ronald Simons, and Rand Conger, "Assessing Neighborhood and

Social Psychological Influences on Childhood Violence in an African-American Sample," *Criminology* 40 (2002): 801–830.

55. Joanne Kaufman, "Explaining the Race/Ethnicity–Violence Relationship: Neighborhood Context and Social Psychological Processes," *Justice Quarterly* 22 (2005): 224–251; David Farrington, Rolf Loeber, and Madga Stouthamer-Loeber, "How Can the Relationship between Race and Violence Be Explained?" in *Violent Crimes: Assessing Race and Ethnic Differences,* ed. D. F. Hawkins (New York: Cambridge University Press, 2003), pp. 213–237.

56. Barbara Warner, "Robberies with Guns: Neighborhood Factors and the Nature of Crime," *Journal of Criminal Justice* 35 (2007): 39–50.

57. Darrell Steffensmeier, Ben Feldmeyer, Casey T. Harris, and Jeffery T. Ulmer, "Reassessing Trends in Black Violent Crime, 1980–2008: Sorting Out the 'Hispanic Effect' in Uniform Crime Reports Arrests, National Crime Victimization Survey Offender Estimates, and U.S. Prisoner Counts," *Criminology* 49 (2011): 197–251.

58. Felton Earls, *Linking Community Factors and Individual Development* (Washington, DC: National Institute of Justice, 1998).

59. Jeffrey B. Bingenheimer, Robert T. Brennan, and Felton J. Earls, "Firearm Violence Exposure and Serious Violent Behavior," *Science* 308 (2005): 1,323–1,326; Harvard University Medical School, "Witnessing Gun Violence Significantly Increases Likelihood that a Child Will Also Commit Violent Crime; Violence May Be Viewed as Infectious Disease," *AScribe Health News Service*, May 26, 2005.

60. Michael Greene, "Chronic Exposure to Violence and Poverty: Interventions that Work for Youth," *Crime and Delinquency* 39 (1993): 106–124.

61. Todd Armstrong, Charles Katz, and Stephen Schnebly, "The Relationship Between Citizen Perceptions of Collective Efficacy and Neighborhood Violent Crime," *Crime and Delinquency,* published online before print November 15, 2010, doi: 10.1177/0011128710386202.

62. Robert Baller, Luc Anselin, Steven Messner, Glenn Deane, and Darnell Hawkins, "Structural Covariates of U.S. County Homicide Rates Incorporating Spatial Effects," *Criminology* 39 (2001): 561–590.

63. Marvin Wolfgang and Franco Ferracuti, *The Subculture of Violence* (London: Tavistock, 1967).

64. David Luckenbill and Daniel Doyle, "Structural Position and Violence: Developing a Cultural Explanation," *Criminology* 27 (1989): 419–436.

65. Robert Sampson and William Julius Wilson, "Toward a Theory of Race, Crime, and Urban Inequality," in *Crime and Inequality*, ed. John Hagan and Ruth Peterson (Stanford, CA: Stanford University Press, 1995), p. 51.

66. Liqun Cao, Anthony Adams, and Vickie Jensen, "A Test of the Black Subculture of Violence Thesis," *Criminology* 35 (1997): 367–379.

67. Eric Baumer, Julie Horney, Richard Felson, and Janet Lauritsen, "Neighborhood Disadvantage and the Nature of Violence," *Criminology* 41 (2003): 39–71.

68. Charis Kubrin and Ronald Weitzer, "Retaliatory Homicide: Concentrated Disadvantage and Neighborhood Culture," *Social Problems* 50 (2003): 157–180.

69. Robert J. Kane, "Compromised Police Legitimacy as a Predictor of Violent Crime in Structurally Disadvantaged Communities," *Criminology* 43 (2005): 469–499.

70. William Wells, Ling Wu, and Xinyue Ye, "Patterns of Near-Repeat Gun Assaults in Houston," *Journal of Research in Crime and Delinquency,* published online before print, May 12, 2011, doi: 10.1177/0022427810397946.

71. Steven Messner, "Regional and Racial Effects on the Urban Homicide Rate: The Subculture of Violence Revisited," *American Journal of Sociology* 88 (1983): 997–1,007; Steven Messner and Kenneth Tardiff, "Economic Inequality and Levels of Homicide: An Analysis of Urban Neighborhoods," *Criminology* 24 (1986): 297–317.

72. Beth Bjerregaard and Alan Lizotte, "Gun Ownership and Gang Membership," *Journal of Criminal Law and Criminology* 86 (1995): 37–58.

73. Rachel Gordon, Benjamin Lahey, Eriko Kawai, Rolf Loeber, Magda Stouthamer-Loeber, and David Farrington, "Antisocial Behavior and Youth Gang Membership," *Criminology* 42 (2004): 55–88.

74. Andrew Papachristos, "Murder by Structure: Dominance Relations and the Social Structure of Gang Homicide," *American Journal of Sociology* 115 (2009): 74–128.

75. Jerome Neapolitan, "A Comparative Analysis of Nations with Low and High Levels of Violent Crime," *Journal of Criminal Justice* 27 (1999): 259–274.

76. Ibid., p. 271.

77. Lonnie Schaible and Lorine Hughes, "Crime, Shame, Reintegration, and Cross-national Homicide: A Partial Test of Reintegrative Shaming Theory," *The Sociological Quarterly* 52 (2011): 104–131.

78. Aki Roberts and Gary Lafree, "Explaining Japan's Postwar Violent Crime Trends," *Criminology* 42 (2004): 179–210.

79. Don Chon, "Contributing Factors for High Homicide Rate in Latin America: A Critical Test of Neapolitan's Regional Subculture of Violence Thesis," *Journal of Family Violence* 26 (2011): 299–307.

80. David Courtwright, "Violence in America," *American Heritage* 47 (1996): 36–52, at 36; David Courtwright, *Violent Land: Single Men and Social Disorder from the Frontier to the Inner City* (Cambridge, MA: Harvard University Press, 1996).

81. William Green, *Rape* (Lexington, MA: Lexington Books, 1988), p. 5.

82. Heidi Zinzow, Heidi Resnick, Ananda Amstadter, Jenna McCauley, Kenneth Ruggiero, and Dean Kilpatrick, "Drug- or Alcohol-Facilitated, Incapacitated, and Forcible Rape in Relationship to Mental Health Among a National Sample of Women," *Journal of Interpersonal Violence* 25 (2010): 2,217–2,236.

83. Susan Randall and Vicki McNickle Rose, "Forcible Rape," in *Major Forms of Crime,* ed. Robert Meyer (Beverly Hills: Sage, 1984), p. 47.

84. Barbara Krah, Renate Scheinberger-Olwig, and Steffen Bieneck, "Men's Reports of Nonconsensual Sexual Interactions with Women: Prevalence and Impact," *Archives of Sexual Behavior* 32 (2003): 165–176.

85. Siegmund Fred Fuchs, "Male Sexual Assault: Issues of Arousal and Consent," *Cleveland State Law Review* 51 (2004): 93–108.

86. Raquel Kennedy Bergen and Paul Bukovec, "Men and Intimate Partner Rape: Characteristics of Men Who Sexually Abuse Their Partner," *Journal of Interpersonal Violence* 21 (2006): 1,375–1,384.

87. Susan Brownmiller, *Against Our Will: Men, Women, and Rape* (New York: Simon & Schuster, 1975).

88. Green, *Rape,* p. 6.

89. Yuri Kageyama, "Court Orders Japan to Pay Sex Slaves," *Boston Globe*, April 28, 1998, p. A2.

90. Marlise Simons, "Bosnian Serb Pleads Guilty to Rape Charge before War Crimes Tribunal," *New York Times,* March 10, 1998, p. 8.

91. Marc Lacey, "Amnesty Says Sudan Militias Use Rape as Weapon," *New York Times,* July 19, 2004, p. A9.

92. Human Rights Watch, *Soldiers Who Rape, Commanders Who Condone: Sexual Violence and Military Reform in the Democratic Republic of Congo* (New York: Author, 2009).

93. FBI, *Crime in the United States, 2010 Preliminary Results.* Crime data in this chapter come from this source. www.fbi.gov/about-us/cjis/ucr/crime-in-the-u.s/2010/preliminary-annual-ucr-jan-dec-2010 (accessed August 11, 2011).

94. Jennifer L. Truman and Michael R. Rand, *Criminal Victimization, 2009* (Washington, DC: Bureau of Justice Statistics, 2010), http://bjs.ojp.usdoj.gov/content/pub/pdf/cv09.pdf (accessed August 11, 2011).

95. Carol Vanzile-Tamsen, Maria Testa, and Jennifer Livingston, "The Impact of Sexual Assault History and Relationship Context on Appraisal of and Responses to Acquaintance Sexual Assault Risk," *Journal of Interpersonal Violence* 20 (2005): 813–822; Arnold Kahn, Jennifer Jackson, Christine

Kully, Kelly Badger, and Jessica Halvorsen, "Calling It Rape: Differences in Experiences of Women Who Do or Do Not Label Their Sexual Assault as Rape," *Psychology of Women Quarterly* 27 (2003): 233–242.

96. Jody Clay-Warner and Jennifer McMahon-Howard, "Rape Reporting: 'Classic Rape' and the Behavior of Law," *Violence and Victims* 24 (2009): 723–743.

97. Sarah Cook, Christine Gidycz, Mary Koss, and Megan Murphy, "Emerging Issues in the Measurement of Rape Victimization," *Violence Against Women* 17 (2011): 201–218.

98. For an analysis of the validity of rape data, see Bonnie S. Fisher, "The Effects of Survey Question Wording on Rape Estimates: Evidence From a Quasi-Experimental Design," *Violence Against Women* 15 (2009): 133–147.

99. Heather Littleton and Craig Henderson, "If She Is Not a Victim, Does That Mean She Was Not Traumatized?: Evaluation of Predictors of PTSD Symptomatology Among College Rape Victims," *Violence Against Women* 15 (2009): 148–167.

100. Mark Warr, "Rape, Burglary, and Opportunity," *Journal of Quantitative Criminology* 4 (1988): 275–288.

101. Maria Testa, Jennifer Livingston, and Carol Vanzile-Tamsen, "The Role of Victim and Perpetrator Intoxication on Sexual Assault Outcomes," *Journal of Studies on Alcohol* 65 (2004): 320–329.

102. Nicholas Groth and Jean Birnbaum, *Men Who Rape* (New York: Plenum Press, 1979).

103. For another typology, see Raymond Knight, "Validation of a Typology of Rapists," in *Sex Offender Research and Treatment: State-of-the-Art in North America and Europe,* ed. W. L. Marshall and J. Frenken (Beverly Hills: Sage, 1997), pp. 58–75.

104. Sarah Ullman, "A Comparison of Gang and Individual Rape Incidents," *Violence and Victimization* 14 (1999): 123–134.

105. Janet Warren, Roland Reboussin, Robert Hazlewood, Natalie Gibbs, Susan Trumbetta, and Andrea Cummings, "Crime Scene Analysis and the Escalation of Violence in Serial Rape," *Forensic Science International* (1998): 56–62.

106. James LeBeau, "Patterns of Stranger and Serial Rape Offending Factors Distinguishing Apprehended and At-Large Offenders," *Journal of Criminal Law and Delinquency* 78 (1987): 309–326.

107. Bonnie Fisher, Francis Cullen, and Leah Daigle, "The Discovery of Acquaintance Rape," *Journal of Interpersonal Violence* 20 (2005): 493–500.

108. Leah Adams-Curtis and Gordon Forbes, "College Women's Experiences of Sexual Coercion," *Trauma, Violence and Abuse* 5 (2004): 91–122.

109. Cassia Spohn, Dawn Beichner, and Erika Davis-Frenzel, "Prosecutorial Justifications for Sexual Assault Case Rejection: Guarding the 'Gateway to Justice,'" *Social Problems* 48 (2001): 206–235.

110. Mary Koss, "Hidden Rape: Sexual Aggression and Victimization in a National Sample of Students in Higher Education," in *Rape and Sexual Assault*, vol. 2, ed. Ann Wolbert Burgess (New York: Garland, 1988), p. 824.

111. R. Lance Shotland, "A Model of the Causes of Date Rape in Developing and Close Relationships," in *Close Relationships*, ed. C. Hendrick (Newbury Park, CA: Sage, 1989), pp. 247–270.

112. Kimberly Tyler, Danny Hoyt, and Les Whitbeck, "Coercive Sexual Strategies," *Violence and Victims* 13 (1998): 47–63.

113. Alan Gross, Andrea Winslett, Miguel Roberts, and Carol Gohm, "An Examination of Sexual Violence Against College Women," *Violence Against Women* 12 (2006): 288–300.

114. Julie A. Allison and Lawrence S. Wrightsman, *Rape: The Misunderstood Crime* (Newbury Park, CA: Sage, 1993), p. 64.

115. Amy Buddie and Maria Testa, "Rates and Predictors of Sexual Aggression Among Students and Nonstudents," *Journal of Interpersonal Violence* 20 (2005): 713–725.

116. Bonnie Fisher, Leah Daigle, Francis Cullen, and Michael Turner, "Reporting Sexual Victimization to the Police and Others: Results from a National-Level Study of College Women," *Criminal Justice and Behavior* 30 (2003): 6–39.

117. Allison and Wrightsman, *Rape: The Misunderstood Crime,* pp. 85–87.

118. Cited in Diana Russell, "Wife Rape," in *Acquaintance Rape: The Hidden Crime,* ed. A. Parrot and L. Bechhofer (New York: Wiley, 1991), pp. 129–139, at 129.

119. David Finkelhor and K. Yllo, *License to Rape: Sexual Abuse of Wives* (New York: Holt, Rinehart & Winston, 1985).

120. Allison and Wrightsman. *Rape: The Misunderstood Crime,* p. 89.

121. Raquel Kennedy Bergen with contributions from Elizabeth Barnhill, "Marital Rape: New Research and Directions," National Online Resource Center for Violence Against Women, www.vawnet.org/Assoc_Files_VAWnet/AR_MaritalRapeRevised.pdf (accessed August 11, 2011); Associated Press, "British Court Rejects Precedent, Finds a Man Guilty of Raping Wife," *Boston Globe,* March 15, 1991, p. 68.

122. Jill Elaine Hasday, "Contest and Consent: A Legal History of Marital Rape," *California Law Review* 88 (2000): 1,373–1,433.

123. Bergen and Barnhill "Marital Rape: New Research and Directions."

124. Sharon Elstein and Roy Davis, *Sexual Relationships between Adult Males and Young Teen Girls: Exploring the Legal and Social Responses* (Chicago: American Bar Association, 1997).

125. Donald Symons, *The Evolution of Human Sexuality* (Oxford: Oxford University Press, 1979).

126. Lee Ellis and Anthony Walsh, "Gene-Based Evolutionary Theories in Criminology," *Criminology* 35 (1997): 229–276.

127. Suzanne Osman, "Predicting Men's Rape Perceptions Based on the Belief that 'No' Really Means 'Yes,'" *Journal of Applied Social Psychology* 33 (2003): 683–692.

128. Martin Schwartz, Walter DeKeseredy, David Tait, and Shahid Alvi, "Male Peer Support and a Feminist Routine Activities Theory: Understanding Sexual Assault on the College Campus," *Justice Quarterly* 18 (2001): 623–650.

129. Diana Russell, *The Politics of Rape* (New York: Stein and Day, 1975).

130. Diana Russell and Rebecca M. Bolen, *The Epidemic of Rape and Child Sexual Abuse in the United States* (Thousand Oaks, CA: Sage, 2000).

131. Rachel Bridges Whaley, "The Paradoxical Relationship between Gender Inequality and Rape: Toward a Refined Theory," *Gender and Society* 15 (2001): 531–555.

132. Paul Gebhard, John Gagnon, Wardell Pomeroy, and Cornelia Christenson, *Sex Offenders: An Analysis of Types* (New York: Harper & Row, 1965), pp. 198–205; Richard Rada, ed., *Clinical Aspects of the Rapist* (New York: Grune & Stratton, 1978), pp. 122–130.

133. Stephen Porter, David Fairweather, Jeff Drugge, Huues Herve, Angela Birt, and Douglas Boer, "Profiles of Psychopathy in Incarcerated Sexual Offenders," *Criminal Justice and Behavior* 27 (2000): 216–233.

134. Brad Bushman, Angelica Bonacci, Mirjam van Dijk, and Roy Baumeister, "Narcissism, Sexual Refusal, and Aggression: Testing a Narcissistic Reactance Model of Sexual Coercion," *Journal of Personality and Social Psychology,* 84 (2003): 1,027–1,040.

135. Schwartz, DeKeseredy, Tait, and Alvi, "Male Peer Support and a Feminist Routine Activities Theory."

136. Groth and Birnbaum, *Men Who Rape,* p. 101.

137. See generally Edward Donnerstein, Daniel Linz, and Steven Penrod, *The Question of Pornography* (New York: Free Press, 1987); Diana Russell, *Sexual Exploitation* (Beverly Hills: Sage, 1985), pp. 115–116.

138. Neil Malamuth and John Briere, "Sexual Violence in the Media: Indirect Effects on Aggression against Women," *Journal of Social Issues* 42 (1986): 75–92.

139. Richard Felson and Marvin Krohn, "Motives for Rape," *Journal of Research in Crime and Delinquency* 27 (1990): 222–242.

140. Laura Monroe, Linda Kinney, Mark Weist, Denise Spriggs Dafeamekpor, Joyce Dantzler, and Matthew Reynolds, "The Experience of Sexual Assault: Findings from a Statewide Victim Needs Assessment,"

Journal of Interpersonal Violence 20 (2005): 767–776.

141. Ibid.

142. Julie Horney and Cassia Spohn, "The Influence of Blame and Believability Factors on the Processing of Simple versus Aggravated Rape Cases," *Criminology* 34 (1996): 135–163.

143. CBS News, "DA: Strauss-Kahn Accuser Cleaned After Encounter," July 1, 2011, www.cbsnews.com/stories/2011/07/01/national/main20076147.shtml (accessed August 11, 2011).

144. Mark Whatley, "The Effect of Participant Sex, Victim Dress, and Traditional Attitudes on Causal Judgments for Marital Rape Victims," *Journal of Family Violence* 20 (2005): 191–200; Spohn, Beichner, and Davis-Frenzel, "Prosecutorial Justifications for Sexual Assault Case Rejection."

145. Patricia Landwehr, Robert Bothwell, Matthew Jeanmard, Luis Luque, Roy Brown III, and Marie-Anne Breaux, "Racism in Rape Trials," *Journal of Social Psychology* 142 (2002): 667–670.

146. "Man Wrongly Convicted of Rape Released 19 Years Later," *Forensic Examiner* (May–June 2003): 44.

147. Gerald Robin, "Forcible Rape: Institutionalized Sexism in the Criminal Justice System," *Crime and Delinquency* 23 (1977): 136–153.

148. Kirk Johnson, "Prosecutors Drop Kobe Bryant Rape Case," *New York Times*, September 2, 2004, www.nytimes.com/2004/09/02/national/02kobe.html (accessed August 11, 2011).

149. Steffen Bieneck and Barbara Krahe, "Blaming the Victim and Exonerating the Perpetrator in Cases of Rape and Robbery: Is There a Double Standard?" *Journal of Interpersonal Violence* 26 (2011): 1,785–1,797.

150. Rodney Kingsworth, Randall MacIntosh, and Jennifer Wentworth, "Sexual Assault: The Role of Prior Relationship and Victim Characteristics in Case Processing," *Justice Quarterly* 16 (1999): 276–302.

151. Associated Press, "Jury Stirs Furor by Citing Dress in Rape Acquittal," *Boston Globe,* October 6, 1989, p. 12.

152. Cassia Spohn and David Holleran, "Prosecuting Sexual Assault: A Comparison of Charging Decisions in Sexual Assault Cases Involving Strangers, Acquaintances, and Intimate Partners," *Justice Quarterly* 18 (2001): 651–688.

153. Susan Estrich, *Real Rape* (Cambridge, MA: Harvard University Press, 1987), pp. 58–59.

154. See, for example, Mich. Comp. Laws Ann. 750.5200-(1); Florida Statutes Annotated, Sec. 794.011; see generally Gary LaFree, "Official Reactions to Rape," *American Sociological Review* 45 (1980): 842–854.

155. Martin Schwartz and Todd Clear, "Toward a New Law on Rape," *Crime and Delinquency* 26 (1980): 129–151.

156. *Michigan v. Lucas* 90-149 (1991); Comment, "The Rape Shield Paradox: Complainant Protection amidst Oscillating Trends of State Judicial Interpretation," *Journal of Criminal Law and Criminology* 78 (1987): 644–698.

157. Andrew Karmen, *Crime Victims* (Pacific Grove, CA: Brooks/Cole, 1990), p. 252.

158. "Court Upholds Civil Rights Portion of Violence Against Women Act," *Criminal Justice Newsletter* 28 (December 1, 1997): 3.

159. This section relies on David John Frank, Tara Hardinge, and Kassia Wosick-Correa, "The Global Dimensions of Rape-Law Reform: A Cross-National Study of Policy Outcomes," *American Sociological Review* 74 (2009): 272–290.

160. Donald Lunde, *Murder and Madness* (San Francisco: San Francisco Book Company, 1977), p. 3.

161. Lisa Baertlein, "HIV Ruled Deadly Weapon in Rape Case," *Boston Globe,* March 2, 1994, p. 3.

162. The legal principles here come from Wayne LaFave and Austin Scott, *Criminal Law* (St. Paul: West, 1986; updated 1993). The definitions and discussion of legal principles used in this chapter lean heavily on this work.

163. LaFave and Scott, *Criminal Law.*

164. Bob Egelko, "State's Top Court OKs Dog Maul Murder Charge: Judge Ordered to Reconsider Owner's Original Conviction," *San Franciso Chronicle* June 1, 2007, www.sfgate.com/cgi-bin/article.cgi?f=/c/a/2007/06/01/BAGIPQ5KE51.DTL (accessed September 21, 2010); Evelyn Nieves, "Woman Gets 4-Year Term in Fatal Dog Attack," *New York Times*, July 16, 2002, p. 1.

165. Pauline Arrillaga, "Jurors Give Drunk Driver 16 Years in Fetus's Death," *Manchester Union Leader,* October 22, 1996, p. B20.

166. *Whitner v. State of South Carolina,* Supreme Court of South Carolina, Opinion Number 24468, July 15, 1996.

167. Christine Vestal and Elizabeth Wilkerson, "States Expand Fetal Homicide Laws," Stateline, August 22, 2006, www.stateline.org/live/details/story?contentId=135873 (accessed August 11, 2011); The National Conference of State Legislatures Fetal Homicide Laws, March 2010, www.ncsl.org/default.aspx?tabid=14386 (accessed August 11, 2011).

168. Dana Haynie and David Armstrong, "Race and Gender-Disaggregated Homicide Offending Rates: Differences and Similarities by Victim-Offender Relations across Cities," *Homicide Studies* 10 (2006): 3–32.

169. Terance Miethe and Wendy Regoeczi ,with Kriss Drass, *Rethinking Homicide: Exploring the Structure and Process Underlying Deadly Situations* (Cambridge, MA: Cambridge University Press, 2004).

170. Todd Shackelford, Viviana Weekes-Shackelford, and Shanna Beasley, "An Exploratory Analysis of the Contexts and Circumstances of Filicide-Suicide in Chicago, 1965–1994," *Aggressive Behavior* 31 (2005): 399–406.

171. Jessie Krienert and Jeffrey Walsh, "Eldercide: A Gendered Examination of Elderly Homicide in the United States, 2000–2005," *Homicide Studies* 14 (2010): 52–71.

172. Philip Cook, Jens Ludwig, and Anthony Braga, "Criminal Records of Homicide Offenders," *JAMA: Journal of the American Medical Association* 294 (2005): 598–601.

173. See, generally, Marc Reidel and Margaret Zahn, *The Nature and Pattern of American Homicide* (Washington, DC: U.S. Government Printing Office, 1985).

174. Angela Browne and Kirk Williams, "Gender, Intimacy, and Lethal Violence: Trends from 1976 through 1987," *Gender and Society* 7 (1993): 78–98.

175. Linda Saltzman and James Mercy, "Assaults between Intimates: The Range of Relationships Involved," in *Homicide: The Victim/Offender Connection,* ed. Anna Victoria Wilson (Cincinnati: Anderson, 1993), pp. 65–74.

176. Angela Browne and Kirk Williams, "Exploring the Effect of Resource Availability and the Likelihood of Female-Perpetrated Homicides," *Law and Society Review* 23 (1989): 75–94.

177. Richard Felson, "Anger, Aggression, and Violence in Love Triangles," *Violence and Victimization* 12 (1997): 345–363.

178. Ibid., p. 361.

179. Scott Decker, "Deviant Homicide: A New Look at the Role of Motives and Victim–Offender Relationships," *Journal of Research in Crime and Delinquency* 33 (1996): 427–449.

180. David Luckenbill, "Criminal Homicide as a Situational Transaction," *Social Problems* 25 (1977): 176–186.

181. Sharon Smith, Kathleen Basile, and Debra Karch, "Sexual Homicide and Sexual Violence–Associated Homicide: Findings From the National Violent Death Reporting System," *Homicide Studies* 15 (2011): 132–153; Vernon J. Geberth, "The Classification of Sex-Related Homicides," www.practicalhomicide.com/Research/sexrelatedhomicides.htm (accessed August 11, 2011).

182. Margaret Zahn and Philip Sagi, "Stranger Homicides in Nine American Cities," *Journal of Criminal Law and Criminology* 78 (1987): 377–397.

183. Jeff Gruenewald, "A Comparative Examination of Homicides Perpetrated by Far-Right Extremists," *Homicide Studies* 15 (2011): 177–203.

184. Tomislav Kovandzic, John Sloan, and Lynne Vieraitis, "Unintended Consequences of Politically Popular Sentencing Policy: The Homicide Promoting Effects of

'Three Strikes' in U.S. Cities (1980–1999)," *Criminology and Public Policy* 3 (2002): 399–424.

185. National Center for Education Statistics, "Indicators of School Crime and Safety: 2008," http://nces.ed.gov/programs/crimeindicators/crimeindicators2008/tables/table_06_1.asp (accessed September 21, 2010).

186. Christine Kerres Malecki and Michelle Kilpatrick Demaray, "Carrying a Weapon to School and Perceptions of Social Support in an Urban Middle School," *Journal of Emotional and Behavioral Disorders* 11 (2003): 169–178.

187. Ibid.

188. Pamela Wilcox and Richard Clayton, "A Multilevel Analysis of School-Based Weapon Possession," *Justice Quarterly* 18 (2001): 509–542.

189. Mark Anderson, Joanne Kaufman, Thomas Simon, Lisa Barrios, Len Paulozzi, George Ryan, Rodney Hammond, William Modzeleski, Thomas Feucht, Lloyd Potter, and the School-Associated Violent Deaths Study Group, "School-Associated Violent Deaths in the United States, 1994–1999," *Journal of the American Medical Association* 286 (2001): 2,695–2,702.

190. Bryan Vossekuil, Marisa Reddy, Robert Fein, Randy Borum, and William Modzeleski, *Safe School Initiative, An Interim Report on the Prevention of Targeted Violence in Schools* (Washington, DC: United States Secret Service, 2000).

191. "BTK Killer Blames 'Demon' for Murders," *USA Today*, July 7, 2005, www.usatoday.com/news/nation/2005-07-07-btk-killings_x.htm (accessed September 21, 2010).

192. Alasdair Goodwill and Laurence Alison, "Sequential Angulation, Spatial Dispersion and Consistency of Distance Attack Patterns from Home in Serial Murder, Rape and Burglary," *Journal of Psychology, Crime and Law* 11 (2005): 161–176.

193. Ronald Holmes and Stephen Holmes, *Murder in America* (Thousand Oaks, CA: Sage, 1994) pp. 13–14.

194. "Killing for Pleasure," Court TV Crime Library, www.crimelibrary.com/serial_killers/weird/swango/pleasure_8.html (accessed September 21, 2010).

195. Aneez Esmail, "Physician as Serial Killer—The Shipman Case," *New England Journal of Medicine* 352 (2005): 1,483–1,844.

196. James Alan Fox and Jack Levin, *Overkill: Mass Murder and Serial Killing Exposed* (New York: Plenum, 1994); James Alan Fox, Jack Levin, and Kenna Quinet, *The Will to Kill: Making Sense of Senseless Murder,* 2nd Ed. (Boston: Allyn & Bacon, 2004).

197. Belea Keeney and Kathleen Heide, "Gender Differences in Serial Murderers: A Preliminary Analysis," *Journal of Interpersonal Violence* 9 (1994): 37–56.

198. Wade Myers, Erik Gooch, and Reid Meloy, "The Role of Psychopathy and Sexuality in a Female Serial Killer," *Journal of Forensic Sciences* 50 (2005): 652–658.

199. Zelda Knight, "Some Thoughts on the Psychological Roots of the Behavior of Serial Killers as Narcissists: An Object Relations Perspective," *Social Behavior and Personality: An International Journal* 34 (2006): 1,189–1,206.

200. Terry Whitman and Donald Akutagawa, "Riddles in Serial Murder: A Synthesis," *Aggression and Violent Behavior* 9 (2004): 693–703.

201. Holmes and Holmes, *Murder in America,* p. 106.

202. Ibid., p. 17; Fox and Levin, *Overkill: Mass Murder and Serial Killing Exposed.*

203. Gabrielle Salfati and Alicia Bateman, "Serial Homicide: An Investigation of Behavioural Consistency," *Journal of Investigative Psychology and Offender Profiling* 2 (2005): 121–144.

204. Jennifer Browdy, "VI-CAP System to Be Operational this Summer," *Law Enforcement News,* May 21, 1984, p. 1.

205. James Alan Fox and Jack Levin, "Multiple Homicide: Patterns of Serial and Mass Murder," in *Crime and Justice: An Annual Edition,* vol. 23, ed. Michael Tonry (Chicago: University of Chicago Press, 1998), pp. 407–455; Fox and Levin, *Overkill: Mass Murder and Serial Killing Exposed;* Fox, Levin, and Quinet, *The Will to Kill: Making Sense of Senseless Murder;* James Allan Fox and Jack Levin, "A Psycho-Social Analysis of Mass Murder," in *Serial and Mass Murder: Theory, Policy, and Research,* ed. Thomas O'Reilly-Fleming and Steven Egger (Toronto: University of Toronto Press, 1993).

206. James Alan Fox and Jack Levin, "Mass Murder: An Analysis of Extreme Violence," *Journal of Applied Psychoanalytic Studies* 5 (2003): 47–64.

207. Grant Duwe, "The Patterns and Prevalence of Mass Murder in Twentieth-Century America," *Justice Quarterly* 21 (2004): 729–761.

208. Fox News, "Gunman in Alabama Massacre Had Hit List," March 11, 2009, www.foxnews.com/story/0,2933,508507,00.html (accessed September 21, 2010).

209. Elissa Gootman, "The Hunt for a Sniper: The Victim; 10th Victim Is Recalled as Motivator on Mission," *New York Times,* October 14, 2002, p. A15; Sarah Kershaw, "The Hunt for a Sniper: The Investigation; Endless Frustration but Little Evidence in Search for Sniper," *New York Times,* October 14, 2002, p. A1.

210. "Mugshots, Court TV's Criminal Biography Series, Profiles Racist Serial Killer Joseph Paul Franklin," www.courttv.com/archive/press/Franklin.html (accessed April 24, 2007).

211. Francis X. Clines, with Christopher Drew, "Prosecutors to Discuss Charges as Rifle Is Tied to Sniper Killings," *New York Times,* October 25, 2002, p. A1.

212. FBI, *Crime in the United States, 2005.*

213. Associated Press, "Woman With HIV Gets 3 Years for Spitting in Face," www.11alive.com/news/watercooler/story.aspx?storyid=118948&catid=186 (accessed September 21, 2010).

214. Keith Harries, "Homicide and Assault: A Comparative Analysis of Attributes in Dallas Neighborhoods, 1981–1985," *Professional Geographer* 41 (1989): 29–38.

215. Kevin Flynn, "Record Payouts in Settlements of Lawsuits against the New York City Police Are Set for Year," *New York Times,* October 1, 1999, p. 12.

216. Peter Lin and James Gill "Homicides of Pregnant Women," *American Journal of Forensic Medicine and Pathology* 32 (2011): 161–163.

217. Etienne Krug, Linda Dahlberg, James Mercy, Anthony Zwi, and Rafael Lozano, *World Report on Violence and Health* (Geneva: World Health Organization, 2002).

218. Ibid., p. 93.

219. See, generally, Ruth S. Kempe and C. Henry Kempe, *Child Abuse* (Cambridge, MA: Harvard University Press, 1978).

220. U.S. Department of Health and Human Services, Administration for Children and Families, Children's Bureau, *Child Maltreatment, 2008* (Washington, DC: U.S. Department of Health and Human Services, 2009), www.acf.hhs.gov/programs/cb/pubs/cm08/index.htm (accessed August 24, 2010).

221. David Finkelhor and Lisa Jones, "Why Have Child Maltreatment and Child Victimization Declined?" *Journal of Social Issues* 62 (2006): 685–716.

222. Glenn Wolfner and Richard Gelles, "A Profile of Violence toward Children: A National Study," *Child Abuse and Neglect* 17 (1993): 197–212.

223. Martin Daly and Margo Wilson, "Violence against Step Children," *Current Directions in Psychological Science* 5 (1996): 77–81.

224. Ruth Inglis, *Sins of the Fathers: A Study of the Physical and Emotional Abuse of Children* (New York: St. Martin's Press, 1978), p. 53.

225. Diana Russell, "The Incidence and Prevalence of Intrafamilial and Extrafamilial Sexual Abuse of Female Children," *Child Abuse and Neglect* 7 (1983): 133–146; see also David Finkelhor, *Sexually Victimized Children* (New York: Free Press, 1979), p. 88.

226. Jeanne Hernandez, "Eating Disorders and Sexual Abuse in Adolescents," paper presented at the annual meeting of the American Psychosomatic Society, Charleston, South Carolina, March 1993; Wolfner and Gelles, "A Profile of Violence toward Children."

227. Lisa Jones and David Finkelhor, *The Decline in Child Sexual Abuse Cases*

(Washington, DC: Office of Juvenile Justice and Delinquency Prevention, 2001).

228. Lisa Jones, David Finkelhor, and Kathy Kopie, "Why Is Sexual Abuse Declining? A Survey of State Child Protection Administrators," *Child Abuse and Neglect* 25 (2001): 1,139–1,141.

229. Eva Jonzon and Frank Lindblad, "Adult Female Victims of Child Sexual Abuse," *Journal of Interpersonal Violence* 20 (2005): 651–666.

230. Jane Siegel and Linda Williams, "Risk Factors for Sexual Victimization of Women," *Violence Against Women* 9 (2003): 902–930.

231. April Chiung-Tao Shen, "Self-Esteem of Young Adults Experiencing Interparental Violence and Child Physical Maltreatment: Parental and Peer Relationships as Mediators," *Journal of Interpersonal Violence* 24 (2009): 770–794.

232. Christina Meade, Trace Kershaw, Nathan Hansen, and Kathleen Sikkema, "Long-Term Correlates of Childhood Abuse among Adults with Severe Mental Illness: Adult Victimization, Substance Abuse, and HIV Sexual Risk Behavior," *AIDS and Behavior* 13 (2009): 207–216.

233. Arina Ulman and Murray Straus, "Violence by Children against Mothers in Relation to Violence between Parents and Corporal Punishment by Parents," *Journal of Comparative Family Studies* 34 (2003): 41–63.

234. R. Emerson Dobash and Russell Dobash, *Violence against Wives* (New York: Free Press, 1979).

235. Julia O'Faolain and Laura Martines, eds., *Not in God's Image: Women in History* (Glasgow: Fontana/Collins, 1974).

236. Laurence Stone, "The Rise of the Nuclear Family in Modern England: The Patriarchal Stage," in *The Family in History*, ed. Charles Rosenberg (Philadelphia: University of Pennsylvania Press, 1975), p. 53.

237. Dobash and Dobash, *Violence against Wives*, p. 46.

238. John Braithwaite, "Inequality and Republican Criminology," paper presented at the annual meeting of the American Society of Criminology, San Francisco, November 1991, p. 20.

239. Richard Gelles and Murray Straus, "Violence in the American Family," *Journal of Social Issues* 35 (1979): 15–39.

240. Jay Silverman, Anita Raj, Lorelei Mucci, and Jeanne Hathaway, "Dating Violence against Adolescent Girls and Associated Substance Abuse, Unhealthy Weight Control, Sexual Risk Behavior, Pregnancy and Suicidality," *Journal of the American Medical Association* 286 (2001): 572–579.

241. Nicole Bell, "Health and Occupational Consequences of Spouse Abuse Victimization Among Male U.S. Army Soldiers," *Journal of Interpersonal Violence* 24 (2009): 751–769.

242. FBI, *Crime in the United States*, 2005.

243. Katie Willis, *Armed Robbery: Who Commits It and Why?* (Canberra: Australian Institute

of Criminology, 2006); Patsy Klaus, *Carjackings in the United States, 1992–96* (Washington, DC: Bureau of Justice Statistics, 1999); Peter J. van Koppen and Robert Jansen, "The Road to the Robbery: Travel Patterns in Commercial Robberies," *British Journal of Criminology* 38 (1998): 230–247.

244. Willis, *Armed Robbery: Who Commits It and Why?*; John Conklin, *Robbery and the Criminal Justice System* (New York: Lippincott, 1972), pp. 1–80.

245. James Calder and John Bauer, "Convenience Store Robberies: Security Measures and Store Robbery Incidents," *Journal of Criminal Justice* 20 (1992): 553–566.

246. Richard Felson, Eric Baumer, and Steven Messner, "Acquaintance Robbery," *Journal of Research in Crime and Delinquency* 37 (2000): 284–305.

247. Ibid., p. 287.

248. Ibid.

249. Heith Copes, Andy Hochstetler, and Michael Cherbonneau, "Getting the Upper Hand: Scripts for Managing Victim Resistance in Carjackings," *Journal of Research in Crime and Delinquency,* published online before print May 3, 2011, doi:10-0022427810397949.

250. Ibid.

251. Peter Van Koppen and Robert Jansen, "The Time to Rob: Variations in Time of Number of Commercial Robberies," *Journal of Research in Crime and Delinquency* 36 (1999): 7–29.

252. Jody Miller, "Up It Up: Gender and the Accomplishment of Street Robbery," *Criminology* 36 (1998): 37–67.

253. Ibid., pp. 54–55.

254. Richard Wright and Scott Decker, *Armed Robbers in Action, Stickups and Street Culture* (Boston: Northeastern University Press, 1997).

255. Manny Fernandez, "Youth Recants Confession in Hate Crime Trial," *New York Times*, April 8, 2010, www.nytimes.com/2010/04/09/nyregion/09patchogue.html (accessed September 21, 2010); "Boy Gets 18 Years in Fatal Park Beating of Transient," *Los Angeles Times*, December 24, 1987, p. 9B.

256. Ewing, *When Children Kill*, pp. 65–66.

257. Mike McPhee, "In Denver, Attacks Stir Fears of Racism," *Boston Globe*, December 10, 1990, p. 3.

258. Jack Levin and Jack McDevitt, *Hate Crimes: The Rising Tide of Bigotry and Bloodshed* (New York: Plenum Press, 1993).

259. Jack McDevitt, Jack Levin, and Susan Bennett, "Hate Crime Offenders: An Expanded Typology," *Journal of Social Issues* 58 (2002): 303–318.

260. Jack Levin, *The Violence of Hate, Confronting Racism, Anti-Semitism, and Other Forms of Bigotry* (Boston: Allyn & Bacon, 2002), pp. 29–56.

261. FBI, *Hate Crime Statistics, 2009* (Washington, DC: FBI, 2010), www2.fbi.gov/ucr/hc2009/abouthcs.html (accessed August 11, 2011).

262. Ibid.

263. Gregory Herek, Jeanine Cogan, and Roy Gillis, "Victim Experiences in Hate Crimes Based on Sexual Orientation," *Journal of Social Issues* 58 (2002): 319–340.

264. Ryan King, Steven Messner, and Robert Baller, "Contemporary Hate Crimes, Law Enforcement, and the Legacy of Racial Violence," *American Sociological Review* 74 (2009): 291–315.

265. New York Police Department Detective Bureau Organization, www.homicidesquad.com/nypd_detective_bureau_organization.htm (accessed August 11, 2011).

266. Brian Levin, "From Slavery to Hate Crime Laws: The Emergence of Race and Status-Based Protection in American Criminal Law," *Journal of Social Issues* 58 (2002): 227–246.

267. Felicia Lee, "Gays Angry Over TV Report on a Murder," *New York Times*, November 26, 2004, p. A3.

268. Frederick M. Lawrence, *Punishing Hate: Bias Crimes under American Law* (Cambridge, MA: Harvard University Press, 1999).

269. Ibid., p. 3.

270. Ibid., p. 9.

271. Ibid., p. 11.

272. Ibid., pp. 39–42.

273. Jack McDevitt, Jennifer Balboni, Luis Garcia, and Joann Gu, "Consequences for Victims: A Comparison of Bias- and Non-Bias-Motivated Assaults," *American Behavioral Scientist* 45 (2001): 697–714.

274. *Virginia v. Black et al.* No. 01-1107. 2003.

275. Donovan Slack and Shelley Murphy, "Amy Bishop Charged with Murder for 1986 Shooting of Brother," *The Boston Globe*, June 16, 2010, www.boston.com/news/local/breaking_news/2010/06/hold_hold_hold_2.html (accessed August 11, 2011).

276. Shelley Murphy, Donovan Slack, and Meghan Irons, "Ala. Suspect Was Questioned in Bomb Case: Officials Thought Woman May Have Had Motive to Target Newton Doctor in 1993," *Boston Globe*, February 15, 2010, www.boston.com/news/local/massachusetts/articles/2010/02/15/more_questions_on_professor_held_in_ala/ (accessed August 12, 2011).

277. James Alan Fox and Jack Levin, "Firing Back: The Growing Threat of Workplace Homicide," *Annals* 536 (1994): 16–30.

278. FBI, *Workplace Violence: Issues in Response* (Quantico, VA: National Center for the Analysis of Violent Crime, 2001) www.fbi.gov/publications/violence.pdf (accessed April 24, 2007).

279. John King, "Workplace Violence: A Conceptual Framework," paper presented at

the annual meeting of the American Society of Criminology, Phoenix, November 1993.

280. Janet R. Copper, "Response to 'Workplace Violence in Health Care: Recognized but Not Regulated,' by Kathleen M. McPhaul and Jane A. Lipscomb (September 30, 2004)," *Online Journal of Issues in Nursing* 10 (2005): 53–55.

281. Associated Press, "Gunman Wounds 3 Doctors in L.A. Hospital," *Cleveland Plain Dealer,* February 9, 1993, p. 1B.

282. Fox and Levin, "Firing Back," p. 5.

283. Michael Mantell and Steve Albrecht, *Ticking Bombs: Defusing Violence in the Workplace* (New York: Irwin, 1994).

284. Centers for Disease Control, National Institute for Occupational Safety and Health, "Workplace Violence," www.cdc.gov/niosh/topics/violence/ (accessed June 23, 2011).

285. Dana Loomis, Stephen Marshall, and Myduc Ta, "Employer Policies Toward

Guns and the Risk of Homicide in the Workplace," *American Journal of Public Health* 95 (2005): 830–832.

286. The following sections rely heavily on Patricia Tjaden, *The Crime of Stalking: How Big Is the Problem?* (Washington, DC: National Institute of Justice, 1997); see also Robert M. Emerson, Kerry O. Ferris, and Carol Brooks Gardner, "On Being Stalked," *Social Problems* 45 (1998): 289–298.

287. Patrick Kinkade, Ronald Burns, and Angel Ilarraza Fuentes, "Criminalizing Attractions: Perceptions of Stalking and the Stalker," *Crime and Delinquency* 51 (2005): 3–25.

288. Kathleen Basile, Monica Swahn, Jieru Chen, and Linda Saltzman, "Stalking in the United States: Recent National Prevalence Estimates," *American Journal of Preventive Medicine* 31 (2006): 172–175.

289. Bonnie Fisher, Francis Cullen, and Michael Turner, "Being Pursued: Stalking

Victimization in a National Study of College Women," *Criminology and Public Policy* 1 (2002): 257–309.

290. Brian Spitzberg and William Cupach, "The State of the Art of Stalking: Taking Stock of the Emerging Literature," *Aggression and Violent Behavior* 12 (2007): 64–86.

291. Reid Meloy, "Stalking: The State of the Science," *Criminal Behaviour and Mental Health* 17 (2007): 1–7.

292. Mary Brewster, "Stalking by Former Intimates: Verbal Threats and Other Predictors of Physical Violence," *Violence and Victims* 15 (2000): 41–51.

293. Spitzberg and Cupach, "The State of the Art of Stalking."

294. Carol Jordan, T. K. Logan, and Robert Walker, "Stalking: An Examination of the Criminal Justice Response," *Journal of Interpersonal Violence* 18 (2003): 148–165.

On May 1, 2011, Osama bin Laden—head of the Al-Qaeda terror network and the world's most wanted man—was killed by members of Seal Team 6 in his secret compound located in Abbottabad, Pakistan. His burial at sea marked the end of the turbulent career of this political criminal. Who was this man who engineered the 9/11 destruction of the World Trade Center in New York City, and what motivated his anger at the United States and the West?

Usamah bin Muhammed bin Awad bin Ladin was born in 1957 or 1958 in Riyadh, Saudi Arabia. He was the seventh son in a family of 52 children. His father, Sheik Mohammed Awad bin Laden, was a poor, uneducated laborer from Hadramout in South Yemen who worked as a lowly porter in Jeddah. In 1930, the elder bin Laden started his own construction business, which became so successful that his family grew to be

(*continued on page 378*)

Political Crime and Terrorism

11

Chapter Outline

Learning Objectives

1. Know what is meant by the term *political crime*
2. Identify the cause of political crime
3. Distinguish between espionage and treason
4. Know the components of state political crime
5. Be able to debate the use and misuse of torture
6. Distinguish among terrorists, insurgents, guerillas, and revolutionaries
7. Understand the various forms of terrorism
8. Know what motivates the terrorist
9. Be familiar with the efforts being made to centralize intelligence gathering
10. Describe the efforts by the FBI and DHS to fight terrorism

known as "the wealthiest non-royal family in the kingdom." Despite his royal associations and great wealth, Mohammed bin Laden remained a humble and devoted Muslim who insisted that his children observe a strict religious and moral code. He went to great pains to teach his children to take charge of their own lives and to maintain their independence. In 1968, this training came into play in a brutal way when Mohammed was killed in a plane crash near San Antonio, Texas, leaving his sons in charge not only of the family business but of their own destinies. Following his death, Mohammed bin Laden's eldest sons continued to expand their late father's company until it employed more than 40,000 people. The bin Laden group also expanded into Egypt, where it is now that country's largest private foreign group.

Osama went on to complete his primary and secondary schooling and joined the Muslim Brotherhood. During this period he expanded his compulsory Islamic studies through a series of meetings that were conducted at the family home by his elder brothers. Among the contacts he made at these meetings were notable Islamic scholars and the leaders of various Muslim movements. Later, he attended King Abdul-Aziz University in Jeddah and completed degrees in public administration and economics. When he wasn't studying, the affluence of his family allowed him to broaden his knowledge through travel to other countries, including Syria, Pakistan, Afghanistan, and Sudan.

In a 1995 interview with a French journalist, bin Laden explained why he chose to join the *mujahideen* fight against the Russians at that time:

> To counter these atheist Russians, the Saudis chose me as their representative in Afghanistan. . . . I did not fight against the communist threat while forgetting the peril from the West. For us, the idea was not to get involved more than necessary in the fight against the Russians, which was the business of the Americans, but rather to show our solidarity with our Islamist brothers. I discovered that it was not enough to fight in Afghanistan, but that we had to fight on all fronts against communist or Western oppression. The urgent thing was communism, but the next target was America. . . . This is an open war up to the end, until victory.[1]

The fortune he used to finance his terrorist activities was derived from an inheritance of more than $300 million from his family. Some analysts note that bin Laden was the only son of his late father's least favorite wife, who was a Syrian and not a Saudi. Bin Laden may have been close to his mother, but he seems to have felt driven to achieve stature in the eyes of his father and the rest of the family. His actions indicate he was willing to do anything to gain power and eclipse his father, who had died when bin Laden was 10 years old.

Bin Laden modeled his behavior after his father in many ways, including working with the Saudi royal family on construction deals. Bin Laden once told an interviewer of his desire to please his father: "My father was very keen that one of his sons should fight against the enemies of Islam. So I am the one son who is acting according to the wishes of his father." Perhaps this need for acceptance explains bin Laden's religious zeal, which was in excess of anyone else's in his large extended family.

After his father's death, bin Laden was mentored by a Jordanian named Abdullah Azzam, whose motto was "Jihad and the rifle alone: no negotiations, no conferences and no dialogues." When Azzam was killed in 1989 by a car bomb in Pakistan, bin Laden vowed to carry on Azzam's "holy war" against the West. He threw himself into the Afghan conflict against the Soviet Union, and when the Russians withdrew, he was convinced that the West was vulnerable. "The myth of the superpower was destroyed not only in my mind, but also in the minds of all Muslims," bin Laden has told interviewers. His masterminding of the 9/11 bombing was not designed to restore his homeland or bring about a new political state but to have his personal value structure adopted by Muslim nations. His attack may have been designed to create a military invasion of Afghanistan, which he hoped to exploit for his particular brand of revolution, a plan that has succeeded, but not with the results he desired.

Bin Laden may have believed his acts would reach the audience that concerned him the most: the *umma*, or universal Islamic community. The media would show Americans killing innocent civilians in Afghanistan, and the *umma* would find it shocking how Americans nonchalantly caused Muslims to suffer and die. The ensuing outrage would open a chasm between the Muslim population of the Middle East and the ruling governments in states such as Saudi Arabia, which were allied with the West. On October 7, 2001, bin Laden made a broadcast in which he said that the Americans and the British "have divided the entire world into two regions—one of faith, where there is no hypocrisy, and another of infidelity, from which we hope God will protect us." Now that he is dead, bin Laden's motivations may never truly be understood. But his impact on the world that was is undeniable.[2]

Does Osama bin Laden's death spell the end of terrorism? Not likely. **Al-Qaeda** cells have now dispersed around the world, helping to offset this loss in leadership. Al-Qaeda cells in the Arabian Peninsula are actively working to topple governments in Yemen and Saudi Arabia. In Somalia an al-Qaeda ally, al-Shabaab, controls significant tracts of territory, and several al-Shabaab leaders have publicly proclaimed loyalty to al-Qaeda. The group is still busily recruiting, even in the United States: In 2009, five Americans from Virginia were arrested in Pakistan on suspicion of terrorist ties. David Headley pleaded guilty in a U.S. court to crimes relating to his role in the November 2008 Lashkar e-Tayyiba attacks in Mumbai, which killed more than 160 people, including six Americans; and Nidal Hasan, facing charges for the Fort Hood attack that killed 13 people and wounded 30 others on November 5, 2009, has been linked to al-Qaeda.[3]

The life and death of Osama bin Laden and the continued activities of his terror organization al-Qaeda have made the study of political crime and terrorism important areas of criminological inquiry in the United States. Many criminologists who previously paid scant attention to the interaction between political motivation and crime have now made it the focus of intense study. This chapter reviews both violent and nonviolent political crime. We briefly discuss the concept of political crime and some of its various forms, and then turn to its most extreme variety, terrorism. Because terrorism now occupies the center stage of both world opinion and government policy, it is important for students of criminology to develop a basic understanding of its definition, history, and structure, and review the steps being taken to limit or eliminate its occurrence.

DEFINING POLITICAL CRIME

Although terrorism now occupies the focal point of public concern, it is merely one of many different types of politically motivated crimes. The term **political crime** is used to signify illegal acts that are designed to undermine an existing government and threaten its survival.[4] Political crimes can include both violent and nonviolent acts and range in seriousness from dissent, treason, and espionage to terrorism and assassination.[5]

When an act becomes a political crime and when an actor is considered a political criminal are often extremely subjective. On June 3, 2011, a federal grand jury indicted two-time presidential candidate John Edwards for allegedly misappropriating for personal use large sums of money given to him as campaign donations. According to the prosecution, Edwards used this money to keep his pregnant mistress Rielle Hunter in hiding during the peak of his 2008 campaign for the White House.[6] Then on June 27, 2011, former governor Rod R. Blagojevich of Illinois was convicted of fraud stemming from his efforts to fill Barack Obama's Senate seat, which became vacant when he was elected president. Blagojevich tried to sell the seat to the highest bidder! Although the crimes of Edwards and Blagojevich seem "political," they actually fall under laws controlling white-collar crimes (see Chapter 13); they are not political crimes in a classic sense, but merely common-law crimes (e.g., larceny, fraud) committed by politicians. In contrast, while some political criminals may profit from their crimes, their activities damage governmental structure and function and undermine the political process.

Because their motivations shift between selfish, personal needs and selfless, noble, or altruistic desires, political crimes often occupy a gray area between conventional and outlawed behavior. It is easy to condemn interpersonal violent crimes such as rape or murder because their goals are typically selfish and self-centered (e.g., revenge or profit). In contrast, political criminals may be motivated by conviction rather than by greed or anger. It is true that some political crime involves profit (such as selling state secrets for money), but most political criminals consider themselves patriotic and altruistic rather than selfish or antisocial. They are willing to sacrifice themselves for what they consider to be the greater good. Some concoct elaborate schemes to hide or mask their actions; others are quite brazen, hoping to provoke the government to overreact in their zeal to crack down on dissent. Because state authorities may engage in a range of retaliatory actions that result in **human rights** violations, even those who support the government may begin to question its activities: maybe the government is corrupt and authoritarian? On the other hand, if the government does nothing, it appears weak and corrupt and unable to protect citizens.

Even those political criminals who profit personally from their misdeeds, such as someone who spies for an enemy nation for financial payoffs, may believe their acts are motivated by a higher calling than common theft. "My ultimate goal is to weaken or overthrow a corrupt government," they reason, "so selling secrets to the enemy is justified." Political criminals may believe that their acts are criminalized only because the group holding power fears them and wants to curtail their behavior. The general public has little objection to laws that control extreme behaviors such as plotting a bloody revolution, but they may have questions when a law criminalizes ordinary political dissent or bans political meetings in an attempt to control suspected political criminals.

In highly repressive nations, any form of nonsanctioned political activity, including writing a newspaper article critical of the regime, may be considered a political crime, punishable by a prison term or even death. Similarly, people labeled as terrorists and insurrectionists by some are viewed as freedom fighters and revolutionaries by others. What would have happened to George Washington and Benjamin Franklin had the British won the Revolutionary War? Would they have been hanged for their political crimes or considered heroes and freedom fighters?

The Goals of Political Criminals

On August 24, 2010, another in a very long line of bombings took place in Iraq. Although the population had gotten used to these attacks, this one was clearly designed to undermine public confidence in the nation's security forces.

The bombers wanted to exploit political uncertainty and undermine the public's trust in Iraq's political parties to form a government. One survivor told reporters, "There may be a state, there may be a government. But what can that state do? What can they do with all the terrorists? Are they supposed to set up a checkpoint in every house?" The bombers may have succeeded in their efforts to create an atmosphere of intimidation and fear designed to oust the government.[7]

Common criminals may be motivated by greed, vengeance, or jealousy, but political criminals have a somewhat different agenda. Rather than personal profit, their acts are aimed at achieving a different set of goals:

- *Intimidation.* Some political criminals want to intimidate or threaten an opponent who does not share their political orientation or views.
- *Revolution.* Some political criminals plot to overthrow the existing government and replace it with one that holds views they find more acceptable.
- *Profit.* Another goal of political crime is profit: selling state secrets for personal enrichment or trafficking in stolen arms and munitions.
- *Conviction.* Some political criminals are motivated by altruism; they truly believe their crimes will benefit society and are willing to violate the law and risk punishment to achieve what they see as social improvement.
- *Pseudo-conviction.* These political criminals conceal conventional criminal motivations behind a mask of conviction and altruism. They may form a revolutionary movement out of a hidden desire to engage in violence rather than their stated goal of reforming society. Pseudo-convictional criminals are particularly dangerous because they convince followers to join them in their crimes without fully revealing their true motivations.[8]

Becoming a Political Criminal

Why does someone become a political criminal? There is no set pattern or reason, and motivations vary widely. Some use political crime as a stepping stone to public office; others use it as a method to focus their frustrations; and still others hope to gain respect from their friends and family. Although the motivations for political crime are complex and varied, political crime expert Randy Borum finds that these criminals share a pattern of thinking that forms a series of cognitive stages:

- Stage 1: *"It's not right."* An unhappy, dissatisfied individual identifies some type of undesirable event or condition. It could be economic (e.g., poverty, unemployment, poor living conditions), social (e.g., government-imposed restrictions on individual freedoms, lack of order, or morality), or personal (e.g., "I am being cheated of what is due me"). Although the conditions may vary, those involved perceive the experience as "things are not as they should be."

- Stage 2: *"It's not fair."* The prospective criminal concludes that the undesirable condition is a product of "injustice"—that is, it does not apply to everyone. A government worker may feel his or her low pay scale is "not right" and that corporate workers with less skill are making more money and getting more benefits. At the same time, government workers are portrayed as lazy and corrupt. This facilitates feelings of resentment and injustice in those who are deprived.
- Stage 3: *"It's your fault."* Someone or some group must be held accountable for the extremist's displeasure. It always helps to identify a potential target. For example, the underpaid worker may become convinced that minorities get all the good jobs while the worker is suffering financially. Extremist groups spread this propaganda to attract recruits. Americans may be portrayed as rich and undeserving by overseas enemies hoping to recruit disenfranchised young men and women to become terrorists.
- Stage 4: *"You're evil."* Because good people would not intentionally hurt others, targeted groups are appropriate objects for revenge and/or violence. The disaffected government worker concludes that his country has let him down so it is only fair that he sells state secrets to foreign nations for profit or joins a terrorist group, or both. Aggression becomes justifiable when aimed against bad people, particularly those who intentionally cause harm to others. In addition, by casting the target as evil, the target is dehumanized, which makes justifying aggression even easier. So it's not so bad to rig an election because the opposing candidates are evil and do not deserve to hold office.[9]

CONNECTIONS

Borum's typology seems similar to the techniques of neutralization discussed in Chapter 7. Is it possible that terrorists must neutralize feelings of guilt and shame before planting their bombs? Or do their religious and political beliefs negate any need for psychological processes to reduce their personal responsibility for violence?

POLITICAL CRIMES

In 2008 a California man named Gladwin Gill was sentenced to a year in prison for making $66,700 in conduit contributions to presidential candidates, two United States Senate candidates, and a political committee endorsing a U.S. House of Representatives candidate. Conduit contributions refer to money a person gives to friends or family members who are directed to contribute it to a specific campaign. This enables the individual to contribute funds in excess of the limit allowed by federal law without seeming to do so. Unlike common-law criminals, political criminals like Gladwin Gill may actually give people money rather than stealing it from them![10] Although the great variety of political crimes seem at first glance to be quite different, they are linked together because, for the most part, they are designed to change, alter, or control the political process and not merely to satisfy individual needs and desires.

Election Fraud

Some political criminals, like Gladwin Gill, want to shape elections to meet their personal needs. In some instances their goal is altruistic: the election of candidates who reflect their personal political views. In others, their actions are motivated by profit: they are paid by a candidate to rig the election.

Whatever the motive, **election fraud** is illegal interference with the process of an election. Acts of fraud tend to involve affecting vote counts to bring about a desired election outcome, whether by increasing the vote share of the favored candidate, depressing the vote share of the rival candidates, or both.

In some third-world dictatorships, election fraud is the norm, and it is common for the ruling party to announce, after party members counted the votes, that they were returned to office with an overwhelming majority. Sometimes allegations of voter fraud by ruling juntas can have disastrous consequences. For example, parliamentary elections took place in Kenya on December 27, 2007, and when it was announced that President Mwai Kibaki had won the presidential election over opposition candidate Raila Odinga, fighting broke out that tore this African nation apart. More than 1,200 Kenyans were reported killed, thousands more injured, and hundreds of thousands made homeless; more than 40,000 houses, farms, and businesses were looted or destroyed.[11] Despite the post-election chaos, Kibaki retained his victory and his power.

Election fraud, a feature of political life since Roman times, includes a variety of behaviors designed to give a candidate or his or her party an unfair advantage:

- *Intimidation.* Voters can be scared away from the polls through threats or intimidation. Having armed guards posted at polling places may convince people it is dangerous to vote. Lists of registered voters can be obtained and people subjected to threatening calls before the election.
- *Disruption.* Bomb threats can be called into voting places in areas that are known to heavily favor the opposing party, with the goal of suppressing the vote. There can be outright sabotage of polling places, ballots, ballot boxes, and voting machines.
- *Misinformation.* Flyers are sent out to voters registered with the opposition party containing misleading

information such as the wrong election date or saying that rules have been changed about who is eligible to vote.

- *Registration fraud.* Political operatives may try to shape the outcome of an election by busing in ineligible voters from other districts. Because many jurisdictions require minimal identification and proof of citizenship, political criminals find it easy to get around residency requirements. They may provide conspirators with "change of address" forms to allow them to vote in a particular election, when in fact no actual change of address has occurred.

- *Vote buying.* Securing votes by payment or other rewards or selling one's vote is an age-old problem. One popular method is to buy absentee ballots from people who are in need of cash. The fraudulent voter can then ensure that the vote goes his or her way, an outcome that cannot be guaranteed if the conspirator casts a secret ballot at a polling place.

Most states have created laws to control and punish vote fraud. The federal government has a number of statutes designed to control and/or restrict fraud, including 18 U.S.C. § 594, which provides:

> Whoever intimidates, threatens, coerces, or attempts to intimidate, threaten, or coerce, any other person for the purpose of interfering with the right of such other person to vote or to vote as he may choose, or of causing such other person to vote for, or not to vote for, any candidate for the office of President, Vice President, Presidential elector, Member of the Senate, Member of the House of Representatives, Delegate from the District of Columbia, or Resident Commissioner, at any election held solely or in part for the purpose of electing such candidate, shall be fined under this title or imprisoned not more than one year, or both.

Another provision that applies to voting is 18 U.S.C. § 245(b)(1)(A):

> Whoever, whether or not acting under color of law, by force or threat of force willfully injures, intimidates or interferes with, or attempts to injure, intimidate or interfere with
>
> (1) any person because he is or has been, or in order to intimidate such person or any other person or any class of persons from
>
> (A) voting or qualifying to vote, qualifying or campaigning as a candidate for elective office, or qualifying or acting as a poll watcher, or any legally authorized election official, in any primary, special, or general election. . . .

This provision is in the Civil Rights section of Title 18, the federal criminal code, and it protects the right of all citizens to vote and campaign for office.

Treason

Few people can forget the image of John Walker Lindh, the so-called *American Taliban*, when he was captured during the American invasion of Afghanistan. Lindh, who had spent his early years in an affluent northern California community, converted to Islam and through a convoluted path wound up first in an al-Qaeda training camp and then fighting with the Taliban on the front lines in Afghanistan. He was captured on November 25, 2001, by Afghan Northern Alliance forces, and questioned by CIA agents. Later that day, there was a violent uprising in the prison in which he was being held and during the attack a CIA agent was killed. Walker escaped only to be recaptured seven days later. At his trial, he apologized for fighting alongside the Taliban, saying, "Had I realized then what I know now . . . I never would have joined them." The 21-year-old said Osama bin Laden is against Islam and that he "never understood jihad to mean anti-American or terrorism." (See Exhibit 11.1.) "I understand why so many Americans were angry when I was first discovered in Afghanistan. I realize many still are, but I hope in time that feeling will change." After a plea agreement, John Walker Lindh was sentenced to 20 years in prison.[12]

Treason involves acts of disloyalty to one's nation. A person who willfully cooperates with an enemy is considered to be a traitor. John Walker Lindh, the so-called American Taliban, is shown being taken into custody at Mazar-i-Sharif, Afghanistan. Calling himself Abdul Hamid, Lindh volunteered to help the enemy. Though some people considered his actions treasonous, in a plea bargain Lindh admitted only to serving in the Taliban army and carrying weapons and received a 20-year sentence for his crimes.

What Is Jihad?

When John Walker Lindh spoke of *jihad,* he used a term that has become all too familiar in contemporary society. Often assumed to mean "holy war," the term is more complex than that simple meaning. According to terror expert Andrew Silke, the term derives from the Arabic for "struggle," and within Islam there are two forms of jihad: the Greater Jihad and the Lesser Jihad. The Greater Jihad refers to a Muslim's personal struggle to live a good and charitable life and adhere to God's commands. In this sense, jihad is a strictly personal and nonviolent phenomenon. The Lesser Jihad refers to violent struggle on behalf of Islam. Jihadists are "those who struggle" and refers to individuals who have volunteered to fight in the Lesser Jihad. The term is used by members of groups such as al-Qaeda to describe themselves and their goals. Jihadists sometimes call themselves *mujahideen,* meaning "holy warriors," and the term is commonly used to refer to Muslims engaged in the Lesser Jihad.

SOURCE: Andrew Silke, "Holy Warriors: Exploring the Psychological Processes of Jihadi Radicalization," *European Journal of Criminology* 5 (2008): 99–123.

Lindh's behavior amounts to what is commonly called **treason**, an act of disloyalty to one's nation or state. Although the crime of treason is well known and the word "traitor" is a generic term, there have been fewer than 40 prosecutions for treason in the entire history of the United States, and most have resulted in acquittal. In fact, though his behavior might be considered *treasonous*, Lindh was not charged or convicted of treason but was charged with serving in the Taliban army and carrying weapons.

The Lindh case grabbed headlines for a while, but the most famous treason case in U.S. history is still the 1807 trial of former Vice President Aaron Burr, a man best known for killing Secretary of the Treasury Alexander Hamilton in 1804 in a duel over a matter of honor. Burr was accused of hatching a plot to separate the western states from the union. When that plot went awry, he conspired to seize Mexico and set up a puppet government with himself as king! Arrested on charges of treason, he was acquitted when the Federal Court, headed by John Marshall, ruled that to be guilty of treason an overt act must be committed; planning is not enough.[13]

Because treason is considered such a heinous crime, and to deter would-be traitors, many nations apply or have applied the death penalty to those convicted of attempting to overthrow the existing government. Treason was considered particularly loathsome under English common law, and until the nineteenth century it was punishable by being "drawn and quartered," a method of execution that involved hanging the offender, removing the intestines while still living, and finally cutting the offender into four pieces for public display. William Wallace, the Scottish patriot made famous in the film *Braveheart,* was so displayed after his execution.

Acts can be considered treasonous in order to stifle political dissent. In eighteenth-century England, it was considered treasonous to merely criticize the king or his behavior, and not surprisingly, the American colonists feared giving their own central government that much power. Therefore, treason is the only crime mentioned in the United States Constitution, which defines treason as levying war against the United States or "in adhering to their Enemies, giving them Aid and Comfort," and requires the testimony of two witnesses or a confession in open court for conviction. The purpose of this was to limit the government's ability to bring charges of treason against opponents and to make it more difficult to prosecute those who are so charged.[14]

Today, the United States Criminal Code codifies treason as "whoever, owing allegiance to the United States, levies war against them or adheres to their enemies, giving them aid and comfort within the United States or elsewhere, is guilty of treason and shall suffer death, or shall be imprisoned not less than five years and fined under this title but not less than $10,000; and shall be incapable of holding any office under the United States."[15] Helping or cooperating with the enemy in a time of war (as Lindh did) would be considered treason; so too would be creating or recruiting a military force to help a foreign nation overthrow the government. After World War II, two women, Iva Ikuko Toguri D'Aquino, a Japanese American born in Los Angeles and known as Tokyo Rose, and Mildred Elizabeth Gillars, born in Portland, Maine, and known as Axis Sally, served prison terms for broadcasting for the Axis powers in an effort to demoralize American troops. The first treason charge in the past 50 years was levied against a California man, Adam Gadahn, whose case is summarized in the Profiles in Crime feature.

Espionage

Robert Hanssen was a counterintelligence agent for the FBI assigned to detect and identify Russian spies. A former Chicago police officer, Hanssen's assignment required him to have access to sensitive top-secret information. In one of the most shocking cases in U.S. history, Hanssen volunteered to become a paid spy for the KGB during the Cold War. He was arrested on February 18, 2001, after leaving a package of classified documents for his Russian handlers under a footbridge in a park outside Washington, D.C. During his years as a double agent, Hanssen not only provided more than 6,000 pages of documents to the Soviet Union but also caused the death of two U.S. double agents whose identities were uncovered with the aid of his secret documents. The Hanssen case was the subject of the 2007 film *Breach* that starred Chris Cooper as the corrupt agent.[16]

Espionage (more commonly called "spying") is the practice of obtaining information about a government, organization, or society that is considered secret or confidential

Azzam the American

AFP/Getty Images/Newscom

The most recent case in which actual treason has been charged involves a 28-year-old California man, Adam Gadahn, also known as Azzam the American, who was indicted in 2006 for making a series of propaganda videotapes for al-Qaeda, including one in which he praised the 9/11 hijackers and referred to the United States as "enemy soil."

Gadahn was raised in a counterculture atmosphere on a rural farm with his father, Philip Pearlstein, the son of a well-known Jewish doctor, and his mother, Jennifer, a computer whiz from Pennsylvania. His parents were self-sufficient and raised their son in a cabin with no running water; they produced their own electricity from solar panels. They hoped that by living in isolation and austerity they could avoid the chaotic and destructive elements of contemporary society. Adam Gadahn became heavily involved in the death metal culture, but still feeling empty and alienated, he began studying Islam at age 17 at the Islamic Society of Orange County. He later moved to Pakistan and married an Afghan woman.

Gadahn appeared in a series of videotaped segments that were broadcast between October 2004 and September 11, 2006. In the first tape, Gadahn is shown wearing black sunglasses and a headdress wrapped around his face. He identified himself as Azzam the American and announced his relationship with al-Qaeda. "The streets of America shall run red with blood," he claimed. In a broadcast in 2005, around the fourth anniversary of the 9/11 attacks, Gadahn called the attacks "blessed raids" and discussed the "jihad against America." In 2006, Gadahn appeared in a videotape that also contained statements from Osama bin Laden and Ayman al-Zawahiri and then made another propaganda broadcast aired on the fifth anniversary of 9/11. On May 29, 2007, Gadahn again made headlines when he issued another video that listed six actions that America must take in order to prevent future terrorist attacks:

- "Pull every last one of your soldiers, spies, security advisors, trainers, attachés . . . out of every Muslim land from Afghanistan to Zanzibar. . . ."
- End "all support and aid, military, political, economic, or otherwise, to the 56-plus apostate regimes of the Muslim world, and abandon them to their well-deserved fate."
- "End all support, moral, military, economic, political, or otherwise, to the bastard state of Israel, and ban your citizens, Zionist Jews, Zionist Christians, and the rest from traveling to occupied Palestine or settling there. Even one penny of aid will be considered sufficient justification to continue the fight."
- "Leave all Muslims alone."
- "Impose a blanket ban on all broadcasts to our region."
- "Free all Muslim captives from your prisons, detention facilities, and concentration camps, regardless of whether they have been recipients of what you call a fair trial or not."

Gadahn warned:

> Your failure to meet our demands . . . means that you and your people will, Allah willing, experience things which will make you forget about the horrors of September 11. . . . This is not a call for negotiations. We do not negotiate with baby killers and war criminals like you.

Gadahn also warned President George W. Bush:

> You will go down in history not only as the president who embroiled his nation in a series of unwinnable and bloody conflicts in the Islamic world, but as the president who set the United States up on its death march.

Gadahn is the first person to be charged with treason against the United States in almost 50 years, and while there have been numerous reports of his death and capture, none have so far proven conclusively valid. On March 7, 2010, the Pakistani government announced that Gadahn had been captured in Karachi, Pakistan; this report has still not been substantiated and Gadahn's whereabouts remain a mystery.

SOURCES: Craig Whitlock, "Converts to Islam Move Up in Cells, Arrests in Europe Illuminate Shift," *Washington Post Foreign Service*, September 15, 2007, p. A10, www.washington-post.com/wp-dyn/content/article/2007/09/14/AR2007091402265.html (accessed November 2, 2010); FBI, "Most Wanted Terrorist: American Charged with Treason," October 11, 2006, www2.fbi.gov/page2/oct2006/gadahn101106.htm (accessed August 16, 2011); Raffi Khatchadourian, "Azzam the American: The Making of an Al Qaeda Homegrown," *New Yorker*, January 22, 2007, www.newyorker.com/reporting/2007/01/22/070122fa_fact_khatchadourian (accessed August 16, 2011).

without the permission of the holder of the information. Espionage involves obtaining the information illegally by covertly entering the area where the information is stored, secretly photographing forbidden areas, or subverting through threat or payoff people who know the information and will divulge it through subterfuge.[17]

Espionage is typically associated with spying on potential or actual enemies by a foreign agent who is working for his or her nation's intelligence service. With the end of the Cold War, the threat of espionage seemed reduced until 2010, when a major Russian spy group was unraveled and 10 people were arrested. These were sleeper agents who had

AP Images/Mark Wilson

Aldrich Hazen Ames was arrested by the FBI in Arlington, Virginia, on espionage charges on February 24, 1994. At the time of his arrest, Ames was a 31-year veteran of the Central Intelligence Agency (CIA) who had been spying for the Russians since 1985. Arrested with him was his wife, Rosario Ames, who had aided and abetted his espionage activities.

Ames was a CIA case officer who spoke Russian and specialized in the Russian intelligence services, including the KGB, the USSR's foreign intelligence service. His initial overseas assignment was in Ankara, Turkey, where he targeted Russian intelligence officers for recruitment. Later, he worked in New York City and Mexico City. On April 16, 1985, while assigned to the CIA's Soviet/East European Division at CIA Headquarters in Langley, Virginia, he secretly volunteered his services to KGB officers at the USSR Embassy in Washington, D.C. Shortly thereafter, the KGB paid him $50,000. During the summer of 1985, Ames met several times with a Russian diplomat to whom he passed classified information about CIA and FBI human sources, as well as technical operations targeting the Soviet Union. In December 1985, Ames met with a Moscow-based KGB officer in Bogota, Colombia. In July 1986, Ames was transferred to Rome.

In Rome, Ames continued his meetings with the KGB, including a Russian diplomat assigned to Rome and a Moscow-based KGB officer. At the conclusion of his assignment in Rome, Ames received instructions from the KGB regarding clandestine contacts in the Washington, D.C. area, where he would next be assigned. In the four years after he volunteered, the KGB paid Ames $1.88 million.

Upon his return to Washington, D.C., in 1989, Ames continued to pass classified documents to the KGB using "dead drops" or prearranged hiding places. He would leave the documents to be picked up later by KGB officers from the USSR Embassy in Washington, and in return the KGB left money and instructions for Ames, usually in other "dead drops."

In the meantime, the CIA and FBI learned that Russian officials who had been recruited by them were being arrested and executed. These human sources had provided critical intelligence information about the USSR, which was used by U.S. policy makers in determining U.S. foreign policy. Following analytical reviews and receipt of information about Ames's unexplained wealth, the FBI opened an investigation in May 1993.

FBI special agents and investigative specialists conducted intensive physical and electronic surveillance of Ames during a 10-month investigation. Searches of Ames's residence revealed documents and other information linking Ames to the Russian foreign intelligence service. On October 13, 1993, investigative specialists observed a chalk mark Ames made on a mailbox confirming to the Russians his intention to meet them in Bogota, Colombia. On November 1, special agents observed him and, separately, his Russian handler in Bogota. When Ames planned foreign travel, including a trip to Moscow, as part of his official duties, a plan to arrest him was approved.

Following guilty pleas by both Ames and his wife on April 28, 1994, Ames was sentenced to incarceration for life without the possibility of parole. Rosario Ames was sentenced on October 20, 1994, to 63 months in prison. Ames also forfeited his assets to the United States, and $547,000 was turned over to the Justice Department's Victims Assistance Fund. Ames is serving his sentence in the federal prison system. Rosario Ames completed her sentence and was released.

SOURCE: FBI, "Famous Cases & Criminals: Aldrich Hazen Ames," www.fbi.gov/about-us/history/famous-cases/aldrich-hazen-ames (accessed August 16, 2011).

---

spent decades fitting seamlessly in their new environment. Neighbors were shocked to find out that "Richard Murphy" and "Cynthia Murphy" were actually spies named Vladimir Guryev and Lydia Guryev, and that "Michael Zottoli" and "Patricia Mills" were in reality Mikhail Kutsik and Natalia Pereverzeva, agents of the Russian Federation. The case was settled when the Russians were exchanged for four American spies being held in Russian prisons.

Not all spies are foreign nationals. There are numerous cases of homegrown spies who are motivated by misguided altruism or belief. Perhaps the most famous international case involved a group of five upper-crust students at prestigious Cambridge University in England who were recruited during the Cold War by the KGB, Russia's foreign intelligence service. The five were motivated by the belief that capitalism was corrupt and that the Soviet Union offered a better model for society. After graduation, they secured sensitive government posts that gave them access to valuable intelligence they then passed on to the Soviet Union. Two of the conspirators, Guy Burgess and Donald Maclean, were exposed in 1951 and defected to the Soviet Union before they could be captured; Kim Philby, who had worked as a high-level intelligence agent, defected to Russia in 1963 but not before passing on information that cost hundreds of lives. The last two members of the ring, Anthony Blunt and John Cairncross, went undetected for many years.[18]

Some spies, like the Cambridge Five, are motivated by ideology; others, like FBI agent Robert Hanssen and CIA operative Harold Nicholson, were looking for profit. In 1997, Nicholson was convicted of selling U.S. intelligence to Russia for $180,000 and was sentenced to 23.5 years imprisonment; Nicholson was the highest ranking CIA official ever convicted for spying for a foreign country. Hanssen sold American secrets to Russia for more than $1.4 million in cash and diamonds over a 22-year period; he is currently serving a life sentence.[19]

Government employees in a position of trust may offer to misappropriate state secrets for a payoff from a foreign government. One of the most infamous of these cases, that of CIA double agent Aldrich Ames, is set out in the Profiles in Crime feature.

Industrial Espionage
Shanshan Du joined GM as an engineer in 2000, signing an agreement to protect proprietary information created or obtained during her employment. Once assigned to the hybrid car division, she copied thousands of secret GM documents and passed them to her husband, Yu Qin, who was secretly running his own company that was involved in hybrid technology. In 2010 Qin contacted a Chinese automotive manufacturer and GM competitor and tried to sell information. His plan was foiled by federal agents before he could peddle the information worth an estimated $40 million.[20]

The concept of espionage has been extended to spying involving corporations, referred to as industrial espionage. This involves such unethical or illegal activities as bribing employees to reveal trade secrets such as computer codes or product formulas. The traditional methods of industrial espionage include recruiting agents and inserting them into the target company or breaking into an office to take equipment and information. It also can involve surveillance and spying on commercial organizations in order to determine the direction of their new product line or even what bid they intend to make on a government contract. Such knowledge can provide vast profits when it allows a competitor to save large sums on product development or to win an undeserved contract by underbidding.[21]

Foreign Industrial Espionage
Not all corporate espionage is homegrown, and some attacks have been carried out by foreign agents. A report of the National Counterintelligence Center lists biotechnology, aerospace, telecommunications, computer software, transportation, advanced materials, energy research, defense, and semiconductor companies as the top targets for foreign economic espionage.[22]

Industrial espionage by foreign agents' efforts has hurt the United States by eroding the U.S. military advantage by enabling foreign militaries to acquire sophisticated capabilities that might otherwise have taken years to develop. Such efforts also undercut the U.S. economy by making it possible for foreign firms to gain a competitive economic edge over U.S. companies.

Many foreign agents did not come to the United States specifically to engage in espionage, but when an opportunity arose they jumped on the chance to satisfy their desire for profits, for academic or scientific acclaim, or out of a sense of patriotism to their home countries.

A number of factors have combined to facilitate private-sector technology theft. Globalization, which has generated major gains for the U.S. economy, has given foreigners unprecedented access to U.S. firms and to sensitive technologies. A proliferation of devices have made it easy for private-sector experts to illegally retrieve, store, and transfer massive amounts of information, including trade secrets and proprietary data; such devices are increasingly common in the workplace.

In addition to private citizens conducting espionage, foreign government organizations also mount their own operations, including:

- Targeting U.S. firms for technology that would strengthen their foreign defense capabilities
- Posting personnel at U.S. military bases to collect classified information to bolster military modernization efforts
- Employing commercial firms in the United States in a cover effort to target and acquire U.S. technology
- Recruiting students, professors, scientists, and researchers to engage in technology collection
- Making direct requests for classified, sensitive, or export-controlled information
- Forming ventures with U.S. firms in the hope of placing collectors in proximity to sensitive technologies or else establishing foreign research[23]

Legal Controls
Until 1996, there was no federal statute that explicitly penalized industrial espionage. Recognizing the increasingly important role that intellectual property plays in the well-being of the American economy, Congress enacted the Economic Espionage Act (EEA) of 1996, which criminalizes the theft of trade secrets. The EEA contains two separate provisions: one that penalizes foreign agents for stealing American trade secrets and one directed at domestic spying.

Convictions of foreign agents under the Economic Espionage Act have been relatively rare. On December 14, 2006, Fei Ye and Ming Zhong pleaded guilty to two counts each of economic espionage. Ye and Zhong were arrested at the San Francisco International Airport on November 23, 2001, with stolen trade secret information from Sun Microsystems and Transmeta Corporation. At their hearing, Ye and Zhong admitted that they intended to utilize the trade secrets in designing a computer microprocessor that was to be manufactured and marketed by a company they had established, known as Supervision, Inc. They would have profited from sales of chips to the city of Hangzhou and the province of Zhejiang in China; their company had applied for funding from the National High Technology Research and Development Program of China. The plea resulted in the first conviction of foreign agents under the Economic Espionage Act more than 10 years after it was enacted into law.[24]

State Political Crime

Some political crimes are committed by people who oppose the state, whereas others are perpetrated by state authorities against the people they are supposed to serve; this is referred to as **state political crime**. Critical criminologists argue that a great deal of political crime arises from the efforts of the state to either maintain governmental power or to uphold the race, class, and gender advantages of those who support the government. In industrial society, the state will do everything to protect the property rights of the wealthy while opposing the real interests of the poor. They might even go to war to support the capitalist classes who need the wealth and resources of other nations. The desire for natural resources such as rubber, oil, and metals was one of the primary reasons for Japan's invasion of China and other Eastern nations that sparked their entry into World War II.

Using Torture

On February 23, 2007, Osama Hassan Mustafa Nasr, an Egyptian cleric, made worldwide headlines when he claimed that he had been kidnapped in Italy by American CIA agents and sent to Egypt for interrogation as part of the CIA's "extraordinary rendition." Nasr claimed, "I was subjected to the worst kind of torture in Egyptian prisons. I have scars of torture all over my body." Italy indicted 26 Americans and five Italian agents accused of seizing him and sending him to Egypt without trial or due process.[25]

Of all state political crimes, the use of **torture** to gain information from suspected political criminals is perhaps the most notorious. Can the torture of a suspected terrorist determined to destroy the government and harm innocent civilians ever be permissible, or is it always an example of state-sponsored political crime? Although most people loathe the thought of torturing anyone, some experts argue that torture can sometimes be justified in what they call the **ticking bomb scenario**: suppose the government found out that a captured terrorist knew the whereabouts of a dangerous explosive device that was set to go off and kill thousands of innocent people. Would it be permissible to engage in the use of torture on this single suspect if it would save the population of a city? The ticking bomb scenario has appeal (see The Criminological Enterprise feature "Want to Torture? Get a Warrant"), but opponents of torture believe that even imminent danger does not justify state violence. There is a danger that such state-sponsored violence would become calculated and premeditated; torturers would have to be trained, ready, and in place for the ticking bomb argument to work. We couldn't be running around looking for torturers with a bomb set to go off, could we? Because torturers would be part of the government bureaucracy, there is no way to ensure that they would use their skills only in certain morally justifiable cases.[26] What happens if a superior officer tells them to torture someone, but they believe the order is unjustified? Should they follow orders or risk a court-martial for being disobedient? Furthermore, there is very little empirical evidence suggesting that *torture* provides any real benefits and much more that suggests it can create serious problems. *It can damage* civil rights and democratic institutions and cause the general public to have sympathy for the victims of torture no matter their evil intent.[27]

Critics have complained that government agencies such as the CIA have used torture without legal authority. Despite its illegality, enemy agents have been detained and physically abused in secret prisons around the world without the benefit of due process. In some cases, suspects have been held in foreign countries simply because their governments are not squeamish about using torture during interrogations. Shocking photo evidence of *torture* from detention facilities at the Guantanamo base in Cuba support these charges. Legal scholars have argued that these tactics violate both international treaties and domestic statutes prohibiting *torture*. Some maintain that the U.S. Constitution limits the authority of an executive agency like the CIA to act against foreigners abroad and also limits physical coercion by the government under the Fifth Amendment due process and self-incrimination clauses and the Eighth Amendment prohibition against cruel and unusual punishments. Legally, it is impermissible for United States authorities to engage in indefinite detention or *torture* regardless of the end, the place, or the victim.[28]

The Waterboarding Controversy

Can a bright line be drawn between what is considered torture and what constitutes firm but legal interrogation methods? This issue made headlines when it was revealed in 2007 that the CIA made routine use of the waterboarding technique while interrogating suspected terrorists.[29] Waterboarding involves immobilizing a person on his or her back, with the head inclined downward, and pouring water over the face and into the breathing passages. It produces an immediate gag reflex and an experience akin to drowning; the subject believes death is imminent.

The use of waterboarding is controversial because there seems to be no agreement on whether it is torture or a relatively harmless instrument of interrogation. The official U.S. government policy and government doctrine is vehemently opposed to torture, but it has condoned harsh interrogation techniques that combine physical and psychological tactics, including head slapping, waterboarding, and exposure to extreme cold. Waterboarding even became an issue during the 2008 presidential campaign when Senator John McCain, a former prisoner of war who had experienced torture firsthand in a North Vietnamese prison camp, told the press, "All I can say is that it was used in the Spanish Inquisition, it was used in Pol Pot's genocide in Cambodia, and there are reports that it is being used against Buddhist monks today. They should know what it is. It is not a complicated procedure. It is torture."[30]

According to the ticking bomb scenario, torture can be justified in order to force a political criminal to reveal the location of an explosive device before it can go off and kill many people. A number of legal and social scholars have debated whether torture can ever be justified in a moral society no matter what the intent, but famed social commentator and legal scholar Alan Dershowitz disagrees. He argues that torture can be justified under some circumstances, especially to prevent damaging terror attacks. Moreover, he believes that the "vast majority" of Americans would expect law enforcement agents to engage in time-honored methods of "loosening tongues" if the circumstances demanded it, even though international bodies such as the United Nations forbid its use no matter how exigent the circumstances. To ensure that torture is not used capriciously, Dershowitz proposes the creation of a "torture warrant" that can only be issued by a judge in cases where (a) there is an absolute need to obtain immediate information in order to save lives and (b) there is probable cause that the suspect has such information and is unwilling to reveal it to law enforcement agents. The suspect would be given immunity from prosecution based on information elicited by the torture; it would only be to save lives. The warrant would limit the torture to nonlethal means, such as sterile needles being inserted beneath the nails to cause excruciating pain without endangering life.

Dershowitz recognizes that it may sound both awful and absurd for a judge to be issuing a warrant to torture a suspect, but in truth every democracy, including our own, has employed torture outside of the law. It is routine for police officers to put tremendous pressure on suspects to get them to talk. The "third degree" is all too common, not only on TV shows but in the back rooms of real police station houses. If it is already used, would it not be better to have it regulated and controlled by the rule of law? If it isn't, law enforcement agents would continue to use torture anyway, only it would fall "below the radar screen of accountability." Which would be more consistent with democratic values?

Dershowitz recognizes that those opposed to the idea of a torture warrant argue that establishing such a precedent would legitimize torture and make it easier to use under any circumstances. But he believes that the opposite would be true: by expressly limiting the use of torture only to the ticking bomb case and by requiring an objective and reasoned judge to approve, limit, and monitor the torture, it will be far more difficult to justify its extension to other institutions. The goal of the warrant would be to reduce and limit the amount of torture that would, in fact, be used in an emergency.

Not everyone agrees that in some extreme cases the "ends justify the means." Human Rights Watch, an international group dedicated to protecting the human rights of people around the world, counters Dershowitz by pointing out that although the ticking bomb scenario makes for great philosophical discussion, it rarely arises in real life. Except in movies and TV, interrogators rarely learn that a suspect in custody knows of a particular, imminent terrorist bombing and that the suspect has the knowledge to prevent a catastrophe. Intelligence is rarely, if ever, good enough to provide such specific advance warning. If terrorists knew their plan could be foiled by information provided by a prisoner, why would they not change the plan? While not practical, the ticking bomb scenario can be dangerous because it expands the use of torture to anyone who might have knowledge of unspecified future terrorist attacks: Why are only the victims of an imminent terrorist attack deserving of protection by torture? Why not also use torture to prevent a terrorist attack tomorrow or next week or next year? And why stop with the alleged terrorists themselves? Why not also torture their families or associates—anyone who might provide life-saving information? The slope is very slippery, Human Rights Watch claims.

CRITICAL THINKING

You are a government agent holding a prisoner who has been arrested on suspicion of being a terrorist. You get a call stating that there is a credible threat that a bomb will go off in two hours unless it can be found and defused. The prisoner has knowledge of the bomb's location. How would you get him to reveal the location? Would you consider using torture? Is there a better method?

SOURCES: Alan M. Dershowitz, *Shouting Fire: Civil Liberties in a Turbulent Age* (New York: Little, Brown, 2002); Dershowitz, "Want to Torture? Get a Warrant," *San Francisco Chronicle*, January 22, 2002; Human Rights Watch, "The Twisted Logic of Torture," January 2005, http://hrw.org/wr2k5/darfurandabughraib/6.htm (accessed August 16, 2011).

TERRORISM

The political crime that many people are most concerned with is terrorism, and the remainder of this chapter focuses on the history, nature, and extent of terrorism and the methods being employed to control it. Terrorism has become so commonplace that the media routinely ignore terror attacks that take many lives. Thousands of incidents occur each year, and the landscape can change at a moment's notice, witness the death of Osama bin Laden. The National Counterterrorism Center estimates that each year approximately 11,000 terrorist attacks occur in 83 countries, resulting in more than 58,000 victims, including nearly 15,000 fatalities. Most attacks occur not in the Middle East but in South Asia, which also has the greatest number of fatalities. Together,

Torture or Not?

As a criminologist, your specialty is terrorism, so it comes as no surprise that the director of the CIA asks you to draw up a protocol setting out the rules for the use of torture with suspected terrorists. The reason for his request is that a series of new articles has exposed the agency's practice of sending suspected terrorists to friendly nations that are less squeamish about using torture. He understands that the American public has mixed feelings about torture. A 2009 *Washington Post*/ABC News poll found that 49 percent of respondents agreed that the United States should not torture, whereas 48 percent believed torture is sometimes acceptable.

A recent Gallup poll found that 55 percent of Americans believe that the use of harsh interrogation techniques is justified, whereas only 36 percent say they are not.

» Write a memo to the CIA director outlining the protocol you recommend for the use of torture with suspected terrorists. In your document, address when torture should be used, who it should be used on, and what tortures you recommend using. Of course, if you believe the use of torture is always unethical, you could let the director know why you have reached this conclusion.

South Asia and the Near East account for almost two-thirds of the high-casualty attacks (those that killed 10 or more people). These data indicate that terrorism has truly reached warlike proportions.[31]

Defining Terrorism

Despite its long history, it is often difficult to precisely define terrorism (from the Latin *terrere*, which means to frighten) and to separate terrorist acts from interpersonal crimes of violence. For example, if a group robs a bank to obtain funds for its revolutionary struggles, should the act be treated as terrorism or as a common bank robbery? In this instance, defining a crime as terrorism depends on the kind of legal response the act evokes from those in power. To be considered **terrorism**, which is a political crime, an act must carry with it the intent to disrupt and change the government and must not be merely a common-law crime committed for greed or egotism.

Because of its complexity, an all-encompassing definition of terrorism is difficult to formulate, although most experts agree that it generally involves the illegal use of force against innocent people to achieve a political objective. According to the U.S. State Department, the term *terrorism* means premeditated, politically motivated violence perpetrated against noncombatant targets by subnational groups or clandestine agents, usually intended to influence an audience. The term *international terrorism* means terrorism involving citizens or the territory of more than one country. A terrorist group is any group practicing, or that has significant subgroups that practice, international terrorism.[32]

Exhibit 11.2 sets out a number of definitions of terrorism drafted or used by prominent governmental agencies or organizations.

Terrorism usually involves a type of political crime that emphasizes violence as a mechanism to promote change. Whereas some political criminals sell secrets, spy, and the like, terrorists systematically murder and destroy or threaten such violence to terrorize individuals, groups, communities, or governments into conceding to the terrorists' political demands.[33] Because the terrorist lacks large armies and formidable weapons, their use of subterfuge, secrecy, and hit-and-run tactics is designed to give them a psychological advantage and the power to neutralize the physical superiority of their opponents.

However, it may be erroneous to assume that terrorists have political goals. Some may try to bring about what they consider to be social reform—for example, by attacking women wearing fur coats or sabotaging property during a labor dispute. Terrorism also must be distinguished from conventional warfare because it requires secrecy and clandestine operations to exert social control over large populations.[34] So terrorist activities may be aimed at promoting an ideology rather than political change.

Terror Cells   Regardless of what organizational structure is used, most groups subdivide their affiliates into **terror cells** for both organizational and security purposes. To enhance security, each cell may be functionally independent so that each member has little knowledge of other cells, their members, locations, and so on. However, individual cell members provide emotional support to one another and maintain loyalty and dedication. Because only the cell leader knows how to communicate with other cells and/or a central command, capture of one cell does not compromise other group members.

Terror cell formations may be based on location, employment, or family membership. Some are formed on the basis of function: some are fighters, others political organizers. The number of cells and their composition depend on the size of the terrorist group: local or national groups will have fewer cells than international terrorist groups that may operate in several countries, such as the al-Qaeda group.

Terrorist and Guerilla

The word *terrorist* is often used interchangeably with the word *guerilla*, but the terms are quite different. **Guerilla** comes from the Spanish term meaning "little war," which developed out of the Spanish rebellion against French troops after Napoleon's 1808 invasion of the Iberian Peninsula.[35] Terrorists have an urban focus. Operating in small bands, or cadres, of three to five members, they target the property or persons of their enemy, such as members of the ruling class.[36] However, terrorists may not have political ambitions, and their actions may be aimed at stifling or intimidating other groups who oppose their political, social, or economic views. For example, terrorists who kill abortion providers in order to promote their "pro-life" agenda are not aiming for regime change. Guerillas, on the other hand, are armed military bands, typically located in rural areas, that attack military, police, and government officials in an effort to destabilize the existing government. Their organizations can grow quite large and eventually take the form of a conventional military force. Some guerilla bands infiltrate urban areas (urban guerillas). For the most part, guerillas are a type of insurgent band.

Terrorist and Insurgent

As commonly used, an **insurgency** is somewhat different from both guerilla warfare and terrorism. The typical goal of an insurgency is to confront the existing government for control of all or a portion of its territory, or force political concessions in sharing political power by competing with the opposition government for popular support.[37] **Insurgents** are organized into covert groups who engage in an organized campaign of extreme violence, which may falsely appear to be random and indiscriminate, such causing the death of innocent civilians, but has a distinct political agenda. Insurgents tend to live isolated and stressful lives and enjoy varying levels of public support.[38]

Although insurgents may engage in violence, they also may use nonviolent methods or political tactics. For example, they may set up food distribution centers and schools in areas in which they gain control in order to provide the population with needed services while contrasting their benevolent rule with the government's incompetence and corruption.

When insurgents use violence, it is designed to inspire support and gain converts while at the same time destroying the government's ability to resist. It is easy to recruit supporters once the population believes that the government is incapable of fighting back. On the other hand, some members of the insurgency might shun violence and create nonviolent splinter groups. They can then operate openly, claiming to sympathize with the violent wing of their organization but just not being part of its structure. They may seek external support from other nations to bring pressure on the government. A terror group, in contrast, neither

The Various Forms of Radical Political Groups

	Terrorist	Guerilla	Insurgent	Revolutionary
Description	Groups who engage in premeditated, politically motivated violence perpetrated against noncombatant targets	Armed groups operating in rural areas who attack the military, the police, and other government officials	Groups who engage in armed uprising, or revolt against an established civil or political authority	Group that engages in civil war against a sovereign power that holds control of the land
Example	Al-Qaeda, Hamas	Mao's People's Liberation Army; Ho Chi Minh's Viet Cong	Iraqi insurgent groups	American Revolution, French Revolution, Russian Revolution
Goals	Personal, criminal or political gain or change	Replace or overthrow existing government	Win over population by showing government's incompetence. Force government into political concessions and/or power sharing	Gain independence or oust existing government or monarchy
Methods	Small, clandestine cells who use systematic violence for purpose of intimidation	Use unconventional warfare and mobile tactics. May grow large and use tactics similar to conventional military force	May use violent (bombings and kidnappings) or nonviolent means (food distribution centers and creating schools)	Can use violent armed conflict or nonviolent methods such as Gandhi used in India

requires nor has active support or sympathy from a large percentage of the population.

Terrorist and Revolutionary

A revolution (from the Latin *revolutio*, "a revolving," and *revolvere*, "turn, roll back") is generally seen as a civil war fought between nationalists and a sovereign power that holds control of the land, or between the existing government and local groups over issues of ideology and power. Historically, the American Revolution may be considered an example of a struggle between nationalistic groups and an imperialistic overseas government. Classic examples of ideological rebellions are the French Revolution, which pitted the middle class and urban poor against the aristocracy, and the Russian Revolution of 1917, during which the Czarist government was toppled by the Bolsheviks. More recent ideological revolutions have occurred in China, Cuba, Nicaragua, and Chile, to name but a few.

Some revolutions (such as the American, French, and Russian) rely on armed force, terror activities, and violence, but others can be nonviolent, depending on large urban protests and threats. Such was the case when the Shah Mohammad Reza Pahlavi was toppled in Iran after a slew of nonviolent demonstrations that ended in the 1979 revolution, which transformed Iran from a constitutional monarchy into an Islamic republic or theocracy under the rule of Ayatollah Ruhollah Khomeini.

Concept Summary 11.1 describes the components of the various types of political groups.

A BRIEF HISTORY OF TERRORISM

Acts of terrorism have been known throughout history. The assassination of Julius Caesar on March 15, 44 BCE is considered an act of terrorism. Terrorism became widespread at the end of the Middle Ages when political leaders were frequently subject to assassination by their enemies.

Religious Roots

The first terrorist activities were committed by members of minority religious groups who engaged in violence to (a) gain the right to practice their own form of religion, (b) establish the supremacy of their own religion over others, or (c) meet the requirements of the blood-thirsty gods they worshipped.[39]

In some instances, a conquered people used force and violence to maintain their right to worship in their own faith. **Zealots**, Hebrew warrior groups, were active during the Roman occupation of Palestine during the first century CE. A subgroup of the Zealots, the Sciari (literally translated as "daggermen"), were so named after the long curved knives they favored as a weapon to assassinate Romans or their sympathizers. The Zealots carried out their attacks in broad daylight, typically with witnesses around, in order to send a message that the Roman authorities and those Jews who collaborated with them would not be safe. Ironically, this tactic is still being used by contemporary terrorists. The Zealots and Sciari led the revolt in 66 CE against Roman occupation of the Holy Land, during which they occupied the fortress of Masada. Here they held out for more than seven months before engaging in mass suicide rather than surrender to the Roman legions. The revolt ended badly, and the Romans destroyed the Jewish temple and sent the population into exile.

Some religious terrorists want to promote the supremacy of their own sect over a rival group. The (Shi'ite) Muslim Order of the Assassins (assassin literally means "hashish-eater," a reference to the commonly held belief that gang members engaged in acts of ritual intoxication and smoked hashish just prior to undertaking their missions) was active in Persia, Syria, and Palestine from 1090 to 1272, killing a great number of their enemies, mainly Sunnis, whom they considered apostates, but also Christians who were then the rulers of the kingdom of Jerusalem.[40] The Assassins also were prone to stabbing their victims in an effort to spread their vision of Islam, and they carried out missions in public places on holy days to publicize their cause. Successful assassinations guaranteed them a place in heaven.

Another form of religious terror is inspired by the requirements of belief. Some religious beliefs have focused on violence, the gods demanding the death of nonbelievers. In India, members of the Thugee cult (from which the modern term "thug" was derived) were devoted to Kali, the goddess of death and destruction. The thugs believed each murder prevented Kali's arrival for 1,000 years, thus sparing the nation from her death and destruction. The thugs traveled in gangs of up to 100 with each member having a defined role—some lured unwary travelers, others strangled the chosen victim. The gang used secret argot and jargon that only they could understand and signs so that members could recognize each other even in the most remote parts of India. Cult members may have killed hundreds of thousands of victims over a 300-year span. They would attach themselves to travelers and when the opportunity arose, strangle them with a noose around their necks, steal their money, and bury their bodies. The killings were highly ritualistic and involved religious rites and prayers. By the mid-nineteenth century the British made it a policy to end Thugee activities, hanged nearly 4,000, and all but eradicated the cult. Thugees represented the last serious religion-inspired terrorist threat until the emergence of Islamic terrorism in the 1980s.

Political Roots

When rulers had absolute power, terrorist acts were viewed as one of the only means of gaining political rights. At times European states encouraged terrorist acts against their enemies. In the sixteenth century, Queen Elizabeth I empowered her naval leaders, including famed captains John Hawkins and Francis Drake, to attack the Spanish fleet and take prizes. These privateers would have been considered pirates had they not operated with government approval. American privateers attacked the British during the Revolutionary War and the War of 1812 and were considered heroes for their actions against the English navy.

The term *terrorist* first became popular during the French Revolution. Use of the word *terrorism* began in 1795 in reference to the **Reign of Terror** initiated by the revolutionary government during which agents of the Committee of Public Safety and the National Convention were referred to as terrorists. In response, royalists and opponents of the Revolution employed terrorist tactics in resistance to the Revolutionists. The widespread use of the guillotine is an infamous reminder of the revolutionary violence; urban mobs demanded blood, and many government officials and aristocrats were beheaded in gruesome public spectacles. From the fall of the Bastille on July 14, 1789, until July 1794, thousands suspected of counterrevolutionary activity were killed on the guillotine. Here again, the relative nature of political crime is documented: most victims of the French Reign of Terror were revolutionaries who had been denounced by rival factions, whereas thousands of the hated nobility lived in relative tranquility. The end of the terror was signaled by the death of its prime mover, Maximilien Robespierre, on July 28, 1794, as the result of a successful plot to end his rule. He was executed on the same guillotine to which he had sent almost 20,000 people.

In the hundred years following the French Revolution, terrorism continued to be a political tool around the world. Terrorist acts became the preferred method of political action for national groups in the early years of the twentieth century. In Eastern Europe, the Internal Macedonian Revolutionary Organization campaigned against the Turkish government, which controlled its homeland (Macedonia became part of the former Yugoslavia). Similarly, the protest of the Union of Death Society, or Black Hand, against the Austro-Hungarian Empire's control of Serbia led to the group's assassination of Archduke Franz Ferdinand, which started World War I. Russia was the scene of left-wing revolutionary activity, which killed the czar in 1917 and gave birth to the Marxist state.

After the war ended, the Treaty of Versailles restructured Europe and broke up the Austro-Hungarian Empire. The result was a hodgepodge of new nations controlled by majority ethnic groups. Self-determination was limited to European nations and ethnic groups and denied to others, especially the colonial possessions of the major European powers, creating bitterness and setting the stage for the long conflicts of the anticolonial period. The Irish Republican Army, established around 1916, steadily battled British forces from 1919 to 1923, culminating in the Republic of Ireland gaining independence.

Between the World Wars, right-wing terrorism existed in Germany, Spain, and Italy. One source of tension, according to author Michael Kellogg, was the virulently anti-Communist exiles who fled Russia after the 1917 Revolution (called White Russians) and took up residence in Germany and other Western nations. According to Kellogg, between 1920 and 1923, Adolf Hitler was deeply influenced by the Aufbau (Reconstruction), the émigrés' organization. Members of the Aufbau allied with the Nazis to overthrow the legitimate German government and thwart German communists from seizing power. The White Russians deep-seated anti-Semitism may have inspired Hitler to go public with his campaign to kill the European Jews, prompting both the Holocaust and the invasion of Russia, which spelled the eventual doom of Hitler and National Socialism.[41]

During World War II, resistance to the occupying German troops was common throughout Europe. The Germans considered the resistors to be terrorists, but the rest of the world considers them heroes. Meanwhile, in Palestine, Jewish terrorist groups—the Haganah, Irgun, and Stern Gang, whose leaders included Menachem Begin, who later became Israel's prime minister—waged war against the British to force them to allow Jewish survivors of the Holocaust to settle in their traditional homeland. Today, of course, many of these alleged terrorists are considered freedom fighters who laid down their lives for a just cause.

After the war, Arab nationalists felt that they had been betrayed. Believing they were promised postwar independence, they were doubly disappointed—first when the French and British were given authority over their lands, and then especially when the British allowed Zionist immigration into Palestine in keeping with a promise contained in the Balfour Declaration.

Since the end of World War II, terrorism has accelerated its development into a major component of contemporary conflict. Primarily in use immediately after the war as a subordinate element of anticolonial insurgencies, it has expanded beyond that role. In the service of various ideologies and aspirations, terrorism sometimes supplanted other forms of conflict completely. It became a far-reaching weapon capable of effects no less global than the intercontinental bomber or missile. It has also proven to be a significant tool of diplomacy and international power for states inclined to use it.

CONTEMPORARY FORMS OF TERRORISM

Today the term *terrorism* encompasses many different behaviors and goals. Some of the more common forms are briefly described here.

Revolutionary Terrorism

Revolutionary terrorists use violence to frighten those in power and their supporters in order to replace the existing government with a regime that holds acceptable political or religious views. Terrorist actions such as kidnapping, assassination, and bombing are designed to draw repressive responses from governments trying to defend themselves. These responses help revolutionaries to expose, through the skilled use of media coverage, the government's inhumane nature. The original reason for the government's harsh response may be lost as the effect of counterterrorist activities is felt by uninvolved people.

Jemaah Islamiyah, an Indonesian terrorist organization aligned with al-Qaeda, is believed to be intent on driving away foreign tourists and ruining the nation's economy so they can usurp the government and set up a pan-Islamic nation in Indonesia and neighboring Malaysia (see Exhibit 11.3).[42]

Political Terrorism

Political terrorism is directed at people or groups who oppose the terrorists' political ideology or whom the terrorists define as "outsiders" who must be destroyed. Political terrorists may not want to replace the existing government but to shape it so that it accepts the terrorists' views.

Right-Wing Political Groups   Domestic terrorists in the United States can be found across the political spectrum. On the right, they tend to be heavily armed groups organized around such themes as white supremacy, anti-abortion, militant tax resistance, and religious revisionism. Identified groups have included, at one time or another, the Aryan Republican Army, the Aryan Nation, the Posse Comitatus, and the Ku Klux Klan. These groups want to shape U.S. government policy over a range of matters, including ending abortion rights, extending the right to bear arms, and eliminating federal taxation. Anti-abortion groups have demonstrated at abortion clinics, attacked clients, bombed offices, and killed doctors who perform abortions. On October 23, 1998, Dr. Barnett Slepian was shot by a sniper and killed in his Buffalo, New York, home; he was one of a growing number of abortion providers believed to be the victims of terrorists who ironically claim to be "pro-life." Although unlikely to topple the government, these individualistic acts of terror are difficult to predict or control. On April 19, 1995, 168 people were killed during the Oklahoma City bombing, the most severe example of political terrorism in the United States so far.

Left-Wing Political Groups   During the turmoil of the 1960s, a number of left-wing political groups emerged to challenge the existing power structure. Some, such as the Black Panther Party—founded in 1966 in Oakland, California, by Bobby Seale and Huey Newton—demanded the right to control community schools, police, and public assistance programs. Many of their activities were productive, such as sponsoring breakfast programs and medical clinics in poor neighborhoods, but they also began to openly carry rifles and shotguns while patrolling areas where the Oakland

EXHIBIT 11.3

Jemaah Islamiyah

Jemaah Islamiyah is a militant Islamic organization located in Southeast Asia devoted to the establishment of fundamentalist Islamic states in countries such as Indonesia, Singapore, Brunei, Malaysia, Thailand, and the Philippines. The name derives from an Arabic phrase meaning "Islamic group" or "Islamic community." The group has its roots in the Darul Islam organization, a violent radical group that advocated the establishment of Islamic law in Indonesia in the 1940s and 1950s as a reaction to Dutch colonial rule and what it perceived as the secular orientation of postcolonial Indonesia.

Jemaah Islamiyah sponsors recruiting, training, indoctrination, and financial support for terror groups in the region and helps link them to kindred organizations such as al-Qaeda, the Abu Sayyaf Group, the Moro Islamic Liberation Front, the Misuari Renegade/Breakaway Group, and the Philippine Raja Solaiman Movement. Jemaah Islamiyah members have been sent to Afghanistan and southern Philippines for military training where they learned bomb-making and other terror skills.

Jemaah Islamiyah operates through cells with a rather loosely organized structure. The top strategists appear to be mostly Indonesian nationals living in Malaysia, many of whom had gone to Afghanistan to fight the Russians during the Soviet occupation in the 1980s. The second level is made up of field coordinators, responsible for delivering money and explosives and for choosing a local subordinate who can effectively act as team leader of the foot soldiers. At the bottom of the organization are the soldiers who drive the cars, survey targets, and deliver the bombs. They are mostly young men from *pesantrens* (religious boarding schools) or Islamic high schools run by teachers who were involved in the Darul Islam rebellions of the 1950s.

Jemaah Islamiyah has been responsible for numerous attacks that have killed hundreds of civilians in the region. The Bali car bombing on October 12, 2002, in which 202 people died, was a coordinated attack designed to destroy the tourist industry, a significant source of income for the government. A suicide bomber using a backpack bomb killed several people in a nightclub frequented by foreign tourists. The survivors ran into the street and were killed by a fertilizer/fuel oil bomb concealed in a parked van. Other attacks linked to Jemaah Islamiyah are the 2003 JW Marriott hotel bombing in Kuningan, Jakarta, the 2004 Australian embassy bombing in Jakarta, and the 2005 Bali terrorist bombing.

Authorities in the region attempted to crack down on the group after the 2002 bombing, arresting more than 200 members. Three of the four main suspects behind the attack were sentenced to death in Indonesia.

SOURCES: Council on Foreign Relations, "Jemaah Islamiyah," www.cfr.org/publication/8948/ (accessed August 16, 2011); Globalsecurity.org, www.globalsecurity.org/military/world/para/ (accessed November 2, 2010).

---

police were rumored to be harassing the community's black citizens. The Panthers' confrontational style led to clashes with police, shootings, and arrests. Because its leaders were faced with criminal charges of varying degrees, the Black Panthers steadily eroded.

Another influential 1960s group, the Students for a Democratic Society (SDS), was founded in Chicago in 1962 and was active on college campuses throughout the sixties protesting the United States' involvement in Vietnam. Though the SDS was nonviolent, a splinter group known as the Weathermen utilized terror tactics to achieve their goals. They were involved in a number of bombings at corporation headquarters and federal institutions, though they typically sent out warnings to evacuate the buildings. The group lost influence when on March 6, 1970, a bomb accidentally exploded in one of their safe houses in New York City. The detonations were so powerful that they collapsed the three-story house, killing three members. The Weathermen disbanded in 1977.

Eco-Terrorism The most active left-leaning domestic political terror groups today are involved in violent actions to protect the environment. Of these groups, the Earth Liberation Front (ELF) is perhaps the best known. Founded in 1994 in Brighton, England, by members of the Earth First! environmental movement, ELF has been active for several years in the United States and abroad. Operating in secret, ELF cells have conducted a series of actions intent on damaging individuals or corporations that they consider a threat to the environment. On October 19, 1998, ELF members claimed responsibility for fires that were set atop Vail Mountain, a luxurious ski resort in Colorado, claiming that the action was designed to stop the resort from expanding into animal habitats (especially that of the mountain lynx); the fires caused an estimated $12 million in damages. On August 22, 2003, members of ELF claimed responsibility for fires that destroyed about a dozen sport utility vehicles at a Chevrolet dealership in West Covina, California.[43] Fires have also been set in government labs where animal research is conducted. Spikes have been driven into trees to prevent logging in fragile areas. Members have conducted arson attacks on property ranging from a Nike shop in a mall north of Minneapolis to new homes on Long Island, New York. On February 7, 2004, ELF group members targeted construction equipment at a 30-acre development site in Charlottesville, Virginia.[44] On March 2, 2008, ELF is believed to have burnt a row of luxury homes in Seattle, causing $7 million in damage. The multimillion dollar homes used green technology such as formaldehyde-free materials, energy-efficient appliances, and landscaping that included native plants in their construction, but the development had drawn opposition because of fear that septic systems could damage critical wetlands needed to protect an aquifer used by about 20,000 people in the area and could harm streams used by Chinook salmon.[45]

You can read about the **Earth Liberation Front** by visiting the Criminal Justice CourseMate at cengagebrain.com, then access the "Web Links" for this chapter.

Another group, the Animal Liberation Front (ALF), focuses their efforts on protecting animals from being used as food, in clothing, or as experimental subjects. Their philosophy is that animals are entitled to the moral right to possess their own lives and control their own bodies. ALF rejects the view that animals are merely capital goods or property intended for the benefit of humans and can be bought, sold, or killed by humans. ALF members conduct actions against scientists who conduct animal research, vandalizing their homes and cars, attacking labs, and setting animals free. They also conduct actions against animal breeding farms and food processing plants. ALF members have raided turkey farms before Thanksgiving and rabbit farms before Easter. Their activities have had significant impact on the commercial aspects of scientific testing, driving up the price of products, such as drugs, which rely on animal experimentation.[46] The ALF position on raising animals in breeding ranches is set out in Exhibit 11.4.

Not surprisingly, the FBI and other law enforcement agencies have targeted eco-terror groups such as ELF and ALF. On January 20, 2006, the FBI announced that its Operation Backfire had led to the arrest of 11 people who were accused of 17 attacks, including the $12 million arson of the Vail Ski Resort in 1998 and the sabotage of a high-tension power line near Bend, Oregon, in 1999.[47]

Nationalist Terrorism

Nationalist terrorism promotes the interests of a minority ethnic or religious group that believes it has been persecuted under majority rule and wishes to carve out its own independent homeland.

In Spain, the Basque Fatherland and Liberty (Euzkadi Ta Askatasuna, or ETA) is devoted to establishing a Basque homeland based on Marxist principles in the ethnically Basque areas in northern Spain and southwestern France. ETA was founded in 1959 by Basque Marxist rebels incensed by the efforts of Spanish dictator Francisco Franco to suppress the Basque language and culture. Since then the group has carried out numerous attacks in Spain and some in France. More than 800 people have been killed in ETA attacks since its founding. The group is best known for

---

EXHIBIT 11.4

Breeding Ranches and Animal Liberation

A common misconception about fur "ranches" is that the animals do not suffer. This is entirely untrue. These animals suffer a life of misery and frustration, deprived of their most basic needs. They are kept in wire-mesh cages that are tiny, overcrowded, and filthy. Here they are malnourished, suffer contagious diseases, and endure severe stress.

On these farms, the animals are forced to forfeit their natural instincts. Beavers, who live in water in the wild, must exist on cement floors. Minks in the wild, too, spend much of their time in water, which keeps their salivation, respiration, and body temperature stable. They are also, by nature, solitary animals. However, on these farms, they are forced to live in close contact with other animals. This often leads to self-destructive behavior, such as pelt and tail biting. They often resort to cannibalism.

The methods used on these farms reflect not the interests and welfare of the animals but the furriers' primary interest—profit. The end of the suffering of these animals comes only with death, which, in order to preserve the quality of the fur, is inflicted with extreme cruelty and brutality. Engine exhaust is often pumped into a box of animals. This exhaust is not always lethal, and the animals sometimes writhe in pain as they are skinned alive. Another common execution practice, often used on larger animals, is anal electrocution. The farmers attach clamps to an animal's lips and insert metal rods into its anus. The animal is then electrocuted. Decompression chambers, neck snapping, and poison are also used.

SOURCE: Animal Liberation Front, www.animalliberationfront.com/ (accessed August 16, 2011).

---

assassinating high-level Spanish officials. In 1973, the group assassinated Admiral Luis Carrero Blanco, the heir-apparent to Franco. Spanish King Juan Carlos was also the target of an unsuccessful plot. In addition, the group has targeted lower-level officials, journalists, and businessmen.

In the Middle East, terrorist activities have been linked to the Palestinians' desire to wrest their former homeland from Israel. At first, the Palestinian Liberation Organization (PLO), led by Yassir Arafat, directed terrorist activities against Israel. Now the group Hamas is perpetuating the conflict with Israel and is behind a spate of suicide bombings and terrorist attacks designed to elicit a sharp response from Israel and set back any chance for peace in the region. Hundreds on both sides of the conflict have been killed during terrorist attacks and reprisals. In Lebanon, Hezbollah, an Iranian-supported group, is dedicated to fighting Israel and seizing control of the government. Their activities are described in Exhibit 11.5.

The Middle East is not the only source of nationalistic terrorism. In Russia, Chechen terrorists have been intent on creating a free Chechen homeland and have been battling the Russian government to achieve their goal.

Hezbollah (from the Arabic, meaning "party of God") is a Lebanese Shi'ite Islamist organization founded in 1982 in response to the presence of Israeli forces in southern Lebanon. At inception, its goals were to both drive Israeli troops out of Lebanon and to form a Shi'ite Islamic republic in Lebanon. Taking its inspiration from Iran, Hezbollah members follow a distinct version of Shia ideology developed by Ayatollah Ruhollah Khomeini, leader of the Islamic Revolution in Iran. Hezbollah has received arms and financial support from Iran, and some observers believe that it is actually a proxy Iranian paramilitary force. Hezbollah is anti-West and anti-Israel and has engaged in a series of terrorist actions including kidnappings, car bombings, and airline hijackings. Some of its most notable attacks directed at U.S. citizens and others include:

- The suicide truck bombings that killed more than 200 U.S. Marines at their barracks in Beirut, Lebanon, in 1983
- The 1985 hijacking of TWA flight 847
- Two major 1990s attacks in Argentina: the 1992 bombing of the Israeli Embassy (killing 29) and the 1994 bombing of a Jewish community center (killing 95)
- A July 2006 raid on a border post in northern Israel in which two Israeli soldiers were taken captive, an action that sparked an Israeli military incursion into Lebanon and the firing of rockets by Hezbollah across the Lebanese border into Israel

In addition to its military/terror campaigns, Hezbollah has attempted to win the hearts and minds of the Lebanese Shi'ite community by providing social services and food to the population. It has also entered the political world, and its candidates have won seats in Lebanon's parliament.

The public face of Hezbollah is Hassan Nasrallah, the group's senior political leader. Originally a military commander, Nasrallah's military and religious training makes him a unique leader. His leadership of Hezbollah's resistance to the Israeli army in the summer of 2006 made him one of the most popular leaders in the Middle East. For over 20 years, Imad Fayez Mugniyah was considered the key planner of Hezbollah's worldwide terrorist operations. On February 13, 2008, Mugniyah was killed in a car bombing in Damascus. Hezbollah officials accused Israel of launching the attacks that killed him, but the Israeli government denied involvement.

SOURCE: Council on Foreign Relations, Hezbollah, www.cfr.org/publication/9155/ (accessed August 16, 2011).

Retributive Terrorism

Some terrorist groups are not nationalist, political, or revolutionary organizations. They do not wish to set up their own homeland or topple a government but rather want to impose their social and religious code on others.[48] **Retributive terrorists** have a number of characteristics that are unique and separate them from guerrillas, revolutionaries, and other terrorists:[49]

- Violence is used as a method of influence, persuasion, or intimidation. The true target of the terrorist act extends far beyond those directly affected by the attack and is designed to lead to some desired behavior on the part of the larger target population or government.
- Victims are usually selected for their maximum propaganda value, usually ensuring a high degree of media coverage. The message is that the target population had better comply with their demands because the terrorists are desperate enough to "do anything." Sometimes this may backfire if the attack results in the death of innocents, especially children, along with the symbolic targets.
- Unconventional military tactics are used, especially secrecy and surprise, as well as targeting civilians, including women and children. Because the goal is to inflict maximum horror, it makes sense to choose targets that contain the largest number of victims from all walks of life. The message: everyone is a target; no one is safe.

How do retributive terror groups use violence to achieve their goals? According to researchers at the RAND Corporation, there are four independent views on this topic:

- *Coercion hypothesis.* Terrorists use violence to cause pain, notably casualties, to frighten the United States and get it to bend to their will (e.g., withdrawing from the Middle East).
- *Damage hypothesis.* Terrorists want to damage the U.S. economy to weaken its ability to intervene in international affairs.
- *Rally hypothesis.* Violence is used to attract the attention of potential recruits and supporters.
- *Franchise hypothesis.* Jihadists use violence to pursue their own, often local, goals and only receive some support and encouragement from international organizations such as al-Qaeda.[50]

RAND researchers have found that the coercion and damage hypotheses are most consistent with prior attack patterns.

Today the retributive terrorist can be categorized into four main groups:

- Al-Qaeda, including the group's strategy, ideology, operations, tactics, finances, changing character, and possible future.
- Terrorist groups that have adopted al-Qaeda's worldview and concept of mass-casualty terrorist attacks, even if the groups are not formally part of al-Qaeda.
- Violent Islamist and non-Islamist terrorist and insurgent groups without known links to al-Qaeda that threaten United States interests, friends, and allies. These include Hezbollah and Hamas, along with insurgencies in Iraq, the Philippines, and other countries.
- The nexus between terrorism and organized crime, including the terrorists and insurgents that use criminal organizations and connections to finance their activities.

Such actions also tend to weaken and corrupt political and social institutions.[51]

Al-Qaeda is the paradigm of the new retributive terrorist organization. Rather than fighting for a homeland or to topple an unpopular government, its message is a call to take up a cause: there is a war of civilizations in which "Jews and Crusaders" want to destroy Islam and must therefore be defeated. Armed jihad is the individual obligation of every Muslim; terrorism and violence are appropriate methods for defeating even the strongest powers. The end product would be a unified Muslim world, the Caliphate, ruled under Muslim law and free of Western influence. These themes are preached in schools, on the Internet, and disseminated in books, cassette tapes, and pamphlets. Videotapes are distributed in which al-Qaeda's leaders expound on political topics, going as far as calling Western leaders liars and drunkards. As a result of this media strategy, al-Qaeda's messages have penetrated deeply into Muslim communities around the world, finding a sympathetic response among many Muslims who have a sense of helplessness both in the Arab world and in the Western Muslim diaspora. Al-Qaeda appears to have had an impact by offering a sense of empowerment to young men who feel lost in their adopted cultures.[52]

This is not to say that al-Qaeda has been universally accepted in the Arab world. There has been backlash and anger due to al-Qaeda's targeting of Muslims in Algeria, Iraq, Saudi Arabia, Pakistan, Indonesia, and elsewhere; and, of course, the death of its founder, Osama bin Laden, has been a blow. Nonetheless, the organization still functions despite repeated attacks by anti-terror forces of the United States and other nations, and it has been dispersed around the world, often partnering with local terror groups.

State-Sponsored Terrorism

State-sponsored terrorism occurs when a repressive government regime forces its citizens into obedience, oppresses minorities, and stifles political dissent. Death squads and the use of government troops to destroy political opposition parties are often associated with political terrorism. Much of what we know about state-sponsored terrorism comes from the efforts of human rights groups such as London-based Amnesty International, whose research shows that tens of thousands of people continue to become victims of security operations that result in disappearances and executions. Political prisoners are now being tortured in about 100 countries, people have disappeared or are being held in secret detention in about 20 countries, and government-sponsored death squads have been operating in more than 35 countries. Countries known for encouraging violent control of dissidents include Brazil, Colombia, Guatemala, Honduras, Peru, Iraq, and Sudan.

State-sponsored terrorism became a world issue when South and Central American dictatorships in the 1970s and 1980s unleashed *state* violence against political dissidents through forced disappearance, political imprisonment, torture, blacklisting, and massive exile. The region-wide *state* repression in this period emerged in response to the rise of the 1960s radical movements, which demanded public reforms and programs to help the lower classes in urban areas and agricultural workers in the countryside. Local authoritarian governments, which used repression to take control of radical political groups, were given financial support by the economic elites who dominated Latin American politics and were fearful of a socialist revolution.[53]

As might be expected, governments claim that repressive measures are needed to control revolutionary groups that routinely use violence. Thus the use of terror is sometimes a way of defending the nation against violence, a conundrum that supports the idea that a state is both protective and destructive.[54]

It is sometimes difficult to assess blame for state terror—is it a few rogue government agents who act on their own authority or the government itself? The issue of responsibility for improper acts hit home during the Abu Ghraib scandal in Iraq. Photos beamed around the world embarrassed the United States when they showed military personnel victimizing suspected insurgents. The government's response was to prosecute and imprison the perpetrators. However, some critics, such as criminologist Mark Hamm, suggest that these images constitute the photographic record of a state-sponsored crime.[55] He argues that rather than being the work of a few rogue officers, the sophisticated interrogation practices at Abu Ghraib were designed and executed by the U.S. Central Intelligence Agency and that the torturing of detainees at Abu Ghraib followed directly from decisions made by top government officials to get tough with prisoner interrogations. So while we condemn state-sponsored violence, it is not easy to identify who is truly responsible.

Cult Terrorism

In 1995, members of Aum Shinrikyo, a radical religious cult, set off poison gas in a Tokyo subway, killing 12 and injuring more than 3,000. The cult members found modern society too complex to understand, with few clear-cut goals and values.[56]

Some cults, like Aum Shinrikyo, may be classified as **cult terror** groups because their leaders demand that followers prove their loyalty through violence or intimidation.[57] These destructive cults are willing to have members commit violence, including murder. Members typically follow a charismatic leader who may be viewed as having godlike powers or even being the reincarnation of an important religious figure. The leader and his or her lieutenants commonly enforce loyalty by severe discipline and by physically preventing members from leaving the group. They may go through doomsday drills and maintain a siege mentality, fearing attacks from the government. It is not uncommon for cult terror groups to begin stockpiling weapons and building defensive barricades. The cult may openly or tacitly endorse individual killings or mass murder, which may be accompanied by mass suicide, either as a further symbolic instrument of their cause or, more commonly, as what they perceive to be justified self-defense, a last resort when the hostile world starts closing in and the leader's authority is threatened.[58]

HOW ARE TERROR GROUPS ORGANIZED?

Terror groups tend to be networked or hierarchical. Newer terrorist organizations tend to be formed as **networks**, loosely organized groups located in different parts of a city, state, or country (or worldwide) that share a common theme or purpose, but have a diverse leadership and command structure and are only in intermittent communication with one another. Although there may be a variety of anti-government groups operating in the United States, there is little evidence that they share a single command structure or organizational fabric. These groups have few resources and little experience, so it is critical that they operate undercover and with as little public exposure as possible.

When needed, networked groups can pull factions together for larger scale operations, such as an attack on a military headquarters, or conversely, they can readily splinter off into smaller groups to avoid detection when a counter-terrorism operation is under way. The advent of the Internet has significantly improved communications among networked terror groups.

As terror organizations evolve and expand, they may eventually develop a hierarchical organization with a commander at the top, captains, local area leaders, and so on. Ideological and religious groups tend to gravitate toward this model because a common creed/dogma controls their operations and a singular leader may be needed to define and disseminate group principles and maintain discipline. In a hierarchical model, the leader has the power to increase or decrease levels of violence for political purposes (e.g., they may order their followers to initiate a bombing campaign to influence an election). Schools may be off limits so that the population is not antagonized, or schools may become a target to show that the government cannot protect their children.

How Are Terror Groups Financed?

Without funding terrorism could not survive. How do these organizations raise the money they need to operate on an international scale. Surprisingly, a great deal of funding came from donations to charities, many of them based in Saudi Arabia. The Saudi government has taken steps to disrupt terrorist financing, but charities continue to play a role in the sponsorship of terrorist groups. In some instances, charities have a benign and legitimate interest in helping people, but they are co-opted by jihadists who then use the funds to buy weapons and fund operations. In addition, some terrorist organizations operate legitimate businesses, which serve the dual purpose of generating profits that can be used for terrorist purposes and for money laundering. Terror groups have been in the agriculture and construction business; Osama bin Laden owned and operated a string of retail honey shops throughout the Middle East and Pakistan.[59]

Sometimes terrorist groups become involved in common-law crimes such as drug dealing and kidnapping, even selling nuclear materials. According to terrorism expert Chris Dishman, these illegal activities may on occasion become so profitable that they replace the group's original focus. In some cases, there has been close cooperation between organized criminal groups and guerillas. In other instances, the relationship is more superficial. For example, the Revolutionary Armed Forces of Colombia imposes a tax on Colombian drug producers, but evidence indicates that the group cooperates with Colombia's top drug barons in running the trade. In some instances, the line between being a terrorist organization with political support and vast resources and being an organized criminal group engaging in illicit activities for profit becomes blurred. What appears to be a politically motivated action, such as the kidnapping of a government official for ransom, may turn out to be merely a crime for profit.[60]

State Financing of Terror

In some cases, terror groups are structured as a front, designed to mislead people about their true purpose or even to conceal the identity of its backers and/or controlling forces. Behind this façade lies the true sponsor whom for political reasons desires to remain hidden. They may even sympathize with the victims all the while being responsible for the terror groups training, weapons, and finance. Iran's financial, material, and logistic support for terrorist and militant groups throughout the Middle East and central Asia is a prime example of a state that funds terrorist groups who serve as a proxy for its political aims.

Iran remained the principal supporter of groups that are implacably opposed to the Middle East peace process. The Qods Force, the external operations branch of the Islamic Revolutionary Guard Corps (IRGC), is the regime's primary mechanism for cultivating and supporting terrorists abroad. Iran provided weapons, training, and funding to Hamas and other Palestinian terrorist groups, including Palestine Islamic Jihad (PIJ) and the Popular Front for the Liberation of Palestine-General Command (PFLP-GC). Iran has provided hundreds of millions of dollars in support to Lebanese Hezbollah and has trained thousands of Hezbollah fighters at camps in Iran. Since the end of the 2006 Israeli-Hezbollah conflict, Iran has assisted Hezbollah in rearming, in violation of UN Security Council Resolution 1701.

The Variety of Terror Groups

Revolutionary terrorists	Use violence to frighten those in power and their supporters in order to replace the existing government with a regime that holds acceptable political or religious views.
Political terrorists	Political terrorism is directed at people or groups who oppose the terrorists' political ideology or whom the terrorists define as "outsiders" who must be destroyed.
Eco-terrorism	Political terror groups involved in violent actions to protect the environment.
Nationalist terrorism	Groups whose actions promote the interests of a minority ethnic or religious group that has been persecuted under majority rule and/or wishes to carve out its own independent homeland.
Retributive terrorism	Groups that use violence as a method of influence, persuasion, or intimidation in order to achieve a particular aim or objective.
State-sponsored terrorism	Carried out by a repressive government regime in order to force its citizens into obedience, oppress minorities, and stifle political dissent.
Cult terrorism	Cults whose leaders demand that followers prove their loyalty through violence or intimidation.

Iran's Qods Force provided training to the Taliban in Afghanistan on small unit tactics, small arms, explosives, and indirect fire weapons. Since at least 2006, Iran has arranged arms shipments to select Taliban members, including small arms and associated ammunition, rocket propelled grenades, mortar rounds, 107 mm rockets, and plastic explosives.

Despite its pledge to support the stabilization of Iraq, Iranian authorities continued to provide lethal support, including weapons, training, funding, and guidance, to Iraqi Shia militant groups that targeted U.S. and Iraqi forces. The Qods Force continued to supply Iraqi militants with Iranian-produced advanced rockets, sniper rifles, automatic weapons, and mortars that have killed Iraqi and Coalition Forces, as well as civilians. Iran was responsible for the increased lethality of some attacks on U.S. forces by providing militants with the capability to assemble explosively formed penetrators that were designed to defeat armored vehicles. The Qods Force, in concert with Lebanese Hezbollah, provided training outside of Iraq and advisers inside Iraq for Shia militants in the construction and use of sophisticated improvised explosive device technology and other advanced weaponry.

Iran remained unwilling to bring to justice senior al-Qaeda (AQ) members it continued to detain, and refused to publicly identify those senior members in its custody. Iran has repeatedly resisted numerous calls to transfer custody of its AQ detainees to their countries of origin or to third countries for trial; it is reportedly holding Osama bin Laden's family members under house arrest.

Senior IRGC, IRGC Qods Force, and Iranian government officials were indicted by the Government of Argentina for their alleged roles in the 1994 terrorist bombing of the Argentine-Jewish Mutual Association (AMIA); according to the Argentine State Prosecutor's report, the attack was initially proposed by the Qods Force. In 2007, INTERPOL issued a "red notice" for six individuals wanted in connection with the bombing. One of the individuals, Ahmad Vahidi, was named as Iran's Defense Minister in August 2009.[61]

The various forms that terror groups take are summarized in Concept Summary 11.2.

WHAT MOTIVATES THE TERRORIST?

Faisal Shahzad, a naturalized U.S. citizen, was born in Pakistan in June 1979. The youngest of four children, he lived a life of privilege by Pakistani standards, attending private secular schools not known for extremist teachings. After moving to the United States, he earned an M.B.A. at the University of Bridgeport in 2005, taking a job as a financial analyst with a cosmetics company. Shortly after his marriage in 2009, Shahzad quit his job, stopped making payments on his house, and then moved to Pakistan with his wife and two children. Before returning to the United States in 2010, he attended a Pakistani training camp where he learned terrorist skills. On May 1, 2010, upon his return to the United States, Shahzad bought a Nissan Pathfinder and tried to blow it up with a makeshift bomb in the Times Square section of New York City. The SUV failed to explode, and Shahzad was promptly captured as he was trying to leave the United States on a Dubai-bound flight. After his apprehension, Shahzad cooperated with authorities and was charged with multiple terrorism-related offenses.[62]

Shahzad, like terror suspect Najibullah Zazi, the admitted leader of a New York City subway bomb plot, seems to be part of a growing group of U.S. citizens to develop extremist religious views and anti-Western values through travels to terrorist hotbeds and visits to websites and chat rooms with connections to terrorist groups. Indeed, of the nearly 1,000 individuals prosecuted for terrorism-related offenses since 9/11, the largest group is American.[63] The government has reacted by passing legislation such as the Prevention of Violent Radicalization and Homegrown Terrorism Act of 2007, but the homegrown threat remains—and continues to grow.[64]

Why would someone like Shahzad attempt to bomb one of the most crowded sections of the city, potentially killing scores of innocent people? He was affluent and successful, not someone bitter because he had been exploited and abused. If he did not like the United States, he could have chosen to return home to Pakistan, a nation whose culture he may have preferred. What made him choose terrorism?

Before terrorism can be effectively fought, controlled, and eradicated, it is important to understand something about the kind of people who become terrorists, what motivates their behavior, and how their ideas are formed. Unfortunately, this is not an easy task. Terrorism researchers have generally concluded that there is no single personality trait or behavior pattern that distinguishes the majority of terrorists or sets them apart so they can be easily identified and apprehended. Some seem truly disturbed, whereas many others have not suffered long-term mental illness or displayed sociopathic traits and/or tendencies; if that were so, bizarre or violent behavior in their early childhood would be a giveaway.[65] A number of competing visions have been put forward to explain why terrorists engage in criminal activities such as bombings, shootings, and kidnappings to achieve a political end. Four views stand out.

Psychological View

Although not all terrorists suffer from psychological deficits, enough do so that the typical terrorist can be described as an emotionally disturbed individual who acts out his or her psychoses within the confines of violent groups. According to this view, terrorist violence is not so much a political instrument as an end in itself; it is the result of compulsion or psychopathology. Terrorists do what they do because of garden variety emotional problems, including but not limited to self-destructive urges and disturbed emotions combined with problems with authority.[66] As terrorism expert Jerrold M. Post puts it, "Political terrorists are driven to commit acts of violence as a consequence of psychological forces, and . . . their special psychology is constructed to rationalize acts they are psychologically compelled to commit."[67]

The view that terrorists suffer psychological abnormality is quite controversial, and some critics suggest that it is spurious; the majority of research on terrorists indicates that most are not psychologically abnormal. Even suicide bombers, a group that should show signs of psychological abnormality, exhibit few signs of the mental problems such as depression that are typically found in people who choose to take their own life. After carefully reviewing existing evidence on the psychological state of terrorists, mental health expert Randy Borum concludes:

- Mental illness is not a critical factor in explaining terrorist behavior. Also, most terrorists are not psychopaths.
- There is no "terrorist personality," nor is there any accurate profile—psychological or otherwise—of the terrorist.
- Histories of childhood abuse and trauma and themes of perceived injustice and humiliation often are prominent in terrorist biographies, but do not really help to explain terrorism.[68]

It is also possible that engaging in stressful terrorist activity results in the development of mental disorders and not vice versa.[69] Charles Ruby reviewed the literature on the psychology of terrorists and found little evidence that *terrorists* are psychologically dysfunctional or pathological. Ruby claims that terrorism is a form of politically motivated violence that is carried out by rational, lucid people who have valid motives; if they had more resources, terrorists would be military officers.[70]

Alienation View

Some experts believe that a lack of economic opportunity and recessionary economies are positively correlated with *terrorism*.[71] Because they are out of the political and social mainstream, young men and women are motivated to join terror groups. Suffering alienation, they lack the tools to compete in a post-technological society. Many are relatively "ordinary" people who, alienated from modern society, believe that a suicide mission will cleanse them from the corruption of the modern world.[72]

According to this view, if terrorists suffer psychological deficiencies, it is because they suffer alienation from friends, family, and society.[73] Many have been raised to hate their opponents and learn at an early age that they have been victimized by some oppressor. Terrorists report that they were estranged from their fathers, whom they viewed as economically, socially, or politically weak and ineffective. They are products of dysfunctional families in which the father was absent or, even if present, was a distant and cold figure.[74] Because of this family estrangement, the budding terrorist may have been swayed to join a group or cult by a charismatic leader who serves as an alternative father figure. Some find it in religious schools run by strong leaders who demand strict loyalty from their followers while indoctrinating them in political causes. This pattern is common among terror groups in Southeast Asia where teachers command strong personal loyalty from their students. This loyalty may be lifelong, as illustrated by the three Jemaah Islamiyah members who testified against their former teacher Abu Bakar

Baasyir during his terror trial. Despite their willingness to testify for the government, two spontaneously started to cry at the sight of their teacher. They repeated that they loved him, but urged him to tell the truth about his activities.[75]

In this sense, terror groups are similar to urban street gangs, which provide a substitute family-like environment that can nurture a heretofore emotionally underprivileged youth.

Socialization View

While alienation and estrangement seem plausible, research shows that terrorist operatives are not poor or lacking in education. Ironically, many terrorists appear to be educated members of the upper class. Osama bin Laden was a multi-millionaire and at least some of his followers are highly educated and trained. The acts of the modern terrorist—using the Internet; organizing logistically complex and expensive assaults; writing and disseminating formal critiques, manifestos, and theories—require the training and education of the social elite, not the poor and the oppressed.

Marc Sageman studied members of extremist Islamist groups and found that most tend to be well educated; about 60 percent had some form of higher education. More than 75 percent came from upper- or middle-class backgrounds. When they joined a terror organization, the majority had professional occupations such as doctor or engineer, or semi-skilled employment, such as a civil servant; fewer than 25 percent were unemployed or working in unskilled jobs. Surprisingly, Sageman found that almost three-quarters were married and that most had children.[76] These findings suggest that terrorists are not suffering from the social problems usually associated with alienation: poverty, lack of education, and ignorance. Sageman found that the vast majority of Islamic terrorists have close social bonds and social networks that supported them when they embraced jihad. They may have felt isolated from the rest of society, but their tight bonds of family and friendship encouraged them to join terror groups.

Many jihadist recruits were living in foreign countries when they got involved with terrorist organizations. Feeling homesick, they sought out people with similar backgrounds, whom they would often find at mosques.[77] If they appeared to be motivated by religious fervor, it was because they were seeking friends in a foreign land. They moved in together to share the rent and to eat together under strict Muslim dietary laws. As a result, they formed groups that solidified their beliefs and created a sense of group solidarity. If one became committed to terror, others would follow rather than let him or her down.

Ideological View

Another view is that terrorists hold extreme ideological beliefs that prompt their behavior. At first they have heightened perceptions of oppressive conditions, believing they are being victimized by some group or government. Once these potential terrorists recognize that these conditions can be changed by an active governmental reform effort that has not happened, they conclude that they must resort to violence to encourage change. The violence need not be aimed at a specific goal. Rather, terror tactics must help set in motion a series of events that enlists others in the cause and leads to long-term change. "Successful" terrorists believe that their "self-sacrifice" outweighs the guilt created by harming innocent people. Terrorism, therefore, requires violence without guilt; the cause justifies the violence.

Some terrorists are motivated by extreme religious beliefs, which often coincide with their ideological views. But how can they justify using violence if they are truly religious? Most of the world's religions eschew violence. Islamic terrorists believe that their commitment to God justifies their extreme actions. They regard the actions of people they trust as a testimony to the righteousness of their acts. They trust significant others, and rely on their wisdom, experience, and testimony and accept their expressions of faith. To the terrorist, someone like Osama bin Laden had demonstrated the strength of his faith by living in poverty and giving up a more luxurious and leisurely life in the name of God. When he called them to jihad, they were likely to follow, even if it meant killing those who denied their faith or beliefs. Perceived miracles, such as the defeat of a superpower through faith alone (e.g., the Soviet/Afghan war or the fight against the United States in Iraq), also increase confidence in the righteousness of the cause. Some have mystical experiences during prayers or dreams that demonstrate the existence of God and reinforce faith. In a videotape in the fall of 2001, Osama bin Laden said that he had banned the reporting of dreams of airplanes flying into buildings prior to September 11 for fear of revealing the plot.[78]

Explaining State Terrorism

How can state-sponsored terrorism be explained? After all, these violent acts are not directed at a foreign government or overseas adversaries but against natives of one's own country. In her book *Reigns of Terror*, Patricia Marchak finds that people willing to kill or maim their fellow countrymen are likely to be highly susceptible to unquestioning submission to authority. They are conformists who want to be part of the central group and who are quite willing to be part of a state regime. They are vulnerable to ideology that dehumanizes their targets and can utilize propaganda to distance themselves psychologically from those they are terrorizing.[79] The Nazis had little trouble recruiting people to carry out horrific acts during the Holocaust because many Germans wanted to be part of the popular social/political movement and were easily indoctrinated by the Nazi propaganda that branded Jews as subhuman. Stalin was able to carry out his reign of terror in Russia because his victims were viewed as state enemies who were trying to undermine the Communist regime. How can these tendencies be neutralized? Marchak sees little benefit to international intervention that results in after-the-fact punishment of the perpetrators, a course of action that was attempted in the former Yugoslavia after death squads had performed "ethnic cleansing" of undesirables. Instead she argues for a prevention strategy that involves international aid and economic development by industrialized nations to those in the third world that are on the verge of becoming collapsed states, the construction of social welfare systems, and the acceptance of international legal norms and standards of human rights.[80]

RESPONSE TO TERRORISM

After the 9/11 attacks, agencies of the criminal justice system began to focus their attention on combating the threat of terror. Even local police agencies created anti-terror programs designed to protect their communities from the threat of attack. How should the nation best prepare itself to thwart potential attacks? The National Commission on Terrorist Attacks Upon the United States (also known as the 9/11 Commission), an independent, bipartisan commission, was created in late 2002 and given the mission of preparing an in-depth report of the events leading up to the 9/11 attacks. Part of their goal was to create a comprehensive plan to ensure that no further attacks of that magnitude take place.

To monitor the more than 500 million people who cross into the United States, the commission recommended that a single agency be created to screen border crossings. They also recommended creation of an investigative agency to monitor all aliens in the United States and to gather intelligence on the way terrorists travel across borders. The commission suggested that people who wanted passports be tagged with biometric measures to make them easily identifiable.

In response to the commission report, a **Director of National Intelligence (DNI)** was created and charged with coordinating data from the nation's primary intelligence-gathering agencies. The DNI serves as the principal intelligence adviser to the president and the statutory intelligence adviser to the National Security Council. On February 17, 2005, President George W. Bush named U.S. Ambassador to Iraq John Negroponte to be the first person to hold the post; he was confirmed on April 21, 2005. The current director is retired Lt. Gen. James R. Clapper.

Among the agencies reporting to the DNI is the staff of the National Counterterrorism Center (NCTC), which is staffed by terrorism experts from the CIA, FBI, and the Pentagon; the Privacy and Civil Liberties Board; and the National Counterproliferation Center. The NCTC serves as the primary organization in the United States government for analyzing and integrating all intelligence possessed or acquired by the government pertaining to terrorism and counterterrorism, excepting purely domestic counterterrorism information.

The 9/11 Commission report outlines what has already been done, what has not been done, and what needs to be done, and agencies of the justice system have begun to respond to the challenge.

Confronting Terrorism with Law Enforcement

In the aftermath of the September 11, 2001, attacks, even before the 9/11 Commission made its report, it became obvious that the nation was not prepared to deal adequately with the threat of terrorism. One reason is the very nature of American society. Because we live in a free and open nation, it is extremely difficult to seal the borders and prevent the entry of terrorist groups. In his book *Nuclear Terrorism*, Graham Allison, an expert on nuclear weapons and national security, describes the almost superhuman effort it would take to seal the nation's borders from nuclear attack. Every day, 30,000 trucks, 6,500 rail cars, and 140 ships deliver more than 50,000 cargo containers into the United States. Fewer than 5 percent ever get screened, and those that do are given inspections using external detectors, which may not detect nuclear weapons or fissile material. The potential for terrorists to obtain bombs is significant: there are approximately 130 nuclear research reactors in 40 countries. Two dozen of these have enough highly enriched uranium for one or more nuclear bombs. If terrorists can get their hands on fissile material from these reactors, they could build a crude but working nuclear bomb within a year. But they may not have to build their own bomb. They may be able to purchase an intact device on the black market. Russia alone has thousands of nuclear warheads and material for many thousands of additional weapons; all of these remain vulnerable to theft. Terrorists also may be able to buy the knowledge to construct bombs. In one well-known incident, Pakistan's leading nuclear scientist, A. Q. Khan, sold comprehensive "nuclear starter kits" that included advanced centrifuge components, blueprints for nuclear warheads, and uranium samples in quantities sufficient to make a small bomb, and even provided personal consulting services to assist in nuclear development.[81]

Recognizing this problem, law enforcement agencies around the country began to realign their resources to combat future terrorist attacks. In response to 9/11, law enforcement agencies undertook a number of steps: increasing the number of personnel engaged in emergency response planning; updating response plans for chemical, biological, or radiological attacks; and reallocating internal resources or increasing departmental spending to focus on terrorism preparedness.[82] Actions continue to be taken on the federal, state, and local levels.

Federal Law Enforcement   One of the most significant changes has been a realignment of the Federal Bureau of Investigation (FBI), the federal government's main law enforcement agency. The FBI has announced a reformulation of its priorities, making protecting the United States from terrorist attack its number one commitment. It is now charged with coordinating intelligence collection with the Border Patrol, Secret Service, and the CIA. The FBI must also work with and share intelligence with the National Counterterrorism Center (NCTC).

To carry out its mission, the FBI has expanded its force of agents. In addition to recruiting candidates with the traditional background in law enforcement, law, and accounting, the bureau is concentrating on hiring agents with scientific and technological skills as well as foreign-language proficiency in priority areas such as Arabic, Farsi, Pashtun, Urdu, all dialects of Chinese, Japanese, Korean, Russian, Spanish, and Vietnamese, and with other priority backgrounds such as foreign counterintelligence, counterterrorism, and military intelligence. Besides helping in counterterrorism activities, these agents staff the Cyber Division, which was created in 2001 to coordinate, oversee, and facilitate FBI investigations in which the Internet, online services, and computer systems and networks are the principal instruments or targets of terrorists.

Department of Homeland Security (DHS)   Soon after the 2001 attack, President George W. Bush proposed the creation of a new cabinet-level agency called the **Department of Homeland Security (DHS)**, which is engaged in:

- Preventing terrorist attacks within the United States
- Reducing America's vulnerability to terrorism
- Minimizing the damage and recovering from attacks that do occur

On November 19, 2002, Congress passed legislation authorizing the creation of the DHS and assigned it the mission of providing intelligence analysis and infrastructure protection, strengthening the borders, improving the use of science and technology to counter weapons of mass destruction, and creating a comprehensive response and recovery division.

Rather than work from ground up, the DHS combined a number of existing agencies into a superagency. Among its components are:

- *Border and transportation security.* The Department of Homeland Security is responsible for securing our nation's borders and transportation systems, which include 350 ports of entry. The department manages who and what enters the country, and works to prevent the entry of terrorists and the instruments of terrorism while simultaneously ensuring the speedy flow of legitimate traffic. The DHS also is in charge of securing territorial waters, including ports and waterways.
- *Emergency preparedness and response.* The department ensures the preparedness of emergency response professionals, provides the federal government's response, and aids America's recovery from terrorist attacks and natural disasters. The department is responsible for reducing the loss of life and property and protecting institutions from all types of hazards through an emergency management program of preparedness, mitigation, response, and recovery.
- *Chemical, biological, radiological, and nuclear countermeasures.* The department leads the federal government's efforts in preparing for and responding to the full range of terrorist threats involving weapons of mass destruction. To do this, the department sets national policy and establishes guidelines for state and local governments. It directs exercises and drills for federal, state, and local chemical, biological, radiological, and nuclear (CBRN) response teams and plans. The department is assigned to prevent the importation of nuclear weapons and material.
- *Information analysis and infrastructure protection.* The department analyzes information from multiple available sources, including the CIA and FBI, in order to assess the dangers facing the nation. It also analyzes law enforcement and intelligence information.[83]

The DHS has numerous and varied duties. It is responsible for port security and transportation systems and manages airport security with its Transportation Security Administration (TSA). It has its own intelligence section, and it covers every special event in the United States, including political conventions.

State Law Enforcement Efforts to Combat Terrorism   In the wake of the 9/11 attacks, a number of states have beefed up their intelligence-gathering capabilities and aimed them directly at homeland security. California has introduced the California Anti-Terrorism Information Center (CATIC), a statewide intelligence system designed to combat terrorism. It divides the state into operational zones, and links federal, state, and local information services in one system. Trained intelligence analysts operate within civil rights guidelines and utilize information in a secure communications system; information is analyzed daily.[84] CATIC combines machine-intelligence with information coming from a variety of police agencies. The information is correlated and organized by analysts looking for trends. Rather than simply operating as an information-gathering unit, CATIC is a synthesizing process. It combines open-source public information with data on criminal trends and possible terrorist activities. Processed intelligence is designed to produce threat assessments for each area and to project trends outside the jurisdiction. The CATIC system attempts to process multiple sources of information to predict threats. By centralizing the collection and analytical sections of a statewide system, California's Department of Justice may have developed a method for moving offensively against terrorism.

Local Law Enforcement   Federal law enforcement agencies are not alone in responding to the threat of terrorism. And, of course, nowhere is the threat of terrorism being taken more seriously than in New York City, one of the main targets of the 9/11 attacks, which has established a Counterterrorism Bureau.[85] After the 9/11 attacks, the NYPD augmented its anti-terrorism forces from 17 to 125 and assigned them to the operational control of the Counterterrorism Bureau. Teams within the bureau have been trained to examine potential targets in the city and attempt to insulate them from possible attack. Viewed as prime targets are the city's bridges, the Empire State Building, Rockefeller Center, and the United Nations. Bureau detectives are assigned overseas to work with the police in several foreign cities, including cities in Canada and Israel. Detectives have been assigned as liaisons with the FBI and with Interpol, in Lyon, France. The city recruits detectives with language skills from Pashtun and Urdu to Arabic, Fujianese, and other dialects. The New York City Police Intelligence Division has been revamped, and agents are examining foreign newspapers and monitoring Internet sites. The department has set up several backup command centers in different parts of the city in case a terror attack puts headquarters out of operation. Backup senior command teams have been created so that if people at the highest levels of the department are killed, individuals will already have been tapped to step into their jobs. For example, The Lower Manhattan Security Initiative (LMSI) is a networked surveillance project designed to detect threats and perform preoperational terrorist surveillance south of Canal Street in Lower Manhattan.

The department is also drawing on the expertise of other institutions around the city. For example, medical specialists have been enlisted to monitor daily developments in the city's hospitals to detect any suspicious outbreaks of illness that might reflect a biological attack. And the police are conducting joint drills with the New York Fire Department to avoid the problems in communication and coordination that marked the emergency response on September 11.

Combating Terrorism in the Courts

In April 2009, the U.S. attorney for the Southern District of New York brought federal charges against Haji Juma Khan, an Afghan who allegedly provided the Taliban with funding through his lucrative (and illegal) opium, morphine, and heroin trafficking organization, dubbed the "Khan Organization."[86] In the same month, Wesam al-Delaema pleaded guilty to conspiring to kill U.S. personnel in Iraq. He is currently serving his sentence in the Netherlands.[87] These are but two of the many terrorism-related cases that have been tried in the nation's court system. Prosecutions began to spike right after 9/11 and continue to grow today; there were 828 prosecutions of suspected terrorists in the United States in the last decade.[88] Some notable terrorism prosecutions in recent years are set out in Exhibit 11.6.

In addition to the trial courts, the Supreme Court has been involved in terror issues ever since Congress authorized President Bush to use "all necessary and appropriate force" against those responsible for the attacks in New York and Washington, D.C. Yaser Hamdi, an American citizen who had left the United States in his youth, was captured in Afghanistan and detained by military forces at Guantanamo Bay, Cuba, for supposedly aiding the Taliban. He was later moved to a military prison in Norfolk, Virginia, where he filed a writ of *habeas corpus*, arguing that, as a U.S. citizen, he was entitled to challenge the constitutionality of his confinement in federal court. In *Hamdi v. Rumsfeld* (2004), the Supreme Court agreed with his argument, holding in a 6–3 decision that the due process clause of the Fifth Amendment requires that U.S. citizens be given the opportunity to challenge their confinement in this way.[90] The Court also decided in *Rasul v. Bush* (2004) that the federal courts have jurisdiction to hear *habeas corpus* petitions from foreign nationals captured outside the United States.[91]

One year later, the Supreme Court heard a case involving Salim Hamdan, a Yemeni and former driver for Osama bin Laden. He was captured by Afghan warlords and turned over to U.S. forces in 2001. He was then transferred in 2002 to Guantanamo Bay and, in 2003, was slated to be tried for various conspiracy offenses before a military tribunal. He filed a *habeas corpus* petition in the U.S. District Court for the Western District of Washington, claiming that he could not legally be tried by a military tribunal. In a 5–3 decision, the Supreme Court agreed.[92] It held that the military commission at issue violated the Uniform Code of Military Justice and the four Geneva Conventions signed in 1949. Charges against him were subsequently dropped, but Hamdan was later deemed an "unlawful enemy combatant," tried once again before a military tribunal, and convicted. He was sentenced to five-and-a-half years in prison, given credit for time served, and sent back to Yemen. He was not named a combatant before going into his first trial, which is partly why the first military tribunal was illegal.

Shortly after Hamdan's case was decided, Congress passed the Military Commissions Act of 2006, which stripped the federal courts of jurisdiction to hear *habeas corpus* petitions from detainees who have been designated as "enemy combatants." In a 5–4 decision, the Supreme Court held that prisoners (even foreign nationals held at Guantanamo Bay) had the right to *habeas corpus* under the U.S. Constitution and that their arguments could be heard in the federal courts.[93] In effect, the Court held that the Military Commissions Act of 2006 was an unconstitutional suspension of the right to *habeas corpus*. In October 2009, President Obama signed into law the Military Commissions Act of 2009, which attempted to improve on—and address some of the deficiencies of—the earlier legislation. For example, the new law does not permit a U.S. citizen to be tried by a military commission.[94]

EXHIBIT 11.6

Notable Terror Prosecutions

- **Toledo terror cell (Northern District of Ohio).** In June 2008, Mohammad Amawi, Marwan El-Hindi, and Wassim Mazloum were convicted of conspiracy to commit terrorist acts against Americans overseas, including U.S. armed forces in Iraq, and conspiracy to provide material support to terrorists. Amawi and El-Hindi were also convicted of distributing information regarding suicide bomb vests and improvised explosive devices.

- **Christopher Paul (Southern District of Ohio).** In June 2008, Paul pleaded guilty to conspiring with members of a German terrorist cell to use a weapon of mass destruction (explosive devices) against Americans vacationing at foreign tourist resorts and against Americans in the United States, as well as against U.S. embassies, diplomatic premises, and military bases in Europe.

- **Hassan Abujihaad (District of Connecticut).** In March 2008, Abujihaad, a former member of the U.S. Navy, was convicted of providing material support to terrorists and delivering classified information on the movements of a U.S. Navy battle group to Azzam Publications, a London-based organization alleged to have provided material support to persons engaged in terrorism.

- **Mohammed Jabarah (Southern District of New York).** In January 2008, Jabarah was sentenced to life in prison after pleading guilty to terrorism charges stemming from his participation in a plot to bomb U.S. embassies in Singapore and the Philippines. Jabarah trained in al-Qaeda camps in Afghanistan and spent time with Osama bin Laden, to whom he swore an oath of allegiance.

- **California prison plot (Central District of California).** In December 2007, Kevin James, who formed a radical Islamic organization while in California state prison, and two of his recruits, Levar Washington and Gregory Patterson, pleaded guilty to terrorism conspiracy charges, admitting they conspired to attack U.S. military facilities and Jewish facilities in Los Angeles.

- **Jose Padilla and co-defendants (Southern District of Florida).** In August 2007, a federal jury convicted Padilla, Adham Hassoun, and Kifah Jayyousi of conspiracy to murder, kidnap, and maim individuals in a foreign country, conspiracy to provide material support, and providing material support to terrorists. Padilla was sentenced to more than 17 years in prison.

- **Zacarias Moussaoui (Eastern District of Virginia).** In May 2006, Moussaoui was sentenced to six consecutive life terms after pleading guilty in April 2005 to various terrorism violations, admitting that he conspired with al-Qaeda to hijack and crash planes into prominent U.S. buildings as part of the 9/11 attacks.

- **Ahmed Omar Abu Ali (Eastern District of Virginia).** In November 2005, Ali was convicted on all counts of an indictment charging him with, among other violations, providing material support to al-Qaeda, conspiracy to assassinate the U.S. president, conspiracy to commit air piracy, and conspiracy to destroy aircraft. Ali was sentenced to 30 years in prison.[89]

SOURCE: U.S. Justice Department, "Fact Sheet: Justice Department Counter-Terrorism Efforts Since 9/11," www.justice.gov/opa/pr/2008/September/08-nsd-807.html (accessed August 16, 2011).

As a result of these cases, detainees, enemy combatants, terror suspects, and the like enjoy greater protection now than they did in the past. Indeed, all but a few of them enjoy the same rights as anyone else, whether or not they are U.S. citizens.

Confronting Terrorism with the Law

Soon after the September 11 terrorist attacks, the U.S. government enacted several laws focused on preventing further acts of violence against the United States and creating greater flexibility in the fight to control terror activity. Most important, Congress passed the **USA Patriot Act (USAPA)** on October 26, 2001. The bill is over 342 pages long, creates new laws, and makes changes to more than 15 existing statutes. Its aim is to give sweeping new powers to domestic law enforcement and international intelligence agencies in an effort to fight terrorism, to expand the definition of terrorist activities, and to alter sanctions for violent terrorism. It is impossible to discuss every provision of this sweeping legislation here, but a few of its more important elements will be examined.

The USA Patriot Act USAPA expands all four traditional tools of surveillance—wiretaps, search warrants, pen/trap orders (installing devices that record phone calls), and subpoenas. The Foreign Intelligence Surveillance Act (FISA), which allows domestic operations by intelligence agencies, is also expanded. USAPA gives greater power to the FBI to check and monitor phone, Internet, and computer records without first needing to demonstrate that they were being used by a suspect or target of a court order.

The government may now serve a single wiretap, or pen/trap order, on any person regardless of whether that person or entity is named in a court order. Prior to this act, telephone companies could be ordered to install pen/trap devices on their networks that would monitor calls coming to a surveillance target and to whom the surveillance target made calls; the USAPA extends this monitoring to the Internet. Law enforcement agencies may now also obtain the e-mail addresses and websites visited by a target, and e-mails of the people with whom they communicate. It is possible to require that an Internet service provider install a device that records e-mail and other electronic communications on its servers, looking for communications initiated or received by the target of an investigation. Under USAPA, the government does not need to show a court that the information or communication is relevant to a criminal investigation, nor does it have to report where it served the order or what information it received.

The act also allows enforcement agencies to monitor cable operators and obtain access to their records and systems. Before the act, a cable company had to give prior notice to the customer, even if that person was a target of an investigation. Information can now be obtained on people with whom the cable subscriber communicates, the content of the person's communications, and the person's subscription records; prior notice is still required if law enforcement agencies want to learn what television programming a subscriber purchases.

The act also expands the definition of "terrorism" and enables the government to monitor more closely those people suspected of "harboring" and giving "material support" to terrorists (Sections 803, 805). It increases the authority of the U.S. attorney general to detain and deport noncitizens with little or no judicial review. The attorney general may certify that he has "reasonable grounds to believe" that a noncitizen endangers national security and is therefore eligible for deportation. The attorney general and secretary of state are also given the authority to designate domestic groups as terrorist organizations and deport any noncitizen who is a member.

Civil Rights and the USA Patriot Act   Although law enforcement agencies may applaud these new laws, civil libertarians are troubled because they view the act as eroding civil rights. Some complain that there are provisions that permit the government to share information from grand jury proceedings and from criminal wiretaps with intelligence agencies. First Amendment protections may be violated because the Patriot Act authority is not limited to true terrorism investigations but covers a much broader range of activity involving reasonable political dissent. Though many critics have called for its repeal, it was reauthorized in 2006 with a slew of provisions ensuring that the act did not violate civil rights by limiting its surveillance and wiretap authorizations.[95]

Combating Terrorism with Politics

In the long run, it may simply be impossible to defeat terror groups and end terrorism using military, law enforcement, or legal solutions. Using force may play into terrorists' hands and convince them that they are freedom fighters valiantly struggling against a better armed and more ruthless foe. No matter how many terrorists are killed and/or captured, military/deterrence-based solutions may be doomed. Aggressive reprisals will cause terrorist ideology to spread and gain greater acceptance in the underdeveloped world. The resulting anger and alienation will produce more terrorists than can be killed off through violent responses. In contrast, if the terrorist ideology is countered and discredited, the appeal of terror groups such as al-Qaeda will wither and die.

One approach suggested by policy experts is to undermine support for terrorist groups by being benevolent nation-builders giving aid to the nations that house terror groups.[96] This is the approach the United States took after World War II to rebuild Germany and Japan (the Marshall Plan) all the while gaining support for its Cold War struggle against the Soviet Union. According to the RAND Corporation, a nonprofit research group, the following steps are required to defeat jihadist groups such as al-Qaeda:

- Attack the ideological underpinnings of global jihadism
- Sever ideological and other links between terrorist groups
- Strengthen the capabilities of front-line states to counter local jihadist threats

This approach may work because al-Qaeda's goal of toppling "apostate" regimes in Saudi Arabia, Egypt, and Pakistan and creating an ultraorthodox pan-Islamic government spanning the world does not sit well with large groups of Muslims; their monolithic vision has no room for other Muslim sects such as Shi'ites and Sunni moderates. Therefore, political and social appeals may help fracture local support for al-Qaeda. In addition, the United States should seek to deny sanctuaries to terrorist groups and strengthen the capabilities of foreign governments to deal with terrorist threats, but in an advisory capacity by providing intelligence. In his recent book *Unconquerable Nation*, Brian Michael Jenkins, a noted expert on the topic, identifies the strategic principles he believes are the key to combating terror in contemporary society. These beliefs are summarized in Exhibit 11.7.

Visit the Criminal Justice CourseMate at cengagebrain.com, then access the "Web Links" to access the following websites:
- The Office of the **Director of National Intelligence**
- The **National Counterterrorism Center** (NCTC)

EXHIBIT 11.7

Countering Terror

- **Destroy the jihadist enterprise.** Jihadists have proven to be flexible and resistant and capable of continued action despite sustained military actions. They remain the primary threat to U.S. national security and will continue to be so for the foreseeable future. Therefore, they must be destroyed and their ability to operate damaged.
- **Conserve resources for a long war.** These include blood, treasure, the will of the American people, and the support of needed allies. This means picking future fights carefully, making security measures both effective *and* efficient, maintaining domestic support, avoiding extreme measures that alienate the people, and cultivating rather than bullying other countries
- **Wage more-effective political warfare.** Political solutions must be pragmatic. We must be ready to compromise. Amnesty should be offered to terrorists who have become disillusioned. Local leaders should be accommodated and deals cut to co-opt enemies.
- **Break the cycle of jihadism.** Jihadism is a cycle beginning with recruitment and ending with death, arrest, or detention. Combating terror must involve neutralizing terror groups' ability to radicalize and indoctrinate potential recruits before the cycle begins and then, at the end of the cycle, deal effectively with terror suspects once they have been captured and detained.

- **Impede recruitment.** Recruitment sites must be identified and made dangerous and therefore unusable. Alternatives to terror must be offered. Former, now disillusioned terrorists can be used to denounce terror and counteract its appeal with potential recruits.
- **Encourage defections and facilitate exits.** Potential defectors must be identified and encouraged to quit through the promise of amnesty, cash, job training, and homes.
- **Persuade detainees to renounce terrorism.** Rehabilitation of known terror suspects may be more important than prosecution and imprisonment.
- **Maintain international cooperation.** International cooperation is a prerequisite to success, a precious commodity not to be squandered by bullying, unreciprocated demands, indifference to local realities, or actions that repel even America's closest friends.
- **Reserve the right to retaliate—a muscular deterrent.** Terror groups and their sponsors should know that any attack using weapons of mass destruction will be met with all-out warfare against any group or government known to be or even suspected of being responsible.

SOURCE: Brian Michael Jenkins, *Unconquerable Nation: Knowing Our Enemy, Strengthening Ourselves* (Santa Monica, CA: RAND Corporation, 2006), www.rand.org/pubs/monographs/2006/RAND_MG454.pdf (accessed November 2, 2010).

SUMMARY

1. **Know what is meant by the term *political crime***
   - Political crime is used to signify illegal acts that are designed to undermine an existing government and threaten its survival. Political crimes can include both violent and nonviolent acts and range in seriousness from dissent, treason, and espionage to violent acts such as terrorism or assassination.

2. **Identify the cause of political crime**
   - The political criminal and political crimes may stem from religious or ideological sources. They often occupy a gray area between conventional and outlawed behavior. Whereas common criminals may be motivated by greed, vengeance, or jealousy, political criminals have a somewhat different agenda. There is no set pattern or reason why someone becomes a political criminal. Some use political crime as a stepping stone to public office; others use it as a method to focus their frustrations.

3. **Distinguish between espionage and treason**
   - Helping or cooperating with the enemy in a time of war would be considered treason. Espionage is the practice of obtaining information about a government, an organization, or a society that is considered secret or confidential without the permission of the holder of the information. Industrial espionage involves unethical or illegal activities such as bribing employees to reveal trade secrets such as computer codes or product formulas.

4. **Know the components of state political crime**
   - Some political crimes are committed by people who oppose the state, whereas others are perpetrated by state authorities against the people they are supposed to serve. State political crime has five components: political corruption, illegal domestic surveillance, human rights violations, state violence, and state-corporate crime.

5. **Be able to debate the use and misuse of torture**
   - The use of torture to gain information from suspected political criminals is highly controversial. The use of waterboarding has become a national issue because there seems to be no agreement on whether it is torture or a relatively harmless instrument of interrogation.

6. **Distinguish among terrorists, insurgents, guerillas, and revolutionaries**
   - Terrorism is generally defined as the illegal use of force against innocent people to achieve a political objective. The term *guerilla* refers to antigovernment forces located in rural areas that attack the military, the police, and government officials. The typical goal of an insurgency is to confront the existing government for control of all or a portion of its territory, or to force political concessions in sharing political power. A revolution is generally seen as a civil war fought between nationalists and a sovereign power that holds control of the land, or between the existing government and local groups over issues of ideology and power.

7. **Understand the various forms of terrorism**
   - Revolutionary terrorists use violence to frighten those in power and their supporters in order to replace the existing government with a regime that holds acceptable political or religious views. Political terrorism is directed at people or groups who oppose the terrorists' political ideology or whom the terrorists define as "outsiders" who must be destroyed. Nationalist terrorism promotes the interests of a minority ethnic or religious group that believes it has been persecuted under majority rule and wishes to carve out its own independent homeland. Retributive terrorists want to impose their social and religious code on others. State-sponsored terrorism occurs when a repressive government regime forces its citizens into obedience, oppresses minorities, and stifles political dissent. Destructive cults are willing to have members commit violence, including murder. Sometimes terrorist groups become involved in common-law crimes such as drug dealing and kidnapping, even selling nuclear materials.

8. **Know what motivates the terrorist**
   - Not all terrorists suffer from psychological deficits, but enough do so that the typical terrorist can be described as an emotionally disturbed individual who acts out his or her psychoses within the confines of violent groups. Another view is that because they are out of the political and social mainstream, young men and women are motivated to join terror groups because they suffer alienation and lack the tools to compete in a post-technological society. Another view is that terrorists hold extreme religious and/or ideological beliefs that prompt their behavior.

9. **Be familiar with the efforts being made to centralize intelligence gathering**
   - The Director of National Intelligence (DNI) is charged with coordinating data from the nation's primary intelligence-gathering agencies. The National Counterterrorism Center (NCTC) serves as the primary organization in the U.S. government for analyzing and integrating all intelligence possessed or acquired by the government pertaining to terrorism and counterterrorism, excepting purely domestic counterterrorism information.

10. **Describe the efforts by the FBI and DHS to fight terrorism**
    - The FBI announced a reformulation of its priorities, making protecting the United States from terrorist attack its number one commitment. It is now charged with coordinating intelligence collection with the Border Patrol, Secret Service, and the CIA. The Department of Homeland Security (DHS) is the federal agency responsible for preventing terrorist attacks within the United States, reducing America's vulnerability to terrorism, and minimizing the damage and recovering from attacks that do occur.

KEY TERMS

al-Qaeda (379)
political crime (379)
human rights (380)
election fraud (381)
treason (383)
espionage (383)
state political crime (387)
torture (388)

ticking bomb scenario (388)
terrorism (389)
terror cells (389)
guerilla (390)
insurgent (390)
Zealot (391)
Reign of Terror (392)
retributive terrorists (396)

state-sponsored terrorism (397)
cult terror (397)
networks (398)
Director of National Intelligence (DNI) (402)
Department of Homeland Security (DHS) (403)
USA Patriot Act (USAPA) (405)

CRITICAL THINKING QUESTIONS

1. Would you be willing to give up some of your civil rights in order to aid the war on terror?
2. Should terror suspects arrested in a foreign land be given the same rights and privileges as an American citizen accused of crime?
3. What groups in America might be the breeding ground for terrorist activity in the United States?
4. In light of the 9/11 attack, should acts of terrorism be treated differently from other common-law violent crimes? Should terrorists be executed for their acts even if no one is killed during their attack?
5. Can the use of torture ever be justified? Is the "ticking bomb" scenario valid?
6. A spy gives plans for a new weapon to the enemy. They build the weapon and use it to kill American soldiers. Is the spy guilty of murder?

NOTES

1. *Frontline*, "Osama bin Laden v. the U.S.: Edicts and Statements," www.pbs.org/wgbh/pages/frontline/shows/binladen/who/edicts.html (accessed November 2, 2010).
2. Michael Scott Doran, "Somebody Else's Civil War," *Foreign Affairs* 81 (2002): 22–25; Peter L. Bergen, *Holy War, Inc.: Inside The Secret World of Osama bin Laden* (New York: Free Press, 2001), pp. 41–50; Yonah Alexander and Michael S. Swetnam, *Usama bin Laden's al-Qaida: Profile of a Terrorist Network* (New York: Transnational Publishers, 2001); Michael Kranish and Anthony Shadid, "Bin Laden Zeal for Stature Used Psychology, Religion," *Boston Globe*, November 19, 2001, p. 3; *Frontline*, "Osama bin Laden v. the U.S.: Edicts and Statements."
3. United States State Department, Country Reports on Terrorism 2009, August 5, 2010, www.state.gov/s/ct/rls/crt/2009/index.htm (accessed August 16, 2011).
4. Jeffrey Ian Ross, *The Dynamics of Political Crime* (Thousand Oaks, CA: Sage, 2003).
5. Ibid.
6. Mike Baker and Nedra Pickler, "John Edwards Charged in Felony Indictment," BreitBart, June 3, 2011, www.breitbart.com/article.php?id=D9NKF7201&show_article=1 (accessed August 12, 2011).
7. Stephen Farrell and Anthony Shadid, "Dozens Killed in Wave of Attacks Across Iraq," *New York Times*, August 25, 2010, www.blogrunner.com/snapshot/D/2/4/dozens_killed_in_wave_of_attacks_across_iraq/ (accessed August 12, 2011).
8. Stephen Schafer, *The Political Criminal, The Problem of Morality and Crime* (New York: Free Press, 1974), pp. 154–157.
9. Randy Borum, "Understanding the Terrorist Mind-Set," *FBI Law Enforcement Bulletin* 72 (2003): 7–10.
10. Veronica Rocha, "Man Sentenced for Donations: Business Owner Gets More Than a Year for Illegal Contributions to Bush and Cheney," *Glendale News Press*, December 11, 2008, http://articles.glendalenewspress.com/2008-12-11/local/gnp-gill11_1_prison-release-contributions-campaigns (accessed August 12, 2011).
11. Amnesty International, "Kenya: Amnesty International Concerned at Police Killings in Election Protests," December 31, 2007, www.amnesty.org/en/for-media/press-releases/kenya-amnesty-international-concerned-police-killings-election-protests (accessed August 12, 2011).
12. BBC news, "Profile of John Walker Lindh," January 24, 2002, http://news.bbc.co.uk/2/hi/americas/1779455.stm (accessed August 12, 2011).
13. University of Missouri–Kansas City School of Law, Douglas Linder, "The Treason Trial of Aaron Burr," www.law.umkc.edu/faculty/projects/ftrials/burr/burraccount.html (accessed August 12, 2011).
14. John Ziff and Austin Sarat, *Espionage and Treason* (New York: Chelsea House, 1999).
15. United States Criminal Code at 18 U.S.C. § 2381.
16. CNN, "Accused FBI Spy Hanssen Pleads Not Guilty," May 31, 2001, http://archives.cnn.com/2001/LAW/05/31/hanssen.arraignment.02/index.html (accessed August 12, 2011).
17. David Owen, *Hidden Secrets: The Complete History of Espionage and the Technology Used to Support It* (Ontario, Canada: Firefly Books, 2002).
18. BBC News, "Key Cases in Soviet-UK Espionage," January 23, 2006, http://news.bbc.co.uk/2/hi/europe/4639130.stm (accessed August 12, 2011).
19. Lawrence Schiller, *Into the Mirror: The Life of Master Spy Robert P. Hanssen* (Darby, PA: Diane Publications, 2004).
20. FBI, "Trade Secret Theft, Couple Conspires to Steal Hybrid Technology," September 24, 2010, www.fbi.gov/news/stories/2010/september/steal-hybrid-technology/steal-hybrid-technology (accessed August 12, 2011).
21. Hedieh Nasheri, *Economic Espionage and Industrial Spying* (Cambridge, England: Cambridge University Press, 2004).
22. Office of the National Counterintelligence Executive, "Annual Report to Congress on Foreign Economic Collection and Industrial Espionage, 2005," www.fas.org/irp/ops/ci/docs/2005.pdf (accessed August 12, 2011).
23. Ibid.
24. Department of Justice, "Two Men Plead Guilty to Stealing Trade Secrets from Silicon Valley Companies to Benefit China," (News release), December 14, 2006, www.justice.gov/criminal/cybercrime/yePlea.htm (accessed August 12, 2011).
25. Nadia Abou El-Magd, "Accuser in Case vs. CIA Agents Tells of Torture: Muslim Cleric Says Egyptians Used Electricity," *Boston Globe*, February 23, 2007, A3.
26. Jessica Wolfendale, "Training Torturers: A Critique of the 'Ticking Bomb' Argument," *Social Theory and Practice* 31 (2006): 269–287.
27. Vittorio Bufacchi and Jean Maria Arrigo, "Torture, Terrorism and the State: A Refutation of the Ticking-Bomb Argument," *Journal of Applied Philosophy* 23 (2006): 355–373.
28. Elizabeth Sepper, "The Ties That Bind: How the Constitution Limits the CIA's Actions in the War on Terror," *New York University Law Review* 81 (2006): 1,805–1,843.
29. Scott Shane, David Johnston, and James Risen, "Secret U.S. Endorsement of Severe Interrogations" *New York Times*, October 4, 2007, www.nytimes.com/2007/10/04/washington/04interrogate.html (accessed August 12, 2011).
30. Michael Cooper and Marc Santora, "McCain Rebukes Giuliani on Waterboarding Remark," *New York Times*, October 26, 2007, www.nytimes.com/2007/10/26/us/politics/26giuliani.html (accessed August 12, 2011).

31. Office of the Director of National Intelligence National Counterterrorism Center, "2009 NCTC Report on Terrorism (2010)," www.nctc.gov/witsbanner/docs/2009_report_on_terrorism.pdf (accessed August 12, 2011).

32. Title 22 of the United States Code section 2656f (d) (1999).

33. Paul Wilkinson, *Terrorism and the Liberal State* (New York: Wiley, 1977), p. 49.

34. Jack Gibbs, "Conceptualization of Terrorism," *American Sociological Review* 54 (1989): 329–340, at 330.

35. Robert Friedlander, *Terrorism* (Dobbs Ferry, NY: Oceana, 1979), p. 14.

36. Daniel Georges-Abeyie, "Political Crime and Terrorism," in *Crime and Deviance: A Comparative Perspective*, ed. Graeme Newman (Beverly Hills: Sage, 1980), pp. 313–333.

37. "Differences between Terrorism and Insurgency," www.terrorism-research.com/insurgency/ (accessed August 12, 2011).

38. Andrew Silke, "Holy Warriors: Exploring the Psychological Processes of Jihadi Radicalization," *European Journal of Criminology* 5 (2008): 99–123.

39. Walter Laqueur, *The New Terrorism: Fanaticism and the Arms of Mass Destruction Terrorism and History* (New York: Oxford University Press, 1999).

40. This section relies heavily on Friedlander, *Terrorism*, pp. 8–20.

41. Michael Kellogg. *The Russian Roots of Nazism: White Russians and the Making of National Socialism, 1917–1945* (New York: Cambridge University Press, 2005).

42. Associated Press, "Malaysia Arrests Five Militants," *New York Times,* October 15, 2002, p. A2.

43. Jocelyn Parker, "Vehicles Burn at Dealership: SUV Attacks Turn Violent," *Detroit Free Press,* August 23, 2003, p. 1.

44. "Brutal Elves in the Woods," *The Economist* 359 (2001): 28–30.

45. Steve Miletich, "Hunt Is On: Who Torched the Street of Dreams?" *Seattle Times,* March 4, 2008, http://seattletimes.nwsource.com/html/snohomishcountynews/2004258337_arson04m.html (accessed August 12, 2011).

46. Fiona Proffitt, "Costs of Animal Rights Terror," *Science* 304 (2004): 1,731–1,739.

47. Department of Justice, "Eleven Defendants Indicted on Domestic Terrorism Charges: Group Allegedly Responsible for Series of Arsons in Western States, Acting on Behalf of Extremist Movements," (News release), January 20, 2006, www.usdoj.gov/opa/pr/2006/January/06_crm_030.html (accessed August 12, 2011).

48. Angel Rabasa, Peter Chalk, Kim Cragin, Sara A. Daly, Heather S. Gregg, Theodore W. Karasik, Kevin A. O'Brien, and William Rosenau, *Beyond al-Qaeda Part 1, The Global Jihadist Movement,* xviii, and *Part 2, The Outer Rings of the Terrorist Universe* (Santa Monica, CA: RAND Corporation, 2006).

49. Lawrence Miller, "The Terrorist Mind: A Psychological and Political Analysis, Part I" *International Journal of Offender Therapy and Comparative Criminology* 50 (2006): 121–138.

50. Martin Libicki, Peter Chalk, and Melanie Sisson, *Exploring Terrorist Targeting Preferences* (Santa Monica, CA: RAND Corporation 2007), www.rand.org/pubs/monographs/MG483/ (accessed August 12, 2011).

51. Mark Mazzetti and David Rohde, "Al Qaeda Chiefs Are Seen to Regain Power," *New York Times*, February 19, 2007, p. 1.

52. Sanjeev Gupta, Benedict Clements, Rina Bhattacharya, and Shamit Chakravarti, "Fiscal Consequences of Armed Conflict and Terrorism in Low- and Middle-Income Countries," *European Journal of Political Economy* 20 (2004): 403–421.

53. Gabriela Fried, "Piecing Memories Together after State Terror and Policies of Oblivion in Uruguay: The Female Political Prisoner's Testimonial Project (1997–2004)," *Social Identities* 12 (2006): 543–562.

54. Martin Miller, "Ordinary Terrorism in Historical Perspective," *Journal for the Study of Radicalism* 2 (2008): 125–154.

55. Mark Hamm, "'High Crimes and Misdemeanors': George W. Bush and the Sins of Abu Ghraib," *Crime, Media, Culture: An International Journal* 3 (2007): 259–284.

56. Haruki Murakami, *Underground* (New York: Vintage Books, 2001).

57. Lawrence Miller, "The Terrorist Mind: A Psychological and Political Analysis, Part II," *International Journal of Offender Therapy and Comparative Criminology* 50 (2006): 255–268.

58. Ibid.

59. Eben Kaplan, "Tracking Down Terrorist Financing" (Washington, DC: Council on Foreign Relations), April 4, 2006, www.cfr.org/international-crime/tracking-down-terrorist-financing/p10356#p2 (accessed August 12, 2011).

60. Chris Dishman, "Terrorism, Crime, and Transformation," *Studies in Conflict and Terrorism* 24 (2001): 43–56.

61. U.S. Department of State, "State Sponsors of Terrorism, 2010," www.state.gov/s/ct/rls/crt/2009/140889.htm (accessed August 12, 2011).

62. Tom Hays, "NYPD Commissioner: NYC Bomb Suspect 'Homegrown'," *Associated Press*, www.journal-news.com/news/nation-world-news/nypd-commissioner-nyc-bomb-suspect-homegrown-698315.html (accessed August 12, 2011).

63. Center on Law and Security, New York School of Law, *Terrorist Trial Report Card: September 11, 2001–September 11, 2009* (New York: Center on Law and Security, 2010), www.lawandsecurity.org/Publications/Terrorism-Trial-Report-Card (accessed August 12, 2011), p. 20.

64. Violent Radicalization and Homegrown Terrorism Prevention Act of 2007, www.govtrack.us/congress/bill.xpd?bill=h110-1955 (accessed August 12, 2011).

65. Stephen J. Morgan, *The Mind of a Terrorist Fundamentalist: The Psychology of Terror Cults* (Awe-Struck E-Books, 2001); Martha Crenshaw, "The Psychology of Terrorism: An Agenda for the 21st Century," *Political Psychology* 21 (2000): 405–420.

66. Andrew Silke, "Courage in Dark Places: Reflections on Terrorist Psychology," *Social Research* 71 (2004): 177–198.

67. Jerrold M. Post, "Terrorist Psycho-Logic: Terrorist Behavior as a Product of Psychological Forces," in *Origins of Terrorism: Psychologies, Ideologies Theologies, States of Mind,* ed. Walter Reich (Cambridge: Cambridge University Press, 1990), p. 12.

68. Randy Borum, *Psychology of Terrorism* (Tampa: University of South Florida, 2004), www.ncjrs.gov/pdffiles1/nij/grants/208552.pdf (accessed August 12, 2011).

69. David Weatherston and Jonathan.Moran, "Terrorism and Mental Illness: Is There a Relationship?" *International Journal of Offender Therapy and Comparative Criminology* 47 (2003): 698–711.

70. Charles Ruby, "Are Terrorists Mentally Deranged?" *Analyses of Social Issues and Public Policy* 2 (2002): 15–26.

71. Ethan Bueno de Mesquita, "The Quality of Terror," *American Journal of Political Science* 49 (2005): 515–530.

72. Murakami, *Underground.*

73. Jerrold Post, "When Hatred Is Bred in the Bone: Psycho-cultural Foundations of Contemporary Terrorism," *Political Psychology* 25 (2005): 615–637.

74. This section leans heavily on Anthony Stahelski, "Terrorists Are Made, Not Born: Creating Terrorists Using Social Psychological Conditioning," *Journal of Homeland Security* (March 2004), www.homelandsecurity.org/journal/Default.aspx?oid=109&ocat=1 (accessed August 12, 2011).

75. Marc Sageman, *Understanding Terror Networks* (Philadelphia: University of Pennsylvania Press, 2004), Chapter 4.

76. Ibid.

77. Ibid.

78. Ibid.

79. Patricia Marchak, *Reigns of Terror* (Montreal: McGill-Queen's University Press, 2003).

80. Ibid., pp. 153–155.

81. Graham Allison, *Nuclear Terrorism: The Ultimate Preventable Catastrophe* (New York: Times Books, 2004).

82. RAND Corporation, "How Prepared Are State and Local Law Enforcement for

Terrorism?" www.rand.org/publications/
RB/RB9093/ (accessed August 12,
2011).

83. Homeland Security, "Information Sharing,"
www.dhs.gov/files/programs/sharing-infor-
mation.shtm (accessed August 12, 2011).
The section on homeland security relies
heavily on "The Department of Homeland
Security," www.whitehouse.gov/infocus/
homeland/index.html (accessed August 12,
2011).

84. California Anti-Terrorism Information
Center (CATIC), http://ag.ca.gov/antiter-
rorism/index.php (accessed August 12,
2011).

85. "NYPD, Counterterrorism Bureau, 2011,"
NYDailyNews.com, www.nydailynews.com/

topics/NYPD+Counterterrorism+Bureau
(accessed August 12, 2011).

86. U.S. Attorney for the Southern District
of New York, press release No. 09-103,
"Afghan Drug Kingpin Charged with
Terrorist Financing for Funding Taliban
Insurgency" April 21, 2009.

87. Del Quentin Wilbur, "U.S. Judge Sentences
Dutch Man to 25 Years for Crimes in Iraq,"
Washington Post, April 17, 2009, A7.

88. Center on Law and Security, New York
School of Law, *Terrorist Trial Report Card.*

89. U.S. Justice Department, "Fact Sheet: Jus-
tice Department Counter-Terrorism Efforts
Since 9/11," www.justice.gov/opa/pr/2008/
September/08-nsd-807.html (accessed
August 12, 2011).

90. *Hamdi v. Rumsfeld,* 542 U.S. 507 (2004).
91. *Rasul v. Bush,* 542 U.S. 466 (2004).
92. *Hamdan v. Rumsfeld,* 548 U.S. 557
(2006).
93. *Boumediene v. Bush,* 553 U.S. 723 (2008).
94. See Section 948c of the Military Commissions Act of 2009, www.defense.gov/
news/2009%20MCA%20Pub%20%20
Law%20111-84.pdf (accessed August 12,
2011).
95. "Senator Feingold on Opposing the U.S.
Patriot Act," www.archipelago.org/vol6-2/
feingold.htm (accessed August 12,
2011).
96. Rabasa et al., *Beyond al-Qaeda Part 1,* www.
jewishpolicycenter.org/100/beyond-al-
qaeda (accessed August 12, 2011).

AP Images/Sergio Dionisio

WHEN

When William M. V. Kingsland died in 2006, New York City newspapers printed glowing obituaries describing him as an urbane upper-class gentleman, an intellectual, and an art expert.[1] His apartment was found to contain a vast and impressive collection of more than 300 works of art—paintings, sketches, sculptures, and other pieces by such artists as Pablo Picasso, John Singleton Copley, Alberto Giacometti, Giorgio Morandi, and Eugene Boudin. Because he left no heirs, New York's Public Administrator office hired two auction houses—Christie's and Stair Galleries—to sell the art. One of his works, a Giacometti, was valued at $900,000 to $1.2 million and a small painting by Morandi would sell for about $600,000. There was hitch, though. As Christie's researched the art to determine its provenance (history of ownership), the famed auction house discovered that many of the works had been reported stolen in the 1960s and 1970s.

(continued on page 414)

Property Crime

12

Chapter Outline

Learning Objectives

1. Be familiar with the history of theft offenses
2. Recognize the differences between professional and amateur thieves
3. Know the similarities and differences between petty and grand larceny
4. Understand the various forms of shoplifting
5. Differentiate between fraud and embezzlement
6. Compare the activities of professional and amateur car thieves
7. Understand what it means to burgle a home
8. Know what it takes to be a "good burglar"
9. Distinguish between the activities of male and female burglars
10. Discuss why people commit arson for profit

Upon further investigation, it turns out that the sophisticated Mr. Kingsland was actually born Melvyn Kohn, and that—counter to his claims—he grew up in a small apartment and not a manor house, he did not attend Groton or Harvard, and he was never actually married to a member of the French royalty.

Kingsland, it turns out, was an art thief, and authorities have been working since his death trying to figure out what was stolen and who were the legitimate owners. When a 1790 Copley portrait of the Second Earl of Bessborough was sold to an art dealer for $85,000, they soon found that it had been stolen in 1971 from the Fogg Art Museum at Harvard. The case had one more bizarre turn: a mover hired by New York's Public Administrator office to transport Kingsland's collection to a warehouse was charged for stealing two Picasso sketches, each valued at approximately $30,000. And that was not the first time those two sketches had been stolen—before they ended up in Kingsland's collection they were actually filched from a New York art gallery![2]

While professional art theft is a specialty, each year millions of people suffer billions in losses to thieves. As a group, these theft offenses can be defined as acts that violate criminal law and are designed to bring financial reward to an offender. The range and scope of U.S. criminal activity motivated by the desire for financial gain are tremendous. Self-report studies show that property crime is widespread among the young in every social class. National surveys of criminal behavior indicate that almost 20 million personal and household thefts occur annually. Though average citizens may be puzzled and enraged by violent crimes, believing them to be both senseless and cruel, they often view economic crimes with a great deal more ambivalence. Society generally disapproves of crimes involving theft and corruption, but the public seems quite tolerant of the "gentleman bandit," such as William Kingsland, even to the point of admiring such figures. They pop up as characters in popular myths and legends—such as the famed English outlaw Robin Hood—and in films such as *Ocean's Eleven* (2001) and *Ocean's Twelve* (2004), and *Ocean's Thirteen* (2007) in which a suave George Clooney and roguish Brad Pitt lead a band of thieves who loot hundreds of millions of dollars from casinos, galleries, and so on.

How can such ambivalence toward thievery be explained? For one thing, if self-report surveys are accurate, national tolerance toward economic criminals may be prompted by the fact that almost every U.S. citizen has at some time been involved in economic crime. Even those among us who would never consider ourselves lawbreakers may have at one time engaged in petty theft, cheated on our income tax, stolen a textbook from a college bookstore, or pilfered from our place of employment. Consequently, it may be difficult for society to condemn economic criminals without feeling hypocritical.

People may also be somewhat more tolerant of economic crimes because they never seem to seriously hurt anyone—banks are insured, large businesses pass along losses to consumers, stolen cars can be easily replaced and, in most cases, are insured. The true pain of economic crime often goes unappreciated. Convicted offenders, especially businesspeople who commit white-collar crimes involving millions of dollars, often are punished rather lightly.

This chapter is the first of two that reviews the nature and extent of economic crime in the United States. It is divided into two principal sections. The first deals with the concept of professional crime and focuses on different types of professional criminals, including the **fence**, a buyer and seller of stolen merchandise. The chapter then turns to a discussion of common theft-related offenses or **street crime**. Included within these general offense categories are such common crimes as auto theft, shoplifting, and credit card fraud. Next, the chapter discusses a more serious form of theft, burglary, which involves forcible entry into a person's home or place of work for the purpose of theft. Finally, the crime of arson is discussed briefly. In Chapter 13, attention will be given to white-collar crimes and economic crimes that involve organizations devoted to criminal enterprise.

A BRIEF HISTORY OF THEFT

Economic crime can be defined as acts in violation of the criminal law designed to bring financial reward to an offender. In U.S. society, the range and scope of criminal activity motivated by financial gain is tremendous: self-report studies show that property crime is widespread among the young in every social class. National surveys of criminal behavior indicate that millions of personal and household thefts occur annually, including auto thefts, shoplifting incidents, embezzlements, burglaries, and larcenies.

Theft, however, is not a phenomenon unique to modern times; the theft of personal property has been known throughout recorded history. The Crusades of the eleventh century inspired peasants and downtrodden noblemen to leave the shelter of their estates to prey on passing pilgrims.[3] Crusaders felt it within their rights to appropriate the possessions of any infidels—Greeks, Jews, or Muslims—they happened to encounter during their travels.

By the thirteenth century, returning pilgrims, not content to live as serfs on feudal estates, gathered in the forests of England and the Continent to poach on game that was the rightful property of their lord or king and, when possible, to steal from passing strangers. By the fourteenth century, many such highwaymen and poachers were full-time livestock thieves, stealing great numbers of cattle and sheep.[4] The fifteenth and sixteenth centuries brought hostilities between England and France in what has come to be known as the Hundred Years' War. Foreign mercenary troops fighting for both sides roamed the countryside; loot and pillage were viewed as a rightful part of their pay. As cities developed and a permanent class of propertyless urban poor was established,[5] theft became more professional. By the eighteenth century, three separate groups of property criminals were active: skilled thieves, smugglers, and poachers.

- **Skilled thieves** typically worked in the larger cities, such as London and Paris. This group included pickpockets, forgers, and counterfeiters, who operated freely. They congregated in **flash houses**—public meeting places, often taverns, that served as headquarters for gangs. Here, deals were made, crimes were plotted, and the sale of stolen goods was negotiated.[6]
- **Smugglers** were the second group of thieves. They moved freely in sparsely populated areas and transported goods, such as spirits, gems, gold, and spices, without bothering to pay tax or duty.
- **Poachers**, the third type of thief, typically lived in the country and supplemented their diet and income with game that belonged to a landlord.

Professional thieves in the larger cities banded together into gangs to protect themselves, increase the scope of their activities, and help dispose of stolen goods. Jack Wild, perhaps London's most famous thief, perfected the process of buying and selling stolen goods and gave himself the title of Thief-Taker General of Great Britain and Ireland. Before he was hanged, Wild controlled numerous gangs and dealt harshly with any thief who violated his strict code of conduct.[7] During this period, individual theft-related crimes began to be defined by the common law. The most important of these categories are still used today.

Theft in the Nineteenth Century: Train Robbery and Safecracking

In the nineteenth century, two new forms of theft appeared. Train robbery hit the nation hard when, in 1866, $700,000 (the equivalent of more than $9 million in today's currency) was taken from an Adams Express car on the New York, New Haven, and Hartford Railroad; it was the first train robbery on record. Also in 1866, the Reno brothers stole $13,000 in their first train holdup. The four brothers and their gang went on to rob a number of banks and trains in southern Indiana and Illinois before being tracked down by the Pinkerton Detective Agency in 1868 (three of the four

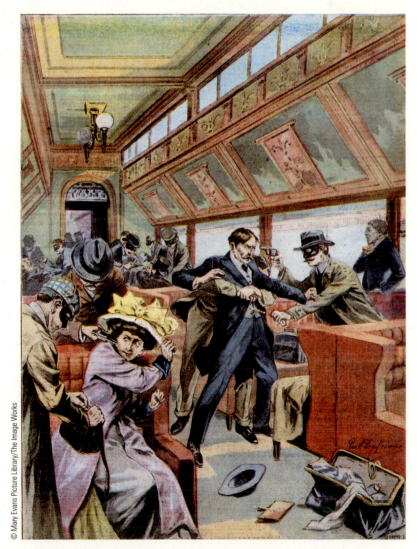

© Mary Evans Picture Library/The Image Works

In this nineteenth-century French lithograph designed to depict the danger of the Wild West, masked and armed train robbers frighten passengers on the Rocky Mountain Line.

brothers were lynched by a gang of vigilantes who attacked the jail where they were being held before trial).[8]

Train robbery flourished toward the end of the nineteenth century because professional robbers considered trains easy pickings.[9] Law enforcement was decentralized, and robbers could escape over the border to a neighboring state to avoid detection. Security arrangements were minimal, and robbers could stop, board, and loot trains with little fear of capture. As the threat to trains increased, improvements were initiated in an effort to deter would-be robbers:

- Plainclothes officers were placed on trains and rode unobtrusively among the passengers.
- Baggage cars were equipped with ramps and stalls containing fleet horses that could be used to immediately pursue bandits.
- Cars were made with finer precision and strength to make them impregnable.
- Forensic science made it easier to identify robbers, and improved communication made it easier to capture them.

Federal involvement in train protection extended the ability of law enforcement beyond the county or state in which the robbery occurred. As a result of these innovations, the number of train robberies decreased from 29 in 1900 to 7 in 1905; by 1920, train robbers had all but disappeared.[10]

Safecracking Secured boxes and safes have existed for centuries, but it wasn't until early in the twentieth century that use of cast iron became widespread and was used to create solid metal boxes. Safecracking also underwent a dramatic change due to technological changes in the design of safes. In the early 1900s, safes were made of manganese steel because it was resistant to drilling and was fireproof. With the invention and distribution of acetylene torches in the latter part of the nineteenth century, safes constructed of manganese became vulnerable and encouraged safecrackers to commit bold crimes. Safe manufacturers fought back by constructing safes with alternating sheets of copper and steel. The copper diffused heat and made the safe resistant to being torched. In response, safecrackers shifted their approach to attacking safes' locks and locking mechanisms. They developed mechanical devices that either dismantled or destroyed locks. Some burglars developed methods of peeling the laminated layers of the safe apart.

After World War II, safecrackers began using carbide and then diamond drill bits, which tore through metal. Safe manufacturers responded by lining safes with new metals designed to chip or break drill bits. They also developed sophisticated security systems featuring light beams, which would trip an alarm if the beam was interrupted by an intruder. When thieves learned how to neutralize these alarms, they were supplanted by motion detectors and ultrasonic systems, which fill the space with sound waves and set

off alarms when they are disturbed. Though these systems can be defeated, it requires expensive electronic gear, which most criminals can neither afford nor operate. As a result, the number of safecrackers has declined, and the crime of safecracking is relatively rare.[11]

> To read more about **Jack Wild** and his times, go to the website of the Old Bailey Court in England by visiting the Criminal Justice CourseMate at cengagebrain. com and accessing the "Web Links" for this chapter.

CONTEMPORARY THEFT

Theft is still a popular criminal pastime, and millions of property and theft-related crimes occur each year. Most are committed by **occasional criminals** who do not define themselves by a criminal role or view themselves as committed career criminals; other theft-offenders are in fact skilled **professional criminals**. The following sections review these two orientations toward property crime.

Occasional Thieves

Occasional offenders are not professional criminals, nor do they make crime their occupation. Many are school-age youths who are unlikely to enter into a criminal career and whose behavior has been described as drifting between conventional and criminal. Added to the pool of amateur thieves are adults who may occasionally violate the criminal law—shoplifters, pilferers, petty thieves—but whose main source of income comes from conventional means and whose self-identity is not criminal. Added together, their behaviors form the bulk of theft crimes.

Occasional thieves do not organize their daily activities around crime nor are they committed to crime as a way of life. Their decision to steal is spontaneous and based on **situational inducements**.[12] These are short-term influences on a person's behavior that increase risk taking. They include psychological factors, such as an immediate and unsolvable financial problem, and social factors, such as peer pressure to commit a spontaneous criminal act—taking a car for a drunken joyride or breaking into a store or home.

While members of every layer of the economy may at some time experience a situational inducement, the opportunity to solve economic crisis through criminal activity is structured by class. While the poor are forced to engage in low-profit, high-risk crimes, members of the upper class have the opportunity to engage in the more lucrative business-related crimes of price fixing, bribery, and embezzlement.

Unlike professionals, occasional thieves do not receive informal peer group support for their crimes. In fact, they will deny any connection to a criminal lifestyle and instead view their transgressions as being "out of character." They may see their crimes as being motivated by necessity. When apprehended, they say they were only "borrowing" the car the police caught them with; they were going to pay for the merchandise they stole from the store, they just "forgot" to go through the checkout line. Because of their lack of commitment to a criminal lifestyle, occasional offenders may be the most likely to respond to the general deterrent effect of the law.

Professional Thieves

In contrast to occasional thieves, professional criminals make a significant portion of their income from crime. Professionals do not delude themselves with the belief that their acts are impulsive, one-time efforts, nor do they employ elaborate rationalizations to excuse the harmfulness of their action ("shoplifting doesn't really hurt anyone"). Consequently, professionals pursue their craft with vigor, attempting to learn from older, experienced criminals the techniques that will earn them the most money with the least risk. Though their numbers are relatively few, professionals engage in crimes that produce the greater losses to society and perhaps cause the more significant social harm.

Professional theft traditionally refers to nonviolent forms of criminal behavior that are undertaken with a high degree of skill for monetary gain and that exploit interests tending to maximize financial opportunities and minimize the possibilities of apprehension. The most typical forms include pocket-picking, burglary, shoplifting, forgery and counterfeiting, extortion, sneak theft, and confidence swindling.[13]

Relatively little is known about the career patterns of professional thieves and criminals. From the literature on crime and delinquency, three patterns emerge:

- Youth come under the influence of older, experienced criminals who teach them the trade.
- Juvenile gang members continue their illegal activities at a time when most of their peers have dropped out to marry, raise families, and take conventional jobs.
- Youth sent to prison for minor offenses learn the techniques of crime from more experienced thieves.

In a classic work, *Box Man: A Professional Thief's Journal*, Harry King, a professional thief, relates this story about his entry into crime after being placed in a shelter-care home by his recently divorced mother:

It was while I was at this parental school that I learned that some of the kids had been committed there by the court for stealing bikes. They taught me how to steal and where to steal them and where to sell them. Incidentally, some of the "nicer people" were the ones who bought bikes from the kids. They would dismantle the bike and use the parts: the wheels, chains, handlebars, and so forth.[14]

Here we can see how would-be criminals may be encouraged in their illegal activities by so-called honest people who are willing to buy stolen merchandise and gain from criminal enterprise.

There is some debate in the criminological literature over who may be defined as a professional criminal. In his classic works, Edwin Sutherland used the term to refer only to thieves who do not use force or physical violence in their crimes and who live solely by their wits and skill.[15] It is more common today for criminologists to use the term to refer to any criminal who identifies with a criminal subculture, who makes the bulk of his or her living from crime, and who possesses a degree of skill in his or her chosen trade.[16] Thus, one can become a professional safecracker, burglar, car thief, or fence. Some criminologists would not consider drug addicts who steal to support their habit as professionals; they lack skill and therefore are amateur opportunists rather than professional technicians. However, some professional criminals take drugs without losing their lofty status in the criminal hierarchy.

Becoming a Professional Thief What we know about the lives of professional criminals has come to us through their journals, diaries, autobiographies, and the first-person accounts they have given to criminologists. The best-known account of professional theft is the life of Chic Conwell, in Edwin Sutherland's classic book *The Professional Thief*.[17] Conwell and Sutherland's concept of professional theft has two critical dimensions.

First, professional thieves engage in limited types of crime, which are described in Exhibit 12.1.[18] Professionals depend solely on their wit and skill. Thieves who use force

---

EXHIBIT 12.1

Sutherland's Typology of Professional Thieves

- Pickpocket (cannon)
- Thief in rackets related to confidence games
- Forger
- Extortionist from those engaging in illegal acts (shakedown artist)
- Confidence game artist (con artist)
- Thief who steals from hotel rooms (hotel prowl)
- Jewel thief who substitutes fake gems for real ones (pennyweighter)
- Shoplifter (booster)
- Sneak thief from stores, banks, and offices (heel)

SOURCE: Chic Conwell, *The Professional Thief*, ed. Edwin Sutherland (Chicago: University of Chicago Press, 1937).

or commit crimes that require little expertise are not considered worthy of the title "professional." Their areas of activity include "heavy rackets," such as bank robbery, car theft, burglary, and safecracking. You can see that Conwell and Sutherland's criteria for professionalism are weighted heavily toward con games and trickery and give little attention to common street crimes.

The second requirement of professional theft is the exclusive use of wits, "front" (a believable demeanor), and talking ability. Manual dexterity and physical force are of little importance. Professional thieves must acquire status in their profession. Status is based on their technical skill, financial standing, connections, power, dress, manners, and wide knowledge base. In their world, "thief" is a title worn with pride. Conwell and Sutherland also argue that professional thieves share common feelings, sentiments, and behaviors. Of these, none is more important than the code of honor of the underworld; even under the threat of the most severe punishment, a professional thief must never inform (squeal) on his or her fellows. Sutherland and Conwell view professional theft as an occupation with much the same internal organization as that characterizing such legitimate professions as advertising, teaching, or police work. They conclude:

> A person can be a professional thief only if he is recognized and received as such by other professional thieves. Professional theft is a group way of life. One can get into the group and remain in it only by the consent of those previously in the group. Recognition as a professional thief by other professional thieves is the absolutely necessary, universal, and definitive characteristic of the professional thief.[19]

The sections below describe two types of professional thieves: fences and cargo thieves.

The Fence

Some experts have argued that Sutherland's view of the professional thief may be outdated because modern thieves often work alone, are not part of a criminal subculture, and were not tutored early in their careers by other criminals.[20] However, some important research efforts show that the principles set down by Sutherland still have value for understanding the behavior of one contemporary criminal type—the **fence**, who earns his or her living solely by buying and reselling stolen merchandise. The fence's critical role in criminal transactions has been recognized since the eighteenth century.[21] They act as middlemen who purchase stolen merchandise—ranging from diamonds to auto hubcaps—and resell them to merchants who market them to legitimate customers.[22]

Much of what we know about fences comes from relatively few in-depth studies of the lives and activities of these specialized professional criminals. Carl Klockars examined the life and times of one successful fence who used the alias Vincent Swaggi. Through 400 hours of listening to and observing Swaggi, Klockars found that this highly professional criminal had developed techniques that made him almost immune to prosecution. During the course of a long and profitable career in crime, Swaggi spent only four months in prison. He stayed in business, in part, because of his sophisticated knowledge of the law of stolen property. To convict someone of receiving stolen goods, the prosecution must prove that the accused was in possession of the goods and knew that they had been stolen. Swaggi had the skills to make sure that these elements could never be proved. Also helping Swaggi stay out of the law's grasp were the close working associations he maintained with society's upper classes, including influential members of the justice system. Swaggi helped them purchase stolen items at below-cost, bargain prices. He also helped authorities recover stolen goods and therefore remained in their good graces. Klockars's work strongly suggests that fences customarily cheat their thief-clients and at the same time cooperate with the law.

Sam Goodman, a fence interviewed by sociologist Darrell Steffensmeier, lived in a world similar to Vincent Swaggi's. He also purchased stolen goods from a wide variety of thieves and suppliers, including burglars, drug addicts, shoplifters, dockworkers, and truck drivers. According to Goodman, to be successful, a fence must meet the following conditions:

- *Upfront cash.* All deals are cash transactions, so an adequate supply of ready cash must always be on hand.
- *Knowledge of dealing—learning the ropes.* The fence must be schooled in the knowledge of the trade, including developing a "larceny sense"; learning to "buy right" at acceptable prices; being able to "cover one's back" and not get caught; finding out how to make the right contacts; and knowing how to "wheel and deal" and how to create opportunities for profit.
- *Connections with suppliers of stolen goods.* The successful fence must be able to engage in long-term relationships with suppliers of high-value stolen goods who are relatively free of police interference. The warehouse worker who pilfers is a better supplier than the narcotics addict, who is more likely to be apprehended and talk to the police.
- *Connections with buyers.* The successful fence must have continuing access to buyers of stolen merchandise who are inaccessible to the common thief. For example, they must make contacts with local pawnshops and other distributors of secondhand goods and be able to move their material without drawing attention from the authorities.[23]
- *Complicity with law enforcers.* The fence must work out a relationship with law enforcement officials who invariably find out about the fence's operations. Steffensmeier found that to stay in business the fence must either bribe officials with good deals on merchandise and cash payments or act as an informer who helps police recover particularly important merchandise and arrest thieves.

The Criminological Enterprise
Confessions of a Dying Thief

In their book *Confessions of a Dying Thief*, Darrell Steffensmeier and Jeffery Ulmer provide a close-up view into the dynamics of career criminal Sam Goodman, a veteran thief and fence and quasi-legitimate businessman. Sam had a criminal career that spanned 50 years, beginning in his mid-teens and ending with his death when he was in his sixties. Steffensmeier and Ulmer find that unlike amateur criminals who age out of crime, professional criminals such as Sam, as well as skilled thieves, dealers in stolen goods, bookmakers, con artists, sex merchants, quasi-legitimate businessmen, local racketeers, and Mafiosi frequently persist in their criminality until they are too old or feeble to do so.

Their interviews with Sam show that criminal opportunity is not merely passive: professional criminals actively seek out and create criminal opportunities that are attractive. They support their careers by gaining different types of criminal knowledge:

- *Civil knowledge.* Widely accessible general knowledge that can be put to criminal use.
- *Preparatory knowledge.* Prior familiarity with criminal orientations, language, attitudes, and skills often gained by hanging around with criminal associates and observing their lifestyles.
- *Technical knowledge.* More esoteric knowledge or skills that can only be obtained by access to more specialized settings and experienced criminal practitioners.

Sam had a strong commitment to crime throughout the course of his life.

The height of his personal commitment to crime was during the middle phase of his career when he was a "big, wide-open" fence. Nonetheless, his favorable attitudes toward crime and other criminals endured into the later "moonlighting" phase of his career when he was less involved in crime. At that point, he also developed more positive attitudes toward legitimate people and associations (such as his employees and legitimate antique dealers). Furthermore, the moonlighting phase of his career saw some changes in Sam's self-definition, as reflected in this assessment in the final weeks of his life (p. 375):

> I never cared how the cops saw me but I wanted the public to see me in a different light. Not as a guy who did time, not as a burglar, not even as a fence, but as a businessman. As a good Joe. In that way I knew what I done was wrong. . . . If they saw me as a crook, that I could handle. But not a [expletive] bum. I wanted the people to respect me as me. As a businessman taking care of business in my shop.

Deviants, even persistent criminals, are seldom deviant in all or even most aspects of their lives. Sam comfortably rubbed shoulders with thieves, gamblers, and quasi-legitimate businessmen but also courted respectability and pledged allegiance to some major normative standards. Sam was unapologetic about his criminal career. While he realized that his behavior may have violated the law, he took pride in the way he conducted himself and did

business, as these deathbed comments illustrate (p. 373):

> I do not feel sad about my life. I did what I thought I had to do at the time. But I would not wish my life on somebody else. I made that very goddamn plain to your students—a life in crime can be a bitch. . . . I done wrong, pulled some very rank shit. But helped a whole lot of people, too. If somebody needed something, came into my shop, I more or less gave it away. Anyone that worked for me, I dealt with fairly. Got paid a good dollar and helped them out in little ways.

The life of Sam Goodman shows that while most criminals age out of crime, some do not and remain active throughout their life span.

CRITICAL THINKING

1. Which of the criminological theories best explains Sam Goodman's life and career? For example, how would Sampson and Laub explain his involvement in fencing? Or is his behavior a matter of rational choice?

2. Speculate on the Internet's impact on professional fencing. How do you suppose stolen merchandise can be sold online?

SOURCE: Darrell Steffensmeier and Jeffery Ulmer, *Confessions of a Dying Thief: Understanding Criminal Careers and Illegal Enterprise* (Piscataway, NJ: Transaction-Aldine, 2005).

For more on Sam Goodman's life, see The Criminological Enterprise feature "Confessions of a Dying Thief."

Fences handle a tremendous variety of products, including televisions, cigarettes, stereo equipment, watches, autos, and cameras.[24] In dealing their merchandise, they operate through many legitimate fronts, including art dealers, antique stores, furniture and appliance retailers, remodeling companies, salvage companies, trucking companies, and jewelry stores. When deciding what to pay the thief for goods, the fence uses a complex pricing policy: professional thieves who steal high-priced items are usually given the highest amounts—about 30 to 50 percent of the wholesale price. Furs valued at $5,000 may be bought for $1,500. However, the amateur thief or drug addict who is not in a good bargaining position may receive only 10 cents on the dollar.

Fencing seems to contain many of the elements of professional theft as described by Sutherland: fences live by their wits, never engage in violence, depend on their skill in negotiating, maintain community standing based on connections and power, and share the sentiments and behaviors of their fellows. The only divergence between Sutherland's thief and the fence is the code of honor; it seems likely that the fence is much more willing to cooperate with authorities than most other professional criminals.

The Occasional Fence Professional fences have attracted the attention of criminologists, but like other forms of theft, fencing is not dominated solely by professional criminals. A significant portion of all fencing is performed by amateur or occasional criminals. Novice burglars, such as juveniles and drug addicts, often find it so difficult to establish relationships with professional fences that they turn instead to nonprofessionals to unload the stolen goods.[25]

One type of occasional fence is the part-timer who, unlike professional fences, has other sources of income. Part-timers are often "legitimate" businesspeople who integrate the stolen merchandise into their regular stock. A rental store manager who buys stolen merchandise and rents it along with his legitimate merchandise is a part-time fence. An added benefit of the illegitimate part of his work is the profit he makes on these stolen items, which is not reported for tax purposes.

Some merchants become actively involved in theft either by specifying the merchandise they want the burglars to steal or by "fingering" victims. Some businesspeople sell merchandise and then describe the customers' homes and vacation plans to known burglars so that they can steal it back!

Associational fences are amateur fences who barter stolen goods for services. These amateurs typically have legitimate professional dealings with known criminals such as bail bond agents, police officers, and attorneys. A lawyer may demand an expensive watch from a client in exchange for legal services. Bartering for stolen merchandise avoids taxes and becomes a transaction in the underground economy.

Neighborhood hustlers buy and sell stolen property as one of the many ways they make a living. They keep some of the booty for themselves and sell the rest in the neighborhood. These dealmakers are familiar figures to neighborhood burglars looking to get some quick cash by selling them stolen merchandise.

Amateur receivers can be complete strangers approached in a public place by someone offering a great deal on valuable commodities. It is unlikely that anyone buying a $2,000 stereo for $200 cash would not suspect that it may have been stolen. Some amateur receivers make a habit of buying suspect merchandise at reasonable prices from a "trusted friend," establishing an ongoing relationship. This practice encourages crime because the criminals know that there will always be someone to buy their merchandise. In addition to the professional fence, the nonprofessional fence may account for a great deal of criminal receiving. Both professional and amateur thieves have a niche in the crime universe.

Professional Cargo Thieves

Some professionals work in highly organized groups, targeting specific items and employing "specialists" who bring a different set of criminal skills to the table. Take for example professional cargo thieves, whose bases of operations are truck yards, hubs for commercial freight carriers, airports, and port cities. These thieves prey upon the huge fleet of cargo ships, planes, and trucks that bring in a daily array of valuable cargoes. While other thieves target cash and jewels, these professionals make off with frozen shrimp, clothing, and electronic goods. Their criminal activities cost the public somewhere between $15 billion and $30 billion a year. Cargo thieves use sophisticated operations with well-organized hierarchies of leadership. They employ specialists who carry out a variety of tasks, including thieves and brokers or fences who help unload the stolen goods on the black market. "Lumpers" physically move the goods, and work with drivers in transporting the stolen merchandise from the docks. Gangs usually employ a specialist who is an expert at foiling the antitheft locks on truck trailers. Cargo thieves heist whole truck loads of merchandise—the average freight on a trailer can be valued at up to $3 million.[26]

Criminologists and legal scholars recognize that common theft offenses fall into several categories linked together because they involve the intentional misappropriation of property for personal gain. In fencing, goods are bought from another who is in illegal possession of those goods. In the case of embezzlement, burglary, and larceny, the property is taken through stealth. In other kinds of theft, such as bad checks, fraud, and false pretenses, goods are obtained through deception. Some of the major categories of common theft offenses are discussed in the next sections in some detail.

LARCENY/THEFT

Larceny/theft was one of the earliest common-law crimes created by English judges to define acts in which one person took for his or her own use the property of another.[27] According to common law, larceny was defined as "the trespassory taking and carrying away of the personal property of another with intent to steal."[28] Most state jurisdictions have incorporated the common-law crime of larceny in their legal codes. Today, definitions of larceny often include such familiar acts as shoplifting, passing bad checks, and other theft offenses that do not involve using force or threats on the victim (robbery) or forcibly breaking into a person's home or place of work (burglary).

When it was originally construed, larceny involved taking property that was in the possession of the rightful owners. For example, it would have been considered larceny for someone to go secretly into a farmer's field and steal a cow. Thus, the original common-law definition required a "trespass in the taking"; this meant that for an act to be considered larceny, goods must have been taken from the physical possession of the rightful owner. In creating this definition of larceny, English judges were more concerned with people disturbing the peace than they were with thefts. If someone tried to steal property from another's possession, they reasoned that the act could eventually lead to a physical confrontation and possibly the death of one party or the other, thereby disturbing the peace! Consequently, the original definition of larceny did not include crimes in which the thief had come into the possession of the stolen property by trickery or deceit. It was therefore not considered larceny if someone entrusted with another person's property decided to keep it for themselves.

The growth of manufacturing and the development of the free enterprise system required greater protection for private property. The pursuit of commercial enterprise often required that one person's legal property be entrusted to a second party; therefore larceny evolved to include the theft of goods that had come into the thief's possession through legitimate means.

To get around the element of "trespass in the taking," English judges created the concept of **constructive possession**. This legal fiction applied to situations in which persons voluntarily and temporarily gave up custody of their property but still believed the property was legally theirs. If a person gave a jeweler her watch for repair, she would still believe she owned the watch even though she had handed it over to the jeweler. Similarly, when a person misplaces his wallet and someone else finds it and keeps it—although identification of the owner can be plainly seen—the concept of constructive possession makes the person who has kept the wallet guilty of larceny.

Larceny Today

Most U.S. state criminal codes separate larceny into **petit (or petty) larceny** and **grand larceny**. The former involves small amounts of money or property and is punished as a misdemeanor. Grand larceny, involving merchandise of greater value, is a felony punished by a sentence in the state prison. Each state sets its own boundary between grand larceny and petty larceny, but $50 to $100 is not unusual. For example, in the Virginia Criminal Code the main distinction between petit and grand larceny is the value of the item taken: larceny of an item with a value of $200 or more is considered grand larceny, while taking something with a value of less than $200 is considered petit larceny. In Virginia, how the larceny is committed may affect its definition: stealing money or property worth $5 or more from a person is considered grand larceny, while theft from the person of money or property with a value of less than $5 is petit

larceny. Taking a firearm from a home or car is automatically considered grand larceny.[29]

How larceny is categorized can have a significant influence on the level of punishment. Looking at Virginia again as an example, grand larceny is a felony with a specific punishment of not less than one year in prison but not more than 20, or at the discretion of a jury (or judge) trying the case, it can also be punished with a jail sentence of not more than 12 months and/or a fine not to exceed $2,500. In contrast, petit larceny is a class 1 misdemeanor punishable by up to 12 months in jail and/or a fine of up to $2,500.[30] The distinction between petit and grand larceny can be especially significant in states such as California that employ three strikes laws mandating that someone convicted of a third felony be given a life sentence. The difference may not be lost on potential criminals: research by John Worrall shows that larceny rates in California have been significantly lowered since passage of the three strikes law.[31]

Larceny/theft is probably the most common criminal offense. According to the FBI, about 6 million larcenies are reported to the police annually, a rate of about 2,100 per 100,000 population.[32] Despite the rather large number of annual larcenies, their number and rate have declined by more than 9 percent during the past decade, and the most recent data indicate that the downward trend seems to be continuing. The average value of property taken during larceny/thefts is now about $864 per offense. When the average value is applied to the estimated number of larceny/thefts, the loss to victims nationally was about $5.5 billion. Thefts of motor vehicle parts, accessories, and contents make up the largest portion of reported larcenies—36 percent.

Types of Larceny

There are many different varieties of larceny. Most involve small items of little value. Many of these go unreported, however, especially if the victims were business owners who do not want to take the time to get involved with police. They simply write off the losses as part of doing business. Hotel owners estimate that guests filch $100 million a year in towels, bathrobes, ashtrays, bedspreads, shower heads, flatware, and even television sets and wall paintings.[33]

Other larcenies involve complex criminal conspiracies, and no one, not even the U.S. government, is immune. Thieves steal millions of dollars worth of government equipment and supplies each year. In one incident, the Department of Energy reported more than $20 million in property missing from its site in Rocky Flats, Colorado, including semi-trailers, forklifts, cameras, desks, radios, and more than 1,800 pieces of computer equipment.[34] The Profiles in Crime feature focuses on the so-called "body snatchers case," a very unusual, albeit horrific, case of larceny.

© Seth Wenig/Landov

In November 2004, New York police investigated the Daniel George and Son Funeral Home in Brooklyn to check out what they considered to be a routine business dispute. But when they began looking around, they found a sealed room outfitted like an operating room, with a surgical table and overhead lights. They also found FedEx receipts made out to companies that purchase human tissue from cadavers for use in surgical procedures. The department's Major Case Squad was called in and they discovered that a former Manhattan dentist named Michael Mastromarino (pictured) and three other men were running a multimillion-dollar body-snatching business that had looted bones and tissue from more than a thousand corpses. The men then sold the body parts to legitimate companies that supplied hospitals around the United States. Hundreds of people in states as far away as Florida, Nebraska, and Texas received tissue and bone carved from looted corpses, including the cadaver of Alistair Cooke, the late host of PBS's *Masterpiece Theatre*. The tissue was used in such procedures as joint and heart-valve replacements, back surgery, dental implants, and skin grafts. Many of the recipients rushed to doctors to be tested for tainted tissue, and some filed civil lawsuits. (One New Jersey lawyer alone signed up some 200 clients.) Mastromarino was charged with opening graves, body stealing, forgery, grand larceny, and racketeering.

Mastromarino had surrendered his dental license in 2000 because he was addicted to the painkiller Demerol. He started a career as a body harvester, opening Biomedical Tissue Services, an FDA-registered company that appeared completely legitimate. However, he got many of the corpses from Joseph Nicelli, who had been hired by funeral directors in New York, New Jersey, and Philadelphia to embalm bodies in his Brooklyn facility. A single harvested body yielded $7,000 in parts. After Nicelli sold the funeral home, he allegedly continued to help Mastromarino sneak into the secret operating room at night to dissect corpses. To hide their crimes, Mastromarino replaced looted bones with plumbing pipes, and stuffed their surgical gloves and gowns into the bodies before stitching them back together. After robbing the bodies, the men allegedly forged death certificates to hide that the tissue had often been stolen from bodies that would have been rejected as donors, being too old or sick. Some of the recipients were subsequently tested for diseases, including hepatitis. While the Food and Drug Administration claims that the risk of serious infection is fairly remote, an agency advisory also mentions that the "actual infectious risk is unknown." A 41-year-old woman who underwent back surgery on Long Island and two patients in New Jersey say they contracted syphilis from stolen bone tissue.

The body snatchers case illustrates the wide variety of schemes that can involve taking the possessions of another. In this case, the possessions were bodily organs and the victims were dead!

SOURCES: Michael Powell and David Segal, "In New York, a Grisly Traffic in Body Parts, Illegal Sales Worry Dead's Kin, Tissue Recipients," *Washington Post*, January 18, 2006, p. A03; William Sherman, "Clients Flee Biz Eyed in Ghoul Probe," *New York Daily News*, October 13, 2005.

Shoplifting

On January 24, 2008, law enforcement officers in Polk County, Florida, announced the arrest of 18 people in connection with a major shoplifting ring. Initial estimates were that the ring had stolen up to $100 million over the past five years! When detectives raided their homes, they found thousands of cosmetics and over-the-counter drugs that the ring had planned to sell at local flea markets or over the Internet. Police found out that the group had worked in pairs and typically cleared about $4,000 in three minutes. They used bags and purses with hidden compartments to conceal the stolen goods. They worked with maps and detailed plans so that they could avoid hitting any one store too often.[35]

While organized theft rings that average $20 million per year are not the norm, **shoplifting** is a very common form of larceny/theft involving the taking of goods from retail stores. Usually shoplifters try to snatch items—jewelry, clothes, records, or appliances—when store personnel are otherwise occupied, hiding the goods on their person. The "five-finger discount" is an extremely common form of crime. Hayes International, a loss prevention/shrinkage control consulting business, does an annual survey of 22 major retailers around the United States and found that these retailers apprehended more than 800,000 shoplifters and recovered more than $100 million in a single year (2008). And these startling data represent a very small percentage of total shoplifting losses, considering that only 22 retail chains were surveyed. Hayes estimates that the total national loss from shoplifting is $37 billion.

Shoplifting is certainly not unique to the United States. In England, about 5 percent of the population is convicted of shoplifting by age 40. Surveys of retailers in the United Kingdom suggest that there are more than 4 million known shoplifting incidents, 1.3 million apprehended shoplifters, and 800,000 shoplifters reported to the police each year. One reason for the popularity of shoplifting may be lax treatment. Although about one in seven apprehended offenders is eventually convicted in court, fewer than one in twenty shoplifting attempts results in apprehension.[36]

Retail security measures add to the already high cost of this crime, all of which is passed on to the consumer. Some studies estimate that about one in every nine shoppers steals from department stores. Moreover, the increasingly popular discount stores, such as Costco, Wal-Mart, and Target, have a minimum of sales help and depend on highly visible merchandise displays to attract purchasers, all of which makes them particularly vulnerable to shoplifters.

Shoplifters: Amateurs and Professionals

In the early 1960s, Mary Owen Cameron conducted a classic study of shoplifting.[37] In her pioneering effort, Cameron found that the majority of shoplifters are amateur pilferers, called **snitches** in thieves' argot. Snitches are usually respectable people who do not conceive of themselves as thieves but are systematic shoplifters who steal merchandise for their own use. Some snitches are simply overcome by an uncontrollable urge to snatch something that attracts them, while others arrive at the store intending to steal. Some adolescents become shoplifters because they have been coerced by older kids into becoming "proxy shoplifters," forced to steal goods with the understanding that if caught their youth will protect them from prosecution.[38]

When caught, they may try to rationalize or neutralize their behavior. When Paul Cromwell and Quint Thurman interviewed 137 apprehended shoplifters, they found widespread use of techniques of neutralizations—statements such as, "I don't know what comes over me. It's like, you know, it's somebody else doing it, not me" (denial of responsibility) or "I like to get nice stuff for my kids, you know. I know it's not O.K., you know what I mean? But I want my kids to dress nice and stuff" (appeal to higher loyalties).[39]

If they are not professionals and want to deny their culpability, why do they steal? Some are impulsive sensation seekers who are driven to shoplift by their psychological need to live on the edge.[40] Others are motivated by rational choice and the desire to get something for nothing. Still another motivation for shoplifting seems to be psychological distress; some amateur shoplifters are looking for a release from anxiety and depression.[41]

Regardless of their motives, snitches are likely to reform if caught because they are not part of a criminal subculture and do not think of themselves as criminals. Cameron reasoned that they are deterred by an initial contact with the law. Getting arrested has a traumatic effect on them, and they will not risk a second offense.

Professional Shoplifters

In her pioneering effort, Cameron found that about 10 percent of all shoplifters were professionals, like the Polk County ring, who derived the majority of their income from shoplifting. Called boosters, or heels, professional shoplifters steal with the intention of reselling stolen merchandise to pawnshops or fences, usually at half the original price.

These professionals can walk into a department store, fill up a cart with expensive medicines, DVDs, iPods, baby formula, and other high-cost items, and use deceptive techniques to slip past security guards.[42] Hitting several stores in a day and the same store once a month, a professional thief can make between $100,000 and $200,000 a year. Some enter a store carrying a "shopping list" provided by a fence who will pay them in cash or drugs. The fence will later sell the merchandise in his or her own discount stores, at flea markets, or through online auctions. Some sell to higher-level fences who repackage—or "scrub"—the goods and pawn them off on retailers at prices that undercut legitimate distributors. Ironically, some stolen merchandise can actually make its way back onto the shelves of the chain store from which it was stolen.[43]

Controlling Shoplifting

One major problem associated with combating shoplifting is that many customers who observe pilferage are reluctant to report it to security agents. Store employees themselves are often loathe to get involved in apprehending a shoplifter. It is also likely that a store owner's decision to prosecute shoplifters will be based on the value of the goods stolen, the nature of the goods stolen, and the manner in which the theft was realized. Shoplifters who planned their crime by using a concealed apparatus, such as a bag pinned to the inside of their clothing, are more apt to be prosecuted than those who impulsively put merchandise into their pockets.[44] The concealment indicates that the crime was premeditated and not a spur of the moment loss of control.

To encourage the arrest of shoplifters, a number of states have passed *merchant privilege laws* designed to protect retailers and their employers from litigation stemming from improper or false arrests of suspected shoplifters. These laws protect but do not immunize merchants from lawsuits. They typically require that arrests be made on reasonable grounds or probable cause, detention be of short duration, and store employees or security guards conduct themselves in a reasonable fashion.

Prevention Strategies

Retail stores initiate a number of strategies designed to reduce or eliminate shoplifting. **Target removal strategies** involve putting dummy or disabled goods on display while the real merchandise is kept under lock and key. Audio equipment with missing parts is displayed, and only after items are purchased are the necessary components installed. Some stores sell from a catalogue while keeping merchandise in stockrooms.

Target hardening strategies involve locking goods in place or having them monitored by electronic systems. Clothing stores may use racks designed to prevent large quantities of garments from being slipped off easily. Store owners may rely on electronic article surveillance (EAS) systems, featuring tags with small electronic sensors that trip sound and light alarms if not removed by employees before the item leaves the store. Security systems now feature source tagging, a process by which manufacturers embed the tag in the packaging or in the product itself. Thieves are hard-pressed to remove or defeat such tags, and retailers save on the time and labor needed to attach the tags at their stores.[45] Situational measures place the most valuable goods in the least vulnerable places, use warning signs to deter potential thieves, and use closed-circuit cameras.

Another approach to shoplifting prevention is to create specialized programs that use methods such as doing community service, paying monetary restitution, writing essays, watching anti-shoplifting videos, writing apology letters, and being placed in individual and/or family counseling. Evaluations indicate that such programs can be successful in reducing recidivism of young shoplifters.[46]

Overzealous Enforcement   These methods may control shoplifting, but stores must be wary of becoming overzealous in their enforcement policies. Those falsely accused have won significant judgments in civil actions.[47] In one case, a woman accused of shoplifting at a J. C. Penney store in Media, Pennsylvania, was awarded $250,000, charging them with false confinement and malicious prosecution after she was mistakenly taken for a shoplifter.[48] Stores may be liable if security guards use excessive force when subduing a suspected shoplifter. There is also the danger of profiling based on gender, age, or racial and ethnic background, resulting in customers being targeted, detained, and searched for inappropriate reasons.[49] And of course, searching and detaining customers based on stereotyping is legally indefensible: in 2009, eight African American plaintiffs sued the Dillard's department store chain, claiming that employees and security workers questioned them while they were shopping in the stores and accused them of stealing merchandise, solely based on their race. In a separate case, Dillard's was ordered to pay a $1.2 million verdict to an African American woman who was detained on suspicion of shoplifting in a store in Overland Park, Kansas.[50]

Bad Checks

Another form of larceny is cashing bad bank checks, knowingly and intentionally drawn on a nonexistent or underfunded bank account, to obtain money or property. In general, for a person to be guilty of passing a bad check, the bank the check is drawn on must refuse payment, and the check casher must fail to make the check good within 10 days after finding out the check was not honored.

Edwin Lemert conducted the best-known study of check forgers more than 40 years ago.[51] Lemert found that the majority of check forgers—he calls them **naive check forgers**—are amateurs who do not believe their actions will hurt anyone. Most naive check forgers come from middle-class backgrounds and have little identification with a criminal subculture. They cash bad checks because of a financial crisis that demands an immediate resolution—perhaps they have lost money at the horse track and have some pressing bills to pay. Lemert refers to this condition as **closure**. Naive check forgers are often socially isolated people who have been unsuccessful in their personal relationships. They are risk prone when faced with a situation that is unusually stressful for them. The willingness of stores and other commercial establishments to cash checks with a minimum of fuss to promote business encourages the check forger to risk committing a criminal act.

Not all check forgers are amateurs. Lemert found that a few professionals—whom he calls **systematic forgers**—make a substantial living by passing bad checks. However, professionals constitute a relatively small segment of the total population of check forgers. It is difficult to estimate the number of such forgeries committed each year or the amounts involved. Stores and banks may choose not to press charges because the effort to collect the money due them is often not worth their while. It is also difficult to separate the true check forger from the neglectful shopper.

Some of the different techniques used in check fraud schemes, which may cost retail establishment upwards of $1 billion per year, are set out in Exhibit 11.2.

Credit Card Theft

In 2008, federal authorities uncovered the largest credit card scam in history. Eleven people, including three from Estonia, three from the Ukraine, two from China, and one from Belarus, stole 40 million credit and debit card numbers from companies such as Marshall's, T.J. Maxx, BJ's Wholesale Club, OfficeMax and Barnes and Noble by hacking into their computer systems and installing "sniffer" programs designed to capture credit card numbers, passwords, and account information as they moved through the retailers' card processing networks. The thieves then concealed the data in encrypted computer servers they controlled in the United States and eastern Europe. Some of the credit and debit card numbers were "cashed out" by encoding the numbers on the magnetic stripes of blank cards and using these cards to withdraw tens of thousands of dollars at a time from automatic teller machines (ATM).[52] This type of international credit card theft is not unique. A card stolen in Amsterdam can be used to make bogus online purchases in Prague within hours. Largely run by former Soviet Union residents, these international cartels cost the financial system billions each year.[53]

EXHIBIT 12.2

Check Fraud Schemes and Techniques

- *Forged signatures.* Legitimate blank checks with an imitation of the payor's signature.
- *Forged endorsements.* The use of a stolen check, which is then endorsed and cashed or deposited by someone other than the payee.
- *Identity assumption.* Identity assumption occurs when criminals learn information about a financial institution customer, such as name, address, financial institution account number, Social Security number, home and work telephone numbers, or employer, and use the information to misrepresent themselves as the valid financial institution customer.
- *Counterfeit checks.* Counterfeit checks are presented based on fraudulent identification or are false checks drawn on valid accounts. Due to the advancement in color copying and desktop publishing capabilities, this is the fastest-growing source of fraudulent checks today.
- *Altered checks.* After a legitimate maker creates a valid check to pay a debt, a criminal then takes the good check and uses chemicals or other means to erase the amount or the name of the payee, so that new information can be entered. The new information can be added by typewriter, in handwriting, or with a laser printer or check imprinter.
- *Closed account fraud.* This is based on checks being written against closed accounts. This type of fraud generally relies upon the float time involved in interfinancial institution transactions.
- *Check kiting.* The process of depositing a check from one bank account into a second bank account without sufficient funds to cover it.

SOURCES: Check Fraud Working Group, "Check Fraud, A Guide to Avoiding Losses," Washington, D.C., http://all.net/books/audit/Check-Fraud/contents.htm (accessed November 3, 2010); National Check Fraud Center, Charleston, SC, 2009, www.ckfraud.org (accessed November 3, 2010).

The use of stolen credit cards is a major problem in U.S. society. It has been estimated that fraud has been responsible for a billion-dollar loss in the credit card industry. Most credit card abuse is the work of amateurs who acquire stolen cards through theft or mugging and then use them for two or three days. However, professional credit card rings may be getting into the act. They collect or buy from employees the names and credit card numbers of customers in retail establishments; then they buy plain plastic cards and have the customers' numbers embossed on them. They create fictitious wholesale companies and apply for and receive authorization to accept credit cards from the customers. They then use the phony cards to charge nonexistent purchases on the accounts of the people whose names and card numbers they collected. One approach is to first obtain the victim's address and card number from a confederate (e.g., a store employee where the victim shops). They may then call the victim, claiming to be from the credit card company, and informing them that their account has been flagged because of suspicious activity. After offering credentials such as a bogus badge ID number, the thief tells them that someone has used the card to purchase a $1,500 television from a local store. When the consumer denies making the purchase, the scammer explains that he is starting a fraud investigation, gives the consumer a "confirmation" number, and asks them for the three-digit security number on the back of the card. The security code allows the thief to make purchases over the Internet or from local merchants.[54]

To combat losses from credit card theft, Congress passed a law in 1971 limiting a person's liability to $50 per stolen card. Some states, such as California, have passed specific statutes making it a misdemeanor to obtain property or services by means of cards that have been stolen, forged, canceled, or revoked, or whose use is for any reason unauthorized.[55]

CONNECTIONS

Similar frauds are conducted over the Internet. These will be discussed in Chapter 15.

The problem of credit card misuse is being compounded by thieves who set up bogus Internet sites strictly to trick people into giving them their credit card numbers, which they then use for their own gain. The Profiles in Crime feature discusses one such Internet credit card scheme.[56] The problem is growing so rapidly that a number of new technologies are aimed at combating credit card number theft over the Internet. One method is to incorporate digital signatures into computer operating systems, which can be accessed with a digital key that comes with each computer. Owners of new systems can present three forms of identification to a notary public and trade a notarized copy of their key for a program that will sign files. The basis of the digital signature is a digital certificate, a small block of data that contains a person's "public key." This certificate is signed, in turn, by a certificate authority. This digital certificate will act like a credit card with a hologram and a photograph and identify the user to the distant website and vice versa.[57]

Auto Theft

Motor vehicle theft is another common larceny offense. Because of its frequency and seriousness, it is treated as a separate category in the Uniform Crime Report (UCR). The FBI now records about 800,000 yearly auto thefts, accounting for a total loss of $7 billion. Like other crimes, there has been a significant reduction in motor vehicle theft rates over the past decade, and the number of car thefts has declined more than 25 percent. UCR projections on auto theft are similar to the projections of the National Crime Victim Survey (NCVS), probably because almost every state requires owners to insure their vehicles, and auto theft is one of the most highly reported of all major crimes (75 percent of all auto thefts are reported to police).

Which Cars Are Taken Most? According to the Highway Loss Data Institute, the rate at which people file insurance claims for theft is highest for models of the 2007–2009 Cadillac Escalade, a luxury SUV, followed by the Ford F-250 crew pickup, Infiniti G37 luxury car, and Dodge Charger with a HEMI engine. Theft rates for these vehicles are three to five times as high as the average for all vehicles.[58] For example, as Table 12.1 indicates, while the overall loss per vehicle on the road is about $14 per year, for Cadillac Escalades it's around $128.

Why these models? Many cars are stolen and then stripped for parts. Thieves target vehicles that can bring them the greatest return in the used-part market.

Amateur Auto Thieves Amateur thieves steal cars for a number of reasons that involve some form of temporary

TABLE 12.1 Stolen Vehicles with Highest Losses

Vehicle	Vehicle size/type	Average loss payment per claim	Overall theft losses per vehicle on the road
Cadillac Escalade	Large/very large luxury SUV	$11,934	$128
Ford F-250 crew 4WD	Very large pickup	$ 9,636	$ 91
Infiniti G37 2-door	Midsize luxury car	$10,324	$ 71
Dodge Charger HEMI	Large family car	$10,118	$ 69
Chevrolet Corvette Z06	Midsize sports car	$41,229	$ 68
Hummer H2 4WD	Very large SUV	$10,324	$ 62
Nissan Pathfinder Armada	Large SUV	$12,458	$ 54
Chevrolet Avalanche 1500	Very large SUV	$ 7,571	$ 54
Chevrolet Silverado 1500 crew	Large pickup	$ 6,814	$ 53
GMC Yukon	Large SUV	$ 9,499	$ 52

SOURCE: Highway Loss Data Institute, www.iihs.org/news/rss/pr080310.html (accessed December 28, 2010).

personal use.[59] Among the reasons why an amateur would steal a car include:

- *Joyriding.* Many car thefts are motivated by teenagers' desire to acquire the power, prestige, sexual potency, and recognition associated with an automobile. Joyriders steal cars not for profit or gain but to experience, even briefly, the benefits associated with owning an automobile.
- *Short-term transportation.* Auto theft for short-term transportation is similar to joyriding. It involves the theft of a car simply to go from one place to another. In more serious cases, the thief may drive to another city or state and then steal another car to continue the journey.
- *Long-term transportation.* Thieves who steal cars for long-term transportation intend to keep the cars for their personal use. Usually older than joyriders and from a lower-class background, these auto thieves may repaint and otherwise disguise cars to avoid detection.
- *Profit.* Auto theft for profit is motivated by the hope of monetary gain. Some amateurs hope to sell the entire car, but most are auto strippers who steal batteries, tires, and wheel covers to sell or to reequip their own cars.
- *Commission of another crime.* A few auto thieves steal cars to use in other crimes, such as robberies and thefts. This type of auto thief desires both mobility and anonymity.

Professional Car Thieves   At one time, most auto theft was the work of amateurs, and most cars were taken by relatively affluent, middle-class teenagers looking for excitement.[60] There appears to be a change in this pattern: fewer cars are being taken today, and fewer stolen cars are being recovered. Part of the reason is that there has been an increase in highly organized professionals who resell expensive cars after altering their identification numbers and falsifying their registration papers. Exporting stolen vehicles has become a global problem, and the emergence of capitalism in eastern Europe has increased the demand for U.S-made cars.[61]

Many cars are now stolen in order to be sold to chop shops for spare parts. Among the most attractive targets are these parts:

- *Global positioning system.* It now costs approximately $1,500 to replace one on a Toyota Camry. The whole unit for a Honda Accord can cost up to $650, navigation included.
- *Air conditioning.* Today, the air conditioning compressor for a Toyota Camry costs up to $1,000. The Chevy Malibu's A/C compressor would net thieves more than $400. Filters and condensers for air conditioning units cost more than $200 each.
- *Air bags.* These life savers do well in the auto-part seller's market. Air bags for a Honda Civic fetch about $900 apiece.

- *Exhaust.* The exhaust system carries emissions from the engine to the atmosphere. According to 2010 data, an overall exhaust system—including catalytic converter in some vehicles—can cost between $500 and $1,000.[62]

Car Cloning   One new form of professional auto theft is called "cloning." After stealing a luxury car from a mall or parking lot, car thieves later visit a large car dealership in another state and look for a car that's the exact make and model (and even the same color) of the stolen one. The thieves jot down the vehicle identification number (VIN) stamped on the top of the dashboard and drive off. The manufacturer-installed VIN plate on the stolen car is removed and replaced with a homemade counterfeit, similar to the original, only this one bears the VIN of the legitimate vehicle. Phony ownership and registration documents complete the cloning. At that point, the stolen vehicle can be easily registered with a motor vehicle agency in another state and sold to an unwary buyer. In one Tampa, Florida, case, more than 1,000 cloned cars were sold to buyers in 20 states and several countries, with estimated losses of more than $25 million to consumers, auto insurers, and other victims.

Carjacking   You may have read about gunmen approaching a car and forcing the owner to give up the keys; in some cases, people have been killed when they reacted too slowly. This type of auto theft has become so common that it has its own name, **carjacking**.[63] Carjacking is legally considered a type of robbery because it involves force to steal.[64]

Both victims and offenders in carjackings tend to be young men. Urban residents are more likely to experience carjacking than suburban or rural residents. About half of all carjackings are typically committed by gangs or groups. These crimes are most likely to occur in the evening, in the central city, in an open area, or in a parking garage. This pattern may reflect the fact that carjacking seems to be a crime of opportunity; it is the culmination of the carjacker's personal needs and desires coinciding with the immediate opportunity for gain. This decision is also shaped by the carjacker's participation in urban street culture.[65]

Weapons, most often guns, were used in about three-quarters of all carjacking victimizations.[66] Despite the presence of weapons, victims resisted the offender in two-thirds of carjackings, and, not surprisingly, about one-third of victims of completed carjackings and about 17 percent of victims of attempted carjackings were injured. Serious injuries, such as gunshot or knife wounds, broken bones, or internal injuries, occurred in about 9 percent of carjackings. More minor injuries, such as bruises and chipped teeth, occurred in about 15 percent of cases.

Combating Auto Theft   Auto theft is a significant target of situational crime prevention efforts. One approach to theft deterrence has been to increase the risks of apprehension. Hotlines offer rewards for information leading to the arrest of car thieves. A Michigan-based program, Operation HEAT

Professional car thieves often prefer older popular models whose parts can easily be sold. They usually turn the cars they steal over to "chop shops," which dismantle them and sell the parts. Some take more expensive luxury cars for export to other countries.

A study by the Highway Loss Data Institute (HLDI) found that most car theft prevention methods, especially alarms, have little effect on theft rates. The most effective methods appear to be devices that immobilize a vehicle by cutting off the electrical power needed to start the engine when a theft is detected.[69] However, car thieves with modest resources—just a few hundred dollars in off-the-shelf equipment—and some computer knowledge can crack the codes of millions of car keys and suborn these security systems.[70]

False Pretenses or Fraud

The crime of **false pretenses**, or **fraud**, involves misrepresenting a fact in a way that causes a victim to willingly give his or her property to the wrongdoer, who then keeps it.[71] In 1757, the English Parliament defined false pretenses to cover an area of law left untouched by larceny statutes. The first false pretenses law punished people who "knowingly and designedly by false pretense or pretenses, [obtained] from any person or persons, money, goods, wares or merchandise with intent to cheat or defraud any person or persons of the same."[72]

False pretense differs from traditional larceny because the victims willingly give their possessions to the offender, and the crime does not, as does larceny, involve a "trespass in the taking." An example of false pretenses would be an unscrupulous merchant selling someone a chair by claiming it was an antique, but knowing all the while that it was a cheap copy. Another example would be a phony healer selling a victim a bottle of colored sugar water as an elixir that would cure a disease.

Swindlers have little shame when defrauding people out of their money; they often target the elderly, sick, and infirm. In the aftermath of Hurricane Katrina, in 2005, swindlers used the tragedy to solicit relief funds from charitable and well-meaning victims and then convert the money for their own usage.[73] Today, about 210,000 people are arrested for fraud schemes each year, though that is probably only the tip of the iceberg.[74]

(Help Eliminate Auto Theft), is credited with recovering more than 900 vehicles, worth $11 million, and resulting in the arrest of 647 people. Another approach has been to place fluorescent decals on windows that indicate that the car is never used between 1 A.M. and 5 A.M.; if police spot a car with the decal being operated during this period, they know it is stolen.[67]

The LoJack system involves installing a hidden tracking device in cars that gives off a signal, enabling the police to pinpoint its location. Research evaluating the effectiveness of this device finds that it has a significant crime reduction capability.[68] Because car thieves cannot tell that LoJack has been installed, it does not reduce the likelihood that a protected car will be stolen. However, cars installed with Lo-Jack have a much higher recovery rate. There may also be a general deterrent effect: areas with high rates of LoJack use experience significant reductions in their auto theft rates. Ironically, LoJack owners actually accrue a smaller than anticipated reward for their foresight than the general public because they have to pay for installation and maintenance of the device. Those without it actually gain more because they benefit from a lower auto theft rate in their community without paying any additional cost.

Other prevention efforts involve making it more difficult to steal cars. Publicity campaigns have been directed at encouraging people to lock their cars. Parking lots have been equipped with theft-deterring closed-circuit TV cameras and barriers. Manufacturers have installed more sophisticated steering column locking devices and other security systems that make theft more difficult.

Confidence Games

Some fraudulent schemes involve getting a **mark** (target) interested in some get-rich-quick scheme, which may have illegal overtones; this is known as a **confidence game** or con game. The criminal's hope is that when victims lose their money, they will be either too embarrassed or too afraid to call the police. There are hundreds of varieties of con games, but the most common is called the **pigeon drop**.[75] Here, a package or shopping bag containing money is "found" by a con man or woman. A passing victim is stopped and asked for advice about what to do, since there is no identification. Another "stranger," who is part of the con, approaches and enters the discussion. The three decide to split the money, but first, to make sure everything is legal, one of the swindlers goes off to consult a lawyer. Upon returning, he or she says that the lawyer claims the money can be split up; first, however, each party must prove he or she is financially stable or has the means to reimburse the original owner, should one show up. The victim then is asked to give some good-faith money for the lawyer to hold. Later, when the victim goes to the lawyer's office to pick up a share of the loot, he or she finds the address bogus and the money gone.

Other cons include:

- A self-proclaimed "contractor" offers an unusually low price for an expensive job such as driveway repair and then uses old motor oil rather than asphalt to make the "repairs." The first rain brings disaster. Some cons offer a free home inspection that turns up several expensive repairs. They then offer a cheap rate to fix the problem, but of course the repairs are actually bogus.
- A business office receives a mailing that looks like an invoice with a self-addressed envelope that makes it look like it comes from the phone company (walking fingers on a yellow background). It appears to be a contract for an ad in the Yellow Pages. On the back, in small print, will be written, "By returning this confirmation, you're signing a contract to be an advertiser in the upcoming, and all subsequent, issues." If the invoice is returned, the business soon finds that it has agreed to a long-term contract to advertise in some private publication that is not widely distributed.
- Con artists read the obituary column and then send a surviving spouse bills supposedly owed by the person deceased. Or they deliver an item, such as a Bible, that they say the deceased relative ordered just before he died.
- A con artist, posing as a bank employee, stops a customer as he or she is about to enter the bank. The con man claims to be an investigator who is trying to catch a dishonest teller. He asks the customer to withdraw cash to see if he or she gets the right amount. After the cash is withdrawn, the conman asks that it be turned over to him so he can check the serial numbers and promises to return the cash in a few minutes, gives the customer a receipt, and escapes through a back exit.
- An old musician carrying his violin enters a restaurant and orders an expensive meal. When asked to pay he claims that he left his wallet at home. He begs the owner to be allowed to retrieve his money and leaves his violin as collateral. While he's gone, another man presents himself to the owner as a rare instrument dealer—he has a personal business card. He wants to have a look at the violin he saw in passing, and as soon as it's produced, he claims it is a valuable antique, perhaps a Stradivarius worth hundreds of thousands of dollars! He asks the owner to give the old violinist his business card as soon as he returns. The old violinist returns and the business owner offers him a thousand dollars for his violin. While the old man seems clueless, he asks for more and they settle on a price of $5,000. He walks out with the money, and when the owner calls the number on the card, ready to resell, he finds out it's a false number. The old man and the "dealer" meet up later, split the cash, and buy another $50 violin. Hence the expression "fiddling around."

Third-Party Fraud

In some instances of false pretenses, the "victim" is a third party, such as an insurance company forced to pay for false claims or the people who have to pay higher claims because of the swindle. Cheating on an entrance exam may be considered third-party fraud because the victims are people who took the test honestly and received lower grades. One example of an innovative third-party cheating scheme was instituted by a man named Po Chieng Ma, who conspired to sell answers to the Graduate Management Administration Test (GMAT), the Graduate Record Examinations (GRE), and the Test of English as a Foreign Language (TOEFL) to an estimated 788 customers, each of whom had paid him between $2,000 and $9,000. In the scheme, people were paid to take the multiple-choice tests in Manhattan and then call California, where the same tests were to be given, with the answers. The answers were passed on to Ma, who, taking advantage of the three-hour time difference, carved the answers in code on the sides of pencils, which were then given to his customers. Ma pleaded guilty to conspiracy and obstruction of justice and received a four-year prison term for his efforts. In this case, there were many victims, including the testing service, universities, and the students who lost places in school because those who inflated their scores through the scheme were admitted instead.[76]

Auto Accident Fraud

Another common scheme involves fake auto accidents, including the ones described below:

- *The "swoop and squat."* A driver is stuck in heavy traffic on a busy highway. A confederate cuts off the driver in front, forcing him or her to slam on the brakes, resulting in a rear-end collision. After the "accident," everyone in the damaged car files bogus injury claims with the driver's insurance company. They may even go to crooked physical therapists, chiropractors, lawyers, or auto repair technicians to further exaggerate their claims.
- *The drive down.* A driver is attempting to merge into a traffic lane. Suddenly, another driver waves her forward, indicating he will allow her to merge. Instead of letting her in, he slams into the car, causing an accident. When the police arrive, the "injured" driver denies ever

motioning, claims serious injury, and files an insurance claim with the victim's company.

- *The sideswipe.* As a driver rounds a corner at a busy intersection with multiple turn lanes, the driver drifts slightly into the next lane. The car in that lane, waiting for such an opportunity, steps on the gas and sideswipes the driver, producing an accident.
- *The t-bone.* A driver is crossing an intersection when a car coming from a side street accelerates and hits the car. When the police arrive, the driver and several planted "witnesses" claim that the driver ran a red light or stop sign.[77]

How common are such fraudulent schemes? Staged accidents cost the insurance industry about $20 billion a year, increasing insurance rates on the average motorist between $100 and $300 extra per car per year.[78]

Embezzlement

On December 14, 2006, Linda Wade Dunn, of Coosada, Alabama, was sentenced to 41 months imprisonment for stealing from her employer, Therapeutic Programs, Inc. (TPI), which provided services to foster children in therapeutic care. From June 1999 through February 2004, Dunn misappropriated approximately $3 million from TPI. How did her scheme work? Dunn, the company bookkeeper, wrote checks on the TPI account and made them payable to herself and to a corporation she controlled. She concealed the theft by altering entries in TPI's records to make it appear that the payees of the checks were legitimate. To cover up her crimes, she intercepted TPI's bank statements, which contained the cancelled checks that would have implicated her in the crime.[79]

Dunn's actions constituted **embezzlement**, a crime that occurs when someone who is trusted with property fraudulently converts it—that is, keeps it for his or her own use or the use of others. It can be distinguished from fraud on the basis of when the criminal intent was formed. Most U.S. courts require that a serious breach of trust must have occurred before a person can be convicted of embezzlement. The mere act of moving property without the owner's consent, or damaging it or using it, is not considered embezzlement. However, using it up, selling it, pledging it, giving it away, or holding it against the owner's will is considered to be embezzlement.

Embezzlement is not a recent crime. It was mentioned in early Greek culture when, in his writings, Aristotle alluded to theft by road commissioners and other government officials.[80] It was first codified in law by the English Parliament during the sixteenth century to fill a gap in the larceny law.[81] Until then, to be guilty of theft, a person had to take goods from the physical possession of another (trespass in the taking). However, as explained earlier, this definition did not cover instances in which one person trusted another and willfully gave that person temporary custody of his or her property. Store clerks, bank tellers, brokers, and merchants gain lawful possession but not legal ownership of other people's money.

Although it is impossible to know how many embezzlement incidents occur annually, the FBI found that about 20,000 people were arrested for embezzlement in probably an extremely small percentage of all embezzlers. However, the number of people arrested for embezzlement has increased more than 40 percent during the past 25 years, indicating that (a) more employees are willing to steal from their employers, (b) more employers are willing to report instances of embezzlement, or (c) law enforcement officials are more willing to prosecute embezzlers. There has also been a rash of embezzlement-type crimes around the world, especially in third world countries where poverty is all too common and the economy is poor and supported by foreign aid and loans. Government officials and businessmen who have their hands on this money are tempted to convert it for their own use—a scenario that is sure to increase the likelihood of embezzlement.[82]

Want to avoid **credit card theft**? The Federal Trade Commission has some important tips; visit the Criminal Justice CourseMate at cengagebrain.com, then access the "Web Links" for this chapter.

BURGLARY

In common law, the crime of burglary is defined as "the breaking and entering of a dwelling house of another in the nighttime with the intent to commit a felony within."[83] Burglary is considered a much more serious crime than larceny/theft because it often involves entering another's home, a situation in which the threat of harm to occupants is great. Even though the home may be unoccupied at the time of the burglary, the potential for harm to the occupants is so significant that most state jurisdictions punish burglary as a felony.

The legal definition of burglary has undergone considerable change since its common-law origins. When first created by English judges during the late Middle Ages, laws against burglary were designed to protect people whose homes might be set upon by wandering criminals. Including the phrase "breaking and entering" in the definition protected people from unwarranted intrusions; if an invited guest stole something, it would not be considered a burglary. Similarly, the requirement that the crime be committed at nighttime was added because evening was considered the time when honest people might fall prey to criminals.[84]

In more recent times, state jurisdictions have changed the legal requirements of burglary, and most have discarded the necessity of forced entry. Many now protect all structures, not just dwelling houses. A majority of states have removed the nighttime element from burglary definitions as well. It is common for states to enact laws creating different degrees of burglary. In this instance, the more serious and heavily punished crimes involve a nighttime forced entry into the home; the least serious involve a daytime entry into a nonresidential structure by an unarmed offender. Several gradations of the offense may be found between these extremes.

The Nature and Extent of Burglary

The FBI's definition of burglary is not restricted to burglary from a person's home; it includes any unlawful entry of a structure to commit theft or felony. Burglary is further categorized into three subclasses: forcible entry, unlawful entry where no force is used, and attempted forcible entry. According to the UCR, about 2 million burglaries occur annually, a decline of about 15 percent from 1996.

Most burglars are amateur occasional thieves rather than professional criminals. Here, Diana Palin, the half-sister of former Alaska Governor Sarah Palin's husband Todd, is shown after her arraignment in Palmer, Alaska, April 3, 2009. Palin was charged with two counts of felony burglary and misdemeanor counts of criminal trespass and theft in connection with break-ins at a home in Wasilla. Palin received a "suspended imposition of sentence." If she maintains a clean record, completes drug treatment, and otherwise complies with the court's orders, she won't have a felony record.

Most occur during daylight hours, in residential structures (about two-thirds), and result in a loss of more than $1,700 per burglary.

The NCVS reports that about 3 million residential burglaries are either attempted or completed annually. Despite this significant number, the NCVS indicates that the number and rate of burglaries has declined significantly during the past decade, down more than 20 percent.

According to the NCVS, those most likely to be burglarized are relatively poor Latino and African American families (annual income under $7,500). Rural owner-occupied and single-family residences have lower burglary rates than urban, renter-occupied, and multiple-family dwellings. Households in the northeast are less likely to experience burglary than households in other regions of the country.

Planning to Burgle

Some burglars are crude thieves who will smash a window and enter a home or structure with minimal preparation; others plan out a strategy. In urban areas and their immediate suburbs, experienced burglars learn to avoid areas of the city in which most residents are renters and not homeowners, reasoning that renters are less likely to be suitable targets than are more affluent homeowners.[85] However, this decision may be shaped by the time of day for which the burglary is planned: when they operate in daylight, experienced burglars minimize the risk of being spotted and apprehended by police by choosing targets in upscale neighborhoods that are set back from the street, provide better cover for their forced entry, and are less likely to be occupied. Homeowners in affluent neighborhoods have higher employment levels, so daylight burglaries are a safer and more lucrative bet. After dark, the patterns seem to change—burglars who operate at night may shift their targets to apartments and townhouses closer to home even though the risk of someone being home is greater.[86] Whether they operate alone or in groups, experienced burglars like to choose targets in neighborhoods they know so they can make their way home undetected if things go awry.[87]

Because it involves planning, risk, and skill, burglary has been a crime long associated with professional thieves who carefully learn their craft. Francis Hoheimer, an experienced professional burglar, has described how he learned the "craft of burglary" from a fellow inmate, Oklahoma Smith, when the two were serving time in the Illinois State Penitentiary. Among Smith's recommendations are these:

> Never wear deodorant or shaving lotion; the strange scent might wake someone up. The more people there are in a house, the safer you are. If someone hears you moving around, they will think it's someone else . . . If

they call, answer in a muffled sleepy voice . . . Never be afraid of dogs, they can sense fear. Most dogs are friendly, snap your finger, they come right to you.[88]

Despite his elaborate preparations, Hoheimer spent many years in confinement.

Burglars must master the skills of their "trade," learning to spot environmental cues nonprofessionals fail to notice.[89] They must learn which targets contain valuables worth stealing and which are most likely to prove to be a dry hole. Research shows that burglary rates for student-occupied apartments are actually much lower than rates for other residences in the same neighborhoods; burglars appear to have learned which apartments to avoid.[90]

Most burglars do not like to travel far from their residence, choosing neighborhoods with single-family homes close by.[91] However, experienced burglars are more willing to travel to find rich targets. They have access to transportation that enables them to select a wider variety of targets than younger, more inexperienced thieves.[92] They also seem to be sensitive to police anticrime efforts: when police are active and forceful, burglary rates decline. Experienced burglars may locate to safer areas or bide their time and wait for the police to reduce their anticrime initiatives as crime rates decline.[93] The Thinking Like a Criminologist feature explores the issue of burglary prevention.

In an important book titled *Burglars on the Job*, Richard Wright and Scott Decker describe the working conditions of active burglars.[94] Most are motivated by the need for cash in order to get high; they want to enjoy the good life, "keeping the party going" without having to work. As Exhibit 12.3 shows, they approach their "job" in a rational workmanlike fashion, but their lives are controlled by their culture and environment. Unskilled and uneducated, urban burglars make the choices they do because there are few conventional opportunities for success.

While most burglars are male, more than 30,000 women are arrested for burglary annually, about 15 percent of the total. What motivates female burglars, and how do they differ from males? These are the topics of the Race, Culture, Gender, and Criminology feature "Are There Gender Differences in Burglary?"

Commercial Burglary

Some burglars prefer to victimize commercial property rather than private homes. Of all business establishments, retail stores are burglars' favorite targets. They display merchandise so that burglars know exactly what to look for, where it can be found, and—because the prices are displayed—how much they can hope to gain in resale to a

---

THINKING LIKE A CRIMINOLOGIST 〉 An Ethical Dilemma

Rational Choice

You are a criminology professor at a local college who is approached by the local police chief, who is quite concerned about high burglary rates in some areas of the city. She is a former student of yours and well aware of recent developments in criminological theory. The chief is a strong advocate of rational choice theory and has already instituted a number of programs based on a deterrence/situational crime prevention model of control. The existing police initiatives include these programs:

© vm/iStockphoto

- The police offer target hardening measures to repeat victims. They install high-tech security equipment in homes so the homes can be monitored on a 24-hour basis. The police plan an advertising campaign to alert would-be offenders that they are on watch at prior target residences.
- A new police initiative identifies repeat burglars in the area and provides intervention designed to supply them with legitimate economic opportunities to reduce their criminal motivation.
- A new school-based program designed to reduce criminal motivation seeks to raise young people's awareness of the dangers of burglary and how it can result in a long prison sentence.

- The police have developed a series of environmental improvements in the target area with a view to minimizing burglary opportunities. These include improved visibility, better access control, and lighting in areas that have relatively high burglary rates. They have also instituted high-visibility police patrols in these areas to deter criminals from committing crimes there.
- A burglary control model house, fitted with low-cost methods of security such as strengthened door/window frames, bolts, locks, and so on, has been built and will be advertised to encourage residents to help themselves avoid burglary.

》 **The chief has asked you to look over these initiatives and write a memo discussing their effectiveness. She wants you to develop a policy plan discussing whether you think there are any possible ethical pitfalls with these initiatives. If you do find problems, she wants you to suggest other policy initiatives that might prove effective in reducing the opportunity to commit burglary and deter potential burglars.**

---

fence. Burglars can legitimately enter a retail store during business hours and gain knowledge about what the store contains and where it is stored; they can also check for security alarms and devices. Commercial burglars perceive retail establishments as quick sources of merchandise that can be easily sold.

Other commercial establishments such as service centers, warehouses, and factories are less attractive targets because it is more difficult to gain legitimate access to plan the theft. The burglar must use a great deal of guile to scope out these places, perhaps posing as a delivery person. In addition, the merchandise is more likely to be used, and it may be more difficult to fence at a premium price.

If burglars choose to attack factories, warehouses, or service centers, the most vulnerable properties are those located far from major thoroughfares and away from pedestrian traffic. Establishments located within three blocks of heavily traveled thoroughfares have been found to be less vulnerable to burglary than those located farther away; commercial establishments in wealthier communities have a higher probability of burglary.[95]

Though alarms have been found to be an effective deterrent to burglary, they are less effective in isolated areas because it takes police longer to respond than on more heavily patrolled thoroughfares, and an alarm is less likely to be heard by a pedestrian who would be able to call for help. Even in the most remote areas, however, burglars are wary of alarms and try to choose targets without elaborate or effective security systems. One study found that the probability of burglary of non-alarmed properties is 4.57 times higher than that of similar property with alarms.[96]

Careers in Burglary

Some criminals make burglary their career and continually develop new and specialized skills to aid their profession. Neal Shover has studied the careers of professional burglars and has uncovered the existence of a particularly successful type which he labels "the **good burglar**."[97] Professional burglars use this title to characterize colleagues who have distinguished themselves as burglars. Characteristics of the good burglar include:

- Technical competence
- Maintenance of personal integrity
- Specialization in burglary
- Financial success
- The ability to avoid prison sentences

To receive recognition as good burglars, Shover found that novices must develop four key requirements of the trade.

First, they must learn the many skills needed to commit lucrative burglaries. This process may include learning how to gain entry into homes and apartment houses; how to select targets with high potential payoffs; how to choose items with a high resale value; how to open safes properly, without damaging their contents; and how to use the proper equipment, including cutting torches, electric saws, explosives, and metal bars.

Second, the good burglar must be able to team up to form a criminal gang. Choosing trustworthy companions is essential if the obstacles to completing a successful job—police, alarms, and secure safes—are to be overcome.

Third, the good burglar must have inside information. Without knowledge of what awaits them inside, burglars can spend a tremendous amount of time and effort on empty safes and jewelry boxes.

Finally, the good burglar must cultivate fences or buyers for stolen wares. Once the burglar gains access to people who buy and sell stolen goods, he or she must also learn how to successfully sell these goods for a reasonable profit. Evidence of these skills was discovered in a study of more than 200 career burglars in Australia. Burglars reported that

Race, Culture, Gender, and Criminology
Are There Gender Differences in Burglary?

Does gender play a role in shaping burglary careers? Are there differences in the way professional male and female burglars approach their craft? Do gender roles influence the burglar lifestyle? To find out, Christopher Mullins and Richard Wright used interviews with 18 active female burglars and 36 males, matched approximately for age. Their findings indicate that significant gender-based differences exist in the way males and females begin and end their offending careers and how they carry out their criminal tasks.

There were similarities in the way most offenders, male or female, were initiated into residential burglary. Burglars of both genders became involved via interaction in intimate groups, such as older friends, family members, or street associates. One told how they got started in burglary:

> [M]e and my brother, we wanted, you know, he came and got me and say he know where a house at to break into. And, uhm, we go there and uh, we just do it . . . me and my brother, he and some more friends.

But there was one key difference between the male and female offenders: the men typically became involved in burglary with male peers; women more often were introduced to crime by their boyfriends. Males are more likely to bring their male peers and family members into their offending networks and resist working with women except their girlfriend or female relative. And when they do include women, they put them in a subservient role, such as a lookout.

Why do they get involved in a burglary career in the first place? Both males and females generally said they got involved in break-ins to finance a party lifestyle centered on drug use and to buy designer clothing and bling-bling jewelry. There were some differences: males reportedly wanted money to pursue sexual conquests; female burglars were far more likely to say that they needed money to buy necessities for their children.

When asked what they were looking for in a prospective residential burglary target, the male and female offenders expressed similar preferences; both wanted to find a dwelling that was (a) unoccupied and (b) contained something of value. Both the men and the women wanted to know something about the people who lived in the residence, be familiar with their day-to-day routine, and to have an idea of the target's valuables. Male offenders used their legitimate jobs as home remodelers, cable television installers, or gardeners to scout potential burglary targets. Female burglars who lacked legitimate entry had to rely on information generated by the men in their immediate criminal social network. Some used sexual attraction to gain the victim's confidence and gather information.

Mullins and Wright also found that men preferred to commit residential burglaries by themselves, while women most often worked with others. Males seemed unwilling to trust accomplices and were also unwilling to share the proceeds. Females, on the other hand, reported that they lacked the knowledge or skills needed to break into a dwelling on their own and were therefore more willing to work with a team.

Finally, when asked what it would take to make them stop committing crime, both male and female offenders claimed that a good job that paid well and involved little or no disciplined subordination to authority would be required to get them to give up their careers in crime. Men also claimed they would probably give up burglary once they settled down and started a family. Because they were dependent on male help, female burglars needed to sever their relationships with criminally involved males in order to reduce their offending. Female burglars were also more sensitive than the males to shaming and ostracism at the hands of their relatives and might quit under family pressure.

Mullins and Wright found that residential burglary is a significantly gender-stratified offense; the processes of initiation, commission, and potential desistance are heavily structured by gender. Women have to negotiate the male-dominated world of burglary to accomplish their crimes. Gender, they found, plays a significant role in shaping opportunity (such as initiation) and the events leading up to residential burglaries (for example, information gathering), while playing a lesser but still important role in molding actual offense commission.

CRITICAL THINKING

1. Do the gender differences in burglary reflect the gender differences found in other segments of society?

2. Do you think gender discrimination helps reduce the female crime rate? If gender equality were achieved, would differences in the crime rate narrow?

SOURCE: Christopher Mullins and Richard Wright, "Gender, Social Networks, and Residential Burglary," *Criminology* 41 (2003): 813–839.

they had developed a number of relatively safe methods for disposing of their loot. Some traded stolen goods directly for drugs; others used fences, legitimate businesses, pawnbrokers, and secondhand dealers as trading partners. Surprisingly, many sold their illegal gains to family or friends. Burglars report that disposing of stolen goods was actually low risk and more efficient than expected. One reason was that in many cases fences and shady businesspeople put in a request for particular items, and the readymade market allowed the stolen merchandise to be disposed of quickly, often in less than one hour. Though the typical markdown was 67 to 75 percent of the price of the goods, most reported that they could still earn a good living, averaging $2,000 per week. Those who benefited most from these transactions were the receivers of stolen property, who make considerable profits and are unlikely to be caught.[98]

According to Shover, a person becomes a good burglar by learning the techniques of the trade from older, more experienced burglars. During this process, the older burglar teaches the novice how to handle such requirements as dealing with defense attorneys, bail bond agents, and other agents of the justice system. Apprentices must be known to have the appropriate character before they are taken under the wing of the old pro. Usually, the opportunity to learn burglary comes as a reward for being a highly respected juvenile gang member, from knowing someone in the neighborhood who has made a living at burglary, or, more often, from having built a reputation for being solid while serving time in prison. Consequently, the opportunity to become a good burglar is not open to everyone.

> **CONNECTIONS**
>
> Shover finds that the process of becoming a professional burglar is similar to the process described in Sutherland's theory of differential association. You can read more about this theory in Chapter 7.

The Burglary "Career Ladder" Paul Cromwell, James Olson, and D'Aunn Wester Avary interviewed 30 active burglars in Texas and found that burglars go through stages of career development. They begin as young *novices* who learn the trade from older, more experienced burglars, frequently siblings or relatives. Novices will continue to get this tutoring as long as they can develop their own markets (fences) for stolen goods. After their education is over, novices enter the *journeyman* stage, characterized by forays in search of lucrative targets and careful planning. At this point, they develop reputations as experienced reliable criminals. Finally, they become *professional* burglars when they have developed advanced skills and organizational abilities that give them the highest esteem among their peers.

The Texas burglars also displayed evidence of rational decision making. Most seemed to carefully evaluate potential costs and benefits before deciding to commit crime. There is evidence that burglars follow this pattern in their choice of burglary sites. Burglars show a preference for corner houses because they are easily observed and offer the maximum number of escape routes.[99] They look for houses that show evidence of long-term care and wealth. Though people may erect fences and other barriers to deter burglars, these devices may actually attract crime because they are viewed as protecting something worth stealing: if there is nothing valuable inside, why go to so much trouble to secure the premises?[100]

Cromwell, Olson, and Avary also found that many burglars had serious drug habits and that their criminal activity was, in part, aimed at supporting their substance abuse.

Repeat Burglary To what extent do burglars strike the same victim more than once? Research suggests that burglars may in fact return to the scene of the crime to repeat their offenses. One reason is that many burgled items are indispensable (for example, televisions and DVD players); therefore, it is safe to assume that they will quickly be replaced.[101] Research shows that some burglars repeat their acts to steal these replacement goods.[102] Graham Farrell, Coretta Phillips, and Ken Pease have articulated why burglars would most likely try to hit the same target more than once:

- It takes less effort to burgle a home or apartment known to be a suitable target than an unknown or unsuitable one.
- The burglar is already aware of the target's layout.
- The ease of entry of the target has probably not changed, and escape routes are known.
- The lack of protective measures and the absence of nosy and intrusive neighbors that made the first burglary a success have probably not changed.
- Goods have been observed that could not be taken out the first time.[103]

The repeat burglary phenomenon should mean that homes in close proximity to a burgled dwelling have an increased burglary risk, especially if they are similar in structure to the initial target. But research shows that lack of diversity in the physical construction and general appearance of dwellings in a neighborhood actually helped reduce repeat victimization. Housing diversity allows offenders a choice of targets, and favored targets will be revisited by burglars. If houses are identical, there is no motive for an offender to favor one property over another, and therefore the risk of repeat victimization is limited.[104]

ARSON

Arson is the willful and malicious burning of a home, public building, vehicle, or commercial building. Close to 60,000 arsons are now recorded each year, with an average loss of about $17,000.

Arson has been a common occurrence in America and was even tried as a weapon during the Civil War. In 1864, a small group of Confederate agents attempted to set New York City ablaze by using a liquid called "solidified Greek fire"; the plot failed because they improperly used the chemical.[105]

There are several motives for arson. Adult arsonists may be motivated by severe emotional turmoil. Some psychologists view fire starting as a function of a disturbed personality. Arson, therefore, should be viewed as a mental health problem and not a criminal act.[106] It is alleged that arsonists often experience sexual pleasure from starting fires and then observing their destructive effects. Although some arsonists may be aroused sexually by their activities, there is little evidence that most arsonists are psychosexually motivated.[107] It is equally likely that fires are started by angry people looking for revenge against property owners or by teenagers out to vandalize property. These findings support the claim that arson should be viewed as a mental health problem, not a criminal act, and that it should be treated with counseling and other therapeutic measures rather than severe punishments.[108]

The Juvenile Fire Starter

Juveniles, the most prolific fire starters, may get involved in arson for a variety of reasons as they mature. Juvenile fire setting has long been associated with psychological abnormality, including depression conduct problems, such as disobedience, aggressiveness, anger, hostility, and resentment over parental rejection.[109] According to research by sociologist Wayne Wooden, juvenile arsonists can be classified in one of four categories:

- *The "playing with matches" fire setter.* This is the youngest fire starter, usually between the ages of 4 and 9, who sets fires because parents are careless with matches and lighters. Proper instruction on fire safety can help prevent fires set by these young children.
- *The "crying for help" fire setter.* This type of fire setter is a 7- to 13-year-old who turns to fire to reduce stress. The source of the stress could be family conflict, divorce, death, or abuse. These youngsters have difficulty expressing their feelings of sorrow, rage, or anger and turn to fire as a means of relieving stress or getting back at their antagonists.
- *The "delinquent" fire setter.* Some youth set fire to school property or surrounding areas to retaliate for some slight experienced at school. These kids may break into the school to vandalize property with friends and later set a fire to cover up their activities.
- *The "severely disturbed" fire setter.* This youngster is obsessed with fires and often dreams about them in "vibrant colors." This is the most disturbed type of juvenile fire setter and the one most likely to set numerous fires with the potential for death and damage.[110]

During the past decade, hundreds of jurisdictions across the nation have established programs to address the growing problem of juvenile fire setting. Housed primarily within the fire service, these programs are designed to identify, evaluate, and treat juvenile fire setters to prevent the recurrence of fire-setting behaviors. A promising approach is the FireSafe Families effort in Rhode Island, which combines a training curriculum for fire-safety educators, a training program for community professionals to identify potential behavior that may lead to arson, and a cognitive-behavioral therapy (CBT) program to treat children who are at risk of becoming juvenile fire starters and their families.[111]

Professional Arson

Other arsons are set by professional arsonists who engage in **arson for profit**. People looking to collect insurance money, but who are afraid or unable to set the fire themselves, hire professional arsonists. These professionals have acquired the skills to set fires yet make the cause seem accidental (for example, like an electrical short). Another form is **arson fraud**, which involves a business owner burning his or her property, or hiring someone to do it, to escape financial problems.[112] Over the years, investigators have found that businesspeople are willing to become involved in arson to collect fire insurance or for various other reasons, including but not limited to these:

- Obtaining money during a period of financial crisis
- Getting rid of outdated or slow-moving inventory
- Destroying outmoded machines and technology
- Paying off legal and illegal debt
- Relocating or remodeling a business; for example, when a theme restaurant has not been accepted by customers
- Taking advantage of government funds available for redevelopment
- Applying for government building money, pocketing it without making repairs, and then claiming that fire destroyed the "rehabilitated" building
- Planning bankruptcies to eliminate debts, after the merchandise supposedly destroyed was secretly sold before the fire
- Eliminating business competition by burning out rivals
- Employing extortion schemes that demand that victims pay up or the rest of their holdings will be burned
- Solving labor–management problems; arson may be committed by a disgruntled employee
- Concealing another crime, such as embezzlement

Some recent technological advances may help prove that many alleged arsons were actually accidental fires. There is now evidence of a fire effect called **flashover**. During the course of an ordinary fire, heat and gas at the ceiling of a room can reach 2,000 degrees. This causes clothes and furniture to burst into flame, duplicating the effects of arsonists' gasoline or explosives. It is possible that many suspected arsons are actually the result of flashover.[113]

SUMMARY

1. **Be familiar with the history of theft offenses**
   - Common theft offenses include larceny, fraud, and embezzlement. These are common-law crimes, originally defined by English judges. Skilled thieves included pickpockets, forgers, and counterfeiters, who operated freely. Smugglers transported goods, such as spirits, gems, gold, and spices, without paying tax or duty. Poachers supplemented their diet and income with game that belonged to a landlord.

2. **Recognize the differences between professional and amateur thieves**
   - Economic crimes are designed to reap financial rewards for the offender. Opportunistic amateurs commit the majority of economic crimes. Economic crime has also attracted professional criminals. Professionals earn most of their income from crime, view themselves as criminals, and possess skills that aid them in their lawbreaking behavior. An example of the professional criminal is the fence who buys and sells stolen merchandise.

3. **Know the similarities and differences between petty and grand larceny**
   - Larceny, the most common theft crime, involves taking the legal possessions of another. Petty larceny is typically theft of amounts under $100 to $500 (depending on state law); grand larceny is theft over that amount. Grand larceny is a felony, petit larceny a misdemeanor.

4. **Understand the various forms of shoplifting**
   - Some shoplifters are amateurs who steal on the spur of the moment. These snitches are otherwise respectable persons who do not conceive of themselves as thieves but systematically steal merchandise for their own use. Some adolescents become shoplifters because they have been coerced by older kids. Called boosters or heels, professional shoplifters steal with the intention of reselling stolen merchandise to pawnshops or fences, usually at half the original price. Boosters know how to hit stores without being detected and have partners who can unload merchandise after it is stolen.

5. **Differentiate between fraud and embezzlement**
   - The crime of false pretenses, or fraud, is similar to larceny in that it involves the theft of goods or money. Fraud differs from common-law larceny because the criminal tricks victims into voluntarily giving up their possessions. Embezzlement involves people taking something that was temporarily entrusted to them. Bank tellers who take money out of the cash drawer and keep it for themselves are committing embezzlement.

6. **Compare the activities of professional and amateur car thieves**
   - Auto theft usually involves amateur joyriders who "borrow" cars for short-term transportation. Some steal cars so they can commit other crimes. Professional auto thieves steal cars to sell the parts that are highly valuable. Car thieves take orders from chop shops and look for particular cars.

7. **Understand what it means to burgle a home**
   - Under common law, the crime of burglary was defined as "the breaking and entering of a dwelling house of another in the nighttime with the intent to commit a felony within." Burglary is a serious crime because it involves entering another's home, which threatens occupants. More recent U.S. state laws have changed the requirements of burglary, and most have discarded the necessity of forced entry.

8. **Know what it takes to be a "good burglar"**
   - Because burglary involves planning and risk, it attracts professional thieves. The most competent have technical skill and personal integrity, specialize in burglary, are financially successful, and avoid prison sentences. Professional burglars size up the value of a particular crime and balance it against the perceived risks. Many have undergone training in the company of older, more experienced burglars.

9. **Distinguish between the activities of male and female burglars**
   - Both male and female burglars engage in other forms of theft, such as shoplifting and assault. Males are more likely to steal cars to supplement their income. Female burglars are much more likely to work with a partner, whereas males are more likely to go it alone. Males also begin their offending careers at an earlier age than females and are more likely to be repeat and recurrent offenders.

10. **Discuss why people commit arson for profit**
    - Arson is the willful, malicious burning of a home, public building, vehicle, or commercial building. Most arsonists are teenage vandals. Professional arsonists specialize in burning commercial buildings for profit. The owners of commercial buildings may resort to arson to get rid of outdated inventory, to qualify for government redevelopment funds, to collect insurance money, to claim the loss of merchandise already sold, or to eliminate business competition (by burning a building owned by a competitor).

KEY TERMS

fence (414)
street crime (414)
economic crime (414)
skilled thieves (415)
flash houses (415)
smugglers (415)
poachers (415)
occasional criminals (416)
professional criminals (416)
situational inducement (416)
professional fence (418)

constructive possession (421)
petit (petty) larceny (421)
grand larceny (421)
shoplifting (422)
snitches (423)
target removal strategies (423)
target hardening strategies (424)
naive check forgers (424)
closure (424)
systematic forgers (424)

carjacking (427)
false pretenses or fraud (428)
mark (428)
confidence game (428)
pigeon drop (429)
embezzlement (430)
good burglar (433)
arson for profit (436)
arson fraud (436)
flashover (436)

CRITICAL THINKING QUESTIONS

1. Differentiate between an occasional and a professional criminal. Which one would be more likely to resort to violence? Which one would be more easily deterred?

2. What crime occurs when a person who owns an antique store sells a client an "original" Tiffany lamp that the seller knows is a fake?

Would it still be a crime if the person selling the lamp was not aware that it was a fake? As an antique dealer, should the seller have a duty to determine the authenticity of the products he or she sells?

3. What are the characteristics of good burglars? Can you compare their career path to any other

professionals, such as doctors or lawyers? Which theory of criminal behavior best predicts the development of the good burglar?

4. You have been the victim of repeat burglaries. What could you do to reduce the chances of future victimization? (Hint: Buying a gun is not an option!)

NOTES

1. Gary Shapiro, "William Kingsland, City 'Gazetteer,' Is Dead," *New York Sun*, April 13, 2006, www.nysun.com/arts/william-kingsland-city-gazetteer-is.../30926/ (accessed November 3, 2010).

2. FBI news release, "Stolen Art Uncovered: Is It Yours?" August 11, 2008.

3. Andrew McCall, *The Medieval Underworld* (London: Hamish Hamilton, 1979), p. 86.

4. Ibid., p. 104.

5. J. J. Tobias, *Crime and Police in England, 1700–1900* (London: Gill and Macmillan, 1979).

6. Ibid., p. 9.

7. Marilyn Walsh, *The Fence* (Westport, CT: Greenwood Press, 1977), pp. 18–25.

8. Don DeNevi, *Western Train Robberies* (Millbrae, CA: Celestial Arts, 1976); Harry Sinclair Drago, *Road Agents and Train Robbers: Half a Century of Western Banditry* (New York: Dodd, Mead, 1973).

9. Neal Shover, *Great Pretenders, Pursuits, and Careers of Persistent Thieves* (Boulder, CO: Westview Press, 1996).

10. Ibid., pp. 50–51.

11. Ibid.

12. John Hepburn, "Occasional Criminals," in *Major Forms of Crime*, ed. Robert Meier (Beverly Hills, CA: Sage, 1984), pp. 73–94.

13. James Inciardi, "Professional Crime," in *Major Forms of Crime*, p. 223.

14. Harry King and William Chambliss, *Box Man: A Professional Thief's Journal* (New York: Harper & Row, 1972), p. 24.

15. Edwin Sutherland, "White-Collar Criminality," *American Sociological Review* 5 (1940): 2–10.

16. Gilbert Geis, "Avocational Crime," in *Handbook of Criminology*, ed. D. Glazer (Chicago: Rand McNally, 1974), p. 284.

17. Chic Conwell, *The Professional Thief*, ed. Edwin Sutherland (Chicago: University of Chicago Press, 1937).

18. Ibid., pp. 197–198.

19. Ibid., p. 212.

20. See, for example, Edwin Lemert, "The Behavior of the Systematic Check Forger," *Social Problems* 6 (1958): 141–148.

21. Cited in Walsh, *The Fence*, p. 1.

22. Carl Klockars, *The Professional Fence* (New York: Free Press, 1976); Darrell Steffensmeier, *The Fence: In the Shadow of Two*

Worlds (Totowa, NJ: Rowman and Littlefield, 1986); Walsh, *The Fence*, pp. 25–28.

23. Simon Fass and Janice Francis, "Where Have All the Hot Goods Gone? The Role of Pawnshops," *Journal of Research in Crime and Delinquency* 41 (2004): 156–179.

24. Walsh, *The Fence*, p. 34.

25. Paul Cromwell, James Olson, and D'Aunn Avary, "Who Buys Stolen Property? A New Look at Criminal Receiving," *Journal of Crime and Justice* 16 (1993): 75–95.

26. FBI, "Cargo Theft's High Cost: Thieves Stealing Billions Annually," July 26, 2006, www2.fbi.gov/page2/july06/cargo_theft072106.htm (accessed November 3, 2010).

27. This section depends heavily on a classic book, Wayne La Fave and Austin Scott, *Handbook on Criminal Law* (St. Paul, MN: West Publishing, 1972).

28. Ibid., p. 622.

29. Virginia Crime Codes, www.vcsc.virginia.gov/VCC_book_MIS.pdf (accessed November 3, 2010).

30. Ibid.

31. John Worrall, "The Effect of Three-Strikes Legislation on Serious Crime in

California," *Journal of Criminal Justice* 32 (2004): 283–296.

32. Data in this chapter on crime rates and trends come from: FBI, Uniform Crime Reports, *Crime in the United States, 2009*, www2.fbi.gov/ucr/cius2009/ (accessed December 28, 2010).

33. Margaret Loftus, "Gone: One TV," *U.S. News and World Report*, July 14, 1997, p. 61.

34. Timothy W. Maier, "Uncle Sam Gets Rolled," *Insight on the News*, March 10, 1997, p. 13.

35. WFTV.Com 9, "Operation 'Beauty Stop' Nabs 18 in $100 Million Theft Ring," January 24, 2008, www.wftv.com/news/15130764/detail.html (accessed November 3, 2010).

36. David Farrington, "Measuring, Explaining and Preventing Shoplifting: A Review of British Research," *Security Journal* 12 (1999): 9–27.

37. Mary Owen Cameron, *The Booster and the Snitch* (New York: Free Press, 1964).

38. Janne Kivivuori, "Crime by Proxy: Coercion and Altruism in Adolescent Shoplifting," *British Journal of Criminology* 47 (2007): 817–833.

39. Paul Cromwell and Quint Thurman, "The Devil Made Me Do It: Use of Neutralizations by Shoplifters," *Deviant Behavior* 24 (2003): 535–550.

40. Ellen Beate Hansen and Gunnar Breivik, "Sensation Seeking as a Predictor of Positive and Negative Risk Behavior Among Adolescents," *Personality and Individual Differences* 30 (2001): 627–640.

41. Yves Lamontagne, Richard Boyer, Celine Hetu, and Celine Lacerte-Lamontagne, "Anxiety, Significant Losses, Depression, and Irrational Beliefs in First-Offense Shoplifters," *Canadian Journal of Psychiatry* 45 (2000): 64–66.

42. FBI, "Organized Retail Theft: New Initiative to Tackle the Problem," April 6, 2007, www2.fbi.gov/page2/april07/retail040607.htm (accessed November 3, 2010).

43. Ibid.

44. Michael Hindelang, "Decisions of Shoplifting Victims to Invoke the Criminal Justice Process," *Social Problems* 21 (1974): 580–595.

45. Jill Jordan Sieder, "To Catch a Thief, Try This," *U.S. News and World Report*, September 23, 1996, p. 71.

46. Thomas Kelley, Daniel Kennedy, and Robert Homant, "Evaluation of an Individualized Treatment Program for Adolescent Shoplifters," *Adolescence* 38 (2003): 725–733.

47. Shaun Gabbidon and Patricia Patrick, "Characteristics and Outcomes of Shoplifting Cases in the U.S. Involving Allegations of False Arrest," *Security Journal* 18 (2005): 7–18.

48. *Ruditys v. J.C. Penney Co.*, No. 02-4114 (Delaware Co., PA, Ct. C.P. 2003).

49. Dean Dabney, Laura Dugan, Volkan Topalli, and Richard Hollinger "The Impact of Implicit Stereotyping on Offender Profiling: Unexpected Results from an Observational Study of Shoplifting," *Criminal Justice and Behavior* 33 (2006): 646–674.

50. Security Information Watch, "Lawsuit Claims Dillard's Used Racial Profiling to Fight Shoplifting," February 6, 2009, www.securityinfowatch.com/root+level/1280619 (accessed November 3, 2010).

51. Edwin Lemert, "An Isolation and Closure Theory of Naive Check Forgery," *Journal of Criminal Law, Criminology and Police Science* 44 (1953): 297–298.

52. CNN Money.com, "11 Charged in Theft of More Than 40M Card Numbers," August 6, 2008, http://money.cnn.com/2008/08/05/news/companies/card_fraud/index.htm (accessed November 3, 2010).

53. Matt Richtell, "Credit Card Theft Is Thriving Online as Global Market," *New York Times*, May 13, 2002, p. A1.

54. Kimberly Palmer, "Beware the Latest Credit Card Scam," *U.S. News and World Report*, May 15, 2008, www.usnews.com/blogs/alpha-consumer/2008/05/15/beware-the-latest-credit-card-scam.html (accessed November 3, 2010).

55. La Fave and Scott, *Handbook on Criminal Law*, p. 672.

56. FBI, "Credit Card Con: Canadian Man Gets 10 Years for $12 Million Telemarketing Scam," www2.fbi.gov/page2/nov03/credit112803.htm (accessed November 3, 2010).

57. Peter Wayner, "Bogus Web Sites Troll for Credit Card Numbers," *New York Times*, February 12, 1997, p. A18.

58. Information provided by Highway Loss Data Institute, www.iihs.org/news/rss/pr080310.html (accessed November 3, 2010).

59. Charles McCaghy, Peggy Giordano, and Trudy Knicely Henson, "Auto Theft," *Criminology* 15 (1977): 367–381.

60. Donald Gibbons, *Society, Crime and Criminal Careers* (Englewood Cliffs, NJ: Prentice Hall, 1977), p. 310.

61. K. Hazelbaker, "Insurance Industry Analyses and the Prevention of Motor Vehicle Theft," in *Business and Crime Prevention*, ed. Marcus Felson and Ronald V. Clarke (Boulder, CO: Lynne Rienner Publishers, 1997).

62. Gregory Robb, "The Most Valuable Salvage Parts of a Car," eHow, October 15, 2010, www.ehow.com/list_7342518_valuable-salvage-parts-car.html (accessed December 6, 2010).

63. Michael Rand, *Carjacking* (Washington, DC: Bureau of Justice Statistics, 1994), p. 1.

64. Patsy Klaus, *Carjacking, 1993–2002* (Washington, DC: Bureau of Justice Statistics, 2004).

65. Bruce Jacobs, Volkan Topalli, and Richard Wright, "Carjacking, Streetlife, and Offender Motivation," *British Journal of Criminology* 43 (2003): 673–688.

66. Klaus, *Carjacking, 1993–2002*.

67. Ronald Clarke and Patricia Harris, "Auto Theft and Its Prevention," in *Crime and Justice: An Annual Review*, ed. N. Morris and M. Tonry (Chicago: University of Chicago Press, 1992).

68. Ian Ayres and Steven D. Levitt, "Measuring Positive Externalities from Unobservable Victim Precaution: An Empirical Analysis of Lojack," *Quarterly Journal of Economics* 113 (1998): 43–78.

69. Hazelbaker, "Insurance Industry Analyses and the Prevention of Motor Vehicle Theft," p. 289.

70. P. Weiss, "Outsmarting the Electronic Gatekeeper: Code Breakers Beat Security Scheme of Car Locks, Gas Pumps," *Science News* 167 (2005): 86.

71. La Fave and Scott, *Handbook on Criminal Law*, p. 655.

72. 30 Geo. III, C. 24 (1975).

73. Internet Crime Complaint Center, "Fraudulent Sites Capitalizing on Relief Efforts of Hurricane Katrina," www.ic3.gov/media/2005/050902.aspx (accessed November 3, 2010).

74. FBI, *Crime in the United States, 2009*, Table 29, www2.fbi.gov/ucr/cius2009/data/table_29.html (accessed December 28, 2010).

75. As described in Charles McCaghy, *Deviant Behavior* (New York: Macmillan, 1976), pp. 230–231.

76. Benjamin Weiser, "4-Year Sentence for Mastermind of Scheme to Cheat on Graduate School Tests," *New York Times*, October 3, 1998, p. 8.

77. FBI, "A Cautionary Tale: Staged Auto Accident Fraud: Don't Let It Happen to You," www.fbi.gov/page2/feb05/stagedauto021805.htm (accessed April, 1, 2009).

78. Ibid.

79. Department of Justice press release, "Local Woman Sentenced for Embezzlement," http://mobile.fbi.gov/dojpressrel/pressrel06/embezzlement121406.htm (accessed June 15, 2007).

80. Jerome Hall, *Theft, Law and Society* (Indianapolis: Bobbs-Merrill, 1952), p. 36.

81. La Fave and Scott, *Handbook on Criminal Law*, p. 644.

82. Dawit Kiros Fantaye, "Fighting Corruption and Embezzlement in Third World Countries," *Journal of Criminal Law* 68 (April 2004): 170–177.

83. La Fave and Scott, *Handbook on Criminal Law*, p. 708.

84. E. Blackstone, *Commentaries on the Laws of England* (London: 1769), p. 224.

85. Elizabeth Groff and Nancy La Vigne, "Mapping an Opportunity Surface of Residential Burglary," *Journal of Research in Crime and Delinquency* 38 (2001): 257–278.

86. Timothy Coupe and Laurence Blake, "Daylight and Darkness Targeting Strategies and the Risks of Being Seen at Residential Burglaries," *Criminology* 44 (2006): 431–464.

87. Wim Bernasco, "Co-Offending and the Choice of Target Areas in Burglary," *Journal of Investigative Psychology and Offender Profiling* 3 (2006): 139–155.

88. Frank Hoheimer, *The Home Invaders: Confessions of a Cat Burglar* (Chicago: Chicago Review, 1975).

89. Richard Wright, Robert Logie, and Scott Decker, "Criminal Expertise and Offender Decision Making: An Experimental Study of the Target Selection Process in Residential Burglary," *Journal of Research in Crime and Delinquency* 32 (1995): 39–53.

90. Matthew Robinson, "Accessible Targets, but Not Advisable Ones: The Role of 'Accessibility' in Student Apartment Burglary," *Journal of Security Administration* 21 (1998): 28–44.

91. Wim Bernasco and Paul Nieuwbeerta, "How Do Residential Burglars Select Target Areas? A New Approach to the Analysis of Criminal Location Choice," *British Journal of Criminology* 45 (2005): 296–315.

92. Brent Snook, "Individual Differences in Distance Travelled by Serial Burglars," *Journal of Investigative Psychology and Offender Profiling* 1 (2004): 53–66.

93. John Worrall, "Does Targeting Minor Offenses Reduce Serious Crime? A Provisional, Affirmative Answer Based on an Analysis of County-Level Data," *Police Quarterly* 9 (2006): 47–72.

94. Richard Wright and Scott Decker, *Burglars on the Job: Streetlife and Residential Break-Ins* (Boston: Northeastern University Press, 1994).

95. Simon Hakim and Yochanan Shachmurove, "Spatial and Temporal Patterns of Commercial Burglaries," *American Journal of Economics and Sociology* 55 (1996): 443–457.

96. Ibid., pp. 443–456.

97. See, generally, Neal Shover, "Structures and Careers in Burglary," *Journal of Criminal Law, Criminology and Police Science* 63 (1972): 540–549.

98. Richard Stevenson, Lubica Forsythe, and Don Weatherburn, "The Stolen Goods Market in New South Wales, Australia: An Analysis of Disposal Avenues and Tactics," *British Journal of Criminology* 41 (2001): 101–118.

99. Paul Cromwell, James Olson, and D'Aunn Wester Avary, *Breaking and Entering: An Ethnographic Analysis of Burglary* (Newbury Park, CA: Sage, 1991), pp. 48–51.

100. See M. Taylor and C. Nee, "The Role of Cues in Simulated Residential Burglary: A Preliminary Investigation," *British Journal of Criminology* 28 (1988): 398–401; Julia MacDonald and Robert Gifford, "Territorial Cues and Defensible Space Theory: The Burglar's Point of View," *Journal of Environmental Psychology* 9 (1989): 193–205.

101. Roger Litton, "Crime Prevention and the Insurance Industry," in *Business and Crime Prevention*, p. 162.

102. Ronald Clarke, Elizabeth Perkins, and Donald Smith, Jr., "Explaining Repeat Residential Burglaries: An Analysis of Property Stolen," in *Repeat Victimization, Crime Prevention Studies*, Vol. 12, ed. Graham Farrell and Ken Pease (Monsey, NY: Criminal Justice Press, 2001), pp. 119–132.

103. Graham Farrell, Coretta Phillips, and Ken Pease, "Like Taking Candy: Why Does Repeat Victimization Occur?" *British Journal of Criminology* 35 (1995): 384–399, at 391.

104. Michael Townsley, Ross Homel, and Janet Chaseling, "Infectious Burglaries," *British Journal of Criminology* 43 (2003): 615–634.

105. Jane Singer, *The Confederate Dirty War: Arson, Bombings, Assassination and Plots for Chemical and Germ Attacks on the Union*, (Jefferson, NC, and London: McFarland & Company, 2005), p. 21.

106. Nancy Webb, George Sakheim, Luz Towns-Miranda, and Charles Wagner, "Collaborative Treatment of Juvenile Firestarters: Assessment and Outreach," *American Journal of Orthopsychiatry* 60 (1990): 305–310.

107. Vernon Quinsey, Terry Chaplin, and Douglas Unfold, "Arsonists and Sexual Arousal to Fire Setting: Correlations Unsupported," *Journal of Behavior Therapy and Experimental Psychiatry* 20 (1989): 203–209.

108. John Taylor, Ian Thorne, Alison Robertson, and Ginny Avery, "Evaluation of a Group Intervention for Convicted Arsonists with Mild and Borderline Intellectual Disabilities," *Criminal Behaviour and Mental Health* 12 (2002): 282–294.

109. Mark Dadds and Jennifer Fraser, "Fire Interest, Fire Setting and Psychopathology in Australian Children: A Normative Study," *Australian and New Zealand Journal of Psychiatry* 40 (2006): 581–586; Pekka Santtila, Helina Haikkanen, Laurence Alison, Laurence Whyte, and Carrie Whyte, "Juvenile Firesetters: Crime Scene Actions and Offender Characteristics," *Legal and Criminological Psychology* 8 (2003): 1–20.

110. Wayne Wooden, "Juvenile Firesetters in Cross-Cultural Perspective: How Should Society Respond?" in *Official Responses to Problem Juveniles: Some International Reflections*, ed. James Hackler (Onati, Spain: Onati Publications, 1991), pp. 339–348.

111. Scott Turner, "Funding Sparks Effort to Cut Juvenile Arson Rate," *George Street Journal* 27 (2003): 1.

112. Leigh Edward Somers, *Economic Crimes* (New York: Clark Boardman, 1984), pp. 158–168.

113. Michael Rogers, "The Fire Next Time," *Newsweek*, November 26, 1990, p. 63.

ROBERT

Robert Allen Stanford was a financier who lived like a king on the tropical island of Antigua.[1] "Sir Robert" (as he liked to be called after being knighted by the Antiguan Prime Minister) ran a renowned investment bank that offered investors high-yielding bank certificates of deposit. Sir Robert's financial activities soon began to raise eyebrows among American authorities: his promises of lucrative returns on relatively safe certificates of deposit were often more than twice the going rate offered by mainstream banks. Stanford's investment opportunities sounded almost too good to be true; unfortunately for investors, they were. Instead of the safe investments promised, Stanford secretly used the money in very risky long-term real estate and private equity investments. Antiguan auditors did not examine the bank's portfolio or verify its assets. Stanford held these facts from investors who were instead told that their money was totally safe thanks to monitoring by a team of more than 20 analysts and yearly audits by Antiguan bank regulators. Before being seized by the government, Stanford's bank had misappropriated $8.5 billion in assets belonging to 30,000 clients in 131 countries.

Enterprise Crime: White-Collar and Green-Collar Crime

13

Learning Objectives

1. Know what is meant by the term *enterprise crime*
2. Link white-collar crime and green-collar crime
3. Define white-collar crime
4. Know what is meant by the term *Ponzi scheme*
5. Be familiar with the various forms of white-collar crime
6. Distinguish between exploitation and influence peddling
7. Know what is meant by the term *payola*
8. Discuss efforts to control white-collar crime
9. Know the basics of green-collar crime
10. Be aware of the assumed cause of enterprise crime

ENTERPRISE CRIMES

Swindlers such as Stanford use their position in the marketplace for illegal gains. Their criminal activities are typically ongoing and typically involve groups of people who provide support, expertise, and so on. Because of their connection to business and commerce and because they conspire to make illegal profits, they are referred to here as business **enterprise crimes**.

While we sometimes think of these business-related crimes as a new phenomenon, they have been around for hundreds of years, ever since the Industrial Revolution began. The period between 1750 and 1850 witnessed the widespread and unprecedented emergence of financial offenses—such as fraud and embezzlement—frequently perpetrated by respectable middle-class offenders as the banking and commercial systems developed. Where there is money, people will steal it, whether it be in the street or in the suite.[2]

In this chapter, we divide these crimes of illicit entrepreneurship into two distinct categories: **white-collar crime** and **green-collar crime**. White-collar crime involves illegal activities of people and institutions whose acknowledged purpose is illegal profit through legitimate business transactions. Green-collar criminology is concerned with the study of environmental harm, environmental laws, and environmental regulation.[3]

White-collar crime and green-collar crime (also called *green crime*) are linked here because in each category offenders twist legal rules to enhance their personal economic position through illicit commercial enterprise. Because they are so connected, these two types of crimes may sometimes overlap. White-collar criminals may engage in the illegal dumping of hazardous waste to increase corporate profits; green-collar criminals may disguise their acts through elaborate corporate structures. Business enterprise crimes taint and corrupt the free market system. They mix and match illegal and legal methods and products in all phases of commercial activity. They involve illegal business practices (embezzlement, price fixing, pollution, dumping, bribery, and

Profiles in Crime
Dumping a Dumper

© Stockbyte/Getty Images

The federal Environmental Protection Agency, the government agency charged with fighting green crime, requires the proper handling and disposal of hazardous wastes. Before such wastes are released into local sewers and wastewater treatment plants, EPA rules require that toxic chemicals be treated in order to protect rivers, lakes, and streams. This rule was lost on Larkin Baggett, who owned and operated Chemical Consultants, Inc., in North Salt Lake City, Utah, a company that mixed and sold chemical products used in the trucking, construction, and concrete industries. Between October 2004 and April 2005, Baggett illegally dumped pollutants onto the ground and into a drain that led to the treatment plant operated by the South Davis Sewer Improvement District in West Bountiful, Utah. The treatment plant had a permit to discharge treated effluent to the Jordan River, which empties into the Great Salt Lake. Baggett instructed his employees to dispose of industrial wastes by dumping them onto the ground and into a sanitary sewer drain, which fed directly to the wastewater treatment plant. One of the wastes, nonylphenol, is a powerful organic chemical and heavy-duty industrial cleaner that is toxic to aquatic life. Baggett's actions caused the plant to violate permit limits for acute toxicity 22 times.

In April 2008, after his indictment for violating environmental laws, and two months before his trial, Baggett became a fugitive. Acting on a tip, EPA agents tracked him down to Marathon, Florida, and when they attempted to arrest him he fought back, assaulting officers. In 2009, Baggett was sentenced to 20 years in prison for illegally dumping pollutants in violation of the federal Clean Water Act and the Resource Conservation and Recovery Act and for assaulting federal officers. Baggett's lengthy sentence is illustrative of the tougher treatment being handed down for enterprise crimes, especially those involving violence.

SOURCE: Environmental Protection Agency, "Utah Man Sentenced to 20 Years in Prison for Environmental, Other Crimes," October 14, 2009, http://yosemite.epa.gov/opa/admpress.nsf/ab-2d81eb088f4a7e85257359003f5339/b250f64c49bd0b378525764f00631c05!OpenDocument (accessed November 4, 2010).

so on) to merchandise what are normally legitimate commercial products (securities, medical care, disposing of computer equipment).[4]

Surprisingly, both forms of enterprise crime can involve violence. Hundreds of thousands of occupational deaths occur each year, many from "corporate violence" such as unsafe working conditions; illegal pollution annually kills and injures more people than all street crimes combined.[5] So while business crimes typically involve stealth and fraud, as the Profiles in Crime feature shows, they may also include violence.

WHITE-COLLAR CRIME

Scholars have long recognized that some unscrupulous businesspeople use their position of trust to fleece the public. In 1907, pioneering sociologist Edward Alsworth Ross recognized the phenomenon when he coined the phrase "the criminaloid" to describe the kind of person who hides behind his or her image as a pillar of the community and paragon of virtue to get personal gain through any means necessary.[6]

In the late 1930s, the distinguished criminologist Edwin Sutherland first used the phrase "white-collar crime" to describe the criminal activities of the rich and powerful. He defined white-collar crime as "a crime committed by a person of respectability and high social status in the course of his occupation."[7] As Sutherland saw it, white-collar crime involved conspiracies by members of the wealthy classes to use their position in commerce and industry for personal gain without regard to the law. Often these actions were handled by civil courts because injured parties were more concerned with recovering their losses than with seeing the offenders punished criminally. Consequently, Sutherland believed that the great majority of white-collar criminals did not become the subject of criminological study. Yet the cost of white-collar crime is probably several times greater than all the crimes customarily regarded as the crime problem. And, in contrast to street crimes, white-collar offenses breed distrust in economic and social institutions, lower public morale, and undermine faith in business and government.[8]

Defining White-Collar Crime

Although Sutherland's work is considered a milestone in criminological history, his focus was on corporate criminality, including the crimes of the rich and powerful. Contemporary definitions of white-collar crime are typically much broader and include both middle-income Americans and corporate titans who use the marketplace for their criminal activity.[9] Included within recent views of white-collar crime are such acts as income tax evasion, credit card fraud, and bankruptcy fraud. Other white-collar criminals use their

positions of trust in business or government to commit crimes. Their activities might include pilfering, soliciting bribes or kickbacks, and embezzlement. Some white-collar criminals set up business for the sole purpose of victimizing the general public. They engage in land swindles (i.e., representing a swamp as a choice building site), securities theft, medical fraud, and so on.

In addition to acting as individuals, some white-collar criminals become involved in criminal conspiracies designed to improve the market share or profitability of their corporations. This type of white-collar crime, which includes antitrust violations, price fixing, and false advertising, is known as **corporate crime**.[10]

Extent of White-Collar Crime

It is difficult to estimate the extent and influence of white-collar crime on victims because all too often those who suffer the consequences of white-collar crime are ignored by victimologists.[11] The most recent national survey conducted by the National White Collar Crime Center found the following:[12]

- Victims were urban dwelling, white male Internet users, with high incomes.
- Nearly one in two households was victimized by white-collar crime within the previous year.
- Well over half of respondents indicated victimization over their lifetime.
- The type of white-collar victimizations that occur most often are nondelivery and auction fraud.
- Increase is seen in crimes involving technology, including credit card fraud.
- While many crimes go unreported, about 30 percent report their victimization to law enforcement or another crime control agency.
- The general public views white-collar crime seriously, calling for increased governmental resource allocations to combat these crimes.

It is not surprising, then, that some estimates of the annual cost of white-collar crime are as high as $660 billion.[13] These losses far outstrip the expense of any other type of crime. Nor is it likely that the full extent of white-collar crime will ever be fully known because many victims (70 percent) are reluctant to report their crime to police, believing that nothing can be done and that getting further involved is pointless.[14]

Beyond the monetary cost, white-collar crime often damages property and kills people. Violations of safety standards, pollution of the environment, and industrial accidents due to negligence can be classified as corporate violence. White-collar crime also destroys confidence, saps the integrity of commercial life, and has the potential for devastating destruction. Think of the possible results if nuclear regulatory rules are flouted or if toxic wastes are dumped into a community's drinking water supply.[15]

COMPONENTS OF WHITE-COLLAR CRIME

White-collar crime today represents a range of behaviors involving individuals acting alone and within the context of a business structure. The victims of white-collar crime can be the general public, the organization that employs the offender, or a competing organization. There have been numerous attempts to create subcategories or typologies of white-collar criminality. The one used here contains seven elements, ranging from an individual using a business enterprise to commit theft-related crimes to an individual using his or her place within a business enterprise for illegal gain, to business enterprises collectively engaging in illegitimate activity.[16]

White-Collar Swindles

A **white-collar swindle** involves the criminal activity of people who use a business proposition to fraudulently trick others out of their money. As you may recall (Chapter 12), fraud is a common-law crime in which someone uses illegal methods to bilk another out of money—for example, a person advertises a real Picasso on eBay and the purchaser discovers it to be a forgery. In contrast, white-collar swindles involve a person using his or her ongoing institutional or business position to commit fraud and fleece a victim.

This distinction can be seen in the sale of sports memorabilia: if a person sells another a baseball allegedly signed by Mickey Mantle and it turns out to be a forgery, that is common-law fraud. If they set up an ongoing business, advertise, and then mix forgeries with real autographs, that is white-collar fraud. In fact, white-collar swindles involving the sale of bogus sports memorabilia have become so widespread that the FBI created *Operation Bullpen*, an ongoing effort aimed at stopping white-collar swindling in the sports memorabilia industry. One culprit turned out to be the largest seller in the world of signed celebrity photos: Truly Unique Collectibles, who through their website made millions of dollars selling forged and fraudulent posters, photos, and items. Their celebrity-signed pictures and posters were obtained by "runners"—people who happen to catch a celebrity at an event and obtain a signed picture there. Though runners may have obtained one or two signatures from famous athletes, they simply forged many more, claiming all were genuine. The investigation found that the overwhelming number of celebrity-signed photographs and posters being sold throughout the world are sold under this pretense; they are almost all forged.[17]

Investment Swindles   The opening vignette told the story of Robert Allen Stanford, a financier whose swindle bilked victims out of more than $8 billion. His crimes are not unique. In the 1990s, the collapse of the Bank of Credit and Commerce International (BCCI) cost depositors an estimated $10 billion. BCCI was the world's seventh largest private bank, with assets of about $23 billion. Bank officials made billions of dollars in loans to confederates who had no intention of repaying them; BCCI officers also used false accounting methods to defraud depositors. The bank's clients included dictators Saddam Hussein and Ferdinand Marcos, and the bank helped them launder money, finance terrorist organizations, and smuggle illegal arms. BCCI officers helped Colombian drug cartel leaders launder drug money so it could be shifted to legitimate banks.[18]

At the time, no one believed that a swindle of this magnitude could ever occur again; they were wrong. The creation of global capital markets has created unprecedented opportunities for U.S. businesses to access capital and investors to diversify their portfolios.[19] Whether through college savings plans or retirement accounts, the number of people investing in securities and commodities has increased 600 percent since 1980.[20] This large-scale investment growth, however, has also led to significant increases in the amount of misconduct seen on Wall Street, and as a result some recent swindles have far exceeded the BCCI scandal. None of these is more notorious than the crimes pulled off by financier Bernard Madoff, who had operated Bernard L. Madoff Investment Securities, LLC, and created the world's greatest **Ponzi scheme** (see Exhibit 13.1). His story is told in the Profiles in Crime feature.

Madoff's Ponzi scheme is not unique. There have been numerous attempts to fraudulently siphon off clients' money, some so great that they have threatened to collapse the world's financial markets (see Exhibit 13.2).

Profiles in Crime
Bernard L. Madoff Investment Securities, LLC

Steven Hirsch/Splash News/Newscom

On March 12, 2009, financier Bernard Madoff pleaded guilty to an 11-count criminal complaint charging him with violations of the antifraud provisions of the Securities Act of 1933, the Securities Exchange Act of 1934, and the Investment Advisers Act of 1940. At his hearing, Madoff admitted that he had defrauded thousands of investors in the nation's most elaborate financial crime. On June 29, 2009, Madoff was sentenced to 150 years in prison, a life sentence.

How did Madoff's scheme unfold? He founded the Wall Street firm Bernard L. Madoff Investment Securities, LLC, in 1960 and it soon became one of Wall Street's largest "specialist" trading firms, specializing in investment management and advice, and managing billions in assets. Madoff became the darling of the jet set and was trusted by many wealthy people, including director Steven Spielberg, actors John Malkovich, Kevin Bacon, and Bacon's wife Kyra Sedgwick, as well as sophisticated financial managers and investors. They were taken in by his promise of high returns and a long track record of success. Things went south when the market crashed and people wanted their money back. It seems the asset management arm of his firm was a giant Ponzi scheme. Madoff had not invested any of the money he had taken in from investors, but instead deposited it in various banks, including New York's Chase Manhattan Bank. He used the interest and principal to pay off investors when they wanted to take money out of their accounts, but few did, because they were making fantastic paper profits. Madoff, of course, convinced them to keep their profits in the account rather than ask for a distribution. When they did ask, his house of cards fell apart. More than $30 billion was missing, and authorities are still trying to figure out where it all went.

When the market melted down in 2007, time ran out and it proved impossible for Madoff to catch up to the paper profits. He finally told his sons what he had done and they contacted the FBI. Madoff later claimed that he merely wanted to satisfy the expectations of high returns his clients demanded and which simply could not be met by legal means. Instead, he resorted to an illegal scheme involving false trading activities, illegal foreign transfers, and false SEC filings. He hoped that clients would simply reinvest their gains without requesting withdrawals until he could figure a way out of investing the money and actually making a profit! Madoff admitted he knew his day of reckoning was inevitable.

Madoff's ponzi scheme has been estimated to cost clients an estimated $65 billion, maybe the largest criminal conspiracy in history. He will spend the rest of his life in prison while authorities try to find out what happened to the cash. In the end, Madoff was regarded as the symbol of the greed run amuck that almost destroyed the nation's financial system.

SOURCES: Securities and Exchange Commission, "SEC Charges Bernard L. Madoff for Multi-Billion Dollar Ponzi Scheme," December 11, 2008, www.sec.gov/news/press/2008/2008-293.htm (accessed November 4, 2010); Joe Lauria, "Life Inside the Weird World of Bernard Madoff," *London Times*, March 22, 2009, http://business.timesonline.co.uk/tol/business/industry_sectors/banking_and_finance/article5949961.ece (accessed November 4, 2010).

EXHIBIT 13.1

What Is a Ponzi Scheme?

A Ponzi scheme is an investment fraud that involves the payment of purported returns to existing investors from funds contributed by new investors. Ponzi scheme organizers often solicit new investors by promising to invest funds in opportunities claimed to generate high returns with little or no risk. In many Ponzi schemes, the fraudsters focus on attracting new money to make promised payments to earlier-stage investors and to use for personal expenses, instead of engaging in any legitimate investment activity. With little or no legitimate earnings, the schemes require a consistent flow of money from new investors to continue. Ponzi schemes tend to collapse when it becomes difficult to recruit new investors or when a large number of investors ask to cash out.

Why are they called "Ponzi schemes"? The term comes from one Charles Ponzi, who duped thousands of New England residents into investing in a postage stamp speculation scheme back in the 1920s. At a time when the annual interest rate for bank accounts was 5 percent, Ponzi promised investors that he could provide a 50 percent return in just 90 days. Ponzi initially bought a small number of international mail coupons in support of his scheme, but quickly switched to using incoming funds to pay off earlier investors.

SOURCE: Securities and Exchange Commission, "Ponzi Schemes," www.sec.gov/answers/ponzi.htm#PonziCollapse (accessed November 4, 2010).

EXHIBIT 13.2

Wall Street Swindles

- *The pyramid scheme.* Similar to Ponzi schemes, the money collected from newer victims of the fraud is paid to earlier victims to provide a veneer of legitimacy. In pyramid schemes, however, the victims themselves are induced to recruit further victims through the payment of recruitment commissions.

- *Prime bank scheme.* Victims are induced to invest in financial instruments, allegedly issued by well-known institutions, which offer risk-free opportunities for high rates of return—benefits which are allegedly the result of the perpetrator's access to a secret worldwide exchange ordinarily open only to the world's largest financial institutions.

- *Advance fee fraud.* This category of fraud encompasses a broad variety of schemes that are designed to induce their victims into remitting up-front payments in exchange for the promise of goods, services, and/or prizes. In the securities and commodities fraud context, victims are informed that in order to participate in a promising investment opportunity, they must first pay various taxes and/or fees.

- *Hedge fund fraud.* Hedge funds are private investment partnerships that have historically accepted only high–net worth clients willing to meet significant minimum investment thresholds. The industry as a whole has been largely unregulated but has become increasingly relevant to middle-class investors through their exposure to hedge fund activities via ancillary investments (e.g., pension funds). The relative lack of regulatory scrutiny has made the industry vulnerable to fraud by fund managers, to include overstatement/misappropriation of fund assets, overcharging for fund management fees, insider trading, market timing, and late trading.

- *Commodities fraud.* These schemes typically involve the deceptive or fraudulent sale of commodities investments. False or deceptive sales practices are used to solicit victim funds for commodities transactions that either never occur or are inconsistent with the original sales pitches. Alternatively, commodities market participants may attempt to illegally manipulate the market for a commodity by such actions as fraudulently reporting price information or cornering the market to artificially increase the price of the targeted commodity.

- *Foreign exchange fraud.* These schemes are characterized by the use of false or deceptive sales practices, alleging high rates of return for minimal risk, to induce victims to invest in the foreign currency exchange market. The touted transactions either never occur, are inconsistent with the original sales pitches, or are executed for the sole purpose of generating excessive trading commissions in breach of fiduciary responsibilities to the victim client.

- *Broker embezzlement.* These schemes involve illicit and unauthorized actions by brokers to steal directly from their clients. Such schemes may be facilitated by the forging of client documents, doctoring of account statements, unauthorized trading/funds transfer activities, or other conduct in breach of the broker's fiduciary responsibilities to the victim client.

- *Late-day trading.* These schemes involve the illicit purchase and sale of securities after regular market hours. Such trading is restricted in order to prevent individuals from profiting on market-moving information that is released after the close of regular trading. Unscrupulous traders attempt to illegally exploit such opportunities by buying or selling securities at the market close price, secure in the knowledge that the market-moving information will generate illicit profits at the opening of trading on the following day.

SOURCE: FBI, "Financial Crimes Report to the Public, Fiscal Year 2008," www.fbi.gov/publications/financial/fcs_report2008/financial_crime_2008.htm#corporate (accessed November 4, 2010).

Mortgage Swindles

During 2008–2009, the nation was rocked by another form of Wall Street fraud that threatened to destroy the financial system, the real estate market, and create a 1929-style depression: the collapse of the subprime mortgage system. As a result of this financial disaster, several prominent financial institutions, including Bear Stearns and Lehman Brothers, went out of business; banks such as IndyMac Bank and Washington Mutual failed, and the federal government was forced to provide over a trillion dollars in relief to keep other companies such as American Insurance Group (AIG) and CitiGroup in business. The American taxpayers will be paying for this bailout over the course of their lives.

The cornerstone of the crisis was the collapse of the subprime mortgage sector. A subprime mortgage is a home loan given to borrowers who, because of their income, would not ordinarily qualify for bank loans. Once the subprime loans have been issued, the vendors typically bundle them into large pools and sell them as securities, a process known as **securitization**. Because they carry risk, they typically pay a higher interest rate than normal securities, making them attractive to investors. By 2006, subprimes had grown to 20 percent of the mortgage market, up from 2 percent a decade earlier; this means an estimated $1.3 trillion of the total $4.5 trillion total mortgage loans outstanding is subprime.

While subprime mortgages can help first-time home buyers of limited means, they also have been the source of fraud by both borrowers and lenders. As opportunities to profit from the housing market grew significantly in the 1990–2008 period, home building and ownership were facilitated by greedy mortgage lenders as well as fraudulent real estate appraisers and borrowers. First-time home buyers were encouraged to borrow almost the full value of their property without regard to their ability to pay back the loans. Artificial financial instruments such as derivatives, and the packaging and sale of mortgages to investors, were used to hedge or transfer risks. Borrowers provided false information to the mortgage broker and/or lender, enabling them to get loans for which they were not qualified. Those involved in mortgage lending, including mortgage brokers, lenders, appraisers, underwriters, accountants, real estate agents, settlement attorneys, land developers, investors, builders, bank account representatives, trust account representatives, investment banks, and credit rating agencies became involved in criminal fraud to maintain or increase their current standard of living. In addition to traditional industry conspirators, there have been instances involving various organized criminal groups and gang members involved in mortgage fraud activity.[21]

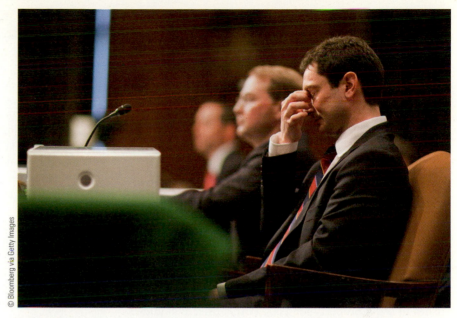

Fabrice Tourre, executive director of structured products group trading with Goldman Sachs Group, rubs his eyes during a Senate Homeland Security and Governmental Affairs subcommittee hearing on Wall Street and the financial crisis in Washington, D.C., on April 27, 2010. Tourre was sued by the Securities and Exchange Commission for fraud. The SEC alleged that Tourre misled investors about Goldman Sachs–backed securities, causing them to lose a billion dollars. He and the firm maintain that they never misled investors, and if they did lose money it was because of their poor judgment in the marketplace.

Subprime lenders made risky loans assuming that real estate values would always be increasing, allowing borrowers to refinance or sell their properties before going into default. However, when sales slowed down in the housing market, loan defaults increased and the securities lost value. As a result, mortgage companies experienced financial distress and bankruptcy.[22]

Desperate for funds, some subprime lenders, in order to stave off regulators, engaged in false accounting entries and fraudulently inflated assets and revenues. Some manipulated their reported loan portfolio risks and used various accounting schemes to inflate their financial reports. And in some cases, before these subprime lenders' stocks rapidly declined in value, executives with insider information sold their equity positions and profited illegally. As a result of these practices, some subprime lenders are being investigated by federal agencies for corporate fraud and insider trading. In one case, officers of Mercury Finance Company were convicted of intentionally misstating the company's financial records: they falsely reported a profit of more than $120 million instead of a loss of $30 million. Executives provided materially false financial statements to more than 20 financial institutions, enabling Mercury to obtain more than $1.5 billion in loan commitments and lines of credit. When the fraud was discovered, Mercury's stock price dropped significantly, costing shareholders nearly $2 billion in market value. A number of company officers went to prison, including former chief executive officer John Brincat, Sr., who pleaded guilty to wire fraud and making a false statement to a bank and was sentenced to 10 years imprisonment.[23]

Foreclosure Rescue Scams Not only has the availability of subprime mortgages presented opportunities for people to commit fraud, but it also created scams designed to prey upon people who obtained mortgages and now cannot make payments. There have been a variety of foreclosure rescue scams:

- *Phantom help.* A desperate homeowner is offered help by a supposed "expert" in avoiding foreclosures. He or she is then saddled with charges for things the homeowner could have done on his or her own (e.g., calling the bank). The phantom helper promises help, collects a fee, and never follows through. Soon it's too late to stop the foreclosure from taking place.
- *Bailout.* In this scam, someone offers to bail out the homeowners by taking the house off their hands with the promise that they can stay on as renters and buy the house back once things have been "fixed." The homeowners soon find

out that they can't buy the house back, and the supposed rescuers get most, if not all, of the equity.

- *Bait and switch.* Scammers tell the victim that he or she is signing documents for a new loan that will solve his or her problems. In reality, the homeowner is signing forged documents that transfer ownership of the home, which the scammers quickly try to sell to a third party at a reduced rate. The victim still owes for the mortgage, but will no longer have the asset.[24]

Builder-Bailout Schemes   The housing crisis has also influenced home builders to engage in fraud in order to unload unsold homes. Builder-bailout schemes occur when a builder or developer experiences difficulty selling his inventory and uses fraudulent means to unload unsold properties. He may offer a buyer an incentive of a mortgage with no down payment in order to get the buyer to buy a house he or she could not normally afford. For example, a builder wishes to sell a property for $300,000, a price that allows him to make a profit. He inflates the value of the property to $360,000 and finds a buyer by offering to give the buyer $60,000 to be used as a down payment. The buyer then goes to a bank and shows that he or she owes $300,000 on a $360,000 property; the lender funds a mortgage loan of $300,000, believing that $60,000 was paid to the builder and the borrower had the required 20 percent home equity. However, the lender is actually funding 100 percent of the home's value. The builder acquires $300,000 from the sale of the home and keeps any profits. If the home goes into foreclosure, the lender who provided the mortgage money finds out that there was actually no equity in the home and loses a fortune.[25]

In addition to the subprime mortgage scandal, a number of other mortgage schemes have been used by unscrupulous lenders and borrowers (Exhibit 13.3).

Religious Swindles   When oil prices skyrocketed in 2003 and 2004, one enterprising swindler, Linda Stetler of the Albany, Kentucky-based Vision Oil Company, lured investors into risky schemes by claiming that God (and not geologists) guided her company's oil exploration: "God gave me a vision of three oil wells," she said in a letter sent to potential investors. State regulators found that Stetler and her company engaged in illegal practices, including inadequate disclosures of risks and selling to unsuitable investors. Vision Oil and its agents were fined by the state and ordered to pay restitution to investors.[26]

Swindlers love to target the religious, taking advantage of their hope. It is estimated that fake religious organizations bilk thousands of people out of $100 million per year.[27] Swindlers take in worshippers of all persuasions: Jews, Baptists, Lutherans, Catholics, Mormons, and Greek Orthodox have all fallen prey to religious swindles. How do religious swindlers operate? Some create fraudulent charitable organizations and convince devout people to contribute to their seemingly worthwhile cause. Some use religious television

---

EXHIBIT 13.3

Common Mortgage Fraud Schemes

- *Illegal property flipping.* Property is purchased, falsely appraised at a higher value, and then quickly sold. What makes property flipping illegal is the appraisal information is fraudulent. The schemes typically involve one or more of the following: fraudulent appraisals, doctored loan documentation, or inflating buyer income. Kickbacks to buyers, investors, property/loan brokers, appraisers, and title company employees are common in this scheme.

- *Silent second.* The buyer of a property borrows the down payment from the seller through the issuance of a nondisclosed second mortgage. The primary lender believes the borrower has invested his own money in the down payment, when in fact it is borrowed. The second mortgage may not be recorded to further conceal its status from the primary lender.

- *Nominee loans/straw buyers.* The identity of the borrower is concealed through the use of a nominee who allows the borrower to use the nominee's name and credit history to apply for a loan.

- *Fictitious/stolen identity.* A fictitious/stolen identity may be used on the loan application. The applicant may be involved in an identity theft scheme: the applicant's name, personal identifying information, and credit history are used without the true person's knowledge.

- *Inflated appraisals.* An appraiser acts in collusion with a borrower and provides a misleading appraisal report to the lender. The report inaccurately states an inflated property value.

- *Foreclosure schemes.* The perpetrator identifies homeowners who are at risk of defaulting on loans, or whose houses are already in foreclosure. Perpetrators mislead the homeowners into believing they can save their homes in exchange for a transfer of the deed and up-front fees. The perpetrator profits from these schemes by remortgaging the property or pocketing fees paid by the homeowner.

- *Equity skimming.* An investor may use a straw buyer, false income documents, and false credit reports to obtain a mortgage loan in the straw buyer's name. Subsequent to closing, the straw buyer signs the property over to the investor in a quit claim deed, which relinquishes all rights to the property and provides no guaranty to title. The investor does not make any mortgage payments, and rents the property until foreclosure takes place several months later.

- *Air loans.* This is a nonexistent property loan where there is usually no collateral. An example of an air loan would be where a broker invents borrowers and properties, establishes accounts for payments, and maintains custodial accounts for escrows. The broker may set up an office with a bank of telephones, each one used as the employer, appraiser, credit agency, etc., for verification purposes.

and radio shows to sell their products. Others place verses from the scriptures on their promotional literature to comfort hesitant investors.

Another particularly cruel swindle is to prey upon couples desperate to adopt children and use religious organizations or local ministries to conduct their scams. In one Indiana case, Victoria Farahan approached the director of a new local adoption ministry and said she could provide healthy newborns from Hospital 31 in Moscow. Couples were provided with pictures of the babies (which turned out to be pictures of Farahan's own children). Because the scam was run through a religious institution people, took it at face value. Before being discovered, Farahan was able to bilk couples out $100,000. On July 17, 2006, she pleaded guilty to two counts of mail fraud and five counts of wire fraud.[28]

White-Collar Chiseling

White-collar **chiseling** involves regularly cheating people or organizations by deception or deceit. Chiseling schemes deprive a buyer or customer of fair treatment by bending the rules of reasonable and familiar business practices. Because the schemes are so subtle, the victims may not even realize they have been cheated.

Chiseling schemes usually involve over-billing or charging for something that the customer never received, such as charging for bogus auto repairs that were not required and never performed. It can also involve substituting cheap off-brand merchandise for higher priced name brands, or short-weighting (intentionally tampering with the accuracy of scales used to weigh products) in supermarkets or dairies. Take for instance the scandal that rocked New York City in 2010 when the Taxi and Limousine Commission revoked the licenses of 633 drivers for overcharging customers as part of a scheme that cost passengers more than a million dollars. The commission found that some cab drivers routinely overcharged customers by activating a switch that charged them out-of-town rates though the ride had taken place within city limits.[29] While 633 culprits does not sound so bad out of thousands of drivers, the commission found that in all, 21,819 taxi drivers had overcharged passengers a total of 286,000 times; the 633 targeted drivers were chronic offenders who had overcharged riders at least 50 or more times.

Professional Chiseling
It is not uncommon for professionals to use their positions to chisel clients. Pharmacists have been known to alter prescriptions or substitute low-cost generic drugs for more expensive name brands.[30] In one of the most notorious cases in the nation's history, Kansas City pharmacist Robert R. Courtney was charged with fraud when it was discovered that he had been selling diluted mixtures of the cancer medications Taxol, Gemzar, Paraplatin, and Platinol, which are used to treat a variety of illnesses

including pancreatic and lung cancer, advanced ovarian and breast cancer, and AIDS-related Kaposi's sarcoma. In one instance, Courtney provided a doctor with only 450 milligrams of Gemzar for a prescription that called for 1,900 mg, a transaction that netted him a profit of $779.[31] After he pleaded guilty, Courtney told authorities that his drug dilution activities were not limited to the conduct he admitted to at the time of his guilty plea. His criminal activities had actually begun in 1992 or even earlier, affected the patients of 400 doctors, involved 98,000 prescriptions, and harmed approximately 4,200 patients.[32] There is no telling how many people died or suffered serious medical complications because of Courtney's criminal conduct.

Securities Chiseling
A great deal of chiseling takes place on the commodities and stock markets, where individuals engage in deceptive practices that are prohibited by federal law.[33] Stockbrokers violate accepted practices when they engage in churning the client's account by repeated, excessive, and unnecessary buying and selling of stock.[34] Other broker fraud includes front running, in which brokers place personal orders ahead of a customer's large order to profit from the market effects of the trade, and bucketing, which is skimming customer trading profits by falsifying trade information.[35] Securities chiseling can also involve using one's position of trust to profit from inside business information, referred to as **insider trading**. The information can then be used to buy and sell securities, giving the trader an unfair advantage over the general public, which lacks this inside information. As originally conceived, insider trading made it illegal for corporate employees with direct knowledge of market-sensitive information to use that information for their own benefit—for example, by buying stock in a company that they learn will be taken over by the larger concern for which they work. In recent years, the definition of insider trading has been expanded by federal courts to include employees of financial institutions, such as law or banking firms, who misappropriate confidential information on pending corporate actions to purchase stock or give the information to a third party so that party may buy shares in the company. Courts have ruled that such actions are deceptive and violate security trading codes.[36] In one well-known case, Robert Moffat, a senior executive at IBM, pleaded guilty to conspiracy and securities fraud for his role in passing information to **hedge fund** managers. His story is set out in the Profiles in Crime feature.

White-Collar Exploitation

White-collar **exploitation** occurs when an individual abuses his or her power or position in an organization to coerce people into making payments to him or her for services to which they are already entitled. If the payments are not made, the services are withheld. In most cases, exploitation occurs when the victim has a clear right to expect a service,

© Bloomberg via Getty Images

In 2010, Robert Moffat, a senior executive with International Business Machines Corporation (IBM), pleaded guilty on three counts of securities-related crimes and received a six-month prison sentence and a $50,000 fine. How did Moffat, a distinguished businessman, married to his college sweetheart, and rumored to be the next CEO of IBM, become embroiled in a securities fraud case that put him behind bars?

Moffat was arrested for sharing company information with billionaire Raj Rajaratnam's New York hedge fund Galleon Group. Moffat provided material and insider information relating to IBM, Advanced Micro Devices, and Lenovo Group Ltd. For his role in the scheme, Rajaratnam was also charged with insider trading in the stocks of several companies, including AMD, Clearwire, and Akamai. He allegedly earned about $20 million through such trades and was charged with giving and receiving nonpublic information on companies such as Polycom, Hilton Hotels, Google, and People Support, and then trading on that information. In all, 20 defendants were charged with more than $40 million worth of alleged insider trading.

Why did Moffat, an up-and-coming and extremely wealthy executive, get involved in such a scheme? In fact, Moffat didn't make a penny from the information he provided, nor did he trade a share of stock. It seems he became involved with Danielle Chiesi, a special friend who worked for New Castle Partners, an equity hedge fund group affiliated with JPMorgan Chase, and served as an information gatherer for Raj Rajaratnam. Chiesi, a former teenage beauty queen, was a woman who used her charms to gain business information. "I love the three S's," she would tell her executive "friends," "sex, stocks, and sports." On August 22, 2008, during a phone call that was intercepted by a government wiretap, Moffat provided Chiesi with information regarding the timing of an upcoming deal involving Advanced Micro; Chiesi used the information and materials to illegally execute securities transactions. Though to be found guilty of insider trading a person must somehow profit from using illegal information, Moffat's profit was not in cash but in terms of the attention and affections of an alluring woman.

SOURCES: United States Department of Justice, "Former IBM Senior Vice President Pleads Guilty in Manhattan Federal Court to Insider Trading," March 29, 2010, http://newyork.fbi.gov/dojpressrel/pressrel10/nyfo032910.htm (accessed November 4, 2010); James Bandler with Doris Burke, "Dangerous Liaisons at IBM: Inside the Biggest Hedge Fund Insider-Trading Ring" July 6, 2010, *Fortune Magazine,* http://money.cnn.com/2010/07/06/news/companies/ibm_insider_trading.fortune/index.htm (accessed November 4, 2010).

and the offender threatens to withhold the service unless an additional payment or bribe is forthcoming. A fire inspector who demands that the owner of a restaurant pay for an operating license is engaging in exploitation.

On the local and state levels, scandals commonly emerge in which liquor license board members, food inspectors, and fire inspectors are named as exploiters. Exploitation can also occur in private industry. Purchasing agents in large companies often demand a piece of the action for awarding contracts to suppliers and distributors. Managing agents in some of New York City's most luxurious buildings have been convicted on charges that they routinely extorted millions of dollars from maintenance contractors and building suppliers. Building managers have been charged with steering repair and maintenance work to particular contractors in exchange for kickbacks totaling millions of dollars.[37]

Extortion is particularly troubling in the criminal justice system when police officers threaten victims with arrest if they do not make payments, or when judges bully defendants, threatening conviction unless they are paid off. In a recent case, Thomas Spargo, a New York state supreme court justice, was convicted of extorting money from a lawyer. If extortion money was not paid, cases handled by his law firm and the lawyer's own personal divorce proceeding would be handled in a biased fashion with negative outcomes![38]

White-Collar Influence Peddling

On February 18, 2010, Bernard Kerik, former commissioner of the New York City Police, was sentenced to four years in prison for accepting gratuities while in office. At Kerik's hearing, U.S. Attorney Preet Bharara said, "It is a very sad day when the former commissioner of the greatest police department in the world is sentenced to prison for base criminal conduct." He added, "Today's sentencing of

Bernard Kerik is one of the most powerful recent reminders that no one in this country is above the law."[39]

Sometimes individuals holding important institutional positions sell power, influence, and information to outsiders who have an interest in influencing the activities of the institution or buying information on what the institution may do in the future. Offenses within this category include government employees taking kickbacks from contractors in return for awarding them contracts they could not have won on merit, or outsiders bribing government officials, such as those in the Securities and Exchange Commission, who might sell information about future government activities. A police officer who sells information on future raids or takes a bribe in lieu of handing out a citation or making an arrest is engaging in influence peddling.

Though they are somewhat similar, **influence peddling** can be distinguished from exploitation. Exploiters force victims to pay for services to which they have a clear right; they are engaging in extortion. In contrast, influence peddlers take bribes in order to use their positions to grant favors and sell information to which their co-conspirators are not entitled. In sum, in crimes of exploitation, the victim is threatened and forced to pay, whereas the victim of influence peddling is the organization compromised by its employees for their own interests.

Influence Peddling in Government

In 2005, Representative Randy "Duke" Cunningham (R-CA) resigned from Congress after confessing to accepting $2.4 million in bribes, including a Rolls-Royce, a yacht, and a nineteenth-century Louis-Philippe commode. As he entered his guilty plea at a federal courthouse in San Diego, he proclaimed: "In my life, I have known great joy and great sorrow. And now I know great shame."[40]

It has become all too common for elected and appointed government officials to be forced to resign or even to be jailed for accepting bribes to use their influence. The Cunningham case is by no means unique. On April 17, 2006, former Governor George Ryan of Illinois was convicted of steering government contracts to people who were willing to give him kickbacks and bribes. The prosecution said Ryan and his family got fancy vacations, money, and other items worth at least $167,000, and in return offered special political favors and state business in the dozen years he served in the state's top roles.[41] On January 3, 2006, influential Washington lobbyist Jack Abramoff pleaded guilty to three felony counts: conspiracy, fraud, and tax evasion for bribing public officials, including Bob Ney, a Republican congressman from Ohio. Caught up in the Abramoff scandal was House

Influence peddlers use their position in a firm or the government for their own personal benefit. Here, former New York City police commissioner Bernard Kerik leaves his car to enter a New York courthouse. On November 5, 2009, the former "top cop" pleaded guilty to eight charges in a plea bargain with prosecutors, who recommended a jail sentence of 27 to 33 months. Kerik was sentenced to four years in federal prison on February 18, 2010.

Majority Leader Tom DeLay, who announced that he was resigning his seat in Congress.[42] On November 24, 2010, a Texas jury convicted the former congressman of money laundering and conspiracy to money launder; he is currently appealing his three-year prison sentence.

Agents of the criminal justice system have also gotten caught up in official corruption, a circumstance that is particularly disturbing because society expects a higher standard of moral integrity from people empowered to uphold the law and judge their fellow citizens. Police officers have been particularly vulnerable to charges of corruption. Thirty years ago, the Knapp Commission found that police corruption in New York City was pervasive and widespread, ranging from patrol officers accepting small gratuities from local businesspeople to senior officers receiving payoffs in the thousands of dollars from gamblers and narcotics violators.[43] Despite years of effort to eradicate police corruption, instances still abound. In New York City more than 20 officers were alleged to have been patrons of prostitutes working at 335 West 39th Street and a nearby massage parlor; some officers were filmed demanding sex.[44]

Influence Peddling in Business

On August 13, 2010, the Apple manager in charge of selecting Asian suppliers, Paul Shin Devine, was arrested for disclosing confidential information to suppliers in exchange for payments. The information helped the suppliers gain an edge when bidding for Apple's business. Devine had the suppliers send payments to his wife's bank account to avoid attracting attention; unfortunately for him, he neglected to delete incriminating e-mails.[45]

Politicians and government officials are not the only ones accused of bribery; business has had its share of scandals. People who hold power in a business may force those wishing to work with the company to pay them some form of bribe or gratuity to gain a contract. In the building industry, a purchasing agent may demand a kickback from contractors hoping to gain a service contract. Sometimes influence peddling can benefit both parties. In the record industry, **payola** is the routine practice of paying radio stations or DJs to play songs. While the recording companies are forced to pay, they also benefit from having their recording artists receive airtime they might not otherwise have gotten. Some large companies have been caught in **payola** scandals; Sony records paid $10 million to the state of New York to settle a claim that its promoters gave gifts to radio station managers to get songs played.[46]

Business-related bribery is not unique to the United States. In some foreign countries, soliciting bribes to do business is a common, even expected, practice. In European countries, such as Italy and France, giving gifts to secure contracts is a routine practice.[47] It is common for foreign officials to solicit bribes to allow American firms to do business in their countries. In 2007, German prosecutors in Munich, along with the Securities and Exchange Commission and the Justice Department in the United States, charged employees of the giant German industrial company Siemens with creating a slush fund worth about $520 million in order to make bribes to secure commercial contracts abroad.[48]

In response to these revelations, Congress passed the Foreign Corrupt Practices Act (FCPA), which makes it a criminal offense to bribe foreign officials or to make other questionable overseas payments. Violations of the FCPA draw strict penalties for both the defendant company and its officers.[49] Moreover, all fines imposed on corporate officers are paid by them, not absorbed by the company. If a domestic company violates the antibribery provisions of the FCPA, a domestic corporation can be fined up to $1 million. Company officers, employees, or stockholders who are convicted of bribery may have to serve a prison sentence of up to five years and pay a $10,000 fine.

Despite the penalties imposed by the FCPA, corporations that deal in foreign trade have continued to give bribes to secure favorable trade agreements.[50] Schering-Plough Corporation agreed to pay a civil penalty of $500,000 for violating provisions of the FCPA when it was revealed that an employee of its Polish subsidiary made a payment to a "charitable foundation" headed by a Polish government official. The government charged that these "charitable" payments were designed to influence the official to purchase Schering-Plough's pharmaceutical products for his region's health fund.[51] Other recent cases have involved the DaimlerChrysler auto company (which was investigated after it was discovered that the firm maintained 40 offshore bank accounts used to fund the payment of bribes) and oil companies Amerada Hess, Marathon, and Chevron (because of

suspicion that money given to charity in Equatorial Guinea goes directly into the hands of the ruling family in exchange for privileges).[52]

White-Collar Pilferage, Embezzlement, and Management Fraud

Another type of white-collar crime involves individuals' use of their positions to steal from the company, embezzle company funds, or appropriate company property for themselves. Here the company or organization that employs the criminal, rather than an outsider, is the victim of white-collar crime.

Pilferage   Is nothing sacred? Three employees and a friend allegedly stole moon rocks from a NASA laboratory in Houston. FBI agents arrested them after they tried to sell the contraband to an undercover agent in Orlando, Florida. The would-be seller reportedly asked $2,000 per gram for the rocks initially but later bumped the price to $8,000 per gram.[53] While the theft of moon rocks does not happen very often, systematic theft of company property by employees, or **pilferage**, is common.[54]

While it is difficult to estimate how much employee pilferage occurs each year, Hayes International, a loss prevention outfit, conducts an annual survey of 24 very large retail firms with over 13,000 stores doing $600 billion in sales. The most recent survey found that the number of employees involved in pilferage is on the rise and so too is the value of the merchandise being stolen. Loss prevention efforts have helped increase the amount of money recovered from dishonest employees:[55]

- One out of every 26 employees was apprehended for theft from their employer in a single year.
- Survey participants now apprehend almost 70,000 dishonest employees each year.
- Dollars recovered from dishonest employee apprehensions now total over $50 million each year.
- The average dishonest employee case value is more than $700.

Employee theft is most accurately explained by factors relevant to the work setting, such as job dissatisfaction and the workers' belief that they are being exploited by employers or supervisors; economic problems play a relatively small role in the decision to pilfer. So, although employers attribute employee fraud to economic conditions and declining personal values, workers themselves say they steal because of strain and conflict.

Management Fraud   Management-level fraud is also quite common. Such acts include converting company assets for personal benefit; fraudulently receiving increases in compensation (such as raises or bonuses); fraudulently increasing personal holdings of company stock; retaining one's present position within the company by manipulating accounts; and concealing unacceptable performance from stockholders.[56]

Management fraud has involved some of the nation's largest companies and richest people. The Criminological Enterprise feature "Tyco, Enron, and WorldCom: Enterprise Crime at the Highest Levels" focuses on three of the most prominent cases of recent years.

White-Collar Client Fraud

White-collar client fraud is theft by a client from an organization that advances credit to its clients or reimburses them for services rendered. These offenses are linked because they involve cheating an organization (such as a government agency, bank, or insurance company) with many individual clients that the organization supports financially (such as insurance policy owners, or loan applicants), reimburses for services provided (such as an insurance company who pays health care providers), covers losses of (such as claims by insurance policyholders), or extends credit to (as the government does to a taxpayer). Included in this category are insurance fraud, bank fraud, credit card fraud, fraud related to welfare and Medicare programs, and tax evasion.

Health Care Fraud On March 21, 2006, Konstantin Grigoryan, his wife, Mayya Leonidovna Grigoryan, and Eduard Gersheli, Aleksandr Treynker, and Haroutyun Gulderyan were all arrested on charges related to a long-running Medicare fraud scheme that federal authorities believe netted them at least $20 million. The scheme involved defrauding Medicare, the federal health care program, by billing for tests that either were unnecessary or were never performed.

The conspirators paid kickbacks to recruit patients and to submit fraudulent billings to Medicare on behalf of medical service providers, such as medical clinics and diagnostic testing centers. The scheme, commonly referred to as "beneficiary-sharing" or "patient-rotating," involved "marketers" who obtained data about Medicare beneficiaries and sold the information to Medicare providers who then engaged in fraudulent billings. Some marketers, known as "cappers," recruited patients with Medicare coverage and brought them to clinics where they were given unnecessary medical services, including ultrasound examinations and blood tests. Once the patients came into a physician's office, the medical providers allegedly billed the patients' Medicare numbers on the dates of their visits and on many other dates—whether or not any services were in fact provided to the beneficiaries. The conspirators would fabricate the tests so that the patients' files could withstand an audit by Medicare. The criminal scheme caused Medicare to pay out at least $20 million in fraudulent claims from 2000 until 2005. Much of the money was deposited into a maze of bank accounts of "management" and "consulting" companies, including a Panamanian shell corporation with a Swiss account.[57]

Crooked health care providers find it lucrative to engage in fraud in obtaining patients and administering their treatment and for patients to try to scam the system for their own benefit. A recent survey of 52 insurers by the National Health Care Antifraud Association (NHCAA) found that they annually recover more than $500 million as a direct result of antifraud activities. While this number is significant, it is only a small fraction of the total estimated loss due to health fraud. The NHCAA estimates that of the nation's annual health care outlay, at least 3 percent—or more than $50 billion—is lost to outright fraud. Other estimates by government and law enforcement agencies place the loss as high as 10 percent of annual expenditures—or $170 billion— lost to fraud each year.[58]

A central target of medical fraud is the federal Medicaid/Medicare program. The Office of Inspector General of the U.S. Department of Health and Human Services estimates that 6 percent of all Medicaid payments (more than $12 billion) should not have been paid due to erroneous billing or payment, inadequate provider documentation of services to back up the claims, or outright fraud.[59] One reason that thieves find Medicaid/Medicare an inviting target is because it operates under a system that pays providers first and investigates later. The so-called "pay and chase method" gives abusers 90 days' lag time to fleece them for millions before authorities are aware a crime has been committed. This system enabled Cuban immigrants Carlos, Luis, and Jose Benitez to make and get paid for fraudulent claims amounting to $119 million for costly HIV drugs that patients never received. After obtaining the proceeds from their crimes, the Benitez brothers transferred millions of dollars in proceeds to sham "marketing" and "management" companies they owned and controlled. They allegedly fled back to Cuba in order to avoid trial.[60]

Statewide Medicaid systems have also been the target of enterprise criminals: New York State officials estimate that 10 percent of the entire program—billions of dollars—has been lost due to fraudulent practices.[61]

There are numerous health care–related schemes. These include:

- Billing for services that were never rendered by using genuine patient information to fabricate entire claims or by adding to claims with charges for procedures or services that did not take place.
- Billing for more expensive services or procedures than were actually provided or performed, commonly known as "upcoding." This practice requires "inflation" of the patient's diagnosis code to a more serious condition consistent with the false procedure code.
- Performing medically unnecessary services solely for the purpose of generating insurance payments. This scheme occurs most often in nerve-conduction and other diagnostic-testing schemes. Some Southern California clinics performed unnecessary, and sometimes harmful, surgeries on patients who were recruited and paid to have these unnecessary surgeries performed.

The Criminological Enterprise
Tyco, Enron, and WorldCom: Enterprise Crime at the Highest Levels

The Tyco Case

Tyco International Ltd. is a gigantic corporate entity that today operates in all 50 U.S. states and over 100 countries and employs more than 250,000 people. Despite its great success, the U.S. government indicted Tyco's chief executive officer, L. Dennis Kozlowski, and chief financial officer, Marc Swartz, on a variety of fraud and larceny charges, including misappropriating $170 million in company funds by hiding unauthorized bonuses and secretly forgiving loans to themselves. Kozlowski and Swartz were also accused of making more than $430 million by lying about Tyco's financial condition in order to inflate the value of their stock.

During their 2004 trial, the government tried to establish a motive by showing jurors elements of their extravagant lifestyle. Kozlowski spent more than $2 million on a party for his wife on the Italian island of Sardinia that featured a performance by singer Jimmy Buffett; young men and women dressed as Roman soldiers and maidens danced and served the guests. He also spent $15 million to furnish an $18 million Tyco-owned apartment on Fifth Avenue in New York City; his expenses included a $15,000 umbrella holder, a $2,200 gilt metal trash basket, and a $6,000 shower curtain.

The defense claimed that the two men were merely highly paid executives and that everything they received was approved by Tyco's board of directors and their

accounting firm, PricewaterhouseCoopers. Because there was no stealth, there could be no embezzlement. However, on September 19, 2005, Kozlowski was convicted of looting the company of $150 million and sentenced to 8.3 to 25 years in prison.

The Enron Case

Enron Corporation, an oil and gas trading firm, was one of the largest companies in the United States before it collapsed and cost thousands of employees their life savings and millions of investors their hard-earned money.

Enron was an aggressive energy company that sought to transform itself into the world's biggest energy trader. Enron's share price collapsed when word got out that the company had been setting up shell companies and limited partnerships to conceal debts so they did not show up in the company's accounts.

In one incident, six Enron executives negotiated complex deals in which they made at least $42 million on personal investments totaling $161,000, all the while knowing that the limited partnerships they sold to retirement plans and private foundations were collapsing in value. It is also suspected that Enron engaged in sham transactions in late 2000 that drove up electricity prices in California and helped worsen the energy crisis that plagued the West for more than a year.

Enron's auditors—Arthur Andersen, a prestigious accounting firm—actually shredded key documents to keep them out

of the hands of the government. One man involved in the incident, David Duncan, a former Andersen partner who was head of the team that audited Enron, agreed to serve as a government witness after pleading guilty to obstruction of justice. Duncan admitted in court that he "knowingly, intentionally, and corruptly persuaded and attempted to persuade" Andersen employees to withhold records, documents, and other objects from an investigation by the Securities and Exchange Commission (SEC).

In the aftermath of the Enron collapse, key company executives, including chief financial officer Andrew Fastow, chief executive officer Jeffrey Skilling, and chairman and CEO Kenneth Lay, were charged with conspiracy, securities fraud, wire fraud, bank fraud, and making false statements. Skilling and chief accounting officer Richard Causey were also charged with money laundering and conspiracy. The government claimed that Lay, Skilling, Fastow, Causey, and others oversaw a massive conspiracy to delude investors into believing that Enron was a growing company when, in fact, it was undergoing business setbacks.

The government charges indicate that between 1999 and 2001, these executives used their position of trust to engage in a wide-ranging scheme to deceive the public and the SEC about the true performance of Enron's businesses. Their fraud helped inflate Enron's stock price from $30 per share in early 1998 to over $80 per share in January 2001. The three allegedly orchestrated

---

■ Misrepresenting noncovered treatments as medically necessary covered treatments for purposes of obtaining insurance payments. This scheme occurs in cosmetic-surgery in which noncovered cosmetic procedures such as nose jobs, tummy tucks, liposuction, or breast augmentations are billed to patients' insurers as deviated-septum repairs, hernia repairs, or lumpectomies.[62]

In addition to individual physicians, some large health care providers have been accused of routinely violating the law to obtain millions in illegal payments. The federal

government filed suit against some of the nation's largest hospital chains, such as Columbia/HCA Healthcare Corporation (320 hospitals) and Quorum Health Group (250 hospitals), alleging that they routinely overstated expenses to bilk Medicare by filing false claims for reimbursement as well as paying kickbacks to doctors for referrals.[63] HCA, the nation's largest for-profit hospital chain, pleaded guilty to defrauding government health care programs and received a combination of civil fines and criminal penalties that totaled $1.7 billion. The government has attempted to tighten control over the industry in order to restrict the opportunity

a series of accounting frauds designed to make up the shortfall between what the company actually earned and what was expected by Wall Street analysts. The government contended that even though the company was losing billions of dollars, executives continued to maintain that the company was doing great and would reach its profit targets.

What would motivate the head of one of the nation's largest companies to commit fraud? The most likely reason is greed: between 1998 and 2001, Lay received approximately $300 million from the sale of Enron stock options and restricted stock and made over $217 million in profit; he was also paid more than $19 million in salary and bonuses. More than 35 individuals were charged in connection with Enron's illegal accounting practices. Of these individuals, 23 have pleaded guilty or been convicted, including Fastow, Skilling, and former chairman and CEO Kenneth Lay (whose conviction was vacated due to his death from natural causes). Fastow was sentenced to six years in prison for his role in the accounting scandal and Skilling was sentenced to 24 years and four months in prison.

The WorldCom Case

WorldCom CEO Bernie Ebbers was found guilty and received a 25-year sentence for falsifying the company's financial statements by more than $9 billion; WorldCom was forced to file for bankruptcy. One of the most important elements of the case was the more than $400 million that WorldCom loaned or guaranteed to loan Ebbers at an interest rate of 2.15 percent.

Ebbers began his career by creating the LDDS (Long Distance Discount Services), which gained many of America's largest corporations as customers for its voice and data network. He then bought IDB Company and renamed it WorldCom. Through a series of acquisitions, WorldCom became one of the largest Internet hookup and networking companies in the United States; its stock value increased 7,000 percent during the 1990s.

When the market collapsed in 2000, WorldCom was heavily in debt and hemorrhaging money. While people were being laid off, the company made its loans to Ebbers so he could hold on to his company stock, for which he had taken out loans to purchase. Then on June 25, 2002, WorldCom announced that it had illegally treated $3.8 billion in ordinary costs as capital expenditures. The bottom dropped out of the stock, creditors began to sue, and Ebbers was in no position to pay back the loans. The company admitted to overstating profits by a whopping $74.4 billion between 2000 and 2001, including at least $10.6 billion that the firm attributed to accounting "errors" as well as "improper" and "inappropriate" accounting. On May 15, 2005, a federal jury in New York convicted Ebbers on all nine counts on which he was charged and Ebbers was sentenced to 25 years in prison.

CRITICAL THINKING

1. Considering the various theories of criminal behavior we have discussed, how would you explain the alleged behavior of millionaire businesspeople such as Bernie Ebbers and Kenneth Lay? Are they impulsive? Do they lack self-control? Is there a personality deficit that can explain their behavior?

2. Should white-collar criminals be punished with a prison sentence or would society be better served if all their ill-gotten gains were confiscated?

SOURCES: Krysten Crawford, CNN, "Ex-WorldCom CEO Ebbers Guilty," March 15, 2006, http://money.cnn.com/2005/03/15/news/newsmakers/ebbers/ (accessed November 4, 2010); MSNBC, "Ebbers Sentenced to 25 Years in Prison, Ex-WorldCom CEO Guilty of Directing Biggest Accounting Fraud," July 13, 2005, www.msnbc.msn.com/id/8474930 (accessed November 4, 2010); Lynne W. Jeter, *Disconnected: Deceit and Betrayal at WorldCom* (New York: Wiley, 2003); Bethany McLean and Peter Elkind, *The Smartest Guys in the Room: The Amazing Rise and Scandalous Fall of Enron* (New York: Penguin, 2003); Kurt Eichenwald, "Ex-Andersen Partner Pleads Guilty in Record-Shredding," *New York Times*, April 12, 2002, p. C1; John A. Byrne, "At Enron, the Environment Was Ripe for Abuse," *Business-Week*, February 25, 2002, p. 12;. Peter Behr and Carrie Johnson, "Govt. Expands Charges Against Enron Execs," *Washington Post*, May 1, 2003, p. 1.

for physicians to commit fraud. Health care companies providing services to federal health care programs are also regulated by federal laws that prohibit kickbacks and self-referrals. The Health Insurance Portability and Accountability Act of 1996 (HIPAA) established health care fraud as an independent federal criminal offense, with the basic crime carrying a federal prison term of up to 10 years in addition to significant financial penalties.[64] HIPAA doubles the prison term to up to 20 years should a perpetrator's fraud result in injury to a patient; if the fraud results in a patient's death, the perpetrator can be sentenced to life in federal prison.

It is a crime, punishable by up to five years in prison, to provide anything of value, money or otherwise, directly or indirectly, with the intent to induce a referral of a patient or a health care service. Liability attaches to both parties in the transaction—the entity or individual providing the kickbacks and the individual receiving payment of the referral. The law also prohibits physicians and other health care providers from referring beneficiaries in federal health care programs to clinics or other facilities in which the physician or health care provider has a financial interest. It is illegal for a doctor to refer her patients to a blood-testing lab in which she has an ownership share. These practices—kickbacks and self-referrals—are prohibited under federal law because they would compromise a medical professional's independent judgment. Congress also mandated the establishment of a nationwide Coordinated Fraud and Abuse Control Program to coordinate federal, state, and local law enforcement efforts against health care fraud and to include "the coordination and sharing of data" with private health insurers.

Health care fraud is expected to continue to rise as people live longer and produce a greater demand for Medicare benefits. In the future, the utilization of long- and short-term care facilities such as skilled nursing, assisted living, and hospice services will expand substantially. Additionally, fraudulent billings and medically unnecessary services billed to health care insurers are now prevalent throughout the country and are expected to grow in the future.[65]

Bank Fraud Encompassing such diverse schemes as check kiting, check forgery, false statements on loan applications, sale of stolen checks, bank credit card fraud, unauthorized use of automatic teller machines (ATMs), auto title fraud, and illegal transactions with offshore banks, bank fraud can cost billions per year.[66] Among the schemes used to defraud banks are mortgage frauds in which a group of conspirators fraudulently obtain loans on overvalued or nonexistent property. Some of the more common schemes are set out in Exhibit 13.4.[67]

To be found guilty of bank fraud, one must knowingly execute or attempt to execute a scheme to fraudulently obtain money or property from a financial institution. A car dealer would commit bank fraud by securing loans on titles to cars it no longer owned. A real estate owner would be guilty of bank fraud if he or she obtained a false appraisal on a piece of property with the intention of obtaining a bank loan in excess of the property's real worth. Penalties for bank fraud include a maximum fine of $1 million and up to 30 years in prison.

Tax Evasion Another important aspect of client fraud is tax evasion. Here the victim is the government that is cheated by one of its clients, the errant taxpayer to whom it extended credit by allowing the taxpayer to delay paying taxes on money he or she had already earned. Tax fraud is a particularly challenging area for criminological study because so many U.S. citizens regularly underreport their income, and it is often difficult to separate honest error from deliberate tax evasion.

The basic law on tax evasion is contained in the U.S. Internal Revenue Code, section 7201, which states:

> Any person who willfully attempts in any manner to evade or defeat any tax imposed by this title or the payment thereof shall, in addition to other penalties provided by law, be guilty of a felony and, upon conviction thereof, shall be fined not more than $100,000 or imprisoned not more than five years, or both, together with the costs of prosecution.

EXHIBIT 13.4

Some Common Bank Fraud Schemes

- *Prime bank investment fraud.* In these schemes, victims are told that certain financial instruments (notes, letters of credit, debentures, or guarantees) have been issued by well-known institutions such as the World Bank and offer a risk-free opportunity with high rates of return. Perpetrators often claim that the unusually high rates of return and low risk are the result of a worldwide secret exchange open only to the world's largest financial institutions. Victims are often drawn into prime bank investment frauds because the criminals use sophisticated terms, legal looking documents, and claim that the investments are insured against loss.

- *Advanced fee schemes.* In these scams, victims are persuaded to advance relatively small sums of money in the hope of realizing a much larger gain. In securities fraud, victims are told that in order to have the opportunity to be an investor in an initial offering of a promising security, investment (business or land development), or commodity, the victim must first send funds to cover taxes or processing fees.

- *Hedge fund fraud.* Hedge funds (HFs) are private investment partnerships that routinely accept only high wealth clients willing to invest at least hundreds of thousands of dollars. Historically, these high wealth investors were deemed "financially sophisticated," and, as a result, HFs have been unregulated and are not required to register with any federal or state regulatory agency. More recently, many middle-class investors have been exposed to HFs through ancillary investments such as pensions and endowments. There are over 8,800 HFs currently operating, with over $1.3 trillion in assets under management.

To prove tax fraud, the government must find that the taxpayer either underreported his or her income or did not report taxable income. No minimum dollar amount is stated before fraud exists, but the government can take legal action when there is a "substantial underpayment of tax." A second element of tax fraud is "willfulness" on the part of the tax evader. In the major case on this issue, willfulness was defined as a "voluntary, intentional violation of a known legal duty and not the careless disregard for the truth."[68] Finally, to prove tax fraud, the government must show that the taxpayer has purposely attempted to evade or defeat a tax payment. If the offender is guilty of passive neglect, the offense is a misdemeanor. Passive neglect means simply not paying taxes, not reporting income, or not paying taxes when due. On the other hand, affirmative tax evasion, such as keeping double books, making false entries, destroying books or records, concealing assets, or covering up sources of income, constitutes a felony.

Although tax cheating is a serious crime, the great majority of major tax cheats (in some categories, four out of five cheaters) are not prosecuted because the IRS lacks the money to enforce the law.[69] Today, the IRS collects more than $2 trillion in revenue and processes more than 224 million tax returns. However, its budget amounts to only 44 cents for each $100 it collects; this is 10 percent less, after adjusting for inflation, than in 1997. In addition, because most IRS resources are devoted to processing tax returns, there is less money for audits, investigations, and collections than there was a decade ago. In 1997, the IRS conducted more than 5,000 tax fraud and other investigations; in 2006, the number dropped to less than 4,000. Not surprisingly, the number of people sentenced for tax evasion and other financial crimes dropped from 3,000 to 2,000 during this span. The problem of tax fraud is significant, and honest taxpayers are forced to bear the costs, which may run into the hundreds of billions.

Corporate Crime

Yet another component of white-collar crime involves situations in which powerful institutions or their representatives willfully violate the laws that restrain these institutions from doing social harm or require them to do social good. This is also known as corporate or **organizational crime**.

Interest in corporate crime first emerged in the early 1900s, when a group of writers, known as muckrakers, targeted the monopolistic business practices of John D. Rockefeller, and other corporate business leaders. In a 1907 article, sociologist E. A. Ross described the "criminaloid": a business leader who while enjoying immunity from the law victimized an unsuspecting public.[70] Edwin Sutherland focused theoretical attention on corporate crime when he began his research on the subject in the 1940s; corporate crime was probably what he had in mind when he coined the phrase "white-collar crime."[71]

Corporate crimes are socially injurious acts committed by people who control companies to further their business interests. The target of their crimes can be the general public, the environment, or even company workers. What makes these crimes unique is that the perpetrator is a legal fiction—a corporation—and not an individual. In reality, it is company employees or owners who commit corporate crimes and who ultimately benefit through career advancement or greater profits. For a corporation to be held criminally liable, the employee committing the crime must be acting within the scope of his employment and must have actual or apparent authority to engage in the particular act in question. **Actual authority** occurs when a corporation knowingly gives authority to an employee; **apparent authority** is satisfied if a third party, such as a customer, reasonably believes the agent has the authority to perform the act in question. Courts have ruled that actual authority may occur even when the illegal behavior is not condoned by the corporation but is nonetheless within the scope of the employee's authority.[72]

Some of the acts included within corporate crime are price fixing and illegal restraint of trade, false advertising, and the use of company practices that violate environmental protection statutes. The variety of crimes contained within this category is great, and they cause vast damage. The following subsections examine some of the most important offenses.

Illegal Restraint of Trade and Price Fixing   A restraint of trade involves a contract or conspiracy designed to stifle competition, create a monopoly, artificially maintain prices, or otherwise interfere with free market competition.[73] The control of restraint of trade violations has its legal basis in the **Sherman Antitrust Act**, which subjects to criminal or civil sanctions any person "who shall make any contract or engage in any combination or conspiracy" in restraint of interstate commerce.[74] For violations of its provisions, this federal law created criminal penalties of up to three years imprisonment and $100,000 in fines for individuals and $10 million in fines for corporations.[75] The act outlaws conspiracies between corporations designed to control the marketplace.

In most instances, the act lets the presiding court judge whether corporations have conspired to "unreasonably restrain competition." However, four types of market conditions are considered so inherently anticompetitive that federal courts, through the Sherman Antitrust Act, have defined them as illegal per se, without regard to the facts or circumstances of the case:

- *Division of markets*. Firms divide a region into territories, and each firm agrees not to compete in the others' territories.
- *Tying arrangement*. A corporation requires customers of one of its services to use other services it offers. For example, it would be an illegal restraint of trade if a railroad required that companies doing business with it or supplying it with materials ship all goods they produce on trains owned by the rail line.[76]
- *Group boycott*. An organization or company boycotts retail stores that do not comply with its rules or desires.
- *Price fixing*. A conspiracy to set and control the price of a necessary commodity is considered an absolute violation of the act.

Deceptive Pricing   Even the largest U.S. corporations commonly use deceptive pricing schemes when they respond to contract solicitations. Deceptive pricing occurs when contractors provide the government or other corporations with incomplete or misleading information on how much it will actually cost to fulfill the contracts on which they are bidding or use mischarges once the contracts are signed.[77] For example, defense contractors have been prosecuted for charging the government for costs incurred on work they are doing for private firms or shifting the costs on fixed-price contracts to ones in which the government reimburses the contractor for all expenses ("cost-plus" contracts). One well-known example of deceptive pricing occurred when the Lockheed Corporation withheld information that its labor costs would be lower than expected on the C-5 cargo plane. The resulting overcharges were an estimated $150 million. Although the government was able to negotiate a cheaper price for future C-5 orders, it did not demand repayment on the earlier contract.[78]

False Claims Advertising   Executives in even the largest corporations sometimes face stockholders' expectations of ever-increasing company profits that seem to demand that sales be increased at any cost. At times executives respond to this challenge by making claims about their products that cannot be justified by actual performance. However, the line between clever, aggressive sales techniques and fraudulent claims is fine. It is traditional to show a product in its best light, even if that involves resorting to fantasy. It is not fraudulent to show a delivery service vehicle taking off into outer space or to imply that taking one sip of beer will make people feel they have just jumped into a freezer. However, it is illegal to knowingly and purposely advertise a product as possessing qualities that the manufacturer realizes it does not have, such as the ability to cure the common cold, grow hair, or turn senior citizens into rock stars (though some rock stars are senior citizens these days).

In 2003, the U.S. Supreme Court, in the case of *Illinois Ex Rel. Madigan v. Telemarketing Associates*, helped define the line separating illegal claims from those that are artistic hyperbole protected by free speech.[79] Telemarketing Associates, a for-profit fundraising corporation, was retained by a charity to solicit donations to aid Vietnam veterans in the state of Illinois. Though donors were told that a significant portion of the money would go to the vets, the telemarketers actually retained 85 percent of all the money collected. The Illinois attorney general filed a complaint in state court, alleging that such representations were knowingly deceptive and materially false. The telemarketers said they were exercising their First Amendment free speech rights when they made their pitch for money.

The Supreme Court disagreed and found that states may charge fraud when fundraisers make false or misleading representations designed to deceive donors about how their donations will be used. The Court held that it is false and misleading for a solicitor to fool potential donors into believing that a substantial portion of their contributions would fund specific programs or services, knowing full well that was not the case.

Worker Safety Violations   Some corporations have endangered the lives of their own workers by maintaining unsafe conditions in their plants and mines. It has been estimated that more than 20 million workers have been exposed to hazardous materials while on the job. Each year about

4 million workers are injured and 4,000 killed on the job. Some industries have been hit particularly hard by complaints and allegations. The control of workers' safety has been the province of the Occupational Safety and Health Administration (OSHA). OSHA sets industry standards for the proper use of such chemicals as benzene, arsenic, lead, and coke. Intentional violation of OSHA standards can result in criminal penalties.

The **National Whistleblower Center** is a nonprofit educational advocacy organization that works for the enforcement of environmental laws, nuclear safety, civil rights, and government and industry accountability through the support and representation of employee whistleblowers. To learn more, visit the Criminal Justice CourseMate at cengagebrain.com, then access the "Web Links" for this chapter.

WHITE-COLLAR LAW ENFORCEMENT SYSTEMS

The Commerce Clause of the U.S. Constitution gives the federal government the authority to regulate white-collar crime. Detection and enforcement are primarily in the hands of administrative departments and agencies, including the FBI, the Internal Revenue Service, the Secret Service, U.S. Customs, the Environmental Protection Agency, and the Securities and Exchange Commission.[80] The decision to pursue criminal rather than civil violations usually is based on the seriousness of the case and the perpetrator's intent, actions to conceal the violation, and prior record. Enforcement generally is reactive (generated by complaints) rather than proactive (involving ongoing investigations or the monitoring of activities). Investigations are carried out by the various federal agencies and the FBI. If criminal prosecution is called for, the case will be handled by attorneys from the criminal, tax, antitrust, and civil rights divisions of the Justice Department. If insufficient evidence is available to warrant a criminal prosecution, the case will be handled civilly or administratively by some other federal agency. The Federal Trade Commission can issue a cease and desist order in antitrust or merchandising fraud cases.

The number of state-funded technical assistance offices to help local prosecutors has increased significantly; more than 40 states offer such services. On the state and local levels, law enforcement officials have made progress in a number of areas, such as controlling consumer fraud. The Environmental Crimes Strike Force in Los Angeles County, California, is considered a model for the control of illegal dumping and pollution.[81] Some of the more common environmental offenses investigated and prosecuted by the task force include:

- The illegal transportation, treatment, storage, or disposal of hazardous waste
- Oil spills
- Fraudulent certification of automobile smog tests[82]

Nonetheless, while local agencies recognize the seriousness of enterprise-type crimes, they rarely have the funds necessary for effective enforcement.[83] Local prosecutors pursue white-collar criminals more vigorously if they are part of a team effort involving a network of law enforcement agencies.[84] National surveys of local prosecutors find that many do not consider white-collar crimes particularly serious problems. They are more willing to prosecute cases if the offense causes substantial harm and if other agencies fail to act. Relatively few prosecutors participate in interagency task forces designed to investigate white-collar criminal activity.[85]

Controlling White-Collar Crime

In years past, it was rare for a corporate or white-collar criminal to receive a serious criminal penalty.[86] White-collar criminals are often considered nondangerous offenders because they usually are respectable older citizens who have families to support. These "pillars of the community" are not seen in the same light as a teenager who breaks into a drugstore to steal a few dollars. Their public humiliation at being caught is usually deemed punishment enough; a prison sentence seems unnecessarily cruel.

The main reason, according to legal expert Stuart Green, is that perception of white-collar crime is clouded by moral ambiguity. White-collar crimes are typically committed by society's success stories, by the rich and the powerful, and frequently have no visible victim at their root. Both the public and the justice system have had trouble distinguishing criminal fraud from mere lawful exaggeration, tax evasion from "tax avoidance," insider trading from "savvy investing," obstruction of justice from "zealous advocacy," bribery from "horse trading," and extortion from "hard bargaining."[87] Hence, white-collar criminals are treated more leniently than lower-class offenders, the topic of the Thinking Like a Criminologist feature.

There have also been charges that efforts to control white-collar crime are biased against specific classes and races: authorities seem to be less diligent when victims are poor or minority group members or the crimes take place in minority areas. When Michael Lynch and his associates studied petroleum refineries' law violations, they found that those polluting black, Latino, and low-income communities receive smaller fines than those refineries in white and affluent communities. They also found that violations of the Clean Air Act, the Clean Water Act, and/or the Resource Conservation and Recovery Act in minority areas received much smaller fines than the same types of violations occurring in white areas ($108,563 versus $341,590).[88]

The prevailing wisdom, then, is that many white-collar criminals avoid prosecution, and those that are prosecuted receive lenient punishment. What efforts have been made to bring violators of the public trust to justice? White-collar criminal enforcement typically involves two strategies designed to control organizational deviance: compliance and deterrence.[89]

Compliance Strategies   Compliance strategies aim for law conformity without the necessity of detecting, processing, or penalizing individual violators. At a minimum, they ask for cooperation and self-policing among the business

community. Compliance systems attempt to create conformity by giving companies economic incentives to obey the law. They rely on administrative efforts to prevent unwanted conditions before they occur. Compliance systems depend on the threat of economic sanctions or civil penalties to control corporate violators.

One method of compliance is to set up administrative agencies to oversee business activity. The Securities and Exchange Commission regulates Wall Street activities, the Food and Drug Administration regulates drugs, cosmetics, medical devices, meats, and other foods, and the Environmental Protection Agency regulates pollution, dumping, and so on. The legislation creating these agencies usually spells out the penalties for violating regulatory standards. This approach has been used to control environmental crimes by levying heavy fines based on the quantity and quality of pollution released into the environment.[90] It is easier and less costly to be in compliance, the theory goes, than to pay costly fines and risk criminal prosecution for repeat violations. Moreover, the federal government bars people and businesses from receiving government contracts if they have engaged in repeated business law violations.

When compliance fails, and businesspeople violate the law, the institution rather than its individual employees are punished. In 2006, for example, employees of the Longley Jones real estate management company illegally removed and disposed of asbestos in 98 buildings they owned or managed. Longley Jones was charged with one count of conspiracy and seven counts of violating the Clean Air Act. The sentence: the company paid a $3,200 special assessment and a $4 million fine, $3 million of which was suspended if it cleaned up the asbestos at various Longley Jones facilities.[91] Compliance rather than punishment is the goal of the court order.

Another compliance approach is to force corporate boards to police themselves and take more oversight responsibility. In the wake of the Enron and WorldCom debacles, the federal government enacted the Sarbanes-Oxley (SOX) legislation in 2002 to combat fraud and abuse in publicly traded companies.[92] This law limits the nonaudit services auditing firms can perform for publicly traded companies in order to make sure accounting firms do not fraudulently collude with corporate officers; as well, it places greater responsibilities on boards to preserve an organization's integrity and reputation, primarily for U.S. publicly traded companies. It also penalizes any attempts to alter or falsify company records in order to delude shareholders:

> Sec. 802(a) Whoever knowingly alters, destroys, mutilates, conceals, covers up, falsifies, or makes a false entry in any record, document, or tangible object with the intent to impede, obstruct, or influence the investigation or proper administration of any matter within the jurisdiction of any department or agency of the United States or any case filed under title 11, or in relation to or contemplation of any such matter or case, shall be fined under this title, imprisoned not more than 20 years, or both.

In sum, compliance strategies attempt to create a marketplace incentive to obey the law. Compliance strategies avoid punishing, stigmatizing, and shaming businesspeople by focusing on the act, rather than the actor, in white-collar crime.[93]

Deterrence Strategies Some criminologists say that the punishment of white-collar crimes should include a retributive component similar to that used in common-law crimes. White-collar crimes, after all, are immoral activities that have harmed social values and deserve commensurate punishment.[94] Even the largest fines and penalties are no more than a slap on the wrist to multibillion-dollar companies. Corporations can get around economic sanctions by moving their rule-violating activities overseas, where legal controls over injurious corporate activities are lax or nonexistent.[95] They argue that the only way to limit white-collar crime is to deter potential offenders through fear of punishment.

Deterrence strategies involve detecting criminal violations, determining who is responsible, and penalizing the offenders to deter future violations.[96] Deterrence systems are oriented toward apprehending violators and punishing them rather than creating conditions that induce conformity to the law.

Deterrence strategies should work—and they have—because white-collar crime by its nature is a rational act whose perpetrators are extremely sensitive to the threat of criminal sanctions. Perceptions of detection and punishment for white-collar crimes appear to be powerful deterrents to future law violations. Although deterrence strategies may prove effective, federal agencies have traditionally been reluctant to throw corporate executives in jail. The government seeks criminal indictments in corporate violations only in "instances of outrageous conduct of undoubted illegality," such as price fixing.[97] The government has also been lenient with companies and individuals that cooperate voluntarily after an investigation has begun; leniency is not given as part of a confession or plea arrangement. Those who comply with the leniency policy are charged criminally for the activity reported.[98]

Is the Tide Turning?

Despite years of neglect, there is growing evidence that white-collar crime deterrence strategies have become normative. In one important case, Adelphia cable operator John Rigas was sentenced to 15 years in prison for bank and securities fraud, and his son Timothy Rigas was sentenced to 20 after their conviction on charges that they used company funds to support their extravagant lifestyle. John Rigas took advantage of a shared line of credit with Adelphia, using the company's money—stockholders' money—for personal extravagances.[99]

This get-tough deterrence approach appears to be affecting all classes of white-collar criminals. Although many people believe affluent corporate executives usually avoid serious punishment, public displeasure with such highly publicized white-collar crimes may be producing a backlash that is resulting in more frequent use of prison sentences.[100] With the Madoff scandal depriving so many people of their life savings, the general public has become educated as to the damage caused by white-collar criminals and may now consider white-collar crimes as more serious offenses than common-law theft offenses.

Considering this changing vision, it is not surprising that the U.S. Department of Justice Antitrust Division is now vigorously pursuing increased jail time for violators as well as more punitive financial penalties. The division has significantly increased the amount of fines it has collected, from $75 million in 2002 to more than $500 million today.

Some commentators now argue that the government may actually be going overboard in its efforts to punish white-collar criminals, especially for crimes that are the result of negligent business practices rather than intentional criminal conspiracy.[101] The U.S. Sentencing Commission has voted to increase penalties for high-dollar fraud and theft offenses.[102] While the Sherman Antitrust Act caps fines at $10 million, the commission's penalties are far more severe. Under these guidelines, corporations convicted of antitrust felonies may result in fines equal to the greater of twice the corporation's illegal financial gain or twice the victim's loss; as a result, both fines and penalties have been increasing.

AP Images/Charlie Riedel, File

On June 3, 2010, a brown pelican covered in oil sits on the beach at East Grand Terre Island along the Louisiana coast in the wake of the BP Deepwater Horizon rig explosion. A permanent cement plug sealed BP's well nearly 2.5 miles below the sea floor in the Gulf of Mexico, five agonizing months after an explosion sank a drilling rig and led to the worst offshore oil spill in U.S. history. Not only were birds, turtles, and fish killed, the spill also damaged grasses that grow on the coast of Louisiana that are crucial to the ecosystem. The oil kills the grass and animals both by releasing poisonous chemicals and by coating them, which causes suffocation.

Since 1999, Florida's Department of Environmental Protection has fielded a multiagency strike force—led by the department's Division of Law Enforcement—to **investigate pollutant discharges and the release of hazardous material statewide**. To learn more, visit the Criminal Justice CourseMate at cengagebrain.com, then access the "Web Links" for this chapter.

GREEN-COLLAR CRIME

On April 20, 2010, an explosion occurred on the *Deepwater Horizon* oil rig, killing 11 platform workers and injuring 17 others.[103] The rig was built by Hyundai Heavy Industries of Korea, owned by the Transocean Drilling Corporation, the drilling overseen by Halliburton, and leased by BP (formerly British Petroleum), in order to drill a deepwater (5,000 feet below the surface) well in the Gulf of Mexico. At first, estimates of the spill were 5,000 barrels a day, but they quickly rose to 60,000. While company officials frantically tried to stem the flow with a variety of failed schemes, millions of barrels of escaping oil created a slick that covered thousands of square miles, devastating wildlife and causing one of the greatest natural disasters in the nation's history. BP, facing billions in civil fines, offered to place $20 billion in an escrow account to cover damages. The leak was finally stopped in August 2010.

On June 1, 2010, the Obama administration announced that it had launched a criminal probe in order to "prosecute to the fullest extent of the law" any persons or companies that broke the law in the time leading up to the spill.[104] Under federal environmental laws, a company may be charged with a misdemeanor for negligent conduct, or a felony if there is evidence that company personnel knowingly engaged in conduct risking injury. It would be a criminal act if, for example, employees of BP or its subcontractors, Transocean and Halliburton:

- Lied in the permit process for obtaining a drilling license
- Tried to cover up the severity of the spill
- Knowing of negligence in construction, chose to ignore the danger it imposed
- Engaged in or approved of unsafe, risky, or dangerous methods to remove the drill, knowing that such methods could injure those on board

To prove a felony, and potentially put BP executives in prison, the government must show that company officials knew in advance that its actions would lead to the explosion and oil spill but chose to ignore the danger; a misdemeanor requires only mere negligence. But even a misdemeanor conviction would amp up the loss to the company, because the Federal Alternative Fines Act allows the government to request monetary fines that are twice the loss associated with an offense.[105] This provision can also have a devastating effect on employees, because fines imposed on individuals under the act may *not* be paid by their employer.[106] A criminal conviction would cost BP more than $60 billion. It would also mean that the company would be prevented from having future sales contracts with the government. Finally, lying to the government during the investigation could bring additional common-law charges of making false statements, obstruction of justice, and conspiracy. At this time, the case has not been resolved.

While some may argue that it is overly harsh to put company executives in prison for what is essentially an accident, civil penalties do not seem to deter companies such as BP. Before the Gulf of Mexico oil spill, BP had already paid hundreds of millions in civil penalties for similar if lesser disasters. One fine of $87 million was paid to the Occupational Safety and Health Administration—the largest fine in OSHA's history— for a Texas refinery explosion; an additional $50 million was paid to the Department of Justice for the same explosion. BP also paid $3 million to OSHA for 42 safety violations at an Ohio refinery and was fined $20 million by the Department of Justice for another spill that violated the Clean Water Act.

Oil spills are just part of the green crime problem. Environmental activists have long called attention to a variety of ecological threats that they feel should be deemed criminal. Green crimes involve a wide range of actions and outcomes that harm the environment and that stem from decisions about what is produced, where it is produced, and how it is produced.[107] Global warming, overdevelopment, population growth, and other changes will continue to bring these issues front and center.[108]

While crimes targeting the environment have received scant attention in the criminological literature, recent events have shifted attention to what is variously called green crime, green criminology, and green-collar crime. The Gulf Coast disaster in 2010 is a powerful and tragic example of how environmental destruction and green crimes may be linked to enterprise systems: the need for corporate profit may outweigh attention to safety, with subsequent catastrophic consequences.

Defining Green Crime

There is no single vision to define the concept of green crimes. Three independent views exist:

- *Legalist*. According to the legalist perspective, environmental crimes are violations of existing criminal laws designed to protect people, the environment or both. This definition would include crimes against workers such as occupational health and safety crimes, as well as laws designed to protect nature and the environment (the Clean Air Act, Clean Water Act, and so on).
- *Environmental justice*. According to the environmental justice view, limiting environmental crimes to actual violations of the criminal law is too narrow. A great deal of environmental damage occurs in third-world nations desperate for funds and willing to give mining and oil companies a free hand to develop resources. These nations have meager regulatory laws and therefore allow businesses wide latitude in environmental contamination that would be forbidden in the United States. In addition, environmental justice advocates believe that corporations themselves have attempted to co-opt or manipulate environmental laws, thereby limiting their scope and reach. Executives fear that the environmental movement will force changes in their production practices and place limits on their growth and corporate power. Some have tried to co-opt green laws by public relations and advertising campaigns that suggest they are doing everything in their power to respect the environment, thereby reducing the need for government regulation. Criminologists must take a broader view of green crimes than the law allows.
- *Biocentric*. According to the biocentric approach, environmental harm is viewed as any human activity that disrupts a biosystem, destroying plant and animal life. This more radical approach would criminalize any intentional or negligent human activity or manipulation that impacts negatively on the earth's natural resources, resulting in trauma to those resources.[109] Environmental harm, according to this view, is much greater than what is defined by law as environmental crimes. As criminologist Rob White points out, this is because some of the most ecologically destructive activities, such as clear felling of old-growth forests, are quite legal. Environmental crimes are typically oriented toward protecting humans and their property and have a limited interest in the interests of animals and plants.[110] Environmental laws protect animal and fish processing plants that treat "nature" and "wildlife" simply and mainly as resources for human exploitation. Human beings are the cause of environmental harm and need to be controlled.

Forms of Green Crime

Green-collar crime can take many different forms, ranging from deforestation and illegal logging to violations of worker safety. A few of the most damaging forms are set out below.

Illegal Logging   Illegal logging involves harvesting, processing, and transporting timber or wood products in violation of existing laws and treaties.[111] It is a universal phenomenon, occurring in major timber-producing countries, especially in the third world where enforcement is lax. Logging violations include taking trees in protected areas such as national parks, going over legally prescribed logging quotas, processing logs without acquiring licenses, and exporting logs without paying export duties. By sidestepping the law, loggers can create greater profits than those generated through legal methods.

The situation is serious because illegal logging can have severe environmental and social impact:

- Illegal logging exhausts forests, destroys wildlife, and damages its habitats. Illegal logging in central Africa is destroying the habitats and threatening the survival of populations of the great apes, including gorillas and chimpanzees.
- It causes ruinous damage to the forests, including deforestation and forest degradation worldwide. The destruction of forest cover can cause flash floods and landslides that have killed thousands of people.
- By reducing forest cover, illegal logging impairs the ability of land to absorb carbon emissions.
- Illegal logging costs billions each year in government revenue, impairing the ability of third-world nations to provide needed social services.
- It creates unsustainable economic devastation in the poorest countries. Vietnam, for example, has lost a third of its forest cover, while in nearby Cambodia illegal logging is at least ten times the size of the legal harvest. These rates of extraction are clearly unsustainable, destroying valuable sources of employment and export revenues for the future.
- The substantial revenues from illegal logging fund national and regional conflict. In Cambodia, for several years Khmer Rouge insurgents were sustained primarily by the revenue from logging areas under their control.[112]

While the scale of illegal logging is difficult to estimate, it is believed that more than half of all logging activities in the most vulnerable forest regions—Southeast Asia, central Africa, South America, and Russia—may be conducted illegally. Worldwide, estimates suggest that illegal activities may account for over a tenth of the total global timber trade, representing products worth at least $15 billion per year.

Illegal Wildlife Exports The smuggling of wildlife across national borders is a serious matter.[113] Exporters find a lucrative trade in the demand for such illicit wildlife commodities as tiger parts, caviar, elephant ivory, rhino horn, and exotic birds and reptiles. Wildlife contraband may include live pets, hunting trophies, fashion accessories, cultural artifacts, ingredients for traditional medicines, wild meat for human consumption (or bush meat), and other products. Illegal profits can be immense.

There are numerous problems presented by illegal wildlife exporting. Poachers imperil endangered species and threaten them with extinction. By evading government controls, they create the potential for introducing pests and diseases into formerly unaffected areas.[114] They import nonnative species, which could harm the receiving habitats. Florida's Everglades have been overrun with nonnative species such as pythons, imported as pets and abandoned in the wild. Illegal wildlife traders range from independent one-person operations that sell a single item to complex, multi-ton, commercial-sized consignments shipped all over the world. Adding all these sources together, the global trade in illegal wildlife is a growing phenomenon and is now estimated to be somewhere between $5 billion and $20 billion annually.

The United States is estimated to purchase nearly 20 percent of all illegal wildlife and wildlife products on the market, perhaps as much as $3 billion annually. The trade is so lucrative because exotic animals and animal parts are enormously expensive (Table 13.1), providing an economic incentive that proves irresistible to smugglers in third-world nations.

TABLE 13.1 Illicit Wildlife Trade and Estimated Retail Value

Illegally Traded Wildlife	Estimated Retail Value
Elephants	$121–$900 per kilogram of ivory
Rhinos	$945–$50,000 per kilogram of rhino horn
Tibetan antelopes	$1,200–$20,000 per shatoosh shawl
Big cats	$1,300–$20,000 per tiger, snow leopard, or jaguar skin; $3,300–$7,000 per set of tiger bones
Bears	$250–$8,500 per gallbladder
Sturgeon	$4,450–$6,000 per kilogram of caviar
Reptiles and insects (often live)	$30,000 per oenpelli python; $30,000 per komodo dragon; $5,000–$30,000 per plowshare tortoise; $15,000 per Chinese alligator; $20,000 per monitor lizard; $20,000 per shingleback skink; $8,500 per pair of birdwing butterflies
Exotic birds (often live)	$10,000 per black palm cockatoo egg ($25,000–$80,000 per mature breeding pair); $5,000–$12,000 per hyacinth macaw; $60,000–$90,000 per lear macaw; $20,000 per Mongolian falcon
Great apes (often live)	$50,000 per orangutan

SOURCE: Liana Sun Wyler and Pervaze A. Sheikh, *International Illegal Trade in Wildlife: Threats and U.S. Policy* (Washington, DC: Congressional Research Service, 2008), http://fpc.state.gov/documents/organization/110404.pdf (accessed November 4, 2010).

ANDREW ROSS/AFP/Getty Images/Newscom

The African nation of Mozambique is a good example of a smaller nation whose thriving fishing industry is being threatened by illegal poachers. In 2007, following an increase in illegal fishing, the United States donated three vessels to Mozambique to increase capacity for surveillance and enforcement of fishing regulations. The commander of Mozambique's navy has ascertained that the "pirate fleets" concentrate their activities around the Bazaruto archipelago, a marine reserve and national park about 20 miles off the mainland. In July 2008, the control ships intercepted a Namibian-flagged fishing boat, *Antillas Reefer*, after it was observed fishing without a license off the central province of Zambezia. On board, authorities found 43 tons of sharks, 4 tons of shark fin, 1.8 tons of shark tail, 11.3 tons of shark liver, and 20 tons of shark oil, with a total value of $5 million. They also seized 65 tons of bait (frozen squid and fish) and illegal deepwater long lines. The *Antillas Reefer* logbook showed that the vessel had been fishing in Mozambique's waters for months in an effort to capture a species of valuable deep-sea sharks banned as a target species in Mozambique. The penalty imposed was $4 million in addition to the confiscation of the vessel, fishing gear, and catch—an appropriate penalty for an IUU (illegal, unreported, and unregulated) fishing vessel and a message for other would-be IUU operators throughout the region.

SOURCE: Ministério das Pescas/Ministry of Fisheries, "Mozambique Ends Up with 2 IUU Cases: *Antillas Reefer* Forfeited to the Government of Mozambique and Payam Released After Paying Fine," www.stopillegalfishing.com/sifnews_article.php?ID=52 (accessed November 4, 2010).

The U.S. Congress has passed numerous laws that regulate and restrict wildlife imports and exports, including the Endangered Species Act of 1973 and the Lacey Act, which protects both plants and wildlife by creating civil and criminal penalties for a wide array of violations. The original act was directed at preserving game and wild birds and prohibiting the introduction of nonnative birds and animals into native ecosystems. The act has been amended and in 1981 was changed to include illegal trade in plants, fish, and wildlife both domestically and abroad. The maximum penalty was increased to $10,000 with possible imprisonment for one year. Additionally, the mental state required for a criminal violation was increased to "knowingly and willfully"; civil penalties were expanded to apply to negligent violations.[115]

These laws and others establish authorities and guidelines for wildlife trade inspection at ports of entry and for wildlife crime law enforcement and prosecution. There are also international laws restricting the wildlife trade. The United Nations Convention on International Trade in Endangered Species of Wild Fauna and Flora (CITES) serves as the primary vehicle for regulating wildlife trade.

Despite such efforts, the trade still flourishes. It has been argued that one way to effectively control the movements of creatures across regions is to allow but closely monitor commercial export of wildlife. However, where legalized trade is allowed, experience shows that this opens up opportunities for forging permits and other documentation, as well as for other types of enabling activity. For example, wild-caught animals can be mixed in with captive-bred animals, making illegal exports even harder to detect.

Illegal Fishing Unlicensed and illegal fishing practices is another billion-dollar green crime. It can take on many forms and involve highly different parties, ranging from huge factory ships operating on the high seas that catch thousands of tons of fish on each voyage, to smaller, locally operating ships that confine themselves to national waters. Illegal fishing occurs when these ships sign on to their home nation's rules but then choose to ignore their scope and boundary, or operate in a country's waters without permission or on the high seas without a flag. Because catches are not reported by the fishing vessels, their illegal fishing can have a detrimental effect on species because government regulators have no idea how many are being caught. Stocks become depleted and species endangered. In addition, illegal fishing techniques, including fishermen using the wrong sized nets or fishing in prohibited areas, can damage fragile marine ecosystems, threatening coral reefs, turtles, and seabirds. In underdeveloped nations, regulators may look the other way because the need for short-term economic, social, or political gains is given more weight than long-term sustainability. As a result, species of whales, abalone, lobsters, and Patagonian toothfish (known in the U.S. as Chilean sea bass) have become endangered.[116] The Profiles in Crime feature focuses on the illegal fishing trade.

Illegal Dumping Some green-collar criminals want to skirt local, state, and federal restrictions on dumping dangerous substances in the environment. Rather than pay expensive processing fees, they may secretly dispose of hazardous wastes in illegal dump sites. Illegally dumped wastes can either be hazardous or nonhazardous materials that are discarded in an effort to avoid either disposal fees or the time and effort required for proper disposal. Materials dumped ranged from used motor oil to waste from construction sites.

One of the largest and fastest growing problems is the disposal of 7 million tons of obsolete high-tech electronics, called e-waste, such as televisions, computers and computer monitors, laptops, VCRs, and so on.[117] According to research by Carole Gibbs, Edmund McGarrell, and Mark Axelrod, while most e-waste in the United States is disposed of in landfills or is incinerated, the toxic material contained in electronic gear (such as lead) encourages illegal dumping in order to avoid recycling costs. Consequently, a considerable amount of e-waste is sent abroad to developing nations for recycling, often in violation of international laws restricting such commerce. All too often, the material overwhelms recycling plants and is instead dumped in local villages near people and water sources. Illegal dump sites have been documented in Nigeria, Ghana, China, the Philippines, Indonesia, Pakistan, and India, and they pose severe threats to both human health and the natural environment.

Illegal Polluting   Long before the Gulf of Mexico disaster, environmental pollution crimes threatened the ecosystem. Prior to the BP spill, the most notorious environmental disaster occurred when the oil tanker *Exxon Valdez* hit a reef in Prince William Sound and devastated Prudhoe Bay on the coast of Alaska. The spill released more than 11 million gallons of crude oil, which covered more than 10,000 miles of ocean. At the time of the disaster, the *Exxon Valdez* was on autopilot; its captain, who may have been drinking, was asleep. Water pollution killed 250,000 sea birds, 2,800 sea otters, 300 harbor seals, 250 bald eagles, up to 22 orcas, and billions of salmon and herring eggs. The spill continues to have an impact on many shore-dwelling animals. Sea otters have yet to reinhabit Herring Bay, and their overall numbers in the area have declined.

Exxon Mobil was fined $150 million and paid an additional $100 million as restitution for damage caused to fish, wildlife, and land, and also agreed to pay $900 million in 10 annual installments to civil claimants. In 1994, a jury found that Exxon acted recklessly, and awarded victims $5 billion in punitive damages. The U.S. Supreme Court cut the amount to $507.5 million in June 2008, hardly a day's pay for the largest company on earth.

Because of the *Exxon Valdez* disaster and other environmental crimes, a great deal of attention is now paid to intentional or negligent environmental pollution caused by many large corporations. The numerous allegations in this area involve almost every aspect of U.S. business. Most environmental crime statutes contain overlapping civil, criminal, and administrative penalty provisions, which gives the government latitude in enforcement. Over time, Congress has elevated some violations from misdemeanors to felonies

and has increased potential jail sentences and fines for those convicted.[118]

Criminal environmental pollution is defined as the intentional or negligent discharge of a toxic or contaminating substance into the biosystem that is known to have an adverse effect on the natural environment or life. It may involve the ground release of toxic chemicals such as kepone, vinyl chloride, mercury, PCBs, and asbestos. Illegal and/or controlled air pollutants include hydrochlorofluorocarbons (HCFCs), aerosols, asbestos, carbon monoxide, chlorofluorocarbons (CFCs), criteria air pollutants, lead, mercury, methane, nitrogen oxides (NO_x), radon, refrigerants, and sulfur oxides (SO_2). Water pollution is defined as the dumping of a substance that degrades or alters the quality of the waters to an extent that is detrimental to their use by humans or by an animal or a plant that is useful to humans. This includes the disposal into rivers, lakes, and streams of:

- Excess fertilizers, herbicides, and insecticides from agricultural lands and residential areas
- Oil, grease, and toxic chemicals from urban runoff and energy production
- Sediment from improperly managed construction sites, crop and forest lands, and eroding streambanks
- Salt from irrigation practices and acid drainage from abandoned mines
- Bacteria and nutrients from livestock, pet wastes, and faulty septic systems

Enforcing Environmental Laws

The United States and most sovereign nations have passed laws making it a crime to pollute or damage the environment. For example, among environmental laws in the U.S. are the following:

- *Clean Water Act (1972).* Establishes and maintains goals and standards for U.S. water quality and purity. It was amended in 1987 to increase controls on toxic pollutants, and in 1990 to more effectively address the hazard of oil spills.
- *Emergency Planning and Community Right-to-Know Act (1986).* Requires companies to disclose information about toxic chemicals they release into the air and water and dispose of on land.
- *Endangered Species Act (1973).* Is designed to protect and recover endangered and threatened species of fish, wildlife, and plants in the United States and beyond. The law works in part by protecting species habitats.
- *Oil Pollution Act (1990).* Enacted in the aftermath of the *Exxon Valdez* oil spill in Alaska's Prince William Sound, this law streamlines federal response to oil spills by requiring oil storage facilities and vessels to prepare spill-response plans and provide for their rapid implementation. The law also increases polluters' liability for cleanup costs and damage to natural resources.

The major enforcement arm against environmental crimes is the Environmental Protection Agency, which was given full law enforcement authority in 1988. The EPA has successfully prosecuted significant violations across all major environmental statutes, including data fraud cases (for instance, private laboratories submitting false environmental data to state and federal environmental agencies); indiscriminate hazardous waste dumping that resulted in serious injuries and death; industry-wide ocean dumping by cruise ships; oil spills that caused significant damage to waterways, wetlands, and beaches; international smuggling of CFC refrigerants that damage the ozone layer and increase skin cancer risk; and illegal handling of hazardous substances such as pesticides and asbestos that exposed children, the poor, and other especially vulnerable groups to potentially serious illness.[119] Its Criminal Investigation Division (EPA CID) investigates allegations of criminal wrongdoing prohibited by various environmental statutes. Such investigations involve, but are not limited to:

- The illegal disposal of hazardous waste
- The export of hazardous waste without the permission of the receiving country
- The illegal discharge of pollutants to a water of the United States
- The removal and disposal of regulated asbestos-containing materials in a manner inconsistent with the law and regulations
- The illegal importation of certain restricted or regulated chemicals into the United States
- Tampering with a drinking water supply
- Mail fraud
- Wire fraud
- Conspiracy and money laundering relating to environmental criminal activities

THE CAUSES OF ENTERPRISE CRIME

Why do people get involved in risky schemes to use their institutional positions to steal money? Why do people risk going to prison because they pollute the environment? Can the same factors that predict other types of criminal offenses also apply to crimes of criminal enterprise? After all, unlike other criminal offenses, white-collar and green-collar crimes are not committed by impoverished teenagers living in the inner city, but by otherwise respectable people, many of whom are educated and financially well off. By their very nature, enterprise crimes require that offenders attain a position of power and trust before they can be committed. Therefore, can the theories that predict and explain common-law crime be applied to enterprise-type crime?

This section describes some of the most prominent views of why people commit crimes of criminal enterprise.

Rational Choice: Greed

When Kansas City pharmacist Robert Courtney was asked after his arrest why he substituted improper doses of drugs instead of what doctors had prescribed, he told investigators he cut the drugs' strength "out of greed."[120]

Courtney is not alone. One view of enterprise crime is that greedy people rationally choose to take shortcuts to acquire wealth, believing that the potential profits far outweigh future punishments. Most believe they will not get caught; they are far too clever to be detected by mere civil servants who work for government agencies.

Greed was rampant in the 1980s. Ivan Boesky was a famous Wall Street trader who had amassed a fortune of about $200 million by betting on corporate takeovers, a practice called *arbitrage*. In 1986, he was investigated by the Securities and Exchange Commission for insider trading. To escape serious punishment, he informed on several associates. In exchange for cooperation, Boesky received a sentence of three and a half years in prison and a $100 million fine. Released after serving two years, Boesky was barred from working in the securities business for the remainder of his life.

Caught in the web was billionaire junk bond trader Michael Milken. Indicted by a federal grand jury, Milken pleaded guilty to five securities and reporting violations and was sentenced to 10 years in prison; he served 22 months. He also paid a $200 million fine and another $400 million to $800 million in settlements relating primarily to civil lawsuits.

Lure Greed unfortunately did not end in the 1980s, and the greed that begat the Wall Street scandals of 2008 to 2010 almost sank the world economy. Recently criminologists Neal Shover and Peter Grabosky introduced the concept of "lure" to help explain why some people succumb to the illegal yet alluring benefits of enterprise crime:[121]

> It may be discomforting to acknowledge, but experience teaches that at any given time there are persons in the larger world that are either bent on breaking the law or are easily tempted to do so. Likewise some organizations are predisposed to transgress. They are distinguished by structural, cultural, or procedural characteristics that increase the odds that their personnel will recognize and exploit lure. Tempted individuals possess qualities or experiences that make them more likely than peers who lack these distinctions to weigh illicit exploitation of lure. The size of the pool of the predisposed and tempted waxes and wanes depending upon a variety of other conditions in their worlds. These include the size of the supply of lure, prevailing estimates of the credibility of external oversight, and

how extensively effective mechanisms of internal oversight and self-restraint are deployed.[122]

Lure is something that is alluring—something that is so attractive and covetable that it can turn the heads of those who are tempted or predisposed. The lure of enterprise crime has diverse sources. When a would-be green-collar criminal sees the wide expanses of uninhabited countryside, they become tempted to dispose of trash quickly and cheaply. When states create loopholes in the law that provide opportunities that can be manipulated easily for criminal purposes—such as tax incentives, subsidies, low-interest loans, and other forms of access to public funds—these benefits may prove too much of a lure for businessmen to resist. As the supply of lure has expanded, so too has the number of privileged citizens and large corporations willing to risk legal censure to acquire its benefits. The lure of crime expands in the absence of capable control systems. When financial oversight was absent in the United States economic markets, the crash of 2008 became inevitable.

Rational Choice: Need

Greed is not the only motivation for white-collar crime; need also plays an important role. Some people turn to crime to fulfill an overwhelming financial or psychological need. Executives may tamper with company books because they feel the need to keep or improve their jobs, satisfy their egos, or support their children. Blue-collar workers may pilfer because they need to keep pace with inflation or buy a new car. Kathleen Daly's analysis of convictions in seven federal district courts indicates that many white-collar crimes involve relatively trivial amounts. Women convicted of white-collar crime typically work in lower-echelon positions, and their acts seem motivated more by economic survival than by greed and power.[123]

Even people in the upper echelons of the financial world, such as Boesky, may carry scars from an earlier needy period in their lives that can be healed only by accumulating ever-greater amounts of money. As one of Boesky's associates put it:

> I don't know what his devils were. Maybe he's greedy beyond the wildest imaginings of mere mortals like you and me. And maybe part of what drives the guy is an inherent insecurity that was operative here even after he had arrived. Maybe he never arrived.[124]

A well-known study of embezzlers by Donald Cressey illustrates the important role need plays in white-collar crime. According to Cressey, embezzlement is caused by what he calls a "nonshareable financial problem." This condition may be the result of offenders' living beyond their means, perhaps piling up gambling debts; offenders feel they cannot let anyone know about such financial problems without ruining their reputations.

Rationalization/Neutralization View

Rationalizing guilt is a common trait of white-collar criminals.[125] What they did was not so bad; what some call crime is merely a "technicality." One offender convicted of price fixing denied the illegality of his actions. "We did not fix prices," he said, "I am telling you that all we did was recover costs."[126] Some white-collar criminals believe that everyone violates business laws, so it is not so bad if they do so themselves.

In his research on fraud, Donald Cressey found that the door to solving personal financial problems through criminal means is opened by the rationalizations people develop for white-collar crime: "Some of our most respectable citizens got their start in life by using other people's money temporarily"; "in the real estate business, there is nothing wrong about using deposits before the deal is closed"; "all people steal when they get in a tight spot."[127] Offenders use these and other rationalizations to resolve the conflict they experience over engaging in illegal behavior.

Some white-collar offenders feel free to engage in business crime because they can easily rationalize its effects. Some convince themselves that their actions are not really crimes because the acts involved do not resemble street crimes.[125] A banker who uses his position of trust to lend his institution's assets to a company he secretly controls may see himself as a shrewd businessman, not as a criminal. A pharmacist who chisels customers on prescription drugs may rationalize her behavior by telling herself that it does not really hurt anyone. Further, some businesspeople feel justified in committing white-collar crimes because they believe government regulators do not really understand the business world or the problems of competing in the free enterprise system. Research shows that speech, occupational, and physical therapists working in hospitals, nursing homes, and with home health agencies engage in Medicaid frauds, including cutting sessions short while charging for the entire session or charging individual session rates for group therapy sessions.[128] When interviewed, the workers used techniques of neutralization to defuse guilt: (a) everyone else does it, (b) it's not my fault or responsibility, and (c) no one is hurt except insurance companies and they are wealthy.

Denying the Victim   It is especially easy for corporate offenders to neutralize wrongdoing when the target is a fellow businessperson or business organization. Because the victim is knowledgeable and sophisticated, he or she should have known better; caveat emptor, as they say: let the buyer beware. Take for instance the 2010 indictment of Goldman Sachs, the respected securities company, charged with "fraudulent misconduct" due to the firm's 2007 sale of $1 billion of repackaged subprime mortgage–backed securities. While Goldman executives did not deny that they packaged and sold the securities, they questioned why their behavior could possibly be considered a criminal act. The deal had been pitched to Goldman by hedge fund operator John Paulson, who offered the firm $15 million to help put together a package of home loans—known in the trade as a collateralized debt obligation (CDO)—and then market the loans to Goldman's clients, including foreign banks. Paulson believed that the American real estate market was about to collapse and he wanted to create a financial bet against what he considered to be distressed properties. In order to make his "bet," he, along with Goldman executives, created a fund called Abacus that was comprised of home mortgages picked personally by Paulson on properties in Arizona, Florida, Nevada, and California, states that were undergoing a collapse in the real estate market. Goldman Sachs then marketed the Abacus fund without disclosing that Abacus fund buyers, including the Royal Bank of Scotland (which lost over $800 million in the deal), lost billions and Paulson made billions.

After the indictment was filed, Goldman Sach's executives claimed they did nothing wrong in marketing the securities because purchasers were sophisticated banks and investment companies who knew what they were doing and should have realized that buying mortgage-backed securities was very risky, especially in a down real estate market. Nor was their behavior unique: marketing derivative securities such as CDOs and the short-selling of assets is a common practice carried out by virtually every major Wall Street firm. In the end, the firm was fined $550 million to settle the claims, prompting the SEC's enforcement director, Robert S. Khuzami, to say, "This settlement is a stark lesson to Wall Street firms that no product is too complex, and no investor too sophisticated, to avoid a heavy price if a firm violates the fundamental principles of honest treatment and fair dealing," While a fine of $550 million seems like a lot, it was considered a victory for Goldman, a firm that earns about $14 billion in profit yearly, because it settled the case without admitting any wrongdoing.[129] Here we can see how the line between smart business practice and corporate crime is typically blurry. When the victim can be denied, it is often difficult to accept blame.

Cultural View

Business culture may also influence white-collar crime. According to this view, some business organizations promote white-collar criminality in the same way that lower-class culture encourages the development of juvenile gangs and street crime. According to the corporate culture view, some business enterprises cause crime by placing excessive demands on employees while at the same time maintaining a business climate tolerant of employee deviance. New employees learn the attitudes and techniques needed to commit white-collar crime from their business peers. Under these circumstances, the attitudes of closest coworkers and the perceived attitudes

of executives have a more powerful control over decision making than the attitudes of outsiders—closest friends and business professors—whose more moderate views might have tempered the decision to commit crime.[130]

Business culture may have been responsible for the collapse of Enron. A new CEO had been brought in to revitalize the company, and he wanted to become part of the "new economy" based on the Internet. Layers of management were wiped out, and hundreds of outsiders were recruited. Huge cash bonuses and stock options were granted to top performers. Young managers were given authority to make $5 million decisions without higher approval. It became common for executives to change jobs two or three times in an effort to maximize bonuses and pay. Seminars were conducted showing executives how to hide profits and avoid taxes.[131]

CONNECTIONS

The view that white-collar crime is a learning process is reminiscent of Edwin Sutherland's description of how gang boys learn the techniques of drug dealing and burglary from older youths through differential association. See Chapter 7 for a description of this process.

Those holding the business culture view would point to the Enron scandal as a prime example of what happens when people work in organizations in which the cultural values stress profit over fair play, government scrutiny is limited and regulators are viewed as the enemy, and senior members encourage newcomers to believe that "greed is good."

Self-Control View

In their *General Theory of Crime*, Travis Hirschi and Michael Gottfredson suggest that the motives that produce white-collar crimes—quick benefits with minimal effort—are the same as those that produce any other criminal behaviors.[132] White-collar criminals have low self-control and are inclined to follow momentary impulses without considering the long-term costs of such behavior.[133] White-collar crime is relatively rare because, as a matter of course, business executives tend to hire people with self-control, thereby limiting the number of potential white-collar criminals. Hirschi and Gottfredson have collected data showing that the demographic distribution of white-collar crime is similar to other crimes. For example, gender, race, and age ratios are the same for crimes such as embezzlement and fraud as they are for street crimes such as burglary and robbery.

SUMMARY

1. **Know what is meant by the term *enterprise crime***
   - Losses from enterprise crime may far outstrip any other type of crime. Enterprise crime involves criminal acts that twist the legal rules of commercial enterprise for criminal purposes.

2. **Link white-collar crime and green-collar crime**
   - White-collar and green-collar crime are linked together because they involve entrepreneurship, and because in both types of crime offenders twist legal rules to enhance their personal economic position through illicit commercial enterprise. Because they are so connected, these two types of crimes may sometimes overlap. Both forms of enterprise crime can involve violence.

3. **Define white-collar crime**
   - Edwin Sutherland first used the phrase "white-collar crime" to describe the criminal activities of the rich and powerful. He defined white-collar crime as "a crime committed by a person of respectability and high social status in the course of his occupation." Included within recent views of white-collar crime are such acts as income tax evasion, credit card fraud, and bankruptcy fraud. Other white-collar criminals use their positions of trust in business or government to commit crimes. Their activities might include pilfering, soliciting bribes or kickbacks, and embezzlement.

4. **Know what is meant by the term *Ponzi scheme***
   - A Ponzi scheme is an investment fraud that involves the payment of purported returns to existing investors from funds contributed by new investors. In many Ponzi schemes, the fraudsters focus on attracting new money to make promised payments to earlier-stage investors and to use for personal expenses, instead of engaging in any legitimate investment activity. The term comes from Charles Ponzi, who duped thousands of New England residents into investing in a postage stamp speculation scheme back in the 1920s.

5. **Be familiar with the various forms of white-collar crime**
   - White-collar fraud involves using a business enterprise as a front to swindle people. Chiseling involves professionals who cheat clients. Embezzlement and employee fraud occur when a person uses a position of trust to steal from an organization. Client fraud involves theft from an organization that advances credit, covers losses, or reimburses for services. Corporate, or organizational, crime involves various illegal business practices such as price fixing, restraint of trade, and false advertising.

6. **Distinguish between exploitation and influence peddling**
   - White-collar exploitation occurs when an individual abuses his or her power or position in an organization to coerce people into making payments to him or her for services to which they are already entitled. If the payments are not made, the services are withheld. In most cases, exploitation occurs when the victim has a clear right to expect a service, and the offender threatens to withhold the service unless an additional payment or bribe is forthcoming. In contrast, influence peddling occurs when individuals holding important institutional positions sell power, influence, and information to outsiders who have an interest in influencing the activities of the institution or buying information on what the institution may do in the future.

7. **Know what is meant by the term *payola***
   - In the record industry, payola is the illegal practice of recording companies paying radio stations or DJs to play songs. While the recording companies are forced to pay, they also benefit from having their recording artists receive air time they might not otherwise have gotten.

8. **Discuss efforts to control white-collar crime**
   - The government has used various law enforcement strategies to combat white-collar crime. Some involve deterrence, which uses punishment to frighten potential abusers. Others involve economic or compliance strategies, which create economic incentives to obey the law. Most offenders do not view themselves as criminals and therefore do not seem to be deterred by criminal statutes. Although thousands of white-collar criminals are prosecuted each year, their numbers are insignificant compared with the magnitude of the problem. The Commerce Clause of the U.S. Constitution gives the federal government the authority to regulate white-collar crime. Detection and enforcement are primarily in the hands of administrative departments and agencies, including the FBI, the Internal Revenue Service, the Secret Service, U.S. Customs, the Environmental Protection Agency, and the Securities and Exchange Commission. On the state and local levels, law enforcement officials have made progress in a number of areas, such as controlling consumer fraud.

9. **Know the basics of green-collar crime**
   - There is no single vision to define the concept of green-collar crimes. Green-collar crime can take many different forms, ranging from deforestation and illegal logging to violations of worker safety. The United States and most sovereign nations have passed laws making it a crime to pollute or damage the environment. The major enforcement arm against environmental crimes is the Environmental Protection Agency, which was given full law enforcement authority in 1988.

10. **Be aware of the assumed cause of enterprise crime**
   - There are numerous explanations for enterprise crime. Some offenders are motivated by greed; others offend due to personal problems. They use rationalizations to allow their financial needs to be met without compromising their values. Corporate culture theory suggests that some businesses actually encourage employees to cheat or cut corners. The self-control view is that white-collar criminals are like any other law violators: impulsive people who lack self-control.

KEY TERMS

enterprise crimes (444)
white-collar crime (444)
green-collar crime (444)
corporate crime (445)
white-collar swindle (446)
Ponzi scheme (446)
securitization (448)

chiseling (451)
insider trading (451)
hedge fund (451)
exploitation (451)
influence peddling (453)
payola (454)
pilferage (454)

white-collar client fraud (455)
organizational crime (459)
actual authority (459)
apparent authority (459)
Sherman Antitrust Act (459)
criminal environmental pollution (467)

CRITICAL THINKING QUESTIONS

1. How would you punish a corporate executive whose product killed people if the executive had no knowledge that the product was potentially lethal? What if the executive did know?

2. What is the difference between white-collar swindles and common-law fraud?

3. Corporate culture theory suggests that some businesses actually encourage employees to cheat or cut corners. Do institutions take on a distinct criminal culture or are the people who work there just greedy?

4. Can you give examples of white-collar exploitation and influence peddling? Have you ever run into one of these problems yourself?

NOTES

1. Clifford Krauss, Phillip L. Zweig, and Julie Creswell, "Texas Firm Accused of $8 Billion Fraud," *New York Times*, February 18, 2009, www.nytimes.com/2009/02/18/business/18stanford.html (accessed November 3, 2010).

2. John Locker and Barry Godfrey, "Ontological Boundaries and Temporal Watersheds in the Development of White-Collar Crime," *British Journal of Criminology* 46 (2006): 976–999.

3. Rob White, "Researching Transnational Environmental Harm: Toward an Eco-Global Criminology," *International Journal of Comparative and Applied Criminal Justice* 33 (2009): 229–248.

4. Mark Haller, "Illegal Enterprise: A Theoretical and Historical Interpretation," *Criminology* 28 (1990): 207–235.

5. Nancy Frank and Michael Lynch, *Corporate Crime, Corporate Violence* (Albany, NY: Harrow & Heston, 1992), p. 7.

6. Edward Alsworth Ross, *Sin and Society: An Analysis of Latter-Day Iniquity* (Boston: Houghton Mifflin, 1907): 45–71.

7. Edwin Sutherland, *White-Collar Crime: The Uncut Version* (New Haven, CT: Yale University Press, 1983).

8. Edwin Sutherland, "White-Collar Criminality," *American Sociological Review* 5 (1940): 2–10.

9. David Weisburd and Kip Schlegel, "Returning to the Mainstream," in *White-Collar Crime Reconsidered*, ed. Kip Schlegel and David Weisburd (Boston: Northeastern University Press, 1992), pp. 352–365.

10. Ronald Kramer and Raymond Michalowski, "State-Corporate Crime," paper presented at the annual meeting of the American Society of Criminology, Baltimore, November 1990.

11. Elizabeth Moore and Michael Mills, "The Neglected Victims and Unexamined Costs of White-Collar Crime," *Crime and Delinquency* 36 (1990): 408–418.

12. 2005 National Public Survey on White-Collar Crime, www.nw3c.org/research/national_public_survey.cfm (accessed April 26, 2010).

13. Ibid.

14. Natalie Taylor, "Under-Reporting of Crime against Small Business: Attitudes Towards Police and Reporting Practices," *Policing and Society* 13 (2003): 79–90.

© Shannon Stapleton/Reuters/Landov

THE

The tastefully crafted *Emperor's Club VIP* website stated: "Our goal is to make life more peaceful, balanced, beautiful and meaningful. We honor commitment to our clients as we covet long-term relationships of trust and mutual benefit. Experience for yourself a service of obvious distinction." It provided its "members" with the companionship of young, beautiful women for "total relaxation massage, entertainment purposes, modeling or private dancing." Site viewers also learned: "We specialize in introductions of fashion models, pageant winners and exquisite students, graduates and women of successful careers (finance, art, media, etc.) to gentlemen of exceptional standards"; the women are primed to "make your dreams come true." The site also showed hourly rates based on how many diamonds the young woman deserved: a seven-diamond companion cost more than $3,000 an hour, or $31,000 per day.

(*continued on page 478*)

gov/-compliance/criminal/index.html (accessed April 26, 2007).

120. Belluck, "Prosecutors Say Greed Drove Pharmacist to Dilute Drugs," p. 3.

121. See also, Neal Shover and Andrew Hochstetler, *Choosing White-Collar Crime* (England: Cambridge University Press, 2006).

122. Neal Shover and Peter Grabosky, "White-Collar Crime and the Great Recession," *Criminology and Public Policy* 9 (2010): 429–433.

123. Kathleen Daly, "Gender and Varieties of White-Collar Crime," *Criminology* 27 (1989): 769–793.

124. Quoted in Tim Metz and Michael Miller, "Boesky's Rise and Fall Illustrate a Compulsion to Profit by Getting Inside Track on Market," *Wall Street Journal*, November 17, 1986, p. 28.

125. Mandeep Dhami, "White-Collar Prisoners' Perceptions of Audience Reaction," *Deviant Behavior* 28 (2007): 57–77.

126. Herbert Edelhertz and Charles Rogovin, eds., *A National Strategy for Containing White-Collar Crime* (Lexington, MA: Lexington Books, 1980), Appendix A, pp. 122–123.

127. Donald Cressey, *Other People's Money: A Study of the Social Psychology of Embezzlement* (Glencoe, IL: Free Press, 1973), p. 96.

128. Rhonda Evans and Dianne Porche, "The Nature and Frequency of Medicare/Medicaid Fraud and Neutralization Techniques among Speech, Occupational, and Physical Therapists," *Deviant Behavior* 26 (2005): 253–271.

129. Sewell Chan and Louise Story, "Goldman Pays $550 Million to Settle Fraud Case," *New York Times*, July 15, 2010, www. nytimes.com/2010/07/16/business/16goldman.html (accessed November 3, 2010).

130. Nicole Leeper Piquero, Stephen Tibbetts, and Michael Blankenship, "Examining the Role of Differential Association and Techniques of Neutralization in Explaining Corporate Crime," *Deviant Behavior* 26 (2005): 159–188.

131. John A. Byrne, "At Enron, the Environment Was Ripe for Abuse," *BusinessWeek*, February 25, 2002, p. 14.

132. Travis Hirschi and Michael Gottfredson, "Causes of White-Collar Crime," *Criminology* 25 (1987): 949–974.

133. Michael Gottfredson and Travis Hirschi, *A General Theory of Crime* (Stanford, CA: Stanford University Press, 1990), p. 191.

Public Order Crime: Sex and Substance Abuse

14

Learning Objectives

1. Be familiar with the association between law and morality

2. Be familiar with the term *social harm*

3. Discuss the activities of moral crusaders

4. Know the various forms of outlawed deviant sexuality

5. Discuss the history of prostitution and what the term means today

6. Distinguish between the different types of prostitutes

7. Be able to discuss what is meant by obscenity and pornography

8. Be able to discuss the cause of substance abuse

9. Compare and contrast the different methods of drug control

10. State the arguments for and against legalizing drugs

The Emperor's Club, as we all know now, was a high-priced call girl ring. One of the young women, known professionally as "Kristin," was 22-year-old Ashley Dupre. Rather than being a highly educated fashion model or career woman, Dupre was a high school dropout who had run away from an abusive home after her sophomore year in high school. She knew what it was like to be broke, homeless, and in need of money. She claimed she became a prostitute because her dream of a singing career hadn't gotten off the ground.

Dupre may have remained an unknown and anonymous "working girl" had it not been for a federal investigation of one of her clients, New York's hard-charging Governor, Eliot Spitzer, who at one time was considered a future presidential candidate. Known in the club as Client #9, Spitzer had paid $80,000 for services rendered. When a federal investigation uncovered his involvement with the Emperor's Club, the scandal rocked the nation, and Spitzer was forced to resign in disgrace.[1] His career took a positive turn June 24, 2010, when CNN announced that Spitzer had been signed to headline a talk show with political columnist Kathleen Parker. (His show was cancelled July 6, 2011.)

Kristin Davis—AKA the Manhattan Madam, who ran the club—did not fare so well: she received a three-month jail sentence.[2] Another employee, Temeka Rachelle Lewis, 32, of Brooklyn, a graduate of the prestigious University of Virginia with a bachelor's degree in English language and literature, received one year's probation. Lewis had been an honor student all her life and grew up in what has been described as "a good church-going family."[3] As for Ashley Dupre, she made thousands of dollars when her recording, "What We Want," was played more than 3 million times on the Internet after the scandal erupted. The *New York Post* hired her to write a weekly advice column dealing with sex and relationships, she appeared in the May 2010 issue of *Playboy*, she has been a guest on *The View*, *The Joy Behar Show*, *Issues with Jane Valez-Mitchell*, and *Geraldo at Large*, and she has a new show on VH1 called *Famous Food*. She was certified through NYU as a New York state real estate salesperson.[4]

The Spitzer case is certainly not unique, and stories have circulated about students and suburban mom's adding to their income by advertising sexual services on Internet sites such as Craigslist, a practice not without its risks. On April 14, 2009, aspiring model Julissa Brisman, who advertised her services on Craigslist as a masseuse, was killed in Boston, Massachusetts, by Philip Markoff, a 23-year-old Boston University medical student. Investigators later found it was not the first time Markoff had attacked a woman he had met via Craigslist and that he may have attacked at least two others.[5] On August 15, 2010, Markoff committed suicide while in custody awaiting trial, so we will never know his motives for these horrendous crimes. A month later, Craigslist announced it would no longer advertise "adult services."

Societies have long banned or limited behaviors believed to run contrary to social norms, customs, and values. These behaviors are often referred to as **public order crimes** or **victimless crimes**, although the latter term can be misleading.[6] Public order crimes involve acts that interfere with the operations of society and the ability of people to function efficiently. Put another way, common-law crimes such as rape or robbery are banned because they cause social harm, whereas other behaviors are outlawed simply because they conflict with social policy, prevailing moral rules, and current public opinion.

Statutes designed to uphold public order usually prohibit the manufacture and distribution of morally questionable goods and services such as erotic material, commercial sex, and mood-altering drugs. They may ban acts that a few people holding political power consider morally tinged, such as homosexual contact. Statutes like these are controversial in part because millions of otherwise law-abiding citizens often engage in these outlawed activities and consequently become criminals. These statutes also are controversial because they selectively prohibit desired goods, services, and behaviors; in other words, they outlaw sin and vice.

This chapter first briefly discusses the relationship between law and morality. Next the chapter addresses public order crimes of a sexual nature: paraphilias, prostitution, and pornography. The chapter concludes by focusing on the abuse of drugs and alcohol.

LAW AND MORALITY

Legislation of moral issues has continually frustrated lawmakers because many of their constituents see little harm in visiting a prostitute or smoking some pot. When a store is robbed or a child assaulted, it is easy to identify the victim and condemn the harm done. It is more difficult to sympathize with or even identify the victims of immoral acts, such as pornography or prostitution, in which the parties involved may be willing participants. Some of the "providers" in the Emperor's Club were paid more for a few days work than a waitress or a teacher makes in a year. The "models" seemed willing and well paid. Can we consider them "victims"? People who employed these women, such as Governor Spitzer, were wealthy and powerful men who freely and voluntarily spent their money for sexual services. Certainly they were not the "victim" here. If there is no victim, can there be a crime?

To answer this question, we might first consider whether there is actually a victim in so-called victimless crimes. Although some young women such as "Kristin" may have voluntarily engaged in highly paid sex work, many others have been coerced into the sex trade and are true victims of it. It is common for young runaways and abandoned children to be coerced into a life on the streets, where they are cruelly treated and held as virtual captives.[7] It has been estimated that women involved in street prostitution are 60 to 100 times more likely to be murdered than the average woman and that most of these killings are the result of a dispute over money rather than being sexually motivated.[8] Clearly, prostitution carries with it significant professional risk. Other sexually related offenses, such as pornography, may involve people who voluntarily perform in "adult films." But as critics such as Andrea Dworkin point out, far from being highly paid stars, women involved in adult films are "dehumanized—turned into objects and commodities."[9]

If public order crimes do not harm their participants, perhaps society as a whole should be considered the victim of these crimes. Is the community harmed when an adult website goes online or a brothel opens down the street? Does this signal that a neighborhood is in decline? Does it teach children that deviance is both tolerated and profitable? If women are degraded and sexualized in adult sex films, does that send a message that it is acceptable to demean and/or harm women?

Debating Morality

In 2011, rising political star Anthony Weiner was forced to resign from office after compromising photos he "tweeted" to young women were posted on the Net. At first, Weiner denied responsibility, telling the media that his account had been hacked and/or that the picture had possibly been altered. Finally, he admitted on June 6, 2011, that he had sent sexually explicit text messages and photographs to several women, both before and after he had gotten married.[10] Did Weiner's behavior cause public harm? After all, he never actually met any of the women with whom he carried on a cyber relationship. All his victims had to do was disconnect or delete his texts, tweets, and e-mails. Some may view Weiner's behavior as odd yet essentially harmless, but others considered his "sexting" to be immoral and unworthy of a public figure. Was Weiner's sexting grossly immoral, or

KAMBOU SIA/AFP/Getty Images/Newscom

A woman who performs genital cutting in her village in Ivory Coast passes by a poster supporting the abolition of female genital mutilation. An estimated 40 percent of women in Ivory Coast undergo this mutilation. Despite efforts to abolish the practice, more than 135 million women worldwide have experienced some form of genital mutilation and more than 2 million girls are estimated to undergo the procedure every year in African and Middle Eastern nations such as Iraq.

merely an example of those harmless human quirks and eccentricities we all possess in some measure?

The debate over morality has existed for all of recorded history: As the Bible tells us, God destroyed "Cities of the Plain," because "The outcry against Sodom and Gomorrah is so great and their sin so grievous."[11] Though Abraham asks God to spare the cities, his request is denied when a posse of angels fails to find 10 righteous people living in the towns.

Punishing immorality with legal sanctions continues today (though not by fire and brimstone). Acts such as pornography, prostitution, and substance abuse are believed to erode the moral fabric of society and are therefore prohibited and punished. They are crimes, according to the great legal scholar Morris Cohen, because "it is one of the functions of the criminal law to give expression to the collective feeling of revulsion toward certain acts, even when they are not very dangerous."[12] In his classic statement on the function of morality in the law, legal scholar Sir Patrick Devlin states:

> Without shared ideas on politics, morals, and ethics no society can exist. . . . If men and women try to create a society in which there is no fundamental agreement about good and evil, they will fail; if having based it on common agreement, the agreement goes, the society will disintegrate. For society is not something that is kept together physically; it is held by the invisible bonds of common thought. If the bonds were too far relaxed, the members would drift apart. A common morality is part of the bondage. The bondage is part of the price of society; and mankind, which needs society, must pay its price.[13]

According to this view, so-called victimless crimes are prohibited because one of the functions of criminal law is to express a shared sense of public morality.[14]

Some influential legal scholars have questioned the propriety of legislating morals. H.L.A. Hart states:

> It is fatally easy to confuse the democratic principle that power should be in the hands of the majority with the utterly different claim that the majority, with power in their hands, need respect no limits. Certainly there is a special risk in a democracy that the majority may dictate how all should live.[15]

Hart may be motivated by the fact that defining morality may be an impossible task: Who defines morality? Are we not punishing differences rather than social harm? As U.S. Supreme Court Justice William O. Douglas once so succinctly put it, "What may be trash to me may be prized by others."[16] After all, many of the great works of Western art depict nude males and females, some quite young. Are the paintings of Rubens or the sculptures of Michelangelo obscene?

Joseph Gusfield argues that the purpose of outlawing immoral acts is to show the moral superiority of those who condemn the acts over those who partake of them. The legislation of morality "enhances the social status of groups carrying the affirmed culture and degrades groups carrying that which is condemned as deviant."[17] Research indicates that people who define themselves as liberals are the most tolerant of sexually explicit material. Demographic attributes such as age, educational attainment, and occupational status also may influence views of pornography: the young and better educated tend to be more tolerant than older, less-educated people.[18] Whose views should prevail?

If a majority of the population chooses to engage in what might objectively be considered immoral or deviant behavior, would it be fair or just to prohibit or control such behavior or render it criminal? Adult websites now account for about 20 percent of all Internet visits by U.S. users. Should all obscenity and pornography be legalized if so many people are active users and wish to enjoy its content?[19] If the law tried to define or limit objectionable material, might it not eventually inhibit free speech and political dissent? Not so, according to social commentator Irving Kristol:

> If we start censoring pornography and obscenity, shall we not inevitably end up censoring political opinion? A lot of people seem to think this would be the case—which only shows the power of doctrinaire thinking over reality. We had censorship of pornography and obscenity for 150 years, until almost yesterday, and I am not aware that freedom of opinion in this country was in any way diminished as a consequence of this fact.[20]

Cultural clashes may ensue when behavior that is considered normative in one society is deplored by those living in another. For example, Amnesty International estimates that more than 135 million of the world's females have undergone genital mutilation.[21] Custom and tradition are by far the most frequently cited reasons for mutilation, and it is often carried out in a ritual during which the young woman is initiated into adulthood.[22] The surgery is done to ensure virginity, remove sexual sensation, and render the females suitable for marriage; a girl in these societies cannot be considered an adult unless she has undergone genital mutilation. Critics of this practice, led by American author Alice Walker (*The Color Purple*), consider the procedure mutilation and torture; others argue that this ancient custom should be left to the discretion of the indigenous people who consider it part of their culture. "Torture," counters Walker, "is not culture." Can an outsider define the morality of another culture?[23] Amnesty International and the United Nations have worked to end the practice. Because of outside pressure, several African nations south of the Sahara have now instituted bans that are enforced with fines and jail terms. The procedure is now forbidden in Senegal, Egypt, Burkina Faso, the Central African Republic, Djibouti, Ghana, Guinea, and Togo. Other countries, among them Uganda, discourage it. In North Africa, the Egyptian Supreme Court upheld a ban on the practice and also ruled it had no place in Islam.[24] Despite these efforts, thousands of girls are still subject to female circumcision every day in Africa and the Middle East and in Muslim areas all over the world.

Social Harm

Most societies have long banned or limited behaviors that are believed to run contrary to social norms, customs, and values. However, many acts that most of us deem highly immoral and objectionable are not, in fact, criminal. There are no laws banning *superbia* (hubris/pride), *avaritia* (avarice/greed), *luxuria* (extravagance or lust), *invidia* (envy), *gula* (gluttony), *ira* (wrath), or *acedia* (sloth), even though they are considered the "seven deadly sins." Nor is it a crime to ignore the pleas of a drowning child, even though to do so might be considered callous, coldhearted, and unfeeling. (Of course, some people—lifeguards, paramedics, firemen, police, and the parents—have a legal duty to help save the child.)

The theory of **social harm** can explain most criminal acts, but it cannot explain them all. Some acts that cause enormous social harm are perfectly legal, whereas others that many people consider virtually harmless are outlawed and severely punished. We are reminded of this irony by 2011 death of funnyman Ryan Dunn of Jackass fame, who died while speeding down the road at more than 130 miles per hour after consuming twice the legal limit of alcohol. It is now estimated that more than 500,000 deaths in the United States each year can be linked to the consumption of tobacco and alcohol, yet these "deadly substances" remain legal to produce and sell. Similarly, sports cars and motorcycles that can accelerate to more than 150 miles per hour are perfectly legal to sell and possess even though almost 40,000 people die each year in car accidents. On the other hand, illegal drugs kill less than 20,000 people annually, and none of these fatalities is linked to marijuana. Yet the sale of marijuana and other recreational drugs is still banned in most states and by the federal government and is heavily punished.[25] According to the theory of social harm, if more people die each year from alcohol-, tobacco-, and automobile-related causes than marijuana, shouldn't marijuana be legalized and Corvettes, Johnny Walker, and Marlboro's be outlawed? But they are not.

Moral Crusades and Crusaders

In the early West, vigilance committees were set up in San Francisco and other boom towns to pursue cattle rustlers and stagecoach robbers and to dissuade undesirables from moving in. These **vigilantes** held a strict standard of morality that resulted in sure and swift justice when they caught their prey.

The avenging vigilante has remained part of popular culture. Fictional do-gooders who take it on themselves to enforce the law, battle evil, and personally deal with those they consider to be immoral have become enmeshed in the public consciousness. From the Lone Ranger to Spiderman, the righteous vigilante is expected to go on moral crusades without any authorization from legal authorities. Who told

Spiderman he could destroy half of New York while fighting Dr. Octopus or the Green Goblin? And what about the Justice League? What gives the Martian Manhunter, Wonder Woman, Plastic Man, and their superhero colleagues the right to fight crime in America? The assumption that it is okay to take matters into your own hands if the cause is right and the target is immoral is not lost on the younger generation. Gang boys sometimes take on the street identity of "Batman" or "Superman" so they can battle their rivals with impunity.

Fictional characters are not the only ones who take it upon themselves to fight for moral decency; members of special interest groups are also ready to do battle.[26] Public order crimes often trace their origin to **moral crusaders** who seek to shape the law toward their own way of thinking; Howard Becker calls them **moral entrepreneurs**. These rule creators, argues Becker, operate with an absolute certainty that their way is right and that any means are justified to get their way: "The crusader is fervent and righteous, often self-righteous."[27] Today's moral crusaders take on such issues as prayer in school, gun ownership, gay marriage, abortion, and the distribution of sexually explicit books and magazines.

During the 1930s, Harry Anslinger, then head of the Federal Bureau of Narcotics, used magazine articles, public appearances, and public testimony to sway public opinion about the dangers of marijuana, which until that time was legal to use and possess.[28] In testimony before the House Ways and Means Committee, considering passage of the Marijuana Tax Act of 1938, Anslinger stated:

> In Florida a 21-year-old boy under the influence of this drug killed his parents and his brothers and sisters. The evidence showed that he had smoked marihuana. In Chicago recently two boys murdered a policeman while under the influence of marihuana. Not long ago we found a 15-year-old boy going insane because, the doctor told the enforcement officers, he thought the boy was smoking marihuana cigarettes. They traced the sale to some man who had been growing marihuana and selling it to these boys all under 15 years of age, on a playground there.[29]

As a result of Anslinger's efforts, a deviant behavior—marijuana use—became a criminal behavior, and previously law-abiding citizens were defined as criminal offenders.

Moral Crusades Today

Moral crusades are sometimes designed to draw a bright line between (a) behavior that is considered morally acceptable and (b) behavior that right-thinking people would consider deviant and unacceptable. Today, popular targets of moral crusaders are abortion clinics, pornographers, gun dealers, and despoilers of the environment.

Of course, what is right and moral is often in the eye of the beholder. For example, in 2004 shock jock Howard Stern was fined by the Federal Communication Commission (FCC) for "repeated, graphic, and explicit sexual descriptions that were pandering, titillating, or used to shock the audience."[30] The government action prompted the Clear Channel Communication Company to drop Stern's show from their stations. In retaliation, Stern posted on his website transcripts from the Oprah Winfrey TV show that used very similar language but was deemed inoffensive by government regulators.[31] Stern was so outraged by the crusade to censor his program that he left public broadcasting for unregulated satellite radio.

One popular target for moral crusaders are anti-smut campaigns that target books considered too "racy" or controversial to be suitable for a public school library. According to the American Library Association, between 2000 and 2006 the Harry Potter series topped the yearly list of books challenged by critics who demanded their removal from school library shelves. Most of the objections to J. K. Rowling's popular series about a young wizard in England centered on the charge that the story promotes Satanism and magic. In the last few years, complaints against Harry and his friends have been outpaced by those lodged against Peter Parnell and Justin Richardson's *And Tango Makes Three*, a children's book that tells the story of two male penguins who find an abandoned egg and raise a baby penguin chick. Because it is geared to a preschool audience, opponents suggest that the underlying theme of the book—learning to accept same-sex relationships (even among penguins)—is morally unacceptable.[32]

In their efforts to protect society, moral crusaders may sometimes engage in illegal and immoral conduct. Abortion foes have resorted to violence and murder to rid the nation of pro-choice health care providers they consider immoral while failing to realize the depravity of their own extreme acts.

Some moral crusaders justify their actions by claiming that the very structure of our institutions and beliefs is in danger because of immorality. Andrea Friedman's analysis of anti-obscenity campaigns during the Cold War era (post–World War II) found that the politics of the times led to images of aggressive or even violent males in comic books and pornography. Moral crusaders argued that this depiction was threatening to family values, which led them to advocate for a ban on violent comics and porn magazines.[33]

The Gay Marriage Crusade

One of the most heated of "moral crusades" has been directed at influencing public acceptance of the gay lifestyle. One group of crusaders is determined to prevent the legalization of gay marriage; their objective is passage of a constitutional amendment declaring that marriage is between one man and one woman. The Defense of Marriage Act in 1996, which defined marriage as a union of one man and one woman for the purposes of federal law, is one of their legal achievements.[34]

Opposing them are groups of activists who have tirelessly campaigned for the civil rights of gay men and women. One of their most important victories occurred in 2003 when the U.S. Supreme Court delivered a historic decision in *Lawrence et al. v. Texas,* which made it impermissible for states to criminalize oral and anal sex and all other forms of intercourse that are not heterosexual under statutes prohibiting sodomy, deviant sexuality, or buggery.[35] The *Lawrence* case involved two gay men who had been arrested in 1998 for having sex in the privacy of their Houston home. In overturning their convictions, the Court said this:

> Although the laws involved . . . here . . . do not more than prohibit a particular sexual act, their penalties and purposes have more far-reaching consequences, touching upon the most private human conduct, sexual behavior, and in the most private of places, the home. They seek to control a personal relationship that, whether or not entitled to formal recognition in the law, is within the liberty of persons to choose without being punished as criminals. The liberty protected by the Constitution allows homosexual persons the right to choose to enter upon relationships in the confines of their homes and their own private lives and still retain their dignity as free persons.

As a result of the decision, sodomy laws banning sexual activity among consenting adults of the same sex were suddenly unconstitutional and unenforceable; acts that were once a crime were now legalized. The *Lawrence* decision paved the way for states to rethink their marriage laws. In 2003 Massachusetts's highest court ruled that same-sex couples are legally entitled to wed under the state constitution, and that the state may not "deny the protections, benefits, and obligations conferred by civil marriage to two individuals of the same sex who wish to marry."[36] Since then five other states have followed along, including New York, which passed a gay marriage law on June 24, 2011; others have created legal unions that are not called marriage but offer all the rights and responsibilities of marriage under state law to same-sex couples. Other states have either granted limited rights or recognize the legality of same-sex marriages performed elsewhere. In California, the State Supreme Court ruled in May 2008 that the state constitution guaranteed gay and lesbian couples the "basic civil right" to marry. Moral crusaders opposed to gay marriage mounted a campaign that resulted in the passage of Proposition 8, adding a new section to the state Constitution that reads: "Only marriage between a man and a woman is valid or recognized in California," thus outlawing gay marriage once again.[37] The battle was not over. On August 4, 2010, a federal judge declared the ban unconstitutional but temporarily stayed the ruling; the issue remains in the courts. Supporters and opponents vow not to give up the fight, and future ballot initiatives are now being formulated.

The debate over gay marriage rages on: Is it fair to prevent one group of loyal tax-paying citizens from engaging in a behavior that is allowed others? Are there objective standards of morality, or should society respect people's differences? After all, opponents charge, polygamy is banned and there are age standards for marriage in every state. If gay marriage is legalized, what about marriage to multiple partners, or with underage minors? How far should the law go in curbing human behaviors that do not cause social harm? Who controls the law, and should the law be applied to shape morality?

The public order crimes discussed in this chapter are divided into two broad areas. The first relates to what conventional society considers deviant sexual practices: paraphilias, prostitution, and pornography. The second area concerns the use of substances that have been outlawed or controlled because of the alleged harm they cause: drugs and alcohol.

SEXUALLY RELATED OFFENSES

On March 3, 2011, Kevin Garfield Ricks pleaded guilty to six counts of production of child pornography and one count of possession of child pornography and was sentenced to more than 25 years in prison. Ricks had engaged in illegal sexual contact with minor boys for more than three decades, beginning as a junior camp counselor in 1979. In 1988, Ricks moved to Japan to teach English, and while he was there he used large quantities of tequila to get victims drunk and then performed sex acts with his incapacitated victims. After leaving Japan in 1995, Ricks moved to Danville, Virginia, and began hosting male foreign exchange students and working in local schools teaching English. In 1997 and 1999, Ricks filmed and photographed himself engaging in sexually explicit conduct with two different 17-year-old exchange students whom he had gotten drunk to the point of passing out. Ricks began teaching in Manassas, Virginia, and in 2009 he engaged in sexually explicit conduct with a 16-year-old former student after getting the boy drunk with beer and approximately 10 shots of tequila. Ricks was arrested February 18, 2010, by the Manassas City Police and pleaded guilty to state charges of indecent liberties, for which he received a sentence of five years with four suspended.[38]

Ricks' behavior is unfortunately not unique. A multinational survey concluded that each year in the United States 325,000 children are subjected to some form of sexual exploitation, which includes sexual abuse, prostitution, use in pornography, and molestation by adults.[39] Because of these alarming statistics and also because some sexual practices are believed to cause social harm, some elements of sexual conduct have been made illegal in the United States and abroad. Three of the most common offenses—paraphilias, prostitution, and pornography—are discussed in some detail in the following sections.

Paraphilias

On June 4, 2009, newspaper headlines around the world told the shocking story of Actor David Carradine, who was found dead in a Thailand hotel. Authorities discovered the 72-year-old actor hanging in his closet, the victim of an autoerotic death resulting from engaging in *asphyxiophilia*, self-strangulation that restricts the supply of oxygen or blood to the brain in order to increase sexual intensity.[40]

Carradine's death was attributed to his involvement with a common form of **paraphilias** (Greek *para*, "to the side of," and *philos*, "loving,")—bizarre or abnormal sexual practices involving recurrent sexual urges focused on (a) nonhuman objects (such as underwear, shoes, or leather), (b) humiliation or the experience of receiving or giving pain (such as in sadomasochism or bondage), or (c) children or others who cannot grant consent. More than 2,000-year-old Buddhist texts contain references to sexually deviant behaviors among monastic communities, including sexual activity with animals and sexual interest in corpses. Richard von Krafft-Ebing's *Psychopathia Sexualis*, first published in 1887, was the first text to discuss such paraphilias as sadism, bestiality, and incest.[41]

When paraphilias, such as wearing clothes normally worn by the opposite sex (transvestite fetishism), are engaged in by adults in the privacy of their homes, they remain outside the law's reach. However, when paraphilias involve unwilling or underage victims, they are considered socially harmful and subject to criminal penalties. Outlawed paraphilias include:

- *Asphyxiophilia (autoerotic asphyxia).* By means of a noose, ligature, plastic bag, mask, volatile chemicals, or chest compression, attempting partial asphyxia and oxygen deprivation to the brain to enhance sexual gratification. Almost all cases of asphyxiophilia involve males.
- *Frotteurism.* Rubbing against or touching a nonconsenting person in a crowd, elevator, or other public area.
- *Voyeurism.* Obtaining sexual pleasure from spying on a stranger while he or she disrobes or engages in sexual behavior with another.
- *Exhibitionism.* Deriving sexual pleasure from exposing the genitals to surprise or shock a stranger.
- *Sadomasochism.* Deriving pleasure from receiving pain or inflicting pain on another.

Pedophilia   Between 2002 and 2004, the archdiocese of Boston was shaken by allegations that a significant number of priests had engaged in sexual relations with minor children. The archdiocese eventually turned over the names of nearly 100 priests to prosecutors. As the scandal spread, clergy elsewhere in the United States and abroad resigned amid allegations that they had abused children or failed to stop abuse of which they had knowledge. In Ireland the Most Rev. Brendan Comiskey, the Bishop of Ferns, offered his resignation to the pope, and an archbishop in Wales was forced to resign because he had ignored complaints about two priests later convicted of sexually abusing children. Responding to the crisis, Pope John Paul II called a special meeting of American Catholic leaders in April 2002 to create new policies on sex abuse. The pope issued a statement in which he said that there is "no place in the priesthood . . . for those who would harm the young." He added that sexual abuse by the clergy was not only an "appalling sin" but a crime, and he noted that "many are offended at the way in which church leaders are perceived to have acted in this matter."[42]

Nowhere did the scandal take on greater proportion than in the Boston area, where Cardinal Bernard Law was forced to step down as leader of the diocese. Numerous churches were closed or sold to help raise money for legal fees and victim compensation. Among the most notorious offenders was Father James Porter, accused of molesting at least 125 children of both sexes over a 30-year period reaching back to the early 1960s. Porter was eventually sentenced to an 18- to 20-year prison term. The church continues to be haunted by charges levied against priests. Recently, it was revealed that Fr. Lawrence Murphy, who taught at St. John's School for the Deaf in a suburb of Milwaukee from 1950 through 1974, sexually abused about 200 boys. The Murphy case (he died in 1998) made national headlines again recently when documents were released showing that then-Cardinal Joseph Ratzinger, now Pope Benedict, knew about the abuse allegations and protected Murphy from being removed from the clergy.[43]

Of all the commonly practiced paraphilias, pedophilia is the one that most concerns the general public. While the cause of pedophilia has not been determined, suspected factors include abnormal brain structure, social maladaption, and neurological dysfunction. Research using brain scans shows that the central processing of sexual stimuli in pedophiles may be controlled by a disturbance in the prefrontal networks of the brain.[44] Brain trauma has also been linked to child molesting. Injury may occur before or at birth, but it is possible that the damage caused by injury and/or accident also can produce the brain malfunctions linked to pedophilia.[45] There is some evidence that pedophilia is heritable and that genetic factors are responsible for the development of pedophilia.[46] Other suspected connections range from cognitive distortions to exposure to pornography.[47]

Whatever the cause, pedophilia is not a limited problem; more than 20 percent of males report sexual attraction to at least one child.[48] However, men are not the only sexual predators; women are also involved. One study of more than 100 adult female sex offenders found that 77 percent of the cases involved child abuse, and in about two-thirds of the cases the women had a male co-offender. Tragically, the women mostly abused their own children together with their male/intimate partner.[49]

One of the most horrific cases of pedophilia involved the kidnapping and death of 9-year-old Jessica Lunsford, which is the subject of the Profiles in Crime feature.

Prostitution

Elliot Spitzer is not the only well-known politician to get caught up in a prostitution scandal. On July 16, 2007, Louisiana's conservative Republican Senator David Vitter apologized to the public after his telephone number showed up in the phone records of Pamela Martin and Associates, the alleged prostitution ring run in the nation's capital by the "D.C. Madam" Deborah Jeane Palfrey. "This was a very serious sin in my past for which I am, of course, completely responsible," Vitter said remorsefully. Soon after he issued his statement, Jeanette Maier, a former madam who ran a house of prostitution in New Orleans, claimed Vitter was also a client in her brothel. She told the press: "As far as the girls coming out after seeing David, all they had was nice things to say. It wasn't all about sex. In fact, he just wanted to have somebody listen to him, you know. And I said his wife must not be listening." Vitter continues to serve as senator, having been re-elected despite the fact that frequenting brothels and employing prostitutes is hardly the behavior expected from a married senator known for his strong advocacy of family values![50] Senator Vitter was not alone in enjoying the services of the D.C. Madam; also on her call list was Randall L. Tobias, who was forced to step down as deputy secretary of state, and Harlan K. Ullman, the military affairs scholar who created the Pentagon's concept known as "shock and awe."[51]

Prostitution has been known for thousands of years. The term derives from the Latin *prostituere*, which means "to cause to stand in front of." The prostitute is viewed as publicly offering his or her body for sale. The earliest record of prostitution appears in ancient Mesopotamia, where priests engaged in sex to promote fertility in the community. All women were required to do temple duty, and passing strangers were expected to make donations to the temple after enjoying its services.[52]

Modern commercial sex appears to have its roots in ancient Greece, where Solon established licensed brothels in 500 BCE. The earnings of Greek prostitutes helped pay for the temple of Aphrodite. Famous men openly went to prostitutes to enjoy intellectual, aesthetic, and sexual stimulation; prostitutes, however, were prevented from marrying.[53]

Prostitution was a sin under canon law during the Middle Ages, but it was widely practiced and considered a method of protecting "respectable" women who might otherwise be attacked by young men. In 1358, the Grand Council of Venice declared that prostitution was "absolutely indispensable to the world."[54] Some church leaders such as

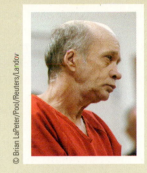

© Brian LaPeter/Pool/Reuters/Landov

On February 24, 2005, 9-year-old Jessica Lunsford was reported missing from her home. When a child is reported missing, the police typically check on all the known sex offenders in the area, which in this case included John Evander Couey, 46, who was not living at the address where he was registered, a legal violation. Police located Couey and searched his room, not finding anything. Couey had a long list of convictions including burglary, carrying a concealed weapon, disorderly intoxication, driving under the influence, indecent exposure, disorderly conduct, fraud, insufficient funds, and larceny. A habitual drug abuser, in 1991 he had been arrested and charged with "fondling a child under the age of 16."

Nineteen days after Jessica Lunsford was first reported missing, detectives returned to Couey's home and this time found blood on the mattress. Couey had fled but was arrested in Georgia. While in police custody, Couey admitted that he had entered the Lunsford home at around 3 A.M. on February 24, 2005, and found Jessica asleep in her bed. He woke her and ordered her to be quiet. "Don't yell or nothing," he said and told her to follow him back to his sister's house, where he raped her repeatedly and kept her in a closet for three days. When he learned that detectives were searching for him, he panicked and buried her even though she was still alive. He showed investigators the shallow grave where they found Jessica's body inside two tied plastic garbage bags. Her wrists were bound, but she had managed to poke two fingers through the plastic in an attempt to free herself.

Couey was found guilty of murder on March 7, 2007, and a death penalty hearing was held soon after. In closing statements, prosecutor Ric Ridgway called the crime "evil" and asked jurors to remember how Jessica died by suffocating in the hole Couey dug, accompanied only by a stuffed toy she had grabbed as she was being abducted. "She was in pain. In the dark. She was certainly terrified," Ridgway said in his closing statement. "If this is not the person who deserves the death penalty, who does?"

Defense lawyers pleaded for mercy, arguing that Couey deserved no more than a life sentence in prison because of mental retardation and mental illness, neglect as a child and the effects of alcohol and drug abuse. "No matter what you do, John Couey is going to die in prison," said defense attorney Alan Fanter. "No child should have to die the way Jessica Lunsford did. But justice is not vengeance." The jury did not buy that argument and sentenced Couey to death on March 14, 2007.

In the aftermath of Jessica Lunsford's abduction, Florida passed legislation that requires increased prison sentences, electronic tracking of all convicted sex offenders on probation, and the mandatory use of state databases by all local probation officials so that known sex offenders cannot avoid the scrutiny of law enforcement. Can such measures control the behavior of pedophiles such as Couey before they kill their innocent victims?

SOURCES: Court TV Crime Library, "Jessica Lunsford," www.crimelibrary.com/serial_killers/predators/jessica_lunsford/9.html (accessed August 12, 2011); *USA Today*, "Judge Throws Out Confession in Jessica Lunsford Case," 30 June 2006, www.usatoday.com/news/nation/2006-06-30-child-confession_x.htm (accessed August 12, 2011); Curt Anderson, "Death Sentence Endorsed in Lunsford Case," *Washington Post*, March 15, 2007, www.washingtonpost.com/wp-dyn/content/article/2007/03/15/AR2007031500518.html (accessed August 12, 2011).

St. Thomas Aquinas condoned prostitution; St. Augustine wrote: "If you expel prostitution from society, you will unsettle everything on account of lusts."[55] Nonetheless, prostitution was officially condemned, and working girls were confined to ply their trade in certain areas of the city and were required to wear distinctive outfits so they could be easily recognized. Any official tolerance disappeared after the Reformation. Martin Luther advocated abolishing prostitution on moral grounds, and Lutheran doctrine depicted prostitutes as emissaries of the devil who were sent to destroy the faith.[56]

During the early nineteenth century, prostitution was tied to the rise of English breweries: saloons controlled by the companies employed prostitutes to attract patrons and encourage them to drink. This relationship was repeated in major U.S. cities, such as Chicago, until breweries were forbidden to own the outlets that distributed their product.

Prostitution Today **Prostitution** is now defined as granting nonmarital sexual access, established by mutual agreement of the prostitute, the client, and the employer (i.e., a pimp) for remuneration. This definition is sexually neutral because prostitutes can be straight or gay and male or female.

Prostitutes are referred to by sociologists as "street-level sex workers" whose activities are similar to any other service industry. The following conditions are usually present in a commercial sexual transaction:

- *Activity that has sexual significance for the customer.* This includes the entire range of sexual behavior, from sexual intercourse to exhibitionism, sadomasochism, oral sex, and so on.

- *Economic transaction.* Something of economic value, not necessarily money, is exchanged for the activity.
- *Emotional indifference.* The sexual exchange is simply for economic consideration. Although the participants may know each other, their interaction has nothing to do with affection.[57] Men believe that the lack of involvement makes hiring a prostitute less of a hassle and less trouble than becoming involved in a romantic relationship.[58]

Sociologist Monica Prasad observed these conditions when she interviewed both men and women about their motivation to employ a prostitute. Although their choice was shaped by sexuality, she found that their decision was also influenced by pressure from friends to try something different and exciting, the wish for a sexual exchange free from obligations, and curiosity about the world of prostitution. Prasad found that most customers who became "regulars" began to view prostitution merely as a "service occupation."[59]

Incidence of Prostitution

It is difficult to assess the number of prostitutes operating in the United States. Fifty years ago, about two-thirds of non–college-educated men and one-quarter of college-educated men had visited a prostitute.[60] It is likely that the number of men who hire prostitutes has declined sharply because the number of arrests for prostitution has remained stable for the past two decades while the population has increased.[61] How can these changes be accounted for? The sexual revolution has liberalized sexuality so that men are less likely to use prostitutes because legitimate alternatives for sexuality are now available. In addition, the prevalence of sexually transmitted diseases has caused many men to avoid visiting prostitutes for fear of irreversible health hazards. Traditional forms of prostitution may be in decline, but **ehooking**, which uses the Internet to shield identities and contact clients, may be responsible for a resurgence in sex for hire, especially in times of economic turmoil.[62]

Despite such changes, the Uniform Crime Report (UCR) indicates that about 80,000 prostitution arrests are made annually, with the gender ratio about 2 to 1 female to male.[63] More alarming is the fact that about 1,200 arrests involved minors under the age of 18, including about 160 kids aged 15 and under. Arguments that criminal law should not interfere with sexual transactions because no one is harmed are undermined by these disturbing statistics.

Prostitution in Other Cultures

Prostitution flourishes abroad and is now an important source of income for global criminal syndicates. In some nations it is legal and regulated by the government; in others prostitution is punished with the death penalty. An example of the former is Germany, which has a flourishing legal sex trade. In 2002, Germany passed a new law removing the prohibition against prostitution and allowed prostitutes to obtain regular work contracts and receive health insurance. In turn, the prostitutes were required to register with the authorities and pay taxes. The city of Cologne made headlines in 2004 when it introduced a sex tax that brings in more than a million dollars per year. Each prostitute pays a tax of 150 euros per month, and sex club owners pay 3 euros per 90 square feet of space in their establishments. The city of Dortmund is considering a fee of 1 euro per day for prostitutes to use the streets, and 15 euros per working day to work as a prostitute.[64] Many sex establishments are quite lavish, and it's estimated that 400,000 people work in the German sex trade.[65] In contrast, many Islamic countries punish prostitution with death. In one incident that made international headlines, three women and three men were stoned to death in Iran after a court found them guilty of adultery and prostitution under Islamic laws. The stoning was carried out by local citizens in public in Khazar Abad, near the Caspian Sea.[66]

There is also a troubling overseas trade in prostitution in which men from wealthy countries frequent semi-regulated sex areas in needy nations such as Thailand to procure young girls forced or sold into prostitution—a phenomenon known as *sex tourism*. In addition to sex tours, there has been

Moonlite BunnyRanch prostitutes (from left) Nadia Ray, Alexis On Fire, Destiny, and Kandi sit at the bar at the brothel in Mound House, Nevada. Should prostitution be legalized and regulated, as it is in Nevada? Why shouldn't adults be allowed to hire Destiny and Kandi in Boston and Cleveland as they do at the BunnyRanch? Before you answer, consider that it is perfectly legal to be a doctor, chiropractor, massage therapist, or personal trainer, and people in these professions have physical contact with their clients. We allow liquor to be sold openly and people to gamble at casinos. Where should the line be drawn? Are these women being harmed by their profession, and does society have a duty to protect them from injury?

AP Images/Brad Horn

a soaring demand for pornography, strip clubs, lap dancing, escorts, and telephone sex in developing countries.[67] To protect children from sex tourism, the Violent Crime Control and Law Enforcement Act of 1994 included a provision, referred to as the Child Sexual Abuse Prevention Act, that made it a criminal offense to travel abroad for the purpose of engaging in sexual activity with a minor.[68] Despite these efforts, prosecuting sex tourists is often tricky due to the difficulty of gathering evidence of crimes that were committed in other countries and that involve minor children.[69]

Types of Prostitutes

Several different types of prostitutes operate in the United States. As you will see, each group operates in a particular venue.

Streetwalkers   Prostitutes who work the streets in plain sight of police, citizens, and customers are referred to as *hustlers*, *hookers*, or *streetwalkers*. Although glamorized by the Julia Roberts character in the film *Pretty Woman* (who winds up with a billionaire played by Richard Gere), streetwalkers are considered the least attractive, lowest paid, most vulnerable men and women in the profession. They are most likely to be impoverished members of ethnic or racial minorities. Many are young runaways who gravitate to major cities to find a new, exciting life and escape from sexual and physical abuse at home.[70] In the United States and abroad, streetwalkers tend to be younger than other prostitutes, start working at a younger age, and have less education. More use money from sex work for drugs and use drugs at work; they are more likely than other prostitutes to be the targets of extreme forms of violence.[71]

Because streetwalkers must openly display their occupation, they are likely to be involved with the police. Streetwalkers wear bright clothing, makeup, and jewelry to attract customers, and they take their customers to hotels. The term "hooker," however, is not derived from the ability of streetwalkers to hook clients on their charms. It actually stems from the popular name given women who followed Union General "Fighting Joe" Hooker's army during the Civil War.[72]

Research shows that there are a variety of working styles among women involved in street-based prostitution. Some are controlled by pimps who demand and receive a major share of their earnings. Others are independent entrepreneurs interested in building stable groups of steady clients. Another group manipulate and exploit their customers and may engage in theft and blackmail.[73]

The street life is very dangerous. Interviews conducted with 325 sex workers in Miami by Hilary Surratt and her colleagues found that more than 40 percent experienced violence from clients in the prior year: 25 percent were beaten, 13 percent were raped, and 14 percent were threatened with weapons.[74] If they survive and gain experience, street workers learn to adopt sex practices that promote their chances of survival, such as refusing to trade sex for drugs and refusing to service clients they consider too dangerous or distasteful for sex.[75] Teela Sanders's research on the everyday life of British sex workers found that street-level sex workers use rational decision making and learning experiences to reduce the risk of violent victimization. Experienced sex workers are able to come up with protective strategies that help them manage the risk of the profession. Most do not randomly accept all clients and eliminate those they consider dangerous or threatening. They also develop methods to deal with the emotional strain of the work as well as techniques to maintain their privacy and keep their "occupation" hidden from family and neighbors.[76]

Bar Girls   B-girls, as they are also called, spend their time in bars, drinking and waiting to be picked up by customers. Although alcoholism may be a problem, B-girls usually work out an arrangement with the bartender so they are served diluted drinks or water colored with dye or tea, for which the customer is charged an exorbitant price. In some bars, the B-girl is given a credit for each drink she gets the customer to buy. It is common to find B-girls in towns with military bases and large transient populations.[77]

Brothel Prostitutes   Also called bordellos, cathouses, sporting houses, and houses of ill repute, **brothels** flourished in the nineteenth and early twentieth centuries. They were large establishments, usually run by madams, that housed several prostitutes. A **madam** is a woman who employs prostitutes, supervises their behavior, and receives a fee for her services; her cut is usually 40 to 60 percent of the prostitute's earnings. The madam's role may include recruiting women into prostitution and socializing them in the trade.[78]

Brothels declined in importance following World War II. The closing of the last brothel in Texas is chronicled in the play and movie *The Best Little Whorehouse in Texas*. Today the most well-known brothels exist in Nevada, where prostitution is legal outside large population centers (one, the Mustang Ranch, has an official website that sells souvenirs!). Despite their decline, some madams and their brothels have achieved national prominence.

Call Girls/Cyberhooking   The aristocrats of prostitution are **call girls**. Like the Emperor's Club VIP girls, some charge customers thousands per night and net hundreds of thousands of dollars per year. Some gain clients through employment in escort services, and others develop independent customer lists. Many call girls come from middle-class backgrounds and service upper-class customers. Attempting to dispel the notion that their service is simply sex for money, they concentrate on making their clients feel important and attractive. Working exclusively via telephone "dates," call girls get their clients by word of mouth or by making arrangements with bellhops, cab drivers, and so on.

They either entertain clients in their own apartments or visit clients' hotels and apartments. Upon retiring, a call girl can sell her "date book" listing client names and sexual preferences for thousands of dollars. Despite the lucrative nature of their business, call girls suffer considerable risk by being alone and unprotected with strangers. They often request the business cards of their clients to make sure they are dealing with "upstanding citizens."

The technological revolution has begun to alter the world of prostitution. Instead of working with a cell phone, cyberprostitutes set up personal websites or put listings on Web boards, such as "Adult Friendfinder," that carry personals. They may use loaded phrases such as "looking for generous older man" in their self-descriptions. When contacted, they ask to exchange e-mails, chat online, or make voice calls with prospective clients. They may even exchange pictures. This allows them to select who they want to be with and avoid clients who may be threatening or dangerous. Some cyberprostitution rings offer customers the opportunity to choose women from their Internet page and then have them flown in from around the country.

Escort Services/Call Houses   Some escort services are fronts for prostitution rings. Both male and female sex workers can be sent out after the client calls an ad in the yellow pages. Las Vegas has more than 1,000 listings for adult services in the yellow pages; New York City lists more than 90 escort agencies. Most escort agencies deny that they are uninvolved in prostitution and claim that their employees never provide sexual services, but very few are exclusively involved in "social companionship." The Internet makes it easy to find escort services for travelers: a recent Google search found more than 300,000 listings under "adult escort services" nationwide.

A relatively new phenomenon, call houses, combines elements of the brothel and call girl rings. A madam receives a call from a prospective customer, and if she finds the client acceptable, she arranges a meeting between the caller and a prostitute in her service. The madam maintains a list of prostitutes who are on call rather than living together in a house. The call house insulates the madam from arrest because she never meets the client or receives direct payment.[79]

Circuit Travelers   Prostitutes known as circuit travelers move around in groups of two or three to lumber, labor, and agricultural camps. They ask the foremen for permission to ply their trade, service the whole crew in an evening, and then move on. Some circuit travelers seek clients at truck stops and rest areas. Sometimes young girls are forced to become circuit travelers by unscrupulous pimps who force them to work as prostitutes in agricultural migrant camps.[80]

Skeezers   Surveys conducted in New York and Chicago have found that a significant portion of female prostitutes have substance abuse problems, and more than half claim that prostitution is how they support their drug habits;

on the street, women who barter drugs for sex are called **skeezers**. Not all drug-addicted prostitutes barter sex for drugs, but those that do report more frequent drug abuse and sexual activity than other prostitutes.[81] In a recent study Jessica Edwards, Carolyn Halpern, and Wendee Wechsberg looked into factors that distinguish female crack cocaine users who become skeezers and found that they (a) engaged in more frequent crack use, (b) were more likely to be homeless and unemployed, and (c) suffered more psychological distress than crack users who steered clear of the sex trade.[82] Other research studies find that skeezers are less likely to have a main sexual partner, and more likely to smoke larger quantities of crack. Skeezers have lower self-esteem, greater depression and anxiety, poorer decision-making confidence, more hostility, less social conformity, greater risk-taking behaviors, and more problems growing up compared to drug users who refrain from trading sex.[83]

Massage Parlors/Photo Studios   Some "working girls" are based in massage parlors and photo studios. Although it is unusual for a masseuse to offer all the services of prostitution, oral sex and manual stimulation are common. Most localities have attempted to limit commercial sex in massage parlors by passing ordinances specifying that the masseuse keep certain parts of her body covered and limiting the areas of the body that can be massaged. Some photo studios allow customers to put body paint on models before the photo sessions start.

Who Becomes a Prostitute?

At 38, Lt. Cmdr. Rebecca Dickinson had risen from the enlisted ranks in the Navy to its officer corps. She started her Navy career in 1986 as an aviation electronics technician, and attended Auburn University and the Naval Supply Corps School. After becoming a commissioned officer, Dickinson served on the support ship *Camden*, the supply ship *Santa Barbara*, and the cruiser *Bunker Hill*. She was assigned to the Naval Academy where she helped teach a leadership course. But faced with money and marital problems, Lt. Cmdr. Dickinson contacted the D.C. Madam Deborah Jeane Palfrey (whose client list included Senator David Vitter) and worked as a prostitute for some of the richest and most powerful men in Washington. When asked why she did it, she replied, "I needed the money, yes, I did." This desperate Navy officer, whose career was destroyed by the scandal, was paid $130 for a 90-minute session.[84]

Why do people like Lt. Cmdr. Dickinson turn to prostitution? A successful career officer earning more than $75,000 per year from the Navy, Dickinson was motivated by an immediate financial need. However, her history is certainly not the norm. It is more common for male and female street-level sex workers to come from troubled homes marked by extreme conflict and hostility.[85] Many of these children experienced sexual trauma at an early age[86] and were initiated into sex by family members when as young as 10 to 12 years old; they have long histories of sexual exploitation and abuse.[87]

Sexual abuse is not the only social problem that is a forerunner to prostitution. Young women involved in prostitution also have extensive histories of substance abuse, health problems, posttraumatic stress disorder (PTSD), social stigmatization, and isolation. Often having little family support, they turn to equally troubled peers for survival: self-medicating with drugs and alcohol and self-mutilation are the norm.[88] One survey of street-level sex workers in Phoenix, Arizona, found that women engaging in prostitution had limited educational backgrounds; most did not complete high school.[89] Girls who get into "the life" report conflict with school authorities, poor grades, and an overly regimented school experience; a significant portion have long histories of drug abuse.[90] Young girls who frequently use drugs and begin using at an early age are most at risk for prostitution to support their habit.[91]

Once they get into the life, personal danger begins to escalate. Girls who may be directed toward prostitution because of childhood sexual abuse also are likely to be revictimized as adults.[92] When sociologist Jolanda Sallmann interviewed women in the Midwest with histories of prostitution, she discovered that they were hurt when people labeled and depersonalized them as "whores" or "hookers."[93] Despite their sensitivity, their lives were chaotic. The majority had suffered physical and/or sexual violence. One woman showed Sallmann the scar across her neck where her pimp literally slit her throat years earlier. Another woman told how she was kidnapped and raped by a client at knifepoint while she was still a juvenile. Despite being told that she "was gonna die," she survived the incident. Considering these problems, why do women remain on the street? Even when street prostitutes try to go straight, they often return to prostitution because their limited education and lack of skills make finding employment very difficult. Without a means to support themselves and their children, they may think staying on the streets is less risky than leaving prostitution. Most self-identified as struggling with a substance use problem throughout most or all of their involvement in prostitution, typically involving crack cocaine, cocaine, and/or heroin.

Considering the linkage between substance abuse and prostitution, it's not surprising that threats of HIV and STDs also are daily worries. Recent research directed at the health risks faced by prostitutes found that many suffer from blood-borne viral infections, sexually transmitted diseases, and mental health symptoms. Prostitution was associated with the use of emergency care for women and the use of inpatient mental health services for men.[94] Although some take precautions, such as using or making their clients use condoms, many forgo protection if their pimps and brothel owners forbid it or clients refuse to cooperate.[95] Their continuous exposure to danger and violence, both as victims and as witnesses, leads many to self-medication with illegal drugs. Prostitutes then find themselves in a vicious cycle of violence, substance abuse, and AIDS risk.[96]

Child Prostitution   Child prostitution is not a recent development. For example, it was routine for poor young girls to serve as prostitutes in nineteenth-century England.[97] In contemporary society, child prostitution has been linked to sexual trauma experienced at an early age.[98] Many have long histories of sexual exploitation and abuse.[99] These early experiences with sex help teach them that their bodies have value and that sexual encounters can be used to obtain affection, power, or money. In a detailed study of child sexual exploitation in North America, Richard J. Estes and Neil Alan Weiner found that the problem of child sexual abuse is much more widespread than previously had been believed or documented.[100] Their research indicated that each year in the United States, 25,000 children are subjected to some form of sexual exploitation, which often begins with sexual assaults by relatives and acquaintances, such as a teacher, coach, or a neighbor. Abusers are nearly always men, and about a quarter of them are married with children.

Once they flee an abusive situation at home, kids are vulnerable to life on the streets. Some get hooked up in the sex trade, starting as strippers and lap dancers and drifting into prostitution and pornography. They remain in the trade because they have lost hope and are resigned to their fate.[101] Some meet pimps who quickly turn them to a life of prostitution and beat them if they do not make their daily financial quotas. Others who fled to the streets exchange sex for money, food, and shelter. Some have been traded between prostitution rings, and others are shipped from city to city and even sent overseas as prostitutes. About 20 percent of sexually exploited children are involved in prostitution rings that work across state lines.

The danger of child prostitution is that it leaves permanent damage. The women Jolanda Sallmann interviewed shared stories of feeling permanently altered by their prostitution and substance use. Although the majority of participants were no longer using substances or exchanging sex, they could not escape their past lives. As one (B.T.) explained:

> **B.T.:** The damage is done.
>
> **Interviewer:** And what do you think the damage is?
>
> **B.T.:** My spirit, my health. Um, my mind, because it's never going to leave me. I'm, you know, even when I'm not selling my body, I was still a prostitute. Before in the past, you know.
>
> **Interviewer:** What does that mean?
>
> **B.T.:** Like once a prostitute always a prostitute. I sold my body. For a long time.
>
> **Interviewer:** So you feel that that is something that doesn't leave you?
>
> **B.T.:** It doesn't go away.[102]

Controlling Prostitution

In the late nineteenth and early twentieth century, efforts were made to regulate prostitution in the United States through medical supervision and by licensing and zoning brothels in districts outside residential neighborhoods.[103] After World War I, prostitution became associated with disease, and the desire to protect young servicemen from harm helped to end almost all experiments with legalization in the United States.[104] Some reformers attempted to paint pimps and procurers as immigrants who used their foreign ways to snare unsuspecting American girls into prostitution. Such fears prompted passage of the federal Mann Act (1925), which prohibited bringing women into the country or transporting them across state lines for the purposes of prostitution. Often called the "white slave act," it carried a $5,000 fine, five years in prison, or both.[105]

Today, prostitution is considered a misdemeanor, punishable by a fine or a short jail sentence. Most states punish both people engaging in prostitution and those who hire people for sexual activities. The Minnesota statute is one example of this:

> Subd. 3. Engaging in, hiring, or agreeing to hire an adult to engage in prostitution; penalties. Whoever intentionally does any of the following may be sentenced to imprisonment for not more than 90 days or to payment of a fine of not more than $1,000, or both:
>   (1) engages in prostitution with an individual 18 years of age or above; or
>   (2) hires or offers or agrees to hire an individual 18 years of age or above to engage in sexual penetration or sexual contact. Except as otherwise provided in subdivision 4, a person who is convicted of violating clause (1) or (2) while acting as a patron must, at a minimum, be sentenced to pay a fine of at least $500.[106]

In practice, clients (known generically as Johns) are rarely arrested even though some studies show that an arrest can deter future involvement.[107] Most law enforcement is uneven and aims at confining illegal activities to particular areas in the city.[108] Some local police agencies concerned about prostitution have used high-visibility patrols to discourage prostitutes and their customers, undercover work to arrest prostitutes and drug dealers, and collaboration with hotel and motel owners to identify and arrest pimps and drug dealers.[109] One novel approach is "John Schools," described in Exhibit 14.1. These schools are attended by arrestees who wish to avoid being labeled as criminals.

Legalize Prostitution?

Although most research depicts prostitutes as troubled women who have lived troubled lives, there may be a trend for some young women to enter the sex trade as a rational

---

EXHIBIT 14.1

John Schools

John Schools focus on male offenders and attempt through education to steer them away from prostitution. One of the first, called the "John Group," is a court-ordered treatment program located in Grand Rapids, Michigan. The treatment program can be required as a condition of probation for men arrested for soliciting prostitutes. The intervention includes four group counseling sessions of about one hour each, and one individual session lasting about two hours. The group sessions convey information about prostitution including legal consequences, health risks, impact on survivors (including testimony from former prostitutes) and communities, sexual addiction, pimping, and healthy relationships. In the individual session offenders develop plans for addressing how they will meet their needs through more prosocial avenues in the future. In addition, the program includes mandatory screening for STDs and HIV.

San Francisco's First Offender Prostitution Program (FOPP) is similar and is offered to eligible arrestees, who are given the choice of paying a fee and attending a one-day class or being prosecuted. The program is a partnership of the San Francisco District Attorney's office, the San Francisco Police Department, and a local nonprofit organization, Standing Against Global Exploitation (SAGE). Client fees support all of the costs of conducting the john school classes, as well as subsidizing police vice operations, screening and processing arrestees, and recovery programs for women and girls involved in commercial sex.

Evaluation by an independent research group (Abt Associates) found that the program has been effective in substantially reducing recidivism among men arrested for soliciting prostitutes. The program has been successfully replicated in 12 other U.S. sites and has been adopted at an additional 25 U.S. sites over the past decade; another 49 jurisdictions are considering adopting similar programs.

SOURCE: Michael Shively, Sarah Kuck Jalbert, Ryan Kling, William Rhodes, Peter Finn, Chris Flygare, Laura Tierney, David Squires, Christina Dyous, Kristin Wheeler, and Dana Hunt, *Final Report on the Evaluation of the First Offender Prostitution Program* (Cambridge, MA: Abt Associates, 2008), www.abtassociates.com/reports/FOPP_Evaluation_FULL_REPORT.pdf (accessed August 12, 2011).

---

choice based on economic need. Changing sexual mores help reduce or eliminate the stigma attached to prostitution. There is even evidence that students turn to prostitution to help pay tuition bills.[110] One recent research study conducted in Australia found that the sex industry has become attractive to college students as a way to supplement their income during a time of reduced government aid and increasing educational costs. They view sex work as a "normal" form of employment for students seeking to obtain a higher education.[111] If this more liberal attitude toward prostitution becomes normative, should the practice become legal?

In some countries, especially in the Muslim world, prostitution carries the death penalty. In others, such as Holland, prostitutes pay taxes and belong to a union. Other countries, such as Australia, allow adults to engage in prostitution but regulate their activities, such as requiring that they receive timely health checkups. Still other countries, such as Brazil, allow women to become prostitutes but criminalize earning money from the work of prostitutes—that is, serving as a pimp. In the United States, prostitution is illegal in all states, although brothels are legal in a number of counties in Nevada (but not in Las Vegas or Reno).

Feminists have staked out conflicting views of prostitution. One position is that women must become emancipated from male oppression and reach sexual equality. The *sexual equality view* considers the prostitute a victim of male dominance. In patriarchal societies, male power is predicated on female subjugation, and prostitution is a clear example of this gender exploitation.[112] In contrast, for some feminists, the fight for equality depends on controlling all attempts by men or women to impose their will on women. The *free choice view* is that prostitution, if freely chosen, expresses women's equality and is not a symptom of subjugation.

Advocates of both positions argue that the penalties for prostitution should be reduced (decriminalized); neither side advocates outright legalization. Decriminalization would relieve already desperate women of the additional burden of severe legal punishment. In contrast, legalization might be coupled with regulation by male-dominated justice agencies. For example, required medical examinations would mean increased governmental control over women's bodies.

Both positions have had significant influence around the world. In Sweden, feminists have succeeded in getting legislation passed that severely restricts prostitution and criminalizes any effort to buy sexual activities.[113] In contrast, Holland legalized brothels in 2001 but ordered that they be run under a strict set of guidelines.[114] The English government is considering licensing brothels and creating managed areas or "toleration zones" to combat street prostitution.[115]

Should prostitution be legalized? In her book *Brothel*, Alexa Albert, a Harvard-trained physician who interviewed young women working at a legal brothel in Nevada, makes a compelling case for legalization. She found that the women remained HIV-free and felt safer working in a secure environment than alone on city streets. Despite long hours and rules that gave too much profit to the owners, the women took pride in their work. In addition to the added security, most earned between $300 and $1,500 per day.[116]

Not all experts agree. Roger Matthews, a British criminologist, opposes legalizing prostitution. It is foolish, he claims, to view prostitution as "sex work" that should either be legalized and/or tolerated and regulated. An example is Holland's "tolerance zones," where women can engage in prostitution without fear of arrest. After studying street prostitution for more than two decades, Matthew finds that women on the street are extremely desperate, damaged, and disorganized and are at frequent risk for beatings, rape, and other forms of violence. Prostitution is, he concludes, the world's most dangerous occupation. His solution is to treat the women forced into prostitution as victims and the men who purchase their services as the criminals. He applauds Sweden's decision to make buying sexual services a crime, thus criminalizing the "johns" rather than the women in prostitution. Sadly, when governments legalize prostitution, Matthews believes it leads to a massive expansion of the trade, both legal and illegal.[117]

Pornography

The term **pornography** derives from the Greek *porne*, meaning "prostitute," and *graphein*, meaning "to write." In the heart of many major cities are stores that display and sell books, magazines, and films depicting every imaginable explicit sex act. Sexually explicit DVDs, sold over the Internet and in stores, make up 15 to 30 percent of all movie sales and rentals. The purpose of this material is to provide sexual titillation and excitement for paying customers. Although material depicting nudity and sex is typically legal, protected by the First Amendment's provision limiting governmental control of speech, most criminal codes prohibit the production, display, and sale of obscene material.

Obscenity, derived from the Latin *caenum*, for "filth," is defined as "deeply offensive to morality or decency . . . designed to incite to lust or depravity."[118] The problem of controlling pornography centers on this definition of obscenity. Police and law enforcement officials can legally seize only material that is judged obscene. But who, critics ask, is to judge what is obscene? At one time, such novels as *Tropic of Cancer* by Henry Miller, *Ulysses* by James Joyce, and *Lady Chatterley's Lover* by D. H. Lawrence were prohibited because they were considered obscene; today they are considered works of great literary value. Thus, what is obscene today may be considered socially acceptable at a future time. After all, *Playboy* and other adult magazines, sold openly on most college campuses, display nude models in all kinds of sexually explicit poses. Though at one time they were considered "racy"; today they are relatively tame and you can buy their stock on the New York Stock Exchange.

Allowing individual judgments on what is obscene makes the Constitution's guarantee of free speech unworkable. Could anti-obscenity statutes also be used to control political and social dissent? The uncertainty surrounding this issue is illustrated by Supreme Court Justice Potter Stewart's famous 1964 statement on how he defined obscenity: "I know it when I see it." Because of this legal and moral ambiguity, a global pornography industry is becoming increasingly mainstream, currently generating up to $60 billion per year in revenue. In fact, some Internet pornography companies are now listed on the NASDAQ stock exchange.[119] Nonetheless, while adult material has gone mainstream, courts have long held that the First

Amendment was not intended to protect indecency; therefore, material considered offensive and obscene can be controlled by the rule of law.[120]

Child Pornography

The use of children in pornography is the most controversial and reprehensible aspect of the business. Each year more than a million children are believed to be used in pornography or prostitution, many of them runaways whose plight is exploited by adults.[121] Sexual exploitation by child pornography rings can devastate victims, causing them physical problems ranging from headaches and loss of appetite to genital soreness, vomiting, and urinary tract infections, and psychological problems including mood swings, withdrawal, edginess, and nervousness. In cases of extreme, prolonged victimization, children may lock onto the sex group's behavior and become prone to further victimization or even become victimizers themselves.

Child pornography has become widespread on the Internet. In *Beyond Tolerance: Child Pornography on the Internet*, sociologist Philip Jenkins argues that activists are focused on stamping out Internet pornography but have not focused on its most dangerous form, kiddie porn, which sometimes involves pictures of 4- and 5-year-old girls in sexual encounters.

When an effort is made to target pedophilic websites, investigators often go in the wrong direction, failing to recognize that most sites are short-lived entities whose addresses are passed around to users. Jenkins suggests that kiddie porn is best combated by more effective law enforcement. Instead of focusing on users, efforts should be directed against suppliers. He also suggests that newsgroups and bulletin boards that advertise and discuss kiddie porn be criminalized.[122]

Virtual Kiddie Porn Computer-generated imagery and other high-tech innovations now make it possible for pornographers to create and distribute pornography using virtual images of children. Fearing the proliferation of kiddie porn over the Internet, Congress enacted the Child Pornography Prevention Act of 1996 (CPPA), which outlaws sexually related material that used or *appeared to use* children under 18 engaging in sexual conduct. In *Ashcroft v. The Free Speech Coalition*, the Supreme Court struck down sections of the CPPA relating to virtual kiddie porn: sexually related material in which an actual child appears is illegal, but possessing "virtual" pornography is legal. The Court reasoned that real children are not harmed with creation of a virtual child.

In response to the Court's decision, Congress passed the PROTECT Act of 2003 (The Prosecutorial Remedies and Other Tools to end the Exploitation of Children Today), which outlawed virtual kiddie porn that makes it almost impossible to distinguish the difference between a real child and a morphed or created image.[123] The Supreme Court reviewed this law in a 2008 case, *United States v. Williams*, which concerned Michael Williams, who was convicted in federal district court of "pandering" (promoting) child pornography under the PROTECT Act. At trial, the district court held that the government can legitimately outlaw the pandering of material as child pornography, even if the images are computer generated, if they are being offered to someone who "thought they were buying images of real children." The Court noted that offers to engage in illegal transactions are excluded from First Amendment protection; therefore, the "speech" of an individual claiming to be in possession of child pornography is not protected by the First Amendment. The Court also stated that the law did not violate due process because its requirements were clear and could be understood by courts, juries, and potential violators.[124] Considering the outcome of Williams, how far should the authorities go to enforce laws against kiddie porn? The Profiles in Crime feature addresses this issue.

Does Pornography Cause Violence?

An issue critical to the debate over pornography is whether viewing it produces sexual violence or assaultive behavior. This debate was given added attention when serial killer Ted Bundy claimed his murderous rampage was fueled by reading pornography.

The evidence is mixed. Some studies indicate that viewing sexually explicit material has little effect on sexual violence. When Neil Malamuth, Tamara Addison, and Mary Koss surveyed 2,972 male college students, they discovered that frequent use of pornography was not related to sexual aggression. There were only relatively minor differences in sexual aggression between men who reported using pornography very frequently when compared to those who said they rarely used it at all. However, men who were both at high risk for sexual aggression and who were very frequent users of pornography were much more likely to engage in sexual aggression than their counterparts who consumed pornography less frequently. Put simply, if a person has relatively aggressive sexual inclinations resulting from various personal and cultural factors, exposure to pornography may activate and reinforce associated coercive tendencies and behaviors. But even high levels of exposure to pornography do not turn nonaggressive men into sexual predators.[125]

How might we account for this surprisingly modest association?[126] It is possible that viewing erotic material may act as a safety valve for those whose impulses might otherwise lead them to violence. Convicted rapists and sex offenders report less exposure to pornography than a control group of nonoffenders.[127] Viewing prurient material may have the unintended side effect of satisfying erotic impulses that otherwise might result in more sexually aggressive behavior.

The pornography–violence link seems modest, but there is more evidence that people predisposed to violence and exposed to material that portrays violence, sadism, and women

Edmund J. Coppa/Splash News/Newscom

In May 2006, U.S. Immigration and Customs Enforcement (ICE) intercepted a mail package coming into the United States from Japan that was addressed to Christopher Handley, 39, of Glenwood, Iowa. Inside the package was sexually explicit material, including books containing visual representations of the sexual abuse of children, specifically Japanese *manga* drawings of minor females being sexually abused by adult males and animals. Handley was indicted after U.S. Postal Inspectors searched his home and seized additional obscene drawings of the sexual abuse of children. On May 20, 2009, Handley pleaded guilty in Des Moines, Iowa, to possessing obscene visual representations of the sexual abuse of children, and on February 11, 2010, he was sentenced to six months in prison, to be followed by three years' supervised release.

What is interesting about the case is that Handley's crime involved his receiving and possessing sexually explicit drawings that were not of actual children but merely imaginary renderings (i.e., virtual kiddie porn). Possession of these images were protected by the 2002 case, *Ashcroft v. The Free Speech Coalition*, and Handley, who was aware of the case, mistakenly believed he had a green light to possess virtual kiddie porn. He was unaware, however, that Congress had passed the PROTECT Act, which carries a five-year mandatory minimum sentence for "receiving" child pornography. With his attorney's advice, Handler plead guilty rather than let a jury decide whether the material he had received was obscene; six months seemed more doable than five years.

Do you think Handler got a raw deal? Does a cartoon image, even if offensive and obscene, really hurt anyone? Is it really kiddie porn, and should it be outlawed?

SOURCES: U.S. Department of Justice, "Iowa Man Pleads Guilty to Possessing Obscene Visual Representations of the Sexual Abuse of Children," May 20, 2009, www.fbi.gov/omaha/press-releases/2009/om052009a.htm/ (accessed August 12, 2011); "Christopher Handley's Attorney Comments on His Case," March 2, 2010, Los Angeles, California, www.tcj.com/beta/news/christopher-handley's-attorney-comments-on-his-case/ (accessed August 12, 2011).

enjoying being raped and degraded are more likely to be sexually aggressive toward female victims.[128] Individuals who are already predisposed to sexually offend may become aroused by pornography exposure and have a greater willingness to undertake sexual coercion.[129] For example, men who engage in domestic violence also tend to watch pornography, and those who do are more controlling and more violent.[130]

Laboratory experiments conducted by a number of leading authorities have found that men exposed to violent pornography are more likely to act aggressively and to hold aggressive attitudes toward women.[131] James Fox and Jack Levin find it common for serial killers to collect and watch violent pornography. Some make their own "snuff" films starring their victims.[132] On a macro level, cross-national research indicates that nations that consume the highest levels of pornography also have extremely high rape rates.[133] However, it is still not certain if such material drives people to sexual violence or whether people predisposed to sexual violence are drawn to pornography with a violent theme. A recent study by Michael Bourke and Andres Hernandez compared a group of men who had been *convicted* of possessing kiddie porn, but had no known history with "hands-on" sexual abuse, with a second group of child pornographers who also had been *convicted* of sexual offending. The goal was to determine whether the former group of offenders were "merely" collectors of child pornography who presented no actual physical risk to children. They found that the Internet offenders were significantly more likely to have sexually abused a child via a hands-on contact even though they had not been caught or convicted and that they were likely to have offended against multiple victims.[134] This research doesn't prove that viewing child pornography is a cause of child molesting per se, but it does indicate there is a high correlation between viewing and acting out, regardless of whether the behavior has been detected or remains hidden.

CONNECTIONS

Chapter 5 discusses the effects of media on violence. As you may recall, some evidence suggests that people exposed to violent media will become violent themselves, but this association is still being debated.

Pornography and the Law

All states and the federal government prohibit the sale and production of pornographic material. Child pornography is usually a separate legal category that involves either the creation or reproduction of materials depicting minors engaged in actual or simulated sexual activity ("sexual exploitation of minors") or the publication or distribution of obscene, indecent, or harmful materials to minors.[135] Under existing federal law, trafficking in obscenity (18 U.S.C. Sec. 1462, 1464, 1466), child pornography (18 U.S.C. Sec. 2252), harassment (18 U.S.C. Sec. 875(c)), illegal solicitation or luring of minors (18 U.S.C. Sec. 2423(b)), and threatening to injure someone (18 U.S.C. Sec. 875(c)) are all felonies punished by long prison sentences.

These laws are designed to control obscene material, whereas the First Amendment of the U.S. Constitution protects free speech and prohibits police agencies from limiting the public's right of free expression. This legal protection has sent the government along a torturous road in the attempt to define when material is criminally obscene and eligible for legal control. For example, the Supreme Court held in the twin cases of *Roth v. United States* and *Alberts v. California* that the First Amendment protects all "ideas with even the slightest redeeming social importance—unorthodox ideas, controversial ideas, even ideas hateful to the prevailing climate of opinion, but implicit in the history of the First Amendment is the rejection of obscenity as utterly without redeeming social importance."[136] In the 1966 case of *Memoirs v. Massachusetts*, the Supreme Court again required that for a work to be considered obscene it must be shown to be "utterly without redeeming social value."[137] These decisions left unclear how obscenity is defined. If a highly erotic movie tells a "moral tale," must it be judged legal even if 95 percent of its content is objectionable? A spate of movies made after the *Roth* decision alleged that they were educational so they could not be said to lack redeeming social importance. Many state obscenity cases were appealed to federal courts so judges could decide whether the films totally lacked redeeming social importance. To rectify the situation, the Supreme Court redefined its concept of obscenity in the case of *Miller v. California*:

> The basic guidelines for the trier of fact must be (a) whether the average person applying contemporary community standards would find that the work taken as a whole appeals to the prurient interest; (b) whether the work depicts or describes, in a patently offensive way, sexual conduct specifically defined by the applicable state law; and (c) whether the work, taken as a whole, lacks serious literary, artistic, political or scientific value.[138]

To convict a person of obscenity under the *Miller* doctrine, the state or local jurisdiction must specifically define obscene conduct in its statute, and the pornographer must engage in that behavior. The Court gave some examples of what is considered obscene: "patently offensive representations or descriptions of masturbation, excretory functions and lewd exhibition of the genitals." In subsequent cases the Court overruled convictions for "offensive" or "immoral" behavior; these are not considered obscene. The *Miller* doctrine has been criticized for not spelling out how community standards are to be determined. Obviously, a plebiscite cannot be held to determine the community's attitude for every trial concerning the sale of pornography. Works that are considered obscene in Omaha might be considered routine in New York, but how can we be sure? To resolve this dilemma, the Supreme Court articulated in *Pope v. Illinois* a reasonableness doctrine: a work is not obscene if a reasonable person applying objective standards would find that the material in question has at least some social value:[139]

> The ideas that a work represents need not obtain majority approval to merit protection, and the value of that work does not vary from community to community based on the degree of local acceptance it has won. The proper inquiry is not whether an ordinary member of any given community would find serious value in the allegedly obscene material, but whether a reasonable person would find such value in the material, taken as a whole.[140]

Controlling Pornography

Sex for profit predates Western civilization. Considering its longevity, there seems to be little evidence that it can be controlled or eliminated by legal means alone. In 1986, the Attorney General's Commission on Pornography advocated a strict law enforcement policy to control obscenity, directing that "the prosecution of obscene materials that portray sexual violence be treated as a matter of special urgency."[141] Since then, there has been a concerted effort by the federal government to prosecute the distribution of obscenity. Law enforcement has been so fervent that industry members have filed suit claiming they are the victims of a "moral crusade" by right-wing zealots.[142]

Although politically appealing, controlling sex for profit is difficult because of the public's desire to purchase sexually related material and services. Law enforcement crusades may not necessarily obtain the desired effect. A get-tough policy could make sex-related goods and services scarce, driving up prices and making their sale even more desirable and profitable. Going after national distributors may help decentralize the adult movie and photo business and encourage local rings to expand their activities, for example, by making and marketing videos as well as still photos or distributing them through computer networks.

An alternative approach has been to restrict the sale of pornography within acceptable boundaries. Some municipal governments have tolerated or even established adult entertainment zones in which obscene material can be openly sold.[143] And since the Internet has become a favored method of delivering adult material, one that defies easy regulation because distribution can be international in scope, it is quite difficult to slow the tide of obscenity.

SUBSTANCE ABUSE

In January of 2008 the media reported that actor Heath Ledger had died in his New York apartment at the age of 28. His big break had been playing opposite Julia Styles in the teen movie *Ten Things I Hate about You*. He became an international star with his stirring performance as a gay cowboy in Ang Lee's acclaimed film *Brokeback Mountain* and as the Joker in the Batman sequel *The Dark Knight*. Some in the media speculated about suicide, but medical examiners later pinned Ledger's death on an accidental overdose of six drugs—painkillers and sedatives—namely, oxycodone, hydrocodone (Vicodin), diazepam (Valium), temazepam (Restoril), alprazolam (Xanax), and doxylamine. Three of the six prescription drugs found in Ledger's apartment had been filled in Europe, where the actor was recently filming, police said.

CONNECTIONS

The debate over dangerous prescription drug use has been intensified because drugs are now easily obtained on the Web, and many suppliers do not require prescriptions. For more on this issue, see the discussion in Chapter 15 on obtaining dangerous drugs via the Web.

Ledger's death is a stark reminder of the dangers of substance abuse, a social problem that spans every segment of society. Large urban areas are beset by drug-dealing gangs, drug users who engage in crime to support their habits, and alcohol-related violence. Rural areas are important staging centers for the shipment of drugs across the country and are often the production sites for synthetic drugs and marijuana farming.[144] Nor is the United States alone in experiencing a problem with substance abuse. Australia reports that almost 20 percent of youths in detention centers and 40 percent of adult prisoners report having used heroin at least once; in Canada, cocaine and crack are considered serious urban problems; South Africa reports increased cocaine and heroin abuse; Thailand has a serious heroin and methamphetamine problem; and British police have found a major increase in heroin abuse.[145]

Another indication of the concern about drugs has been the increasing number of drug-related arrests: from less than half a million in 1977 to more than 1.8 million today.[146] Similarly, the proportion of prison inmates incarcerated for drug offenses has increased by 600 percent since 1986.[147] Clearly the justice system views drug abuse as a major problem and is taking what decision makers regard as decisive measures for its control.

Despite the scope of the drug problem, some still view drug use as another type of victimless public order crime. There is great debate over the legalization of drugs and the control of alcohol. Some consider drug use a private matter and drug control another example of government intrusion into people's private lives. Furthermore, legalization could reduce the profit of selling illegal substances and drive suppliers out of the market.[148] Others see these substances as dangerous and believe that the criminal activity of users makes the term "victimless" nonsensical. Still another position is that the possession and use of all drugs and alcohol should be legalized but that the sale and distribution of drugs should be heavily penalized. This would punish those profiting from drugs and would enable users to be helped without fear of criminal punishment.

When Did Drug Use Begin?

The use of chemical substances to change reality and to provide stimulation, relief, or relaxation has gone on for thousands of years. The opium poppy was first cultivated more than 5,000 years ago and was used by the Persians, Sumerians, Assyrians, Babylonians, and Egyptians. Users discovered the bliss that could be achieved by smoking the extract derived from crushing the seed pods, which yielded a pleasurable, peaceful feeling throughout the body. Known as the Hul Gil, or "plant of joy," its use spread quickly around the fertile crescent.[149] The ancient Greeks knew and understood the problem of drug use. At the time of the Crusades, the Arabs were using marijuana. In the Western Hemisphere, natives of Mexico and South America chewed coca leaves and used "magic mushrooms" in their religious ceremonies.[150] Drug use was also accepted in Europe well into the twentieth century. Recently uncovered pharmacy records circa 1900 to 1920 showed sales of cocaine and heroin solutions to members of the British royal family; records from 1912 show that Winston Churchill, then a member of Parliament, was sold a cocaine solution while staying in Scotland.[151]

In the early years of the United States, opium and its derivatives were easily obtained. Opium-based drugs were used in various patent medicine cure-alls. Morphine was used extensively to relieve the pain of wounded soldiers in the Civil War. By the turn of the century, an estimated 1 million U.S. citizens were opiate users.[152]

Several factors precipitated the current stringent U.S. drug laws. The rural religious creeds of the nineteenth century—especially those of the Methodists, Presbyterians, and Baptists—emphasized individual human toil and self-sufficiency while designating the use of intoxicating substances as an unwholesome surrender to the evils of urban morality. Religious leaders were thoroughly opposed to the use and sale of narcotics. The medical literature of the late 1800s began to designate the use of morphine and opium as a vice, a habit, an appetite, and a disease. Nineteenth- and early twentieth-century police literature described drug users as habitual criminals. Moral crusaders in the nineteenth century defined drug use as evil and directed that local and national entities should outlaw the sale and possession of drugs. Some well-publicized research efforts categorized drug use as highly dangerous.[153] Drug use was also associated with the foreign immigrants recruited to work in factories and mines; they brought with them their national drug habits. Early antidrug legislation appears to have been tied to prejudice against immigrating ethnic minorities.[154]

After the Spanish-American War of 1898, the United States inherited Spain's opium monopoly in the Philippines. Concern over this international situation, along with the domestic issues just outlined, led the U.S. government to participate in the First International Drug Conference, held in Shanghai in 1908, and a second one at The Hague in 1912. Participants in these two conferences were asked to strongly oppose free trade in drugs. The international pressure, coupled with a growing national concern, led to the passage of the antidrug laws discussed here.

Alcohol and Its Prohibition

The history of alcohol and the law in the United States also has been controversial and dramatic. Early in the twentieth century, a drive was mustered to prohibit the sale of alcohol. This **temperance movement** was fueled by the belief that the purity of the U.S. agrarian culture was being destroyed by the growth of the city. Urbanism was viewed as a threat to the lifestyle of the majority of the nation's population, then living on farms and in villages. The forces behind the temperance movement were such lobbying groups as the Anti-Saloon League led by Carrie Nation, the Women's Christian Temperance Union, and the Protestant clergy of the Baptist, Methodist, and Congregationalist faiths.[155] They viewed the growing city, filled with newly arriving Irish, Italian, and eastern European immigrants, as centers of degradation and wickedness. The propensity of these ethnic people to drink heavily was viewed as the main force behind their degenerate lifestyle. The eventual prohibition of the sale of alcoholic beverages brought about by ratification of the Eighteenth Amendment in 1919 was viewed as a triumph of the morality of middle- and upper-class Americans over the threat posed to their culture by the "new Americans."[156]

Prohibition failed. It was enforced by the Volstead Act, which defined intoxicating beverages as those containing one-half of 1 percent, or more, alcohol.[157] What doomed Prohibition? One factor was the use of organized crime to supply illicit liquor. Also, the law made it illegal only to sell alcohol, not to purchase it; this cut into the law's deterrent

capability. Finally, despite the work of Eliot Ness and his "Untouchables," law enforcement agencies were inadequate, and officials were likely to be corrupted by wealthy bootleggers.[158] In 1933 the Twenty-First Amendment to the Constitution repealed Prohibition, signaling the end of the "noble experiment."

The Extent of Substance Abuse

What is the extent of the substance abuse problem today? This question can be answered from both a macro and a micro level: What quantity of drugs is being produced and shipped? How many people are drug users?

Drug Production and Importation   The most recent reports on the world drug problem indicate that the drug epidemic may be abating, that drug cultivation is in decline, and that law enforcement agencies have become more adept at seizing drug shipments. There is evidence that drug cultivation (opium and coca) is flat or down. Major markets for opiates (Europe and Southeast Asia), cocaine (North America), and cannabis (North America, Oceania, and Europe) are in decline. For example, the global area under opium poppy cultivation has declined by 23 percent since 2007, and during the same period coca cultivation declined by 13 percent.[159] This decline was mainly due to sustained success in reducing cultivation in Southeast Asia. Poppy cultivation in the so-called Golden Triangle has fallen by some 80 percent since 2000; the region is now almost opium free.

Individual Drug Use   Not only has the cultivation and importation of banned substances been in decline, but so too has individual drug use patterns in the United States and around the world.

Some of the most important information on drug use among young people, the annual Monitoring the Future (MTF) survey, is conducted by the Institute of Social Research (ISR) at the University of Michigan.[160] Data collected from the self-report responses of nearly 50,000 high school students in the 8th, 10th, and 12th grades (8th and 10th graders were added to the survey in 1991) in almost 400 schools across the United States asks students about their yearly and lifetime drug use experiences.

The most recent MTF surveys show that individual drug use has fallen significantly in the past 30 years or so. In 1975, when the MTF began surveying students, a majority of high school students (55 percent) had used an illicit drug by the time they graduated. As Figure 14.1 shows, drug use peaked in 1981 (66 percent of seniors reported using drugs) before a long and gradual decline to 41 percent in 1992—the low point. After 1992 the proportion of youth who used some illegal substance rose considerably, reaching a recent high point of 55 percent in 1999; it then declined gradually to slightly less than half (48 percent) by 2010.

Percent who used any illicit drug in lifetime

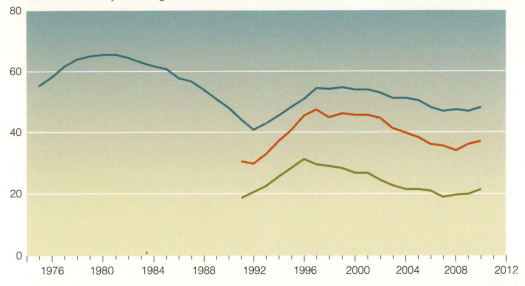

Percent who used any illicit drug in last 12 months

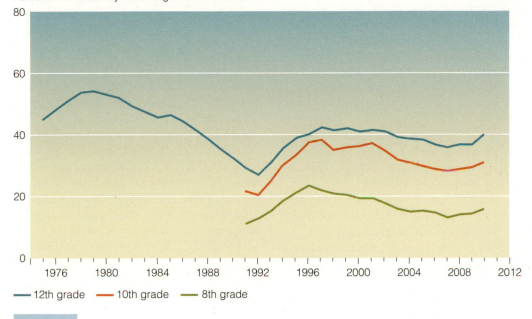

—— 12th grade   —— 10th grade   —— 8th grade

FIGURE 14.1
Trends in Annual Prevalence of Illicit Drug Use

SOURCE: Lloyd Johnston, Jerald Bachman, Patrick O'Malley, and John Schulenberg, *Monitoring the Future National Results on Adolescent Drug Use: Overview of Key Findings, 2010* (Ann Arbor: Institute for Social Research, The University of Michigan), www.monitoringthefuture.org/pubs/monographs/mtf-overview2010.pdf.

Overall drug usage has stabilized, but for the past few years marijuana use has risen for all three grades, reversing a long, gradual decline over the preceding decade. Daily marijuana use increased significantly in all three grades, and by 12th grade, about 6 percent of American high school students say that they are daily, or near-daily, marijuana users. One reason for the uptick may be that kids are now reporting a decline in their perception of the risk associated with marijuana use; similarly, disapproval

of drug use has begun to decline. It is possible that changing attitudes—less fear, less disapproval—are harbingers of increased usage.

Although the improvement has been impressive, more than 10 percent of 8th graders and more than 30 percent of 12th graders have used some type of illicit drug during the past year. Drug use may be down, but many kids continue to use drugs and have no problem finding illegal drugs on campus.[161]

National Survey on Drug Use and Health A second source of drug use data comes from surveys taken by the Substance Abuse and Mental Health Services Administration (SAMHSA), a division of the Department of Health and Human Services, which conducts the National Survey on Drug Use and Health (NSDUH) (the survey was called the National Household Survey on Drug Abuse—NHSDA—prior to 2002).[162] The NSDUH collects information from all U.S. residents of households, noninstitutional group quarters (such as shelters, rooming houses, dormitories), and civilians living on military bases (it excludes homeless people who do not use shelters, military personnel on active duty, and residents of institutional group quarters, such as jails and hospitals).

The most recent NSDUH survey indicates that, like the MTF survey, drug use trends have been relatively stable during the past few years with slight declines in the use of most illegal substances. Nonetheless, an estimated 20 million Americans aged 12 or older had used an illicit drug in the past year, including marijuana/hashish, cocaine (including crack), heroin, hallucinogens, inhalants, or prescription-type psychotherapeutics used nonmedically. About half of all people who said they used a single drug smoked marijuana. Illicit drugs other than marijuana were used by about 10 million people, or 47 percent of illicit drug users aged 12 or older; about 20 percent used both marijuana and other drugs.

Alcohol Abuse The national survey also tells us something about alcohol abuse. Users and usage are divided into three groups based on their frequency of drinking:

- *Current (past month) use.* At least one drink in the past 30 days. Slightly more than half of Americans aged 12 or older report current alcohol usage; this means an estimated 130 million people are drinkers.
- *Binge use.* Five or more drinks on the same occasion (i.e., at the same time or within a couple of hours of each other) on at least 1 day in the past 30 days. Nearly one-quarter of the population aged 12 or older participated in binge drinking at least once in the past 30 days. This translates to about 60 million binge drinkers.
- *Heavy use.* Five or more drinks on the same occasion on each of 5 or more days in the past 30 days. About 7 percent of the population aged 12 or older, or 17 million people, can be classified as heavy drinkers, binging at least five times per month.

In addition to these disturbing data, there is evidence that very young children are involved in alcohol consumption: about 4 percent of kids aged 12 or 13 used alcohol; by the time they hit 18 and 19, more than 70 percent were drinkers. More than one-third of teens 18 and older were binge drinkers.

What Causes Substance Abuse?

What causes people to abuse substances? Although there are many different views on the causes of drug use, most can be characterized as seeing the onset of an addictive career as being either an environmental or a personal matter.

Subcultural View Those who view drug abuse as having an environmental basis concentrate on lower-class addiction. Because a disproportionate number of drug abusers are poor, the onset of drug use can be tied to such factors as racial prejudice, devalued identities, low self-esteem, poor socioeconomic status, and the high level of mistrust, negativism, and defiance found in impoverished areas. Residents feel trapped in a cycle of violence, drug abuse, and despair.[163] Youths in these disorganized areas may join peers to learn the techniques of drug use and receive social support for their habit. Research shows that peer influence is a significant predictor of drug careers that actually grow stronger as people mature.[164] Drug use splits some communities into distinct groups of relatively affluent abstainers and desperately poor abusers.[165]

Psychological View Not all drug abusers reside in lower-class slum areas; the problem of middle-class substance abuse is very real. Consequently, some experts have linked substance abuse to psychological deficits such as impaired cognitive functioning, personality disturbance, and emotional problems that can strike people in any economic class.[166] Research on the psychological characteristics of drug abusers does, in fact, reveal the presence of a significant degree of personal pathology. Studies have found that addicts suffer personality disorders characterized by low frustration tolerance, anxiety, and fantasies of omnipotence. Many addicts exhibit psychopathic or sociopathic behavior characteristics, forming what is called an addiction-prone personality.[167]

What is the connection between psychological disorder and drug abuse? Drugs may help people deal with unconscious needs and impulses and relieve dependence and depression. People may turn to drug abuse as a form of self-medication to reduce the emotional turmoil of adolescence, deal with troubling impulses, or cope with traumatic life experiences such as institutional child abuse (kids who were sexually or physically abused in orphanages, mental institutions, juvenile detention centers, day care centers, etc.).[168] Survivors of sexual assault and physical abuse in the home also have been known to turn to drug and alcohol abuse as a coping mechanism.[169] Depressed people may use drugs as an alternative to more radical solutions to their pain such as suicide.[170] Kids with low self-esteem, or those who are self-conscious about their body image or who have a poor self-image may turn to drugs to ease psychological turmoil.[171]

Genetic Factors Research shows that substance abuse may have a genetic basis.[172] For example, a number of studies comparing alcoholism among identical twins and fraternal twins have found that the degree of concordance (both siblings behaving identically) is twice as high among the identical twin groups.[173]

Taken as a group, studies of the genetic basis of substance abuse suggest that people whose parents were alcoholic or drug dependent have a greater chance of developing a problem than the children of nonabusers, and this relationship occurs regardless of parenting style or the quality of the parent–child relationship.[174] However, not all children of abusing parents become drug dependent themselves, suggesting that even if drug abuse is heritable, environment and socialization must play some role in the onset of abuse.[175]

Social Learning Social psychologists suggest that drug abuse may result from observing parental drug use. Parental drug abuse begins to have a damaging effect on children as young as 2 years old, especially when parents manifest drug-related personality problems such as depression or poor impulse control.[176] Children whose parents abuse drugs are more likely to have persistent abuse problems than the children of nonabusers.[177]

People who learn that drugs provide pleasurable sensations may be the most likely to experiment with illegal substances; a habit may develop if the user experiences lower anxiety, fear, and tension levels.[178] Having a history of family drug and alcohol abuse has been found to be a characteristic of violent teenage sexual abusers.[179] Heroin abusers report an unhappy childhood that included harsh physical punishment and parental neglect and rejection.[180]

Problem Behavior Syndrome (PBS) For many people, substance abuse is just one of many problem behaviors.[181] Longitudinal studies show that drug abusers are maladjusted, alienated, and emotionally distressed and that drug use is only one among many social problems.[182] Having a deviant lifestyle begins early in life and is punctuated with criminal relationships, family history of substance abuse, educational failure, and alienation. Crack cocaine use has been linked to sexual abuse as children and social isolation as adults.[183] There is robust support for the interconnection of problem drinking and drug abuse, delinquency, precocious sexual behavior, school failure, running away, homelessness, family conflict, and other similar social problems.[184]

Rational Choice Not all people who abuse drugs do so because of personal pathology. Some may use drugs and alcohol because they want to enjoy their effects: get high, relax, improve creativity, escape reality, and increase sexual responsiveness. Research indicates that adolescent alcohol abusers believe that getting high will make them powerful, increase their sexual performance, and facilitate their social behavior; they care little about negative future consequences.[185] Claire Sterk-Elifson's research on middle-class drug-abusing women shows that most were introduced by friends in the context of "just having some fun."[186]

Substance abuse, then, may be a function of the rational but mistaken belief that drugs can benefit the user. The decision to use drugs involves evaluations of personal consequences (such as addiction, disease, and legal punishment) and the expected benefits of drug use (such as peer approval, positive affective states, heightened awareness, and relaxation). Adolescents may begin using drugs because they believe their peers expect them to do so.[187]

Is There a Drug Gateway?

Some experts believe that, regardless of its cause, most people fall into drug abuse slowly, beginning with alcohol and then following with marijuana and more serious drugs as the need for a more powerful high intensifies. A number of research efforts have confirmed this **gateway model**. James Inciardi, Ruth Horowitz, and Anne Pottieger found a clear pattern of adult involvement in adolescent drug abuse. Kids on crack started their careers with early experimentation with alcohol at age 7, began getting drunk at age 8, had alcohol with an adult present by age 9, and became regular drinkers by the time they were 11 years old.[188] Drinking with an adult present, presumably a parent, was a significant precursor of future substance abuse and delinquency. "Adults who gave children alcohol," they argue, "were also giving them a head start in a delinquent career."[189] Other research efforts support this view when they find that the most serious drug users have a history of recreational drug and alcohol abuse.[190] Kids who begin using alcohol in adolescence become involved in increasing levels of deviant behavior as they mature.[191] However, a recent longitudinal analysis by Cesar Rebellon and Karen Van Gundy found evidence that marijuana users are up to five times more likely to escalate their drug abuse and try cocaine and heroin than are nonusers.[192] In sum, although most marijuana smokers do not become hard drug users, some do, and the risk of using dangerous substances may be increased by first engaging in recreational drugs.

The drug gateway vision is popular, but not all research efforts find that users progress to ever-more potent drugs, and some show that, surprisingly, many hard-core drug abusers never smoked pot or used alcohol.[193] In addition, although many American youths have tried marijuana, few progress to crack or heroin abuse.[194]

Types of Drug Users and Abusers

The general public often groups all drug users together without recognizing that there are many varieties, ranging from adolescent recreational drug users to adults who run large smuggling operations.[195]

- *Adolescents who distribute small amounts of drugs.* Some dealers began their involvement in the drug trade by using and distributing small amounts of drugs; they do not commit any other serious criminal acts. Some start out as "stash dealers" who sell drugs to maintain a consistent access to drugs for their own consumption; their customers are almost always personal acquaintances, including friends and relatives.[196] They are insulated from the legal system because their activities rarely result in apprehension and sanction.

- *Adolescents who frequently sell drugs.* A small number of adolescents, most often multiple-drug users or heroin or cocaine users, are high-rate dealers who bridge the gap between adult drug distributors and the adolescent user. Frequent dealers often have adults who "front" for them—that is, loan them drugs to sell without upfront cash. The teenagers then distribute the drugs to friends and acquaintances, returning most of the proceeds to the supplier while keeping a commission for themselves. Frequent dealers are more likely to sell drugs in public and can be seen in known drug user hangouts in parks, schools, or other public places. Deals are irregular, so the chances of apprehension are slight.

- *Teenage drug dealers who commit other delinquent acts.* A more serious type of drug-involved youth comprises those who use and distribute multiple substances and also commit both property and violent crimes; many are gang members.[197] Although these youngsters make up only about 2 percent of the teenage population, they commit 40 percent of the robberies and assaults and about 60 percent of all teenage felony thefts and drug sales.

  These youths are frequently hired by older dealers to act as street-level drug runners. Each member of a crew of 3 to 12 boys will handle small quantities of drugs, perhaps three bags of heroin, which are received on consignment and sold on the street; the supplier receives 50 to 70 percent of the drug's street value. The crew members also act as lookouts, recruiters, and guards. Between drug sales, the young dealers commit robberies, burglaries, and other thefts.[198]

- *Adolescents who cycle in and out of the justice system.* Some drug-involved youths are failures at both dealing and crime. They do not have the savvy to join gangs or groups and instead begin committing unplanned, opportunistic crimes that increase their chances of arrest. They are heavy drug users, which both increases apprehension risk and decreases their value for organized drug distribution networks. Drug-involved "losers" can earn a living steering customers to a seller in a "copping" area, "touting" drug availability for a dealer, or acting as a lookout. However, they are not considered trustworthy or deft enough to handle drugs or money. They may bungle other criminal acts, which solidifies their reputation as undesirable.

- *Drug-involved youth who continue to commit crimes as adults.* Although about two-thirds of substance-abusing youths continue to use drugs after they reach adulthood, about half desist from other criminal activities.

Those who persist in both substance abuse and crime as adults exhibit a garden variety of social and developmental problems. Some evidence also exists that these drug-using persisters have low nonverbal IQs and poor physical coordination.

- *Outwardly respectable adults who are top-level dealers.* A few outwardly respectable adult dealers sell large quantities of drugs to support themselves in high-class lifestyles. Outwardly respectable dealers often seem indistinguishable from other young professionals. Upscale dealers drift into dealing from many different walks of life. Some begin as campus dealers whose lifestyle and outward appearance are indistinguishable from other students (though they are more frequently involved in illegal behavior outside of drug dealing).[199] Frequently they are drawn from professions and occupations that are unstable, have irregular working hours, and accept drug abuse. Former graduate students, musicians, performing artists, and barkeepers are among those most likely to fit the profile of the adult who begins dealing drugs in his or her 20s. Some use their business skills and drug profits to get into legitimate enterprises or illegal scams. Others drop out of the drug trade because they are the victims of violent crime committed by competitors or disgruntled customers; a few wind up in jail or prison.

- *Smugglers.* Smugglers import drugs into the United States. They are generally men, middle-aged or older, who have strong organizational skills, established connections, capital to invest, and a willingness to take large business risks. Smugglers are a loosely organized, competitive group of individual entrepreneurs. There is a constant flow in and out of the business as some sources become the target of law enforcement activities, new drug sources become available, older smugglers become dealers, and former dealers become smugglers.

- *Adult predatory drug users who are frequently arrested.* Many users who begin abusing substances in early adolescence continue in drugs and crime in their adulthood. Getting arrested, doing time, using multiple drugs, and committing predatory crimes are a way of life for them. They have few skills, did poorly in school, and have long criminal records. The threat of conviction and punishment has little effect on their criminal activities. These "losers" have friends and relatives involved in drugs and crime. They specialize in robberies, burglaries, thefts, and drug sales. They filter in and out of the justice system and begin committing crimes as soon as they are released. In some populations, at least one-third of adult males are involved in drug trafficking and other criminal acts well into their adulthood.[200]

  If they make a "big score," perhaps through a successful drug deal, they may significantly increase their drug use. Their increased narcotics consumption then destabilizes their lifestyle, destroying family and career ties. When their finances dry up, they may become *street junkies*, people whose traditional lifestyle has been destroyed, who turn to petty crime to maintain an adequate supply of drugs. Cut off from a stable source of quality heroin, not knowing from where their next fixes or the money to pay for them will come, looking for any opportunity to make a buck, getting sick or "jonesing," being pathetically unkempt and unable to maintain even the most primitive routines of health or hygiene, street junkies live a very difficult existence. Because they are unreliable and likely to become police informants, street junkies pay the highest prices for the poorest quality heroin; lack of availability increases their need to commit habit-supporting crimes.[201]

- *Adult predatory drug users who are rarely arrested.* Some drug users are "winners." They commit hundreds of crimes each year but are rarely arrested. On the streets, they are known for their calculated violence. Their crimes are carefully planned and coordinated. They often work with partners and use lookouts to carry out the parts of their crimes that have the highest risk of apprehension. These "winners" are more likely to use recreational drugs, such as coke and pot, than the more addicting heroin or opiates. Some become high-frequency users and risk apprehension and punishment. But for the lucky few, their criminal careers can stretch for up to 15 years without interruption by the justice system. These users are sometimes referred to as *stabilized junkies* who have learned the skills needed to purchase and process larger amounts of heroin. Their addiction enables them to maintain normal lifestyles, although they may turn to drug dealing to create contacts with drug suppliers. They are employable, but earning legitimate income does little to reduce their drug use or dealing activities.[202]

- *Less predatory drug-involved adult offenders.* Most adult drug users are petty criminals who avoid violent crime. These occasional users are people just beginning their addiction, who use small amounts of narcotics, and whose habit can be supported by income from conventional jobs; narcotics have relatively little influence on their lifestyles.[203] They are typically high school graduates and have regular employment that supports their drug use. They usually commit petty thefts or pass bad checks. They stay on the periphery of the drug trade by engaging in such acts as helping addicts shoot up, bagging drugs for dealers, operating shooting galleries, renting needles and syringes, and selling small amounts of drugs. These petty criminal drug users do not have the stomach for a life of hard crime and drug dealing. They violate the law in proportion to the amount and cost of the drugs they are using. Pot smokers have a significantly lower frequency of theft violations than daily heroin users, whose habit is considerably more costly.

- *Outwardly respectable adults who are frequent users.* Some drug users continue their activities into their adulthood, and others may initiate drug use as part of a new lifestyle developed in adulthood. These users may be successful college graduates who become caught up in the club scene in major cities and get involved in recreational drug use. Surveys of urban young adults find that almost 40 percent report use of at least one club drug.[204]

Another element of the outwardly respectable adult drug abuser use illegal substances to enhance their professional careers. The sports world has been rocked with stories of famed athletes who have admitted taking performance-enhancing drugs. Recent research shows that professional ballet dancers, a group not usually suspected of being drug involved, routinely use banned substances to improve performance.[205]

The number of outwardly respectable drug users is expected to rise as the aging baby boomers, who grew up in the drug culture, both live longer and continue to use banned substances. Evidence shows that this group, who may number 70 million people by 2030, will continue to use illegal substances in amounts unheard of for people of their age and lifestyle.[206]

- *Drug-involved female offenders.* Women who are drug-involved offenders constitute a separate type of substance abuser. Although women are far less likely than men to use addictive drugs, research conducted by CASA found that 15 million girls and women use illicit drugs or abuse controlled prescription drugs, 32 million smoke cigarettes, and 6 million are alcohol abusers and alcoholics. Substance abuse is nondiscriminatory and affects all women—rich, poor, young, old, urban, rural, professional, and homemaker.[207]

  Though infrequently violent criminals, women who abuse substances are more likely to get involved in prostitution and low-level drug dealing; a few become top-level dealers. Many are pregnant or are already mothers, and because they share needles, they are at high risk of contracting AIDS and passing the HIV virus to their newborn children. They maintain a high risk of victimization. One study of 171 women using crack cocaine found that since initiating crack use, 62 percent of the women reported suffering a physical attack and 32 percent suffered rape; more than half were forced to seek medical care for their injuries.[208]

Drugs and Crime

One of the main reasons for the criminalization of particular substances is the assumed association between drug abuse and crime. Substance abuse appears to be an important precipitating factor in a variety of criminal acts, especially income generating crimes such as burglary.[209] A number of sources indicate a strong connection between drug use and crime.

User Surveys Numerous self-report studies have examined the criminal activity of drug users. As a group, they show that people who take drugs also have extensive involvement in crime.[210] Youths who abuse alcohol are the most likely to engage in violence during their life course; violent adolescents report histories of alcohol abuse; adults with long histories of drinking also are more likely to report violent offending patterns.[211] Surveys show that youths who self-report delinquent behavior are more likely to use illicit drugs. Kids who were involved in serious brawls or theft were significantly more likely to use drugs than those who did not engage in such antisocial behaviors.[212]

Arrestee Data According to the National Survey on Drug Use and Health:

- Adults who were arrested in the past year for any serious violent or property offense were more than four times as likely to have used an illicit drug in the past year than those who were not arrested for a serious offense (60 percent versus 14 percent).
- Adults who had been arrested for serious violent or property offenses in the past year were more likely than those not arrested for serious offenses to have used marijuana (and cocaine, crack cocaine, hallucinogens, methamphetamines, heroin, and prescription drugs) nonmedically.[213]

Correctional Surveys Another indication of a drug–crime connection are correctional surveys that disclose that many convicted criminals are lifelong substance abusers.[214] The most recent surveys show that the drug use rate among parolees is double that of the general population. Similarly, about 24 percent of adults on probation reported drug abuse, more than double the rate of the general population.[215]

A 2010 survey by researchers at the National Center on Addiction and Substance Abuse (CASA) at Columbia University found that approximately 85 percent of current inmates could benefit from drug abuse treatment. CASA estimates that 1.5 million of the current 2.3 million prison inmates meet the clinical criteria for substance abuse or addiction. Another 458,000 inmates have a history of substance abuse and either:

- Were under the influence of alcohol or other drugs at the time of their crime,
- Committed their offense to get money to buy drugs, or
- Were incarcerated for an alcohol or drug law violation

The CASA study also found that alcohol and drugs are significant factors in the commission of many crimes. Alcohol and drugs are involved in the following:

- 78 percent of violent crimes
- 83 percent of property crimes
- 77 percent weapon offenses
- 77 percent of probation or parole violations[216]

These data seem to show a powerful connection between drug abuse, crime, and punishment.

Is There a Drug–Crime Connection? It is of course possible that most criminals are not actually drug users but that police are more likely to apprehend muddle-headed substance abusers than clear-thinking abstainers. A second, and probably more plausible, interpretation is that most criminals are, in fact, substance abusers.

Although the drug–crime connection is powerful, the true relationship remains uncertain because many users have had a history of criminal activity before the onset of their substance abuse. It is possible that:

- Chronic criminal offenders begin to abuse drugs and alcohol *after* they have engaged in crime; that is, crime causes drug abuse.
- Substance abusers turn to a life of crime to support their habits; that is, the economics of drug abuse causes crime. Rich drug users don't commit crime.
- Drug use and crime co-occur in individuals; that is, both crime and drug abuse are caused by some other common factor. For example, risk takers may abuse drugs and also commit crime.[217]
- Drug users engage in activities that involve them with peers who encourage them to commit crime or support their criminal activity.[218] Kids who join gangs are more likely later to abuse substances and commit crime.
- Drug abusers face social problems that lead them to crime. They are more likely to drop out of school, be underemployed, engage in premarital sex, and become unmarried parents.[219] Social problems and not drug use are the cause of crime.

Considering these scenarios, it is impossible to make a definitive statement such as "drugs cause crime."[220]

Even though we cannot assume that "drugs cause crime," there is no question that a strong link exists and that people involved in crime tend to be drug users. One way of assessing the drug–crime association is through data collected by the Arrestee Drug Abuse Monitoring (ADAM II) program, which conducts interviews and determines drug usage of adult male arrestees within 48 hours of their arrest in 10 U.S. counties. The most recent data show that while only 8 percent of males in the general population 18 years or older had used marijuana in the past 30 days, arrestee usage ranged from 34 percent (in Washington, D.C.) to 52 percent (in Chicago). Similarly, about 20 percent of males in the general population admitted to ever having used cocaine powder and 5 percent to ever having used crack, whereas anywhere from 17 percent (Sacramento) to 44 percent (Chicago) of arrestees tested positive for cocaine in their system at the time of arrest (indicating use in the past few days). Heroin, a drug rarely reported in the general population (0.2 percent among males), was detected in anywhere from 1 percent (Charlotte) to 29 percent (Chicago) of arrestees. These data not only show a clear drug–crime association but that arrestees used drugs just prior to their involvement in crime.[221]

In sum, although there is no conclusive evidence that taking drugs turns otherwise law-abiding citizens into criminals, there are indications that people who commit crime also use drugs significantly more than the average citizen. As addiction levels increase, so too do the frequency and seriousness of criminality. Even if the crime rate of drug users was only half that reported in the research literature, drug users would be responsible for a significant portion of the total criminal activity in the United States.

Drugs and the Law

The federal government first initiated legal action to curtail the use of some drugs early in the twentieth century. In 1906 the Pure Food and Drug Act required manufacturers to list the amounts of habit-forming drugs in products on their labels but did not restrict their use. However, the act prohibited the importation and sale of opiates except for medicinal purposes. In 1914 the Harrison Narcotics Act restricted importation, manufacture, sale, and dispensing of narcotics. It defined *narcotic* as any drug that produces sleep and relieves pain, such as heroin, morphine, and opium. The act was revised in 1922 to allow importation of opium and coca (cocaine) leaves for qualified medical practitioners. The Marijuana Tax Act of 1937 required registration and payment of a tax by all who imported, sold, or manufactured marijuana. Because marijuana was classified as a narcotic, those registering would also be subject to criminal penalty.

In later years, other federal laws were passed to clarify existing drug statutes and revise penalties. For example, the Boggs Act of 1951 provided mandatory sentences for violating federal drug laws. The Durham-Humphrey Act of 1951 made it illegal to dispense barbiturates and amphetamines without a prescription. The Narcotic Control Act of 1956 increased penalties for drug offenders. In 1965 the Drug Abuse Control Act set up stringent guidelines for the legal use and sale of mood-modifying drugs, such as barbiturates, amphetamines, LSD, and any other "dangerous drugs," except narcotics prescribed by doctors and pharmacists. Illegal possession was punished as a misdemeanor and manufacture or sale as a felony. And in 1970 the Comprehensive Drug Abuse Prevention and Control Act set up unified categories of illegal drugs and associated penalties with their sale, manufacture, or possession. The law gave the U.S. attorney general discretion to decide in which category to place any new drug.

Since then, various federal laws have attempted to increase penalties imposed on drug smugglers and limit the manufacture and sale of newly developed substances. For example, the 1984 Controlled Substances Act set new, stringent penalties for drug dealers and created five categories of narcotic and non-narcotic substances subject to federal laws.[222] The Anti-Drug Abuse Act of 1986 again set new standards for minimum and maximum sentences for drug offenders,

increased penalties for most offenses, and created a new drug penalty classification for large-scale offenses (such as trafficking in more than 1 kilogram of heroin), for which the penalty for a first offense was 10 years to life in prison.[223] With then-President George H. W. Bush's endorsement, Congress passed the Anti-Drug Abuse Act of 1988, which created a coordinated national drug policy under a "drug czar," set treatment and prevention priorities, and, symbolizing the government's hard-line stance against drug dealing, imposed the death penalty for drug-related killings.[224]

For the most part, state laws mirror federal statutes. Some states now apply extremely heavy penalties for selling or distributing dangerous drugs, involving long prison sentences of up to 25 years.

Drug-Control Strategies

Substance abuse remains a major social problem in the United States. Politicians looking for a safe campaign issue can take advantage of the public's fear of drug addiction by calling for a war on drugs. These wars have been declared even when drug usage is stable or in decline.[225] Can these efforts pay off? Can illegal drug use be eliminated or controlled?

A number of different drug-control strategies have been tried with varying degrees of success. Some aim to deter drug use by stopping the flow of drugs into the country, apprehending and punishing dealers, and cracking down on street-level drug deals. Others focus on preventing drug use by educating potential users to the dangers of substance abuse (convincing them to "say no to drugs") and by organizing community groups to work with the at-risk population in their area. Still another approach is to treat known users so they can control their addictions. Some of these efforts are discussed in the following sections.

Source Control   One approach to drug control is to deter the sale and importation of drugs through the systematic apprehension of large-volume drug dealers, coupled with the enforcement of strict drug laws that carry heavy penalties. This approach is designed to capture and punish known international drug dealers and deter those who are considering entering the drug trade. A major effort has been made to cut off supplies of drugs by destroying overseas crops and arresting members of drug cartels in Central and South America, Asia, and the Middle East, where many drugs are grown and manufactured. The federal government has been in the vanguard of encouraging exporting nations to step up efforts to destroy drug crops and prosecute dealers. Translating words into deeds is a formidable task. Drug lords are willing and able to fight back through intimidation, violence, and corruption when necessary. Nonetheless global drug production and distribution has been in decline.

Attempts to reduce the quantity of illegal drugs produced and imported each year may be working, but this seems to have little effect on U.S. consumption. Drug users in the United States are more able and willing to pay for drugs than anyone else in the world. Even if the supply were reduced, whatever drugs there were would find their way to the United States.

Adding to control problems is the fact that the drug trade is an important source of foreign revenue, and destroying the drug trade undermines the economies of third-world nations. Even if the government of one nation were willing to cooperate in vigorous drug suppression efforts, suppliers in other nations, eager to cash in on the sellers' market, would be encouraged to turn more acreage over to coca or poppy production. Today, almost every Caribbean country is involved with narcotrafficking and, in the case of Jamaica, large-scale production and export of marijuana. Illicit drug shipments in the region are worth more money than the top five legitimate exports combined. Drug gangs are able to corrupt the political structure and destabilize countries. Drug addiction and violent crime are now common in Jamaica, Puerto Rico, and even small islands like St. Kitts. The corruption of the police and other security forces has reached a crisis point in Jamaica, where an officer can earn the equivalent of half a year's salary by simply looking the other way on a drug deal.[226] There also are indications that the drug syndicates may be planting a higher yield variety of coca and improving refining techniques to replace crops lost to government crackdowns.

Adding to the problem of source control is the fact that the United States has little influence in some key drug-producing areas.[227] War and terrorism make source control strategies problematic. After the United States toppled Afghanistan's Taliban government, the remnants began to grow and sell poppy to support their insurgency; Afghanistan now supplies 90 percent of the world's opium.[228] Similarly, cocaine production is surging in Peru's remote tropical valleys, helping to make it a contender to surpass Colombia as the world's largest exporter of cocaine. One reason is that the anti-government Shining Path guerrillas are competing with outside groups from Mexico and Colombia to control the cocaine trade. Despite government efforts, Peruvian traffickers export almost 300 tons of cocaine each year.[229]

Interdiction Strategies Law enforcement efforts have also been directed at intercepting drug supplies as they enter the country. Border patrols and military personnel using sophisticated hardware have been involved in massive interdiction efforts; many impressive multimillion-dollar seizures have been made. Government sources indicate that cocaine movement into the United States has declined significantly in the past few years. Reports of reduced street-level availability in many cities, higher prices and lower purity, and indications of decreased abuse support the judgment that there is a downward trend in cocaine availability: more than 500 metric tons of cocaine are now being seized by law enforcement agents each year.[230]

Although law enforcement efforts are impressive, U.S. borders are so vast and unprotected that total interdiction is impossible. Drug importers have dug cross-border tunnels to evade detection, use go-fast boats and constantly changing transshipment points, use an army of "drug mules" to transship narcotics, and may be bribing border guards to look the other way when drug shipments pass through their checkpoints.[231]

If all importation were shut down, homegrown marijuana and laboratory-made drugs, such as "ice," LSD, and PCP, could become the drugs of choice. Even now, their easy availability and relatively low cost are increasing their popularity among the at-risk population.

Law Enforcement Strategies Local, state, and federal law enforcement agencies have been actively fighting against drugs. One approach is to direct efforts at large-scale drug rings. The long-term consequence has been to decentralize drug dealing and encourage new groups to become major suppliers. Asian, Latin American, and Jamaican groups, motorcycle clubs, and local gangs such as the Crips and Bloods are all now involved in large-scale dealing. Colombian syndicates have established cocaine distribution centers on every continent, and Mexican organizations are responsible for large methamphetamine shipments to U.S., Russian, Turkish, Italian, Nigerian, Chinese, Lebanese, and Pakistani heroin trafficking syndicates, which are now competing for dominance.

Police also target, intimidate, and arrest street-level dealers and users in an effort to make drug use so much of a hassle that consumption is cut back and the crime rate reduced. Among the approaches that have been tried are reverse stings, in which undercover agents pose as dealers and arrest users who approach them for a buy.

In terms of weight and availability, there is still no commodity more lucrative than illegal drugs. They cost relatively little to produce and provide large profit margins to dealers and traffickers. At an average street price of $118 per gram in the United States (the current price according to the Office of National Drug Control Policy), a metric ton of pure cocaine is worth more than $100 million; cutting it and reducing purity can double or triple the value.[232] For example, from January 2007 through March 2009, extensive law enforcement efforts resulted in disruption of the drug market in the United States. As a result, the price per pure gram of cocaine increased 75 percent, from $98 to $172, while the purity sold on the street decreased 29 percent, to less than half.[233]

It is difficult for law enforcement agencies to counteract the inducement of drug profits. When large-scale drug busts are made, supplies become scarce and market values increase, encouraging more people to enter the drug trade. There are also suspicions that a displacement effect occurs: stepped-up efforts to curb drug dealing in one area or city simply encourage dealers to seek out friendlier territory.[234]

Punishment Strategies Even if law enforcement efforts cannot produce a general deterrent effect, the courts may achieve the required result by severely punishing known drug dealers and traffickers. A number of initiatives have made the prosecution and punishment of drug offenders a top priority. State prosecutors have expanded their investigations into drug importation and distribution and created special prosecutors to focus on drug dealers. Once convicted, drug dealers can get very long sentences.

However, these efforts often have their downside. Defense attorneys consider delay tactics to be sound legal maneuvering in drug-related cases. Courts are so backlogged that prosecutors are anxious to plea bargain. The consequence of this legal maneuvering is that about 25 percent of people convicted on federal drug charges are granted probation or some other form of community release. Even so, prisons have become jammed with inmates, many of whom were involved in drug-related cases. Many drug offenders sent to prison do not serve their entire sentences because they are released in an effort to relieve prison overcrowding. The mean sentence for drug trafficking is 55 months, but the actual time served is 24 months or about half of the original sentence.[235]

It is unlikely that the public would approve of a drug-control strategy that locks up large numbers of traffickers; research indicates that the public already believes drug trafficking penalties are too harsh (while supporting the level of punishment for other crimes).[236] And some critics are disturbed because punishment strategies seem to have a disproportionate effect on minority group members and the impoverished. Some have gone as far as suggesting that government agencies are either ignoring or covering up the toll harsh drug penalties have on society's disadvantaged because it is politically expedient to be a tough defender of the nation's moral climate.[237]

Community Strategies Another type of drug-control effort relies on the involvement of local community groups to lead the fight against drugs. Representatives of various local government agencies, churches, civic organizations, and similar institutions are being brought together to create drug prevention and awareness programs.

Citizen-sponsored programs attempt to restore a sense of community in drug-infested areas, reduce fear, and promote conventional norms and values.[238] These efforts can be classified into one of four distinct categories:[239]

- Law enforcement–type efforts, which may include block watches, cooperative police–community efforts, and citizen patrols. Some of these citizen groups are nonconfrontational: they simply observe or photograph dealers, write down their license plate numbers, and then notify police. On occasion, telephone hotlines have been set up to take anonymous tips on drug activity. Other groups engage in confrontational tactics that may even include citizens' arrests. Area residents have gone as far as contracting with private security firms to conduct neighborhood patrols.
- Use the civil justice system to harass offenders. Landlords have been sued for owning properties that house

drug dealers; neighborhood groups have scrutinized drug houses for building code violations. Information acquired from these various sources is turned over to local authorities, such as police and housing agencies, for more formal action.

- Community-based treatment efforts. Some of these programs utilize citizen volunteers who participate in self-help support programs. Some such as Narcotics Anonymous or Cocaine Anonymous have more than 1,000 chapters nationally. Other programs provide youths with martial arts training, dancing, and social events as an alternative to the drug life.
- Enhance the quality of life, improve interpersonal relationships, and upgrade the neighborhood's physical environment. Activities might include the creation of drug-free school zones (which encourage police to keep drug dealers away from the vicinity of schools). Consciousness-raising efforts include demonstrations and marches to publicize the drug problem and build solidarity among participants. Politicians have been lobbied to get better police protection or tougher laws passed; New York City residents even sent bags filled with crack collected from street corners to the mayor and police commissioner to protest drug dealing. Residents have cleaned up streets, fixed broken streetlights, and planted gardens in empty lots to broadcast the message that they have local pride and do not want drug dealers in their neighborhoods.

These community crime-prevention efforts seem appealing, but there is little conclusive evidence that they are an effective drug-control strategy. Some surveys indicate that most residents do not participate in the programs. There is also evidence that community programs work better in stable, middle-income areas than in those that are crime ridden and disorganized.[240] Although these findings are discouraging, some studies do find that on occasion deteriorated areas can sustain successful antidrug programs.[241] Future evaluations of community control efforts should determine whether they can work in the most economically depressed areas.

Education Strategies According to this view, substance abuse would decline if kids could be taught about the dangers of drug use. The most widely known drug education program, Drug Abuse Resistance Education (D.A.R.E.), is an elementary school course designed to give students the skills for resisting peer pressure to experiment with tobacco, drugs, and alcohol. It is unique because it employs uniformed police officers to carry the antidrug message to the students before they enter junior high school. More than 40 percent of all school districts incorporate assistance from local law enforcement agencies in their drug prevention programming, but reviews of the program have not been supportive. Dennis Rosenbaum and his associates found that it had only a marginal impact on student drug use and attitudes.[242] A longitudinal study by psychologist Donald Lynam and his colleagues found that D.A.R.E. had no effect on students' drug use at any time through 10th grade, and a 10-year follow-up failed to find any hidden or delayed "sleeper" effects. At age 20, there were no differences in drug use between those who received D.A.R.E. and those who did not; the only difference was that those who received D.A.R.E. reported slightly lower levels of self-esteem at age 20, an effect that proponents were not aiming for.[243] These evaluations caused D.A.R.E. to revise its curriculum; it is now aimed at older students and relies more on having them question their assumptions about drug use than on listening to lectures on the subject.

Drug-Testing Strategies Drug testing of students, private employees, government workers, and criminal offenders is believed to deter substance abuse. In the workplace, employees are tested to enhance on-the-job safety and productivity. In some industries, such as mining and transportation, drug testing is considered essential because abuse can pose a threat to the public. Mandatory drug-testing programs in government and industry have become routine. The federal government requires employee testing in regulated industries such as nuclear energy and defense contracting. About 4 million transportation workers are subject to testing.

Drug testing is also part of the federal government's Drug-Free Workplace Program, which has the goal of improving productivity and safety. Employees most likely to be tested include presidential appointees, law enforcement officers, and people in positions of national security.

Criminal defendants are now routinely tested at all stages of the justice system, from arrest to parole. The goal is to reduce criminal behavior by detecting current users and curbing their abuse. Can such programs reduce criminal activity? Two evaluations of pretrial drug-testing programs found little evidence that monitoring defendants' drug use influenced their behavior.[244]

Schools have adopted drug testing of students, and there is some evidence that random tests can reduce drug use among youth. Those who favor student testing believe it may also help improve the learning environment in schools by diminishing the culture of drugs without sacrificing school morale.[245]

Drug Treatment Strategies A number of approaches are taken to treat known users, getting them clean of drugs and alcohol and thereby reducing the at-risk population. One approach rests on the assumption that each user is an individual and successful treatment must be geared to the using patterns and personality of the individual offenders in order to build a sense of self.[246] Some programs have placed abusers in regimens of outdoor activities and wilderness training to create self-reliance and a sense of accomplishment.[247] Others focus on problem-solving skills, helping former and current addicts to deal with their real-world issues.[248] Providing supportive housing for formerly homeless drug addicts also may lead to better access to medical care, food, and job opportunities—all of which result in lower levels of addiction.[249]

More intensive efforts use group therapy approaches relying on group leaders who have been substance abusers; through such sessions users get the skills and support to help them reject social pressure to use drugs. These programs are based on the Alcoholics Anonymous approach, which holds that users must find within themselves the strength to stay clean and that peer support from those who understand their experiences can help them achieve a drug-free life.

Some detoxification efforts use medical procedures to wean patients from the more addicting drugs to others, such as methadone, that can be more easily regulated. Methadone is a drug similar to heroin, and addicts can be treated at clinics where they receive methadone under controlled conditions. However, methadone programs have been undermined because some users sell their methadone on the black market, and others supplement their dosages with illegally obtained heroin. Other programs utilize drugs such as Naxalone, which counter the effects of narcotics and ease the trauma of withdrawal.[250] Naltrexone is used in conjunction with counseling and social support in some programs to help people who have already terminated their substance abuse avoid drinking or using drugs. Naltrexone works by blocking the effects of heroin or other opioids at their receptor sites. Medications also have been developed that are designed to ease withdrawal symptoms and help the transition to a drug-free life.

Other therapeutic programs attempt to deal with the psychological causes of drug use. Hypnosis, aversion therapy (getting users to associate drugs with unpleasant sensations, such as nausea), counseling, biofeedback, and other techniques are often used.

Some treatment programs are delivered on an outpatient basis, and others rely on residential care. Which approach is better is still being debated. A stay in a residential program may stigmatize people as addicts, and they may be introduced to other users while in treatment with whom they will associate after release. Users do not often enter these programs voluntarily and have little motivation to change.[251]

The best treatment for drug use may be a continuum of care that includes a customized treatment regimen—addressing all aspects of an individual's life, including medical and mental health services—and follow-up options (e.g., community or family-based recovery support systems), which can be crucial to a person's success in achieving and maintaining a drug-free lifestyle.[252] Exhibit 14.2 covers the most commonly used and relevant treatment strategies. However, relatively few drug-dependent people receive the treatment efforts they so desperately need. Many people who need treatment are unaware or are in denial. And even those who could be helped soon learn that there are simply more users who need treatment than there are beds in treatment facilities. Many facilities are restricted to users whose health insurance will pay for short-term residential care; when their insurance coverage ends, patients are often released, even though their treatment is incomplete.

EXHIBIT 14.2

Effective Treatment Approaches

- *Medications*. Medications can be used to help with different aspects of the treatment process.
- *Withdrawal*. Medications offer help in suppressing withdrawal symptoms during detoxification. Patients who go through medically assisted withdrawal but do not receive any further treatment show drug abuse patterns similar to those who were never treated.
- *Treatment*. Medications can be used to help reestablish normal brain function and to prevent relapse and to diminish cravings. Medications are now available for treating opioids (heroin, morphine), tobacco (nicotine), and alcohol addiction; other are being developed for treating stimulant (cocaine, methamphetamine) and cannabis (marijuana) addiction. A significant problem: many addicts are polydrug users, requiring multiple medications.
- *Behavioral treatments*. Behavioral treatments help patients engage in the treatment process, modify their attitudes and behaviors related to drug abuse, and increase healthy life skills. These treatments can enhance the effectiveness of medications and help people stay in treatment longer. Outpatient behavioral treatment encompasses a wide variety of programs for patients who visit a clinic at regular intervals. Most of the programs involve individual or group drug counseling. Some programs also offer other forms of behavioral treatment such as
  - *Cognitive–behavioral therapy*, which seeks to help patients recognize, avoid, and cope with the situations in which they are most likely to abuse drugs.
  - *Multidimensional family therapy*, which was developed for adolescents with drug abuse problems—as well as

their families—and addresses a range of influences on their drug abuse patterns and is designed to improve overall family functioning.
  - *Motivational interviewing*, which capitalizes on the readiness of individuals to change their behavior and enter treatment.
  - *Motivational incentives* (contingency management), which uses positive reinforcement to encourage abstinence from drugs.
- *Residential treatment* programs can be very effective, especially for those with more severe problems.
- *Therapeutic communities* (TCs) are highly structured programs in which patients remain at a residence, typically for 6 to 12 months. TCs differ from other treatment approaches principally in their use of the community—treatment staff and those in recovery—as a key agent of change to influence patient attitudes, perceptions, and behaviors associated with drug use. Patients in TCs may include those with relatively long histories of drug addiction, involvement in serious criminal activities, and seriously impaired social functioning. TCs are now also being designed to accommodate the needs of women who are pregnant or have children. The focus of the TC is on the resocialization of the patient to a drug-free, crime–free lifestyle.

SOURCE: National Institute on Drug Abuse, "NIDA InfoFacts: Treatment Approaches for Drug Addiction," www.nida.nih.gov/infofacts/treatmeth.html (accessed August 12, 2011).

Supporters of treatment argue that many addicts are helped by intensive in- and outpatient treatment. As one District of Columbia program shows, clients who complete treatment programs are less likely to use drugs than those who drop out.[253] Although such data support treatment strategies, it is possible that completers are motivated individuals who would have stopped using drugs even if they had not been treated.

To aid in dispensing treatment, state jurisdictions have developed specialized drug courts. These are described in the Policy and Practice in Criminology feature.

Employment Programs Research indicates that drug abusers who obtain and keep employment will end or reduce the incidence of their substance abuse.[254] Not surprisingly, then, there have been a number of efforts to provide vocational rehabilitation for drug abusers. One approach is the supported work program, which typically involves job-site training, ongoing assessment, and job-site intervention. Rather than teach work skills in a classroom, support programs rely on helping drug abusers deal with real work settings. Other programs that have merit provide training to overcome the

barriers to employment and improve work skills, including help with motivation, education, experience, the job market, job-seeking skills, and personal issues.[255]

Concept Summary 14.1 summarizes the various drug-control efforts.

Drug Legalization

While the massive effort to control drugs may have been responsible for the downward trend in drug use, hundreds of thousands of American citizens remain routine drug abusers. It is difficult to get people out of the drug culture because of the enormous profits involved in the drug trade. It also is difficult to control drugs by convincing known users to quit; few treatment efforts have been successful. The problem may lie in the fact that there are multiple efforts to control drugs, some relying on enforcement and punishment and others on treatment and rehabilitation. Whereas the former requires drug users to be secretive and discreet in order to avoid detection, the latter demands openness and receptivity to treatment.[256]

The mission of drug courts is to stop the abuse of alcohol and other drugs and related criminal activity by offenders. Drug courts handle cases involving drug-addicted offenders through an extensive supervision and treatment program. In exchange for successful completion of the program, the court may dismiss the original charge, reduce or set aside a sentence, offer some lesser penalty, or offer a combination of these. The aim is to place nonviolent first offenders into intensive treatment programs rather than in jail or prison.

The drug court movement began in 1989, when the Dade County (Miami) Circuit Court developed an intensive, community-based, treatment, rehabilitation, and supervision program for felony drug defendants designed to reduce recidivism rates. There are now more than 2,100 drug courts in operation with close to 300 more being planned or developed.

Drug courts divert nonviolent, substance abusing offenders from prison and jail into treatment. By increasing direct supervision of offenders, coordinating public resources, and expediting case processing, drug court can help break the cycle of criminal behavior, alcohol and drug use, and incarceration. A decade of research indicates that a drug court experience reduces crime by lowering rearrest and conviction rates, improving substance abuse treatment outcomes, and reuniting families; they also produce measurable cost benefits.

Drug courts address the overlap between the public health threats of drug abuse and crime. Crimes are often drug related; drug abusers are frequently involved with the criminal justice system. Drug courts provide an ideal setting to address these problems by linking the justice system with health services and drug treatment providers while easing the burden on the already overtaxed correctional system.

Are Drug Courts Effective?

The U.S. government has a great deal of confidence in drug courts and points to most recent research on programs around the nation, which taken in sum confirm that drug courts are successful. According to more than a decade of research, drug courts significantly improve substance abuse treatment outcomes, substantially reduce crime, and produce greater cost benefits than any other justice strategy. For example, one study of nine adult drug courts in California reported that rearrest rates over a four-year period were 29 percent for drug court clients (and only 17 percent for those completing the program) as compared to 41 percent for similar drug offenders who did not participate in a drug court program. Another study of four adult drug courts in Massachusetts found that drug court participants were 13 percent less likely to be rearrested, 34 percent less likely to be reconvicted, and 24 percent less likely to be reincarcerated than probationers who had been carefully matched to the drug court participants. These evidence-based evaluations support the utility of the drug court concept.

Not Everyone Agrees

Although this research is reassuring, drug courts have been criticized by the influential Drug Policy Alliance, a nonprofit organization dedicated to reforming the nation's drug laws. According to the Alliance, drug courts often "cherry pick" people expected to do well anyway, many of whom are in drug court because of a petty drug law violation, including marijuana. As a result, drug courts do not typically divert people from lengthy prison terms. Because they focus on low-level offenses, even positive results for individual participants translate into little public safety benefit to the community. Treatment in the community, whether voluntary or probation-supervised, often produces better results. The Alliance also finds that drug courts leave many people worse off than if they had received drug treatment outside the criminal justice system, had been left alone, or even had been conventionally sentenced. The successes represent only some of those who pass through drug courts and only a tiny fraction of people arrested. One reason is that drug court participants spend more days in jail *while in drug court* than if they had been conventionally sentenced, and participants deemed "failures" may actually face longer sentences than those who did not enter drug court in the first place (often because they lost the opportunity to plead to a lesser charge). The participants, they conclude, who stand the best chance of succeeding in drug courts are those without a drug problem, whereas those struggling with compulsive drug use are more likely to end up incarcerated.

CRITICAL THINKING

1. Are drug courts inherently coercive? Should drug users be forced to go into treatment?

2. Are drug treatment programs doomed to failure because there are so many different types of drug abusers, with entirely different motivations?

SOURCES: C. West Huddleston III, Douglas Marlowe, and Rachel Casebolt, *Painting the Current Picture: A National Report Card on Drug Courts and Other Problem-Solving Court Programs in the United States* (Washington, DC: National Drug Court Institute, Bureau of Justice Assistance, 2008), www.ndci.org/sites/default/files/ndci/PCPII1_web%5B1%5D.pdf (accessed August 12, 2011); Drug Policy Alliance, "Drug Courts Are Not the Answer: Toward a Health-Centered Approach to Drug Use, 2011," www.drugpolicy.org/sites/default/files/Drug%20Courts%20Are%20Not%20the%20Answer_Final2.pdf (accessed August 12, 2011).

CONCEPT SUMMARY 14.1

Drug-Control Strategies

Control Strategy	Main Focus	Problems/Issues
Source control	Destroy overseas crops and drug labs	Drug profits are hard to resist; drug crops in hostile nations are off limits
Interdiction	Seal borders; arrest drug couriers	Extensive U.S. borders are hard to control
Law enforcement	Police investigation and arrest of dealers	New dealers are recruited to replace those in prison
Punishment	Deter dealers with harsh punishments	Crowded prisons promote bargain justice
Community programs	Help community members deal with drug problems on the local level	Relies on community cohesion and efficacy
Drug education	Teach kids about the harm of taking drugs	Evaluations do not show programs are effective
Drug testing	Threaten employees with drug tests to deter use	Evaluations do not show drug testing is effective; people cheat on tests
Treatment	Use of therapy to get people off drugs	Expensive, requires motivation; clients associate with other users
Employment	Provide jobs as an alternative to drugs	Requires that former addicts become steady employees
Legalization	Decriminalize or legalize drugs	Political hot potato; danger of creating more users

The so-called war on drugs is expensive, costing more than $500 billion over the past 20 years—money that could have been spent on education and economic development. Drug enforcement and treatment now cost federal, state, and local governments about $100 billion per year.[257] Considering these problems, some commentators have called for the legalization or decriminalization of restricted drugs. Legalization is warranted, according to drug expert Ethan Nadelmann, because the use of mood-altering substances is customary in almost all human societies; people have always wanted, and will find ways of obtaining, psychoactive drugs.[258] Nadelmann heads the Drug Policy Alliance, a national organization dedicated to ending the "war against drugs," which the alliance believes has become overzealous in its effort to punish drug traffickers.[259]

Nadelmann reminds us that federal, state, and local governments have spent hundreds of billions of dollars trying to make America "drug free," yet heroin, cocaine, methamphetamine, and other illicit drugs are still readily available. The number of Americans behind bars on drug charges is greater than the number of Europeans incarcerated for *all* charges, despite the fact that our population is 500 million less than Europe's population.

Nadelmann also reminds us that the effort to control drugs creates more problems than it solves. Public health problems like HIV and hepatitis C are exacerbated by draconian laws that keep users in hiding and restrict their access to clean needles. And when they get caught and go to prison, their families suffer: children of inmates are at risk of educational failure, joblessness, addiction, and delinquency. People suffering from cancer, AIDS, and other debilitating illnesses are regularly denied access to or even arrested and prosecuted for using medical marijuana.

Banning drugs creates networks of manufacturers and distributors, many of whom use violence as part of their standard operating procedures. Although some believe that drug use is immoral, Nadelmann questions whether it is any worse than the unrestricted use of alcohol and cigarettes, both of which are addicting and unhealthful. Far more people die each year because they abuse these legal substances than are killed in drug wars or from abusing illegal substances.

Nadelmann also states that just as Prohibition failed to stop the flow of alcohol in the 1920s, while it increased the power of organized crime, the policy of prohibiting drugs is similarly doomed to failure. When drugs were legal and freely available in the early twentieth century, the proportion of Americans using drugs was not much greater than today. Most users led normal lives, probably because of the legal status of their drug use.

If drugs were legalized, the argument goes, price and distribution could be controlled by the government. This would reduce addicts' cash requirements, so crime rates would drop because users would no longer need the same cash flow to support their habits. Drug-related deaths would decline because government control would reduce needle sharing and the spread of AIDS. Legalization would also destroy the drug-importing cartels and gangs. Because drugs would be bought and sold openly, the government would reap a tax windfall both from taxes on the sale of drugs and from income taxes paid by drug dealers on profits that have been part of the hidden economy. Of course, drug distribution would be regulated, like alcohol, keeping drugs away

Medical Marijuana

The national drug czar asks you to review this policy statement by the Drug Policy Alliance, on the potential legalization of marijuana:

Since the 1970s pressure has been building to move away from the total prohibition of cannabis. Over the past century, numerous reports from independent, government-sponsored commissions have documented the drug's relative harmlessness and recommended the elimination of criminal sanctions for consumption-related offenses. Opinion polls show growing support for cannabis reform, and scientific, medical, and patient communities consistently provide evidence of the drug's therapeutic potential. As the public increasingly demands legal access to cannabis for both medicinal and other responsible uses,

policy makers are being forced to consider how to regulate the drug.

❯❯ **As the coordinator of the nation's efforts to control drugs, the czar who heads the Office of Drug Control Policy wants your opinion on continuing the ban on marijuana possession and use. Is it ethical, he wants to know, to prohibit a drug that has medicinal applications and can relieve suffering? Or is marijuana too dangerous to legalize for any reason? Divide the class into two groups, one taking the legalization of medical marijuana position and the other supporting the continued ban on marijuana even for medical purposes. Have an in-class debate with members of each side presenting arguments for and against medical marijuana.**

from adolescents, public servants such as police and airline pilots, and known felons.

The Consequences of Legalization Critics claim the legalization approach might have the short-term effect of reducing the crime rate, but it might also have grave social consequences. Legalization would increase the nation's rate of drug usage, creating an even larger group of nonproductive, drug-dependent people who must be cared for by the rest of society.[260] If drugs were legalized and freely available, drug users might significantly increase their daily intake. In countries like Iran and Thailand, where drugs are cheap and readily available, the rate of narcotics use is quite high. Historically, the availability of cheap narcotics has preceded drug-use epidemics, as was the case when British and American merchants sold opium in nineteenth-century China. Furthermore, if the government tried to raise money by taxing legal drugs, as it now does with liquor and cigarettes, that might encourage drug smuggling to avoid tax payments, creating a black market supply chain; these "illegal" drugs might then fall into the hands of adolescents.

There are also health problems. Because women may more easily become dependent on crack than men, the number of drug-dependent babies could begin to match or exceed the number delivered with fetal alcohol syndrome.[261] Drunk-driving fatalities, which today number about 12,000 per year, might be matched by deaths due to driving under the influence of pot or crack. And although distribution would be regulated, it is likely that adolescents would have the same opportunity to obtain potent drugs as they now have to obtain alcoholic beverages.

Decriminalization or legalization of controlled substances is unlikely in the near term, but further study is warranted. What effect would a policy of partial decriminalization (for example, legalizing small amounts of marijuana) have on drug use rates? Would a get-tough policy help to "widen the net" of the justice system and actually deepen some youths' involvement in substance abuse? Can society provide alternatives to drugs that will reduce teenage drug dependency?[262] The answers to these questions have proven elusive.

SUMMARY

1. **Be familiar with the association between law and morality**
   - Public order crimes are acts considered illegal because they conflict with social policy, accepted moral rules, and public opinion. There is usually great debate over public order crimes. Some charge that they are not really crimes at all and that it is foolish to legislate morality. Others view such morally tinged acts as prostitution, gambling, and drug abuse as harmful and therefore subject to public control.

2. **Be familiar with the term *social harm***
   - According to the theory of social harm, acts become crimes when they cause injury and produce harm to others. However, some dangerous activities are not considered crimes and

others that do not appear harmful are criminalized.

3. **Discuss the activities of moral crusaders**
   - Moral crusaders seek to shape the law toward their own way of thinking. These moral entrepreneurs take on such issues as prayer in school, gun ownership, gay marriage, abortion, and the distribution of sexually explicit books. One group of crusaders is determined to prevent the legalization of gay marriage; their objective is passage of a constitutional amendment declaring that marriage is between one man and one woman. Opposing them are groups of activists who have tirelessly campaigned for the civil rights of gay men and women.

4. **Know the various forms of outlawed deviant sexuality**
   - Outlawed sexual behavior, known as paraphilias, include such acts as frotteurism: rubbing against or touching a nonconsenting person in a crowd, elevator, or other public area; voyeurism: obtaining sexual pleasure from spying on a stranger while he or she disrobes or engages in sexual behavior with another; exhibitionism: deriving sexual pleasure from exposing the genitals to surprise or shock a stranger; sadomasochism: deriving pleasure from receiving pain or inflicting pain on another; and pedophilia: attaining sexual pleasure through sexual activity with prepubescent children.

5. **Discuss the history of prostitution and what the term means today**
   - Prostitution has been known for thousands of years. The earliest record of prostitution appears in ancient Mesopotamia, where priests engaged in sex to promote fertility in the community. Modern commercial sex appears to have its roots in ancient Greece. Today, prostitution can be defined as granting nonmarital sexual access, established by mutual agreement of the prostitutes, their clients, and their employers, for remuneration.

6. **Distinguish between the different types of prostitutes**
   - Prostitutes who work the streets in plain sight of police, citizens, and customers are referred to as hustlers, hookers, or streetwalkers. B-girls spend their time in bars, drinking and waiting to be picked up by customers. Brothel prostitutes live in a house with a madam who employs them, supervises their behavior, and receives a fee for her services; call girls work via telephone "dates" and get their clients by word of mouth or by making arrangements with bellhops, cab drivers, and so on. Some escort services are fronts for prostitution rings. Prostitutes known as circuit travelers move around in groups of two or three to lumber, labor, and agricultural camps. Prostitutes set up personal websites or put listings on Web boards, such as Craigslist, that carry personals.

7. **Be able to discuss what is meant by obscenity and pornography**
   - Pornography involves the production, distribution and sale of sexually explicit material intended to sexually excite paying customers. The depiction of sex and nudity is not illegal, but it does violate the law when it is judged obscene. "Obscenity" is a legal term that today is defined as material offensive to community standards. Legally, something is considered obscene if the average person applying contemporary community standards would find that the work taken as a whole appeals to the prurient interest; that the work depicts or describes prohibited sexual conduct; and whether the work, taken as a whole, lacks serious literary, artistic, political, or scientific value. Thus, each local jurisdiction must decide what pornographic material is obscene. A growing problem is the exploitation of children in obscene materials (kiddie porn), which has been expanded through the Internet.

8. **Be able to discuss the cause of substance abuse**
   - The onset of drug use can be tied to such factors as racial prejudice, devalued identities, low self-esteem, poor socioeconomic status, and the high level of mistrust, negativism, and defiance found in impoverished areas. Some experts have linked substance abuse to psychological deficits such as impaired cognitive functioning, personality disturbance, and emotional problems. Substance abuse may have a genetic basis. Social psychologists suggest that drug abuse also may result from observing parental drug use. Substance abuse may be just one of many social problem behaviors. Some may use drugs and alcohol because they want to enjoy their effects: get high, relax, improve creativity, escape reality, and increase sexual responsiveness.

9. **Compare and contrast the different methods of drug control**
   - A number of different drug-control strategies have been tried, with varying degrees of success. Some aim to deter drug use by stopping the flow of drugs into the country, apprehending and punishing dealers, and cracking down on street-level drug deals. Others focus on preventing drug use by educating potential users to the dangers of substance abuse (convincing them to "say no to drugs") and by organizing community groups to work with the at-risk population in their area.

Still another approach is to treat known users so they can control their addictions.

10. **State the arguments for and against legalizing drugs**
    - Drugs should be legalized because the money spent on control could be used on education and economic development.

People have always wanted, and will find ways of obtaining, psychoactive drugs. The drug war causes many health problems, such as HIV and hepatitis C, because users are in hiding and their access to clean needles is restricted. If drugs were legalized, price and distribution could be controlled by the government. Those opposed to legalization argue that if drugs were readily available it would lead to increased use, and a large group of nonproductive, drug-dependent people might significantly increase their daily intake.

KEY TERMS

public order crimes (478)
victimless crimes (478)
social harm (481)
vigilantes (481)
moral crusaders (481)
moral entrepreneurs (481)

paraphilias (483)
prostitution (485)
ehooking (486)
brothels (487)
madam (487)
call girls (487)

skeezers (488)
pornography (491)
obscenity (491)
temperance movement (496)
gateway model (499)

CRITICAL THINKING QUESTIONS

1. Under what circumstances, if any, might the legalization or decriminalization of drugs be beneficial to society?

2. Do you consider alcohol a drug? Should greater control be placed on the sale of alcohol?

3. Do TV shows and films glorify drug usage and encourage youths to enter the drug trade? Should all images on TV of drugs and alcohol be banned?

4. Is prostitution really a crime? Should a man or a woman have the right to sell sexual favors if he or she so chooses?

5. Do you believe there should be greater controls placed on the distribution of sexually explicit material on the Internet? Would you approve of the online sale of sexually explicit photos of children if they were artificial images created by computer animation?

6. Which statement is more accurate? (a) Sexually aggressive men are drawn to pornography because it reinforces their preexisting hostile orientation to sexuality. (b) Reading or watching pornography can make men become sexually aggressive.

7. Are there objective standards of morality? Does the existing criminal code reflect contemporary national moral standards? Or are laws banning sexual behaviors and substance abuse the product of a relatively few "moral entrepreneurs" who seek to control other people's behaviors?

NOTES

1. "Emperors Club: All About Eliot Spitzer's Alleged Prostitution Ring," *Huffington Post*, March 10, 2008, www.huffingtonpost.com/2008/03/10/emperors-club-all-about-_n_90768.html (accessed August 12, 2011).

2. United States Attorney for the Southern District, press release, "Booker for Prostitution Ring Pleads Guilty to Federal Prostitution Conspiracy and Money Laundering Offenses," May 14, 2008, www.docstoc.com/docs/42215420/BOOKER-FOR-PROSTITUTION-RING-PLEADS-GUILTY-TO-FEDERAL-PROSTITUTION (accessed August 12, 2011).

3. Rich Schapiro and Adam Nichols, "Hooker Booker's Family Can't Understand Her Fall into Life of Sleaze," *New York Daily News*, March 13, 2008, http://articles.nydailynews.com/2008-03-13/news/17893478_1_spitzer-emperors-club-vip-ashley-alexandra-dupr (accessed August 12, 2011).

4. Ashley Alexandra Dupré, official page, www.myspace.com/ashleydupre (accessed August 12, 2011).

5. Emily Friedman and Michele McPhee, "'Craigslist Killer' Appears in Court, Shouts 'Not Guilty,'" ABC News, June 22, 2009, http://abcnews.go.com/US/story?id=7897975 (accessed August 12, 2011).

6. Edwin Schur, *Crimes without Victims* (Englewood Cliffs, NJ: Prentice Hall, 1965).

7. Jennifer Williard, *Juvenile Prostitution* (Washington, DC: National Victim Resource Center, 1991).

8. C. Gabrielle Salfati, Alison James, and Lynn Ferguson, "Prostitute Homicides: A Descriptive Study," *Journal of Interpersonal Violence* 23 (2008): 505–543.

9. Andrea Dworkin, quoted in "Where Do We Stand on Pornography?" *Ms* (January–February 1994): 34.

10. Raymond Hernandez, "Weiner Resigns in Chaotic Final Scene," *New York Times*, June

16, 2011, www.nytimes.com/2011/06/17/nyregion/anthony-d-weiner-tells-friends-he-will-resign.html (accessed August 12, 2011).

11. *The Bible*, New International Version, Genesis 18:20.

12. Morris Cohen, "Moral Aspects of the Criminal Law," *Yale Law Journal* 49 (1940): 1,017.

13. Sir Patrick Devlin, *The Enforcement of Morals* (New York: Oxford University Press, 1959), p. 20.

14. See Joel Feinberg, *Social Philosophy* (Englewood Cliffs, NJ: Prentice Hall, 1973), Chapters 2 and 3.

15. H.L.A. Hart, "Immorality and Treason," *Listener* 62 (1959): 163.

16. *United States v. 12 200-ft Reels of Super 8mm Film,* 413 U.S. 123 (1973), at 137.

17. Joseph Gusfield, "On Legislating Morals: The Symbolic Process of Designating Deviancy," *California Law Review* 56 (1968): 58–59.

18. John Franks, "The Evaluation of Community Standards," *Journal of Social Psychology* 139 (1999): 253–255.

19. Information provided by Hitwise, Inc., June 4, 2004, www.hitwise.com (accessed April 26, 2007).

20. Irving Kristol, "Liberal Censorship and the Common Culture," *Society* 36 (September 1999): 5.

21. Amnesty International, www.amnesty.org/en/library/info/POL10/012/2011/en (accessed August 12, 2011).

22. Barbara Crossette, "Senegal Bans Cutting of Genitals of Girls," *New York Times*, January 18, 1999, p. A11.

23. David Kaplan, "Is It Torture or Tradition?" *Newsweek,* December 20, 1993, p. 124.

24. Crossette, "Senegal Bans Cutting of Genitals of Girls."

25. Ali Mokdad, James Marks, Donna F. Stroup, and Julie Gerberding, "Actual Causes of Death in the United States, 2000," *Journal of the American Medical Association* 291 (2004): 1,238–1,241.

26. Howard Becker, *Outsiders* (New York: Macmillan, 1963), pp. 13–14.

27. Ibid.

28. Edward Brecher, *Licit and Illicit Drugs* (Boston: Little, Brown, 1972), pp. 413–416.

29. Hearings on H.R. 6385, April 27, 28, 29, 30, and May 4, 1937, www.hempfarm.org/Papers/Hearing_Transcript_1.html (accessed August 12, 2011).

30. Federal Communications Commission, "In the Matter of Clear Channel Broadcasting," File No. EB-03-IH-0159 Washington, DC, April 7, 2004, www.fcc.gov/eb/Orders/2004/FCC-04-88A1.html (accessed August 12, 2011).

31. Howard Stern, http://tv.gawker.com/5737271/%7CcommentLink%7C (accessed August 12, 2011).

32. American Library Association, "Top Ten Most Frequently Challenged Books of 2010," www.ala.org/ala/issuesadvocacy/banned/frequentlychallenged/21stcenturychallenged/2010/index.cfm (accessed August 12, 2011).

33. Andrea Friedman, "Sadists and Sissies: Anti-Pornography Campaigns in Cold War America," *Gender and History* 15 (2003): 201–228.

34. U.S. Code, Title 1 §7. Definition of "marriage" and "spouse."

35. *Lawrence et al. v. Texas*, No. 02-102, June 26, 2003.

36. *Hillary Goodridge et al. vs. Department of Public Health and Another*, SJC-08860, November 18, 2003.

37. CNN News, "California Ban on Same-sex Marriage Struck Down," May 16, 2008, www.cnn.com/2008/US/05/15/same.sex.marriage/index.html (accessed August 12, 2011); The Huffington Post, "California Gay Marriage Banned As Proposition 8 Passes," Nov. 5, 2008, www.huffingtonpost.com/2008/11/05/california-gay-marriage-b_n_141429.html (accessed August 12, 2011).

38. United States Attorney's Office, Eastern District of Virginia, "Former Manassas School Teacher Sentenced to 25 Years for Producing Child Pornography," press release, May 26, 2011, www.fbi.gov/washingtondc/press-releases/2011/former-manassas-school-teacher-sentenced-to-25-years-for-producing-child-pornography (accessed August 12, 2011).

39. Richard Estes and Neil Alan Weiner, *The Commercial Sexual Exploitation of Children in the U.S., Canada, and Mexico* (Philadelphia: University of Pennsylvania Press, 2001).

40. Associated Press, "David Carradine Found Dead in Thailand Hotel," MSNBC.com, June 4, 2009, www.msnbc.msn.com/id/31103217/ (accessed August 12, 2011).

41. W. P. de Silva, "Sexual Variations," *British Medical Journal* 318 (1999): 654–655.

42. Richard Owen, "Pope Calls for Continuous Prayer to Rid Priesthood of Paedophilia," *Sunday Times*, January 7, 2008, www.timesonline.co.uk/tol/comment/faith/article3142511.ece.

43. CNN, "Archbishop: Mistakes Made in Priest Sex Abuse Case," March 31, 2010, www.cnn.com/2010/US/03/31/wisconsin.church.abuse/index.html (accessed August 12, 2011).

44. Boris Schiffer, Thomas Paul, Elke Gizewski, Michael Forsting, Norbert Leygraf, Manfred Schedlowski, and Tillmann H. C. Kruger, "Functional Brain Correlates of Heterosexual Paedophilia," *NeuroImage* 41 (2008): 80–91.

45. Ray Blanchard, Bruce K. Christensen, Scott M. Strong, James M. Cantor, Michael E. Kuban, Philip Klassen, Robert Dickey, and Thomas Blak, "Retrospective Self-reports of Childhood Accidents Causing Unconsciousness in Phallometrically Diagnosed Pedophiles," *Archives of Sexual Behavior* 31 (2002): 111–127.

46. Michael Allan and Randolph Grace, "Psychometric Assessment of Dynamic Risk Factors for Child Molesters," *Sexual Abuse: A Journal of Research* 19 (2007): 347–367.

47. For an analysis of this issue, see Theresa Gannon and Devon Polaschek, "Cognitive Distortions in Child Molesters: A Re-examination of Key Theories and Research," *Clinical Psychology Review* 26 (2006): 1,000–1,019.

48. Kathy Smiljanich and John Briere, "Self-Reported Sexual Interest in Children: Sex Differences and Psychosocial Correlates in a University Sample," *Violence and Victims* 11 (1996): 39–50.

49. Miriam Wijkman, Catrien Bijleveld, and Jan Hendriks, "Women Don't Do Such Things! Characteristics of Female Sex Offenders and Offender Types," *Sexual Abuse: A Journal of Research and Treatment* 22 (2010): 135–156.

50. Fox News, "Louisiana Senator David Vitter Apologizes Again for Connection to D.C. Madam Scandal," July 16, 2007, www.foxnews.com/story/0,2933,289531,00.html (accessed August 12, 2011).

51. Ginger Thompson and Philip Shenon, "Navy Officer Describes Working as a Prostitute," *New York Times*, April 12, 2008, www.nytimes.com/2008/04/12/us/12officer.html?ex=1365652800&en=65a734ab30a26c33&ei=5088&partner=rssnyt&emc=rss (accessed August 12, 2011).

52. See, generally, V. Bullogh, *Sexual Variance in Society and History* (Chicago: University of Chicago Press, 1958), pp. 143–144.

53. Spencer Rathus, *Human Sexuality* (New York: Holt, Rinehart & Winston, 1983), p. 463.

54. Jeffery Richards, *Sex, Dissidence and Damnation: Minority Groups in the Middle Ages* (New York: Routledge, 1994), p. 125.

55. Ibid., p. 118.

56. Annette Jolin, "On the Backs of Working Prostitutes: Feminist Theory and Prostitution Policy," *Crime and Delinquency* 40 (1994): 60–83.

57. Charles McCaghy, *Deviant Behavior* (New York: Macmillan, 1976), pp. 348–349.

58. Marian Pitts, Anthony Smith, Jeffrey Grierson, Mary O'Brien, and Sebastian Misson, "Who Pays for Sex and Why? An Analysis of Social and Motivational Factors Associated with Male Clients of Sex Workers," *Archives of Sexual Behavior* 33 (2004): 353–358.

59. Monica Prasad, "The Morality of Market Exchange: Love, Money, and Contractual Justice," *Sociological Perspectives* 42 (1999): 181–187.

60. Cited in McCaghy, *Deviant Behavior*.

61. FBI, *Crime in the United States, 2005* (Washington, DC: U.S. Government Printing Office, 2006), updated with data from FBI,

Crime in the United States, 2006.

62. Scott Shuger "Hookers.com, How E-commerce Is Transforming the Oldest Profession," *Slate Magazine,* www.slate.com/id/73797/ (accessed August 12, 2011).

63. FBI, *Crime in the United States, 2009,* (Washington, DC: U.S. Government Printing Office, 2010) table 29.

64. DerWesten, "Minister will grünes Licht für Sex-Steuer geben," March 25, 2010, www.derwesten.de/nachrichten/politik/Minister-will-gruenes-Licht-fuer-Sex-Steuer-geben-id2781309.html (accessed August 12, 2011).

65. Mark Landler, "World Cup Brings Little Pleasure to German Brothels," *New York Times,* July 3, 2006, www.nytimes.com/2006/07/03/world/europe/03berlin.html?ex=1309579200&en=e28e47eba8978d37&ei=5089&partner=rssyahoo&emc=rss (accessed August 12, 2011).

66. Associated Press, "Iran Stones Six to Death," October 26, 1997, www.uri.edu/artsci/wms/hughes/stoned_to_death (accessed August 12, 2011).

67. Elizabeth Bernstein, "The Meaning of the Purchase: Desire, Demand, and the Commerce of Sex," *Ethnography* 2 (2001): 389–420.

68. 18 U.S.C. [section] 2423(b) (2000).

69. Sara K. Andrews, "U.S. Domestic Prosecution of the American International Sex Tourist: Efforts to Protect Children from Sexual Exploitation," *Journal of Criminal Law and Criminology* 94 (2004): 415–453.

70. Mark-David Janus, Barbara Scanlon, and Virginia Price, "Youth Prostitution," in *Child Pornography and Sex Rings,* ed. Ann Wolbert Burgess (Lexington, MA: Lexington Books, 1989), pp. 127–146.

71. Teela Sanders and Rosie Campbell, "Designing Out Vulnerability, Building in Respect: Violence, Safety and Sex Work Policy," *British Journal of Sociology* 58 (2007): 1–19.

72. Charles Winick and Paul Kinsie, *The Lively Commerce* (Chicago: Quadrangle Books, 1971), p. 58.

73. Celia Williamson and Lynda Baker, "Women in Street-based Prostitution: A Typology of Their Work Styles," *Qualitative Social Work* 8 (2009): 27–44.

74. Hilary Surratt, James Inciardi, Steven Kurtz, and Marion Kiley, "Sex Work and Drug Use in a Subculture of Violence," *Crime and Delinquency* 50 (2004): 43–60.

75. Lisa Maher, "Hidden in the Light: Occupational Norms among Crack-Using Street-Level Sex Workers," *Journal of Drug Issues* 26 (1996): 143–173.

76. Teela Sanders, *Sex Work: A Risky Business* (Devon, England: Willan, 2005).

77. Winick and Kinsie, *The Lively Commerce,* pp. 172–173.

78. Paul Goldstein, "Occupational Mobility in the World of Prostitution: Becoming a Madam," *Deviant Behavior* 4 (1983): 267–279.

79. Ibid., pp. 267–270.

80. Mireya Navarro, "Group Forced Illegal Aliens into Prostitution, U.S. Says," *New York Times,* April 24, 1998, p. A10.

81. Paul Goldstein, Lawrence Ouellet, and Michael Fendrich, "From Bag Brides to Skeezers: A Historical Perspective on Sex-for-Drugs Behavior," *Journal of Psychoactive Drugs* 24 (1992): 349–361.

82. Jessica Edwards, Carolyn Halpern, and Wendee Wechsberg, "Correlates of Exchanging Sex for Drugs or Money Among Women Who Use Crack Cocaine," *AIDS Education and Prevention* 18 (2006): 420–429.

83. Jan Risser, Sandra Timpson, Sheryl McCurdy, Michael Ross, and Mark Williams, "Psychological Correlates of Trading Sex for Money Among African American Crack Cocaine Smokers," *American Journal of Drug and Alcohol Abuse* 32 (2006): 645–653.

84. Thompson and Shenon, "Navy Officer Describes Working as a Prostitute."

85. Alyson Brown and David Barrett, *Knowledge of Evil: Child Prostitution and Child Sexual Abuse in Twentieth Century England* (Devon, England: Willan, 2002).

86. Jocelyn Brown, Patricia Cohen, Henian Chen, Elizabeth Smailes, and Jeffrey Johnson, "Sexual Trajectories of Abused and Neglected Youths," *Journal of Developmental and Behavioral Pediatrics* 25 (2004): 77–83.

87. Gerald Hotaling and David Finkelhor, *The Sexual Exploitation of Missing Children* (Washington, DC: U.S. Department of Justice, 1988).

88. Tammy Heilemann and Janaki Santhiveeran, "How Do Female Adolescents Cope and Survive the Hardships of Prostitution? A Content Analysis of Existing Literature," *Journal of Ethnic & Cultural Diversity in Social Work* 20 (2011): 57–76.

89. Lisa Kramer and Ellen Berg, "A Survival Analysis of Timing of Entry into Prostitution: The Differential Impact of Race, Educational Level, and Childhood/Adolescent Risk Factors," *Sociological Inquiry* 73 (2003): 511–529.

90. John Potterat, Richard Rothenberg, Stephen Muth, William Darrow, and Lynanne Phillips-Plummer, "Pathways to Prostitution: The Chronology of Sexual and Drug Abuse Milestones," *Journal of Sex Research* 35 (1998): 333–342.

91. Sheila Royo Maxwell and Christopher Maxwell, "Examining the 'Criminal Careers' of Prostitutes within the Nexus of Drug Use, Drug Selling, and Other Illicit Activities," *Criminology* 38 (2000): 787–809.

92. Michael Miner, Jill Flitter, and Beatrice Robinson, "Association of Sexual Revictimization with Sexuality and Psychological Function," *Journal of Interpersonal Violence* 21 (2006): 503–524.

93. Jolanda Sallmann, "Living With Stigma: Women's Experiences of Prostitution and Substance Use," *Afilia Journal of Women and Social Work* 25 (2010): 146–159.

94. Mandi Burnette, Emma Lucas, Mark Ilgen, Susan Frayne, Julia Mayo, and Julie Weitlauf, "Prevalence and Health Correlates of Prostitution Among Patients Entering Treatment for Substance Use Disorders," *Archives of General Psychiatry* 65 (2008): 337–344.

95. Michael Rekart, "Sex-Work Harm Reduction," *The Lancet* 366 (2005): 2,123–2,134.

96. Nancy Romero-Daza, Margaret Weeks, and Merrill Singer, "Nobody Gives a Damn if I Live or Die: Violence, Drugs, and Street-Level Prostitution in Inner-City Hartford, Connecticut," *Medical Anthropology* 22 (2003): 233–259.

97. Brown and Barrett, *Knowledge of Evil.*

98. Jocelyn Brown, Patricia Cohen, Henian Chen, Elizabeth Smailes, and Jeffrey Johnson, "Sexual Trajectories of Abused and Neglected Youths," *Journal of Developmental and Behavioral Pediatrics* 25 (2004): 77–83.

99. Gerald Hotaling and David Finkelhor, *The Sexual Exploitation of Missing Children* (Washington, DC: U.S. Department of Justice, 1988).

100. Richard Estes and Neil Alan Weiner, *The Commercial Sexual Exploitation of Children in the U.S., Canada, and Mexico* (Philadelphia: University of Pennsylvania Press, 2001).

101. Shu-ling Hwang and Olwen Bedford, "Juveniles' Motivations for Remaining in Prostitution," *Psychology of Women Quarterly* 28 (2004): 136–137.

102. Sallmann, "Living With Stigma: Women's Experiences of Prostitution and Substance Use," p. 153.

103. Barbara G. Brents and Kathryn Hausbeck, "State-Sanctioned Sex: Negotiating Formal and Informal Regulatory Practices in Nevada Brothels," *Sociological Perspectives* 44 (2001): 307–335.

104. Ibid.

105. Mara Keire, "The Vice Trust: A Reinterpretation of the White Slavery Scare in the United States, 1907–1917," *Journal of Social History* 35 (2001): 5–42.

106. Minnesota Statute 609.324, "Other Prostitution Crimes; Patrons, Prostitutes, and Individuals Housing Individuals Engaged in Prostitution; Penalties," www.revisor.leg.state.mn.us/bin/getpub.php?type=s&year=current&num=609.324 (accessed August 12, 2011).

107. Devon Brewer, John Potterat, Stephen Muth, John Roberts, Jr., Jonathan Dudek, and Donald Woodhouse, *Clients of Prostitute Women: Deterrence, Prevalence, Characteristics, and Violence* (Washington, DC: National Institute of Justice, 2007), www.ncjrs.gov/pdffiles1/nij/grants/218253.pdf (accessed August 12, 2011).

108. Ronald Weitzer, "The Politics of Prostitution in America," in *Sex for Sale,* ed.

Ronald Weitzer (New York: Routledge, 2000): 159–180.

109. Sherry Plaster Carter, Stanley Carter, and Andrew Dannenberg, "Zoning Out Crime and Improving Community Health in Sarasota, Florida: Crime Prevention through Environmental Design," *American Journal of Public Health* 93 (2003): 1,442–1,445.

110. Ron Roberts, Sandra Bergström, and David La Rooy, "UK Students and Sex Work: Current Knowledge and Research Issues," *Journal of Community and Applied Social Psychology* 17 (2007): 141–146.

111. Sarah Lantz, "Students Working in the Melbourne Sex Industry: Education, Human Capital and the Changing Patterns of the Youth Labour Market," *Journal of Youth Studies* 8 (2005): 385–401.

112. Andrea Dworkin, *Pornography* (New York: Dutton, 1989).

113. Arthur Gould, "The Criminalisation of Buying Sex: The Politics of Prostitution in Sweden," *Journal of Social Policy* 30 (2001): 437–438.

114. Suzanne Daley, "New Rights for Dutch Prostitutes, but No Gain," *New York Times,* August 12, 2001, p. A4.

115. James Morton, "Legalising Brothels," *Journal of Criminal Law* 68 (2004): 87–90.

116. Alexa Albert, *Brothel: Mustang Ranch and Its Women* (New York: Random House, 2001).

117. Roger Matthews, *Prostitution, Politics and Policy* (London, Routledge-Cavendish, 2008).

118. *Merriam-Webster Dictionary* (New York: Pocket Books, 1974), p. 484.

119. Neil Malamuth, Tamara Addison, and Mary Koss, "Pornography and Sexual Aggression: Are There Reliable Effects and Can We Understand Them?" *Annual Review of Sex Research* 11 (2000): 26–94.

120. Lynn Morgan, "Indecency, Pornography, and the Protection of Children," *Georgetown Journal of Gender and the Law* 7 (2006): 701–721.

121. Albert Belanger et al., "Typology of Sex Rings Exploiting Children," in *Child Pornography and Sex Rings,* ed. Ann Wolbert Burgess (Lexington, MA: Lexington Books, 1984), pp. 51–81.

122. Philip Jenkins, *Beyond Tolerance: Child Pornography Online* (New York: New York University Press, 2001).

123. The Prosecutorial Remedies and Other Tools to End the Exploitation of Children Today, 18 USC 1466A (2003).

124. *United States v. Williams,* 553 U.S. 285 (2008).

125. Neil Malamuth, Tamara Addison, and Mary Koss, "Pornography and Sexual Aggression: Are There Reliable Effects and Can We Understand Them?" *Annual Review of Sex Research* 11 (2000): 26–94.

126. Berl Kutchinsky, "The Effect of Easy Availability of Pornography on the Incidence of Sex Crimes," *Journal of Social Issues* 29 (1973): 95–112.

127. Michael Goldstein, "Exposure to Erotic Stimuli and Sexual Deviance," *Journal of Social Issues* 29 (1973): 197–219.

128. Joetta Carr and Karen VanDeusen, "Risk Factors for Male Sexual Aggression on College Campuses," *Journal of Family Violence* 19 (2004): 279–289; see Edward Donnerstein, Daniel Linz, and Steven Penrod, *The Question of Pornography* (New York: Free Press, 1987).

129. Michael Seto, Alexandra Maric, and Howard Barbaree, "The Role of Pornography in the Etiology of Sexual Aggression," *Aggression and Violent Behaviour* 6 (2001): 35–53.

130. Catherine Simmons, Peter Lehmann, and Shannon Collier-Tenison, "Linking Male Use of the Sex Industry to Controlling Behaviors in Violent Relationships: An Exploratory Analysis," *Violence Against Women* 14 (2008): 406–417.

131. Edward Donnerstein, "Pornography and Violence against Women," *Annals of the New York Academy of Science* 347 (1980): 277–288; E. Donnerstein and J. Hallam, "Facilitating Effects of Erotica on Aggression against Women," *Journal of Personality and Social Psychology* 36 (1977): 1,270–1,277.

132. James Alan Fox and Jack Levin, "Multiple Homicide: Patterns of Serial and Mass Murder," in *Crime and Justice: An Annual Edition,* vol. 23, ed. Michael Tonry (Chicago: University of Chicago Press, 1998): 418–419.

133. John Court, "Sex and Violence: A Ripple Effect," *Pornography and Aggression,* ed. Neil Malamuth and Edward Donnerstein (Orlando: Academic Press, 1984).

134. Michael Bourke and Andres Hernandez, "The 'Butner Study' Redux: A Report of the Incidence of Hands-on Child Victimization by Child Pornography Offenders," *Journal of Family Violence* 24 (2009): 183–191.

135. "State Laws on Obscenity, Child Pornography, and Harassment," www.lorenavedon.com/laws.htm (accessed April 26, 2007).

136. *Roth v. United States,* 354 U.S. 476 (1957).

137. *A Book Named "John Cleland's Memoirs of a Woman of Pleasure" v. Attorney General of Massachusetts* 383 U.S. 413 (1966).

138. *Miller v. California,* 413 U.S. 15 (1973).

139. *Pope v. Illinois,* 481 U.S. 497 (1987).

140. Ibid.

141. Attorney General's Commission on Pornography, "Final Report," July 1986 (Nashville, TN: Rutledge Hill Press, 2nd printing edition, 1986), pp. 376–377.

142. Bob Cohn, "The Trials of Adam and Eve," *Newsweek,* January 7, 1991, p. 48.

143. 427 U.S. 50 (1976).

144. Ralph Weisheit, "Studying Drugs in Rural Areas: Notes from the Field," *Journal of Research in Crime and Delinquency* 30 (1993): 213–232.

145. "British Officials Report Skyrocketing Heroin Use," *Alcoholism and Drug Abuse Weekly* 10 (August 17, 1998): 7; National Institute on Drug Abuse, Community Epidemiology Work Group, *Epidemiological Trends in Drug Abuse, Advance Report* (Washington, DC: National Institute on Drug Abuse, 1997).

146. FBI, Uniform Crime Report, *Crimes in the United States, 2005,* Table 29, www2.fbi.gov/ucr/05cius/data/table_29.html (accessed August 16, 2011).

147. Heather West, William Sabol, and Sarah Greenman, *Prisoners, 2009* (Washington, DC: Bureau of Justice Statistics, 2010), http://bjs.ojp.usdoj.gov/content/pub/ascii/p09.txt.

148. Arnold Trebach, *The Heroin Solution* (New Haven, CN: Yale University Press, 1982).

149. James Inciardi, *The War on Drugs* (Palo Alto, CA: Mayfield, 1986), p. 2.

150. See, generally, David Pittman, "Drug Addiction and Crime," in *Handbook of Criminology,* ed. D. Glazer (Chicago: Rand McNally, 1974), pp. 209–232; Board of Directors, National Council on Crime and Delinquency, "Drug Addiction: A Medical, Not a Law Enforcement, Problem," *Crime and Delinquency* 20 (1974): 4–9.

151. Associated Press, "Records Detail Royals' Turn-of-Century Drug Use," *Boston Globe,* August 29, 1993, p. 13.

152. See Edward Brecher, *Licit and Illicit Drugs* (Boston: Little, Brown, 1972).

153. James Inciardi, *Reflections on Crime* (New York: Holt, Rinehart & Winston, 1978), p. 15.

154. William Bates and Betty Crowther, "Drug Abuse," in *Deviants: Voluntary Actors in a Hostile World,* ed. E. Sagarin and F. Montanino (New York: Foresman, 1977), p. 269.

155. Inciardi, *Reflections on Crime,* pp. 8–10. See also A. Greeley, William McCready, and Gary Theisen, *Ethnic Drinking Subcultures* (New York: Praeger, 1980).

156. Joseph Gusfield, *Symbolic Crusade* (Urbana: University of Illinois Press, 1963), Chapter 3.

157. McCaghy, *Deviant Behavior,* p. 280.

158. Ibid.

159. Office of Supply Reduction, "ONDCP New Data: Cocaine Market Remains under Significant Stress," June 20, 2011, http://ofsubstance.gov/blogs/pushing_back/archive/2011/06/20/51905.aspx (accessed August 16, 2011).

160. The Monitoring the Future survey is conducted by Lloyd Johnston, Jerald Bachman, Patrick O'Malley, and John Schulenberg, for the Institute for Social Research, University of Michigan, Ann Arbor, www.isr.umich.edu/home/ (accessed August 16, 2011).

161. Kristin Finn, "Patterns of Alcohol and Marijuana Use at School," *Journal of Research on Adolescence* 16 (2006): 69–77.

162. Department of Health and Human Services, "Results from the 2009 National

Survey on Drug Use and Health," http://oas.samhsa.gov/NSDUH/2k9NSDUH/2k9ResultsP.pdf (accessed August 16, 2011).

163. Susan James, Janice Johnson, and Chitra Raghavan, "I Couldn't Go Anywhere," *Violence Against Women* 10 (2004): 991–1,015.

164. Marvin Krohn, Alan Lizotte, Terence Thornberry, Carolyn Smith, and David McDowall, "Reciprocal Causal Relationships among Drug Use, Peers, and Beliefs: A Five-Wave Panel Model," *Journal of Drug Issues* 26 (1996): 205–428.

165. Kellie Barr, Michael Farrell, Grace Barnes, and John Welte, "Race, Class, and Gender Differences in Substance Abuse: Evidence of Middle-Class/Underclass Polarization among Black Males," *Social Problems* 40 (1993): 314–326.

166. Peter Giancola, "Constructive Thinking, Antisocial Behavior, and Drug Use in Adolescent Boys with and without a Family History of a Substance Use Disorder," *Personality and Individual Differences* 35 (2003): 1,315–1,331.

167. Jerome J. Platt, *Heroin Addiction and Theory, Research and Treatment: The Addict, the Treatment Process and Social Control* (Melbourne, FL: Krieser, 1995), p. 127.

168. Alan Carr, Barbara Dooley, Mark Fitzpatrick, Edel Flanagan, Roisin Flanagan-Howard, Kevin Tierney, Megan White, Margaret Daly, and Jonathan Egan, "Adult Adjustment of Survivors of Institutional Child Abuse in Ireland," *Child Abuse & Neglect* 34 (2010): 477–489.

169. Daniel Smith, Joanne Davis, and Adrienne Fricker-Elhai, "How Does Trauma Beget Trauma? Cognitions About Risk in Women with Abuse Histories," *Child Maltreatment* 9 (2004): 292–302.

170. Sean Kidd, "The Walls Were Closing In, and We Were Trapped," *Youth and Society* 36 (2004): 30–55.

171. David Black, Steve Sussman, Jennifer Unger, Pallay Pokhrel, and Ping Sun, "Gender Differences in Body Consciousness and Substance Use Among High-Risk Adolescents," *Substance Use & Misuse* 45 (2010): 1,623–1,635.

172. Tracy Hampton, "Genes Harbor Clues to Addiction, Recovery," *Journal of the American Medical Association* 292 (2004): 321–323.

173. D. W. Goodwin, "Alcoholism and Genetics," *Archives of General Psychiatry* 42 (1985): 171–174.

174. Martha Vungkhanching, Kenneth Sher, Kristina Jackson, and Gilbert Parra, "Relation of Attachment Style to Family History of Alcoholism and Alcohol Use Disorders in Early Adulthood," *Drug and Alcohol Dependence* 75 (2004): 47–54.

175. For a thorough review of this issue, see John Petraitis, Brian Flay, and Todd Miller, "Reviewing Theories of Adolescent Substance Use: Organizing Pieces in the Puzzle," *Psychological Bulletin* 117 (1995): 67–86.

176. Judith Brooks and Li-Jung Tseng, "Influences of Parental Drug Use, Personality, and Child Rearing on the Toddler's Anger and Negativity," *Genetic, Social and General Psychology Monographs* 122 (1996): 107–128.

177. Thomas Ashby Wills, Donato Vaccaro, Grace McNamara, and A. Elizabeth Hirky, "Escalated Substance Use: A Longitudinal Grouping Analysis from Early to Middle Adolescence," *Journal of Abnormal Psychology* 105 (1996): 166–180.

178. Denise Kandel and Mark Davies, "Friendship Networks, Intimacy, and Illicit Drug Use in Young Adulthood: A Comparison of Two Competing Theories," *Criminology* 29 (1991): 441–471.

179. J. S. Mio, G. Nanjundappa, D. E. Verlur, and M. D. DeRios, "Drug Abuse and the Adolescent Sex Offender: A Preliminary Analysis," *Journal of Psychoactive Drugs* 18 (1986): 65–72.

180. D. Baer and J. Corrado, "Heroin Addict Relationships with Parents During Childhood and Early Adolescent Years," *Journal of Genetic Psychology* 124 (1974): 99–103.

181. Chie Noyori-Corbett and Sung Seek Moon, "Multifaceted Reality of Juvenile Delinquency: An Empirical Analysis of Structural Theories and Literature," *Child and Adolescent Social Work Journal* 27 (2010): 245–268.

182. John Wallace and Jerald Bachman, "Explaining Racial/Ethnic Differences in Adolescent Drug Use: The Impact of Background and Lifestyle," *Social Problems* 38 (1991): 333–357.

183. Amy Young, Carol Boyd, and Amy Hubbell, "Social Isolation and Sexual Abuse among Women Who Smoke Crack," *Journal of Psychosocial Nursing* 39 (2001): 16–19.

184. Xiaojin Chen, Kimberly Tyler, Les Whitbeck, and Dan Hoyt, "Early Sexual Abuse, Street Adversity, and Drug Use Among Female Homeless and Runaway Adolescents in the Midwest," *Journal of Drug Issues* 34 (2004): 1–20; John Donovan, "Problem-Behavior Theory and the Explanation of Adolescent Marijuana Use," *Journal of Drug Issues* 26 (1996): 379–404.

185. A. Christiansen, G. T. Smith, P. V. Roehling, and M. S. Goldman, "Using Alcohol Expectancies to Predict Adolescent Drinking Behavior after One Year," *Journal of Counseling and Clinical Psychology* 57 (1989): 93–99.

186. Claire Sterk-Elifson, "Just for Fun? Cocaine Use Among Middle-Class Women," *Journal of Drug Issues* 26 (1996): 63–76, at 69.

187. Icek Ajzen, *Attitudes, Personality and Behavior* (Homewood, IL: Dorsey Press, 1988).

188. James Inciardi, Ruth Horowitz, and Anne Pottieger, *Street Kids, Street Drugs, Street Crime: An Examination of Drug Use and Serious Delinquency in Miami* (Belmont, CA: Wadsworth, 1993), p. 43.

189. Ibid.

190. Cesar Rebellon and Karen Van Gundy, "Can Social Psychological Delinquency Theory Explain the Link Between Marijuana and Other Illicit Drug Use? A Longitudinal Analysis of the Gateway Hypothesis," *Journal of Drug Issues* 36 (Summer 2006): 515–539; Mary Ellen Mackesy-Amiti, Michael Fendrich, and Paul Goldstein, "Sequence of Drug Use among Serious Drug Users: Typical vs. Atypical Progression," *Drug and Alcohol Dependence* 45 (1997): 185–196.

191. Bu Huang, Helene White, Rick Kosterman, Richard Catalano, and J. David Hawkins, "Developmental Associations between Alcohol and Interpersonal Aggression during Adolescence," *Journal of Research in Crime and Delinquency* 38 (2001): 64–83.

192. Cesar Rebellon and Karen Van Gundy, "Can Social Psychological Delinquency Theory Explain the Link Between Marijuana and Other Illicit Drug Use? A Longitudinal Analysis of the Gateway Hypothesis," *Journal of Drug Issues* 36 (2006): 515–540.

193. Andrew Golub and Bruce Johnson, "The Multiple Paths Through Alcohol, Tobacco and Marijuana to Hard Drug Use among Arrestees," paper presented at the annual meeting of the American Society of Criminology, San Diego, November 1997.

194. Andrew Golub and Bruce D. Johnson, *The Rise of Marijuana as the Drug of Choice among Youthful Adult Arrestees* (Washington, DC: National Institute of Justice, 2001).

195. These lifestyles are described in Marcia Chaiken and Bruce Johnson, *Characteristics of Different Types of Drug-Involved Offenders* (Washington, DC: National Institute of Justice, 1988).

196. Kenneth Tunnell, "Inside the Drug Trade: Trafficking from the Dealer's Perspective," *Qualitative Sociology* 16 (1993): 361–381.

197. Lening Zhang, John Welte, and William Wieczorek, "Youth Gangs, Drug Use and Delinquency," *Journal of Criminal Justice* 27 (1999): 101–109.

198. Carolyn Rebecca Block, Antigone Christakos, Ayad Jacob, and Roger Przybylski, *Street Gangs and Crime* (Chicago: Illinois Criminal Justice Information Authority, 1996).

199. Richard Tewksbury and Elizabeth Ehrhardt Mustaine, "Lifestyle of the Wheelers and Dealers: Drug Dealing among American College Students," *Journal of Crime and Justice* 21 (1998): 37.

200. Hilary Saner, Robert MacCoun, and Peter Reuter, "On the Ubiquity of Drug Selling among Youthful Offenders in Washington, D.C., 1985–1991: Age, Period, or Cohort Effect?" *Journal of Quantitative Criminology* 11 (1995): 362–373.

201. Charles Faupel and Carl Klockars, "Drugs–Crime Connections: Elaborations from the Life Histories of Hard-Core Heroin Addicts," *Social Problems* 34 (1987): 54–68.
202. Charles Faupel, "Heroin Use, Crime and Unemployment Status," *Journal of Drug Issues* 18 (1988): 467–479.
203. Faupel and Klockars, "Drugs–Crime Connections."
204. Jeffrey T. Parsons, Perry N. Halkitis, and David S. Bimbi, "Club Drug Use among Young Adults Frequenting Dance Clubs and Other Social Venues in New York City," *Journal of Child and Adolescent Substance Abuse* 15 (2006): 1–14.
205. Damir Sekulic, Mia Peric, and Jelena Rodek, "Substance Use and Misuse Among Professional Ballet Dancers," *Substance Use & Misuse* 45 (2010): 1,420–1,430.
206. David Duncan, Thomas Nicholson, John White, Dana Burr Bradley, and John Bonaguro, "The Baby Boomer Effect: Changing Patterns of Substance Abuse Among Adults Ages 55 and Older," *Journal of Aging & Social Policy* 22 (2010): 237–248.
207. The National Center on Addiction and Substance Abuse (CASA), *Women Under the Influence* (Baltimore, MD: Johns Hopkins University Press, 2006).
208. Russel Falck, Jichuan Wang, and Robert Carlson, "The Epidemiology of Physical Attack and Rape among Crack-Using Women," *Violence and Victims* 16 (2001): 79–89.
209. Denise Gottfredson, Brook Kearley, and Shawn Bushway, "Substance Use, Drug Treatment, and Crime: An Examination of Intra-Individual Variation in a Drug Court Population," *Journal of Drug Issues* 38 (Spring 2008): 601–630.
210. Ibid.
211. Bu Huang, Helene White, Rick Kosterman, Richard Catalano, and J. David Hawkins, "Developmental Associations between Alcohol and Interpersonal Aggression during Adolescence," *Journal of Research in Crime and Delinquency* 38 (2001): 64–83; Helene Raskin White and Stephen Hansell, "The Moderating Effects of Gender and Hostility on the Alcohol–Aggression Relationship," *Journal of Research in Crime and Delinquency* 33 (1996): 450–470.
212. "Overview of Findings from the 2002 National Survey on Drug Use and Health," www.oas.samhsa.gov/nhsda/2k2nsduh/Overview/2k2Overview.htm#chap5 (accessed August 16, 2011).
213. National Surveys on Drug Use and Health, "Illicit Drug Use among Persons Arrested for Serious Crimes," www.oas.samhsa.gov/2k5/arrests/arrests.cfm (accessed August 16, 2011).
214. Jerome Cartier, David Farabee, and Michael Prendergast, "Methamphetamine Use, Self-Reported Violent Crime, and Recidivism among Offenders in California Who Abuse Substances," *Journal of Interpersonal Violence* 21 (2006): 435–445.
215. Bureau of Justice Statistics, "Drugs and Crime Facts," http://bjs.ojp.usdoj.gov/content/dcf/duc.cfm (accessed August 16, 2011).
216. The National Center on Addiction and Substance Abuse (CASA), *Behind Bars II: Substance Abuse and America's Prison Population*. February 2010, www.casacolumbia.org/templates/publications_reports.aspx (accessed August 16, 2011).
217. Evelyn Wei, Rolf Loeber, and Helene White, "Teasing Apart the Developmental Associations between Alcohol and Marijuana Use and Violence," *Journal of Contemporary Criminal Justice* 20 (2004): 166–183.
218. Susan Martin, Christopher Maxwell, Helene White, and Yan Zhang, "Trends in Alcohol Use, Cocaine Use, and Crime," *Journal of Drug Issues* 34 (2004): 333–360.
219. Marvin Krohn, Alan Lizotte, and Cynthia Perez, "The Interrelationship between Substance Use and Precocious Transitions to Adult Sexuality," *Journal of Health and Social Behavior* 38 (1997): 87–103, at 88.
220. Arielle Baskin-Sommers and Ira Sommers, "Methamphetamine Use and Violence among Young Adults," *Journal of Criminal Justice* 34 (2006): 661–674.
221. "2009 Annual Report, Arrestee Drug Abuse Monitoring Program II" (Washington, DC: Office of National Drug Control Policy, Executive Office of the President, 2010), www.whitehousedrugpolicy.gov/publications/pdf/adam2009.pdf (accessed August 16, 2011).
222. Controlled Substance Act, 21 U.S.C. 848 (1984).
223. Anti-Drug Abuse Act of 1986, PL 99-570, U.S.C. 841 (1986).
224. Anti-Drug Abuse Act of 1988, PL 100-690; 21 U.S.C. 1501; Subtitle A–Death Penalty, Sec. 7001, Amending the Controlled Substances Abuse Act, 21 U.S.C. 848.
225. Eric Jensen, Jurg Gerber, and Ginna Babcock, "The New War on Drugs: Grass Roots Movement or Political Construction?" *Journal of Drug Issues* 21 (1991): 651–667.
226. Orlando Patterson, "The Other Losing War," *New York Times*, January 13, 2007.
227. George Rengert, *The Geography of Illegal Drugs* (Boulder, CO: Westview Press, 1996), p. 2.
228. Information provided by the Office of National Drug Control Policy, www.whitehouse.gov/ondcp.
229. Simon Romero, "Coca Production Makes a Comeback in Peru," *New York Times*, June 13, 2010, www.nytimes.com/2010/06/14/world/americas/14peru.html?th&emc=th (accessed August 16, 2011).
230. Office of National Drug Control Policy, "Cocaine Smuggling in 2009," www.whitehousedrugpolicy.gov/publications/pdf/Cocaine_Smuggling_in_2009.pdf (accessed June 25, 2011).
231. CNN, "Official: Mexican Cartels Use Money, Sex to Bribe U.S. Border Agents," June 9, 2011, http://articles.cnn.com/2011-06-09/us/mexico.border.corruption_1_corrupt-agents-border-agents-drug-cartels?_s=PM:US (accessed June 25, 2011).
232. Office of National Drug Control Policy, "Cocaine," www.whitehousedrugpolicy.gov/drugfact/cocaine/index.html (accessed April 26, 2011).
233. Preface to Chapter 5, "Disrupting Street Drug Gangs—Operation Knock Out," www.whitehousedrugpolicy.gov/publications/policy/ndcs10/chapter5.pdf (accessed April 26, 2011).
234. Mark Moore, *Drug Trafficking* (Washington, DC: National Institute of Justice, 1988).
235. Matthew Durose and Patrick Langan, *Felony Sentences in State Courts, 2002* (Washington, DC: Bureau of Justice Statistics, 2004).
236. Peter Rossi, Richard Berk, and Alec Campbell, "Just Punishments: Guideline Sentences and Normative Consensus," *Journal of Quantitative Criminology* 13 (1997): 267–283.
237. Michael Welch, Russell Wolff, and Nicole Bryan, "Recontextualizing the War on Drugs: A Content Analysis of NIJ Publications and Their Neglect of Race and Class," *Justice Quarterly* 15 (1998): 719–742.
238. Robert Davis, Arthur Lurigio, and Dennis Rosenbaum, eds., *Drugs and the Community* (Springfield, IL: Charles C Thomas, 1993), pp. xii–xv.
239. Saul Weingart, "A Typology of Community Responses to Drugs," in Davis, Lurigio, and Rosenbaum, *Drugs and the Community*, pp. 85–105.
240. Davis, Lurigio, and Rosenbaum, *Drugs and the Community*, pp. xii–xiii.
241. Marianne Zawitz, *Drugs, Crime and the Justice System* (Washington, DC: Bureau of Justice Statistics, 1992), pp. 109–112.
242. Dennis Rosenbaum, Robert Flewelling, Susan Bailey, Chris Ringwalt, and Deanna Wilkinson, "Cops in the Classroom: A Longitudinal Evaluation of Drug Abuse Resistance Education (D.A.R.E.)," *Journal of Research in Crime and Delinquency* 31 (1994): 3–31.
243. Donald R. Lynam, Rich Milich, Rick Zimmerman, Scott Novak, T. K. Logan, Catherine Martin, Carl Leukefeld, and Richard Clayton, "Project D.A.R.E.: No Effects at 10-Year Follow-Up," *Journal of Consulting and Clinical Psychology* 67 (1999): 590–593.
244. John Goldkamp and Peter Jones, "Pretrial Drug-Testing Experiments in Milwaukee and Prince George's County: The Context of Implementation," *Journal of Research in Crime and Delinquency* 29 (1992): 430–465; Chester Britt, Michael Gottfredson, and John Goldkamp, "Drug Testing and

Pretrial Misconduct: An Experiment on the Specific Deterrent Effects of Drug Monitoring Defendants on Pretrial Release," *Journal of Research in Crime and Delinquency* 29 (1992): 62–78.

245. Joseph R. McKinney, "The Effectiveness and Legality of Random Student Drug Testing Programs Revisited," *West's Education Law Reporter* 196 (2006); "Effectiveness of Random Student Drug-Testing Programs, 2005," www.studentdrugtesting. org/2005%20McKinney%20survey%20 results.pdf (accessed April 26, 2007).

246. Katherine Theall, Kirk Elifson, Claire Sterk, and Eric Stewart, "Criminality Among Female Drug Users Following an HIV Risk-Reduction Intervention," *Journal of Interpersonal Violence* 22 (2007): 85–107.

247. See, generally, Peter Greenwood and Franklin Zimring, *One More Chance* (Santa Monica, CA: RAND, 1985).

248. Daniel Rosen, Jennifer Q. Morse, and Charles F. Reynolds, "Adapting Problem-solving Therapy for Depressed Older Adults in Methadone Maintenance Treatment," *Journal of Substance Abuse Treatment* 40 (2011): 132–141.

249. Audrey Hickert and Mary Jane Taylor, "Supportive Housing for Addicted, Incarcerated Homeless Adults," *Journal of Social Service Research* 37 (2011): 136–151.

250. Tracy Beswick, David David, Jenny Bearn, Michael Gossop, Sian Rees, and John Strang, "The Effectiveness of Combined Naloxone/Lofexidine in Opiate Detoxification: Results from a Double-Blind Randomized and Placebo-Controlled Trial," *American Journal on Addictions* 12 (2003): 295–306.

251. Eli Ginzberg, Howard Berliner, and Miriam Ostrow, *Young People at Risk: Is Prevention Possible?* (Boulder, CO: Westview Press, 1988), p. 99.

252. National Institute on Drug Abuse, "NIDA InfoFacts: Treatment Approaches for Drug Addiction," www.nida.nih.gov/infofacts/ treatmeth.html (accessed August 16, 2011).

253. National Evaluation Data and Technical Assistance Center, *The District of Columbia's Drug Treatment Initiative (DCI)* (Washington, DC: Author, February 1998).

254. The following section is based on material found in Jerome Platt, "Vocational Rehabilitation of Drug Abusers," *Psychological Bulletin* 117 (1995): 416–433.

255. Celia Lo, "Sociodemographic Factors, Drug Abuse, and Other Crimes: How They Vary among Male and Female Arrestees," *Journal of Criminal Justice* 32 (2004): 399–409.

256. Barry Goetz, "Pre-Arrest/Booking Drug Control Strategies: Diversion to Treatment, Harm Reduction and Police Involvement," *Contemporary Drug Problems* 33 (2006): 473–520.

257. Office of National Drug Control Policy, "National Drug Control Strategy, FY 2009 Budget Summary February 2008," www. whitehousedrugpolicy.gov/publications/ policy/09budget/index.html (accessed August 16, 2011).

258. Ethan Nadelmann, "An End to Marijuana Prohibition," *National Review*, July 12, 2004; Peter Andreas and Ethan Nadelmann, *Policing the Globe: Criminalization and Crime Control in International Relations* (London: Oxford University Press, 2006).

259. Drug Policy Alliance, "What's Wrong with the Drug War?" www.drugpolicy.org/drug-war/ (accessed August 14, 2010).

260. David Courtwright, "Should We Legalize Drugs? History Answers No," *American Heritage* (February–March 1993): 43–56.

261. James Inciardi and Duane McBride, "Legalizing Drugs: A Gormless, Naive Idea," *Criminologist* 15 (1990): 1–4.

262. Kathryn Ann Farr, "Revitalizing the Drug Decriminalization Debate," *Crime and Delinquency* 36 (1990): 223–237.

FBI - LOS ANGELES
UNITED STATES ATTORNEY'S OFFICE – LOS ANGELES
FBI LEGAL ATTACHE - CAIRO
OPERATION PHISH PHRY

The FBI called it Operation Phish Phry, a play on words for the popular cybercrime of phishing, fraudulently collecting personal information from victims that can be used to defraud financial institutions by creating dummy accounts or bogus credit cards. However, this phish phry was not a "mom and pop" scam but an international conspiracy involving more than 100 people in the United States and Egypt. An elaborate global conspiracy designed to steal identities by targeting American-based financial institutions, phish phry victimized account holders by fraudulently using their personal financial information. Egyptian-based hackers obtained bank account numbers and related personal identification information from bank customers by sending e-mail messages that appeared to be official correspondence from banks or credit card vendors. The bank customers were directed to fake websites purporting to be linked to financial

(continued on page 522)

15

Crimes of the New Millennium: Cybercrime and Transnational Organized Crime

Learning Objectives

1. Be familiar with the concept of cybercrime
2. Know the basic forms cybercrime takes
3. Discuss the distribution of illicit materials via the Net
4. Be able to discuss the concept of stealing intellectual property
5. Know what is meant by the terms *identity theft* and *phishing*
6. Be familiar with the different types of cybervandalism
7. Understand the concept of cyberterrorism
8. Discuss efforts to control cybercrime
9. Trace the evolution of organized crime
10. Be familiar with transnational organized crime

institutions, where the customers were asked to enter their account numbers, passwords, and other personal identification information. Because the websites appeared to be legitimate—complete with bank logos and legal disclaimers—the customers did not realize that the websites did not belong to legitimate financial institutions.

Armed with the bank account information, members of the conspiracy hacked into accounts at two banks. Once they accessed the accounts, the Egyptians communicated via text messages, telephone calls, and Internet chat groups with co-conspirators in the United States. Through these communications, members of the criminal ring coordinated the illicit online transfer of funds from compromised accounts to newly created fraudulent accounts. In the United States conspirators directed associates to recruit "runners," who set up bank accounts where the funds stolen from the compromised accounts could be transferred and withdrawn. A portion of the illegally obtained funds were then transferred via wire services to individuals operating in Egypt who had originally provided the bank account information obtained via phishing.

After the case was blown open by American and Egyptian law enforcement agents, the conspirators were charged with a variety of crimes, including conspiracy to commit wire fraud and bank fraud; aggravated identity theft; and conspiracy to commit computer fraud, specifically unauthorized access to protected computers in connection with fraudulent bank transfers and domestic and international money laundering.[1] In all, 100 people were indicted—the largest number of defendants ever charged in a cybercrime case—and by 2011 there had been 46 convictions as a result of Phish Phry.[2] The plot's prime mover, Nichole Michelle Merzi, was found guilty of conspiracy, computer fraud, bank fraud, and aggravated identity theft; two other leaders, Kenneth Joseph Lucas and Jonathan Preston Clark, pleaded guilty to conspiracy and bank fraud, and Lucas also pleaded guilty to aggravated identity theft. The conspiracy and bank fraud counts carry maximum sentences of 30 years in prison, and aggravated identity theft adds a minimum of 2 years.

Just a few years ago, complex, global criminal financial enterprises like phish phry could not have been contemplated let alone transacted. Innovation brings change and with it new opportunities to commit crime. The technological revolution has provided new tools to misappropriate funds, damage property, and sell illicit material. It has created **cybercrime**, a new breed of offenses that can be singular or ongoing but typically involve the theft and/or destruction of information, resources, or funds utilizing computers, computer networks, and the Internet. The Internet age also has provided new tools and opportunities for organized criminals who have morphed from local gangs into transnational criminal organizations whose illegal activities span not only national borders but continents. Drug gangs may move their product from one nation to another, and human traffickers ply their trade across continents.

CONNECTIONS

Chapter 13 reviewed the concept of enterprise crime and its motivations, and Chapter 14 covered public order crimes. Cybercrime can be viewed as a type of enterprise crime employing sophisticated technology to achieve illegal profits. It also can involve public order crimes such as the online purchase and sale of pornography and controlled substances. The Internet now enables these previously localized crimes to be conducted on a global scale.

Criminals are becoming more technologically sophisticated, routinely using the Internet to carry out their criminal conspiracies. The widespread use of computers and the

Internet has ushered in the age of **information technology (IT)** and made it an intricate part of daily life in most industrialized societies. IT involves computer networking, the Internet, and advanced communications. It is the key to the economic system and will become more important as major industries shift their manufacturing plants to areas of the world where production is much cheaper. IT is responsible for the **globalization** phenomenon, the process of creating transnational markets, politics, and legal systems—in other words, creating a global economy. The Internet, coupled with ever-more powerful computers, is now the chosen medium for providing a wide range of global services, ranging from entertainment and communication to research and education.

The cyber age has generated an enormous amount of revenue. Worldwide enterprise IT spending is forecast to reach $2.5 trillion in 2011; it will reach $2.8 trillion in 2014.[3] Today more than 1.4 billion people are using e-mail, sending 90 trillion messages per year. Social media sites like Facebook and Twitter are expanding exponentially. As of 2011,

- *Twitter* had 175 million registered users and was adding 15 million new users per month.
- *Linkedin* had 100 million active users globally.
- *Facebook* had more than 800 million users—50 percent of active users logging in each day and 65 million users accessing the site through a mobile device. The site has now overtaken Google as the number one site visited on the Web globally.[4]

Magnifying the importance of the Internet is the fact that many critical infrastructure functions are now being conducted online, ranging from banking to control of shipping on the Mississippi River.[5] Because of its scope, depth, and usage, the Internet has opened up a broad new avenue for illegal activity; cybercrime has become a feature of the new millennium.

In addition to cybercrime, the IT revolution has increased the scope of organized criminal enterprises. Criminal organizations originally local in scope and activity can now extend their operations from coast to coast and across international borders, hence the term transnational crime. Integrating IT into their plans and schemes, these criminal organizations now compete with, and in some instances have replaced, traditional organized crime groups. They are able to carry out criminal schemes on a global basis while confounding law enforcement agents who seek to disrupt their criminal efforts.

This new array of crimes presents a compelling challenge because (a) it is rapidly evolving with new schemes being created daily, (b) it is difficult to detect through traditional law enforcement channels, and (c) its control demands that agents of the justice system develop technical skills that match those of the perpetrators.[6] It is even possible that the recent decrease in the crime rate is a result of cybercrime replacing traditional street crime. Instead of robbing a bank at gunpoint, a new group of contemporary thieves finds it easier to hack into accounts and transfer funds to offshore banks. Instead of shoplifting from a brick and mortar store, the contemporary cyberthief devises clever schemes to steal from etailers. And instead of limiting their criminal escapades to the local population, transnational gang members now find a whole world of opportunity.

Cybercrime and transnational organized crimes present a significant challenge for criminologists because they defy long-held assumptions about the cause of crime. How can we say that crime is a function of social forces, the social environment, or the social structure, when these contemporary criminals are typically highly educated and technologically sophisticated and commit their crimes in places far removed from their victims? These criminal conspiracies demand a high degree of self-control and dedication—something a truly impulsive or mentally unstable person would have difficulty achieving.[7]

CYBERCRIME

In 2010 Americans became very familiar with the previously little-known website WikiLeaks, an international organization that publishes classified and secret documents submitted to it by unnamed and anonymous sources. Launched in 2006 and run by Julian Assange, an Australian who emigrated to Sweden, Wikileaks has supporters around the globe. In April of 2010 the site began to post videos and documents that had been illegally appropriated from U.S. diplomatic and military computers by unknown hackers. For example, one video showed a 2007 incident in which Iraqi civilians and journalists were killed by U.S. forces. It also leaked more than 76,000 classified war documents from Afghanistan, and in November of 2010 it released U.S. State Department cables. Both the U.S. and foreign governments were embarrassed when the confidential cables hit the Net.

In the aftermath of the leaks, Army Specialist Bradley Manning, 22, was arrested when an informant told federal authorities that he had overheard Manning bragging about giving WikiLeaks a video of a helicopter assault in Iraq plus more than 260,000 classified U.S. diplomatic cables taken from government computers. Assange has been accused of sexual misconduct in Sweden, but so far no charges have been filed against him for the WikiLeaks disclosures.[8]

Cybercrimes come in three forms and involve billions of dollars in lost revenue and vandalized property each year. Some cybercriminals use modern technology to accumulate goods and services. **Cybertheft** schemes range from illegally copying material under copyright protection to using technology to commit traditional theft-based offenses such as larceny and fraud. Other cybercriminals are motivated less by profit and more by the urge to commit **cybervandalism**, or technological destruction. They aim their malicious attacks at disrupting, defacing, and destroying technology they find offensive. A third type of cybercrime is **cyberwar**, which consists of acts aimed at undermining the social, economic, and political system of an enemy nation by destroying its electronic infrastructure and disrupting its economy. This can range from stealing secrets from foreign nations to destroying an enemy's Web-based infrastructure.

Thus some cybercriminals are high-tech thieves and others are high-tech vandals; the property the latter destroy is electronic rather than physical. And some may combine theft and vandalism in cyberterror attacks.

CYBERTHEFT: CYBERCRIMES FOR PROFIT

Many of us have encountered "scareware"—those pop-up messages you see on your computer screen saying you've got a virus and all you have to do to get rid of it is buy the antivirus software being advertised. Who would fall for such a scheme? Well, in 2011 a scareware scam attributed to a group based in Kiev, Ukraine, claimed an estimated 960,000 victims who lost a total of $72 million.[9]

It is ironic that technological breakthroughs since the dawn of the Industrial Revolution—such as telephones and automobiles—not only brought with them dramatic improvements for society but also created new opportunities for criminal wrongdoing: criminals use the telephone to place bets or threaten victims; cars can be stolen and sold for big profits.[10] The same pattern is now occurring during the IT revolution. The computer and Internet provide opportunities for socially beneficial endeavors—such as education, research, commerce, and entertainment—while at the same time serving as a tool to facilitate illegal activity. Criminals can operate in a more efficient and effective manner using computer-based technologies. Cyberthieves have the luxury of remaining anonymous, living in any part of the world (such as the three hackers discussed at the beginning of the chapter), conducting their business during the day or in the evening, working alone or in a group, and reaching a much wider number of potential victims than ever before. No longer are con artists or criminal entrepreneurs limited to fleecing victims in a particular geographic locale; the whole world can be their target. The technology revolution has opened novel methods for cybertheft that heretofore were nonexistent, ranging from the unlawful distribution of computer software to Internet security fraud.

Cyberthieves conspire to use cyberspace either to distribute illegal goods and services or to defraud people for quick profits. Some of the most common methods are discussed here.

Computer Fraud

It was not a major case and did not make national headlines, but in 2011 Catherine Griffin, a Georgia woman, was indicted by a federal grand jury on charges of computer fraud for accessing information on government computers for private financial gain. It seems that Catherine was paid to fraudulently obtain the federal government's "First-Time Home Buyer Tax Credits" for friends and relatives who were not eligible to receive the credits and had not purchased homes during the eligible time period. How did she do it? Simple, she was hired as a seasonal employee by the IRS, which gave her access to the IRS computer system. In exchange for $2,000, she used her access to alter her co-conspirators' taxpayer information, making them eligible for the government grants. The computer fraud charges each carry a maximum sentence of five years in prison and a fine of up to $250,000.[11]

Catherine's crime falls under the general category of computer fraud, which can be prosecuted as a larceny or under special laws that criminalize the theft of electronic and/or magnetic impulse property. Some common computer-based thefts include:

- *Theft of information.* The unauthorized obtaining of information from a computer (hacking), including software that is copied for profit.
- *The "Salami" fraud.* With this type of fraud the perpetrator carefully skims small sums from the balances of a large number of accounts in order to bypass internal controls and escape detection.
- *Software theft.* The comparative ease of making copies of computer software has led to a huge illegal market, depriving authors of very significant revenues.
- *Manipulation of accounts/banking systems.* This is similar to a "Salami" fraud, but on a much larger and usually more complex scale, and is sometimes perpetrated as a "one-off kamikaze" fraud.

These are but a few of the most common forms of cybertheft; the full list is as long as the imagination of the criminal mind.

Theft from ATMs   Automatic teller machines (ATMs) are now attracting the attention of cybercriminals looking for easy profits.[12] One approach is to use a thin, transparent-plastic overlay on an ATM keypad that captures a user's identification code as it is entered. Though the plastic covering looks like some sort of cover to protect the keys, in fact, microchips in the device record every keystroke. Another transparent device inside the card slot captures card data. While the user completes the transaction, a computer attached to the overlay records all the data necessary to clone the card. In one recent South Florida case, three people made "skimming devices" that captured the information stored on the magnetic stripe of bank debit cards when the debit cards were placed into ATMs throughout Broward, Palm Beach, and Miami-Dade counties. The skimming devices, and hidden micro-video cameras, were placed on the

An international investigation begun in Australia, and called Operation Joint Hammer by the authorities, resulted in the rescue of 14 girls—some as young as 3 years old—who were being sexually abused by pornographers. Approximately 170 people were arrested, more than 60 of them U.S. citizens. Seven major child pornography rings were been dismantled.

It started when authorities in Queensland, Australia, came across a pornographic video online showing a young victim, determined to be Dutch with a Flemish accent. Authorities in Belgium were contacted, and the ensuing European investigation became known as Operation Koala. Belgian police identified and arrested the molester, who provided information about the video's producer, an Italian national who ran a pornographic website. When Italian police arrested the producer and shut down his website, they retrieved 50,000 e-mails to the porn site. They were routed to the 28 countries from which they originated—with more than 11,000 coming from the United States. A joint federal and state investigation led to the prosecution of some dangerous sexual predators:

- A New Jersey man pleaded guilty to producing sexual images of his 9-year-old daughter. Evidence seized during the search of his home revealed that he had nearly 130,000 images of child pornography. He was sentenced to almost 20 years in prison.
- An Arizona fifth-grade schoolteacher was a customer of the Italian pornography website. A search of his home resulted in allegations of sexual contact with female students at his school. He faces multiple charges of sexual exploitation of children.
- A convicted sex offender from Philadelphia who spent 15 years in prison for molesting children was charged with advertising, distributing, and receiving child pornography. Evidence indicates that he administered two major global online child pornography bulletin boards.

One of the men indicted, 54-year-old Raymond Roy of San Juan Capistrano, California, posted videos of Thai children "to give everyone something to do for an afternoon." Another posting made on July 10, 2007, stated "This one may offend here, so a word of caution, these girls are heavily drugged, Not much action to speak of, the girls are (sic) to (expletive deleted) up to move, or resist. Three girls, the first one being the youngest, around 8 or 9 yo." "Yo" stands for "years old."

SOURCES: FBI News Release, "Rescuing Our Children: Seven Massive Porn Rings Dismantled," February 9, 2009, www.fbi.gov/news/stories/2009/february/jointhammer_020909 (accessed August 15, 2011); Associated Press, "International Child Porn Ring Uncovered," *New York Times*, March 4, 2008.

ATMs to record customers' personal identification numbers (PINs) as they conducted their transactions. The defendants and their co-conspirators subsequently removed the skimming devices and micro-video cameras from the ATMs and downloaded the stolen information. They created false bank debit cards by encoding the magnetic stripes of gift cards and other plastic cards with magnetic stripes containing the customer's stolen banking information. Using these false cards and the customers' PINs, the defendants withdrew customers' funds from ATMs. The defendants sent some of the funds fraudulently obtained to individuals across the United States, Romania, and elsewhere, using Western Union and other money transmitting services. Rather than rob an ATM user at gunpoint, the cybercriminal relies on stealth and technological skill to commit the crime.

Distributing Illicit or Illegal Services and Material

The Internet has become a prime source for the delivery of illicit or legally prohibited material. Included within this market are pornography and obscene material, such as kiddie porn, and dangerous drugs.

Distributing Obscenity   The IT revolution has revitalized the porn industry. The Internet is an ideal venue for selling and distributing obscene material, which can be stored and viewed on a personal computer. It is difficult to count the vast number of websites featuring sexual content, including nude photos, videos, live sex acts, and webcam strip sessions among other forms of "adult entertainment."[13] However, it is estimated that the revenue generated from adult sites each year is greater than all movie box office sales.[14] The number of visits to pornographic sites (mostly by men, though women make up about 30 percent of the viewers) surpasses those made to Internet search engines; some individual sites report as many as 50 million hits per year.

How do adult sites operate today? A number of different schemes are in use:[15]

- A large firm sells annual subscriptions in exchange for unlimited access to content.
- Password services charge an annual fee to deliver access to hundreds of small sites, which share the subscription revenues.
- Large firms provide free content to smaller affiliated sites. The affiliates post the free content and then try to channel visitors to the large sites, which give the smaller sites a percentage of the fees paid by those who sign up.

- Webmasters forward traffic to another porn site in return for a small per-consumer fee. In many cases, the consumer is sent to the other sites involuntarily, which is known in the industry as *mousetrapping*. Web surfers who try to close out a window after visiting an adult site are sent to another web page automatically. This can repeat dozens of times, causing users to panic and restart their computers in order to escape.
- Adult sites cater to niche audiences looking for specific kinds of adult content.

Many of these sites cater to adult tastes, but others cross the legal border by peddling access to obscene material or even kiddie porn.

Despite some successful prosecutions, it has been difficult to control Internet pornography. Various federal legislative efforts, including the Communications Decency Act (1996), the Child Online Protection Act (1998), and the Children's Internet Protection Act (2000), have been successfully challenged in the courts under the First Amendment. Filtering devices used extensively in schools and libraries fail to block a lot of obscene material, giving youngsters the opportunity to use computers away from home to surf the Net for adult content. Although in *United States v. Williams* the Supreme Court upheld the ban on selling virtual kiddie porn as real images, it is unlikely that any law enforcement efforts will put a dent in the Internet porn industry.[16]

CONNECTIONS

Pornography was discussed more fully in Chapter 14. The ability to access pornographic material over the Internet has helped expand the sale of sexually related material. People wishing to purchase sexually related material no longer face the risk of public exposure in adult book stores or movie theaters. Sellers of adult films and photos can now reach a much wider international audience.

Distributing Dangerous Drugs In addition to sexual material, the Internet has become a prime purveyor of prescription drugs, some of which can be quite dangerous when used to excess or when they fall into the hands of minors. The National Center on Addiction and Substance Abuse (CASA) at Columbia University conducts surveys on the sale of prescription drugs on the Net, and the most recent survey identified a total of 365 sites, including 206 advertising sites and 159 sites offering drugs for sale. Only 2 of the selling sites were certified by the National Association of Boards of Pharmacy as legitimate Internet pharmacy practice sites; the other 157 were rogue sites.[17] Of the 15 percent of sites offering drugs for sale that indicated a prescription is required, half simply ask that the prescription be faxed—increasing the risk of multiple use of one prescription or other fraud. This is a particularly serious problem because the number of people who admit abusing controlled prescription drugs has increased from 7.8 million in 1992 to about 16 million today—more than the combined number who reported abusing cocaine, hallucinogens, inhalants, and heroin.

Another problem: there are no controls preventing children from ordering drugs. Children are especially at risk, and it is feared that more than 2 million kids abused a prescription drug in the past year. More teens have abused prescription drugs than have abused many illegal drugs, such as Ecstasy, cocaine, crack, and methamphetamine. With access to a credit card, which most teenagers have, teens can order opioid-based drugs (e.g., Codeine, Demerol, OxyContin, Percocet, and Darvon), depressants (e.g., Xanax, Librium, and Valium), and stimulants (e.g., Adderall, Dexedrine, and Ritalin).[18]

Denial-of-Service Attack

Some students go to football games, but not Mitchell Frost, a University of Akron student who spent his time plotting cybercrimes. As an undergraduate student at Akron, Frost used the university's computer network to control other computer networks via computers he intentionally infected and had taken over, known as "BotNet" zombies. He then used the compromised computers to spread malicious computer codes, commands, and information to even more computers, all for the purpose of harvesting and obtaining information and data from the compromised computer networks, including user names, passwords, credit card numbers, and security codes. Using these networks, Frost initiated attacks on numerous Internet sites, including those of Bill O'Reilly and Ann Coulter, temporarily interrupting operation of these websites, which required the site owners to intervene and repair their computer systems. He then launched attacks against the University of Akron computer server, which caused the entire network to be knocked offline for approximately 8½ hours, preventing all students, faculty, and staff members from accessing the network. For his efforts, Frost received a 30-month prison sentence. The moral: you may not like Bill O'Reilly, but blocking his computer site will send you to prison.[19]

Frost's efforts are known as a **denial-of-service attack**, which are typically designed to harass or extort money from legitimate users of an Internet service by threatening to prevent access to the service.[20] Examples include the following:

- Attempts to flood a computer network, thereby preventing legitimate network traffic
- Attempts to disrupt connections within a computer network, thereby preventing access to a service
- Attempts to prevent a particular individual from accessing a service
- Attempts to disrupt service to a specific system or person

A denial-of-service attack may involve threatening or actually flooding an Internet site with millions of bogus messages or orders so that the website will be tied up and unable to perform as promised. Unless the site operator pays extortion, the attackers threaten to keep up the interference until real consumers become frustrated and abandon the site. Even so-called respectable businesspeople have been accused of launching denial-of-service attacks against rival business interests.[21]

Online gambling casinos—a $7 billion a year industry—have proven particularly vulnerable to attack. Hundreds of attacks have been launched against online casinos located in Costa Rica, the Caribbean, and Great Britain. If the attack coincides with a big sporting event such as the Super Bowl, the casinos may give in and make payments rather than lose revenue and fray customer relations.[22]

Illegal Copyright Infringement

For the past decade, groups of individuals have been working together to illegally obtain software and then "crack" or "rip" its copyright protections before posting it on the Internet for other members of the group to use; this is called **warez**. Frequently, these new pirated copies reach the Internet days or weeks before the legitimate product is commercially available.

Because cyberspace has no borders, software pirates can ply their trade from anywhere in the world, and the effects can be devastating to developers. In 2011 Microsoft estimated that it lost $4 billion in yearly revenue from illegal copies of Windows software pirated in China alone; Apple and Oracle face similar threats.[23]

The government has actively pursued members of the warez community, and some have been charged and convicted under the Computer Fraud and Abuse Act (CFAA), which criminalizes accessing computer systems without authorization to obtain information,[24] and the Digital Millennium Copyright Act (DMCA), which makes it a crime to circumvent antipiracy measures built into most commercial software and also outlaws the manufacture, sale, or distribution of code-cracking devices used to illegally copy software.[25]

File Sharing   Another form of illegal copyright infringement involves file-sharing programs that enable Internet users to download music and other copyrighted material without paying the artists and record producers their rightful royalties. Theft through the illegal reproduction and distribution of movies, software, games, and music is estimated to cost U.S. industries around $20 billion worldwide each year.

Although some students routinely share files and download music, criminal copyright infringement represents a serious economic threat. The United States Criminal Code provides penalties for a first-time offender of five years incarceration and a fine of $250,000.[26] Other provisions provide for the forfeiture and destruction of infringing copies and all equipment used to make the copies.[27]

On June 27, 2005, copyright protection of music and other types of entertainment distributed via the Internet was upheld by the Supreme Court in the case of *MGM Studios, Inc. v. Grokster*, 125 S. Ct. 2764 (2005). The Court unanimously held that software distributors such as Grokster could be sued for inducing copyright infringement if they market file-sharing software that might encourage people to illegally copy protected material even if that software also could be used for legitimate purposes. Justice Souter wrote:

> We hold that one who distributes a device with the object of promoting its use to infringe copyright, as shown by the clear expression or other affirmative steps taken to foster infringement, is liable for the resulting acts of infringement by third parties.

As a result of the opinion, on November 7, 2005, Grokster announced that it would suspend its file-sharing service; it also was required to pay $50 million to the music and recording industries.

Internet Securities Fraud

Fifteen-year-old Jonathan Lebed was charged with securities fraud by the SEC after he repeatedly bought low-cost, thinly traded stocks and then spread hundreds of false and misleading messages concerning them—generally baseless price predictions. After their values were artificially raised, Lebed sold the securities at an inflated price. His smallest one-day gain was $12,000, and one day he made $74,000. Lebed agreed to findings of fraud but later questioned whether he had done anything wrong; he was forced to hand over his illicit gains, plus interest, which came to $285,000.[28]

Though he might not agree, young Lebed's actions are considered Internet fraud because they involve using the Internet to intentionally manipulate the securities marketplace for profit. There are three major types of Internet securities fraud today:

- *Market manipulation.* Stock market manipulation occurs when an individual tries to control the price of stock by interfering with the natural forces of supply and demand. There are two principal forms of this crime: the "pump and dump" and the "cyber smear." In a pump and dump scheme, erroneous and deceptive information is posted online to get unsuspecting investors interested in a stock while those spreading the information sell previously purchased stock at an inflated price. The cyber smear is a reverse pump and dump: negative information is spread online about a stock, driving down its price and enabling people to buy it at an artificially low price before rebuttals by the company's officers reinflate the price.[29]

- *Fraudulent offerings of securities.* Some cybercriminals create websites specifically designed to fraudulently sell securities. To make the offerings look more attractive than they are, assets may be inflated, expected returns overstated, and risks understated. In these schemes, investors are promised abnormally high profits on their investments. No investment is actually made. Early investors are paid returns with the investment money received from the later investors. The system usually collapses, and the later investors do not receive dividends and lose their initial investment. For example, the Tri-West Investment Company solicited investments in "prime bank notes."[30] Visitors to their website were promised an annualized rate of return of 120 percent plus return of their principal at the end of a year, as well as substantial referral fees of 15 percent on all referred investments. The website, which contained alleged testimonials describing instant wealth from early investors, also told visitors that their investments were "guaranteed." Investors contributed $60 million in funds to Tri-West, and some "dividends" were paid. However, no money was actually invested, the dividends were paid from new investments, and most of the cash was siphoned off by the schemers.

- *Illegal touting.* This crime occurs when individuals make securities recommendations and fail to disclose that they are being paid to disseminate their favorable opinions. Section 17(b) of the Securities Act of 1933 requires that paid touters disclose the nature, source, and amount of their compensation. If those who tout stocks fail to disclose their relationship with the company, information misleads investors into believing that the speaker is objective and credible rather than bought and paid for.

Phishing and Identity Theft

Identity theft occurs when a person uses the Internet to steal someone's identity and/or impersonate the victim to open a new credit card account or conduct some other financial transaction. It is a type of cybercrime that has grown at surprising rates over the past few years.[31] In fact, the threat is so real that a recent survey found that the general public would be willing to have their taxes increased to fund a program that reduced identity theft.[32]

Identity theft can destroy a person's life by manipulating credit records or stealing from his or her bank accounts. Identity thieves use a variety of techniques to steal information. They may fill out change of address cards at the post office and obtain people's credit card bills and bank statements. They may then call the credit card issuer and, pretending to be the victim, ask for a change in address on the account. They then charge numerous items over the Internet and have the merchandise sent to the new address. It may take months for the victim to realize the fraud because the victim is not getting bills from the credit card company.

What are the most common goals of credit card thieves? Surveys have found that *opening new lines of credit* remains the most frequently occurring use for a victim's identity, followed by using personal information to make *charges on stolen credit cards and debit cards, obtaining utilities, applying for bogus* personal loans and business loans, and *check fraud* (personal information is used to access an existing account via theft or the creation of false checks).[33]

Phishing   Some identity thieves create false e-mails or websites that look legitimate but are designed to gain illegal access to a victim's personal information; this is known as **phishing** (also known as *carding* and *spoofing*).

Some phishers send out e-mails that look like they come from a credit card company or online store telling the victims there is a problem with their account credit or balance. To fix the problem and update their account, they are asked to submit their name, address, phone numbers, personal information, credit card account numbers, and Social Security number (SSN). Or the e-mail may direct them to a phony website that purports to be a legitimate company or business enterprise. Once victims access the website, they are asked to provide personal information or financial account information so that the problem can be fixed. Some phishing schemes involve job offers. Once unsuspecting victims fill out the "application," answering personal questions and including their Social Security number, the phisher has them in their grasp. One ingenious scam is referred to as reshipping (see Exhibit 15.1).

Once phishers have a victim's personal information, they can do three things. They can gain access to preexisting bank and credit card accounts and buy things using those accounts. Or phishers can use the information to open brand new bank and credit card accounts without the victim's knowledge. Finally, phishers can implant viruses in their software that forward the phishing e-mail to other recipients once one person responds to the original e-mail, thereby luring more potential victims into their nets. Some common phisher scams are listed in Exhibit 15.2.

Phishing e-mails and websites have become even more of a problem now that cybercriminals can easily copy brand names, logos, and corporate personnel insignia directly into the e-mail. The look is so authentic that victims believe the e-mail comes from the advertised company. Most phishers send out spam e-mails to a large number of recipients knowing that some of those recipients will have accounts with the company that they are impersonating.

EXHIBIT 15.1

Reshipping

- The "reshipping" scheme requires individuals in the United States to receive packages at their residence and subsequently repackage the merchandise for shipment, usually abroad.

- "Reshippers" are recruited in various ways, but most often through employment offers and Internet chat rooms.

- "Employers" post help-wanted advertisements at popular Internet job search sites, and respondents quickly reply to the online advertisement. As part of the application process, the prospective employee is required to complete an employment application, which requires the applicant to divulge sensitive personal information, such as date of birth and Social Security number. The "employer" then uses this information to get a credit card in the victim's name.

- The applicant is informed he or she has been hired and will be responsible for forwarding, or reshipping, merchandise purchased in the United States to the company's overseas home office. The packages quickly begin to arrive, and as instructed, the employee dutifully forwards the packages to their overseas destination. Unbeknownst to the "reshipper," the recently received merchandise was purchased with a fraudulent credit card, something the victim only learns when charged for the merchandise he or she just shipped out of the country!

SOURCE: Internet Crime Complaint Center, www.ic3.gov/crimeschemes.aspx#item-16 (accessed August 15, 2011).

EXHIBIT 15.2

Common Phishing Scams

1. *Account verification scams.* Individuals purchase domain names that are similar to those of legitimate companies, such as *Amazon.Accounts.net.* The real company is Amazon, but it does not have *Accounts* in its domain name. These con artists then send out millions of e-mails asking consumers to verify account information and request Social Security numbers. The victim is directed to a bogus website by clicking the legitimate-looking address.

2. *Sign-in rosters.* Some companies and governmental agencies (colleges, EDD, state-sponsored programs) ask you to put your name and SSN on a sign-in roster. Identity thieves may sign up toward the end of a page so they can copy and collect personal identifying information.

3. *"Help move money from my country," aka Nigerian 419 scam.* A bogus e-mail is sent from an alleged representative of a foreign government asking the victim to help move money from one account to another. Some forms include requests to help a dying woman or free a political prisoner. Some claim that the victim has been the recipient of a legacy or a winning lottery ticket. Nigerian money offers now account for about 12 percent of the scam offers.

4. *Canadian/Netherlands lottery.* Originating from the Netherlands and other foreign countries, these scams usually ask for money to hold the prize until the victim can collect in person.

5. *"Free credit report."* Almost all "free credit report" e-mails are scams. Either the person is trying to find out the victim's Social Security number or the victim is billed for services later on.

6. *"You have won a free gift."* The victim receives an e-mail about a free gift or prize. The victim just has to send his or her credit card information to take care of shipping and handling. Responding may result in hundreds of spams or telemarketing calls.

7. *E-mail chain letters/pyramid schemes.* Victims are sent an official looking e-mail requesting cooperation by sending a report to five friends or relatives. Those who respond are then contacted for money in order to keep the chain going.

8. *"Find out everything on anyone."* This e-mail is trying to solicit money by offering a CD or program that victims can use to find out personal information on another person. However, the information is actually in the public domain and can be easily accessed without the program.

9. *Job advertisement scams.* Phishers spoofing legitimate Internet job websites (for instance spoofing Monster.com) contact a victim promising a high-paying job. They solicit personal information, including Social Security numbers.

10. *VISA/MasterCard scam.* A VISA or MasterCard "employee" sends an e-mail asking to confirm unusual spending activity and asks the victim for the code on the back of his or her credit card.

SOURCE: Identity Theft Resource Center (ITRC), "Scams and Consumer Alerts," www.idtheftcenter.org (accessed August 15, 2011).

To meet the increasing threat of phishing and identity theft, Congress passed the Identity Theft and Assumption Deterrence Act of 1998 (Identity Theft Act) to make it a federal crime when anyone:

> Knowingly transfers or uses, without lawful authority, a means of identification of another person with the intent to commit, or to aid or abet, any unlawful activity that constitutes a violation of Federal law, or that constitutes a felony under any applicable State or local law.[34]

Violations of the act are investigated by federal investigative agencies such as the U.S. Secret Service, the FBI, and the U.S. Postal Inspection Service. In 2004 the Identity Theft Penalty Enhancement Act was signed into law; the act increases existing penalties for the crime of identity theft, establishes aggravated identity theft as a criminal offense, and establishes mandatory penalties for aggravated identity theft. According to the new law, anyone who knowingly "transfers, possesses, or uses, without lawful authority" someone else's identification will be sentenced to an extra prison term of two years with no possibility of probation. Committing identity fraud while engaged in crimes associated with terrorism—such as aircraft destruction, arson, airport violence, or kidnapping top government officials—will receive a mandatory sentence enhancement of five years.[35]

Vishing Voice over Internet Protocol (VoIP) is a technology that allows people to make voice calls using a broadband Internet connection instead of a regular (or analog) phone line.[36] Some VoIP services only allow subscribers to call other people using the same service, but others allow you to call anyone who has a telephone number—including local, long distance, mobile, and international numbers. Also, while some VoIP services only work over a computer or a special VoIP phone, others allow traditional phone hookups connected to a VoIP adapter. Cyberthieves have already employed this technology in identity theft schemes.

In one version, the victim receives an e-mail that provides a number to call. Those who call this "customer service" number (a VoIP account, not a real financial institution) are led through a series of voice-prompted menus that ask for account numbers, passwords, and other critical information. In another version the victim is contacted over the phone instead of by e-mail. The call is either a live person or a recorded message directing the victim to take action to protect a personal account. The visher may have collected some personal information, including account or credit card numbers, which can create a false sense of security for the victim.[37]

Botnets One attack method is to release a *botnet* or software robot, also known as a zombie or drone, that allows an unauthorized user to remotely take control of a host computer without the victim's knowledge or permission.[38] Infected computers can be used to launch denial-of-service attacks, send spam and spyware, or commit cyberextortion. Botnets are networks of virus-infected computers controlled remotely by an attacker. They can be used to steal funds, hijack identities, and commit other crimes. One botnet, the Coreflood virus, is a key-logging program that enables cyberthieves to steal personal and financial information by recording unsuspecting users' every keystroke. Once a computer or network of computers is infected by Coreflood—infection may occur when users open a malicious e-mail attachment—thieves control the malware through remote servers. The government has seized and "disinfected" computer servers in an effort to control Coreflood.[39]

Etailing Fraud

New fraud schemes are evolving to reflect the fact that billions of dollars in goods are sold on the Internet each year. **Etailing fraud** can involve both illegally buying and selling merchandise on the Net.

Not only do etail frauds involve selling merchandise, they can also involve buyer fraud. One scam involves purchasing top-of-the-line electronic equipment over the Net and then purchasing a second, similar looking but cheaper model of the same brand. The cheaper item is then returned to the etailer after switching bar codes and boxes with the more expensive unit. Because etail return processing centers don't always check returned goods closely, they may send a refund for the value of the higher-priced model.

In another tactic, called *shoplisting*, a person obtains a legitimate receipt from a store either by buying it from a customer or finding it in the trash and then returns to the store and picks up an identical product while casually shopping. He then takes the product and receipt to the returns department and attempts to return it for either cash, store credit, or a gift card. The thief then sells the gift card on the Internet at a discount for quick cash. Not surprisingly, the underground market for receipts has been growing as stores have liberalized return policies.[40] Some of the most common fraud schemes are included in Exhibit 15.3. Before you say, "how could anyone fall for this stuff?" remember that more than 200,000 people file complaints with the government's Internet fraud center each year, and these scams create more than $240 million in losses each year![41]

Twenty-five-year-old Robert Beck of O'Fallon, Missouri, ignored his distrust of online auctions and paid $1,900 for a top-of-the-line home theater speaker system. It never arrived. He was not the sole victim of this scheme: the sellers scammed at least 500 people of more than $100,000. Etailing schemes vary widely and are hard to control because many scam artists operate from overseas locations. What can be done to reduce etailing fraud?

AP Images/Kyle Ericson

EXHIBIT 15.3

Common Internet Fraud Schemes

Telephone Collection Scam

A caller claims that the victim is delinquent in a payday loan and must repay the loan to avoid legal consequences. The caller purports to be a representative of the FBI, Federal Legislative Department, various law firms, or another legitimate-sounding agency. The caller claims to be collecting debts for companies such as United Cash Advance, U.S. Cash Advance, U.S. Cash, U.S. Cash Net, and other Internet check-cashing services. The fraudster relentlessly calls the victim's home, cell phone, and place of employment. The caller refuses to provide the victim with any details of the alleged payday loan and becomes abusive when questioned. The caller threatens the victim with legal action, arrest, and in some cases physical violence if the victim refuses to pay. In many cases, the caller even resorts to harassment of the victim's relatives, friends, and employer.

Hitman Scam

The victim receives an e-mail from a member of an organization such as the "Ishmael Ghost Islamic Group." The e-mailer claims to have been sent to assassinate the victim and the victim's family members. The e-mailer asserts that the reason for the impending assassination resulted from an alleged offense, by the victim, against a member of the e-mailer's gang. In a bizarre twist, however, the e-mailer reveals that upon obtaining the victim's information, another member of the gang (purported to know a member of the victim's extended family) pleaded for the victim's pardon. The e-mailer alleges that an agreement was reached with the pleading gang member to allow the victim pardon from assassination if the victim takes some action, such as sending $800 to a receiver in the United Kingdom for the migration of Islamic expatriates from the United States. Victims of this e-mail are typically instructed to send the money via Western Union® or Money Gram® to a receiver in the United Kingdom. The e-mailer often gives the victim 72 hours to send the money or else pay with his or her life.

Pet Scams

- An online (or offline) ad selling a pet asks that the buyer send in his or her money, plus a little extra for delivery costs. But the buyer never gets the pet; the scam artist simply takes the money and runs.

- A person is selling a pet and receives a check for more than the asking price. When the seller asks about the overpayment, he or she is told it's meant for someone else who will be caring for the pet temporarily. The seller is asked to deposit the check and to wire the difference to this other person. But the check bounces, and the seller loses any money he or she sent.

Secret Shoppers and Funds Transfer Scams

- A person is hired via the Web to rate experiences while shopping or dining. The person is paid by check and is asked to wire a percentage of the money to a third party. Like the pet scam, the check is bad and the victim is out the money he or she sent. As part of the scam, the fraudsters often use (illegally) real logos from legitimate companies.

- When renting out a property, a person is sent a check that is more than the rental fee and asked to wire the difference to someone else.

- A person takes a job that requires him or her to receive money from a company and redistribute these funds to affiliates via wire transfer.

Adoption and Charity Fraud

A person is sent an e-mail that tugs on the heartstrings, asking for a pressing donation to a charity and often using the subject header, "Urgent Assistance Is Needed." The name of a real charity is generally used, but the information provided sends the money to a con artist. One set of scams used the name of a legitimate British adoption agency to ask for money for orphaned or abandoned children.

Romance Fraud

A person encounters someone in an online dating or social networking site who lives far away or in another country. That person strikes up a relationship with the victim and then wants to meet, but needs money to cover travel expenses. Typically, that's just the beginning—the person may claim to have taken ill or been injured during the journey and ask for money to pay the hospital expenses.

SOURCE: FBI, "Internet Crime Report 2010," www.ic3.gov/media/annual-report/2010_IC3Report.pdf (accessed August 15, 2011); FBI, "Internet Crime Report 2008 and 2009," www.ic3.gov/media/annualreport/2009_IC3Report.pdf (accessed August 15, 2011).

CYBERVANDALISM: CYBERCRIME WITH MALICIOUS INTENT

Some cybercriminals may not be motivated by greed or profit but by the desire for revenge and destruction or to achieve a malicious intent. Cybervandalism ranges from sending destructive viruses and worms to stalking or bullying people using cyberspace as a medium. Cybervandals may want to damage or deface websites or even, as Exhibit 15.4 reveals, pull a virtual fire alarm!

Cybervandals are motivated more by malice than by greed:

- Some cybervandals target computers and networks seeking revenge for some perceived wrong.
- Some want to exhibit their technical prowess and superiority.

EXHIBIT 15.4

Swatting

Cybervandals have developed a new form of "entertainment" called swatting, which involves calling 9-1-1 and faking an emergency that draws a response from law enforcement—usually a SWAT team. The callers often tell tales of hostages about to be executed or bombs about to go off. The community is placed in danger as responders rush to the scene, taking them away from real emergencies. And the officers are placed in danger as unsuspecting residents may try to defend themselves. In one case a swatter in Washington State was charged with pretending to be calling from the home of a married California couple, saying he had just shot and murdered someone. A local SWAT team arrived on the scene, and the husband, who had been asleep in his home with his wife and two young children, heard something and went outside to investigate—after first stopping in the kitchen to pick up a knife. What he found was a group of SWAT assault rifles aimed directly at him. Fortunately, the situation didn't escalate, and no one was injured.

Swatters have become more sophisticated in their targets and use of technology. Consider the following Texas case:

■ Five swatters in several states targeted people who were using online telephone party chat lines (or their family or friends).

■ The swatters found personal details on the victims by accessing telecommunication company information stored on protected computers.

■ Then, by manipulating computer and phone equipment, they called 9-1-1 operators around the country. By using "spoofing technology," the swatters even made it look like the calls were actually coming from the victims!

■ Between 2002 and 2006, the five swatters called 9-1-1 lines in more than 60 cities nationwide, affecting more than 100 victims, causing a disruption of services for telecommunications providers and emergency responders, and resulting in up to $250,000 in losses.

■ "Swats" that the group committed included bomb threats at sporting events, causing the events to be delayed; claiming that hotel visitors were armed and dangerous, causing an evacuation of the entire hotel; and making threats against public parks and officials.

SOURCE: FBI, "Don't Make the Call: The New Phenomenon of 'Swatting'," www.fbi.gov/page2/feb08/swatting020408.html (accessed August 15, 2011).

■ Some wish to highlight the vulnerability of computer security systems.
■ Some want to spy on other people's private financial and personal information (computer voyeurism).
■ Some want to destroy computer security because they believe in a philosophy of open access to all systems and programs.[42]

Cybervandalism takes many different forms. Some common forms are discussed in the following sections.

Worms, Viruses, Trojan Horses, Logic Bombs, and Spam

The typical use of cyberspace for destructive intent is from sending or implanting disruptive programs—viruses, worms, trojan horses, logic bombs, and spam.

Viruses and Worms A **computer virus** is one type of malicious software program (also called **malware**) that disrupts or destroys existing programs and networks, causing them to perform the task for which the virus was designed.[43] The virus is then spread from one computer to another when a user sends out an infected file through e-mail, a network, or a disk. **Computer worms** are similar to viruses but use computer networks or the Internet to self-replicate and send themselves to other users, generally via e-mail, without the aid of the operator.

The damage caused by viruses and worms can be considerable. On March 26, 1999, the Melissa virus disrupted e-mail service around the world when it was posted to an Internet newsgroup, causing more than $80 million in damage. Its creator, David Smith, pleaded guilty to state and federal charges and was later sentenced to 20 months in prison (leniency was granted because he cooperated with authorities in thwarting other hackers).[44] Another damaging piece of malware was the MS Blaster worm—also known as W32. Blaster and W32/Lovsan—which took advantage of a vulnerability in a widely used feature of Microsoft Windows and infected more than 120,000 computers worldwide.[45]

Trojan Horses Some hackers introduce a **Trojan horse** program into a computer system. The Trojan horse looks like a benign application but contains illicit codes that can damage the system operations. Sometimes hackers with a sense of irony will install a Trojan horse and claim that it is an antivirus program. When it is opened, it spreads viruses in the computer system. Though Trojan horses do not replicate themselves like viruses, they can be just as destructive.

Logic Bombs A fourth type of destructive attack that can be launched on a computer system is the **logic bomb**, a program that is secretly attached to a computer system, monitors the network's work output, and waits for a particular signal such as a date to appear. Also called a *slag code*, it is a type of delayed-action virus that may be activated when a program user makes certain input that sets it in motion. A logic bomb may cause a variety of problems ranging from displaying or printing a spurious message to deleting or corrupting data. For example, William Shea was convicted of placing malicious computer code on the network of Bay Area Credit Services, Inc., of San Jose, California, that caused the deletion and modification of financial records and disruption of the proper functioning of the company's computer network.[46] Shea's bomb affected more than 50,000 debtor accounts and caused the company more than $100,000 in damages. Shea, a disgruntled former employee, still had administrative level access to and familiarity with the company's computer systems, including the database server. Company officials did not know that Shea had placed malicious code on the computer network before he left the company that was set to modify and delete data at the end of the month.

Spam An unsolicited advertisement or promotional material, **spam** typically comes in the form of an unwanted e-mail message; *spammers* use electronic communications to send unsolicited messages in bulk. Although e-mail is the most common form of spam, it can be sent via instant messaging, Usenet newsgroup, and mobile phone messaging as well as via other media.

Spam can simply be in the form of an unwanted and unwelcome advertisement. For example, it may advertise sexually explicit websites and get into the hands of minors. A more dangerous and malicious form of spam contains a Trojan horse disguised as an e-mail attachment, which advertises some commodity such as free software or an electronic game. If the recipient downloads or opens the attachment, a virus may be launched that corrupts the victim's computer; the Trojan horse also may be designed to capture important data from the victim's hard drive and send it back to the hacker's e-mail address.

Sending spam can become a crime and even lead to a prison sentence when it causes serious harm to a computer or network.

Website Defacement

Cybervandals may aim their attention at the websites of their victims. **Website defacement** is a type of cybervandalism that occurs when a computer hacker intrudes on another person's website by inserting or substituting codes that expose visitors to the site to misleading or provocative information. Defacement can range from installing humorous graffiti to sabotaging or corrupting the site. In some instances, defacement efforts are not easily apparent or noticeable—for example, when they are designed to give misinformation by substituting or replacing authorized text on a company's web page. The false information may mislead customers and frustrate their efforts to utilize the site or make it difficult for people using search engines to find the site as they surf the Net.

Almost all defacement attacks are designed to vandalize web pages rather than bring profit or gain to the intruders (though some defacers may eventually extort money from their targets). Some defacers are simply trying to impress the hacking community with their skills. Others may target a corporation when they oppose its business practices and policies (such as oil companies, tobacco companies, or defense contractors). Some defacement has political goals such as disrupting the website of a rival political party or fund-raising group. Soon after the war in Iraq began, there were approximately 20,000 website defacements, both pro- and antiwar, with most taking place within the first few days of the onset of conflict.[47]

Content analysis of web page defacements indicate that about 70 percent are pranks instituted by hackers; the rest have a political motive. Defacers are typically members of an extensive social network who are eager to demonstrate their reasons for hacking and often leave calling cards, greetings, and taunts on web pages.[48]

Website defacement is a significant and major threat to online businesses and government agencies. It can harm the credibility and reputation of the organization and demonstrate that its security measures are inadequate. As a result, clients lose trust and may be reluctant to share information such as credit card numbers and personal information. An e-tailer may lose business if potential clients believe the site is not secure. Financial institutions, such as Web-based banks and brokerage houses, are particularly vulnerable because they rely on security and credibility to protect their clients' accounts.[49]

Cyberstalking

For two years, Georges DeBeir contacted adolescent girls he met in Internet chat rooms and promised them gifts and money in exchange for sex. Finally, he went too far. DeBeir initiated a conversation in a "teensex" chat room with a 14-year-old Baltimore girl named Kathy. After weeks of trading explicit e-mail messages, DeBeir asked Kathy to meet him in person for sex, all the while stressing the importance of keeping their relationship confidential. Unfortunately for DeBeir, "Kathy" was an undercover FBI agent working for Innocent Images, a computer crimes unit targeting sexual predators and child pornographers on the Internet. DeBeir was arrested at a Baltimore shopping mall where he had arranged to meet Kathy. He pleaded guilty to one count of traveling interstate with the intent to have sex with a minor, a federal charge that carries with it a maximum sentence of 10 years in prison.[50]

Cyberstalking refers to the use of the Internet, e-mail, or other electronic communication devices to stalk another person.[51] Traditional stalking involves repeated harassing or threatening behavior, such as following a person, appearing at a person's home or place of business, making harassing phone calls, leaving written messages or objects, or vandalizing a person's property. In the Internet age, stalkers, such as Georges DeBeir, can pursue victims through online chat rooms. Pedophiles can use the Internet to establish a relationship with the child, and later make contact for the purpose of engaging in criminal sexual activities. Research by Janis Wolak and her colleagues found that publicity about online "predators" who prey on naive children using trickery and violence is largely inaccurate. Today, Internet predators are more likely to meet, develop relationships with at-risk adolescents, and beguile underage teenagers rather than use coercion and violence.[52]

Not all cyberstalkers are sexual predators. Some send repeated threatening or harassing messages via e-mail and use programs to send messages at regular or random intervals without being physically present at a computer terminal. A cyberstalker may trick other people into harassing or threatening a victim by impersonating the victim on Internet bulletin boards or chat rooms and posting messages that are provocative, such as "I want to have sex." The stalker then posts the victim's name, phone number, or e-mail address, hoping that other chat participants will stalk or hassle the victim without the stalker's personal involvement.

AP Images/Family Handout

Megan Meier, 13, committed suicide after receiving cruel messages on Myspace in St. Charles, Missouri, from Lori Drew, the mother of one of Megan's former friends. Drew was convicted November 26, 2008, of three minor offenses but the conviction was later set aside on technical grounds. Ironically, in the national outrage over the case, the Drews have had their home and work addresses, phone and cell phone numbers, and aerial photos of their home posted on the Internet; their property was vandalized. In response to the case, a number of jurisdictions passed laws making it easier to prosecute people for Internet harassment.

Cyberbullying

On May 15, 2008, a federal grand jury in Los Angeles indicted Lori Drew, a Missouri woman, for her alleged role in a MySpace hoax on a teenage neighbor who later committed suicide. Drew, along with others, created a fake online boy named Josh Evans, who established a cyber-romance with 13-year-old Megan Meier. Later, after being spurned by "Josh," Megan took her own life. She had received several messages from "Josh" suggesting that she kill herself and that the "world would be better off without her." Drew was charged with one count of conspiracy and three counts of accessing protected computers without authorization to obtain information to inflict emotional distress. On November 26, 2008, Drew was found guilty on three lesser charges (reduced from felonies to misdemeanors by the jury); her conviction was later overturned on appeal.[53]

This case of cyberbullying, though unusual in its tragic outcome, illustrates one of the newest challenges facing the justice system. Experts define bullying among children as repeated negative acts committed by one or more children against another. These negative acts may be physical or verbal in nature—for example, hitting or kicking, teasing or taunting—or they may involve indirect actions such as manipulating friendships or purposely excluding other children from activities. Implicit in this definition is an imbalance in real or perceived power between the bully and the victim. It may come as no surprise that 30 to 50 percent of gay, lesbian, and bisexual young people experience harassment in an educational setting.[54]

Studies of bullying suggest that there are short- and long-term consequences for both the perpetrators and the victims of bullying. Students who are chronic victims of bullying experience more physical and psychological problems than their peers who are not harassed by other children, and they tend not to grow out of the role of victim. Young people mistreated by peers may not want to be in school and may thereby miss out on the benefits of school connectedness as well as educational advancement. Longitudinal studies have found that victims of bullying in early grades also reported being bullied several years later.[55] Chronically victimized students may, as adults, be at increased risk for depression, poor self-esteem, and other mental health problems, including schizophrenia.[56]

Bullying is a problem that remains to be solved, but it has now morphed from the physical to the virtual. In cyberspace physical distance is no barrier to the frequency and depth of harm doled out by a bully to his or her victim.[57] **Cyberbullying** is the willful and repeated harm inflicted through the medium of electronic text. Like their real-world counterparts, cyberbullies are malicious aggressors who seek implicit or explicit pleasure or profit through the mistreatment of other individuals. Although power in traditional bullying might be physical (stature) or social (competency or popularity), online power may simply stem from Net proficiency. Cyberbullies are able to navigate the Net and utilize technology in a way that puts them in a position of power relative to their victims.

Cyberbullies employ two major formats when harassing their victims: (1) using a computer to send harassing e-mails or instant messages, posting obscene, insulting, and slanderous messages to online bulletin boards, or developing websites to promote and disseminate defamatory content; or (2) using a cell phone to send harassing text messages to the victim.[58]

How common is cyberbullying? Drs. Sameer Hinduja and Justin Patchin, leading experts on cyberbullying, have conducted yearly surveys using large samples of high school youth. Their most recent effort finds that about 20 percent of the more than 4,000 high school middle school students they surveyed report having been the target of some form of Internet harassment; similarly, about 20 percent of the students said they have harassed someone via the Internet. When asked about specific types of cyberbullying in the previous 30 days (Figure 15.1), mean or hurtful comments (14 percent) and rumors spread online (13 percent) are the most commonly cited. In all, about 17 percent of the sample reported being cyberbullied two or more times over the course of the previous 30 days. Adolescent girls are significantly more likely to have experienced cyberbullying in their lifetimes. The type of cyberbullying tends to differ by gender; girls are more likely to spread rumors whereas boys are more likely to post hurtful pictures or videos.[59]

Cyberspying

On July 21, 2005, Carlos Enrique Perez-Melara, the creator and marketer of a spyware program called Loverspy, was indicted by a federal grand jury and charged with such crimes as manufacturing a surreptitious interception device, sending a surreptitious interception device, and advertising a surreptitious interception device.[60]

Loverspy is a computer program designed and marketed by Perez for people to use to spy on others. Purchasers can select from a menu an electronic greeting card to send to up to five different victims' e-mail addresses. Unbeknownst to the victims, once the e-mail greeting card is opened, Loverspy secretly installs itself on their computer and records all their activities, including e-mails sent and received, websites visited, and passwords entered. Loverspy also gave the purchaser the ability to remotely control the victim's computer, including accessing, changing, and deleting files, and turning on Web-enabled cameras. More than 1,000 people from the United States and elsewhere purchased Loverspy and used it against more than 2,000 victims.[61]

Perez was indicted for engaging in **cyberspying**, illegally using the Internet to gather information that is considered private and confidential. Cyberspies have a variety of motivations. Some are people involved in marital disputes who may want to seize the e-mails of their estranged spouse. Business rivals might hire disgruntled former employees, consultants, or outside contractors to steal information from their competitors. These commercial cyberspies target upcoming bids, customer lists, product designs, software source code, voice mail messages, and confidential e-mail messages.[62] Some of the commercial spying is conducted by foreign competitors who seek to appropriate trade secrets in order to gain a business advantage.[63]

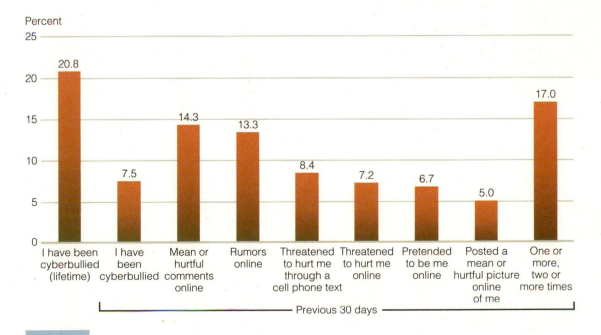

FIGURE 15.1
Cyberbullying Victimization

SOURCE: Sameer Hinduja and Justin W. Patchin (2011). Cyberbullying Research Center (www.cyberbullying.us). Used by permission.

Big Brother Is Watching You

The president's national security advisor approaches you with a problem. It seems that a tracking device has been developed that can be implanted under the skin that will allow people to be constantly monitored. Implanted at birth, the data surveillance device could potentially cover *everyone*, with a record of every transaction and activity they engage in entered into databases monitored by powerful search engines that would keep them under constant surveillance. The surveillance device would enable the government to keep tabs on their whereabouts as well as monitoring biological activities such as brain waves, heart rate, and so on. The benefits are immense. Once a person becomes a suspect in a crime or is believed to be part of a terrorist cell, he or she could be monitored from a distance without danger to any government agent. The person cannot hide or escape detection. Physical readings could be made to determine if the person is under stress, using banned substances, and so on.

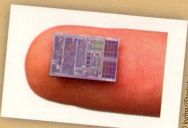

© kydna/iStockphoto

❯❯ The director wants you to write a paper for the NSA expressing your opinion on this device. You begin by reading what the American Civil Liberties Union has to say: "The United States is at risk of turning into a full-fledged surveillance society. The tremendous explosion in surveillance-enabling technologies, combined with the ongoing weakening in legal restraints that protect our privacy mean that we are drifting toward a surveillance society. The good news is that it can be stopped. Unfortunately, right now the big picture is grim."

Is this device worthwhile considering the threats faced by the United States from terrorists and criminals, or, as the ACLU suggests, would it be unethical because it violates the personal privacy and freedom of people before they have broken any law?

CYBERWARFARE: CYBERCRIME WITH POLITICAL MOTIVES

Will future warfare be conducted in cyberspace as well as on the ground? Destroying an enemy's computer network, incapacitating their defense systems, may soon become the opening salvo of hostilities. Sounds fanciful, but there already have been efforts to compromise the United States' defense industry and military establishment. On May 28, 2011, Lockheed Martin Corp., the world's largest aerospace company, announced that it detected and thwarted "a significant and tenacious attack" on its information systems.[64] Not to worry this time, a company spokesman claimed, because swift action protected the company's secrets. While this attempt at **cyberespionage** did not damage America's military capability, there have been other incidents in which agents have been able to steal top-secret government secrets. In 2005, agents of the Chinese espionage ring known as Titan Rain were able to penetrate computers, enter hidden sections of a hard drive, zip up as many files as possible, and transmit the data to way stations in South Korea, Hong Kong, or Taiwan before sending them to mainland China. Titan Rain was able to penetrate the Redstone Arsenal military base and NASA; the U.S. Army's flight-planning software was electronically stolen.[65] In 2008 the Pentagon issued a report on China's "cyberwarfare capabilities,"

acknowledging that hackers in China had penetrated the Pentagon's computer system.[66] The United States may be engaging in cyberwar as well. In 2010 Iran announced that the computers at its nuclear facility in Natanz was under attack by an outside enemy, presumably the United States and/or Israel. The Stuxnet computer worm, a destructive program, was used to wipe out roughly a fifth of Iran's nuclear centrifuges, delaying though not destroying Tehran's ability to make its first nuclear arms. The Stuxnet attack may be the most effective use of cyberwar to date.[67]

Responding to these threats, the United States government announced in 2011 that computer sabotage by another country could constitute an act of war, However, not every attack would lead to retaliation, only those so serious that it would threaten American lives, commerce, infrastructure, or worse; and there would have to be indisputable evidence leading to the nation-state involved.[68] On June 23, 2009, the Secretary of Defense directed the Commander of U.S. Strategic Command to establish USCYBERCOM, whose duties are summarized as follows:

> USCYBERCOM will fuse the Department's full spectrum of cyberspace operations and will plan, coordinate, integrate, synchronize, and conduct activities to: lead day-to-day defense and protection of DoD information networks; coordinate DoD operations providing support to military missions; direct the operations and defense of specified DoD information networks and; prepare to, and when directed, conduct full spectrum military cyberspace operations. The command is charged with pulling together existing cyberspace

resources, creating synergy that does not currently exist and synchronizing war-fighting effects to defend the information security environment.[69]

U.S. Cybercommand went operational on May 21, 2010.

Cyberterrorism

Cyberspace also serves as a venue for terrorism. **Cyberterrorism** can be seen as any effort by covert forces to disrupt the intersection where the virtual electronic reality of computers meets the physical world.[70] FBI expert Mark Pollitt defines cyberterrorism as "the premeditated, politically motivated attack against information, computer systems, computer programs, and data which results in violence against noncombatant targets by subnational groups or clandestine agents."[71]

Terrorist organizations are beginning to understand the power that disruption of cyberspace can inflict on their enemies even though, ironically, they may come from a region where computer databases and the Internet are not widely used. Terrorist organizations are adapting IT into their arsenal of terror, and agencies of the justice system have to be ready for a sustained attack on the nation's electronic infrastructure.

Why Terrorism in Cyberspace?

Cyberspace is a handy battlefield for the terrorist because an attack can strike directly at a target that bombs won't affect: the economy. Technological change plays a significant role in the development of critical infrastructures, and they are particularly vulnerable to attack. With rapid technological change, and the interdependence of systems, it is difficult to defend against efforts to disrupt services.[72]

Cyberterrorists have many advantages. There are no borders of legal control, making it difficult for prosecutors to apply laws to some crimes. Criminals can operate from countries where cyber laws barely exist, making them almost untouchable. Cyberterrorists can use the Internet and hacking tools to gather information on targets.[73] There is no loss of life and no need to infiltrate "enemy" territory. Terrorists can commit crimes from anyplace in the world, and the costs are minimal. Nor do terror organizations lack for skilled labor to mount cyber attacks. There are a growing number of highly skilled computer experts who are available at reasonable costs in developing countries.

Cyber Attacks

Has the United States already been the target of cyber attacks? It may be difficult to separate the damage caused by hackers from deliberate attacks by terrorists, but the Center

In April 2007, two suicide car bomb attacks rocked the city of Algiers in Algeria, damaging the prime minister's office, killing at least 23 people, and injuring more than 160. Al-Qaeda's branch in North Africa claimed responsibility for the attacks, publishing photographs of what it said were the three suicide bombers in an Internet statement. This picture allegedly shows one of the suicide bombers responsible for the attack. The Arabic writing says, "The Martyr al-Zubair Abu Sajda." Cyberterror and the use of the Internet to further the interests of terror groups and publicize their activities has become a reality of contemporary life.

for Strategic and International Studies has uncovered attacks on the National Security Agency, the Pentagon, and a nuclear weapons laboratory; operations were disrupted at all of these sites.[74] The financial service sector is a prime target and has been victimized by information warfare.

Here are some possible scenarios:

- Logic bombs are implanted in an enemy's computer. They can go undetected for years until they are instructed through the Internet to overwhelm a computer system.
- Programs are used to allow terrorists to enter "secure" systems and disrupt or destroy the network.
- Using conventional weapons, terrorists overload a network's electrical system thereby threatening computer security.[75]
- The computer system of a corporation whose welfare is vital to national security—such as Boeing or Raytheon—is breached and disrupted.
- Internet-based systems used to manage basic infrastructure needs—such as an oil pipeline's flow or water levels in dams—are attacked and disrupted, posing a danger of loss of life and interruption of services.

Cyberterrorists may directly attack the financial system. In ever-increasing numbers people are spending and investing their money electronically, using online banking, credit card payment, and online brokerage services. The banking/financial system transacts billions of dollars each day through a complex network of institutions and systems. Efficient and secure electronic functioning is required for people to be willing to conduct credit and debit card purchases, money transfers, and stock trading. A cyber attack can disrupt these transactions and interfere with the nation's economic well-being.[76]

Terrorists can use the Internet to recruit new members and to disseminate information. For example, Islamic militant organizations use the Internet to broadcast anti-Western slogans and information. An organization's charter and political philosophy can be displayed on its website, which can also be used to solicit funds.

Some experts question the existence of cyberterrorism, going so far as to claim that not a single case of cyberterrorism has yet been recorded, that hackers are regularly mistaken for terrorists, and that cyber defenses are more robust than is commonly supposed.[77]

Funding Terrorist Activities

In Chapter 11, we noted that obtaining funds is a key to terrorist activity. Terrorist groups are using the Internet to raise funds to buy arms and carry out operations.[78] One method of funding is through fraudulent charitable organizations claiming to support a particular cause, such as disaster relief or food services. Charitable organizations in the United States raise more than $130 billion per year. Using bogus charities to raise money is particularly attractive to cyberterrorists because they face far less scrutiny from the government than for-profit corporations and individuals. They may also qualify for financial assistance from government-sponsored grant programs. One such bogus group, Holy Land Foundation for Relief and Development (HLFRD), provided more than $12 million to the terrorist group Hamas; in total, HLFRD raised more than $57 million but only reported $36.2 million to the IRS.[79]

Bogus companies are used by terrorist groups to receive and distribute money. These shell companies may engage in legitimate activities to establish a positive reputation in the business community but produce bills for nonexistent products that are "paid" by another party with profits from illegal activities, such as insurance fraud or identity theft.[80] If a shell company generates revenues, funds can be distributed by altering financial statements to hide profits and then depositing the profits in accounts that are used directly or indirectly to support terrorist activities. In 2001, a U.S. telecommunications company was indicted on charges of aiding members of al-Qaeda in preparation for the 9/11 terrorist attacks by handling more than $500,000 in transfers monthly.

Another source of terrorist funding, which is discussed less often in the literature, is intellectual property (IP) crime. The illegal sale of counterfeited goods and the illegal use of IP to commit other crimes, such as stock manipulation, have been used to support terrorist activities.[81]

The various branches of cybercrime are set out in Concept Summary 15.1.

THE EXTENT AND COSTS OF CYBERCRIME

How common are cybercrimes, and how costly are they to American businesses and the general public? The Internet has become a vast engine for illegal profits and criminal entrepreneurs. An accurate accounting of cybercrime will probably never be made because so many offenses go unreported, but there is little doubt that its incidence is growing rapidly.

Though thousands of breaches occur each year, most are not reported to local, state, or federal authorities. Some cybercrime goes unreported because it involves low-visibility acts—such as copying computer software in violation of copyright laws—that simply never get detected.[82] Some businesses choose not to report cybercrime because they fear revealing the weaknesses in their network security systems. However, the information that is available indicates that the profit in cybercrime is vast and continually growing.[83] Losses are now in the billions and rising with the continuing growth of e-commerce. A number of watchdog groups have attempted to decipher estimated costs due to theft, loss of work product, damage to computer networks, and so on.

- *Illegal copying.* The Business Software Alliance (BSA), a professional watchdog group, found in a recent survey that 36 percent of the software installed on computers worldwide (including operating systems, consumer software, and local market software) was pirated, representing a loss of nearly $29 billion. The study found that $80 billion in software was installed on computers, but only $51 billion was legally purchased.[84]

- *Payment fraud.* Credit card fraud on the Internet has increased from $1.6 billion in 2000 to more than $15 billion today.[85]
- *Computer security breaches.* When the Computer Security Institute (CSI) contacted 700 computer security practitioners in U.S. corporations, government agencies, financial institutions, medical institutions, and universities, it found that the average loss from computer security breaches was now more than $200,000.[86] The survey showed that such crimes as unauthorized access of computer systems and theft of information have undergone a dramatic increase in recent years. Ironically, while computer theft is increasing, the percentage of organizations reporting computer intrusions to law enforcement has been in decline, presumably because companies fear negative publicity about their security systems!
- *Phishing and identity theft.* The cost of phishing and identity theft now runs in the billions in the United States. Fifty-seven million U.S. adults think they have received a phishing e-mail. Nearly 1 million users have suffered from identity theft fraud, costing banks and card issuers more than $1 billion each year.[87] The Anti-Phishing Working Group reports that more than 15,000 phishing attempts, which used different legitimate brand names, occur each year. The United States is not alone in experiencing losses due to identity theft. In Britain, identity fraud is one of the fastest-growing criminal trends and costs the British economy around £1.3 billion per year (more than $2 billion); it takes victims up to 300 hours of effort to regain their former status with banks and credit reference agencies.[88]
- *Cybervandalism.* Corporations are often the target of cybervandals, but the costs and the damage caused is not significant.[89] However, Symantec Corp. conducts an annual Internet Security Threat Report. The latest effort, which is based on data from more than 24,000 security devices deployed in more than 180 countries, shows that online attackers are increasingly using stealthy attacks on personal computers in the pursuit of profit rather than simply to vandalize computer networks. Hackers and malicious-software writers unleashed huge numbers of low-grade attacks designed to advance identity theft, spamming, extortion, and other schemes. There has been a significant increase in attack programs using malicious codes, as cybervandals hope at least some will get past defenses. Attackers also are targeting their assaults more carefully and using less familiar methods, such as lacing websites with attacks. Personal computers are increasingly the target of attacks because they are considered the weak links in corporate network security and at the same time contain valuable consumer data, such as financial account numbers, passwords, and identifying information.[90]

CONTROLLING CYBERCRIME

The proliferation of cybercrime and its cost to the economy have created the need for new laws and enforcement processes specifically aimed at controlling its new and emerging formulations. Because technology evolves so rapidly, the enforcement challenges are particularly vexing. Numerous organizations provide training and support for law enforcement agents, and new federal and state laws have been aimed at particular areas of high-tech crimes.

Congress has treated computer-related crime as a distinct federal offense since the passage of the Counterfeit Access Device and Computer Fraud and Abuse Law in 1984.[91] The 1984 act protected classified U.S. defense and foreign relations information, financial institution and consumer reporting agency files, and access to computers operated for the government. The act was supplemented in 1996 by the National Information Infrastructure Protection Act (NIIPA), which significantly broadens the scope of the law.[92]

Because cybercrime is new, existing laws sometimes are inadequate to address the problem. Therefore, new legislation has been drafted to protect the public from this new breed of cybercriminal. For example, before October 30, 1998, when the Identity Theft and Assumption Act of 1998 became law, there was no federal statute that made identity theft a crime. Today, federal prosecutors are making substantial use of the statute and are actively prosecuting cases of identity theft.[93] All states except Vermont and the District of Columbia now have passed laws related to identity theft.

In the wake of the 9/11 attacks, the NIIPA has been amended by sections of the USA Patriot Act to make it easier to enforce crimes by terrorists and other organized enemies against the nation's computer systems. Subsection 1030(a)(5)(A)(i) of the act criminalizes "knowingly causing the transmission of a program, code, or command, and as a result, intentionally causing damage to a protected computer." This section applies regardless of whether the user had authorization to access the protected computer; company insiders and authorized users can be culpable for intentional damage to a protected computer. The act also prohibits intentional access without authorization that results in damage but does not require intent to damage; the attacker can merely be negligent or reckless.

In addition to these main acts, computer-related crimes can also be charged under at least 40 different federal statutes. In addition to some of the statutes discussed earlier in the chapter, these include the Copyright Act and Digital Millennium Copyright Act, the National Stolen Property Act, the mail and wire fraud statutes, the Electronic Communications Privacy Act, the Communications Decency Act of 1996, the Child Online Protection Act, the Child Pornography Prevention Act of 1996, and the Internet False Identification Prevention Act of 2000.[94] Movie pirates who use the Internet to sell illegally copied films have led the federal

Theft of intellectual property has become an international issue, and nations around the globe are organizing to thwart cyberthieves. Here, a visitor walks past a salesperson displaying an original copy of antivirus software at the Computers Fair in Kuala Lumpur, Malaysia. Malaysia said it will launch surprise raids on companies nationwide to ferret out illegal software and bring the country's copyright piracy rate down to at least the global average. From 2008 to 2009, despite installations of unlicensed software on personal computers in Asia-Pacific falling from 61 percent to 59 percent, the commercial value of illegal software rose to over US$16.5 billion, according to the Business Software Alliance (BSA).

government to create the Family Entertainment and Copyright Act of 2005. One part of that statute, known as the ART Act (Artists' Rights and Theft Prevention Act of 2005), criminalizes the use of recording equipment to make copies of films while in movie theaters. The statute also makes it illegal to make a copy of a work in production and put it on the Internet so it will be accessible to members of the public when the individual making the copy knew or should have known the work was intended for commercial distribution.[95]

International Treaties   Because cybercrime is essentially global, international cooperation is required for its control. The Convention on Cybercrime, ratified by the U.S. Senate in August 2006, is the first international treaty that addresses the definition and enforcement of cybercrime. Now signed by 43 nations, it focuses on improving investigative techniques and increasing cooperation among nations. The convention includes a list of crimes that each signatory state must incorporate into its own law, including such cyber offenses as hacking, distribution of child pornography, and protection of intellectual property rights. It also gives law enforcement agencies new powers, including the ability to require that an Internet service provider monitor a person's online viewing and search choices in real time. The convention also requires signatory states to cooperate whenever possible in the investigations and prosecution of cybercriminals. The vision is that a common legal framework will eliminate jurisdictional hurdles to facilitate the law enforcement of borderless cybercrimes.[96]

Cybercrime Enforcement Agencies

To enforce these laws, the federal government now has a number of organizations focusing on control of cyberfraud. One approach is to create working groups that coordinate the activities of numerous agencies involved in investigating cybercrime. For example, the Interagency Telemarketing and Internet Fraud Working Group brings together representatives of numerous U.S. attorneys' offices, the FBI, the Secret Service, the Postal Inspection Service, the Federal Trade Commission, the Securities and Exchange Commission, and other law enforcement and regulatory agencies to share information about trends and patterns in Internet fraud schemes.[97]

Specialized enforcement agencies have been created. The Internet Fraud Complaint Center, based in Fairmont, West Virginia, is run by the FBI and the National White-Collar Crime Center. It brings together about 1,000 state and local law enforcement officials and regulators. Its goal is to analyze fraud-related complaints in order to find distinct patterns, develop information on particular cases, and send investigative packages to law enforcement authorities in the jurisdiction that appears likely to have the greatest investigative interest in the matter. The center now receives more than 200,000 complaints each year, including auction fraud, nondelivery, and credit/debit card fraud, as well as nonfraudulent complaints, such as computer intrusions, spam/unsolicited e-mail, and child pornography.[98] Law enforcement has made remarkable strides in dealing with identity theft as a crime problem over the last several years.

One of the most successful federal efforts is the New York Electronic Crimes Task Force (NYECTF), a partnership between the U.S. Secret Service and a host of other public safety agencies and private corporations. Today, the task force consists of more than 250 individual members representing federal, state, and local law enforcement, the private sector, and computer science specialists from 18 different universities. Since 1995, the New York task force has charged more than 1,000 individuals with electronic crime losses exceeding $1 billion. It has trained more than 60,000 law enforcement personnel, prosecutors, and private industry representatives in cybercrime prevention. Its success has prompted similar electronic crime task forces to be set up in Boston, Miami, Charlotte, Chicago, Las Vegas, San Francisco, Los Angeles, and Washington, D.C.[99]

TRANSNATIONAL ORGANIZED CRIME

On June 10, 2010, the Department of Justice announced the arrest of more than 2,200 individuals on narcotics-related charges in the United States.[100] The two-year investigation, involving more than 3,000 agents and officers, targeted the transportation infrastructure of Mexican drug trafficking organizations in the United States, especially along the Southwest border, through coordination between federal, state, and local law enforcement. One of those seized was Carlos Ramon Castro-Rocha, an alleged heroin trafficker who was designated a Consolidated Priority Organization Target (CPOT), a designation reserved by federal enforcement agencies for significant narcotics traffickers who are believed to be the leaders of drug trafficking organizations responsible for the importation of large quantities of narcotics into the United States. Overall, Project Deliverance led to the arrest of 2,266 individuals and the seizure of approximately $154 million in U.S. currency and approximately 1,262 pounds of methamphetamine, 2.5 tons of cocaine, 1,410 pounds of heroin, 69 tons of marijuana, 501 weapons, and 527 vehicles.

The investigative efforts in Project Deliverance were coordinated by the multiagency Special Operations Division, comprised of agents and analysts from the DEA, FBI, ICE, Internal Revenue Service, U.S. Customs and Border Protection, U.S. Marshals Service, and the Bureau of Alcohol, Tobacco, Firearms, and Explosives, as well as attorneys from the Criminal Division's Narcotic and Dangerous Drug Section. More than 300 federal, state, local, and foreign law enforcement agencies contributed investigative and prosecutorial resources to Project Deliverance, many of which were through the High Intensity Drug Trafficking Area (HIDTA) Task Forces and the Organized Crime Drug Enforcement Task Forces (OCDETFs). Significant assistance for Project Deliverance was also provided by the Criminal Division's Office of International Affairs.

Project Deliverance gives a glimpse into the national and global reach of organized crime groups. These criminal conspiracies involve ongoing criminal enterprise groups whose ultimate purpose is personal economic gain through illegitimate means. Here a structured enterprise system is set up to continually supply consumers with merchandise and services banned by criminal law but for which a ready market exists: prostitution, pornography, gambling, and narcotics. The system may resemble a legitimate business run by an ambitious chief executive officer, his or her assistants, staff attorneys, and accountants, with thorough, efficient accounts receivable and complaint departments.[101] Cross-national gangs are large criminal organizations, some with more than 20,000 members whose activities are bi-coastal; the criminal activities of transnational gangs are global and have no borders. Both groups make use of contemporary technology to aid in their criminal enterprise.

Gangs and Cyberspace

Cross-national and transnational gangs are a product of the cyber age, and gang members often use cell phones and the Internet to communicate and to promote their illicit activities.[102] Gangs typically use the voice and text messaging capabilities of cell phones to conduct drug transactions and prearrange meetings with customers. Prepaid cell phones are used when conducting drug trafficking operations. Internet-based methods such as social networking sites, encrypted e-mail, Internet telephony, and instant messaging are commonly used by gang members to communicate with one another and with drug customers. Gang members use social networking Internet sites such as MySpace, YouTube, and Facebook as well as personal web pages to communicate and boast about their gang membership and related activities. Some use the Internet to intimidate rival gang members and maintain websites to recruit new members. Gang members flash gang signs and wear gang colors in videos and photos posted on the Web. Sometimes rivals "spar" on Internet message boards.[103]

This section briefly defines transnational organized crime, reviews its history, and discusses its economic effect and control.

Mexican marines escort drug kingpin Sergio Villarreal Barragan, aka "El Grande," during his presentation to the press in Mexico City, September 13, 2010. Before his capture, Barragan was a leader of the Beltran Leyva drug cartel. Despite setbacks such as this, the cartels continue to flourish and dominate the international drug trade. More than 28,000 people have been killed in Mexico in the past four years, many in drug-related incidents.

AP Images/Miguel Tovar

Characteristics of Transnational Organized Crime

A precise description of the characteristics of **transnational organized crime** is difficult to formulate, but here are some of its general traits:[104]

- Transnational organized crime is a conspiratorial activity, involving the coordination of numerous people in the planning and execution of illegal acts or in the pursuit of a legitimate objective by unlawful means (e.g., threatening a legitimate business to get a stake in it).
- An offense is transnational if—
  - It is committed in more than one state.
  - It is committed in one state but a substantial part of its preparation, planning, direction, or control takes place in another state.
  - It is committed in one state but involves an organized criminal group that engages in criminal activities in more than one state.
  - It is committed in one state but has substantial effects in another state.[105]
- Transnational organized crime involves continuous commitment by primary members, although individuals with specialized skills may be brought in as needed. Organized crime is usually structured along hierarchical lines—a chieftain supported by close advisors, lower subordinates, and so on.
- Transnational organized crime has economic gain as its primary goal, although power and status may also be motivating factors. Economic gain is achieved through global supply of illegal goods and services, including drugs, sex slaves, arms, and pornography.
- In addition to providing illegal material such as narcotics, contemporary global syndicates engage in enterprise crimes such as laundering illegal money through legitimate businesses, land fraud, and computer crime.
- Transnational criminal syndicates employ predatory tactics, such as intimidation, violence, and corruption.
- Transnational organized crime groups are quick and effective in controlling and disciplining their members, associates, and victims and will not hesitate to use lethal violence against those who flout organizational rules.
- Transnational crime depends heavily on the instruments of the IT age: the Internet, global communications, rapid global transportation systems, universal banking system, global credit card and payment systems.
- Transnational organized crime groups do not include terror organizations, though there may be overlap. Some terror groups are involved in criminality to fund their political objectives, and others have morphed from being politically motivated to being solely involved in for-profit criminal activity. Transnational criminal organizations may aid terror groups with transportation and communication.

Activities of Transnational Organized Crime

What are the main activities of organized crime? The traditional sources of income are derived from providing illicit materials and using force to enter into and maximize profits in legitimate businesses. Most organized crime income comes from such activities as human trafficking, narcotics distribution, illegal gambling, theft rings, Internet pornography, and cargo theft. The international trade in human trafficking and prostitution is the subject of the Race, Culture, Gender, and Criminology feature "International Trafficking in Persons."

Organized crime groups have branched out into computer crime and other white-collar activities as well. Transnational crime figures have entered the information age, using computers and the Internet to sell illegal material, recruit members, and contact each other to engage in criminal conspiracies.

Contemporary organized crime cartels have also branched out into securities fraud. They target "small cap" or "micro cap" stocks, over-the-counter stocks, and other types of thinly traded stocks that can be easily manipulated and sold to elderly or inexperienced investors. The conspirators use offshore bank accounts to conceal their participation in the fraud scheme and to launder the illegal proceeds in order to avoid paying income tax.[106]

Origins of Organized Crime

While transnational gangs themselves are a recent phenomenon, organized crime gangs have been around for more than 400 years. In the 1600s, London was terrorized by organized gangs that called themselves Hectors, Bugles, Dead Boys, and other colorful names. In the seventeenth and eighteenth centuries, English gang members wore distinctive belts and pins marked with serpents, animals, stars, and the like. The first mention of youth gangs in America occurred in the late 1780s when prison reformers noted the presence of gangs of young people hanging out on Philadelphia's street corners. By the 1820s, New York's Bowery and Five Points districts, Boston's North End and Fort Hill, and the outlying Southwark and Moyamensing sections of Philadelphia were the locales of youth gangs with colorful names like the Roach Guards, Chichesters, the Plug Uglies, and the Dead Rabbits.[107]

At the turn of the twentieth century, "La Mano Nera" ("The Black Hand"), an offshoot of Sicilian criminal groups, established themselves in northeastern urban centers. Gangsters demanded payments from local businessmen in return for "protection"; those who would not pay were beaten and their shops vandalized. Eventually the Black Hand merged with gangs of Italian heritage to form larger urban-based gangs and groups.

A turning point in the development of organized gangs occurred on January 16, 1919, when the Eighteenth

Attacks," www.cert.org/tech_tips/denial_of_service.html (accessed March 1, 2008).

21. Saul Hansell, "U.S. Tally in Online-Crime Sweep: 150 Charged," *New York Times*, August 27, 2004, p. C1.

22. Stephen Baker and Brian Grow, "Gambling Sites, This Is a Holdup," *BusinessWeek*, August 9, 2004, pp. 60–62.

23. Douglas A. McIntyre, "How Much Are China Sales Worth to Microsoft?" *24/7 Wall St.*, May 27, 2011, http://247wallst.com/2011/05/27/how-much-are-china-sales-worth-to-microsoft/ (accessed May 30, 2011).

24. The Computer Fraud and Abuse Act (CFAA), 18 U.S.C. §1030 (1998).

25. The Digital Millennium Copyright Act, Public Law 105-304 (1998).

26. Title 18, United States Code, Section 2319.

27. Title 17, United States Code, Section 506.

28. This section is based on Richard Walker and David M. Levine, "'You've Got Jail': Current Trends in Civil and Criminal Enforcement of Internet Securities Fraud," *American Criminal Law Review* 38 (2001): 405–430.

29. Jim Wolf, "Internet Scams Targeted in Sweep: A 10-Day Crackdown Leads to 62 Arrests and 88 Indictments," *Boston Globe*, May 22, 2001, p. A2.

30. U.S. Department of Justice, "Alleged Leaders of $60 Million Internet Scam Indicted on Fraud and Money Laundering Charges: Massive Internet Investment Fraud Case Involves 15,000 Investors from 60 Countries," January 3, 2003, www.cybercrime.gov/waagePlea.htm.

31. These sections rely on "Phishing Activity Trends Report, June 2005," www.anti-phishing.org/reports/APWG_Phishing_Activity_Report_Jun_05.pdf (accessed August 15, 2011), and "Anti-Phishing Working Group," www.antiphishing.org/ (accessed August 15, 2011).

32. Nicole Leeper Piquero, Mark A. Cohen, and Alex R. Piquero, "How Much Is the Public Willing to Pay to Be Protected from Identity Theft?" *Justice Quarterly* 28 (2011): 437–459.

33. Linda Foley, Karen Barney, and Jay Foley, "Identity Theft: The Aftermath 2009," Identity Theft Resource Center (ITRC), www.idtheftcenter.org/artman2/uploads/1/Aftermath_2009_20100520.pdf (accessed August 15, 2011).

34. Identity Theft and Assumption Deterrence Act, as amended by Public Law 105-318, 112 Stat. 3007 (October 30, 1998).

35. Public Law 108-275 (2004).

36. Federal Communications Commission, "Voice Over Internet Protocol," www.fcc.gov/voip/ (accessed August 15, 2011).

37. FBI, "Something Vishy: Be Aware of a New Online Scam," February 23, 2007, www.fbi.gov/page2/feb07/vishing022307.htm (accessed August 15, 2011).

38. Frank Hayes, "Botnet Threat," *Computerworld* 40 (2006): 50.

39. FBI, "Botnet Operation Disabled: FBI Seizes Servers to Stop Cyber Fraud," April 14, 2011, www.fbi.gov/news/stories/2011/april/botnet_041411/botnet_041411 (accessed August 15, 2011).

40. Elizabeth Woyke and Dan Beucke, "Many Not-So-Happy Returns," *BusinessWeek*, August 15, 2005, p. 10.

41. FBI, "Internet Crime Report: The Top Scams of 2007," April 3, 2008, www.fbi.gov/page2/april08/ic3_report040308.html (accessed August 15, 2011).

42. Anne Branscomb, "Rogue Computer Programs and Computer Rogues: Tailoring Punishment to Fit the Crime," *Rutgers Computer and Technology Law Journal* 16 (1990): 24–26.

43. Heather Jacobson and Rebecca Green, "Computer Crimes," *American Criminal Law Review* 39 (2002): 272–326.

44. U.S. Department of Justice, "Creator of 'Melissa' Computer Virus Pleads Guilty to State and Federal Charges," December 9, 1999, www.cybercrime.gov/melissa.htm (accessed August 15, 2011); see also Jacobson and Green, "Computer Crimes," pp. 273–275.

45. Robert Lemos, "'MSBlast' Worm Widespread But Slowing," *CNET News.com*, August 12, 2003, http://news.com.com/2100-1002-5062655.html (accessed April 27, 2007).

46. U.S. Department of Justice, Northern District of California, "Federal Jury Convicts Former Technology Manager of Computer Hacking Offense: Defendant Found Guilty of Placing Computer 'Time Bomb' on Employer's Network Following Employment Dispute," September 8, 2005, www.cybercrime.gov/sheaConvict.htm.

47. "Cyber Threat!" *Middle East* 335 (2003): 38–41.

48. Hyung-jin Woo, Yeora Kim, and Joseph Dominick, "Hackers: Militants or Merry Pranksters? A Content Analysis of Defaced Web Pages," *Media Psychology* 6 (2004): 63–82.

49. Yona Hollander, "Prevent Web Page Defacement," *Internet Security Advisor* 2 (2000): 1–4.

50. Debra Baker, "When *Cyber* Stalkers Walk," *American Bar Association Journal* 85 (1999): 50–54.

51. U.S. Department of Justice, "Cyberstalking: A New Challenge for Law Enforcement and Industry," a Report from the Attorney General to the Vice President, 1999, www.usdoj.gov/criminal/cybercrime/cyberstalking.htm (accessed April 27, 2007).

52. Janis Wolak, David Finkelhor, Kimberly Mitchell, and Michele Ybarra, "Online 'Predators' and Their Victims: Myths, Realities, and Implications for Prevention and Treatment," *American Psychologist* 63 (2008): 111–128.

53. Fox News, "Missouri Woman Indicted in MySpace Cyber-Bullying Case That Ended in Teen's Suicide," May 15, 2008, www.foxnews.com/printer_friendly_story/0,3566,356056,00.html (accessed August 15, 2011).

54. Kate Gross, "Homophobic Bullying and Schools—Responding to the Challenge," *Youth Studies Australia* 25 (2006): 60.

55. Jane Ireland and Rachel Monaghan, "Behaviors Indicative of Bullying Among Young and Juvenile Male Offenders: A Study of Perpetrator and Victim Characteristics," *Aggressive Behavior* 32 (2006): 172–180.

56. Dan Olweus, "A Useful Evaluation Design, and Effects of the Olweus Bullying Prevention Program," *Psychology, Crime and Law* 11 (2005): 389–402.

57. This section leans heavily on **Justin** Patchin and Sameer Hinduja, "Bullies Move Beyond the Schoolyard: A Preliminary Look at Cyberbullying," *Youth Violence and Juvenile Justice* 4 (2006): 148–169.

58. Sameer Hinduja and Justin Patchin, "Cyberbullying: An Exploratory Analysis of Factors Related to Offending and Victimization," *Deviant Behavior* 29 (2008): 129–156.

59. Data from Cyberbullying Research Center, August 25, 2010, http://cyberbullying.us/index.php (accessed August 15, 2011).

60. Manufacturing a Surreptitious Interception Device, Title 18, United States Code, Section 2512(1)(b); Advertising a Surreptitious Interception Device, Title 18, United States Code, Section 2512(1)(c)(i).

61. U.S. Department of Justice, Southern District of California, "Creator and Four Users of Loverspy Spyware Program Indicted," www.cybercrime.gov/perezIndict.htm (accessed August 15, 2011).

62. Tom Yager, "Cyberspying: No Longer a Crime for Geeks Only," *InfoWorld* 22 (2000): 62.

63. Nathan Vardi, "Chinese Take Out," *Forbes* 176 (2005), www.forbes.com/global/2005/0725/022.html.

64. Reuters, "Lockheed Martin Hit by Computer Attack," *Los Angeles Times*, May 29, 2011, www.latimes.com/news/nation-world/nation/la-na-lockheed-martin-20110529,0,5490207.story (accessed August 8, 2011).

65. Nathan Thornburgh, Matthew Forney, Brian Bennett, Timothy Burger, and Elaine Shannon, "The Invasion of the Chinese Cyberspies (and the Man Who Tried to Stop Them)," *Time*, September 5, 2005, p. 10.

66. Andrew Gray, "Chinese Hackers Worry Pentagon: A recent report expresses concerns about technological advances in both cyberspace and space," *PC World*, March 9, 2008, www.gyre.org/node/5061 (accessed August 15, 2011).

67. William J. Broad, John Markoff, and David E. Sanger, "Israeli Test on Worm Called Crucial in Iran Nuclear Delay," *New York Times*, January 15, 2011, www.nytimes.com/2011/01/16/world/middleeast/16stuxnet.html (accessed August 8, 2011).

68. MSNBC, "Sources: US Decides Cyber Attack Can Be 'Act of War'," May 29, 2011, www.msnbc.msn.com/id/43224451/ns/us_news-security/t/sources-us-decides-cyber-attack-can-be-act-war/ (accessed August 8, 2011).

69. U.S. Cyber Command, www.stratcom.mil/factsheets/cyber_command/ (accessed August 8, 2011).

70. Barry Collin, "The Future of CyberTerrorism: Where the Physical and Virtual Worlds Converge," http://afgen.com/terrorism1.html (accessed August 8, 2011).

71. Mark Pollitt, "Cyberterrorism—Fact or Fancy?" FBI Laboratory, www.cs.georgetown.edu/~denning/infosec/pollitt.html (accessed August 8, 2011).

72. Tomas Hellström, "Critical Infrastructure and Systemic Vulnerability: Towards a Planning Framework," *Safety Science* 45 (2007): 415–430.

73. Mathieu Gorge, "Cyberterrorism: Hype or Reality?" *Computer Fraud and Security* 2 (2007): 9–12.

74. Daniel Benjamin, *America and the World in the Age of Terrorism* (Washington, DC: CSIS Press, 2005), pp. 1–216.

75. Yael Shahar, "Information Warfare," IWS: The Information Warfare Site, www.iwar.org.uk/cyberterror/resources/CIT.htm (accessed August 8, 2011).

76. General Accounting Office, "Critical Infrastructure Protection: Efforts of the Financial Services Sector to Address Cyber Threats."

77. Gabriel Weimann, "Cyberterrorism: The Sum of All Fears?" *Studies in Conflict and Terrorism* 28 (2005): 129–150.

78. This section leans heavily on John Kane and April Wall, "Identifying the Links between White-Collar Crime and Terrorism," National White Collar Crime Center, 2004, www.ncjrs.gov/pdffiles1/nij/grants/209520.pdf (accessed August 8, 2011).

79. *United States v. Holy Land Foundation for Relief and Development*, www.law.com/jsp/tx/LawDecisionTX.jsp?id=1202473830008&slreturn=1&hbxlogin=1 (accessed August 8, 2011).

80. Kane and Wall, "Identifying the Links between White-Collar Crime and Terrorism."

81. Loretta Napoleoni, *Modern Jihad: Tracing the Dollars Behind the Terror Networks* (Sterling, VA: Pluto Press, 2003).

82. Clyde Wilson, "Software Piracy: Uncovering Mutiny on the Cyberseas," *Trial* 32 (1996): 24–31.

83. Deloitte, "2010 Global Security Survey," www.deloitte.com/view/en_GX/global/industries/financial-services/2ac300d256409210VgnVCM100000ba42f00aRCRD.htm (accessed August 8, 2011).

84. Business Software Alliance, "BSA Eighth Annual Global Software Piracy Study," 2010, www.bsa.org/globalstudy/loader.cfm?url=/commonspot/security/getfile.cfm&pageid=16947 (accessed August 8, 2011).

85. Jeanne Capachin and Dave Potterton, "Online Card Payments, Fraud Solutions Bid to Win," *Meridien Research Report,* January 18, 2001.

86. Computer Security Institute, "CSI/FBI Computer Crime and Security Survey, 2005," www.gocsi.com (accessed August 8, 2011).

87. Avivah Litan, "Phishing Victims Likely Will Suffer Identity Theft Fraud," Gartner Group, May 14, 2004, www.gartner.com/DisplayDocument?doc_cd=120804 (accessed August 8, 2011).

88. David Porter, "Identity Fraud: The Stealth Threat to UK PLC," *Computer Fraud and Security* (2004): 4–7.

89. Lorine Hughes and Gregory DeLone, "Viruses, Worms, and Trojan Horses: Serious Crimes, Nuisance, or Both?" *Social Science Computer Review* 25 (2007): 78–98.

90. "Symantec Internet Security Threat Report Trends for January–June 07," Vol. 12, September 2007, http://eval.symantec.com/mktginfo/enterprise/white_papers/ent-whitepaper_internet_security_threat_report_xii_exec_summary_09_2007.en-us.pdf (accessed August 8, 2011).

91. Public Law 98-473, Title H, Chapter XXI, [sections] 2102(a), 98 Stat. 1837, 2190 (1984).

92. Public Law 104-294, Title II, [sections] 201, 110 Stat. 3488, 3491–94 (1996).

93. Heather Jacobson and Rebecca Green, "Computer Crime," *American Criminal Law Review* 39 (2002): 273–326; Identity Theft and Assumption Act of 1998 (18 U.S.C. S 1028(a)(7)).

94. Comprehensive Crime Control Act of 1984, PL 98-473, 2101-03, 98 Stat. 1837, 2190 (1984), Adding 18 USC 1030 (1984); Counterfeit Active Device and Computer Fraud and Abuse Act, Amended by PL 99-474, 100 Stat. 1213 (1986), Codified at 18 U.S.C. 1030 (Supp. V 1987); Computer Abuse Amendments Act 18 U.S.C. Section 1030 (1994); Copyright Infringement Act 17 U.S.C. Section 506(a) 1994; Electronic Communications Privacy Act of 1986 18 U.S.C. 2510–2520 (1988 and Supp. II 1990).

95. Family Entertainment and Copyright Act of 2005, Title 18 United States Code Section 2319B.

96. U.S. State Department, "Fact Sheet," September 29, 2006, Council of Europe Convention on Cybercrime, www.law.fsu.edu/journals/transnational/vol12_2/keyser.pdf (accessed August 8, 2011); Council of Europe Convention on Cybercrime, CETS No. 185, http://conventions.coe.int/Treaty/Commun/QueVoulezVous.asp?NT=185&CL=ENG (accessed August 8, 2011).

97. Bruce Swartz, Deputy Assistant General, Criminal Division, Justice Department, "Internet Fraud Testimony before the House Energy and Commerce Committee," May 23, 2001.

98. "IC3 Annual Internet Crime Report 2006," www.ic3.gov/media/annualreport/2006_IC3Report.pdf (accessed August 8, 2011).

99. "Statement of Mr. Bob Weaver, Deputy Special Agent in Charge, New York Field Office, United States Secret Service, Before the House Financial Services Committee Subcommittee on Financial Institutions and Consumer Credit and the Subcommittee on Oversight and Investigations," U.S. House of Representatives, April 3, 2003, www.iwar.org.uk/ecoespionage/resources/fraud/040303bw.pdf (accessed August 8, 2011).

100. Department of Justice, press release, "'Project Deliverance' Results in More Than 2,200 Arrests During 22-Month Operation, Seizures of Approximately 74 Tons of Drugs and $154 Million in U.S. Currency: Joint Effort with Mexican Law Enforcement Results in Arrest of High Priority Target," June 10, 2010, www.fbi.gov/news/pressrel/press-releases/201cproject-deliverance201d-results-in-more-than-2-200-arrests-during-22-month-operation-seizures-of-approximately-74-tons-of-drugs-and-154-million-in-u.s.-currency (accessed August 8, 2011).

101. See, generally, President's Commission on Organized Crime, *Report to the President and the Attorney General, The Impact: Organized Crime Today* (Washington, DC: U.S. Government Printing Office, 1986). Herein cited as *Organized Crime Today*.

102. Information in this section comes from the National Gang Intelligence Center, "National Gang Threat Assessment," 2009, www.justice.gov/ndic/pubs32/32146/index.htm (accessed August 8, 2011).

103. Ibid.

104. *Organized Crime Today*, pp. 7–8.

105. James O. Finckenauer and Ko-lin Chin, *Asian Transnational Organized Crime: Its Impact on the United States* (Washington, DC: National Institute of Justice, 2007), www.ncjrs.gov/pdffiles1/nij/214186.pdf (accessed August 8, 2011).

106. Statement for the record of Thomas V. Fuentes, Chief, Organized Crime Section, Criminal Investigative Division, Federal Bureau of Investigation, "Organized Crime before the House Subcommittee on Finance and Hazardous Materials." September 13, 2000.

107. Christopher Adamson, "Defensive Localism in White and Black: A Comparative History of European-American and African American Youth Gangs," *Ethnic and Racial Studies* 23 (2000): 272–298.

108. Donald Cressey, *Theft of the Nation* (New York: Harper & Row, 1969).

109. National Legal Policy Center, "Bonanno Crime Boss Gets Two Life Terms," August 17, 2005, http://nlpc.org/stories/2005/07/04/bonanno-crime-boss-gets-two-life-terms (accessed August 8, 2011).

110. FBI, "Mafia Takedown: Philadelphia Boss Charged," May 25, 2011, www.fbi.gov/news/stories/2011/may/mafia_052511/mafia_052511 (accessed August 8, 2011).

111. CBS News, "Notorious Mobster James 'Whitey' Bulger Arrested," June 23, 2011, www.cbsnews.com/stories/2011/06/22/national/main20073558.shtml (accessed August 8, 2011).

112. Selwyn Rash, "A Battered and Ailing Mafia Is Losing Its Grip on America," *New York Times,* October 22, 1990, p. B7.

113. National Gang Intelligence Center, "National Gang Threat Assessment 2009," www.fbi.gov/stats-services/publications/national-gang-threat-assessment-2009-pdf (accessed August 8, 2011).

114. FBI, "African Criminal Enterprises," www.fbi.gov/about-us/investigate/organized-crime/african (accessed August 8, 2011).

115. FBI, "Balkan Criminal Enterprises," www.fbi.gov/about-us/investigate/organized-crime/balkan (accessed August 8, 2011).

116. FBI, "Operation Power Outage: Armenian Organized Crime Group Targeted," March 3, 2011, www.fbi.gov/news/stories/2011/march/armenian_030311/armenian_030311 (accessed August 8, 2011).

117. Louise I. Shelley, "Crime and Corruption: Enduring Problems of Post-Soviet Development," *Demokratizatsiya* 11 (2003): 110–114; James O. Finckenauer and Yuri A. Voronin, *The Threat of Russian Organized Crime* (Washington, DC: National Institute of Justice, 2001).

118. Omar Bartos, "Growth of Russian Organized Crime Poses Serious Threat," *CJ International* 11 (1995): 8–9.

119. Bilyana Tsvetkova, "Gangs in the Caribbean," *Harvard International Review* June 2009, http://hir.harvard.edu/index.php?page=article&id=1863 (accessed August 8, 2011).

120. This section leans heavily on Finckenauer and Chin, *Asian Transnational Organized Crime.*

121. National Institute of Justice, "Major Transnational Organized Crime Groups," 2010, www.ojp.usdoj.gov/nij/topics/crime/transnational-organized-crime/major-groups.htm (accessed August 8, 2011).

122. Drug Enforcement Administration New Release, "DEA Announces Largest Single U.S. Strike Against Mexican Drug Cartels," October 22, 2009, www.justice.gov/dea/pubs/pressrel/pr102209ap.html (accessed August 8, 2011).

123. 18 U.S.C. 1952 (1976).

124. Public Law 91-452, Title IX, 84 Stat. 922 (1970) (codified at 18 U.S.C. 1961–68, 1976).

125. William Booth, "Mexican Azteca Gang Leader Arrested in Killings of 3 Tied to U.S.," *Washington Post*, March 30, 2010, www.washingtonpost.com/wp-dyn/content/article/2010/03/29/AR2010032903373.html (accessed August 8, 2011).

126. Angela Kocherga, "Zeta Leader Captured in Mexico," KVUE News, July 4, 2011, www.kvue.com/home/Zeta-leader-captured-in-Mexico--124979219.html (accessed August 8, 2011).

127. Orlando Patterson, "The Other Losing War," *New York Times*, January 13, 2007.

128. George Rengert, *The Geography of Illegal Drugs* (Boulder, CO: Westview Press, 1996), p. 2.

129. Office of National Drug Control Policy, www.whitehousedrugpolicy.gov/ (accessed August 15, 2011).

130. Francisco Gutierrez, "Institutionalizing Global Wars: State Transformations in Colombia, 1978–2002: Colombian Policy Directed at Its Wars, Paradoxically, Narrows the Government's Margin of Maneuver Even as It Tries to Expand It," *Journal of International Affairs* 57 (2003): 135–152.

Glossary

acquaintance rape Forcible sex in which offender and victim are acquainted with each other.

acquaintance robbery Robbers who focus their thefts on people they know.

active precipitation The view that the source of many criminal incidents is the aggressive or provocative behavior of victims.

actual authority The authority a corporation knowingly gives to an employee.

adolescent-limited offender Offender who follows the most common criminal trajectory, in which antisocial behavior peaks in adolescence and then diminishes.

age-graded theory A developmental theory that posits that (a) individual traits and childhood experiences are important to understand the onset of delinquent and criminal behavior; (b) experiences in young adulthood and beyond can redirect criminal trajectories or paths; (c) serious problems in adolescence undermine life chances; (d) positive life experiences and relationships can help a person knife off from a criminal career path; (e) positive life experiences such as gaining employment, getting married, or joining the military create informal social control mechanisms that limit criminal behavior opportunities; (f) former criminals may choose to desist from crime because they find more conventional paths more beneficial and rewarding.

aggravated rape Rape involving multiple offenders, weapons, and victim injuries.

aging out The process by which individuals reduce the frequency of their offending behavior as they age. It is also known as spontaneous remission, because people are believed to spontaneously reduce the rate of their criminal behavior as they mature. Aging out is thought to occur among all groups of offenders.

alexithymia A deficit in emotional cognition that prevents people from being aware of their feelings or being able to understand or talk about their thoughts and emotions; they seem robotic and emotionally dead.

al-Qaeda (Arabic for "the base") An international fundamentalist Islamist organization comprising independent and collaborative cells, whose goal is reducing Western influence upon Islamic affairs.

American Dream The goal of accumulating material goods and wealth through individual competition; the process of being socialized to pursue material success and to believe it is achievable.

anal stage In Freud's schema, the second and third years of life, when the focus of sexual attention is on the elimination of bodily wastes.

androgens Male sex hormones.

anomie A condition produced by normlessness. Because of rapidly shifting moral values, the individual has few guides to what is socially acceptable. According to Robert Merton, anomie is a condition that occurs when personal goals cannot be achieved by available means. In Agnew's revision, anomie can occur when positive or valued stimuli are removed or negative or painful ones applied.

antithesis An opposing argument.

apparent authority Authority that a third party, such as a customer, reasonably believes the agent has to perform the act in question.

arousal theory A view of crime suggesting that people who have a high arousal level seek powerful stimuli in their environment to maintain an optimal level of arousal. These stimuli are often associated with violence and aggression. Sociopaths may need greater than average stimulation to bring them up to comfortable levels of living; this need explains their criminal tendencies.

arson for profit People looking to collect insurance money, but who are afraid or unable to set the fire themselves, hire professional arsonists. These professionals have acquired the skills to set fires, yet make the cause seem accidental.

arson fraud A business owner burns his or her property, or hires someone to do it, to escape financial problems.

at risk Children and adults who lack the education and skills needed to be effectively in demand in modern society.

atavistic anomalies According to Lombroso, the physical characteristics that distinguish born criminals from the general population and are throwbacks to animals or primitive people.

attachment theory The belief that the ability to form attachments—that is, emotionally bond to another person—has important lasting psychological implications that follow people across the life span.

attention deficit hyperactivity disorder (ADHD) A psychological disorder in which a child shows developmentally inappropriate impulsivity, hyperactivity, and lack of attention.

authority conflict pathway The path to a criminal career that begins with early stubborn behavior and defiance of parents.

behavior modeling Process of learning behavior (notably aggression) by observing others. Aggressive models may be parents, criminals in the neighborhood, or characters on television or in video games and movies.

behaviorism The branch of psychology concerned with the study of observable behavior rather than unconscious motives. It focuses on the relationship between particular stimuli and people's responses to them.

biological determinism A belief that criminogenic traits can be acquired through indirect heredity from a degenerate family whose members suffered from such ills as insanity, syphilis, and alcoholism, or through direct heredity—being related to a family of criminals.

biophobia Sociologists who held the view that no serious consideration should be given to biological factors when attempting to understand human nature.

biosocial theory An approach to criminology that focuses on the interaction between biological and social factors as they relate to crime.

bipolar disorder An emotional disturbance in which moods alternate between periods of wild elation and deep depression.

blameworthy Basing punishment solely on whether a person is responsible for wrongdoing and deserving of censure or blame.

booking Fingerprinting, photographing, and recording of personal information of a suspect in police custody.

boosters Professional shoplifters who steal with the intention of reselling stolen merchandise.

brothel A house of prostitution, typically run by a madam who sets prices and handles "business" arrangements.

California Personality Inventory (CPI) A frequently administered personality test used to distinguish deviant groups from nondeviant groups.

call girls Prostitutes who make dates via the phone and then service customers in hotel rooms or apartments. Call girls typically have a steady clientele who are repeat customers.

capable guardians Effective deterrents to crime, such as police or watchful neighbors.

capitalist bourgeoisie The owners of the means of production.

career criminal A person who repeatedly violates the law and organizes his or her lifestyle around criminality.

carjacking Theft of a car by force or threat of force.

cerebral allergies A physical condition that causes brain malfunction due to exposure to some environmental or biochemical irritant.

chemical restraints or chemical straitjackets Antipsychotic drugs such as Haldol, Stelazine, Prolixin, and Risperdal, which help control levels of neurotransmitters (such as serotonin/dopamine), that are used to treat violence-prone people.

child abuse Any physical, emotional, or sexual trauma to a child for which no reasonable explanation, such as an accident, can be found. Child abuse can also be a function of neglecting to give proper care and attention to a young child.

chiseling Crimes that involve using illegal means to cheat an organization, its consumers, or both, on a regular basis.

chivalry hypothesis The idea that low female crime and delinquency rates are a reflection of the leniency with which police treat female offenders.

chronic offender According to Wolfgang, a delinquent offender who is arrested five or more times before he or she is 18 stands a good chance of becoming an adult criminal; such offenders are responsible for more than half of all serious crimes.

chronic victimization Those who have been crime victims maintain a significantly higher chance of future victimization than people who have remained nonvictims. Most repeat victimizations occur soon after a previous crime has occurred, suggesting that repeat victims share some personal characteristic that makes them a magnet for predators.

civil law The set of rules governing relations between private parties, including both individuals and organizations (such as business enterprises and/or corporations). The civil law is used to resolve, control, and shape such personal interactions as contracts, wills and trusts, property ownership, and commerce.

classical criminology Eighteenth-century social thinkers believed that criminals choose to commit crime and that crime can be controlled by judicious punishment.

cleared crimes Crimes are cleared in two ways: when at least one person is arrested, charged, and turned over to the court for prosecution; or by exceptional means, when some element beyond police control precludes the physical arrest of an offender (for example, the offender leaves the country).

closure A term used by Lemert to describe people from a middle-class background who have little identification with a criminal subculture but cash bad checks because of a financial crisis that demands an immediate resolution.

cognitive theory The study of the perception of reality and of the mental processes required to understand the world in which we live.

cohort A sample of subjects whose behavior is followed over a period of time.

collective efficacy Social control exerted by cohesive communities, based on mutual trust, including intervention in the supervision of children and maintenance of public order.

college boy A disadvantaged youth who embraces the cultural and social values of the middle class and actively strives to be successful by those standards. This type of youth is embarking on an almost hopeless path, because he is ill-equipped academically, socially, and linguistically to achieve the rewards of middle-class life.

commitment to conformity A strong personal investment in conventional institutions, individuals, and processes that prevents people from engaging in behavior that might jeopardize their reputation and achievements.

common law Early English law, developed by judges, that incorporated Anglo-Saxon tribal custom, feudal rules and practices, and the everyday rules of behavior of local villages. Common law became the standardized law of the land in England and eventually formed the basis of the criminal law in the United States.

Communist Manifesto In this document, Marx focused his attention on the economic conditions perpetuated by the capitalist system. He stated that its development had turned workers into a dehumanized mass who lived an existence that was at the mercy of their capitalist employers.

concentration effect As working-class and middle-class families flee inner-city poverty areas, the most disadvantaged population is consolidated in urban ghettos.

conduct disorder (CD) Children with ADHD who continually engage in aggressive and antisocial behavior in early childhood.

conduct norms Behaviors expected of social group members. If group norms conflict with those of the general culture, members of the group may find themselves described as outcasts or criminals.

confidence game A swindle, usually involving a get-rich-quick scheme, often with illegal overtones, so that the victim will be afraid or embarrassed to call the police.

conflict view The view that human behavior is shaped by interpersonal conflict and that those who maintain social power will use it to further their own needs.

conscience One of two parts of the superego; it distinguishes between what is right and wrong.

consensus view of crime The belief that the majority of citizens in a society share common ideals and work toward a common good and that crimes are acts that are outlawed because they conflict with the rules of the majority and are harmful to society.

consent In prosecuting rape cases, it is essential to prove that the attack was forced and that the victim did not give voluntary consent to her attacker. In a sense, the burden of proof is on the victim to show that her character is beyond question and that she in no way encouraged, enticed, or misled the accused rapist. Proving victim dissent is not a requirement in any other violent crime.

constructive possession In the crime of larceny, willingly giving up temporary physical possession of property but retaining legal ownership.

contagion effect Genetic predispositions and early experiences make some people, including twins, susceptible to deviant behavior, which is transmitted by the presence of antisocial siblings in the household.

containment theory The idea that a strong self-image insulates a youth from the pressures and pulls of criminogenic influences in the environment.

contextual discrimination A practice in which African Americans receive harsher punishments in some instances (as when they victimize whites) but not in others (as when they victimize other blacks).

continuity of crime The view that crime begins early in life and continues throughout the life course. Thus, the best predictor of future criminality is past criminality.

corner boy According to Cohen, a role in the lower-class culture in which young men remain in their birth neighborhood, acquire families and menial jobs, and adjust to the demands of their environment.

corporate crime White-collar crime involving a legal violation by a corporate entity, such as price fixing, restraint of trade, or hazardous waste dumping.

covert pathway A path to a criminal career that begins with minor underhanded behavior and progresses to fire starting and theft.

crackdowns The concentration of police resources on particular problem areas, such as street-level drug dealing, to eradicate or displace criminal activity.

crime discouragers Discouragers can be grouped into three categories: guardians, who monitor targets (such as store security guards); handlers, who monitor potential offenders (such as parole officers and parents); and managers, who monitor places (such as homeowners and doorway attendants).

crime typology The study of criminal behavior involving research on the links between different types of crime and criminals. Because people often disagree about types of crimes and criminal motivation, no standard exists within the field. Some typologies focus on the criminal, suggesting the existence of offender groups, such as professional criminals, psychotic criminals, occasional criminals, and so on. Others focus on the crimes, clustering them into categories such as property crimes, sex crimes, and so on.

criminal anthropology Early efforts to discover a biological basis of crime through measurement of physical and mental processes.

criminal environmental pollution A crime involving the intentional or negligent discharge of a toxic waste into the biosystem that destroys plant or animal life.

criminal justice The study of the agencies of social control—police, courts, and corrections.

criminality A personal trait of the individual as distinct from a "crime," which is an event.

criminological enterprise The areas of study and research that taken together make up the field of criminology. Criminologists typically specialize in one of the subareas of criminology, such as victimology or the sociology of law.

criminologists Researchers who use scientific methods to study the nature, extent, cause, and control of criminal behavior.

criminology The scientific study of the nature, extent, cause, and control of criminal behavior.

crisis intervention Emergency counseling for crime victims.

critical criminologists Researchers who view crime as a function of the capitalist mode of production and not the social conflict that might occur in any society regardless of its economic system.

critical criminology The view that capitalism produces haves and have-nots, each engaging in a particular branch of criminality. The mode of production shapes social life. Because economic competitiveness is the essence of capitalism, conflict increases and eventually destabilizes social institutions and the individuals within them.

critical feminism Scholars, both male and female, who focus on the effects of gender inequality and the unequal power of men and women in a capitalist society.

cross-sectional survey Survey data derived from all age, race, gender, and income segments of the population measured simultaneously. Because people from every age group are represented, age-specific crime rates can be determined. Proponents believe this is a sufficient substitute for the more expensive longitudinal approach that follows a group of subjects over time to measure crime rate changes.

crusted over Children who have been victims of or witnesses to violence and do not let people inside, nor do they express their feelings. They exploit others and in turn are exploited by those older and stronger; as a result, they develop a sense of hopelessness.

cult terrorists Cults that can be classified as terror groups because their leaders demand that followers prove their loyalty through violence or intimidation. Members typically follow a charismatic leader who may be viewed as having godlike powers or even being the reincarnation of an important religious figure. The leader and his or her lieutenants commonly enforce loyalty by severe discipline and by physically preventing members from leaving the group. They may go through doomsday drills and maintain a siege mentality, fearing attacks from the government. The cult may openly or tacitly endorse individual killings or mass murder, which may be accompanied by mass suicide.

cultural deviance theory Branch of social structure theory that sees strain and social disorganization together resulting in a unique lower-class culture that conflicts with conventional social norms.

cultural transmission The concept that conduct norms are passed down from one generation to the next so that they become stable within the boundaries of a culture. Cultural transmission guarantees that group lifestyle and behavior are stable and predictable.

culture conflict According to Sellin, a condition brought about when the rules and norms of an individual's subcultural affiliation conflict with the role demands of conventional society.

culture of poverty The view that people in the lower class of society form a separate culture with its own values and norms that are in conflict with conventional society; the culture is self-maintaining and ongoing.

cumulative disadvantage A condition in which repeated negative experiences in adolescence undermine life chances and reduce employability and social relations. People who increase their cumulative disadvantage risk continued offending.

cyberbullying Willful and repeated harm inflicted through the medium of electronic text.

cybercrime The theft and/or destruction of information, resources, or funds via computers, computer networks, or the Internet.

cyberespionage Efforts by intelligence agencies to penetrate computer networks of an enemy nation in order to steal important data.

cyberspying Illegally using the Internet to gather information that is considered private and confidential.

cyberstalking Use of the Internet, e-mail, or other electronic communications devices to stalk another person. Some cyberstalkers pursue minors through online chat rooms; others harass their victims electronically.

cyberterrorism Internet attacks against an enemy nation's technological infrastructure.

cybertheft The use of computer networks for criminal profits. Copyright infringement, identity theft, and Internet securities fraud are examples of cybertheft.

cybervandalism Malicious attacks aimed at disrupting, defacing, and destroying technology.

cyberwar Politically motivated attacks designed to compromise the electronic infrastructure of an enemy nation and disrupt its economy.

cycle of violence The idea that victims of crime, especially childhood abuse, are more likely to commit crimes themselves.

date rape Forcible sex during a courting relationship.

defective intelligence Traits such as feeblemindedness, epilepsy, insanity, and defective social instinct, which Goring believed had a significant relationship to criminal behavior.

defensible space The principle that crime prevention can be achieved through modifying the physical environment to reduce the opportunity individuals have to commit crime.

deliberation Planning a homicide after careful thought, however brief, rather than acting on sudden impulse.

delinquent boy A youth who adopts a set of norms and principles in direct opposition to middle-class values, engaging in short-run hedonism, living for today and letting tomorrow take care of itself.

demystify To unmask the true purpose of law, justice, or other social institutions.

Department of Homeland Security (DHS) An agency of the federal government charged with preventing terrorist attacks within the United States, reducing America's vulnerability to terrorism, and minimizing the damage and aiding recovery from attacks that do occur.

deterrence theory The view that if the probability of arrest, conviction, and sanctioning increases, crime rates should decline.

developmental criminology A view of criminal behavior that emphasizes the changes people go through over the life course. It presents a criminal career as a dynamic process involving onset, continuity, persistence, acceleration, and eventual desistance from criminal behavior, controlled by individual level traits and conditions.

deviant behavior Behavior that departs from the social norm.

deviant place theory People become victims because they reside in socially disorganized, high-crime areas where they have the greatest risk of coming into contact with criminal offenders.

dialectic method For every idea, or thesis, there exists an opposing argument, or antithesis. Because neither position can ever be truly accepted, the result is a merger of the two ideas, a synthesis. Marx adapted this analytic method for his study of class struggle.

differential association theory According to Sutherland, the principle that criminal acts are related to a person's exposure to an excess amount of antisocial attitudes and values.

differential opportunity The view that lower-class youths, whose legitimate opportunities are limited, join gangs and pursue criminal careers as alternative means to achieve universal success goals.

differential reinforcement Behavior is reinforced by being either rewarded or punished while interacting with others; also called direct conditioning.

differential reinforcement theory An attempt to explain crime as a type of learned behavior. First proposed by Akers in collaboration with Burgess in 1966, it is a version of the social learning view that employs differential association concepts as well as elements of psychological learning theory.

diffusion of benefits Efforts to prevent one crime help prevent another; in other instances, crime control efforts in one locale reduce crime in another area.

direct conditioning Behavior is reinforced by being either rewarded or punished while interacting with others; also called differential reinforcement.

Director of National Intelligence (DNI) Government official charged with coordinating data from the nation's primary intelligence-gathering agencies.

discouragement Crime control efforts targeting a particular locale help reduce crime in surrounding areas and populations.

disorders Any type of psychological problems (formerly labeled neuroses or psychoses), such as anxiety disorders, mood disorders, and conduct disorders.

displacement A program that helps lower crime rates at specific locations or neighborhoods may be redirecting offenders to alternative targets.

disputatiousness Behavior within culturally defined conflict situations in which an individual who has been offended by a negative outcome in a dispute seeks reparations through violent means.

diversion programs Programs of rehabilitation that remove offenders from the normal channels of the criminal justice system, thus avoiding the stigma of a criminal label.

dramatization of evil As the negative feedback of law enforcement agencies, parents, friends, teachers, and other figures amplifies the force of the original label, stigmatized offenders may begin to reevaluate their own identities. The person becomes the thing he is described as being.

drift According to Matza, the view that youths move in and out of delinquency and that their lifestyles can embrace both conventional and deviant values.

dropout factories High schools in which the completion rate is consistently 40 percent or less.

early onset A term that refers to the assumption that a criminal career begins early in life and that people who are deviant at a very young age are the ones most likely to persist in crime.

economic crime An act in violation of the criminal law that is designed to bring financial gain to the offender.

edgework The excitement or exhilaration of successfully executing illegal activities in dangerous situations.

egalitarian families Families in which spouses share similar positions of power at home and in the workplace.

ego The part of the personality, developed in early childhood, that helps control the id and keep people's actions within the boundaries of social convention.

ego ideal Part of the superego; directs the individual into morally acceptable and responsible behaviors, which may not be pleasurable.

ehooking Using the Internet to advertise sexual services and make contact with clients.

elder abuse A disturbing form of domestic violence by children and other relatives with whom elderly people live.

eldercide The murder of a senior citizen.

election fraud Illegal interference with the process of an election. Acts of fraud tend to involve affecting vote counts to bring about a desired election outcome, whether by increasing the vote share of the favored candidate, depressing the vote share of the rival candidates, or both. Varieties of election fraud include intimidation, disruption of polling places, distribution of misinformation such as the wrong election date, registration fraud, and vote buying.

Electra complex A stage of development when girls begin to have sexual feelings for their fathers.

electroencephalograph (EEG) A device that can record the electronic impulses given off by the brain, commonly called brain waves.

embezzlement A type of larceny that involves taking the possessions of another (fraudulent conversion) that have been placed in the thief's lawful possession for safekeeping, such as a bank teller misappropriating deposits or a stockbroker making off with a customer's account.

Enlightenment A philosophical, intellectual and cultural movement of the seventeenth and eighteenth centuries that stressed reason, logic, criticism, education and freedom of thought over dogma and superstition.

enterprise crimes The use of illegal tactics to gain profit in the marketplace. Enterprise crimes can involve both the violation of law in the course of an otherwise legitimate occupation or the sale and distribution of illegal commodities.

equipotentiality View that all individuals are equal at birth and are thereafter influenced by their environment.

eros The instinct to preserve and create life; eros is expressed sexually.

espionage The practice of obtaining information about a government, organization, or society that is considered secret or confidential without the permission of the holder of the information. Commonly called spying.

exploitation (of criminals) Using others to commit crimes: for example, as contract killers or drug runners.

exploitation (of victims) Forcing victims to pay for services to which they have a clear right.

expressive crimes Crimes that have no purpose except to accomplish the behavior at hand, such as shooting someone.

expressive violence Violence that is designed not for profit or gain but to vent rage, anger, or frustration.

false pretenses or fraud Misrepresenting a fact in a way that causes a deceived victim to give money or property to the offender.

felony murder A homicide in the context of another felony, such as robbery or rape; legally defined as first-degree murder.

fence A buyer and seller of stolen merchandise.

feticide Endangering or killing an unborn fetus.

filicide Murder of an older child.

fixated An adult who exhibits behavior traits characteristic of those encountered during infantile sexual development.

flash houses Public meeting places in England, often taverns, that served as headquarters for gangs.

flashover An effect in a fire when heat and gas at the ceiling of a room reach 2,000 degrees, and clothes and furniture burst into flame, duplicating the effects of arsonists' gasoline or explosives. It is possible that many suspected arsons are actually the result of flashover.

focal concerns According to Miller, the value orientations of lower-class cultures; features include the needs for excitement, trouble, smartness, and personal autonomy.

gang rape Forcible sex involving multiple attackers.

gateway model An explanation of drug abuse that posits that users begin with a more benign drug (alcohol or marijuana) and progress to more potent drugs.

general deterrence A crime control policy that depends on the fear of criminal penalties. General deterrence measures, such as long prison sentences for violent crimes, are aimed at convincing the potential law violator that the pains associated with crime outweigh its benefits.

general strain theory (GST) According to Agnew, the view that multiple sources of strain interact with an individual's emotional traits and responses to produce criminality.

General Theory of Crime (GTC) According to Gottfredson and Hirschi, a developmental theory that modifies social control theory by integrating concepts from biosocial, psychological, routine activities, and rational choice theories.

gentrification A residential renewal stage in which obsolete housing is replaced and upgraded; areas undergoing such change seem to experience an increase in their crime rates.

globalization The process of creating transnational markets, politics, and legal systems in an effort to form and sustain a global economy.

good burglar Professional burglars use this title to characterize colleagues who have distinguished themselves as burglars. Characteristics of the good burglar include technical competence, maintenance of personal integrity, specialization in burglary, financial success, and the ability to avoid prison sentences.

grand larceny Theft of money or property of substantial value, punished as a felony.

green-collar crime Acts involving illegal environmental harm that violate environmental laws and regulations.

guerilla The term means "little war" and developed out of the Spanish rebellion against French troops after Napoleon's 1808 invasion of the Iberian Peninsula. Today the term is used interchangeably with the term "terrorist."

hate or bias crimes Acts of violence or intimidation designed to terrorize or frighten people considered undesirable because of their race, religion, ethnic origin, or sexual orientation.

hedge fund A stock fund that uses aggressive strategies, including selling short, using leverage, interest rate swaps, arbitrage, and derivatives to hopefully earn above-average profits.

hot spots Places or areas in the city that have significantly higher crime rates than other areas and where crime is regular and frequent, rather than random and uncommon.

human rights Those personal, social, and economic rights and freedoms that should belong to all people.

humanistic psychology A branch of psychology that stresses self-awareness and "getting in touch with feelings."

id The primitive part of people's mental makeup, present at birth, that represents unconscious biological drives for food, sex, and other life-sustaining necessities. The id seeks instant gratification without concern for the rights of others.

identity crisis A psychological state, identified by Erikson, in which youth face inner turmoil and uncertainty about life roles.

imperatively coordinated associations These associations are composed of two groups: those who possess authority and use it for social domination, and those who lack authority and are dominated.

incapacitation effect The idea that keeping offenders in confinement will eliminate the risk of their committing further offenses.

incivilities Rude and uncivil behavior; behavior that indicates little caring for the feelings of others.

index crimes The eight crimes that, because of their seriousness and frequency, the FBI reports the incidence of in the annual Uniform Crime Report. Index crimes include murder, rape, assault, robbery, burglary, arson, larceny, and motor vehicle theft.

infanticide The murder of a very young child.

inferiority complex People who have feelings of inferiority and compensate for them with a drive for superiority.

influence peddling Using an institutional position to grant favors and sell information to which their co-conspirators are not entitled.

informal sanctions Disapproval, stigma, or anger directed toward an offender by significant others (parents, peers, neighbors, teachers), resulting in shame, embarrassment, and loss of respect.

information processing A branch of cognitive psychology that focuses on the way people process, store, encode, retrieve, and manipulate information to make decisions and solve problems.

inheritance school Advocates of this view trace the activities of several generations of families believed to have an especially large number of criminal members.

insider trading Illegal buying of stock in a company based on information provided by someone who has a fiduciary interest in the company, such as an employee or an attorney or accountant retained by the firm. Federal laws and the rules of the Securities and Exchange Commission require that all profits from such trading be returned and provide for both fines and a prison sentence.

institutional anomie theory The view that anomie pervades U.S. culture because the drive for material wealth dominates and undermines social and community values.

instrumental crimes Offenses designed to improve the financial or social position of the criminal.

instrumental theory The view that criminal law and the criminal justice system are capitalist instruments for controlling the lower class.

instrumental violence Violence used in an attempt to improve the financial or social position of the criminal.

insurgent The typical goal of an insurgency is to confront the existing government for control of all or a portion of its territory, or force political concessions in sharing political power. While terrorists may operate in small bands with a narrow focus, insurgents represent a popular movement and may also seek external support from other nations to bring pressure on the government.

integrated theories Models of crime causation that weave social and individual variables into a complex explanatory chain.

intelligence A person's ability to reason, comprehend ideas, solve problems, think abstractly, understand complex ideas, learn from experience, and discover solutions to complex problems.

interactionist view The view that one's perception of reality is significantly influenced by one's interpretations of the reactions of others to similar events and stimuli.

involuntary manslaughter A homicide that occurs as a result of acts that are negligent and without regard for the harm they may cause others, such as driving under the influence of alcohol or drugs.

just desert The philosophy of justice that asserts that those who violate the rights of others deserve to be punished. The severity of punishment should be commensurate with the seriousness of the crime.

justice The quality of being fair under the law. Justice is defined by the relationship that exists between the individual and the state; justice demands that the state treats every person as equally as possible without regard to their gender, religion, race, or any other personal status.

latency A developmental stage that begins at age 6. During this period, feelings of sexuality are repressed until the genital stage begins at puberty; this marks the beginning of adult sexuality.

latent delinquency A psychological predisposition to commit antisocial acts because of an id-dominated personality that renders an individual incapable of controlling impulsive, pleasure-seeking drives.

latent trait A stable feature, characteristic, property, or condition, present at birth or soon after, that makes some people crime prone over the life course.

latent trait theories Theoretical views that criminal behavior is controlled by a master trait, present at birth or soon after, that remains stable and unchanging throughout a person's lifetime.

learning disability (LD) A disorder in one or more of the basic psychological processes involved in understanding or using spoken or written languages.

left realism An approach that views crime as a function of relative deprivation under capitalism and that favors pragmatic, community-based crime prevention and control.

liberal feminism theory Theory suggesting that the traditionally lower crime rate for women can be explained by their second-class economic and social position. As women's social roles have changed and their lifestyles have become more like those of men, it is believed that their crime rates will converge.

life course persisters One of the small group of offenders whose criminal career continues well into adulthood.

life course theories Theoretical views studying changes in criminal offending patterns over a person's entire life.

lifestyle theory People may become crime victims because their lifestyle increases their exposure to criminal offenders.

lumpen proletariat The fringe members at the bottom of society who produce nothing and live, parasitically, off the work of others.

madam A woman who employs prostitutes, supervises their behavior, and receives a fee for her services.

mala in se Acts that are outlawed because they violate basic moral values, such as rape, murder, assault, and robbery.

mala prohibitum Acts that are outlawed because they clash with current norms and public opinion, such as tax, traffic, and drug laws.

manslaughter A homicide without malice.

marginal deterrence The concept that a penalty for a crime may prompt commission of a marginally more severe crime because that crime receives the same magnitude of punishment as the original one.

marginalization Displacement of workers, pushing them outside the economic and social mainstream.

marital exemption The practice in some states of prohibiting the prosecution of husbands for the rape of their wives.

marital rape Forcible sex between people who are legally married to each other.

mark The target of a con man or woman.

masculinity hypothesis The view that women who commit crimes have biological and psychological traits similar to those of men.

mass murder The killing of a large number of people in a single incident by an offender who typically does not seek concealment or escape.

mechanical solidarity A characteristic of a preindustrial society, which is held together by traditions, shared values, and unquestioned beliefs.

meta-analysis A research technique that uses the grouped data from several different studies.

middle-class measuring rods According to Cohen, the standards by which teachers and other representatives of state authority evaluate lower-class youths. Because they cannot live up to middle-class standards, lower-class youths are bound for failure, which gives rise to frustration and anger at conventional society.

minimal brain dysfunction (MBD) An abruptly appearing, maladaptive behavior that interrupts an individual's lifestyle and life flow. In its most serious form, MBD has been linked to serious antisocial acts, an imbalance in the urge-control mechanisms of the brain, and chemical abnormality.

Minnesota Multiphasic Personality Inventory (MMPI) A widely used psychological test that has subscales designed to measure many different personality traits, including psychopathic deviation (Pd scale), schizophrenia (Sc scale), and hypomania (Ma scale).

mission hate crimes Violent crimes committed by disturbed individuals who see it as their duty to rid the world of evil.

moral crusaders People who strive to stamp out behavior they find objectionable. Typically, moral crusaders are directed at public order crimes, such as drug abuse or pornography.

moral development The way people morally represent and reason about the world.

moral entrepreneurs Interest groups that attempt to control social life and the legal order in such a way as to promote their own personal set of moral values. People who use their influence to shape the legal process in ways they see fit.

motivated offenders The potential offenders in a population. According to rational choice theory, crime rates will vary according to the number of motivated offenders.

Multidimensional Personality Questionnaire (MPQ) A test that allows researchers to assess such personality traits as control, aggression, alienation, and well-being. Evaluations using this scale indicate that adolescent offenders who are crime prone maintain negative emotionality, a tendency to experience aversive affective states such as anger, anxiety, and irritability.

murder The unlawful killing of a human being (homicide) with malicious intent.

naive check forgers Amateurs who cash bad checks because of some financial crisis but have little identification with a criminal subculture.

narcissistic personality disorder A condition marked by a persistent pattern of self-importance, need for admiration, lack of empathy, and preoccupation with fantasies of unlimited success, power, brilliance, beauty, or ideal love.

National Crime Victimization Survey (NCVS) The ongoing victimization study conducted jointly by the Justice Department and the U.S. Census Bureau that surveys victims about their experiences with law violation.

National Incident-Based Reporting System (NIBRS) A program that requires local police agencies to provide a brief account of each incident and arrest within 22 crime patterns, including incident, victim, and offender information.

nature theory The view that intelligence is largely determined genetically and that low intelligence is linked to criminal behavior.

negative affective states According to Agnew, anger, depression, disappointment, fear, and other adverse emotions that derive from strain.

negative reinforcement Using either negative stimuli (punishment) or loss of reward (negative punishment) to curtail unwanted behaviors.

neglect Not providing a child with the care and shelter to which he or she is entitled.

negligent manslaughter A homicide that occurs as a result of acts that are negligent and without regard for the harm they may cause others, such as driving under the influence of alcohol or drugs; also called involuntary manslaughter.

neocortex A part of the human brain; the left side of the neocortex controls sympathetic feelings toward others.

networks When referring to terrorist organizations, networks are loosely organized groups located in different parts of the city, state, or country (or world) that share a common theme or purpose, but have a diverse leadership and command structure and are only in intermittent communication with one another.

neuroallergies Allergies that affect the nervous system and cause the allergic person to produce enzymes that attack wholesome foods as if they were dangerous to the body. They may also cause swelling of the brain and produce sensitivity in the central nervous system—conditions that are linked to mental, emotional, and behavioral problems.

neurophysiology The study of brain activity.

neutralization theory Neutralization theory holds that offenders adhere to conventional values while "drifting" into periods of illegal behavior. In order to drift, people must first overcome (neutralize) legal and moral values.

nonnegligent manslaughter A homicide committed in the heat of passion or during a sudden quarrel; although intent may be present, malice is not; also called voluntary manslaughter.

nurture theory The view that intelligence is not inherited but is largely a product of environment. Low IQ scores do not cause crime but may result from the same environmental factors.

obscenity According to current legal theory, sexually explicit material that lacks a serious purpose and appeals solely to the prurient interest of the viewer. While nudity per se is not usually considered obscene, open sexual behavior, masturbation, and exhibition of the genitals is banned in most communities.

obsessive-compulsive disorder An extreme preoccupation with certain thoughts and compulsive performance of certain behaviors.

occasional criminals Offenders who do not define themselves by a criminal role or view themselves as committed career criminals.

Oedipus complex A stage of development when males begin to have sexual feelings for their mothers.

offender-specific crime The idea that offenders evaluate their skills, motives, needs, and fears before deciding to commit crime.

offense-specific crime The idea that offenders react selectively to the characteristics of particular crimes.

oral stage In Freud's schema, the first year of life, when a child attains pleasure by sucking and biting.

organic solidarity Postindustrial social systems, which are highly developed and dependent upon the division of labor; people are connected by their interdependent needs for one another's services and production.

organizational crime Crime that involves large corporations and their efforts to control the marketplace and earn huge profits through unlawful bidding, unfair advertising, monopolistic practices, or other illegal means.

overt pathway Pathway to a criminal career that begins with minor aggression, leads to physical fighting, and eventually escalates to violent crime.

paranoid schizophrenics Individuals who suffer complex behavior delusions involving wrongdoing or persecution—they think everyone is out to get them.

paraphilias Bizarre or abnormal sexual practices that may involve recurrent sexual urges focused on objects, humiliation, or children.

parental efficacy Parenting that is supportive, effective, and noncoercive.

Part I crimes Another term for index crimes; eight categories of serious, frequent crimes.

Part II crimes All crimes other than index and minor traffic offenses. The FBI records annual arrest information for Part II offenses.

passive precipitation The view that some people become victims because of personal and social characteristics that make them attractive targets for predatory criminals.

paternalistic families Traditional family model in which fathers assume the role of breadwinners, while mothers tend to have menial jobs or remain at home to supervise domestic matters.

patriarchy A society in which men dominate public, social, economic, and political affairs.

payola Bribery of an influential person in exchange for the promotion of a product or service, such as giving radio disc jockeys payments to play songs.

peacemaking An approach that considers punitive crime control strategies to be counterproductive and favors the use of humanistic conflict resolution to prevent and control crime.

permeable neighborhood Areas with a greater than usual number of access streets from traffic arteries into the neighborhood.

persistence The idea that those who started their delinquent careers early and who committed serious violent crimes throughout adolescence were the most likely to persist as adults.

personality The reasonably stable patterns of behavior, including thoughts and emotions, that distinguish one person from another.

petit (petty) larceny Theft of a small amount of money or property, punished as a misdemeanor.

phallic stage In Freud's schema, the third year, when children focus their attention on their genitals.

pigeon drop A con game in which a package or wallet containing money is "found" by a con man or woman. A passing victim is stopped and asked for advice about what to do, and soon another "stranger," who is part of the con, approaches and enters the discussion. The three decide to split the money; but first, one of the swindlers goes off to consult a lawyer. The lawyer claims the money can be split up, but each party must prove he or she has the means to reimburse the original owner, should one show up. The victim then is asked to give some good-faith money for the lawyer to hold. When the victim goes to the lawyer's office to pick up a share of the loot, he or she finds the address bogus and the money gone. In the new millennium, the pigeon drop has been appropriated by corrupt telemarketers, who contact typically elderly victims over the phone to bilk them out of their savings.

pilferage Theft by employees through stealth or deception.

pleasure principle According to Freud, a theory in which id-dominated people are driven to increase their personal pleasure without regard to consequences.

poachers Early English thieves who typically lived in the country and supplemented their diet and income with game that belonged to a landlord.

political crime Illegal acts that are designed to undermine an existing government and threaten its survival. Political crimes can include both violent and nonviolent acts and range in seriousness from dissent, treason, and espionage to violent acts such as terrorism or assassination.

Ponzi scheme An investment fraud that involves the payment of purported returns to existing investors from funds contributed by new investors.

population All people who share a particular personal characteristic, such as all high school students or all police officers.

pornography Sexually explicit books, magazines, films, or tapes intended to provide sexual titillation and excitement for paying customers.

positivism The branch of social science that uses the scientific method of the natural sciences and suggests that human behavior is a product of social, biological, psychological, or economic forces.

posttraumatic stress disorder (PTSD) Psychological reaction to a highly stressful event; symptoms may include depression, anxiety, flashbacks, and recurring nightmares.

power–control theory The view that gender differences in crime are a function of economic power (class position, one-earner versus two-earner families) and parental control (paternalistic versus egalitarian families).

premeditation Consideration of a homicide before it occurs.

premenstrual syndrome (PMS) The stereotype that several days prior to and during menstruation

females are beset by irritability and poor judgment as a result of hormonal changes.

primary deviance According to Lemert, deviant acts that do not help redefine the self-image and public image of the offender.

primary prevention programs Treatment programs that seek to correct or remedy personal problems before they manifest themselves as crime.

problem behavior syndrome (PBS) A cluster of antisocial behaviors that may include family dysfunction, substance abuse, smoking, precocious sexuality and early pregnancy, educational underachievement, suicide attempts, sensation seeking, and unemployment, as well as crime.

procedural criminal law Those laws that set out the basic rules of practice in the criminal justice system. Some elements of the law of criminal procedure are the rules of evidence, the law of arrest, the law of search and seizure, questions of appeal, jury selection, and the right to counsel.

productive forces Technology, energy sources, and material resources.

productive relations The relationships that exist among the people producing goods and services.

professional criminals Offenders who make a significant portion of their income from crime.

professional fence An individual who earns his or her living solely by buying and reselling stolen merchandise.

proletariat A term used by Marx to refer to the working-class members of society who produce goods and services but who do not own the means of production.

prostitution The granting of nonmarital sexual access for remuneration.

psychoanalytic or psychodynamic perspective Branch of psychology holding that the human personality is controlled by unconscious mental processes developed early in childhood.

psychopath A person with an antisocial personality disorder, who is aggressive, violent, criminal, amoral, and who lacks empathy with other people.

psychopathic personality A personality characterized by a lack of warmth and feeling, inappropriate behavior responses, and an inability to learn from experience. Some psychologists view psychopathy as a result of childhood trauma; others see it as a result of biological abnormality.

psychosis A mental state in which the perception of reality is distorted. People experiencing psychosis hallucinate, have paranoid or delusional beliefs, change personality, exhibit disorganized thinking, and engage in unusual or bizarre behavior.

public (or administrative) law The branch of law that deals with the government and its relationships with individuals or other governments. It governs the administration and regulation of city, county, state, and federal government agencies.

public order crimes Acts that are considered illegal because they threaten the general well-being of society and challenge its accepted moral principles. Prostitution, drug use, and the sale of pornography are considered public order crimes.

racial profiling Selecting suspects on the basis of their ethnic or racial background.

racial threat hypothesis The belief that as the percentage of minorities in the population increases, so too does the amount of social control that police direct at minority group members.

rational choice The view that crime is a function of a decision-making process in which the potential offender weighs the potential costs and benefits of an illegal act.

reaction formation According to Cohen, rejecting goals and standards that seem impossible to achieve. Because a boy cannot hope to get into college, for example, he considers higher education a waste of time.

reactive (defensive) hate crimes Perpetrators believe they are taking a defensive stand against outsiders whom they believe threaten their community or way of life.

reality principle According to Freud, the ability to learn about the consequences of one's actions through experience.

reasoning criminal According to the rational choice approach, law-violating behavior occurs when an offender decides to risk breaking the law after considering both personal factors (such as the need for money, revenge, thrills, and entertainment) and situational factors (how well a target is protected and the efficiency of the local police force).

reciprocal altruism According to sociobiology, acts that are outwardly designed to help others but that have at their core benefits to the self.

recruiters Experienced criminals who seek out younger, less-experienced novices to train and mentor in criminal activity.

reflected appraisals When parents are alienated from their children, their negative labeling reduces their children's self-image and increases delinquency.

Reign of Terror The origin of the term "terrorism," the French Revolution's Reign of Terror began in 1795 and was initiated by the revolutionary government during which agents of the Committee of Public Safety and the National Convention were referred to as terrorists.

reintegrative shaming A method of correction that encourages offenders to confront their misdeeds, experience shame because of the harm they caused, and then be reincluded in society.

relative deprivation The condition that exists when people of wealth and poverty live in close proximity to one another. Some criminologists attribute crime rate differentials to relative deprivation.

restitution agreements Conditions of probation in which the offenders repay society or the victims of crime for the trouble the offenders caused. Monetary restitution involves a direct payment to the victim as a form of compensation. Community service restitution may be used in victimless crimes and involves work in the community in lieu of more severe criminal penalties.

restorative justice Using humanistic, nonpunitive strategies to right wrongs and restore social harmony.

retaliatory hate crimes A hate crime motivated by revenge for another hate crime, either real or imaginary, which may spark further retaliation.

retributive terrorists Terror groups who refrain from tying specific acts to direct demands for change. They want to instead redirect the balance between what they believe is good and evil. They see their revolution as existing on a spiritual plane; their mission is to exact retribution against sinners.

retrospective cohort study A study that uses an intact cohort of known offenders and looks back into their early life experiences by checking their educational, family, police, and hospital records.

retrospective reading The reassessment of a person's past to fit a current generalized label.

road rage A term used to describe motorists who assault each other.

role exit behaviors In order to escape from a stifling life in male-dominated families, girls may try to break away by running away and or even attempting suicide.

routine activities theory The view that the volume and distribution of predatory crime are closely related to the interaction of suitable targets, motivated offenders, and capable guardians.

sadistic personality disorder A repeat pattern of cruel and demeaning behavior. People suffering from this type of extreme personality disturbance seem prone to engage in serious violent attacks, including homicides motivated by sexual sadism.

sampling Selecting a limited number of people for study as representative of a larger group.

schizophrenia A type of psychosis often marked by bizarre behavior, hallucinations, loss of thought control, and inappropriate emotional responses. Schizophrenic types include catatonic, which characteristically involves impairment of motor activity; paranoid, which is characterized by delusions of persecution; and hebephrenic, which is characterized by immature behavior and giddiness.

scientific method Using verifiable principles and procedures for the systematic acquisition of knowledge; typically involves formulating a problem, creating a hypothesis, and collecting data through observation and experiment to verify the hypothesis.

secondary deviance According to Lemert, accepting deviant labels as a personal identity. Acts become secondary when they form a basis for self-concept, as when a drug experimenter becomes an addict.

secondary prevention programs Treatment programs aimed at helping offenders after they have been identified.

second-degree murder A homicide with malice but not premeditation or deliberation, as when a desire to inflict serious bodily harm and a wanton disregard for life result in the victim's death.

securitization The process in which vendors take individual subprime loans and bundle them into large pools and sell them as securities.

self-control A strong moral sense that renders a person incapable of hurting others or violating social norms.

self-control theory According to Gottfredson and Hirschi, the view that the cause of delinquent behavior is an impulsive personality. Kids who are impulsive may find that their bond to society is weak.

self-report survey A research approach that requires subjects to reveal their own participation in delinquent or criminal acts.

sentencing circle A peacemaking technique in which offenders, victims, and other community members are brought together in an effort to formulate a sanction that addresses the needs of all.

serial killer The killing of a large number of people over time by an offender who seeks to escape detection.

serial rape Multiple rapes committed by one person over time.

sexual abuse Exploitation of a child through rape, incest, or molestation by a parent or other adult.

shame The feeling we get when we don't meet the standards we have set for ourselves or that significant others have set for us.

Sherman Antitrust Act Law that subjects to criminal or civil sanctions any person "who shall make any contract or engage in any combination or conspiracy" in restraint of interstate commerce.

shield laws Laws designed to protect rape victims by prohibiting the defense attorney from inquiring about their previous sexual relationships.

shoplifting The taking of goods from retail stores.

siege mentality Residents who become so suspicious of authority that they consider the outside world to be the enemy out to destroy the neighborhood.

situational crime prevention A method of crime prevention that stresses tactics and strategies to eliminate or reduce particular crimes in narrow settings, such as reducing burglaries in a housing project by increasing lighting and installing security alarms.

situational inducement Short-term influence on a person's behavior, such as financial problems or peer pressure, that increases risk taking.

skeezers Prostitutes who trade sex for drugs, usually crack.

skilled thieves Thieves who typically work in the larger cities, such as London and Paris. This group includes pickpockets, forgers, and counterfeiters, who operated freely.

smugglers Thieves who move freely in sparsely populated areas and transport goods, such as spirits, gems, gold, and spices, without bothering to pay tax or duty.

snitches Amateur shoplifters who do not self-identify as thieves but who systematically steal merchandise for personal use.

social bond Ties a person has to the institutions and processes of society. According to Hirschi, elements of the social bond include commitment, attachment, involvement, and belief.

social capital Positive relations with individuals and institutions that are life sustaining.

social control theory The view that people commit crime when the forces that bind them to society are weakened or broken.

social disorganization theory Branch of social structure theory that focuses on the breakdown of institutions such as the family, school, and employment in inner-city neighborhoods.

social harm A view that behaviors harmful to other people and society in general must be controlled. These acts are usually outlawed, but some acts that cause enormous amounts of social harm are perfectly legal, such as the consumption of tobacco and alcohol.

social learning theory The view that human behavior is modeled through observation of human social interactions, either directly from observing those who are close and from intimate contact, or indirectly through the media. Interactions that are rewarded are copied, while those that are punished are avoided.

social process theory The view that criminality is a function of people's interactions with various organizations, institutions, and processes in society.

social reaction theory (labeling theory) The view that people become criminals when significant members of society label them as such and they accept those labels as a personal identity. Also known as labeling theory.

social structure theory The view that disadvantaged economic class position is a primary cause of crime.

socialization The interactions people have with various organizations, institutions, and processes of society.

sociobiology The scientific study of the determinants of social behavior, based on the view that such behavior is influenced by both the individual's genetic makeup and interactions with the environment.

sociological social psychology The study of human interactions and relationships, emphasizing such issues as group dynamics and socialization.

sociopath Personality disorder characterized by superficial charm and glibness, a lack of empathy for others, amoral conduct, and lack of shame, guilt, or remorse for antisocial behavior. The term may be used interchangeably with *psychopath*, but both terms have been replaced by *antisocial behavior disorder*.

somatotype A system developed for categorizing people on the basis of their body build.

specific deterrence A crime control policy suggesting that punishment be severe enough to convince convicted offenders never to repeat their criminal activity.

stalking A pattern of behavior directed at a specific person that includes repeated physical or visual proximity, unwanted communications, and/or threats sufficient to cause fear in a reasonable person.

stalking statutes Laws that prohibit "the willful, malicious, and repeated following and harassing of another person."

state dependence The propensity to commit crime profoundly and permanently disrupts normal socialization. Early rule breaking strengthens criminal motivation and increases the probability of future rule breaking.

state (organized) crime Acts defined by law as criminal and committed by state officials, both elected or appointed, in pursuit of their jobs as government representatives.

state political crime Political crime that arises from the efforts of the state to either maintain governmental power or to uphold the race, class, and gender advantages of those who support the government. It is possible to divide state political crimes into five varieties: (1) political corruption, (2) illegal domestic surveillance, (3) human rights violations, (4) state violence such as torture, illegal imprisonment, police violence and use of deadly force, and (5) state corporate crime committed by individuals who abuse their state authority or who fail to exercise it when working with people and organizations in the private sector.

state-sponsored terrorism Terrorism that occurs when a repressive government regime forces its citizens into obedience, oppresses minorities, and stifles political dissent.

status frustration A form of culture conflict experienced by lower-class youths because social conditions prevent them from achieving success as defined by the larger society.

statutory rape Sexual relations between an underage individual and an adult; though not coerced, an underage partner is considered incapable of giving informed consent.

stigma An enduring label that taints a person's identity and changes him or her in the eyes of others.

strain The emotional turmoil and conflict caused when people believe they cannot achieve their desires and goals through legitimate means. Members of the lower class might feel strain because they are denied access to adequate educational opportunities and social support.

strain theory Branch of social structure theory that sees crime as a function of the conflict between people's goals and the means available to obtain them.

stratified society Grouping according to social strata or levels. American society is considered stratified on the basis of economic class and wealth.

street crime Common theft-related offenses such as larcenies and burglaries, embezzlement, and theft by false pretenses.

street efficacy A concept in which more cohesive communities with high levels of social control and social integration foster the ability for kids to use their wits to avoid violent confrontations and to feel safe in their own neighborhood. Adolescents with high levels of street efficacy are less likely to resort to violence themselves or to associate with delinquent peers.

structural theory The view that criminal law and the criminal justice system are means of defending and preserving the capitalist system.

subculture of violence Norms and customs that, in contrast to society's dominant value system, legitimize and expect the use of violence to resolve social conflicts.

subcultures Groups that are loosely part of the dominant culture but maintain a unique set of values, beliefs, and traditions.

substantive criminal law The branch of the law that defines crimes and their punishment. It involves such issues as the mental and physical elements of crime, crime categories, and criminal defenses.

subterranean values Morally tinged influences that have become entrenched in the culture but are publicly condemned. They exist side by side with conventional values and while condemned in public may be admired or practiced in private.

sufferance The aggrieved party does nothing to rectify a conflict situation; over time, the unresolved conflict may be compounded by other events that cause an eventual eruption.

suitable target According to routine activities theory, a target for crime that is relatively valuable, easily transportable, and not capably guarded.

superego Incorporation within the personality of the moral standards and values of parents, community, and significant others.

supranational criminology Comprising the study of war crimes, crimes against humanity, and the penal system in which such crimes are prosecuted and tried.

symbolic interaction theory The sociological view that people communicate through symbols. People interpret symbolic communication and incorporate it within their personality. A person's view of reality, then, depends on his or her interpretation of symbolic gestures.

synthesis A merger of two opposing ideas.

systematic forgers Professionals who make a living by passing bad checks.

systematic review A research technique that involves collecting the findings from previously conducted studies, appraising and synthesizing the evidence, and using the collective evidence to address a particular scientific question.

target hardening strategies Making one's home or business crime proof through the use of locks, bars, alarms, and other devices.

target removal strategies Displaying dummy or disabled goods as a means of preventing shoplifting.

temperance movement An effort to prohibit the sale of liquor in the United States that resulted in the passage of the Eighteenth Amendment to the Constitution in 1919, which prohibited the sale of alcoholic beverages.

terror cells Divisions of terrorist group affiliates, each of which may be functionally independent so that each member has little knowledge of other cells, their members, locations, and so on. The number of cells and their composition depend on

the size of the terrorist group. Local or national groups will have fewer cells than international terrorist groups that may operate in several countries, such as the al-Qaeda group.

terrorism The illegal use of force against innocent people to achieve a political objective.

tertiary prevention programs Crime control and prevention programs that may be a requirement of a probation order, part of a diversionary sentence, or aftercare at the end of a prison sentence.

testosterone The principal male steroid hormone. Testosterone levels decline during the life cycle and may explain why violence rates diminish over time.

thanatos According to Freud, the instinctual drive toward aggression and violence.

theory of anomie A modified version of the concept of anomie developed by Merton to fit social, economic, and cultural conditions found in modern U.S. society. He found that two elements of culture interact to produce potentially anomic conditions: culturally defined goals and socially approved means for obtaining them.

thesis In the philosophy of Hegel, an original idea or thought.

three strikes Policies whereby people convicted of three felony offenses receive a mandatory life sentence.

thrill-seeking hate crimes Acts by hatemongers who join forces to have fun by bashing minorities or destroying property; inflicting pain on others gives them a sadistic thrill.

ticking bomb scenario A scenario that some experts argue in which torture can perhaps be justified if the government discovers that a captured terrorist knows the whereabouts of a dangerous explosive device that is set to go off and kill thousands of innocent people.

torture An act that causes severe pain or suffering, whether physical or mental, that is intentionally inflicted on a person for such purposes as obtaining a confession, punishing them for a crime they may have committed, or intimidating or coercing them into a desired action.

trait theory The view that criminality is a product of abnormal biological and/or psychological traits.

trajectory theory A view of criminal career formation that holds there are multiple paths to crime.

transitional neighborhood Areas undergoing a shift in population and structure, usually from middle-class residential to lower-class mixed use.

treason An act of disloyalty to one's nation or state.

truly disadvantaged Wilson's term for the lowest level of the underclass; urban, inner-city, socially isolated people who occupy the bottom rung of the social ladder and are the victims of discrimination.

turning points According to Laub and Sampson, the life events that alter the development of a criminal career.

underclass The lowest social stratum in any country, whose members lack the education and skills needed to function successfully in modern society.

Uniform Crime Report (UCR) Large database, compiled by the Federal Bureau of Investigation, of crimes reported and arrests made each year throughout the United States.

USA Patriot Act (USAPA) Legislation giving U.S. law enforcement agencies a freer hand to investigate and apprehend suspected terrorists.

victim compensation The victim ordinarily receives compensation from the state to pay for damages associated with the crime. Rarely are two

compensation schemes alike, however, and many state programs suffer from lack of both adequate funding and proper organization within the criminal justice system. Compensation may be made for medical bills, loss of wages, loss of future earnings, and counseling. In the case of death, the victim's survivors can receive burial expenses and aid for loss of support.

victim precipitation theory The idea that the victim's behavior was the spark that ignited the subsequent offense, as when the victim abused the offender verbally or physically.

victimization (by the justice system) While the crime is still fresh in their minds, victims may find that the police interrogation following the crime is handled callously, with innuendos or insinuations that they were somehow at fault. Victims have difficulty learning what is going on in the case; property is often kept for a long time as evidence and may never be returned. Some rape victims report that the treatment they receive from legal, medical, and mental health services is so destructive that they cannot help but feel "re-raped."

victimless crimes Crimes that violate the moral order but in which there is no actual victim or target. In these crimes, which include drug abuse and sex offenses, it is society as a whole and not an individual who is considered the victim.

victimologists People who study the victim's role in criminal transactions.

victim-witness assistance programs Government programs that help crime victims and witnesses; may include compensation, court services, and/or crisis intervention.

vigilantes Individuals who go on moral crusades without any authorization from legal authorities. The assumption is that it is okay to take matters into your own hands if the cause is right and the target is immoral.

violentization process According to Lonnie Athens, the process by which abused children are turned into aggressive adults. This process takes violent youths full circle from being the victims of aggression to its initiators; they are now the same person they grew up despising, ready to begin the process with their own children.

virility mystique The belief that males must separate their sexual feelings from needs for love, respect, and affection.

white-collar client fraud Theft by a client from an organization that advances credit or reimburses for services rendered. These offenses involve cheating an organization that supports, reimburses, or extends credit to clients.

white-collar crime Illegal acts that capitalize on a person's status in the marketplace. White-collar crimes can involve theft, embezzlement, fraud, market manipulation, restraint of trade, and false advertising.

white-collar swindle A crime in which people use a business proposition to trick others out of their money.

workplace violence Irate employees or former employees attack coworkers or sabotage machinery and production lines; now considered the third leading cause of occupational injury or death.

Zealot The original Zealots were Hebrew warrior groups active during the Roman occupation of Palestine during the first century BCE. Today the term commonly refers to a fanatical or over-idealistic follower of a political or religious cause.

Case Index

Name Index

Blankenship, Michael, 261n117; 475n130
Blanton, Zachariah, 165
Blau, Judith, 66n70; 225n154
Blau, Peter, 66n70; 225n154
Blevins, Kristie R., 327n58; 330n153
Blickle, Gerhard, 181n263
Block, Carolyn Rebecca, 358; 516n198
Block, Richard, 66n70; 225n156
Blodget, Henry, 473n45
Blokland, Arjan, 329n152
Blount, William, 369n46
Blumer, Herbert, 26n18; 249–250; 262n166
Blumstein, Alfred, 45; 66n41; 137n201
Boba, Rachel, 85
Boehm, Christopher, 368n13
Boehnke, Klaus, 226n170
Boesky, Ivan, 468, 469
Bogaerts, Jef, 259n30
Bohm, Robert, 271; 292n26
Boland, John, 473n36
Bolen, Rebecca M., 371n130
Bolland, Patrick, 278
Bonacci, Angelica, 371n134
Bonaguro, John, 517n206
Bond, Dale, 330n179
Bonett, Douglas, 177n95
Bonger, William, 269
Bonkiewicz, Luke, 336–337; 369n30
Bonn, Scott, 275
Bonnie, Richard, 161
Bonta, James, 179n191; 180n221
Bontrager, Sephanie, 263n198
Bookless, Clara, 180n224
Booth, Alan, 67n101; 176nn54, 59
Booth, William, 555n125
Borgatta, E., 67n89
Boruch, Victor, 27n44
Borum, Randy, 26n12; 180n228; 373n190; 380–381; 400; 409n9; 410n68
Bosket, Willie, 59
Botchkovar, Ekaterina, 67n84; 259n45
Bothwell, Robert, 372n145
Botsis, A., 178n138
Bottcher, Jean, 67n103
Bottomore, P. B., 292n7
Bouchard, Thomas, 179n164
Boudin, Eugene, 412
Boudreau, Abbie, 174n4
Bouffard, Jeffrey, 133nn31, 34
Boulerice, Bernard, 177n96
Bourgois, Philippe, 106; 133n33
Bourke, Michael, 493; 515n134
Boutwell, Brian, 178n148; 328n99
Bowden, Blake Sperry, 94n40
Bowlby, John, 158–159; 180nn195, 196
Bowling, Benjamin, 327n55
Box, Steven, 67n110; 292n40
Boyd, Carol, 516n183
Boyer, Richard, 439n41
Brack, Duncan, 474nn111, 112
Bradshaw, Catherine, 327n46
Bradley, Dana Burr, 517n206

Braga, Anthony A., 135nn144, 147; 136n175; 369n31; 372n172
Bragason, Ólafur Örn, 171
Braithwaite, John, 225n152; 286–287; 292n20; 294nn131, 132, 134, 136; 374n238; 473n30; 474nn90, 93
Braithwaite, Valerie, 294n134
Brame, Robert, 67n79; 263nn205, 210; 318; 326n22; 327nn51, 62; 328n82; 329nn114, 130, 144, 151; 330n169
Brammer, Michael, 171
Branch, Kathryn, 358
Branscomb, Anne, 553n42
Brantingham, Patricia, 134nn98, 110
Brantingham, Paul, 134nn98, 110
Bratton, William, 34
Brauer, Jonathan, 261n105
Braukmann, C., 328n80
Brecher, Edward, 513n28; 515n152
Breiling, James, 259n55
Breivik, Gunnar, 439n40
Brems, Christiane, 37; 65n27
Brennan, Patricia, 177n101; 178n142; 180n217; 369n40
Brennan, Robert T., 370n59
Brents, Barbara G., 514nn103, 104
Breslin, Beau, 295n145
Breverlin, Matt, 122–123
Brewer, Devon, 514n107
Brewer, Robert, 369n24
Brewer, Victoria, 66n67; 123; 136n200; 326n31
Brewster, Mary, 366; 375n292
Brezina, Timothy, 132n22; 176n58; 216; 226nn192, 194, 195, 202; 259nn48, 49; 330n162
Briar, Scott, 245; 261nn121, 124
Briere, John, 371n138; 513n48
Briken, Peer, 148; 177n99; 181nn264, 265
Brisman, Julissa, 478
Brison, Susan, 74; 94n31
Britain, R. P., 177n106
Britton, Lee, 69n161; 137n204
Broad, William J., 554n67
Broder, Paul, 178n117
Broidy, Lisa, 67n105; 180n207; 226nn201, 204, 205; 327n51
Bronner, Augusta, 169; 182n272
Bronte-Tinkew, Jacinta, 259n31
Brookman, Fiona, 112; 134n80
Brooks, Judith, 326n32; 516n176
Brooks-Gunn, Jeanne, 222nn22–25
Browdy, Jennifer, 373n204
Brown, Alan, 177n91
Brown, Alyson, 514nn85, 97
Brown, Charles, 135n137
Brown, Christopher M., 474n97
Brown, Garrett, 292n25
Brown, Jocelyn, 514nn86, 98
Brown, Roy, III, 372n145
Brown, Sandra, 260n74
Brown, Thomas, 178n119
Browne, Angela, 372nn174, 176

Browne, C., 180n216
Browne, Derek, 180n224
Brownfield, David, 95n79; 223n43; 261n107; 262n159; 328n104; 329n117
Browning, Christopher, 227n209
Brownmiller, Susan, 370n87
Brownstein, Henry, 369n22
Bruce, Marie, 28, 30; 30
Bryan, Nicole, 517n237
Bryant, Kobe, 348
Bryant, Susan Leslie, 94n21
Buchanan, Christy Miller, 176n57
Bucher, Jean-Luc, 120
Buchsbaum, Monte, 177n108; 178n115
Buck, Andrew, 97n142; 133n73
Buck, Philip, 369n26
Buddie, Amy, 371n115
Budtz-Jorgensen, E., 175n31
Bueno de Mesquita, Ethan, 410n71
Bufacchi, Vittorio, 409n27
Buffet, Warren, 207
Buitelaar, Jan, 176n61
Buker, Hasan, 176n55
Bukovec, Paul, 370n86
Bukowski, William, 95n87; 259n56
Bulger, James, 543
Bullogh, V., 513n52
Bulten, Erik, 175n37
Bundy, Theodore, 353
Burger, Timothy, 553n65
Burgess, Ann Wolbert, 371n110
Burgess, Ernest W., 188; 196; 197; 222nn13, 14
Burgess, Guy, 385
Burgess, P., 180n216
Burgess, Robert, 240; 260n96
Burke, Doris, 452
Burke, Jeffrey, 180n199
Burnette, Mandi, 514n94
Burns, Barbara, 180n228
Burns, John F., 552n8
Burns, Ronald, 375n287; 474nn83, 88
Burr, Aaron, 383
Burrell, Amy, 96nn99, 110; 133n28
Bursik, Robert, 135nn128, 152, 153; 223nn56, 61; 224nn105, 111; 225nn129, 138, 149; 328n104; 329n132
Burt, Callie Harbin, 329n126
Burton, Thomas, 473n50
Burton, Velmer, 67nn83, 102; 133n78; 226n184; 260n66; 262nn153, 155
Bush, George W., 120; 275; 384; 402; 404; 503
Bushman, Brad J., 45; 66n57; 162–163; 371n134
Bushway, Shawn D., 51; 67nn79, 81; 259nn42, 43; 263n210; 303–304; 327nn54, 64; 517nn209, 210
Buswell, Brenda, 67n102
Butcher, Kristin F., 68n150
Butterfield, Fox, 59; 68n135

Bynum, Timothy, 223n42; 224n79
Byrne, Donn, 179n189
Byrne, James, 135n122; 223n59; 224n81; 225nn122, 156
Byrne, John A., 456–457; 475n131

C

Cadoret, R. J., 179n170
Caeti, Tory, 134n108; 135n145
Cain, C., 179n170
Cain, Kevin, 136n187
Calafat, Antonia, 176n81
Calder, James, 374n245
Caldwell, Roslyn, 258n8
Calnon, Jennifer, 68nn119, 122
Calvan, Bobby Caina, 136n196
Cameron, Mary Owen, 423; 439n37
Campa, Mary, 327n46
Campbell, Alec, 517n236
Campbell, Anne, 67n111; 179n180; 328nn101, 102
Campbell, Doris, 358
Campbell, Jacquelyn, 358
Campbell, Luther, 16
Campbell, Neve, 365
Campbell, Rebecca, 96n126
Campbell, Rosie, 514n71
Campbell, Suzanne, 135n140
Campo-Flores, Arian, 222n1
Cancino, Jeffrey Michael, 66n73; 224nn113, 116
Canela-Cacho, Jose, 137n201
Canfield, Richard L., 176n81; 177n90
Cannon, Robert, 320
Cantor, David, 97n142
Cantor, James M., 513n45
Cao, Liqun, 370n66
Capachin, Jeanne, 554n85
Capaldi, Deborah, 259n55; 326n25; 369n39
Caplan, Joel, 89; 96n135
Capowich, George E., 225n130; 226n185
Carbonell, Joyce, 181n260
Cardona, George, 107
Cardoso, Maria R. A., 177n83
Carey, Gregory, 178n149; 179n165
Caringella-MacDonald, Susan, 294n105
Carlen, Pat, 293n90
Carlson, Robert, 517n208
Carney, Cormac J., 315
Carr, Alan, 516n168
Carr, Joetta, 515n128
Carradine, David, 483
Carrano, Jennifer, 259n31
Carrington, Frank, 97n153
Carrington, Tim, 474nn77, 78
Carrizo, Daniel, 176n80
Carrozza, Mark, 262n149
Carter, Ricki, 321
Carter, Sherry Plaster, 515n109
Carter, Stanley, 515n109
Cartier, Jerome, 517n214
Cartwright, Desmond, 261n114
Casebolt, Rachel, 508

Casey, Annie E., 190
Casey, Teresa, 308
Caspi, Avshalom, 66n72; 156; 179nn161, 184, 193; 182n270; 325n14; 326nn24, 31; 327n50; 330n165; 330nn174, 175
Cassell, Paul, 137n206
Castro-Rocha, Carlos Ramon, 541
Catalano, Richard, 259n50; 261n130; 305; 330n177; 516n191; 517n211
Catalano, Shannan, 65n8
Catan, Thomas, 474n103
Cauce, Mari, 95n76
Caudy, Michael S., 330n158
Cauffman, Elizabeth, 67n105; 180n207; 181n239; 329n138
Causey, Richard, 456
Cavanagh, Kevin, 177n86
Cecchi, Matthew, 112; 114
Cecil, Joe, 27n44
Cederblad, Marianne, 182n291
Cernkovich, Stephen, 65n31; 207–208; 226nn168, 188; 262n150; 303; 326n17; 327n53; 328n77; 330n176
Cetin, Mesut, 171
Chafetz, Janet Saltzman, 293nn93, 94
Chaiken, Marcia, 516n195
Chakravarti, Shamit, 410n52
Chalk, Peter, 410nn48, 50
Chambers, Robert, 168
Chambliss, William, 270; 292n15; 438n14
Chamlin, Mitchell, 135n128; 316–317; 329n134
Chan, Sewell, 475n129
Chan, Siu-Ching, 8; 26n10
Chan, Tony, 175n27
Chancer, Lynn, 293n87
Chaplin, Terry, 440n107
Chapman, Duane "Dog," 156
Chapman, Jane Roberts, 294n98
Chappell, Duncan, 65n9
Chard-Wierschem, Deborah, 66n76
Charlebois, P., 69n165
Chaseling, Janet, 440n104
Chayet, Ellen, 136n185
Chazan, Guy, 474n103
Chen, Bing Yi, 549
Chen, C.-Y., 224n83
Chen, Henian, 514nn86, 98
Chen, Jieming, 260n81
Chen, Jieru, 375n288
Chen, Xiaojin, 330n154; 516n184
Chen, Yi Fu, 226n178
Cheng, Zhongqi, 175n34
Cherbonneau, Michael, 361; 374nn249, 250
Chermak, Steven, 68n129
Chesney-Lind, Meda, 293nn90, 92; 294n105
Cheuk, D. K. L., 145; 175n35
Chiesi, Danielle, 452
Chilcoat, Howard, 326n39
Chilton, Roland, 262n178
Chin, Ko-lin, 554nn105, 120

Chiricos, Theodore, 67n80; 135nn128, 151; 200; 224nn91, 92, 94; 263n198; 293n64
Cho, Adrian, 473n53
Cho, Seung-Hui, 84; 138, 140; 354
Chon, Don, 370n79
Choudhury, Muhtashem, 473n33
Christakos, Antigone, 516n198
Christensen, Bruce K., 513n45
Christenson, Cornelia, 371n132
Christenson, R. L., 259n42
Christiansen, A., 516n185
Christodoulou, G., 178n138
Chronis, Andrea, 258n27
Chung, He Len, 326n37
Chung, Ick-Joong, 329nn146, 150
Churchill, Winston, 495
Cirillo, Kathleen, 181nn250, 255; 182n290
Clapper, James R., 402
Clark, John, 65n35
Clark, Jonathan Preston, 522
Clark, Richard D., 135n156
Clark-Daniels, Carolyn, 135nn130, 135
Clarke, Amory, 171
Clarke, Gregory N., 180n202
Clarke, Ronald V., 97n140; 116; 117; 132n19; 133n36; 134nn102, 104, 105, 107, 115, 117; 135n122; 439nn61, 67; 440n102
Clarke-Stewart, K. Alison, 175n27
Clason, Dennis L., 261n104
Classen, Gabriele, 226n170
Clay-Warner, Jody, 371n96
Clayton, Richard, 373n188; 517n243
Clear, Todd, 372n155
Cleckley, Hervey, 170–171
Clements, Benedict, 410n52
Cleveland, H. Harrington, 182n273
Clinard, Marshall, 473n47
Clines, Francis X., 373n211
Clingempeel, Glenn, 327n45
Clinton, Monique, 369n26
Clooney, George, 414
Cloward, Richard, 217–218; 219; 227nn227–233
Coatsworth, Douglas, 94n40
Cocchetti, Dante, 259n34
Cochran, John, 133n26; 134n95; 261n141; 328n104; 358
Cogan, Jeanine, 374n263
Cohen, Albert, 214–217; 225n162
Cohen, Jacqueline, 26n7; 66n41; 95n83; 133n61; 135n143; 137n201
Cohen, Lawrence, 83, 84–85; 96nn97, 108; 179n171
Cohen, Mark A., 93nn5, 8; 474n101; 553n32
Cohen, Morris, 480; 513n12
Cohen, Patricia, 326n32; 514nn86, 98
Cohen, Robert, 95n86; 260n64
Cohen-Bendahan, Celina, 176n61
Cohen-Kettenis, Peggy, 176n61
Cohn, Albert, 227nn218–221, 223–225
Cohn, Bob, 515n142

Cohn, Ellen, 66nn55, 59, 61
Cohn, Steven, 224n112
Cole, Christopher, 474n118
Coley, Rebekah Levine, 225n127
Coll, Xavier, 326n23
Colletti, Patrick, 177n97
Collier-Tenison, Shannon, 515n130
Collin, Barry, 554n70
Collins, James, 369n25
Collins, Mark, 327n65
Collins, Randall, 336; 369n17
Colony, Catherine, 368n3
Colvin, Mark, 382n86
Colwell, Brian, 181n250; 182n290
Colwell, Lori, 65n26
Comer, James, 68n134
Comiskey, Brendan, 484
Comstock, George, 162–163
Comte, Auguste, 141
Conger, Katherine, 232
Conger, Rand D., 232; 258n7; 259n36; 329n128; 369nn45, 54
Conklin, John, 176n73
Conoscenti, Lauren M., 343
Conroy, Jeffrey, 362
Conway, Kevin P., 330n170
Conwell, Chic, 417–418; 438nn17–19
Cook, Kimberly, 132n18
Cook, Philip, 369n31; 372n172
Cook Sarah, 371n97
Cook Wesley, 278
Cook William, 278
Cooke, Alistair, 422
Cooley, Charles Horton, 14; 249–250; 262n166
Coomer, Brandi Wilson, 66n40
Coontz, Phyllis, 176nn64, 65
Cooper, Alison, 175n41
Cooper, Cary, 66n60; 176n62
Cooper, Chris, 383
Cooper, Helene, 474n104
Cooper, Kylie, 474n73
Cooper, Michael, 409n30
Cooper, Roy, 347
Copes, Heith, 260n82; 361; 374nn249, 250
Copley, John Singleton, 412, 414
Copper, Janet R., 375n280
Copping, Lee, 328n101
Coren, S., 178n137
Corill, Dean, 354
Cork, Daniel L., 65n25
Cornish, Derek, 116; 132n19; 133n36; 134n104
Corrado, J., 516n180
Corrigan, Patrick, 250; 262n170
Cortese, Samuele, 175n31
Cory-Slechta, Deborah A., 177n90
Costa, Francis, 326n23
Costanzo, Michael, 133n58
Costello, Jane, 180n212
Cota-Robles, Sonia, 259n29
Couey, John Evander, 485
Coulter, Ann, 526
Coupe, Richard Timothy, 96n104; 440n86

Court, John, 515n133
Courtney, Robert R., 451; 468
Courture, Heather, 132n16
Courtwright, David, 340; 370n80; 518n260
Couzens, Michael, 65n13
Covington, Jeanette, 224nn90, 106; 225n156
Cox, Louis, 104; 132n11
Cragin, Kim, 410n48
Cram, Lisa, 304
Crane, D. Russell, 232
Crane, Jonathan, 223n46
Craven, Wes, 365
Crawford, Charles, 293n64
Crawford, Krysten, 456–457
Creamer, Vicki, 260n74
Crenshaw, Martha, 410n65
Cressey, Donald, 4–5; 12; 26n3, 16; 237; 260n73; 469; 475n127; 555n108
Creswell, Julie, 472n1
Cretacci, Michael, 262n143
Crews, F. T., 175n30
Crinella, Francis, 175n27
Croisdale, Tim, 69n161; 137n204
Cromwell, Paul, 133nn56, 57, 72; 423; 435; 438n25; 439n39; 440n99
Crosby, L., 327n48
Crosby, Rick, 326n27
Crosnoe, Robert, 261n129
Cross, Catherine, 328n101
Crossette, Barbara, 513nn22, 24
Crouch, Ben, 136n200
Crow, Matthew, 56; 68n127
Crowder, Kyle, 223n67
Crowe, R. R., 179n170
Crowther, Betty, 515n154
Cruise, Keith, 368n8
Cui, Ming, 258n7
Cullen, Charles, 353
Cullen, Francis T., 67nn83, 102; 94n38; 95nn63, 75, 80, 81; 133n78; 180n213; 216; 226nn184, 192, 195; 258nn13, 19, 25; 260nn66, 78; 261n133; 262nn149, 153, 167; 295n154; 327n58; 329nn134–136; 330n153; 371nn107, 116; 375n289; 474nn84, 85
Culpepper, Thomas, 30
Cummings, Andrea, 134n92; 371n105
Cumpler, Debbie, 175n41
Cunningham, Randy "Duke," 453
Cupach, William, 366; 375nn290, 293
Currie, Elliott, 280; 293n82
Curry, David, 223n74; 224n95
Curry, Mary Ann, 358
Cuvelier, Steven, 133n78
Czaja, Ronald, 65n34

D

Dabney, Dean, 439n49
Dadds, Mark, 440n109
Dafeamekpor, Denise Spriggs, 371n140; 372n141
Dahlberg, Linda, 8–9; 373nn217, 218
Dahrendorf, Ralf, 269

Daigle, Leah E., 94n38; 95n63; 260n78; 329nn135, 136; 330n167; 371nn107, 116
Dal Forno, Gloria, 329n124
Dalen, Lindy, 175n41
D'Alessio, Stewart, 67n87; 122–123; 248–249; 262n152; 330n171
Daley, Suzanne, 515n114
Dalton, Katharina, 147; 176n70
Daly, Eileen, 171
Daly, Kathleen, 293nn90, 92, 96; 294nn105, 127; 469; 475n123
Daly, Margaret, 516n168
Daly, Martin, 67n92; 95n70; 155; 179nn172–176; 224n87; 225n153; 329n123; 373n223
Daly, Sara A., 410n48
Daniels, Brant, 87
Daniels, Leona, 87
Daniels, R. Steven, 135nn130, 135
Dann, Robert, 122–123
Dannefer, Dale, 68n115
Dannenberg, Andrew, 515n109
Dantzler, Joyce, 371n140; 372n141
Darrow, William, 514n90
Darwin, Charles, 140–141
Das, Shyamal, 176n55
Davey, Monica, 473n41
David, David, 518n250
Davidson, Laura, 67n82
Davies, Garth, 223n47
Davies, Mark, 260nn87, 90; 262n151; 516n178
Davies, Priscilla, 182n283
Davies, Susan, 326n27
Davies-Netley, Sally, 94n21
Davis, Joanne, 516n169
Davis, John, 175n27
Davis, Kristin, 478
Davis, Robert C., 94n30; 95n55; 96nn118, 134; 97n141; 517nn238, 240
Davis, Roy, 371n124
Davis-Frenzel, Erika, 371n109; 372n144
Davison, Elizabeth, 134n86
Day, H. D., 182n283
De Coster, Stacy, 180n223; 223n60; 226n182
De Gruchy, John W., 295n149
De Li, Spencer, 136n191; 260n68; 327n63; 328n75
de Silva, W. P., 513n41
Dean, Charles, 136n193; 326n22; 330n169
Deane, Glenn, 65n7; 330n156; 369n20; 370n62
DeBaryshe, Barbara, 326n19
DeBeir, Georges, 533–534
Deboutte, Dirk, 259n30
Decker, Scott, 134n89; 262n154; 360; 372n179; 374n254; 432, 433; 440nn89, 94
Dedjinou, Adrienne, 474n73
Deeley, Quinton, 171
Defillipis, James, 292n6
DeFronzo, James, 225n140; 227n240

Gagnon, C., 69n165
Gagnon, John, 371n132
Gainey, Randy, 225n128; 263n198
Gajewski, Francis, 135nn144, 147
Galaway, Burt, 97n153
Gale, Nathan, 133n58
Gall, Franz Joseph, 141
Galvin, Jim, 262n178
Galway, Roberta, 426
Gamble, Wendy, 259n29
Gannon, Theresa, 513n47
Gans, Dian, 176n46
Gant, Charles, 178n126
Garcia, Luis, 225n122; 374n273
Gardner, Carol Brooks, 375n286
Garfinkel, Robin, 176n82
Garner, Connie Chonoweth, 261n133
Garner, Joel H., 136n193
Garnier, Helen, 261n136
Garofalo, James, 95n90; 97n150
Garofalo, Raffaele, 142; 175n13
Gartner, Rosemary, 95n72; 123
Gary, Faye, 358
Gates, Bill, 207
Gatzke-Kopp, Lisa M., 144; 175n29
Gau, Jacinta M., 260n78
Gaylor, Rita, 180n206
Ge, Xiaojia, 67n86
Geberth, Vernon J., 372n181
Gebhard, Paul, 371n132
Geis, Gilbert, 65n9; 438n16; 473nn15, 56
Geller, Susan Rose, 330n178
Gelles, Richard, 358; 373nn222, 226; 374n239
George, David, 177n109
Georges-Abeyie, Daniel, 68n120; 410n36
Gerber, Jurg, 517n225
Gerberding, Julie, 513n25
Gere, Richard, 487
Gerges, Abraham, 72
Gersheli, Eduard, 455
Gerstein, Dean, 326n32
Gertz, Marc, 48–49, 51; 66n64; 134n84; 224nn91, 92, 94; 293n63; 369n33
Giacometti, Alberto, 412
Giampietro, Vincent, 171
Giancola, Peter, 516n166
Gibbons, Donald, 181n257; 439n60
Gibbs, Carole, 467; 474n117
Gibbs, Jack, 135n151; 263n208; 293n71; 410n34
Gibbs, Jennifer, 281
Gibbs, John, 67n102; 133n75
Gibbs, Natalie, 134n92; 371n105
Gibson, Chris, 94n32; 224n113; 330n167
Gidycz, Christine, 371n97
Giever, Dennis, 328n95
Gifford, Robert, 440n100
Giffords, Gabrielle, 124; 140
Gilchrist, Lewayne, 329n146
Gill, Gladwin, 381
Gill, James, 373n216
Gillars, Mildred Elizabeth, 383
Gillis, A. R., 294n108

Gillis, Roy, 374n263
Gillman, Matthew W., 177n93
Ginzberg, Eli, 518n251
Ginzburg, E., 66n72; 326n24
Giordano, Peggy, 65n31; 226nn168, 188; 260nn79, 85; 262nn150, 157; 303; 326n17; 327n53; 328n77; 329n122; 330n176; 439n59
Giroux, Bruce, 330n160
Gisli, Gudjonsson, 171
Gizewski, Elke, 513n44
Gjeruldsen, Susanne Rogne, 369n28
Glass, Nancy, 358
Glazer, D., 515n150
Gleyzer, Roman, 368n9
Glick, Barry, 65n12
Glueck, Eleanor, 166–167; 181n258; 258n5; 298–299; 310–311; 325nn4, 6
Glueck, Sheldon, 166–167; 181n258; 258n5; 298–299; 310–311; 325nn4, 6
Goddard, Henry H., 142; 169; 175n15
Godfrey, Barry, 472n2
Goetz, Barry, 518n256
Goffman, Alice, 56–57
Gold, Martin, 67n108
Golding, Jean, 175n27
Goldkamp, John, 135n140; 517n244
Goldman, M. S., 516n185
Goldstein, Michael, 515n127
Goldstein, Paul, 369n22; 369n29; 514nn78, 79, 81; 516n190
Golub, Andrew, 516nn193, 194
Gonzales, Martha Denise, 243
Gonzales, Nancy, 258n6
Gooch, Erik, 373n198
Gooch, Teresa, 66n48
Goodman, Robert, 180n201
Goodman, Sam, 418–419
Goodstein, Laurie, 262n174
Goodwill, Alasdair, 373n192
Goodwin, D. W., 516n173
Gootman, Elissa, 373n209
Gordon, Kristina Coop, 94n25
Gordon, Leslie, 369n45
Gordon, Rachel, 370n73
Gordon, Robert, 261n114
Gorge, Mathieu, 554n73
Goring, Charles, 157; 179n186
Gorr, Wilpen, 26n7; 135n143
Gossop, Michael, 518n250
Gottfredson, Denise, 95n78; 96n100; 225nn126, 150; 517nn209, 210
Gottfredson, Gary, 95n78; 225nn126, 150
Gottfredson, Michael, 52; 65n21; 67nn85, 90; 95n90; 114; 133n37; 134n97; 177n100; 246; 309–317; 326n30; 329n116; 382nn87–89, 92, 93, 100, 112; 470; 475nn131, 132
Gottfredson, Stephen, 133n74
Gottschalk, Earl, 473n27
Gould, Arthur, 515n113
Gould, Leroy, 67n114
Gould, Stephen Jay, 175n16

Gove, Walter, 133n26; 134n95; 176n53; 178n140
Grabosky, Peter, 468–469; 475n122
Grace, Randolph, 513n46
Grandison, Terry, 93n10
Grandjean, P., 175n31
Grann, Martin, 369n28
Grasmick, Harold G., 135nn138, 152, 153; 224n105; 225nn129, 138, 149; 328n104; 329nn125, 132
Graves, Robert M., 65n25
Gray, Andrews, 553n66
Gray, Gregory, 176n44
Gray, Louis N., 132n20; 181n243
Gray-Ray, Phyllis, 262nn169, 183
Graziano, Joseph, 175n34; 177n91
Greeley, A., 515n155
Green, Aisa, 177n110
Green, Donald, 135n151
Green, Lorraine. *See* Mazerolle, Lorraine Green
Green, Rebecca, 553nn43, 44; 554n93
Green, Stuart P., 474n87
Green, William, 370nn81, 88
Greenbaum, Robert, 368n2
Greenberg, David, 293n70
Greenberg, Stephanie, 224n81
Greene, Michael, 370n60
Greenfeld, Lawrence, 95n65; 136n182
Greenhouse, Joel, 177n89
Greening, Leilani, 181n251
Greenman, Sarah, 515n147
Greenwood, Peter, 518n247
Gregg, Heather S., 410n48
Gregory, Alice, 179n167
Gregory, Carol, 67n113
Grierson, Anthony, 513n58
Griffin, Catherine, 524
Griffiths, Curt Taylor, 295n147
Grigoryan, Konstantin, 455
Grigoryan, Mayya Leonidovna, 455
Grimalt, Joan O., 176n80
Grimes, Tom, 162–163
Grimshaw, Kate, 175n41
Griswold, David, 261n132; 262n159
Groff, Elizabeth, 439n85
Grohm, Carol, 371n113
Gross, Alan, 371n113
Gross, Kate, 553n54
Gross, Samuel, 11; 26n13
Groth, A. Nicholas, 344; 346; 371nn102, 136
Grove, H., 473n56
Groves, W. Byron, 225nn126, 150; 271; 292nn2, 29
Grow, Brian, 553n22
Grubesic, Tony, 369n21
Gruenewald, Jeff, 352; 372n183
Gruenewald, Paul, 224n100
Grus, Catherine, 94n16
Gu, Joann, 374n273
Guerry, André-Michel, 188
Guess, Teresa, 293n68
Guijarro, Margarita, 326n30
Gulderlyan, Haroutyun, 455

Jones, Donald, 154; 179nn168, 169
Jones, Heather, 258n27
Jones, Jamie Leigh, 74
Jones, Lisa, 373nn221, 227; 374n228
Jones, Marshall, 154; 179nn168, 169
Jones, Peter, 69n159; 517n244
Jones, Shayne, 224nn82, 119
Jonzon, Eva, 374n229
Jordan, Carol, 375n294
Jordan, Lamar, 95n53
Jorgensen, Jenel S., 180n202
Jorgensen, P. J., 175n31
Joubert, S. J., 474n109
Joyce, James, 491
Juan Carlos, Spain, 395
Judah, Richard, 178n126
Júlvez, Jordi, 176n80
Junger, Marianne, 262n146; 326n30; 328n109
Junger-Tas, Josine, 262n146
Jusko, Todd A., 177n90
Jussim, Lee, 259n38

K

Kadleck, Colleen, 134n113
Kageyama, Yuri, 370n89
Kahler, Christopher, 94n25
Kahn, Arnold, 370n95
Kakoulidis, Christos, 368n5
Kalb, Larry, 326n21
Kaloupek, Danny, 94n43
Kalpoe, Deepak, 2, 4
Kalpoe, Satish, 2, 4
Kaltiala-Heino, Riittakerttu, 180n203
Kandel, Denise, 260nn87, 90; 262n151; 516n178
Kandel, Elizabeth, 177n95
Kane, John, 554nn78, 80
Kane, Robert J., 225n136; 370n69
Kanka, Maureen, 90
Kanka, Megan, 10; 19–20; 90
Kanka, Richard, 90
Kanth, Sarita, 8–9
Kaplan, David, 513n23
Kaplan, Eben, 410n59
Kaplan, Howard, 263nn192, 193, 201
Karasik, Theodore W., 410n48
Karch, Debra, 372n181
Karmaus, Wilfried, 177n86
Karmen, Andrew, 33; 96n131; 372n157
Karp, David R., 295n145
Kassin, Saul, 65n26
Kasza, Kristen, 175n28
Kates, Don, 133n64
Katz, Basil, 473n39
Katz, Charles, 370n61
Katz, James, 105
Kauffman, K., 181n232
Kaufman, Joanne, 68n137; 226n187; 370n55; 373n189
Kauzlarich, David, 292n43
Kawai, Eriko, 370n73
Kay, Barbara, 261n126
Kaysen, Debra, 67n106; 95n82

Kazemian, Lila, 66n39; 69n160
Kazmierczak, Steven, 138, 140
Kearley, Brook, 517nn209, 210
Keckler, Charles N. W., 135n157
Keeler, Gordon, 180n212
Keels, Micere, 224n102
Keen, Bradley, 68n124
Keenan, Kate, 259n52; 330n160
Keeney, Belea, 354; 373n197
Keilitz, Ingo, 178n117
Keire, Mara, 514n105
Keith, Bruce, 258n18
Keith, H., 474n116
Kellam, Sheppard, 326n39
Kelley, Thomas, 439n46
Kelling, George, 135n137
Kellogg, Michael, 392–393; 410n41
Kelly, Kathryn, 179n189
Kempe, C. Henry, 373n219
Kempe, Ruth S., 373n219
Kempf-Leonard, Kimberly, 62; 67n97; 69nn163, 164; 136n181; 262nn148, 154
Kennedy, Daniel, 439n46
Kennedy, David M., 369n31
Kennedy, John, 296, 298
Kennedy, John F., 219
Kennedy, Leslie, 97n139; 328n91
Kenney, T. J., 177n112
Kerbs, Jodi, 180n206
Kercher, Kyle, 67n89
Kerich, Michael, 177n109
Kerik, Bernard, 452–453
Kerner, Hans-Jürgen, 66n76; 259n51; 330n164
Kershaw, Sarah, 373n209
Kershaw, Trace, 374n232
Kessler, Daniel, 121; 135n149
Kethineni, Sesha, 262n153
Kevorkian, Jack, 19
Keys, David, 293n68
Khadafi, Muammar, 264
Khan, A. Q., 402
Khan, Haji Juma, 404
Khatchadourian, Raffi, 384
Khomeini, Ayatollah Ruhollah, 391; 396
Khuzami, Robert S., 470
Kibaki, Mwai, 381
Kidd, Sean, 516n170
Kiley, Marion, 514n74
Kilias, Martin, 45
Killip, Steve, 96n129
Kilpatrick, Dean G., 94nn14, 27; 96n114; 343; 369n25; 370n82
Kim, D., 175n30
Kim, Julia Yun Soo, 65n33
Kim, KiDeuk, 136n161
Kim, Min Jung, 94n42
Kim, Sang-Weon, 225n157
Kim, Yeora, 553n48
King, Harry, 417; 438n14
King, John, 374n279
King, Kate, 137n202
King, Ryan, 67n96; 363; 374n264

Kingery, Paul M., 181n250; 182n290
Kingree, J. B., 180n205
Kingsland, William M. V., 412, 414
Kingsworth, Rodney, 372n150
Kinkade, Patrick, 375n287
Kinlock, Timothy, 326n38
Kinney, Linda, 371n140; 372n141
Kinscherff, Robert, 180n208
Kinsey, Richard, 293n83
Kinsie, Paul, 514nn72, 77
Kipp, Heidi, 258n27
Kiritsy, Mary, 176n45
Kitchin, Elizabeth, 175n41
Kivivuori, Janne, 26n6; 65n2; 94nn28, 36; 180n203; 439n38
Kjelsberg, Ellen, 180n200
Klackenberg-Larsson, Ingrid, 182n283
Klassen, Philip, 513n45
Klaus, Patsy, 439nn64, 66
Kleck, Gary, 48–49, 51; 66n64; 67n80; 90; 97nn146–149; 133n64; 134n84; 293n64; 337; 369nn32, 33
Klein, Andrew, 126; 136n194
Klein, Uwe, 181n263
Kleinman, Ken P., 177n93
Kletschka, H. K., 178n131
Kline, Jennie, 175n34
Kling, Kristen, 67n102
Kling, Ryan, 490
Klinger, David, 135n133; 225n134
Klockars, Carl, 293n74; 418; 438n22; 517nn201, 203
Knight, Raymond, 371n103
Knight, Zelda, 373n199
Knoller, Marjorie, 349
Knottnerus, G. Mark, 177n86
Knowles, Gordon, 133n49
Kobrin, Solomon, 219; 224nn107, 108; 227n241
Kochel, Tammy Rinehart, 277; 293n61
Kocherga, Angela, 555n126
Kocieniewski, David, 473n44
Kohlberg, Lawrence, 164; 181nn231, 232
Kohn, Robert, 94n25
Kolbo, Jerome, 94n40
Konofal, Eric, 175nn31, 34
Koons, Barbara, 223n64
Koops, Willem, 181n244
Kopie, Kathy, 374n228
Kornhauser, Ruth, 223n45; 227n235
Koroloff, Nancy, 180n206
Kort-Butler, Lisa, 226n182
Koss, Mary, 344–345; 371n97; 371n110; 492; 515nn119, 125
Kosterman, Rick, 259n35; 326n40; 330n177; 516n191; 517n211
Kovandzic, Tomislav V., 121; 135nn138, 139; 337; 352; 369n36; 372n184
Koziol-McLain, Jane, 358
Kozlowski, L. Dennis, 456
Krafft-Ebing, Richard von, 483
Krah, Barbara, 370n84; 372n149
Krahn, Harvey, 262n160
Kramer, Lisa, 514n89

Mayo, Julia, 514n94
Mazerolle, Lorraine Green, 134nn113, 118, 119; 135nn144, 147
Mazerolle, Paul, 180n207; 226nn177, 183–185; 326nn16, 22; 329n114; 330n169
Mazloum, Wassim, 405
Mazzetti, Mark, 410n51
McAuslan, Pam, 369n26
McBride, Duane, 518n261
McCaffrey, Shannon, 258n3
McCaghy, Charles, 26n17; 439nn59, 75; 473n54; 513nn57, 60; 515nn157, 158
McCain, John, 387
McCall, Andrew, 438nn3, 4
McCall, Patricia, 68n138; 224n110; 329nn147, 148
McCann, Donna, 175n41
McCarthy, Bill, 95n72; 132n23; 136n172; 260nn75, 76; 294n109; 308
McCauley, Elizabeth, 326n40
McCauley, Jenna, 343; 370n82
McClelland, Gary, 26n15
McCluskey, Cynthia Perez. *See* Perez, Cynthia
McCluskey, John, 223n42
McCord, Joan, 216; 326n15; 330n170
McCready, William, 515n155
McCue, Colleen, 66nn48, 49
McCurdy, Sheryl, 514n83
McDevitt, Jack, 362; 363; 364; 374nn258, 259, 273
McDonel, E. D., 181n252
McDowall, David, 66n76; 94n35; 95n92; 516n164
McEntire, Ranee, 224n94
McFall, R., 181n252
McFarland, Christine, 177n89
McFarlane, Alexander, 180n224
McFarlane, Judith, 358
McGahey, Richard, 223n74
McGarrell, Edmund F., 467; 474n117
McGee, Rob, 179n193
McGloin, Jean Marie, 181n238; 328n106; 329n121; 330nn157–159
McGuire, Kathleen, 66n53
McGuire, Stryker, 368n4
McGuree, Patrick, 292n3
Mchugh, Suzanne, 179n160
McIntyre, Douglas A., 553n23
McKay, Henry D., 196–198; 199; 223nn51, 53, 54
McKenzie, Roderic, 222nn13, 14
McKibben, André, 134n93
McKinney, Aaron, 363
McKinney, Joseph R., 518n245
McLanahan, Sara, 258n15
McLean, Bethany, 456–457
McLean, W. Graham, 175n40
McLendon, Michael, 355
McLeod, Jane, 326n33
McLeod, Maureen, 97n150
McMackin, Robert, 94n43
McMahon-Howard, Jennifer, 371n96

McMillan, Richard, 66n77; 96n109; 223n72
McMorris, Barbara J., 327n68
McMurray, Scott, 473n35
McNamara, Grace, 516n177
McNeill, Richard, 225nn126, 150
McNulty, Thomas, 223n40; 225n143
McPhaul, Kathleen M., 375n280
McPhee, Michele, 512n5
McPhee, Mike, 374n257
McQuarie, Donald, 292n3
McVeigh, Timothy, 21
Mdzinarishvili, A., 175n30
Mead, George Herbert, 14; 249–250; 262n166
Meade, Christina, 374n232
Meagher, Chris, 115
Mears, Daniel, 67n104; 260nn93, 94
Measelle, Jeffrey, 179n161
Medina-Ariza, Junajo, 95n55
Medlicott, Sandra, 313
Mednick, Sarnoff, 69n155; 175n25; 176nn42, 66, 68; 177nn95, 101, 106; 178nn142, 143, 146; 179nn182, 183; 180n217; 369n40
Meehan, Albert, 293n60
Meeker, James, 224n93
Meesters, Cor, 178n123; 329n133
Megargee, Edward, 181n269
Meier, Megan, 534
Meier, Robert, 96n111; 223n44; 258n4
Meissner, Christian, 65n26
Melde, Chris, 94n45; 327n59
Mellingen, Kjetil, 176n42
Meloy, Reid, 373n198; 375n291
Meltzer, Howard, 180n201
Menard, Scott, 223n75; 329n119
Mendenhall, Ruby, 224n102
Mendes, Silvia, 135n125
Mercy, James, 8–9; 97n144; 373nn217, 218
Mergon, Robert, 225n158
Merkens, Hans, 226n170
Mero, Richard, 327n72
Merton, Robert K., 205–207
Merzi, Nichole Michelle, 522
Meseck-Bushey, Sylvia, 179n159
Messer, Julie, 180n201
Messerschmidt, James, 282–283; 293n95; 294n101
Messerschmidt, Pamela, 369n25
Messner, Steven, 65n7; 66nn75, 75; 85; 96n109; 134nn82, 90; 207–208; 222n4; 223nn72, 73; 225nn123, 162–166; 226n199; 369n20; 370nn62, 71; 374nn246–248, 264
Metz, Tim, 475n124
Mezey, Gill, 171
Michalowski, Raymond, 292n43; 472n10; 474nn95, 96
Michelson, N., 177n95
Miech, Richard, 66n72; 326n24
Miethe, Terance, 95n92; 96nn95, 111; 293n66; 372n169
Milan, Stephanie, 325n13

Miles, William, 65n32
Miletich, Steve, 410n45
Mileusnic, Darinka, 26n15
Milich, Rich, 517n243
Milken, Michael, 468
Miller, Alan, 226n177
Miller, Bobbi Viegas, 95nn89, 91
Miller, Brenda, 94n21
Miller, Henry, 491
Miller, Jody, 109; 133nn50–54; 374nn252, 253
Miller, Joshua, 181nn240, 260
Miller, Kirk, 65n34
Miller, L. E., 178n145
Miller, Lawrence, 410nn49, 57, 58
Miller, Lisa, 225n148
Miller, Martin, 410n54
Miller, Michael, 475n124
Miller, Susan, 67n113
Miller, Ted R., 93n8
Miller, Thomas, 369n29
Miller, Todd, 133n77; 326n30; 516n175
Miller, Walter, 213; 227nn214, 215; 260n70
Mills, Michael, 472n11
Milman, Harold, 175n33
Milner, Trudie, 135n155
Mincy, Ronald, 223n39
Miner, Michael, 94n23; 514n92
Ming, Kwan Kin, 549
Minor, M. William, 136n168; 261n114
Mio, J. S., 516n179
Miodovnik, Amir, 176n81
Mirowsky, John, 224n97
Mischel, Walter, 181n256
Misson, Sebastian, 513n58
Mitchell, Derek, 171
Mitchell, Kimberly, 553n52
Mitchell, Nick, 263n212
Moch, Annie, 222n26
Modzeleski, William, 373nn189, 190
Moffat, Robert, 451, 452
Moffitt, Terrie, 66n72; 69n166; 176n66; 177nn94, 106; 178n121; 179nn161, 182, 184; 181n262; 182nn270, 278; 315; 318; 321; 325n14; 326nn24, 31; 327nn41, 50, 51; 329nn113, 115, 145, 149, 153; 330nn163–165, 174, 175
Moilanen, Irma, 258n10
Mokdad, Ali, 513n25
Mokherjee, Jessica, 226n172
Mokhiber, Russell, 474n102
Momenan, Reza, 177n109
Monachesi, Elio, 181nn267, 268
Monaghan, Rachel, 553n55
Money, J., 176n67
Monhan, John, 180n219
Monroe, Laura, 371n140; 372n141
Monroe, R. E., 177n113
Monson, Candice, 96n115
Montada, Leo, 94n44
Montanino, F., 515n154
Montgomery, Nicholas, 26n13

Powell, Andrea, 223n63
Powell, Michael, 422
Pradai-Prat, D., 175n39
Pranis, Kay, 294n142
Prasad, Monica, 486; 513n59
Pratt, Travis C., 181n238; 260n78; 328n106; 330n157
Prendergast, Michael, 517n214
Presser, Lois, 295n152
Preston, Julia, 215
Pribesh, Shana, 224n97
Price, Jamie, 223n74
Price, Virginia, 514n70
Pridemore, William Alex, 225n157; 369n21
Prince, Emily, 175n41
Prinz, Ronald, 175n38
Priyadarsini, S., 260n89
Proffitt, Fiona, 410n46
Proietti, Lua, 329n124
Proulx, Jean, 134n93; 327n4nn, 46
Pruitt, B. E., 181n250; 182n290
Pruitt, Matthew, 222n32
Prunella, Jill, 177n110
Przybylski, Roger, 516n198
Pugh, M. D., 66n71; 262n150
Pugh, Meredith, 65n31
Pullmann, Michael, 180n206

Q

Qin, Yu, 386
Quetelet, Adolphe (L. A. J.), 187–188; 222nn7, 8
Quinet, Kenna Davis, 95n57; 373n196
Quinney, Richard, 270; 284; 292nn16, 36, 37; 294n125; 473n30
Quiñones, Alan, 215
Quinsey, Vernon, 440n107
Quisenberry, Neil, 224n82

R

Raaijmakers, Quinten, 181n235
Rabasa, Angel, 410n48; 411n96
Rada, Richard, 371n132
Rader, Dennis, 353
Radosevich, Marcia, 68n114
Radosh, Polly, 294n140
Raffalovich, Lawrence, 66n77; 96n109; 223n72
Rafter, Nicole Hahn, 175nn6, 7, 11, 12; 325n3
Raghavan, Chitra, 516n163
Raine, Adrian, 8; 26n10; 145; 149; 152; 175n26; 176n42; 177nn97, 101, 108, 111; 178nn115, 142, 143; 179n183; 181n237; 330n165; 369n40
Raitt, F. E., 176n71
Raj, Anita, 374n240
Rajaratnam, Raj, 452
Raley, R. Kelly, 68n143
Ramírez, Stephany Tatiana Flores, 4
Ramsey, Elizabeth, 326n19
Ramsey, Susan, 94n25
Rand, Michael R., 75–76; 93n3; 94n48; 370n94; 439n63

Randall, Susan, 370n83
Range, Lillian, 94n21
Rankin, Bruce, 225nn139, 144
Rankin, Joseph, 65n24; 258n14
Rapin, J., 175n39
Rapp, Geoffrey, 123
Rappley, Marsha D., 177n86
Rash, Selwyn, 555n112
Rashbaum, William K., 65n14
Ratchford, Marie, 328nn97, 99
Ratcliffe, Jerry, 66n50
Rathouz, Paul, 258n27
Rathus, Spencer, 65n35; 181n268; 261n116; 513n53
Ratzinger, Joseph, 484
Raudenbush, Stephen W., 223n68; 224n114
Rauh, Virginia, 147; 176n82
Rawlings, Robert, 177n109
Ray, James V., 330n158
Ray, Melvin, 262nn169, 183, 187
Reagan, Ronald, 87; 105; 162
Realmuto, George, 260n87
Rebellon, Cesar, 226nn175, 186, 187; 258n12; 262n161; 499; 516nn190, 192
Reboussin, Roland, 134n92; 371n105
Rebovich, Donald, 135n122
Reckless, Walter, 123; 245–246; 261nn125, 126
Reddy, Marisa, 373n190
Reed, Elizabeth, 95n82
Reed, M. D., 262n165
Rees, Sian, 518n250
Regnerus, Mark, 261n142
Regoeczi, Wendy, 372n169
Regoli, Robert, 261n115
Reich, Walter, 410n67
Reidel, Marc, 372n173
Reiman, Jeffery, 29n30
Reisig, Michael, 224nn99, 116
Reiss, Albert, 133n74; 178n134; 181n254; 182n289; 223n74; 224nn86, 107, 108; 245; 261n123; 369n23; 474n89
Reitzel, Deborah, 96n129
Rekart, Michael, 514n95
Remy, Nicholas, 103
Ren, Xin, 259n51
Rengert, George, 97n142; 125; 133nn35, 55, 73; 136n170; 517n227; 555n127
Rengifo, Andres, 45
Rennison, Callie Marie, 65n23
Renzetti, Claire M., 341; 544–545
Resig, Michael, 316; 329n131
Resnick, Heidi S., 94n27; 343; 369n25; 370n82
Resnick, Patricia, 67n106; 96nn113, 115
Restifo, Nicholas, 368n6
Reuter, Peter, 516n200
Reynolds, B. J., 177n112
Reynolds, Charles F., 518n248
Reynolds, Matthew, 371n140; 372n141
Reynolds, Morgan, 132n19
Rheingold, Alyssa, 94n27
Rhodes, William, 490

Ribas-Fitó, Núria, 176n80
Rice, Frances, 178n147
Rice, Harvey, 243
Rich, William, 178n117
Rich-Edwards, Janet W., 177n93
Richard, Chris, 552n12
Richards, Jeffery, 513nn54, 55
Richards, Maryse, 95nn89, 91
Richardson, Alexandra, 175n36
Richardson, Deborah, 96n101
Richardson, Samuel, 341
Richman, Kimberly, 65n26
Richmond, F. Lynn, 227n238
Richter, Linda, 132n21
Ricketts, Melissa L., 329n143
Ricks, Kevin Garfield, 483
Ridder, Elizabeth, 326n35
Riddle, David, 175n38
Riddle, James, 328n78
Rideout, Greta, 345
Rideout, John, 345
Ridgway, Ric, 485
Riess, Julie, 177n89
Rigas, John, 462
Rigas, Timothy, 462
Riggs, Shelley, 180n197
Rijsdijk, Fruhling, 179n161
Rimland, Bernard, 143; 175n22
Rimpela, Matti, 180n203
Ringwalt, Chris, 517n242
Risen, James, 409n29
Risser, Jan, 514n83
Ritakallio, Minna, 180n203
Ritchell, Matt, 439n53
Ritz, Christina E., 222n3
Rivera, Craig, 262n184; 263n190
Rizvi, Shireen, 67n106; 96n115
Roache, Declan, 290
Robb, Gregory, 439n62
Roberton, Alison, 440n108
Roberts, Aki, 370n78
Roberts, Albert, 96n121
Roberts, Charles, 354
Roberts, Jennifer, 65n38
Roberts, John, Jr., 514n107
Roberts, Julia, 487
Roberts, Kathleen, 328n99
Roberts, Mary K., 261n132; 262n159
Roberts, Miguel, 371n113
Roberts, Ron, 515n110
Robertson, Craig, 262nn169, 183
Robertson, Dene, 171
Robertson, Richard T., 175n27
Robespierre, Maximilien, 392
Robin, D. R., 177n112
Robin, Gerald, 372n147
Robins, Lee, 69n166
Robinson, Beatrice, 94n23; 514n92
Robinson, Matthew, 133n71; 440n90
Robles, Albert, 107
Rocha, Veronica, 409n9
Roche, Declan, 295n153
Roche, M., 175n39
Rocques, Michael, 293n58

Spelman, William, 135nn144, 147; 136n197; 223n62
Spergel, Irving, 223n74; 224n95
Spielberg, Steven, 447
Spillane, Frank H., 127
Spitzberg, Brian, 366; 375nn290, 293
Spitzer, Eliot, 476, 478; 484
Spohn, Cassia, 253–254; 263n200; 293n67; 348; 371n109; 372nn142, 144, 152
Spracklen, Kathleen, 259n55
Springett, Gwynneth, 180n211
Spruzheim, Johann K., 141
Spunt, Barry, 369n29
Squires, David, 490
Squires, Gregory, 223n65
St. Guillen, Aljandra, 72
St. Guillen, Imette, 70, 72
St. Hilaire, Maureen, 72
Stack, Steven, 122–123
Stack, Susan, 176n66; 177n106; 179n182
Stafford, Mark C., 132n20; 181n243
Stahelski, Anthony, 410n74
Stalin, Josef, 401
Stanford, Robert Allen, 442; 446
Stark, Rodney, 96nn93, 94; 225n135; 235; 260n67
Starles, R. M., 177n112
Stattin, Hakan, 182n283
Steele, Tracy, 122–123
Steen, Sara, 263n198
Steer, Colin, 175n27
Steffensmeier, Darrell, 54; 67nn89, 100, 110, 112; 223nn66, 74; 293n65; 370n57; 418–419
Steffensmeier, Renee Hoffman, 67n110
Stegink, Lewis, 176n45
Stein, Judith, 261n136
Stein, Nancy, 294n103
Steinberg, Laurence, 181n239; 329n138
Steiner, Hans, 180n207
Stephan, James, 137n207
Stephens, Gene, 294n140
Sterk, Claire, 518n246
Sterk-Elifson, Claire, 40; 66nn43, 44; 499; 516n186
Stermac, Lana, 94n24
Stern, Howard, 513n31
Stetler, Linda, 450
Stetson, Barbara, 260n74
Steury, Ellen Hochstedler, 180n213
Stevens, Bradley, 93n5
Stevens, Tomika, 369n25
Stevenson, Jim, 175n41
Stevenson, Richard, 440n98
Stewart, Claire, 181n242
Stewart, Eric, 94n47; 95n74; 293n63; 369n54; 518n246
Stewart, Martha, 461
Stewart, Potter, 491
Stice, Eric, 259n37
Stigler, George J., 132n7
Stoddart, Clare, 176n44
Stoff, David, 259n55

Stolzenberg, Lisa, 67n87; 122–123; 248–249; 262n152; 330n171
Stone, Emily, 66n48
Stone, Laurence, 374n236
Stone, Sharon, 248
Storr, C. L., 224n83
Story, Louise, 475n129
Stotland, E., 473n56
Stout, Ronnie, 368n5
Stouthamer-Loeber, Magda, 93n5; 95n83; 182nn270, 278; 259n52; 326nn21, 23, 31, 33; 330nn160, 165; 370nn55, 73
Stowell, Jacob, 66n73
Strang, Heather, 295nn148, 150
Strang, John, 518n250
Strate, John, 27n33
Stratton, Howard, 330n180
Straus, Murray A., 259n32; 337; 358; 369nn44, 51; 374nn233, 239
Strauss-Kahn, Dominique, 346–347
Stretesky, Paul, 177n84; 474nn88, 107
Streuning, Elmer, 262n167
Strodtbeck, Fred, 261n114
Strong, Scott M., 513n45
Stroosma, Luwe, 175n37
Stroup, Donna F., 513n25
Strueber, Daniel, 368n11
Stuart, Gregory, 94n25; 368n8
Stumbo, Phyllis, 176n45
Styles, Julia, 495
Su, S. Susan, 226n202; 326n32
Suarez, Juan, 340
Sudermann, Marlies, 96n129
Suleiman, Daniel, 27n25
Sullivan, Christopher J., 180n226; 258n26; 328n106; 330nn157, 158
Sullivan, Dennis, 284; 294nn121, 123, 124
Sumaila, U. R., 474n116
Sun, Ivan, 225n128
Sun, Ping, 516n171
Sung, Hung-en, 132n21
Sunstein, Cass R., 129; 137n208
Sunyer, Jordi, 176n80
Surguladze, Simon, 171
Surratt, Hilary, 487; 514n74
Susser, Ezra S., 177n91
Sussman, Steve, 516n171
Sutherland, Edwin H., 4–5; 9; 12; 26nn3, 16; 169; 182nn271, 275; 237–240; 245; 260nn71–73; 417–418; 438n15; 445; 470; 472n7, 8; 474n71
Swaggi, Vincent, 418
Swahn, Monica, 369n24; 375n288
Swango, Michael, 353
Swartz, Bruce, 554n97
Swartz, James A., 136n164
Swartz, Marc, 456
Swartz, Marvin, 180n228
Sweeten, Gary, 259nn42, 43; 262n186; 308; 327n58
Swetnam, Michael S., 409n2
Sykes, Gresham, 241–242; 244; 261nn109, 111–113; 292n33
Symons, Donald, 371n125

Thornburgh, Nathan, 553n65
Thorne, Ian, 440n108
Thrasher, Frederick, 188; 222n12
Thurman, Quint, 423; 439n39
Tibbetts, Stephen, 261n117; 328n90; 330n167; 475n130
Tice, Peter, 326n33
Tierney, Kevin, 516n168
Tierney, Laura, 490
Tifft, Larry, 65n35; 284; 294nn121, 122
Tillyer, Marie Skubak, 94n49; 95n73; 133n68
Timberlake, Justin, 248
Timmendequas, Jesse, 10; 90
Timpson, Sandra, 514n83
Tita, George, 95n83; 368n2
Titchener, Edward, 164
Titterington, Victoria, 95n51; 294n100
Tittle, Charles R., 66n69; 67n84; 135n134; 223n44; 227n236; 254; 258n4; 259n45; 263nn204, 209; 316; 328n104; 329nn118, 125, 132; 382n86
Tjaden, Patricia, 375n286
Tobias, Aurelio, 326n23
Tobias, J. J., 438nn5, 6
Tobias, Randall L., 484
Tobin, Kimberly, 134n88
Tobin, Michael, 177n89
Tobin, Terri, 126; 136n194
Tobler, Nancy, 330n180
Toby, Jackson, 293n72
Todd, Peter, 68n118
Toguri D'Aquino, Iva Ikuko, 383
Tomas, Joseph, 326n23
Tomaskovic-Devey, Donald, 65n34
Tomasovic, Elizabeth, 369n27
Tonry, Michael, 95nn59, 60; 97n140; 132nn15, 19; 133n74; 135n121; 136n177; 175n25; 177n94; 179n172; 223n74; 224nn86, 107, 108; 258n22; 259n39; 292n17; 293n73; 310–311; 325n8; 373n205; 439n67; 515n132
Topalli, Volkan, 244; 439nn49, 65
Torrent, Maties, 176n80
Tourre, Fabrice, 449
Towns-Miranda, Luz, 440n106
Townsley, Michael, 440n104
Tracy, Paul, 62; 67n97; 68n116; 69nn155, 163, 164; 136n181
Traub, Leah Goldman, 180n227
Trebach, Arnold, 515n148
Treiber, Kyle, 225n147
Tremblay, Pierre, 133n40; 260nn75, 76
Tremblay, Richard, 69n165; 177n96; 327nn42, 51; 328n104
Trendle, Giles, 552n5
Treno, Andrew, 224n100
Treynker, Aleksandr, 455
Trickett, Alan, 95n58
Triplett, Ruth, 225n128; 263n202
Tripodia, Stephen, 327n71
Tristan, Jennifer, 259n37
Truman, Jennifer L., 75–76; 370n94

Trumbetta, Susan, 134n92; 371n105
Trump, Donald, 207
Tseng, Li-Jung, 516n176
Tsvetkova, Bilyana, 555n119
Tuch, Steven, 68n131
Tunnell, Kenneth, 133n62; 239; 260n91; 516n196
Tunstall, Nigel, 171
Turic, Darko, 178n147
Turner, Charles, 326n30
Turner, Heather, 94n15; 95n52
Turner, Michael, 95nn75, 81; 135n141; 371n116; 375n289
Turner, Scott, 440n111
Turpin-Petrosino, Carolyn, 27n45
Tyler, Kimberly, 81; 95n77; 371n112; 516n184
Tzavaras, Nikos, 368n5

U

Uggen, Christopher, 108; 133nn32, 39; 294nn112, 117; 327nn65, 71
Ullman, Harlan K., 484
Ullman, Sarah, 371n104
Ullrich, Simone, 180n218
Ulman, Arina, 358; 374n233
Ulmer, Jeffery T., 370n57; 419
Ulrich, Yvonne, 358
Umaña, Alcides, 187
Umhau, John, 177n109
Unfold, Douglas, 440n107
Unger, Jennifer, 516n171
Unnever, James, 258nn13, 19
Urbina, Ian, 174n1

V

Vaccaro, Donato, 516n177
Vaillant, George, 310–311
Valiente, Carlos, 178n144
Valier, Claire, 223n55
van den Bergle, Pierre, 175n18
van den Bree, Marianne, 178n147
van Den Haag, Ernest, 136n163
van den Oord, Edwin, 182n273
van der Geest, Victor, 329n152
van der Laan, Peter, 330n168
Van der Sloot, Joran, 2, 4
van der Staak, Cees, 175n37
Van Deusen, Karen, 515n128
van Dijk, Jan, 8–9
van Dijk, Mirjam, 371n134
van Duesen, Katherine Teilmann, 69n155
van Geen, Alexander, 175n34
van Goozen, Stephanie, 176n61
Van Gundy, Karen, 262n161; 499; 516nn190, 192
van Hoof, Anne, 181n235
Van Kammen, Wemoet, 259n52; 330n160
van Kesteren, John, 8–9
van Koppen, Peter J., 134n85; 374nn243, 251
Van Loh, Timothy, 328n109
van Mastrigt, Sarah, 322; 330n172

Van Voorhis, Patricia, 261nn133, 138; 295n152
Van Wormer, Katherine, 368n10
Vance, Jonathan Wryn, 80
Vander Ven, Thomas, 262n149
Vanzile-Tamsen, Carol, 370n95; 371n101
Varano, Sean, 223n42
Vardi, Nathan, 553n63
Vargas, Elizabeth, 363
Vashista, Anish, 473n33
Vásquez, Bob Edward, 134n116
Vatis, Michael A., 552n6
Vaughn, Michael, 308; 314; 328n108
Vazonyi, Alexander, 67n108; 179nn178, 179; 314; 328nn81, 109
Veach-White, Ernie, 180n206
Vega, Hector, 215
Velez, Maria, 222n31; 225n132
Venables, Peter, 176n42; 178n143; 181n237
Veneziano, Carol, 181n234
Veneziano, Louis, 181n234
Venkatesh, Sudhir Alladi, 125; 136n171; 317; 329nn139, 140
Venziale, James, 18
Verhulst, Frank, 330n168
Verlur, D. E., 516n179
Vermeiren, Robert, 259n30; 330n169
Vermeule, Adrian, 129; 137n208
Verona, Edelyn, 181n260
Veronen, Lois, 96n114
Vestel, Christine, 372n167
Veysey, Bonita, 66n75; 180n226
Vicomandi, David, 329n124
Victor, Timothy, 27n44
Victorino, Troy, 320
Viding, Essi, 181n262
Vieraitis, Lynne, 372n184
Villaume, Alfred, 294n130
Villemez, Wayne, 66n69
Virkkunen, Matti, 176n51; 177n95; 178nn135, 136
Visher, Christy, 262n175; 369n37
Vitaro, Frank, 327n51
Vitter, David, 484; 488
Volavka, Jan, 175n25; 176n68; 177n106; 178n146
Vold, George, 269
Von, Judith, 96n114
von Hentig, Hans, 26n14; 95n66
Von Hirsch, Andrew, 129–130; 137nn209–211
Voronin, Yuri A., 555n117
Voss, Harwin, 67n114
Vossekuil, Bryan, 373n190
Vowell, Paul, 260n81
Vucinich, S., 327n48
Vungkhanching, Martha, 516n174

W

Wade, Emily, 259n37
Wadsworth, Tim, 45; 222n34
Wagner, Charles, 440n106
Wagner, H. Ryan, 180n228

Wish, Eric, 261n120
Wislar, Joseph S., 65n33
Wissow, Lawrence, 259n34; 369n42
Wittebroode, Karin, 95n57; 96n102
Wittekind, Janice Clifford, 328n109
Wittrock, Stacy, 223n60
Wolak, Janis, 534; 553n52
Wolbert, Ann, 515n121
Wolf, Jim, 553n29
Wolfe, Barbara, 151; 178n124
Wolfe, Linda, 168
Wolfendale, Jessica, 409n26
Wolfers, Justin, 123
Wolff, Mary, 176n81
Wolff, Russell, 517n237
Wolfgang, Marvin E., 9; 26nn5, 11; 39; 61–62; 68n116; 69nn153–155, 162; 95n67; 132n8; 299; 325n7; 339; 370n63
Wolfner, Glenn, 373nn222, 226
Wolraich, Mark, 176n45
Won, Christopher Wong, 16
Wong, Virginia, 145; 175n35
Woo, Hyung-jin, 553n48
Wood, Eric, 180n197
Wood, Peter, 133n26; 134n95; 136n188; 328n104
Wooden, Wayne, 436; 440n110
Woodhouse, Donald, 514n107
Woods, Katherine, 68n139
Wooldredge, John, 263n199
Woolford, Andrew, 292n4
Wooton, Barbara, 179n151
Wormith, J. Stephen, 181n257
Worrall, John, 121; 135n139; 225n141; 438n31; 440n93
Wosick-Correa, Kassia, 372n159
Woyke, Elizabeth, 553n40
Wozniak, John F., 294n120; 295n154
Wright, Bradley Entner, 66n72; 260n68; 322; 325n14; 326n24; 330nn174, 175
Wright, Cynthia Pfaff, 65n34
Wright, James, 95n56; 113; 134n83
Wright, John Paul, 177n100; 216; 226nn192, 195; 258n25; 259n57; 262n149; 308; 316–317; 327n58; 328n98; 329n134; 330n153
Wright, Joy, 180n211
Wright, Richard, 83; 110; 133nn54, 66; 360; 374n254; 432, 433; 434; 439n65; 440nn89, 94
Wright, Robert O., 177n93
Wrightsman, Lawrence S., 371nn114, 117, 120
Wrinkle, Robert, 123
Wu, Chyi-In, 369n45
Wu, Lawrence, 226n197
Wu, Ling, 370n70
Wunderlich, Ray, 176n76
Wundt, Wilhelm, 164
Wung, Phen, 330n160
Wuornos, Aileen, 354
Wyler, Liana Sun, 474n113

X

Xie, Min, 94n35
Xu, Xiao, 358

Y

Yager, Tom, 553n62
Yamamoto, T., 177n105
Yang, Yaling, 177n97
Yar, Majid, 552n7
Yaryura-Tobias, J. A., 176n50
Ybarra, Michele, 553n52
Ye, Fei, 386–387
Ye, Xinyue, 370n70
Yeager, Peter, 473n47
Yeudall, Lorne T., 177n113; 178nn129, 130; 182n283
Yeung, W. Jean, 222nn24, 25
Yili, Xu, 224n80
Yin, Yip Pak, 549
Yllo, K., 371n119
Yodanis, Carrie, 294n99
Yost, Berwood, 96n128
Young, Amy, 516n183
Young, Jock, 270; 279–280; 292nn13, 36, 37; 293nn78, 79, 83
Young, Kimball, 182n275

Young, Lawrence, 181n268
Younts, Wesley, 260n84
Yunger, James, 122–123

Z

Zaalberg, Ap, 175n37
Zaff, Jonathan, 262n145
Zahn, Margaret, 372nn173, 182
Zalman, Marvin, 27n33
Zamaro, Nereo, 226n189
Zamost, Scott, 174n4
Zapp, Alexandra, 127
Zatz, Marjory, 262n176
Zavala, Egberg, 369n43
Zawacki, Tina, 369n26
Zawitz, Marianne, 517n241
Zayed, Z. A., 177n106
Zazi, Najibullah, 399–400
Zeedyk, M. S., 176n71
Zehr, Howard, 285; 294n128
Zeibel, John, 204
Zgoba, Kristen, 10
Zhang, Lening, 263n203; 516n197
Zhang, Quanwu, 259n52
Zhang, Yan, 517n218
Zhao, Jihong, 224n113
Zheng, Wei, 177n91
Zheng, Yan, 175n34
Zhong, Hua, 67n112
Zhong, Ming, 386–387
Zhu, Chenbo, 176n81
Zielinski, David, 327n46
Ziff, John, 409n14
Zimmerman, Grégoire, 180n204
Zimmerman, Gregory, 222n5; 313; 328n103
Zimmerman, Joel, 178n117
Zimmerman, Rick, 517n243
Zimring, Franklin, 48; 66nn62, 63; 135n150; 518n247
Zinkhan, George, 28, 30
Zinzoq, Heidi, 370n82
Zlotnick, Caron, 94n25
Zorbaugh, Harvey, 188; 222n12
Zweig, Phillip L., 472n1
Zwi, Anthony, 8–9; 373nn217, 218

Subject Index

Conduct disorder (CD), 159
   ADHD children and, 150
Conduct norms, 213
Conduit contributions, 381
Confessions of a Dying Thief (Steffensmeier
   & Ulmer), 419
Confidence games, 428–430
   fraud, 429
   types of, 429
Conflict
   social conflict, 266
   view of crime, 13
Conflict gangs, 218
Conflicts of interest in research, 23–24
Conformity
   commitment to, 245
   social adaptations and, 205
Conscience, 157
Consensus view of crime, 12–13
Consent and rape, 347–348
Consolidated Priority Organization Target
   (CPOT), 541
Conspiracy
   defined, 17
   example of, 18
Constitutional limits on criminal law,
   16–17
Constructive possession, 421
Contagion effect, 154
Containment theory, 245–246
Contextual discrimination, 253–254
Continuity of crime, 62
Contractual relationship, *actus reus* and, 20
Control. *See* Crime control
Controlled Substances Act of 1984, 503
Convention on Cybercrime, 540
Convention on International Trade in
   Endangered Species of Wild Fauna and
   Flora (CITES), 466
Conviction, political crime for, 380
Copyright Act, 539
Copyright infringement, 527
Coreflood virus, 530
Corner boy role, 216–217
Corporate crime, 459–460
   advertising, false claims in, 460
   deceptive pricing, 459–460
   restraint of trade, 459
   worker safety violations, 460
Corporations
   critical criminology and, 271
   globalization and, 273–274
   state-corporate crime, 276
   structural theory and, 272
Costco, 423
Costs and benefits
   incapacitation effect and, 128
   of situational crime prevention, 118–119
   victimization, social costs of, 73
Counseling for victims, 88
Counterfeit Access Device and Computer
   Fraud and Abuse Law of 1984, 539
Counterfeit checks, 425
Counterterrorism activities, 403

Courts
   cohort data from records, 39
   drug courts, 508
   escorts for victims, 88
   race and ethnicity and, 56–57
   restorative justice and, 288
   terrorism and, 404–405
Covert pathway to crime, 318–320
Crack cocaine. *See* Cocaine/crack cocaine
Crackdowns by police, 121
Credit cards
   cybertheft and, 528
   phishing and, 528
   theft, 424–425, 426
Crime. *See also* Crime control; Criminal
      law; Patterns in crime
   conflict view of, 13
   consensus view of, 12–13
   critical criminology defining, 271–272
   defined, 14–15
   drug use and, 501–503
   economic gain, criminality for, 108–109
   families, crime-prone, 142
   interactionist view of, 14
   left realism and, 280–281
   legal definition of, 20
   Marxist view of, 269
   measurement, 6–7
   rational choice theory, criminality in,
      108–110
   social harm concept, 12–13
   and social institutions, 276–279
   structuring of, 110
   supernatural crimes, 271
   valid measures, development of, 7
"Crime, Corrections, and California:
      What Does Immigration Have to Do
      with It?" (Public Policy Institute of
      California), 60
Crime and Personality (Eysenck), 298
Crime and the American Dream (Messner &
      Rosenfeld), 207
Crime control, 5
   policies, development of, 7
   and violent crime, 113
Crime discouragers, 116, 117, 119
*Crime in Context: A Critical Criminology of
      Market Societies* (Taylor), 280
Crime in the Making (Sampson & Laub), 304
Crime mapping, 41
   CATCH (Crime Analysis Tactical Clearing
      House) program, 43
   Providence, Rhode Island map, 42
*Crime Prevention through Environmental
      Design* (Jeffery), 116
Crimes Against Children Research Center,
      University of New Hampshire, 73
Crime trends. *See* Trends in crime
Crime typologies, 9–10
Crime Victims Board of New York, 78
Crime Victims' Rights Act of 2004, 87
Criminal anthropology, 142
Criminal Division and Project
      Deliverance, 541

Criminal environmental pollution, 467
Criminal justice, 4, 6
   criminology compared, 5
Criminal law, 16–17
   common law, 15
   consensus view and, 12
   constitutional limits on, 16–17
   in contemporary society, 16
   elements of, 20
   environment, protection of, 22
   evolution of, 19–20
   history of, 15
   judicial decisions and, 16
   marijuana, legalization of, 22–23
   rape, definition of, 20–21
   sex offender registration and, 20
   substantive criminal law, 18–19
   technology and, 21–22
   and terrorism, 23
Criminal statistics, 6–7
Criminal techniques, knowledge of, 109
Criminogenic traits, 142
Criminologists, 4
Criminology. *See also* Research
   areas of study, 23–24
   criminal justice compared, 5
   defined, 4–5
   deviance and, 5–7
   ethical issues in, 23–24
   sociology of law and, 7
   subjects of study, 23–34
Crips gang, 543
Crisis intervention for victims, 88–89
Critical criminologists, 266
Critical criminology, 266–271
   branches of, 267
   on causes of crime, 272–279
   contemporary critical criminology,
      270–271
   critical feminism, 281–284
   critique of, 279
   defining crime and justice, 271–272
   globalization, view of, 273–274
   history of, 266–269
   instrumental theory and, 272
   left realism, 279–281
   peacemaking criminology, 284–285
   on political crime, 387
   restorative justice and, 285
   social institutions and crime, 276–279
   on state (organized) crime, 274–276
   structural theory and, 272
Critical feminism, 281–284, 285
   exploitation and criminality, 283
   power-control theory, 283–284
Cross burning, 364
Cross-national surveys on social bond
      theory, 248
Cross-sectional surveys, 35
Cruel and unusual punishments, 17, 104
The Crusades
   rape during, 342
   theft during, 415
Crusted over children, 338–339

Crying for help fire setters, 436
Cult of domesticity, 283
Cult terrorism, 397–398
Cultural deviance theory, 193,
    212–219, 239
  code of the streets, 216
  conduct norms and, 213
  delinquent subcultures, theory of,
    214–215
  drug trade, life in, 215
  focal concerns and, 213–214
  formation of subcultures, 216–217
  middle-class measuring rods, 215
Cultural retaliatory homicide, 339
Culture. *See also* Race and ethnicity
  anomie and, 207–208
  bias, cultural, 57–59
  closed-circuit television (CCTV)
    surveillance and, 118
  code of the streets, 216
  conflict and, 213
  crime and, 8–9
  differential association theory and, 239
  General Theory of Crime (GTC) and, 316
  globalization and crime, 274
  homicide and, 8
  honor killing and, 341
  morality and, 480
  of Philadelphia underclass, 56–57
  prostitution and, 486–487
  rape and, 8–9
  strain theory and, 209
  trends in crime and, 45
  violence and, 339–340
  white-collar crime, cultural view of, 470
Culture, Conflict and Crime (Sellin), 213
Culture of poverty, 189–190
Cumulative disadvantage, 307
  in age-graded theory, 304
Curfew laws, 116
  gang violence and, 121
Cyberbullying, 534–535
Cybercrime, 522–523, 523–540
  controlling, 539–540
  cost of, 538–539
  cyberbullying, 534–535
  cyberspying, 535
  enforcement agencies, 540
  extent of, 538–539
  international treaties on, 540
  summary of, 538
Cyber Division (FBI), 403
Cyberespionage, 536
Cyberhooking, 487–488
Cyberspying, 535
Cyberstalking, 7, 533–534
Cyberterrorism, 537–539
  funding of, 538
Cybertheft, 523, 524–531, 538. *See also*
    Phishing
  botnets, 530
  computer fraud, 524–525
  copyright infringement, 527
  denial-of-service attacks, 526–527

drugs, distribution of, 526
  etailing fraud, 530–531
  file sharing infringements, 527
  identity theft, 528–530
  illicit/illegal services or material,
    distributing, 525–526
  reshipping scheme, 529
  securities fraud on, 527–528
  vishing, 530
Cybervandalism, 523–524, 531–536, 538
  cyberstalking, 533–534
  extent and cost of, 539
  logic bombs, 532–533
  spam, 533
  swatting, 532
  Trojan horses, 532
  viruses, 532
  website defacement, 533
  worms, 532
Cyberwarfare, 524, 536–538
Cycle of violence, 75

D

DaimlerChrysler company, 454
Dark Ages, criminal law in, 15
Darul Islam organization, 394
Data mining, 41
Dating violence, 359
  date rape, 344–345
  date rape drug, 156
Day of week, crime patterns and, 48
DEA (Drug Enforcement Administration), 18
  Project Deliverance and, 541
  transnational organized crime and, 549
Dead Boys gang, 542
Dead Rabbits gang, 542
Death penalty. *See* Capital punishment
Death squads, 276
  in Russia, 277
  state-sponsored terrorism and, 397
Decent values, 216
Deceptive pricing, 459–460
Declaration of the Rights of Man
    (France), 104
Decriminalization of prostitution, 491
Defenses, 21
Defensible space, 116
Defensive hate crimes, 362
Defiance, 167
Deliberate indifference murder, 349
Deliberation and murder, 349
Delinquency and Opportunity (Cloward &
    Ohlin), 217
Delinquency in a Birth Cohort (Wolfgang,
    Figlio, & Sellin), 61
Delinquent boy role, 217
Delinquent Boys (Cohen), 214
Delinquent fire setters, 436
Delinquent subcultures, theory of,
    214–215
Deltona massacre, 320
Democratic Republic of Congo (DRC), 273
  rape in, 342
Demystifying law and justice, 272

Denial-of-service attacks, 526–527
Denying the victim, 242
  white-collar crime and, 469–470
Depression
  brain tumors and, 151
  psychosis and, 159
Deprivation
  relative deprivation, 59, 204, 281
  and terrorism, 281
Desert theory, 129–130
Desisting from crime
  life course theory and, 303–304
  persistence and, 310
  reasons for, 310–311
Destructiveness, 167
Deterrence. *See also* General deterrence;
    Specific deterrence
  criminal law and, 19
  incapacitation effect and, 128
  reintegrative shaming and, 287
  restrictive/partial deterrence, 124
  violent crime and, 113
  of white-collar crime, 462
Developmental theory, 296–330. *See also*
    General Theory of Crime (GTC);
    Latent trait theory; Life course theory;
    Trajectory theory
  evaluation of, 322
  public policy implications of, 322–323
Deviance, 5–7. *See also* Cultural
    deviance theory
  cliques, joining, 252
  cultural deviance critique, 239
  family deviance, 232–233
  interactionist view of crime and, 14
  learning-deviant behavior link, 240–241
  primary deviance, 253
  secondary deviance, 253
  social bond theory, deviant involvement
    and, 249
  social harm and, 12
Deviant-oriented murder, 352
Deviant place theory, 82–83, 86
Dialectic method, 268–269
Diet
  and biosocial theory, 145
  food allergies, 147
Differential association theory, 237–240
  analysis of, 239–240
  principles of, 237–238
  summary of, 255
  testing, 238–239
Differential opportunity theory, 217–218
Differential reinforcement theory, 240–241
  summary of, 255
  testing, 240–241
Diffusion and situational crime prevention,
    118–119
Digital Millennium Copyright Act (DMCA),
    527, 539
Dionysian temperament, 142
Direct association
  genetics and, 153
  neurological deficits and, 148

Genitals
  female genital mutilation, 480, 479
  stage of development, 158
Genocide, 271
Genovese family, 543
Gentrification, 200
Germany, Marshall Plan in, 406
Get tough policies and left realism, 281
GHB (date rape drug), 156
The Ghetto (Wirth), 188
Glass-eating scam, 33
Globalization
  critical criminology and, 273–274
  information technology (IT) and, 523
Glucose metabolism, 145–146
Goals
  and general strain theory (GST), 208
  of political crime, 380
The Gold Coast and the Slum (Zorbaugh), 188
Golden Triangle, 496
Goldman Sachs Group, 449
  Abacus fund, 470
  denying the victim by, 469–470
Good burglars, 433–434
Good Samaritans program, 88–89
Google, 452
Government. *See also* specific agencies
  drug-testing strategies, 506
  influence peddling and, 453
  tax evasion, 458–459
GPS, motor vehicle theft for, 427
Grand Council of Venice, 484–485
Grand larceny, 421
Gratifiability as target, 78
Great Depression, crime after, 42
Greater Jihad, 383
Greece
  drug use in, 495
  embezzlement in ancient Greece, 430
  prostitution in, 484
Greed, 102
  enterprise crime and, 468–469
  general deterrence and, 125
  South Gate scandal and, 107
Green-collar crime, 463–468
  biocentric view of, 464
  defined, 444–445, 464
  dumping, illegal, 466–467
  enforcing environmental laws, 467–468
  environmental justice view of, 464
  fishing, illegal, 466
  legalist view of, 464
  logging, illegal, 464–465
  polluting, illegal, 467
  wildlife exports, illegal, 465–466
Grokster case, 527
Group boycotts, 459
Guantanamo Bay, Cuba, 387, 404
Guardianship, 84
Guerillas, 390, 391
Guillotine, 392
Guilt
  inducing guilt for crime, 117
  in neutralization theory, 241, 244

Guilty by Reason of Insanity (Lewis), 335
Gulf drug cartel, 547
Guns. *See* Firearms

H

Habeas corpus and terrorism, 404
Haganah, 393
Haldol, 152
Halliburton, 463
Hallucinations and violence, 335
Hamas, 395
  charitable funding for, 538
  Iran, financing by, 398
  as retributive terrorists, 396
Hammurabi, Code of, 15
Handguns. *See* Firearms
Happy Feet, 40
Hardcores, 244
Harrison Narcotics Act of 1914, 503
Hate crimes, 10–11, 360–364
  controlling, 363–364
  factors predicting, 362
  legal controls on, 364
  murder and, 352
  nature and extent of, 363
  roots of, 362–363
Hate Crimes (McDevitt & Levin), 362
Hayes International, 422
HCFCs (hydrochlorofluorocarbons), 467
Head Start program, 220
  social process theory and, 256
Health/health care. *See also* Mental illness
  fraud, health care, 455–458
  hospitals, cohort data from, 39
  life course persisters and, 321
  problem behavior syndrome (PBS) and, 301–302
  trends in crime and, 45
Health Insurance Portability and
    Accountability Act of 1996 (HIPPA), 457
Heart rate, arousal theory and, 152
Hebraic law
  Mosaic Code, 15
  on rape, 341
Hectors gang, 542
Hedge funds, 448
  bank fraud schemes, 458
  IBM scam, 452
Heijin, 547, 548
Heiress stealing, 341–342
Help move money from my country
    scam, 529
Hezbollah, 395–396
  Iran, financing by, 398
  as retributive terrorists, 396
High Intensity Drug Trafficking Area
    (HIDTA) Task Forces, 541
High loyalties, appeal to, 242
High school students
  dropout factories, 276–277
  dropping out, 234
  drug use by, 496
  trends in crime by, 46
Highway Loss Data Institute (HLDI), 428

Highwaymen, 415
Hilton Hotels, 452
Hispanic Americans. *See* Race and ethnicity
Hitman scam, 531
HIV/AIDS
  John Schools and, 490
  prostitution and, 489
  social costs of, 73
Holland, prostitution in, 491
Hollowed out communities, 195
Holocaust, 393
  explanation of, 401
Holy Land Foundation for Relief and
    Development (HLFRD), 538
Homelessness
  lifestyle theory of victimization and, 81
  murder and, 352
Homicide. *See also* Manslaughter; Murder
  cultural retaliatory homicide, 339
  culture and, 8
  evolution theory and, 155
  feticide, 349–350
  as Part I crime, 31
  race-specific differences in, 60
Homicide (Daly & Wilson), 155
Homosexuality. *See also* Hate crimes
  sodomy laws and, 19
  victimization and, 78
Honor killing, 341
Hookers, 487
Hooks for change, 303
Hormones
  biosocial theory and, 146–147
  PMS (premenstrual syndrome), 147
Hospitals, cohort data from, 39
Hostility, 167
  domestic violence and, 358
Hotmail, predators on, 80
Hot spots of crime, 41, 84
Household victimization rates, 76
Hul Gil, 495
Human agency, desistance and, 305
The Human Centipede, 40
Humanistic psychology, 164
Humanity, crimes against, 271
Human nature
  General Theory of Crime (GTC) and, 316
  latent trait theory and, 309–310
Human rights violations, 271, 380. *See also*
    Political crime
  state (organized) crime and, 276
Human Rights Watch, 264, 266
  on torture, 388
  United Arab Emirates, violations in, 276
Human smuggling, 22
Human trafficking, 544–545
Humiliation. *See* Shame
Hundred Years' War, 415
Hunter/gatherers, violence and, 335
Huntington's chorea, 151
Hurricane Katrina, swindlers after, 428
Husband and wife. *See also* Divorce;
    Domestic violence; Family
  age-graded theory and, 307–308

Islamic Revolutionary Guard Corps
(IRGC), 398
Isolation
child abuse and, 357
prostitution and, 489

J

Jacob Wettring Crimes Against Children
Law, 91
Jamaica, drug dealing in, 504, 550
Jao Pho gang, 548
Japan
Aum Shinrikyo, 397
Marshall Plan, 406
transnational organized crime in, 547–548
violence in, 339
J.C. Penny's, 424
Jealousy, 102
Jemaah Islamiyah, 393, 394, 400–401
Jihad, 383
combating, 406–407
Job advertisement scam, 529
Job Corps, 220
John lists, 117
John Schools, 490
Joyriding, 416, 427
Juárez drug cartel, 547
Judaism. *See also* Holocaust
Argentine-Jewish Mutual Association
(AMIA), 399
terrorism and, 393
Zealots, 391–392
Justice. *See also* Restorative justice
critical criminology defining, 271–272
demystifying, 272
restorative justice, 284, 285
Justice for All Act, 87
Justice system
advocates for victims and, 88
costs of, 72–73
Philadelphia underclass and, 56–57
race and ethnicity and, 56–57
trends in crime and, 45
Justification defense, 21
Juvenile delinquency
chronic offenders and, 61–62
fire setters, 436
self-report surveys on, 36
subcultures, theory of, 214–215
unemployment rates and, 85

K

Kahn Organization, 404
Kali, 392
Kenya, election fraud in, 381
Kepone pollution, 467
KGB and espionage, 385
Kickbacks, 453, 454
in Medicare fraud, 455
Kiddie porn, 492, 493, 526
Kidnapping
by Asian transnational gangs, 547
terrorist groups and, 398
Kiting checks, 425

Knapp Commission, 453
Known group method, 38
Kosovar, rape in, 342
Ku Klux Klan (KKK), 363, 364, 393

L

Labeling theory. *See* Social reaction theory
Labor. *See also* Migrant workers
human trafficking for, 544–545
markets and crime patterns, 51
Lacey Act, 466
Lack of concern for others, 167
La Cosa Nostra, 543
Lady Chatterley's Lover (Lawrence), 491
La Familia Michoacana, 547, 549
La Mano Nera gang, 542
Larceny/fraud
auto accident fraud, 429–430
embezzlement, 430
Larceny/theft, 420–430. *See also* Motor
vehicle theft; Shoplifting
bad checks as, 424–425
body snatchers case, 422
clearance rates for, 32
in common law, 15
confidence games, 428–430
credit card theft, 424–425, 426
defined, 17
false pretenses or fraud, 428
grand larceny, 421
as misdemeanor, 18
as Part I crime, 31
petit/petty larceny, 421
types of, 421–422
The Last House on the Left, 341
Late bloomers, trajectory theory and, 318
Late-date trading, 448
Latency, 158
Latent delinquency, 158
Latent trait theory, 308–317
aging out process and, 309
evaluation of, 322
human nature and, 309
Latin American gangs, 547
Latin Kings gang, 340
Latino Americans. *See* Race and ethnicity
Law, Order and Power (Chambliss &
Seidman), 270
Law enforcement. *See also* Police
cybercrime enforcement agencies, 540
drug use and, 504
reporting of crimes by, 33–34
terrorism and, 402–404
train robbery and, 415–416
trends in crime and policy of, 45
white-collar crime systems, 460–463
Laws. *See also* Common law; Criminal law;
Curfew laws
actus reus and imposition by, 20
Bentham, Thomas on, 103
categories of, 16
civil law, 16
demystifying, 272
differential association theory and, 237

drug use and, 503
on election fraud, 382
immigration laws, 60
on pornography, 494
and rape, 346–347
sociology of, 7
three strikes policies, 63
transnational organized crime and,
549–550
Lead
biosocial theory and, 147–148
pollution, 467
League of Nations Convention on
terrorism, 390
Learning and crime, 109
Learning disabilities, 149–150
Lebanon, Hezbollah in, 395–396
Left realism, 279–281, 285
criticism of, 281
and terrorism, 281
Left-wing political terrorism, 393–394
Lehman Brothers, 448
Lenovo Group Ltd., 452
Lesions in brain, 151
Lesser Jihad, 383
Lethal injections, 17
Life course persisters, 321
Life course theory, 299–308
age-graded theory, 304–308
age of criminal onset, 302–303
changing influences and, 301
concepts in, 301–304
desisting from crime, 303–304
evaluation of, 322
gender and, 302–303
problem behavior syndrome (PBS),
301–302
Life event calendar (LEC), 38
Life in Prison (Williams), 314
Lifestyles
routine activities and, 85
victimization, lifestyle theory of, 11, 78,
82, 86
Linkedin, 523
Liquor license scams, 452
Lithium, 172
Live from Death Row (Abu-Jamal), 278
Lobbyists, influence peddling by, 453
Local law enforcement and terrorism, 404
Local unemployment, 199
Lockdown society, 285
Lockheed Martin Corporation, 460, 536
Logging, illegal, 464–465
Logic bombs, 532–533
as cyberterrorism, 537
LoJack system, 116, 119, 428
Lone wolves, 321–322
Longley Jones real estate management
company, 462
Long-term care facilities, victimization
in, 77
Los Angeles gangs, 184, 186
Los Juaritos gang, 40
Los Sureños gang, 543

The New Jim Crow: Mass Incarceration in the Age of Colorblindness (Alexander), 280

New York City. *See also* 9/11 attacks
  Counterterrorism Bureau, 404
  organized gangs in, 542

New York Electronic Crimes Task Force (NYECTF), 540

New York State's Sex Offender Registration Act, 91

NIBRS (National Incident-Based Reporting System), 34–35

Nickerson Gardens Housing Project, 50

Nigerian 419 scam, 529

9/11 attacks, 376, 378–379
  New York Police Department and, 404
  response to, 402–407

9/11 Commission, 402

99 Cents Only stores scam, 546

Nitrogen oxide pollution, 467

No frills theory, 130

Nominee loans/straw buyers scams, 450

Nonnegligent manslaughter, 349

Non-starters, trajectory theory and, 318

Nonylphenol, 444

Norepinephrine, 151

Nuclear Terrorism (Allison), 402

Nuclear weapons, terrorism and, 403

Nurture theory, 169

NutraSweet, 145

O

Oaxaca drug cartel, 547

Obitiatry, 19

Obscenity, 491. *See also* Pornography
  defined, 480
  interactionist view of crime and, 14
  Internet, distribution on, 525–526
  sociology of law and, 7

Observational research, 40

Obsessive-compulsive disorder (OCD), 74

Occasional theft, 416–417

Ocean's movies, 414

Oedipus complex, 158

Offender-specific crime, 107–108

Offense-specific crime, 107–108

Office for Victims of Crime (OVC), 82

OfficeMax, credit card theft from, 424

Office on National Drug Control Policy (ONDCP), 5, 504

Oil Pollution Act of 1990, 467

Older persons. *See* Elderly persons

Old Testament law. *See* Hebraic law

Omnibus Victim and Witness Protection Act, 87

On Aggression (Lorenz), 335–336

"On Crimes and Punishment" (Beccaria), 103

Online predators, 80

Open area robbery, 358–359

Operation Backfire, 395

Operation Bullpen (FBI), 446

Operation Hammerhead, 201

Operation HEAT, 427–428

Operation Joint Hammer, 525

Operation Phish Phry, 520, 522

Operation Weed and Seed, 220

Opium
  Afghanistan and, 504
  in ancient world, 495
  cultivation of, 496
  in nineteenth century, 496

Opportunist robbers, 359

Opportunity
  differential opportunity theory, 217–218
  General Theory of Crime (GTC) and, 313
  reducing opportunities for crime, 116
  storylines and, 211

Oppositional defiant disorder (ODD), 159

Oracle and copyright infringement from, 527

Oral stage, 158

Organic solidarity, 204

Organizational crime, 459–460

Organized crime. *See also* Transnational organized crime
  history of, 542–543

Organized Crime Control Act, 549–550

Organized Crime Drug Enforcement Task Forces (OCDETFs), 541

OSHA (Occupational Safety and Health Administration), 460
  BP violations and, 464

Outpatient drug treatment programs, 506

Outwardly respectable adult drug users, 501

Over-billing/over-charging, 451

Overt pathway to crime, 318–320

P

Pakistan, nuclear weapons in, 402

Palestine. *See also* Hamas
  nationalist terrorism in, 395–396, 398
  terrorism in, 393

Palestine Islamic Jihad (PIJ), 398

Palestine Liberation Organization (PLO), 395

Panic disorder, 74

Paper and pencil interviewing (PAPI), 37

Paraguay, rape laws in, 348

Paranoia and violence, 335

Paranoid schizophrenia, 159

Paraphilias, 483–484

Parental abuse, 357

Parental efficacy, 233

Parenting. *See* Family

Partial deterrence, 124

Part I and II crimes (UCR), 30–31

Particular deterrence. *See* Specific deterrence

Part-time fences, 420

Passive precipitation, 80–81

Paternalistic families, 283

Pathways to crime, 318–320

Patriarchy, 282

Patriot Act. *See* USA Patriot Act

Patterns in crime, 47–63
  age and, 52–53
  ecology of crime and, 48
  firearms and, 48–49
  gender and, 53–54
  immigration and, 60–61
  SES (socioeconomic status) and, 49–52

Payola scandals, 454

PCP, violence and, 336

Peacemaking criminology, 284–285

Pedophilia, 483–484
  child pornography and, 492

Peep game, 110

Peers
  differential association theory and, 239
  differential reinforcement theory and, 240–241
  General Theory of Crime (GTC) and, 316
  and social bond theory, 248–249
  socialization and, 234–235
  strain theory and, 210
  terrorism, peer support and, 281

Pemoline, 172

Penology, 11

Pentagon
  cyber attacks on, 537
  cyberespionage and, 536

People Support, 452

Perception
  general deterrence and, 120
  shaping of, 165–166

Permeable neighborhoods, 111

Persian Gulf War, 275

Persistence, 62
  desistance and, 310
  life course persisters, 321
  life course theory and, 302–303
  trajectory theory and, 318

Person, crimes against the, 17

Personal factors, life course theory and, 304

Personal horrification stage of violentization process, 338

Personality. *See also* Developmental theory
  antisocial personality, 167
  defined, 166–167
  problem behavior syndrome (PBS) and, 302
  rape and, 346
  research on, 167–168
  terrorist personality, 10–11
  trait theories and, 143
  of victims, 81

Personality traits, 166–172

Peru, drug trafficking and, 504

PET (positron-emission tomography), 149
  scams, 531

Petit/petty larceny, 421

Phallic stage, 158

Phantom help offers, 449

Pharmacies
  chiseling by, 451
  Internet, distributing dangerous drugs on, 526

Phenytoin, 172

Philadelphia
  cohort research, 299
  distribution of offenses in, 61
  organized gangs in, 542
  underclass in, 56–57

Philippine Raja Solaiman Movement, 394

The Philippines, Jemaah Islamiyah in, 394

Phishing, 21–22, 528–530
  common scams, 529
  extent and cost of, 539
  Operation Phish Phry, 520, 522
Photo studios, 488
Phrenology, 141
Phthalates, 147
Pico Norte 19th Street Gang, 40
Pigeon drop, 429
Pilferage, 454
Pinkerton Detective Agency, 415–416
Place of crime, choosing, 110
Playboy, 491
Playing with matches fire setters, 436
Plea negotiations and general
    deterrence, 124
Pleasure principle, 157
Plug Uglies gang, 542
PMS (premenstrual syndrome), 147
Poaching, 415, 465–466
Police
  cohort data from, 39
  crackdowns by, 121
  data mining by, 41
  drug dealing and, 504
  extortion by, 452
  influence peddling and, 453
  left realism and, 280
  reporting of crimes by, 33–34
  restorative justice and, 288
  state violence and, 276
  system bias and, 55–57
  and terrorism, 404
  tipping point, adding police and, 120–121
  trends in crime and policy of, 45
  variations of patrols and crime, 121
Political crime, 379–387. *See also*
    Espionage; Terrorism
  election fraud, 381–382
  goals of, 380
  state political crime, 387–388
  thinking patterns for, 380–381
  torture as, 387–388
Political terrorism, 393–394
Politics. *See also* Political crime
  critical criminology and, 270–271
  terrorism and, 392–393
Pollution, criminal environmental, 467
Polycom, 452
Ponzi schemes, 315, 446–447
Poor personal skills, 167
Popular Front for the Liberation of
    Palestine-General Command
    (PFLP-GC), 398–399
Population
  moral panic and, 275
  rape and density of, 342–343
Pornography, 13, 491–495. *See also* Child
    pornography
  controlling, 494–495
  Internet, distribution on, 525–526
  laws on, 494
  morality and, 480
  Operation Joint Hammer, 525

  and rape, 346
  restricting sale of, 494–495
  sociology of law and, 7
  violence and, 492–493
  women and, 479
Positivism, 141
  biological positivism, 141
  social positivism, 188
Posse Comitatus, 393
Poverty
  child poverty, 190
  concentration effect, 198–199
  costs of crime and, 192
  crime rates and, 231
  cultural deviance theory and, 213–214
  minority group poverty, 190–192
  patterns in crime and, 50
  peacemaking criminology and, 284–285
  problem behavior syndrome (PBS) and,
    301–302
  in social disorganization theory, 193–196
  substance abuse and, 336
  trait theories and, 143
  underclass and, 189–190
  victimization and, 78
  victims, assistance for, 87
  War on Poverty, 219–220
Power-control theory, 283, 285
  evaluation of, 283–284
Powerlessness, critical feminism and, 282
Power rape, 344
Predatory criminals
  drug users, 500–501
  targets for, 110
Pregnancy. *See also* Abortion
  and feticide, 349–350
Premeditation and murder, 349
Preppie Murder Case, 168
Present-orientation and crime, 317
Pretty Woman, 487
Prevention of Violent Radicalization
    and Homegrown Terrorism Act of
    2007, 400
Price fixing, 459
PricewaterhouseCoopers, 456
Primary deviance, 253
Primary prevention programs, 172
Primary sources of crime data, 30–39. *See*
    also UCR (Uniform Crime Report)
  evaluating, 38–39
  NCVS (National Crime Victimization
    Survey), 35–36
  NIBRS (National Incident-Based
    Reporting System), 34–35
  self-report surveys, 36–38
  survey research, 35
Prime bank schemes, 448, 458
The Princess Diaries, 40
Principles of Criminality (Sutherland), 237
Prisons and prisoners. *See also*
    Incarceration; Recidivism
  demographics of prisoners, 58
  left realism and, 280–281
  no frills theory, 130

  psychopathy and, 170
  trends in crime and prison policy, 45
Private premises robbery, 359
Problem behavior syndrome (PBS),
    301–302
  in life course persisters, 321
  and substance abuse, 499
Procedural criminal law, 16
Productive forces, 268
Productive relations, 268
Productivity, loss of, 73
Profaci family, 543
Professional chiseling, 451
Professional robbers, 359
Professional theft, 416, 417–418
The Professional Thief (Sutherland), 417–
    418
Profiling, 55
  DWB (driving while black), 55
  racial threat hypothesis, 277
  social reaction theory and, 251
Profit
  arson for, 436
  mass murder for, 355
  motor vehicle theft for, 427
  political crime for, 380
Prohibition, 496
  organized gangs and, 542–543
Project Coronado, 549
Project Deliverance, 541
Project on Human Development in Chicago
    Neighborhoods, 338
Project Safe Neighborhoods, 120
Proletariat, 268
Prolixin, 152
Property crime, 412–441. *See also* Burglary;
    Larceny/theft; Theft
  arson, 435–436
  culture and, 8
  defined, 17
  peak age for, 52
  trends in, 43, 46
  victimization trends, 76
Property flipping, illegal, 450
Prostitution, 13, 484–491
  child prostitution, 489
  controlling, 490
  culture and, 486–487
  defined, 485–486
  for economic reasons, 108
  Emperor's Club scandal, 476, 478–479
  feminist theory on, 491
  human trafficking for, 544–545
  incidence of, 486
  John lists and, 117
  John Schools, 490
  legalization of, 486, 490–491
  rings, breaking up, 47
  risks of, 479
  types of prostitutes, 487–488
PROTECT Act of 2003, 492, 493
Provocation for crime, reducing, 117
Pseudo-conviction, political crime for, 380
Psychoanalytic theory, 157–158

Psychodynamic theory, 157–158
  and antisocial behavior, 158
  elements of, 157
  psychosexual stages of development, 158
Psychological sociology, 230–231
Psychological trait theories, 156–166
  attachment theory, 158–159
  behavioral theory, 161–164
  cognitive theory, 164–166
  history of, 157
  mental disorders and crime, 159–161
  psychodynamic theory, 157–158
  social learning theory and, 161–164
Psychological view
  of drug use, 498–499
  of substance abuse, 498–499
Psychopathia Sexualis (Krafft-Ebing), 483
Psychopathic deviation (Pd) scale, 167
Psychopaths, 167, 170–171
  causes of, 170
  as killers, 353–354
  neurophysiology of, 171
  personality of, 141
  terrorists as, 10–11
Psychosexual stages of development, 158
Psychosis
  and crime, 159–161
  violence and, 335
Psychosurgery, 172
Psychotic killing, 352
PTSD (posttraumatic stress disorder)
  adolescent victims and, 73
  prostitution and, 489
  victims suffering, 73
Puberty and genital stage, 158
Public law, 16
Public opinion, 18–19
Public order crimes, 13, 478–479
Public policy
  and capital punishment, 129
  and developmental theory, 322–323
  and rational choice theory, 128–130
  and social process theory, 256
  and social structure theories, 219–220
  and trait theories, 172
Public social control, 202–203
Public stigma, 250
Puerto Rico, drug crime in, 504, 550
Pump and dump stock market schemes, 102
Punishing Hate: Bias Crimes under American Law (Lawrence), 363–364
Punishment, 11. *See also* Capital punishment; General deterrence
  Beccaria, Cesare on, 103
  criminal law and, 19
  cruel and unusual punishments, 17, 104
  for drug dealers/dealing, 504–505
  history of, 15
  of immorality, 480
  just desert policy and, 129–130
  lag between crime and, 124
  in Middle Ages, 103
  parental punishment and violence, 337
  peacemaking criminology and, 284–285

perception and general deterrence, 120
  specific deterrence and, 125–126
Purchasing agent fraud, 452
Pure Food and Drug Act of 1906, 503
Pyramid schemes, 448
  Internet scams, 529

Q

Qods Force, 398–399
Quakerism, 284
Quasi-experimental design, 40
Quorum Health Group, 456

R

Race and ethnicity. *See also* Bias and prejudice; Hate crimes; Profiling; Racism
  community change and, 201
  contextual discrimination, 253–254
  convergence, possibility of, 60
  cultural bias and, 57–59
  family dissolution and, 60
  fear, race and, 199–200
  General Theory of Crime (GTC) and, 316
  incarceration rates and, 58, 105
  income and crime, 191–192
  murder and, 350
  patterns in crime and, 55–57
  poverty, minority group, 190–192
  racial threat hypothesis, 277
  rape cases and, 347
  reporting accuracy and, 38
  robbery and, 360
  shoplifting, stereotyping and, 424
  slavery and, 57, 59
  social reaction theory and, 253–254
  structural bias, 59–60
  system bias and, 55–57
  trends in crime and, 45
  and truly disadvantaged, 194–195
  victimization and, 59, 78, 79
Racial threat effect, 55, 201, 277
Racism, 60. *See also* Profiling
  critical criminology and, 266
  problem behavior syndrome (PBS) and, 301–302
  trait theories and, 143
  and truly disadvantaged, 195
Racketeer Influenced and Corrupt Organization Act (RICO), 549–550
Radical political groups, 391
Radiological weapons, terrorism and, 403
Radon pollution, 467
RAND Corporation
  on jihadist groups, 406
  on retributive terrorism, 396
Rape, 340–348
  aggravated rapes, 346
  in America, 343
  causes of, 345–346
  clarifying definition of, 20–21
  clearance rates for, 32
  compensation of victims, 87
  consent factor and, 347–348
  culture and, 8–9

defined, 17
  Duke rape case, 347
  as felony, 18
  history of, 340–342
  honor killing and, 341
  incidence of, 342–343
  international trends in, 348
  laws and, 347–348
  minimal brain dysfunction (MBD) and, 149
  murder related to, 351–352
  as Part I crime, 31
  PTSD (posttraumatic stress disorder) and, 73
  rational choice and, 114
  reforms in laws, 348
  sexual motivation for, 346
  shield laws, 348
  socialization factors and, 346
  varieties of, 344–345
  victim blaming and, 348
  victim precipitation theory and, 80–81
  and warfare, 342
The Rape of Lucrece (Shakespeare), 341
Rape of the Sabine Women (Poussin), 340, 342
Rational choice theory, 101–137. *See also* General deterrence
  Beccaria, Cesare on, 103
  burglary and, 111, 432
  concepts of, 105–110
  contemporary theory, 104–105
  crime, structuring of, 110
  development of, 102–105
  and drug use, 111–112, 499
  and eliminating crime, 114–115
  on enterprise crime, 468–469
  just desert policies, 129–130
  and murder, 114
  on offense and offender, 107–108
  public policy and, 128–130
  reasons for crime, 106
  risk evaluation and, 106–107
  robbery and, 113–114
  and sex crimes, 114
  situational crime prevention, 115–119
  on substance abuse, 499
  summary of, 129
  target of crime, choosing, 110
  and theft, 111
  time and place of crime, choosing, 110
  type of crime, choosing, 110
Rationalization and white-collar crime, 469–470
Reaction formation, 217
Reactive hate crimes, 362
Reality principle, 157
Reasoning criminals, 106
Rebellion and anomie, 206
Recidivism
  domestic violence, specific deterrence and, 126
  for prostitution, 490
  of sex offenders, 10
  specific deterrence and, 126
  trends in crime and, 45

Social institutions and crime, 276–279
Socialization, 230–236
  commitment to conformity and, 245
  cultural deviance theory and, 213–214
  education and, 234
  family and, 231–234
  gender differences in crime and, 53–54
  latent traits and, 309
  life course theory and, 304
  peer relations and, 234–235
  rape, male socialization and, 346
  religion and, 235
  self-control and, 311–312
  terrorism and, 401
  violence and, 337–338
Social learning theory, 161–164, 236–245
  differential association theory, 237–240
  differential reinforcement theory,
    240–241
  domestic violence and, 358
  neutralization theory, 241–244
  on rape, 346
  on substance abuse, 499
  validity of, 245
Social networking sites and predators, 80
Social order and criminal law, 19
Social phenomenon, crime as, 5
Social positivism, Durkheim, Émile on, 188
Social process theory, 231. *See also* Social
    control theory; Social learning theory;
    Social reaction theory
  evaluating, 254–256
  public policy implications of, 256
  summary of, 255
Social reaction theory, 236, 249–254
  consequences of labeling, 252–253
  differential enforcement and, 251–252
  dramatization of evil, 252–253
  effects of labeling, 254
  interpreting crime and, 251
  primary deviance, 253
  process of labeling in, 250
  research on, 253–254
  retrospective reading process, 252
  secondary deviance, 253
  summary of, 255
  validity of, 254
The Social Reality of Crime (Quinney), 270
Social Security number (SSN) and
    phishing, 528
Social structure theories, 192–203. *See also*
    Cultural deviance theory
  differential opportunity theory, 217–218
  evaluation of, 218–219
  public policy implications, 219–220
  social disorganization theory, 193–198
  strain theory, 193
  three branches of, 193
  truly disadvantaged, 194–195
Social support, reporting crime and, 33
Sociobiology, 142–143
Sociobiology (Wilson), 143
Socioeconomic status (SES). *See* SES
    (socioeconomic status)

Sociological criminology
  Chicago School, 188–189
  development of, 187–189
Sociological social psychology, 230–231
Sociology, 141
  of law, 7
  sociobiology, 142–143
Sociopaths, 167
  serial killers as, 354
Sodomy
  criminal law and, 19
  murder related to, 351–352
Software
  copyright infringement, 527
  illegal copying of, 538–539
  theft, 524
Solicitation, defined, 17
Somalia, al-Shabaab in, 379
Somatotype school, 142
Son of Sam murderer, 354
South Africa
  rape laws in, 348
  restorative justice and, 288–289
Southeast European Cooperative
    Initiative, 549
South Gate scandal, 107
Spain
  nationalist terrorism in, 395
  Spanish-American War, 496
Spam, 533
Spanish-American War, 496
Special deterrence. *See* Specific
    deterrence
Specialization and trajectory theory, 318
Specific deterrence, 125–126
  domestic violence studies on, 126
  summary of, 129
SPECT (single photon emission computed
    tomography), 149
Speed of punishment and deterrence,
    123–124
Spoofing. *See* Phishing
Sports memorabilia swindling, 446
Spousal abuse. *See* Domestic violence
Spouses. *See* Husband and wife
Spree killers, 355
Spurious association, victimization and, 75
Spying. *See* Espionage
SQUID (superconducting quantum
    interference device), 149
Sri Lanka, 276
St. Kitts, drug crime and, 504, 550
Stability-instability, 167
Stabilized junkies, 501
Stalking, 10–11, 81, 365–366
  cyberstalking, 533–534
  laws, 19
Standard of living and globalization, 273
Standing Against Global Exploitation
    (SAGE), 490
Stand your ground laws, 90
Stanford Law Review on capital punishment,
    129
Stashing, 109

State-corporate crime, 276
State (organized) crime, 274–276
State dependence, 309
State law enforcement and terrorism, 403
State political crime, 387–388
State terrorism, 397
  explanation of, 401–402
State violence, 276
Status crimes, 17
Status frustration, 214
Statutory rape, 344, 345
STDs (sexually transmitted diseases)
  John Schools and, 490
  prostitution and, 489
Stealth retaliation in drug market, 112
Stelazine, 152
Stepfamilies, 232
  child abuse and, 357
  domestic violence and, 358
Stern Gang, 393
Stigma
  prostitution and, 489
  reducing programs, 256
  reintegrative shaming and, 286
  restorative justice and, 285
  social reaction theory and, 250
Storylines, 210, 211
Strain theory, 193, 204–212. *See also*
    Anomie
  chronic offenders and, 210
  coping with strain, 210
  general strain theory (GST), 208–212
  sources of strain, 209–210
  storylines and, 210, 211
Strangers
  and crime, 79
  and murder, 352
  and rape, 344
Stratified society, 189
Street Corner Society (Whyte), 40
Street crimes, 13
Street junkies, 501
Street-level sex workers, 485–486
Streetwalkers, 487
Stress. *See also* PTSD (posttraumatic stress
    disorder)
  family, economic stress and, 232
  victims and victimization, 73, 75
Strict liability, 16, 21
Structural strain, 204
Structural theory, 272
Students. *See also* High school students
  college lifestyle and victimization, 82
  murder, student relations and, 352–353
Students for a Democratic Society
    (SDS), 394
Stuxnet computer worm, 536
Subcultural norms, 213
Subcultures
  in cultural deviance theory, 193
  cultural deviance theory and, 213–214
  delinquent subcultures, theory of, 214–215
  substance abuse, subcultural view of, 498
  of violence, 339–340

Torture
at Abu Ghraib, 397
defined, 389–390
female genital mutilation as, 480
justification for, 388
in Middle Ages, 103
as political crime, 387–389
waterboarding, 387
Tough love programs, 63
Toughness as focal concern, 214
Touting of securities, illegal, 528
Tracking systems and motor vehicle
theft, 116
Track system in education, 234
Train robbery, 415–416
Trait theories, 138–182. *See also* Biosocial
theory
contemporary trait theories, 143–144
foundations of, 140–144
Lombroso, Cesare and, 141–142
personality traits and, 166–172
psychological trait theories, 156–166
public policy implications of, 172
sociobiology, 142–143
Trajectory theory, 51, 317–322
adolescent-limited offenders, 321
age-graded theory and, 305–306
early-onset offending and, 318
evaluation of, 322
generalization of offenders, 318
life course persisters, 321
lone wolves, 321–322
pathways to crime, 318–320
recruiters, 321–322
specialization of offenders, 318
Transitional neighborhoods, 196
Transitions and age-graded theory,
305–306
Transmeta Corporation espionage case, 386
Transnational organized crime, 523,
541–550
activities of, 542
Asian transnational groups, 547–548
characteristics of, 542
controlling, 548–549
cyberspace and, 541
Eastern European gangs, 545–547
eradication of, 550
Latin American gangs, 547
laws on, 549–550
Mexican drug cartels, 547
origins of, 542–543
Project Deliverance, 541
Racketeer Influenced and Corrupt
Organization Act (RICO) and,
549–550
rise of, 543–544
Russian organized crime, 546–547
sex trafficking and, 544–545
Transocean Drilling Corporation, 463
Transportation Security Administration
(TSA), 403
Transvestitism, 483
Traumatic brain injury, 148

Traumatic socialization, 170
Treason, 382–383
Treaty of Versailles, 392
Trends in crime, 41–46
factors influencing, 44–45
future trends, 46–47
self-reporting, trends in, 46
victimization trends, 75–76
Triads gangs, 548
Trial by combat, 15
Trial by ordeal, 15
Tri-West Investment Company fraud, 528
Trojan horses, 532
Tropic of Cancer (Miller), 491
Trouble as focal concern, 214
Truly disadvantaged, 194–195
Truth and Reconciliation Commission
(Mandela), 288–289
Turkey, Internal Macedonian Revolutionary
Organization in, 392
Turning points, 305–306
age-graded theory and, 305–306
marriage as, 308
Twenty-First Amendment, 496
Twin studies
contagion effect, 154
genetic theories and, 153–154
on self-control, 312
Twitter, 523
2 Live Crew, 16
"Two Nations" (Wilson), 105
Tyco case, 456
Tying arrangements, 459

U

UCR (Uniform Crime Report), 30–34
on burglary, 431
clearance rates, 32
evaluating data, 38–39
on juvenile murders, 350
law enforcement practices and, 33–34
methods for compiling, 31–32, 34
on motor vehicle theft, 428–429
Part I crimes, 30–31
Part II crimes, 30–31
on prostitution, 486
rape, incidence of, 342–343
reporting practices and, 32–33
trends in crime and, 42
validity of, 32–34
Uganda, violence in, 339
Ulysses (Joyce), 491
Unappreciated, feelings of, 167
The Unborn Victims of Violence Act of
2004, 350
Unconquerable Nation (Jenkins), 407
Underclass, 189–190
general deterrence and, 125
Underreporting of crime, 33–34
Unemployment
chronic unemployment, 199
juvenile delinquency and, 85
minority group unemployment, 191
patterns in crime and, 51

problem behavior syndrome (PBS) and,
301–302
structural bias and, 59
substance abuse and, 336
Uniform Code of Military Justice, 404
Uniform Crime Report (UCR). *See* UCR
(Uniform Crime Report)
Union of Death Society, 392
United Arab Emirates, 276
United Nations
Convention on International Trade in
Endangered Species of Wild Fauna and
Flora (CITES), 466
United Nations
and female genital mutilation, 480
International Study on the Regulation of
Firearms, 8
Survey of Crime Trends and Operations
of Criminal Justice Systems (UNCJS), 8
on terrorism, 390
and torture, 388
United States. *See also* specific agencies
Al-Qaeda in, 379
domestic terrorism, 393
rape in, 343
values and violence, 340
University of Michigan Institute for Social
Research (ISR), 37
"Untouchables," 496
Upward Bound, 220
Urban areas
as natural areas for crime, 188–189
patterns of crime in, 48, 50
victimization and, 76
U.S. Bureau of Alcohol, Tobacco,
Firearms, and Explosives' Project
Deliverance, 541
U.S. Bureau of Justice Statistics, 30
U.S. Bureau of Labor Statistics' Census
of Fatal Occupational Injuries
(CFOI), 365
U.S. Census Bureau and NCVS (National
Crime Victimization Survey), 35
U.S. Customs and Border Protection
Project Deliverance and, 541
white-collar crime and, 460
U.S. Department of Energy, larceny/theft
from, 421
U.S. Department of Health and Human
Services, 256
on child abuse, 356
on Medicaid fraud, 455
Substance Abuse and Mental
Health Services Administration
(SAMHSA), 498
U.S. Department of Homeland Security
(DHS), 403
U.S. Department of Justice
Antitrust Division, 463
National Institute of Justice, 23
on transnational organized crime, 541
Violent Criminal Apprehension Program
(VICAP), 354
white-collar crime and, 460

Wealth. *See* SES (socioeconomic status)

Weapons. *See also* Firearms
  chemical weapons, terrorism and, 403
  of mass destruction (WMD), 275
  nuclear weapons, terrorism and, 403

Weather and patterns in crime, 48

The Weathermen, 394

Website defacement, 533

Weed and Seed sites, 220

Welfare and social structure theories, 219

Wernicke-Korsakoff's syndrome, 151

What Is to Be Done About Law and Order?
  (Lea & Young), 280

When Work Disappears (Wilson), 194

White-collar crime, 237, 379–380,
  445–463. *See also* Political crime
  bank fraud, 458
  causes of, 468–470
  chiseling, 451
  client fraud, 455–459
  compliance strategies, 461–462
  corporate crime, 459–460
  critical criminology and, 270
  cultural view of, 470
  defined, 444–445
  denying the victim and, 469–470
  deterrence strategies, 462
  exploitation, 451–452
  extent of, 445
  greed and, 468–469
  health care fraud, 455–458
  influence peddling, 452–454

law enforcement systems, 460–463
management fraud, 454–455
mortgage swindles, 448–450
need and, 469
neutralization theory and, 243,
  469–470
patriarchy and, 282
pilferage, 454
rationalization and, 469–470
religious swindles, 450–451
self-control and, 314, 470
in social reaction theory, 252
specific deterrence and, 126
state law enforcement and, 460–461
swindles, 446–447
tax evasion, 458–459

White-collar swindles, 446–447

WHO (World Health Organization)
  on domestic violence, 356
  global violence surveys, 8

Wife beating. *See* Domestic violence

WikiLeaks, 523

Wildlife exports, illegal, 465–466

Wiretaps under USA Patriot Act, 405–406

Withdrawal from drug use, 507

Women's Christian Temperance Union, 496

Workplace violence, 364–365
  controlling, 365
  extent of, 365
  factors predicting, 365

World Bank, 274

WorldCom case, 457, 462

A World of Gangs (Hagedorn), 196

World Trade Organization, 271

World War I
  crime after, 41–42
  prostitution after, 490
  rape during, 342
  Union of Death Society and, 392

World War II
  Marshall Plan, 406
  terrorism in, 393
  treason and, 383

Worms, computer, 532
  Stuxnet computer worm, 536

X

Xbox murders, 320, 354

XY chromosomes, 152–153

XYY chromosomes, 152–153

Y

Yahoo, predators on, 80

Yakuza gang, 547

Yemen, Al-Qaeda in, 379

Yugoslavia
  Bosnia, rape in, 342
  state terrorism in, 402

Z

Zealots, 391–392

Zen, 284

Zetas gang, 550

Zimbabwe, rape laws in, 348

Credits

This page constitutes an extension of the copyright page. We have made every effort to trace the ownership of all copyrighted material and to secure permission from copyright holders. In the event of any question arising as to the use of any material, we will be pleased to make the necessary corrections in future printings. Thanks are due to the following authors, publishers, and agents for permission to use the material indicated.

Preface. xvii: AP Images/via Scanpix

Chapter 1. 2: AP Images/Karel Navarro, File; **11:** © David Robinson/Corbis; **13:** © jokilica/Fotalia; **18:** AP Images/ Philadelphia Police Department; **22:** AP Images/Jane Rosenberg

Chapter 2. 28: AP Images/*Athens Banner–Herald Athens,* David Manning; **37:** © Ace Stock Limited/Alamy; **40:** © Hector Mata/AFP/Getty Images; **48:** AP Images/ Nashville Police Department; **50:** © Robert Nickelsberg/Getty Images; **55:** AP Images/ Steve Yeater; **63:** © luoman/iStockphoto

Chapter 3. 70: AP Images/Tina Fineberg; **74:** © Chip Somodevilla/Getty Images; **79:** AP Images/Sam Horton; **81:** Image of Sport/Newscom; **84:** AP Images/Alex Wong; **87:** AP Images/Rich Pedroncelli; **90:** © Rich Seymour/iStockphoto

Chapter 4. 100: © Reuters/Jeff Zelevansky/ Landov; **107:** AP Images/Nick Ut; **108:** © Francesco Guidicini/NI Syndication ZUMA; **114:** AP Images/Lenny Ignelzi; **120:** AP Images/*Minnesota Daily*/Lauren Desteno; **127:** AP Images/Robert E. Klein; **130:** © Lou Oates/Shutterstock

Chapter 5. 138: Sipa USA/Sipa/Sipa Press/ Newscom; **144:** AP Images/Mike Derer, Pool; **148:** AP Images/Jim Cole; **151:** Dr. Alan Zametkin/Clinical Brain Imaging, courtesy of Office of Scientific Information, NIMH; **161:** © crabshack photos/Fotalia; **165:** AP Images/Michael Conroy; **168:** (left) AP Images/Mario Suriani, (right) AP Images/Louis Lanzano; **172:** AP Images/ *Daily Press,* Sangjib Min

Chapter 6. 184: AP Images/*La Prensa,* Delmer Martinez; **187:** AP Images/Luis Romero; **192:** © Kevin Fleming/Corbis; **197:** © Ralf-Finn Hestoft/Corbis; **201:** © Catherine Yeulet/iStockphoto; **204:** AP Images/Bob Child; **206:** © Joe Raedle/Getty Images; **213:** © Robert Nickelsberg/Getty Images; **218:** © Spencer Platt/Getty Images

Chapter 7. 228: AP Images/John Bazemore; **233:** AP Images/Steve Helber; **235:** AP Images/John Amis; **241:** © Simon Wheatley; **248:** AP Images/Federal Police/ HO; **249:** AP Images/John Miller; **251:** © Chris Schmidt/iStockphoto

Chapter 8. 264: © Holly Pickett/Redux; **274:** © Richard Clement/Reuters/Landov; **277:** © Konstantin Zavrazhin/Getty Images; **278:** AP Images/Chris Gardner; **282:** © A. Ramey/PhotoEdit Inc.; **284:** AP Images/Harry Cabluck; **286:** © Rachael Rush/iStockphoto; **288:** © Charles Ommanney/Getty Images

Chapter 9. 296, 304: ZUMA Press/ Newscom; **312:** David Hoffman/UPPA/ Photoshot/Newscom; **314:** © David McNew/Getty Images; **318:** AP Images/ Consignment Gallery release via Bedford, N.H., Police Dept.; **320:** AP Images/Peter Bauer, Barbara Perez, David Tucker, Pool, File; **321:** © Jacom Stephens/iStockphoto

Chapter 10. 332: AP Images/Joe Burbank, Pool; **335:** AP Images/Gwen Mayor; **340:** © Eddie Green/iStockphoto; **342:** © Nicolas Poussin, c. 1637–38. *The Rape of the Sabines,* Louvre, Paris, France/ Bridgeman Art Library; **353:** AP Images/ *Morning Call,* Frank Wiese; **359:** AP Images/FBI; **362:** © Stephen Barcelo/*Daily News L. P.*

Chapter 11. 376: © Michael Appleton/ *New York Times*/Redux; **382:** AP Images/ APTN; **384:** AFP/Getty Images/Newscom; **385:** AP Images/Mark Wilson; **388:** © Konstantins Visnevskis/iStockphoto; **392:** AFP/Getty Images/Newscom

Chapter 12. 412: AP Images/Sergio Dionisio; **415:** © Mary Evans Picture Library/The Image Works; **422:** © Seth Wenig/Landov; **428:** © Daniel Allan/Getty Images/Taxi; **431:** AP Images/Al Grillo; **432:** © vm/iStockphoto

Chapter 13. 442: © Dave Einsel/Getty Images; **444:** © Stockbyte/Getty Images; **447:** Steven Hirsch/Splash News/Newscom; **449, 452:** © Bloomberg via Getty Images; **453:** © Spencer Platt/Getty Images; **461:** © Rich Legg/iStockphoto; **463:** AP Images/ Charlie Riedel, File; **466:** Andrew Ross/ AFP/Getty Images/Newscom

Chapter 14. 476: © Shannon Stapleton/ Reuters/Landov; **479:** Kambou Sia/AFP/ Getty Images/Newscom; **485:** © Brian LaPeter/Pool/Reuters/Landov; **486:** AP Images/Brad Horn; **493:** Edmund J. Coppa/ Splash News/Newscom; **510:** © Nicholas Belton/iStockphoto

Chapter 15. 520: AP Images/Nick Ut; **530:** AP Images/Kyle Ericson; **534:** AP Images/ Family Handout; **536:** © kydna/iStockphoto; **537:** © DSK/AFP/Getty Images; **540:** AP Images/Andy Wong; **541:** AP Images/Miguel Tovar; **544:** Paul Faith/PA URN:7357910 (Press Association via AP Images)

Time Line of Criminological Theories

ORIGIN
Classical Theory

CONTEMPORARY THEORY
(Rational) Choice Theory (p.102)

Beccaria
On Crimes and Punishment (1764)

Kant
Philosophy of Law (1887)

Brockway
The American Reformatory (1910)

Mabbott
Punishment (1939)

Bentham
Moral Calculus (1789)

Bentham
The Rationale of Punishment (1830)

ORIGIN
Positivist Theory

CONTEMPORARY THEORY
Biosocial Theory (p.144)

Gall
Cranioscopy/Phrenology (1800)

Lombroso
Criminal Man (1863)

Garofalo
Criminology (1885)

Kretschmer
Physique and Character (1921)

Hooton
American Criminal (1939)

Dugdale
The Jukes (1877)

Ferri
Criminal Sociology (1884)

Goring
The English Convict (1913)

ORIGIN
Positivist Theory

CONTEMPORARY THEORY
Psychological Trait Theory (p.156)

Maudsley
Pathology of Mind (1867)

Tarde
Penal Philosophy (1912)

Freud
General Introduction to Psychoanalysis (1920)

Pinel
Treatise on Insanity (1800)

Healy
The Individual Deliquent (1915)

ORIGIN
Marxist Theory

CONTEMPORARY THEORY
Critical Criminology (p.266)

Marx
Communist Manifesto (1848)

Bonger
Criminality and Economic Conditions (1916)

Rusche & Kircheimer
Punishment and Social Structure (1939)

ORIGIN
Sociological Theory

CONTEMPORARY THEORY
Social Structure Theory (p.192)

Quetelet
The Propensity of Crime (1831)

Durkheim
The Division of Labor in Society (1893)

Park, Burgess, & McKenzie
The City (1925)
Shaw et al. (1925)
Delinquency Areas
Thrasher
The Gang (1926)

Merton
Social Structure and Anomi (1938)

Sellin
Culture, Conflict and Crime (1938)

ORIGIN
Sociological Theory

CONTEMPORARY THEORY
Social Learning Theory (p.236)

Mead
The Psychology of Punitive Justice (1917)

Sutherland
Criminology (1924)

Sutherland
Principles of Criminology (1939)

Sutherland
The Professional Thief (1937)

ORIGIN
Multifactor/Integrated Theory

CONTEMPORARY THEORY
Life Course Theory (p.300)

Glueck & Glueck
500 Criminal Careers (1930)

ORIGIN
Multifactor/Integrated Theory

CONTEMPORARY THEORY
Latent Trait Theory (p.308)

1775 1800 1825 1850 1875 1900 1925 1939

Time Line of Criminological Theories (continued)

Andenaes
General Preventive Effects of Punishment (1966)

Martinson
What Works (1974)

Cohen & Felson
Routine Activities (1979)

Clarke
Situational Crime Prevention (1992)

Packer
The Limits of Criminal Sanction (1968)

Newman
Defensible Space (1973)

J. Q. Wilson
Thinking About Crime (1975)

Katz
Seductions of Crime (1988)

Montagu
Man and Aggression (1968)

Jeffery
Crime Prevention (1971)

E. O. Wilson
Sociobiology (1975)

Mednick & Volavka
Biology and Crime (1980)

Rowe
The Limits of Family Influence (1995)

Sheldon
Varieties of Delinquent Youth (1949)

Dalton
The Premenstrual Syndrome (1971)

Ellis
Evolutionary Sociobiology (1989)

Friedlander
Psychoanalytic Approach to Delinquency (1947)

Eysenck
Crime and Personality (1964)

Bandura
Aggression (1973)

Hirschi & Hindelang
Intelligence and Delinquency (1977)

Henggeler
Delinquency in Adolescence (1989)

Moffitt
Neuropsychology of Crime (1992)

Wilson & Daly
Evolutionary Psychology (1997)

Murray & Herrnstein
The Bell Curve (1994)

Vold
Theoretical Criminology (1958)

Chambliss & Seidman
Law, Order and Power (1971)

Lea & Young
Left Realism (1984)

Hagan
Structural Criminology (1989)

Braithwaite
Crime, Shame, and Reintegration (1989)

Dahrendorf
Class and Class Conflict in Industrial Society (1959)

Taylor, Walton, & Young
The New Criminology (1973)

Daly & Chesney-Lind
Feminist Theory (1988)

Quinney & Pepinsky
Criminology as Peacemaking (1991)

Cloward & Ohlin
Delinquency and Opportunity (1960)

Kornhauser
Social Sources of Delinquency (1978)

Wilson
The Truly Disadvantaged (1987)

Agnew
General Strain Theory (1992)

Courtwright
Violent Land (1996)

Lewis
The Culture of Poverty (1966)

Blau & Blau
The Cost of Inequality (1982)

Messner & Rosenfeld
Crime and the American Dream (1994)

Lemert
Social Pathology (1951)

Hirschi
Causes of Delinquency (1969)

Schur
Labeling Deviant Behavior (1972)

Akers
Deviant Behavior (1977)

Kaplan
General Theory of Deviance (1992)

Becker
Outsiders (1963)

Heimer & Matsueda
Differential Social Control (1994)

Glueck & Glueck
Unraveling Juvenile Delinquency (1950)

West & Farrington
Delinquent Way of Life (1977)

Thornberry
Interactional Theory (1987)

Sampson & Laub
Crime in the Making (1993)

Weis
Social Development Theory (1981)

Moffitt
Adolescence-Limited and Life-Course Persistent Antisocial Behavior (1995)

Hathaway & Monachesi
Analyzing and Predicting Juvenile Delinquency with the MMPI (1953)

Wolfgang, Figlio, & Sellin
Delinquency in Birth Cohorts (1972)

Wilson & Herrnstein
Crime and Human Nature (1985)

Tittle
Control Balance: Toward a General Theory of Deviance (1995)

Eysenck
Crime and Personality (1964)

Gottfredson & Hirschi
General Theory of Crime (1990)

| 1947 | 1969 | 1975 | 1980 | 1991 | 1995 | 1997 |